ICPP 2002

Proceedings

International Conference on Parallel Processing

18-21 August 2002
Vancouver, B.C., Canada

Sponsored by

The International Association for Computers and Communications (IACC)

In cooperation with

The Ohio State University, USA

IBM Research, USA

Microsoft Research, USA

Research Division of The Commonwealth Information Security Center
at James Madison University, USA

Edited by

Tarek S. Abdelrahman

Los Alamitos, California

Washington   •   Brussels   •   Tokyo

IEEE Computer Society Order Number PR01677
ISBN 0-7695-1677-7
ISBN 0-7695-1678-5 (case)
ISBN 0-7695-1679-3 (microfiche)
ISSN 0190-3918

Additional copies may be ordered from:

IEEE Computer Society	IEEE Service Center	IEEE Computer Society
Customer Service Center	445 Hoes Lane	Asia/Pacific Office
10662 Los Vaqueros Circle	P.O. Box 1331	Watanabe Bldg., 1-4-2
P.O. Box 3014	Piscataway, NJ 08855-1331	Minami-Aoyama
Los Alamitos, CA 90720-1314	Tel: + 1 732 981 0060	Minato-ku, Tokyo 107-0062
Tel: + 1 714 821 8380	Fax: + 1 732 981 9667	JAPAN
Fax: + 1 714 821 4641	http://shop.ieee.org/store/	Tel: + 81 3 3408 3118
http://computer.org/	customer-service@ieee.org	Fax: + 81 3 3408 3553
csbooks@computer.org		tokyo.ofc@computer.org

Editorial production by Danielle C. Martin

Cover art production by Alex Torres

Printed in the United States of America by Victor Graphics, Inc.

Table of Contents

International Conference on Parallel Processing (ICPP 2002)

Keynote Address

Proteins, Petaflops and Algorithms
  Dr. William Pulleyblank, IBM Research, USA

Session 1A: Instruction-Level Parallelism

Session 1B: Parallelizing Compilers

Session 1C: Grid Computing

Session 2A: Interconnection Networks

Keynote Address

Session 4A: Network Routing I

Session 4B: Programming Methodologies

Session 4C: Web Servers

Preface

It is with pleasure that I present you with the proceedings of the 2002 International Conference on Parallel Processing (ICPP-2002). Strong in its 31st year, ICPP remains the leading forum for the presentation of forefront research in the field of parallel processing.

This year the conference received 188 submissions from over 22 countries. Each submission was assigned to one of the conference's 9 Vice Chairs (VCs) to obtain at least 3 reviews. A meeting of the VCs was held in Toronto on April 20-21, 2002 to discuss the submissions. The VCs thoroughly evaluated the papers and produced an outstanding program with the 67 papers contained in these proceedings. These papers present state-of-the-art work in both traditional and emerging areas of parallel processing, including architecture, compilers, scheduling, parallel programming, grid computing, mobile computing, and middleware systems, just to name a few. I am thankful to all the authors who submitted their papers to the conference. I am also thankful to the members of the program committee and to the reviewers for taking the time to read and evaluate the papers. The high quality of the papers in these proceedings is a testament to the hard work and dedication of all the authors and of all the reviewers.

The conference program features three distinguished keynote speakers: William Pulleyblank, Ian Foster, and John Gustafson. I am grateful to all of them for sharing their insights and experiences with the conference attendees. The conference program also features a panel session on how to fire enthusiasm back into parallel processing research. I am grateful to Rudolf Eigenmann for organizing this panel, and to all the panelists for participating.

The achievement of a successful conference relies on many, whose efforts and hard work must be acknowledged. David Lilja, the conference's General Chair, provided invaluable guidance and constant encouragement. The VCs, Angelos Bilas, Rudolf Eigenmann, Oscar Ibarra, Andreas Moshovos, Jose Moreira, Jon Weissman, Chu-Sing Yang, Yuanyuan Yang, and Albert Zomaya, all made a superb effort in forming the program committee, and have all put in many hours of their valuable time to evaluate and discuss the submissions. Michael Voss, Eduard Ayguade, and Yu-Chee Tseng did a wonderful job of publicizing the conference. Lionel Ni and Mateo Valero provided valuable help in making best paper and travel awards. Kelly Chan made local arrangements for the meeting of the VCs in Toronto. Finally, Danielle Martin provided invaluable assistance in the production of these proceedings.

This year, ICPP is fortunate to have received support from a number of sponsors. IBM Research provided a contribution to reduce the conference registration fees for student attendees. Microsoft Research sponsored student travel grants. Finally, the Computer Security Center at James Madison University provided travel support for the workshop keynote speaker and support for the publication of the workshop proceedings. I am grateful to them all for their generous contributions.

Last, and by no means least, I would like to express my gratitude to Professor Tse-yun Feng, Professor Ming T. Liu, and Professor Ten H. Lai for their support of this conference in particular, and of the field of parallel processing in general.

Tarek S. Abdelrahman

Program Chair

University of Toronto

Organizing Committee

General Chair

David J. Lilja, University of Minnesota, USA

Program Chair

Tarek Abdelrahman, University of Toronto, Canada

Program Vice-Chairs

Architecture

Andreas Moshovos, University of Toronto, Canada

Compilers and Languages

Rudolf Eigenmann, Purdue University, USA

Algorithms and Applications

Oscar Ibarra, University of California at Santa Barbara, USA

OS/Resource Management

Jon Weissman, University of Minnesota, USA

Programming Methodologies & Tools

José Moreira, IBM, T.J. Watson, USA

Network-Based and Cluster Computing

Angelos Bilas, University of Toronto, Canada

Networking and Protocols

Yuanyuan Yang, SUNY at Stony Brook, USA

Wireless and Mobile Computing

Albert Zomaya, University of Sydney, Australia

Web and Multimedia

Chu-Sing Yang, National Sun Yat-Sen University, Taiwan

Workshops Chair

Stephan Olariu, Old Dominion University, USA

Awards Co-Chairs

Lionel Ni, Michigan State University, USA

Mateo Valero, Universitat Politècnica de Catalunya, Spain

Publicity Co-Chairs

Michael Voss, University of Toronto, Canada

Yu-Chee Tseng, National Chiao-Tung University, Taiwan

Eduard Ayguade, Universitat Politècnica de Catalunya, Spain

International Liaison Chair

Steve Lai, The Ohio State University, USA

Local Arrangements Chair

Robert Ito, University of British Columbia, Canada

Registration Chair

Elizabeth O'Neill, The Ohio State University, USA

Treasurer

Mike Liu, The Ohio State University, USA

Steering Committee Chair

Tse-yun Feng, Penn State University, USA

Program Committee

Tarek Abdelrahman, University of Toronto, Canada
Tarek F. Abdelzaher, University of Virginia, USA
Dharma P. Agrawal, University of Cincinnati, USA
George Almasi, IBM T. J. Watson Research Center, USA
Nancy Amato, Texas A&M University, USA
Eduard Ayguade, Universitat Politècnica de Catalunya, Spain
Prithviraj Banerjee, Northwestern University, USA
Ricardo Bianchini, Rutgers University, USA
Azzedine Boukerche, University of North Texas, USA
Mats Brorsson, Royal Institute of Technology, Sweden
Steve Chapin, Syracuse University, USA
Barbara Chapman, University of Houston, USA
Tzi-cker Chiueh, State University of New York at Stony Brook, USA
Edith Cohen, AT&T Labs-Research, USA
Michele Colajanni, University of Modena, Italy
Sajal Das, University of Texas at Arlington, USA
Jose Duato, Universitat Politècnica de Valencia, Spain
Sandhya Dwarkadas, University of Rochester, USA
Tarek El-Ghazawi, The George Washington University, USA
David Everitt, Swinburne University of Technology, Australia
Thomas Fahringer, University of Vienna, Austria
Babak Falsafi, Carnegie Mellon University, USA
Mike Feeley, University of British Columbia, Canada
Wu-chi Feng, Oregon Health and Science University, USA
Silvia Figueira, Santa Clara University, USA
Efstratios Gallopoulos, University of Patras, Greece
Michael Gerndt, Technische Universität München, Germany
Vladimir Getov, University of Westminster, UK
Qianping Gu, University of Aizu, Japan
Mary Hall, University of Southern California, USA
Hossam Hassanein, Queen's University, Canada
Jeff Hollingsworth, University of Maryland at College Park, USA
Tsan-sheng Hsu, Academia Sinica, Taiwan
Marty Humphrey, University of Virginia, USA
David Kaeli, Northeastern University, USA
Hironori Kasahara, Waseda University, Japan
Hironori Kasahara, Waseda University, Japan
Peter J. Keleher, University of Maryland at College Park, USA
Myung Kim, Ewha Womans University, Korea
Uli Kremer, Rutgers University, USA
Mohan Kumar, The University of Texas at Arlington, USA

Reviewers

Tarek Abdelrahman

Tarek Abdelzaher

Dharma Agrawal

Kento Aida

Tomas Akenine-Möller

George Almasi

Nancy Amato

Stergios Anastasiadis

Iosif Antochi

Christos D. Antonopoulos

George Apostolopoulos

Eduard Ayguade

Reza Azimi

Mark Baker

Prith Banerjee

Ioana Banicescu

Bill Barekas

Douglas Bass

Anindya Basu

Birgit Baum-Waidner

R. Bettati

Ricardo Bianchini

Angelos Bilas

Jean-Camille Birget

Rajendra V. Boppana

Jacir L. Bordim

Azzedine Boukerche

Dmitry Brodsky

Mats Brorsson

Darius Buntinas

Enrique V. Carrera

Rafael Casado

Cheng-Shang Chang

Ye-In Chang

Steve Chapin

Barbara Chapman

Ryan Chapman

Baoquan Chen

G. H. Chen

Gen-Huey Chen

Jianer Chen

Loon-Been Chen

Ming-Syan Chen

Xiao Chen

Yunli Chen

Sheng-Tzong Cheng

Dmitry Cheresiz

Tzi-cker Chiueh

Sung-Eun Choi

Wahid Chrabakh

Peter Christen

Rosalia Christodoulopoulou

Lingkun Chu

Chung-Ping Chung

Edith Cohen

Michele Colajanni

Jesus Corbal

Toni Cortes

Dan Crisu

Fei Dai

Chita R. Das

Sajal K. Das

Kei Davis

Marios Dikaiakos

Allen Downey

Steve Dropsho

David Du

Jose Duato

Sandhya Dwarkadas

Rudolf Eigenmann

Eric Eilertson

Tarek El-Ghazawi

Darin England

Mike Erlinger

Levent Ertoz

Abdol-Hossein Esfahanian

David Everitt

Thomas Fahringer

Babak Falsafi

Karl-Filip Faxen

Rainer Feldmann

Wu-chi Feng

Silvia Figueira

J. Flich

Michail Flouris

X. Fu

Yun Fu

Satoshi Fujita

Nathalie Furmento

E. Gallopoulos

Colin Gan

Maria J. Garzaran

Georgi N. Gaydadjiev

Peng Ge

Alex Gerbessiotis

Michael Gerndt

Vladimir Getov

Ananth Grama

LeMonte' Green

Gheorghe Grigoras
Qianping Gu
Amitav Gupta
Vijay K. Gurbani
Panagiotis E. Hadjidoukas
Erik Hagersten
Mary Hall
Hossam Hassanein
Aaron Hawkins
Wai Hong Ho
Jeff Hollingsworth
Cynthia Hood
Madhusudan Hosaagrahara
Akira Hosoi
Hung-Chang Hsiao
Lih-Hsing Hsu
Tsan-sheng Hsu
Y. Charlie Hu
Chung-Ming Huang
Nen-Fu Huang
Tsung-i Mark Huang
Marty Humphrey
Ren-Hung Hwang
Oscar Ibarra
Kazuhisa Ishizaka
Peter Jamieson
Dongming Jiang
Tianyi Jiang
Alex Jones
Y. Joon
David Kaeli
Iyad Kanj
Vijay Karamcheti
Sven Karlsson
Hironori Kasahara
Lami Kaya
Pete Keleher
Chamath Keppitiyagama
Darren J. Kerbyson

Thilo Kielmann
Eun Jung Kim
Myung Kim
Soo-Hwan Kim
Sung Kwon Kim
Keiji Kimura
Hiroshi Koide
Demetres Kouvatsos
Nectarios Koziris
Ulrich Kremer
Ajay Kshemkalyani
Sanjeev Kumar
Vipin Kumar
Georgi Kuzmanov
Aage Kvalnes
Jesus Labarta
Casper Lageweg
Wei Kuang Lai
Francis Lau
Byoung-Dai Lee
Shie-Jue Lee
Mike Lewis
Keqin Li
Xiang-Yang Li
Ran Libeskind-Hadas
Hwa-Chun Lin
Xiaola Lin
Ying-Dar Lin
Markus Lindermeier
Jiuxing Liu
Pu Liu
Darrell Long
David Lopez
Ulf Lorenz
Wei Lou
Bruce Lowekamp
Honghui Lu
Matthew Luckie
Pedro López

Takashi Maeba
Yoshitaka Maekawa
Naraig Manjikian
Evangelos Markatos
Philip K. McKinley
Avi Mendelson
Sam Midkiff
Prasant Mohapatra
José Moreira
Andreas Moshovos
Irene Moulitsas
Amy L. Murphy
Koji Nakano
David Nassimi
Thu D. Nguyen
Jari Nikara
Dimitrios S. Nikolopoulos
Motoki Obata
Eunseuk Oh
Hiroshi Ohta
Stephen Olariu
A. Yavuz Oruc
Ming Ouhyoung
Mohamed Ould-Khaoua
Marius Padure
Michael Palis
Elena Panainte
Cherri Pancake
Dhabaleswar K. Panda
Hyun Seok Park
Kunsoo Park
Sung-Soon Park
Sanjay J. Patel
Li-Shiuan Peh
Fabrizio Petrini
Michael Philippsen
Keshav Pingali
Timothy M. Pinkston
Dionisios Pnevmatikatos

Eleftherios D. Polychronopoulos

Cheng Qian

Sanguthevar Rajasekaran

Yansong (Jennifer) Ren

Umit Rencuzogullari

Celso Ribeiro

David Robinson

Antonio Robles

Steven Roos

Vilho Räisänen

Robert Rönngren

Ahmed Safwat

Sartaj Sahni

George Sapunjis

Mitsuhisa Sato

Makoto Satoh

Andreas Schmidt

Jennifer Schopf

Jennifer M. Schopf

Assaf Schuster

Loren Schwiebert

Dimitrios N. Serpanos

Sanjeev Setia

André Seznec

Gary Shao

Shashi Shekhar

Kai Shen

Tsang-Ling Sheu

Jeonghee Shin

Piyush Shivam

Bujor Silaghi

Federico Silla

Mihai Sima

Ambuj Singh

Rajeev Sivaram

Arun Somani

S. W. Song

Yong Ho Song

Matthew Sottile

Evan Speight

Pyrrhos Stathis

Per Stenstrom

Ivan Stojmenovic

Craig Stunkel

Jaspal Subhlok

Xian-He Sun

Yeali S. Sun

Zehra Sura

Martin Swany

Chunqiang Tang

Hong Tang

X. Tang

Xiaoyong Tang

Brian Tierney

Savio Tse

Chien-Chao Tseng

Yu-Chee Tseng

Georgios C. Tsolis

George Tsouloupas

Dean Tullsen

Pavel Tvrdik

Amin Vahdat

Amitabh Varshney

Ioannis E. Venetis

Vlad Vlassov

Michael Voss

Chien-Min Wang

Dajin Wang

Jianchao Wang

Kuochen Wang

Yongge Wang

Jon Weissman

Craig Wills

Roland Wismüller

Stephan Wong

I-Chen Wu

Jie Wu

Jiesheng Wu

Kui Wu

Peng Wu

Dong Xiang

Hirozumi Yamaguchi

Hayato Yamana

Chu-Sing Yang

M. K. Yang

Tao Yang

Yuanyuan Yang

Chihsiang Yeh

Akimasa Yoshida

P. Yu

Xin Yuan

Ki Hwan Yum

Javier Zalamea

Marcia Zangrilli

Qing-An Zeng

Dali Zhang

Xiaodong Zhang

Zhao Zhang

Jian Zhao

Yuanyuan Zhou

Sotirios G. Ziavras

Hitay Özbay

Keynote Address

Session 1A

Instruction-Level Parallelism

Hardware Schemes for Early Register Release

Teresa Monreal[†], Víctor Viñals[†], Antonio González* and Mateo Valero*

[†]Departamento de Informática e Ing. de Sistemas
Universidad de Zaragoza
e-mail: {tmonreal,victor}@posta.unizar.es

*Departament d'Arquitectura de Computadors
Universitat Politècnica de Catalunya
e-mail: {antonio,mateo}@ac.upc.es

Abstract

Register files are becoming one of the critical components of current out-of-order processors in terms of delay and power consumption, since their potential to exploit instruction-level parallelism is quite related to the size and number of ports of the register file. In conventional register renaming schemes, register releasing is conservatively done only after the instruction that redefines the same register is committed. Instead, we propose a scheme that releases registers as soon as the processor knows that there will be no further use of them. We present two early-releasing hardware implementations with different performance/complexity trade-offs. Detailed cycle-level simulations show either a significant speedup for a given register file size, or a reduction in register file size for a given performance level.

1. Introduction

Dynamic scheduling, also known as out-of-order execution, allows instructions to be executed as soon as their operands are ready bypassing prior instructions in the sequential program order. This is achieved by means of register renaming [11][21], which remove false register-dependences (output and anti dependences) creating a new register *version* for each register destination. Register versions are written only once, and read as many times as needed to satisfy flow dependences. Among the versions of a given register kept inside the processor, all but the oldest one are speculative and could become useless if an exception or a branch misprediction occurs.

Register versions can either be centralized in a single file, or distributed among different data structures. In this work, we are interested in improving the utilization of *merged* register files [21]. That is, register files that merge together committed and non-committed versions, as happens in processors such as MIPS R10K [25]. To differentiate ISA registers from rename registers (holding versions), they are called logical and physical registers, respectively.

To keep pace with the general processor trend (increasing number of in-flight instructions and functional units), register files are required to offer more registers, to be reachable in a single cycle and from more ports [18][19]. All of this, should be done ideally without compromising the growing frequencies of the out-of-order execution core, and further consuming a reasonable amount of power [26]. In fact, Simultaneous Multithreading, a feasible path for such future processors, can only achieve all its performance potential with large register files able to keep values from several threads [23].

Many works assume that the register file can impact on the processor cycle time [1][5][6][7] and is one of the most power-consuming structures [26]. Its size (P registers) and number of ports (T read and write ports) determine silicon area, power consumption and access time [20]. Therefore, a *direct* way to reduce register file delay is reducing P, T, or both. To do that, common approaches trade off IPC decrease against IPS (instructions per second) increase.

A first approach address the internal file organization basically without modifying the interface with the functional units. Some examples are the Minimally-Ported Banked register file [1] or the two-level register hierarchy managed in an inclusive [5] or exclusive [1] way.

A second approach suggest clustered microarchitectures, where the register file is sliced in banks, each bank directly feeding a functional unit cluster. Many of these solutions have been targeted to decentralize several critical structures, not only the register file. One example is the Dependence-Based architecture [18], where each bank is a complete copy of the register file as in the Alpha 21264 two-cluster case [12]. Other examples are the Multicluster architecture [7] (each bank is assigned a subset of the ISA registers) and related optimizations on assignment heuristics [2][4], or the Energy-Efficient Multicluster architecture [26] (each bank contains a subset of physical registers).

Finally, a third approach aims to act on the mechanism that controls the allocation or release of physical registers, trying to reduce the average number of required registers. In general, after applying some control improvement, a reduction in P is enabled without any IPC loss. Some works suggest delaying the allocation of registers until the functional units supply the results, either in a restricted form (dynamic result renaming [24]) or in a more flexible way (virtual registers [16]).

It is known that the conventional way of releasing is inefficient since registers are retained longer than strictly needed [17][6]. A previous approach to release registers early was suggested by Moudgill et al. in [17]. Their implementation is based on counters of pending reads but does not support precise exceptions. Afterward, Farkas et al. measured the gains of an imprecise early release policy, but no implementation was proposed [6].

Our contribution is to introduce and evaluate, hardware-only mechanisms devoted to release physical registers earlier, which take into account branch speculation and enable precise exception recovery. Our proposals can be applied to reduce the register file size, and so its access time, at the expense of introducing overhead structures that are not on critical timing paths. Alternatively, for register files that are already small enough to fit in the cycle time we can maintain P and use early release to increase IPC.

The paper is structured as follows: Section 2 presents the background for building the mechanisms and evaluates their potential gain. Section 3 focuses on a simple but limited mechanism, and Section 4 extends it taking into account control speculation. Methodology and results are presented in Section 5. We discuss related work in Section 6 and offer concluding remarks in Section 7.

2. Conventional Release Policy

First, we point out that register files can be dimensioned either in a *loose* or in a *tight* way. Next, we review the conventional policy for allocating and releasing registers and then, we give experimental evidence of its low efficiency.

To exemplify, we show four processors with merged register files, namely MIPS R10/12K [25][8], Alpha 21264 [12], and Intel P4 [9]. Table 1 shows their number of physical registers (P) and ports (T). It also shows the size (N) and name of the structure that reorders the uncommitted instructions.

Table 1. Out-of-order processors with merged register files.

	MIPS R10K	MIPS R12K	ALPHA 21264	INTEL P4
P = # of Phys. Registers in **Int** File T = # of Read and Write Ports	64 7R 3W		2x 80 2x (4R 6W)[a]	128 n.a.
P = # of Phys. Registers in **FP** File T = # of Read and Write Ports	64 5R 3W		72 6R 4W	128 n.a.
N = Reorder Structure *Size* Reorder Structure *Name*	32 Active List	48 Active List	80 In-Flight Window	126 µops Reorder Buffer

a. The integer register file has been replicated because a single file with 14 ports (8 read plus 6 write) could not be implemented without compromising performance.

MIPS R10K supports up to N=32 uncommitted instructions in its Active List. Since MIPS ISA has L=32 logical integer registers and P=64 physical registers, this processor never stalls because of the lack of physical registers ($P = L + N$). By contrast, in MIPS R12K and Alpha 21264 a long enough instruction sequence without branches and stores can stall decoding ($P < L + N$). If this situation

arises IPC may temporarily drop. We say that a loose register file has $P \approx L + N$. On the other hand, we call the second alternative a tight register file because a sequence with less than N instructions writing P-L registers runs out of physical registers, forcing the processor to stop filling the issue window. Intel P4 has a loose register file (128 phys. $\approx$ 8 logical + 126 uncomm.) unless the inflight flag registers were renamed using physical registers. In this case the file could become very tight.

Loose designs exploit all the ILP attainable by allowing the whole instruction window to be filled under any condition, whereas tight designs may contribute to reduce processor cycle time if the register file is located in a critical timing path.

We assume a renaming mechanism similar to that of processors in Table 1. Figure 1 shows the involved components: Map Table, Reorder Structure, Free List, and In-Order Map Table. The Map Table (MT) keeps the logical to physical mapping [11]. The destination physical register identifiers (pd) are supplied by the Free List.

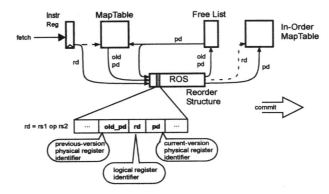

Figure 1. Allocate/release mechanism. Detail of a ROS entry.

The Reorder Structure (ROS) keeps information about all uncommitted instructions in program order. We assume a FIFO behavior implemented with SRAM and read/write pointers. Therefore, a ROS address can be used as a unique instruction identifier.

While instructions are decoded, three fields are written into the ROS bottom entry: <old_pd, rd, pd>. The identifier of the physical register containing the *previous* version (old_pd) is read from MT. The logical and physical identifiers of the destination register (the *current* version) are, respectively, rd and pd[1].

As instructions commit, the pd and rd entries are used for updating the In-Order Map Table (IOMT), and the old_pd identifier is added to the Free List. This is the way *conventional release* acts [17]. The IOMT keeps the logical to physical architectural mapping. When an exception has

---

1. Each ROS entry stores the result identifier, as in an indirect *Reorder Buffer*. But it also has the previous-version identifier, as in an indirect *History Buffer* [22]. So we adopt ROS as a more general term.

to be serviced, the IOMT avoids rolling back the ROS to recover the architectural state. In Intel P4, the IOMT is called Retirement Register Alias Table [9].

Physical registers can be Free or Allocated, and Allocated registers can be either *Empty, Ready,* or *Idle* according to the usefulness of their content (Figure 2a). We say a physical register is Empty from the moment it is allocated until it is actually written. We say a register is Idle from the commit of the instruction using that register for the last time, until the commit of the instruction producing the next version. An Allocated register is Ready when it is neither Empty nor Idle.

Figure 2b shows the execution of a program sample, where the physical register p7 experiences every state. Instruction *i* writes logical register r1, which is renamed to physical register p7. Later on, instruction LU (last-use) reads r1 for the last time. Finally, instruction NV (next-version) rewrites r1. As Figure 2b shows, p7 will not be released until instruction NV commits, being it Allocated and Idle from LU commit to NV commit.

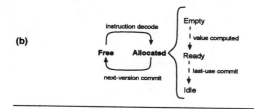

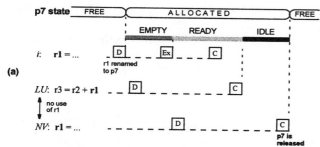

Figure 2. Breakdown of the ALLOCATED state and example of state evolution of the physical register p7.

This policy performs poorly because of two reasons:
- Registers are allocated too early. Empty registers do not contain information. Mechanisms which delay allocation try to remove this state [24][16].
- Registers are released too late. Idle registers are useless. Section 3 and Section 4 focus on mechanisms directed to release registers entering the Idle state quickly. Precise recovery will be covered in detail in Section 4.3.

Figure 3 shows the average number of Allocated registers being either in Empty, Ready or Idle states in conventional renaming for a SPEC 95 subset. We assume a processor with a tight register file with 96 physical registers (L=32, P=96int + 96FP, N=128). We consider only integer registers for integer programs and FP registers for FP

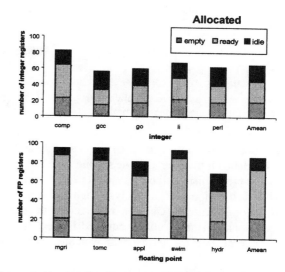

Figure 3. Number of *Allocated* registers being either in *Empty, Ready,* or *Idle* states in a conventional renaming.

programs. The experimental framework is detailed in Section 5.

On average, for our workload, the late release policy of conventional renaming increases the number of used registers (empty + ready) by 45.8% for integer programs, and by 16.8% for FP programs, as shown by the idle bar in Figure 3.

3. Basic Mechanism

Figure 4.a shows an example where LU instruction reads for the last time r1. Figure 4.b shows the less frequent case where LU instruction writes r3 without further use until the NV instruction comes.

The basic idea is to tie up the physical register release with the commit of the instruction using it for the last time in program order. To do so, first we identify the LU instruction (when decoding the NV instruction) and second, an early release of the physical register is scheduled for the LU instruction *commit*. Note that, if the LU instruction is already committed when decoding its NV pair, the corresponding physical register can be released *immediately*.

If a speculative NV instruction has to be squashed we need to undo its scheduling. Here, two distinct cases arise:
- **Case 1.** There are no pending branches between instructions LU and NV. This occurs if both LU and NV instructions belong to the same basic block. It can also occur if LU and NV instructions are in different basic blocks but all the intervening branches are already executed and their conditions and target addresses verified at NV decode time.
- **Case 2.** When decoding the NV instruction, there are still pending branches between it and its previous LU instruction pair.

7

```
i:  r1 = ...      ;r1 renamed to p7    LU: r3 = r5 + r9 ;r3 renamed to p7

LU: r3 = r2 + r1                          no use
     no use                               of r3
     of r1                            NV: r3 = ...
NV: r1 = ...
          (a)                                    (b)
```

Figure 4. Two examples where the physical register p7 can be released when the LU instruction commits.

This Section introduces an implementation of a basic mechanism dealing only with the first case. Later on, Section 4 extends it to cover also the second case.

The basic mechanism will only schedule early releases if an LU-NV instruction pair is safely recognized when the NV instruction is decoded (Case 1). In the remaining cases, the conventional releasing policy outlined in Section 2 is applied. To implement the basic mechanism any instruction should have the ability to release its physical source (Figure 4.a) and destination (Figure 4.b) registers at commit time. The ability to disconnect the (conventional) release of the previous-version register is also needed, in case such register is going to be released early.

3.1. Hardware Resources

Figure 5 shows an implementation based on adding fields to the Reorder Structure (ROS) and Map Table (MT). The extended ROS has now the following fields:

- **r1, r2, rd:** logical register identifiers.
- **p1, p2, pd:** physical register identifiers.
- **old_pd:** physical identifier of the previous-version destination register.
- **rel_old:** previous-version release bit. If reset at commit time, old_pd will not be released.
- **rel1, rel2, reld:** early-release bits for p1, p2, and pd, respectively. When set at commit time, they force the corresponding physical register release.

At decode/rename time the previous-version release bit is set and all the early-release bits are reset.

The MT extension is better described as a separate structure called Last-Uses Table (LUs Table). LUs Table identifies instructions using a given register for the last time. Every entry has the following fields:

- **ROSid:** for each logical register, it keeps the identifier of the instruction using it for the last time, that is, the LU instruction.
- **Kind:** kind of register use: src1, src2, dst.
- **C:** reports whether the LU instruction is still in the pipeline (C=0) or has already been committed (C=1).

Once this table supplies the ROS identifier of an LU instruction, an early release can be scheduled by setting the corresponding early-release bit. As is the case for MT, we assume that an LUs Table copy is made at each branch prediction, so that a branch misprediction recovery can retrieve the proper copy [10].

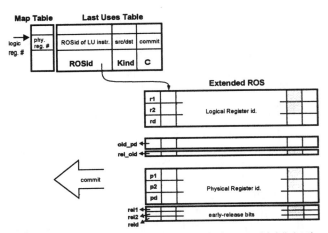

Figure 5. Basic mechanism. The shaded areas highlight the fields added to extend the ROS.

3.2. Control

Control steps are located at decode, rename and commit stages. We describe them in reverse order.

Commit: C bit update and register release. When instruction i commits, its logical register identifiers are available in the ROS head. We index LUs Table with these identifiers and read the ROSid fields comparing them with the i identifier and, where a match is found, the commit bit is set (C=1).

So, we record that a potential LU instruction has been committed[2]. Note that this action on bit C has to be extended to all LUs Table copies to achieve a proper branch misprediction recovery.

In parallel, the release bits drive physical register release. Up to four identifiers can be supplied to Free List: p1, p2, pd (early release) and old_pd (conventional release).

Renaming 1: LUs Table update. To record register uses properly, up to three LUs table entries have to be updated for each renamed instruction. The instruction ROS address is kept in ROSid, the register role is kept in Kind (src1, src2 or dst), and the C bit is reset. So, the identity of the instruction using a given logical register for the last time is recorded in program order. Figure 6.a shows an example of this step.

Renaming 2: release scheduling or register reuse. For each instruction having a destination register -a NV instruction-, this step ends either scheduling an early release or reusing the previous-version physical register.

To do so, the logical destination register of NV is used to look up the LUs Table. Let's call LU the found instruction, and LUid its ROS address. Next, if there are no branches pending verification between the NV and LU instructions, we proceed as follows:

---

2. Alternatively, we can access *associatively* to all ROSid fields with the i identifier, setting bits C in the entries where a match is found. With this support, the r1 and r2 fields in the ROS would no longer be needed.

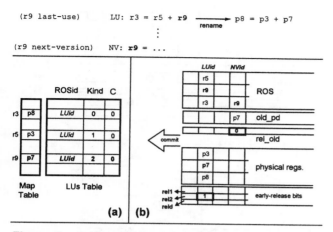

Figure 6. a) Map Table and LUs Table after renaming instruction *LU*. **b)** Decoding of instruction *NV*: the LUs Table is looked up, *NV* disables itself p7 release by resetting rel_old, and an early release of p7 is scheduled for instruction *LU*.

- If LU instruction is still in the pipeline (C=0), we set in ROS the suitable early-release bit: rel<u>x</u>[LUid]=1, where <u>x</u> is 1, 2 or d. We also reset the previous-version release bit for NV: rel_old[NVid]=0. Figure 6.b illustrates this step.
- Otherwise, if LU instruction is already committed (C=1) we can release immediately the physical register indicated in the Map Table, resetting as before the rel_old release bit. In fact, we can *reuse* the same physical register leaving the mapping untouched and not reclaiming any new register.

3.3. Performance

The basic mechanism is simple but its ability to release register earlier is limited. Its performance is noticeable with tight register files. With 64int+64FP and 48int+48FP physical registers, it achieves an average speedup over conventional release of around 3% and 6%, respectively, for numerical programs. For integer programs, the average speedup is negligible. However, processors with very tight register files benefit from early release in both application types: a 40int+40FP register configuration experiences 5% speedup for integer codes, and 9% for floating-point. Simulation details are shown in Section 5.

4. Extended mechanism

In the basic mechanism any time a register redefinition is decoded with some previous unresolved branch, the early-release opportunity is lost. We show next an extended mechanism that overcomes this problem by handling *conditional* releases. The idea is quite similar to that of a branch stack of Map Table copies used to recover from branch misprediction. The proposed implementation definitively disconnects the register release from the commit of the NV instruction. This saves the storage required for the old_pd and rel_old fields in the ROS.

4.1. Hardware resources

Figure 7 shows all the components making up the extended mechanism. From the basic mechanism, we maintain the Physical Register Identifiers and the Early-Release bit array, calling them PRid and RwC0 (<u>R</u>elease <u>w</u>hen <u>C</u>ommit), respectively.

The key structure is a Release Queue (RelQue). In the vertical dimension this queue acts as a FIFO with as many *levels* occupied as branches pending confirmation are. Therefore, it has to be sized with as many levels as pending branches the processor supports.

A given RelQue level keeps schedulings of *conditional* releases. A release is conditional whenever the originating NV instruction is speculative. Level number n keeps the schedulings depending on the validation of the n oldest pending branches. Each level in the RelQue comprises two structures: a bit-vector RwNS<u>x</u> (RwNS1, RwNS2, ...) and a 3-bit array RwC<u>x</u> (RwC1, RwC2, ...).

RwNS<u>x</u> (Release when Non-Speculative), keeps the conditional releases for the already committed LU instructions in a decodified form (1 physical reg. = 1 bit).

RwC<u>x</u> (Release when Commit), keeps the conditional releases to be synchronized with the commit of LU instructions still in the pipeline. The identity of the physical register to be released is kept codified in PRid. To deal with the in-order commit requirement, all the RwC<u>x</u> structures have to support right to left shift operation in the horizontal dimension, as the ROS has.

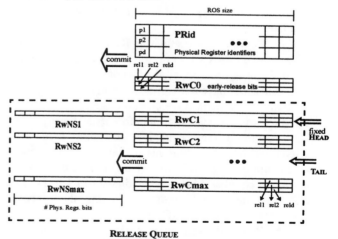

Figure 7. Extended mechanism.

4.2. Control

The basic idea is to stack up a new level in the RelQue each time a branch is decoded. The NV instructions which are decoded after that branch look up the LUs table, identifying LU instructions and scheduling releases, in RwNS<u>x</u> if the

LU instruction is already committed, otherwise in RwC<u>x</u>. As branch predictions are confirmed, the conditional releases on both RwNS<u>x</u> and RwC<u>x</u> move towards RwC0. In a misprediction the corresponding entry in the RelQue and all the younger ones are cleared, squashing the conditional releases previously scheduled by the mispredicted path.

Next we show in detail the control steps needed to manage the RelQue and release registers. We assume branches can be verified out of order. For the sake of clarity, we assume that the RelQue FIFO head is at a fixed location, marking the last occupied level with the pointer TAIL.

- Step 1. **Branch instruction decode.** A new level with all its bits reset is appended to the RelQue by simply increasing the TAIL pointer.
- Step 2. **Speculative NV instruction decode.** The RelQue level pointed by TAIL is marked with a conditional release for a given physical register p. Two cases can arise for an NV instruction with n pending branches in front of it: first, if the LU instruction is already committed, the bit vector RwNSn is marked (RwNSn[p]=1). Second, the bit array RwCn is marked (RwCn[LUid]rel<u>x</u>=1, where <u>x</u> = 1, 2 or d).
- Step 3. **Branch misprediction.** The prediction for the branch number n was wrong. All levels in the RelQue from n to TAIL are cleared. Therefore, TAIL is left pointing to the $n-1$ level.
- Step 4. **Branch confirmation.** The prediction for the pending branch number n is found to be correct. All the releases located between the entries n and TAIL are moved towards RwC0 (see example in Figure 8.a). At the same time entry n is ored with entry $n-1$. There is some additional work to case $n=1$ which will be dealt with later on.
- Step 5. **Commit effects in the Release Queue.** The RelQue, also needs a FIFO right-to-left management in the RwC<u>x</u> structures. So, all the bits of every level in the RwC<u>x</u> bit arrays have to be shifted left any cycle as many positions as instructions are committing.

An LU instruction can commit before its NV instruction pair becomes non-speculative. In this case, all schedulings of committing instructions are moved from the commit head of RwC<u>x</u> to RwNS<u>x</u> because the branch prediction could still be confirmed (see *Mark* in Figure 8.b). This movement requires decoding the register identifiers located at the ROS head.

- Step 6. **Physical register releasing.** Putting all the previous steps together, registers can be released at the commit stage of LU instructions and each time the oldest branch is confirmed.

In the first case, the registers scheduled in the RwC0 entries of the committing instructions are released (see *Commit Release* in Figure 8.b). In the second case, the registers scheduled in RwNS1 are released when the

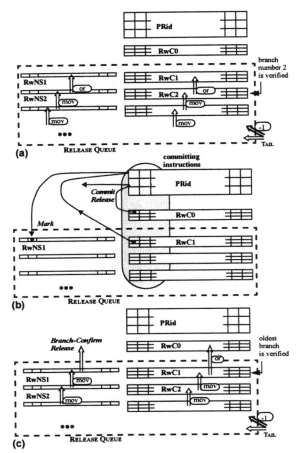

Figure 8. a) The second oldest branch is confirmed, **b)** RwNS<u>x</u> marking and Commit Release, **c)** oldest branch confirmation triggers a branch-confirm release.

oldest branch prediction is confirmed (see *Branch-Confirm Release* in Figure 8.c). This is the additional work we mentioned for $n=1$ in Step 4.

With regard to non-speculative NV instruction decoding, the same rules as in he basic mechanism apply: if the LU instruction found is already committed, then releasing proceeds immediately, otherwise the release is scheduled in the RwC0 level.

Finally, note that the total number of set bits in the whole RelQue is bound by the ROS size. Indeed, there are exactly as many bits set as non-committed instructions with destination registers are. Therefore, if we implement the RelQue as a true two-dimension shift register, most of the time the shifted values are zeroes. This is because when estimating the consumption of the mechanism we can safely neglect the RelQue contribution (Section 4.4).

4.3. Precise exceptions

Between the last-use of a logical register r (LU instr.) and its closest redefinition (NV instr.), an exception can appear once the current version of r has been lost by an early release action.

The exception handler saves the PC of the instruction to execute (or re-execute) it later. It also saves all the logical registers into the Process Control Block if the exception requires a context switch. In doing this, the handler could store for r a value that may be different from the last value stored in that logical register. Later on, when context is restored the same -incorrect- value is stored back in r. The point here is that the value attached to r does not really matter because the early releasing hardware only discards a version if it is guaranteed that the first use of r is a write. Therefore, we can conclude that our system does not strictly hold the usual condition to be precise:

"An interrupt is precise if the saved process state corresponds with a sequential model of program execution where one instruction completes before the next begins" [22].

However, this definition of precise exceptions is sufficient but not necessary to guarantee a proper recovery. The optimization we propose is safe in that these incorrect values are guaranteed not to be used by the program. Similar optimizations in software were proposed elsewhere [13].

4.4. Implementation remarks

The key structure of the Extended mechanism is the LUs Table. It can be implemented as a heavily ported SRAM, requiring 32 read and 24 write ports for an 8-way superscalar processor (P=32 entries, T=56 ports, word size= 9 bits). To assess its impact on cycle time and consumption, we use the delay and power model of Rixner et al. for a 0.18μm technology [20]. Figure 9 shows the access time and energy for the LUs Table. The same figures are also computed for the integer and FP register files considered for the aggressive processor evaluated in the next Section (T_{int} = 44, T_{fp} =50), varying P from 40 to 160 physical registers.

As can be seen, the LUs Table delay is clearly below any register size. In particular, it is a 26% less than that of the smaller integer file. With regard to consumption, the LUs Table requires only a 20% of the least demanding file.

We can use early release as a means to reduce register file requirements for a given performance level. For

example, we can move from a 64int+79fp to a 56int+72fp configuration while maintaining IPC (see next Section). When comparing the energy consumption of these two alternatives, we have the following:

E_{conv} (RF$_{64int}$+RF$_{79fp}$) = 3850pJ,
and for early release:

E_{early} (RF$_{56int}$+RF$_{72fp}$+2xLUsTable) = 3851pJ.
Therefore, the energy balance is neutral. Regarding storage cost, it is quite affordable in the context of a high-performance microprocessor. As an example, an Alpha 21264 will need about 1.22 KBytes to support the extended mechanism (ROSsize = 80, physical identifier = 8bits, # of physical regs. = 80+72 = 152, # of pending branches = 20). The int+fp LUs Tables will further add around 128B.

5. Evaluation and results

Early register releasing has been evaluated by using SimpleScalar v3.0 [3]. The out-of-order simulator has been modified to include physical register files (integer and FP) which are handled by the considered release policies. The main parameters of the microarchitecture are in Table 2.

Table 2. Processor parameters.

Parameter	Value
Fetch width	8 instructions (up to 2 taken branches)
L1 I-cache	32 KB, 2-way set-associative, 32 byte lines, 1 cycle hit time
Branch prediction	18-bit gshare, speculative updates, up to 20 pending branches
ROS size	128 entries
Functional Units (latency)	8 Simple int (1); 4 int mult (7); 6 simple FP (4); 4 FP mult (4); 4 FP div (16); 4 load/store
Load/Store Queue	64 entries with store-load forwarding
Issue mechanism	out-of-order issue. Loads are executed when all previously store addresses are known
Physical Registers	40-160 int / 40-160 FP (32 int / 32 FP logical)
L1 D-cache	32 KB, 2-way set-associative, 64 byte lines, 1 cycle hit time
L2 Unified Cache	1 MB, 2-way set-associative, 64 byte lines, 12 cycles hit time
Main Memory	unbounded size, 50 cycles access time
Commit width	8 instructions

Ten randomly-chosen benchmarks from the Spec95 suite are used: five integer and five FP programs. All programs were simulated to completion (by changing the reference inputs) excepting *tomcatv*, for which the initial part reading a huge input file was skipped. Table 3 lists the programs, inputs, and the number of executed instructions.

Table 3. Used benchmarks. We ran Compaq/Alpha Fortran and C compilers with -O5 for Fortran and -O4 -migrate for C.

	Application	Inputs	exec inst (M)
int	compress	40000 e 2231	170
	gcc	genrecog.i	145
	go	9 9	146
	li	7 queens	243
	perl	scrabbl.in	47
FP	mgrid	test, replacing two first lines to 5 and 18	169
	tomcatv	test	191
	applu	train, changing dt=1.5e-03 and nx=ny=nz=13	398
	swim	train	431
	hydro2d	test (replacing ISTEP=1)	472

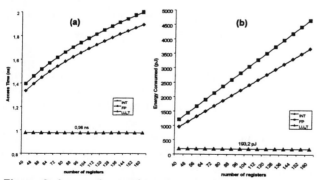

Figure 9. Access time and energy consumption of LUs Table and register file vs number of registers.

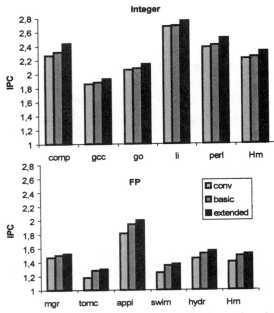

Figure 10. IPC of early releasing (*basic* and *extended* mechanisms) vs. conventional (*conv*) for 48+48 register file.

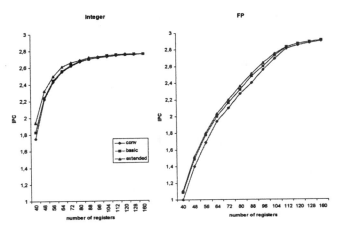

Figure 11. IPC harmonic mean vs number of physical registers for *conv*, *basic*, and *extended*.

5.1. Results

First, we observe the performance impact of early releasing in a processor with very tight register files of 48int + 48FP registers. Figure 10 shows the average number of instructions committed per cycle (IPC) for each benchmark, as well as the harmonic mean (Hm) for integer and FP programs. Conventional releasing (*conv*) is compared with our basic and extended mechanisms (*basic* and *extended*, respectively).

The performance gains with early releasing for FP codes are much more significant than for integer programs. *Basic* provides an average speedup over *conv* of 6% for FP codes, whereas for integer benchmarks the speedup is negligible. However, *extended* provides an average speedup over *conv* of 8% and 5% for FP and integer codes, respectively.

These are expected results, since in general FP programs have a much higher register pressure and integer programs are branch-intensive. Remember that branches limit the effectiveness of early releases by delaying their effects until the corresponding verification is done.

Next, we will show how early release performs under different conditions of register pressure. We consider a wide range of register file sizes, plotting the achieved IPC for all policies in Figure 11.

A first remarkable point is the low register pressure in integer codes. For them, a loose register file has no sense, with or without early release.

Excluding loose designs, early release always has a performance advantage, being the difference more sustained for FP codes. Moreover, when comparing *basic*

with *extended*, we can realize that *extended* is specially well suited for integer codes, whereas for FP codes both mechanisms behave similarly.

FP codes experience significant gains with tight register files between 40 and 104 registers. In this range, *extended* gives a speedup smoothly decreasing from 10% to 2% (from 9% to 1% in *basic*). However, programs with high register pressure can experience much larger figures with *extended*; for instance *hydro2d* gets 12% with 40 registers and *tomcatv* gets (16%, 12%, 8%) with (40, 56, 88) registers, respectively.

Integer codes benefit from early release, but only for very tight register files, roughly between 40 and 64 registers. Within this range, *extended* gives a speedup decreasing from 11% to 2% (from 5% to 0% in *basic*).

Alternatively, we can use early release as a means to reduce register requirements for a given performance level. Table 4 shows several register configurations giving the same IPC, along with the saved storage.

Table 4. Register file sizes giving equal IPC.

FP codes			int codes		
conv	extended	**saved %**	conv	extended	**saved %**
69	64	7.2%	64	56	12.5%
79	72	8.9%	72	64	11.1%

6. Related Work

Another approach intended to release registers early was suggested by Moudgill et al. in [17]. In that work, they suggest releasing physical registers eagerly, as soon as LU instructions complete out of order. Last-use tracking is based on counters which record the number of pending reads for every physical register. This initial proposal does not support precise exceptions since counters are not correctly recovered when instructions are squashed, and was not evaluated. Later on in the same paper, they present the simplified approach which we are referring to all the time as "conventional release".

Farkas et al. compare an imprecise early release model to the conventional one [6]. They propose conditions to free registers that are quite similar to the ones we use for the basic mechanism. However, they are imprecise because the register release is done when the LU instruction completes execution, instead of waiting for its commit. Besides, no implementation was proposed for this model.

Lozano and Gao [14] suggest an extension to register renaming in which the compiler identifies some LU instructions. So, their mechanism prevents register versions from updating the register file if they have short lifetimes. The compiler identifies such last-uses and the mechanism allows a register file traffic reduction, but the concepts are not applied to register releasing. Moreover, they apply their solutions only inside basic blocks.

Other researchers also use the compiler to detect LU instructions in order to release physical registers [13][15]. The compiler can identify registers containing dead values and inform the hardware. To do this, a change in the ISA is required, either defining extra instruction bits or adding new instructions, so that the compiler can schedule releases. Besides, the compiler has a limited knowledge of the dynamic control flow, and the release scheduling must be conservative. By contrast, hardware solutions have the potential to dynamically change a LU identification, releasing more registers early.

7. Conclusions

Current register renaming schemes release physical registers in a conservative way, which unnecessarily increases the register requirements of out-of-order processors. We envision early release as another design tool to either shrink the register file and adjust its access time to the cycle time (both for tight and loose systems), or increase IPC while maintaining size (for tight systems).

We have introduced two mechanisms of increasing complexity and performance in order to release registers early. Such mechanisms support precise exception recovery and are out of critical timing paths.

Our evaluation shows promising speedups, especially in numerical codes, for a wide size range of tight register files. On average, these speedups vary from 10% to 2% as register file size is increased until reaching the loose status and, in some programs, a speedup of up to 16% is attained for tight register files. In integer codes our proposal is only effective for very tight register files, where speedups of up to 11% can be obtained.

Alternatively, we can use early release to tighten the register file while maintaining IPC. As regards typical microarchitectures we have found that register file sizes can be reduced by 12.5% and 8.9%, respectively for integer and FP codes, without reducing IPC. This is an important point, since register file reduction translates directly to lower access time.

8. Acknowledgments

Work supported by CICYT TIC01-0995 grant and by the computing resources of CEPBA. We would like to thank Elena Castrillo for her contributions in editing this paper.

9. References

[1] R. Balasubramanian, S. Dwarkadas, and D.H. Albonesi. "Reducing the Complexity of the Register File in Dynamic Superscalar Processors", *MICRO-34*, Dec. 2001.

[2] A. Baniasadi and A. Moshovos. "Instruction Distribution Heuristics for Quad-Cluster, Dinamically Scheduled, Superscalar Processors", *MICRO-33*, pp. 337-347, Dec. 2000.

[3] D. Burger and T.M. Austin. "The Simplescalar Tool Set v2.0", *TR 1342*, U. of Wisconsin-Madison, CS Department, June 1997.

[4] R. Canal, J.M. Parcerisa, and A. González. "Dynamic Cluster Assignment Mechanisms", *HPCA-6*, Jan. 2000.

[5] J. Cruz, A. González, M. Valero, and N.m Topham. "Multiple-Banked Register File Architectures", *27th ISCA*, pp. 316-325, June 2000.

[6] K. Farkas, N. Jouppi, and P. Chow. "Register File Considerations in Dynamically Scheduled Processors", *HPCA-2*, pp. 40-51, 1996.

[7] K. Farkas, P. Chow, N. Jouppi, and Z. Vranesic. "The Multicluster Architecture: Reducing Cycle Time Through Partitioning", *MICRO-30*, pp. 149-159, Dec. 1997.

[8] L. Gwennap. "MIPS R12000 to Hit 300 MHz", *Microprocessor Report*, Micro Design Resources, 11(13):1-4 Oct, 1997.

[9] G. Hinton et al. "The Microarchitecture of the Pentium 4 Processor", *Intel Technology Journal Q1*, 2001.

[10] W.W. Hwu and Y.N. Patt. "Checkpoint Repair for Out-of-order Execution Machines", *14th ISCA*, pp. 18-26, June 1987.

[11] R.M. Keller. "Look-Ahead processors", *ACM Computing Surveys*, 7(4):177-195, Dec 1975.

[12] R.E. Kessler. "The Alpha 21264 Microprocessor", *IEEE Micro*, 19(2):24-36, March-April 1999.

[13] J.L. Lo, S. S. Parekh, S.J. Eggers, H. M. Levy, and D.M. Tullsen. "Software-Directed Register Deallocation for Simultaneous Multithreaded Processors", *IEEE T. on PDS*, 10(9):922-933, Sept 1999.

[14] L.A. Lozano and G.R. Gao. "Exploiting Short-Lived Variables in Superscalar Processors", *MICRO-28*, pp. 292-302, Nov. 1995.

[15] M.M. Martin, A. Roth, and C.N. Fischer. "Exploiting Dead Value Information", *MICRO-30*, pp. 125-135, Dec. 1997.

[16] T. Monreal, A. González, M. Valero, J. González, and V. Viñals. "Delaying Physical Register Allocation Through Virtual-Physical Registers", *MICRO-32*, pp. 186-192, Nov. 1999.

[17] M. Moudgill, K. Pingali, and S. Vassiliadis. "Register Renaming and Dynamic Speculation: an Alternative Approach", *MICRO-26*, pp. 202-213, Nov. 1993.

[18] S. Palacharla, N. Jouppi, and J. Smith. "Complexity-Effective Superscalar Processors", *24th. ISCA*, pp. 206-218, June 1997.

[19] Y. Patt, S. Patel, M. Evers, D. Friendly, and J. Stark., "One Billion Transistors, One Uniprocessor, One Chip", *IEEE Computer*, 30(9):51-57, Sept. 1997.

[20] S. Rixner, W. J. Dally, B. Khailany, P. Mattson, U.J. Kapasi and J. D. Owens. "Register Organization for Media Processing", *HPCA-6*, pp. 375-386, January 2000.

[21] D. Sima. "The Design Space of Register Renaming Techniques", *IEEE Micro*, 20(5):70-83, Sept-Oct 2000.

[22] J. E. Smith and A.R. Pleszkun. "Implementation of Precise Interrupts in Pipelined Processors", *12th. ISCA*, pp. 36-44, 1985.

[23] D. Tullsen, S. Eggers, and H. Levy. "Simultaneous Multithreading: Maximizing On-Chip Parallelism", *22th. ISCA*, pp. 392-403, June 1995.

[24] S. Wallace, N. Bagherzadeh. "A Scalable Register File Architecture for Dinamically Scheduled Processors", *PACT-5*, pp. 179-184, Oct. 1996.

[25] K.C. Yeager. "The MIPS R10000 Superscalar Microprocessor", *IEEE Micro*, 16(2):28-40, 1996.

[26] V.V. Zyuban and P.M. Kogge. "Inherently Lower-Power High-Performance Superscalar Architectures", *IEEE T. on C.*, 50(3):268-285, March 2001.

Out-of-Order Instruction Fetch using Multiple Sequencers

Paramjit Oberoi and Gurindar Sohi

Computer Sciences Department, University of Wisconsin - Madison
1210 West Dayton Street, Madison, WI 53706-1685, USA
`{param,sohi}@cs.wisc.edu`

Abstract

Conventional instruction fetch mechanisms fetch contiguous blocks of instructions in each cycle. They are difficult to scale since taken branches make it hard to increase the size of these blocks beyond eight instructions. Trace caches have been proposed as a solution to this problem, but they use cache space inefficiently.

We show that fetching large blocks of contiguous instructions, or wide fetch, is inefficient for modern out-of-order processors. Instead of the usual approach of fetching large blocks of instructions from a single point in the program, we propose a high-bandwidth fetch mechanism that fetches small blocks of instructions from multiple points in a program.

In this paper, we demonstrate that it is possible to achieve high-bandwidth fetch by using multiple narrow fetch units operating in parallel. Our mechanism performs as well as a trace cache, does not waste cache space, is more resilient to instruction cache misses, and is a natural fit for techniques that require fetching multiple threads, like multithreading, dual-path execution, and speculative threads.

1 Introduction

Modern processors need a large instruction window to ensure that many independent instructions are available for execution at any time. As processors with more functional units are built, it is also necessary to increase the instruction fetch bandwidth so that the instruction window size can be correspondingly increased.

Increasing the instruction fetch bandwidth beyond eight instructions per cycle poses special problems. Typical programs contain taken branches every eight instructions on average [6]. At every taken branch in a program, the fetch unit must be redirected to fetch instructions from a new address. Since most instruction caches can only supply data from contiguous memory locations in one cycle, instructions from the branch target address cannot be fetched in the same cycle as the instructions up to the branch. This restricts instruction fetch bandwidth to the average number of instructions between taken branches. The wider the fetch unit, the more likely it is that fetch slots will be wasted because of discontinuities in the instruction stream.

Proposed solutions to this problem can be divided into two categories: (a) augmenting the branch predictor to predict multiple branches per cycle [21] and the instruction cache to supply multiple discontinuous lines per cycle [4], and (b) storing instructions in dynamic execution order in the cache (i.e. using a *trace* cache) [11,12,16]. The first solution makes the branch predictor and the cache more complex, potentially increasing the cycle time; the second solution leads to inefficient use of cache space, potentially increasing cache miss rates.

Both classes of solutions work by fetching a large number of contiguous instructions from a single point in the program every cycle. In this paper, we propose a high-bandwidth fetch mechanism that fetches a small number of contiguous instructions from multiple points in the program, as opposed to fetching a large number of contiguous instructions from a single point.

Fetching a large block of contiguous instructions, or *wide fetch*, is inefficient for out-of-order processors. Figure 1 illustrates how fetch and execution of consecutive instructions overlaps in time. This data is from a 16-wide processor augmented with a trace cache. Traces are variable length, up to a maximum of 16 instructions. The trace selection algorithm is described in Section 2.4.1, and the simulated machine configuration is discussed in Section 3. On average, the processor fetches one trace every two cycles. The first instruction of a typical trace starts execution three cycles after the trace has been completely fetched, and it takes about 20 cycles for all instructions in the trace to begin executing.

As clearly illustrated by the figure, traces are fetched consecutively but their execution is almost entirely concurrent. This is not an entirely unexpected result: previous work has shown that significant parallelism exists between instructions of different traces [20]. Therefore, the actual order in which instructions are executed is very different from their order in the program. First, a small number of data-independent instructions in both traces get

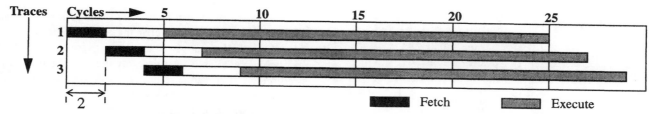

Figure 1. Temporal relationship between instructions in consecutive traces

executed, followed by the rest of the instructions in the traces in dataflow order.

Even though a trace cache can fetch an entire trace in one cycle, all instructions in the trace are *not needed* in that cycle since only a small fraction will be executed immediately. Wide fetch is inefficient for out-of-order processors since instructions are not needed in sequential order. A few instructions from each trace that are first in dataflow order are the ones needed earliest, followed later by the rest of the instructions in the trace. Wide fetch mechanisms must fetch not only the critical instructions that are first in dataflow order, but also all the intervening instructions.

We propose a fetch mechanism that fetches multiple traces concurrently using multiple narrow instruction sequencers instead of one wide sequencer. Since multiple traces are fetched concurrently, the individual instructions are fetched out-of-order. Narrow sequencers use the available bandwidth more effectively since fewer fetch slots are wasted due to branches and cache-line boundaries. Moreover, just like out-of-order execution is able to overlap long latency operations with other useful instructions, out-of-order fetch can tolerate instruction supply delays like I-cache misses by fetching other useful instructions while the miss is resolved. This mechanism can be thought of as just-in-time trace constructor [8] that can build multiple traces concurrently.

We also observed that programs display a remarkably large amount of trace locality. In some benchmarks as many as 70% of the dynamic traces repeat within the next sixteen traces. It may be better to reuse the constructed traces rather than discarding them immediately after use. This turns our mechanism into a small trace cache with a very fast trace construction mechanism. Whereas a trace cache can exploit almost all the locality that is available, it is slow at constructing traces; this mechanism can exploit a smaller amount of locality, but can construct traces quickly. Reusing trace buffers also has the advantage of reducing accesses to the instruction cache by more than 80% in some cases and 50% on average.

Multiple sequencers also make it possible to use the fetch unit in far more flexible ways than a monolithic fetch unit would allow. It is much easier to implement

techniques like dual-path execution [5,10], speculative threads [22], etc., that require fetching multiple threads. In a multithreaded processor, multiple sequencers enable a much finer grained control over allocation of fetch resources to threads than is possible otherwise.

The next section describes our mechanism in detail. Section 3 contains an evaluation of the proposed mechanism. We discuss some related work in Section 4. Section 5 concludes the paper with a summary and some future research directions.

2 Instruction Fetch with Multiple Sequencers

The conventional approach of fetching instructions from the location pointed to by the program counter is insufficient for fetching instructions from multiple points in the program. To be able to fetch from multiple locations, we must know the addresses of multiple instructions in the near future rather than just a single current address.

Instead of keeping track of control flow at the granularity of individual instructions we divide the instruction stream into coarser units called traces. A *trace* is a dynamic sequence of instructions in program order, potentially spanning control instructions. Control flow can be predicted on the granularity of traces using a trace predictor [11,16]. It has been demonstrated that trace predictors can achieve equivalent or higher prediction accuracies than conventional branch predictors [7].

Once future control flow can be predicted at trace granularity, multiple traces can be fetched concurrently by using multiple instruction sequencers. This parallelizes instruction fetch: the latency and the width of a single instruction sequencer are no longer the primary determinants of the fetch bandwidth since it is straightforward to add more instruction sequencers to increase the total raw fetch bandwidth.

2.1 Design Details

The architecture we are proposing is illustrated in Figure 2. The instruction fetch queue (IFQ) between the fetch and decode stages is preceded by a set of trace buffers. The fetch unit is replicated, and fetched instructions are placed in trace buffers rather than directly

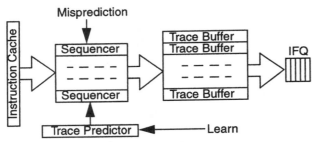

Figure 2. Multiple Sequencers

in the IFQ. A trace predictor is used for control prediction instead of a branch predictor. The L1 instruction cache is banked so that multiple sequencers can fetch instructions concurrently. Bank accesses are controlled by a bank access controller that receives requests for cache accesses, converts these requests into a sequence of bank accesses, and schedules the accesses in order to avoid conflicts. All pipeline stages after the IFQ are unchanged.

Each trace buffer is a small FIFO queue of instructions. Associated with it is a set of registers that describe its *fetch context*: a starting address, a program counter (PC), branch prediction bits, and bits indicating whether the buffer is valid and active. A buffer is *valid* when it contains a trace not completely consumed by the IFQ. A valid buffer is *active* if instructions are still being fetched into it, i.e., if the trace being fetched into it has not been constructed completely. All valid trace buffers are linked to each other by a sequence of next-trace pointers.

Instructions are fetched into active trace buffers starting at the address pointed to by each buffer's PC. Each trace buffer's PC is updated as usual when instructions are fetched into it. The IFQ reads instructions out of the oldest trace buffer and follows the next trace pointer when it encounters the end of the current trace. Once all instructions in the trace are inserted into the IFQ, the trace buffer is marked invalid.

2.2 Fetch Unit

When a program starts executing, the fetch unit fetches instructions sequentially, as usual, and places them in an available trace buffer instead of the instruction fetch queue. It also checks each instruction fetched for trace termination conditions. At the end of the trace, it obtains a new trace buffer, links it to the old one, and marks the old buffer inactive. Then, it continues fetching instructions sequentially into the new trace buffer.

On a trace prediction, the fetch unit obtains a new trace buffer and adds it to the end of the chain of valid buffers. When multiple trace buffers are active, instructions are fetched into all of them simultaneously if enough sequencers are available.

A new trace buffer can be created in the following ways: first, when the trace predictor makes a prediction, and second, by fall through from the previous trace if no prediction is available. A third way is when the fetch unit is redirected after a misprediction—this will be discussed in Section 2.6. Branches are assumed not-taken if predictions are not available.

Instruction fetch into different buffers is completely decoupled. Stalls in one buffer do not affect the other active buffers. Trace end points may be reached in an order completely different from program order. The IFQ still receives the instructions in program order, so no changes are needed to the machine beyond the IFQ, except for some mechanisms for recovering from mispredictions and training the trace predictor.

2.3 Banked Instruction Cache

To enable multiple sequencers to fetch instructions concurrently, the instruction cache must be able to supply multiple cache lines in the same cycle. Although this can be achieved by multiporting the cache so that multiple lines can be read out of a single bank in the same cycle, that would substantially increase the size of the cache, slow it down, and increase its power consumption. We instead achieve the same effect by banking the cache and adding a bank access controller that schedules access to the banks.

Lines are mapped to banks using standard low-order interleaving. The bank access controller services requests in oldest-trace-first order, servicing at most one request from each sequencer in a cycle.

2.4 Trace Selection and Prediction

Good trace selection involves balancing several contradictory requirements. First, the traces must be reasonably long. At the same time, traces should be terminated at the end of control structures like loops and functions to increase the prediction accuracy and decrease the number of unique traces. However, we don't want to stop traces at each control instruction since being able to fetch past control instructions is one of the primary motivations for building traces.

We use function boundaries as the primary division, along with some other constraints to ensure reasonable size, high prediction accuracy, and a small working set. The reader is referred to other papers [11,17] for a more detailed exploration of trace selection techniques.

2.4.1 Trace Selection. We limit the size of traces to 16 instructions. Traces are terminated if (1) they are too long, (2) a call, return, or indirect branch is encountered, or (3) the trace is longer than eight instructions and an unconditional branch is encountered.

Table 1: Trace Characteristics of SPEC 2000 Benchmarks

Benchmark	Dynamic Instructions	Traces	Average Trace Size	Dynamic Traces	Traces Contributing 95% instructions
Integer					
bzip2	8822 M	1819	12.79	690 M	109 (6%)
crafty	4265 M	7541	12.02	355 M	909 (12%)
gap	1246 M	9074	10.70	117 M	972 (11%)
gcc	2016 M	38180	11.26	179 M	7165 (19%)
gzip	3367 M	1942	12.06	279 M	58 (3%)
mcf	260 M	1424	9.84	26 M	132 (9%)
parser	4203 M	6496	10.35	406 M	692 (11%)
Floating Point					
ammp	5491 M	2932	13.11	419 M	332 (11%)
equake	1443 M	2182	11.10	130 M	356 (16%)
lucas	3689 M	1090	15.68	235 M	130 (7%)
mesa	2845 M	2543	11.30	252 M	110 (4%)

Terminating traces at calls/returns and indirect branches enables using a return address stack (RAS) and an indirect branch predictor to supplement the trace predictor, significantly increasing prediction accuracy (see Section 2.4.3 for details). Terminating traces at all unconditional branches when the trace is longer than eight instructions reduces the number of unique traces in the program since traces tend to start at fewer points. This leads to higher prediction accuracy and smaller trace cache miss rate.

Table 1 lists the trace characteristics of the SPEC CPU 2000 benchmarks used in this study. Most benchmarks have a fairly small number of static traces. Integer benchmarks have more traces, as well as smaller traces, than floating point benchmarks. As the last column shows, the number of traces that execute frequently is a small percentage of the number of traces in all benchmarks, and a relatively small absolute number for all benchmarks except gcc.

2.4.2 Trace Prediction. We use the trace predictor proposed by Jacobson et al. [7]. Each trace is assigned a trace identifier obtained by combining bits from the starting address of the trace and its branch history. The predictor consists of a correlated table indexed by trace identifiers of the previous traces, and a smaller filtering table to eliminate the easy to predict traces from the primary table. The trace predictor is based on the Multiscalar task predictor named "DOLC" [1].

Each entry in the predictor contains the starting address of the trace, a bitmap encoding the directions of conditional branches, and bits indicating whether the trace ends with a function call, return, or indirect branch. In case of a trace ending with a call or indirect branch, the predictor also contains the address of the last instruction. The predictor is indexed by a hash function applied to the

trace history buffer. The predictor is updated in the commit stage as instructions retire.

The letters D, O, L, and C in the name of the predictor stand for the four parameters that define the predictor: the size of the history buffer (or **D**epth), the number of bits extracted from the identifier of **C**urrent trace, the number of bits extracted from the identifier of **L**ast trace, and the number of bits extracted from the identifiers of **O**lder traces. We use the values D=9, C=9, L=7, and O=4. The primary table contains 64k lines and the secondary table 16k lines. Figure 3 shows both the trace prediction accuracy and the branch prediction accuracy of the predictor.

2.4.3 Returns and Indirect Branches. Since instructions are being fetched out of order, it is possible for a later return instruction to be fetched before an earlier return instruction. However, return instructions must access the RAS in program order for its predictions to be correct. A similar argument holds for the indirect branch predictor.

We access the RAS or the indirect predictor when traces are predicted. Traces can contain at most one call, return, or indirect branch since these instructions end traces. The trace predictor predicts whether a trace will end with these instructions, and the address of the instruction if required. Since traces are predicted in program order, the RAS and the indirect branch predictor are accessed in program order as well.

Restoring predictor state on mispredictions is handled by making a copy of any data that is modified, just like in conventional out-of-order processor. When the last instruction of a trace is fetched, the prediction is verified. On mispredictions, the predictor state is repaired by restoring it to the backed up value and then redoing the modifications made by future traces.

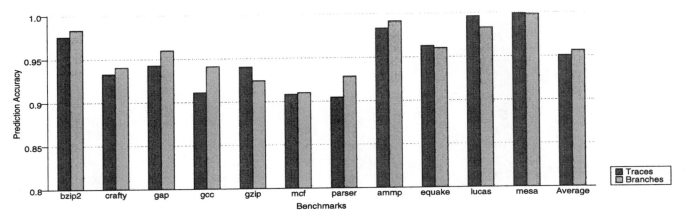

Figure 3. Trace and Branch Prediction Accuracy

2.5 Trace Reuse

The technique as described above discards instructions in trace buffers once they have been decoded. An alternative is to keep instructions in the buffer and to reuse buffers if control flow reaches the same trace again. If there is sufficient locality in the instruction stream, trace reuse could lead to an improvement in performance as well as a reduction in cache/memory traffic.

Reduced cache traffic makes the performance much more robust in the presence of bank conflicts. It also reduces the power consumed by the L1 instruction cache. However, it may not lead to an net reduction in power usage as compared to a processor without multiple sequencers, since the reduction is offset by the power consumed by trace buffers.

2.6 Recovering from Branch Mispredictions

On a branch misprediction, in addition to simply redirecting the fetch unit, the current fetch context must be restored so that (1) the trace selection algorithm does not get misaligned, and (2) the trace identifier history remains accurate. This can be done with mechanisms that already exist in all processors for restoring the global branch history after mispredictions.

Some mispredictions can be detected in the fetch stage itself by comparing the PC following the last instruction in a trace to the predicted next trace. In case of a mismatch, all future traces are marked invalid. Early detection of such mispredictions allows earlier recovery, and reduces the number of spurious instructions fetched and executed.

2.7 Out-of-Order Renaming

Once the instructions are being fetched out of order, it is desirable to be able to execute independent instructions from a later trace before previous traces have been fetched completely. This requires renaming instructions out of

order. We believe that a solution similar to those proposed by Stark et al. [19] and Cher et al. [3] can be used to solve this problem.

The trace predictor can be augmented to predict a *rename mask* that identifies independent instructions. This mask can be used to selectively execute only these instructions until all prior traces have been fetched. Delayed instructions can be renamed when all their sources are available. Alternatively, they can be renamed speculatively, and on a misspeculation the source register values can copied into the predicted physical registers after execution of the source instructions.

This paper concentrates only on the fetch component of the instruction supply problem. We do not evaluate out-of-order renaming in this paper.

3 Experimental Evaluation

We used a simulator based on the SimpleScalar toolset [2] to model a multiple sequencer based fetch mechanism. Parameters of the base-case processor are shown in Table 2. We simulate a 16-wide processor with large caches to ensure that it can achieve high IPC, and can therefore benefit from high bandwidth instruction fetch. Large caches also ensure that the conventional instruction fetch mechanism works as well as possible, which shows that the performance improvement due to multiple sequencers cannot simply be achieved by enlarging the instruction cache.

All benchmarks were taken from the SPEC CPU 2000 suite and compiled with optimization using the Compaq/Alpha vendor compiler (version 6.4-214). Test inputs were used, and the programs were simulated for at most one billion instructions. Table 1 lists some characteristics of the benchmarks. We used only a subset of the benchmarks because of limitations in the simulator: (1) many floating point programs produced output that did not match the

Table 2: Simulation Parameters

Width	Fetch, decode and commit at most 16 instructions per cycle
Functional Units	16 integer ALUs, 4 integer multipliers, 4 floating point ALUs, 1 floating point multiplier, 4 load/store units
In-flight Instructions	256 entry instruction window 128 entry load/store queue
L1 Caches (Insn & Data)	64K, 2-way set-associative, 1 cycle access time, 64b blocks
L2 Cache (Unified)	256K, 4-way set-associative, 10 cycle access time, 128 byte blocks
Memory	100 cycle access time

reference output because of differences in the behavior of floating point instructions, (2) no support for the exec system call, and (3) problems related to Fortran runtime libraries.

We compare three different instruction fetch mechanisms: conventional 16-wide fetch (**W16**), trace cache (**TC**), and multiple sequencers (**MS**). **W16** fetches instructions sequentially, stopping at the first taken branch or cache line boundary. The number of branch predictions per cycle is unlimited. **TC** models a 2-way set associative trace cache with 16 instructions per trace. On a cache hit, the entire trace can be fetched in one cycle if there are sufficient slots in the instruction fetch queue. On a cache miss, instructions are fetched from the L1 instruction cache using the **W16** mechanism. The processor contains an L1 instruction cache of the same size as the trace cache. We found that this division gave better results than a large trace cache without an L1 instruction cache. In one cycle, instructions can be fetched from either the trace cache, or the L1 instruction cache, but not both. The trace predictor is described in Section 2.4. The total size of the level one instruction storage is kept the same whenever two schemes are compared (i.e. when **TC** is compared to **W16**, the sum of the size of the trace cache and L1 instruction cache in **TC** is equal to the size of the L1 instruction cache in **W16**).

The various **MS** configurations are labeled using the convention **MS-NxMw** where N is the number of sequencers and M the width of each sequencer. For example, **MS-2x8w** denotes two 8-wide sequencers. There are 16 trace buffers of 16 instructions each. The instruction cache is divided into eight banks as described in Section 2.3. The trace predictor and the trace selection algorithm are identical to those used by **TC**. The trace predictor can make one prediction every cycle. New trace buffers are activated on predictions made by the predictor regardless of the number of buffers already active.

Sequencers are assigned to trace buffers in oldest first order. The L1 instruction cache is the same as in **W16**.

The results section is structured as follows. First, in Section 3.1, we study the effect of multiple sequencers on instruction cache traffic. In Section 3.2 we compare the performance of multiple sequencers with conventional instruction sequencing and trace caches. Finally, in Section 3.3 we study the behavior of these mechanisms under high cache miss rates.

3.1 Instruction Cache Traffic

When building a high bandwidth fetch unit, it is inevitable that the number of instructions fetched will be much greater than the number of committed instructions, due to fetching down mispredicted paths. An over-eager fetch mechanism may increase memory traffic and worsen instruction cache performance, doing more harm than good.

Figure 4 shows the number of instructions fetched by **W16**, **TC**, and **MS** without trace reuse, normalized by the number of committed instructions. The number of instructions fetched is equal to the total number of instructions read from the L1 cache for **W16** and **MS**, and the sum of the number of instructions fetched from the L1 cache and the trace cache for **TC**. Floating point benchmarks show only a small increase in the number of instructions fetched. Integer benchmarks show a relatively higher increase of 40% on average. This is comparable to the number of extra instructions fetched by a trace cache.

Figure 5 presents the same data as Figure 4, except that trace reuse is now enabled. Trace reuse directly translates into reduced cache traffic, since the instructions corresponding to reused traces do not have to be fetched from the instruction cache. Cache traffic is reduced dramatically—by 50% over all benchmarks on average, and by more than 80% for four benchmarks (bzip2, gzip, mcf, and ammp). The trace buffers act as a filter cache [9,15] making the number of instructions fetched from the cache smaller than the number of instructions executed in most cases.

Interestingly, two benchmarks that benefit the most from trace reuse, gzip and mcf, are also the ones that had the most wasted instructions without trace reuse. This suggests that most of the mispredictions in them are due to a small number of traces that occur frequently, but are hard to predict—for example, an unpredictable switch statement in a long running loop.

3.2 Performance

As discussed earlier, one way of thinking about this technique is that it constructs traces *just in time* so that by the time control reaches a trace the entire trace has already been constructed. If this happens often, this scheme will

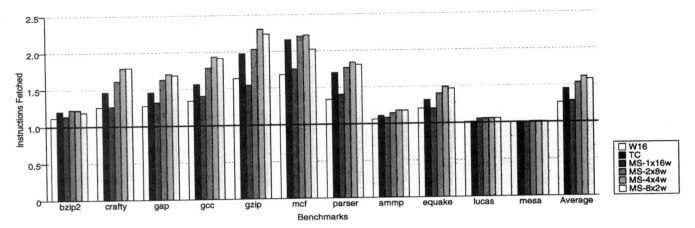

Figure 4. Extra Instructions fetched (without Trace Reuse)

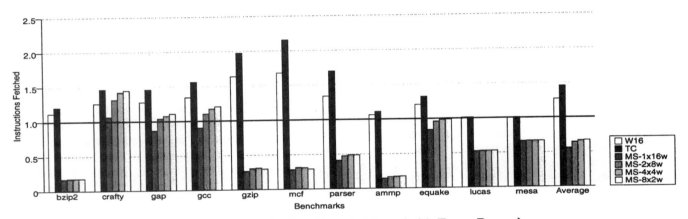

Figure 5. Extra Instructions fetched (with Trace Reuse)

provide the illusion of a trace cache, and therefore will perform as well as a trace cache. In fact, it is likely that in that case **MS** will perform better than a trace cache, since a trace cache requires both predictability as well as locality in the sequence of traces, whereas **MS** requires only predictability since traces are constructed on the fly.

Figure 6 shows the fraction of traces pre-constructed completely before they are needed. On average, 85% of the traces are successfully pre-constructed. The graph also demonstrates the effectiveness of multiple narrow sequencers: **MS-1x16w** is able to construct only 60% of the traces in time, and as the number of sequencers increases the number of successfully constructed traces increases.

Figure 7 directly compares the performance of different fetch mechanisms, normalized by the performance of **W16**. **MS-2x8w** performs better than **TC** on the average, and **MS-4x4w** performs as well as **TC**. **TC** performs poorly on the benchmarks `gcc` and `crafty` since both these benchmarks have a large number of frequently executed

traces, whereas **MS**, which uses cache space more efficiently, performs well. **TC** performs comparably to **MS** on both these benchmarks if the trace cache size is increased.

Performance decreases as the width of the fetch unit decreases, especially when the fetch unit is narrower than four. Multiple narrow fetch units rely on being able to predict future traces ahead of time, and the probability of misprediction increases as traces are predicted further into the future. For example, eight two-wide fetch units would be able to maintain instruction supply only if it were possible to accurately predict the next eight traces at all points in the program. If the trace prediction accuracy is 95%, the eighth trace has a one in three ($1 - 0.95^8 = 0.34$) chance of being mispredicted.

The integer benchmarks show more benefit from high bandwidth fetch than floating point programs. Improving instruction fetch bandwidth does not help floating point programs since they are usually limited by large instruction latencies (cache misses, floating point operations).

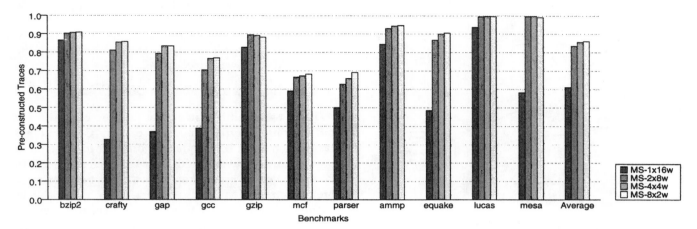

Figure 6. Pre-constructed traces

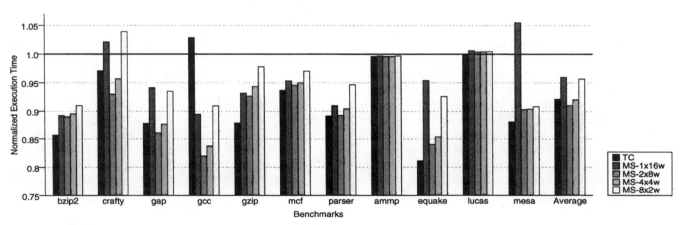

Figure 7. Performance

3.3 Instruction Cache Size

Figure 8 shows the performance of **W16**, **TC** and **MS** over a range of instruction cache sizes. The figure plots execution time normalized to **W16** with a 64K instruction cache. **TC** suffers the most as the cache becomes smaller, since efficient use of cache space is more critical with small caches. **W16** outperforms **TC** at cache sizes of less than 16K.

The four **MS** schemes provide the most robust performance, slowing down less than 10% even when the cache is one-eighth in size. Multiple sequencers are able to utilize the available cache space more efficiently since they do not have the storage overheads associated with trace caches. In case an L1 cache miss does occur, they are better at tolerating the miss latency since other instructions can be fetched while the miss is handled, and multiple misses can be overlapped with each other.

MS-1x16w behaves as robustly as the other **MS** schemes, even though it cannot fetch multiple traces in parallel. This suggests that it is the ability to initiate multiple cache misses in parallel that is the important factor in tolerating small cache sizes.

4 Related Work

Stark et al. [19] proposed a limited form of out-of-order instruction fetch for tolerating instruction cache misses, and proposed several ways of out-of-order renaming. Unlike the technique described in this paper, instruction fetch proceeded normally during most of the execution. Instructions were fetched out-of-order only on cache misses.

Trace preconstruction was proposed by Jacobson et al. [8] to decrease the number of trace cache misses on programs with large working sets. Their focus was constructing a set of traces well ahead of the current trace so that when control reached that point in the future it would suffer no trace cache misses. Their technique maintains a stack containing entries corresponding to the

21

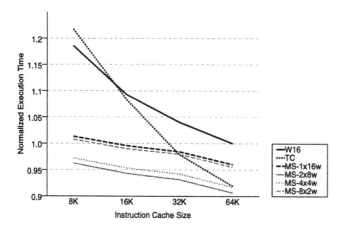

Figure 8. Performance variation with I-cache size

hierarchical structure of functions and loops in the program. The stack is used to identify potential preconstruction points many cycles ahead of when they are needed. In contrast, our scheme uses a standard trace predictor to make predictions and tries to stay just a little ahead of the processor. These two factors are related: the reason we are able to use a standard trace predictor is that we only predict control flow in the immediate future. Unlike the aim of trace preconstruction—prefetching potential trace cache misses—our scheme takes the idea to its limit by making the cache very small and constructing all the traces just before control flow reaches them.

Fetch Target Queue [14] was proposed by Reinman et al. to decouple instruction fetch from the rest of the execution pipeline. Their scheme predicts targets of future branches in advance of when the branches are fetched and inserts the target addresses in the fetch target queue. This queue can then be used for prefetching cache blocks that are not present in the level one instruction cache. However, the fetch bandwidth of the processor is still limited by the density of taken branches in the instruction stream.

Speculative multithreading architectures like Multiscalar [1,18] come closest to this technique as far as the nature of instruction fetch is concerned. They typically consist of multiple execution cores, each of which has a fetch unit and a trace/task predictor that assigns traces to cores. Since each execution core fetches instructions it needs by itself, instructions are fetched as and when they are needed, in an order different from program order. The technique proposed in this paper decouples the decision to build clustered fetch units from the decision to build clustered execution cores.

Another approach to high bandwidth fetch is changing the code layout to correspond more closely to the desired fetch order. Ramirez et al. proposed a profile based compiler optimization called a *Software Trace Cache* [13]

that rearranges basic blocks in the program so that the instruction cache stores continuous traces of instructions, just like a trace cache. Their results show that the best performance is achieved by a combination of both the hardware and software trace cache.

5 Conclusions and Future Directions

High bandwidth instruction fetch is essential for building high performance processors. Conventional instruction fetch techniques are difficult to scale up to provide this extra bandwidth since the fetch unit needs to be redirected on each taken branch. Trace caches are a brute force solution to this problem. They are capable of supplying instructions at a very high rate but are expensive in terms of their area requirements since they utilize cache space inefficiently.

Sequencing through the program at the granularity of traces and fetching multiple traces simultaneously by using a replicated fetch unit can be used to get the best of both worlds: fetch bandwidth of a trace cache, and the storage efficiency of an instruction cache. Trace-granularity sequencing decouples the fetch of different parts of the program from each other, and this decoupling enables parallelizing instruction fetch by using multiple sequential instruction sequencers. We described the design of such a fetch unit in detail and demonstrated that it is capable of achieving similar fetch bandwidth to a trace cache, and, at the same time, decreasing the number of instructions fetched from the instruction cache.

Our results also suggest that multiple sequencers are more resilient to larger I-cache miss rates than a trace cache. An important area of future work is evaluating this mechanism in the context of future technology trends like variable latency caches, longer access times and power consumption restrictions. We expect that multiple sequencers will turn out to be a good fit for the requirements of future processors.

Fetching instructions out of order is only half the battle, since even when instructions are fetched out of order they simply wait in a buffer for instructions before them to be fetched before they can be executed. In the future, we plan to relax this restriction as well by renaming instructions out-of-order and issuing them to execution units without requiring all prior instructions to be fetched.

6 Acknowledgements

We would like to thank Adam Butts, Brian Fields, Manoj Plakal, and Ravi Rajwar for commenting on drafts of this paper. This work was supported in part by National Science Foundation grants CCR-9900584 and EIA-0071924, donations from Intel and Sun Microsystems, and the University of Wisconsin Graduate School.

7 References

[1] S. Breach. *Design and Evaluation of a Multiscalar Processor*. PhD thesis, University of Wisconsin-Madison, 1998.

[2] D. C. Burger and T. M. Austin. The SimpleScalar Tool Set, Version 2.0. Technical Report CS-TR-97-1342, University of Wisconsin-Madison, Jun. 1997.

[3] C-Y. Cher and T. N. Vijaykumar. Skipper: A Microarchitecture For Exploiting Control-flow Independence. In *Proceedings of the 34th Annual International Symposium on Microarchitecture*, Austin, Texas, Dec. 2–5, 2001.

[4] T. M. Conte, K. N. Menezes, P. M. Mills, and B. A. Patel. Optimization of Instruction Fetch Mechanisms for High Issue Rates. In *Proceedings of the 22nd Annual International Symposium on Computer Architecture*, pages 333–344, Santa Margherita Ligure, Italy, June 22–24, 1995.

[5] T. Heil and J. E. Smith. Selective Dual Path Execution. Technical report, University of Wisconsin-Madison, Nov. 1996.

[6] J. L. Hennessy and D. A. Patterson. *Computer Architecture: A Quantitative Approach*. Morgan Kaufmann, second edition, 1996.

[7] Q. Jacobson, E. Rotenberg, and J. E. Smith. Path-Based Next Trace Prediction. In *Proceedings of the 30th Annual International Symposium on Microarchitecture*, pages 14–23, Research Triangle Park, North Carolina, Dec. 1–3, 1997.

[8] Q. Jacobson and J. E. Smith. Trace Preconstruction. In *Proceedings of the 27th Annual International Symposium on Computer Architecture*, pages 37–46, Vancouver, British Columbia, June 12–14, 2000.

[9] J. Kin, M. Gupta, and W. H. Mangione-Smith. The Filter Cache: An Energy Efficient Memory Structure. In *Proceedings of the 30th Annual International Symposium on Microarchitecture*, pages 184–193, Research Triangle Park, North Carolina, Dec. 1–3, 1997.

[10] M. J. Knieser and C. A. Papachristou. Y-Pipe: A Conditional Branching Scheme without Pipeline Delays. In *Proceedings of the 25th Annual International Symposium on Microarchitecture*, pages 125–128, Portland, Oregon, Dec. 1–4, 1992.

[11] S. J. Patel, D. H. Friendly, and Y. N. Patt. Critical Issues Regarding the Trace Cache Fetch Mechanism. Technical Report CSE-TR-335-97, Department of Electrical Engineering and Computer Science, University of Michigan, May 1997.

[12] A. Peleg and U. Weiser. Dynamic Flow Instruction Cache Memory Organized Around Trace Segments Independent of Virtual Address Line, March 30, 1994. US Patent 5,381,533.

[13] A. Ramirez, J-L. Larriba-Pey, C. Navarro, J. Torrellas, and M. Valero. Software Trace Cache. In *Proceedings of the 1999 international conference on Supercomputing*, pages 119–126, Rhodes, Greece, 1999.

[14] G. Reinman, B. Calder, and T. M. Austin. Optimizations Enabled by a Decoupled Front-End Architecture. *IEEE Transactions on Computers*, 50(4):338–355, Apr. 2001.

[15] R. Rosner, A. Mendelson, and R. Ronen. Filtering Techniques to Improve Trace-Cache Efficiency. In *Proceedings of the 10th International Conference on Parallel Architectures and Compilation Techniques*, Barcelona, Spain, Sep. 8–12, 2001.

[16] E. Rotenberg, S. Bennett, and J. E. Smith. Trace Cache: A Low Latency Approach to High Bandwidth Instruction Fetching. In *Proceedings of the 29th Annual International Symposium on Microarchitecture*, pages 24–34, Paris, France, Dec. 2–4, 1996.

[17] E. Rotenberg, Q. Jacobson, Y. Sazeides, and J. E. Smith. Trace Processors. In *Proc. 30th International Symposium on Microarchitecture*, pages 138–148, Dec. 1997.

[18] G. S. Sohi, S. Breach, and T. N. Vijaykumar. Multiscalar Processors. In *Proc. 22nd International Symposium on Computer Architecture*, pages 414–425, Jun. 1995.

[19] J. Stark, P. Racunas, and Y. N. Patt. Reducing the Performance Impact of Instruction Cache Misses by Writing Instructions into the Reservation Stations Out-of-Order. In *Proceedings of the 30th Annual International Symposium on Microarchitecture*, pages 34–43, Research Triangle Park, North Carolina, Dec. 1–3, 1997.

[20] S. Vajapeyam and T. Mitra. Improving Superscalar Instruction Dispatch and Issue by Exploiting Dynamic Code Sequences. In *Proceedings of the 24th Annual International Symposium on Computer Architecture*, pages 1–12, Denver, Colorado, June 2–4, 1997.

[21] T-Y. Yeh, D. T. Marr, and Y. N. Patt. Increasing the Instruction Fetch Rate via Multiple Branch Prediction and a Branch Address Cache. In *Conference Proceedings, 1993 International Conference on Supercomputing*, pages 67–76, Tokyo, July 20–22, 1993.

[22] C. B. Zilles and G. S. Sohi. Execution-Based Prediction Using Speculative Slices. In *Proceedings of the 28th Annual International Symposium on Computer Architecture*, pages 2–13, Göteborg, Sweden, Jun. 30–July 4, 2001.

Session 1B

Parallelizing Compilers

Exploiting Locality in the Run-Time Parallelization of Irregular Loops *

María J. Martín[‡], David E. Singh[†], Juan Touriño[‡], and Francisco F. Rivera[†]

[‡]Dept. of Electronics and Systems, University of A Coruña, Spain

[†]Dept. of Electronics and Computer Science, University of Santiago de Compostela, Spain

mariam@udc.es, david@dec.usc.es, juan@udc.es, fran@dec.usc.es

Abstract

The goal of this work is the efficient parallel execution of loops with indirect array accesses, in order to be embedded in a parallelizing compiler framework. In this kind of loop pattern, dependences can not always be determined at compile-time as, in many cases, they involve input data that are only known at run-time and/or the access pattern is too complex to be analyzed. In this paper we propose run-time strategies for the parallelization of these loops. Our approaches focus not only on extracting parallelism among iterations of the loop, but also on exploiting data access locality to improve memory hierarchy behavior and, thus, the overall program speedup. Two strategies are proposed: one based on graph partitioning techniques and other based on a block-cyclic distribution. Experimental results show that both strategies are complementary and the choice of the best alternative depends on some features of the loop pattern.

1. Introduction

The aim of this work is the parallelization of loops with indirect array accesses, which commonly appear in scientific and engineering applications: sparse matrix programs, fluid flow and molecular dynamics simulations, finite element codes... A generic case of such loop is shown in Figure 1, where arrays $I1$ and $I2$ can take any integer value. Any dependence can appear inside the loop: RAW (true data dependence), WAW (output dependence) or WAR (anti-dependence). On the one hand, if there are no loop-carried dependences, we have a DOALL loop, which can be easily parallelized to achieve the desired speedup. On the other hand, DOACROSS loops have dependences across iterations and they have to be executed in succession or, if we want to extract some parallelism, synchronization primitives should be inserted at appropriate points in the code to guarantee the order of accesses imposed by dependences.

```
DO i = 1,N
    ...
    ... = A(I1(i)) op ...
    ...
    A(I2(i)) = ...
    ...
ENDDO
```

Figure 1. Loop with indirect array accesses

There are, in the literature, a number of run-time approaches for the parallelization of this kind of loops. All of them focus on extracting the maximum degree of parallelism from the loop and reducing the overhead of the run-time analysis. Our approach not only maximizes parallelism, but also increases data locality to better exploit memory hierarchy in order to improve code performance. The target computer assumed throughout this paper is a CC-NUMA shared memory machine. We intend to increase cache line reuse in each processor and to reduce false sharing of cache lines, which is an important factor of performance degradation in CC-NUMA architectures.

Although for illustrative purposes the loop of Figure 1 (with one read and one write per iteration) will be used as case study, our method is a generic approach that can also be applied to loops with more than one indirect read access per iteration. One particular case of our scope is the irregular reduction pattern. However, as it frequently appears in real codes and it presents special characteristics, it is better to use efficient specific strategies for the parallel execution of this kind of pattern, such as the ones described in [6][19].

The work is organized as follows: in Section 2 we review other approaches for the parallelization of loops with indirect array accesses, stressing similarities and differences between those strategies and our proposals. Next, we describe in Section 3 our methods, based on an inspector-executor strategy. In Section 4 the performance of the strategies are analyzed and compared with another method through detailed experimental results. Section 5 presents related work; specifically, we focus on related research on data locality exploitation and improvement in memory hierarchy performance. Finally, concluding remarks are given in Section 6.

*This work was funded by the Ministry of Science and Technology of Spain and FEDER funds of the European Union (ref. TIC2001-3694-C02)

2. Previous works

The methods to parallelize this kind of loops can be basically classified into two major groups: speculative execution and inspector-executor strategies.

In the speculative execution methods [5] [16], the loop is executed in parallel at the same time that dependences are analyzed. If the analysis determines that the loop is not parallel, the whole computation is rolled back and the loop is executed serially. The main drawback of this strategy is the associated overhead when the loop is not parallel.

In the inspector-executor strategy, the inspector determines data dependences at run-time, and the executor runs loop iterations in parallel following the order fixed by the dependences. One of the first inspector-executor approaches was proposed by Zhu and Yew [23]: loop iterations are divided into subsets called *wavefronts*, which contain iterations that can be executed in parallel. This approach has two limitations: first, inspector and executor are tightly coupled and, thus, the inspector is not reused across invocations of the same loop, even if the dependences do not change. Second, the execution of consecutive reads to the same array entry is serialized (RAR). Midkiff and Padua [15] improve this strategy by allowing concurrent reads of the same entry. Saltz et al. [18] propose an alternative solution but restricted to the particular case of loops with no output dependences. In this strategy, inspector and executor are uncoupled. Leung and Zahorjan [12] extend the previous work to consider output dependences and propose different strategies to parallelize the inspector.

These proposals exploit iteration-level parallelism. A different approach can be found in [2], where finer grain parallelism (operation-level) is exploited also using an inspector-executor method called CYT algorithm. Dependences are analyzed in the inspector phase; if the indirection arrays do not change between invocations of the loop, then the inspector can be reused. In the executor stage, iterations are cyclically distributed among the processors, and each processor goes on with the execution as dependences are fulfilled. Operation-level synchronizations are performed to guarantee a correct execution order. The advantage of this algorithm is the extraction of a higher degree of parallelism.

The goal of all these inspector-executor approaches is to maximize parallelism and minimize the overhead of the analysis phase. A comparison between strategies based on iteration-level and operation-level parallelism is presented in [21]. The strategies were evaluated for loops with different structures, memory access patterns and computational workloads. This work shows experimentally that operation-level methods outperform iteration-level methods.

This paper describes two new operation-level algorithms: Local-CYT (LCYT from now on) and Low Overhead LCYT (LO-LCYT). They are based on the approach developed in [2], but they use different iteration distribution schemes to exploit data locality. The effectiveness of our algorithms is assessed on an SGI Origin 2000 and the results are compared with those obtained with the CYT proposal.

3. LCYT algorithms

Our methods are split in two phases: inspector, where memory accesses are analyzed and an iteration distribution is performed accordingly; and executor, where the assigned iterations are executed in parallel. Both phases are independent, which allows to reuse the dependence information of the inspector if the same loop is executed several times.

3.1. LCYT inspector phase

In this stage memory access and data dependence information is collected. The access information, which determines the iteration partition approach, is stored in a graph structure. Dependence information is stored in a table called *Ticket Table* [2]. The inspector phase consists of three parts:

1. Construction of a graph representing memory accesses. It is a non-directed weighted graph; both nodes and graph edges are weighted. Each node represents m consecutive elements of array A, m being the number of elements of A that fit in a cache line. The weight of each node is the number of iterations that access that node for write. Moreover, each node is assigned a table which contains the indices of those iterations. The edges join nodes that are accessed in the same iteration. Each edge has a weight that corresponds to the number of times that the pair of nodes is accessed in an iteration.

2. Graph partitioning. The graph partitioning will result in a node distribution (and, therefore, an iteration distribution) among processors. Our aim is to partition the graph so that a good node balance is achieved and the number of edges being cut is minimum. Node balance results in load balance and cut minimization involves a decrease in the number of cache invalidations, as well as an increase in cache line reuse. Besides, as each node represents a cache line with consecutive elements of A, false sharing is eliminated. We have used the *pmetis* program [10] from the METIS software package to distribute the nodes among the processors according to the objectives described above. The *pmetis* partitioning algorithm is based on multilevel recursive bisection. The algorithm consists of three stages: in the first stage the size of the graph is reduced by collapsing nodes and edges (*coarsening*). Next, the smaller graph is partitioned. In the third stage the partition is successively projected back towards the original graph (*uncoarsening*).

3. Creation of a Ticket Table containing data dependence information: it is a table $N \times r$, N being the number of loop iterations, and r the number of accesses per iteration to the

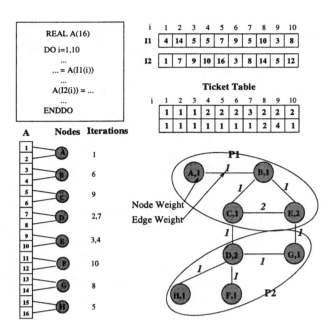

Figure 2. Example of LCYT graph partitioning

target array. In the loop of Figure 1 $r = 2$ because array A has one write and one read access. The table stores the number of times each array entry is accessed. So, for the loop of Figure 1, $TABLE(i, 1)$ represents the number of accesses to element $A(I1(i))$ from the first up to the ith iteration. The creation of the Ticket Table is independent of the graph construction and partitioning, and thus these stages can be performed in parallel.

Figure 2 shows an example of the three steps of the inspector for $N = 10$, an array A of 16 elements, a cache line size of 2 elements and two array accesses per loop iteration ($r = 2$). The figure shows the mapping of array entries in nodes, the generation of the graph using access information, and the graph partitioning for two processors. The corresponding Ticket Table is also depicted.

The graph partitioning is the most costly part of the LCYT inspector. This overhead strongly depends on the number of nodes ($\lceil M/m \rceil$, M being the number of entries of array A) and can be reduced by increasing the number of cache lines of A elements per node (and thus reducing the number of nodes) at the expense of load imbalance.

3.2. LO-LCYT inspector phase

We propose an inspector with lower overhead, named LO-LCYT, that considers a simpler iteration partitioning to optimize memory accesses (although not as good as LCYT). Unlike LCYT, only write accesses are considered for the iteration distribution. The graph construction and partitioning stages of LCYT are then replaced by the following procedure in LO-LCYT. Array A is split into blocks of $m \times l$

consecutive elements of A, l being the number of cache lines considered in the block. Blocks are cyclically assigned and each processor executes the iterations that access the elements of its blocks for write; that is, the iteration distribution is driven by a block-cyclic assignment of array A. The number of iterations assigned to each block are not taken into account for the distribution of blocks; nevertheless, in general, the cyclic distribution provides a good balance. This balance is worse as l increases but, in contrast, data locality is better exploited. The value of l is chosen as a tradeoff between both parameters. The LO-LCYT inspector overhead depends on the number of iterations N and, in general, it is lower than the LCYT partitioning overhead, except for those cases in which $M \ll N$. As in LCYT, the iteration partitioning and the Ticket Table can be calculated in parallel because they are independent tasks.

3.3. Executor phase

The executor is the same for both algorithms and uses the dependence information recorded in the Ticket Table to execute, in each processor, the iterations assigned in the inspector phase. An array reference can be performed if and only if the preceding references are finished. The executor uses a shared variable ($Ready$) to count the number of times each entry of A is accessed. In the course of the executor, before accessing the xth entry of A in the ith iteration for read ($r = 1$) or write ($r = 2$), it is checked if $Ready(x) = TABLE(i, r)$. If not, the processor will wait until the condition is fulfilled and just then, the access is performed and $Ready(x)$ is incremented by one. All array accesses are performed in parallel except for the dependences specified in the Ticket Table. Iterations with dependences can be partially overlapped because we consider dependences between accesses instead of between iterations.

RAR occurrences are serialized, which introduces pseudo-dependences among truly concurrent iterations. Xu and Chaudhary [22] have proposed an improvement to the CYT algorithm that allows concurrent reads of the same array entry. The inclusion of this improvement in our LCYT proposals would be straightforward.

4. Performance evaluation

In this section, the CYT, LCYT and LO-LCYT strategies are compared experimentally. We begin with a description of the experimental conditions in Section 4.1. Our primary concern is to quantitatively assess the improvement in the executor stage by taking into account the access locality. Thus, in Section 4.2 we mainly focus on the executor evaluation in terms of the comparison of performance, cache line reuse, false sharing and load balancing. The effect of the inspector overhead on the results is also discussed.

```
REAL A(M)
DO i = 1,N
    tmp1 = A(INDEX(i*2-1))
    A(INDEX(i*2)) = tmp2
    DO j = 1,W
       dummy loop simulating useful work
    ENDDO
ENDDO
```

Figure 3. Experimental workload

4.1. Experimental conditions

The parallel performance of the irregular loop is mainly characterized by three parameters: loop size, workload cost and access pattern. In order to evaluate their influence on performance, we use the loop pattern shown in Figure 3, following the same approach taken by other authors [2] [22]; N represents the problem size, the computational cost of the loop is simulated by the parameter W and the access pattern is determined by array $INDEX$ and the size of array A.

Examples of this loop pattern appear in the solution of sparse linear systems (e.g. routines $lsol$, $ldsol$ and $ldsoll$ of the Sparskit library [17]), where the loop size and the access pattern depend on the sparse coefficient matrix. These systems are solved in a wide variety of codes: linear programming applications, process simulation, finite element and finite difference applications, optimization problems... Therefore, we have used in our experiments as indirection arrays the patterns of sparse matrices that appear in real codes. These matrices were extracted from the Harwell-Boeing (HB) collection [4]. We have also considered synthetic access patterns to cover a wider range of cases. The patterns (5 HB and 4 synthetic) are characterized in Table 1, where $2 \times N$ is the size of the indirection array $INDEX$ and M is the size of array A. The parameter CP (Critical Path, $1 \leq CP \leq N$) is the length of the longest dependence chain in the loop and gives an estimate of how parallel the loop is (if $CP = 1$ the loop is fully parallel; if $CP = N$ it is fully serial). The rightmost column of Table 1 normalizes CP with respect to the number of iterations N.

Two kinds of synthetic patterns were considered: uniform and non-uniform. The uniform pattern assumes all array elements have the same probability of being accessed. It is denoted as xxx_U in Table 1, xxx being the size of array $INDEX$. The non-uniform pattern (denoted as xxx_90_10) was generated so that 90% of references are only to 10% of array elements. This pattern reflects hot spots in memory accesses and results in longer dependence chains. In all synthetic patterns, $M = 2 \times N$.

The target machine is an SGI Origin 2000 with R10K at 250 MHz. The R10K has a 2-level cache hierarchy with L1 instruction and data caches of 32KB each, and L2 unified cache of 4MB (L2 cache line of 128 bytes). The tests were written in Fortran+OpenMP directives (MIPSpro compiler

Table 1. Benchmark matrices

Matrix	$2 \times N$	M	CP	$CP*100/N$
gemat1	47368	4929	4938	20.85
gemat12	33110	4929	49	0.30
mbeacxc	49920	496	487	1.95
beaflw	53402	507	500	1.87
psmigr_2	540022	3140	2626	0.97
25600_U	25600	25600	9	0.07
25600_90_10	25600	25600	45	0.35
51200_U	51200	51200	11	0.04
51200_90_10	51200	51200	46	0.18

with -O3 optimization level), and executed in single-user mode. All data structures were cache aligned. In our experiments, the cost per iteration, W, of loop i of Figure 3 can be modeled as $T(W) \approx 8 \times 10^{-5} \times (1 + W)$ ms. W depends on the application; typical values range from 5 to 30 using HB matrices for the loop patterns of the aforementioned Sparskit routines that solve sparse linear systems.

4.2. Experimental results

Figure 4 shows the reduction in the execution times by applying the LCYT and LO-LCYT algorithms as compared to the CYT method for some of the matrices. LCYT(n) means that each node represents n cache lines of A elements; LO-LCYT(n) takes blocks of size n cache lines. As expected, LCYT partitioning is better for a finer node definition (that is, only one line per node). Regarding LO-LCYT, the best results are obtained, in general, for blocks of two lines, being a tradeoff between load balancing and memory reuse. It can also be observed that, as the LCYT partitioning analyzes not only write accesses, but also read accesses, it improves the results of the LO-LCYT method.

The largest reductions are obtained in loops with small computational cost per iteration (W) because, in this kind of loops, memory accesses to array A have a greater influence on the overall execution time. As W increases, the improvement falls (it can even be negative) because load balancing and waiting times become critical factors for performance.

We define the load balancing parameter for p processors as $bal = N/(p \times itmax)$, $0 < bal \leq 1$, where N is the number of iterations and $itmax$ the maximum number of iterations assigned to one processor. As CYT distributes iterations cyclically, load is always balanced. Table 2 presents bal values for $p=8$ using the different algorithms. In general, load balancing obtained for our test matrices is very good, except for those ones with small M. For instance, the size of array A is over 500 elements for matrices $mbeacxc$ and $beaflw$, which results in a small number of nodes (in LCYT) and blocks (in LO-LCYT) and, therefore, it is difficult to obtain an optimal distribution.

The reduction in the execution times illustrated in Figure 4 is a consequence of the improvement in data locality

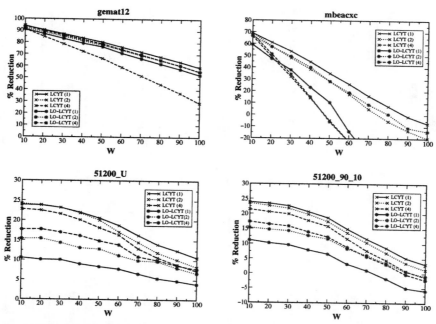

Figure 4. Percentage of reduction in execution times on 8 processors for some test matrices

Table 2. Load balancing of LCYT/LO-LCYT

	LCYT(n)			LO-LCYT(n)		
	$n=1$	$n=2$	$n=4$	$n=1$	$n=2$	$n=4$
gemat1	.971	.912	.854	.948	.941	.920
gemat12	.985	.918	.822	.956	.953	.922
mbeacxc	.639	.550	.331	.555	.643	.336
beaflw	.582	.553	.332	.568	.644	.338
psmigr_2	.919	.853	.768	.797	.711	.699
25600_U	.997	.988	.956	.972	.973	.958
25600_90_10	.982	.981	.947	.913	.925	.926
51200_U	.997	.992	.977	.968	.983	.975
51200_90_10	.998	.983	.985	.909	.963	.953

of our approaches. We used the R10K event counters to measure L1 and L2 cache misses, as well as the number of L2 invalidations. Figure 5 shows the results (normalized with respect to the CYT algorithm) for each matrix on 8 processors using LCYT(1) and LO-LCYT(2). The reduction in the number of cache misses and invalidations is very significant, mainly for the HB matrices, since $M << N$ in these matrices, and thus the probability of reuse is higher. The best memory hierarchy optimization achieved by *gemat12* results in the highest reduction in execution time.

Figure 6 shows the executor speedups on 8 processors for different workloads using the CYT, LCYT(1) and LO-LCYT(2) algorithms. In general, LCYT has a better behavior, although LO-LCYT achieves acceptable results in almost all cases. Our proposals work better for loops with low W because in this case memory hierarchy performance has a greater influence on the overall execution time. The maximum achievable speedup is limited by the degree of

parallelism of the loop. Loops with long dependence chains prevent parallelism. The CYT algorithm obtains the best speedups for the synthetic matrices, which have a shorter CP; and the worst speedup is for *gemat1*, which has the longest CP of the test suite of Table 1. Although matrix *gemat12* has a short CP, the speedup achieved by CYT is very low. Note that the critical path is only an estimate of parallelism degree and speedup is strongly influenced by the iteration distribution among processors, so that the number of waits is minimized. Moreover, speedup increases with W because the executor overhead becomes negligible.

In order to represent the impact of the inspector overhead, Figure 7 shows, for an HB and a synthetic matrix, the overall execution time of the algorithms CYT, LCYT(1) and LO-LCYT(2), given by $T = T_i + N_{it} \times T_e$ ms, where T_i and T_e are the inspector and executor times, respectively, and N_{it} is the number of times the inspector is reused in the code (from 1 to 100 times in our experiments). In many applications, the loop to be parallelized is contained in one or more sequential loops. In this case, if access patterns to array A do not change across iterations, the inspector can be reused (e.g. iterative sparse linear system solvers).

The overall execution times of LCYT and LO-LCYT are always lower than those of CYT for the HB matrix and the difference increases as W diminishes. LCYT achieves the best results in *gemat12* for all parameter combinations because M is relatively small and it results in a low graph partitioning cost. Regarding the synthetic matrix, as M is much higher, the LCYT inspector overhead is more significant and, therefore, this algorithm is only advantageous as compared with CYT if the inspector is reused a certain

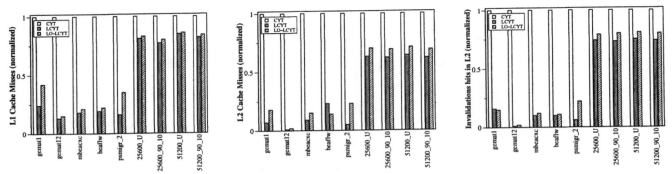

Figure 5. Cache behavior of the three strategies

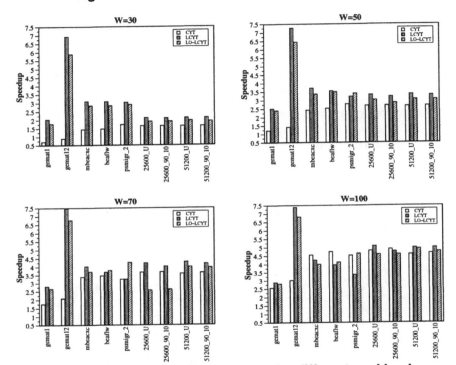

Figure 6. Speedups on 8 processors for different workloads

number of times (from N_{it}=20 for W=30, and N_{it}=26 for W=70). As in this case the inspector overhead of LO-LCYT is less, LCYT performance is better from N_{it}=49 for W=30, and N_{it}=64 for W=70. Below that threshold, the best overall performance is achieved by LO-LCYT.

Matrices *gemat12* and *51200_U* represent the behavior of the HB and the synthetic test matrices, respectively. Table 3 shows the overall behavior of all test matrices for different W. It contains the number of iterations (N_{it}) from which the overall execution times of LCYT and LO-LCYT (LO in the table) are lower than those of CYT. If this number is 1, it means that the execution time is always lower, and it is not necessary to reuse the inspector to improve the results. This is the case for the HB matrices using both LCYT and LO-LCYT and for the synthetic matrices using LO-LCYT (except for W=70). The entry with a dash means that the

overall execution time is never improved because the executor time of CYT is lower (the only case is matrix *psmigr_2* using LCYT for $W \geq 70$). The number in parentheses in the LCYT columns is the value of N_{it} from which LCYT outperforms LO-LCYT. The results show that LCYT is better than LO-LCYT for most HB matrices, but for the synthetic matrices LCYT is better only if the inspector is reused because, as $M = 2N$, the graph partitioning cost is high.

5. Related work

Cache misses are becoming increasingly costly due to the widening gap between processor and memory performance. Therefore, it is a primary goal to increase the performance of each memory hierarchy level. Much research

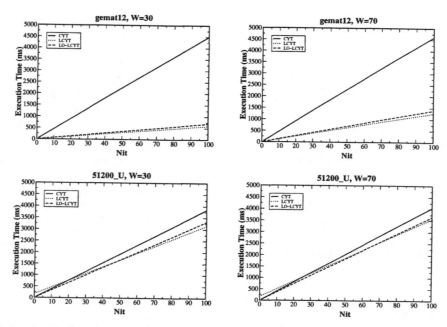

Figure 7. Overall execution times on 8 processors for some benchmark matrices

Table 3. Threshold N_{it} for outperforming CYT

	W=30		W=50		W=70	
	LCYT	LO	LCYT	LO	LCYT	LO
gemat1	1 (2)	1	1 (1)	1	1 (2)	1
gemat12	1 (1)	1	1 (1)	1	1 (1)	1
mbeacxc	1 (1)	1	1 (1)	1	1 (1)	1
beaflw	1 (1)	1	1 (1)	1	1 (1)	2
psmigr_2	1 (1)	1	1 (-)	1	- (-)	1
25600_U	18 (49)	1	21 (49)	1	31 (56)	2
25600_90	17 (48)	1	23 (56)	1	46 (75)	3
51200_U	20 (49)	1	22 (56)	1	26 (64)	1
51200_90	18 (47)	1	22 (56)	1	33 (71)	2

has been devoted to enhancing data locality of dense arrays with regular access patterns, by means of loop and/or data transformations [9] [13] [20]. Regarding irregular codes, there are different proposals to improve locality of sequential codes on uniprocessors. Al-Furaih and Ranka [1] focus on data reordering using METIS [10] and BFS (*Breadth First Search*). Ding and Kennedy [3] propose two transformations: one reorders data accesses to improve temporal locality (locality grouping) and the other reorders data layout to enhance spatial reuse (dynamic data packing). They also assess the performance improvement of applying a combination of both techniques. Mellor-Crummey et al [14] use space-filling curves to reorder data and/or computation.

There is much less research on the improvement of locality on multiprocessors, an important issue on NUMA systems. Han and Tseng evaluate in [7] the effect on the parallel execution of codes of uniprocessor techniques that improve locality, focusing on reduction operations. In [11]

Leung and Zahorjan treat locality in the specific context of the parallel execution of a loop with no output dependences. Their strategy is based on array reordering to improve spatial locality. A recent proposal also based on data reordering using space-filling curves to enhance spatial locality of irregular codes on shared memory systems can be found in [8]. Our LCYT proposals, in contrast, are based on loop restructuring and their primary objective is to exploit both spatial and temporal locality, as well as avoid false sharing of data. Moreover, our strategies can be applied to any loop that follows the general pattern represented in Figure 1.

6. Conclusions

Kernels of grand challenge applications that use irregular structures make poor use of memory hierarchy on multiprocessors and performance degrades as a result. As techniques to enhance memory performance have become increasingly important, we have proposed two methods (LCYT and LO-LCYT) to parallelize loops with indirect array accesses using run-time support. Compared to existing research on irregular codes, our algorithms are designed not only to enhance parallelism, but also data locality, improving temporal and spatial locality and eliminating false sharing.

Experimental results show the effectiveness of both methods, which reduce the number of cache misses and invalidations. It results in a significant reduction in the execution times of the executor (except for high workloads), LCYT being the method that achieves the best results in this phase. The main drawback of LCYT is the overhead of the

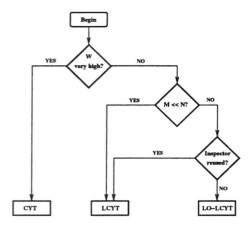

Figure 8. Choice of the parallelization strategy

graph partitioning when the size of the indirectly accessed array is not much less than the number of loop iterations. In these cases, the method is only advantageous if the inspector is reused in the code and thus the overhead is partially amortized. This is not the case of LO-LCYT, which obtains good results in almost all circumstances. We can conclude that, excepting very high workloads, the best overall results are achieved by the proposals LCYT or LO-LCYT depending on the input code, as shown in Figure 8.

Our techniques are in the domain of automatic parallelization and the final goal is to include the algorithms in a parallelizing compiler. Thus, the compiler would select the best strategy according to the loop and matrix parameters, following the decision diagram of Figure 8. The parameter thresholds should be empirically determined.

References

[1] I. Al-Furaih and S. Ranka. Memory Hierarchy Management for Iterative Graph Structures. In *12th Int'l Parallel Processing Symposium*, Orlando, FL, 1998.

[2] D.-K. Chen, J. Torrellas, and P.-C. Yew. An Efficient Algorithm for the Run-Time Parallelization of DOACROSS Loops. In *Supercomputing Conference*, pages 518–527, Washington DC, 1994.

[3] C. Ding and K. Kennedy. Improving Cache Performance in Dynamic Applications through Data and Computation Reorganization at Run Time. In *ACM SIGPLAN'99 Conference on Programming Language Design and Implementation*, pages 229–241, Atlanta, GA, 1999.

[4] I. S. Duff, R. G. Grimes, and J. G. Lewis. User's Guide for the Harwell-Boeing Sparse Matrix Collection. Technical Report TR-PA-92-96, CERFACS, 1992.

[5] M. Gupta and R. Nim. Techniques for Speculative Run-Time Parallelization of Loops. In *Supercomputing Conference*, Orlando, FL, 1998.

[6] H. Han and C.-W. Tseng. Efficient Compiler and Run-Time Support for Parallel Irregular Reductions. *Parallel Computing*, 26(13-14):1861–1887, 2000.

[7] H. Han and C.-W. Tseng. Improving Locality for Adaptive Irregular Scientific Codes. In *13th Int'l Workshop on Languages and Compilers for Parallel Computing*, pages 173–188, Yorktown Heights, NY, 2000.

[8] Y. C. Hu, A. L. Cox, and W. Zwaenepoel. Improving Fine-Grained Irregular Shared-Memory Benchmarks by Data Reordering. In *Supercomputing Conference*, Dallas, TX, 2000.

[9] M. T. Kandemir, A. N. Choudhary, J. Ramanujam, and P. Banerjee. Improving Locality Using Loop and Data Transformations in an Integrated Framework. In *31st Annual IEEE/ACM Int'l Symposium on Microarchitecture*, pages 285–297, Dallas, TX, 1998.

[10] G. Karypis and V. Kumar. A Fast and High Quality Multilevel Scheme for Partitioning Irregular Graphs. *SIAM Journal on Scientific Computing*, 20(1):359–392, 1999.

[11] S.-T. Leung and J. Zahorjan. Restructuring Arrays for Efficient Parallel Loop Execution. Technical Report 94-02-01, Department of Computer Science and Engineering, University of Washington, 1994.

[12] S.-T. Leung and J. Zahorjan. Extending the Applicability and Improving the Performance of Runtime Parallelization. Technical Report 95-01-08, Department of Computer Science and Engineering, University of Washington, 1995.

[13] K. S. McKinley, S. Carr, and C.-W. Tseng. Improving Data Locality with Loop Transformations. *ACM Trans. on Programming Languages and Systems*, 18(4):424–453, 1996.

[14] J. M. Mellor-Crummey, D. B. Whalley, and K. Kennedy. Improving Memory Hierarchy Performance for Irregular Applications. In *ACM Int'l Conference on Supercomputing*, pages 425–433, Rhodes, Greece, 1999.

[15] S. P. Midkiff and D. A. Padua. Compiler Algorithms for Synchronization. *IEEE Transactions on Computers*, 36(12):1485–1495, 1987.

[16] D. Patel and L. Rauchwerger. Implementation Issues of Loop-Level Speculative Run-Time Parallelization. In *8th Int'l Conference on Compiler Construction*, pages 183–197, Amsterdam, The Netherlands, 1999.

[17] Y. Saad. *SPARSKIT: a Basic Tool Kit for Sparse Matrix Computations (Version 2)*, 1994.

[18] J. H. Saltz, R. Mirchandaney, and K. Crowley. Run-Time Parallelization and Scheduling of Loops. *IEEE Transactions on Computers*, 40(5):603–612, 1991.

[19] D. E. Singh, F. F. Rivera, and M. J. Martín. Run-Time Characterization of Irregular Accesses Applied to Parallelization of Irregular Reductions. In *30th Int'l Conference on Parallel Processing Workshops*, pages 17–22, Valencia, Spain, 2001.

[20] M. E. Wolf and M. S. Lam. A Data Locality Optimizing Algorithm. In *ACM SIGPLAN'91 Conference on Programming Language Design and Implementation*, pages 30–44, Toronto, Canada, 1991.

[21] C. Xu. Effects of Parallelism Degree on Run-Time Parallelization of Loops. In *31st Hawaii Int'l Conference on System Sciences*, Kohala Coast, HI, 1998.

[22] C. Xu and V. Chaudhary. Time Stamp Algorithms for Runtime Parallelization of DOACROSS Loops with Dynamic Dependences. *IEEE Transactions on Parallel and Distributed Systems*, 12(5):433–450, 2001.

[23] C.-Q. Zhu and P.-C. Yew. A Scheme to Enforce Data Dependence on Large Multiprocessor Systems. *IEEE Transactions on Software Engineering*, 13(6):726–739, 1987.

Analysis of Memory Hierarchy Performance of Block Data Layout*

Neungsoo Park, Bo Hong, and Viktor K. Prasanna
Department of Electrical Engineering - Systems
University of Southern California
Los Angeles, CA 90089-2562
{neungsoo,bohong,prasanna}@halcyon.usc.edu
http://advisor.usc.edu

Abstract

Recently, several experimental studies have been conducted on block data layout as a data transformation technique used in conjunction with tiling to improve cache performance. In this paper, we provide a theoretical analysis for the TLB and cache performance of block data layout. For standard matrix access patterns, we derive an asymptotic lower bound on the number of TLB misses for any data layout and show that block data layout achieves this bound. We show that block data layout improves TLB misses by a factor of $O(B)$ compared with conventional data layouts, where B is the block size of block data layout. This reduction contributes to the improvement in memory hierarchy performance. Using our TLB and cache analysis, we also discuss the impact of block size on the overall memory hierarchy performance. These results are validated through simulations and experiments on state-of-the-art platforms.

1. Introduction

The increasing gap between memory latency and processor speed is a critical bottleneck in achieving high performance. The gap is typically bridged through a multi-level memory hierarchy that can hide memory latency. The performance of this memory hierarchy system is severely impacted by the locality of data references. To improve memory hierarchy performance, compiler optimization techniques (e.g. loop permutation, fusion, and tiling) [13, 14, 21] have received considerable attention, which improve the locality of the data reference. These techniques, called *control transformations*, change the loop iteration order, thereby changing the data access pattern [4, 8, 19, 25]. Most

previous optimizations concentrate on single-level cache [8, 11, 15, 19, 23]. Multi-level caches in memory hierarchy were considered by a few researchers [20, 25]. However, most of these approaches target mainly the cache performance, paying less attention to the Translation Look-aside Buffer (TLB) performance. As the problem sizes become larger, the overall performance can drastically degrade because of TLB thrashing [22]. Hence, both TLB and cache must be considered in optimizing application performance. In [12], cache and TLB performance were considered *in concert*. In this analysis, TLB and cache were assumed to be fully-set associative. However, cache is direct mapped or small set-associative in most of state-of-the-art platforms.

Some recent work [11, 17, 18, 23] proposed *data transformations* that change the data layout in memory to match the data access pattern. It was proposed in [10] that both data and loop transformation can be applied to loop nests for optimizing cache locality. In [5, 6], a matrix is partitioned into small blocks of data. Data elements within one block are mapped onto contiguous memory. These blocks were laid out in memory by different space-filling curves. These data layouts have shown performance improvement over canonical row or column major layouts. Block data layout is one such layout where blocks are arranged in row-major order. ATLAS [2, 24] uses block data layout with tiling to exploit temporal and spatial locality. The combination of block data layout and tiling has shown high performance on various platforms. However, these results were confirmed through experiments; we are not aware of any formal analysis that addresses TLB performance..

In this paper, we study the impact of *block data layout*[1], with and without tiling, on the performance of both TLB and caches. First, we analyze the intrinsic TLB performance of block data layout. The TLB and cache performance for block data layout with tiling are analyzed. The block data

---

*Supported by the DARPA Data Intensive Systems Program under contract F33615-99-1-1483 monitored by Wright Patterson Air force Base, in part by NSF CCR-9900613, and in part by an equipment grant from Intel Corporation.

---

[1] To avoid confusion, in this paper, 'block' is used in the context of a data transformation technique, e.g. block data layout. 'tiling' is used to represent a control transform technique.

layout with tiling shows better TLB performance compared with other state-of-the-art techniques like copying [11, 23] and padding [15, 19]. Simulations and experiments are conducted to verify this analysis.

Similar to the importance of tile size selection for tiling, appropriate block size selection for block data layout is critical to achieve high performance. In ATLAS, the selection of the optimal block size is done *empirically* at compile time by running several experiments with different block sizes [24]. The selection criteria does not have any supporting formal analysis. In [5, 6], it is observed that the block size should not be too small nor too large. However, no analytical bounds for block size were presented. In this paper, we propose an analytical bound for optimal block size in block data layout, on the basis of our TLB and cache analysis.

The contributions of this paper are as follows:

- We present a lower bound analysis for TLB performance. Further, we show that block data layout intrinsically has better TLB performance than canonical layouts (Section 2). Compared with row major layout, the number of TLB misses for block data layout is improved by $O(\sqrt{P_v})$ where P_v is the page size.
- We analyze the TLB and cache performance of tiling with block data (Section 3.1 and 3.2). In tiled matrix multiplication, block data layout improves the number of TLB misses by a factor of B, where B is the block size.
- On the basis of our cache and TLB analysis, we propose a block size selection algorithm that provides a tight analytical bound for block size (Section 3.3). The best block sizes found by ATLAS fall in the range given by our algorithm.
- We validate our analysis through simulations and experiments on real platforms using matrix multiply, LU decomposition and Cholesky factorization (Section 4).

The rest of this paper is organized as follows. Section 2 describes block data layout and gives analysis of its TLB performance. Section 3 discusses the TLB and cache performance when tiling and block data layout are used in concert. A block size selection algorithm is described based on this analysis. Section 4 shows simulation based as well as experimental results. Concluding remarks are presented in Section 5.

2. Block Data Layout and TLB Performance

In Section 2, we analyze the TLB performance of block data layout. We show that block data layout has better intrinsic TLB performance than conventional data layouts. Without loss of generality, the canonical layout is assumed to be row major.

0	1	2	3	4	5	6	7
8	9	10	11	12	13	14	15
16	17	18	19	20	21	22	23
24	25	26	27	28	29	30	31
32	33	34	35	36	37	38	39
40	41	42	43	44	45	46	47
48	49	50	51	52	53	54	55
56	57	58	59	60	61	62	63

(a) Row-major layout

0	1	4	5	8	9	12	13
2	3	6	7	10	11	14	15
16	17	20	21	24	25	28	29
18	19	22	23	26	27	30	31
32	33	36	37	40	41	44	45
34	35	38	39	42	43	46	47
48	49	52	53	56	57	60	61
50	51	54	55	58	59	62	63

(b) Block data layout

Figure 1. Various data layouts: block size 2×2 for (b)

The following notations are used in this paper. P_v denotes virtual page size. S_{tlb} denotes the TLB entry capacity. In general, $S_{tlb} \ll P_v$. Block size is $B \times B$, where it is assumed $B^2 = kP_v$. Cache is assumed to be direct-mapped. S_{ci} is the size of the ith level cache. Its line size is denoted as L_{ci}. We assume that TLB is fully set-associative and Least-Recently-Used(LRU) replacement policy is used.

2.1. Block Data Layout

To support multi-dimensional array representations in current programming languages, the default data layout is *row-major* or *column-major*, denoted as canonical layouts [7]. Both row-major and column-major layouts have similar drawbacks. For example, consider a large matrix stored in row-major layout. Due to large stride, column accesses can cause cache conflicts. Further, if every row in a matrix is larger than the size of a page, column accesses can cause TLB trashing, resulting in drastic performance degradation. In block data layout, a large matrix is partitioned into sub-matrices. Each sub-matrix is a $B \times B$ matrix and all elements in the sub-matrix are mapped onto contiguous memory locations. The blocks are arranged in row-major order. Figure 1 shows block data layout with block size 2×2.

2.2. TLB Performance of Block Data Layout

In this subsection, we present a lower bound on the TLB misses for any data layout. We discuss the intrinsic TLB performance of block data layout. We present an analysis on the TLB performance of block data layout and show that its performance is improved when compared with conventional layouts. Throughout this paper, we consider an $N \times N$ array. Also it is assumed that N is large enough that $N \geq P_v \gg S_{tlb}$.

2.2.1 A Lower Bound on TLB Misses

In general, most matrix operations consist of row and column accesses, or permutations of row and column accesses, which are called *generic access pattern* [2] in this paper. In this section, we consider an access pattern where an array is accessed first along *all* rows *and* then along *all* columns. The lower bound analysis of TLB misses incurred in accessing the data array along all the rows and then all the columns is as follows.

Theorem 2.1 *For accessing an array along all the rows and then along all the columns, the asymptotic [3] minimum number of TLB misses is given by $2\frac{N^2}{\sqrt{P_v}}$.*

Proof: Consider an arbitrary mapping of array elements to pages. Let $A_k = \{i|$ at least one element of row i is in page k $\}$. Similarly, let $B_k = \{j|$ at least one element of column j is in page k $\}$. Let $a_k = |A_k|$ and $b_k = |B_k|$. Note that $a_k \times b_k \geq P_v$. Using the mathematical identity that the arithmetic mean is greater than or equal to the geometric mean ($a_k + b_k \geq 2\sqrt{a_k \times b_k} \geq 2\sqrt{P_v}$), we have:

$$\sum_{k=1}^{\frac{N^2}{P_v}} (a_k + b_k) \geq 2\frac{N^2}{P_v}\sqrt{P_v}.$$

Let x_i (y_j) denote the number of pages where elements in row i (column j) are scattered. The number of TLB misses in accessing all rows consecutively and then all columns consecutively is given by $T_{miss} \geq \sum_{i=1}^{N}(x_i - O(S_{tlb})) + \sum_{j=1}^{N}(y_j - O(S_{tlb}))$. $O(S_{tlb})$ is the number of page entries required for accessing row i (column j) that are already present in the TLB. Page k is accessed a_k times by row accesses, thus, $\sum_{i=1}^{N} x_i = \sum_{k=1}^{\frac{N^2}{P_v}} a_k$. Similarly, $\sum_{j=1}^{N} y_j = \sum_{k=1}^{\frac{N^2}{P_v}} b_k$. Therefore, the total number of TLB misses is given by

$$T_{miss} \geq \sum_{k=1}^{\frac{N^2}{P_v}} (a_k + b_k) - 2N \cdot O(S_{tlb}) \geq 2 \times \frac{N^2}{\sqrt{P_v}} - 2N \cdot O(S_{tlb}). \tag{1}$$

As the problem size (N) increases, the number of pages accessed along a row (column) becomes larger than the size of TLB (S_{tlb}). Thus the number of TLB entries that are reused is reduced between two consecutive row (column) accesses. Therefore the asymptotic minimum number of TLB misses is given by $2\frac{N^2}{\sqrt{P_v}}$. ⊙

---

[2] In the rest of this paper, we refer to the access pattern of all rows and all columns as generic access pattern

[3] This asymptotic [9] bound holds true when N is large. Also, the impact of S_{tlb} becomes negligible when N is large and hence does not appear in the bound.

We obtained a lower bound on TLB misses for any layout when data are accessed along all rows and then along all columns. This lower bound of TLB misses also holds when data is accessed along an arbitrary permutation of all rows and columns.

Corollary 2.1 *For accessing an array along an arbitrary permutation of row and column accesses, the asymptotic minimum number of TLB misses is given by $2\frac{N^2}{\sqrt{P_v}}$.*

2.2.2 TLB Performance

In this section, we consider the same access pattern as discussed in Section 2.2.1. Consider a given $N \times N$ array stored in a canonical layout. During the first pass (row accesses), the memory pages are accessed consecutively. Therefore, TLB misses caused by row accesses is equal to $\frac{N^2}{P_v}$. During the second pass (column accesses), elements along the column are assigned to N different pages. Hence, a column access causes N TLB misses, since $N \gg S_{tlb}$. All N column accesses result in N^2 TLB misses. The total number of TLB misses caused by all row accesses and all column accesses is thus $\frac{N^2}{P_v} + N^2$. Therefore, in canonical layout, TLB misses drastically increase due to column accesses.

Compared with canonical layout, block data layout has better TLB performance. The following theorem shows that block data layout minimizes the number of TLB misses.

Theorem 2.2 *For accessing an array along all the rows and then along all the columns, block data layout with block size $\sqrt{P_v} \times \sqrt{P_v}$ minimizes the number of TLB misses.*

Detailed proof for this theorem can be found in [16]. In general, the number of TLB misses for a $B \times B$ block data layout is $k\frac{N^2}{B} + \frac{N^2}{B}$. It is reduced by a factor of $\frac{(P_v+1)B}{P_v(k+1)} (\approx \frac{B}{k+1})$ when compared with canonical layout. When $B = \sqrt{P_v}$ ($k = 1$), this number approaches the lower bound shown in Theorem 2.1.

This theorem holds true even when data in block data layout is accessed along an arbitrary permutation of all rows and columns.

Corollary 2.2 *For accessing an array along an arbitrary permutation of rows and columns, block data layout with block size $\sqrt{P_v} \times \sqrt{P_v}$ minimizes the number of TLB misses.*

Even though block data layout has better TLB performance compared with canonical layouts for generic access patterns, it alone does not reduce cache misses. The data access pattern of tiling matches well with block data layout. In the following section, we discuss the performance improvement of TLB and caches when block data layout is used in conjunction with tiling.

```
for kk=0 to N by B
    for jj=0 to N by B
        for i=0 to N
            for k=kk to min(kk+B-1,N)
                r = X(i,k)
                for j=jj to min(jj+B-1,N)
                    Z(i,j) += r*Y(k,j)
```

(a) 5-loop tiled matrix multiplication

```
for jj=0 to N by B
    for kk=0 to N by B
        for ii=0 to N by B
            for i=ii to min(ii+B-1,N)
                for k=kk to min(kk+B-1,N)
                    r = X(i,k)
                    for j=jj to min(jj+B-1,N)
                        Z(i,j) += r*Y(k,j)
```

(b) 6-loop tiled matrix multiplication

Figure 2. Tiled matrix multiplication

3. Performance Analysis of Block Data Layout with Tiling

Tiling is a well-known optimization technique that improves cache performance. Tiling transforms the loop nest so that temporal locality can be better exploited for a given cache size. Consider an $N \times N$ matrix multiplication represented as $\mathbf{Z} = \mathbf{XY}$. For large problems, its performance can suffer from severe cache and TLB thrashing. To reduce cache and TLB misses, tiling transforms the matrix multiplication to a 5-loop nest tiled matrix multiplication (TMM) as shown in Figure 2(a). To efficiently utilize block data layout, we consider a 6-loop TMM as shown in Figure 2(b).

3.1. TLB Performance

In this section, we show the TLB performance improvement of block data layout with tiling. To illustrate the effect of block data layout on tiling, we consider a generic access pattern abstracted from tiled matrix operations. The access pattern is shown in Figure 3, where the whole matrix is accessed first along the rows then along the columns, in a tiled pattern. The tile size is equal to B.

With canonical layout, TLB misses will not occur when accessing consecutive tiles in the same row, if $B \leq S_{tlb}$. Hence, the tiled accesses along the rows generate $\frac{N^2}{P_v}$ TLB misses. However, tiled accesses along columns cause considerable TLB misses. B page table entries are necessary for accessing each tile. For all tiled column accesses, the total number of TLB misses is $T_{col} = B \times \frac{N}{B} \times \frac{N}{B} = \frac{N^2}{B}$. It is reduced by a factor of B compared with the number of TLB misses for all column accesses without tiling (see Section 2.2).

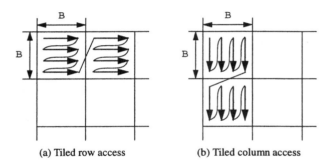

(a) Tiled row access   (b) Tiled column access

Figure 3. Tiled accesses

(a) over 2 pages   (b) over 3 pages

Figure 4. Blocks extending over page boundaries

The total number of TLB misses are further reduced when block data layout is used in concert with tiling [4]. This is formally stated in Theorem 3.1. To analyze TLB misses for tiled accesses using block data layout, we need to know the number of pages that a block of data is mapped onto. This is stated in Lemma 3.1.

Lemma 3.1 *Consider an array stored in block data layout with block size $B \times B$, where $B^2 = kP_v$. The average number of pages that one block of data is mapped onto is $k + 1$.*

Proof: For block size kP_v, assume that $k = n + f$, where n is a non-negative integer and $0 \leq f < 1$. An illustrative example of a block extending over page boundaries is shown in Figure 4. The probability that a block extends over $n + 1$ contiguous pages is $1 - f$. The probability that a block extends over $n + 2$ contiguous pages is f. Therefore, the average number of pages per block in block data layout is given by: $(1 - f) \times (n + 1) + f \times (n + 2) = k + 1$. ⊙

Theorem 3.1 *Assume that an $N \times N$ array is stored using block data layout. For tiled access along the rows and then the columns, the total number of TLB misses is $\left(2 + \frac{1}{k}\right)\frac{N^2}{P_v}$.*

Proof: Blocks in block data layout are arranged in row-major order. So, a page overlaps between two consecutive blocks that are in the same row. The page is continuously accessed. The number of TLB misses caused by all tiled row accesses is thus $\frac{N^2}{P_v}$, which is the minimum number of TLB misses. However, no page overlaps between two consecutive blocks in the same column. Therefore, each block along

---

[4] Throughout this paper, the block size of block data layout is assumed to be the same as the tile size so that the tiled access pattern matches the block data layout.

the same column goes through $(k + 1)$ different pages according to Lemma 3.1. The number of TLB misses caused by all tiled column accesses is thus $T_{col} = (k + 1) \times \frac{N}{B} \times \frac{N}{B} = (k + 1)\frac{N^2}{kP_v}$. Therefore, the total TLB misses caused by all row and all column accesses is $T_{miss} = (2 + \frac{1}{k})\frac{N^2}{P_v}$. $\odot$

For tiled access, the number of TLB misses using canonical layout is $\frac{N^2}{P_v} + \frac{N^2}{B}$, where $B = \sqrt{kP_v}$. Using Theorem 3.1, compared with canonical layout, block data layout reduces the number of TLB misses by $\frac{\sqrt{kP_v} + \sqrt{k}}{2k+1} = \frac{B+\sqrt{k}}{2k+1}$.

A similar analytical result can be derived for real applications. Consider the 5-loop TMM with canonical layout in Figure 2 (a). Array **Y** is accessed in a tiled row pattern. On the other hand, arrays **X** and **Z** are accessed in a tiled column pattern. A tile of each array is used in the inner loops (i, k, j). The number of TLB misses for each array is equal to the average number of pages per tile, multiplied by the number of tiles accessed in the outer loops (kk, jj). The average number of pages per tile is $B + \frac{B^2}{P_v}$. Therefore, the total number of TLB misses is given by: $2N^3(\frac{1}{B^2} + \frac{1}{BP_v}) + N^2(\frac{1}{B} + \frac{1}{P_v})$.

Consider the 6-loop TMM on block data layout as shown in Figure 2 (b). A $B \times B$ tile of each array is accessed in the inner loops (i, k, j) with block layout. The number of TLB misses for each array is equal to the average number of pages per block multiplied by the number of blocks accessed in the outer loops (ii, kk, jj). According to Lemma 3.1, the average number of pages per block is $\frac{B^2}{P_v} + 1 (= k + 1)$. Therefore, the total number of TLB misses (TM) is

$$TM = 2N^3 \left(\frac{1}{BP_v} + \frac{1}{B^3}\right) + N^2 \left(\frac{1}{P_v} + \frac{1}{B^2}\right). \quad (2)$$

Compared with the 5-loop TMM with canonical layout, TLB misses decrease by a factor of $O(B)$ using the 6-loop TMM with block data layout.

3.2. Cache Performance

For a given cache size, tiling transforms the loop nest so that the temporal locality can be better exploited. This reduces capacity misses. However, since most of the state-of-the-art architectures have direct-mapped or small set-associative caches, tiling can suffer from considerable conflict misses as shown in Figure 5 (a). This degrades the overall performance.

We can reorganize a canonical layout to a block layout for tiled computations. Then as shown in Figure 5 (b), a self interference miss does not occur since all elements in a block can be mapped into contiguous locations in cache without any conflict.

In general, cache miss analysis for direct mapped cache with canonical layout is complicated because the self in-

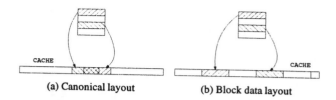

(a) Canonical layout   (b) Block data layout

Figure 5. Example of conflict misses

terference misses cannot be quantified easily. Cache performance analysis of tiled algorithm was discussed in [11]. The cache performance of tiling with copying optimization was also presented. We observe that the behavior of cache misses for tiled access patterns on block layout is similar to that of tiling with copying optimization on canonical layout. Also, self-interference misses can be easily quantified when block data layout is used. According to these, we have derived the total number of cache misses for 6-loop TMM with block data layout. Detailed proof can be found in [16]. For i^{th} level cache with line size L_{ci} and cache size S_{ci}, the total number of cache misses (CM_i) is:

$$CM_i \approx \begin{cases} \frac{N^3}{L_{ci}} \left\{ \frac{1}{B} \left(2 + \frac{(3L_{ci} + 2L_{ci}^2)}{S_{ci}} \right) + \frac{1}{N} + \frac{4B + 6L_{ci}}{S_{ci}} \right\} \\ \qquad \text{for } B < \sqrt{S_{ci}} \\ \frac{N^3}{L_{ci}} \left\{ \frac{4B}{S_{ci}} + \frac{2}{B} - \frac{2S_{ci}}{B^2} + 2 - \frac{1}{N} + \frac{6L_{ci}}{S_{ci}} \right\} \\ \qquad \text{for } \sqrt{S_{ci}} \leq B < \sqrt{2S_{ci}} \\ \frac{N^3}{L_{ci}} \left\{ 1 + \frac{2}{B} + \left(1 + \frac{L_c}{B}\right) \left(\frac{B + 2L_c}{S_{ci}}\right) \right\} \\ \qquad \text{for } \sqrt{2S_{ci}} \leq B \end{cases}$$

$$(3)$$

3.3. Block Size Selection

To achieve high performance, it is significant to select the block size of block data layout. In this section, we describe an approach for selecting the block size. In a multi-level memory hierarchy system, it is difficult to predict the execution time (T_{exe}) of a program. But, T_{exe} is proportional to the total miss cost of TLB and cache. In order to minimize T_{exe}, we will evaluate and minimize the total miss cost for both TLB and l-level caches. We have:

$$MC = TM \cdot M_{tlb} + \sum_{i=1}^{l} CM_i H_{i+1} \quad (4)$$

where MC denotes the total miss cost, CM_i is the number of misses in the ith level cache, TM is the number of TLB misses, H_i is the cost of a hit in the ith level cache, and M_{tlb} is the cost of a TLB miss. The $(l + 1)^{th}$ level cache is the main memory. It is assumed that all data reside in the main memory $(CM_{l+1} = 0)$.

For a simple 2-level memory hierarchy that consists of only one level cache and TLB, the total miss cost (denoted

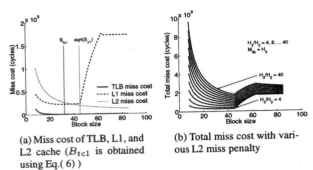

(a) Miss cost of TLB, L1, and L2 cache (B_{tc1} is obtained using Eq.(6))

(b) Total miss cost with various L2 miss penalty

Figure 6. Miss cost estimation for 6-loop TMM (UltraSparc II parameters)

as MC_{tc1}) in Eq. (4) reduces to:

$$MC_{tc1} = TM \cdot M_{tlb} + CM \cdot H_2, \qquad (5)$$

where H_2 is the access cost of main memory. In the above estimation, M_{tlb} and CM are substituted with Eq.(2) and Eq.(3), respectively. Using the derivative of MC_{tc1}, the optimal block size, B_{tc1}, which minimizes the total miss cost caused by L1 cache and TLB misses is given as

$$B_{tc1} \approx \sqrt{\frac{\left(\frac{2L_{1c}M_{tlb}}{P_v} + \left[2 + \frac{3L_{c1}+2L_{c1}^2}{S_{c1}} \right] H_2 \right) S_{c1}}{4H_2}}. \qquad (6)$$

We now extend this analysis to determine a range for optimal block size in a multi-level memory hierarchy that consists of TLB and two levels of cache. The miss cost is classified into two groups: miss cost caused by TLB and L1 cache misses and miss cost caused by L2 misses. Figures 6 (a) and (b) show the miss cost estimated through Eqs.(2) and (3). Figure 6(a) represents the individual cost of TLB, L1, and L2 miss, using UltraSparc II parameters. Figure 6(b) shows the change of estimated total miss costs based on different ratios of L1 cache miss penalty (H_2) and L2 cache miss penalty (H_3). Using Eq.(6), we discuss the total miss cost for 3 ranges of block size:

Lemma 3.2 For $B < B_{tc1}$, $MC(B) > MC(B_{tc1})$.

Proof: According to the derivatives, $\frac{dMC_{tc1}}{dB} < 0$ and $\frac{dCM_2}{dB} < 0$ for $B < B_{tc1}$, TLB, L1, and L2 miss costs increase as block size decreases. This is shown in Figure 6(a), thereby increasing the total miss cost. Therefore, the optimal block size cannot be in the range $B < B_{tc1}$. ⊙

Lemma 3.3 For $B > \sqrt{S_{c1}}$, $MC(B) > MC(\sqrt{S_{c1}})$.

Proof: In the range $B > \sqrt{S_{c1}}$, the change in TLB miss cost is negligible as the block size increases. Since block size is larger than L1 cache size, self-interferences occur in this range. The number of L1 cache misses drastically increases as shown in Figure 6(a). For $\sqrt{S_{c1}} \le B < \sqrt{2S_{c1}}$, although the number of L2 cache misses decreases ($\frac{dCM_2}{dB} < 0$), the ratio of derivatives of Eq.(3) for L1 and L2 misses is as follows:

$$\left| \frac{H_2 \frac{dCM_1}{dB}}{H_3 \frac{dCM_2}{dB}} \right| = \frac{H_2}{H_3} \left| \frac{\frac{N^3}{L_{c1}} \left[\frac{4}{S_{c1}} + \frac{4S_{c1}}{B^3} - \frac{2}{B^2} \right]}{\frac{N^3}{L_{c2}} \left[\frac{4}{S_{c2}} - \left(2 + \frac{3L_{c2}+2L_{c2}^2}{S_{c2}} \right) \frac{1}{B^2} \right]} \right| > 1.$$

Therefore, the total miss cost increases for $\sqrt{S_{c1}} \le B < \sqrt{2S_{c1}}$. For $B \ge \sqrt{2S_{c1}}$, there is no reuse in L1 cache. Thus, the L1 cache miss cost saturates. As shown in Figure 6(b), $TM(B) > TM(\sqrt{S_{c1}})$ for $B \ge \sqrt{2S_{c1}}$, because L1 miss cost is dominantly larger than L2 miss cost and TLB miss cost for $B \ge \sqrt{2S_{c1}}$. Therefore, the optimal block size cannot be in the range $B > \sqrt{S_{c1}}$. ⊙
Detailed proof of Lemma 3.3 can be found in [16].

Theorem 3.2 The optimal block size B_{opt} satisfies $B_{tc1} \le B_{opt} < \sqrt{S_{c1}}$.

Proof: This follows from Lemma 3.2 and 3.3. Therefore, an optimal block size that minimizes the total miss cost is located in $B_{tc1} \le B_{opt} < \sqrt{S_{c1}}$. We select a block size that is a multiple of L_{c1} (L1 cache line size) in this range. ⊙

4 Experimental Results

To verify our TLB performance analysis, simulations for the generic access pattern (accessing along all rows and then all columns) were performed. Furthermore, three applications (matrix multiplication, LU decomposition, and Cholesky factorization) are tested through simulations and executions on real platforms to confirm our analysis.

4.1 Simulations of generic access pattern

To verify our TLB performance analysis, simulations were performed using the SimpleScalar simulator [3]. It is assumed that the page size is $8KByte$ and the data TLB is fully set-associative with 64 entries (similar to the data TLB in UltraSparc 2.) Double precision data points are assumed. A 32×32 block size is considered for block data layout.

Table 1 compares the TLB misses of block data layout with canonical layout when the matrix is accessed with a generic access pattern. Table 1 (a) shows the TLB misses for accesses along all rows and then all columns. For small problem sizes, TLB misses with block data layout are considerably less than those with canonical layout. For problem size 1024×1024, TLB entries used in a column(row) access are almost fully reused in the next column(row) access, thereby $O(S_{tlb})$ in Eq.(1) becoming relatively large.

Table 1. Comparison of TLB misses

Layout	1024	2048	4096
Block Layout	2081	81794	1196033
Canonical Layout	1049601	4198401	16793601

(a) Along all rows and then all columns

Layout	1024	2048	4096
Block Layout	64140	273482	1080986
Canonical Layout	1053606	4208690	16822675

(b) Arbitrary permutation of row and column accesses

Layout	1024	2048	4096
Block Layout	64501	274473	1080465
Canonical Layout	1053713	4208681	16822395

(c) Arbitrary permutation of all rows followed by arbitrary permutation of all columns accesses

The number of TLB misses using block data layout is 504.37 times less than that using canonical layout. It is also less than the lower bound obtained from Theorem 2.1. For larger problem sizes, $O(S_{tlb})$ in Eq.(1) becomes negligible, since the TLB entries cannot be reused. Hence the total number of TLB misses approaches the lower bound. As shown in Table 1 (a), TLB misses with block data layout are upto 16 times less compared with canonical layout. Table 1 (b) and (c) confirm Corollary 2.1 and 2.2. With these access patterns, TLB entries referenced during one row(column) access are not reused when accessing the next row(column). The number of TLB misses with block data layout approaches the lower bound on TLB misses.

Table 2 shows simulation results for tiled row and column accesses. Block size is set to be the same as the tile size. As shown in Table 2, the number of TLB misses conform our analysis from Theorem 3.1. The number of TLB misses with block data layout is 91% less than that with canonical layout.

4.2 Experimental results for various applications

To show the effect of block data layout, we performed simulations and experiments on the following applications: tiled matrix multiplication(TMM), LU decomposition, and Cholesky factorization(CF). The performance of tiling with

Table 2. TLB misses for all tiled row accesses followed by all tiled column accesses

Layout	1024	2048	4096
Block Layout	2081	12289	49153
Canonical Layout	33794	139265	561025

block data layout (tiling+BDL) is compared with other optimization techniques: tiling with copying(tiling+copying), and tiling with padding(tiling+padding). For tiling+BDL, the tile size (in tiling) is chosen to be the same as the block size in block data layout. Initial and final data layouts are canonical layouts. All the costs in performing data layout transformations (from canonical layout to block data layout and vice versa) are included in the reported results. As stated in [11], we observed that the copying technique cannot be applied efficiently to LU and CF applications, since copying overhead offsets the performance improvement. Hence we do not consider tiling+copying for these applications. In all our simulations and experiments, the data elements are double-precision.

4.2.1 Simulation results

To show the performance of TLB and caches using tiling+BDL, simulations were performed using the SimpleScalar simulator [3]. The problem size was 1024×1024.

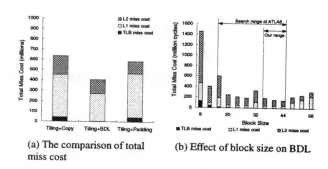

(a) The comparison of total miss cost

(b) Effect of block size on BDL

Figure 8. Total miss cost for TMM using UltraSparc II parameters

Figures 7 and 8 show the TMM simulation results, based on UltraSparc II parameters. As shown in Figure 7(a), Tiling+BDL reduced 91–96% of TLB misses. This confirms our analysis presented in Section 3.1. Figure 8 shows the total miss cost (calculated from Eq. (4)) for TMM. L1, L2, and TLB miss penalties were assumed to be 6, 24, and 30 cycles, respectively. Figure 8(a) shows the comparison of the total miss cost of tiling+BDL with that of tiling+copying and tiling+padding. The comparison shows that tiling+BDL results in the smallest total miss cost. Specifically, the TLB miss cost of tiling+BDL is negligible compared with L1 and L2 miss costs. Figure 8(b) shows the effect of block size on the total miss cost for TMM using tiling+BDL. As discussed in Section 3.3, $B_{tc1} = 32.2$, $\sqrt{S_{c1}} = 45.3$, and $L_{c1} = 4$ using this architecture parameters. Theorem 3.2 suggests the range for optimal block size to be 36–44. Simulation results show that the optimal block size for this architecture was 44.

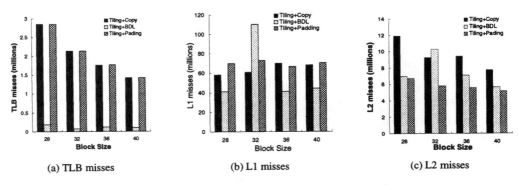

(a) TLB misses   (b) L1 misses   (c) L2 misses

Figure 7. Simulation results for TMM using UltraSparc II parameters

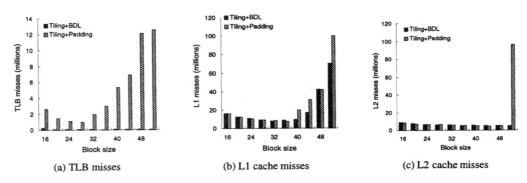

(a) TLB misses   (b) L1 cache misses   (c) L2 cache misses

Figure 9. Simulation results for LU using Pentium III parameters

As shown in Figure 8(b), our proposed range is much tighter than the search range of ATLAS.

Figure 9 and 10 present simulation results for LU using Intel Pentium III parameters. Similar to TMM, the number of TLB misses for tiling+BDL was almost negligible compared with that for tiling+padding as shown in Figure 9(a). For both techniques, L1 and L2 cache misses were reduced considerably because of 4-way set-associativity. For tiling+padding, when the block size was larger than L1 cache size, the padding algorithm in [15] suggested a pad size of 0. There is essentially no padding effect, thereby drastically increasing L1 and L2 cache misses. Figure 10 shows the block size effect on total miss cost using tiling+padding and tiling+BDL. Tiling+padding reduced L1 and L2 cache miss costs considerably. However, TLB miss costs were still significantly high, affecting the overall performance. As discussed in Section 3.3, the suggested range for optimal block size is 32–44. Simulations validate that the optimal block size achieving the smallest miss cost locates in the range selected using our approach.

4.2.2 Application execution results on real platforms

To verify our block size selection and the performance improvements using block data layout, we

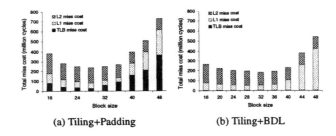

(a) Tiling+Padding   (b) Tiling+BDL

Figure 10. Effect of block size on LU decomposition using Pentium III parameters

performed experiments on several platforms. The parameters are tabulated in Table 3. gcc compiler was used in these experiments. The compiler optimization flags were set to "-fomit-frame-pointer -O3 -funroll-loops". Execution time was the user processor time measured by sys-call clock(). The problem sizes ranged from 1000×1000 to 1600×1600.

The experimental results of TMM using tiling+BDL on UltraSparc II is shown in Fig. 11. Fig. 11(a) shows the best block size for TMM with respect to different problem sizes. For each problem size, we performed experiments by test-

Table 3. Features of various experimental platforms

Platforms	Speed (MHz)	L1 cache			L2 cache			TLB		
		Size (KB)	Line (Byte)	Ass.	Size (KB)	Line (Byte)	Ass.	Entry	page (KB)	Ass.
Alpha 21264	500	64	64	2	4096	64	1	128	8	128
UltraSparc II	400	16	32	1	2048	64	1	64	8	64
UltraSparc III	750	64	32	4	4096	64	4	512	8	2
Pentium III	800	16	32	4	512	32	4	64	4	4

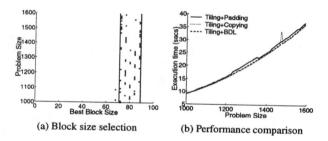

(a) Block size selection   (b) Performance comparison

Figure 11. Experimental results for TMM on Ultra-SPARC II

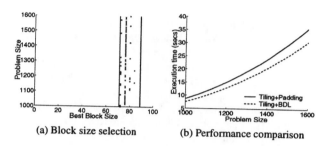

(a) Block size selection   (b) Performance comparison

Figure 13. Experimental results for LU on Ultra-SPARC III

(a) Block size selection   (b) Performance comparison

Figure 12. Experimental results for TMM on Alpha 21264

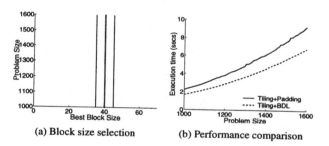

(a) Block size selection   (b) Performance comparison

Figure 14. Experimental results for Cholesky factorization on Pentium III

ing block sizes ranging from 8–80. In all these tests, we found that the optimal block size for each problem size was in the range given by Theorem 3.2. This is shown in Figure 11(a). We also tested ATLAS. Through a wide search ranging from 16 to 44, ATLAS found 36 and 40 as the optimal block sizes. These blocks lie in the range given by Theorem 3.2. These experiments confirm that our approach proposes a reasonably good range for block size selection. Figures 11(b) show the execution time comparison of tiling+BDL with tiling+copying and tiling+padding. Figure 12–14 show experimental results for 3 different applications on 3 different platforms. Tiling+BDL technique is faster than using other optimization techniques, for almost all problem sizes and on all the platforms. These results confirm our analysis. More experimental results are available in [16].

5 Concluding Remarks

This paper studied a critical problem in understanding the performance of algorithms on state-of-the-art machines that employ multi-level memory hierarchy. We presented a lower bound on the number of TLB misses for any data layout and showed that block data layout achieves this bound. The number of TLB misses using tiling and block data layout were considerably reduced compared with copying or padding techniques. We showed that block data layout with tiling leads to improved overall memory hierarchy performance compared with other techniques. Further, we proposed a tight range for block size in ATLAS using our performance analysis. Our analysis was verified using simulations as well as actual execution results.

This work is part of the Algorithms for Data IntensiVe

Applications on Intelligent and Smart MemORies (ADVISOR) Project at USC [1]. In this project we focus on developing algorithmic design techniques for mapping applications to architectures. Through this we understand and create a framework for application developers to exploit features of advanced architectures to achieve high performance.

References

[1] ADVISOR Project. http://advisor.usc.edu.

[2] Automatically Tuned Linear Algebra Software (ATLAS). http://math-atlas.sourceforge.net/.

[3] D. Burger and T. M. Austin. The SimpleScalar Tool Set, Version 2.0. Technical Report 1342, University of Wisconsin-Madison Computer Science Department, June 1997.

[4] J. Chame, M. Hall, and J. Shin. Compiler Transformations for Exploiting Bandwidth in PIM-Based Systems. *Proceedings of Solving the Memory Wall Workshop, held in conjunction with the ISCA 2000*, June 2000.

[5] S. Chatterjee, V. V. Jain, A. R. Lebeck, S. Mundhra, and M. Thottethodi. Nonlinear Array Layouts for Hierarchical Memory Systems. *Proceedings of the 13th ACM ICS '99*, June 1999.

[6] S. Chatterjee, A. R. Lebeck, P. K. Patnala, and M. Thottethodi. Recursive Array Layouts and Fast Parallel Matrix Multiplication. *Proceedings of the 11th ACM SPAA*, pages 222–371, June 1999.

[7] M. Cierniak and W. Li. Unifying Data and Control Transformations for Distributed Shared-Memory Machines. *Proceedings of the SCM SIGPLAN PLDI 1995*, pages 205–217, June 1995.

[8] S. Coleman and K. S. McKinley. Tile Size Selection Using Cache Organization and Data Layout. *Proceedings of the SIGPLAN PLDI 1995*, June 1995.

[9] E. Horowitz, S. Sahni, and S. Rajasekaran. *Computer Algorithms in Pseudocode: The Human Dimension*. W. H. Freeman Press, 1998.

[10] M. Kandemir, A. Choudhary, J. Ramanujam, and P. Banerjee. Improving Locality Using Loop and Data Transformations in an Integrated Framework. *Proceedings of the 31st IEEE/ACM International Symposium on Microarchitecture*, November 1998.

[11] M. Lam, E. Rothberg, and M. E. Wolf. The Cache Performance and Optimizations of Blocked Algorithms. *Proceedings of ASPLOS-IV*, April 1991.

[12] N. Mitchell, K. Högstedt, L. Carter, and J. Ferrante. Quantifying the Multi-Level Nature of Tiling Interactions. *International Journal of Parallel Programming*, 1998.

[13] D. Padua. Outline of a Roadmap for Compiler Technology. *IEEE Computing in Science & Engineering*, Fall 1996.

[14] D. Padua. The Fortran I Compiler. *IEEE Computing in Science & Engineering*, January/Febrary 2000.

[15] P. R. Panda, H. Nakamura, N. Dutt, and A. Nicolau. Augmenting Loop Tiling with Data Alignment for Improved Cache Performance. *IEEE Transactions on Computers*, 48(2), Feburary 1999.

[16] N. Park, B. Hong, and V. K. Prasanna. Tiling, Block Data Layout, and Memory Hierarchy Performance. Technical Report USC-CENG 01-05, Department of Electrical Engineering, USC, September 2001.

[17] N. Park, D. Kang, K. Bondalapati, and V. K. Prasanna. Dynamic Data Layouts for Cache-conscious Factorization of DFT. *Proceedings of IPDPS 2000*, April 2000.

[18] N. Park and V. K. Prasanna. Cache Conscious Walsh-Hadamard Transform. *ICASSP 2001*, May 2001.

[19] G. Rivera and C.-W. Tseng. Data Transformations for Eliminating Conflict Misses. *ACM SIGPLAN PLDI 1998*, June 1998.

[20] G. Rivera and C.-W. Tseng. Locality Optimizations for Multi-Level Caches. *Proceedings of IEEE SC'99*, November 1999.

[21] J. Sanchez, A. Gonzalez, and M. Valero. Static Locality Analysis for Cache Management. *PACT 1997*, November 1997.

[22] A. Saulsbury, F. Dahgren, and P. Stenström. Receny-based TLB Preloading. *ISCA 2000*, June 2000.

[23] O. Temam, E. D. Granston, and W. Jalby. To Copy or Not to Copy: A Comile-Time Technique for Assessing When Data Copying Should be Used to Eliminate Cache Conflicts. *Proceedings of IEEE SC'93*, November 1993.

[24] R. C. Whaley and J. Dongarra. Automatically Tuned Linear Algebra Software (ATLAS). *Proceedings of SC'98*, November 1998.

[25] Q. Yi, V. Adve, and K. Kennedy. Transforming Loops to Recursion for Multi-Level Memory Hierarchies. *ACM SIGPLAN PLDI 2000*, June 2000.

Session 1C

Grid Computing

Integrating Trust into Grid Resource Management Systems

Farag Azzedin and Muthucumaru Maheswaran

University of Manitoba and TR*Labs*
Winnipeg, Manitoba
Canada
E-mail: {fazzedin, maheswar}@cs.umanitoba.ca

Abstract

Grid computing systems that have been the focus of much research activities in recent years provide a virtual framework for controlled sharing of resources across institutional boundaries. Security is one major concern in any system that enables remote execution. Several techniques can be used for providing security in Grid systems including sandboxing, encryption, and other access control and authentication mechanisms. The additional overhead caused by these mechanisms may negate the performance advantages gained by Grid computing. Hence, we contend that it is essential for the scheduler to consider the security implications while performing resource allocations. In this paper, we present a trust model for Grid systems and show how the model can be used to incorporate the security implications into scheduling algorithms. Three scheduling heuristics that can be used in a Grid system are modified to incorporate the trust notion and simulations are performed to evaluate the performance.

Keywords: Grid computing, resource management system, security, trust.

1. Introduction

Resource management in Grid systems [5, 9] is challenging due to: (a) geographical distribution of resources, (b) resource heterogeneity, (c) autonomously administered Grid domains having their own resource policies and practices, and (d) Grid domains using different access and cost models.

In previous generation *distributed computing environments* (DCEs), *resource management systems* (RMSs) were primarily responsible for allocating resources for tasks. They also performed functions such as resource discovery and monitoring that supported their primary role. In Grid systems, with distributed ownership for the resources and tasks, it is important to consider *quality of service* (QoS) and security while allocating resources. Integration of QoS into RMS has been examined by several researchers [7, 11]. However, security is implemented as a separate subsystem of the Grid [6] and the RMS makes the allocation decisions oblivious of the security implications.

Our study on integrating trust into resource management algorithms is motivated by the following scenarios. Grid computing systems provide a facility that enable large-scale controlled sharing and interoperation among resources that are distributively owned and managed. Trust is a major concern of the consumers and producers of services that participate on a Grid. Some resource consumers may not want their applications mapped onto resources that are owned and/or managed by entities they do not trust. Similar concerns apply from the resource producer side as well. Current generation of distributed systems addresses these concerns by providing security at different levels. Suppose resource M is allocated task T. Resource M can employ sandboxing techniques to prevent task T from eavesdropping or interfering with other computation or activities ongoing on M. Similarly, task T may employ encryption, data hiding, intelligent data encoding, or other mechanisms to prevent M from snooping into the sensitive information carried by task T.

Based on the above scenarios we hypothesize that if the RMS is aware of the security requirements of the resources and tasks it can perform the allocations such that the security overhead is minimized. This is the goal of the *trust-aware resource management system* (TRMS) studied here. The TRMS achieves this goal by allocating resources considering a trust relationship between the *resource provider* (RP) and the *resource consumer* (RC). If an RMS maps a resource request strictly according to the trust, then there can be a severe load imbalance in a large-scale wide area system such as the Grid. On the other hand, considering just the load balance or resource-task affinities, as in existing RMSs, causes inefficient overall operation due to the introduction of the overhead caused by enforcing the required level of security. Mapping according to load balance or trust considerations results in diverging schedules. The former spreads the requests for the sake of load balance while the latter segregates them for security considerations. In the TRMS algorithms examined here, the minimization criterion is derived from load balancing and security considerations.

This paper is organized as follows. Section 2, defines the notions of trust and reputation and outlines mechanisms for computing them. A trust model for Grid systems is presented in Section 3. Trust-aware resource management algorithms are presented in Section 4. The performance and the analysis of the proposed algorithms are examined in Section 5. Related work is briefly discussed in Section 6.

2. Trust and Reputation

2.1. Definition of Trust and Reputation

The notion of trust is a complex subject relating to a *firm belief* in attributes such as reliability, honesty, and competence of the trusted entity. There is a lack of consensus in the literature on the definition of trust and on what constitutes trust management [12, 8, 1]. The definition of trust that we will use in this paper is as follows:

> *Trust is the firm belief in the competence of an entity to act as expected such that this firm belief is not a fixed value associated with the entity but rather it is subject to the entity's behavior and applies only within a specific context at a given time.*

That is, the *firm belief* is a dynamic value and spans over a set of values ranging from *very trustworthy* to *very untrustworthy*. The *trust level* (TL) is built on past experiences and is given for a specific context. For example, entity y might trust entity x to use its storage resources but not to execute programs using these resources. The TL is specified for a given time frame because the TL today between two entities is not necessarily the same TL a year ago.

When making trust-based decisions, entities can rely on others for information pertaining to a specific entity. For example, if entity x wants to make a decision of whether to have a transaction with entity y, which is unknown to x, x can rely on the reputation of y. The definition of reputation that we will use in this paper is as follows:

> *The reputation of an entity is an expectation of its behavior based on other entities' observations or the collective information about the entity's past behavior within a specific context at a given time.*

2.2. Computing Trust and Reputation

In computing trust and reputation, several issues have to be considered. First, the trust decays with time. For example, if x trusts y at level p based on past experience five years ago, the trust level today is very likely to be lower unless they have interacted since then. Similar time-based decay also applies for reputation. Second, entities may form alliances and as a result would tend to trust their allies more than they would trust others. Finally, the TL that x holds about y is based on x's direct relationship with y as well as the reputation of y, i.e., the trust model should compute the eventual trust based on a combination of direct trust and reputation and should be able to weigh the two components differently.

Let x and y denote two entities. The trust relationship for a specific context c at a given time t between the two entities, expressed as $\Gamma(x, y, t, c)$, is computed based on the direct relationship for the context c at time t between x and y, expressed as $\Theta(x, y, t, c)$, as well as the reputation of y for context c at time t expressed as $\Omega(y, t, c)$. Let the weights given to direct and reputation relationships be α and β, respectively. The trust relationship is a function of direct trust and reputation. If the "trustworthiness" of y, as far as x is concerned, is based more on direct relationship with x than the reputation of y, α will be larger than β.

The direct relationship is computed as a product of the TL in the *direct-trust table* (DTT) and the *decay function* ($\Upsilon(t - t_{xy}, c)$), where c is the context, t the current time, and t_{xy} the time of the last transaction between x and y. The reputation of y is computed as the average of the product of the TL in the *reputation-trust table* (RTT), the *decay function* ($\Upsilon(t - t_{zy}, c)$), and the recommender trust factor ($R(z, y)$) for all entities $z \neq x$. In practical systems, entities will use the same information to evaluate direct relationships and give recommendations, i.e., RTT and DTT will refer to the same table. Because reputation is based primarily on what other entities say about a particular entity, we introduced the *recommender trust factor R* to prevent cheating via collusions among a group of entities. Hence, R is a value between 0 and 1 and will have a higher value if the recommender does not have an alliance with the target entity. In addition, we assume that R is an internal knowledge that each entity has and is learned based on actual outcomes.

$$\Gamma(x, y, t, c) = \alpha \times \Theta(x, y, t, c) + \beta \times \Omega(y, t, c)$$
$$\Theta(x, y, t, c) = DTT(x, y, c) \times \Upsilon(t - t_{xy}, c)$$

And $\forall z \neq x$, we have:

$$\Omega(y, t, c) = \frac{\sum_{k=1}^{n} RTT(z, y, c) \times R(z, y) \times \Upsilon(t - t_{zy}, c)}{\sum_{k=1}^{n}(z)}$$

Currently, we are developing a trust management architecture that can evolve and maintain the trust values based on the concepts explained above. The rest of this paper is concerned with using the trust values maintained by such a system to perform efficient resource allocation.

3. A Trust Model for Grid Systems

3.1. Trust Model for Grid Systems

In our model, the overall Grid system is divided into *Grid domains* (GDs). The GDs are autonomous administrative entities consisting of a set of resources and clients managed by a single administrative authority. By organizing a Grid as a collection of GDs, issues such as scalability, site autonomy, and heterogeneity can be easily addressed. In our model, we associate two virtual domains with each GD: (a) a *resource domain* (RD) to signify the resources within the GD and (b) a *client domain* (CD) to signify the clients within the GD. As RDs and CDs are virtual domains mapped onto GDs, some instances of RDs and CDs can map onto the same GD.

An RD has the following attributes that are relevant to the TRMS: (a) ownership, (b) set of *type of activity* (ToA) it supports, and (c) *trust level* (TL) for each ToA. The set of ToAs determine the functionalities provided by the resources that are part of the RD. Some example activities a task can engage at an RD include printing, storing data, and using display services. Associating a TL with each ToA provides the flexibility to selectively open services to clients.

Similarly, the CDs have their own trust attributes relevant to the TRMS. The CD trust attributes include: (a) ownership, (b) ToAs sought, and (c) TLs associated with ToAs. The ToA field indicates the type and number of activities a client is requesting. The ToAs can be atomic or composed. A client with an atomic ToA requires just one activity whereas a client with a composed ToA requires multiple activities.

A trust level table exists between a set of RDs and CDs. The entries in the trust level table are *symmetric* quantifiers for the trust relationships that are asymmetric. For example, let the trust relationship between client domain CD_i and resource domain RD_j be defined by $f(i, j)$. Because trust is an asymmetric function the reverse relationship between RD_j and CD_i, in general, is not given by $f(i, j)$. However, in this study, we denote the current value of the two functions using a single value, i.e., TL_{ij}^k for CD_i and RD_j engaging in activity A_k. The entry TL_{ij}^k in a trust level table denotes the trust value for an activity of a client from CD_i on a resource in RD_j. Suppose we have client X from CD_i wanting to engage in activities A_p, A_q, and A_r on resource Y at RD_j. From the trust level table, we can compute the *offered trust level* (OTL), TL_{ij}^o for the composite activity between X and Y, i.e., $TL_{ij}^o = \min(\text{TL for } A_p, \text{TL for } A_q, \text{TL for } A_r)$. There are two *required trust levels* (RTLs), one from the client side and the other from the resource side. If the OTL is greater than or equal to the maximum of client and resource RTLs, then the activity can proceed with no additional overhead. Otherwise, there will be additional security overhead involved in supplementing the OTL to meet the requirements.

The trust level values used in Table 1 range from *very low trust level* denoted as A, to *extremely high trust level* denoted as F. Table 1 shows the *expected trust supplement* (ETS) for different RTL and OTL values. The ETS values are given by RTL − OTL. The ETS value is zero, when RTL − OTL < 0. It can be noted from Table 1 that the RTL

Table 1. Expected trust supplement values.

requested TL	offered TL				
	A	B	C	D	E
A	0	0	0	0	0
B	B - A	0	0	0	0
C	C - A	C - B	0	0	0
D	D - A	D - B	D - C	0	0
E	E - A	E - B	E - C	E - D	0
F	F	F	F	F	F

has a value F that is not provided by OTL. This is supported in the model so that client or resource domains can enforce enhanced security by increasing their RTL value to F.

A straight forward approach to creating and maintaining the trust level table can result in an inefficient process in a very large-scale system such as the Grid. This process is made efficient in our model by various methods. First, as mentioned previously, we divide the Grid system into GDs. The resources and clients within a GD inherit the parameters associated with the RD and CD that are associated with the GD. This increases the scalability of the overall approach. Second, trust is a slow varying attribute, therefore, the update overhead associated with the trust level table is not significant. A value in the trust level table is modified by a new trust level value that is computed based on a *significant* amount of transactional data.

Figure 1 shows a block diagram of a trust-aware RMS. The CDs and RDs have agents associated with them that monitor the Grid level transactions and form the trust notions. These agents have access to the trust level table. If the new trust values they form are different from the existing values in the tables, the agents update the table. In this study, we maintain a single table in a centrally organized RMS. The table may, however, be replicated at different domains for reading purposes.

4. Trust-Aware Resource Management Algorithms

4.1. Overview

In this section, we present three *trust-aware resource management* (TRM) algorithms as example applications of integrating trust into the RMS where clients belonging to different CDs present the requests for task executions and the TRM algorithms allocate the resources. Different requests belonging to the same CD may be mapped onto different RDs. The TRM algorithms presented here are based on the following assumptions: (a) scheduler is organized centrally, (b) tasks are mapped non-preemptively, and (c) tasks are indivisible (i.e., a task cannot be distributed over multiple machines).

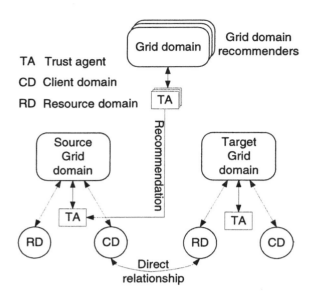

TA Trust agent
CD Client domain
RD Resource domain

Figure 1. Components of a Grid resource management trust model.

Our three TRM algorithms are implemented using three heuristics based on [10]: (a) trust-aware *minimum completion time* (MCT) heuristic, (b) trust-aware Min-min heuristic, and (c) trust-aware Sufferage heuristic. The MCT is an on-line or immediate mode mapping heuristic whereas the Min-min and Sufferage are batch mode mapping heuristics.

For the on-line mode mapping heuristic, the TRM schedules client requests as they arrive. This scheduling is done by the `TRM-scheduler` algorithm based on the MCT on-line mapping heuristic. For the batch mode mapping heuristics, the TRM collects client requests for a predefined time interval to form batch of requests, called a `meta-request`. The `TRM-scheduler` algorithm schedules the `meta-request` based on the two batch heuristics namely trust-aware Min-min, and trust-aware Sufferage heuristics.

Let $t(r_i)$ denote the task being executed by request r_i and $c(r_i)$ denote the originating client. Furthermore, let R_i be the ith meta-request and α_i be the available time of machine M_i after executing all requests assigned to it. Further, α_i^j be the available time α_i after executing all requests that belong to meta-request R_j. Also, let $EEC(M_i, t(r_j))$ be the *expected execution cost* for $t(r_j)$ on machine M_i and $ESC(M_i, t(r_j))$ be the *expected security cost* if $t(r_j)$ is assigned to machine M_i. The ESC value is a function of the *trust cost* (TC) value obtained from ETS (Table 1) and the task under consideration. When the RMS is considering the trust notion while allocating resources, the following equation is used to calculate the ESC table:

$$ESC(M_i, t(r_j) \quad = \quad EEC(M_i, t(r_j) \times (TC \times 15)/100$$

If the RMS is not considering the trust notion while allocating resources, the following equation is used to calculate the ESC table:

$$ESC(M_i, t(r_j) \quad = \quad EEC(M_i, t(r_j) \times 50/100$$

The trust levels A to F are assigned corresponding numeric values that range from 1 to 6, respectively. As shown in Table 1, TC ranges from 0 to 6. Hence the average TC value is 3. In our model, the ESC values are computed by multiplying the EEC values by a weighted TC value. We arbitrarily choose the weight for TC as 15. Therefore, when trust is considered, on average the ESC values are calculated as 45% of the EEC. On the other hand, when trust is not considered the ESC values are calculated as 50% of the EEC.

Finally, let $ECC(M_i, t(r_j))$ denotes the *expected completion cost* of $t(r_j)$ on machine M_i which is computed as the EEC of $t(r_j)$ on machine M_i plus the ESC of $t(r_j)$ on machine M_i. The goal of TRM algorithm is to assign $R_i = \{r_0 \dots r_{n-1}\}$ such that $\{max_m\{\alpha_m^i\}\}$ is minimized $\forall_m$ where n is the number of requests and m is the number of machines.

The Trust-Aware Minimum Completion Time Algorithm: The MCT heuristic [10] assigns each task to the machine that results in that task's earliest completion time. This causes some tasks to be assigned to machines that do not have the minimum execution time for them. As a task arrives, all the machines are examined to determine the machine that gives the earliest completion time for the task.

The trust-aware MCT algorithm starts by computing the ESC in terms of the trust cost which is the difference between the $c(r_j)$ requested TL and the offered TL by a machine M_i in RD_k. The trust cost is an indicator of how well is the trust relationship between an RD and a CD. For example, if the trust cost is 0, then the two parties completely trust each other. After that, the ECC table is initialized and the request r_j is assigned to the machine with the lowest completion cost. The task $t(r_j)$ that was successfully assigned to machine M_i is used to update machine M_i available time α_i which in turn is used to compute or update the expected completion cost for all requests yet to be assigned to machime M_i.

The Trust-Aware Min-min Algorithm: The `TRM-scheduler` algorithm schedules a batch of requests called *meta-request*. To map the meta-requests, we introduce a heuristic based on [10] called the trust-aware Min-min heuristic. Min-min begins by scheduling the tasks that change the expected machine available time by the least amount.

The initialization phase of he trust-aware Min-min algorithm is similar to the ones in the MCT heuristic. The request scheduled on machine M_i is deleted from the meta-request R_v. The task $t(r_j)$ that was successfully assigned

Table 2. Secure versus regular transmission for a 100 Mbps network.

File size/MB	Using rcp/(sec)	Using scp/(sec)	Overhead
1	0.19	0.63	69.84%
10	1.37	2.45	44.08%
100	9.77	15.34	36.31%
500	48.88	77.56	36.70%
1000	97.00	155.07	37.45%

Table 3. Secure versus regular transmission for a 1000 Mbps network.

File size/MB	Using rcp/(sec)	Using scp/(sec)	Overhead
1	0.34	0.65	47.69%
10	0.50	2.18	77.06%
100	4.98	14.23	65.00%
500	22.44	69.86	67.88%
1000	46.05	138.30	66.70%

to machine M_i is used to update machine M_i available time α_i which in turn is used to compute or update the expected completion cost for all requests yet to be assigned to machime M_i.

The Trust-Aware Sufferage Algorithm: The TRM-scheduler algorithm schedules a batch of requests called meta-request based on [10] called the trust aware Sufferage heuristic. The Sufferage heuristic is based on the idea that better mappings can be generated by assigning a machine to a task that would "suffer" most in terms of expected completion time if that particular machine is not assigned to it.

The initialization of the trust-aware Sufferage algorithm is similar to the Min-min heuristic. However, for each iteration, the algorithm picks an arbitrary request r_i from the meta-request and aasigns it to a machine m_j that gives the earliest completion cost for request r_i. If however there was another request r_k that was assigned to machine m_j previously, the algoeithm chooses the request (among r_i and r_k) that suffers the most if not assigned to machine m_j. It shoud be noted that the unchosen request (among r_i and r_k) will not be considered again for execution until the next iteration.

5. Performance Evaluation

5.1. Evaluation of Security Overheads

We conducted a study to examine the overhead of securing data transmissions for 100 Mbps and 1000 Mbps

networks. The machines used were base on an Intel Pentium III processor running at 866 MHz with memory size of 256 MB and a level 2 cache of size 256 KB. Tables 2 and 3 show the security overhead for secure transmissions using *secure copy* (scp) versus the regular transmission using *remote copy* (rcp) for different network speeds and with different file sizes. As illustrated in Tables 2 through 3, using scp introduces an overhead caused by the addition of security to the file transfer.

From Table 3, we observe that the security overhead negates the benefits of using the high speed network. Also, the security overhead as shown in Table 3 is significant for the secure transmission when compared to the regular transmission using rcp.

Furthermore, a performance study was done in [4] where three target benchmark applications are processed by *Minimal i386 Software Fault Isolation Tool* (MiSFIT) [13] and *Security Automata SFI Implementation* (SASI x86SFI) [4] sandboxing systems. *Software fault isolation* (SFI) is a sandboxing technique for transforming code written in unsafe language into safe compiled code. MiSFIT specializes the SFI technique to transform C++ code into safe binary code whereas SASI x86SFI specializes SFI to transform x86 assembly language output of the GNU gcc C compiler to safe binary code. The three target applications used are: (a) a memory intensive application benchmark called *page-eviction hotlist*, (b) *logical log-structured disk*, and (c) a command line message digest utility called MD5.

Page-eviction hotlist has the highest runtime overhead of 137% on MiSFIT and 264% on SASI x86SFI compared to the execution of the target applications on the target systems with no sandboxing. The other two benchmark applications performed as follows (compared to their execution on the target systems with no sandboxing): the *logical log-structured disk* has runtime overhead of 58% on MiSFIT and 65% on SASI x86SFI, whereas MD5 has runtime overhead of 33% on MiSFIT and 36% on SASI x86SFI.

The additional overhead caused by techniques such as sandboxing may negate the performance advantages gained by the Grid computing and hence we contend that it is essential for the scheduler to consider the security implications while performing resource allocations.

5.2. Analysis of the Trust-Aware Schemes

The goal of the three mapping heuristics (MCT, Min-min, and Sufferage) is to minimize the makespan, where makespan is defined as the maximum among the available times of all machines after they complete the tasks assigned to them. Initially $\alpha_m = 0, \forall_m$. The scheduler assigns request r_n to machine M_m such that the scheduling criterion is minimized. The heuristics considered in this paper use makespan minimization as their scheduling criterion.

Let X_{km} be the mapping function computed by the scheduler, where $X_{km} = 1$, if request r_k is assigned to machine M_m and 0, otherwise. The makespan $\Lambda = max_{M_m}\{\alpha_m\}$, where α_m is the available time of machine M_m after completing all the tasks assigned to it by the scheduler. The value of α_m is given by:

$$\alpha_m = \sum_{k=0}^{n-1} ECC(t(r_k), m) \times X_{km}$$

$$= \sum_{k=0}^{n-1} [EEC(t(r_k), m) + ESC(t(r_k), m)] \times X_{km}$$

A given scheduling heuristic computes a value of X_{km} such that the makespan is minimized. It should be noted that due to the non-optimality of the heuristics, the makespan value may not be the globally minimal one.

Theorem: The makespan obtained a trust-aware scheduler is always less than or equal to the makespan obtained by the trust-unaware scheduler that uses the same assignment heuristic.

Proof: Let the makespan obtained by the trust-aware heuristic be:

$$\Lambda_T^n = max\{\sum_{k=0}^{n-1}(EEC(t(r_k), m) +$$
$$ESC(t(r_k), m)) \times X_{km}^T\}$$

Let the makespan obtained by the trust-unaware heuristic be:

$$\Lambda_{UT}^n = max\{\sum_{k=0}^{n-1}(EEC(t(r_k), m) +$$
$$ESC(t(r_k), m)) \times X_{km}^{UT}\}$$

For $n = 1$, i.e., for the first task,

$$\Lambda_T^1 = (EEC(t(r_k), m) + ESC(t(r_k), m)) \times X_{km}^T$$
$$\Lambda_{UT}^1 = (EEC(t(r_k), m) + ESC(t(r_k), m)) \times X_{km}^{UT}$$

Suppose, $\Lambda_T^1 > \Lambda_{UT}^1$, and thus we will have the following inequality:

$$(EEC(t(r_k), m) + ESC(t(r_k), m)) \times X_{km}^T >$$
$$(EEC(t(r_k), m) + ESC(t(r_k), m)) \times X_{km}^{UT}$$

X_{km}^T was chosen to minimize $(EEC(t(r_k), m) + ESC(t(r_k), m)) \times X_{km}^T)$ while X_{km}^{UT} was chosen to minimize $(EEC(t(r_k), m) + ESC(t(r_k), m)) \times X_{km}^{UT})$. The above inequality, implies another choice that further minimizes the sum exists that was not selected by the heuristic. This is a contradiction. Hence, $\Lambda_T^1 < \Lambda_{UT}^1$.

Let $\Lambda_T^i < \Lambda_{UT}^i$ (i.e., assume the trust-aware scheme provides a smaller makespan after mapping i tasks). Following the above process, we can show that $\Lambda_T^{i+1} < \Lambda_{UT}^{i+1}$. Therefore, by induction $\Lambda_T^n < \Lambda_{UT}^n$.

5.3. Evaluation of the Trust-Aware Schemes

Simulations were performed to investigate the performance of the trust aware resource management algorithms. The resource allocation process was simulated using a discrete event simulator with the requests arrivals modeled using a Poisson random process. The number of CDs and RDs were randomly generated from [1, 4]. The ToAs required for each request were randomly generated from [1, 4] meaning that each $t(r_i)$ involves at least one ToA but no more than four ToAs. The two RTL values were randomly generated from [1, 6] representing trust levels A to F, respectively. Whereas, the OTL values were randomly generated from [1, 5] representing trust levels A to E, respectively.

In an ECC matrix, the numbers along a row indicate the estimated expected completion cost of the corresponding request on different machines. The average variation along the rows is referred as the *machine heterogeneity*. Similarly, the numbers along a column of the ECC matrix indicate the estimated expected completion cost of the machine for different requests. The average variation along columns is referred to as *task heterogeneity*. Two classes of EEC matrices were used in the simulation. The first class is the consistent *low task and low machine heterogeneity* (LoLo). This class of ECCs model network computing systems that have related machines that are similar in performance. The tasks that are submitted to the system have similar resource requirements as well. The second class is the inconsistent LoLo. In this class, the machines are not related.

Table 4. Comparison of average completion time for inconsistent LoLo heterogeneity using the MCT heuristic.

# of tasks	Using trust	Machine utilization	Ave. completion time (sec)	Improvement
50	No	92.86%	5,817.38	36.99%
	Yes	93.56%	3,665.23	
100	No	96.29%	11,244.77	37.59%
	Yes	96.12%	7,018.38	

When not using trust, the idea is to map a task belonging to request r_i to machine M_j that gives us the earliest completion time without considering the security overhead. Although the completion time was calculated in terms of the execution time of $t(r_i)$ on M_j plus the security overhead of executing $t(r_i)$ on M_j, the security overhead is not considered when mapping $t(r_i)$ to M_j. For the trust-aware heuristics, the security overhead is considered when mapping as well as when calculating the completion time of executing $t(r_i)$ on M_j.

Tables 4 and 5, show the benefit of integrating the trust

Table 5. Comparison of average completion time for consistent LoLo heterogeneity using the MCT heuristic.

# of tasks	Using trust	Machine utilization	Ave. completion time (sec)	Impro-vement
50	No	93.90%	4,786.27	34.44%
	Yes	93.96%	3,137.78	
100	No	96.51%	9,117.53	34.26%
	Yes	96.81%	5,994.25	

notion into an MCT-based RMS. Table 4 was run for the inconsistent LoLo heterogeneity with 5 machines. In Table 4, the completion time was reduced by about 38%. Table 5 was run for the consistent LoLo heterogeneity with 5 machines. In Table 5, the completion time was reduced by about 35%.

Table 6. Comparison of average completion time for inconsistent LoLo heterogeneity using the Minmin heuristic.

# of tasks	Using trust	Machine utilization	Ave. completion time (sec)	Impro-vement
50	No	90.56%	3,983.04	23.51%
	Yes	90.87%	3,046.79	
100	No	93.71%	7,227.78	23.34%
	Yes	94.35%	5,540.47	

Table 7. Comparison of average completion time for consistent LoLo heterogeneity using the Minmin heuristic.

# of tasks	Using trust	Machine utilization	Ave. completion time (sec)	Impro-vement
50	No	93.17%	3,750.59	25.28%
	Yes	92.53%	2,802.27	
100	No	96.15%	6,712.27	25.32%
	Yes	95.91%	5,012.39	

Tables 6 and 7 show the benefit of integrating the trust notion into a Minmin-based RMS. Table 6 was run for the inconsistent LoLo heterogeneity with 5 machines. In Table 6, the completion time was reduced by almost 24%. Table 7 was run for the consistent LoLo heterogeneity with 5 machines. In Table 7, the completion time was reduced by almost 26%.

Tables 8 and 9 show the benefit of integrating the trust notion into a Sufferage-based RMS. Table 8 was run for the inconsistent LoLo heterogeneity with 5 machines. In Table 8, the completion time was reduced by almost 40%.

Table 8. Comparison of average completion time for inconsistent LoLo heterogeneity using the Sufferage heuristic.

# of tasks	Using trust	Machine utilization	Ave. completion time (sec)	Impro-vement
50	No	92.59%	5,257.31	39.66%
	Yes	93.96%	3,172.09	
100	No	96.60%	9,609.78	38.40%
	Yes	97.08%	5,919.49	

Table 9. Comparison of average completion time for consistent LoLo heterogeneity using the Sufferage heuristic.

# of tasks	Using trust	Machine utilization	Ave. completion time (sec)	Impro-vement
50	No	94.14%	4,473.05	32.67%
	Yes	95.32%	3,011.81	
100	No	97.11%	8,356.33	33.19%
	Yes	97.33%	5,582.56	

Table 9 was run for the consistent LoLo heterogeneity with 5 machines. In Table 9, the completion time was reduced by almost 33%.

In summary, the simulation results indicate that incorporating trust into resource management heuristics can improve the overall quality of the schedules obtained by the resource allocation process.

6. Related Work

To the best of our knowledge, no existing literature directly addresses the issues of trust aware resource management. In this section, we examine several papers that examine issues that are peripherally related.

In [6], a security architecture for a Grid system is designed and implemented in the context of the Globus system. In [6] the security policy focuses on authentication and a framework to implement this policy have been proposed.

A design and implementation of a secure service discovery service (SDS) is presented in [2]. SDS can be used by service providers as well as clients. Service providers use SDS to advertise their services that are available or already running while clients use SDS to discover these services.

A model for supporting trust based on experience and reputation is proposed in [1]. This trust-based model allows entities to decide which other entities are trustworthy and also allows entities to tune their understanding of another entity's recommendations.

A survey of trust in Internet applications is presented in [8] and as part of this work a policy specification language called Ponder [3] was developed. Ponder can be used to define authorization and security management policies. Ponder is being extended Ponder to allow for more abstract and potentially complex trust relationships between entities across organizational domains.

7. Conclusions

Resource management is the central part Grid computing system. In a large-scale wide-area system such the Grid, security is a prime concern. One approach is to be conservative and implement techniques such as sandboxing, encryption, and other access control mechanisms on all elements of the Grid. However, the overhead caused by such a design may negate the advantages of Grid computing. This study examines the integration of the notion of "trust" into resource management such that the allocation process is aware of the security implications. In this paper we presented three scheduling heuristics that incorporated the trust notion while scheduling the resource requests. The performance evaluation involved two phases: (a) determining the overhead in securing common operations and (b) performing simulations to evaluate the benefit of incorporating trust in the scheduling heuristics.

The experiments performed to evaluate the overhead of securing remote computation indicate that the overhead is significant and techniques for minimizing such overhead by eliminating redundant application of secure operations can greatly enhance the overall performance.

The simulations performed to evaluate the effectiveness of the modifications indicate that the performance can be improved by about 40%. Several further issues remain to be addressed before the trust notion can be included in practical RMSs. Some of these include techniques for managing and evolving trust in a large-scale distributed system, and mechanisms for determining trust values from ongoing transactions.

Acknowledgement

A preliminary version of this paper appeared in the *First IEEE International Workshop on Security and Grid Computing*.

References

[1] A. Abdul-Rahman and S. Hailes, "Supporting trust in virtual communities," *Hawaii Int'l Conference on System Sciences*, Jan. 2000.

[2] S. E. Czerwinski, B. Y. Zhao, T. D. Hodes, A. D. Joseph, and R. H. Katz, "An architecture for a secure service discovery service," *5th Annual Int'l Conference on Mobile Computing and Networks (Mobicom '99)*, 1999.

[3] N. Damianou, N. Dulay, E. Lupu, and M. Sloman, "The Ponder policy specification language," *Workshop on Policies for Distributed Systems and Networks*, 2001.

[4] U. Erlingsson and F. B. Schneider, "SASI enforcement of security policies: A retrospective," *New Security Paradigms Workshop*, 1999.

[5] I. Foster, C. Kesselman, and S. Tuecke, "The anatomy of the Grid: Enabling scalable virtual organizations," *Int'l Journal on Supercomputer Applications*, 2001.

[6] I. Foster, C. Kesselman, G. Tsudik, and S. Tuecke, "A security architecture for computational Grids," *ACM Conference on Computers and Security*, 1998, pp. 83–91.

[7] I. Foster, A. Roy, and V. Sander, "A quality of service architecture that combines resource reservation and application adaptation," *8th Int'l Workshop on Quality of Service (IWQoS '00)*, June 2000.

[8] T. Grandison and M. Sloman, "A survey of trust in Internet applications," *IEEE Communications Surveys & Tutorials*, Vol. 3, No. 4, 2000.

[9] K. Krauter, R. Buyya, and M. Maheswaran, "A taxonomy and survey of Grid resource management systems," *Software Practice and Experiance*, Vol. 32, No. 2, Feb 2002, pp. 135–164.

[10] M. Maheswaran, S. Ali, H. J. Siegel, D. Hensgen, and R. F. Freund, "Dynamic mapping of a class of independent tasks onto heterogeneous computing systems," *Journal of Parallel and Distributed Computing*, Vol. 59, No. 2, Nov. 1999, pp. 107–131.

[11] M. Maheswaran, "Quality of service driven resource management algorithms for network computing," *1999 Int'l Conference on Parallel and Distributed Processing Technologies and Applications (PDPTA '99)*, June 1999, pp. 1090–1096.

[12] B. Misztal, "Trust in modern societies," *Polity Press, Cambridge MA*, Polity Press, Cambridge MA, 1996.

[13] C. Small and M. Seltzer, "MiSFIT: A tool for constructing safe extensible C++ systems," *IEEE-Concurrency*, Vol. 6, No. 3, 1998, pp. 33–41.

A System for Monitoring and Management of Computational Grids

Warren Smith
Computer Sciences Corporation
NASA Ames Research Center
wwsmith@nas.nasa.gov

Abstract

As organizations begin to deploy large computational grids, it has become apparent that systems for observation and control of the resources, services, and applications that make up such grids are needed. Administrators must observe resources and services to ensure that they are operating correctly and must control resources and services to ensure that their operation meets the needs of users. Users are also interested in the operation of resources and services so that they can choose the most appropriate ones to use. In this paper we describe a prototype system to monitor and manage computational grids and describe the general software framework for control and observation in distributed environments that it is based on.

1. Introduction

A recent trend in government and academic research is the development and deployment of computational grids [14, 22]. Computational grids are large-scale distributed systems that typically consist of high-performance compute, storage, and networking resources. Examples of such computational grids are the DOE Science Grid [3], the NSF Partnerships for Advanced Computing Infrastructure [6, 7], and the NASA Information Power Grid [29]. Most of the work to deploy these grids is in developing the software services to allow users to execute applications on large and diverse sets of distributed resources. These services include security, execution of remote applications, managing remote data, access to information about resources and services, and so on. There are several toolkits that provide these services, such as Globus [21], Legion [26], and Condor [30].

NASA is building a computational grid called the Information Power Grid (IPG) that is based upon the Globus toolkit. The IPG currently consists of resources and users at four NASA centers and our attempt to deploy a production grid of this size has highlighted the need for systems to observe and control the resources, services, and applications that make up such grids. We have found it difficult to ensure that the many resources in the IPG and the grid services executing on those resources are performing correctly. We have also found it cumbersome to perform administrative tasks such as adding grid users to our resources. These observations have led to our development of a system to address these needs.

This paper provides an overview of our system for monitoring and managing a computational grid. It allows administrators to observe the status of the resources and services that make up a Globus-based computational grid, to perform actions to correct failures, and perform day-to-day administrative functions. This system is constructed using the CODE toolkit [35] that provides a secure, scalable, and extensible framework for making observations on remote computer systems, transmitting this observational data to where it is needed, performing actions on remote computer systems, and analyzing observational data to determine what actions should be taken. We begin our discussion with an overview of the CODE framework. Section 3 describes the current functionality of our grid monitoring and management system. Section 4 describes related work and Section 5 summarizes our work and presents future work.

2. CODE Framework

We have developed a software framework for Control and Observation in Distributed Environments, called CODE for obvious reasons [35]. We are using this framework to implement several useful grid services, including our grid monitoring and management system. This section provides an overview of the framework.

2.1. Architecture

We call CODE a framework because it contains the core code that is necessary for performing monitoring and management. Users only need to add components to this framework and start the framework running. For example, if a user wants to create a host monitor, she would create components to monitor processes, files, network communications, and so on. The user would then add these components to the framework and tell the framework to begin monitoring the host. This same process is used for adding components to perform management actions. In fact, the typical process will be

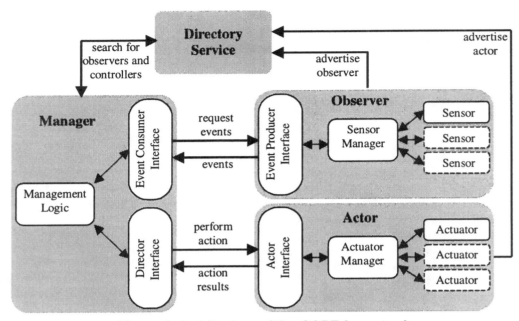

Figure 1. Architecture of the CODE framework.

easier because CODE provides a set of commonly used components for observing various properties and performing various actions and all a user will have to do is select which of these components to use.

The CODE architecture is shown in Figure 1. The components that are shown with a solid outline are those that are supplied by our framework, the components that are shown with a dashed outline are provided by the user, and the gray boxes show the logical grouping of the components in our framework into entities that may be on different hosts. The logical components of our framework are *observers* that perform and report observations, *actors* that perform actions, *managers* that receive observations, make decisions, and request actions, and a *directory service* for locating observers and actors.

An observer is a process on a computer system that provides information that can be measured from the system it is executing on. This could be information about the computer system, services or applications running on that computer system, or information that is not related to the computer system but that is accessible from it. Examples of this last type of information are scheduling queue information from a front-end system and the current use of a local area network. An observer provides information in the form of *events*. An event has a type and contains data in the form of <name, value> pairs. The values are typically of simple types such as string or integers, but can also be structures. An observer allows a manager to query for an event or to subscribe for a set of events. A subscription is useful, for example, if a user wants to be notified of the load on a system periodically or notified whenever some fault condition occurs. Access

to events is controlled based on user identity and user location on both a per-observer and a per-event type basis.

An observer consists of the following components:

- **Sensor**. A sensor is used to sense or measure some property. For example, a CPU load sensor would measure the CPU load of a host. A sensor is a passive component that performs measurements only when the sensor manager requests them. We are providing a set of sensors as part of our framework, but users will most likely need to implement sensors for their specific purposes.

- **Sensor Manager**. The sensor manager receives event requests or subscriptions from the event producer interface, uses the appropriate sensor at the appropriate time to perform a measurement, and sends the result of the measurement to the event producer interface in the form of an event.

- **Event Producer Interface**. The event producer interface provides an interface for observers to access a distributed event service. This event service allows event subscriptions to be established between producers and consumers, allows consumers to query for events from producers, and allows producers to send events to consumers.

An actor is a process on a computer system that can be asked to perform actions. These actions are made from the actor process and could affect local or remote resources, services, and applications. Access to actions is controlled based on user identity and user location on both a per-actor and a per-action type basis. An actor consists of the following components:

- **Actuator**. An actuator is a component that can be used to perform a specific action. For example, an actuator can be used to start a daemon. An actuator is a passive component that performs actions only when the actuator manager requests them. We are providing a set of actuators as part of our framework, but users will most likely need to implement actuators for their own specific purposes.
- **Actuator Manager**. The actuator manager receives requests to perform actions from the actor interface, uses the appropriate actuator to perform the action, and sends the results of the action back to the actor interface.
- **Actor Interface**. The actor interface provides an interface to a distributed action service that transmits requests for actions and their results.

A manager is a process that asks observers for information, reasons upon that information, and asks actors to take actions when the observations indicate that actions need to be taken. A manager consists of the following components:

- **Management Logic**. The management logic receives events from the event consumer interface, reasons upon this information to determine if any actions need to be taken, and then takes any actions using the director interface. There are two ways to implement the management logic:
  - Write C++ or Java code that contains a series of if and case statements, a state machine, or whatever code is needed to decide what actions to perform.
  - Use an expert system and write management rules. We are experimenting with using the CLIPS expert system [25] to simplify the writing of managers.
- **Event Consumer Interface**. The event consumer interface is used to request events from observers and receive those events.
- **Director Interface**. The director interface is used to request that actors perform actions and to receive the results of those actions.

A common component of a computational grid is a directory service or grid information service [20]. For our purposes, a directory service is a distributed database that is accessed using the Lightweight Directory Access Protocol (LDAP) [28]. We use a directory service to store the locations of observers and actors, describe what types of observations and actions they provide, and allow managers to search for the observers and actors.

2.2. Implementation

We have implemented the CODE framework in C++ and in Java so that it can be used from a variety of programming languages. At this point, the CODE framework supports communication using TCP, UDP, and SSL. The SSL communication is implemented using the Globus Grid Security Infrastructure [23]. The CODE framework is an implementation of the Grid Monitoring Architecture [40] defined in the Global Grid Forum and supports encoding of communication messages with extension of the event protocol [37, 38] that is being defined in the Global Grid Forum. This protocol encodes data using the eXtensible Markup Language (XML) and CODE uses the Xerces XML parsers to decode messages. Further, the format of the data CODE places in the directory service is compatible with the LDAP schemas [36] being defined in the Global Grid Forum.

3. Grid Management System

As computational grids grow, it becomes very difficult to ensure the correct operation of the large number of resources and services that make up a grid and to configure the services that are available on a grid. We have developed a prototype Grid Management System (GMS) to assist with these tasks in a Globus-based grid such as the NASA Information Power Grid. Figure 2 shows the high-level architecture of this system and we will describe the components of this architecture next.

3.1. GRAM Management Agent

The Globus toolkit includes a service called the Globus Resource Allocation Manager (GRAM) [17] that allows remote users to execute applications on a computer system. Our system has an agent on each host that has a GRAM server. The purpose of this agent is to ensure that the GRAM service is available to users, that the computer system it is associated with is operating correctly, and that there is network connectivity to other GRAM hosts. The GRAM management agent contains a CODE observer, actor, and manager. The observer is used to monitor the following properties:

1. The network latency between the GRAM host and other GRAM hosts. These latencies are used in this situation to detect any network problems. The ping sensor measures round trip times using the Unix ping command.
2. The available network bandwidth between the GRAM host and other GRAM hosts. These bandwidth measurements are also used to detect network problems and help users select resources. The IPerf [42] network measurement tool is used to make these measurements.
3. The CPU load is measured to determine if the computer system is overloaded and unusable. This measurement is made using three different sensors. One sensor uses the Unix uptime program, a second uses the PBS qstat command, and the third uses the

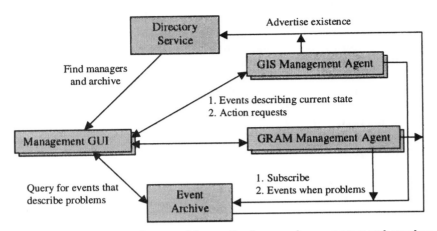

Figure 2. Architecture of our grid monitoring and management system.

LSF bjobs command. The sensor that is used depends on how access to the computer system is scheduled.

4. The memory statistics are measured using the Unix vmstat command, or similar commands, to determine if the memory subsystem is overloaded.

5. The available disk space is measured using the Unix df command. The GRAM servers require some minimal amount of disk space to operate.

6. The status of the GRAM reporter. The IPG is currently running the Globus MDS in classic mode. In that mode, a GRAM reporter daemon is executing on each GRAM host and writing data into a remote LDAP server.

7. The GRAM log files. These log files contain information about usage of the GRAM service and information about any problems that occur. These log files are observed for any problems.

8. The GRAM grid map file. This file specifies which grid users can execute applications through the GRAM service and also maps grid user identifiers to local Unix user identifiers. This information is provided so that remote administrators can determine and modify which grid users can use the GRAM service.

The actor has actuators to perform the following actions:

1. Start and stop the Iperf server. An Iperf server is needed so that Iperf clients can connect and perform Iperf experiments.

2. Send email. The email actuator is used to send email to administrators when a problem cannot be handled automatically, but must be corrected immediately.

3. Modify the GRAM gridmap file. This actuator is used by the remote management GUI so that access to the GRAM service on the host can be given to or taken away from grid users and the mapping of grid users to local user identities can be modified

4. Start, stop, or restart the GRAM reporter. If the GRAM reporter is not running or is not responding it can be stopped or started.

The GRAM management agent also includes a CODE manager. At this time, this manager does not receive any observations nor perform any actions. This approach assumes that the management of a grid takes place in the management GUIs. In the future, this manager will receive observations and perform actions so that management functionality will be offloaded to the GRAM manager and that the system will be more scalable.

When this agent begins executing, it locates the event archive (described further in Section 3.3) using the directory service and initiates subscriptions with the archive as the producer of events. These subscriptions indicate that the GRAM management agent will send events to the archive when problems occur. These problems include excessive CPU or memory use, failure of the GRAM reporter, or problems in the GRAM log files. At any time, management GUIs can contact this agent to receive information or request that actions be performed.

3.2. GIS Management Agent

A Globus-based computational grid also has a distributed database, called a Grid Information Service (GIS) that contains information about the resources, users, services, and applications that are part of the computational grid. The Globus GIS is the called the Metacomputing Directory Service [16]. A GIS typically consists of multiple servers running on multiple hosts. Our architecture includes an agent to monitor the operation of GIS servers, to determine if there are any problems, and to take actions to attempt to address any problems. Similarly to the GRAM agent, this agent provides observational data to remote agents and allows authorized remote agents to request actions. The GIS management agent for each

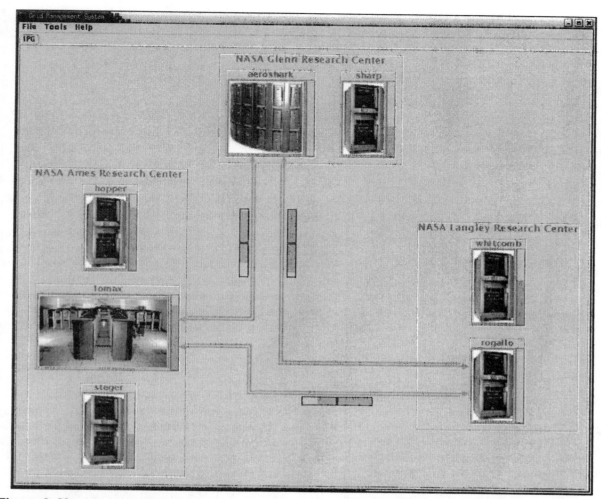

Figure 3. Management GUI displaying the status of a subset of the resources on the NASA IPG.

GIS server consists of an observer, an actor, and a manager. The observer monitors the following properties:
1. The network connectivity between the GIS hosts. LDAP servers typically refer searches for information to other LDAP servers.
2. The CPU load of the host.
3. The available memory of the host.
4. The available disk space.
5. The status of the LDAP server itself. This is measured in two ways. First, the existence of the LDAP server process is observed. Second, the time to request a search and receive a reply is measured.

The actor that is part of a GIS management agent is relatively simple: It only has two actuators at the current time. One actuator is used to send emails. The other actuator is used to start, stop, and restart the LDAP server. The GIS management agent also includes a CODE manager. At this time, this manager does not receive any observations nor perform any actions.

When the GIS management agent begins executing, it locates the event archive using the directory service and initiates subscriptions with the archive as the producer of events. These subscriptions indicate that the GIS management agent will send events to the archive when problems occur.

3.3. Event Archive

The event archive stores events so that management GUIs can obtain information about problems that have occurred in the past. The archive acts as an event consumer for events generated by GRAM and GIS management agents and acts as a producer of events for management GUIs. GRAM and GIS management agents use the directory service to find the archive and then they initiate a subscription to the archive. The agents then send events to the archive whenever problems occur. Management GUIs also find the archive using the directory service. They then query for events from the

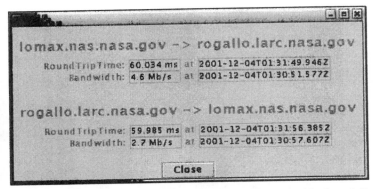

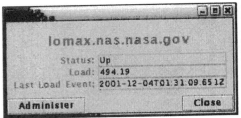

Figure 4. Detailed information about the load on the SGI Origin lomax.nas.nasa.gov and about the connection between lomax.nas.nasa.gov (in California) and rogallo.larc.nasa.gov (in Virginia).

archive. This query contains an event filter that is used to select which events to return. At the current time, we are using the Xpath [15] language as our filter language and the Xindice [12] XML database to store our events.

3.4. Directory Service

As described in Section 2.1, the observers and actors on the GRAM and GIS hosts register themselves in the directory service so that managers can find them. The event archive also registers itself so that management GUIs, GRAM managers, and GIS managers can find it.

3.5. Management GUI

The final component of our grid monitoring and management system is a graphical user interface that is used by grid administrators. Instances of this interface can be started and stopped at any time by multiple administrators. This interface allows grid administrators to view the current status of a grid, be notified when problems occur on the grid, examine problems that have occurred in the past, and perform grid administrative tasks. Figure 3 shows the management GUI being used to show the status of a subset of the resources on the NASA IPG. While the colors can't be seen here, the boxes around each computer system icon indicate whether status information from the machine has been received recently. The boxes are colored green when information has been received recently, yellow when an expected event has not been received, and red when two expected events have not been received. The vertical progress bars next to each computer system icon show what fraction of the CPUs in that computer system is being used. The lines between computer systems indicate whether the machines can ping each other. They are also colored green, yellow, and red to indicate if pings have been successful. The progress bars next to the lines show the fraction of maximum measured bandwidth, in both directions, that was available during the last bandwidth experiment. The computers and

networks to monitor along with icon selection and placement of all of the graphical components are stored in a configuration file that is loaded when the GUI starts.

As you can see from the figure, a user of the management GUI can quickly understand the status of some of the major IPG systems and the networks that connect them. Users can also click on any of the machines or network connections to display more detailed information such as that shown in Figure 4.

This interface can also be used to perform administrative tasks. At the current time, the interface allows an administrator to add, remove, and modify users in the GRAM grid map files on the remote computer systems. This interface provides several different ways to view user access. One display shows the grid user to local user name mappings for a single computer system and allows modifications to these mappings. Another display shows all of the computers that a grid user has access to and all of the local user names the grid user maps to. An administrator can use this display to add or remove access to computer systems and specify which local user name a grid user should map to.

4. Related Work

There are many existing systems for remote monitoring and management of networks and computer systems. A few commercial systems are OpenView [4] from Hewlett Packard, ManagementCenter [10] from Sun, Works2000 [2] from Cisco, Unicenter Networks and Systems Management [11] from Computer Associates, Tivoli Enterprise Console [5] and related products from IBM, PATROL [8] from BMC Software, and SiteAssure [9] from Platform Computing. These systems typically provide a wide range of monitoring and management services for a variety of resources. There are several problems with using these tools in our current grid environments. First, these products do have a cost associated with them, which may be difficult to afford for all of the participants in a multi-institution research grid.

Other problems are the lack of standards and compatibility between products and the lack of portability because of the unavailability of source code. Further, such tools do not support the grid security infrastructure. There are other systems that are free for noncommercial use or open source, but these tools tend to lack the functionality of the commercial tools previously mentioned and would need to be extended to manage grid services. Examples of such tools are NetSaint [24] and Big Brother [1]. Many of these types of tools are based on the Simple Network Management Protocol [39] that can provide information on networking and other types of resources, services, and so on.

Another area of related work is distributed event services, one of the core components of our framework. There has also been a large amount of work in this area. CORBA has defined an event service [31] and a notification service [32]. The problem with these services is that they are part of CORBA, which is not commonly used in grid computing. There Java Messaging Service [27] has support for distributed event services, but this only supports the Java language. There are also research projects to develop distributed event services such as Sienna [13], Elvin [33], Echo [18], OIF [19], and XEvents [34] and research projects to perform various types of monitoring such as NWS [43], JAMM [41], and MDS [16]. Many of these services are quite usable, the main advantage of the one that is part of our framework is that it will continue to be compatible with the standards defined in the Grid Forum. The benefit of this is that each implementation of an event service or monitoring system will have positives and negatives in terms of programming language, performance, and usability. Standards allow users to select the best implementations for their needs and still communicate with other implementations that are optimized for different purposes.

5. Summary and Future Work

Our efforts to deploy a computational grid at NASA have demonstrated the need for tools to observe and control the resources, services, and applications that make up grids. This has led to our development of CODE which provides a secure, scalable, and extensible framework for making observations from remote computer systems, transmitting this observational data to where it is needed, performing actions from remote computer systems, and analyzing observational data to determine what actions should be taken.

A prototype of our framework is complete and we are continuing to improve it. In addition to the core framework, we have implemented sensors for measuring various properties such as process status, file characteristics, disk space, CPU load, network interface characteristics, and LDAP search performance. We have also implemented a few simple actuators. We have used this framework to develop a prototype grid management system that allows administrators to observe the current status of the resources and services that make up a grid, to correct problems when they appear, and to perform administrative tasks such as modifying which grid users can access which computer systems. The grid management system also records failures that occur so that they can be examined at a later time.

In the future we will continue to improve and extend the CODE framework and we will also improve our Grid Management System as we gain experience from its use. Further, we will track the standards for grid event services that are being developed in the Global Grid Forum and will strive to be compatible with those standards.

Acknowledgments

We gratefully acknowledge the help of Abdul Waheed who participated in the early phases of this project and of Jerry Yan who provided the initial motivation. We also wish to thank Dan Gunter, Ruth Aydt, Brian Tierney, Dennis Gannon, and Valerie Taylor for the many useful discussions we have had related to this work both inside and outside of the Grid Forum. This work has been supported by the NASA HPCC and CICT programs.

References

[1]   "Big Brother," http://bb4.com/.
[2]   "CiscoWorks2000," http://www.cisco.com/warp/public/44/jump/ciscoworks.shtml.
[3]   "The DOE Science Grid," http://www-itg.lbl.gov/Grid.
[4]   "HP OpenView," http://www.openview.hp.com.
[5]   "IBM Tivoli Enterprise Console," http://www.tivoli.com/products/index/enterprise-console/.
[6]   "The National Computational Science Alliance," http://www.ncsa.uiuc.edu/access/index.alliance.html.
[7]   "The National Partnership for Advanced Computing Infrastructure," http://www.npaci.edu/.
[8]   "PATROL Console," http://www.bmc.com/products/.
[9]   "Platform SiteAssure," http://www.platform.com/products/rm/SiteAssure/index.asp.
[10]   "Sun Management Center," http://wwws.sun.com/software/solaris/sunmanagementcenter/.
[11]   "Unicenter Network and Systems Management," http://www3.ca.com/solutions/product.asp?id=2869.
[12]   "Xindice," http://xml.apache.org/xindice.
[13]   A. Carzaniga, D. S. Rosenblum, and A. L. Wolf, "Achieving Scalability and Expressiveness in an Internet-Scale Event Notification Service." In Proceedings of the Ninteenth ACM Symposium on Principles of Distributed Computing, Portland, OR, 2000.

[14] C. Catlett and L. Smarr, "Metacomputing," in *Communications of the ACM*, vol. 35, 1992, pp. 44-52.

[15] J. Clark and S. DeRose, "XML Path Language (XPath) Version 1.0," World Wide Web Consortium November 16 1999.

[16] K. Czajkowski, S. Fitzgerald, I. Foster, and C. Kesselman, "Grid Information Services for Distributed Resource Sharing." In Proceedings of the The 10th IEEE International Symposium on High Performance Distributed Computing, 2001.

[17] K. Czajkowski, I. Foster, N. Karonis, C. Kesselman, S. Martin, W. Smith, and S. Tuecke, "A Resource Management Architecture for Metasystems," *Lecture Notes on Computer Science*, vol. 1459, 1998.

[18] G. Eisenhauer, F. Bustamante, and K. Schwan, "Event Services for High Performance Computing." In Proceedings of the 9th IEEE International Symposium on High Performance Distributed Computing, 2000.

[19] R. E. Filman and D. D. Lee, "Managing Distributed Systems with Smart Subscriptions." In Proceedings of the International Conference on Parallel and Distributed Processing Techniques and Applications, Las Vegas, NV, 2000.

[20] S. Fitzgerald, I. Foster, C. Kesselman, G. v. Laszewski, W. Smith, and S. Tuecke, "A Directory Service for Configuring High-Performance Distributed Computations." In Proceedings of the 6th IEEE International Symposium on High Performance Distributed Computing, 1997.

[21] I. Foster and C. Kesselman, "Globus: A Metacomputing Infrastructure Toolkit," *International Journal of Supercomputing Applications*, vol. 11, pp. 115-128, 1997.

[22] I. Foster and C. Kesselman, "The Grid: Blueprint for a New Computing Infrastructure,".: Morgan Kauffmann, 1999.

[23] I. Foster, C. Kesselman, G. Tsudik, and S. Tuecke, "A Security Architecture for Computational Grids." In Proceedings of the 5th ACM Conference on Computer and Communications Security, 1998.

[24] E. Galstad, "NetSaint Network Monitor," http://www.netsaint.org/.

[25] J. Giarratano, *Expert Systems: Principles and Programming*: Brooks and Cole Publishing, 1998.

[26] A. Grimshaw, W. Wulf, J. French, A. Weaver, and P. R. Jr., "Legion: The Next Logical Step Toward A Nationwide Virtual Computer," Department of Computer Science, University of Virginia CS-94-21, June, 1994 1994.

[27] M. Hapner, R. Burridge, R. Sharma, J. Fialli, and K. Stout, "Java Message Service Specification v1.1," Sun Microsystems June 2002.

[28] T. Howes and M. Smith, *LDAP: Programming Directory-Enabled Applications with Lightweight Directory Access Protocol*: Macmillan Technical Publishing, 1997.

[29] W. Johnston, D. Gannon, and B. Nitzberg, "Grids as Production Computing Environments: The Engineering Aspects of NASA's Information Power Grid." In Proceedings of the 8th IEEE International Symposium on High Performance Distributed Computing, 1999.

[30] M. Litzkow and M. Livny, "Experience with the Condor Distributed Batch System." In Proceedings of the IEEE Workshop on Experimental Distributed Systems, 1990.

[31] OMG, "Event Service Specification v1.1,", 2001-03-01, March 2001.

[32] OMG, "Notification Service Specification v1.0,", 2000-06-20, June 2000.

[33] B. Segall, D. Arnold, J. Boot, M. Henderson, and T. Phelps, "Content Based Routing with Elvin4." In Proceedings of the AUUG2k, Canberra, Australia, 2000.

[34] A. Slominski, M. Govindaraju, D. Gannon, and R. Bramley, "SoapRMI Events: Design and Implementation," Computer Science Department, Indiana University TR549, May 2001.

[35] W. Smith, "A Framework for Control and Observation in Distributed Environments," NASA Advanced Supercomputing Division, NASA Ames Research Center, Moffett Field, CA NAS-01-006, June 2001.

[36] W. Smith and D. Gunter, "Simple LDAP Schemas for Grid Monitoring," The Global Grid Forum GWD-Perf-13-1, 2001.

[37] W. Smith, D. Gunter, and D. Quesnel, "A Simple XML Producer-Consumer Protocol," The Global Grid Forum GWD-Perf-8-2, 2001.

[38] W. Smith, D. Gunter, and D. Quesnel, "An XML-Based Protocol for Distributed Event Services." In Proceedings of the The 2001 International Conference on Parallel and Distributed Processing Techniques and Applications, Las Vegas, NV, 2001.

[39] W. Stallings, *SNMP, SNMPv2, and CMIP: The Practical Guide to Network-Management Standards*. Reading, Massachusetts: Addison-Wesley, 1993.

[40] B. Tierney, R. Aydt, D. Gunter, W. Smith, Valerie Taylor, R. Wolski, and M. Swany, "A Grid Monitoring Service Architecture," Global Grid Forum Performance Working Group 2001.

[41] B. Tierney, B. Crowley, D. Gunter, M. Holding, J. Lee, and M. Thompson, "A Monitoring Sensor Management System for Grid Environments." In Proceedings of the 9th IEEE Symposium on High Performance Distributed Computing, Pittsburgh, PA, 2000.

[42] A. Tirumala and J. Ferguson, "Iperf Version 1.2," http://dast.nlanr.net/Projects/Iperf/.

[43] R. Wolski, "Forecasting Network Performance to Support Dynamic Scheduling Using the Network Weather Service." In Proceedings of the 6th IEEE Symposium on High Performance Distributed Computing, 1997.

Session 2A

Interconnection Networks

Hypercube Network Fault Tolerance: A Probabilistic Approach*

Jianer Chen
Dept. of Computer Science
Texas A&M University
College Station, TX 77843
chen@cs.tamu.edu

Iyad A. Kanj
School of CTI
DePaul University
Chicago, IL 60604
ikanj@cs.depaul.edu

Guojun Wang
College of Information Eng.
Central-South University
ChangSha, Hunan 410083, China
Gordon434@163.net

Abstract

Extensive experience has shown that hypercube networks are highly fault tolerant. What is frustrating is that it seems very difficult to properly formulate and formally prove this important fact, despite extensive research efforts in the past two decades. Most proposed fault tolerance models for hypercube networks are only able to characterize very rare extreme situations thus significantly underestimating the fault tolerance power of hypercube networks, while for more realistic fault tolerance models, the analysis becomes much more complicated. In this paper, we develop new techniques to analyze a realistic fault tolerance model and derive lower bounds for the probability of hypercube network fault tolerance. Our results are both theoretically significant and practically important. Theoretically, our method offers very general and powerful techniques for formally proving lower bounds on the probability of network connectivity, while practically, our results provide formally proven and precisely given upper bounds on node failure probabilities for manufacturers to achieve a desired probability for network connectivity. Our techniques are also useful for analysis of the performance of routing algorithms.

1. Introduction

With the continuous increase in network size, dealing with large size networks with faults has become unavoidable. In particular, the problem of keeping all non-faulty nodes in a network connected and developing efficient and reliable routing algorithms in a network with faults has been extensively studied in the last two decades.

The current paper focuses on the study of fault tolerance of hypercube networks. Hypercube networks are among the earliest proposed network models and still remain as one of the most important and attractive ones. A number of research and commercial large-scale parallel machines have been built based on the hypercube topology [9, 16, 18]. Recent research has also shown that fault tolerant hypercube networks of large size can be used as an effective control topology in supporting large-scale multicast applications in the Internet [14].

Extensive experience has shown that hypercube networks can tolerate a large number of faulty nodes while still remain functioning. What is frustrating is that it seems very difficult to properly formulate and formally prove this important fact, despite extensive research efforts in the past two decades (see [5, 10] for comprehensive surveys). It is easy to see that the n-dimensional hypercube network H_n can tolerate no more than $n - 1$ faulty nodes: H_n becomes disconnected when all n neighbors of a non-faulty node become faulty. However, this is the only way that n faulty nodes disconnect H_n [13, 17] and in practice the situation is very unlikely. Moreover, the ratio $(n - 1)/2^n$ of faulty nodes over the total nodes in H_n is impractically too small, which requires, for example for $n = 20$, the average failure probability of each individual node to be not larger than 0.002%. Much effort has been devoted attempting to introduce more realistic definitions to measure hypercube networks' ability of tolerating faults. Concepts such as *forbidden set* [4, 11, 12] and *cluster fault tolerance model* [6, 7] have been proposed. The concept of forbidden sets suggests to prohibit certain "very unlikely" failure patterns. A special model for forbidden sets, the *k-safeness* of networks, insists that each non-faulty node has at least k non-faulty neighbors [4, 8, 12]. However, routing algorithms on the model of k-safe networks seem to become more complicated, and efficient routing algorithms have only been developed for 1-safe and 2-safe hypercube networks [4, 8]. Since in the worst case a k-safe hypercube network H_n can tolerate no more than $2^k(n - k) - 1$ faulty nodes [12, 20], this line of research still assumes a bound $O(n)$ on the number of faulty nodes in H_n.

An alternative approach, which seems to more reason-

*This work is supported in part by the USA NSF Grant CCR-0000206, and by the China NNSF Grants for Distinguished Young Scholars and for the Changjiang Scholar Reward Project.

65

ably characterize "normal" failure situations and avoid being trapped by the unlikely rare situations, is to study the probability of connectivity of a network under an assumed probabilistic distribution of individual node failures. Najjar and Gaudiot [15] have studied this model using the following approach. Let Q be an N node network in which all nodes have degree n. An *h-cluster* in Q is a connected subgraph of h nodes in Q. We say that a disconnection is *caused by an h-cluster* C if all nodes in C are non-faulty but all nodes adjacent to C are faulty. Najjar and Gaudiot [15] conjectured that the probability of network disconnection caused by 1-clusters should be much larger than that caused by other situations. Based on this conjecture, they studied the probability of disconnection caused by 1-clusters and used it to approximate the probability of real network disconnection. They also verified their conjecture based on a variety of assumptions, including that the number of possible h-clusters in Q must be bounded by $O(N)$ and that the number of nodes adjacent to an h-cluster must be bounded by $O(n)$. Obviously, hypercube networks (and actually most hierarchical networks) do not satisfy these assumptions: an n-dimensional hypercube H_n has $N = 2^n$ nodes and each node in H_n has degree n, while the number of edges in H_n, each of which makes a 2-cluster, is $nN/2$ (thus not $O(N)$), and the number of nodes in H_n adjacent to a k-dimensional subcube, which makes a 2^k-cluster, is $2^k(n-k)$ (thus can be much larger than $O(n)$).

Therefore, the conjecture given in [15] was not firmly verified and formally proved for hypercube networks, and an approximation of the probability of connectivity derived from this conjecture for hypercube networks will not be convincing. On the other hand, a precise calculation or a good approximation of the connectivity probability for hypercube networks seems to be very difficult. The hypercube networks may have a very large variety of different kinds of connected subgraphs of variant structures. A good approximation of the probability would require an effective characterization of these subgraphs, while it is known that even identifying a single connected subgraph of a hypercube network is already NP-hard [19].

The main contribution of the current paper is the development of systematic and powerful techniques for formal analysis of the above probabilistic fault tolerance model, which enables us to develop effective lower bounds for connectivity probability for hypercube networks. Our techniques make use of the concept of "local subcube connectivity" introduced in [1]. The study of local subcube connectivity shows a very nice and important property for the hypercube networks: a properly defined local connectivity of small subcubes implies the global connectivity of the entire network. Since small subcubes have much smaller size, a probabilistic analysis on the local subcube connectivity becomes possible and feasible. From the probability derived

for the local subcube connectivity, we then are able to obtain effective lower bounds on the probability for the global connectivity for the entire hypercube network. Our results are both theoretically significant and practically important. Theoretically, our method offers very general and powerful techniques for formally proving lower bounds on the probability for network connectivity. Practically, our results provide formally proven and precisely given upper bounds on node failure probability for manufacturers to achieve a desired network connectivity probability. For example, our techniques give *formal proofs* that as long as the individual node failure probability is not larger than 10%, an nCUBE machine of 1024 nodes [16] remains connected with probability at least 99%, while when individual node failure probability is bounded by 1.7%, a Thinking Machines' CM-2 computer of 65, 536 nodes [18] remains connected with probability larger than 99.99%. To our knowledge, these are the first group of *precisely stated* and *formally proven* conclusions that show the high fault tolerance of hypercube networks, although they had been previously "observed" by extensive practical experience and experiments.

To further illustrate the power of our techniques, we study the success probability of a simple routing algorithm on hypercube networks, which is a slight modification of the "dimension-order" algorithm [5]. This simple routing algorithm is deterministic and local-information-based, running in optimal time, and constructing a routing path of length bounded by a small constant plus twice of the optimal length. Compared to most routing algorithms proposed in the extensive literature (see [3, 5, 10, 13] and their bibliographies), this algorithm is simpler and weaker. However, our new techniques enable us to formally prove that even with such a simple algorithm, and with a very large fraction of faulty nodes, the hypercube networks can still route successfully with a very high probability.

Finally, we point out that our techniques can be extended to other node failure probabilities, to other hierarchical network structures, and to other network applications.

2. The probability of hypercube connectivity

The *n-dimensional hypercube* H_n (or shortly the *n-cube*) consists of 2^n nodes, each is labeled by a distinguished binary string of length n. Two nodes in H_n are adjacent if the binary labels of them differ by exactly one bit. Each binary string $b_1 b_2 \cdots b_{n-k}$ of length $n - k$ corresponds to a *k-dimensional subcube* H_k in H_n (or shortly a *k-subcube*) of 2^k nodes whose labels are of the form $b_1 b_2 \cdots b_{n-k} x_{n-k+1} \cdots x_n$, where each x_j is either 0 or 1. The subcube H_k will also be written as $H_k = b_1 b_2 \cdots b_{n-k} * *$. It is easy to see that each k-subcube of H_n is isomorphic to the k-cube. Note that there are other subgraphs of H_n that are isomorphic to the k-cube. However, in this paper, we only consider "basic" k-subcubes of the form $b_1 b_2 \cdots b_{n-k} * *$.

The concept of *local k-subcube connectivity* of a hypercube network has been proposed in [1]. We first give a quick review on the related definitions and results.

Definition ([1]) The n-cube H_n is *locally k-subcube connected* if in every k-subcube H_k of H_n, less than half of the nodes in H_k are faulty and the non-faulty nodes of H_k make a connected graph.

In particular, a k-subcube H_k of the n-cube is k-subcube connected if less than half of the nodes in H_k are faulty, and the non-faulty nodes in H_k make a connected graph.

Theorem 2.1 ([1]) *The non-faulty nodes in a locally k-subcube connected n-cube make a connected graph for all $k \leq n$.*

Throughout this paper, we assume that in the n-cube H_n, the node failures are independent, and every node has the same failure probability p. For a given event $\mathbf{E}$, we denote by Prob[$\mathbf{E}$] the probability of the event $\mathbf{E}$. We first derive lower bounds, in terms of p and the size 2^n of the n-cube, on the probability that the n-cube H_n is locally k-subcube connected. For a fixed k-subcube H_k, We define the following event:

Event NL(H_k)

The k-subcube H_k is not locally k-subcube connected.

We have the following lemma.

Lemma 2.2 Prob[**NL**(H_k)] $= p^k U_k(p)$, *where*

$$U_k(p) = \sum_{i=k}^{2^{k-1}-1} B_{k,i} p^{i-k} (1-p)^{2^k-i}$$
$$+ \sum_{j=2^{k-1}}^{2^k} \binom{2^k}{j} p^{j-k} (1-p)^{2^k-j}$$

and $B_{k,i}$, $k \leq i \leq 2^{k-1}-1$, is the number of ways to remove i nodes from the k-subcube H_k so that the remaining nodes in H_k do not make a connected graph.

Lemma 2.2 implies the following important theorem immediately.

Theorem 2.3 *Suppose that each node in the n-cube H_n has a uniform and independent failure probability p and that $k \leq n$. Then the probability that the non-faulty nodes in H_n remain connected is at least $1 - 2^{n-k} p^k U_k(p)$, where $U_k(p)$ is the polynomial of p given in Lemma 2.2.*

PROOF. Let H_k be any k-subcube of the n-cube H_n. By Lemma 2.2, the probability that the k-subcube H_k is not locally k-subcube connected is equal to $p^k U_k(p)$. Thus, the probability that the k-subcube H_k is locally k-subcube connected is equal to $1 - p^k U_k(p)$. In consequence, the probability that the n-cube H_n is locally k-subcube connected, i.e., the probability that all 2^{n-k} k-subcubes in H_n are locally k-subcube connected is equal to $(1 - p^k U_k(p))^{2^{n-k}}$, which is at least as large as $1 - 2^{n-k} p^k U_k(p)$.

Now the theorem follows since by Theorem 2.1, the local k-subcube connectivity of H_n implies that the non-faulty nodes in H_n are connected. $\qquad \square$

It turns out that Theorem 2.3 is very powerful in the discussion of fault tolerance of hypercube networks. Consider the local 3-subcube connectivity. It is not hard to see that $B_{3,3} = 8$ since the only way to remove 3 nodes to disconnect the 3-cube H_3 is to remove the 3 neighbors of a node in H_3, and there are totally 8 nodes in H_3. Therefore, the polynomial $U_3(p)$ is given by

$$\begin{aligned} U_3(p) &= B_{3,3}(1-p)^5 + \sum_{j=4}^{8} \binom{8}{j} p^{j-3}(1-p)^{8-j} \\ &= 8(1-p)^5 + 70p(1-p)^4 + 56p^2(1-p)^3 \\ &\quad + 28p^3(1-p)^2 + 8p^4(1-p) + p^5 \end{aligned}$$

Using the standard techniques in calculus, we can check that in the interval $[0,1]$, the polynomial $U_3(p)$ is positive and reaches its maximum $9.881\cdots$ at point $p = 0.14119\cdots$. Now applying Theorem 2.3 enables us to conclude that the probability that the non-faulty nodes in the n-cube H_n remain connected is at least

$$1 - 2^{n-3} p^3 U_3(p) \geq 1 - 10 \cdot 2^{n-3} p^3$$

This implies that, for example, if the failure probability of each individual node is bounded by 0.1%, then a 20-cube, which has about a million nodes, can sustain up to $2^{20} \cdot 0.1\% > 1,000$ faulty nodes while still keeping its non-faulty nodes connected with a probability larger than 99.8%. Note that this is a very significant improvement over the traditional definition of fault tolerance, which allows the 20-cube to tolerate at most 19 faulty nodes, and over the concepts of 1-safeness and 2-safeness, which allow the 20-cube to tolerate at most 37 and 71 faulty nodes, respectively.

The above example shows that Theorem 2.3 can be used as a scheme in evaluating the power of hypercubes' fault tolerance. In general, by considering local k-subcube connectivity, we try to derive an upper bound c_k for the polynomial $U_k(p)$ in the interval $[0,1]$, which will immediately make us able to conclude that the probability that the non-faulty nodes of an n-cube H_n, where $n \geq k$, remain connected is at least $1 - c_k 2^{n-k} p^k$. This gives us a potential to derive a larger and larger probability for the connectivity for the n-cube H_n if $c_k 2^{n-k} p^k$ is decreasing when k increases. Unfortunately, even for local 4-subcube connectivity, the analysis for deriving a precise formula for the polynomial $U_4(p)$ becomes extremely tedious. On the other hand, the construction of the polynomial $U_k(p)$ is routine: for each i, $k \leq i \leq 2^{k-1} - 1$, simply enumerate all possible removals of i nodes from H_k, and count the number of removals that disconnect H_k. This will directly give us the number $B_{k,i}$, and hence the polynomial $U_k(p)$. This procedure can obviously be automated and fed to a computer. Based on this idea, we have programmed this procedure for local 5-subcube connectivity and run the program on a parallel Sun workstation system, which gives us the polynomial $U_5(p)$ as follows.

$$
\begin{aligned}
U_5(p) = \\
& 32(1-p)^{27} + 832p(1-p)^{26} + 10400p^2(1-p)^{25} \\
+ \ & 83120p^3(1-p)^{24} + 476640p^4(1-p)^{23} \\
+ \ & 2086896p^5(1-p)^{22} + 7251584p^6(1-p)^{21} \\
+ \ & 20524992p^7(1-p)^{20} + 48190080p^8(1-p)^{19} \\
+ \ & 95095920p^9(1-p)^{18} + 159252160p^{10}(1-p)^{17} \\
+ \ & 601080390p^{11}(1-p)^{16} + 565722720p^{12}(1-p)^{15} \\
+ \ & 471435600p^{13}(1-p)^{14} + 347373600p^{14}(1-p)^{13} \\
+ \ & 225792840p^{15}(1-p)^{12} + 129024480p^{16}(1-p)^{11} \\
+ \ & 64512240p^{17}(1-p)^{10} + 28048800p^{18}(1-p)^{9} \\
+ \ & 10518300p^{19}(1-p)^{8} + 3365856p^{20}(1-p)^{7} \\
+ \ & 906192p^{21}(1-p)^{6} + 201376p^{22}(1-p)^{5} \\
+ \ & 35960p^{23}(1-p)^{4} + 4960p^{24}(1-p)^{3} \\
+ \ & 496p^{25}(1-p)^{2} + 32p^{26}(1-p) + p^{27}
\end{aligned}
$$

Again using the standard techniques in calculus, we verify that the polynomial $U_5(p)$ in the interval $[0, 1]$ is positive and bounded by 32. This computation, together with Theorem 2.3, enables us to conclude the following.

Theorem 2.4 *Suppose that each node in the n-cube H_n has a uniform and independent failure probability p and that $n \geq 5$. Then the probability that the non-faulty nodes in H_n remain connected is at least $1 - 32 \cdot 2^{n-5} p^5 = 1 - 2^n p^5$.*

We give a few remarks on Theorem 2.4.

From the theoretical point of view, Theorem 2.4 has developed powerful techniques for formally proving lower bounds on the probability of hypercube connectivity in terms of the probability of individual node failures. As described in the introductory section, although it was well observed that the hypercube networks are highly fault tolerant,

there was no formal proofs for this important fact. Theorem 2.4 provides a formal proof of a precisely stated bound for this measure.

From the practical point of view, Theorem 2.4 provides a formally proven threshold on the node failure probability for manufacturers to achieve a desired probability for the connectivity of hypercube networks. In particular, when the dimension n of the hypercube network and a designated probability p' for network connectivity are given, by setting $1 - 2^n p^5 \geq p'$, we can derive an upper bound for the individual node failure probability p in terms of n and p', which will guarantees the desired probability for network connectivity. For example, if we want to build an nCUBE machine of 1024 nodes [16], which is a 10-cube, and achieve connectivity of probability at least 99%, we can derive from $1 - 2^{10} p^5 \geq 99\%$ that $p \leq 10\%$. Thus, as long as the manufacturers ensure that the individual node failure probability is not larger than 10%, the probability of network connectivity of the nCUBE machine of 1024 nodes is at least 99%. Similarly, if we want to achieve connectivity of probability 99.99% for a Thinking Machines' CM-2 computer with 65,536 processors [18], we just need to ensure that the individual node failure probability is not larger than 1.7%. Note that the above required individual node failure probabilities are feasibly achievable by today's manufacturing technology, which thus provide formal proofs for the possibilities of building highly fault tolerant hypercube computers. To the authors' knowledge, Theorem 2.4 provides the first *formally proven* conclusion for this important fact, although previous extensive experience and experiments have given people strong impression that the hypercube networks "should be" very highly fault tolerant.

3. Analysis for a simple routing algorithm

One important reason to require the connectivity of non-faulty nodes in a network is to ensure the existence of fault-free routing paths between any two non-faulty nodes in the network. Using the scheme we established in the previous section (Theorem 2.1 and Theorem 2.3), we have been able to show the high probability of connectivity of a hypercube network with faulty nodes. In this section, we show that our scheme is also very useful and powerful in the analysis of routing algorithms on hypercube networks.

We consider a routing algorithm that is a slight modification of the simplest *dimension-order* routing algorithm. Given two nodes $u = u_1 u_2 \cdots u_n$ and $v = v_1 v_2 \cdots v_n$ in the n-cube, the dimension-order algorithm routes from u to v by "converting" each bit u_i into v_i, in the order $i = 1, 2, \ldots, n$ [5]. It has been well known that the dimension-order routing algorithm, though simple, is extremely vulnerable to network faults [5].

We modify the dimension-order routing scheme as fol-

Algorithm. H-Router

Input: an n-cube H_n and two non-faulty nodes $u = u_1 u_2 \cdots u_n$
and $v = v_1 v_2 \cdots v_n$ in H_n

Output: a path of non-faulty nodes in H_n from u to v

1. $w = u$, and initialize the path $P = [w]$;

2. **for** $i = 1$ to $n - k$ **do**

       if $w_i \neq v_i$ {so $v_i = \overline{w_i}$} **then**

         if $w' = w_1 \cdots w_{i-1} \overline{w_i} w_{i+1} \cdots w_n$ is non-faulty

         then extend the path P to w';   let $w = w'$;

         else if there is a j, $n - k + 1 \leq j \leq n$ such that

           $q = w_1 \cdots w_{j-1} \overline{w_j} w_{j+1} \cdots w_n$ and

           $q' = w_1 \cdots w_{i-1} \overline{w_i} w_{i+1} \cdots w_{j-1} \overline{w_j} w_{j+1} \cdots w_n$

           are both non-faulty

         then extend the path P to q then to q';   let $w = q'$;

         else STOP('routing fails');

3. apply BFS in k-subcube $w_1 \cdots w_{n-k} * *$ to convert the last k bits

Figure 1. A routing algorithm

lows. We start by converting the first $n - k$ bits u_i into v_i, in the order $i = 1, 2, \ldots, n - k$. In case a bit u_i cannot be directly converted into v_i because of network faults, we try to flip a bit among the last k bits to make the ith bit convertible. After converting the first $n - k$ bits, we apply a Breadth First Search process in a k-subcube to convert the last k bits. The formal algorithm is presented in Figure 1.

The algorithm **H-Router** is deterministic and local-information-based, requiring no global network faulty information. Compared to most routing algorithms proposed in the extensive literature (see [3, 5, 10, 13] and their bibliographies for references), this algorithm is simpler and looks weaker. However, in the rest of this section, using our new techniques, we formally prove that even with such a simple routing algorithm, and with a very large fraction of faulty nodes, the hypercube networks can still route successfully with a very high probability.

Note that the loop body of step 2 in the algorithm **H-Router** is executed only when $u_i \neq v_i$. Let $H_{n-k}(u, v)$ be the Hamming distance between the substrings $u_1 u_2 \cdots u_{n-k}$ and $v_1 v_2 \cdots v_{n-k}$, then the loop body in step 2 is executed exactly $H_{n-k}(u, v)$ times. During each execution of the loop body, at most 2 bits are flipped. Thus, step 2 of the algorithm runs in time $O(n)$ and increases the path length by at most $2H_{n-k}(u, v)$. Finally, step 3 of the algorithm **H-Router** runs in time $O(2^k)$ and extends the routing path to the destination node v in the k-subcube $v_1 v_2 \cdots v_{n-k} * *$.

Thus, the algorithm **H-Router**, if succeeds, runs in optimal time and, when k is small, constructs routing paths of length bounded by a small constant plus twice of the optimal length. The algorithm **H-Router** may fail when fault-free routing paths exist between the two given nodes. In the following, we use our new developed techniques to show that this happens with very small probability.

We say that two k-subcubes $b_1 b_2 \cdots b_{n-k} * *$ and $b'_1 b'_2 \cdots b'_{n-k} * *$ in the n-cube H_n are *neighboring k-subcubes* if the two binary strings $b_1 b_2 \cdots b_{n-k}$ and $b'_1 b'_2 \cdots b'_{n-k}$ differ by exactly one bit. Note that each k-subcube in H_n has exactly $n - k$ neighboring k-subcubes.

Let w be a node in a k-subcube H_k and let H'_k be a neighboring k-subcube of H_k. We say that *the k-subcube H'_k is not reachable from w in two steps* if every path in $H_k \cup H'_k$ of length bounded by 2 from w to a node in H'_k contains at least one faulty node $q \neq w$ (note that the node w could be either faulty or non-faulty). For a k-subcube H_k we define the following events.

Event L2(H_k)

There are a node w in H_k and a neighboring k-subcube H'_k of H_k such that H'_k is not reachable from w in two steps.

Event FN(H_k)

H_k has at least $2k - 2$ faulty nodes.

We can prove the following lemma.

Lemma 3.1 Prob[**L2**(H_k)] *is bounded by* $4^k (n - k) p^{k+1}$, *and* Prob[**FN**(H_k)] *is bounded by* $p^{2k-2} \binom{2^k}{2k-2}$.

Theorem 3.2 *Suppose that each node in the n-cube H_n has a uniform and independent failure probability p, then for any $k \leq n$ and for any two given non-faulty nodes u and v in H_n, with probability at least $1 - 2^{n-k} p^k [U_k(p) + 4^k (n - k) p + p^{k-2} \binom{2^k}{2k-2}]$, where the polynomial $U_k(p)$ is given in Lemma 2.2, the algorithm **H-Router** runs in time $O(kn + 2^k)$ and constructs a routing path from u to v of length bounded by $2H_{n-k}(u, v) + k + 2$.*

PROOF. Let H_k be a fixed k-subcube in the n-cube H_n. Recall that $\mathbf{NL}(H_k)$ is the event that H_k is not locally k-subcube connected, $\mathbf{L2}(H_k)$ is the event that there exist a node w in H_k and a neighboring k-subcube H'_k of H_k such that H'_k is not reachable from w in two steps, and $\mathbf{FN}(H_k)$ is the event that H_k has at least $2k - 2$ faulty nodes. Now let $\mathbf{Bad}(H_k)$ be the union of these events:

$$\mathbf{Bad}(H_k) = \mathbf{NL}(H_k) \cup \mathbf{L2}(H_k) \cup \mathbf{FN}(H_k)$$

then we have

$$
\begin{aligned}
&\text{Prob}[\mathbf{Bad}(H_k)] \\
\leq\ & \text{Prob}[\mathbf{NL}(H_k)] + \text{Prob}[\mathbf{L2}(H_k)] + \text{Prob}[\mathbf{FN}(H_k)] \\
\leq\ & p^k U_k(p) + 4^k (n - k) p^{k+1} + p^{2k-2} \binom{2^k}{2k-2} \\
=\ & p^k \left[U_k(p) + 4^k (n - k) p + p^{k-2} \binom{2^k}{2k-2} \right] \quad (1)
\end{aligned}
$$

where the second inequality is by Lemma 2.2 and Lemma 3.1, and the polynomial $U_k(p)$ is given in Lemma 2.2.

Let the complement event of the event **Bad**(H_k) be **Good**(H_k), which is stated as:

Event Good(H_k)

(1) the k-subcube H_k is locally k-subcube connected; (2) for every node w in H_k, every neighboring k-subcube H_k' of H_k is reachable from w in two steps; and (3) the number of faulty nodes in H_k is bounded by $2k - 3$.

Then the probability of the event **Good**(H_k) is

$$\text{Prob}[\textbf{Good}(H_k)] = 1 - \text{Prob}[\textbf{Bad}(H_k)]$$

Now we define **GOOD** to be the intersection of the events **Good**(H_k) over all k-subcubes H_k in the n-cube H_n, thus

Event GOOD

For every k-subcube H_k in the n-cube H_n: (1) H_k is locally k-subcube connected; (2) for every node w in H_k, every neighboring k-subcube H_k' of H_k is reachable from w in two steps; and (3) the number of faulty nodes in H_k is bounded by

$$2k - 3.$$

Since there are totally 2^{n-k} k-subcubes in the n-cube H_n, the node failure probability is independent, and any two k-subcubes in H_n are disjoint (thus the events **Good**(H_k) and **Good**(H_k') are independent for two different k-subcubes H_k and H_k'), we have

$$
\begin{aligned}
\text{Prob}[\textbf{GOOD}] &= (\text{Prob}[\textbf{GOOD}(H_k)])^{2^{n-k}} \\
&= (1 - \text{Prob}[\textbf{Bad}(H_k)])^{2^{n-k}} \\
&\geq 1 - 2^{n-k}\text{Prob}[\textbf{Bad}(H_k)] \quad (2)
\end{aligned}
$$

Combining (1) and (2), we get immediately

$$\text{Prob}[\textbf{GOOD}] \geq$$
$$1 - 2^{n-k}p^k\left[U_k(p) + 4^k(n-k)p + p^{k-2}\binom{2^k}{2k-2}\right]$$

Therefore, it suffices to show that under the conditions of the event **GOOD**, the algorithm **H-Router** achieves the performance described in the theorem.

Consider step 2 of the algorithm. In case the ith bit w_i of the node $w = w_1 w_2 \cdots w_n$ is not equal to the ith bit v_i of the destination node $v = v_1 v_2 \cdots v_n$, we look for a subpath from the node w in the k-subcube $H_k = w_1 \cdots w_{i-1} w_i w_{i+1} \cdots w_{n-k} * *$ to the neighboring k-subcube $H_k' = w_1 \cdots w_{i-1} v_i w_{i+1} \cdots w_{n-k} * *$. Under the conditions of the event **GOOD**, the neighboring k-subcube H_k' of the k-subcube H_k is reachable from the node

w in H_k in two steps. That is, either w's neighbor $w' = w_1 \cdots w_{i-1} v_i w_{i+1} \cdots w_n$ in H_k' is non-faulty, or a neighbor $q = w_1 \cdots w_{i-1} w_i w_{i+1} \cdots w_{n-k} \cdots w_{j-1} \overline{w_j} w_{j+1} \cdots w_n$ of w in H_k and q's neighbor $q' = w_1 \cdots w_{i-1} v_i w_{i+1} \cdots w_{n-k} \cdots w_{j-1} \overline{w_j} w_{j+1} \cdots w_n$ in H_k' are both non-faulty. Thus, the path P can be extended to the k-subcube H_k' by adding at most two edges. Finally, since the loop body in step 2 is executed only when $u_i \neq v_i$, we conclude that the length of the path P after step 2 of the algorithm is bounded by $2H_{n-k}(u, v)$. Moreover, the running time of step 2 is bounded by $O(kH_{n-k}(u,v) + (n-k)) = O(kn)$.

Finally, we consider step 3 of the algorithm. Now the node w and the destination node v are in the same k-subcube $H_k = v_1 v_2 \cdots v_{n-k} * *$. Under the conditions of the event **GOOD**, the k-subcube H_k is locally k-subcube connected and the number of faulty nodes in H_k is bounded by $2k - 3$. Since the non-faulty nodes in H_k are connected, every non-faulty node in H_k has at least one non-faulty neighbor in H_k. Latifi [11] has shown that if each non-faulty node in H_k has at least one non-faulty neighbor and the total number of faulty nodes in H_k is bounded by $2k-3$, then every pair of non-faulty nodes in H_k are connected by a path of length bounded by $k + 2$ that consists of only non-faulty nodes. Therefore, the Breadth First Search process from the node w will construct a path from w to v in H_k whose length is bounded by $k + 2$. This completes the routing path from the source node u to the destination node v in the n-cube H_n. Moreover, the Breadth First Search in step 3 of the algorithm runs in time $O(2^k)$.

Therefore, under the conditions of event **GOOD**, whose probability is at least $1 - 2^{n-k}p^k[U_k(p) + 4^k(n-k)p + p^{k-2}\binom{2^k}{2k-2}]$, the routing algorithm **H-Router** runs in time $O(kn + 2^k)$ and constructs a routing path of length bounded by $2H_{n-k}(u,v) + k + 2$. □

Remark. The running time of the algorithm **H-Router** in Theorem 3.2 can be further improved to $O(kn + k^2)$. In fact, Latifi [11] has described a construction that runs in time $O(k^2)$ and constructs a routing path of length bounded by $k + 2$ for any two non-faulty nodes in a k-cube, under the conditions that each non-faulty node has at least one non-faulty neighbor and that the total number of faulty nodes in H_k is bounded by $2k - 3$. In consequence, the running time of step 3 of the algorithm **H-Router** can be reduced to $O(k^2)$, which gives the improved running time $O(kn + k^2)$ for the algorithm **H-Router**.

Corollary 3.3 *Suppose that each node in the n-cube H_n has a uniform and independent failure probability p, then for any two given non-faulty nodes u and v in H_n, with probability at least $1 - 2^{n-5}p^5[32 + 1024(n - 5)p + 10518300p^3]$, the algorithm H-Router runs in time $O(n)$*

and constructs a routing path from u to v of length bounded by $2H_{n-5}(u,v) + 7$.

PROOF. Let $k = 5$ in Theorem 3.2, we conclude that with probability at least $1 - 2^{n-5}p^5[U_5(p) + 4^5(n-5)p + p^3\binom{32}{8}]$, the routing algorithm **H-Router** constructs in time $O(n)$ a routing path from u to v of length bounded by $2H_{n-5}(u,v) + 5 + 2 = 2H_{n-5}(u,v) + 7$, where the polynomial $U_5(p)$ is given in Lemma 2.2.

As we have verified in section 2, in the interval $[0, 1]$, the polynomial $U_5(p)$ is bounded by 32. This, plus $\binom{32}{8} = 10518300$, proves the corollary. □

Again Corollary 3.3 provides explicitly stated and formally proven upper bounds on the individual node failure probability in order to achieve a designated success probability for the routing algorithm **H-Router**. For instance, as long as the individual node failure probability is not larger than 4.7%, the routing algorithm **H-Router** routes successfully in an nCUBE machine of $1,024$ processors [16] with probability at least 99%, while when the individual node failure probability is bounded by 1.7%, the routing algorithm **H-Router** routes successfully in a Thinking Machines' CM-2 computer with $65,536$ processors [18] with probability larger than 99.9%. Again since the required individual node failure probabilities are feasible in today's manufacturing technology, Corollary 3.3 provides formally proven conclusions showing that the simple routing algorithm **H-Router** works practically well.

4. Conclusions and final remarks

Fault tolerance and network routing have been among the most studied topics in the research of parallel processing and computer networking. In this paper, we have established a scheme that enables us to study the probability of network fault tolerance in terms of individual node failure probability. Our results are both theoretically significant and practically important. Theoretically, the scheme offers very general and powerful techniques for establishing lower bounds on the probability for network connectivity, while practically, our scheme has provided formally proven threshold on the node failure probability that guarantees very high probability for network connectivity and efficiency and effectiveness of routing algorithms. Before closing this paper, we make a few remarks.

The scheme established in this paper is not only restricted to hypercube networks. In fact, the technique developed here is very general and can be applied to any hierarchical network structures in which larger networks can be decomposed into smaller sub-networks of similar structure. Examples of hierarchical networks include mesh networks, a variety of hypercube variations, and many network structures based on Cayley graphs [13, 17]. Roughly speaking, the scheme suggests that for hierarchical network structures, the study of global connectivity and routings can be reduced to the study of smaller substructures. In most cases, the study of small substructures is much easier since they have much fewer nodes and simpler structure. Sometimes certain properties of the small substructures can even be obtained using exhaustive enumerations.

Our scheme should also suggest a possible approach for the study of network fault tolerance under other probability distributions of node failures. For example, clustered node failure distributions have also become very popular under the belief that a node tends to fail when many of its neighbors have failed. We believe that based on our approach, the probabilistic study of network fault tolerance in terms of this kind of node failure distributions should become possible. Other extensions of our scheme include the study of other network communication problems, such as broadcasting, multicasting, and parallel routing.

We would also like to remark on our scheme for more technical details. To make our discussion more specific, we will concentrate on hypercube networks. However, the readers are reminded that most of these discussions are also applicable to other hierarchical network structures.

Theorem 2.4 could be further improved. In fact, since every locally k-subcube connected n-cube is also locally $(k+1)$-subcube connected [1], under the same node failure distribution, the probability that an n-cube is locally $(k+1)$-subcube connected is at least as large as the probability that the n-cube is locally k-subcube connected. Therefore, deriving the probability for, say, local 6-subcube connectivity will most likely improve the bound given in Theorem 2.4. Therefore, Theorem 2.4 is really an example of an application of Theorem 2.3, which offers a very general scheme for the study of hypercube fault tolerance. On the other hand, it does require to overcome certain analysis and computational difficulties in order to improve Theorem 2.4: when k increases, the construction of the polynomial $U_k(p)$ quickly becomes computationally infeasible. For example, to construct the polynomial $U_6(p)$ using a routine method needs to enumerate about half of the $2^{2^6} > 10^{19}$ subsets of nodes in the 6-cube. For further larger k, this enumeration becomes even less feasible. Better and deeper mathematical analysis seems needed for deriving and estimating the value for the polynomial $U_k(p)$.

There is another reason that we may not want to consider local k-subcube connectivity for large k. Consider Theorem 3.2, the running time of the algorithm **H-Router** is bounded by $O(kn + 2^k)$, which will become inefficient when k is very large. Indeed, the local n-subcube connectivity of an n-cube basically just tells that the non-faulty nodes in the n-cube are connected without giving any other useful information. Thus, what a routing algorithm can do is to exhaustively search among the non-faulty nodes, which obviously takes time $O(2^n)$. Note that Latifi's method [11], which routes in a k-subcube in time $O(k^2)$, cannot help for large k either since it requires the number of faulty nodes to be bounded by $2k - 3$. When k is large, the ratio $(2k - 3)/2^k$ will require an impractically small bound for individual node failure probability p.

Finally, we would like to explain the advantage of our scheme over the previously proposed fault tolerance models. Compared to Najjar and Gaudiot's results [15], our results are precisely stated and formally proved, while the results in [15] are approximations based on an unverified conjecture. Now consider the model of k-safe networks [4, 8, 12]. The k-safe networks require that each non-faulty node have at least k non-faulty neighbors. Using the techniques developed in this paper, it is possible to prove that for small k, a hypercube network is k-safe with high probability. However, the k-safeness of the hypercube does not guarantee the connectivity of the network unless we also bound the number of faulty nodes by $2^k(n - k) - 1$ [12, 20]. This constraint then significantly bounds the node failure probability to the order $2^k(n - k)/2^n$, which would be impractically small even for a reasonable value k and a moderate value n. On the other hand, our scheme allows a much larger percentage of faulty nodes and guarantees the connectivity of the entire network.

References

[1] J. CHEN, G. WANG, AND S. CHEN, Locally subcube-connected hypercube networks: theoretical analysis and experimental results, *IEEE Transactions on Computers 51*, (2002), pp. 530-540.

[2] T. H. CORMEN, C. E. LEISERSON, AND R. L. RIVEST, *Introduction to Algorithms*, McGraw-Hill Book Company, New York, 1992.

[3] J. DUATO, S. YALAMANCHILI, AND L. NI, *Interconnection Networks: An Engineering Approach*, IEEE Comput. Soc., Los Alamitos, 1997.

[4] A. H. ESFAHANIAN, Generalized measures of fault tolerance with application to n-cube networks, *IEEE Transactions on Computers 38*, (1989), pp. 1586-1591.

[5] M. D. GRAMMATIKAKIS, D. F. HSU, M. KRAETZL, AND J. F. SIBEYN, Packet routing in fixed-connection networks: a survey, *Journal of Parallel and Distributed Computing 54*, (1998), pp. 77-132.

[6] Q.-P. GU AND S. PENG, Optimal algorithms for node-to-node fault tolerant routing in hypercubes, *The Computer Journal 39*, (1996), pp. 626-629.

[7] Q.-P. GU AND S. PENG, k-pairwise cluster fault tolerant routing in hypercubes, *IEEE Transactions on Computers 46*, (1997), pp. 1042-1049.

[8] Q.-P. GU AND S. PENG, Unicast in hypercubes with large number of faulty nodes, *IEEE Transactions on Parallel and Distributed Systems 10*, (1999), pp. 964-975.

[9] INTEL CORP., *Intel iPSC/2*, Intel Scientific Computers, 1988.

[10] S. LAKSHMIVARAHAN AND S. K. DHALL, Ring, torus and hypercube architectures/algorithms for parallel computing, *Parallel Computing 25*, (1999), pp. 1877-1906.

[11] S. LATIFI, Combinatorial analysis of the fault diameter of the n-cube, *IEEE Transactions on Computers 42*, (1993), pp. 27-33.

[12] S. LATIFI, M. HEDGE, AND M. NARAGHI-POUR, Conditional connectivity measures for large multiprocessor systems, *IEEE Transactions on Computers 43*, (1994), pp. 218-222.

[13] F. T. LEIGHTON, *Introduction to Parallel Algorithms and Architectures: Arrays, Trees, Hypercubes*, Morgan Kaufmann, San Mateo, CA, 1992.

[14] J. LIEBEHERR AND B. S. SETHI, A scalable control topology for multicast communications, *Proc. IEEE INFOCOM'98*, (1998), pp. 1197-1203.

[15] W. NAJJAR AND J. L. GAUDIOT, Network resilience: a measure of network fault tolerance, *IEEE Transactions on Computers 39*, (1990), pp. 174-181.

[16] NCUBE CORPORATION, *nCUBE 2 Processor Manual*, Dec. 1990.

[17] Y. SAAD AND M. H. SCHULTZ, Topological properties of hypercubes, *IEEE Transactions on Computers 37*, (1988), pp. 867-872.

[18] THINKING MACHINES CORPORATION, Connection Machine, Model CM-2 Technical Summary, Version 6.0 edition, November 1990.

[19] A. WAGNER AND D. CORNEIL, Embedding trees in a hypercube is NP-complete, *SIAM J. Computing 19*, (1990), pp. 570-590.

[20] J. WU AND G. GUO, Fault tolerance measures for m-ary n-dimensional hypercubes based on forbidden faulty sets, *IEEE Transactions on Computers 47*, (1998), pp. 888-893.

A Class of Multistage Conference Switching Networks for Group Communication

Yuanyuan Yang
Department of Electrical & Computer Engineering
State University of New York, Stony Brook, NY 11794, USA
Jianchao Wang
DataTreasury Corporation, Melville, NY 11747, USA

Abstract— **Many emerging network applications, such as tele-conferencing and information services, require group communication, in which messages from one or more sender(s) are delivered to a large number of receivers. In this paper, we consider efficient network support for a key type of group communication, conferencing. A conference refers to a group of members in a network who communicate with each other within the group. In our recent work [5], we proposed a design for a conference network which can support multiple disjoint conferences. The major component of the network is an enhanced multistage switching network which interconnects switch modules with fan-in and fan-out capability. The multistage network used is modified from an indirect binary cube network by relaying all internal outputs at each stage through multiplexers to the outputs of the network. Each conference is realized in an indirect binary cube-like subnetwork depending on its location. A natural question here is: Can we directly adopt a class of multistage networks such as a baseline, an omega, or an indirect binary cube network to obtain a conference network with more regular network structure, simpler self-routing algorithm and less hardware cost? This paper aims to answer this question. The key issue in designing a conference network is to determine the multiplicity of routing conflicts, which is the maximum number of conflict parties competing a single interstage link when multiple disjoint conferences simultaneously present in the network. Our results in this paper show that for a network of size $n \times n$, the multiplicities of routing conflicts are small constants (between 2 and 4) for an omega network or an indirect binary cube network; while it can be as large as $\frac{\sqrt{n}}{3} + 1$ for a baseline network. Thus, our design for conference networks is based on an omega network or an indirect binary cube network but not a baseline network. We also develop fast self-routing algorithms for setting up routing paths in the newly designed conference networks. As can be seen, such an $n \times n$ conference network has $O(\log n)$ routing time and communication delay and $O(n \log n)$ hardware cost. The conference networks are superior to existing designs in terms of routing complexity, communication delay and hardware cost. The conference network proposed is rearrangeably nonblocking in general, and is strictly nonblocking under some conference service policy. It can be used in applications that require efficient or real-time group communication.**

I. INTRODUCTION AND PREVIOUS WORK

Many emerging network applications, such as tele-conferencing and information services, require *group communication*, in which messages from one or more sender(s) are delivered to a large number of receivers. The demand for group communication from these appli-

Research supported in part by the U.S. National Science Foundation under grant numbers CCR-0073085 and CCR-0207999.

cations has been growing at an accelerated pace. As a result, efficient support for group communication will become a critical networking issue in the near future. It has received a considerable amount of attention in networking and parallel and distributed computing research communities in recent years, see, for example, [1]-[14].

In this paper, we consider efficient network support for a key type of group communication, conferencing. A *conference* refers to a group of members in a network who communicate with each other within the group. In a conference, any one or more members can broadcast their messages simultaneously to every member in the group. Each member is called a *conferee* of the conference. The maximum number of conferees in a conference is called *the size of the conference*.

A *conference network* can support any simultaneous multiple conferences of various conference sizes, in which each conference can be formed among any members in the network while each member can only be allowed to join at most one conference at a time. Conference networks can be used in many applications that require efficient or real-time group communication. An immediate application is audio/video-conferencing among a group of people. Another example is to support arbitrary communication within a cluster of processors collaborating on a common computing task. In addition, a conference network can be used to transport text, image, audio and video information in a multimedia conference, and enables multiple parties in a conference to collaborate on textual and graphic documents.

A *multiconnection*, also called many-to-many connection, is a collective communication operation between a subset of network inputs and a subset of network outputs in which the inputs in the input subset can broadcast their messages to the outputs in the output subset simultaneously. A crossbar with fan-in and fan-out capability can be used to realize such multiconnections. Fig. 1(a) shows an example of a multiconnection from input set $\{0, 1, 3\}$ to output set $\{1, 2\}$. Clearly, this type of crossbar switch itself can serve as a conference network. However, using a single crossbar to build a large size conference network is very expensive because that an $n \times n$ crossbar has $O(n^2)$ hardware cost. Thus, the crossbar implementation is only suitable for a network of a small size.

Hwang and Jajszczyk [1] considered using a three-stage Clos-type network composed of crossbar switches with multiconnection capability for supporting multiconnection communication. Fig. 1(b) shows a routing for a multiconnection in a three-stage Clos-type network. However, their results on this type of network still yielded $O(n^2)$ hardware cost.

Another approach to constructing a conference network is to adopt so-called sandwich network structure. As illustrated in Fig. 2, an $n \times n$ conference network is the concatenation of three networks. The first and the third networks are simply $n \times m$ and $m \times n$ permutation networks respectively, where $m(\geq n)$ is one of key factors which determine the network cost. The first network, called presentation net-

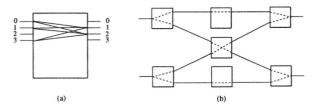

(a)   (b)

Fig. 1. (a) A example of multiconnection, or a many-to-many connection, in a crossbar. (b) An example of multiconnection routing in a three-stage network.

work, connects each conferee at any location to an input of the second network. The third network, called distribution network, routes each conferee at an output of the second network to its original location, i.e. the outputs of the third network are fed back to the inputs of the first network. The second $m \times m$ network , called *conference component network*, performs conference functionality which allows conferees in the same conference to communicate with each other, and handles multiple conferences simultaneously. Since the second network in the sandwich network structure is the only component which requires conference capability, this type of network structure has the potential to reduce network cost.

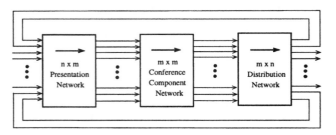

Fig. 2. The sandwich network structure for a conference network.

There have been several conference network designs in the literature which fall into this category. Yang and Masson [2] proposed a sandwich network using a sequential ring as the second network, in which $m = O(n)$. The network was originally designed for a rearrangeable multicast network but can also be used for a rearrangeable conference network. Houlahan, Cowen, and Masson [3] designed a nonblocking conference network, in which the conference component network is a hypercube with $m = O(n\sqrt{\log n})$. Du and Masson [4] also proposed a nonblocking conference network, in which the conference component adopted is an r-dimensional mesh with $m = O(n^{\frac{r+1}{r}})$. A common feature of these designs is that the conference component network is a direct network in which each node has a dedicated link to each of its neighboring nodes, and the key idea for realizing a conference is to find a group of connected idle nodes in the direct network. However, due to the nature of the conference component networks adopted, these designs suffer the following drawbacks: (1) The subnetwork allocated for a conference is usually an irregular network, and no efficient all-to-all broadcast algorithm exists for irregular networks; (2) the connections among different conferees have different delays; (3) the maximum delay in a conference may be as large as the conference size.

Recently, in [5] we proposed a new conference network which adopts both existing technologies and overcomes the drawbacks mentioned above. The overall conference network is implemented as a sandwich network structure, and the conference component network is a specially designed multistage network with $m = n$. We now

briefly review this conference network. Functionally, we can view the conference component network as an $n \times n$ crossbar network. To realize a conference request with conference size c, we first allocate some c consecutive idle inputs as well as the idle outputs with the same labels as the inputs in the conference component network; then permute the c conferees in the presentation network to the c inputs of the conference component network, and permute the c outputs of the conference component network through the distribution network to its c outputs which is equivalent to the original c conferees. A routing example is shown in Fig. 3.

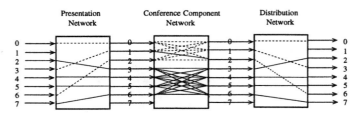

Fig. 3. An example of realizing conferences in a conference network. The two conferences are $\{0, 3, 6\}$ and $\{1, 2, 5, 7\}$

The conference component network is a multistage network which interconnects basic switch modules with fan-in and fan-out capability as shown in Fig. 4. Each $k \times k$ ($k \geq 2$) basic module is actually a $(k + 4) \times (k + 4)$ crossbar switch, in which k input links and k output links are internal links and are used for internal communication within the switch, and the extra four input links and four output links are external links and are used to connect to other basic modules in adjacent stages. All the internal outputs at each stage with the same label are relayed through multiplexers to the outputs of the network. All the external links of basic switch modules act as interstage links between adjacent stages according to the interconnecting function of an indirect binary cube network. Clearly, if we remove all the internal links as well as multiplexers in Fig. 4, the network would become an indirect binary cube network with duplicated interstage links.

A natural question may arise here: Can we directly adopt a class of multistage networks such as a baseline, an omega, or an indirect binary cube network to get a conference network with more regular network structure, simpler self-routing algorithm and less hardware cost? The key issue is to determine the multiplicities of routing conflicts, which is the maximum number of connection requests from different confer-

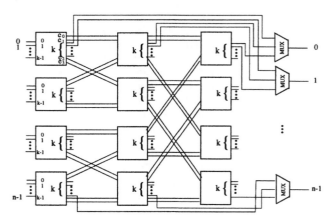

Fig. 4. The structure of an $n \times n$ conference component network designed in [5], where $\lceil \frac{n}{k} \rceil = 4$.

74

ences competing for a single interstage link, for each of these known multistage networks.

Our results in this paper will show that for a network of size $n \times n$, the multiplicities of routing conflicts are small constants (between 2 and 4) for an omega network or an indirect binary cube network; while it can be as large as $\frac{\sqrt{n}}{3} + 1$ for a baseline network. Thus our design for conference networks is based on an omega network or an indirect binary cube network but not a baseline network. We will also develop fast self-routing algorithms for setting up routing paths in the conference networks. For such an $n \times n$ conference network, the routing time and communication delay are $O(\log n)$, and the hardware cost is $O(n \log n)$. As can be seen, the newly designed conference networks are superior to existing designs in terms of routing complexity, communication delay and hardware cost. The conference network proposed is rearrangeably nonblocking in general, and is strictly nonblocking under some conference service policy. It can be used in applications that require efficient or real-time group communication.

II. A CLASS OF MULTISTAGE NETWORKS

Multistage interconnection networks such as baseline, omega, and indirect binary m-cube networks, have been proposed and widely used in various communication systems (see [15], [6] for an overview). Notice that there are several different definitions for each of these networks in the literature. In this paper, we follow the definitions used in [15], [11], which will be given formally in the following. A typical network structure for this class of networks is that each network has $n(= 2^m)$ inputs and outputs and $\log n(= m)$ stages, with each stage consisting of $\frac{n}{2}$ 2×2 switches and any two adjacent stages connected by n interstage links. Fig. 5(a), (b) and (c) illustrate an 8×8 baseline network, omega network and indirect binary 3-cube network, respectively.

In an $n \times n$ network, the m stages are labeled as $0, 1, \ldots m - 1$, and any one of n input (output) links of a stage can be expressed in m bits binary address as $a_{m-1}a_{m-2}\ldots a_1 a_0$. The mapping functions of these networks are determined by the interstage permutation functions for each network.

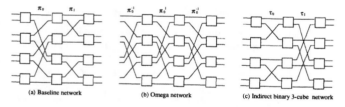

(a) Baseline network   (b) Omega network   (c) Indirect binary 3-cube network

Fig. 5. Three typical multistage networks for $n = 8$.

In a baseline network, the interstage permutation between stage i and stage $i + 1$ is denoted as π_i, for $0 \le i \le m - 2$, which represents the following mapping,

$$a_{m-1} \ldots a_1 a_0 \xrightarrow{\pi_i} a_{m-1} \ldots a_{m-i}a_0 a_{m-i-1} \ldots a_2 a_1. \quad (1)$$

This mapping corresponds to a 1-bit circular-right-shift among the $m - i$ least significant bits while keeping the i most significant bits unchanged.

In an omega network, all interstage permutations as well as the permutation between the network inputs and the inputs of stage 0 are the same mapping which is the reverse permutation of π_0 and is denoted as π_0^{-1}. It has the following form,

$$a_{m-1}a_{m-2} \ldots a_1 a_0 \xrightarrow{\pi_0^{-1}} a_{m-2}a_{m-3} \ldots a_1 a_0 a_{m-1}, \quad (2)$$

which is in fact a 1-bit circular-left-shift operation.

In an indirect binary m-cube network, the interstage permutation between stage i and stage $i + 1$ is denoted as τ_i, for $0 \le i \le m - 2$, which represents the following mapping,

$$a_{m-1}a_{m-2} \ldots a_{i+2}a_{i+1}a_i \ldots a_1 a_0 \xrightarrow{\tau_i}$$
$$a_{m-1}a_{m-2} \ldots a_{i+2}a_0 a_i \ldots a_1 a_{i+1}. \quad (3)$$

Clearly, it is the function of swapping bit a_0 for bit a_{i+1}.

This class of multistage network has a common feature that there is a unique path between each pair of network input and network output. This feature enables the network to have self-routing capability which makes a very fast routing algorithm possible. We will elaborate it in the next subsections.

A. Point-to-Point Self-Routing Algorithms for the Class of Multistage Networks

In general, routing in a multistage network is to establish a path from a source to a destination by setting up the switches along the path. In traditional point-to-point routing, there are two switch settings for a 2×2 switch: parallel and cross as shown in Fig. 6(a) and (b) (we will extend the switch settings to conference routing later). When the switch setting is 0, the switch is set to parallel; when the switch setting is 1, the switch is set to cross. For the class of multistage networks, there exist very simple routing algorithms called self-routing algorithms, in which switch settings depend only on the source and destination addresses.

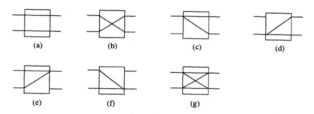

Fig. 6. Switch settings in a 2×2 switch: (a) Parallel (b) Cross (c) Upper broadcast (d) Lower broadcast (e) Upper merge (f) Lower merge (g) Butterfly.

In an $n \times n$ multistage network where $n = 2^m$, let a pair of source and destination addresses be s and d in binary $s_{m-1}s_{m-2}\cdots s_1 s_0$ and $d_{m-1}d_{m-2}\cdots d_1 d_0$, respectively. The switch setting for the switches at stage i of a baseline network can be represented as

$$s_i \oplus d_{m-i-1}; \quad (4)$$

that for an omega network is

$$s_{m-i-1} \oplus d_{m-i-1}; \quad (5)$$

and that for an indirect binary m-cube network is

$$s_i \oplus d_{(i+1) \bmod m}, \quad (6)$$

where $\oplus$ is the bitwise exclusive-or operation.

B. Simpler Point-to-Point Self-Routing Algorithms

For self-routing (i.e. setting switches while routing), we can have simpler switch settings for these multistage networks. As can be seen in the following, the new switch settings affect one input/output pair of each switch on the routing path, and the switch settings depend only on the destination address. The new switch settings are: When routing reaches an input of some switch at stage i, make a single connection from the input to the output with local address $\sigma_i(d) \in \{0, 1\}$ in the switch. The one bit value $\sigma_i(d)$ is a function of destination address d as defined below.

For a baseline network

$$\sigma_i(d) = d_{m-i-1}; \qquad (7)$$

for an omega network

$$\sigma_i(d) = d_{m-i-1}; \qquad (8)$$

and for an indirect binary m-cube network

$$\sigma_i(d) = d_{(i+1) \bmod m}. \qquad (9)$$

These switch settings can be easily extended to other multistage networks. We now verify that the switch settings do yield correct routings for the multistage networks. We use a baseline network as an example and other networks can be similarly verified. Let the mapping in the switch at stage i corresponding to switch settings (7)-(9) simply be σ_i. Notice that under mapping σ_i the input link with address $a_{m-1}a_{m-2}\ldots a_1 a_0$ at stage i is mapped to the output link with address $a_{m-1}a_{m-2}\ldots a_1\sigma_i(d)$ at the stage, where bit values $\sigma_i(d)$ is set to the least significant bit of the address.

The ith step of self-routing in a baseline, an omega, or an indirect binary cube network is given in (10), (11), and (12), respectively.

$$\begin{aligned} &\overset{\sigma_i}{\rightarrow} \quad d_{m-1}\ldots d_{m-i}s_{m-1}\ldots s_{i+1}d_{m-i-1} \\ &\overset{\pi_i}{\rightarrow} \quad d_{m-1}\ldots d_{m-i}d_{m-i-1}s_{m-1}\ldots s_{i+1} \end{aligned} \qquad (10)$$

$$\begin{aligned} &\overset{\pi_0^{-1}}{\rightarrow} \quad s_{m-i-2}\ldots s_0 d_{m-1}\ldots d_{m-i}s_{m-i-1} \\ &\overset{\sigma_i}{\rightarrow} \quad s_{m-i-2}\ldots s_0 d_{m-1}\ldots d_{m-i}d_{m-i-1} \end{aligned} \qquad (11)$$

$$\begin{aligned} &\overset{\sigma_i}{\rightarrow} \quad s_{m-1}\ldots s_{i+1}d_i\ldots d_1 d_{i+1} \\ &\overset{\tau_i}{\rightarrow} \quad s_{m-1}\ldots s_{i+2}d_{i+1}d_i\ldots d_1 s_{i+1} \end{aligned} \qquad (12)$$

It can be verified that in the above self-routing processes, the destination is reached from the source. As will be seen next, the self-routing using switch settings in (7)-(9) for point-to-point connections can be easily extended to the case of many-to-many connections.

III. THE EXTENSION OF SWITCHING SETTINGS FOR MANY-TO-MANY CONNECTIONS

Assume that the 2×2 switches used in a multistage network have fan-in and fan-out capability, that is, such a switch can support the extended switch settings of one-to-two (broadcast), two-to-one (merge), and two-to-two (butterfly) connections as shown in Fig. 6. Notice that in any 2×2 switch, the local addresses of two inputs (outputs) are 0 and 1 and we can use $i \rightarrow j$ ($i, j \in \{0, 1\}$) to represent that the input with local address i connects to the output with local address j in a switch setting. Thus a switch setting can be expressed as a set of such single connections within the switch. We can simply refer to the switch setting as a *switch setting set*. For example, the switch settings of parallel and cross used in point-to-point routing are $\{0 \rightarrow 0, 1 \rightarrow 1\}$ and $\{0 \rightarrow 1, 1 \rightarrow 0\}$, respectively; the switch setting of upper broadcast is $\{0 \rightarrow 0, 0 \rightarrow 1\}$; the switch setting of lower merge is $\{0 \rightarrow 1, 1 \rightarrow 1\}$; and the switch setting of butterfly is $\{0 \rightarrow 0, 0 \rightarrow 1, 1 \rightarrow 0, 1 \rightarrow 1\}$.

Clearly, in many-to-many routing, the switch settings in a 2×2 switch actually have the additive property, that is, two switch settings to the same switch yield a new switch setting which, as a switch setting set, is the union of the two previous switch setting sets. Therefore, we can decompose a many-to-many connection to some simpler connections, then route these decomposed connections in the network, and

the final switch setting on a switch is the "addition" (or "union") of all the switch settings of the decomposed connections, if applicable.

In this paper, we decompose a many-to-many connection to multiple one-to-many (or multicast) connections.

IV. MULTIPLICITY OF ROUTING CONFLICTS IN A MULTISTAGE NETWORK

A. Routing Conflicts

Routing conflict stands for the situation that more than one different connection requests compete the same link (as a resource) in the network at a time in their routing processes. In the case of a routing conflict, only one connection request wins the competition, i.e. occupies this competed resource, and other connection requests either wait until this resource is released, or find another alternative path for continued routing, or simply abort the current routing.

In a routing conflict, we define the number of connection requests which request the same link as *multiplicity* of the routing conflict. We are interested in the maximum multiplicity of routing conflicts for a certain type of multiple connections in a network. In the rest of the paper, we will always consider the maximum multiplicity and simply refer to it as multiplicity. For the sake of easy presentation, given a link l in the network, we denote the set of network inputs from which link l is reachable as $fromSet(l)$, and the set of network outputs to which link l can reach as $toSet(l)$.

Notice that in conference connection routing, the subconnections within a conference can share links in the network; while connections from different conferences are not allowed to share any links, since more than one conference connections attempting to acquire a single link at the same time is considered as a routing conflict as described above.

The class of multistage networks, such as baseline, omega and indirect binary cube, are unique-path networks, which have many nice properties such as low hardware cost, low network latency, and self-routing capability. However, a drawback of this class of network is that concurrently routing multiple connections (even one-to-one connections) in the network usually causes many routing conflicts.

B. Multiplicities of Routing Conflicts for Permutations

We now analyze the multiplicity of routing conflicts for multiple conferences. For comparison purpose, we first give the result on the multiplicity of routing conflicts for multiple one-to-one connections which has been studied by several researchers, see, for example, [16] [17].

The following lemma gives the results for multiple one-to-one connections for the class of multistage networks, which reveals that the multiplicities of routing conflicts are large and are the same for all multistage networks in the class.

Lemma 1: For an $n \times n$ multistage network (baseline, indirect binary cube, omega, or their reverse networks, etc), the multiplicity of routing conflicts for multiple one-to-one connections is $\sqrt{n}$.

Proof: omitted. ∎

C. Multiplicity of Routing Conflicts for Conference Connections

When using any of these multistage networks as a conference component network, we assume that a conference connection request is a many-to-many connection from source set C to destination set C, where C is a set of conferees with consecutive addresses on the input side and output side of the network, and we simply denote the conference connection as C. In addition, we assume that the multiple conference connections in the network, $C_1, C_2, C_3, \ldots$ are mutually disjoint.

A conference connection is actually an all-to-all connection within a group of consecutive conferees. For practical reasons, we assume a conference has at least three conferees. Similar to the case of one-to-one connections, we are interested in the maximum number of disjoint conferences which need to pass a single interstage link in the network. In the following we analyze each individual network one by one. As will be seen, although the class of multistage networks have been shown to be topologically equivalent (e.g. see [15]), they behave quite differently in realizing conference connection requests.

C.1 Multiplicity of Routing Conflicts for a Baseline Network

The following results show that the multiplicity of conference routing conflicts for a baseline network is rather large.

Lemma 2: For an $n \times n$ baseline network (or its reverse network), the multiplicity of routing conflicts for multiple conferences is $\frac{\sqrt{n}}{3}+1$.

Proof: Recall that the interstage permutations π's for an $n \times n$ baseline network are given in (1). For a given pair of source and destination addresses $s_{m-1}s_{m-2}\cdots s_1 s_0$ and $d_{m-1}d_{m-2}\cdots d_1 d_0$, and under self-routing (7), the ith step self-routing process is shown in (10).

Without loss of generality, let m be even. As can be seen, after mapping $\pi_{\frac{m}{2}-1}$, the routing reaches an input link, say, l (at stage $\frac{m}{2}$), with address $d_{m-1}\ldots d_{\frac{m}{2}}s_{m-1}\ldots s_{\frac{m}{2}}$. Also notice that any routing path from an input (of the network) with address $s_{m-1}\ldots s_{\frac{m}{2}}\times\times\ldots\times$ to an output with address $d_{m-1}\ldots d_{\frac{m}{2}}\times\times\ldots\times$ will pass through link l, where each $\times$ can be either 0 or 1.

We can see that the $fromSet(l)$ is the set of $2^{\frac{m}{2}}$ consecutive network inputs in the form $s_{m-1}\ldots s_{\frac{m}{2}}\times\times\ldots\times$. and the $toSet(l)$ is the set of $2^{\frac{m}{2}}$ consecutive network outputs in the form $d_{m-1}\ldots d_{\frac{m}{2}}\times\times\ldots\times$. In particular, when $s_{m-1}=d_{m-1}, s_{m-2}=d_{m-2},\ldots$, and $s_{\frac{m}{2}}=d_{\frac{m}{2}}$, the two segments have the same address space on the input side and output side of the network (see Fig. 7). Since a conference consists of at least 3 conferees (otherwise, no need to use conference network) and all conferees in a conference are consecutive, we immediately have that there are at most $2^{\frac{m}{2}}/3+1=\frac{\sqrt{n}}{3}+1$ disjoint conferences each of which contains at least one conferee falling into that address space. Therefore, the maximum multiplicity of routing conflicts for a baseline network is $\frac{\sqrt{n}}{3}+1$. ∎

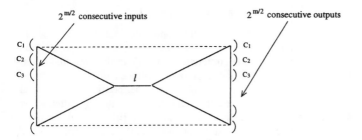

Fig. 7. In an $n \times n$ baseline network, when *fromSet(l)* and *toSet(l)* are the same $2^{m/2}$ consecutive addresses, there can be $\frac{\sqrt{n}}{3}+1$ disjoint conferences passing through link l in the routing.

However, as will be seen shortly, the multiplicities of conference routing conflicts for an indirect binary cube network or an omega network are constant.

C.2 Multiplicity of Routing Conflicts for an Omega Network

Lemma 3: For an $n \times n$ omega network (or its reverse network), the multiplicity of routing conflicts for multiple conferences is 3.

Proof: Recall that the interstage connections for an omega network are given in (2). For a pair of source and destination addresses $s_{m-1}s_{m-2}\cdots s_1 s_0$ and $d_{m-1}d_{m-2}\cdots d_1 d_0$, under self-routing (8), the ith step self-routing process is shown in (11). After switch mapping σ_i, the routing reaches an output link, say, l (at stage i), with address $s_{m-i-2}\ldots s_0 d_{m-1}\ldots d_{m-i-1}$. Notice that any routing path from an input (of the network) with address $\times\ldots\times s_{m-i-2}\ldots s_0$ to an output with address $d_{m-1}\ldots d_{m-i-1}\times\ldots\times$. will pass through link l.

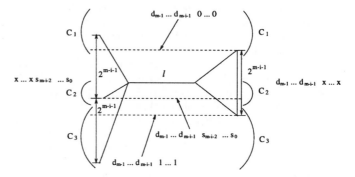

Fig. 8. In an Omega network, *fromSet(l)* contains 2^{i+1} inputs, which are not consecutive at all (with 2^{m-i-1} apart), and *toSet(l)* contains 2^{m-i-1} consecutive outputs. There are three disjoint conferences C_1, C_2, C_3 which can pass through l in the routing.

We can see that all the 2^{i+1} inputs in the form $\times\ldots\times s_{m-i-2}\ldots s_0$ (which represents *fromSet(l)*) are not consecutive at all, where two adjacent elements are 2^{m-i-1} apart; while all the 2^{m-i-1} outputs in the form $d_{m-1}\ldots d_{m-i-1}\times\ldots\times$ (which represents *toSet(l)*) are consecutive output links of the network as illustrated in Fig. 8. Also the intersection of $\times\ldots\times s_{m-i-2}\ldots s_0$ and $d_{m-1}\ldots d_{m-i-1}\times\ldots\times$ is $d_{m-1}\ldots d_{m-i-1}s_{m-i-2}\ldots s_0$, which is a one-element set. We denote the element as a. Clearly, a conference has a routing path passing through link l if and only if it has a conferee with address in the form $\times\ldots\times s_{m-i-2}\ldots s_0$ and a conferee with address in the form $d_{m-1}\ldots d_{m-i-1}\times\ldots\times$, since in the conference each conferee must have a routing path to all conferees. Also, notice that a conference has conferees with consecutive addresses. Denote a conferee with address form $\times\ldots\times s_{m-i-2}\ldots s_0$ as an S-type node, and a conferee with address form $d_{m-1}\ldots d_{m-i-1}\times\ldots\times$ as a D-type node. Now we show that there are no more than three disjoint conferences which have a routing path passing through link l. If this is not true, suppose there are four disjoint conferences C_1, C_2, C_3 and C_4 competing link l in the routing. Then each conference has at least an S-type node and a D-type node. Let them be $S_1, D_1; S_2, D_2; S_3, D_3;$ and S_4, D_4 for C_1, C_2, C_3 and C_4, respectively. We have that S_1, S_2, S_3, S_4 are distinct, D_1, D_2, D_3, D_4 are distinct, but S_j and D_j may be identical. By the definitions of an S-type node and a D-type node, we have that

$$|S_j - S_k| \geq 2^{m-i-1} \text{ for } j \neq k, \text{ and } |D_j - D_k| < 2^{m-i-1}.$$

Since each conference has consecutive conferees, we can assume addresses in C_1, C_2, C_3 and C_4 are in an increasing order by conference (e.g. all conferee addresses in C_1 is less than those in C_2). We immediately have that

$$|D_4 - D_1| > |S_3 - S_2| \geq 2^{m-i-1},$$

which contradicts with $|D_4 - D_1| < 2^{m-i-1}$. That is, there are at most three disjoint conferences with a path passing through link l.

77

For a slightly large n, we can actually construct the case that three disjoint conferences compete link l. Among them, one conference covers $d_{m-1} \ldots d_{m-i-1} s_{m-i-2} \ldots s_0$, and other two each covers one of the two ends of the consecutive segment $d_{m-1} \ldots d_{m-i-1} \times \ldots \times$ and at least one address in $\times \ldots \times s_{m-i-2} \ldots s_0$. In Fig. 8, C_2, C_1 and C_3 are three such conferences. Therefore, the multiplicity of conference routing conflicts for an omega network is at most 3. ∎

C.3 Multiplicity of Routing Conflicts for an Indirect Binary Cube Network

Lemma 4: For an $n \times n$ indirect binary cube network (or its reverse network), the multiplicity of routing conflicts on an interstage link for multiple conferences is either 4 or 2, depending on the link is horizontal or oblique.

Proof: Suppose the source and destination addresses are $s_{m-1} s_{m-2} \cdots s_1 s_0$ and $d_{m-1} d_{m-2} \cdots d_1 d_0$, respectively. By the ith step self-routing in an indirect binary network (12), after switch mapping σ_i, the routing reaches an output link, say, l (at stage i), with address $s_{m-1} \ldots s_{i+1} d_i \ldots d_1 d_{i+1}$. Also, notice that any routing path from an input (of the network) with address $s_{m-1} \ldots s_{i+1} \times \times \ldots \times$ to an output with address $\times \ldots \times d_{i+1} \ldots d_1 \times$ will pass through link l.

We can see that all the 2^{i+1} inputs in the form $s_{m-1} \ldots s_{i+1} \times \times \ldots \times$ (which represents $fromSet(l)$) are consecutive input links of the network. However, all the 2^{m-i-1} outputs in the form $\times \ldots \times d_{i+1} \ldots d_1 \times$ (which represents $toSet(l)$) are sparsely distributed on the output side of the network. In fact, they are 2^{m-i-2} 2-element segments with adjacent two $2^{i+2} - 1$ apart (see Fig. 9).

To see how many disjoint conferences can pass through link l, we have two different cases depending on the intersection of $s_{m-1} \ldots s_{i+1} \times \times \ldots \times$ and $\times \ldots \times d_{i+1} \ldots d_1 \times$, which are the address spaces on the input side and output side of the network, respectively.

If $s_{i+1} \neq d_{i+1}$, the intersection (of $fromSet(l)$ and $toSet(l)$) is empty. In this case, we claim that there are at most two disjoint conferences that have a path passing through link l. The proof is similar to that in Lemma 3, and is omitted. We now give the construction of the two disjoint conferences having a path passing through link l. They can be constructed by letting each of the conferences cover one of the two ends of $s_{m-1} \ldots s_{i+1} \times \times \ldots \times$ and at least one address in the form $\times \ldots \times d_{i+1} \ldots d_1 \times$. As shown in Fig. 9(a), C_1 and C_3 are such conferences whose routing passes through link l. However, the routing for the conference such as C_2 never passes through link l. Clearly, the multiplicity of routing conflicts for link l is 2 in this case.

If $s_{i+1} = d_{i+1}$, the intersection (of $fromSet(l)$ and $toSet(l)$) becomes $s_{m-1} \ldots s_{i+1} d_i \ldots d_1 \times$ which consists of two elements, say, $a_1 = s_{m-1} \ldots s_{i+1} d_i \ldots d_1 0$ and $a_2 = s_{m-1} \ldots s_{i+1} d_i \ldots d_1 1$. Then, we claim that at most four conferences have a path passing through link l. The proof is also omitted. For a slightly large n, we can construct four disjoint conferences each having a routing path passing through link l as follows: two conferences each covers one of the two elements of the intersection and the other two conferences each covers one of the two ends of the consecutive segment $s_{m-1} \ldots s_{i+1} \times \times \ldots \times$ and at least one address in the form $\times \ldots \times d_{i+1} \ldots d_1 \times$. As shown in Fig. 9(b), C_1, C_2, C_3 and C_5 are such conferences. Therefore, the multiplicity of routing conflicts on link l is 4 in this case.

In addition, notice that from the interstage mapping τ_i in point-to-point self-routing of an indirect binary cube network, when $s_{i+1} = d_{i+1}$ the interstage link (between stage i and stage $i + 1$) starting from l is a horizontal link, and when $s_{i+1} \neq d_{i+1}$ it is an oblique

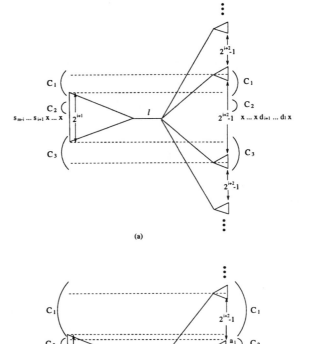

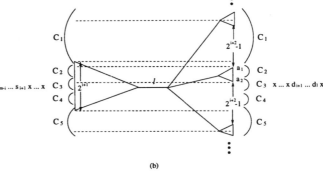

Fig. 9. In an $n \times n$ indirect binary m-cube, $fromSet(l)$ contains 2^{i+1} consecutive inputs, and $toSet(l)$ is sparsely distributed 2 consecutive segments ($2^{i+2} - 1$ apart). (a) $s_{i+1} \neq d_{i+1}$. (b) $s_{i+1} = d_{i+1}$.

link. In conclusion, the maximum multiplicity of conference routing conflicts on an interstage link in an indirect binary cube network is 4 or 2 depending on the link is horizontal or oblique. ∎

V. CONFERENCE NETWORK DESIGNS

In this section, we describe the conference network architecture. Given n potential conferees with labels $0, 1, \ldots, n - 1$, they are connected by an $n \times n$ conference network in the way that potential conferee i links to both input i and output i of the network, for $i \in \{0, 1, \ldots, n - 1\}$. A *conference* is defined as a subset of all potential conferees, where each member of the subset is called a *conferee* of the conference. In a conference $C \subseteq \{0, 1, \ldots, n - 1\}$, any conferee in C can broadcast its message to all the conferees of C. A conference network allows multiple disjointed conferences coexist at a time, and keeps the communication private within each individual conference.

The conference network proposed in this paper adopts the sandwich structure as described in Section 1 in Fig. 2 with $m = n$. For an $n \times n$ conference network, both presentation network and distribution network are ordinary $n \times n$ permutation networks, and the network in the middle is an $n \times n$ conference component network. Since there are many excellent designs for permutation networks, the main focus of this paper is to design the conference component network by adopting the class of multistage networks.

A. Conflict-free Conference Component Network Design based on the Class of Multistage Networks

The design criteria for a conference component network are short communication delay, simple routing algorithm, low network cost, and equal communication delay for every conferee in a conference. As can be seen in the following, these goals can be achieved by using multistage networks modified from the traditional multistage networks discussed earlier.

In a conference component network, conferees in a conference are always in consecutive addresses, although they can be in any addresses in the overall conference network. We have seen in the last section that multiple disjoint conference connections in a multistage network such that a baseline, an omega, and an indirect binary cube network may cause routing conflicts. However, the analysis of the multiplicity of conference routing conflicts in the multistage networks can be used for designing a conflict-free conference component network as follows.

Theorem 1: Given any multistage network MIN, a conference component network (CCN) is constructed by multiplying each interstage link of the MIN to multiple copies with the number of copies equal to the maximum multiplicity of conference routing conflicts on the link in the MIN. Thus, any multiple disjoint conference requests in such a conference component network can be realized conflict-free.

The proof is straight-forward, but the theorem is very important to constructing a conflict-free conference component network in this paper.

By applying Theorem 1 and Lemma 3, the omega type conflict-free conference component network is obtained by tripling each interstage link in the original omega network. As a result, the switches used in the conference component network are 6×6 now instead of 2×2 in the original network as shown in Fig. 10 (a). An omega type conference component network is shown in Fig. 11 (a).

By applying Theorem 1 and Lemma 4, the indirect binary cube type conference component network is constructed as follows: each oblique interstage link is doubled and each horizontal interstage link is quadruplicated in the original indirect binary cube network. Thus, the switches also become 6×6 ones as shown in Fig. 10 (b), and an indirect binary cube type conference component network is shown in Fig. 11 (b).

Fig. 10. (a) In an Omega network, each interstage link is tripled. (b) In an indirect binary cube network, each horizontal link is quadruplicated, and each oblique link is doubled.

Although we can do the same thing for a baseline type conference network, it is not a feasible solution in reality because it yields a very high hardware cost due to the fact that it requires $\frac{\sqrt{n}}{3} + 1$ times interstage links than that of the original network.

Finally, it is worth mentioning that in the optical domain we can employ wavelength-division-multiplexing (WDM) technology to solve the same problem. In that case, instead of making multiple copies of a link, a link with multiple wavelengths will be used.

VI. CONFERENCE SELF-ROUTING ALGORITHM IN CONFERENCE COMPONENT NETWORKS

In this section, we develop a self-routing algorithm for a conference component network.

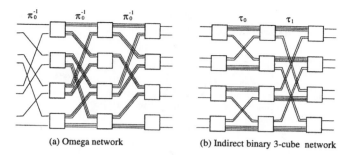

(a) Omega network (b) Indirect binary 3-cube network

Fig. 11. Conference component networks based on multistage networks. (a) Omega type network. (b) Indirect binary cube type network.

Assume that each conference has a unique identifier, called *conference-id*. This identifier should be included in the routing message to the switch. Needless to say, each switch must know its own stage number. Also, the self-routing algorithm is required to reset the switch setting when a conference is terminated.

The self-routing algorithm for conference routing, **conf-self-routing**(), is described in Table 1. This algorithm is loaded into every switch in the network. It waits for any message from the inputs of the switch it resides. The routing message from some local input (of the switch) is a three tuple $< f, g, C' >$ where f is the routing flag indicating "routing" or "reset-routing", g is the conference-id of the conference, and C' is a set of network outputs which represent a subset of conferees reachable from the local input. In the case of "reset-routing", C' is not required and can be passed as ϕ.

Since we introduce multiple copies of interstage links to the conference component network, in the routing algorithm we need to represent local addresses for switch inputs and outputs. To keep routing as easy as in the original multistage network, we use 2-tuple $[v, u]$ to represent a local address of an input link or an output link in a switch, where $v \in \{0, 1\}$ is the local address in a switch in the original network, and u is the index in the set of multiplied copies of the link with $0 \leq u < p$, where p is the number of the multiplied copies of the link. For an interstage link, which is linked from an output link (expressed as $[v', u']$) of a switch in the current stage to an input link (expressed as $[v, u]$) of a switch in the next stage, we always assume the indexes of the input link and output link are the same, i.e. $u = u'$.

For a conference C, initially, a message $< f, g, C >$ is sent from each network input $c \in C$ (the initialization step is not shown in the algorithm). Then each switch receiving the message executes the functions in algorithm **conf-self-routing**.

The switch setting part of **conf-self-routing** follows (7)-(9) for point-to-point connections. For a routing message $< f, g, C' >$, if for all $c' \in C'$ $\sigma_s(c')$'s yield the same value, a single connection is contributed to the current switch setting; otherwise a broadcast connection is contributed to the switch setting.

The algorithm also handles multiple conferences for their routing and reset-routing processes. It can be easily verified that algorithm **conf-self-routing** correctly performs conference routing in all cases.

VII. COMPLEXITY ANALYSIS AND COMPARISONS

In this section, we analyze the hardware cost, switch setting time, and communication delay of the newly proposed conference component network, and compare it with existing designs. Suppose the networks considered are $n \times n$ networks.

For hardware cost, since the proposed conference component network is obtained simply by replacing each 2×2 switch in the original multistage network by a 6×6 switch, the hardware cost is $18n \log_2 n$

TABLE 1

CONFERENCE SELF-ROUTING ALGORITHM IN THE CONFERENCE COMPONENT
NETWORK

```
conf-self-routing()
{ /* Suppose current switch is at stage s. */
  waiting to receive a message from a local input of this switch;
  suppose the received message is < f, g, C' > from a local input [v, u];
  case f =="routing": {
    if (for all different c' ∈ C', σ_s(c')'s are equal) {
      /* contribute a single connection to switch setting*/
      let σ_s(c') be v', and choose an output [v', u'] (of the switch)
        which has been assigned a conference-id g, or is inactive
        thus hasn't been assigned any conference-id;
      add {[v, u] → [v', u']} to the switch setting set of this
        switch; /* [v', u'] is now active */
      if (output [v', u'] has not been assigned a conference-id) {
        assign conference-id g to output [v', u'];
        if s < m − 1
          send message < f, g, C' > along output [v', u'];
      }
    }
    else { /* among σ_s(c')'s for c' ∈ C' some are 0, and others are 1. */
      /* contribute two connections to switch setting */
      choose outputs [0, u'_0] and [1, u'_1] (of the switch) which
        have been assigned a conference-id g, or are inactive
        thus have not been assigned any conference-id;
      add {[v, u] → [0, u'_0], [v, u] → [1, u'_1]} to the switch setting
        set of this switch; /* [0, u'_0] and [1, u'_1] are now active */
      if (outputs [0, u'_0] and [1, u'_1] have not been assigned a conference-id) {
        assign conference-id g to outputs [0, u'_0] and [1, u'_1];
        if s < m − 1 {
          C'_0 = {c'|σ_s(c') = 0 for c' ∈ C'};
          C'_1 = {c'|σ_s(c') = 1 for c' ∈ C'};
          send message < f, g, C'_0 > along output [0, u'_0];
          send message < f, g, C'_1 > along output [1, u'_1];
        }
      }
    }
  }
  case f =="reset-routing": {
    let T' be the local output set that local input [v, u] is
      connected to this switch;
    if (outputs in T' have been assigned a conference-id) {
      /* if true, must be g */
      unassign conference-id from outputs in T';
      if (s < m − 1)
        for each [v', u'] ∈ T' send message < f, g, φ > along output [v', u'];
    }
    reset switch setting of connection ([v, u], T') in the switch;
  }
}
```

crosspoints compared with $2n \log_2 n$ crosspoints in the original multistage network.

Since the network has $\log_2 n$ stages, the communication delay is $O(\log_2 n)$ as in the original multistage network. For switch setting time, suppose the conference size is c, from the self-routing algorithm, the switch settings in switches at the same stage are performed in parallel, and those in switches at different stages are performed in a pipelined fashion. Thus, the total switch setting time by all the switches on the routing paths is at most $O(c \log_2 n)$.

Now we compare the new design with previous design in [5], which has $n(k+10) \log_2 \frac{n}{k}$ (for $k \geq 16$) hardware cost, $O(\log_2 \frac{n}{k})$ communication delay, and $O(c \max\{k, \log_2 \frac{n}{k}\})$ switch setting time. As can be seen, the new design has less hardware cost than the design in [5] with large k, and has a comparable communication delay and switch-

ing time to those in [5]. Thus, the new design has all characteristics (of [5]) which are superior to other existing designs in [1]-[4]. The major advantages of this network over the previous design [5] are that the new network has a more regular network structure and much simpler self-routing algorithm so that the implementation is much easier.

VIII. CONCLUSIONS

The class of self-routing multistage networks, such as baseline, omega, or indirect binary cube networks, are well-known to have nice properties for routing permutations. However, more and more emerging network applications require efficient group communication. In this paper, we consider using this class of networks for a type of group communication called conferencing. The key issue in designing a conference network is to determine the multiplicity of routing conflicts on an interstage link in such a network so that we can choose a network with the minimum cost for conferencing. We have shown that for a network of size $n \times n$, the multiplicities of routing conflicts are small constants (between 2 and 4) for an omega network or an indirect binary cube network; while it can be as large as $\frac{\sqrt{n}}{3} + 1$ for a baseline network. We then designed conference networks based on an omega network or an indirect binary cube network. A similar method can be used for analyzing other multistage networks. We have also developed fast self-routing algorithms for setting up routing paths in the newly designed conference networks. As can be seen, such an $n \times n$ conference network has $O(\log n)$ routing time and communication delay and $O(n \log n)$ hardware cost. The conference networks are superior to existing designs in terms of routing complexity, communication delay and hardware cost. The conference network proposed is rearrangeably nonblocking in general, and is strictly nonblocking under some conference service policy. It can be used in applications that require efficient or real-time group communication. Interesting future work may include further study of various rearrangement strategies mentioned in this paper and comparing their performance.

REFERENCES

[1] F.K. Hwang and A. Jajszczyk "On Nonblocking Multiconnection Networks," *IEEE Trans. Comm.*, vol. 34, no. 10, pp. 1038-1041, 1986.

[2] Y. Yang and G.M. Masson, "Broadcast Ring Sandwich Networks," *IEEE Trans. Computers*, vol. 44, no. 10, pp. 1169-1180, 1995.

[3] J.F. Houlahan, et al., "Hypercube Sandwich Approach to Conferencing," *Journal of Supercomputing*, vol. 10, no. 3, pp. 271-283, 1996.

[4] Y. Du and G.M. Masson, "Strictly Nonblocking Conference Networks Using High-Dimensional Meshes," *Networks*, vol. 33, no. 4, pp. 293-308, July 1999.

[5] Y. Yang "A New Conference Network for Group Communication," *Proc. 2001 International Conference on Parallel Processing (ICPP '01)*, pp. 141-148, Valencia, Spain, Sept. 2001.

[6] J. Duato, S. Yalamanchili, and L.M. Ni, *Interconnection Networks: An Engineering Approach*, Morgan Kaufmann Publishers, 2002.

[7] C.K. Wong, et al., "Secure Group Communications Using Key Graphs," *IEEE/ACM Trans. Networking*, vol 8, no. 1, pp. 16-30, 2000.

[8] M. Baldi, et al., "Adaptive Group Multicast with Time-Driven Priority," *IEEE/ACM Trans. Networking*, vol 8, no. 1, pp. 31-43, 2000.

[9] A. Gopal, et al., "Fast Broadcast in High-Speed Networks," *IEEE/ACM Trans. Networking*, vol 7, no. 2, pp. 262-275, 1999.

[10] Y. Yang and J. Wang, "Optimal All-to-All Personalized Exchange in a Class of Optical Multistage Networks," *IEEE Trans. Parallel and Distributed Systems*, vol. 12, no. 6, pp. 567-582, 2001.

[11] Y. Yang and J. Wang, "Optimal All-to-All Personalized Exchange in Self-Routable Multistage Networks," *IEEE Trans. Parallel and Distributed Systems*, vol. 11, no. 3, pp. 261-274, 2000.

[12] Y. Yang and J. Wang, "Pipelined All-to-All Broadcast in All-Port Meshes and Tori," *IEEE Trans. Computers*, vol. 50, no. 10, 2001.

[13] Y. Suh and K.G. Shin, "All-to-All Personalized Communication in Multidimensional Torus and Mesh Networks," *IEEE Trans. Parallel and Distributed Systems*, vol. 12, no. 1, pp. 38-59, 2001.

[14] D. Xuan, et al., "A Routing Protocol for Anycast Messages," *IEEE Trans. Parallel and Distributed Systems*, vol. 11, no. 6, pp. 571-588, 2000.

[15] C.-L. Wu and T.-Y. Feng, "On a Class of Multistage Interconnection Networks," *IEEE Trans. Computers*, vol. 29, no. 8, pp. 694-702, 1980.

[16] D.P. Agrawal, "Graph Theoretic Analysis and Design of Multistage Interconnection Networks," *IEEE Trans. Computers*, vol. 32, no. 7, 1983, pp. 637-648.

[17] F.T. Leighton, *Introduction to Parallel Algorithms and Architectures: Arrays, Trees, Hypercubes*, Morgan Kaufmann Publishers, 1992.

A New Mechanism for Congestion and Deadlock Resolution*

Yong Ho Song and Timothy Mark Pinkston
University of Southern California
Los Angeles, CA 90089-2562, USA
E-mail: {yongho,tpink}@charity.usc.edu

Abstract

Efficient and reliable communication is essential for achieving high performance in a networked computing environment. Limited network resources bring about unavoidable competition among in-flight packets, resulting in network congestion and, possibly, deadlock. Many techniques have been proposed to improve performance by efficiently handling network congestion and deadlock. However, none of them provide an efficient way of accelerating the movement of packets involved in congestion onward to their destinations. In this paper, we propose a new mechanism for the detection and resolution of network congestion and deadlocks. The proposed mechanism is based on increasing the scheduling priority of packets involved in congestion and providing necessary resources for those packets to make forward progress. Simulation results show that the proposed technique outperforms previously proposed techniques by effectively dispersing network congestion.

1 Introduction

The interconnection network is the communication backbone for both tightly coupled multiprocessor servers and loosely coupled (and, oftentimes, heterogeneous) distributed network-based multicomputer clusters. The performance of the interconnection network —measured, in part, by packet delivery time from source to destination (i.e., latency) and by the number of packets delivered per unit time (i.e., throughput)— has a substantial impact on overall system performance. Finiteness in network resources inevitably brings about contention on network resources that may delay or prevent packet transmission in the network. Such contention causes packets to block which, eventually, can lead to network congestion and, possibly, deadlock.[1] Deadlocks reduce communication

efficiency and reliability, consequently degrading network and system performance considerably. Thus, it is vitally important to guard against congestion and deadlock in such a way as not to impose overly restrictive measures that under-utilize network resources.

Much research has been conducted toward increasing the performance of interconnection networks by handling network congestion and deadlock in an efficient way. Avoidance-based deadlock handling techniques [2, 15, 16] prevent cyclic dependencies on all the network resources from occurring by forcing packets to use a subset of the resources, or even all the resources in a partially or totally ordered fashion. These techniques trade off routing flexibility for deadlock freedom. On the contrary, recovery-based techniques [3, 5, 6, 7, 10, 13] allow deadlocks to form, and recover from them when detected. Considering that deadlocks rarely occur for typical traffic loads and network parameters [14, 19, 21], recovery techniques allow for better utilization of network resources. For either deadlock handling approach, no way of *accelerating* the movement of packets already involved in congestion or deadlock is provided. Avoidance-based techniques such as Duato's adaptive routing [2] only provide a way for packets to evade congestion already formed along some links toward their destinations. Recovery-based techniques such as Disha [6, 7] resolve deadlocks by rescuing one of the packets in a detected potential deadlock to its destination, but the remaining packets are still susceptible to deadlocking again before making any progress.

What is desirable is the development of mechanisms that address the problem at its source: namely, the blocked packets—whether they are within the network or at network endpoints. Under certain circumstances of network loading, traffic bursts and pathological communication behavior, blockage on a single resource can easily grow into paths of blockage dependencies, cyclic blocking, and even knotted cyclic blocking across many network resources by packets [19, 20, 21]. To increase performance, it is important to detect such blocking behavior and quickly disperse it, allowing packets involved in congestion and deadlock-precipitating situations to accelerate movement out of those regions, particularly when deadlock is handled based on recovering from it [5, 6, 7, 10, 13]. Conges-

---

*This research was supported by an NSF grant, CCR-9812137.

[1] Deadlocks occur as a result of cyclical hold-and-wait dependencies on network resources by in-flight messages (or packets) that block packets from making progress indefinitely.

tion dispersion is possible because real traffic typically is not uniform; some areas in the network are more heavily loaded—regions where hot spots form—while other neighboring areas have available resources to route packets.

In this paper, we propose a new mechanism for detecting and dispersing cyclic as well as non-cyclic blocking dependencies on network resources. In essence, the mechanism detects the configuration of network congestion by propagating a special control packet over suspected resources. Router resources marked by such control packets get reserved such that chained reservations of network resources can result. The availability of a reserved resource triggers packets along resource dependency chains (or cycles, if they exist) to shift by at least one buffer position toward their destinations. For this, an empty buffer space that could hold at least one packet will be made available at one end of a non-cyclic dependency chain, or at a node in a cyclic dependency chain. Even though this shifting operation alone does not immediately remove packets out of congested areas, it effectively decreases the coupling among packets involved in dependency relations on congested resources. In effect, it allows packets the opportunity to disperse out of congested areas after each "shift" operation. This reduces the probability of recurrence of the dependency relation that causes congestion to persist, since new routing candidates could arise as a result of the shift, e.g., some packets being routed could use alternative resources or even arrive at their destination after the shift.

The remainder of this paper is structured as follows. Section 2 describes previous work on techniques to improve network performance. Section 3 presents our new mechanism for detection and resolution of cyclic dependencies as a way to efficiently handle network congestion and potential deadlocks. Section 4 discusses the performance of the mechanism, and, finally, Section 5 draws some conclusions.

2 Problem Background and Motivation

A high-performance network allows the maximum number of packets to make forward progress toward their destinations in minimal time usually along shortest paths. Consider for the moment the forward movement of packets in the network. Each time a packet moves forward, an empty buffer in a queue associated with a router port within the network or a network interface port at the network endpoint is consumed by the head of the packet. Likewise, an occupied buffer is released by the tail of the packet. Assuming that the unit of an empty buffer space for a packet is defined as a *bubble*, each forward movement of a packet in one direction is equivalent to the backward propagation of a bubble in the opposite direction. Thus, the movement of packets in a network can be characterized simply by considering the availability of bubbles in resources needed by packets and how those bubbles flow through those network resources: the more bubbles flowing within needed network re-

sources, the greater the number of packets that make forward progress.

All of the previously proposed deadlock handling techniques in some way affect the availability and/or flow of bubbles in a network to increase performance. Deadlock-free routing techniques based on avoiding deadlock restrict bubble flow such that all bubbles supplied by network endpoints always flow through some defined subset (or the entire set) of network resources in some total or partial order [2, 3, 15, 16]. Alternatively, recovery-based deadlock handling techniques always make some bubble(s) available within any set of network resources on which a path of cyclic dependencies can form [5, 6, 7, 10, 13].

Adaptivity relaxes restrictions by allowing bubbles to flow more freely among network resources, but some restrictions are still enforced to ensure deadlock freedom. The challenging problem becomes how to apply the fewest restrictions on bubble flow to maintain deadlock freedom while selectively controlling the orientation of bubbles so that they migrate to specific areas of the network when such action is needed. Previous research has mostly addressed only the first part of this problem—increasing adaptivity. Only recently has both parts received attention, mainly in the context of deadlock recovery [3, 13]. A complete solution would support, when the need arises, accelerated dispersal of packets out of congested areas and restricted entry into those areas by packets not involved in congestion to achieve predefined system goals. This acts to quickly dispel congestion and deadlock-precipitating resource dependencies while still allowing packets to route adaptively along more profitable (less congested) paths. Addressing this challenge essentially reduces to solving a scheduling problem: How should freed resources (bubbles) be locally allocated to contending packets which may have multiple routing options such that resource contention is minimized not only locally, but also globally throughout the network? Doing this requires exploiting some amount of global knowledge intelligently.

Many techniques have been proposed to preserve enough bubbles inside a network by identifying potential network congestion and, if needed, limiting the injection of new packets [1, 17, 18]. Detected congestion on network resources is notified to source nodes of the congested packets or to adjacent nodes neighboring the congestion. However, the dispersion of network congestion still remains up to the routing function used in normal packet delivery only. That is, the movement of preserved bubbles is controlled only by the routing algorithm.

True fully adaptive routing (TFAR) techniques [5, 6, 7, 13] enable routers to exploit the maximum level of routing adaptivity by not imposing any restrictions on bubble movement. Because deadlocks are allowed to form in networks using these techniques, efficient deadlock detection and recovery techniques should be provided in order to decide whether packets suffer from the lack of bubbles and, if so, how enough bubbles should be supplied to those packets. The performance of TFAR networks mostly depends on the accuracy in detecting deadlock and on the efficiency of the recovery mechanism. Some TFAR techniques eliminate unnecessary re-transmission of packets under recovery by delivering them to their destinations through the exclusive use of deadlock buffers in intermediate routers. However, such progressive recovery techniques may incur unnecessary overhead due to those recovered packets bypassing packets preceding them in the network. In the worst case, an entire transaction involving packets delivered out-of-order during recovery may have to be repeated in order to guarantee consistency and accuracy at the application level.

When network routers forward packets over their internal crossbars, they can prioritize the scheduling of candidate packets from the head of input ports based on one or more packet properties such as packet size, estimated hop count to destination, waiting time in the router, etc [9]. In addition, quality of service requirements can be taken into consideration such that packets may be prioritized based on bandwidth usage by their communication streams [8, 11, 22, 23]. To the best of our knowledge, however, no router scheduling techniques have provisions for directing incoming bubbles to blocked packets at input ports in such a way that congestion is dispersed. That is, no speculation is done for predicting which input port should switch the packet from the head of the associated buffer to a locally congested output port in order to relieve congestion more globally. The speculation proposed in [12] speculates only on the output port or output queue (i.e., availability of a bubble, which, in their case, is a free output virtual channel), not on the input port or input queue as we propose here.

3 The Proposed Technique

3.1 The Basic Idea

The principal idea of the proposed technique is to precisely identify the sources of network congestion (i.e., blocked packets), temporarily increase the scheduling priorities for them, and allocate *acceleration bubbles* to them in order to allow them to make forward progress toward their destinations. The proposed technique consists of a congestion detection mechanism and an accompanying resolution mechanism.

Congestion detection can be initiated by any router in the network which fails to forward packets from an input port to any of the *routing-candidate output ports* supplied by the routing function under certain conditions (see Section 3.2). More than one router may start detection simultaneously. The router generates a special control packet, called a *ping*, to probe the configuration of network congestion and sends it on the congested link to the attached neighboring router for further investigation. If the neighbor finds the congestion to continue from the ping-receiving input port to its candidate output ports, it propagates the ping further to its neighbor(s) along those output ports. This process is repeated by downstream routers until

either no more congestion exists or the ping returns to the point where it was generated. In the latter case, it is determined that the network has a cyclic congestion dependency (as opposed to a path of congestion as in the former case).

When propagating a ping, routers exclusively reserve the internal path between the input and output ports of the router through which the ping proceeds, called the *ping path*, for later backward propagation of a bubble. Likewise, a total sequence of ping paths that a ping follows, referred to as the *ping trace*, is maintained by the associated routers in a distributed fashion. One of the challenges of ping propagation is in determining how pings should reserve network resources exclusively in such a way as not to incur further deadlocks due to the reservation. The problem is that each router uses only locally available information on making decisions on further ping propagation without having a global view on resource reservation by pings. The ping path information is referenced by the router scheduler to ensure that the first bubble in the associated output port should be consumed by the leading packet at the head of the paired input port in an attempt to resolve the detected congestion. The propagation of one bubble on a ping path deletes the recorded path information, and returns those related router resources to the normal router scheduling algorithm. Alternatively, the information on ping paths could be cleared upon receiving cancellation requests as described in the next section.

Once the ping terminates by detecting either cyclic or acyclic congestion dependencies, at least one acceleration bubble should be provided into those ping traces to resolve the detected congestion by advancing all the associated packets by at least one buffer position. For acyclic dependencies, the *ping-terminating router* is responsible for drawing a bubble into the ping trace from outside the acyclic dependency. To accomplish this, the router gives the highest scheduling priority to a packet from the input port where the ping trace ends. The routed packet transfers an *external bubble* (that is, a bubble that originated from outside the router) to its input port which is propagated backward along the ping trace. For cyclic dependencies, such external bubbles may not be available. Specifically, in networks using a recovery-based deadlock handling technique, detected cyclic dependencies could be a part of knotted cycles, forming deadlocks in the network. Considering this pathological case, the *ping-initiating router* must generate an internal bubble for the detected ping trace. The recovery technique proposed in this paper creates the internal bubble by use of a router-local *acceleration buffer* in a way such that a leading packet from the input port of the ping path is *sheltered* in a special buffer in the router. The bubble then traverses the cyclic ping trace in the opposite direction, and, upon its return to the ping-initiating router, it is used by the sheltered packet from the acceleration buffer. Irrespective of the source of acceleration bubbles, the packets in the cyclic or acyclic ping trace can eventually advance toward their destination at least by one buffer position. Such a packet-advancing operation via bubbles, referred to as a *shift operation*, may or may not provide immediate relief for those packets already involved in congestion or deadlock. However, new leading packets that emerge after the shift operation may require a different set of candidate output ports or sink at the new router due to arriving at its destination, possibly breaking the chained dependencies. In any event, the repeated detection of congestion and re-use of acceleration buffers will disperse congestion eventually.

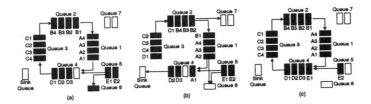

Figure 1. Importance of controlling bubble flow in one of possibly many logical networks with adaptive routing. (a) Packets A1 and E1 compete for a bubble in Queue 4, the only one in the cycle. (b) If allocated to A1, deadlock is prevented. (c) If allocated to E1, the bubble exits the cycle, intensifying congestion and possibly causing deadlock.

To illustrate our idea, consider the simplistic example shown in Figure 1. After detecting congestion (alternatively, potential deadlock as in Figure 1(c)), the schedulers in all of the routers (not shown) speculatively determine that the preferred path through which bubbles should flow is counter to the cycle shown in Figure 1(a) or (c). Instead of randomly choosing between A1 and E1 (alternatively, E2) or naively selecting based solely on packet lifetime, the scheduler more intelligently grants an acceleration bubble to A1—one of the culprit packets acting to sustain congestion (alternatively, potential deadlock) along the cyclic resource dependency relation. If an external bubble is unavailable due to potential deadlock (as in Figure 1(c)), our proposed cyclic congestion resolution mechanism creates an internal bubble available to A1. After all of the culprit packets have been allocated the bubble once it reaches the other routers, new packets are in position for being routed, as shown in Figure 1(b) (for cyclic congestion resolution, the bubble in Queue 4 would be replaced by E1). The routing function may supply different or additional routing options to these packets, allowing congestion to be dissipated with the additional bubbles introduced to those packets resulting from the speculative scheduling, i.e., the bubbles in Queue 7 and the Sink Queue.

3.2 Congestion and Potential Deadlock Detection

Congestion can occur along acyclic paths, cyclic paths, or trees within the network; potential deadlock can occur only along cyclic paths. No matter its form, packets occupying con-

gested and/or potentially deadlocked resources can be identified and tracked by their dependency relation along those resources. The detection technique we propose does this tracking using pings that probe resources suspected of such behavior within the network. These congestion/deadlock-detecting control packets are transmitted on the same control channels used to send other control signals.

Pings can be generated by a router (the ping initiator) for a given input port when the following conditions are satisfied: (1) the occupation of the queue(s) associated with the port is above a certain threshold, i.e., $O_{threshold}$; (2) the packet at the head of the queue(s) cannot advance for a threshold period of time, i.e., T_{time_out}; (3) the output port(s) needed for forwarding the packet at the head of the queue(s) is blocked, i.e., no bubbles are available; and (4) the input port is not an injection port.[2] An input port meeting these conditions is detected as being congested or potentially deadlocked, and used as a starting point of ping propagation. The ping initiator probes the network for congested and/or potentially deadlocked resources. A ping may be sent to more than one output port as long as the above conditions are met. The maximum number of output ports to send a ping is defined as *ping fan-out*, which could vary depending on the network organization and the use of the ping mechanism. Each ping path is recorded in a router's *ping table*, which is indexed by an output port number (see Figure 2). This table is referenced not only during detection of congestion, but also during the resolution process to ensure precise control over bubble movement. For the sake of scalability, each output port is associated with at most one ping path.

Output Port #	Ping ID (hex)	Origin	Valid	Input Port #
0	12340021	External	Yes	1
1	ABCD0007	Internal	Yes	3
n-1	-	-	No	-

Figure 2. Possible organization of router ping table.

On receiving pings from neighbors, routers perform a *propagation eligibility test* to decide whether the pings should be propagated to other routers or terminated in completion of the detection process. To minimize possible overhead for accomplishing a global consensus on network congestion, the propagation eligibility test is done on locally available information only: the buffer occupancy of input and output ports, and the resource dependencies among the ports imposed by the routing function. The test result is used in conjunction with the first three conditions mentioned above for generating a ping to make a final decision. Basically, a ping is propagated only

---

[2]With this, our proposed scheduling mechanism causes throttling to occur on injection channels.

if it has not completed a cycle and will not *collide* with previously generated pings. Ping collision happens when all the candidate output ports have been reserved by other pings. Except for some specific cases of ping collision described below, incoming pings should not be further propagated to ensure successful circulation of an internal bubble over a detected cyclic dependency. If a ping trace previously reserved by a ping is allowed to be altered by other pings, an internal bubble generated by a ping-initiating router could get derailed from the detected cycle as it travels backward along the ping trace. This could cause the acceleration buffer in that router to remain occupied indefinitely, preventing recovery from deadlock. Alternatively, it is possible to avoid such ping collision by allowing the same output port to be reserved by more than one ping arriving through other input ports. In this case, the organization of the ping table would need to be augmented in such a way that the table provides a sufficient number of entries for each output port. However, this approach may result in poor scalability.

When an incoming ping collides with other pings at candidate output ports, the router is in one of the following three situations, depending on the reservation status as shown in Figure 3: (1) all the candidate output ports have been reserved by different pings and are associated with other input ports, (2) the same ping path has been reserved by a different ping that was initiated at the router, and (3) the same path has been reserved by a different ping, but not initiated at this router.

In Case 1, all the candidate output ports are reserved previously by other ping(s). Correct ping operation requires that any existing ping paths reserved by different pings with different input ports should not be altered by later pings. Therefore, the new incoming ping which is *interlocked* should be squashed, and the prior resource reservations made along its trace should be cleared.

In Case 2, the router where the ping just arrived had generated a different ping along the same ping path as the incoming one needs to reserve. This happens when more than one router initiates the detection of the same acyclic or cyclic congestion. Due to the requirement that a cycle should be detected by at most one ping, all the reservations done by other pings should be cancelled. In order to elect one ping to finish detection, the router compares the detection priority of the incoming ping against that which was generated before, where the detection priority is represented by the ping identification (Ping ID, see Section 3.4 for detail). If the incoming ping has higher priority, it outranks the ping generated at the router and propagates along the previously charted ping path.

In Case 3, ping propagation eligibility occurs only when the incoming ping outranks the previously transmitted ping. Therefore, all the ping paths previously reserved by the outranked ping are safely overridden.

Cancellation plays a crucial role in preventing network resources from remaining reserved due to unsuccessful detec-

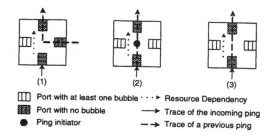

Figure 3. Possible collision situations of router upon the arrival of a new ping.

tion of network congestion. Cancellation packets are basically similar to ping packets in that they are control packets sharing the same packet format. When a router creates a cancellation packet, it specifies the identification of the ping to cancel. When receiving a cancellation, a router first references its ping table to locate the proper entry with the same Ping ID, then forwards the cancellation further to the input port recorded in the ping table entry and clears the entry. This continues until cancellation packet reaches the point where the corresponding ping was created.

When an incoming ping has just completed a cyclic traversal but at a *ping-propagating router*—one which is within a ping trace—a shift operation can start at that router. In this special case, the cancellation needs to be initiated by that router to clear the partial ping trace from it to the ping-initiating router; Otherwise, the partial ping trace remains reserved with no guaranteed provision of internal or external bubbles.

3.3 Congestion and Potential Deadlock Resolution

The resolution technique proposed in this section resolves temporal and spatial resource dependencies by speculatively scheduling bubbles to needed input ports before those bubbles actually arrive at router output ports. For this idea to work, precise control over bubble movement is required such that priority for bubble flow is along the links which most contribute to congestion and/or potential deadlock. Speculation is therefore based on congestion and potential deadlock information obtained from our proposed pinging detection mechanism.

Let us first consider networks which always avoid deadlock. In these networks, only congestion can occur which should be resolved quickly after being detected. External bubbles are guaranteed to be supplied eventually to network resources that need them. Reservations on a ping path made for each pinged output port indicate that the next bubble which eventually comes to that port should be allocated to an input port that is either (1) detected as closing a dependency cycle or (2) detected simply as being congested. When a bubble arrives at an output, the scheduler looks up the ping table to see if a reservation has been made for the output. If so and the grant signal for the output port is accepted, the corresponding entry in the ping table is cleared. In this way, arriving bubbles are coerced to flow along a pre-detected path of congestion, allowing the opportunity for packets along that path to disperse out of congestion by shifting forward, as shown in Figure 1(b).

Now consider the case of deadlock recovery networks. In these networks, both congestion and potential deadlock situations can occur which should be resolved quickly after being detected. Internal bubbles must be introduced into the network resources that need them by removing at least one of the packets involved [20], i.e., packet A1 in Figure 1(c). This can be done by sheltering in the acceleration buffer the culprit packet at the head of the input port identified as closing the dependency cycle. The buffer should be large enough to hold an entire packet without loss of information. When the internal bubble completes circulation along the cyclic ping trace, it returns to the router and evacuates the culprit packet from the acceleration buffer. It is also possible for one or more external bubbles to be drawn to ping traces during the circulation of internal bubbles. This is because it is possible for ping-propagating routers to route packets from the input port of the ping path to one of the output ports outside of the ping path upon receiving external bubbles on those ports. However, once drawn to ping traces, external bubbles are handled in the same way as internal ones, and, therefore, can be used to evacuate acceleration buffers faster with no harm.

3.4 Router Architecture

Figure 2 shows a pipelined router architecture that supports our proposed mechanism. The additional hardware for a traditional router architecture includes two tables (Routing Failure Table and Ping Table), two registers, and a packet-sized acceleration buffer for generating an internal bubble.

The routing failure table—indexed by an input port number—caches stalled routing options due to congestion at the corresponding output ports. This makes it possible for the ping propagation eligibility test to acquire outstanding dependency relations between input and output ports without having to consult the routing table. Depending on the actual implementation, each routing failure table entry contains 1 to n output ports, where n is the maximum number of output ports. The size complexity of the table is calculated as $O(mn)$ in the maximal configuration, where m and n are the number of input and output ports, respectively. Each entry should be cleared upon progress made by a packet in the corresponding input port.

As mentioned earlier, the ping table (see Figures 2 and 4) records the reservation status of ping paths. Because an output port is associated with at most one ping path, the ping table can be organized such that each entry is indexed by an output port number. The ping table has one input port per entry, which limits the size complexity to $O(n)$, where n is the number of output ports.

The Ping ID register and the Ping Status register are used only when the associated router generates a ping to initiate net-

work congestion. The former records the Ping ID of a newly generated ping. Each router can have a maximum of one outstanding ping at a time. The information in this register is used to compare detection priorities with any incoming pings. Ping ID consists of the random number portion and the identification portion of ping initiator. For fair distribution of detection priorities over ping initiators, the random number portion goes into the most significant part of Ping ID. The Ping Status register indicates the current status in congestion detection and resolution. Possible states include idle state, detection state and resolution state. This register is mainly used to prevent routers in recovery mode from being outranked by other pings.

Overall, augmentation of the router architecture imposes a minimal impact on the critical path. Most of the added hardware is used only when routers experience enough network congestion to initiate or assist detection activities. In addition, it works in parallel with existing router hardware (e.g., routing table look-up and crossbar arbitration).

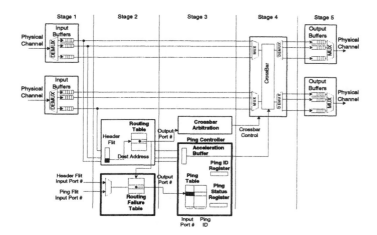

Figure 4. A pipelined router architecture which incorporates the additional hardware (shown in bold boxes) for detection and resolution of cyclic dependencies in the network.

4 Performance Evaluation

4.1 Simulation Methodology

The simulator used for evaluation is based on a flit-level network simulator, Flexsim 1.2, developed by the SMART Interconnects Group at USC. The simulator is augmented to incorporate the ping mechanism as a congestion/deadlock detection technique and the bubble mechanism as a recovery technique. Pings are assumed to traverse the network through physically separated links. They could, however, have been implemented on the same physical links as used for data transmission. In either case, since pings are transferred only when the links are unable to make progress in packet delivery due to congestion, the bandwidth consumption by ping propagation should have minimal impact on the transmission of data packets. Our preliminary simulations show that in-band ping transmission uses only a small fraction (less than 2%) of data transmission bandwidth. In this study, regular (k-ary n-cube toroidal) networks with the following default parameters are simulated: 8-ary 2-cube, bidirectional channels, virtual cut-through flow control, 4 virtual channels per physical link and random traffic patterns. Each virtual channel is assumed to hold one packet at a time. In addition, the default threshold occupancy of the queue ($O_{threshold}$) is set to 100%, and the default threshold timeout for initiating ping navigation (T_{time_out}) is set to 25 cycles. The ping propagation latency through a router is assumed to be one cycle.

4.2 Simulation Results

4.2.1 Congestion and Deadlock Handling

To be used as an alternative to previously proposed techniques for handling deadlock anomalies in networks, the ping-based congestion detection technique and the bubble-based resolution technique are merged to form a ping and bubble mechanism (PB, in short). Note that this PB mechanism indirectly handles deadlock anomalies by detecting and resolving network congestion. For this experiment, three deadlock handling techniques are compared in terms of network throughput and packet delivery latency: true fully adaptive routing with the PB technique, true full adaptive routing with the Disha technique and avoidance-based routing using Duato's adaptive protocol.

Figure 5 shows the simulation results for the three techniques with varying network loads. As can be seen, PB and Disha techniques yield similar performance in terms of maximum network throughput, outperforming the avoidance-based technique. The difference in network throughput increases as the network load increases beyond the saturation point, as shown in Figure 5(b). Both Disha and Duato significantly suffer from degradation in network throughput, while PB effectively tolerates such degradation. Among these techniques only PB can actively disperse network congestion through speculative scheduling. Once accelerated toward their destinations, some packets may leave the network instead of remaining congested, creating new bubbles into the network which could be used for making forward progress in delivering other packets.

The major contribution to congestion dispersion comes from the detection of acyclic resource dependencies. Results show that 85% of newly generated pings terminate after detecting acyclic dependencies, and 14.95% of them are cancelled due to the ping interlocking and outranking situation. Only 0.05% of the pings successfully complete cyclic traversal on network resources to track the existence of cyclic dependencies. This observation indicates that PB tends to handle dead-

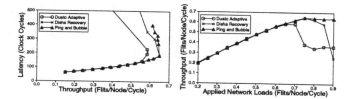

Figure 5. Network throughput and latency for the networks with deadlock avoidance and recovery routing. (a) Network performance in throughput and latency plotted in Burton Normal Form[4], and (b) measured network throughput vs. applied network loads.

lock anomalies at very early stages by dispersing network congestion, which could be considered a preventive approach to the deadlock problem.

The impact of the shift operation on network performance could be affected by routing flexibility, average distance to destination, and many other network parameters. In particular, the first affects how shifted packets differ from their predecessors in terms of resource dependency, while the second impacts how many packets could sink at their destinations after shift operations. Simulation results show that after shift operations, 10% of the shifted packets sink, another 10% of them have routing dependencies on non-pinged output ports, and about 2-3% of them become free from congestion by having bubbles at needed output ports.

The PB technique, in addition to achieving better performance than Disha, does not cause out-of-order delivery of packets during recovery operations. Even though Disha is capable of progressively recovering from potential deadlocks, the packets recovered via the resources for deadlock-recovery may bypass their preceding packets which are in the same communication stream. These packets, in the worst case, may cause re-transmission of a large chunk of packets due to the execution consistency enforced by applications or higher level network protocols. Our simulation results show that in Disha-based networks around 10% of the packets are delivered out-of-order through deadlock recovery resources when network load is beyond 80% of maximum network capacity. In networks with PB, packets in chained dependencies are shifted toward destinations by one buffer position, while maintaining their relative order in the network.

4.2.2 Effect of Congestion Detection

The ping technique, implemented in networks with deadlock avoidance-based approaches, could be used to help disperse temporal and spatial network congestion. It is enabled by the deadlock-avoiding routing function which guarantees the delivery of packets in the network and the creation of external bubbles for further congestion dispersion. Therefore, the main role of the ping technique is to efficiently deliver those external bubbles to where they are needed most. For this experiment, we use torus networks with Duato's adaptive routing protocol with 4 virtual channels per physical link: two channels for escape paths and two for adaptive paths. For simplicity, ping generation and propagation are all based on the congestion status of adaptive paths only.

Figure 6 illustrates the performance of the two networks, only one of them implementing the PB technique. As shown in the figure, the network can be improved by 5% in maximum throughput by incorporating the PB technique. For network loads of 0.75 or larger, network throughput is improved by up to 100%. These results show that having bubbles in networks is not sufficient to efficiently resolve network congestion. Instead, bubble movement in the network should be properly controlled for achieving better performance. It is also shown that the PB technique can be used even in deadlock-free networks in order to efficiently disperse network congestion.

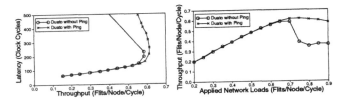

Figure 6. Network throughput and latency for the networks with and without the ping-based congestion sensitive scheduling. (a) Network performance in throughput and latency plotted in Burton Normal Form and (b) measured network throughput vs. applied network loads.

4.2.3 Effect of Injection Limitation

The performance improvement via the proposed techniques is mostly from efficient dispersion of network congestion. But, it is also partially due to the capability of the ping mechanism to limit injection of new packets by end nodes. In fact, this capability is provided as a by-product of ping generation and propagation: first, packet congestion at an injection port is not allowed to trigger ping generation, which prohibits active dispersion of the congestion formed at injection ports; second, resource reservations via ping operations give priority to the associated input ports for the potential bubbles at the outputs, throttling packet injection toward those output ports from end nodes.

To observe the effect of the injection-limiting capability of our ping technique, two networks with true fully adaptive routing are simulated using the PB technique, one of them implementing relaxed injection limitation by allowing injection ports to trigger ping operations. Note that it is impossible to precisely turn off the injection limiting effect due to resource reservation by pings.

Figure 7 shows the effect of injection throttling implicitly provided in the proposed ping technique. As shown in the figure, networks yield better performance when injection ports are prohibited from triggering ping operations, although the effect is not significant (see the curves with the labels of *PB with No InjLim* and *PB with InjLim*). When injection ports are allowed to trigger pinging, the network bubbles leave the network, which in turn increases the congestion level in the network. One of the reasons for having less significant difference in the performance is that such implicit limitation itself is not efficient enough to prevent networks from being deeply saturated. The networks with fully adaptive routing can provide more than one routing path for new packets waiting for injection, which enables those packets to enter the network via non-reserved router ports.

The figure also shows the impact of deadlock handling techniques on the performance of networks using a previously proposed injection limitation technique, called ALO [1]. As indicated in the figure, the Disha-based networks benefit less from the ALO technique. ALO is reported to be effective in wormhole networks [1], but it is less efficient for throttling packet injection in virtual cut-through networks. This is because by buffering entire packets at the routers virtual cut-through networks slowly propagate congestion to end nodes, which could mislead end nodes to believe that the network is not congested yet. In other words, when ALO starts to limit packet injection, the network is saturated to a certain extent, but not fully. In this case, while the Disha-based networks suffer from overhead due to deadlock handling, the PB technique can efficiently utilize the remaining bubbles to make progress in packet delivery.

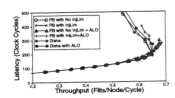

Figure 7. Network throughput and latency for the networks with injection-limiting techniques with PB-based true fully adaptive routing protocol.

4.2.4 Performance over varying network loads

We experimented with 16×16 tori to observe the performance behavior of the proposed congestion control techniques in larger scaled networks. Figure 8 shows the performance of two deadlock handling techniques: PB and Disha. As can be seen, the performance of the two techniques is almost the same: both suffer from performance degradation when the network is deeply saturated. The reasons for this are the following. In Disha, once a network is fully saturated, more routers experience timeouts on packet delivery and compete for the use of recovery resources which are not abundant, resulting in recovery resources becoming the performance bottleneck. However, in PB, as the size of the networks increases, the length of chained congestion tends to increase accordingly, which causes pings to travel longer paths (more routers) before discovering cyclic dependencies or sinking at the end of acyclic dependencies. The longer pings travel, the higher the probability of interference with the propagation of other pings and to cause pings to be cancelled. Therefore, in order for networks to gracefully degrade in performance under high network load, they should have an efficient way of reducing the average length of the ping paths.

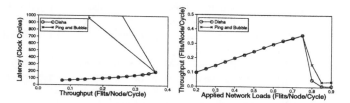

Figure 8. Network throughput and latency for PB and Disha deadlock handling techniques. (a) Network performance in throughput and latency plotted in Burton Normal Form and (b) measured network throughput vs. applied network loads.

In a realistic network environment, network loads vary over time based on applications' need for communication. To observe the effectiveness of congestion/deadlock handling techniques in such environments, we simulated two 16×16 networks: one with the PB technique and the other with the Disha technique. The network load linearly increases from 0% to the 100% for a pre-specified amount of time, called a *cycle time*, and then repeats the pattern after being reset to 0%. The cycle time is parameterized in this experiment to observe the impact of the duration of congestion on the performance of the two techniques.

Table 1 shows the network performances compared in terms of network throughput, packet delivery latency and other important metrics. As shown in the table, both techniques perform almost equally well when the cycle times are small. However, the PB technique outperforms Disha by 340% in throughput and 500% in latency when the cycle time is 2000. When simulated with short cycle time, the network congestion does not last long enough to make networks remain fully saturated. The short-term congestion can be easily dispersed by either technique. However, when longer cycle times are used, the network could experience enough congestion up to saturation. In this case, the PB-based network can disperse network congestion by the simultaneous use of multiple pings, while the Disha-based network experiences a performance bottleneck on recovery resources. In summary, the PB technique can more

efficiently disperse temporal congestion than Disha, especially when networks experience severe time-varying congestion.

5 Conclusion

In this paper, we propose a novel technique for efficiently handling network congestion and deadlock anomalies. The proposed technique not only precisely identifies congested resources but also actively disperses detected congestion by providing bubbles for blocked packets due to such congestion. This technique can be deployed in networks with recovery-based routing algorithms such as true fully adaptive routing or with avoidance-based routing. In the former case, acceleration buffers implemented in routers are used to create necessary bubbles for deadlock resolution.

The techniques proposed in this paper provide several advantages for system and network designers. First, the techniques make true fully adaptive routing approaches more practically applicable to real environments by providing an efficient way to handle network congestion and deadlock. Unlike other recovery-based deadlock handling techniques, the ping and bubble technique does not cause out-of-order delivery of packets during recovery even when networks are deeply saturated. Second, no single point of failure exists because token mechanism is no more necessary. Third, PB is able to actively disperse network congestion by precisely controlling the movement of bubbles in a network. Fourth, congestion dispersion may take place in more than one place simultaneously, which enables packets to experience less blockage during the transmission, thus increasing the network performance. Fifth, PB implicitly provides injection-limiting capability for networks such that when networks are saturated the ping technique prevents packets from being injected into the network. If used conjunctively with explicit injection-limiting techniques such as ALO, the PB technique can yield better performance by effectively throttling new packet injections and thus keeping the network from being fully saturated.

Acknowledgements

We are very appreciative of the insightful and invaluable comments made by anonymous reviewers and, especially, José Duato which have greatly improved the quality of the paper.

References

[1] E. Baydal, P. López, and J. Duato. A simple and efficient mechanism to prevent saturation in wormhole networks. In *Proceedings of the 14th Intl Conf on Parallel and Distributed Processing Symposium*, pages 617–622, May 2000.

[2] J. Duato. A New Theory of Deadlock-free Adaptive Routing in Wormhole Networks. *IEEE Trans on Parallel and Distributed Systems*, 4(12):1320–1331, 1993.

Table 1. Performance of the two congestion / deadlock handling techniques in resolving temporal network congestion.

Technique	PB	Disha	PB	Disha	PB	Disha	PB	Disha
Cycle Time	200		500		1000		2000	
Throughput	0.253	0.254	0.237	0.236	0.246	0.057	0.189	0.0557
Latency	177.89	182.06	207.71	210.5	374.16	4928.77	1254.74	6458.15
Packets Delivered	40560	40786	75893	75806	177657	41167	288143	84756

[3] J. Duato and T. M. Pinkston. A General Theory for Deadlock-Free Adaptive Routing Using a Mixed Set of Resources. *IEEE Trans on Parallel and Distributed Systems*, 12(12), Dec 2001.

[4] J. Duato, S. Yalamanchili, and L. Ni. *Interconnection Networks: An Engineering Approach*. IEEE Computer Society Press, 1997.

[5] J. Kim, Z. Liu, and A. Chien. Compressionless Routing: A Framework for Adaptive and Fault-tolerant Routing. *IEEE Transactions on Parallel and Distributed Systems*, 8(3):229–244, March 1997.

[6] A. K.V. and T. M. Pinkston. An Efficient, Fully Adaptive Deadlock Recovery Scheme: DISHA. In *Proceedings of the 22nd Intl Symp on Computer Architecture*, pages 201–210, June 1995.

[7] A. K.V., T. M. Pinkston, and J. Duato. Generalized Theory for Deadlock-Free Adaptive Wormhole Routing and its Application to Disha Concurrent. In *Proc of the 10th Intl Parallel Processing Symposium*, pages 815–821, April 1996.

[8] N. McKeown. The iSLIP scheduling algorithm for input-queued switches. *IEEE/ACM Transactions on Networking*, 7(2):188–201, Apr. 1999.

[9] N. Ni and L. N. Bhuyan. Fair Scheduling for Input Buffered Switches. *Proceedings of the 15th International Parallel and Distributed Processing Symposium*, pages 1682–1689, April 2001.

[10] P. Palazzari and M. Coli. Virtual Cut-Through Implementation of the Hole-Based Packet Switching Routing Algorithm. In 6th *Euromicro Workshop on Parallel and Distributed Processing*, pages 416–421, Jan 1998.

[11] A. K. Parekh and R. G. Gallager. A generalized processor sharing approach to flow control in integrated services networks: the single-node case. *IEEE/ACM Transactions on Networking*, 1(3):344–357, June 1993.

[12] L.-S. Peh and W. J. Dally. A Delay Model and Speculative Architecture for Pipelined Routers. In *Proceedings of the 7th International Symposium on High Performance Computer Architecture*, January 2001.

[13] T. M. Pinkston. Flexible and Efficient Routing Based on Progressive Deadlock Recovery. *IEEE Transactions on Computers*, 48(7), July 1999.

[14] T. M. Pinkston and S. Warnakulasuriya. On Deadlocks in Interconnection Networks. In *Proc of the 24th Intl Symp on Computer Architecture*, pages 38–49, June 1997.

[15] V. Puente, C. Izu, R. Beivide, J. A. Gregorio, F. Vallejo, and J. M. Prellezo. The adaptive bubble router. *Journal of Parallel and Distributed Computing*, 61(9):1180–1208, Sept. 2001.

[16] L. Schwiebert and D. N. Jayasimha. A Necessary and Sufficient Condition for Deadlock-free Wormhole Routing. *Journal of Parallel and Dist Computing*, 32(1):103–117, Jan 1996.

[17] M. Thottethodi, A. R. Lebeck, and S. S. Mukherjee. Self-Tuned Congestion Control for Multiprocessor Networks. In *Proceedings of the 7th International Symposium on High Performance Computer Architecture*, January 2001.

[18] W. Vogels, D. Follett, J. Hsieh, D. Lifka, and D. Stern. Tree-saturation in the AC3 Velocity Cluster Interconnect. In *Proceedings of the Symposium on Hot Interconnects*. IEEE Computer Society, August 2000.

[19] S. Warnakulasuriya and T. M. Pinkston. Characterization of Deadlocks in k-ary n-cube Networks. *IEEE Trans on Parallel and Distributed Systems*, 10(9):904–921, Sep 1999.

[20] S. Warnakulasuriya and T. M. Pinkston. A Formal Model of Message Blocking and Deadlock Resolution in Interconnection Networks. *IEEE Transactions on Parallel and Distributed Systems*, 11(3):212–229, March 2000.

[21] S. Warnakulasuriya and T. M. Pinkston. Characterization of Deadlocks in Irregular Networks. *Journal of Parallel and Distributed Computing*, December 2001.

[22] K. Yum, A. Vaidya, C. Das, and A. Sivasubramaniam. Investigating QoS support for traffic mixes with the mediaworm router. In *Sixth International Symposium on High-Performance Computer Architecture*, pages 97–108, Jan. 1999.

[23] L. Zhang. VirtualClock: A new traffic control algorithm for packet-switched networks. *ACM Transactions on Computer Systems*, 9(2):101–124, May 1991.

Session 2B

Programming Environments

ZEN: A Directive-based Language for Automatic Experiment Management of Distributed and Parallel Programs*

Radu Prodan and Thomas Fahringer
Institute for Software Science, University of Vienna
Liechtensteinstr. 22, A-1090 Vienna, Austria
{radu,tf}@par.univie.ac.at

Abstract

So far there exists very little support to specify and to control execution of a large number of experiments on distributed and parallel architectures. This paper describes ZEN, a directive-based language for the specification of arbitrarily complex program executions by varying problem, system, or machine parameters for parallel and distributed applications. ZEN introduces directives to substitute strings and to insert assignment statements inside arbitrary files, such as program, input, script, or makefiles. The programmer thus can invoke experiments for arbitrary value ranges of any problem parameter, including program variables, file names, compiler options, target machines, machine sizes, scheduling strategies, data distributions, etc. The number of experiments can be controlled through ZEN constraint directives. Finally, the programmer may request a large set of performance metrics to be computed for any code region of interest. The scope of ZEN directives can be restricted to arbitrary file or code regions. We have implemented a prototype tool for automatic experiment management that is based on ZEN. We will report results for performance analysis of an ocean simulation application and for parameter study of a computational finance code.

1. Introduction

The development and execution management of scientific and engineering applications on complex, heterogeneous, and non-dedicated distributed architectures, ranging from cluster architectures to widely distributed GRID structures is a tedious, time-consuming and error-prone undertaking. On one hand, scientists, and engineers perform complex parameter studies for large applications to obtain solution information for a wide variety of input parameter values. On the other hand, the development of performance-oriented applications involves many cycles of code editing, performance tuning, code execution, testing and performance analysis. Some performance metrics, such as scalability or speedup, may require the testing of numerous problem and machine sizes for different compiler options and target architectures. To this date, researchers are commonly forced to manually create their parameter studies, manage many different sets of input data, launch large number of program compilations and executions, administer corresponding result files, invoke performance analysis tools to derive performance metrics, relate performance data back to experiments and code regions, etc.

In this paper we describe ZEN, a directive-based language for the specification of complex parameter and performance studies. ZEN directives are employed to annotate arbitrary files and specify value ranges for any problem, system or machine parameters. Such parameters may include program variables, file names, compiler options, target machines, machine sizes, scheduling strategies, data distributions, etc. Performance behaviour directives can be used to gather performance metrics. The scope of ZEN directives can be restricted to arbitrary file or code regions. Constraint directives restrict the number of experiments to a subset of meaningful parameter combinations.

We have implemented ZENTURIO, a tool for automatic experiment management of distributed and parallel programs that parses application files annotated with ZEN directives and generates appropriate application codes, based on the semantics of the directives. The applications are then transferred to the target machine for compilation and execution. Upon their completion, the output files and performance data are stored into a database for analysis and visualisation. ZENTURIO employs SCALEA [9] for code instrumentation and computation of performance overheads.

The rest of this paper is organised as follows. The next section discusses related work. Section 3 describes the ZEN language in detail. Experiments are presented in Section 4. Finally, some concluding remarks are made and future work is outlined in Section 5.

*This research is supported by the Austrian Science Fund as part of the Aurora project under contract SFBF1104.

2. Related Work

The Paradyn performance analysis tools [5] supports experiment management by techniques for quantitatively comparing experiments and performance diagnosis. Experiments have to be set up manually, whereas performance analysis is done automatically.

The ZOO project [4] has been initiated to support scientific experiment management by providing an experiment specification language and by supporting automatic experiment execution and data exploration. Parametrisation is limited to input and output files.

Nimrod [1] is a tool that manages parameter studies by generating one job for each unique combination of parameter values and by taking the cartesian product of all values. The set of possible parameter value combinations cannot be restricted, and string substitution in program files is not allowed.

Instead of using a language based approach, the ILAB [10] project tries to control parameter studies through a graphical user interface. ILAB is restricted to input files.

In the framework of the IST APART working group (Workpackage 3: Implementation Issues) [6] a design of an automatic performance analysis system has been developed. The ideas of this workpackage have stimulated some of the functionality provided by ZENTURIO.

3. ZEN Language Description

In this section, we give an introduction to ZEN sets and directives and discuss all individual ZEN directives in detail.

3.1. ZEN Sets

ZEN enables the specification of value ranges for arbitrary parameters, variables, or strings in any text file before experiments are invoked. ZEN introduces the so-called ZEN sets to efficiently describe these value ranges. A *ZEN set* is a totally ordered set of (integer or real) numbers or strings with a well-defined syntax and a well-defined evaluation function ε. The following syntax based on regular expressions is used to specify ZEN sets:

zen-set	is	"{" *elem-list* "}"
elem	is	*num* **or** *comp-elem*
num	is	*low:up[:stride]* **or** *number*
comp-elem	is	(*zen-num-set* | *zen-string*)+
low	is	*number*
up	is	*number*
stride	is	*number*
number	is	*integer* **or** *real*
zen-num-set	is	"{" *num-list* "}"
zen-string	is	([^\n{},:] | "\{" | "\}" | "\," | "\:")*

A term *elem-list* corresponds to a list of *elem* terms, separated by commas (the same holds for *num-list*).

Let $\cdot$ denote the string concatenation operator which is also referred in the following by using one blank character, and let $\mathcal{P}$ denote the power set, and $\mathbb{R}$ the set of real numbers. The semantics (i.e. the concrete set of elements) of a ZEN set, is given by the evaluation function: $\varepsilon: zen\text{-}set \to \mathcal{P}(\mathbb{R} \cup string)$, $\varepsilon(\{ elem_1, \ldots, elem_n \}) = \bigcup_{1 \leq i \leq n} \overline{\varepsilon}(elem_i)$, where function $\overline{\varepsilon}$ is defined in Fig. 1. The pattern *low:up:stride* has by default $stride = 1$, therefore, $\overline{\varepsilon}(low:up) = \overline{\varepsilon}(low:up:1)$. *zen-strings* must obey the syntax defined by the evaluation function $\overline{\varepsilon}_s$. Commas, braces and colons inside *zen-strings* must be prefixed with one '\' character. Thus commas can be distinguished from the value delimiters of a *zen-num-set*, *zen-num-set*s inside *zen-strings* can be avoided, and the pattern *low:up:stride* can be a *zen-string*.

A totally ordered set $\mathcal{S}$ with an ordering operation $\prec$ is denoted by $(\mathcal{S}, \prec)$. A single element of a ZEN set is called *ZEN element*. The *total order* of ZEN elements in a ZEN set, denoted by the operator $\prec$, is given by the ordering rules expressed in Fig. 2. The total order of ZEN sets is used by the ZEN index constraint directive (see Section 3.6).

3.2. ZEN Directives

A *ZEN directive* is a comment line starting with the prefix ZEN$. The characters which mark the begin (and eventually the end) of a comment is the only programming language specific feature of ZEN. In order to define a ZEN directive, a comment line must have the ZEN$ prefix immediately after the special character(s) which mark its begin. For instance, !ZEN$ A={1,2,3} and //ZEN$ A={1,2,3} denote a ZEN directive in the context of the Fortran and the Java/C++ programming languages, respectively.

There are four categories of ZEN directives. *Substitute* (see Section 3.3) and *assignment directives* (see Section 3.4) assign a ZEN set to a *ZEN variable* (defined as a sequence of characters). Each ZEN element in the ZEN set represents an experimental value for the corresponding ZEN variable. The *constraint directives* (see Section 3.6) define boolean conditions over ZEN variables, thus restricting the set of possible experiments. The *performance measurement directives* (see Section 3.7) are used to request a large number of performance metrics for specific code regions.

Every ZEN directive d, except the assignment directive, is associated with a scope denoted by *scope(d)*, which refers to the code region in which the directive holds.

The ZEN variable name must obey the following syntax rules: (1) equality characters must be prefixed with a '\' character which distinguishes them from the value assignment characters inside a ZEN directive (e.g. PARAMETER::\=0); (2) arithmetical (+, −, *, /, %, ^), relational (==, !=, <, >, <=, >=) and logical (!, &&,\|\|) operators, as well as left and right parenthesis must be prefixed with a '\' character, which distinguishes them from the parenthesis and operators in a ZEN constraint (e.g. threads\(4\), see Ex. 4.2); (3) a ZEN variable must not be an integer or real number which avoids ambiguities in-

$$\bar{\varepsilon} : elem \to \mathcal{P}(\mathbb{R} \cup string), \ \bar{\varepsilon}(e) = \begin{cases} \{low + k * stride \mid k \in \mathbb{N}, k \in [0 .. \frac{up - low}{stride}]\}, & e \text{ is } low\text{:}up\text{:}stride; \\ \{e\}, & e \text{ is } number; \\ X, & e \text{ is } (zen\text{-}num\text{-}set \mid zen\text{-}string)+, \end{cases}$$

$$(zen\text{-}num\text{-}set \mid zen\text{-}string)+ = zen\text{-}string_1 \{num_{11}, \ldots, num_{1n_1}\} \ldots zen\text{-}string_p \{num_{p1}, \ldots, num_{pn_p}\} \ zen\text{-}string_{p+1},$$

$$X = \{\bar{\varepsilon}_s(zen\text{-}string_1) \ n_1 \ldots \bar{\varepsilon}_s(zen\text{-}string_p) \ n_p \ \bar{\varepsilon}_s(zen\text{-}string_{p+1}) \mid$$
$$\forall (n_1, \ldots, n_p) \in \varepsilon(\{num_{11}, \ldots, num_{1n_1}\}) \times \ldots \times \varepsilon(\{num_{p1}, \ldots, num_{pn_p}\})\},$$

$$\bar{\varepsilon}_s : string \to string, \ \bar{\varepsilon}_s(s) = \begin{cases} s, & \forall e \in \{``\backslash", \ ``\backslash\{", \ ``\backslash\}", \ ``\backslash:"\}, \ e \notin s; \\ \bar{\varepsilon}_s(s_l) \ c \ \bar{\varepsilon}_s(s_r), & s = s_l \backslash c \ s_r, \ \forall c \in \{`,`, `\{`, `\}`, `:`, \ ``\}; \end{cases}$$

Figure 1. The ZEN set element evaluation function.

- $\forall \ elem_i, elem_j \in \varepsilon(\{elem_1, \ldots, elem_n\}), \ i, j \in [1 .. n], \ elem_i \prec elem_j \iff i < j;$
- $\forall \ e_i, e_j \in \bar{\varepsilon}(low\text{:}up\text{:}stride), e_i \prec e_j \iff e_i = low + k_i * stride \wedge e_j = low + k_j * stride \wedge k_i < k_j;$
- $\forall \ (n_1, \ldots, n_p), (n'_1, \ldots, n'_p) \in \varepsilon(\{num_{11}, \ldots, num_{1n_1}\}) \times \ldots \times \varepsilon(\{num_{p1}, \ldots num_{pn_p}\}),$
  $string_1 \ n_1 \ldots string_p \ n_p \ string_{p+1} \prec string_1 \ n'_1 \ldots string_p \ n'_p \ string_{p+1} \iff$
  $\exists \ i \in [1 .. n] \text{ such that } (\forall j \in [1 .. i - 1] : n_j = n'_j) \wedge n_i \prec n'_i;$
- $\forall \ (A, \prec), \ (B, \prec) \text{ totally ordered sets} \implies (A \cup B, \prec) \text{ totally ordered set, where:}$
  $\forall a, b \in A \cup B, \ a \prec b \iff a \in A \wedge b \in B \backslash A \ \vee \ (a, b \in A \ \vee \ a, b \in B \backslash A) \wedge a \prec b.$

Figure 2. Rules for expressing the total order of elements in ZEN sets.

side of ZEN constraint boolean expressions.

The *value set* of a ZEN variable z, denoted by $\mathcal{V}^z$, is the totally ordered ZEN set $(S, \prec)$ associated with z: $\mathcal{V}^z = \varepsilon(S)$ (see Section 3.1), where $\prec$ is defined in Fig. 2.

The *index domain* of a ZEN variable z, denoted by $\mathcal{I}^z$, is the totally ordered set of elements $\mathcal{I}^z = (S, <)$, where $S = \{ i \in \mathbb{N}^* \mid i \leq |\mathcal{V}^z| \}$ and $\mathbb{N}$ denotes the natural numbers. The total order of elements in $\mathcal{I}^z$ is the natural order.

The *value function* of a ZEN variable z is the total bijective function: $\vartheta : \mathcal{I}^z \to \mathcal{V}^z$ which associates each element $i \in \mathcal{I}^z$ with the ith element $e \in \mathcal{V}^z$, such that: $\forall \ i, i_1, i_2 \in \mathcal{I}^z, \ i_1 < i < i_2 \iff \vartheta(i_1) \prec \vartheta(i) \prec \vartheta(i_2)$. We denote i to be the *index* of $e \in \mathcal{V}^z$. The *index function* $\vartheta^{-1} : \mathcal{V}^z \to \mathcal{I}^z$ is the inverse of the value function. The value and index functions are used by the index domain constraints in Section 3.6.

An arbitrary file $\mathcal{F}$ (e.g. source, input data, and make-file) augmented with a set of ZEN directives is called a *ZEN file*. The ZEN file is denoted by $\mathcal{F}(z_1, \ldots, z_n)$, where $z_i, \ i \in [1..n]$, are the ZEN variables corresponding to the ZEN directives in $\mathcal{F}$. A *ZEN file instance*, denoted by $\mathcal{F}'(e_1, \ldots, e_n)$, where $e_i \in \mathcal{V}^{z_i}, \ i \in [1..n]$, is an instantiation of the ZEN file $\mathcal{F}$, obtained by instantiating each ZEN variable with one ZEN element from its value set.

The translation of a ZEN file to a ZEN file instance is done by the *ZEN Transformation System (ZTS)*, depicted in

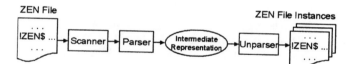

Figure 3. ZEN Transformation System (ZTS).

Fig. 3. ZTS can be considered a source-to-source compiler which generates ZEN file instances based on the ZEN directives encountered. The number of the ZEN file instances is given by the cardinality of the value set of a ZEN file, as defined in Section 3.5. ZEN variables can be of three different types: *integer*, *real* and *string*, determined by ZTS in the parsing phase, based on the values of the ZEN elements.

3.3. ZEN Substitute Directive

The *ZEN substitute directive* is used to replace strings in ZEN files, which is expressed by assigning a ZEN set to a ZEN variable. This directive is commonly employed to examine different problem and machine sizes, data or work distributions, scheduling strategies, etc. The scope of the *global substitute directive* comprises the entire ZEN file in which the directive occurs. It has the following syntax:

substitute-directive	**is**	SUBSTITUTE *zen-var = zen-set*
zen-var	**is**	*string*

Let $\nu(z)$ denote the textual name of a ZEN variable. ZTS replaces all occurrences of the name $\nu(z)$ of a ZEN substi-

95

tute variable z in a directive d with one element $e \in \mathcal{V}^z$ in the entire file which contains d. The user must ensure that the substitution does not change the semantics of the code.

Example 3.1 (OpenMP Loop Distribution)
```
d1: !ZEN$ SUBSTITUTE STATIC={STATIC\,{1,10:50:10},
                             DYNAMIC\,{1,10:50:10}}
    !$OMP DO SCHEDULE(STATIC)
    ...
d2: !ZEN$ SUBSTITUTE STATIC = {
                    GUIDED\,{1, 10:50:10} } BEGIN
    !$OMP DO SCHEDULE(STATIC)
    !ZEN$ END SUBSTITUTE
```

The ZEN directive $d1$ in Ex. 3.1 allows the programmer to examine various loop scheduling strategies combined with chunk sizes. The original OpenMP scheduling clause STATIC is replaced with every ZEN element in the set $\mathcal{V}^{STATIC}$ with cardinality 12. Note that the code shown in this example is semantically valid for both ZEN aware (understands ZEN syntax and semantics) and ZEN unaware (ignores ZEN directives) systems.

Similarly, one could vary other OpenMP parameters such as the number of threads within a parallel region.

The local ZEN substitute directive restricts the scope of a directive to a specific region of a ZEN file. It has the following syntax:

local-subst-dir **is** SUBSTITUTE *zen-var = zen-set* BEGIN
code-region
END SUBSTITUTE

The code fragment in Ex. 3.1 contains two ZEN directives $d1$ and $d2$, which assign different ZEN sets to two ZEN variables with the identical name STATIC. Despite the identical name, the two ZEN variables are distinct, each one having its own scope and value set. If the textual names of two or more ZEN variables in a ZEN file are identical, then these ZEN variables are called *homonym*.

The impact of the homonym ZEN variables to the semantics of global and local ZEN substitution directives is as follows. No homonym global ZEN substitute variables are allowed within one ZEN file. A local substitute directive d_i with a substitution variable z_i overrides any global or local ZEN substitute directive d_j with an associated substitution variable z_j, where z_i and z_j are homonym. In this case the value set of z_i is augmented with the value set of z_j. The union of two ordered value sets is defined in Fig. 2.

A ZEN variable z is therefore characterised by the: (1) textual *name* $\nu(z)$; (2) associated *ZEN directive d* which assigns a value set to z; (3) *ZEN file* $\mathcal{F}$ which contains the directive d; and (4) *line number* of the directive in $\mathcal{F}$.

The following naming conventions for ZEN variables hold in the remainder of this paper: (1) if no homonym ZEN variable has been defined, we use the textual name of the ZEN variable; (2) if other homonym ZEN variables have been defined, we use the ZEN variable name subscripted with a ZEN directive identifier.

The value sets cardinalities for the homonym ZEN variables from Ex. 3.1 are: $|\mathcal{V}^{STATIC_{d1}}| = 12$, $|\mathcal{V}^{STATIC_{d2}}| = 18$.

The substitution directive must be used with care, as it might replace undesired occurrences of the ZEN variable in the corresponding scope (see Ex. 3.2). For instance, if a variable D must be substituted in a given scope, then every occurrence of this character is replaced, even in keywords such as DO or END. To avoid this problem, we introduced the ZEN assignment directive, described in the next section.

3.4. ZEN Assignment Directive

The *ZEN assignment directive* is used to insert assignment statements into files. This directive is commonly used to indicate all values of interest for specific problem or machine size parameters (variables) occurring in a program. Formally, a ZEN assignment directive assigns a ZEN set to a ZEN variable, which must be a valid program variable in the context of a ZEN file. The ZEN assignment directive has the following syntax:

assign-directive **is** ASSIGN *zen-var = zen-set*

The ZTS textually replaces a ZEN assignment directive with an assignment statement, which assigns one element $e \in \mathcal{V}^z$ to the ZEN variable z. The assignment statement inserted by ZTS must conform to the programming language of the associated ZEN file. For example, if the ZEN file represents a C program, the assignment statement adheres to the C syntax. ZTS does not apply any type checking or examine whether the (ZEN) variable has been declared in the program. A possible syntax error will be detected by a subsequent compilation process of the ZEN file instance.

Example 3.2 (ZEN Assignment and Global Value Set Constraint)
```
     INTEGER D, P, i
     !ZEN$ ASSIGN P = { {2:8:2}**2 }
s:   D = 50
d:   !ZEN$ ASSIGN D = { 2**{6:12} }
     DO i = 1, D
     !ZEN$ CONSTRAINT VALUE N^3 / P < 10000000
```

The ZEN directive d in Ex. 3.2 assigns 7 values to a ZEN variable D, representing the upper bound of the following DO loop. The value set of the ZEN variable D is: $\mathcal{V}^D = \{ 2**6, 2**7, 2**8, 2**9, 2**10, 2**11, 2**12 \}$, the index domain: $\mathcal{I}^D = \{ 1, 2, 3, 4, 5, 6, 7 \}$, and the value function: $\vartheta: \mathcal{I}^D \rightarrow \mathcal{V}^D$, $\vartheta(i) = 2**(i+5)$. Note that the code is semantically valid for both ZEN aware and ZEN unaware systems. ZEN aware systems replace the ZEN directive with an assignment of the (ZEN) variable D with one of the elements in $\mathcal{V}^D$. In this case, the assignment s becomes redundant and is subject to dead-code elimination. Also note that using a substitution instead of the assignment directive would also replace the character D in the keyword DO. The consequence would be an erroneous program.

3.5. Multi-dimensional Value Set

So far we have mostly described ZEN files with a single ZEN directive that generates a number of ZEN file instances equal to the cardinality of its value set. The ZEN file instances refer to the set of experiments implied by the ZEN directives in the ZEN file. In this section we describe how to deal with multiple ZEN directives and how to define the corresponding ZEN file instances that must be generated to conduct all experiments.

The *multi-dimensional value set* of n ZEN variables $z_1, \ldots, z_n$, denoted by $\mathcal{V}(z_1, \ldots, z_n)$, is the cartesian product of their value sets: $\mathcal{V}(z_1, \ldots, z_n) = \mathcal{V}^{z_1} \times \ldots \times \mathcal{V}^{z_n}$.

The *value set* of a ZEN file $\mathcal{F}(z_1, \ldots, z_n)$, denoted by $\mathcal{V}(\mathcal{F}(z_1, \ldots, z_n))$, or simply by $\mathcal{V}^{\mathcal{F}}$, is the set of all ZEN file instances generated from the multi-dimensional value set of its ZEN variables: $\mathcal{V}(\mathcal{F}(z_1, \ldots, z_n)) = \{ \mathcal{F}'(e_1, \ldots, e_n) \mid (e_1, \ldots, e_n) \in \mathcal{V}(z_1, \ldots, z_n) \}$.

Ex. 3.1 defines two ZEN directives *d1* and *d2* which, respectively, assign two homonym ZEN variables STATIC_{d1} and STATIC_{d2}. The multi-dimensional value set is given by the cartesian product of their value sets: $\mathcal{V}(\text{STATIC}_{d1}, \text{STATIC}_{d2}) = \mathcal{V}^{\text{STATIC}_{d1}} \times \mathcal{V}^{\text{STATIC}_{d2}}$, with the cardinality $|\mathcal{V}(\text{STATIC}_{d1}, \text{STATIC}_{d2})| = 12 \cdot 18 = 216$.

A *ZEN application*, denoted by $\mathcal{A}(\mathcal{F}_1, \ldots, \mathcal{F}_n)$, or simply by $\mathcal{A}$, is a set of ZEN files $\mathcal{F}_1, \ldots, \mathcal{F}_n$. A *ZEN application* is commonly a full application with a set of source files, annotated with ZEN directives. A *ZEN application instance*, denoted by $\mathcal{A}'(\mathcal{F}'_1, \ldots, \mathcal{F}'_n)$, or simply by $\mathcal{A}'$, is a set of ZEN file instances which instantiate each ZEN file of the ZEN application: $\mathcal{A}'(\mathcal{F}'_1, \ldots, \mathcal{F}'_n) = \{ \mathcal{F}'_i \in \mathcal{V}^{\mathcal{F}_i} \mid i \in \mathbb{N}, i \in [1..n] \}$.

The *value set* of a ZEN application, denoted by $\mathcal{V}(\mathcal{A}(\mathcal{F}_1, \ldots, \mathcal{F}_n))$ or simply by $\mathcal{V}^{\mathcal{A}}$, is the set of application instances generated by the cartesian product of the value sets of its constituent ZEN files: $\mathcal{V}(\mathcal{A}(\mathcal{F}_1, \ldots, \mathcal{F}_n)) = \{ \mathcal{A}'(\mathcal{F}'_1, \ldots, \mathcal{F}'_n) \mid (\mathcal{F}'_1, \ldots, \mathcal{F}'_n) \in \mathcal{V}^{\mathcal{F}_1} \times \ldots \times \mathcal{V}^{\mathcal{F}_n} \}$.

The value set of a ZEN application represents the complete set of ZEN application instances. An application instance corresponds to a set of files that are compiled by a target compiler and executed on a target machine. The execution of a specific application instance, during which performance and output data are collected, is called *experiment*.

3.6. ZEN Constraint Directive

Multi-dimensional value sets are likely to produce a large number of combinations of ZEN elements that result in experiments with no useful meaning. The consequence can be a dramatic increase in the time needed to conduct all experiments required by a parameter study. In order to reduce the multi-dimensional value set to a meaningful and interesting subset, we introduce the ZEN constraint directives.

The *ZEN constraint directive* defines a boolean expression over the value sets of several (assign and substitute) ZEN variables. The purpose is to reduce the number of ZEN file instances generated. Depending on the type of the ZEN variables (see Section 3.2) to be included in a constraint, we have to use an appropriate constraint directive: (1) a *value set constraint* restricts the value sets of one or more ZEN variables of type integer or real, based on a boolean expression defined over the associated ZEN elements; (2) an *index domain constraint* restricts the value sets of one or more ZEN variables of any type (including string) based on a boolean function defined over their index domains (see Section 3.2).

Similar to the substitute directive, ZEN provides constraint directives with global and local scopes. Local ZEN constraint directives can be nested too.

global-constraint	**is**	CONSTRAINT *type b-expr*
b-expr	**is**	*bool-expr(zen-var-list)*
type	**is**	VALUE
	or	INDEX
local-constraint	**is**	CONSTRAINT *type b-expr* BEGIN
		code-region
		END CONSTRAINT

The term *b-expr* refers to a boolean expression with constants and ZEN variables as operands.

A ZEN constraint directive d which defines the boolean expression *bool-expr*$(zen\text{-}var_1, \ldots, zen\text{-}var_n)$, holds in the scope of d for every ZEN variable whose name is included in $\{ zen\text{-}var_1, \ldots, zen\text{-}var_n \}$. This means that if there exist homonym ZEN variables in the scope of d with the name in $\{zen\text{-}var_1, \ldots, zen\text{-}var_n\}$, then the following set of constraints are generated: $\{ bool\text{-}expr(z_1, \ldots, z_n) \mid \forall \{ z_1, \ldots, z_n \} \subset scope(d), \text{ such that } \nu(z_i) = zen\text{-}var_i, i \in [1..n] \}$, where $\nu(z_i)$ is the name of a ZEN variable.

Let $z_1, \ldots, z_n$ denote a set of ZEN variables. The tuple $(e_1, \ldots, e_n) \in \mathcal{V}^{z_1} \times \ldots \times \mathcal{V}^{z_n}$ is *valid* iff $\forall$ value set constraints with a *bool-expr*$(z_1, \ldots, z_n)$: *bool-expr*$(e_1, \ldots, e_n) = true$. The tuple $(i_1, \ldots, i_n) \in \mathcal{I}^{z_1} \times \ldots \times \mathcal{I}^{z_n}$ is valid iff $\forall$ index domain constraints with a *bool-expr*$(z_1, \ldots, z_n)$: *bool-expr*$(i_1, \ldots, i_n) = true$.

Taking the ZEN constraints into account, we redefine the *multi-dimensional value set* for a set of ZEN variables $z_1, \ldots, z_n$ as follows:
$$\mathcal{V}(z_1, \ldots, z_n) = \{ (e_1, \ldots, e_n) \in \mathcal{V}^{z_1} \times \ldots \times \mathcal{V}^{z_n} \mid (e_1, \ldots, e_n) \text{ is valid} \wedge (\vartheta^{-1}(e_1), \ldots, \vartheta^{-1}(e_n)) \text{ is valid} \}.$$

In Ex. 3.2, the ZEN variable P defines the square numbers from 2^2 to 8^2 with stride 2 and D defines the powers of 2 ranging from 2^6 to 2^{12}: $\mathcal{V}^P = \{ 2**2, 4**2, 6**2, 8**2 \}$, $\mathcal{V}^D = \{ 2**6, 2**7, 2**8, 2**9, 2**10, 2**11, 2**12 \}$. The value set constraint directive filters the ZEN elements of $\mathcal{V}^D \times \mathcal{V}^P$, such that the boolean expression defined yields true. Assuming that D is the size of a 3-dimensional array and P the number of processors onto which the array is distributed, the constraint restricts the value set to the combinations which need less than 10MB on each processor.

Index-domain constraint directives are exemplified in Ex. 4.1 and Ex. 4.3 of Section 4.1.

3.7. ZEN Performance Behaviour Directive

For performance-oriented program development the user commonly requires information about the performance behaviour for specific code regions, such as the number of cache misses, communication time, or floating-point operations per second, etc. ZEN supports the specification of performance metrics to be measured for specific code regions through the *ZEN performance behaviour directive*. The scope of this directive can be limited to the entire file or to local code regions through the following syntax:

```
glob-meas  is  CR cr_mnems PMETRIC pm_mnems
loc-meas   is  CR cr_mnems PMETRIC pm_mnems BEGIN
               code-region
               END CR
```

Two sets of mnemonics can be used to specify code regions (*cr_mnem*) and performance metrics (*pm_mnem*). Overall ZEN supports approximately 50 code regions (e.g. CR_P = entire program, CR_L = all loops, CR_OMPPA = all OpenMP parallel loops) and 40 performance metric mnemonics (e.g. ODATA = data movement, OSYNC = synchronisation, ODATA_L2 = number of level 2 cache misses) for various programming paradigms, including OpenMP, HPF, and MPI. A complete list of mnemonics supported by ZEN can be found in [9]. In order to obtain the performance data for the chosen code regions, an interface to an external performance tool has to be provided.

A global performance directive d collects performance metrics for all code regions in the ZEN file that contains d. The performance metrics are specified in the PMETRIC part and the code regions in the CR part of d. The local performance directive restricts performance information to the corresponding code region. There can be nested performance measurement directives with arbitrary combinations of global and local directives. If different performance metrics are requested for a specific code region by several nested directives, then the union of these metrics is determined. An example of using the performance behaviour directives is given in Section 4, Ex. 4.2.

4. Experiments

We have developed ZENTURIO [7] which is a experiment management system whose basic architecture is illustrated in Fig. 4. In order to evaluate ZENTURIO, we have conducted two different experiments: a performance study for an ocean simulation application and a parameter study for a backward pricing application.

4.1. Experiment-1: Performance Study for an Ocean Simulation Application

In the first experiment we studied the scalability behaviour of an OpenMP/MPI Fortran90 version of a code that

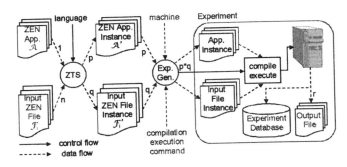

Figure 4. The ZENTURIO Experiment Management System Architecture, where $p = |\mathcal{V}^{\mathcal{A}}|$, $q = |\mathcal{V}^{\mathcal{F}_1} \times \ldots \times \mathcal{V}^{\mathcal{F}_n}|$.

simulates the ocean in order to explain the westward intensification of wind-driven ocean currents [8]. Jobs are scheduled on dedicated nodes using the PBS (Portable Batch queuing System). We employed ZEN to specify the application parameters and performance metrics of interest. ZENTURIO automatically invoked all the corresponding experiments and stored the output results and performance data in a database.

The scalability of the code was examined by varying two parameters: (1) the machine size which consists of two dimensions: (i) the number of SMP nodes controlled by directives inserted in the PBS script (see Ex. 4.1); (ii) the number of threads per node controlled by the input parameter to the omp_set_num_threads OpenMP library routine (see Ex. 4.2); (2) the problem size by varying the grid (ocean) size and the number of iterations on the grid (see Ex. 4.3).

Example 4.1 (PBS Script)
```
#ZEN$ SUBSTITUTE nodes\=2 = { nodes={1:10} }
#PBS -l walltime=1:00:00,nodes=2:fourproc:ppn=4
#PBS -q @gescher.vcpc.univie.ac.at
#PBS -N stommel
cd $PBS_O_WORKDIR
#ZEN$ SUBSTITUTE $4 = { 1:10 }
mpirun -np $4 omp_02 < st.in
#ZEN$ CONSTRAINT INDEX nodes\=2 == $4
```

Example 4.2 (Source Code Excerpt)
```
!ZEN$ CR CR_P PMETRIC ODATA, WTIME
...
!ZEN$ SUBSTITUTE threads\(4\)= { threads({1:4}) }
      CALL omp_set_dynamic(.true.)
      CALL omp_set_num_threads(4)
```

Example 4.3 (Input Data File – st.in)
```
!ZEN$ SUBSTITUTE points = { 200, 400 }
      points points
      2000000, 40000000
      1.0e-9 2.25e-11 3.0e-6
!ZEN$ SUBSTITUTE iters = { 20000, 40000 }
      iters
!ZEN$ CONSTRAINT INDEX points == iters
```

Only 8 ZEN directives have been included in three files of this application to generate 80 experiments:

$|\mathcal{V}(nodes=2, \$4, threads(4), points, iters)| = 80$. In addition, the compilation and execution command had to be provided. The remainder, including the performance visualisations shown in Fig. 5, has been done automatically by ZENTURIO. For each experiment the overall execution time and the communication overhead are measured (denoted by the `ODATA` and `WTIME` mnemonics in Ex. 4.2). After completing an experiment, performance data is processed and stored in the experiment database. We use the SCALEA [9] performance tool for instrumenting codes and for computing and storing performance overheads.

For a 200 × 200 grid, the program does not scale (see Fig. 5(a)) which is due to the poor communication behaviour (see Fig. 5(b)) of this problem size. We also observe that this problem size scales well with the number of threads on a single SMP node. For larger number of nodes the number of threads does not improve the overall performance. The reason is the large MPI communication overhead which dominates the overall execution time.

The 400 × 400 grid problem size implies a very reasonable scaling behaviour for up to 4 SMP nodes (see Fig. 5(c)). Using more than 4 SMP nodes does not substantially decrease the execution time anymore. This is due to an increased communication overhead and a decreasing ratio of execution to communication time (see Fig. 5(d)). For smaller number of nodes, the computation to communication time ratio is high and effective parallelisation of OpenMP loops onto a set of threads yields a very satisfying scaling behaviour. Increasing the number of threads decreases the execution time as expected.

4.2. Experiment-2: Parameter Study for the Backward Pricing Application

The backward pricing kernel [2] is a parallel implementation of the backward induction algorithm to compute the price of an interest rate dependent financial product, such as a variable coupon bond. We studied the total price output parameter, by varying three input parameters: (1) the coupon bond (0.01 to 0.1); (2) the number of time steps, over which the price is computed (5 to 60); (3) the coupon bond's end time, which must be equal to the number of time steps;

Example 4.4 (Input Parameter Assignment)
```
read(10,*) nr_steps
!ZEN$ ASSIGN nr_steps = { 5:60:5 }
read(10,*) bond%end
!ZEN$ ASSIGN bond\%end = { 5:60:5 }
!ZEN$ CONSTRAINT VALUE nr_steps == bond\%end
...
read(10, *) bond%coupon
!ZEN$ ASSIGN bond\%coupon = { 0.01:0.1:0.001 }
```

The application was encoded such that all input parameters are read from different input data files. We annotated a single source file with 3 ZEN assignment directives immedi-

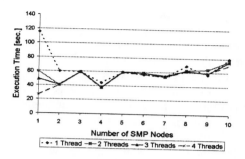

(a) 200 × 200 Grid, 20000 Iterations

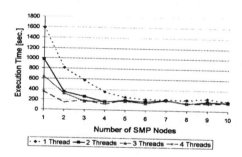

(b) 200 × 200 Grid, 20000 Iterations

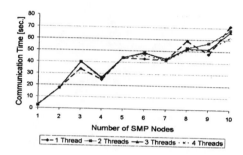

(c) 400 × 400 Grid, 40000 Iterations

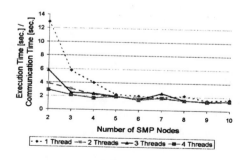

(d) 400 × 400 Grid, 40000 Iterations

Figure 5. Performance study for an ocean simulation application with varying problem and machine sizes.

ately after the corresponding `read` statements (see Ex. 4.4). Thus, the original `read` statement is made redundant. An additional constraint directive is used to guarantee that the coupon bond's end time is identical with the number of time steps for every experiment. Note that for this experiment we are not interested in performance aspects, but concentrated only on examining the effects of different input parameters on the corresponding output results.

The 3D surface in Fig. 4.2 shows the evolution of the total price (output parameter of the backward pricing code) as a function of the number of time steps and the coupon.

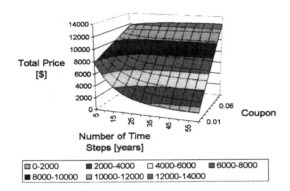

Figure 6. Evolution of the total price with the number of steps.

5. Conclusions and Future Work

We have described ZEN, a new directive based language for automatic experiment management. By inserting ZEN directives into arbitrary files (e.g. program, input and script makefiles), we enable the specification of arbitrarily complex program executions for parameter studies, performance analysis and tuning, and software testing, for a wide variety of parallel and distributed architectures. ZEN directives are interpreted as comments and therefore ignored by non-ZEN-aware systems, whereas ZEN-aware systems can employ these directives to generate appropriate experiments.

We have implemented a prototype experiment management system (ZENTURIO) that includes a ZEN Transformation System (ZTS), an interface to a performance instrumentation and monitoring system, and an experiment generator and monitor. This system shields users from intimate details of job scheduling, code instrumentation for performance analysis, transferring codes and input files to various target architectures, application compiling, and job launching and monitoring. Thus, scientists and engineers can concentrate on the science of the underlying experiments. We have demonstrated the usefulness of ZENTURIO for a performance analysis of an ocean simulation application and for a parameter study of a computational finance code.

ZEN and ZENTURIO are part of the ASKALON pro-

gramming environment and tool set for cluster and Grid architectures [3]. ASKALON comprises various other tools that support performance instrumentation and measurement, automatic bottleneck analysis, and performance prediction. We are currently extending ZENTURIO for larger classes of target systems including Grid infrastructures.

References

[1] D. Abramson, R. Sosic, R. Giddy, and B. Hall. Nimrod: A tool for performing parameterised simulations using distributed workstations high performance parametric modeling with nimrod/G: Killer application for the global grid? In *Proceedings of the 4th IEEE Symposium on High Performance Distributed Computing (HPDC-95)*, pages 520–528, Virginia, Aug. 1995. IEEE Computer Society Press.

[2] E. Dockner and H. Moritsch. Pricing Constant Maturity Floaters with Embeeded Options Using Monte Carlo Simulation. Technical Report AuR_99-04, AURORA Technical Reports, University of Vienna, January 1999.

[3] T. Fahringer, A. Jugravu, S. Pllana, R. Prodan, C. Seragiotto, and H.-L. Truong. ASKALON - A Programming Environment and Tool Set for Cluster and Grid Computing. www.par.univie.ac.at/project/askalon, Institute for Software Science, University of Vienna.

[4] Y. E. Ioannidis, M. Livny, S. Gupta, and N. Ponnekanti. ZOO : A desktop experiment management environment. In T. M. Vijayaraman, A. P. Buchmann, C. Mohan, and N. L. Sarda, editors, *VLDB'96, Proceedings of 22th International Conference on Very Large Data Bases*, pages 274–285, Mumbai (Bombay), India, 3–6 Sept. 1996. Morgan Kaufmann.

[5] K. L. Karavanic and B. P. Miller. Experiment management support for performance tuning. In ACM, editor, *Proceedings of the SC'97 Conference*, San Jose, California, USA, Nov. 1997. ACM Press and IEEE Computer Society Press.

[6] B. Mohr. Design of Automatic Performance Analysis Systems, APART Workpackage 3: Implementation Issues. APART technical report, Forschungszentrum Jülich, Zentralinstitut für Angewandte Mathematik (ZMG), D-52425 Jülich, May 2000. www.kfa-juelich.de/apart.

[7] R. Prodan and T. Fahringer. ZENTURIO: An Experiment Management System for Cluster and Grid Computing. Institute for Software Science, University of Vienna. http://www.par.univie.ac.at/project/zenturio.

[8] H. Stommel. The western intensification of wind-driven ocean currents. *Transactions American Geophysical Union*, 29:202–206, 1948.

[9] H.-L. Truong and T. Fahringer. SCALEA: A Performance Analysis Tool for Distributed and Parallel Program. In *8th International Europar Conference(EuroPar 2002)*, Lecture Notes in Computer Science, Paderborn, Germany, August 2002. Springer-Verlag. To appear.

[10] M. Yarrow, K. M. McCann, R. Biswas, and R. F. V. der Wijngaart. Ilab: An advanced user interface approach for complex parameter study process specification on the information power grid. In *Proceedings of Grid 2000: International Workshop on Grid Computing*, Bangalore, India, Dec. 2000. ACM Press and IEEE Computer Society Press.

Dead Timestamp Identification in Stampede *

Nissim Harel [†]   Hasnain A. Mandviwala [†]   Kath Knobe [‡]   Umakishore Ramachandran [†]

Abstract

Stampede *is a parallel programming system to support computationally demanding applications including interactive vision, speech and multimedia collaboration. The system alleviates concerns such as communication, synchronization, and buffer management in programming such real-time stream-oriented applications. Threads are loosely connected by channels that hold timestamped data items. There are two performance concerns when programming with Stampede. The first is space, namely, ensuring that memory is not wasted on items that are not fully processed. The second is time, namely, ensuring that processing resource is not wasted on a timestamp that is not fully processed. In this paper we introduce a single unifying framework, dead timestamp identification, that addresses both the space and time concerns simultaneously. Dead timestamps on a channel represent garbage. Dead timestamps at a thread represent computations that need not be performed. This framework has been implemented in the Stampede system. Experimental results showing the space advantage of this framework are presented. Using a color-based people tracker application, we show that the space advantage can be significant (up to 40%) compared to the previous garbage collection techniques in Stampede.*

1 Introduction

There is a class of emerging stream-oriented applications spanning interactive vision, speech, and multimedia collaboration that are computationally demanding and dynamic in their communication characteristics. Such applications are good candidates for the scalable parallelism exhibited by clusters of SMPs.

A major problem in parallel implementation of these kinds of application is "buffer management", since (1) threads may not access their input in a strict stream-like manner, (2) newly created threads may have to re-analyze earlier data, (3) datasets from different sources need to be correlated temporally, and (4) not all the data produced at earlier stages of the processing pipeline will necessarily be used at the later stages due to the differential (higher) processing times for later stages compared to the earlier ones.

These features imply two requirements. First, data items must be meaningfully associated with time, and second, there must be a discipline of time that allows systematic reclamation of storage for data items (*garbage collection*).

Stampede is a parallel programming system designed and developed to simplify programming of such applications. The programming model of Stampede is simple and intuitive. A Stampede program consists of a dynamic collection of threads communicating timestamped data items through *channels* [1]. Threads can be created to run anywhere in the cluster. Channels can be created anywhere in the cluster and have cluster-wide unique names. Threads can *connect* to these channels for doing input/output via *get/put* operations. A timestamp value is used as a *name* for a data item that a thread puts into or gets from a channel. The run-time system of Stampede takes care of the synchronization and communication inherent in these operations, as well as managing managing the storage for items put into or gotten from the channels.

1.1 Live and dead timestamps

Every item on a channel is uniquely indexed by a *timestamp*. Typically a thread will *get* an item with a particular timestamp from an input connection, perform some processing [2] on the data in the item, and then *put* an item with that same timestamp onto one of its output connections. Items with the same timestamp in different channels represent various stages of processing of the same input.

The time to process an item varies from thread to thread. In particular, earlier threads (typically faster threads that

---

*The work has been funded in part by an NSF ITR grant CCR-01-21638, NSF grant CCR-99-72216, Compaq Cambridge Research Lab, the Yamacraw project of the State of Georgia, and the Georgia Tech Broadband Institute. The equipment used in the experimental studies is funded in part by an NSF Research Infrastructure award EIA-99-72872, and Intel Corp.

[†]College of Computing, Georgia Institute of Technology, {nissim, mandvi, rama}@cc.gatech.edu

[‡]HP Cambridge Research Lab, kath.knobe@hp.com

---

[1]Stampede also provides another cluster-wide data abstraction called *queues*. Queues also hold timestamped data items and differ in some semantic properties from the channels. From the point of view of the focus of this paper these differences are immaterial and hence we will not mention them in the rest of the paper.

[2]We use "processing a timestamp", "processing an item", and "processing a timestamped item" interchangeably to mean the same thing.

perform low level processing) may be producing items *dropped* by later threads doing higher level processing at a slower rate. Only timestamps that are completely processed affect the output of the application, while a timestamp that is dropped by any thread during the application execution is *irrelevant*. The metric for efficiency in these systems is the rate of processing *relevant* timestamps (*i.e.,* timestamps that make it all the way through the entire pipeline). The work done processing irrelevant timestamps represents an inefficient use of processing resources.

At a coarse grain time marches forward in this class of applications. That is, the timestamps being processed, in general, tend to monotonically increase with time. Old items (no longer needed by any thread) should be eliminated to free storage. However, since at a fine grain, a thread may be examining individual timestamps out of order, it is not trivial to determine when an item can be eliminated.

The algorithm developed in this paper determines a *timestamp guarantee* for each node (thread or channel). For a given timestamp T, the guarantee will indicate whether T is *live* or whether it is guaranteed to be *dead*. A timestamp T is live at a node N if (a) T is a relevant timestamp, *and* (b) there is some further processing at N on T (*i.e.,* T is still in use at N). Otherwise T is a dead timestamp at node N. If the node is a thread, "in use" signifies that the node is still processing the timestamp; if the node is a channel, "in use" signifies that the timestamp has not been processed by all the threads connected to that channel.

A timestamp may be live at a node at some execution time but dead at a later time. A timestamp may be live at one node but dead at another. Dead timestamps are interpreted differently depending on the node type. If the node is a channel, items in that channel with dead timestamps are garbage and can be removed. If the node is a thread, dead timestamps that have not yet been produced by the thread represent dead computations and can be eliminated. Note that dead computation elimination is distinct from dead code elimination. It is not the static code that we eliminate but rather an instance of its dynamic execution.

A unified view of garbage collection and dead computation elimination results from a single algorithm that determines dead timestamps at all nodes (thread and channels). This identification of dead timestamps is used on channels to indicate dead data (garbage) and at threads to indicate dead computations.

1.2   Background

There are two apparently unrelated technologies in Stampede, scheduling [8] and garbage collection [9]. Our earlier garbage collection work calculates lowerbounds for timestamp values of interest to any of the application threads. Using these lower bounds, the runtime system can *garbage collect* the storage space for useless data items on

Analysis	Scheduling	Dead timestamp identification	Garbage collection
State	Prior work	This paper	Prior work
Task graph restrictions	Static graph graph and predictive time per item	All potential threads and connections known at compile time	None
Aggressiveness	High	Medium	Low
Focus	Elimination of irrelevant work	Elimination of of **irrelevant** work and garbage	Elimination of garbage

Figure 1. Summary of three optimizations

channels. This algorithm which we refer to as *transparent GC*, is general and does not use any application-specific property.

Our earlier scheduling work computes an ideal schedule at compile-time. It generates a schedule that will pick a timestamp and complete the processing of that timestamp through the entire application pipeline. Thus only relevant timestamps are processed in the entire pipeline. Garbage collection is trivial in this environment. The schedule is totally static and the last use of each item on every channel is clear at compile-time. However, it only works on a restricted class of programs. The task graph must be static and further, the time for a thread to process a timestamp is fixed and predictable at compile-time.

The dead timestamp identification and elimination work presented in this paper develops a *single unified* technique that is used for both garbage collection and scheduling. The focus, type of task graph for which this technique is applicable, and the aggressiveness of the technique are in between those of static scheduling and transparent GC, as described in figure 1.

The rest of the paper is organized as follows. We present a new unified algorithm for dead timestamp identification in Section 2. Implementation details of this algorithm in Stampede are given in Section 3. Performance results showing the reduction in memory footprint of the new algorithm compared to the previous garbage collection techniques in Stampede are shown in Section 4. Comparison of the dead timestamp identification algorithm to other related research is presented in Section 5. Concluding remarks and future directions are discussed in Section 6.

2   Dead Timestamp Identification

We can describe an application in Stampede in terms of a task graph. This task graph is a bipartite directed graph of *nodes*, each of which is either a *thread*, which performs a certain computation, or a *channel*, which serves

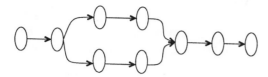

Figure 2. An abstract task graph

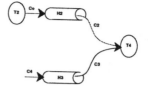

Figure 3. A sample dependent task graph

as a medium for buffer management between two or more threads. Directed edges between nodes are called *connections*. A connection describes the direction of the data flow between two nodes. Both types of nodes, threads and channels, have input and output edges called input and output connections (figure 2).

Dead timestamp identification is a process by which the runtime system identifies for each node what timestamps are provably of no use. This forms the basis of both garbage collection and dead computation elimination.

The information that is propagated among the nodes is a guarantee that can be used to *locally* separate live timestamps from dead ones. The dead timestamp algorithm generates two types of guarantees: forward and backward. The *forward guarantee* for a connection identifies timestamps that might cross that connection in the future. The *backward guarantee* for a connection identifies timestamps that are dead on that connection.

Both forward and backward processing are local in that, based on guarantees available locally, they compute a new guarantee to propagate forward or backward along a connection to neighboring nodes.

Next we will describe how possible dependences between connections, in general, and the monotonic property of a connection, in particular, help in determining guarantees on each connection. Then, we will discuss how forward and backward guarantees on a specific node are determined. Finally, transfer functions that help optimize the basic algorithm are described at the end of this section.

2.1 Monotonic and dependent connections

Monotonicity is an attribute of a connection that indicates the forward direction of time. The progression of time is, of course, controlled by the code in the threads. Monotonicity occurs, for example, in the common case of a thread's input connection, where the thread issues a command to get the latest timestamp on an input channel. Assume the timestamp it gets is T. Then as part of managing its own virtual time, it may issue a command that guarantees it is completely done with any timestamp below T on that channel. Such a guarantee from a thread on an input connection from a channel indicates that timestamps less than T are irrelevant (and can be gotten rid of from the channel) so far as this thread is concerned. Both thread to channel and channel to thread connections can be monotonic.

Consider the task graph in Figure 3. Assume that thread T4 gets a timestamp from C2 only if it gets the same timestamp from C3. This happens, for example, in stereo vision, where a thread gets the latest timestamp from one channel and then looks in the other for the matching timestamp. Connection C2 is said to be a *locally dependent* on connection C3. This relationship is not commutative, that is, the relationship (C2 depends on C3) does not imply that (C3 depends on C2). Notice that in this example, for a timestamp TS, $Next\_TS(C2) = Last\_TS(C3)$, because the thread T4 gets a timestamp from C2 only if it gets the same timestamp from C3.

We may also view monotonicity as a type of dependency where a connection, say C, is loosely dependent on itself. In the case of a strictly monotonic connection, the next timestamp to be processed must be greater than the last one processed, or, $Next\_TS(C) > Last\_TS(C)$. But this view is not limited to strictly monotonic connections. In fact, we can describe any level of monotonic guarantee in terms of a dependency. Every connection is, therefore, locally dependent, either on itself or on some other connection. A local dependence results in a *local guarantee*. Dependences in general and monotonicity in particular form the basis of the algorithm, which takes local guarantees and combines and propagates them to produce *transitive guarantees*.

2.2 Forward and backward processing

Dead timestamp identification algorithm has two components: forward and backward processing. The input to this algorithm is the application specified task graph (such as the one in Figure 2) that gives the connectivity among threads and channels, along with the associated monotonicity and dependence properties of the connections. Forward processing at a node N computes the forward guarantee as the set of timestamps that are likely to leave N. Similarly, backward processing at a node N computes the backward guarantee as the set of timestamps that are dead so far as N is concerned. Dependences in general, and monotonicity in particular, are the basis for these guarantees. These properties allow associating a *timestamp marker* on each connection that separates good (higher) timestamps from bad

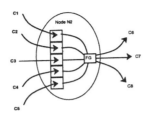

Figure 4. ForwardGuaranteeVec

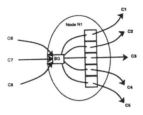

Figure 5. BackwardGuaranteeVec

(equal or lower) ones. Forward processing and backward processing algorithms use these markers available locally at each node on the connections that are incident at that node to generate the guarantees. These algorithms execute at run-time at the time of item transfers. Thus, the process of updating of the guarantees is associated with the flow of items through the system. In particular, as a timestamped item is transferred from node N1 to node N2, we update the forward guarantee at node N2 and the backward guarantee at node N1. This enables continual and aggressive identification of dead timestamps.

Figure 4 provides an example for the components involved in this processing In this example, node N2 has input connections, C1-C5 and output connections C6-C8. Each node maintains a vector of forward guarantees *ForwardGuaranteeVec*. There is a slot in this vector for each input connection, in this case C1-C5. Slot C_i of the vector holds the last forward guarantee communicated to the node over C_i. These are simply the timestamp markers associated with these connections. Forward processing at a node N involves computing the MIN of the elements of this vector and maintaining it as the *ForwardGuarantee* for this node N, labeled FG in the figure.

Figure 5 provides an example for the components involved in this processing In this example, node N1 has input connections, C6-C8 and output connections C1-C5. Each node, maintains a vector of backward guarantees *BackGuaranteeVec*. There is a slot in this vector for each output connection, in this case C1-C5. Slot C_i of the vector holds the last backward guarantee communicated to the node over C_i. These are once again the timestamp markers associated

with these connections. Backward processing at a node N involves computing the MIN of the elements of this vector and maintaining it as the *BackwardGuarantee* for this node N, labeled BG in the figure.

BackwardGuarantee for node N identifies dead timestamps for that node. If the node is a channel, items in the channel with timestamps that are dead can be removed as garbage. Timestamps that arrive at a channel where they have been previously determined to be dead are *dead on arrival* and need not be placed in the channel. If the node is a thread, dead timestamps that have not yet been computed by that thread are dead computations and need not be computed.

2.3 Transfer Functions Optimization

The basic framework uses the application specified task graph and the properties of the connections to generate the forward and backward guarantees. We can go further and use additional knowledge about the application to more aggressively expose dead timestamps. For example, it is conceivable that not all input connections to a thread node play a role in determining the timestamps on one of its output connection. If this application knowledge were to be made available to the forward and backward processing algorithms, then the guarantees produced would be more optimistic.

The machinery used to capture this application knowledge is *Transfer functions*. A forward transfer function is defined for each "out" connection from a node, and a backward transfer connection is defined for each "in" connection to a node. $\mathcal{T}_f$ and $\mathcal{T}_b$ indicate the forward and backward transfer functions respectively. $\mathcal{T}_f(C_{out}) = \{C1_{in}, C2_{in}, \dots Cn_{in}\}$ where node N is the (unique) source of the output connection C_{out} and $\{C1_{in}, C2_{in}, \dots Cn_{in}\}$ is a subset of the input connections of N such that the timestamps put to C_{out} are determined only by the connections in this set. A connection, C_i for example, might not be in this set if C_i is a dependent connection or if timestamps for some output connection other than C_{out} are determined by C_i. $\mathcal{T}_b(C_{in}) = \{C1, C2, \dots Cn\}$ where node N is the (unique) target of the input connection C_{in} and $\{C1, C2, \dots Cn\}$ is a subset of the input and output connections of N such that relevant timestamps for N are determined only by connections in this set.

For a thread node, the forward and backward transfer functions for connections incident at that node are determined by the thread code itself (and assumed to be made available in some form to the runtime system). For a channel node, the forward transfer function for any "out" connection is the set of all input connections; the backward transfer function for any "in" connection is the set of all input and output connections incident at that channel node.

These transfer functions are used by the forward and

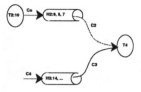

Figure 6. Dead timestamp elimination example

backward processing algorithms to generate tighter bounds for dead timestamps. This is illustrated via an example. In Figure 3, assume that input connection C2 depends on C3. Thus $C3 \in \mathcal{T}_b(C2)$, but $C2 \notin \mathcal{T}_b(C3)$. Let T4 get the latest timestamp from C3 (say this is t); it then executes a *get* from C2 for the same timestamp t. Figure 6 shows a dynamic state of Figure 3. The highest timestamp on channel H3 is 14. H2 contains timestamps 7, 8 and 9. T2 is about to compute timestamp 10. When T4 gets timestamp 14 from C3 it will then wait for timestamp 14 from C2. The backward transfer function will help backward processing at node T4 to compute the backward guarantee on C2 as 14, thus allowing H2 to eliminate timestamps less than 14 as garbage (*i.e.,* timestamps 7, 8, and 9); this in turn will tell T2 to eliminate as dead computations, thread steps that produce timestamps 10, 11, 12 and 13.

3 Implementation Issues

We have completed implementation of the dead timestamp identification algorithm described in the earlier section within Stampede. This new implementation allows a node (which can be a channel or a thread) to propagate timestamp values of interest forward and backward through the dataflow graph (of channels and threads) that represents the application. The new implementation assumes that the application dataflow graph is fully specified at application startup (*i.e.,* static).

Forward propagation is instigated by the runtime system upon a put/get operation on a channel. For example, when a thread does a put on a channel, a lowerbound value for timestamps that that thread is likely to generate in the future is enclosed by the runtime system and sent to the channel. Similarly upon a get from a channel, the runtime system calculates a lowerbound for timestamp values that could possibly appear in that channel and piggybacks that value on the response sent to the thread.

Backward propagation is similarly instigated by put/get operations. In fact, backward propagation is likely to be more beneficial in terms of performance due to the properties of monotonicity and dependence on other connections which we described in Section 2.1. These properties come

into play during a get operation on a channel. We have extended the Stampede API to enable a thread to enquire the forward and backward guarantees so that it may incorporate these guarantees in its computation.

There is very minimal application level burden to use the extended implementation of Stampede. Specifically, the application has to provide a few handler codes that the runtime system can call during execution to determine the forward and backward transfer functions for a given connection, the monotonicity and the dependence (if any) of a given connection on other ones.

Compared to the original implementation the new one offers two specific avenues for performance enhancement. First it provides a unified framework for both eliminating unnecessary computation from the thread nodes and the unnecessary items from the channel nodes as compared to the old one which does only the latter. Secondly, the new one allows getting rid of items from the channels more aggressively compared to the old one using the application level guarantees of monotonicity and dependence for a connection.

4 Performance Results

The Stampede cluster system supports three different garbage collection strategies: a simple reference count based garbage collector (REF), a transparent garbage collector (TGC), and the new dead timestamps based garbage collector (DGC). In REF, an application thread explicitly encodes the reference count when it does a *put* operation. The item is garbage collected when the reference count goes to zero. In TGC, the runtime system computes a global virtual time (GVT) using a distributed algorithm [9], which runs concurrent with the application. Subsequently, in each node of the cluster all items with timestamps lower than GVT are garbage collected. The GVT value thus computed is necessarily a safe lower bound for timestamps not needed by any thread. Clearly, REF is the most aggressive in terms of eliminating garbage as soon as it is recognized, while TGC is the most conservative. Neither REF nor TGC offer any help for removing dead computations. DGC is intended to help eliminate both dead computations and dead items. However, in this study we show the relative performance of the three techniques with respect to garbage collection only.

We use a real-time color-based people tracker application developed at Compaq CRL [10] for this study. Given a color histogram of a model to look for in a scene, this application locates the model if present. The application task graph and its connection dependencies are provided at [5]. As we mentioned earlier in Section 2, these connection dependencies are provided by the application and used by the dead timestamp identification algorithm to compute the forward and backward guarantees. A digitizer produces a new image every 30 milliseconds, giving each image a timestamp equal to the current frame number, The target detection algorithm cannot process at the rate at which the digitizer produces images. Thus not every image produced by the digitizer makes its way through the entire pipeline. At every stage of the pipeline, the threads get the latest available timestamp from their respective input channels. To enable a fair comparison across the three GC algorithms, the digitizer reads a pre-recorded set of images from a file; two target detection threads are used in each experiment; and the same model file is supplied to both the threads. Under the workload described above, the average message sizes delivered to the digitizer, motion mask, histogram, and target detection channels are 756088, 252080, 1004904, and 67 bytes respectively.

We have developed an elaborate measurement infrastructure that helps us to accumulate the memory usage as a function of time in the Stampede channels, and the latency for Stampede put/get/consume operations during the execution of the application. A post-mortem analysis program generates metrics of interest. Details of this measurement infrastructure are outside the scope of this paper.

The metrics for evaluating the three different strategies are the following: *memory footprint, space-time, currency,* and *latency per relevant timestamp*. Memory footprint is the amount of memory used by the application as a function of real time. This metric is indicative of the instantaneous memory pressure of the application. Space-time is the product of the memory usage and time for which a particular chunk of memory is used. This can be considered as the integral of the memory footprint over time. Currency is the value of relevant timestamp (that made its way through the entire pipeline) as a function of real time. This metric is indicative of the real-time performance of the application. The higher the currency value for a given real-time the better the performance. Latency is the elapsed time for a relevant timestamp to make it through the entire pipeline. This metric is the determinant of the real-time performance of the application.

The experiments are carried out on a cluster of 17, 8-way 550 MHz P-III Xeon SMP machines with 4GB of main memory running Redhat Linux 7.1. The interconnect is Gigabit Ethernet. The Stampede runtime uses a reliable messaging layer called CLF implemented on top of UDP. We use two configurations: (1) all the threads and channels execute on one node within a single address space. This configuration represents one extreme, in which all computation is mapped onto a single node, and does not require the runtime system to use the messaging layer. (2) the threads and channels are distributed over 5 nodes of the cluster. This configuration represents the other extreme, where threads and channels do not share the same address space. In this scenario, the messaging layer (CLF), as well as the physical network latencies, come into play. CPU resources, however,

$Config\ 1:$ 1 node	Total frames	Average Latency (ms)	Mean memory usage (kB)	Total space − time usage (kB ∗ ms)
DGC	4802	505,594	16,913	2,380,869,326
TGC	4801	491,946	24,043	3,402,019,615
REF	4802	489,610	23,755	3,229,459,927

Figure 7. Metrics (1-node). Performance of the three GC algorithms for the tracker application with all the threads executing within a single address space on one node. All experiments were run for the same period of time. Transparent GC (TGC) and Reference Counting (REF) on average consume around 40% more memory than dead-timestamps based GC (DGC). The space-time usage of TGC is 42.9% and that of REF is 35.6% greater than DGC. On the other hand, DGC is 2.7% and 3.2% slower in terms of average latency than TGC and REF, respectively.

are not shared.

Figures 7 and 8 show latency per processed timestamp reaching the end of the application pipeline. Although the latency has increased for DGC due to inline execution of transfer functions on puts and gets, the percentage increase is only marginal (2.7% and 0.5% compared to TGC, 3.2% and less than 0.1% compared to REF for 1-node and 5-node configurations respectively). However, the memory footprint of the application as shown in Figure 9 is very much in favor of DGC. Furthermore, Figures 7 and 8 show a low mean for memory usage compared to both TGC and REF. The low memory usage compared to TGC is expected due to the aggressive nature of our algorithm. However, the performance advantage compared to REF is quite interesting. REF makes local decisions on items in a channel once the consumers have explicitly signaled a set of items to be garbage. DGC has an added advantage over REF in that it propagates guarantees to upstream channels thus enabling dead timestamps to be identified much earlier, resulting in a smaller footprint compared to REF. This trend can also be seen in the space-time metric column of Figures 7 and 8.

Figure 10 shows the currency metric for the three GC algorithms, for the first (1-node) configuration. The y-axis is the value of the timestamp that reaches the end of the pipeline and the x-axis is the real time. The higher the currency value for a given real time the better, since this is indicative of how recent the processed information is with respect to real time. The dead-timestamp based GC algorithm gives almost the same currency (Figure 10) despite the small increase in latency we observed earlier (average latency column in Figures 7 and 8). The currency metric results for the second (5-node) configuration is almost indistinguishable for the three algorithms and hence not shown in the paper. An interesting question for future work is investigating how the three algorithms behave in a resource

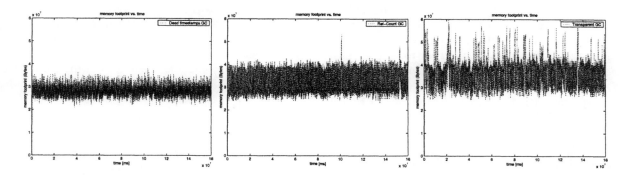

Figure 9. **Memory Footprint.** The three graphs represent the memory footprint of the application (distributed over 5 nodes) for the three GC algorithms: DGC-Dead timestamps (left), REF-Reference Counting (center), and TGC-Transparent (right). We recorded the amount of memory the application uses on every allocation and deallocation. All three graphs are to the same scale, with the y-axis showing memory use (bytes x 10^7), and the x-axis representing time (milliseconds). The graphs clearly show that DGC has a lower memory footprint than the other two. In addition, it deviates much less from the mean, thereby requiring a smaller amount of memory during peak usage.

$Config\ 2:$ 5 nodes	$Total$ $frames$	$Average$ $Latency$ (ms)	$Mean$ $memory$ $usage$ (kB)	$Total$ $space-time$ $usage$ $(kB*ms)$
DGC	5509	557,502	28,096	4,842,436,910
TGC	5489	554,584	36,911	6,276,379,274
REF	5510	556,964	32,764	5,606,728,841

Figure 8. **Metrics (5-node).** Performance of three GC algorithms for the tracker application with the threads distributed on 5 nodes of the cluster. All configurations were run for the same period of time. Transparent GC (TGC) and Reference Counting (REF) on average consume respectively 31.4% and 16.6% more memory than dead-timestamps based GC (DGC). The space-time usage of Transparent GC is 29.6% and that of REF is 15.8% greater than DGC. On the other hand, the average latency of DGC is only 0.5% and 0.1% slower than that of TGC and REF, respectively.

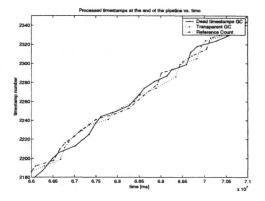

Figure 10. **Currency of Processed Timestamps (1-node).** There is no substantial difference in the currency of processed timestamps using any of the three GC algorithms.

constrained environment.

We noted earlier that the new GC algorithm can aid both in eliminating dead items from channels and dead computations from threads. Clearly, dead computations can only result if later stages of the pipeline indicate during execution their lack of interest for some timestamp values to earlier stages. Thus for dead computation elimination one or more of the following conditions need to hold: (1) variability in processing times for items, (2) higher processing time for at least one earlier stage of the pipeline, (3) dependences on connections that change with time, and (4) variability in resource availability over time. The first three are properties of the application and workload, while the fourth is a property of the computational infrastructure. These properties do not hold in the application, the workload, and the hardware environment used in this study. We are currently exploring possible scenarios for illustrating the performance

advantage of dead computation elimination.

5 Related Work

The traditional GC problem [11, 7] concerns reclaiming storage for heap-allocated objects (data structures) when they are no longer "reachable" from the computation. On the other hand, Stampede's GC problem deals with determining when timestamped items in channels can be reclaimed. The runtime system determines that a specific timestamp (which is not a memory pointer but an index or a tag) will not be used anymore. Thus storage associated with all items that are tagged with this timestamp can be reclaimed.

The problem of determining the interest set for timestamp values in Stampede has similarity to the garbage collection problem in Parallel Discrete Event Simulation (PDES) systems [3]. However, PDES systems require that repeated executions of an application program using the same input data and parameters produce the same results [4]. Thus, *every* timestamp must *appear* to be processed *in order* by the PDES system. To insure this property, the PDES literature proposes both conservative synchronization algorithms (such as CMB - Chandy-Misra-Bryant [1, 2]) and optimistic ones (such as Time Warp [6]). The latter must support roll backs if processing of a timestamp out of order by a node results in violating causality. These systems do not have the notion of dead computation elimination (because every timestamp must be processed).

On the other hand, the Stampede programming model requires neither in-order execution, nor processing of every timestamp. Consequently, roll backs are irrelevant. As with PDES, if nothing is known about the application task graph, Stampede must compute GVT to enable garbage collection [9]. In this paper, we developed the algorithmic machinery to enable garbage collection based entirely on local events with no reliance on any global mechanism. This is somewhat akin to the approach taken by the (CMB) algorithm for PDES. Yet, we show in Section 4, that our new algorithm acheives comparable latency as our earlier algorithm (in [9]), while accruing all the benefits of space reduction. The key to the success of this new algorithm is access to an application level task graph, as well as properties of the connections.

Dead code elimination is a common optimization technique in compilers for high level languages. However, we are not aware of any other work that provides a unified framework and implementation for eliminating dead computations and dead items at runtime.

6   Conclusions

Stampede is a cluster programming system for interactive stream-oriented applications such as vision and speech. Space management (in the form of eliminating unnecessary items) and time management (in the form of eliminating unnecessary computations) are crucial to enhance the performance of such applications. Stampede provides threads and channels as computational abstractions for mapping the dataflow graph of the application to the cluster. In this paper, we have proposed a novel unified framework for dynamically eliminating both dead computations and dead items from such a computational pipeline. The framework defines a simple and intuitive machinery for applications to specify the properties of the computational pipeline. This information is used by the runtime to dynamically generate guarantees (lower bounds on timestamp values) to the threads and channels, that are then used in the dynamic elimination of dead items and computations. Stampede system has been implemented and runs on several different cluster platforms. Experimental results show that the memory footprint of the new algorithm for a color-based vision tracker application is reduced anywhere from 16% to 40% compared to previous techniques. Future work includes more elaborate experimentation to illustrate the dead computation elimination capabilities of the unified framework.

References

[1] R. E. Bryant. Simulation of Packet Communication Architecture Computer Systems. Technical Report MIT-LCS-TR-188, M.I.T, Cambridge, MA, 1977.

[2] K. Chandy and J. Misra. Asynchronous distributed simulation via a sequence of parallel computation. *Communications of the ACM*, 24:198–206, 1981.

[3] R. M. Fujimoto. Parallel Discrete Event Simulation. *Comm. of the ACM*, 33(10), October 1990.

[4] R. M. Fujimoto. Parallel and distributed simulation. In *Winter Simulation Conference*, pages 118–125, December 1995.

[5] N. Harel, H. Mandviwala, K. Knobe, and U. Ramachandran. Dead timestamp identification in stampede. Technical Report GIT-CC-02-08, College of Computing, Georgia Institute of Technology, February 2002.

[6] D. R. Jefferson. Virtual time. *ACM Transactions on Programming Languages and Systems*, 7(3):404–425, July 1985.

[7] R. Jones and R. Lins. *Garbage Collection : Algorithms for Automatic Dynamic Memory Management*. John Wiley, August 1996. ISBN: 0471941484.

[8] K. Knobe, J. M. Rehg, A. Chauhan, R. S. Nikhil, and U. Ramachandran. Scheduling constrained dynamic applications on clusters. In *Proc. SC99: High Performance Networking and Computing Conf*, Portland, OR, November 1999. Technical paper.

[9] R. S. Nikhil and U. Ramachandran. Garbage Collection of Timestamped Data in Stampede. In *Proc.Nineteenth Annual Symposium on Principles of Distributed Computing (PODC 2000)*, Portland, Oregon, July 2000.

[10] J. M. Rehg, M. Loughlin, and K. Waters. Vision for a Smart Kiosk. In *Computer Vision and Pattern Recognition*, pages 690–696, San Juan, Puerto Rico, June 17–19 1997.

[11] P. R. Wilson. Uniprocessor garbage collection techniques, Yves Bekkers and Jacques Cohen (eds.). In *Intl. Wkshp. on Memory Management (IWMM 92)*, St. Malo, France, pages 1–42, September 1992.

Iterative Grid-Based Computing Using Mobile Agents

Hairong Kuang, Lubomir F. Bic, Michael B. Dillencourt
Information and Computer Science
University of California, Irvine, CA 92697-3425, USA
{hkuang, bic, dillenco}@ics.uci.edu

Abstract

We describe an environment for the distributed solution of iterative grid-based applications. The environment is built using the MESSENGERS mobile agent system. The main advantage of paradigm-oriented distributed computing is that the user only needs to specify application-specific sequential code, while the underlying infrastructure takes care of the parallelization and distribution. The two paradigms discussed in this papers are the finite difference method, and individual-based simulation. These paradigms present some interesting challenges, both in terms of performance (because they require frequent synchronized communication between nodes) and in terms of repeatability (because the mapping of the user space onto the network may change due to load balancing or due to changes in the underlying logical network). We describe their use, implementation, and performance within a mobile agent-based environment.

Keywords: *mobile agents, programming paradigms, grid-based computing, finite difference methods, individual-based simulations*

1. Introduction

Developing distributed application is significantly more difficult than developing sequential applications. Paradigm-oriented distributed computing greatly simplifies the task of distributed computing. It makes use of the computation and communication skeletons, while the application programmer only has to provide the application-specific components. The advantage of this approach is that it hides the details of distributed computing such as task partitioning, communication, and synchronization.

We have built a paradigm-oriented distributed computing environment on top of the MESSENGERS mobile agent infrastructure [2, 3]. The autonomous migration ability of agents makes them capable of utilizing a dynamically changing network. Their inherent portability allows them

to handle the distribution of tasks in a heterogeneous environment in a transparent manner. Agent mobility can also be exploited for load balancing and fault tolerance. Because of these features, mobile agents lend themselves naturally to paradigm-oriented distributed computing.

In previous research, we investigated three common paradigms: bag-of-tasks, branch-and-bound, and genetic programming [9, 10]. The reason for choosing those paradigms was that applications that fit those paradigms can be easily divided into multiple, highly independent tasks. In the bag-of-tasks paradigm, there is no communication at all between tasks. In the branch-and-bound and genetic-programming paradigms, exchanges of information between tasks are *non-essential communications*, in the sense that they do not affect the correctness although they may be quite useful for optimization purposes.

In this paper, we investigate more complicated paradigms in the area of iterative grid-based computing. Iterative grid-based applications are suitable candidates for distributed computing. They usually require large amounts of computation, which makes it worth distributing tasks over multiple computers. Spatially oriented computations make it easy to partition the simulation space. Near neighbor computations demand only near neighbor communications, which reduces the communication cost. The paradigms we investigated are the finite difference method for solving partial differential equations [14] and spatially oriented individual-based simulations in which the behavior of entities is based solely on their interactions with nearby entities [13].

Unlike the three paradigms discussed in [9, 10], iterative grid-based paradigms require frequent synchronized communications that are also *essential communications*, meaning that they are necessary for correctness. The presence of essential communications increases the challenge of providing a distributed implementation with reasonable performance characteristics. In this paper, we describe an implementation that addresses that challenge. We describe the two iterative paradigms in detail in Section 2, and then present, in Section 3, the underlying implementation using

```
1.   FDM() {
2.     double vals1[XSIZE][YSIZE], vals2[SIZE][YSIZE];
3.     double *oldVals, *newVals;
4.     double △X = XLEN/XSIZE, △Y = YLEN/YSIZE;

5.     // initialization
6.     for ( every element ⟨X, Y⟩ ) {
7.       vals1[X][Y] = Init( X, Y, XSIZE, YSIZE, △X, △Y );
8.     }
9.     oldVals = vals1;
10.    newVals = vals2;

11.    // iterative computation
12.    until ( Termination_condition ) {
13.      for ( every element ⟨X, Y⟩ ) {
14.        newVals[X][Y] = Compute( X, Y, oldVals, △X,
                   △Y, △t );
15.      }
16.      newVals ↔ oldVals;
17.    }
18.    // output
19.    for ( every element ⟨X, Y⟩ ) {
20.      WriteResult( outFile, X, Y, oldVals );
21.    }
22.  }
```

Figure 1. The finite difference paradigm specification

MESSENGERS. Performance results are discussed in Section 4.

2. Paradigms

2.1. Finite difference paradigm

The finite difference method [14] is a common approach for solving differential equations. In the finite difference method, we have a discrete d-dimensional grid of element locations, and we want to compute a value $u_{x,t}$ at each grid location x and for a regular sequence of times t. The value of $u_{x,t+\triangle t}$ is a function of $u_{x,t}$ and the values of u at the neighbors of x at time t.

Figure 1 shows the structure of the finite difference paradigm for a 2D problem. The algorithm starts by initializing the values of all elements (lines 6–8), and pointers to element buffers (lines 9–10). It then repeatedly computes the new values of all elements for each time step until the termination condition is satisfied (lines 12–17). In each iteration of the computation, the value of each element gets updated (lines 13–15), and the pointers to the two element buffers are swapped (line 16). Finally, element values are written into the output file (lines 19–21).

Specifying a finite difference paradigm problem requires four functions.

1. **Init**: this is the initialization function that initializes the value of each element.

2. **Termination_condition**: this specifies the criteria for terminating the computation. A few special termination condition routines are provided, such as terminating after a user-specified number of iteration or terminating when the L_1, L_2, or L_∞ difference between successive arrays of grid values is below a user-specified tolerance.

3. **Compute**: this is the main function of the paradigm. Given its own value and its neighbors' values in the previous time step, it will produce the new value for the current time step.

4. **WriteResult**: this is an output function, which writes the value of an element to an output file.

In addition, users need to specify several parameters. The geometry parameters include the dimension of the grid, the number of nodes (**SIZE**) in each dimension, the length (**LEN**) of each dimension, and whether the grid is toroidal or not. The time interval ($\triangle t$) is also required, as are parameters required by the termination condition. These parameters are specified through a graphical user interface, which is an extension of the interface described in [9].

2.2. Individual-Based Simulation Paradigm

Individual-based simulation programs are widely used to simulate the behaviors of a collection of entities, for example, the movements of molecule particles [5], the schooling behavior of fish or birds [7, 13], and the evolution of an ecology environment [6]. The simulated entities move in a specified space over a period of time. At each time step, an entity decides its own behavior by interacting with its nearby environment and surrounding entities. Typically, an entity has an associated *radius of visibility*, and its behavior is affected only by entities within this radius. The state of an environment may include information, such as the temperature, the speed of a current, the amount of food, or the shape and the size of an obstacle. The state of an entity may include its position, moving speed, moving orientation, age, and so on.

The individual-based simulation paradigm is similar in several respects to the finite difference paradigm. First, in both paradigms, the simulated space is partitioned into a grid. Secondly, both are time-dependent iterative computations. Lastly, both are near-neighbor computations: the computation on each grid cell depends on only the states of the neighboring grid cells. Nevertheless, these two paradigms also have differences. The finite difference computation is static, while the individual-based simulation is dynamic. In a finite difference computation, each grid has only one element, which is not moving. In an individual-based simulation, each grid cell has zero or more entities, moving around and interacting with the environment and with each other.

A typical individual-based simulation program starts by initializing the environment and the entities and then repeatedly executing simulation steps. In each step, the state of each entity and the state of the environment are updated. The state of each entity is updated based on its surrounding environment and its interactions with nearby entities, all of which lie within its radius of visibility. As a result of these interactions, an entity may move to a new position, new entities may be spawned, and old entities may be killed or die.

Variants of the individual-based simulation paradigm arise depending on how the *collision problem* is handled. This problem arises because entities share resources (including space), and hence must contend for resources. For example, two entities may move to the same position, their paths may intersect, or they may decide to eat the same food. Collision detection and resolution is an important issue in individual-based simulation.

Our individual-based simulation paradigm supports two frameworks of collision detection and resolution: the immediate state update method and the delayed state update method. In the delayed state update method, each entity makes a tentative decision based on the old state of the previous time step. After all the entities are finished, possible collisions are detected and resolved. The advantage of the delayed state update method is that the decision making is easy, but the collision detection and resolution are complicated, and sometimes will cause a domino effect.

An individual-based simulation program using the delayed state update method needs to keep two sets of states. The old state stores the snapshot of the simulated space and the entities at the end of the previous time step, while the current state stores the snapshot in the current time step. The structure of individual-based simulation programs using the delayed state update method is very similar to that of finite difference programs, which can be deduced in a straightforward way. We omit its details here.

In the immediate state update method, each entity makes a collision-free decision based on the current state. After an entity's own state and its surrounding environment are updated, the old states are thrown away. Because an entity uses the most current states, collision detection and resolution is much easier to conduct. Collision detection and resolution can be combined with the process of state update, so that a global collision detection and resolution stage is no longer needed. The immediate state update method requires less memory compared to the delayed state update method since the old state does not need to be kept.

Figure 2 shows the structure of the individual-based simulation paradigm using the immediate state update method. It solves a 2D problem. First, the environment and all the entities get initialized (line 8–16). The while loop (line 17–31) is the main body of the program, which simulates the behavior of entities for a fixed number of iterations. At each iteration, all the entities update their states separately (line 20–26). The program keeps only the most current state. Before an entity's state is updated, it is dequeued (line 21). The entity's state is modified in place and the environment is updated incrementally (line 23). An entity can detect and resolve possible collisions while updating its state. Any updating of the environment that is independent of the effect of the entities is performed on lines 27–30.

The individual-based simulation paradigm is quite complicated and even has many variants. However, the details of the paradigm can be hidden from users. Specifying an individual-based simulation application requires specifying only four functions:

1. **newEnv**: this initializes the environment in a grid cell.

2. **newEntity**: this initializes an entity.

3. **updateEntity**: this updates the state of an entity at a time step.

4. **updateEnv**: this updates the state of an environment on a grid cell at a time step.

Users also need to specify the geometry of the simulation space. **XLEN** is the width of the space, while **YLEN** is the length of the space. **XSIZE** is the number of grid cells at dimension x, while **YSIZE** is the number of grid cells at dimension y. $\triangle t$ is the time interval between time steps. **NUM_OF_ENTITIES** is the initial number of entities in the space. **MAX_TIME_STEPS** specifies the number of simulation steps. **R** is the radius of visibility for an entity; this must be smaller than both **XLEN/XSIZE** and **YLEN/YSIZE**.

In addition, two data structure definitions must be provided, one describing an environment (**Env**), the other describing an entity (**Entity**). The data structures are defined by the user, but the **Entity** structure must include the following fields:

```
{
    ...
    long id;
    double x;
    double y;
    ...
}
```

```
1.  IBS() {
2.     Env env[XSIZE][YSIZE];
3.     School entityGroup[XSIZE][YSIZE];
4.     School *entityList;
5.     Entity entities[NUM_OF_ENTITIES];
6.     Entity *curEntity;
7.     double △X=XLEN/XSIZE, △Y=YLEN/YSIZE;

8.     // initialize fish school and environment
9.     for ( all the grid cell ⟨i, j⟩ ){
10.       newEnv( &env[i][j], i, j, XSIZE, YSIZE, △X, △Y );
11.       newEntityList( &entityGroup[i][j] );
12.     }
13.     for( i=0; i<NUM_OF_ENTITIES; i++ ) {
14.       newEntity(&entities[i], i );
15.       add entity i to the corresponding current grid cell;
16.     }

17.     // iterative simulation
18.     while( t<MAX_TIME_STEPS ) {
19.       t++;
20.       for ( each grid cell ⟨i, j⟩ ) {
21.         while( (curEntity = popEntity(
                   &entityGroup[i][j] )) != NULL ) {
22.           entityList = getNeighbors( curEntity,
                   entityGroup, R);
23.           ⟨entityList, env⟩ = updateEntity( t, curEntity,
                   env, entityList, △X, △Y, △t );
24.           add each entity in entityList to entityGroup;
25.         }
26.       }
27.       for ( each grid cell ⟨i, j⟩ ) {
28.         entityList = updateEnv( t, &env[i][j], i, j,
                   △X, △Y, △t );
29.         add each entity in entityList to entityGroup;
30.       }

31.     }
32.  }
```

Figure 2. The individual-based simulation paradigm specification

The field *id* contains an identifier which uniquely identifies an entity. The fields *x* and *y* specify the position of the entity in the 2-D simulated space. The visibility of these two fields allows the system to transparently manage entity lists. The entity list management issue is common to all the individual-based simulation applications and also independent of specific applications. When an entity adjusts its position, we need to know if it has moved out of the current grid cell. If the entity has moved out of the grid, it will be deleted from the old list and added to a new list. In our individual-based simulation paradigm, we provide an entity list management library, which includes a data structure describing an entity list, and a list of operations to manipulate an entity list. For example, *getNeighbors()* function returns a list of entities within a specific radius of a given entity, *newEntityList()* creates an empty entity list with a default size, *AddEntity()* adds an entity to an existing entity list, and *PopEntity()* pops the first entity from an entity list. Functions are also provided to navigate an entity list. These entity list operations can be called by the user-defined functions.

3. Implementation of Paradigms Using MESSENGERS

3.1. Finite difference paradigm

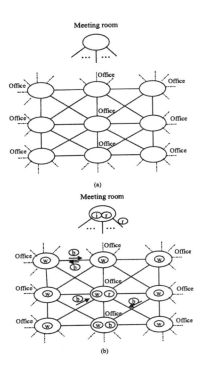

Figure 3. Logical network for the finite difference paradigm in MESSENGERS System

Figure 3(a) shows a logical network to support the distributed implementation of the finite difference paradigm. Each node represents a place to which a messenger can hop. The "Meeting room" node is where the tolerance is gathered and computed. If the termination condition is satisfied, a termination notification will be sent to all the "Office" nodes. An "Office" node is where the element values assigned to the node get iteratively updated. At each iteration, a new value for each of the elements is computed, and boundary information is exchanged with its neighbors when all the boundaries become obsolete. The "Office" nodes can be connected either as a two-dimensional grid (as shown in the figure) or as a ring, depending on how the user grid is partitioned. If the user grid is partitioned into strips, the "Office" nodes are connected as a ring. The advantage of this type partition is that each partition has only two neighboring strips, which simplifies the boundary exchange and synchronization. If the user grid is partitioned into rectangular blocks, the "Office" nodes are connected as a 2D grid. The advantage of this partition technique is that each partition exchanges less boundary message with its neighbors.

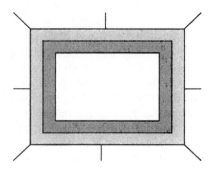

Figure 4. The structure of a rectangular partition

The implementation uses four types of messengers as shown in Figure 3(b). The initialization messenger (i) builds the logical network and injects the worker (w) messengers into offices, one per office. Each worker messenger initializes its partition and starts boundary messengers (b). Then each partition is repeatedly updated by the worker messenger and the boundary messengers until the termination condition is satisfied. Figure 4 shows a structure of a partition when the user grid is partitioned into rectangular blocks, in which the light gray area is the ghost boundary, the dark gray area is the boundary of the partition, and the white area is the inner part of the partition. At each iteration, the worker messenger updates the grid cells in the white area, which do not depend on the values of the grid cells in the neighboring partitions. Each partition has eight boundary messengers, one per side and one per corner. Each boundary messenger alternates between two neighboring "Office" nodes. At each iteration, a boundary messenger updates the grid cells on the portion of the boundary it takes care of. It then carries its boundary information, hops to a neighboring "Office", and deposits the data at the ghost boundary. At the next step, it works at the neighboring "Office" node, updates a portion of its boundary, and then carries the boundary information back to the departure node. Each "Office" node also has a messenger that gathers the tolerance information at the end of each iteration and carries it

to the "Meeting room". These are called "report" messengers (r). Once all the ant messengers have carried their information to the meeting room, the tolerance is computed. If the termination condition is met, the ant messenger will hop back to its "Office" and notify the workers.

The above implementation uses several strategies to improve the performance. In principle, it attempts to update each boundary and send it to its neighbor as early as possible. In this way the communication and computation can be overlapped, and the idle waiting time can be avoided. At the beginning of each iteration, the worker messenger sends out a signal, which wakes up incoming boundary messengers and allows them to update the boundary and carry the boundary data to its neighboring node. However, if some of the neighboring nodes are slower and the boundary messengers have not arrived yet, the worker messenger does not wait for the slower nodes. Instead it goes ahead and updates the inner part of the partition, but it interrupts itself periodically to give late incoming boundary messengers a chance to work. As a result, it eliminates the necessity of a barrier at each step, and therefore squeezes out the idle waiting time.

3.2. Individual-based simulation paradigm

Our distributed implementation of the individual-based simulation paradigm is similar to that of the finite difference paradigm, reflecting the similarities in the paradigms themselves. They have the same possible logical networks and similar types of messengers, and near neighbor boundary exchange is also required for each time step. One major difference arises because of the dynamic migration of the entities in individual-based simulations. Because of this migration, near-neighbor communication in the distributed implementation requires two steps: first the emigrating entities move to the neighboring nodes, then the boundary information is exchanged. Another difference arises because of the more dynamic nature of the individual-based simulation paradigm. In the finite difference paradigm, once the partition of the user grid is fixed, the load on each machine and the message size exchanged remains constant for the duration of the simulation. In the individual-based simulation paradigm, because entities are moving in the space, the load on each machine and the message sizes are dynamically changing.

Our implementation of the individual-based simulation paradigm supports the same logical network structures as in the individual-based simulation paradigm. The "Meeting room" node is where the positions of all the entities are gathered and sent to the client to be visualized. An "Office" node is where a worker iteratively updates the states of the entities and environment assigned to the node. At each time step, a worker updates entities and environments, sends the entities migrating to the neighboring spaces away, and exchanges boundary information.

The system has three types of messengers. The initialization messenger (i) builds the logical network and injects the worker (w) messengers into offices, one per office. Each worker messenger initializes its partition. It then repeatedly updates its grid cell until the termination condition is satisfied. At each iteration, it receives its neighbors' boundaries, computes entities' new states, sends emigrating entities to its neighbors, receives immigrating entities, and sends the boundary to its neighbors. A shuttle messenger (s) carries emigrating entities to its neighboring node and brings the neighbor's boundary back.

An important issue in mobile agent-based implementations of individual-based systems is the representation of migrating entities. In [2], each entity is represented as a separate agent. This allows an entity to freely migrate to its destination, but it means that each migrating entity is a separate hop of an agent from one node to another. In our implementation, we use shuttle agents that synchronously carry dynamic clusters of entities from one node to another. This is arguably a less natural way to address entity migration, but it decreases network traffic considerably and hence increases performance and scalability considerably. What is really needed is an increase in the number of agents that can hop in a short period of time without degrading system performance. Some work in this direction is described by Fukuda et al. [4].

3.3. Repeatability

An important goal of a simulation is *repeatability*: a user should have the option of rerunning a simulation and obtaining exactly the same results. This can be very important for validating changes made at the application level or for tracking down elusive application bugs. Achieving repeatability in distributed implementations presents some interesting challenges, due to the repartitioning of the user grid (i.e., changes if the mapping of the user grid onto the logical nodes). Repartitioning may occur within a run due to load balancing, and it may also occur from one run to another if the user runs the same simulation but changes the configuration (e.g., changes the logical network or the number of machines).

One issue that must be addressed to achieve repeatability is random number generation. In order for two simulations to achieve the same result, the random choice made during the second run must be exactly the same as the corresponding random choice made during the first run. This can be achieved in various ways: for example, a stream of random numbers can be associated with each entity, or a stream of random numbers can be associated with each user grid cell. The paper [11] contains a comparison of these two approaches and a few others as well.

The second issue that affects repeatability is the order in which entities are processed. This order affects the result of the simulation when the immediate state update method is used. We introduce an odd-even labeling scheme to specify a particular order in which entities are updated. This scheme ensures that entities are processed in the same order, irrespective of the partitioning of the user grid.

The scheme works as follows: we label each user grid cell with its index (x, y), and then label the cell with a number in the range 0–3. The label is 0 if both x and y are even, 1 if x is even and y is odd, 2 if x is odd and y is even, and 3 if both x and y are odd. At each time step, we update the states of all entities located at user grid cells with a particular label (starting with 0) before proceeding on the next label. The odd-even scheme is shown in Figure 5.

In order to make this labeling scheme work correctly, the boundary exchange between neighboring partitions needs to be expanded, and a condition must be imposed on the size of the user grid. The reason for the expanded boundary exchange is illustrated in Figure 5. The white area is the collection of user cells that are allocated to the machine, and the gray area is the ghost boundary (i.e., the boundary data obtained from the neighbor as part of the boundary exchange). In order to correctly update the cell with label 3 in the lower left corner of the area allocated to the machine, we must have the updated contents of the cell with label 2 immediately below it, which in turn requires the cell with label 1 below it and to its left, which in turn requires the cell with label 0 below it. To update this last cell, we need all its neighbors. It is not hard to see that this example implies that to correctly update the white area in all cases, the exchanged boundary must consist of a layer of 4 cells around the white area. In other words, this scheme requires expanding the size of the exchanged boundary by a factor of 4.

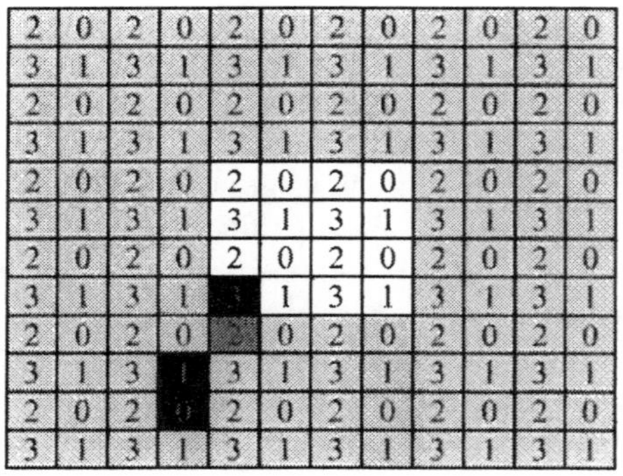

Figure 5. Distributed odd-even individual-based simulation paradigm

The odd-even labeling scheme represents a coloring of the user grid in the graph-theoretical sense, namely that two cells that touch, either along an edge or at a corner, are assigned different labels. In fact, if two entities are located in two different grid cells that are assigned the same label, the distance between them is at least as large as the length of the shortest side of a grid cell. In a typical individual-based system model, there are parameters r_v and r_m, which respectively represent the *radius of visibility* and the *radius of motion*. An entity's behavior in a time step can only be affected by another entity if the second entity is within a distance of r_v of the first, and an entity can move a distance of at most r_m in one time unit. Generally it is assumed $r_m \leq r_v$. It must be true that the length of a user cell must be at least r_v (note that this is enforced as described in Section 2.2). If we strengthen this constraint by requiring that the length of the shortest side a user grid cell is at least $(r_v + r_m)$, then an entity in a grid cell cannot affect an entity in a different grid cell with the same label. Hence, with this strengthened constraint, the odd-even labeling scheme will guarantee repeatability when the immediate-update method is used.

4. Performance Evaluation

4.1. Finite difference paradigm

We tested the finite difference paradigm using Metropolis Monte Carlo algorithm, which solves the Ising model [1, 8]. The Ising model is one of the pillars of statistical mechanics. It consists of an array of spins which can be pointing "up" or "down", and interact with neighboring spins. Each spin and its neighboring spins have an energetic preference to be the same value. Energy is given by

$$E = -J \sum_{i \neq j} S_i S_j$$

where S is equal to +1 or -1 as spin state, $\langle i, j \rangle$ are nearest neighbors, and J is the interaction strength. The Metropolis Monte Carlo algorithm uses Boltzman's rejector for energy fluctuation.

In our experiments, the simulated space is a 2-D toroidal grid, of which spin states are initialized randomly and changed for 500 steps. At each step, each spin makes a tentative flip and uses Boltzman's rejector to decide if this change is accepted or not. We varied the grid size to see how the problem size influenced the speedup.

Figure 6 shows the speedup of the distributed finite difference programs running on 9 machines. The horizontal axis represents the size of the user grid, while the vertical axis represents the speedup, which is the ratio of the execution time of the distributed programs running on 1 machine

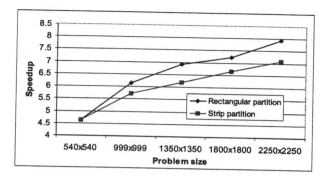

Figure 6. Performance of the distributed finite difference programs running on 9 machines

to the execution time of the distributed program running on 9 machines. The figure shows that the speedup of the distributed programs increases as the user grid size increases. This is because a program with a larger user grid has a larger program size, which represents a bigger computation-to-communication ratio. We can also see that programs with a rectangular partition consistently have better speedup than those with a strip partition. This is because programs with a rectangular partition have a smaller boundary than programs with a strip partition. Therefore, programs with a rectangular partition has smaller amount of communication data, which leads to a better speedup.

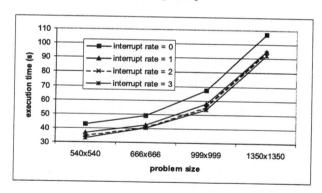

Figure 7. Performance of the distributed finite difference programs running on 9 machines when interrupt rate varies

In our implementation of the distributed finite difference paradigm, the worker messenger interrupt itself periodically to give boundary messengers a chance to work. Another type of experiments has been performed to see how the interrupt rate influences the performance. We use programs with a rectangular partition since they have a better speedup.

115

Figure 7 shows the performance of the distributed finite difference programs running on 9 machine when the interrupt rate varies. The horizontal axis represents the size of the user grid, while the vertical axis represents the execution time in seconds. Different lines represent the performance of the programs with different interrupt rates. When the interrupt rate is equal to zero, the worker messenger does not interrupt itself during its computation at each iteration, while when the interrupt rate, denoted as r, is greater than zero, the worker messenger interrupts itself r times. The figure shows that the performance of the distributed programs improves as the interrupt rate increases no matter the size of the program size. When the interrupt rate increases from zero to one, the performance improves the largest. As the interruption gets more frequent, the performance still improves but not as significant. This is because the interruption of a computation brings extra context switch cost.

4.2. Individual-based simulation paradigm

We tested the individual-based simulation paradigm using a fish schooling model described in [7]. This model assumes a 2-dimensional space where each fish periodically adjusts its position and velocity by coordinating its movement with up to four of its neighbors. We tested the paradigm using both the delayed state method and the odd-even immediate state update method. To make the programs using these two methods comparable, we made a few changes to the fish schooling model. After each fish calculates its new velocity by coordinating with its neighbors, it will discard the effort and adjust its position by moving a random angle. As a result, each fish moves around independently. Whatever method is used, each fish will move at the same trace, which guarantees the amount of computation will be the same. The simulation space is a 2- dimensional 300 by 300 toroid in which fish move as a single school of fish for 500 simulation steps. The positions of all the fish are logged in output files. Because of the uncertainty of distributed programs, we run each program three times. The execution time presented is the average of three runs.

Figure 8 compares the performance of the delayed state update method and the immediate state update method using the odd-even process order. The horizontal axis represents the number of simulated fish, i.e., the problem size, while the vertical axis represents the execution time. The figure shows that the delayed state update method performs better than the odd-even immediate state update method if run in the distributed way. This is because the odd-even immediate state update method has larger communication volume. While in the sequential situation, the odd-even immediate state update method runs faster when the problem size becomes larger. This is because the odd-even immediate state update method uses less memory compared to the

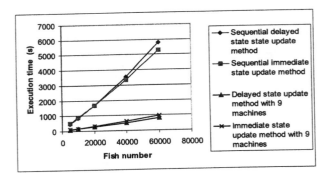

Figure 8. Performance of the individual-based simulation programs

delayed state update method.

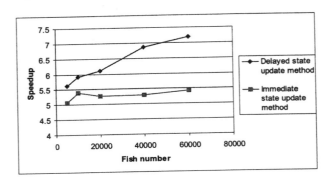

Figure 9. Speedup for the individual-based simulation experiments

Figure 9 shows the speedup of distributed fish schooling simulation programs. The horizontal axis represents the number of simulated fish, while the vertical axis represents the speedup, which is the ratio of the execution time of the sequential program to the execution time of distributed programs which run on 9 machines. The figure shows that the speedup of the distributed programs increases as the problem size increases. This is because the computation-to-communication ratio increases with the increase of the problem size. From the figure, we can also see that the distributed delayed state update programs have better speedup than the distributed odd-even immediate state update programs. This is because distributed odd-even immediate state update programs send and receive four times message size as large as distributed delayed state update programs each time when the boundary information is exchanged. Distributed odd-even programs also need to duplicate redundant computations.

Another issue related to the performance of distributed individual-based simulation programs is the load imbalance on each machine. As we discussed in the previous section of the paper, because the simulated entities move around the space, the load on each machine will dynamically change accordingly. In the experiments we performed, as the fish randomly walks in the space, the load statistically should be balanced. However, in a snap shot of a experiment with 5000 fish performed on 9 machines, we found the most heavily loaded machine has 622 fish, while the least loaded machine has 490 fish. The most heavily loaded machine has 25.5% more load than the least loaded machine. Therefore, a load balance scheme which can dynamically balance the load on each machine will increase the performance of distributed individual simulation. Although we did not present the performance of the load-balanced distributed individual-based simulated programs in this paper, our group has investigated the load balance mechanism in [12].

5. Final Remarks

Paradigm-oriented computing simplifies distributed implementation by providing a coordination layer that insulates the application programmer from the details of the distributed computation. We have described the specification and implementation of environments supporting paradigms for solving finite difference equations and simulating individual-based systems. Our performance evaluations have shown that significant speedups can be achieved on a network of workstations, cooperating with each other using a system of mobile agents.

References

[1] K. Binder and D. Heermann. *Monte Carlo Simulation in Statistical Physics*. Springer-Verlag, Berlin, 1988.

[2] M. Fukuda, L. F. Bic, and M. B. Dillencourt. Messages versus messengers in distributed programming. *Journal of Parallel and Distributed Computing*, 57:188–211, 1999.

[3] M. Fukuda, L. F. Bic, M. B. Dillencourt, and F. Merchant. Distributed coordination with messengers. *Science of Computer Programming*, 31(2), 1998.

[4] M. Fukuda, N. Suzuki, L. M. Campos, and S. Kobayashi. Programmability and performance of M++ self-migrating threads. In *Proceedings of the 3rd IEEE International Conference on Cluster Computing (CLUSTER'01)*, Oct. 2001.

[5] L. Greengard and V. Rokhlin. A fast algorithm for particle simulation. *Journal of Computational Physics*, 73:325–348, 1987.

[6] G. Hartvigsen and S. Levin. Evolution and spatial structure interact to influence plant-herbivore population and community dynamics. In *Proceedings of the Royal Society of London, Series B 264*, pages 1677–1685, 1997.

[7] A. Huth and C. Wissel. The simulation of the movement of fish schools. *Journal of Theoretical Biology*, 156:365–385, 1992.

[8] M. Kalos and P. Whitlock. *Monte Carlo Methods, Vol. I. Basics*. Wiley, New York, 1986.

[9] H. Kuang, L. F. Bic, and M. B. Dillencourt. PODC: Paradigm-oriented distributed computing. In *Proceedings of the 7th IEEE Workshop on Future Trends of Distributed Computing Systems (FTDCS'99)*, pages 169–175, Dec. 1999.

[10] H. Kuang, L. F. Bic, and M. B. Dillencourt. Paradigm-oriented distributed computing using mobile agents. In *Proceedings of the 20th IEEE International Conference on Distributed Computing Systems (ICDCS'00)*, pages 11–19, Apr. 2000.

[11] H. Kuang, L. F. Bic, and M. B. Dillencourt. Repeatability, programmability, and performance of iterative grid-based computing. Technical report, Information and Computer Science, University of California, Irvine, 2001.

[12] F. Merchant, L. F. Bic, and M. B. Dillencourt. Load balancing in individual-based spatial applications. In *Proceedings of the International Conference on Parallel Architectures and Compilation Techniques (PACT'98)*, Oct. 1998.

[13] C. Reynolds. Flocks, herds, and schools: A distributed behavioral model. *Computer Graphics*, 21(4):25–34, July 1987.

[14] E. F. Van de Velde. *Concurrent Scientific Computing*. Springer-Verlag, 1994.

Session 2C

Tolerating Network Failures in System Area Networks

Jeffrey Tang
Department of Computer Science
University of Toronto
Toronto, Ontario M5S 3G4, Canada
jtang@cs.toronto.edu

Angelos Bilas
Dept. of Electrical and Computer Engineering
University of Toronto
Toronto, Ontario M5S 3G4, Canada
bilas@eecg.toronto.edu

ABSTRACT

In this paper, we investigate how system area networks can deal with transient and permanent network failures. We design and implement a firmware–level retransmission scheme to tolerate transient failures and an on–demand network mapping scheme to deal with permanent failures. Both schemes are transparent to applications and are conceptually simple and suitable for low–level implementations, e.g. in firmware. We then examine how the retransmission scheme affects system performance and how various protocol parameters impact system behavior. We analyze and evaluate system performance by using a real implementation on a state–of–the art cluster and both micro–benchmarks and real applications from the SPLASH-2 suite.

1. INTRODUCTION

Recently there has been a lot of progress in providing low–latency, high–bandwidth access in commodity clusters by using system area networks (SANs). These advances in the interconnection network technology both at the hardware and architectural levels have resulted in efficient SANs [6, 16] and higher, user–level communication protocols [27, 11, 3, 17, 32, 31]. System area networks usually connect high–end workstations within a computer room or building and have evolved from the interconnection network technologies used in parallel systems. They are widely used in commodity clusters, which are currently being deployed in a wide spectrum of areas, e.g. as replacements to more expensive parallel computing [5] and storage systems [33]. Despite the improvements on the performance side, very little work has been done on tolerating transient and permanent failures in the SAN interconnects. The underlying assumption is that transient errors, such as packet corruption, as well as permanent failures, such as switch errors, are rare events. As these networks are finding commercial applications, besides performance, fault tolerance and availability are also becoming important issues. However, due to cost and complexity reasons, system area networks do not necessarily provide reliability at the hardware level. Moreover, most of the recent work in system area networks has not studied the performance implications of tolerating network errors. Thus, little is known today about these aspects of SANs, and especially their commercial versions [18, 6, 16] and the effects on real applications.

In this paper we investigate how failures can be toler-

ated in system area networks. We demonstrate how modern network interface controllers (NICs), such as Infiniband adapters, can incorporate in firmware a retransmission protocol to tolerate transient network failures and an on–demand mapping scheme to discover alternate routes when permanent network failures occur. Our retransmission scheme avoids all copies, has low memory and computational requirements, and imposes low overhead in the common path. Our on–demand mapping scheme only uncovers paths to nodes where messages need to be sent, and imposes overhead only when re–mapping is necessary. Both of these schemes are transparent to any layers above the network interface in general and to the application layer in particular.

Besides proposing the above solutions, this work also attempts to answer the following performance–related questions: What is the performance impact associated with providing reliability in firmware? What is the effect of error rate on system performance? What are the most important parameters in the reliability protocol, what is their effect on application performance, and what values are the best compromise between fast recovery and low overheads in the absence of errors?

We implement our schemes on a state–of–the–art cluster of Intel–based PCs with a programmable system area network. We run both micro–benchmarks and real life applications from the SPLASH–2 shared–memory application suite. We find that: (i) Adding reliable transmission at the firmware level increases one–way latency for small messages by at most $2.1\mu s$ for message sizes up to 64 bytes (at most 20% increase) and reduces bandwidth by less than 4% for all message sizes above 4 KBytes. (ii) Our retransmission scheme is very robust. Application performance degrades significantly only at very high error rates of 10^{-3} and upwards. Application performance is practically unaffected with all but these very high error rates. (iii) For the specific retransmission protocol parameters we find that: The best value to use for the retransmission timer in setups similar to our system is 1ms. Longer timer intervals result in slower recovery times and shorter timer intervals result in higher communication overheads. The NIC send queue size has little effect on applications performance. Queue sizes of 4 or greater work well in all applications and error rates that we examine. (iv) Our on–demand dynamic mapping scheme is orthogonal to the network mapping algorithm and does not introduce any overhead in the common case.

The rest of the paper is organized as follows. Section 2 provides the necessary background and discusses related work. Section 3 describes our experimental platform. Section 4 presents the protocol design. Section 5 discusses our evaluation methodology. Section 6 presents our results. Finally, Section 7 draws our conclusions.

2. BACKGROUND AND RELATED WORK

In this work we examine how transient and permanent *network* failures can be tolerated in System Area Networks (SANs). Previous work has examined these problems in the context of other types of networks, mainly local area networks (LANs) [30, 28] and parallel interconnection networks [9, 21, 1]. However, existing solutions for other types of networks are not directly applicable to SANs. Modern SANs are different from both of these types of networks. Compared to LANs: SANs offer much higher bandwidth and lower latency. Applications running on SANs are much more demanding in terms of network resources and are less tolerant to latencies. SANs typically have smaller diameters (a few feet) and use source routing rather than store–and–forward for message exchanges. The error rate in SANs is lower, resulting in different tradeoffs. SANs exhibit lower round–trip latencies and thus require less buffering. Compared to parallel interconnection networks, SANs exhibit the reciprocal behaviors. In addition, SANs support arbitrary topologies and have lower cost.

Research projects in system area networks and user–level communication systems have taken different approaches in dealing with network errors. The authors in [20] demonstrate the need for providing reliability in lower layers (the NIC) as opposed to the library or the application level. A preliminary version of our schemes was presented in [11] in the context of VMMC–2. However, that work focuses on support for streaming communication as opposed to tolerating network failures. AM–II [8] provides reliability guarantees similar to our system using acknowledgments and time-outs. However, their approach differs in a number of ways: The retransmission scheme is implemented at the host (library) level. Timers are managed on a per packet basis. Sending a packet schedules a timer event, and receiving an acknowledgment stops the associated timer. In contrast, we maintain only one timer in our system for all packets. AM–II provides receiver–side buffering combined with negative acknowledgments (NACKs) to provide flow control. Our scheme does not use NACKs. PM [31] provides flow control using a modified ACK/NACK mechanism. In this scheme, the sender does not free any packets until a positive acknowledgment is received, and the receiver is free to discard incoming data, i.e. when its buffer pool is exhausted. The sender retransmits upon receiving negative acknowledgments. This protocol guarantees in–order message delivery. However, PM assumes the network to be reliable and the acknowledgments to always reach their destination. BIP [15] and FM [27] assume that the underlying network is reliable and treat network errors as catastrophic. The authors in [4] present LCI, a Low-level Communication Interface, that supports reliability and multicast. They study the relationship of communication protocol decomposition (between the NIC and the host) with application character-

istics. Similar to our work, they find that NIC support for both reliability and multicast performs best for the applications they examine. However, although the overhead of reliability on small–message latency is similar to our solution, the impact on bandwidth performance is significantly higher. Maximum bandwidth performance in LCI is about 70MBytes/s compared to 120 MBytes/s in our scheme. Finally, in our work we also examine the retransmission protocol characteristics with respect to various system parameters and the network error rate. BDM/Pro [17] provides reliability in the communication library. All sent packets are retransmitted if the acknowledgments do not arrive within a certain amount of time. The receiver only acknowledges groups of N packets as well the last packet of each message. However, BDM/PRO buffers data on the host side rather than on the NIC as in our approach. When packets must be retransmitted, they are re–DMAed from the host memory. The Virtual Interface (VI) specification [12] defines three levels of reliability: Unreliable delivery, reliable delivery, and reliable reception. VI NICs are only required to support the unreliable delivery mode. Our work shows that reliability in VI networks can be implemented at the NIC level with minimal overhead. Similarly, Infiniband [18] specifies reliability levels for different types of communication and provides a number of guidelines on how these should be implemented. In our work we design, implement, and evaluate a firmware-level retransmission scheme that serves as a guide for similar implementations in Infiniband NICs.

Tightly coupled multiprocessors have traditionally implemented reliability at the hardware level. The hardware scheme used in most Cray systems [9] is the single bit error correction, double bit error detection (SECDED) scheme. SECDED is more appropriate for implementation in the memory controller. SANs usually operate at the PCI bus level and packet based schemes are more appropriate as opposed to memory–level based schemes. The interconnect employed in the Origin 2000 System [21] is based on the SGI SPIDER router chip [14]. To achieve high availability, the interconnect fabric isolates each module so that a failure in one module does not affect other modules. Furthermore, all high–speed router and I/O links are protected by a full cyclic redundancy check (CRC) code and a hardware link–level protocol that detects and automatically retries faulty packets. The flexible routing network supports multiple paths between nodes, partial population of the interconnect, and hot swapping of links for servicing faulty hardware. Their hardware scheme is similar to our approach in that corrupted or lost packets are retransmitted based on a Go–Back–N sliding window protocol. In contrast, however, our implementation assumes a slower processor on the NIC and a more loosely–coupled interconnect, e.g. higher system latencies and arbitrary topologies. The micro–channel adapter interconnects nodes to switch boards in IBM SP2 [1] and generates a CRC code for each packet. To tolerate permanent errors, each switching element is shadowed by a duplicate switching element. Each switch also contains at least one stage more than necessary for full connectivity, and this extra stage guarantees that there are at least four different paths between every pair of nodes. The redundant paths also reduce congestion in the network. Furthermore, the error-detection support in hardware is coupled with error recovery capability in the communication software, which supports end–to–end packet acknowledgment and retransmission if an acknowledgment is not received promptly.

With respect to tolerating permanent network failures, the most common approach has been to either use routing schemes that statically account for redundant routes and use an alternative route in case of permanent failures [2, 1] or to fully re–map the network when a failure occurs [6, 28, 22]. Previous research in SANs aimed at finding cost-effective, efficient algorithms for determining full network maps and deadlock–free routing paths in SANs. In some cases it also considered the quality of the generated routes. The authors in [6, 28, 22] provide schemes for discovering full network maps and use the UP*/DOWN* algorithm to determine deadlock–free routes. UP*/DOWN*, proposed in [10, 29], is a popular algorithm for finding deadlock–free network routes. However, the selected paths are generally not shortest paths. The authors in [13] examine several variations of the UP*/DOWN* algorithms by exploiting the fact that more than a single route is possible for a given source–destination pair. Virtual Channels [23] (VCs) can be used to deadlock–free routing algorithms and to increase link utilization. The authors in [24] study the sensitivity to failures of two routing algorithms, UP*/DOWN* and minimal adaptive routing. These two algorithms are also examined in the context of fiber channel storage area networks [25]. Our work leverages the derived mapping algorithms. It takes advantage of the retransmission scheme we design as a deadlock recovery mechanism to avoid computing full network maps and deadlock–free routes that greatly complicate the network mapping process. Although our scheme has the potential of improving on the quality of routes, in this work we do not investigate this any further.

3. EXPERIMENTAL PLATFORM

Our experimental environment consists of Intel–based PCs connected with a Myrinet network [6]. Each PC is equipped with two Pentium II processors clocked at 450MHz and 512 MBytes of main memory. The communication layer we use in the system is VMMC [11].

3.1 Myrinet

Figure 1 shows the block diagram of the Myrinet NIC architecture. In this work we use the Myrinet M2M-PCI64A-2 adapters. The PCI–based NIC is composed of a 32–bit control processor (LANai 7) with 2 MBytes of SRAM. This memory is used for network buffers as well as for firmware code and data. The LANai 7 is clocked at 66 MHz and executes a loadable Myrinet control program (MCP). The MCP controls the NIC resources, e.g., DMA engines, and implements the low–level communication protocols. Each NIC has three DMA engines: two for transferring data between the network and the SRAM and one for transferring data between the SRAM and the host main memory over the PCI bus. The DMA engines can be controlled either by the host or the LANai processor. The host can also access the SRAM using programmed I/O. Each network link is full duplex with 1.28 GBits/s bandwidth in each direction.

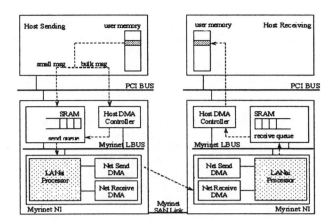

Figure 1: Message exchanges in VMMC. The arrow points to the direction of data flow, for a typical send operation.

All the switches we use are full crossbars. Myrinet uses wormhole routing and the entire route needs to be stored in each packet header.

3.2 Virtual Memory Mapped Communication

The communication model used by VMMC provides protected user–level communication between the sender's and the receiver's virtual address spaces. Before communication can take place, the receiving process exports areas of its address space where it is willing to accept incoming data with a set of permissions. The sending process must import remote buffers before directly depositing data to remote memory. Communication is protected in that the exporter can restrict the processes and hosts that can import a buffer.

Figure 1 illustrates how messages are exchanged in VMMC. On the send side, messages are transferred to the NIC in one of two ways: programmed I/O for small messages ($\leq$ 32 bytes) and DMA for medium and large messages ($>$ 32 bytes). Programmed I/O involves the host CPU transferring data directly to the NIC address space as opposed to data movement by the DMA engine. Messages larger than 4 KBytes are segmented into chunks by the MCP. On the receive side, the packet is first deposited in a receiving queue on the NIC. Since the NIC also maintains the translations between physical and virtual addresses of receive buffers [11], the MCP DMAs the incoming packet into host memory directly without having to interrupt the host processor.

3.3 Error Handling

The transient network errors that can occur are packet corruption and packet loss. Different types of interconnects may experience different sources for these errors. In Myrinet the sources of these errors are: (i) Hardware problems that can cause both packet corruption and loss. Although the hardware error rate in Myrinet is very low (10^{-15}), the possibility of hardware error is still present and cannot be ignored, especially in cases of commercial applications. (ii) Network timeouts that can cause both packet corruption and loss. As a deadlock detection and recovery mechanism, Myrinet provides a user configurable timer ($62.5ms$ to $4s$) [6]. If the send path is blocked for more than this amount of time (for any reason), the sender resets the path. The reset empties all hardware queues along the path and drops any stored packets or parts of packets. (iii) Communication software behavior that should only cause packet loss, e.g., by voluntarily dropping packets. For instance, the communication software may drop packets for flow control reasons.

The Myrinet hardware (and other SANs) provides mechanisms to detect packet corruption errors using CRC checksums. On the send side, the network DMA computes a 32–bit CRC and appends it to the end of each packet. On the receive side, the network DMA computes the CRC of the incoming packet. To detect any packet corruption, the MCP needs to check the two CRCs. Intermediate switches recompute CRCs on the fly to take account for the modified packet headers. Currently, there is no hardware mechanism to detect packet loss.

4. PROTOCOL DESIGN

For the purpose of our work we define network failures as any failures that occur on the communication path between a pair of nodes after a packet has left the sending NIC and before it is delivered to the receiving NIC. We consider NIC failures, not as part of the interconnection network, but rather the end–nodes themselves. In our system, end-node failures are dealt at a higher level [7]. Network failures are categorized as either *transient* or *permanent*. Transient network failures are temporary, and the failing components return to normal operation after a fixed and usually small amount of time. Permanent network failures occur when a system component, e.g., link or switch, cannot recover from a failure and usually needs to be replaced. Transient network failures are tolerated with a packet retransmission scheme. Permanent network failures require the existence and discovery of alternate routes in the interconnect. The main challenge is to perform these tasks without introducing high overheads in the common case, when there are no failures, and to minimize the recovery time in case of failures.

To distinguish between transient and permanent failures we simply use a time interval threshold. If a failure on a path between two nodes is remedied (by a successful packet delivery) within this interval the failure is treated as transient. If the failure persists for longer than this threshold, without any successful packet deliveries, the path is considered to have a permanent failure and is marked as invalid.

4.1 Tolerating Transient Failures

A challenging issue in the design and implementation of user–level communication systems is where and how to incorporate a retransmission protocol in order to provide low–overhead reliable communication. Retransmission can be incorporated either in the user–level library running on the host or in the communication library running on the network interface as firmware. Implementing the reliability protocol on the host may impact application performance significantly as explained later. Our approach to reliable communication is to implement the retransmission method on the NIC. However, providing reliability on the NIC requires careful resource management. The NIC processor is significantly slower when compared to the host processor. Furthermore, the amount of memory available on the NIC is limited.

In our scheme, each packet is assigned a unique sequence number. After the packet is transmitted to the destination node, instead of freeing the packet buffer, it is placed in a retransmission queue. When the receiver receives a packet, it sends back an acknowledgment. When the sender receives the acknowledgment, it frees the packet buffer. The sender employs a timeout mechanism, where it periodically checks the retransmission queues for packets that have not been acknowledged for an extended period of time. These packets are then retransmitted. Any network error will result in the receiver not acknowledging one or more packets, and the sender retransmitting a set of packets.

4.1.1 Design choices

Within this general scheme there is a wide range of design and implementation decisions that need to be made, based on the semantics of the communication layer (VMMC provides in order, point–to–point delivery), the overhead of implementing each choice, and the behavior of the resulting retransmission scheme in the presence and absence of networks errors. In our particular implementation: The full retransmission scheme is implemented in firmware on the NIC. Each acknowledgment carries a single sequence number and acknowledges *all* packets up to (and including) that particular sequence number. Also, to reduce NIC occupancy, there are no negative acknowledgments. On the sender, each remote node has its own retransmission queue. This is a critical issue for system scalability. Using retransmission queues per pair of user processes would result in high resource requirement in the firmware. A similar solution to our work is adapted in Infiniband [18]. When the receiver does not receive a particular sequence number, it will drop immediately *all* subsequent packets from that remote node until it receives the expected sequence number. Thus, there is no packet buffering at the receiver. Upon retransmission, the sender retransmits (in order) *all* packets in the retransmission queue for the particular node. Acknowledgments are not critical, in the sense that they can be dropped. Sequence numbers and retransmission information are maintained on a per–node and not per–connection basis.

These design choices result in a number of advantages: We push functionality towards the NIC with little additional complexity to reduce the performance and complexity impact on higher layers [20]. We take advantage of packet buffering that takes place on the NIC and we do not introduce extra packet copies in the retransmission code. This is not the case in schemes that are implemented on the host side, at the library level. In those cases, either a copy of each packet/message needs to be made or the user is not allowed to reuse the buffer until the acknowledgment is received. Moreover, these overheads always occur in the common path. None of these limitations exist in our scheme. Our implementation is lightweight, requires very little resources, and is appropriate for implementation at the firmware or hardware level. On the send side, storing a packet after transmission, retransmitting a packet, and freeing acknowledged packets involves simply moving packet buffers between queues (the global NIC transmission queue, the individual node retransmission queue, and the global NIC free queue). The retransmission timer can be relatively long so that a small overhead is imposed. On the receive side, the only additional operations needed are either acknowledging a packet or dropping out of order packets. Acknowledging packets involves sending a simple acknowledgment message including a sequence number. Dropping a packet is a simple dequeue operation.

4.1.2 Optimizations

We apply a number of optimizations on this basic scheme. First, instead of sending explicit acknowledgments, we use piggy–backed acknowledgments in regular data packets in cases of two–way traffic. Explicit acknowledgments are still needed in cases where there is one–way traffic for extended periods of time or the sender will run out of send–buffer space. Second, we do not need to acknowledge every packet. Instead, a single acknowledgment can be used to acknowledge a set of consecutive packets. Upon receiving an acknowledgment, the sender frees all related packets with a single operation. Third, to vary the frequency of acknowledgments we employ sender–based feedback. Each packet, from the sender to the receiver, contains a bit stating whether an acknowledgment is needed so that buffer space can be freed. This approach allows the sender control over how fast its NIC buffers should be released based on the amount of available system resources. When the number of available NIC buffers is small, the sender would request for an explicit acknowledgment so that the buffers can be freed in a timely fashion. When the number of available NIC buffers is adequate, the sender could afford to wait for return traffic and requests for piggy–backed acknowledgments. When the number of available NIC buffers is large, the sender reduces the frequency of acknowledgment requests. These optimizations create a trade–off between the amount of buffer space required at the sender and the frequency of acknowledgments, which we examine later.

4.2 Tolerating Permanent Failures

The retransmission scheme can tolerate transient failures but is not able to deal with permanent network failures, such as permanent link and switch faults. To transparently deal with these types of errors we propose and use a simple extension to existing infrastructure. The Myrinet firmware includes a mapping component [6] that can discover the full topology of a system area network by performing a breadth first search. It forms a spanning tree and extracts the routes between all host pairs in the network using the UP*/DOWN* algorithm [26].

We propose extending this mapping scheme in two ways: To compute only partial maps of the network and to dynamically compute new routes as they are needed. When a NIC needs to communicate with another NIC or if packets cannot be delivered over an existing route, it starts mapping the network to find a new route to the destination node. The NIC returns to normal operation as soon as a route is found.

If no alternative route to a node exists, the node is labeled as unreachable and any pending packets are dropped. If an alternative path exists, sequence numbers are reset, a

new generation of sequence numbers is started, and communication is resumed. With these extensions it is not clear anymore when a node joins the network, i.e. if this node is a new node or a reincarnation of a previously existing node. The sequence number management scheme clearly distinguishes between packet generations and drops packets in the network that belong to previous generations as soon as a new generation is started.

This approach has a number of benefits compared to mapping techniques that compute full system maps. The effect of permanent errors is localized. When a permanent error occurs, only the affected NICs will invalidate the failing routes and discover new ones (if they exist) on demand. Moreover, while computing each route in the network, there is no need to stop the rest of the traffic in the system. Computing a route happens concurrently with other traffic in the network, localizing the delay mostly to a single pair of nodes. Each node only needs a partial set of routes to the nodes that it is communicating with and does not need to maintain full routing tables. Moreover, whenever a fault occurs, the initial recovery overhead is lower, since only the necessary routes will be recomputed and this cost is amortized over a longer period of time. Furthermore, no overhead is added to the common path (when routes are already computed and no failures occur). Besides tolerating permanent failures, this scheme allows for dynamic network reconfiguration. Nodes can move in the network and routes will be recomputed dynamically as they are needed. There is no need for a central map manager that performs the mapping. Any node can discover routes to other nodes. This is an important feature of the scheme, since requiring a central map manager usually means that additional care needs to be taken to deal with failures of the map manager. Since deadlock–free routes are not needed, the quality of the routes may be improved. However, we do not explore this direction any further and improving the quality of the computed routes by load balancing the induced traffic or in other ways is beyond the scope of this work.

A key issue is that our scheme relies on retransmission for correctness. Since we do not compute the full network map and we do not take into account any existing routes in the system, it is possible that deadlock situations may arise. The final set of routes computed is not deadlock free. Our mapping scheme relies on the retransmission protocol to deal with deadlocks. When there is no progress in a specific path, the sender resets the path to the receiver and clears all hardware buffers. Then, our retransmission protocol will retransmit each packet. Thus, instead of computing deadlock–free routes to avoid deadlocks, we rely on deadlock detection and recovery.

The main disadvantage of our scheme is that since the network is mapped independently by all nodes, work is replicated. This may result in longer times for mapping the full network. Although various techniques, e.g., caching, may be used to improve this, we do not explore this direction any further in this work.

5. EVALUATION METHODOLOGY

Our main goal in the rest of the paper is to identify the most important parameters of our retransmission scheme

Parameters	Values			
# NIC Send Buffers	2	8	32	128
Timeout Interval	10 μs	1 ms	100 ms	1 s
Error Rates	0	10^{-3}	10^{-4}	10^{-5}

Table 1: Range of system parameters studied in this work.

and examine the performance sensitivity as these parameters change. We would further like to use this knowledge and tune such retransmission schemes to incur minimal overheads in the absence of networks errors.

5.1 Retransmission Protocol

The most important parameters in our retransmission scheme are: The NIC send queue size, the retransmission timeout interval, and the network error rate. Table 1 shows the ranges of the parameter values that we examine.

5.1.1 Number of send buffers

The NIC send queue size affects the amount of concurrency and the cost of recovery in the system. Since the NIC send buffers are not released until acknowledgments are received, this parameter determines the number of packets that can be pipelined across the network before the sender blocks due to a lack of send buffers. The amount of memory that is available for send buffers on the NIC can vary significantly, from a few KBytes to a few MBytes or so in the most aggressive, high–end NICs. This memory needs to be shared among the firmware code, data structures, receive, and send buffers. In our system we use NICs that are relatively aggressive with 2 MBytes of memory. Thus, we have the ability to vary the number of send buffers in a wide range of values. The values that we choose are between about 8 KBytes and 512 KBytes (each buffer has a fixed size of about 4 KBytes).

We should mention that receive–side buffering is not as important for this work. We make sure that there are enough NIC receive buffers available so that multiple senders can never overwhelm a receiver. This is based on two features of our system: First, the number of receive buffers available on each NIC is about the same as the number of nodes in the system. Thus, each sender is guaranteed at least one receive buffer regardless of the packet destination. With the current technology, a cluster of SMPs with 128 processors is considered a relative large system [19] and requires at most a few tens of receive buffers. Furthermore, current trends indicate that the NIC memory increases faster than the scaling of the system. Second, the receive path is considerably faster than the send path. In particular, the sender side needs to perform operations such as address translation, preparing packet headers, transferring data from host to the NIC, and managing retransmission buffers. On the other hand, the receiver only needs to move data directly to host memory upon packet arrival.

5.1.2 Retransmission timer interval

The retransmission timer imposes a trade–off between the overhead in the common case (no errors) and the recovery time when errors occur. A small timeout interval increases the processing overhead and may lead to false retransmissions in cases of high network contention. A large timeout interval incurs long recovery delays when a packet is lost. We are interested in determining a timeout interval that recovers well from errors and at the same time introduces little overhead to the common path. Since the minimum round–trip time in our system is about $16\mu s$ we choose a range of values between $10\mu s$ and 1s for the retransmission time. The $10\mu s$–value, although practically not realistic, is chosen as one extreme of the spectrum to force very frequent retransmissions. The 1s–value is chosen as the other end of the spectrum.

5.1.3 Network error rate

Since we do not have access to switches (no firmware), to simulate network errors in a controlled manner, we model network errors by dropping packets on the send side NIC, right before they are injected to the network. At predefined packet counts, the dropping mechanism on the NIC inserts the next packet in the retransmission queue without actually transmitting it onto the network. Since packet is not delivered, the receiver does not acknowledge this and any subsequent packets from this source node. When the retransmission timer expires on the send side, the sender retransmits all unacknowledged packets, starting with the dropped packet. By changing the dropping interval, we are able to control the rate at which packets are dropped. Detection of lost packets on the receive side includes the cost of detecting packet corruption. Thus, dropping packets to simulate network errors (as opposed to, e.g., inserting corrupted packets) incurs the highest possible overhead on the receive side. We perform experiments with varying error rates and contrast our results with the case where no errors occur. To reduce the amount of time it takes to run experiments, we start with error rates of 10^{-5} (i.e. drop one packet every 10^5 packets) and increase the error rate by a factor of 10 at each step, i.e. $10^{-4}, 10^{-3}$. Finally, we do not experiment with bursty errors, since high, uniform errors rates are a more stressful test.

5.1.4 Evaluation workload

We use both micro–benchmarks and real applications. At the micro–benchmark level we use a simple latency test, a ping–pong bandwidth test, and a unidirectional bandwidth test. Unlike the ping–pong bandwidth test, in the unidirectional bandwidth test data flows only in one direction. The sender does not wait for the receiver to acknowledge a message before sending the next one. This type of bandwidth test measures how fast data can be put onto the network.

Application	Problem Size	Other Parameter
FFT	1 M points	18 iterations
RadixLocal	4M keys	5 iterations
WaterNSquared	4096 molecules	15 steps

Table 2: SPLASH application problem sizes.

We also use a subset of the SPLASH–2 application suite as modified in [19]: FFT, RadixLocal, and WaterNSquared. FFT performs a six–step FFT algorithm that minimizes interprocess communication. It is a single–writer application in that a given word of data is written only by the pro-

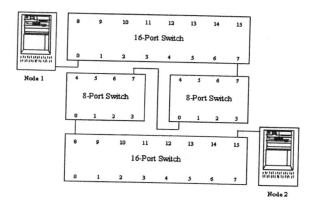

Figure 2: System setup for dynamic mapping.

cessor assigned, and it incurs high communication (band-width limited). RadixLocal performs an integer radix sort, and it is a variation of the Radix program from the original SPLASH suite. Radix performs fine–grain accesses to shared data (latency sensitive). The version under study is an improvement over the original version to reduce the irregularity of accesses [19]. WaterNSquared evaluates the forces and potentials in a system of water molecules. It is an $O(n^2)$ algorithm with a small communication to computation ratio but uses lock synchronization heavily.

We perform the micro–benchmark tests on a pair of nodes connected with a switch and the applications tests on a sub-cluster of 4 nodes with 8 processors total. In all cases we generate enough packets to allow at least ten packets to be dropped at the lower error rate (and more in the higher error rates). In FFT and RadixLocal we modify the programs to perform the computation for more iterations and increase the run time. In WaterNSquared, we increase the problem input size. Table 2 shows the exact input parameters and problem sizes for each application.

5.2 Dynamic System Mapping

Our dynamic mapping scheme does not interfere at all with NIC operations when there are no failures. It is only triggered when a node cannot be reached after a number of retransmissions. For this reason we only present basic measurements of the number of messages and the time it takes to map a single node in our system. The mapping time depends on the system topology and network size that is used. We consider our setup to be representative of many real–life SANs used either in clusters that perform parallel computations or in storage area networks. In all these cases nodes are connected in a tree with redundant links to avoid single–points of failures. We configure our system to include four switches: two 16–port and two 8–port, full–crossbar switches. We connect two of the system nodes at various locations of the system, as shown in Figure 2. We present both the time and the number of probe messages it takes to map a single pair of nodes in our setup.

6. RESULTS

We explore the entire parameter space as presented in Table 1. However, due to time and space constraints we present results for only a subset of the parameter values.

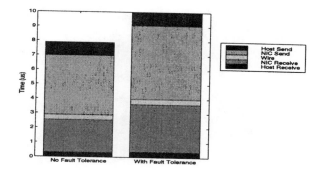

Figure 3: Latency breakdown for 4–byte messages.

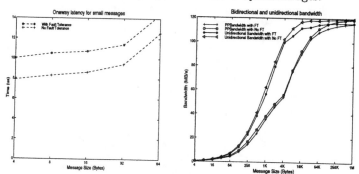

Figure 4: System latency and bandwidth with and without the retransmission protocol.

We extract the more important observations and then present the data that support these observations.

6.1 Reliable Transmission Protocol

6.1.1 Overhead

We find that adding reliable transmission exhibits a 20% overhead in the absence of errors. Figure 3 compares the one–way latency breakdown of a 4–byte message with and without retransmission. The retransmission protocol overhead is divided almost equally between the send and the receive sides, i.e. about $1.0\mu s$ in each case. The overhead in the send path results primarily from the management of retransmission queues. The overhead in the receive path results primarily from the processing of acknowledgments. These overheads are fairly low considering that the NIC processor is relatively slow. Overall, the highly–optimized initial latency for a 4–byte message is increased from about $8\mu s$ to $10\mu s$. Figure 4 illustrates the cost of the reliability protocol in terms of micro–benchmarks. In particular, the latency overhead is less than $2.1\mu s$ for messages up to 64–bytes, and the bandwidth overhead is less than 4%, for all messages sizes above 4 KBytes in both the bidirectional and unidirectional cases. The system bandwidth for large messages is limited by the 32–bit PCI bus at around 120 MB/s.

Finally, we should note that these measurements for the overall overhead of the retransmission protocol have been performed for a retransmission interval of 1ms and a NIC send queue size of 32, since these are the best values for our

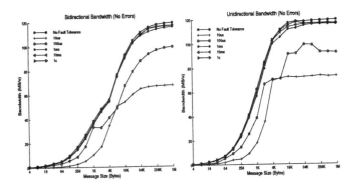

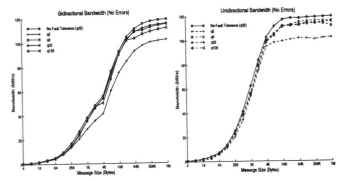

Figure 5: The effect of retransmission interval on bandwidth with no errors. The NIC send queue size is set to 32.

Figure 7: The effect of NIC send queue size on bandwidth with no errors. The retransmission interval is set to 1ms.

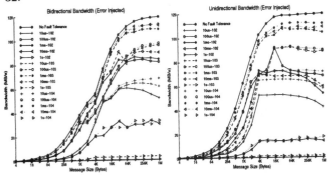

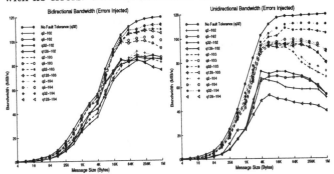

Figure 6: The effect of retransmission interval on bandwidth with errors injected. The NIC send queue size is set to 32. The error rates presented are: 10^{-2}, 10^{-3}, and 10^{-4}.

setup as will be explained next.

6.1.2 Effect of retransmission timer interval

Figure 5 shows the effect of the retransmission timer in the absence of errors and a network queue size of 32. We see that a retransmission interval of $100\mu s$ or less incurs a high overhead (bandwidth drops by more than 17% across all messages sizes), whereas an interval of 1ms or longer introduces a much lower overhead.

Figure 6 shows the same statistics in the presence of varying errors. The curves in the figure correspond to the various retransmission intervals under selected error rates. We observe that using a timer value of 1ms results in robust behavior as the error rate varies. Even at the high error rate of 10^{-4}, system bandwidth is still within 10% of the case were no network errors occur for messages sizes of 4 KBytes and up. As the retransmission interval becomes shorter or longer system bandwidth drops significantly, by more than 18% for $100\mu s$ and 72% for 1s, for the same message sizes.

6.1.3 Effect of network send queue size

Figure 7 shows the effect of the NIC send queue size in the absence of network errors and a retransmission interval of 1ms. We see that only very small queue sizes have an effect on system performance. Any queue size above 8 results in the close-to-maximum bandwidth. Figure 8 shows that in the presence of errors the same trends are still valid. Any

Figure 8: The effect of NIC send queue size on bandwidth with errors injected. The retransmission interval is set to 1ms. The error rates presented are: 10^{-2}, 10^{-3}, and 10^{-4}.

network send queue size above 8 or so results in bandwidth close to the best case when the error rate is 10^{-4} or less. For higher error rates (i.e. 10^{-2}), however, the performance for large queue size degrades more. In particular, a large send queue size of 128 in the unidirectional bandwidth results in more than 30% reduction in bandwidth. This behavior is the result of sender–based feedback that attempts to reduce the number of acknowledgments when there is plenty of resources (i.e. send buffers) and the fact that the system does not support selective retransmission. As a sender with a large queue size slows down the rate of freeing NIC buffers by not requesting ACKs, the performance degrades faster at higher error rates.

6.1.4 Real applications

Figure 9 shows the execution time breakdowns for selected parameters values for each of the three applications we examine. The SVM protocol we use is GeNIMA [5], which leverages NIC support to eliminate all synchronous communication operations and exhibits relatively high latencies and increased network traffic. The results are grouped by error rates, with each group consisting of 4 bars. Each bar represents the application execution time for a particular parameter configuration. Our results are very close to that of the micro–benchmark results. First we notice that WaterNSquared is rather insensitive to most of the parameter changes. This is due to the high computation to communication ratio that it exhibits. Second we notice that

128

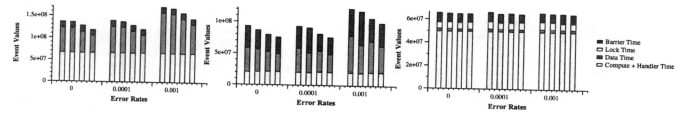

Figure 9: FFT (left), RadixLocal (middle) and WaterNSquared (right) execution time breakdowns, grouped by error rates. Each group consists of 4 bars that correspond, from left to right, to the following parameters: r100μs–q2, r100μs–q32, r1ms–q2, and r1ms–q32.

for error rates up to 10^{-4}, changes in system performance are very small for FFT and RadixLocal as well. Both FFT and Radix exhibit similar performance for each parameter configuration for 0 and 10^{-3} error rates. However, in each error rate performance varies up to 19%. Finally, at high error rates (10^{-3} or above), performance starts to deteriorate significantly (by more than 20%) when compared to the failure–free case.

6.2 Dynamic System Mapping

Table 3 shows the mapping time and the breakdown of the different types of probe messages exchanged in the event of a network topology change. In particular, a node is reconnected to a different location of the system and the first packet exchange triggers the mapping process. The different types of probe messages serve the purpose of locating hosts, locating switches, and distinguishing new switches from old ones, if necessary (i.e. unlike hosts, Myrinet switches do not have identities) [22]. The number of probe messages exchanged is linear with respect to the size of the network due to the breadth–first search. The number of probe messages, and thus the overall mapping time, may be further reduced [22], but we do not pursue this direction here.

7. CONCLUSIONS

System area networks have been the subject of extensive research, especially with respect to performance issues. However, little work has been done in the areas of fault tolerance and system availability. Our work is a first step towards this direction. We investigate how reliability can be incorporated in modern SANs and how they behave under errors. As such, this work is especially relevant for commercial SANs, which are now being deployed in applications with reliability demands, such as storage systems [33]. We demonstrate how reliability schemes can be incorporated in modern NICs and we investigate the performance implications.

We use a reliability protocol implemented in the NIC that takes advantages of sender–side buffering to tolerate transient network failures. We also propose an extension to existing network mapping schemes for dealing with permanent network failures transparently at the NIC level. Our scheme performs on–demand mapping of system nodes and does not require full system mapping. It relies on the retransmission mechanism to deal with deadlocks, if they occur, and it does not require a central map manager.

We study the retransmission protocol behavior with re-

# Hops (i.e. Links)	Host	Switch	Total	Mapping Time (ms)
1	28	0	28	3.054
2	53	20	73	25.855
3	83	41	124	48.488
4	113	73	186	83.567

Table 3: Dynamic routing performance summary. The columns labeled *Host* and *Switch* refer to host and switch probe messages respectively.

spect to various system parameters and determine a set of values for these parameters that offer fast recovery time in the presence of high network errors while limiting the overhead in the absence of network errors. Our retransmission protocol imposes a 20% overhead on system latency for small messages in the failure–free case, increasing latency from 8 to 10 μs. The overhead imposed on bandwidth is less than 4% for all message sizes above 4 KBytes. The parameter space exploration for our retransmission scheme shows that it is very robust with respect to error rate. System performance, both with micro–benchmarks and real applications, starts to degrade significantly only when error rates are higher than 10^{-3}. Finally, the retransmission scheme is rather insensitive to the network send queue size and even relatively small numbers of buffers on the send side result in little or no performance degradation.

8. ACKNOWLEDGMENTS

The authors would like to thank Peter Jamieson and Eugenia Distefano for helpful hints on setting up and using the experimental testbed. We would like to thank the members of the ATHLOS project for the useful discussions during the course of this work. Also, we thankfully acknowledge the support of Natural Sciences and Engineering Research Council of Canada, Canada Foundation for Innovation, Ontario Innovation Trust, the Nortel Institute of Technology, and Communications and Information Technology Ontario.

9. REFERENCES

[1] T. Agerwala, J. L. Martin, J. H. Mirza, D. C. Sadler, D. M. Dias, and M. Snir. SP2 system architecture. *IBM Systems Journal*, 34(2):152–184, 1995.

[2] W. E. Baker, R. W. Horst, D. P. Sonnier, and W. J. Watson. A flexible servernet-based fault-tolerant architecture. In *Proc. of the 25th International Symposium on Fault-Tolerant Computing*, Pasadena, CA, 1995.

[3] R. A. F. Bhoedjang, T. Ruhl, and H. E. Bal. Lfc: A communication substrate for myrinet. In *Fourth Annual Conference of the Advanced School for Computing and Imaging*, Lommel, Belgium, June 1998.

[4] R. A. F. Bhoedjang, K. Verstoep, T. Ruhl, H. E. Bal, and R. Hofman. Evaluating design alternatives for reliable communication on high-speed networks. In *Proc. of The 9th International Conference on Architectural Support for Programming Languages and Operating Systems (ASPLOS9)*, Cambridge, MA, Nov. 2000.

[5] A. Bilas, C. Liao, and J. P. Singh. Using network interface support to avoid asynchronous protocol processing in shared virtual memory systems. In *Proc. of the 26th International Symposium on Computer Architecture (ISCA26)*, May 1999.

[6] N. J. Boden, D. Cohen, R. E. Felderman, A. E. Kulawik, C. L. Seitz, J. N. Seizovic, and W. Su. Myrinet: A gigabit-per-second local area network. *IEEE Micro*, 15(1):29–36, Feb. 1995.

[7] R. Christodoulopoulou and A. Bilas. Dynamic data replication for tolerating single node failures in shared virtual memory clusters of workstations. In *Proc. of The Workshop on Caching, Coherence and Consistency (WC3 2001)*, June 2001.

[8] B. N. Chun, A. M. Mainwaring, and D. E. Culler. Virtual network transport protocols for myrinet. In *Proc. of The 1997 IEEE Symposium on High Performance Interconnects (HOT Interconnects V)*, August 1997.

[9] Cray. Cray t3e data sheets. http://www.cray.com/products/systems/index.html, 2001.

[10] W. J. Dally and C. L. Seitz. Deadlock-free message routing in multiprocessor interconnection networks. *IEEE Transactions on Computers*, 36(5):547–553, 1987.

[11] C. Dubnicki, A. Bilas, Y. Chen, S. Damianakis, and K. Li. VMMC-2: efficient support for reliable, connection-oriented communication. In *Proc. of The 1997 IEEE Symposium on High Performance Interconnects (HOT Interconnects V)*, Aug. 1997. A short version of this appears in IEEE Micro, Jan/Feb, 1998.

[12] D. Dunning and G. Regnier. The Virtual Interface Architecture. In *Proc. of The 1997 IEEE Symposium on High Performance Interconnects (HOT Interconnects V)*, Aug. 1997.

[13] J. Flich, M. P. Malumbres, P. Lopez, and J. Duato. Improving routing performance in myrinet networks. In *Proc. of the 14th International Parallel and Distributed Processing Symposium (IPDPS'00)*, Cancun, Mexico, 2000.

[14] M. Galles. Scalable pipelined interconnect for distributed endpoint routing: The SGI SPIDER chip. In *Proc. of The 1996 IEEE Symposium on High Performance Interconnects (HOT Interconnects IV)*, 1996.

[15] P. Geoffray, L. Prylli, and B. Tourancheau. BIP-SMP: High performance message passing over a cluster of commodity SMPs. In *Proc. of The 1999 Supercomputing Conference on High Performance Networking and Computing (SC98)*. IEEE, Nov. 1999.

[16] R. Gillett, M. Collins, and D. Pimm. Overview of network memory channel for PCI. In *Proc. of the IEEE Spring COMPCON '96*, Feb. 1996.

[17] H. Gregory, J. Thomas, P. McMahon, A. Skjellum, and N. Doss. Design of the BDM family of myrinet control programs, 1998.

[18] InfiniBand Trade Association. Infiniband architecture specification, version 1.0. http://www.infinibandta.org, Oct. 2000.

[19] D. Jiang, H. Shan, and J. P. Singh. Application restructuring and performance portability on shared virtual memory and hardware-coherent multiprocessors. In

[20] V. Karamcheti and A. A. Chien. Software overhead in messaging layers: where does the time go? *ACM SIGPLAN Notices*, 29(11):51–60, Nov. 1994.

[21] J. Laudon and D. Lenoski. The SGI origin: A ccNUMA highly scalable server. In *Proc. of the 24th International Symposium on Computer Architecture (ISCA24)*, volume 25 of *ACM SIGARCH Computer Architecture News*, pages 241–251. ACM Press, 1997.

[22] A. M. Mainwaring, B. N. Chun, S. Schleimer, and D. S. Wilkerson. System area network mapping. In *Proc. of the 7th Annual ACM SIGPLAN Symposium on Parallel Algorithms and Architectures (SPAA97)*, pages 116–126, Newport, Rhode Island, June 22–25, 1997. SIGACT/SIGARCH and EATCS.

[23] J. C. Martinez, F. Silla, P. Lopez, and J. Duato. On the influence of the selection function on the performance of networks of workstations. In *Proc. of the 3rd International Symposium on High Performance Computing (ISHPC 2000)*, pages 292–299, Tokyo, Japan, 2000.

[24] J. Molero, F. Silla, V. Santonja, and J. Duato. Performance sensitivity of routing algorithms to failures in networks of workstations. In *Proc. of the 3rd International Symposium on High Performance Computing (ISHPC 2000)*, pages 230–242, Tokyo, Japan, 2000.

[25] X. Molero, F. Silla, V. Santonja, and J. Duato. On the effect of link failures in fibre channel storage area networks. In *Proc. of the 2000 International Symposium on Parallel Architectures, Algorithms, and Networks (I-SPAN 2000)*, Dallas, Texas, 2000.

[26] S. S. Owicki and A. R. Karlin. Factors in the performance of the AN1 computer network. Technical Report 88, DEC System Research Center, 130 Lytton Ave., Palo Alto, CA 94301, June 1992.

[27] S. Pakin, V. Karamcheti, and A. A. Chien. Fast Messages: Efficient, portable communication for workstation clusters and massively parallel processors (MPP). *IEEE Concurrency*, 5(2):60–73, April-June 1997. University of Illinois.

[28] M. D. Schroeder, A. D. Birrell, M. Burrows, H. Murray, R. M. Needh, T. L. Rodeheffer, E. H. Satterthwaite, and C. P. Thacker. Autonet: a high-speed, self-configuring local area network using point-to-point links. Technical Report 59, Digital Equipment Corporation, Systems Research Center, Palo Alto, CA, Apr. 1990.

[29] M. D. Schroeder, A. D. Birrell, M. Burrows, H. Murray, R. M. Needham, T. L. Rodeheffer, E. H. Satterthwaite, and C. P. Thacker. Autonet: a high-speed, self-configuring local area network using point-to-point links. Technical Report 59, Digital Equipment Corporation, Systems Research Center, Palo Alto, CA, Apr. 1990.

[30] A. S. Tanenbaum. *Computer Networks*. Prentice Hall, Inc., Upper Saddle River, NJ, 3rd edition, 1996.

[31] H. Tezuka, A. Hori, and Y. Ishikawa. PM: A high-performance communication library for multi-user parallel environments. Technical Report TR-96015, Real World Computing Partnership, Nov. 1996.

[32] T. von Eicken, A. Basu, V. Buch, and W. Vogels. U-net: a user-level network interface for parallel and distributed computing. In *Proc. of the Fifteenth Symposium on Operating Systems Principles (SOSP15)*, pages 40–53, Dec. 1995.

[33] Y. Zhou, A. Bilas, S. Jagannathan, C. Dubnicki, J. Philbin, and K. Li. Experiences with vi communication for database storage. In *Proc. of the 29th International Symposium on Computer Architecture (ISCA29)*, May 2002.

Multi-level Shared State for Distributed Systems *

DeQing Chen, Chunqiang Tang, Xiangchuan Chen,
Sandhya Dwarkadas, and Michael L. Scott

Computer Science Department, University of Rochester
{*lukechen,sarrmor,chenxc,sandhya,scott*} @*cs.rochester.edu*

Abstract

As a result of advances in processor and network speeds, more and more applications can productively be spread across geographically distributed machines. In this paper we present a transparent system for memory sharing, InterWeave, developed with such applications in mind. InterWeave can accommodate hardware coherence and consistency within multiprocessors (level-1 sharing), *software distributed shared memory (S-DSM) within tightly coupled clusters* (level-2 sharing), *and version-based coherence and consistency across the Internet* (level-3 sharing). *InterWeave allows processes written in multiple languages, running on heterogeneous machines, to share arbitrary typed data structures as if they resided in local memory. Application-specific knowledge of minimal coherence requirements is used to minimize communication. Consistency information is maintained in a manner that allows scaling to large amounts of shared data. In C, operations on shared data, including pointers, take precisely the same form as operations on non-shared data. We demonstrate the ease of use and efficiency of the system through an evaluation of several applications. In particular, we demonstrate that InterWeave's support for sharing at higher (more distributed) levels does not reduce the performance of sharing at lower (more tightly coupled) levels.*

1 Introduction

Advances in processing speed and network bandwidth are creating new interest in such ambitious distributed applications as interactive data mining, remote scientific visualization, computer-supported collaborative work, and intelligent environments. These applications are characterized both by the need for high-end parallel computing and by the need to coordinate widely distributed users, devices, and data repositories. Increasingly, the parallel computing part can make productive use of the parallelism afforded by comparatively inexpensive and widely available clusters of

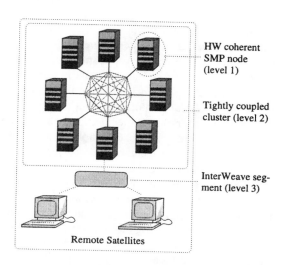

Figure 1. InterWeave's target environment.

symmetric multiprocessors (SMPs). The more distributed components may need to span the Internet.

Conceptually, many of these applications seem easiest to describe in terms of some sort of *shared state*. Many programmers—particularly those who are connecting together components developed for small and mid-size multiprocessors—would like to capture shared state with a shared-memory programming model. In order to meet this demand, we are developing a system, known as InterWeave [8], that allows the programmer to map shared data into program components regardless of location or machine type, and to transparently access that data once mapped.

InterWeave represents a merger and extension of our previous Cashmere [19, 20] and InterAct [15] projects. Once shared data has been mapped, InterWeave can support hardware coherence and consistency within multiprocessors (*level-1* sharing), Cashmere-style software distributed shared memory (S-DSM) within tightly coupled clusters (*level-2* sharing), and InterAct-style version-based coherence and consistency across the Internet (*level-3* sharing). Figure 1 provides a pictorial representation of the target environment.

InterWeave has been designed to maximize the lever-

*This work was supported in part by NSF grants CCR–9702466, CCR–9705594, EIA–9972881, CCR–9988361, EIA–0080124, and CCR–0204344.

age of available hardware support, and to minimize the extent to which sharing at the higher (more distributed) levels might impact the performance of sharing at the lower (more tightly coupled) levels. At levels 1 and 2, InterWeave inherits Cashmere's integration of intra-SMP hardware cache coherence with cluster-level VM-based lazy release consistency. In particular, it employs *two-way diffing* to avoid the need for TLB shootdown when processes synchronize across nodes [19], and relies on low-latency user-level messages for efficient synchronization, directory management, and write-notice propagation [20]. In a similar vein, consistency at level 3 employs the twins, diffs, write notices, and home-node copies already maintained at level 2.

At the third level, data in InterWeave evolves through a series of consistent versions. Application-specific knowledge of minimal coherence requirements is used to minimize communication. When beginning a read-only critical section on a logical grouping of data (a *segment*), InterWeave uses a programmer-specified predicate to determine whether the currently cached version, if any, is "recent enough" to use. Several coherence models (notions of "recent enough") are built into the InterWeave system; others can be defined by application programmers. When the application desires consistency across segment boundaries, to avoid causality loops, we invalidate mutually-inconsistent versions using a novel hashing mechanism that captures the history of a segment in a bounded amount of space. S-DSM-like twins and diffs allow us to update stale segments economically.

In keeping with wide-area distribution, InterWeave allows processes at level 3 to be written in multiple languages and to run on heterogeneous machine architectures, while sharing arbitrary typed data structures as if they resided in local memory [21]. In C, operations on shared data, including pointers, take precisely the same form as operations on non-shared data. Like CORBA and many older RPC systems, InterWeave employs a type system based on a machine- and language-independent interface description language (IDL).[1] When transmitting data between machines, we convert between the local data format (as determined by language and machine architecture) and a standard *InterWeave wire format*. We also *swizzle* pointers [23] so that they can be represented locally using ordinary machine addresses.

Recognizing that the performance tradeoffs between function shipping and data migration/caching are application-dependent, we have designed InterWeave to complement existing RPC and RMI systems. Programmers can choose on a function-by-function basis whether to access data directly or to invoke an operation on a machine

at which the data is believed to reside. When choosing the latter option, the presence of the InterWeave library allows a program to use genuine reference parameters as an alternative to deep-copy value parameters.

We describe the design of InterWeave in more detail in Section 2. We then describe our implementation in Section 3, with an emphasis on the coherence, consistency, and communication mechanisms. Performance results for applications in iterative, interactive data mining; remote scientific visualization; and multi-user collaboration appear in Section 4. We compare our design to related work in Section 5 and conclude with a discussion of status and plans in Section 6.

2 InterWeave Design

The InterWeave programming model assumes a distributed collection of servers and clients. Servers maintain persistent copies of shared data, and coordinate sharing among clients. Clients in turn must be linked with a special InterWeave library, which arranges to map a cached copy of needed data into local memory, and to update that copy when appropriate.

2.1 Data Allocation

The unit of sharing in InterWeave is a self-descriptive data *segment* (a heap) within which programs allocate strongly typed *blocks* of memory.[2] Every segment is specified by an Internet URL. The blocks within a segment are numbered and optionally named. By concatenating the segment URL with a block name or number and optional offset (delimited by pound signs), we obtain a *machine-independent pointer (MIP)*: "foo.org/path#block#offset". To accommodate heterogeneous data formats, offsets are measured in primitive data units—characters, integers, floats, etc.—rather than in bytes.

Every segment is managed by an InterWeave server at the IP address corresponding to the segment's URL. Different segments may be managed by different servers. Assuming appropriate access rights, the IW_open_segment() library call communicates with the appropriate server to open an existing segment or to create a new one if the segment does not yet exist.[3] The call returns an opaque *han-*

---

[1] InterWeave's IDL is currently based on Sun XDR, but this is not an essential design choice. InterWeave could easily be modified to work with other IDLs.

[2] Like distributed file systems and databases, and unlike systems such as PerDiS [11], InterWeave requires manual deletion of data; there is no automatic garbage collection. A web-based perusal tool, comparable to a file-system browser, will allow a user or system administrator to search for orphaned data.

[3] Authentication and access control in InterWeave are currently based on a simple public key mechanism. Access keys can be specified at segment creation time or changed later by any client that successfully acquires write access.

dle that can be passed as the initial argument in calls to `IW_malloc()`:

```
IW_handle_t h = IW_open_segment(url);
IW_wl_acquire(h);        /* write lock */
my_type* p = (my_type*)
    IW_malloc(h, my_type_desc);
*p = ...
IW_wl_release(h);
```

As in multi-language RPC systems, the types of shared data in InterWeave must be declared in IDL. The Inter-Weave IDL compiler translates these declarations into the appropriate programming language(s) (C, C++, Java, Fortran). It also creates initialized *type descriptors* that specify the layout of the types on the specified machine. The descriptors must be registered with the InterWeave library prior to being used, and are passed as the second argument in calls to `IW_malloc()`. These conventions allow the library to translate to and from wire format, ensuring that each type will have the appropriate machine-specific byte order, alignment, etc. in locally cached copies of segments.

Level-3 synchronization takes the form of reader-writer locks. A process must hold a writer lock on a segment in order to allocate, free, or modify blocks. The lock routines take a segment handle as parameter. Within a tightly coupled cluster or a hardware-coherent node, a segment that is locked at level 3 may be shared using data-race-free [1] memory semantics.

Given a pointer to a block in an InterWeave segment, or to data within such a block, a process can create a corresponding MIP:

```
IW_mip_t m = IW_ptr_to_mip(p);
```

This MIP can then be passed to another process through a message, a file, or an argument of a remote procedure in RPC-style systems. Given appropriate access rights, the other process can convert back to a machine-specific pointer:

```
my_type *p = (my_type*) IW_mip_to_ptr(m);
```

The `IW_mip_to_ptr` call reserves space for the specified segment if it is not already locally cached (communicating with the server if necessary to obtain layout information for the specified block), and returns a local machine address. Actual data for the segment will not be copied into the local machine until the segment is locked.

It should be emphasized that `IW_mip_to_ptr()` is primarily a bootstrapping mechanism. Once a process has one pointer into a data structure, any data reachable from that pointer can be directly accessed in the same way as local data, even if embedded pointers refer to data in other segments. InterWeave's pointer-swizzling and data-conversion

mechanisms ensure that such pointers will be valid local machine addresses. It remains the programmer's responsibility to ensure that segments are accessed only under the protection of reader-writer locks.

2.2 Coherence

InterWeave's goal is to support seamless sharing of data using ordinary reads and writes, regardless of location. Unfortunately, given the comparatively high and variable latencies of even local-area networks, traditional hardware-inspired coherence and consistency models are unlikely to admit good performance in a distributed environment. Even the most relaxed of these models guarantees a consistent view of *all* shared data among *all* processes at synchronization points, resulting in significant amounts of communication. To reduce this overhead, InterWeave exploits the fact that processes in a distributed application can often accept a significantly more relaxed—and hence less communication-intensive—notion of coherence. Depending on the application, it may suffice to update a cached copy of a segment at regular (temporal) intervals, or whenever the contents have changed "enough to make a difference," rather than after every change. When updating data, we require that a process have exclusive write access to the most recent version of the segment. When reading, however, we require only that the currently cached version be "recent enough" to satisfy the needs of the application.

InterWeave currently supports six different definitions of "recent enough". It is also designed in such a way that additional definitions (coherence models) can be added easily. Among the current models, *Full* coherence always obtains the most recent version of the segment; *Strict* coherence obtains the most recent version *and* excludes any concurrent writer; *Null* coherence always accepts the currently cached version, if any (the process must explicitly override the model on an individual lock acquire in order to obtain an update); *Delta* coherence [17] guarantees that the segment is no more than x versions out-of-date; *Temporal* coherence guarantees that it is no more than x time units out of date; and *Diff-based* coherence guarantees that no more than $x\%$ of the primitive data elements in the segment are out of date. In all cases, x can be specified dynamically by the process. All coherence models other than Strict allow a process to hold a read lock on a segment even when a writer is in the process of creating a new version.

When a process first locks a shared segment, the Inter-Weave library obtains a copy from the segment's server. At each subsequent read-lock acquisition, the library checks to see whether the local copy of the segment is "recent enough". If not, it obtains a version update from the server. An adaptive polling/notification protocol, described in Section 3.3, often allows the implementation to avoid communication with the server when updates are not required.

Twin and diff operations [6], extended to accommodate heterogeneous data formats, allow the implementation to perform an update in time proportional to the fraction of the data that has changed.

Unless otherwise specified, lock acquisitions default to Full coherence. The creator of a segment can specify an alternative coherence model if desired, to be used by default whenever any process locks that particular segment. An individual process may also establish its own default for a given segment, and may override this default for individual critical sections. Different processes (and different fragments of code within a given process) may therefore use different coherence models for the same segment. These models are entirely compatible: the server for a segment always has the most recent version; the model used by a given process at a given time simply determines how it decides if its own cached copy is recent enough.

The server for a segment need only maintain a copy of the segment's most recent version. The API specifies that the current version of a segment is always acceptable as an update to a client, and since processes cache whole segments, they never need an "extra piece" of an old version. To minimize the cost of segment updates, the server maintains a timestamp on each block of each segment, so that it can avoid transmitting copies of blocks that have not changed. As partial protection against server failure, InterWeave periodically checkpoints segments and their metadata to persistent storage. The implementation of real fault tolerance is a subject of future work.

As noted in Section 1, an SDSM-style "level-2" sharing system such as Cashmere can play the role of a single node at level 3. Any process in a level-2 system that obtains a level-3 lock does so on behalf of its entire level-2 system, and may share access to the segment with its level-2 peers. If level-3 lock operations occur in more than one level-2 process, the processes must coordinate their activities (using ordinary level-2 synchronization) so that operations are seen by the server in an appropriate order. Working together, Cashmere and InterWeave guarantee that updates are propagated consistently, and that protocol overhead required to maintain coherence is not replicated at levels 2 and 3. Further details appear in Section 3.

2.3 Consistency

Without additional mechanisms, in the face of multiversion relaxed coherence, the versions of segments currently visible to a process might not be mutually consistent. Specifically, let A_j refer to version j of segment A. If B_k was created using information found in A_j, then previous versions of A are causally incompatible with B_k; a process that wants to use B_k (and that wants to respect causality) should invalidate any cached segment version A_i, $i < j$.

To support this invalidation process, we would ideally like to tag each segment version, automatically, with the names of all segment versions on which it depends. Then whenever a process acquired a lock on a segment the library would check to see whether that segment depends on newer versions of any other segments currently locally cached. If so, the library would invalidate those segments. The problem with this scheme, of course, is that the number of segments in the system—and hence the size of tags—is unbounded. In Section 3.2 we describe a mechanism based on hashing that achieves the same effect in bounded space, at modest additional cost.

To support operations on groups of segments, we allow their locks to be acquired and released together. Locks that are acquired together are acquired in a predefined total order to avoid deadlock. Write locks released together make each new segment version appear to be in the logical past of the other, ensuring that a process that acquires the locks together will never obtain the new version of one without the other. To enhance the performance of the most relaxed applications, we allow an individual process to "opt out" of causality on a segment-by-segment basis. For sharing levels 1 and 2 (hardware coherence within SMPs, and software DSM within clusters), consistency is guaranteed for data-race-free programs.

3 Implementation

The underlying implementation of InterWeave can be divided into four relatively independent modules:

- the memory management module, which provides address-independent storage for segments and their associated metadata;

- the modification detection module, which creates wire-format diffs designed to accommodate heterogeneity and minimize communication bandwidth;

- the coherence and consistency module, which obtains updates from the server when the cached copy of a segment is no longer recent enough, or is inconsistent with the local copies of other segments; and

- the communication module, which handles efficient communication of data between servers and clients.

The memory management and modification detection modules are described in detail in a companion paper [21]. We describe them briefly in the first subsection below, and then focus in the remaining subsections on the coherence/consistency and communication modules.

3.1 Memory Management and Modification Detection

As described in Section 2, InterWeave presents the programmer with two granularities of shared data: *segments* and *blocks*. Each block must have a well-defined type, but this type can be a recursively defined structure of arbitrary complexity, so blocks can be of arbitrary size. Every block has a serial number within its segment, assigned by `IW_malloc()`. It may also have a symbolic name, specified as an additional parameter. There is no a priori limit on the number of blocks in a segment, and blocks within the same segment can be of different types and sizes.

When a process acquires a write lock on a given segment, the InterWeave client library asks the operating system to write protect the pages that comprise the local copy of the segment. When a page fault occurs, the `SIGSEGV` signal handler, installed by the library at program startup time, creates a pristine copy, or *twin* [6], of the page in which the write fault occurred. It saves a pointer to that twin for future reference, and then asks the operating system to re-enable write access to the page.

When a process releases a write lock, the library performs a word-by-word diff of modified pages and their twins. It then converts this diff to a machine-independent wire format that expresses changes in terms of segments, blocks, and primitive data unit offsets, rather than pages and bytes, and that compensates for byte order, word size, and alignment. When a client acquires a lock and determines that its copy of the segment is not recent enough, the server builds a similar diff that describes the data that have changed between the client's outdated copy and the master copy at the server.

Both translations between local and wire format—for updates to the server at write lock release and for updates to the client at lock acquisition—are driven by type descriptors, generated by the InterWeave IDL compiler, and provided to the InterWeave library via the second argument to `IW_malloc()` calls. The content of each descriptor specifies the substructure and machine-specific layout of its type.

To accommodate reference types, InterWeave relies on pointer swizzling [23]. Briefly, swizzling uses type descriptors to find all (machine-independent) pointers within a newly-cached or updated segment, and converts them to pointers that work on the local machine. Pointers to segments that are not (yet) locally cached point into reserved but unmapped pages where data will lie once properly locked. The set of segments currently cached on a given machine thus displays an "expanding frontier" reminiscent of lazy dynamic linking.

3.2 Coherence and Consistency

Each server maintains an up-to-date copy of each of the segments for which it is responsible, and controls access to those segments. For each segment, the InterWeave server keeps track of blocks and *subblocks*. Each subblock comprises a small contiguous group of primitive data elements from the same block. For each modest-sized block in each segment, and for each subblock of a larger block, the server remembers the version number of the segment in which the content of the block or subblock was most recently modified. This convention strikes a compromise between the size of server-to-client diffs and the size of server-maintained metadata.

At the time of a lock acquire, a client must decide whether its local copy of the segment needs to be updated. (This decision may or may not require communication with the server; see Section 3.3.) If an update is required, the client sends the server the (out-of-date) version number of the local copy. The server then identifies the blocks and subblocks that have changed since the last update to this client, constructs a wire-format diff, and returns it to the client.

Hash-Based Consistency. To ensure inter-segment consistency, we use a simple hash function to compress the dependence history of segments. Specifically, we tag each segment version S_i with an n-slot vector timestamp, and choose a global hash function h that maps segment identifiers into the range $[0..n-1]$. Slot j in the vector indicates the maximum, over all segments P whose identifiers hash to j, of the most recent version of P on which S_i depends. When acquiring a lock on S_i, a process checks each of its cached segment versions Q_k to see whether k is less than the value in slot $h(Q)$ of S_i's vector timestamp. If so, the process invalidates Q_k. Hash collisions may result in unnecessary invalidations, but these affect performance only, not correctness.

To support the creation of segment timestamps, each client maintains a local master timestamp. When the client acquires a lock on any segment (read or write) that forces it to obtain a new version of a segment from a server, the library updates the master timestamp with any newer values found in corresponding slots of the timestamp on the newly obtained segment version. When releasing a write lock (thereby creating a new segment version), the process increments the version number of the segment itself, updates its local timestamp to reflect that number, and attaches this new timestamp to the newly-created segment version.

Integration with 2-Level System. When a tightly coupled cluster, such as a Cashmere-2L system, uses an InterWeave segment, the cluster appears as a single client to the segment server. The client's local copy of the segment is kept in cluster-wide shared memory.

Figure 2 pictorially represents a sequence of actions performed by a level-2 system. (Details on our level-2 coherence protocol can be found in previous work [19].) The timelines in the figure flow from left to right, and represent three processors within a tightly coupled cluster. In the current implementation, we designate a single node within the cluster to be the segment's *manager* node (in this case processor P0). All interactions between the level-2 system and

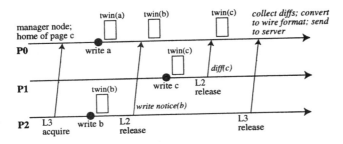

Figure 2. Coherence actions at levels 2 and 3.

the segment's InterWeave server go through the manager node. During the period between a level-3 (InterWeave) write lock acquire and release, the manager node ensures that modifications made within the level-2 system can be identified through the use of twins and diffs.

InterWeave achieves its goal of minimizing additional coherence actions by piggybacking as far as possible on existing level-2 operations. Three different scenarios are illustrated in the figure. First, as illustrated on the P0 timeline, the manager node creates a twin for a page if it experiences a write fault. If the manager is not the level-2 home node for the page, then this twin is used for both level-2 and level-3 modification detection purposes. If the manager node is the level-2 home node, then this twin is needed for level 3 only. Second, as illustrated by page *b*, the manager creates a level-3 twin if it receives a write notice from another node in the cluster (P2) and must invalidate the page. Third, as illustrated by page *c*, the manager creates a twin for level-3 purposes (only) if it receives a level-2 diff from another node in the cluster (P1).

On a level-3 release, the manager node compares any level-3 twins to the current content of the corresponding pages in order to create diffs for the InterWeave server. Overhead is thus incurred only for those pages that are modified and, in practice, the number of additional twins created is fairly low.

3.3 Communication

In our current implementation each InterWeave server takes the form of a daemon process listening on a well-known port at a well-known Internet address for connection requests from clients. The server keeps metadata for each active client of each segment it manages, as well as a master copy of the segment's data.

Each InterWeave client maintains a pair of TCP connections to each server for which it has locally cached copies of segments. One connection is used for client requests and server responses. The other is used for server notifications. Separation of these two categories of communication allows them to be handled independently. All communication between clients and servers is aggregated so as to minimize

the number of messages exchanged (and thereby avoid extra per-message overhead).

Servers use a heartbeat mechanism to identify dead clients. If a client dies while holding a write lock or a read lock with Strict coherence, the server reverts to the previous version of the segment. If the client was not really dead (its heartbeat was simply delayed), its subsequent release will fail.

Several protocol optimizations minimize communication between clients and servers in important common cases. (Additional optimizations, not described here, minimize the cost of modification detection and conversion to and from wire format [21].) First, when only one client has a copy of a given segment, the client will enter *exclusive* mode, allowing it to acquire and release locks (both read and write) an arbitrary number of times, with no communication with the server whatsoever. This optimization is particularly important for high-performance clients such as Cashmere clusters. If other clients appear, the server sends a message requesting a summary diff, and the client leaves exclusive mode.

Second, a client that finds that its local copy of a segment is usually recent enough will enter a mode in which it stops asking the server for updates. Specifically, every locally cached segment begins in *polling* mode: the client will check with the server on every read lock acquire to see if it needs an update (temporal coherence provides an exception to this rule: no poll is needed if the window has yet to close). If three successive polls fail to uncover the need for an update, the client and server will switch to *notification* mode. Now it is the server's responsibility to inform the client when an update is required (it need only inform it once, not after every new version is created). If three successive lock acquisition operations find notifications already waiting, the client and server will revert to polling mode.

Third, the server maintains a cache of diffs that it has received recently from clients, or collected recently itself, in response to client requests. These cached diffs can often be used to respond to future requests, avoiding redundant collection overhead.

Finally, as in the TreadMarks SDSM system [4], a client that repeatedly modifies most of the data in a segment will switch to a mode in which it simply transmits the whole segment to the server at every write lock release. This *no-diff* mode eliminates the overhead of mprotects, page faults, and the creation of twins and diffs.

4 Performance Results

InterWeave currently runs on Alpha, Sparc, x86, and MIPS processors, under Windows NT, Linux, Solaris, Tru64 Unix, and IRIX. Together, the server and client library comprise approximately 31,000 lines of heavily commented C++ code. Our uniprocessor results were collected on Sun Ultra 5 workstations with 400 MHz Sparc v9 processors and 128 MB of memory, running SunOS 5.7, and on 333 MHz Celeron PCs with 256 MB of memory, running Linux 6.2. Our Cashmere cluster is a collection of AlphaServer 4100 5/600 nodes, each with four 600 MHz 21164A processors, an 8 MB direct-mapped board-level cache with a 64-byte line size, and 2 GBytes of memory, running Tru64 Unix 4.0F. The nodes are connected by a Memory Channel 2 system area network, which is used for tightly-coupled sharing. Connection to the local area network is via TCP/IP over 100Mb Ethernet.

4.1 Coherence Model Evaluation

We use a data mining application [16] to demonstrate the impact of InterWeave's relaxed coherence models on network bandwidth and synchronization latency. Specifically, the application performs incremental sequence mining on a remotely located database of *transactions* (e.g. retail purchases). Each transaction in the database (not to be confused with transactions *on* the database) comprises a set of *items*, such as goods that were purchased together. Transactions are ordered with respect to each other in time. The goal is to find sequences of items that are commonly purchased by a single customer in order over time.

In our experimental setup, the database server (itself an InterWeave client) reads from an active database whose content continues to grow. As updates arrive the server incrementally maintains a summary data structure (a lattice of item sequences) that is used by mining queries. Each node in the lattice represents a sequence that has been found with a frequency above a specified threshold. The lattice is represented by a single InterWeave segment; each node is a block in that segment. Each data mining client, representing a distributed, interactive interface to the mining system, is also an InterWeave client. It executes a loop containing a reader critical section in which it performs a simple query.

Our sample database is generated by tools from IBM research [18]. It includes 100,000 customers and 1000 different items, with an average of 1.25 transactions per customers and a total of 5000 item sequence patterns of average length 4. The database size is 20MB.

The summary structure is initially generated using half the database. The server then repeatedly updates the structure using an additional 1% of the database each time. Because the summary structure is large, and changes slowly over time, it makes sense for each client to keep a local cached copy of the structure and to update only the modified data as the database evolves. Moreover, since the data in the summary are statistical in nature, their *values* change slowly over time, and clients do not need to see each incremental change. Delta or diff coherence will suffice, and can dramatically reduce communication overhead. To illustrate

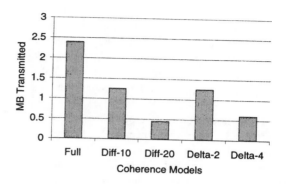

Figure 3. Sequence mining: bandwidth required under different coherence models.

these effects, we measure the network bandwidth required by each client for summary data structure updates as the database grows and the database server finds additional sequences.

Figure 3 shows the total bandwidth requirement as the client relaxes its coherence model. The leftmost bar represents the bandwidth requirement if the client uses the Full coherence model (Section 2.2). The other four bars show the bandwidth requirements if the client uses Diff and Delta coherence with different thresholds. Using Diff coherence with a threshold of 20% (i.e., consider a cached copy to be "recent enough" if no more than 20% of its primitive data elements are out of date), we see a savings of almost 75%.

4.2 3-Level System for Parallel Applications

To illustrate the interaction between InterWeave shared state, managed across the Internet, and software distributed shared memory, running on a tightly coupled cluster, we collected performance measurements for remote visualization and steering of two pre-existing scientific simulations: the Splash-2 Barnes-Hut N-body benchmark, and a CFD stellar dynamics application known as Astroflow [10]. Barnes-Hut is written in C. Astroflow is written in Fortran. Both simulations run on four nodes of our AlphaServer cluster. Barnes-Hut repeatedly computes new positions for 16,384 bodies. Astroflow computes on a 256×256 discretized grid. In both cases, the progress of the simulation can be observed and modified using a visualization and steering "satellite" that runs on a remote workstation. The Astroflow satellite is a pre-existing Java program, originally designed to read from a checkpoint file, but modified for our purposes to share data with the simulator via InterWeave. The Barnes-Hut satellite was written from scratch (in C) for this experiment.

In both applications, the simulator uses a write lock to update the segment that it shares with the satellite. The Barnes-Hut satellite uses a relaxed read lock with Temporal coherence to obtain an effective frame rate of 15 frames per second. In Astroflow the simulation proceeds slowly enough that Full coherence requires negligible bandwidth.

To assess the baseline overhead of InterWeave we linked both simulators with the InterWeave library, but ran them without connecting to a satellite. Though the cluster must communicate with the InterWeave server to create its initial copy of the simulation data, the *exclusive mode* optimization (Section 3.3) eliminates the need for further interaction, and the overall impact on performance is negligible.

To assess the overhead of InterWeave in the presence of a satellite, we constructed, by hand, versions of the simulators that use explicit messaging over TCP/IP to communicate with the satellite (directly, without a server). We then ran these versions on the standard Cashmere system, and compared their performance to that of Cashmere working with InterWeave. Results for Barnes-Hut appear in Figure 4. (For Astroflow, both the messaging and InterWeave versions have such low communication rates that the impact on performance is negligible.) In all cases the satellite was running on another Alpha node, communicating with the cluster and server, if any, via TCP/IP over 100Mb Ethernet. Each bar gives aggregate wall-clock time for ten iteration steps. The labels on pairs of bars indicate the number of nodes and the total number of processors involved in each experiment. In the first three pairs a single processor was active in each node. In the final pair, four processors per node were active. The "C" bars are for explicit messaging code running on standard Cashmere; the "IW" bars are for Cashmere working with InterWeave. The C bars are subdivided to show the overhead of communication; the IW bars also show the (comparatively small) overhead of data translation and the coherence protocol. For this particular sharing scenario, much of the shared data is modified in every interval. InterWeave therefore switches, automatically, to *no-diff* mode to minimize the cost of tracking modifications.

4.3 API Ease-of-Use

The changes required to adapt Barnes-Hut and Astroflow to work with InterWeave were small and isolated. No special code is required to control the frequency of updates (one can adjust this in the satellite simply by specifying a temporal bound on relaxed coherence). No assumptions need to be embedded regarding the number of satellites (one can launch an arbitrary number of them, on multiple workstations, and each will connect to the server and monitor the simulation). No knowledge of networking or connection details is required, beyond the character-string name of the segment shared between the simulator and the satellite. While the matter is clearly subjective, we find the InterWeave code to be significantly simpler, easier to understand, and faster to write than the message-passing version.

In a separate experiment, we used InterWeave to de-

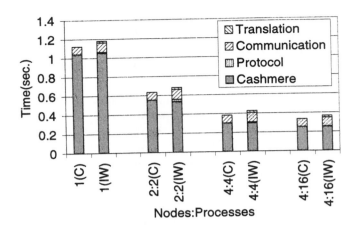

Figure 4. Overhead of InterWeave library and communication during Barnes-Hut remote visualization.

velop, from scratch, a distributed calendar program. The program was originally written with about two weeks of part-time effort by a first-year graduate student. Subsequent minor modifications served primarily to cope with changes in the API as InterWeave evolved.

The program maintains appointment calendars for a dynamically changing group of individuals. Users can create or delete a personal calendar; view appointments in a personal calendar or, with permission, the calendars of others; create or delete individual appointments; propose a group meeting, to be placed in the calendars of a specified group of users; or accept or reject a meeting proposal.

A single global segment, accessed by all clients, contains a directory of users. For each user, there is an additional segment that contains the user's calendar. Within each user calendar there is a named block for each day on which appointments (firm or proposed) exist. The name of the block is a character string date. To obtain a pointer to Jane Doe's calendar for April 1, we say `IW_mip_to_ptr("iw.somewhere.edu/cal/jane #04-01-2001")`.

The calendar program comprises 1250 lines of C++ source, approximately 570 of which are devoted to a simple command-line user interface. There are 68 calls to InterWeave library routines, spread among about a dozen user-level functions. These calls include 3 reader and 10 writer lock acquire/release pairs, 17 additional lock releases in error-checking code, and a dozen `IW_mip_to_ptr` calls that return references to segments.

In comparison to messaging code, the InterWeave calendar program has no message buffers, no marshaling and unmarshaling of parameters, and no management of TCP connections. (These are all present in the InterWeave library, of course, but the library is entirely general, and can be reused by other programs.) Instead of an application-specific protocol for client-server interactions, the InterWeave code has reader-writer locks, which programmers, in our experience, find significantly more straightforward and intuitive.

5   Related Work

InterWeave finds context in an enormous body of related work—far too much to document in this paper. We focus here on some of the most relevant systems in the literature; additional discussion can be found in the TR version of this paper [9].

Dozens of object-based systems attempt to provide a uniform programming model for distributed applications. Many are language specific; many of the more recent of these are based on Java. Language-independent distributed object systems include PerDiS [11], Legion [13], Globe [22], Microsoft's DCOM, and various CORBA-compliant systems. Globe replicates objects for availability and fault tolerance. PerDiS and a few CORBA systems (e.g. Fresco [14]) cache objects for locality of reference. Unfortunately, object-oriented update propagation, typically supported either by invalidate and resend on access or by RMI-style mechanisms, tends to be inefficient (re-sending a large object or a log of operations). Equally significant from our point of view, there are important applications (e.g. compute intensive parallel applications) that do not employ an object-oriented programming style.

At least two early S-DSM systems provided support for heterogeneous machine types. Toronto's Mermaid system [25] allowed data to be shared across more than one type of machine, but only among processes created as part of a single run-to-completion parallel program. All data in the same VM page was required to have the same type, and only one memory model—sequential consistency—was supported. CMU's Agora system [5] supported sharing among more loosely-coupled processes, but in a significantly more restricted fashion than in InterWeave. Pointers and recursive types were not supported, all shared data had to be accessed indirectly through a local mapping table, and only a single memory model (similar to processor consistency) was supported.

Friedman [12] and Agrawal et al. [2] have shown how to combine certain pairs of consistency models in a non-version-based system. Alonso et al. [3] present a general system for relaxed, user-controlled coherence. Khazana [7] also proposes the use of multiple consistency models. The TACT system of Yu et al. [24] allows coherence and consistency requirements to vary continuously in three orthogonal dimensions. Several of InterWeave's built-in coherence models are similarly continuous, but because our goal is to reduce read bandwidth and latency, rather than to increase availability (concurrency) for writes, we insist on strong se-

mantics for writer locks. To the best of our knowledge, InterWeave is the first system to provide a general framework in which the user can define application-specific coherence models.

6   Conclusions and Future Work

We have described a run-time system, InterWeave, that allows processes to access shared data transparently using ordinary reads and writes. InterWeave is, to the best of our knowledge, the first such system to seamlessly and efficiently span the spectrum from hardware cache coherence within SMP nodes, through software distributed shared memory on tightly-coupled clusters, to relaxed, version-based coherence across the Internet. It is also, we believe, the first to fully support shared memory across heterogeneous machine types and languages.

We have demonstrated the efficiency and ease of use of the system through an evaluation on both real applications and artificial benchmarks. Experience to date indicates that users find the API conceptually appealing, and that it allows them to build new programs significantly more easily than they can with RPC or other message passing paradigms. For applications in which RPC-style function shipping is required for good performance, InterWeave provides enhanced functionality via genuine reference parameters.

Quantitative measurements indicate that InterWeave is able to provide sharing in a distributed environment with minimal impact on the performance of more tightly-coupled sharing. InterWeave facilitates the use of relaxed coherence and consistency models that take advantage of application-specific knowledge to greatly reduce communication costs, and that are much more difficult to implement in hand-written message-passing code. We are actively collaborating with colleagues in our own and other departments to employ InterWeave in three principal application domains: remote visualization and steering of high-end simulations (enhancing the Astroflow visualization described in Section 4.2), incremental interactive data mining (Section 4.1), and human-computer collaboration in richly instrumented physical environments.

Acknowledgments

Srinivasan Parthasarathy developed the InterAct system, and participated in many of the early design discussions for InterWeave. Eduardo Pinheiro wrote an earlier version of InterWeave's heterogeneity management code. We are grateful to Amy Murphy and Chen Ding for their insightful suggestions on the content of this paper.

References

[1] S. V. Adve and M. D. Hill. A Unified Formulation of Four Shared-Memory Models. *IEEE Trans. on Parallel and Distributed Systems*, 4(6):613–624, June 1993.

[2] D. Agrawal, M. Choy, H. V. Leong, and A. K. Singh. Mixed Consistency: A Model for Parallel Programming. In *Proc. of the 13th ACM Symp. on Principles of Distributed Computing*, Los Angeles, CA, Aug. 1994.

[3] R. Alonso, D. Barbara, and H. Garcia-Molina. Data Caching Issues in an Information Retrieval System. *ACM Trans. on Database Systems*, 15(3):359–384, Sept. 1990.

[4] C. Amza, A. Cox, S. Dwarkadas, and W. Zwaenepoel. Software DSM Protocols that Adapt between Single Writer and Multiple Writer. In *Proc. of the 3rd Intl. Symp. on High Performance Computer Architecture*, San Antonio, TX, Feb. 1997.

[5] R. Bisiani and A. Forin. Multilanguage Parallel Programming of Heterogeneous Machines. *IEEE Trans. on Computers*, 37(8):930–945, Aug. 1988.

[6] J. B. Carter, J. K. Bennett, and W. Zwaenepoel. Implementation and Performance of Munin. In *Proc. of the 13th ACM Symp. on Operating Systems Principles*, pages 152–164, Pacific Grove, CA, Oct. 1991.

[7] J. Carter, A. Ranganathan, and S. Susarla. Khazana: An Infrastructure for Building Distributed Services. In *Intl. Conf. on Distributed Computing Systems*, pages 562–571, May 1998.

[8] D. Chen, S. Dwarkadas, S. Parthasarathy, E. Pinheiro, and M. L. Scott. InterWeave: A Middleware System for Distributed Shared State. In *Proc. of the 5th Workshop on Languages, Compilers, and Run-time Systems for Scalable Computers*, Rochester, NY, May 2000.

[9] D. Chen, C. Tang, X. Chen, S. Dwarkadas, and M. L. Scott. Beyond S-DSM: Shared State for Distributed Systems. TR 744, Computer Science Dept., Univ. of Rochester, Mar. 2001.

[10] G. Delamarter, S. Dwarkadas, A. Frank, and R. Stets. Portable Parallel Programming on Emerging Platforms. *Current Science Journal*, 78(7), Indian Academy of Sciences, Apr. 2000.

[11] P. Ferreira, M. Shapiro, X. Blondel, O. Fambon, J. Garcia, S. Kloosterman, N. Richer, M. Roberts, F. Sandakly, G. Coulouris, J. Dollimore, P. Guedes, D. Hagimont, and S. Krakowiak. PerDiS: Design, Implementaiton, and Use of a PERsistent DIstributed Store. Research Report 3525, INRIA, Rocquencourt, France, Oct. 1998.

[12] R. Friedman. Implementing Hybrid Consistency with High-Level Synchronization Operations. In *Proc. of the 12th ACM Symp. on Principles of Distributed Computing*, Ithaca, NY, Aug. 1993.

[13] A. S. Grimshaw and W. A. Wulf. Legion — A View from 50,000 Feet. In *Proc. of the 5th Intl. Symp. on High Performance Distributed Computing*, Aug. 1996.

[14] R. Kordale, M. Ahamad, and M. Devarakonda. Object Caching in a CORBA Compliant System. *Computing Systems*, 9(4):377–404, Fall 1996.

[15] S. Parthasarathy and S. Dwarkadas. InterAct: Virtual Sharing for Interactive Client-Server Applications. In *4th Workshop on Languages, Compilers, and Run-time Systems for Scalable Computers*, May 1998.

[16] S. Parthasarathy, M. J. Zaki, M. Ogihara, and S. Dwarkadas. Incremental and Interactive Sequence Mining. In *Intl. Conf. on Information and Knowledge Management*, Nov. 1999.

[17] A. Singla, U. Ramachandran, and J. Hodgins. Temporal Notions of Synchronization and Consistency in Beehive. In *Proc. of the 9th Annual ACM Symp. on Parallel Algorithms and Architectures*, Newport, RI, June 1997.

[18] R. Srikant and R. Agrawal. Mining Sequential Patterns. IBM Research Report RJ9910, IBM Almaden Research Center, Oct. 1994. Expanded version of paper presented at the Intl. Conf. on Data Engineering, Taipei, Taiwan, Mar. 1995.

[19] R. Stets, S. Dwarkadas, N. Hardavellas, G. Hunt, L. Kontothanassis, S. Parthasarathy, and M. Scott. Cashmere-2L: Software Coherent Shared Memory on a Clustered Remote-Write Network. In *Proc. of the 16th ACM Symp. on Operating Systems Principles*, St. Malo, France, Oct. 1997.

[20] R. Stets, S. Dwarkadas, L. I. Kontothanassis, U. Rencuzogullari, and M. L. Scott. The Effect of Network Total Order, Broadcast, and Remote-Write Capability on Network-Based Shared Memory Computing. In *Proc. of the 6th Intl. Symp. on High Performance Computer Architecture*, Toulouse, France, Jan. 2000.

[21] C. Tang, D. Chen, S. Dwarkadas, and M. L. Scott. Support for Machine and Language Heterogeneity in a Distributed Shared State System. Submitted for publication, May 2002. Expanded version available as TR 783, Computer Science Dept., Univ. of Rochester.

[22] M. van Steen, P. Homburg, and A. S. Tanenbaum. Globe: A Wide-Area Distributed System. In *IEEE Concurrency*, pages 70–78, Jan.-Mar. 1999.

[23] P. R. Wilson. Pointer Swizzling at Page Fault Time: Efficiently and Compatibly Supporting Huge Address Spaces on Standard Hardware. In *International Workshop on Object Orientation in Operating Systems*, page 244ff, Paris, France, Sept. 1992.

[24] H. Yu and A. Vahdat. Design and Evaluation of a Continuous Consistency Model for Replicated Services. In *Proc. of the 4th Symp. on Operating Systems Design and Implementation*, San Diego, CA, Oct. 2000.

[25] S. Zhou, M. Stumm, K. Li, and D. Wortman. Heterogeneous Distributed Shared Memory. In *IEEE Trans. on Parallel and Distributed Systems*, pages 540–554, 1992.

Honey, I Shrunk the Beowulf!*

W. Feng[†], M. Warren[‡], E. Weigle[†]
{feng, msw, ehw}@lanl.gov

[†] Computer & Computational Sciences Division
[‡] Theoretical Physics Division

Los Alamos National Laboratory
Los Alamos, NM 87545

Abstract

In this paper, we present a novel twist on the Beowulf cluster — the Bladed Beowulf. Designed by RLX Technologies and integrated and configured at Los Alamos National Laboratory, our Bladed Beowulf consists of compute nodes made from commodity off-the-shelf parts mounted on motherboard blades measuring 14.7″× 4.7″× 0.58″. Each motherboard blade (node) contains a 633-MHz Transmeta TM5600™CPU, 256-MB memory, 10-GB hard disk, and three 100-Mb/s Fast Ethernet network interfaces. Using a chassis provided by RLX, twenty-four such nodes mount side-by-side in a vertical orientation to fit in a rack-mountable 3U space, i.e., 19″ in width and 5.25″ in height.

A Bladed Beowulf can reduce the total cost of ownership (TCO) of a traditional Beowulf by a factor of three while providing Beowulf-like performance. Accordingly, rather than use the traditional definition of price-performance ratio where price is the cost of acquisition, we introduce a new metric called ToPPeR: Total Price-Performance Ratio, where total price encompasses TCO. We also propose two related (but more concrete) metrics: performance-space ratio and performance-power ratio.

Keywords: Beowulf, cluster, blade server, RLX, Transmeta, code morphing, VLIW, NAS benchmarks, price-performance ratio, ToPPeR, performance-space ratio, performance-power ratio, n-body code, treecode.

1 Introduction

In a relatively short time, Beowulf clusters [9, 12] have revolutionized the way that scientists approach high-performance computing. In contrast to tightly-coupled supercomputers, Beowulfs primarily use commodity off-the-shelf (COTS) technologies to deliver computational cycles at the lowest price, where price is defined as the cost of acquisition. However, when price is defined as the total cost of ownership (TCO), the advantages of Beowulfs, while still apparent, are not as compelling due to the added costs of system integration, administration, and maintenance (although many software tools have become available to reduce the impact of these added costs).

In this paper, we present our novel "Bladed Beowulf" cluster. Designed by RLX Technologies and integrated and configured at Los Alamos National Laboratory, our Bladed Beowulf cluster consists of compute nodes made from COTS parts mounted on motherboard blades called RLX ServerBlades™ (see Figure 1). Each motherboard blade (node) contains a 633-MHz Transmeta TM5600™ CPU [5], 256-MB memory, 10-GB hard disk, and three 100-Mb/s Fast Ethernet network interfaces. Twenty-four such ServerBlades mount into a chassis, shown in Figure 2, to form a "Bladed Beowulf" called the RLX System 324™ that fits in a rack-mountable 3U space, i.e., 19″ in width and 5.25″ in height.[1]

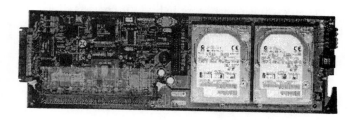

Figure 1. The RLX ServerBlade

*This work was supported by the U.S. Dept. of Energy's *Los Alamos Computer Science Institute* and *Information Architecture - Linux* Programs through Los Alamos National Laboratory contract W-7405-ENG-36. Also available as Los Alamos Unclassified Report 02-1210, March 2002.

[1]While the blade-to-chassis interface is RLX proprietary, the remainder of the cluster is COTS. However, a recent announcement (Feb. 5, 2002) by HP provides for an open enhancement of the CompactPCI (cPCI) specification to standardize blade servers across manufacturers.

Figure 2. The RLX System 324

The rest of the paper is organized as follows. In Section 2, we discuss the architecture and technology behind our Bladed Beowulf. Next, Section 3 presents the performance evaluation of our Bladed Beowulf via a gravitational microkernel benchmark, an N-body parallel simulation, NAS parallel benchmarks, and a treecode benchmark. With these performance numbers in hand, we then propose a new performance metric for the high-performance computing community — Total Price-Performance Ratio (ToPPeR), where Total Price encompasses the total cost of ownership — and discuss two related metrics, namely performance-space ratio and performance-power ratio.

2 Architecture of a Bladed Beowulf

The Crusoe family of processors takes a radically different approach to microprocessor design. In contrast to the traditional transistor-laden, and hence, power-hungry CPUs from AMD and Intel, the Transmeta Crusoe TM5600 CPU is a software-hardware hybrid. It consists of a 128-bit VLIW hardware engine surrounded by a software layer called code morphing. This code morphing software (CMS) presents an x86 interface to the BIOS, operating system (OS), and applications.

2.1 VLIW Engine

Having CMS handle x86 compatibility frees hardware designers to create a very simple, high-performance VLIW engine with two integer units, a floating-point unit, a memory (load/store) unit, and a branch unit. Each of the integer units is a 7-stage pipeline, and the floating-point unit is a 10-stage pipeline.

In Transmeta's terminology, the Crusoe processor's VLIW is called a *molecule*. Each molecule can be 64 bits or 128 bits long and can contain up to four RISC-like instructions called *atoms*, which are executed in parallel. The format of the molecule directly determines how atoms get routed to functional units, thus greatly simplifying the decode and dispatch hardware. And unlike superscalar architectures, molecules are expected in order, eliminating the need for complex out-of-order hardware which currently accounts for approximately 20% of the transistor count in a superscalar architecture.

This last issue has resulted in the current crop of *complex* RISC chips. For instance, the MIPS R10000 and HP PA-8000 are arguably much more complex than today's standard CISC architecture — the Pentium II. Furthermore, because modern CPUs are more complex, have more transistors, and perform more functions than their early RISC predecessors, the hardware requires *lots* of power, and the more power a CPU draws, the hotter it gets. The hotter that a CPU gets, the more likely it will fail, and perhaps, cause other components to fail (which is what happens in our traditional Beowulf clusters). In fact, unpublished (but reliable) empirical data from two leading vendors indicates that the failure rate of a component doubles for every 10°-C increase in temperature.

Due to the complexity of the x86 instruction set, the decode and dispatch hardware in superscalar out-of-order x86 processors (such as the Pentium 4) require a large number of transistors that increase power consumption significantly. At load, the Transmeta TM5600 and Pentium 4 CPUs generate approximately 6 and 75 watts, respectively, while an Intel IA-64 generates over 130 watts![2] Because of this substantial difference, the TM5600 requires no active cooling whereas a Pentium 4 (and most definitely, an Intel IA-64) processor can heat to the point of failure if it is not aggressively cooled. Consequently, as in our Bladed Beowulf (24 CPUs in a 3U), Transmetas can be packed closely together with no active cooling, thus resulting in a tremendous savings in the total cost of ownership with respect to reliability, electrical usage, cooling requirements, and space usage.

The current generation of Crusoe processors *eliminates* roughly 75% of the transistors traditionally found in all-hardware CPU designs to dramatically reduce power requirements and die size. CMS then "replaces" the functionality that the eliminated transistors would have provided. And because CMS typically resides in standard flash ROMs on the motherboard, improved versions can be downloaded into already-deployed CPUs. This ability to change CMS provides two huge advantages over traditional microprocessor fabrication. First, optimizing and fixing bugs amounts

---

[2]At the end of 2001, the fastest Crusoe CPU (i.e., TM5800) at load dissipated less than 1 watt (on average) with a 366-MHz TM5800 and approximately 2.5 watts (on average) with an 800-MHz TM5800 [2].

to replacing CMS in Transmetas whereas it may result in a costly hardware re-design and/or re-fabrication in Intels and AMDs. Second, changing to a different instruction set, e.g., from x86 to SPARC, simply involves a change in CMS rather than a complete change from one hardware microprocessor to another.

2.2 Code Morphing Software (CMS)

While the VLIW's native instruction set bears no resemblance to the x86 set, the CMS layer gives x86 programs the illusion that they are running on x86 hardware. That is, CMS dynamically "morphs" x86 instructions into VLIW instructions.

CMS consists of two main modules that work in tandem to create the illusion of running on an x86 processor: (1) the interpreter and (2) the translator. The interpreter module interprets x86 instructions one at a time, filters infrequently executed code from being needlessly optimized, and collects run-time statistical information about the x86 instruction stream to decide if optimizations are necessary.

When CMS detects critical and frequently used x86 instruction sequences, CMS invokes the translator module to re-compile the x86 instructions into optimized VLIW instructions called *translations*. These native translations reduce the number of instructions executed by packing atoms into VLIW molecules, thus resulting in better performance.

Caching the translations in a *translation cache* allows CMS to re-use translations. When a previously translated x86 instruction sequence is encountered, CMS skips the translation process and executes the cached translation directly out of the translation cache. Thus, caching and re-using translations exploits the locality of instruction streams such that the initial cost of the translation is amortized over repeated executions.

2.3 The RLX System 324: Bladed Beowulf

The RLX System 324 comes in three sets of easy-to-integrate pieces: the 3U system chassis, 24 ServerBlades, and bundled cables for communication and power.

The system chassis fits in the industry-standard 19-inch rack cabinet and measures 5.25″ high, 17.25″ wide, and 25.2″ deep. It features two hot-pluggable 450-watt power supplies that provide power load-balancing and auto-sensing capability for added reliability. Its system midplane integrates the system power, management, and network signals across all RLX ServerBlades. The ServerBlade connectors on the midplane completely eliminate the need for internal system cables and enable efficient hot-pluggable ServerBlade support.

The chassis also includes two sets of cards: the Management Hub card and the Network Connect cards. The former provides connectivity from the management network

interface of each RLX ServerBlade to the external world. Consolidating 24 ServerBlade management networks in the hub card to one "RJ45 out" enables system management of the entire chassis through a single standard Ethernet cable. The latter provides connectivity to the public and private network interfaces of each RLX ServerBlade.

3 Experimental Study

We evaluate our Bladed Beowulf (internally dubbed *MetaBlade*, or short for Trans*meta*-based *blade*s) in four contexts. First, we use a gravitational microkernel benchmark based on an N-body simulation to evaluate the performance of instruction-level parallelism in commodity off-the-shelf processors — two of which are comparably clocked to the 633-MHz Transmeta TM5600 (i.e., 500-MHz Intel Pentium III and 533-MHz Compaq Alpha EV56) and two others which are not (i.e., 375-MHz IBM Power3 and 1200-MHz AMD Athlon MP). Second, we run a full-scale N-body simulation to obtain a Gflop rating for our *MetaBlade* Bladed Beowulf and take a brief look at the scalability of the simulation code on *MetaBlade*. Third, we use the NAS Parallel Benchmarks (NPB) 2.3 [1] to evaluate the task-level parallelism of the above processors. And lastly, we run a treecode simulation to compare the performance of *MetaBlade* to past and current clusters and supercomputers.

3.1 Experimental Set-Up

Our *MetaBlade* Beowulf cluster consists of twenty-four compute nodes with each node containing a 633-MHz Transmeta TM5600 CPU (100% x86 compatible), 256-MB SDRAM, 10-GB hard disk, and 100-Mb/s network interface. We connect each compute node to a 100-Mb/s Fast Ethernet switch, resulting in a cluster with a star topology.

3.2 Gravitational Microkernel Benchmark

The most time-consuming part of an N-body simulation is computing components of the accelerations of particles. For example, the x-component of the acceleration for particle j under the gravitational influence of particle k is given by

$$\frac{Gm_k(x_j - x_k)}{r^3} \quad (1)$$

where G is the gravitational constant, m_k is the mass of particle k, and r is the separation between the particles, i.e.,

$$r = \sqrt{(x_j - x_k)^2 + (y_j - y_k)^2 + (z_j - z_k)^2} \quad (2)$$

Evaluating $r^{-3/2}$ is the slowest part of computing the acceleration, particularly when the square root must be performed in software.

Because of the importance of the above calculation to our N-body codes at Los Alamos National Laboratory, we evaluate the instruction-level parallelism of the Transmeta TM5600 using two different implementations of a reciprocal square root function. The first implementation uses the *sqrt* function from a math library while the second implementation uses Karp's algorithm [4]: table lookup, Chebychev polynomial interpolation, and Newton-Raphson iteration. To simulate Eq. (1) in the context of an N-body simulation (and coincidentally, enhance the confidence interval of our floating-point evaluation), our microkernel benchmark loops 500 times over the reciprocal square-root calculation.

Table 1 shows the Mflops ratings for five commodity processors over the two different implementations of the gravitational microkernel benchmark. Considering that the Transmeta TM5600 is a software-hardware hybrid and the other CPUs are all-hardware designs, the Transmeta performs quite well. In the "Math *sqrt*" benchmark, the Transmeta performs as well as (if not better than) the Intel and Alpha, relative to clock speed. The performance of the Transmeta suffers a bit with the "Karp *sqrt*" benchmark, primarily because the other processor implementations of the code have been optimized to their respective architectures whereas the Transmeta was not due to the lack of knowledge on the internal details of the Transmeta TM5600.

Processor	Math *sqrt*	Karp *sqrt*
500-MHz Intel Pentium III	87.6	137.5
533-MHz Compaq Alpha EV56	76.2	178.5
633-MHz Transmeta TM5600	115.0	144.6
375-MHz IBM Power3	298.5	379.1
1200-MHz AMD Athlon MP	350.7	452.5

Table 1. Mflop Ratings on an Gravitational Microkernel Benchmark

3.3 Gravitational N-body Simulation

Raw Performance Benchmark: In November 2001, we ran a simulation with 9, 753, 824 particles on the 24 processors of our Bladed Beowulf (i.e., *MetaBlade*) for about 1000 timesteps. The latter half of the simulation was performed on the showroom floor of the SC 2001 conference. Figure 3 shows an image of this simulation. Overall, the simulation completed about 1.3×10^{15} floating-point operations sustaining a rate of 2.1 Gflops during the entire simulation.[3] With a peak rating of 15.2 Gflops, this real application code running on our Bladed Beowulf achieves 2.1 / 15.2 = 14% of peak.

---

[3]We achieved a 3.3-Gflop rating when running the simulation on *MetaBlade2*, a 24-processor chassis with 800-MHz Transmetas and a newer version of CMS, i.e., 4.3.x., courtesy of RLX Technologies.

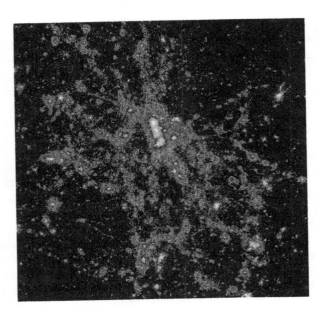

Figure 3. Intermediate Stage of a Gravitational N-body Simulation with 9.7 Million Particles.
The region shown is about 150 million light years across.

Scalability Benchmark: Here we run our N-body simulation code on different numbers of processors to evaluate the scalability of the simulation code over our *MetaBlade* Bladed Beowulf. Table 2 shows the results of these runs.

The scalability results for our Bladed Beowulf are in line with those for traditional clusters. And although the N-body code is highly parallel, the communication overhead is enough to cause the drop in efficiency.

# CPUs	Time (sec)	Speed-Up
1	1367.22	1.00
2	713.60	1.92
4	368.50	3.71
8	210.45	6.50
16	112.71	12.13
24	78.91	17.33

Table 2. Scalability of an N-body Simulation on the *MetaBlade* Bladed Beowulf

3.4 NAS Parallel Benchmarks

The results shown in Table 3 use the NAS Parallel Benchmarks, Version 2.3 [1]. These benchmarks, based on Fortran 77 and the MPI standard, approximate the performance that a typical user can expect for a portable parallel program on a distributed memory computer.

Briefly, the benchmarks are

- BT: simulated computational-fluid dynamics (CFD) application that solves block-tridiagonal systems of 5x5 blocks.

- SP: simulated CFD application that solves scalar pentadiagonal systems.

- LU: simulated CFD application that solves a block lower triangular-block upper triangular system of equations.

- MG: multigrid method to compute the solution of the three-dimensional scalar Poisson equation.

- EP: embarrassingly parallel benchmark to generate random numbers.

- IS: parallel sort over small integers.

Code	Athlon MP	Pentium 3	TM5600	Power3
BT	191.9	71.9	65.9	180.5
SP	167.6	52.7	43.6	155.6
LU	206.3	78.1	80.2	387.3
MG	180.1	41.9	61.6	249.3
EP	4.7	1.4	1.4	3.9
IS	36.4	6.6	12.4	11.0

Table 3. Single Processor Performance (Mops) for Class W NPB 2.3 Benchmarks.

Based on these results, we see that the 633-MHz Transmeta Crusoe TM5600 performs as well as the 500-MHz Intel Pentium III and about one-third as well as the Athlon and Power3 processors.

3.5 Treecode Benchmark

In this section, we run a treecode benchmark on our *MetaBlade* and *MetaBlade2* Bladed Beowulf clusters and compare it to the historical performance of the benchmark running on other Beowulf clusters and supercomputers.

3.5.1 Background on the Treecode Library

N-body methods are widely used in a variety of computational physics algorithms where long-range interactions are important. Several proposed methods allow N-body simulations to be performed on arbitrary collections of bodies in $O(N)$ or $O(N \log N)$ time. These methods represent a system of N bodies in a hierarchical manner by the use of a spatial tree data structure, hence the "treecode" connotation.

Isolating the elements of data management and parallel computation in a treecode library dramatically reduces the amount of programming required to implement a particular physical simulation [10]. For instance, only 2500

lines of code external to the library are required to implement a gravitational N-body simulation. The vortex particle method [7] requires only 2500 lines interfaced to the same treecode library. Smoothed particle hydrodynamics [11] takes 3000 lines. As a point of comparison, the treecode library itself runs nearly 20,000 lines of code.

3.5.2 Treecode Benchmark Results

Table 4 shows the relative placing of the *MetaBlade* (633-MHz Transmetas with CMS 4.2.x) and *MetaBlade2* (800-MHz Transmetas with CMS 4.3.x) Bladed Beowulfs with respect to Mflops/processor. The latter only places behind the SGI Origin 2000 supercomputer. So, although the RLX System 324 was designed for web-server farms, it demonstrates prowess as a supercomputing cluster. Per processor, the performance of the Transmeta Crusoe TM5600 is about twice that of the Intel Pentium Pro 200 which was used in the Loki Beowulf cluster that won the Gordon Bell price/performance prize in 1997 [12] and performs about the same as the 533-MHz Compaq Alpha processors used in the Avalon cluster.

Machine	CPU	Gflop	Mflop/proc
LANL SGI Origin 2000	64	13.10	205.0
SC'01 MetaBlade2	24	3.30	138.0
LANL Avalon	128	16.16	126.0
LANL MetaBlade	24	2.10	87.5
LANL Loki	16	1.28	80.0
NAS IBM SP-2(66/W)	128	9.52	74.4
SC'96 Loki+Hyglac	32	2.19	68.4
Sandia ASCI Red	6800	464.9	68.4
Caltech Naegling	96	5.67	59.1
NRL TMC CM-5E	256	11.57	45.2
Sandia ASCI Red	4096	164.3	40.1
JPL Cray T3D	256	7.94	31.0

Table 4. Historical Performance of Treecode on Clusters and Supercomputers

4 Performance Metrics

Although Hennessy and Patterson [3] have shown the pitfalls of using processor clock speed, instructions per second (ips), and floating-point operations per second (flops) as performance metrics, scientists still tend to evaluate the performance of computing platforms based on floating-point operations per second (and even worse, some scientists compare processor clock speeds across different families of processors) despite the introduction of benchmark suites such as NAS [1] and SPEC [6]. In fact, since June

1993, the most prominent benchmarking list in the high-performance computing community has been the Top500 list at http://www.top500.org. This list is based on the "flop" rating of a single benchmark, i.e., Linpack, which solves a dense system of linear equations.

4.1 The ToPPeR Metric

The use of "flops" remains and will continue. Even at SC, the world's premier supercomputing conference, the Gordon Bell Awards are based on performance (where performance is measured in "flops") and price-performance ratio (where price is the cost of acquisition and performance is in "flops"). In contrast, we propose a new (but related) performance metric: <u>to</u>tal <u>p</u>rice-<u>p</u>erformance <u>r</u>atio (ToPPeR) where total price is the total cost of ownership.

Our *MetaBlade* Bladed Beowulf turns out to be approximately twice as expensive as a similarly performing traditional Beowulf cluster. So, based solely on price-performance ratio (where price encompasses only the cost of acquisition), there exists no reason to use a Bladed Beowulf other than for its novelty. However, we argue that there is more to price than just the cost of acquisition, and hence, propose the notion of <u>T</u>otal <u>P</u>rice-<u>P</u>erformance <u>R</u>atio (ToPPeR) where total price encompasses the total cost of ownership. We will demonstrate that the ToPPeR metric for Bladed Beowulf clusters is a factor of three times better than traditional Beowulf clusters.

Total cost of ownership (TCO) refers to all the expenses related to buying, owning, and maintaining a computer system within an organization. We break TCO into two components: acquisition cost (AC) and operating cost (OC), i.e., TCO = AC + OC.

The AC simply consists of hardware costs (HWC) and software costs (SWC), i.e., AC = HWC + SWC. This cost is generally a *fixed, one-time* cost at the time of purchase. The OC, however, is much more difficult to quantify as it tends to be highly variable and recurring; this cost includes, but is not necessarily limited to, system-administration costs (SAC) such as installation, configuration, maintenance, upgrading, and support, power-consumption costs (PCC), space-consumption costs (SCC), and downtime costs (DTC).[4] The system administration costs (SAC) of a Beowulf cluster can be particularly onerous as they involve the recurring costs of labor and materials.

In sum, using the notation defined above, we propose the following equations as steps towards defining the total cost

---

of ownership in high-performance computing.

$$TCO = AC + OC$$

where

$$AC = HWC + SWC$$
$$OC = SAC + PCC + SCC + DTC$$

and

$$SAC = \sum \text{labor costs} + \sum \text{recurring material costs}$$

Table 5 presents a summary of the total cost of ownership (TCO) on five comparably-equipped, 24-node clusters based on AMD Athlons, Compaq/DEC Alphas, Intel Pentium IIIs (PIIIs) and Pentium 4s (P4s), and Transmeta Crusoe TM5600s, respectively, where each compute node has a 500 to 650-MHz CPU, 256-MB memory, and 10-GB hard disk. The exception is the Pentium 4 CPU which can only be found at 1.3 GHz and above.

For the purposes of our TCO calculation, we assume that the operational lifetime of each cluster to be four years. Based on our own empirical data from our Bladed Beowulf and four traditional Beowulf clusters that support small application-code teams, the system administration cost (SAC) of a traditional Beowulf runs about $15K/year or $60K over four years when operating in typical office environment where the ambient temperature hovers around 75°-F. In contrast, our Bladed Beowulf (in a dusty 80°-F environment) has been highly reliable with zero hardware failures and zero software failures in nine months; this translates to zero additional labor and zero additional hardware costs. And if there were a failure, we would leverage the bundled management software to diagnose a hardware problem immediately. Our only system administration cost incurred thus far was the initial 2.5-hour assembly, installation, and configuration of our Bladed Beowulf; at $100/hour, that amounts to $250 in the first year. Although there have been no failures thus far, we will assume that one major failure will occur per year, e.g., a compute node fails. The cost of the replacement hardware and the labor to install it amounts to $1200/year. Thus, over a four-year period, SAC runs $5050.

We estimate the power drawing and cooling costs of the clusters based on the power dissipation of each node. For example, a complete Intel P4 node (with memory, disk, and network interface) generates about 85 watts under load, which translates to 2.04 kW for 24 nodes. Assuming a typical utility rate of $0.10/kWh over 8760 hours per year (or 35,040 hours over four years), the cost runs $7,148. In addition, the traditional Beowulfs require power to cool the nodes from overheating, which typically amounts to half a watt per every watt dissipated, thus pushing the total

---

[4]Other OC components that may be seen more in an enterprise environment rather than a high-performance computing (HPC) environment include centralization, standardization, evaluation for re-investment, training, and auditing. In our calculation for TCO, we only use the OC components relevant to HPC but note that the calculation can be extended for other environments.

Cost Parameter	Alpha	Athlon	PIII	P4	TM5600
Acquisition	$17K	$15K	$16K	$17K	$26K
System Admin	$60K	$60K	$60K	$60K	$5K
Power & Cooling	$11K	$6K	$6K	$11K	$2K
Space	$8K	$8K	$8K	$8K	$2K
Downtime	$12K	$12K	$12K	$12K	$0K
TCO	$108K	$101K	$102K	$108K	$35K

Table 5. Total Cost of Ownership for a 24-node Cluster Over a Four-Year Period

power cost 50% higher to $10,722. In contrast, our 24-node *MetaBlade* Bladed Beowulf based on the Transmeta TM5600 dissipates 0.4 kW at load and requires no fans or active cooling, which results in a total power cost of $2,102 over four years.

Space costs are rarely considered in the TCO of a computer system. Given that Pittsburgh Supercomputing Center leased space from Westinghouse and spent $750,000 to renovate the facilities in order to house its new 6-Tflop Terascale Computing System [8], these costs ought to be included as part of the total cost of ownership. In our space-cost calculation, however, we make the more conservative assumption that space is being leased at a cost of $100 per square foot per year. For example, a 24-node Alpha cluster takes up 20 square feet, which translates to a four-year space cost of $8000, whereas the 24-node Bladed Beowulf takes up 6 square feet for a four-year cost of $2400.[5]

Based on how supercomputing centers charge for time on their clusters and supercomputers, we can estimate the cost of downtime based on the amount of lost revenue. We assume a conservative $5.00 charged per CPU hour (although a recent keynote speech at IEEE IPDPS 2001 indicates that the downtime cost per hour for a NYC stockbroker is $6,500,000). In the case of a 24-node cluster, these costs are relatively small even when we assume that a single failure causes the entire cluster to go down. Specifically, we experience a failure and subsequent four-hour outage (on average) every two months on traditional Beowulf clusters. Thus, the cost of the downtime is 96 hours over four years for the cluster; with 24 nodes, the total CPU downtime is 96 hours × 24 = 2304 hours. The total downtime cost is then $11,520. In contrast, our Bladed Beowulf has yet to fail after nine months of operation; so, the downtime cost has been $0 thus far. Assuming one failure will occur by the end of the year and is diagnosed in an hour using to the bundled management software, the annual downtime is one hour or four hours over four years for a total cost of $20.

For the five comparably-equipped and comparably-

performing, 24-node CPUs, the TCO on our *MetaBlade* Bladed Beowulf is approximately three times better than the TCO on a traditional Beowulf. In a larger-scale supercomputing environment, the results are even more dramatic, e.g., for a 240-node cluster, the space costs differ by a factor of 33. However, the biggest problem with this metric is identifying the hidden costs in the operational costs; furthermore, the magnitude of most of these operational costs is institution-specific. To address this issue more definitively, we propose two related (but more concrete) metrics — performance/space ratio and performance/power ratio — in the next section.

Before we do that, however, we conclude that with the TCO of our 24-node Bladed Beowulf being three times smaller than a traditional cluster and its performance being 75% of a comparably-clocked traditional Beowulf cluster; the ToPPeR value for our Bladed Beowulf is less than half that of a traditional Beowulf. In other words, the total price-performance ratio for our Transmeta-based Bladed Beowulf is over twice as good as a traditional Beowulf.

4.2 Performance/Space

As we noted earlier, space costs money. Thus, it is important to simultaneously maximize performance and minimize space. This provides the motivation for the "performance/space" metric. With respect to this metric, Table 6 compares a traditional 128-node Beowulf called Avalon (which won the Gordon Bell price/performance award in 1998) with our 24-node *MetaBlade* (MB) Beowulf and a recently-ordered 240-node Bladed Beowulf (dubbed *Green Destiny* or GD) that would fit in the same footprint as *MetaBlade*, i.e., six square feet. Even without a rack full of RLX System 324s, our 24-node *MetaBlade* Beowulf beats the traditional Beowulf with respect to performance/space by a factor of two. With a fully-loaded rack of ten RLX System 324s and associated network gear, our *Green Destiny* Bladed Beowulf would result in an over twenty-fold improvement in the performance/space metric when compared to a traditional Beowulf.

---

[5]It is very important to note that if we were to scale up our Bladed Beowulf to 240 nodes, i.e., cluster in a rack, the cost per square foot over four years would *remain* at $2400 while the traditional Beowulfs' cost would increase ten-fold to $80,000, i.e., 33 times more expensive!

Machine	Avalon	MB	GD
Performance (Gflop)	16.2	2.1	21.0
Area (ft^2)	120	6	6
Perf/Space (Mflop/ft^2)	135	350	3500

Table 6. Performance-Space Ratio of a Traditional Beowulf vs. Bladed Beowulfs

Machine	Avalon	MB	GD
Performance (Gflop)	17.6	2.1	21.4
Power (kW)	18.0	0.52	5.2
Perf/Power (Gflop/kW)	0.98	4.12	4.12

Table 7. Performance-Power Ratio for a Traditional Beowulf vs. Bladed Beowulfs

4.3 Performance/Power

Because the electricity needed to power (and cool) machines costs money, we also introduce the "performance/power" metric. Table 7 shows that the Bladed Beowulfs outperform the traditional Beowulf by a factor of four with respect to this metric.

5 Conclusion

In this paper, we presented our *MetaBlade* Bladed Beowulf cluster. Although the acquisition cost of this cluster is approximately 50%-75% more than a comparably-equipped but traditional Beowulf cluster, our experiences and calculations predict that the total cost of ownership of a Transmeta-based Bladed Beowulf will be three times cheaper than a traditional Beowulf cluster. This observation prompted us to propose a new metric called ToPPeR: Total Price-Performance Ratio, where total price encompasses TCO.

The disparity in power dissipation and space usage as well as for ToPPeR will increase in size as Intel pushes forward with its even more voracious IA-64 while Transmeta moves in the other direction, i.e., even lower power consumption but competitive performance. For instance, the 800-MHz Transmeta Crusoe TM5800 that we demonstrated at SC 2001 (http://www.sc2001.org) alongside the 633-MHz Transmeta Crusoe TM5600 produces a "flop" rating of 3.3 Gflops (about 50% better than the 633-MHz TM5600) while generating only 3.5 watts per CPU. The TM6000, expected in volume in the last half of 2002, is expected to improve "flop" performance over the TM5800 by another factor of two to three while reducing power requirements in half again.

Acknowledgements

The authors wish to thank the DOE Los Alamos Computer Science Institute and Information Architecture - Linux Programs for supporting this project, IEEE/ACM SC 2001 and Los Alamos National Laboratory for providing a venue to garner visibility for an earlier version of the project, and Gordon Bell and Linus Torvalds for their encouragement on this endeavor.

This research is part of a larger project called *Supercomputing in Small Spaces*. For more information, go to http://sss.lanl.gov.

References

[1] D. Bailey, T. Harris, W. Saphir, R. van der Wijngaart, A. Woo, and M. Yarrow. The NAS Parallel Benchmarks 2.0. *The International Journal of Supercomputer Applications*, December 1995.

[2] D. Ditzel. The TM6000 Crusoe: 1-GHz x86 System on a Chip. 2001 Microprocessor Forum, October 2001.

[3] J. Hennessy and D. Patterson. *Computer Architecture: A Quantitative Approach*. Morgan Kaufmann Publishers, 1995.

[4] A. Karp. Speeding Up N-body Calculations on Machines Lacking a Hardware Square Root. *Scientific Programming*, 1(2), 1992.

[5] A. Klaiber. The Technology Behind Crusoe Processors. *White Paper*, January 2000.

[6] SPEC Newsletter. SPEC Benchmark Suite Release, 1990.

[7] J. Salmon, M. Warren, and G. Winckelmans. Fast Parallel Treecodes for Gravitational and Fluid Dynamical N-body Problems. *Intl. J. Supercomputer Appl.*, 8:129–142, 1994.

[8] B. Spice. Wiring, Air-Cooling Systems Go In As Assembly of Terascale Approaches: Setting the Stage for the Supercomputer. *The Pittsburgh Post-Gazette*, April 2001.

[9] T. Sterling, D. Becker, D. Savarese, J. Dorband, U. Ranawake, and C. Packer. Beowulf: A Parallel Workstation for Scientific Computation. In *Proc. of the Int'l Conf. on Parallel Processing (ICPP)*, August 1995.

[10] M. Warren and J. Salmon. A Parallel Hashed Oct-Tree N-Body Algorithm. In *Supercomputing '93*, November 1993.

[11] M. Warren and J. Salmon. A Portable Parallel Particle Program. *Computer Physics Communications*, 87:266–290, 1995.

[12] M. Warren, J. Salmon, D. Becker, M. Goda, T. Sterling, and G. Winckelmans. Pentium Pro Inside: I. A Treecode at 430 Gigaflops on ASCI Red, II. Price/Performance of $50/Mflop on Loki and Hyglac. In *Proc. of SC 1997*, November 1997. Gordon Bell Awards for Both Performance and Price/Performance.

Session 3A

Networks & Routers

Randomized Broadcast Channel Access Algorithms
for Ad Hoc Networks

Zhijun Cai   Mi Lu   Xiaodong Wang

Department of Electrical Engineering
Texas A&M University
College Station, TX 77843
PH: 979-845-9578, FAX: 979-845-2630, EMAIL: czjhh@ee.tamu.edu

Abstract

The problem of broadcast channel access in single-hop and multihop ad hoc networks is considered. Two novel randomized and distributed channel access algorithms are developed and analyzed for single-hop and multihop networks, respectively. These algorithms are designed based on maximizing the worst-case channel efficiency, by optimizing some key parameters, including the backoff probability distribution and the slot length. The proposed algorithm for single-hop networks offers significantly higher throughput than the CSMA methods when the traffic load is heavy, while still achieving good performance when the load is light or medium. The proposed algorithm for multihop networks can flexibly adapt to the traffic load, and offers much better throughput performance than the existing broadcast scheduling algorithms in light or medium load.

1   Introduction

An ad hoc network [1, 2] is a distributed system consisting of many mobile stations (MSs) with no predetermined topology and central control. The MSs in an ad hoc network communicate wirelessly in a self-organized manner. Efficient broadcast channel access is one of the fundamental problems for ad hoc networks. Considerable research has been done on this problem for both single-hop networks and multihop networks. In single-hop networks, since any MS can directly communicate with all other MSs, broadcast channel access is identical to the traditional medium access control (MAC). If an MS can transmit the packet successfully through the channel, all other MSs can receive the packet successfully. The typical existing methods include Aloha and Carrier Sensing Multiple Access (CSMA), etc. For the problem of broadcasting in multihop networks, to cope with the hidden terminal problem [1], a number of broadcast scheduling algorithms have been proposed [3, 4, 5]. In these methods, the time slots are pre-reserved by different MSs for broadcasting according to the scheduling algorithms. The problem of determining schedules with maximum throughput has been shown to be NP-complete [3, 5]. Since the slots are pre-reserved, the adaptivity of the scheme is poor, i.e., the maximum broadcast throughput of an MS is not adaptive to the network traffic load. Furthermore, most of the existing broadcast scheduling algorithms make use of the network topology information. When the topology changes, the previous schedule will expire, and a new schedule should be generated. Such a topology-dependent characteristic incurs significant overhead, especially in highly dynamic environments. In this paper, we develop randomized broadcast channel access algorithms for both single-hop and multihop ad hoc networks to maximize the worst-case channel efficiency. The rest of this paper is organized as follows. In Section 2, some background materials are given. The proposed randomized broadcast channel access methods for single-hop and multihop ad hoc networks are given and analyzed in Sections 3 and 4, respectively. Section 5 contains the conclusions.

2   Background

It is assumed that each MS in the ad hoc network is equipped with a single transceiver to communicate with other MSs and the transmission radius is identical. Due to the limited transmission radius, the packets may be relayed over multiple MSs before the destination MS is reached. The neighbors of an MS A are the MSs which can directly

---

[1] If one MS is in the range of the receiver, but not the transmitter, the MS is termed a *hidden terminal* to the transmitter.

communicate with A (within A's transmission range). The MSs are assumed to have the busy tone detection capability [6]. During its data transmission or reception, the MS can not detect the busy tone. Time is divided into equal-length slots, and the transmission channel is assumed to be error-free. Each slot is divided into the Sensing Period (SP), the Packet Period (PP) and the Acknowledgment Period (AP). The length of the PP is designed to accommodate one fixed-length data packet. When the MSs communicate, two types of conflicts may arise [7]. The primary conflict refers to the situation that when an MS transmits in a given slot, it cannot receive a packet in the same slot and vise versa. The secondary conflict refers to the situation that an MS can not receive more than one packets in one slot. In both cases, all packets are rendered useless [8]. The AP is used for busy tone transmission to acknowledge the broadcast packets, with a duration no less than the sum of maximum propagation delay and maximum transition time between the receiving state and the transmission state for an MS. Compared with the sum of the SP and the PP, the length of AP is negligible. Hence, the slot length is approximately the sum of the SP and the PP. Suppose that $X_1, X_2, \ldots, X_n$ are independent and identically distributed (i.i.d.) random variables with a probability density function (pdf) $f(x)$ and the corresponding cumulative distribution function (cdf) $F(x)$. Let $X_{(1)} \le X_{(2)} \le \ldots \le X_{(n)}$ be their ordered values. Then, the joint pdf of $X = X_{(j)}$ and $Y = X_{(k)}$, where $j < k$ is given by [9]

$$f_{jk}(x,y) = F(x)^{(j-1)} f(x) [F(y) - F(x)]^{(k-j-1)} f(y)$$
$$[1 - F(y)]^{(n-k)} \frac{n!}{(j-1)!(k-j-1)!(n-k)!}$$

for $x < y$.

3 Proposed Channel Access Algorithm for Single-hop Networks

Given an n-MS single-hop ad hoc network, any MS can directly communicate with other MSs; that is, any MS is a neighbor of all other MSs. Assume that the number of MSs in the network is upper bounded by U, and the data packet is of fixed length. In this paper, the packet length is normalized to 1. Denote β as the normalized SP length, and λ as the normalized maximum propagation delay in the network. Due to the limited transmission radius for the MSs in ad hoc networks, typically $\lambda \ll 1$. Denote $\tau = \frac{\lambda}{\beta}$, which represents the normalized maximum propagation delay with respect to the SP length.

3.1 Channel Access Algorithm

All the MSs that have packets in buffer will transmit over the channel *with probability* 1. For an MS that will transmit the packet in a certain slot, a backoff value δ will be generated following a predetermined pdf $g(x)$ on $[0, 1]$ (the determination of $g(x)$ will be discussed in Section 3.2). Then the MS will listen to the channel at time $\beta\delta$ (normalized value with respect to the packet length). If no carrier is detected, it will transmit the packet immediately. Otherwise, it will cancel the transmission attempt in the current slot. For an MS that does not transmit the packet during the slot, it should listen to the PP. If the packet collision occurs, the MS will transmit the busy tone in the AP. For an MS that transmits the packet during the slot, it should listen to the AP. If the busy tone is not detected, then the MS will realize that its packet has been successfully broadcast. The following distributed algorithm should be running in each MS.

Algorithm: Broadcast channel access algorithm for single-hop ad hoc networks ;

Determine the optimal $g(x)$;
for *Each slot* **do**
  if *Packet buffer is not empty* **then**
    Fetch the packet;
    Generate a backoff value δ following $g(x)$ on $[0, 1]$;
    Listen to the channel at time $\beta\delta$ (slot starts at time 0);
    if *No carrier is detected* **then**
      Transmit the packet immediately;
    else
      Cancel the packet transmission in this slot;
    end
  end
  if *I did not transmit the packet during this slot* **then**
    Listen to the slot;
    if *Packet collision occurs* **then**
      Transmit the busy tone in the AP;
    end
  end
  if *I have transmitted the packet during this slot* **then**
    Listen to the AP;
    if *No busy tone is detected* **then**
      Delete the packet from the packet buffer;
    else
      Keep the packet in the packet buffer;
    end
  end
end

3.2 Optimal Backoff pdf $g^*(x)$

Suppose the cdf of $g(x)$ is $G(x)$. During a certain slot, assume there are m MSs that will transmit the packets, and the backoff values they generate are $\delta_1, \delta_2, \ldots, \delta_m$.

Suppose the ordered values of the above m values are $\delta_{(1)}, \delta_{(2)}, \ldots, \delta_{(m)}$, with $\delta_{(1)} \leq \delta_{(2)} \leq \cdots \leq \delta_{(m)}$. Moreover, suppose the MS corresponding to $\delta_{(i)}$ is S_i.

If $\delta_{(2)} - \delta_{(1)} \geq \tau$, S_1 will transmit its packet successfully, since when S_i ($2 \leq i \leq m$) listens to the channel, the carrier can be detected, and S_i will cancel the packet transmission in this slot. Otherwise, a collision will occur. The probability that the slot is a successful slot when m MSs attempt to transmit in the slot is $P_s(m, g(x), \tau) = P(\delta_{(2)} - \delta_{(1)} \geq \tau)$ for $m \geq 2$ and is 1 for $m = 1$. By (1), the joint pdf of $\delta_{(1)}$ and $\delta_{(2)}$ is given by

$$f_{12}(x, y) = m(m-1)g(x)g(y)[1 - G(y)]^{m-2} .$$

Then we have

$$P_s(m, g(x), \tau) = \int_0^{1-\tau} \int_{x+\tau}^1 f_{12}(x, y) \, dy dx$$

$$= \begin{cases} 0, & \\ \quad \text{if } m \geq 2 \text{ and } \tau > 1, & \\ m \int_0^{1-\tau} g(x)[1 - G(x+\tau)]^{m-1} \, dx, & \\ \quad \text{if } m \geq 2 \text{ and } \tau \leq 1, & \\ 1, \text{ if } m = 1. & \end{cases}$$

Since if $\tau > 1$, for any $m \geq 2$, the slot success probability is 0, we are interested in the case $\tau \leq 1$ (the optimization of τ will be described in Section 3.3).

Given $g(x)$ and τ, since the slot success probability will decrease when the number of MSs attempting the slot increases, $P_s(m, g(x), \tau) \geq P_s(U, g(x), \tau), 1 \leq m \leq U$. We are interested in determining the optimal $g(x)$ to maximize the worst-case slot success probability, i.e.,

$$g^*(x) = \arg\max_{g(x)} P_s(U, g(x), \tau)$$

$$= \arg\max_{g(x)} \left(\int_0^{1-\tau} g(x)[1 - G(x+\tau)]^{U-1} \, dx \right) .$$

We should determine a suitable $g(x)$ family in order to simplify the above function optimization problem. The interested case is $U \geq 2$. When U is large, we would like most MSs to select larger backoff values, which makes the number of MSs selecting smaller backoff values fewer. Hence, the possibility that $\delta_{(2)} - \delta_{(1)} \geq \tau$ will be larger. In other words, when U is large, we would like the probability mass of $g(x)$ to adaptively concentrate on the vicinity close to 1 to increase the success probability. Moreover, the larger the value of U, the more the probability mass should concentrate on bigger backoff values. Hence, $g(x)$ should be adaptive to U, and have the capability to adaptively concentrate its probility mass on the vicinity close to 1. On the other hand, when U is small, for example, $U = 2$. We would like $g(x)$ close to the uniform distribution. Therefore, $g(x)$ should be a parameterized pdf on $[0, 1]$, which can adaptively change from uniform distribution to the pdf which concentrates its

major probability mass on the vicinity close to 1. A simple cdf family of the above natures is $G(x) = x^{r+1}$, $0 \leq x \leq 1$, where r is a non-negative real number. Therefore, we suggest to use the following backoff pdf

$$g(x) = (r+1)x^r, 0 \leq x \leq 1 \quad (1)$$

where r is a non-negative real number. Clearly, $g(x)$ in (1) is a pdf on $[0, 1]$, and when $r = 0$, $g(x)$ is the uniform pdf. With the increase of r, the probability mass of $g(x)$ will adaptively concentrate on the bigger backoff values. Hence, we can choose the parameter r adaptive to U and τ to maximize the worst-case slot success probability. Substituting (1) into (1), we obtain

$$r^* = \arg\max_r P_s(U, r, \tau)$$

$$= \arg\max_r \left((r+1) \int_0^{1-\tau} x^r [1 - (x+\tau)^{r+1}]^{U-1} \, dx \right)$$

For fixed U and τ, r^* can be obtained by numerically maximizing (2). Denote $P_s^*(U, \tau) \equiv \max_r P_s(U, r, \tau)$.

Figure 1 illustrates the relationship between m and $P_s(m, r, \tau)$ given $\tau = 0.01$, $r = 6$, $U = 1000$. It is seen that $P_s(m, r, \tau) \geq P_s(U, r, \tau) = 0.8345, 1 \leq m \leq U$. Interestingly, $P_s(m, r, \tau)$ is not very sensitive to m, which is a useful property for this application since it implies when the actual load is light, that our design based on the worst-case performance (i.e., $m = U$) will incur little attendant loss. In Figure 2, we illustrate the relationship between r and $P_s(U, r, \tau)$ given $\tau = 0.01$ and $U = 1000$. In this case, $r^* = 5.72$ and $P_s^*(U, \tau) = 0.8356$.

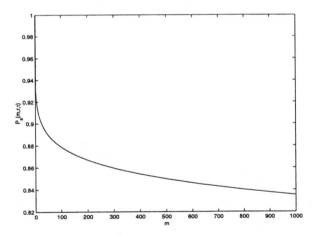

Figure 1: The relationship between m and $P_s(m, r, \tau)$ ($\tau = 0.01$, $r = 6$).

3.3 Optimal SP Length β^*

Given an ad hoc network, the transmission radius for an MS and the packet length can be determined, which means

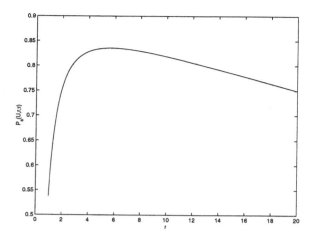

Figure 2: The relationship between r and $P_s(U, r, \tau)$ ($\tau = 0.01$, $U = 1000$).

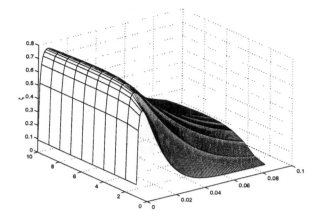

Figure 3: The Relationship between r, τ and ζ ($U = 1000$ and $\lambda = 0.001$).

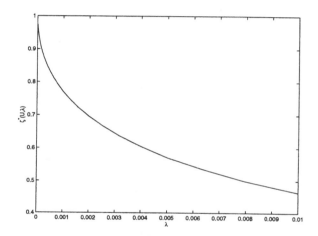

Figure 4: The Relationship between λ and $\zeta^*(U, \lambda)$ ($U = 1000$).

that λ can be determined. We next address the optimization of SP length β to maximize the worst-case slot efficiency. Given m, λ and τ, since $\tau = \frac{\lambda}{\beta}$, then $\beta = \frac{\lambda}{\tau}$, and the slot efficiency is given by

$$\zeta(m, \lambda, \tau) = \frac{P_s^*(m, \tau)}{\beta + 1} = \frac{P_s^*(m, \tau)\tau}{\lambda + \tau} , \qquad (2)$$

which measures the fraction of the slot used for successful data transmission.

For fixed U and λ, we choosed τ to maximize the worst-case slot efficiency $\zeta(U, \lambda, \tau)$

$$\tau^* = \arg\max_\tau \frac{P_s^*(U, \tau)\tau}{\lambda + \tau} . \qquad (3)$$

The optimal SP length is then

$$\beta^* = \frac{\lambda}{\tau^*} , \qquad (4)$$

and denote $\zeta^*(U, \lambda) \equiv \max_\tau \zeta(U, \lambda, \tau)$.

In Figure 3, when $U = 1000$ and $\lambda = 0.001$, the relationship between r, τ and ζ is illustrated. In this case, $r^* = 5.69$, $\tau^* = 0.0071$, $\beta^* = 0.1353$ and $\zeta^*(U, \lambda) = 0.7758$. In Figure 4, we illustrate the relationship between λ and $\zeta^*(U, \lambda)$ given $U = 1000$. As seen in Figure 4, $\zeta^*(U, \lambda)$ increases to its limit 1 as $\lambda \to 0$.

Typically, in ad hoc networks, due to the limited transmission radius for each MS, we have $\lambda \ll 1$. For example, assume packet length is 255 bytes, and the network bandwidth is $1M$ bps. Suppose the transmission radius is 100 meters. Then $\lambda \approx 0.00016$, and the corresponding $\zeta^*(U, \lambda) = 0.8997$ for $U = 1000$.

3.4 Comparisons with CSMA

Denote the offered load G as the average number of packets arrived at the network per unit time (recall that the packet length is normalized to 1, the unit time), and the throughput S as the average number of packets that are transmitted successfully per unit time in the network. Assume the offered load is uniformly distributed among all MSs. As discussed above, for fixed U and λ, we can obtain r^*, τ^* and β^* according to (2), (3) and (4) respectively. Since the normalized length of each slot is $1 + \beta^*$, given the slot success probability P_s, the throughput is then $\frac{P_s}{1+\beta^*}$. By determining the slot success probability, the throughput is given by

$$S = \begin{cases} \dfrac{P_s(\lceil \frac{G}{1+\beta^*} \rceil, r^*, \tau^*)}{1+\beta^*} , & \text{if } G \le \lfloor \frac{U}{1+\beta^*} \rfloor , \\ \dfrac{P_s(U, r^*, \tau^*)}{1+\beta^*} , & \text{if } G > \lceil \frac{U}{1+\beta^*} \rceil . \end{cases} \qquad (5)$$

We next compare the throughput performance of the proposed algorithm with the well known CSMA methods [10, 8]. In particular, for non-persistent slotted CSMA, the throughput is given by

$$S = \frac{\lambda G e^{-\lambda G}}{1 + \lambda - e^{-\lambda G}} ; \qquad (6)$$

and for non-persistent non-slotted CSMA, the throughput is given by

$$S = \frac{G e^{-\lambda G}}{(1 + 2\lambda)G + e^{-\lambda G}} . \qquad (7)$$

In Figure 5, the performance comparison between the proposed method and the different CSMA methods (non-persistent slotted CSMA and non-persistent non-slotted CSMA) is illustrated for $U = 10000, \lambda = 0.001$. It is seen that the proposed method offers much better performance when the load is heavy, while still keeping good performance under the light and medium load.

$$S = \begin{cases} G, & \text{if } G \leq 1, \\ 1, & \text{if } G > 1. \end{cases} \qquad (8)$$

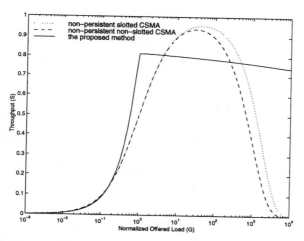

Figure 5: Performance comparison ($U = 10000, \lambda = 0.001$).

4 Proposed Channel Access Algorithm for Multi-hop Networks

In a multihop ad hoc network consisting of n MSs, the packets may be relayed over multiple MSs before the destination MS is reached. For a given MS A, if the shortest number of hops between A and a particular MS is equal to h, then that MS is an h-hop neighbor of A. Denote $\rho_h(A)$ as the set of all h-hop neighbors of A. The definitions of β, λ and τ are the same as those in Section 3.

When designing the broadcast channel access algorithm for multihop ad hoc networks, we should pay attention to

the hidden terminal problem [1, 6, 11, 12, 13]. The hidden terminals can lead to the increase of packet conflicts, since they can not sense the on-going data transmission. We next propose a randomized broadcast channel access method to maximize the worst-case channel efficiency for all MSs while still keeping good performance in the light and medium load.

4.1 Channel Access Algorithm

Two busy tones, a primary busy tone and a secondary busy tone with sufficient spectral separation, will be used in the proposed algorithm. During any slot, all the MSs that have packets in buffer will transmit over the channel *with probability* 1. For an MS that will transmit the packet in a certain slot, a backoff value δ will be generated following a predetermined pdf $g(x) = (r + 1)x^r$ on $[0, 1]$ (the determination of optimal r^* will be discussed in Section 4.2). Then the MS will listen to the channel at time $\beta\delta$ (normalized value with respect to the packet length). If no busy tone is detected, it will transmit the primary busy tone until the end of the SP, and will transmit the packet in the PP. If the primary busy tone is detected, the MS will transmit the secondary busy tone until the end of the SP, and will cancel the packet transmission in the PP. If the secondary busy tone is detected, the MS will cancel the packet transmission in the PP. If both busy tones are detected, the MS will transmit the secondary busy tone until the end of the SP, and will cancel the packet transmission in the PP. For an MS that does not transmit the packet during the slot, it should listen to the PP. If the packet collision occurs, the MS will transmit the primary busy tone in the AP. For an MS that transmits the packet during the slot, it should listen to the AP. If no busy tone is detected, the MS will conclude that its packet has been successfully broadcast; otherwise the packet is unsuccessful and will be retransmitted in later slots. Note that different from the algorithm for single-hop networks, here the packets are transmitted only in the PP. The following distributed algorithm should be running in each MS.

A successful packet transmission scenario is as follows. After an MS A transmits the primary busy tone, all the MSs in $\rho_1(A)$ will be aware of that, and each of them will transmit the secondary busy tone. Hence, all the MSs in $\rho_2(A)$ will cancel their data transmission in this slot, thus the hidden terminal problem is avoided (the MSs in $\rho_2(A)$ can not sense the primary busy tone). The primary busy tone is used for avoiding the primary conflict, and the secondary busy tone is used for avoiding the secondary conflict. Note that with only one busy tone the hidden terminal problem can not be resolved efficiently in the distributed environment. After all the MSs in $\rho_1(A)$ have received the packet successfully, they will remain silent during the AP. By sensing the AP, A will realize that its packet is successful.

Algorithm: Broadcast channel access algorithm for multihop networks ;

Determine the optimal r;
for *Each slot* **do**

  if *Packet buffer is not empty* **then**

    Fetch the packet;
    Generate a backoff value δ following $(r+1)x^r$ on $[0,1]$;
    Listen to the channel at time $\beta\delta$ (slot starts at time 0);
    switch *Listening* **do**

      case *No busy tone is detected*

        Transmit the primary busy tone until the end of the SP;
        Transmit the packet in the PP;

      case *The primary busy tone is detected*

        Transmit the secondary busy tone until the end of the SP;
        Cancel the packet transmission in this slot;

      case *Only the secondary busy tone is detected*

        Cancel the packet transmission in this slot;

    end

  end

  if *I did not transmit the packet during the slot* **then**

    Listen to the PP;
    if *Packet collision occurs* **then**

      Transmit the primary busy tone in the AP;

    end

  end

  if *I have transmitted the packet during the slot* **then**

    Listen to the AP;
    if *No busy tone is detected* **then**

      Delete the packet from the packet buffer;

    else

      Keep the packet in the packet buffer;

    end

  end

end

4.2 Optimal Backoff Parameter r^*

Assume an MS A will attempt to transmit in a given slot, and generate a backoff value δ_A. Suppose K_1 MSs in $\rho_1(A)$ and K_2 MSs in $\rho_2(A)$ attempt the same slot, and the backoff values are $\delta_1, \delta_2, \ldots, \delta_{K_1}$ and $\delta_1', \delta_2', \ldots, \delta_{K_2}'$. Denote $\delta_{\min} = \min_{1 \le i \le K_1} \delta_i$ and $\delta_{\min}' = \min_{1 \le i \le K_2} \delta_i'$. From the proposed algorithm, if $\delta_{\min} - \delta_A \ge \tau$ and $\delta_{\min}' - \delta_A \ge 2\tau$, A will broadcast its packet to all MSs in $\rho_1(A)$ successfully. By (1), and following the method in Section 3.2, the probability that A can broadcast its packet successfully in this slot is given by

$$
\begin{aligned}
&P_s \; (K_1, K_2, r, \tau) \\
&= P(\{\delta_{\min} - \delta_A \ge \tau\} \cap \{\delta_{\min}' - \delta_A \ge 2\tau\}) \\
&= \begin{cases}
1, & \text{if } K_1 = K_2 = 0, \\
0, & \text{if } K_1 \ge 1 \text{ and } \tau > 1, \\
0, & \text{if } K_2 \ge 1 \text{ and } \tau > 0.5, \\
(r+1)\int_0^{1-2\tau} x^r[1-(x+2\tau)^{r+1}]^{K_2}\, dx, \\
\qquad \text{if } K_1 = 0, K_2 \ge 1 \text{ and } \tau \le 0.5, \\
(r+1)\int_0^{1-\tau} x^r[1-(x+\tau)^{r+1}]^{K_1}\, dx, \\
\qquad \text{if } K_2 = 0, K_1 \ge 1 \text{ and } \tau \le 1, \\
(K_1+1)(K_2+1)(r+1)^2 \int_0^{1-2\tau} \\
x^r[1-(x+2\tau)^{r+1}]^{K_2}\, dx \\
\int_0^{1-\tau} x^r[1-(x+\tau)^{r+1}]^{K_1}\, dx/(K_1+K_2), \\
\qquad \text{otherwise}.
\end{cases}
\end{aligned} \tag{9}
$$

If $\tau > 0.5$, then $2\tau > 1$. For any $K_2 \ge 1$, $\delta_{\min}' - \delta_A < 1$, which implies the success probability is 0. We are interested in the case $\tau \le 0.5$ (the optimization of τ will be described in Section 4.3).

Denote γ_1 and γ_2 as the upper bounds of the number of 1-hop neighbors and 2-hop neighbors for all MSs [14, 15]. The success probability will decrease when the number of MSs attempting the slot increases, $P_s(K_1, K_2, r, \tau) \ge P_s(\gamma_1, \gamma_2, r, \tau)$, $0 \le K_1 \le \gamma_1$, $0 \le K_2 \le \gamma_2$. We are interested in determining the optimal r to maximize the worst-case slot success probability for any MS

$$
r^* = \arg\max_r P_s(\gamma_1, \gamma_2, r, \tau). \tag{10}
$$

For fixed γ_1, γ_2 and τ, r^* can be obtained by numerically maximizing (10), denote $P_s^*(\gamma_1, \gamma_2, \tau) \equiv \max_r P_s(\gamma_1, \gamma_2, r, \tau)$.

Figure 6 illustrates the relationship between K_1, K_2 and $P_s(K_1, K_2, r, \tau)$ given $\tau = 0.01$, $r = 3$, $\gamma_1 = 10$, $\gamma_2 = 60$. It is seen that $P_s(K_1, K_2, r, \tau) \ge P_s(\gamma_1, \gamma_2, r, \tau) = 0.0137$, $0 \le K_1 \le \gamma_1$, $0 \le K_2 \le \gamma_2$. In Figure 7, we illustrate the relationship between r and $P_s(\gamma_1, \gamma_2, r, \tau)$ given $\tau = 0.01$, $\gamma_1 = 10$ and $\gamma_2 = 60$. In this case, $r^* = 2.56$ and $P_s^*(\gamma_1, \gamma_2, \tau) = 0.0117$, which means that for any MS, the worst-case slot success probability is no less than 0.0117.

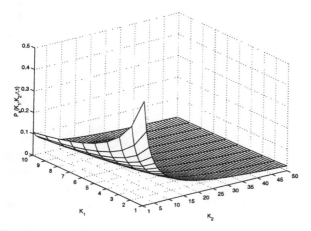

Figure 6: The relationship between K_1, K_2 and $P_s(K_1, K_2, r, \tau)$ ($\tau = 0.01$, $r = 3$).

4.3 Optimal SP Length β^*

Since $\tau = \frac{\lambda}{\beta}$, then $\beta = \frac{\lambda}{\tau}$. Given γ_1, γ_2 and τ, the maximum worst-case slot efficiency is

$$\zeta(\gamma_1, \gamma_2, \lambda, \tau) = \frac{P_s^*(\gamma_1, \gamma_2, \tau)}{\beta + 1} = \frac{P_s^*(\gamma_1, \gamma_2, \tau)\tau}{\lambda + \tau} . \quad (11)$$

For fixed γ_1, γ_2 and λ, we choose τ to maximize the worst-case slot efficiency $\zeta(\gamma_1, \gamma_2, \lambda, \tau)$

$$\tau^* = \arg\max_\tau \frac{P_s^*(\gamma_1, \gamma_2, \tau)\tau}{\lambda + \tau} . \quad (12)$$

The optimal SP length is then

$$\beta^* = \frac{\lambda}{\tau^*} , \quad (13)$$

and denote $\zeta^*(\gamma_1, \gamma_2, \lambda) \equiv \max_\tau \zeta(\gamma_1, \gamma_2, \lambda, \tau)$.

In Figure 8, given $\gamma_1 = 10$, $\gamma_2 = 60$ and $\lambda = 0.001$, the relationship between r, τ and ζ is illustrated. In this case,

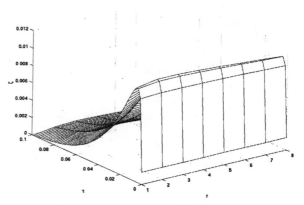

Figure 8: The Relationship between r, τ and ζ ($\gamma_1 = 10$, $\gamma_2 = 60$ and $\lambda = 0.001$).

$r^* = 2.49$, $\tau^* = 0.0061$, $\beta^* = 0.1639$ and $\zeta^*(\gamma_1, \gamma_2, \lambda) = 0.0112$, which means that the worst-case channel efficiency for any MS is no less than 0.0112. In Figure 9, we illustrate the relationship between λ and $\zeta^*(\gamma_1, \gamma_2, \lambda)$ given $\gamma_1 = 10$ and $\gamma_2 = 60$. It is seen that $\zeta^*(\gamma_1, \gamma_2, \lambda)$ increases to its limit $\frac{1}{\gamma_1 + \gamma_2} \approx 0.0143$ as $\lambda \to 0$.

5 Conclusion

We have designed and analyzed two distributed and randomized broadcast channel access methods for single-hop and multihop ad hoc networks respectively. These algorithms are designed based on maximizing the worst-case channel efficiency, by optimizing some key parameters, including the backoff probability distribution and the slot

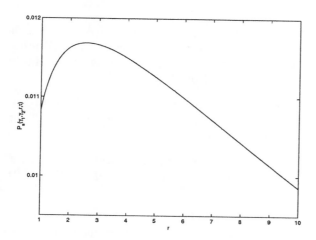

Figure 7: The relationship between r and $P_s(\gamma_1, \gamma_2, r, \tau)$ ($\tau = 0.01$, $\gamma_1 = 10$, $\gamma_2 = 60$).

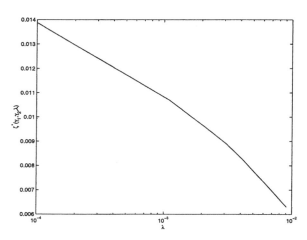

Figure 9: The Relationship between λ and $\zeta^*(\gamma_1, \gamma_2, \lambda)$ ($\gamma_1 = 10$ and $\gamma_2 = 60$).

length. Since the parameter optimization process occurs during the system initialization, no additional overhead is incurred on the processors of the MSs after initialization. The proposed algorithm for single-hop networks offers significantly higher throughput than the CSMA methods when the traffic load is heavy, while still achieving good performance when the load is light or medium. The proposed algorithm for multihop networks employs two busy tones to resolve the hidden terminal problem. It can flexibly adapt to the traffic load, and offers much better performance than the existing broadcast scheduling algorithms in light or medium load.

(This research was supported by the Texas Advanced Technology Program under Grant No. 000512-0039-1999.)

References

[1] D. Newman and K. Tolly, "Wireless LANs: How far? How fast?," in *Data Comm.*, March 1995, pp. 77–87.

[2] A. I. Elwalid and D. Mitra, "Effective Bandwidth of General Markovian Traffic Sources and Admission Control of High Speed Networks," *IEEE/ACM Trans. Networking*, vol. 1, no. 3, pp. 329–343, Jun 1993.

[3] A. Ephremides and T. V. Truong, "Scheduling Broadcasts in Multihop Radio Networks," *IEEE Trans. Commun.*, vol. 38, no. 4, pp. 456–460, 1990.

[4] B. Hajek and G. Sasaki, "Link Scheduling in Polynomial Time," *IEEE Trans. Inform. Theory*, vol. 34, pp. 910–917, 1988.

[5] R. Ramaswami and K. K. Parhi, "Distributed Scheduling of Broadcasts in a Radio Network," in *Proc. of IEEE INFOCOM'89*, 1989, pp. 497–504.

[6] Z. J. Haas and J. Deng, "Dual Busy Tone Multiple Access (DBTMA) - Performance Evaluation," in *Proc. of VTC'99*, 1999, vol. 1, pp. 314–319.

[7] I. Chlamtac and A. Farago, "Making Transmission Schedules Immune to Topology Changes in Multi-hop Packet Radio Networks," *IEEE Trans. Networking*, vol. 2, no. 1, pp. 23–29, 1994.

[8] Raphael Rom and Moshe Sidi, *Multiple Access Protocols*, Springer-Verlag, 1990.

[9] Peter Clifford, "http://www.jesus.ox.ac.uk/~clifford/a5/chap2/r May 2000.

[10] F. A. Tobagi and L. Kleinrock, "Packet Switching in Radio Channels: Part I – Carrier Sense Multiple Access Modes and Their Throughput Delay Characteristics," *IEEE Trans. Commun.*, vol. 23, no. 12, pp. 1400–1416, 1975.

[11] F. A. Tobagi and L. Kleinrock, "Packet Switching in Radio Channels: Part II – The Hidden Terminal Problem in Carrier Sence Multiple-Access and the Busy-Tone Solution," *IEEE Trans. Commun.*, vol. 23, no. 12, pp. 1417–1433, 1975.

[12] S. Kishore, P. Agrawal, K. M. Sivalingam, and J. C. Chen, "MAC Layer Scheduling Strategies during Handoff for Wireless Mobile Multimedia Networks," in *Proc. of IEEE International Conference on Personal Wireless Communications (ICPWC)*, Dec 1997, pp. 100–104.

[13] D. J. Baker and A. Ephremides, "The Architecture Organization of A Mobile Radio Network via a Distributed Algorithm," *IEEE Trans. Commun.*, vol. COM-29, pp. 1694–1701, Nov 1981.

[14] T. Hou and V. O. K. Li, "Transmission Range Control in Multihop Packet Radio Networks," *IEEE Trans. Commun.*, vol. COM-34, pp. 38–44, 1986.

[15] L. Hu, "A Novel Topology Control for Multihop Packet Radio Networks," in *Proc. of IEEE INFOCOM'91*, 1991, pp. 1084–1093.

[16] A. M. Chou and V. O. K. Li, "Slot Allocation Strategies for TDMA protocols in Multihop Packet Radio Networks," in *Proc. of IEEE INFOCOM'92*, 1992, pp. 710–716.

[17] K. Hung and T. Yum, "Fair and Efficient Transmission Scheduling in Multihop Packet Radio Networks," in *Proc. of IEEE GLOBECOM'92*, 1992, pp. 6–10.

BPA: A Fast Packet Scheduling Algorithm for Real-Time Switched Ethernet Networks

Jinggang Wang and Binoy Ravindran
Real-Time Systems Laboratory
The Bradley Department of Electrical and Computer Engineering
Virginia Tech, Blacksburg, VA 24061
Phone: 540-231-3777, Fax: 540-231-3362, E-mail: jiwang5@vt.edu, binoy@vt.edu

Abstract

In this paper, we present a MAC-layer packet scheduling algorithm called BPA, for real-time switched Ethernet networks. BPA considers a message model where trans-node application-level messages have end-to-end timeliness requirements that are specified using Jensen's benefit functions. The objective of BPA is to maximize the aggregate message-level benefit. The algorithm reasons that this objective can be achieved by maximizing aggregate packet-level benefit, where packets of messages are allowed to inherit benefit functions of their parent messages. BPA thus solves a non-preemptive packet scheduling problem. Since this problem is NP-hard, BPA heuristically computes packet schedules to maximize aggregate benefit, incurring a worst-case computational complexity of $O(n^2)$. This is better than the $O(n^3)$ complexity of the previously known best algorithm (called CMA) for the same problem. Further, our experimental studies show that BPA performs as good as CMA for a broad set of benefit functions, and significantly outperforms CMA for some benefit functions. Furthermore, we observe that BPA yields lower missed-deadline ratio than CMA when message arrival density increases.

1. Introduction

The IEEE 802.3 Ethernet standard is unsuited for real-time applications due to the non-determinism that is inherent in Ethernet's CSMA/CD MAC protocol. The CSMA/CD protocol conceptually employs a non-deterministic distributed message scheduling algorithm, where hosts that attempt to simultaneously transmit messages and thus contend for the network medium, "backs-off" for a random period of time, before

attempting to transmit again. The back-off strategy is repeated where the randomly determined waiting time exponentially increases with each subsequent collision, until the host is able to transmit.

Implementations of the 802.3 standard is usually done using a hub, where hosts are connected to the different ports of the hub. The hub simply broadcasts each message that it receives from any host at any of its ports, to every host that is connected to one of its ports. This significantly increases the likelihood of message collisions, triggering the CSMA/CD protocol.

Such a non-deterministic scheduling of the network medium is antagonistic toward satisfying the scheduling objectives of real-time applications such as the hard real-time objective of "always meet all timing constraints." However, Ethernet is attractive for real-time applications due to its wide availability, low cost, and high performance such as that offered by the emerging 10 Gigabit Ethernet standard [1]. This has motivated research on circumventing the non-determinism of Ethernet CSMA/CD so that Ethernet networks can be used for building real-time distributed applications.

In [13], the authors present Rether, a software component that is integrated into the device drivers of end-hosts. Rether regulates the access of a host to the network by passing a control-token among the hosts, and thus prevents hosts from arbitrarily transmitting messages (and thereby triggering CSMA/CD). Rether provides a "per connection" real-time guarantee, similar to that provided by ATM networks. An application requests a real-time connection that has a given bandwidth requirement. If the request can be honored, Rether admits the request and continuously honors the request as long as the requested bandwidth is not exceeded by the application.

The CSMA/DDCR protocol presented in [5] on the other hand, emulates a distributed, non-preemptive version of the Earliest Deadline First (EDF) algorithm [8]. When message collisions occur, the protocols at the collided hosts initiate a deterministic search that is guaranteed to complete earlier for the host with the earliest deadline message. The host that completes the search earlier is then allowed to access the network. Furthermore, CSMA/DDCR has formally proven timeliness feasibility conditions. The feasibility conditions are established in [5] under upper bounds for message arrival densities (i.e., application workloads) that are postulated at design-time. Thus, given a hard real-time distributed application, a designer can easily verify the schedulability of the application by assigning numerical values to the protocol's feasibility condition and get an "yes" or "no" answer (on the application feasibility).

Another alternative to circumventing the non-determinism of CSMA/CD is to use switched Ethernet networks, where each host is connected to the output port of a switch using a full-duplex Ethernet segment. Though switches are traditionally used (and intended) for interconnecting multiple Ethernet network segments (that are internally built using hubs), there is an increasing trend toward using switches for building a single-segment network itself.

Thus, unlike in hub-based Ethernet networks (that is envisaged in IEEE 802.3), a switch can determine the destination host of each incoming message that arrives at one of its ports. If the network segment from the switch output port to the destination host is "busy," the switch can buffer the message in internal buffers, and later route the message on the output port when the segment becomes free. Thus, the switch avoids collisions by "directing" the network traffic.

The switched network approach is presented in EtheReal [12] and SIXNET's SIXNET Industrial Ethernet Switch [11]. EtheReal provides the same per connection guarantee as that provided by Rether. Furthermore, the switch-based approach is gaining support in the real-time industry, with several companies developing Ethernet switches that are now in widespread usage [11, 10].

As switched Ethernet networks are thus increasingly used for building real-time distributed systems, real-time systems that are emerging for the purpose of strategic mission management are "asynchronous" in the sense that processing and communication latencies do not necessarily have known upper bounds, and event and task arrivals may be non-deterministically distributed [6, 7]. This emerging generation of real-time distributed systems are very important for real-time control in many domains, including defense, industrial automation, and telecommunications.

Thus, the non-determinism inherent in asynchronous real-time distributed systems generally makes it difficult or impossible to obtain upper bounds on application parameters such as message arrival densities and bandwidth needs. Therefore, it becomes difficult or impossible to perform the classical hard real-time schedulability analysis either off-line or on-line (as part of an admission control mechanism) and obtain the hard real-time guarantee of "always meet all timing constraints" on the application behavior [6].

In this paper, we advance the real-time Ethernet switch-based technology by presenting a packet scheduling algorithm called Best-Effort Packet Scheduling Algorithm (or BPA) for constructing asynchronous real-time distributed systems. BPA considers a message model where trans-node application-level messages have end-to-end timeliness requirements that are specified using Jensen's benefit functions [6]. Thus, delivering an end-to-end message at its destination host at anytime will yield a benefit that is specified by the message benefit function. Furthermore, the algorithm considers a switched Ethernet network where end-hosts are connected to ports of a switch through full-duplex Ethernet segments. Thus, BPA schedules outgoing packets from source end-hosts to the switch and from the switch to destination hosts.

Given such a timeliness model and system model, the objective of BPA is to maximize the aggregate message-level benefit. Thus, BPA is a "best-effort" algorithm in the sense that it seeks to provide the best benefit to the application, where the best benefit that the application can accrue is application-specified (using benefit functions).

To maximize aggregate message-level benefit, the algorithm decomposes the benefit function of a message into benefit functions for packets of the message, since packets form the input to the algorithm. Furthermore, the algorithm reasons that by maximizing aggregate packet-level benefit, the message-level benefit can be maximized as much as possible. BPA thus solves a non-preemptive packet scheduling problem, since packet transmission is non-preemptive. This problem is equivalent to the non-preemptive task scheduling problem solved in [2].

In [2], Chen and Muhlethaler show that this scheduling problem is NP-hard. Further, Chen and Muhlethaler present a heuristic algorithm, which has a computational complexity of $O(n^3)$. For convenience, we call this Chen and Muhlethaler's Algorithm (or CMA). Furthermore, the authors experimentally show that CMA performs very well with respect to the best optimal algorithm for this problem.

BPA heuristically solves the same problem as that solved by CMA. However, we show that the complexity of BPA is only $O(n^2)$. To study how well BPA performs, we conduct simulation studies. Our simulation results indicate that BPA performs as good as CMA, and sometimes better than CMA. Furthermore, we observe that BPA yields lower missed-deadline ratio than CMA when message arrival density increases.

Thus, the contribution of the paper is the BPA packet scheduling algorithm that seeks to maximize aggregate message benefit in real-time distributed systems.

The rest of the paper is organized as follows: We discuss the message model and the system model that we are considering in this work in Section 2. We formally describe the problem that we are addressing and state our objectives in Section 3. We describe the BPA algorithm, the heuristics employed by the algorithm, and the rationale behind the heuristics in Section 4. In Section 5, we discuss BPA's performance in a single processor environment. We describe BPA's performance in a switched network environment in Section 6. Finally, the paper concludes with a summary of the work and its contributions in Section 7.

2. The Message and System Model

2.1. The Message Model

We denote the set of messages of the application by the set $M = \{M_1, M_2, \ldots, M_n\}$. Each message has an end-to-end timing requirement that is expressed using Jensen's benefit function [6]. We denote the benefit function of a message M_i as $B_i(t)$. Thus, the arrival of a message M_i at its destination host (since the release of the message at the source host) at a time t will yield a benefit $B_i(t)$. Example benefit functions are shown in Figure 1.

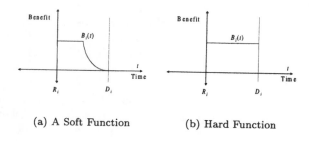

(a) A Soft Function   (b) Hard Function

Figure 1. Jensen's Benefit Functions

Though benefit functions can take arbitrary shapes, we restrict our focus to *unimodal* functions i.e., those benefit functions that never increase when time advances. Unimodal functions allow the specification of

a broad range of timing constraints encompassing the entire spectrum of hard and soft timing constraints.

2.2. The System Model

We consider a single-segment switched Ethernet network, where hosts are interconnected through a centralized switch as our target platform (see Figure 2). Each host is connected to the switch using a full-duplex Ethernet segment (IEEE 802.3) and to a port at the switch that is dedicated for the host. Thus, the link between each host and the switch is a dedicated link for simultaneous two-way communication between the host and the switch.

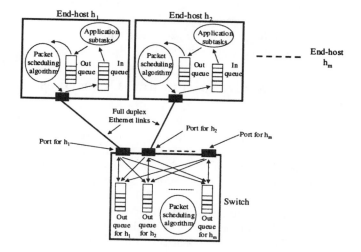

Figure 2. The Switched Ethernet Real-Time Network System Model

A message that is sent from an application process is first packetized on the host of the process. The message packets are then deposited into the MAC-layer of the host. When packets arrive at the MAC-layer of the host, they are queued in the outgoing packet queue of the host. Whenever the network segment from the host to the switch becomes free for transmission, it triggers the packet scheduling algorithm at the end-host, which then executes and schedules a packet from the packet queue for transmission.

The switch is assumed to maintain a list of packet ready-queues, one queue per host. Each queue stores the packets that are destined for the corresponding host. When packets arrive at the switch, they are queued in the outgoing packet queue at the switch for the corresponding destination host. Whenever the network segment from the switch to an end-host becomes free for transmission, it triggers the packet scheduling algorithm at the switch, which then executes and schedules a packet from the packet queue of the destination host for transmission (on the corresponding output port).

We denote the set of packets of a message M_i as $P_i = \{p_1^i, p_2^i, \ldots, p_m^i\}$. For convenience, we denote the set of all message packets of the application as the set $P = \bigcup_{i=1}^n P_i$. From now on, for convenience, we will drop the superscript i of a packet p_j^i, unless i is needed. Thus, we will simply denote the set of all packets as $P = \{p_1, p_2, \ldots, p_{m \times n}\}$.

The bit length of a packet p_i is denoted as b_i. Thus, the transmission latency of a packet p_i is given by $l_i = b_i/\psi$, where ψ denotes the nominal throughput of the underlying Ethernet network segment (e.g., 10^9 bits/s for Gigabit Ethernet).

We assume that the clocks of the end-hosts are synchronized using a protocol such as [9].

3. Problem Definition and Objectives

Given the timeliness model and the system model described in Section 2, our objective is to maximize the aggregate benefit accrued by the arrival of all application messages at their destination hosts. Thus, the problem that we are addressing in this paper can be described as $Maximize \sum_{k=1}^n B_k(t_k)$, where t_k is the time at which message M_k arrives at its destination host.

The BPA algorithm is a packet scheduling algorithm. Thus, packets constitute the "input" to the algorithm. Therefore, if packets have benefit functions, that will enable the algorithm to reason about scheduling packets such that it will maximize the aggregate message-level benefit. This requires us to translate benefit functions of messages into benefit functions for packets.

Since the packets of a message do not have any precedence relations, the packets can be transmitted in any order from the source host of the message. Furthermore, the benefit of a message is accrued only when all packets of the message arrive at the destination host and are reassembled. Thus, the packets of a message can simply inherit the benefit function of its parent message.

Thus, BPA reasons that by scheduling packets at outgoing queues of end-hosts and at the switch such that the aggregate packet benefit is maximized, the algorithm can maximize the aggregate message benefit.

We now formalize the objective of BPA as follows: Let $\mathcal{A} \subseteq P$ denote the set of packets in the outgoing packet queue at an end-host or at the switch at a time t. (Note that the switch has one outgoing queue per host). Let $\alpha \subseteq (m \times n)$ denote the number of packets

in the set $\mathcal{A}$. Let $\mathcal{S}(\mathcal{A})$ denote all possible sequences of packets of the set $\mathcal{A}$, and let $\sigma \in \mathcal{S}(\mathcal{A})$ denotes one of the possible packet sequence—or a packet schedule—of the packets in $\mathcal{A}$. Let $\sigma(i)$ denotes the packet occupying the ith position in the schedule σ. Then, the objective of BPA is to: $Maximize_{\sigma \in \mathcal{S}(\mathcal{A})} B(\sigma) = \sum_{k=1}^{\alpha} B_{\sigma(k)}(t + t_k)$, where $t_k = \sum_{i=1}^k l_{\sigma(i)}$.

Thus, the objective of BPA is to determine a packet schedule that will maximize the aggregate packet benefit in terms of the sum of the individual benefits of each packet that is accrued when the packet arrives at its destination host.

This optimization problem is equivalent to the non-preemptive task scheduling problem addressed by Chen and Muhlethaler in [2]. In [2], Chen and Muhlethaler show that their task scheduling problem is NP-hard by establishing the equivalence of their problem to the scheduling problem addressed in [3]. Thus, the problem that we are addressing in this paper is NP-hard.

In [2], Chen and Muhlethaler present a heuristic algorithm to solve this problem. As discussed in Section 1, we refer to this algorithm as CMA, for convenience. Given, n tasks (i.e., $\alpha = n$ packets in our case), the complexity of CMA is shown to be $O(n^3)$ in [2]. Through simulation studies, Chen and Muhlethaler show that CMA yields an aggregate benefit that is generally close to the maximum possible—or the optimal—aggregate benefit. To determine the optimal aggregate benefit, they use Held and Karp's dynamic programming solution for the same problem presented in [4]. Held and Karp's solution has an exponential complexity of $O(n2^n)$.

We believe that $O(n^3)$ is too high for a scheduling algorithm, especially for an on-line algorithm such as a packet scheduling algorithm. This is because, higher the cost of the algorithm, higher will be the scheduling overhead. Thus, when used in the switch, the algorithm will "slow down" the routing of packets at the switch and thereby reduce the utilization of the network segments. Furthermore, a faster scheduling algorithm will require less buffer space for storing the outgoing packet queues. If the scheduler is slow, packets will quickly queue-up over a short period of time.

Thus, in designing BPA, our objective is twofold: (1) compute scheduling decisions faster than CMA's $O(n^3)$ time, and (2) compute scheduling decisions that will yield an aggregate packet benefit that is as close as possible to that of CMA, if not better.

4. The BPA Algorithm: Heuristics and Rationale

4.1. Sort Packets In Decreasing Order Of "Return of Investments"

The potential benefit that can be obtained by spending a unit amount of network transmission time for a packet defines a measure of the "return of investment" for the packet. Thus, by ordering packets in the schedule in the decreasing order of their return of investments, we "greedily" collect as much "high return" packets into the schedule as early as possible. Furthermore, since a packet included in the schedule at any instant in time is always the one with the next "highest-return" packet among the set of non-examined packets, we increase our chance of collecting as much "high return" packets into the schedule as early as possible. This will increase the likelihood of maximizing the aggregate packet benefit as packets yield greater benefit if they arrive earlier at their destinations, since unimodal benefit functions are non-increasing.

The return of investment for a packet can be determined by computing the slope of the packet benefit function. However, computing slopes of arbitrary unimodal benefit functions can be computationally expensive. Thus, we determine the return of investment for a packet as simply the ratio of the maximum possible packet benefit (specified by the packet benefit function) to the packet deadline. This is just a single division, costing $O(1)$ time. We call this ratio, the "pseudo-slope" of a packet. The slope is "pseudo" as it does not represent the correct slope and only gives a crude measure of the slope.

4.2. Move Infeasible Packets Toward Schedule End

Infeasible packets are packets that cannot arrive at their destination before their deadlines, no matter what. This is because, the transmission time of such packets are longer than the time interval between the scheduling instant—the arrival time of a packet into the outgoing packet queue at a host or the switch—and the packet deadlines.

By moving infeasible packets to the end of the schedule, we collect as much feasible packets to the beginning of the schedule as possible. This will increase the likelihood of maximizing the aggregate packet benefit as feasible packets yield greater benefit if they arrive earlier at their destinations since unimodal benefit functions are non-increasing. Furthermore, infeasible packets yield zero benefit when they arrive at their destinations after their deadlines. Thus, there is no reason for

transmitting them early and jeopardize the potential benefit that can be accrued from feasible packets.

```
BPA_Algorithm(𝒜, α, t)
/* 𝒜: set of packets in outgoing packet queue; α: # of packets
   in 𝒜; t: time of scheduling event */
1. σ = ∅; /* Intialize packet schedule to empty; */
2. For each packet pᵢ ∈ 𝒜
      2.1 PseudoSlope(pᵢ) = Bᵢ(0)/Dᵢ; /* Max benefit occurs
          at time 0, since functions are unimodal; */
3. Sort packets in 𝒜 in decreasing order of their pseudo-slopes;
   /* 𝒜 is now sorted */
4. σ = 𝒜; /* packet schedule σ is set equal to sorted set 𝒜 */
5. For k = 1 to α
      5.1 InOrder = TRUE;
      5.2 For i = 1 to α − 1
            5.2.1 j = i + 1; /* pⱼ: packet that follows pᵢ in σ */
            5.2.2 If (t + lᵢ > Dᵢ) /* Check for feasibility of pᵢ */
                  • Move pᵢ to end of schedule σ;
                  • Continue; /* Skip to another iteration */
            5.2.3 If (t + lⱼ > Dⱼ) /* Check for feasibility of pⱼ */
                  • Move pⱼ to end of schedule σ;
                  • Continue; /* Skip to another iteration */
            5.2.4 Δᵢ,ⱼ(t) = [Bᵢ(t + lᵢ) + Bⱼ(t + lᵢ + lⱼ)] −
                  [Bⱼ(t + lⱼ) + Bᵢ(t + lⱼ + lᵢ)]; /* Compute Δ */
            5.2.5 If (Δᵢ,ⱼ(t) < 0) /* Out of order, so swap */
                  • σ(i) = pⱼ;
                  • σ(j) = pᵢ;
                  • t = t + lⱼ;
                  • InOrder = FALSE;
            5.2.6 Else
                  • t = t + lᵢ;
      5.3 If (InOrder = TRUE) /* No swaps; all packets inorder */
            • 5.3.1 Break;
6. σ is the final schedule; return σ(1) as the packet selected
   for transmission;
```

Figure 3. Pseudo-Code of BPA Algorithm

4.3. Maximize Local Aggregate Benefit As Much As Possible

We derive the notion of local aggregate benefit from the *precedence-relation* property presented by Chen and Muhlethaler in [2]. For completeness, we summarize this here.

Consider two schedules $\sigma_a = \langle \sigma_1, p_i, p_j, \sigma_2 \rangle$ and $\sigma_b = \langle \sigma_1, p_j, p_i, \sigma_2 \rangle$ of a packet set $\mathcal{A}$, such that $\sigma_1 \neq 0$, $\sigma_2 \neq 0$, $\sigma_1 \bigcup \sigma_2 = \mathcal{A} - \{p_i, p_j\}$, and $\sigma_1 \bigcap \sigma_2 = \emptyset$. Consider a (scheduling) time instant $t = \sum_{k \in \sigma_1} l_k$, when a scheduling decision has to be made. That is, t is the instant in time after all packets in the schedule σ_1 has been transmitted.

Now, the scheduling decision at time t can be made by determining $\Delta_{i,j}(t)$, where: $\Delta_{i,j}(t) = [B_i(t + l_i) + B_j(t + l_i + l_j)] - [B_j(t + l_j) + B_i(t + l_j + l_i)]$. Thus, if $\Delta_{i,j}(t) \geq 0$, then schedule σ_a will yield a higher aggregate benefit than schedule σ_b. Otherwise, σ_b is better than σ_a. This is the precedence-relation property presented by Chen and Muhlethaler in [2].

Now, by examining adjacent packets p_i and p_j in a schedule $\langle \sigma_1, p_i, p_j, \sigma_2 \rangle$ and ensuring that $\Delta_{i,j}(t) \geq 0$, we can maximize the *local* aggregate benefit of packets p_i and p_j. If all adjacent packets in the schedule have such locally maximized aggregate benefit, this will increase the likelihood of maximizing the global aggregate benefit.

The maximization of the local aggregate benefit can be done in a manner similar to that of Bubble sort. We can examine adjacent pairs of packets in the schedule, compute Δ, and swap the packets, if the reverse order can lead to higher local aggregate benefit. Furthermore, the procedure can be repeated until no swaps are required.

Thus, BPA computes packet schedules according to the heuristics discussed here. Pseudo-code of BPA at a high-level of abstraction is shown in Figure 3.

4.4. Computational Complexity of BPA

The computational complexity of BPA depends upon the complexity of Step (5). The complexity of all other steps are dominated by this step.

The complexity of Step (5) is dominated by that of Step (5.2); all other sub-steps of Step (5) take $O(1)$ time. Step (5.2) can iterate a maximum of α times, and therefore costs $O(\alpha)$. Step (5) can iterate a maximum of α times, and thus costs $O(\alpha^2)$. Given m application messages, where each message can be packetized into at most n packets, $\alpha = O(mn)$. Thus, the complexity of BPA is $O(m^2n^2)$.

To compare the complexity of BPA with that of CMA, we need to uniformly express the problem size. Thus, given n application packets, BPA has a complexity $O(n^2)$. Given n non-preemptable tasks, which form the input to CMA, CMA has a complexity of $O(n^3)$ [2]. Thus, BPA is an order of magnitude faster than CMA.

5. Performance in a Single Processor Environment

To study how well BPA performs with respect to CMA, and with respect to the optimal algorithm, we first consider a single processor environment, where all three algorithms are used as task scheduling algorithms for scheduling non-preemptive tasks. Note that non-preemptive task scheduling is equivalent to packet scheduling on end-hosts and at the switch. We consider a single processor environment for its simplicity.

5.1. Experiment Setup and Parameters

To study the performance of the algorithms in a large data space, we randomly generate all task parameters such as execution times, deadlines, and maximum benefit of the benefit functions using probability distribution functions. We consider six benefit functions for

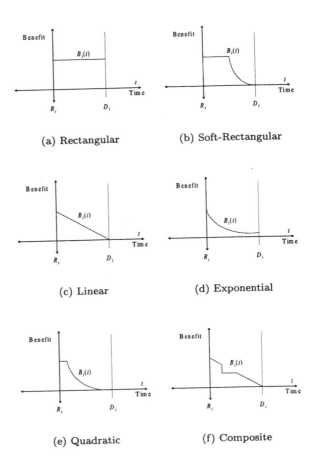

Figure 4. Example Benefit Functions

our experimental study. The functions are shown in Figure 4. These include rectangular, soft-rectangular, linear, exponential, quadratic, and composite.

5.2. Performance Results

We considered several task sets and measured the aggregate benefit yielded by BPA, CMA, and the optimal algorithm for the task sets. The optimal algorithm determines optimal schedules through an exhaustive search.

Since the input task workload to BPA and CMA is randomly generated, the absolute value of the aggregate benefit produced by the algorithms is not of much significance. Thus, we compute the ratio of the aggregate benefit produced by BPA and CMA to that produced by the optimal algorithm. We call this ratio, the *normalized aggregate benefit*.

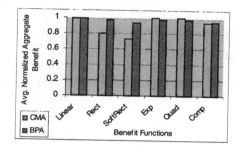

Figure 5. Performance of BPA and CMA With Respect to Optimal Algorithm

Figure 5 shows the average values of the normalized aggregate benefit for BPA and CMA. The measurements were obtained from repeated experiments—2500 times for a 9 task-set— for each of the six benefit functions.

From Figure 5, we observe that the performance of BPA is very close ($\geq$ 93%) to that of the optimal algorithm for all six benefit functions. Furthermore, we observe that CMA performs quite close to that of the optimal algorithm for some benefit functions such as quadratic, linear, and exponential, but performs poorly for functions such as the rectangular and soft-rectangular benefit functions.

We also observe that the performance of BPA is close to that of CMA for linear, exponential, quadratic, and composite benefit functions. However, BPA outperforms CMA for rectangular and soft-rectangular benefit functions. We observed similar, consistent results for other task sets that were considered in our study.

6. Performance in a Switched Network Environment

6.1. Experiment Setup and Parameters

Similar to the single processor experimental setup, we randomly generate all message parameters in the network environment using probability distribution functions. The parameters include destination address of messages, message lengths, message deadlines, maximum benefit of message benefit functions, and message inter-arrival times.

Besides BPA and CMA, we also considered EDF and the First-In-First-Out (FIFO) algorithms for a broader comparative study. However, we excluded the optimal algorithm from this study, as we observed that the actual execution time of the optimal algorithm was extremely large even for moderately loaded situations. Thus, the optimal algorithm is not practically feasible.

6.2. Performance Results

Since we excluded the optimal algorithm from this study, we normalize the aggregate benefit by computing the ratio of the aggregate benefit produced by the algorithms to that produced by FIFO. We believe that it is reasonable to use FIFO as a baseline algorithm, since FIFO has the least scheduling cost of $O(1)$ time.

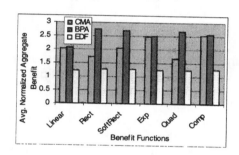

Figure 6. Performance of BPA, CMA, and EDF With Respect to FIFO

Figure 6 shows the average of the normalized aggregate benefit produced by BPA, CMA, and EDF for all experiments that were conducted for the algorithms, for each of the six benefit functions. From Figure 6, we observe that BPA performs the best and EDF performs the worst, for all six benefit functions. The performance of CMA lies in between BPA and EDF.

Further, we observe that BPA maintains an average normalized aggregate benefit of 2.5. Furthermore, we note that the performance of BPA and CMA is just about the same for linear, exponential, and composite benefit functions. However, BPA significantly outperforms CMA for rectangular, soft-rectangular, and quadratic benefit functions. These results are consistent with that of the single processor environment presented in Section 5.2, except for quadratic functions.

6.2.1 Performance Under Increasing Arrival Density

We were also interested to determine how BPA and CMA perform when the arrival density of messages increase. The arrival density of a message—and thus packets of the message—is simply the number of times the message arrives during an interval of time. Thus, a larger arrival density implies a larger message traffic.

We repeated the experiments described in Section 6.2 for 16 message arrival densities that are progressively increasing. Figure 7 shows the (end-to-end) message missed-deadline ratio of BPA, CMA, EDF, and FIFO for quadratic benefit functions.

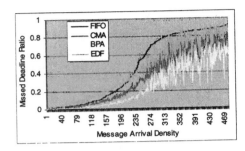

Figure 7. Performance Under Increasing Arrival Density and Quadratic Functions

From Figure 7, we observe that the missed-deadline ratio of all algorithms increase as the message arrival density increases. Furthermore, we observe that the missed-deadline ratio of BPA is the smallest. This is followed by the ratios of CMA and EDF. FIFO has the largest missed-deadline ratio. We observed similar consistent results for all other benefit functions. These are not shown here due to space limitations.

7. Conclusions

In this paper, we present a MAC-layer packet scheduling algorithm called BPA, for real-time switched Ethernet networks. BPA considers a message model where trans-node application-level messages have end-to-end timeliness requirements that are specified using Jensen's benefit functions. The objective of BPA is to maximize the aggregate message-level benefit. To achieve this objective, the algorithm allows packets of messages to directly inherit benefit functions of their parent messages. Furthermore, the algorithm reasons that by maximizing aggregate packet-level benefit, the aggregate message-level benefit can be maximized as much as possible.

BPA thus solves a non-preemptive packet scheduling problem. Since this problem is NP-hard, BPA heuristically computes packet schedules with a worst-case complexity of $O(n^2)$. This is better than the $O(n^3)$ CMA algorithm — the best known algorithm for the same problem. Further, our experimental studies show that BPA performs as good as CMA for a broad set of

benefit functions, and significantly outperforms CMA for some benefit functions. Furthermore, we observe that BPA yields lower missed-deadline ratio than CMA when message arrival density increases. We believe that these results are significant as BPA's scheduling cost is an order of magnitude less than that of CMA.

8. Acknowledgements

This work was supported by the U.S. Office of Naval Research under Grant N00014-00-1-0549.

References

[1] 10GEA. 10 gigabit ethernet technology overview white paper. Available at: www.10gea.org, September 2001.

[2] K. Chen and P. Muhlethaler. A scheduling algorithm for tasks described by time value function. *Journal of Real-Time Systems*, 10(3):293–312, May 1996.

[3] M. R. Garey, R. E. Tarjan, and G. T. Wilfong. One-processor scheduling with symmetric earliness and tardiness penalties. *Math. Oper. Res.*, 13(2):330–348, May 1988.

[4] M. Held and R. M. Karp. A dynamic programming approach to sequencing problems. *Journal of SIAM*, 10(1):196–210, March 1962.

[5] J.-F. Hermant and G. L. Lann. A protocol and correctness proofs for real-time high-performance broadcast networks. In *Proceedings of the Eighteenth International Conference on Distributed Computing Systems*, pages 360–369, 1998.

[6] E. D. Jensen. Asynchronous decentralized real-time computer systems. In W. A. Halang and A. D. Stoyenko, editors, *Real-Time Computing*, Proceedings of the NATO Advanced Study Institute. Springer Verlag, October 1992.

[7] E. D. Jensen and B. Ravindran. Special issue on asynchronous real-time distributed systems. Call for papers available at: www.ee.vt.edu/~tocsi/, 2000.

[8] J. W. S. Liu. *Real-Time Systems*. Prentice Hall, New Jersey, 2000.

[9] D. L. Mills. Improved algorithms for synchronizing computer network clocks. *IEEE/ACM Transactions on Networking*, pages 245–254, June 1995.

[10] Z. Networks. Multiport ethernet adaptors product zx340q series. Available at: www.znyx.com/products/netblaster/zx340q.htm.

[11] SIXNET. The sixnet industrial ethernet switch. Available at: www.sixnetio.com/.

[12] S. Varadarajan and T. Chiueh. Ethereal: A host-transparent real-time fast ethernet switch. In *Proceedings of The International Conference on Network Protocols*, October 1998.

[13] C. Venkatramani. *Design, Implementation and Evaluation of RETHER: A Real-Time Ethernet Protocol*. PhD thesis, State University of New York at Stony Brook, December 1996.

Design and Evaluation of Scalable Switching Fabrics for High-Performance Routers

Nian-Feng Tzeng and **Ravi C. Batchu**

Center for Advanced Computer Studies
University of Louisiana at Lafayette
Lafayette, LA 70504, USA

Abstract

This work considers switching fabrics with distributed packet routing to achieve high scalability and low costs. The considered switching fabrics are based on a multistage structure with different re-circulation designs, where adjacent stages are interconnected according to the indirect n-cube connection style. They all compare favorably with an earlier multistage-based counterpart according to extensive simulation, in terms of performance measures of interest and hardware complexity. When queues are incorporated in the output ports of switching elements (SE's), the total number of stages required in our proposed fabrics to reach a given performance level can be reduced substantially. The performance of those fabrics with output queues is evaluated under different "speedups" of the queues, where the speedup is the operating clock rate ratio of that at the SE core to that over external links. Our simulation reveals that a small speedup of 2 is adequate for buffered switching fabrics comprising 4×8 SE's to deliver better performance than their unbuffered counterparts with 50% more stages of SE's, when the fabric size is 256. The buffered switching fabrics under our consideration are scalable and of low costs, ideally suitable for constructing high-performance routers with large numbers of line cards.

1. Introduction

Rapidly growing demand for high-speed networks has prompted the investigation into scalable routers that are capable of forwarding data at the aggregate rate of multi-terabits per second. Such a router contains many line cards (LC's) for admitting external links of various speeds. Those LC's are interconnected by a switching fabric to provide paths for packets to travel from arrival LC's to their respective departure LC's. Routers serve to connect external links with various data rates through its line cards (LC's). On receiving a packet, an LC transmits it, based on the packet destination, to the outgoing LC through which the packet is to be delivered forward. The outgoing LC is determined by a table lookup, performed either locally at the arrival LC or via a remote forwarding engine (FE). Any router with multiple LC's (common in a current high-performance router) employs a switching fabric to interconnect its constituent LC's, providing paths among LC's for packets to move from their arrival LC's toward their destined LC's. Switching fabrics naturally affect overall router performance and dictate router scalability.

It is highly desirable to devise scalable fabrics for future high-performance routers which may contain large numbers of LC's. A multistage switching structure is referred to as the space-division architecture and comprises multiple stages of switching elements (SE's) with or without buffers. Different multistage-based configurations have been introduced, and the Shuffleout has been shown to outperform others [1]. A variation of the Shuffleout, formed by providing paths from its primary outputs back to its primary inputs, was considered. It is known as the closed-loop Shuffleout [2], which allows for packets to be re-circulated back, when they fail to reach their destinations at the primary outputs. Both the Shuffleout and the closed-loop Shuffleout are unbuffered. An unbuffered multistage structure enjoys the advantage of hardware simplicity.

Buffers can be introduced to SE's in a multistage structure to enhance its throughput, because they can hold packets which head for the same output port simultaneously and which otherwise have to be dropped or deflection routed [7]. Packets held in the buffers are delivered in sequence later on. For a multistage-based switching fabric, incorporating buffers in its constituent SE's can lower the number of stages required to achieve a given performance level. Buffers may be incorporated in the output (or input) ports of SE's, forming output (or input) queues. It has been shown that output queuing outperforms input queuing [5], but output queuing requires a "speedup," where the core of SE's runs faster than the connected links. Output queuing does not suffer from the *head-of-line* problem. Previous simulation and analytical studies indicated that a small speedup (say, 2 – 4) was enough in practice for output queuing to deliver packets quickly to their output ports [4].

In this article, we propose and evaluate switching fabric designs, dubbed the *I-Cubeout* [11], for scalable routers. Our proposed fabrics comprise multiple stages of SE's interconnected following the indirect *n*-cube connection style [9], with different approaches for re-circulating packets from their primary outputs back into the fabrics. The

This work was support in part by the National Science Foundation under Grants EIA-9871315 and CCR-0105529, by the Army Research Office under Grant/Cooperative Agreement No. DAAG55-98-1-0240, and by the Board of Regents of the State of Louisiana under Contract No. LEQSF(2000-2001)-ENH-TR-90.

simplest re-circulation design requires little control logics for re-circulating paths but exhibits relatively lower performance. Other two approaches make use of more control logics to arrive at better performance. Our simulation has unveiled that the proposed switching fabrics all outperform their compatible closed-loop Shuffleout. When buffers are introduced to output ports of SE's, it is found that the number of stages for our proposed fabrics to yield a given performance level is reduced substantially, even for the speedup of only 2. Since the costs of our switching fabrics are likely to be proportional to the number of stages involved, buffered fabrics appear more attractive than their unbuffered counterparts and are better applicable to large sized routers with hundreds of LC's.

2. Related Work

An I-Cubeout switch with size N (= 2^n) is denoted by ICO_N, where each SE is a small crossbar of size $b \times 2b$ to provide b outlets for terminating packets at their destination queues as soon as they reach their destined rows [11]. For a 2×4 SE (i.e., $b = 2$), it has two remote outlets (for connecting SE's in the next stage) and two local outlets (for terminating packets at destination queues). Adjacent stages are interconnected according to an indirect n-cube connecting pattern [9]. Specifically, the two remote outlets of any SE in the same stage differ in their addresses by a constant; those in stage 1 (i.e., the leftmost stage) differ by $N/2$, those in stage 2 differ by $N/4$, and so on, for ICO_N. At the nth stage, the two remote outlets of any SE differ by 1. A copy of the indirect n-cube connection spans from stage 1 to stage n. In stage $n+1$, the two remote outlets of an SE differ by $N/2$, identical to the situation of stage 1. This stage begins another copy of the indirect n-cube connection, which covers the next n stages. ICO_N may contain any number of stages, not necessary an integer multiple of n. For example, ICO_8 may contain five (5) stages, while a copy of the indirect 3-cube covers three (3) stages.

Packets in ICO are self-routed in a distributed manner, with the routing tag of each packet computed at the primary input according to its source and destination addresses via a bit-wise XOR operation [11]. The tag is carried along with the packet to guide its traversal across ICO. The first tag bit is used by SE's in Stage 1 of any copy, and the second tag bit is by SE's in Stage 2 of any copy, etc. If a tag bit, say in position p, is "1", the packet takes a "cross" state at the visited SE in stage p of any copy, signifying that the upper (or lower) inlet of the SE is connected to the lower (or upper) remote outlet. It reflects that the packet is "corrected" at position p, and the correction can be done in stage p of any copy. After it is done, the pth tag bit is reset to "0". If the tag bit is "0", the visited SE is set to the "straight" state, since no correction is then needed. After a packet advances one stage, its tag is rotated leftward by one bit position, so that the tag bit to be examined at any stage is always the leftmost one. When the tag bits all become "0", the packet has reached its destined row and may take the associated local outlet to reach its destination queue.

If two packets at an SE in stage p have distinct values in their p^{th} tag bits, a conflict occurs and only one of the two conflicting packets is forwarded to its destined outlet, with the other being deflection-routed [11]. This is because the SE can be set to either the cross or the straight state at a time, but not both. The packet with a smaller distance to its destination is given priority, where the distance is defined as the minimum number of stages a packet has to travel before getting to its destination. The distance of a packet can be told directly from its current tag. A simple priority resolution logic is devised for this purpose [11]. For SE with output queues and with a speedup of k, up to k competing packets are accepted by any output queue and deflection-routing happens only if there are more than k packets competing for one output port or if the targeted output queue has a capacity less than what is needed to hold k packets.

While ICO explained so far is composed of 2×4 SE's, it is obvious that ICO in general can be built by $b \times 2b$ SE's, each connecting to b SE's in the next stage and terminating at b destination queues. When a packet has not reached its destined row at an SE, it is forwarded to the next stage through the remote outlet decided by the leftmost $\log_2 b$ routing tag bits. If a packet fails to reach its destined row after traversing all the stages, the packet is dropped at the output side of the last stage (called the primary outputs). It is found that ICO exhibits lower hardware complexity than its (open-loop) Shuffleout counterpart [11] mainly because every SE in the Shuffleout switch is equipped with b distance computing blocks, one for each input. The complexity of such a computing block grows in the order of approximately $O(m^3)$, where m equals $\log_b N$ for a switching fabric of size N comprising $b \times 2b$ SE's [3]. This rapid growth in hardware complexity makes it prohibitively expensive to construct a large Shuffleout switch, restricting its scalability.

The closed-loop Shuffleout [2] was formed by adding re-circulation paths to the open-loop structure so that packets may travel through all the stages several times until they reach their destined output queues eventually (or get dropped when storage at each primary input for holding re-entered packets is fully exhausted), where a primary input is an input of the first stage. Storage is provided at each primary input for holding concurrently arrived packets, but there is no queue at the input or output ports of its constituent SE's.

3. Proposed Switching Fabrics —
NONBUFFERED CASES

Our proposed switching fabrics without buffers for scalable routers are based on ICO with appropriate re-circulating connections from the primary outputs back to the fabrics. These connections enable the packets to re-enter the fabrics when they fail to reach their destined rows in the primary output side, instead of being dropped otherwise. They aim to lower the number of stages required in ICO for a given performance level, when compared with ICO without such re-circulating connections, in order to simplify the destination queues logics and to reduce the total number of stages (of SE's). For efficient utilization of fabric resources, the re-circulating connections in ICO are to be fed to the *last* copy of fabrics either statically or dynamically, unlike the closed-loop Shuffleout which re-circulates connections back to the fabric primary input side statically. Our ICO's all lead to fewer conflicts and thus less resource wastage when using the last copy of stages for routing re-entered packets to their destined rows. This is because traffic is consistently lighter in a later stage of ICO_N, and one full copy (of $log_b N$ stages) is needed to route any packet to its destination. From this point onward, a packet is designated as a *fixed-length data unit* which can be delivered from one SE to another SE in a subsequent stage in one cycle. Messages are of varying sizes and are partitioned into packets (of fixed length) before being injected into switching fabrics for delivery. At their destinations, packets are put back to their original messages before being processed at the outgoing line cards (e.g., producing appropriate headers and performing needed fragmentation according to the protocols employed therein). Different re-circulation designs for ICO's are described next.

A. Static Re-circulating Connections

The simplest form of re-circulation is realized by connecting each primary output (at the last stage) back to the input of $log_b N$ stages ahead in the same row, for ICO_N composed of $b \times 2b$ SE's. It has a *static* re-entry point for each re-circulating connection, denoted as ICO_N^S, irrespective of whether or not there is a packet arriving from a prior stage at that re-entry point. ICO_8^S with five stages of 2×4 SE's is illustrated in Fig. 1, where the re-entry point of each re-circulating connection is 3 stages ahead (of the primary output side). Making re-circulating connections this way involves the least amount of extra logics. Each re-entry point is equipped with a 2-to-1 multiplexor, denoted by "M" in the figure, to accommodate the re-circulating connection.

The routing tag of each packet sent along a re-circulating connection back to the switching fabric *need not* be recomputed or modified, as the re-circulated packet is treated as if it advances to a next stage. There is no buffer provided at each re-entry point, and the packet can be fed through a re-circulating connection back to ICO^S only if there is *no packet arriving* from the prior stage to that re-entry point concurrently. This means a re-entered packet has lower priority, and resources are made available to re-entered packets only if they are otherwise not utilized. Note that if re-circulated packets are fed back to the first stage of fabrics, like the closed-loop Shuffleout, all such packets are dropped when the load equals 1.0 where a new packet is always injected into every primary input in each cycle, causing the re-circulated packets (which are older) to be discarded. After a packet gets re-entered into the fabric but conflicts with

another packet later at any SE (in the last copy of $log_b N$ stages), the one closer to its destination is given priority, irrespective of its age. If their distances are identical, the older packet (i.e., the re-entered one) gets priority. This is so desired to keep the *worst packet latency* small in ICO with re-circulating connections and is the only additional logic added in SE's in the presence of re-circulating connections.

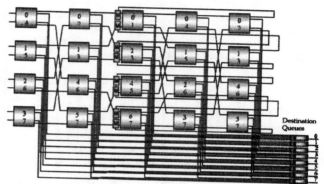

Fig. 1. ICO_8 with static re-circulating connections, ICO_8^S.

B. Dynamic Re-circulating Connections – First Avail

In order to lower the possibility of dropping re-entered packets due to conflicting with other concurrent packets from the prior stage, every re-circulating connection is provided with $log_b N$ entry points, one for each stage of the last copy, as shown in Fig. 2(a). Each entry point is equipped with a 2-to-1 multiplexor to accommodate a re-circulating connection. When a packet is to re-enter the fabric, it utilizes the entry point which corresponds to the *first* available inlet, where an inlet is available (at the time when a packet is to re-enter the fabric) if the prior stage delivers no packet to the inlet simultaneously. As the outlet of each SE has a latch to hold one packet at the end of each cycle, the availability of an inlet can be told directly using the latch indicator of the outlet (in the prior stage) which is connected to the inlet. If none of the inlets in the last copy is available, the packet is dropped. This fabric design re-circulates packets back via the <u>f</u>irst <u>a</u>vailable entry points dynamically, referred to as ICO^{FA}. Such a design is expected to get more packets re-circulated successfully back to the fabric at the expense of more multiplexors and their control logics.

Consider a given re-circulating connection. Let the availability of an inlet at stage i of the last copy be denoted by a_i (with $a_i = 1$ signifying that the inlet is available), the control signal for loading the packet via the entry point at stage i along the re-circulating connection shown in Fig. 2(a) is expressed as

$$l_i = \underline{a}_1 \underline{a}_2 \dots \underline{a}_{i-1} a_i,$$

where $\underline{a}_j$ represents $-a_j$ for $1 \le j \le i-1$. Note that Fig. 2(a) provides only the top re-circulating connection for clarity, leaving out the remaining connections. These control signals ensure that a re-circulated packet re-enters the fabric through the first available entry point (and only that one). When a packet is fed back at stage *f*, its tag has to be rotated leftward by (*f*-1)×log₂*b* bit positions before re-entry. A fast, simple logic to achieve such tag rotation is depicted in Fig. 2(b). The logic involves $\log_b N$ registers of length $\log_2 N$, with an appropriate control signal for data paths between a pair of adjacent registers, as given in the figure. After the packet re-enters the fabric with its proper tag accompanied, it is routed following the same routing algorithm. If it conflicts with another packet in an SE, the associated priority resolution logic is invoked to decide the one to be routed to its desired outlet, with the other being deflection-routed.

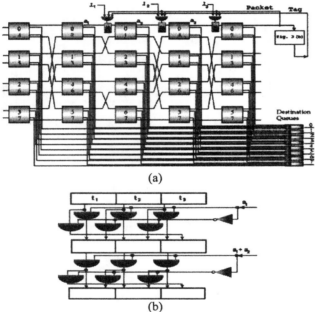

(a)

(b)

Fig. 2. (a) ICO_8 with dynamic re-circulating connections, ICO_8^{FA}, (b) Tag rotation logic for a re-circulating connection.

In general, ICO^{FA} does not have to provide entry points for *all* stages in the last copy, but just the early few stages, to restrict hardware overhead with almost no impact on performance measures of interest. It is found by our simulation that providing three (a constant number of) entry points is almost as good as providing $\log_b N$ entry points for any ICO_N^{FA}, presenting good scalability. We thus refer to ICO_N^{FA} as the design with *three entry points* per re-circulating connection (which translates to constant hardware overhead) subsequently. Note that ICO_N^S may be viewed as a special case of ICO_N^{FA} where only one entry point is provided for each re-circulating connection; in this case, no tag rotation is necessary.

The additional two entry points along each re-circulating connection in ICO_N^{FA} enhance throughput (or equivalently, offered load) noticeably, in comparison to that

of ICO_N^S. In this article, the terms of throughput and offered load are used interchangeably. The throughput gain is more pronounced when the total number of stages is smaller. Simulation results of ICO^{FA} with different total stages will be presented in the next section. For the cases of buffered ICO (as will be treated in the next section), however, ICO_N^{FA} is found to exhibit only negligibly better performance than ICO_N^S.

C. Dynamic Re-circulating Connections – First "1" Bit

While ICO^{FA} provides three entry points per re-circulating connection and allows a packet to re-enter the fabric at the first available stage, it does not check if the routing bit(s) corresponding to that re-entry stage is (are all) "0". This is not the best point for the packet to re-enter the fabric, unless the routing bit(s) for that stage is not (are not all) "0". The reason is two-fold: (1) the packet stays in the same row after that stage if the routing bit(s) is (are all) "0", and having the packet re-enter the fabric there costs one extra cycle unnecessarily, and (2) the re-entered packet may conflict with another packet in the re-entry stage and get deflection-routed, taking an extra (otherwise unneeded) re-circulating trip to "correct" this deflection-routing. The throughput gain out of ICO^{FA} may be offset somewhat by an increased mean latency.

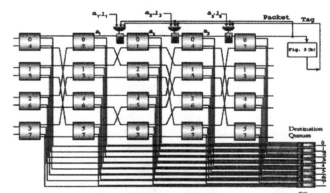

Fig. 3. ICO_8 with dynamic re-circulating connections, ICO_8^{FO}.

The best entry point for a re-circulated packet obviously corresponds to the *first* "1" bit in its routing tag, dubbed ICO^{FO}. This is because the packet has to get "corrected" in that corresponding stage before it can reach its destined row. To this end, an entry point is provided at every stage of the last copy for each re-circulating connection, as demonstrated in Fig. 3. The control signal for the entry point at stage *i* shown in the figure is given by

$$l_i = \underline{t}_1 \underline{t}_2 \ldots \underline{t}_{i-1} t_i,$$

where $\underline{t}_j$ (or t_i) is the 'NOR' (or 'OR') result of the routing bit(s) for stage *j*, $1 \leq j \leq i-1$ (or stage *i*). If the re-entered packet happens to conflict with another packet at the entry point, the former packet is dropped. This is done simply by making use of the availability indicator of an inlet at stage *i* of the last copy, a_i, as shown in Fig. 3. If the packet re-enters the fabric via the entry point of stage f, its tag is to be rotated leftward by $(f-1) \times \log_2 b$ bit positions before re-entry, using the same logic as depicted in Fig. 2(b), with control signals produced using t_j rather than a_j, for $1 \leq j \leq 2$. After a packet re-enters the fabric, it is routed in the same way as that described for ICO^{FA}. Unlike ICO_N^{FA}, ICO_N^{FO} requires *exactly* $\log_b N$ entry points for each re-circulating connection, since the first "1" tag bit may correspond to the last stage (of the last copy). As ICO^{FO} selects the best entry point for each re-entered packet, it is expected to exhibit the highest performance measures of interest for a given number of total stages, most suitable (among the three designs) for scalable router construction.

4. Buffered Switching Fabrics

Buffers are commonly introduced to the SE's of switching fabrics for performance improvement, in addition to their needs in packet switches for offering quality-of-service guarantees by establishing separate queues at each switch port for different traffic flows with various priority levels [10]. Buffers can be placed at the output (or input) ports of SE's to constitute output (or input) queues. Output queuing is known to exhibit better performance and be spared from the head-of-line blocking problem, but it often requires a "speedup" to achieve its peak throughput (of 100% potentially), where a speedup refers to that the switch core runs faster than the external links, so that multiple packets competing for an output port can be accepted by its associated output queue in one cycle [5]. In this work, we intend to explore the potential savings in total numbers of stages (of SE's) resulting from incorporating output queues in our proposed switching fabrics. This savings translates to cost reduction because the cost of a multistage-based fabric is largely proportional to the total number of stages (which dictates the overall chip count). In addition, few stages make the concentration logics in front of each destination queue simpler, further lowering the hardware cost.

Let the speedup at an output queue (of SE's) be denoted by ζ. For a fabric constructed out of $b \times 2b$ SE's, ζ is clearly no greater than ζ since there are at most ζ packets competing for an output queue (at an SE) in one cycle. While the number of lines terminating at each destination queue for a proposed fabric is equal to the number of stages in the fabric, a simple selector is placed in front of each destination queue in order to choose up to ζ packets in each cycle for acceptance by the queue, and those packets chosen are from the *last ζ active* stages (with respect to the destination), where an active stage has a packet to be delivered to the destination queue. More details about the selector design are provided in the next section. Destination queues are thus assumed to have a speedup of ζ in our switching fabrics. As will be illustrated by the simulation results later, performance of all the proposed fabrics is sensitive to ζ, and

an increase in ζ leads to better performance for any given ICO_N^S, ICO_N^{FA}, or ICO_N^{FO}. When a fabric is composed of 4×8 SE's, it is possible to run at a rate of 200 MHz, which is deemed rather moderate with the current manufacturing technology (given that the spider chip which employs a full 6×6 crossbar is operating at 200 MHZ [12]). With this clock rate, ζ may be pushed to 4, when each output queue takes one packet in 1.25 ns. This is realizable practically, since the current on-chip SRAM (static RAM) can have an access time as little as 1 ns.

The routing procedure in SE's with output queues is identical to that explained in Section II for SE's without queues, except for deflection-routing decision. Specifically, in a $b \times 2b$ SE with the speedup of ζ ($\leq b$) at output queues, if there are more than ζ packets heading for an output port in one cycle, the associated output queue can accept up to ζ such competing packets in a cycle, provided that the queue has capacity to hold them. Note that each queue has a specified capacity which can hold a number of packets (of fixed length). In each cycle, the packet, if any, at the head of each queue is moved to the next stage, say stage p, as follows. If the packet has reached its destined row in stage p, it is sent to the queue associated with the local port connected to its destination queue (referred to as a local queue), provided that the queue has capacity to take it and there are no more than ζ packets competing for the same queue at the same cycle. If the queue has no capacity left, the packet is sent to the queue associated with the remote output port connecting to the same row (called a remote queue) in stage $p+1$; the packet then attempts to reach its destined local queue in stage $p+1$ during the next cycle. If there are more than ζ competing packets, ζ of them are randomly chosen for reaching the destined local queue, with the rest directed to the associated remote queue (for delivery to their destined local queue in the next stage).

If a packet has not reached its destined row in stage p, it is forwarded to a remote queue determined by the routing bit(s) of the packet. When there are more than ζ packets competing for the remote queue, the distance of each packet dictates if the packet is to be sent to the desired queue or to be deflection-routed: the packet which is closer to its destination is given priority, like in the nonbuffered cases. The priority resolution logic devised for the nonbuffered SE's [11] can be employed for this purpose after a minor modification. For the speedup of ζ, the SE core is operating ζ times faster. However, the resolution logic, being a simple combinational circuit, in an SE can arrive at one decision in less than $(1/\zeta)$ cycle time (called a phase); for example, with the cycle time of 5 ns and $\zeta = 2$, we have $(1/\zeta)$ cycle time equal to 2.5 ns and the resolution logic is expected to produce one decision in a fraction of 2.5 ns. After a packet is chosen as a winner, the logic input corresponding to the winner packet is changed to all "1" (reflecting a farthest distance) so that the packet with the second smallest distance is selected in the next decision phase. This process repeats ζ times in a cycle to choose ζ winners for reaching the desired queue. All losers, if any, are deflection-routed to other remote queue(s) in the SE.

5. Performance Evaluation

Different types of $b \times 2b$ SE's for building various sizes (N) of proposed switching fabrics have been examined via simulation, including $b = 2, 4, 8$ and $N = 64, 256$. As the simulation results point to a similar trend, this section presents only the results of switching fabrics comprising 4×8 SE's with $N = 256$. We illustrate and discuss the results for unbuffered switching fabrics first, followed by those for switching fabrics with output queues operating under different speedups. As will be seen, a buffered switching fabric requires much fewer stages to deliver a given performance level than its unbuffered counterpart, even when the speedup is only 2.

A. Simulation Model

A copy of such a fabric composed of $\log_4(256) = 4$ stages. Each primary input is assumed to generate packets of fixed length randomly with their destinations uniformly distributed between 0 and 255 under different loads. A packet moves from one SE to another in the next stage in one cycle, based on the routing algorithm. A re-circulated packet in any of the three fabric designs also takes one cycle to get re-admitted. Each data value given in Figs. 4-7 is the result after 200,000 clock cycles in our simulation, where this number of cycles is found to yield steady-state outcomes. The performance measures of interest include *mean latency*, *offered load* (or *throughput*), and *packet drop rate*. Mean latency signifies the average number of cycles for a packet to reach its destination queue after it is generated. The number of packets arriving at a typical destination queue per cycle is defined as offered load (or throughput), whereas the probability of a packet gets dropped in the switching fabric under a given load reflects the packet drop rate. For buffered switching fabrics, each SE output queue (either local or remote one) is equipped with a buffer for holding 12 packets. When an output queue runs out of its capacity (i.e., unable to keep those selected ζ packets in one cycle, where ζ is the speedup), some packets which otherwise should reach the queue are deflection-routed. Each queue has a bypass provision such that a packet entering the queue does not have to take 12 cycles to exit unless there are 11 packets situated in front of it. This provision allows a packet which enters an empty queue to leave the queue immediately in the next cycle. A small queue capacity degrades performance for the fabrics under consideration, in particular, when ζ is 4; on the other hand, an excessively large queue does not enhance performance noticeably. As a result, we present only results for the queue capacity equal to 12 slots (i.e., packets) here.

B. Results and Discussion – Unbuffered Cases

Let k denote the total number of stages involved in a switching fabric. The mean latency versus offered load for $k = 7$ under ICO_{256}^{S}, ICO_{256}^{FA}, and ICO_{256}^{FO} is depicted in Fig. 4. The performance results of a compatible closed-loop Shuffleout (denoted by CSO_{256}) are also included for comparison. As can be observed, ICO_{256}^{S} under $k = 7$ exhibits considerably better performance than its CSO_{256} counterpart. For a given offered load, ICO_{256}^{S} enjoys sizable reduction in mean latency, by up to almost 20%. The maximum sustained throughput is slightly higher under ICO_{256}^{S} than under CSO_{256} for $k = 7$. This performance advantage is achieved, even though the constituent switching elements are less complicated in ICO than in CSO, as elaborated in Section II. It results directly from the fact that re-entered packets in ICO travel through the last 4 stages (i.e., last copy) where traffic is far lighter than that in earlier stages. When k grows, the performance gaps shrink, as can be found for the case of $k = 10$ in Fig. 4, since fewer packets then need to be re-circulated.

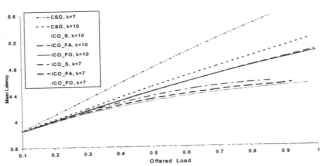

Fig. 4. Mean latency versus offered load for $k = 7$ and $k = 10$.

The re-circulation designs are expected to have substantial impacts on overall performance, in particular, for a relatively small k, say, $k < 2*\log_b N$. When k equals 7, for example, ICO_{256}^{S} achieves the maximum offered load of 0.87 only, whereas ICO_{256}^{FO} can sustain the offered load of 0.97. In addition, for any given throughput, ICO_{256}^{FO} results in slightly lower mean latency than the other two designs, for both $k = 7$ and $k = 10$. From the performance standpoint, ICO_{256}^{FO} is clearly superior. While ICO_{256}^{FO} requires hardware for rotating the tag of every re-entered packet properly along each re-circulating connection (as described in Section III), it takes fewer stages when compared with ICO_{256}^{S} to achieve the same performance level. For example, ICO_{256}^{FO} needs only 7 stages to yield the maximum offered load achievable by ICO_{256}^{S} with $k = 9$ (derived from the results in Fig. 5 below). These savings in the reduced stage count and in simplifying interfaces to the destination queues more than offset the added hardware amount, since four pieces of tag rotation logics (needed for the four outlets of an SE in the last stage) are clearly far simpler than a 4×8 unbuffered SE (consult Fig. 2(b) for a tag rotation logic). On the other hand, ICO_{256}^{FO} possesses slightly more hardware than ICO_{256}^{FA} but delivers a marked gain in the maximum offered load for $k = 7$.

The switching fabric of a router often employs a back-pressure mechanism to refrain packets from entering the fabric once its resources are exhausted [6, 8], instead of dropping packets after they are admitted. When no back-pressure mechanism is adopted, the drop rate performance measure serves as a good indicator of the probability that the backpressure mechanism is engaged. The packet drop rate versus k under the load of 1.0 is demonstrated in Fig. 5. For any given k, ICO_{256}^{S} is found to enjoy consistently a smaller drop rate than its CSO_{256} counterpart, as expected. Likewise, ICO_{256}^{FO} outperforms ICO_{256}^{S} and ICO_{256}^{FA} for all k values examined. The gap between the drop rate of ICO_{256}^{FO} and that of ICO_{256}^{S} (or ICO_{256}^{FA}) is particularly large for $k < 8$. This is mainly because the switching fabric with $k < 8$ does not have a full copy of stages to route packets without competing with re-entered ones (since less than two full copies of stages are involved), making it especially crucial to conserve fabric resources by admitting re-circulated packets only through their best entry points, as done by ICO_{256}^{FO}. When k grows, fewer packets are re-circulated and the performance gain due to ICO_{256}^{FO} decreases accordingly, as shown in Fig. 5.

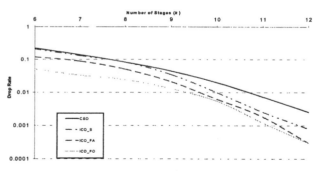

Fig. 5. Packet drop rate versus k under the load of 1.0.

C. Results of Buffered Switching Fabrics

A buffered switching fabric is expected to exhibit better performance than its unbuffered counterpart for any given number of stages of SE's. In Fig. 6, mean latency versus offered load for the three buffered switching fabrics is demonstrated under $k = 4$ and $k = 6$ with the speedup of $\zeta = 2$. It should be noted that the minimum number of stages of 4×8 SE's required for any multistage-based fabric of size $N = 256$ is 4 (referring to as one copy of stages earlier). With $k = 4$, ICO^S exhibits the maximum offered load of 0.85, almost identical to what ICO^{FA} does. In addition, ICO^S and ICO^{FA} are found to yield roughly the same mean latency throughout the entire range of the offered load, signifying that they offer almost identical performance (despite more complicated re-circulating connections for ICO^{FA}). On the other hand, ICO^{FO} reaches

the maximum throughput exceeding 0.98 for $k = 4$, and its corresponding performance curve is noticeably lower than those of ICO^S and ICO^{FA}. This indicates that ICO^{FO} clearly outperforms its two counterparts when buffers are introduced to SE's, like unbuffered cases demonstrated previously. If the number of stages grows to 6 (i.e., $k = 6$), ICO^S and ICO^{FA} again exhibit almost identical performance, with their maximum offered loads beyond 0.98, as illustrated in Fig. 6.

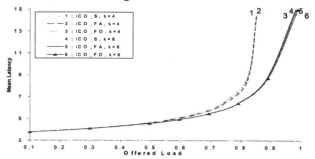

Fig. 6. Mean latency versus offered load for buffered switching fabrics under $k = 4$ and $k = 6$ with $\zeta = 2$.

Under this speedup (of $\zeta = 2$), it appears that $k = 6$ is adequate for ICO^S and ICO^{FA} to sustain satisfactory performance levels. As expected, ICO^{FO} again exhibits better performance than ICO^S and ICO^{FA}, but the performance gap shrinks in this case than in the case of $k = 4$. The maximum offered load for ICO^{FO} with $k = 6$ approaches 0.99. For ICO^S and ICO^{FA}, the increase of k from 4 to 6 substantially enhances its performance, whereas for ICO^{FO}, the performance improvement amount is negligible since its performance under $k = 4$ is very good already. In general, ICO_N^{FO} is a superior design choice among the three buffered switching fabrics (composed of $b \times 2b$ SE's), in particular when k is equal to, or only slightly more than, $\log_b N$.

The packet drop rate as a function of k is shown in Fig. 7 for the three switching fabrics with different speedups (ζ) under the load of 1.0. Under a speedup of $\zeta = 2$, all switching fabrics experience reduced drop rates as k grows. The drop rate reduction accelerates when k goes beyond 6, because the re-circulated packets not only are few but also are fed back into the fabrics through a stage whose traffic is expected to be very light. For any k, buffered ICO^{FO} always maintains a smaller drop rate than its ICO^S and ICO^{FA} counterparts. If the speedup is pushed up aggressively to $\zeta = 4$, the drop rates for the three switching fabrics not only are consistently much lighter for any k but also go down quicker as k increases, when compared with those under $\zeta = 2$. As might be expected, ICO^{FO} is observed to outperform its two counterparts by a wide margin. Under $k = 6$, for example, ICO^{FO} gives rise to a drop rate less than 10^{-4}, in contrast to 10^{-3} exhibited by ICO^S and ICO^{FA}. When k exceeds 6, ICO^{FA} starts to outperform ICO^S noticeably and the drop rate gap between them expands as k grows further.

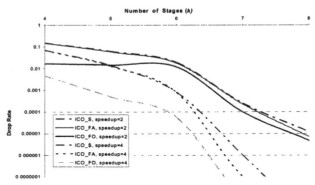

Fig. 7. Packet drop rate versus k for buffered switching fabrics under the load of 1.0.

Comparing these results with those of unbuffered cases reveals that the introduction of buffers to SE's yields considerable performance enhancement for a given k. As an instance, ICO^S with $k = 6$ delivers a maximum offered load of 0.79 (from Fig. 5) without buffers in SE's, as opposed to more than 0.98 with buffers. Likewise, ICO^{FO} under $k = 6$ arrives at the maximum offered load of 0.95 without buffers, in contrast to 0.99 with buffers. Alternatively, the switching fabrics with buffers need far fewer stages to achieve a given performance level than their compatible unbuffered ones. For example, the drop rate of our buffered ICO^{FO} (or ICO^S) with $k = 6$ is smaller than that of its unbuffered counterpart with $k = 9$ according to Fig. 5, reflecting a significant savings in the total number of SE's involved. While an SE with buffers is more complex than a corresponding SE without buffers, the overall cost of a switching fabric is likely to depend mostly on the number of stages (or SE's), because the number of stages dictates the chip count of a fabric. This reduction in the number of stages also translates to a simpler circuit (i.e., selector) for terminating packets at each destination queue. As a result, a buffered switching fabric appears to be more attractive than its unbuffered counterpart due to its potentially lower cost.

6. Conclusion

This article has introduced scalable switching fabrics based on a multistage structure with different re-circulating designs, referred to as ICO^S, ICO^{FA}, and ICO^{FO}, respectively. With distributed routing, these fabrics aim to interconnect large numbers of line cards (LC's) in high-performance routers. They employ far simpler switching elements (SE's) than an earlier multistage-based switch, known as the closed-loop Shuffleout (CSO), since no distance computing logics are needed. They all outperform a compatible CSO, resulting from re-circulating packets to the last copy of

stages where traffic is far lighter. In particular, ICO^{FO} is demonstrated to prevail among all the fabric designs, made possible by employing simple logics to re-circulate packets through best entry points in the last copy (of stages) without wasting resources or causing unnecessary conflicts. It leads to considerable savings in hardware complexity.

When buffers are incorporated in SE's to create a queue for each output port, the number of stages (of SE's) required for a proposed switching fabric to achieve a given performance level is lowered significantly when compared with its unbuffered counterpart, even for a small speedup of 2. This reduction in the number of stages also leads to a simpler logic for terminating packets at each destination queue. As a result, buffered switching fabrics seem to have lower costs than compatible unbuffered ones, because the overall cost of a fabric is determined largely by the stage count (which affects the chip count). Our simulation results reveal that buffered ICO$_N^S$ and ICO$_N^{FA}$ exhibit roughly identical performance for any given k and ζ (speedup), but buffered ICO$_N^{FO}$ clearly prevails, in particular when k is close to $\log_b N$ and ζ is small (say, 2). While buffered ICO^S, ICO^{FA}, and ICO^{FO} all possess good scalability and low overall costs, buffered ICO^{FO} is especially suitable for large sized construction, in particular, under speedup = 2.

References

[1] S. Bassi et al., "Multistage Shuffle Networks with Shortest Path and Deflection Routing for High Performance ATM Switching: The Open-Loop Shuffleout," *IEEE Trans. on Communications*, vol. 42, pp. 2881-2889, Oct. 1994.
[2] S. Bassi et al., "Multistage Shuffle Networks with Shortest Path and Deflection Routing for High Performance ATM Switching: The Closed-Loop Shuffleout," *IEEE Trans. on Communications*, vol. 42, pp. 3034-3044, Nov. 1994.
[3] M. Decina, P. Giacomazzi, and A. Pattavina, "Shuffle Interconnection Networks with Deflection Routing for ATM Switching: the Open-Loop Shuffleout," *Proc. 13th Int'l Teletraffic Conf.*, June 1991, pp. 27-34.
[4] A. L. Gupta and N. D. Georganas, "Analysis of a Packet Switch with Input and Output Buffers and Speed Constraints," *Proceedings of IEEE INFOCOM'91*, Apr. 1991, pp. 694-700.
[5] M. G. Hluchyj and M. J. Karol, "Queueing in High-Performance Packet Switching," *IEEE J. on Selected Areas in Communications*, vol. 6, pp. 1587-1597, Dec. 1988.
[6] M. Katevenis, D. Serpanos, and E. Spyridakis, "Switching Fabrics with Internal Backpressure Using the ATLAS I Single-Chip ATM Switch," *Proceedings of IEEE GLOBECOM'97*, Nov. 1997, pp. 242-246.
[7] N. F. Maxemchuk, "Comparison of Deflection and Store-and-Forward Techniques in the Manhattan Street and Shuffle-Exchange Networks," *Proceedings of IEEE INFOCOM'89*, Apr. 1989, pp. 800-809.
[8] N. McKeown et al., "The Tiny Tera: A Packet Switch Core," *IEEE Micro*, vol. 17, pp. 26-33, Jan./Feb. 1997.
[9] M. Pease, III, "The Indirect Binary n-Cube Microprocessor Array," *IEEE Trans. on Computers*, vol. C-26, pp. 250-265, May 1977.
[10] S. Moon, J. Rexford, and K. G. Shin, "Scalable Hardware Priority Queue Architectures for High-Speed Packet Switches," *IEEE Trans. on Computers*, vol. 49, pp. 1215-1227, Nov. 2000.
[11] N. Tzeng, K. Ponnuru, and K. Vibhatavanij, "A Cost-Effective Design for ATM Switching Fabrics," *Proceedings of 1999 IEEE Int'l Conf. on Communications (ICC)*, June 1999, pp. S37.4.1-5.
[12] M. Galles, "Spider: A High-Speed Network Interconnect," *IEEE Micro*, vol. 17, pp. 34-39, Jan./Feb. 1997.

Session 3B

Systems and Infrastructures

The Tracefile Testbed - A Community Repository for Identifying and Retrieving HPC Performance Data

Ken Ferschweiler[1], Scott Harrah[2], Dylan Keon[1], Mariacarla Calzarossa[3],
Daniele Tessera[3], Cherri Pancake[2]

[1]*Northwest Alliance for Computational Science & Engineering, Oregon State University*
[2]*Department of Computer Science, Oregon State University*
[3]*Dipartimento di Informatica e Sistemistica, Università di Pavia*
kennino/keon@nacse.org, harrahsc/pancake@cs.orst.edu, mcc/tessera@alice.unipv.it

Abstract

HPC programmers utilize tracefiles, which record program behavior in great detail, as the basis for many performance analysis activities. The lack of generally accessible tracefiles has forced programmers to develop their own testbeds in order to study the basic performance characteristics of the platforms they use. Since tracefiles serve as input to performance analysis and performance prediction tools, tool developers have also been hindered by the lack of a testbed for verifying and fine-tuning tool functionality. We have created a community repository that meets the needs of both application and tool developers. In this paper, we describe how the Tracefile Testbed was designed to facilitate flexible searching and retrieval of tracefiles based on a variety of characteristics. Its Web-based interface provides a convenient mechanism for browsing, downloading, and uploading collections of tracefiles and tracefile segments, as well as viewing statistical summaries of performance characteristics.

1. Background and motivation

A high-performance computing (HPC) application is characterized by many variables that control its execution and determine its performance. Variables such as algorithm type, problem size, input parameters, programming languages and paradigms, libraries, hardware architecture, etc., can have very significant effects on program behavior. It is important to understand the role played by each variable and the ways they combine to influence the performance achieved, or achievable, by the application.

Two approaches are commonly used for the purpose of understanding these effects: performance profiling and performance prediction. Profiling [7, 8] captures the behavior of an application by monitoring its execution. Monitoring can be based on hardware counter sampling or it can require the instrumentation of the application's source code or its binary executable. The data produced by monitoring may be analyzed on-the-fly or stored as tracefiles for post-mortem analysis. Many of the tools currently available for HPC performance analysis are based on tracefiles. Examples include:

- Jumpshot [10] analyzes tracefiles and provides multiple time-space diagrams of program behavior.
- Continuous Monitoring [6] captures logs of appropriately instrumented applications while they are being executed with the objective of automating the testing of performance properties of complex systems.
- Paradyn [4] employs historical performance data, gathered in previous executions of an application, to improve the effectiveness of automated performance diagnosis. The Paradyn's Performance Consultant extracts knowledge from all the performance data collected over the life of an application [3].

Performance prediction [2] takes a different approach. These techniques attempt to provide estimates of the performance achievable by an application by analyzing its structure and the influences of compiler transformations and the system architecture, using symbolic analysis, simulation, or other model-based methods. Prediction tools often rely directly or indirectly on tracefiles. The data from tracefiles can serve as the basis for constructing or validating the performance model, or can be used directly by the tool to adjust the model to the characteristics of a particular application (e.g., [9]).

Tracefiles are typically generated by the application programmer as part of the performance tuning process. Our field studies of HPC programmers indicate that many experienced programmers also create suites of simple pseudo-benchmark codes and generate tracefiles to help establish basic performance characteristics when they move to new HPC platforms. The intent in both cases is to help the user better understand and tune his/her applications.

The developers of trace-based tools also generate suites of tracefiles. In this case, the objective is to assist in the process of testing and fine-tuning tool functionality. According to the subjects interviewed in our field studies, tool developers do not often have access to "real" applications for these activities; rather, they construct artificial codes designed to generate tracefiles that will stress the tool's boundary conditions or generate demonstration visualizations.

Tracefiles are a valuable source of information about the properties and behavior both of applications and of the systems on which they are executed. Tool users and developers alike have indicated in several public forums (e.g., Parallel Tools Consortium meetings, BOF sessions at the SC conference, community workshops on parallel debugging and performance tuning tools) that it would be useful to construct a generally accessible testbed for tracefile data. This would make it possible for users to see if tracefiles from related applications can be of use in the design and tuning of their own application. It would also provide a more realistic foundation for testing new performance tools. Further, since tracefiles are typically large and unwieldy to store (the recording of key program events during one application run can generate gigabytes of data), a centralized repository could encourage programmers to archive their tracefiles rather than deleting them when they are no longer of immediate use.

2. The Tracefile Testbed

With support from DOD's HPC Modernization Program, we undertook the creation of a community repository, the Tracefile Testbed. The objective was to develop a database that not only supports convenient and flexible searching of tracefile data generated on HPC systems, but also maximizes the benefit to others of performance data that was collected by a particular programmer or tool developer for his/her own purposes.

The Tracefile Testbed was implemented as a joint project of NACSE and the Università di Pavia. It was structured according to a data model that describes both the static and dynamic behavior of parallel applications, as captured in tracefiles. The tracefiles are maintained as separate file units. The source code that generated the tracefiles is also available (unless that code is proprietary). Metadata encapsulating the performance behavior and run-time environment characteristics associated with the tracefiles are maintained in a relational database using Oracle8i.

A key aspect of tracefile storage is their size. While our organization has committed to maintaining the repository as a contribution to the HPC community, size was also considered from the perspective of the users, who will find that storing many downloaded copies is quite resource-intensive. We accommodated this usability consideration in the following way. Within the Tracefile Testbed, all file locations are maintained in the metadata database as URLs. This allows users – if they choose – to "maintain" their own subsets of tracefiles by simply storing links or shortcuts to the files, rather than the files themselves. A secondary advantage of this approach is that it allows us to distribute the repository itself. That is, the actual tracefiles may be located on multiple servers, which can be different from the server(s) hosting the tool interface and the metadata database. The initial implementation involves three servers: a Web server maintains the interface, a relational database server hosts the metadata, and the tracefiles are stored on a separate file server. The general architecture of the Tracefile Testbed browser is illustrated in Figure 1.

A Web-based interface allows users to navigate through the repository, select tracefiles and segments from one or more applications, browse their characteristics, and download the data. Performance data can be identified and extracted based on various selection criteria, such as "all data related to a given application," "data related to a class of applications," "data from programs executed on a particular system architecture," "data from runs that performed global broadcast operations," etc. The Tracefile Testbed provides performance summaries of selected trace data; alternatively, the tracefile data may be downloaded for analysis using available tools in order to derive detailed performance figures.

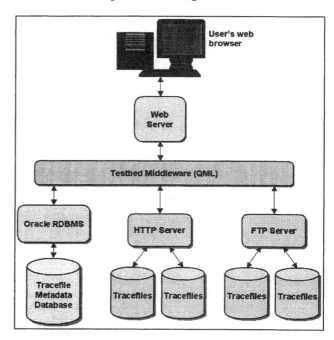

Figure 1. Architecture of the Tracefile Testbed

There are several significant challenges to be addressed in creating a repository of this nature:

- How can we represent the characteristics of a parallel application and its associated tracefile(s) in such a way that testbed users can easily find and select appropriate performance data?

- How much metadata can be gleaned from the tracefiles themselves, versus supplied by the user submitting the files?

- How can tracefiles be subdivided into smaller segments to minimize the amount of data that must be downloaded for a particular purpose? What is the proper abstraction for those segments, given that we cannot guarantee events on different processors occurred near-simultaneously (or even that they occurred at all)?

- How can we ensure that download operations always yield useful data? How can we reduce the need to download tracefiles? Can we allow users to maintain shortcuts to the appropriate files, without having to copy the files themselves?

- How can tracefile segments be structured so that they can serve as input to trace-based tools when the user hasn't downloaded the complete file?

- Can the repository reduce the need for programmers to write simple analysis routines? Is there a way to provide a "snapshot" view that compares the performance recorded in multiple tracefiles?

- How can the effort required to enter metadata be minimized, in order to encourage fully annotated submissions?

- What mechanisms for searching, selecting, and browsing tracefile data are powerful and flexible enough to help programmers understand application behavior?

- Are the same mechanisms appropriate for use by tool developers? If not, what type of specialized support is required?

- To what extent can the user interface guide the user through the repository, so that totally unfamiliar users can quickly arrive at the most useful information?

Clearly, many of the issues are related to the usability of the repository, rather than structural aspects of the database itself. The sections below discuss how each issue was addressed in developing the Tracefile Testbed.

3. Data model

In order to categorize and maintain tracefile data, we require a data model with the power to describe the characteristics of parallel applications and the performance measurements collected during their execution. In large part, the framework chosen to describe tracefiles derives from user needs in searching the tracefile collection. Based on previous usability studies, we determined that users wish to select entire tracefiles (or segments thereof) on the basis of machine architecture types and parameters, information related to the tracefile itself, and information related to the tracefile segments. Users should also be able to perform searches based on arbitrary keywords reflecting system platforms, problem types, and user-defined events.

The model must capture not just parallel machine characteristics, but also the design strategies and implementation details of the application. For this purpose, the information describing a parallel application has been grouped into three layers: the *system layer* provides a coarse-grained description of the parallel machine on which the application is executed. The other two layers comprise information derived from the application itself; the *application layer* describes its static characteristics, whereas the *execution layer* deals with the dynamic characteristics directly related to measurements collected at run time. Most of the information comprising the system and application layers is not available in the tracefile, but must be supplied by the application programmer in the form of metadata. Execution layer information can be harvested directly from the tracefiles.

The system layer description includes machine architecture (e.g., shared memory, virtual shared memory, distributed memory, cluster of SMPs), number of processors, clock frequency, amount of physical memory, cache size, communication subsystem, I/O subsystem, communication and numeric libraries, and parallelization tools.

The static characteristics of the application layer range from the disciplinary domain (e.g., computational fluid dynamics, weather forecasting, simulation of physical and chemical phenomena) to the algorithms (e.g., partial differential equation solvers, spectral methods, Monte Carlo simulations) and programming languages employed. They also include information about the application program interface (e.g., MPI, OpenMP, PVM) and links to the source code. Problem size, number of allocated processors, and work and data distributions are further examples of static characteristics.

The execution layer provides a description of the behavior of a parallel application in terms of measurements generated at run time. These measurements are typically timestamped descriptions that correspond to specific events (I/O operation, cache miss, page fault, etc.) or to instrumentation of the source code (e.g., beginning or end of an arbitrary section of code, such as a subroutine or loop). The type and number of measurements associated with each event depend on the event type and on the monitoring methods used to collect the measurements. Application behavior might be described by the time to execute a particular program section or the number of events recorded in a particular time span.

4. Describing tracefile content

To maintain the system, application, and execution information describing the tracefile repository, we implemented a database of descriptive metadata. These exist at multiple levels: they include descriptions of individual tracefiles, sets of tracefiles, and segments of tracefiles. The use of off-the-shelf rDBMS software allows us to maintain and search these metadata with a great deal of power, flexibility, and robustness, and with a minimum of investment in software development.

As discussed previously, the choice of which metadata to maintain – the data model – was based on our assessment of user needs in searching the tracefile collection. The Tracefile Testbed provides the ability to search on machine, application, or execution parameters. The versatility of the database allows us to search based on flexible combinations of these parameters, but careful database design was required to make full use of the power of the rDBMS. Figure 2 presents a conceptual view of the database schema supporting user searches.

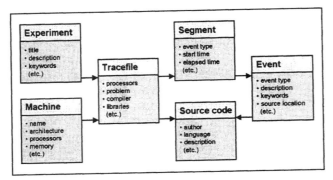

Figure 2. General structure of tracefile metadata

Note that tracefiles do not typically stand alone; they are usually generated as *sets* of related files pertaining to a larger project, or experiment. The metadata database allows us to maintain this information about the origin of tracefiles. The sets of tracefiles provide a convenient grouping mechanism, and allow users to view information on all tracefiles generated during a *physical experiment*, or suite of related executions. In other cases, a number of tracefiles that were not generated together may still form a naturally cohesive set (e.g., they may demonstrate a common computational approach, or illustrate the effects of varying a particular parameter). Since cohesion of such sets would not always be apparent from the metadata described above, the system allows specification of *virtual experiments* – groups of tracefiles, which, though not related in origin, have an *ex post facto* relationship that is

useful to a researcher. This structure allows tracefiles to belong to multiple sets that cut across each other, allowing individual users to superimpose organizational schemes that fit their particular needs.

A key requirement for the Tracefile Testbed is that it be easy for members of the HPC community to add new tracefiles to the repository. We were fortunate in having access to a sizeable collection of tracefiles, from a variety of machine and problem types, to use as the initial population of the repository. We have gathered on the order of 100 files over the last few years in our benchmarking work with the SPEC suite [1]. Given the number of files we anticipate gathering from the APART (Automated Performance Analysis: Resources and Tools) working group and other members of the HPC community, it was important to be able to parse the files in batch mode, and our initial parser reflects this bias. A Web-based tool for uploading tracefiles has also been implemented.

To ensure that metadata are available for all tracefiles in the Testbed, they must be supplied as part of the uploading mechanism. As discussed previously, information such as system- and application-level metadata does not exist *a priori* in the tracefiles, but must be provided by the programmer or benchmarker. The originator of the tracefiles is also the source of descriptive information about user-defined events in the execution-level metadata. To facilitate the input of that information, we developed a tracefile metadata format and a corresponding parser. Most of the metadata elements are likely applicable to a whole series of tracefiles, so the format and uploading tools were designed to facilitate metadata reuse and ease the task of uploading multiple tracefiles.

5. Identifying tracefile events and segments

While tracefiles are typically quite large, the portion of a tracefile that is of interest for a particular purpose may be only a small fragment of the file. For instance, a researcher wishing to compare the performance of FFT implementations may want to work with a fragment that brackets the routine(s) in which the FFT is implemented. Similarly, a tool developer may be interested in testing tool functionality in the presence of broadcast operations; the remainder of the trace may be largely irrelevant. If the source code is appropriately instrumented at the time of tracefile creation, the sections of interest will be easily identifiable, but locating them in a large corpus of tracefile data may still be an onerous task. In order to simplify identification of tracefile fragments that are of interest, it is convenient to maintain a description of the internal structure of tracefiles. Some of this structure may be automatically generated from information in the tracefile, but the remainder must be supplied as metadata, typically by the programmer who contributes the file to the repository.

Since a tracefile is essentially a list of timestamped events (with some descriptive header information), it is easy to identify a subset of a tracefile corresponding to the events occurring during a particular time interval. The obvious choice for definition of such a time interval are the begin and end timestamps of a user-defined event (such as the FFT routine mentioned above). We discuss user-defined events because system-defined events in MPI are atomic; that is, they do not have start and end markers. However, such a view may be an oversimplification that does not capture the behavior of interest during the time interval. Since the tracefile is a straightforward list of per-processor events, it is considerably more difficult to define events that pertain to the entire parallel machine. The idealized view of a data-parallel application would have all processors participating in all events (i.e., executing the same segment of code) approximately simultaneously; however, there is no guarantee in an actual application that any event will include all processors, simultaneously or not.

Consequently, a user who wishes to extract a subset of a tracefile to capture system performance during a particular event is faced with a difficulty. Although the user may know that particular events on one processor correspond to events on other processors, it is not clear from the tracefile how these correspondences can be automatically inferred. We have used a heuristic approach to identifying machine-wide events. A machine-wide event includes all of the same-type per-processor events whose starting markers in the tracefile are separated by fewer than K*N events, where N is the number of processors in the machine, and K is a definable constant (currently set to 4). The per-processor events that comprise a machine-wide event may or may not overlap in time, but discussion with users of parallel performance evaluation systems indicate that they expect this criterion to effectively capture the corresponding events.

The machine-wide event, defined as a starting timestamp (and, for user-defined events, an ending timestamp) in a particular tracefile, is the basic unit of tracefile data that our system maintains; we allow users to attach descriptions, keywords, and source code references to these events. Further, it is possible to search, browse, and download just the portions of a tracefile that are of interest to a particular user. A *tracefile segment* is defined as the portion of the tracefile between where a machine-wide event begins and ends. A given tracefile may have thousands of segments; they can be accessed individually or in groups sharing some characteristic (e.g., all segments corresponding to global summation operations).

6. Using tracefile segments

The principal reason many HPC users create and maintain tracefiles is to be able to use them as input to per-

formance-analysis software. To support this requirement, the Tracefile Testbed provides single-keystroke operations for downloading tracefiles to the user's local machine via http or ftp.

The issue of tracefile segments introduces problems with respect to tool compatibility. Trace-based performance tools require "legal" tracefiles as input; while there is no single standard for tracefile format, we assume that a tracefile that is usable by popular performance analysis packages will also be suitable for HPC users who write their own analysis tools. A fragment naively extracted from a tracefile will not, in general, be of a legal format. In particular, it will lack header information and will probably contain unmatched markers of entry to and exit from instrumented program regions. To make segments useful, the Tracefile Testbed modifies the fragment in order to generate a legal tracefile that describes as closely as possible the behavior of the application in the region that the user has selected.

7. Performance summaries

In many cases, the information that a user wants from a tracefile or set of tracefiles may be easily summarized without recourse to other performance analysis software. This is particularly the case when an application programmer wishes to compare some measure of "overall" performance across several different tracefiles. To simplify such tasks, the Tracefile Testbed provides some simple performance summary functions that may be performed on selected sets of tracefiles or tracefile segments. Available summary functions include:

- Mean and standard deviation of segment length (in elapsed time, in a particular set of tracefile segments)
- Identification and length of the shortest and longest segments (in a particular set of tracefile segments)
- Number of identifiable segments in a tracefile
- Elapsed time of a tracefile
- Per-processor mean and standard deviation of the elapsed time of a particular type of event (e.g., I/O operation, cache miss)
- Processor utilization during a parallel event (e.g., how much processor time is spent waiting during a barrier synchronization)

8. The user interface

The user interface to the Tracefile Testbed was implemented using Web technology to emphasize portability and convenience. Two interfaces were created: one for searching the Testbed and downloading performance data, the other for uploading tracefiles and corresponding metadata. Perhaps the most important concern in the design of the interfaces was scalability to the potential size of the testbed; our goal was to enable users to search and locate performance data in the most efficient manner possible, then seamlessly download the appropriate files or segments.

The search and upload interfaces both permit users to move freely among querying, downloading, uploading, and help activities. Definitions for all operations are available in pop-up windows activated when the mouse is positioned over instances of the term in the interface. Although the relational nature of the Testbed would allow users to query and view the values of all data fields, our previous experiences in usability of database interfaces [5] indicated that presenting the user with so many choices at once would be confusing. Instead, we applied a "drill-down" approach, where users are presented with a subset of the selectable fields at each step, allowing us to develop a comprehensive, yet concise and intuitive user interface.

Throughout the interface, users have the option of returning to previous stages in their search by using the "Return" buttons. The advantage of providing these rather than simply using the "Back" button provided by the Web browser is that we can provide a descriptive label for the button (e.g., "Return to Tracefile Listing") so that users can know to exactly which step in the search sequence they will be moved.

The search interface was developed using QML (Query Markup Language), a Web-to-database middleware package developed and distributed by NACSE. QML facilitates the dynamic generation of selectable lists by pre-fetching values from the Testbed, meaning that the interface does not require updating to accommodate additions to the database. The initial query screen is displayed in Figure 3.

The selection criteria available on the initial query interface page are those identified by representative users as the most useful in terms of facilitating discrimination among tracefiles in the Testbed. Criteria are displayed in three logical groupings to improve legibility and selection efficiency. Tracefile-related choices include tracefile format and event types. Selectable machine environment variables are machine type, number of processors, memory per processor, processor speed, and cache size. The query choices relating to the application are experiment name (both physical and virtual experiments are displayed), source code language, and algorithm. The user can make multiple selections from any of the lists, in which case the *union* (logical OR) of the matching records will be returned. After making arbitrary selections, the user can choose to narrow the search by eliminating choices that are unavailable due to constraints imposed by other selections. This drill-down operation repopulates the lists with data reflecting the selected constraints. The

procedure can be repeated as many times as the user chooses before the actual search is activated.

In subsequent screens, the user can browse the search results. Tracefiles are grouped into *tracefile classes* based on the unique combinations of language, source size, machine type, algorithm, compiler, and number of processors found. This helps users restrict the number of results before they view individual tracefiles, since queries may easily return hundreds of tracefiles (see Figure 4).

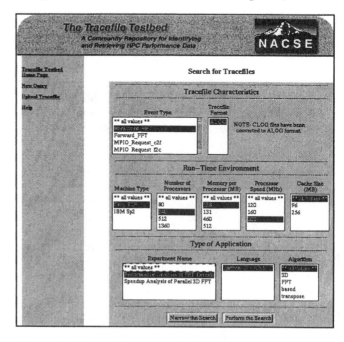

Figure 3. Query interface starting page

Initial Results: Tracefile Classes

To view results, select one or more classes.

Select Class	Tracefiles in Class	Language	Source Size	Algorithm	Compiler	Machine Type	Number of Processors
☐	4	Fortran 77 + ANSI C	600	3D	f90	Cray T3E	1360
☐	4	Fortran 77 + ANSI C	600	FFT	f90	Cray T3E	1360
☐	4	Fortran 77 + ANSI C	600	based	f90	Cray T3E	1360
☐	4	Fortran 77 + ANSI C	600	transpose	f90	Cray T3E	1360

| View Class Performance | View Tracefile List | Return to Query |

Figure 4. Search results, grouped by class

When one or more tracefiles have been selected, the user may download them for use with a performance analysis tool. To allow users to view summary information without special tools, and to allow users to download tracefiles exhibiting particular performance characteristics, three types of performance summaries can be generated. One compares performance across tracefile classes, while the other two present timing information on individual events and segments within the selected tracefile(s). The performance summary screen for tracefile classes is shown in Figure 5. From this point, the user can choose to download one or more entire classes or view more information on tracefiles within the class(es).

Performance Summary: Tracefile Classes

To view or download results, select one or more tracefiles.

Select Class	Tracefiles in Class	Experiment	Algorithm	Machine Type	Elapsed Time per Processor				
					# Proc-essors	Avg. Time	St. Dev.	Min	Max
☑	4	Speedup Analysis of Parallel 3D FFT	3D	Cray T3E	1360	6626.64	182.87	362	1098922
☑	4	Speedup Analysis of Parallel 3D FFT	FFT	Cray T3E	1360	6626.64	182.87	362	1098922
☐	4	Speedup Analysis of Parallel 3D FFT	based	Cray T3E	1360	6626.64	182.87	362	1098922
☐	4	Speedup Analysis of Parallel 3D FFT	transpose	Cray T3E	1360	6626.64	182.87	362	1098922

View Tracefile List	Download Tracefile Class	Return to Class List

Figure 5. Performance summary, by tracefile class

Performance tool developers will want to use the tracefiles for testing their own tool functionalities; they may also be interested in graphical or more detailed performance summary information than the Testbed offers. The Tracefile Testbed provides facilities for downloading tracefiles or relevant segments of tracefiles. Downloading entire tracefiles is accomplished through the "Individual Tracefiles" portion of the interface, which provides a link to the tracefile in the Testbed's ftp server. Additionally, users may download selected tracefile segments. To download selected segments, users mark the appropriate segments in the Segment Performance screen and select "Download Segments." This prompts a cgi program to parse the tracefile and create a new file containing only the original file's header information and the desired segments.

An upload interface was designed with the goal of encouraging users to supply adequate amounts of quality metadata, without being discouraged by the level of effort required. This was a challenge, given the number of metadata elements required for the Testbed. While creating a virtual experiment is easy, since most metadata are already available in the database, the uploading of new tracefiles requires a significant amount of new metadata

to be entered. In addressing this problem, we chose to put the form on as few pages as possible, rather than breaking it into smaller components over multiple pages. That way, it is immediately clear how much information is required. In addition, we endeavored to minimize the amount of typing required by allowing users to copy and modify the metadata from an existing tracefile.

9. Summary

Responding directly to a requirement that has been expressed in a variety of community forums, the Tracefile Testbed provides HPC programmers and tool developers with Web access to a repository of tracefiles. A database of metadata describing the systems, applications, and execution-level information of each tracefile supports a variety of search approaches. Performance summaries assist users to assess the relevance of files and segments before they are examined in detail. Individual files and/or segments may be downloaded to the user's local system for further analysis and comparison. Application programmers should find this community repository useful both in predicting the behavior of existing programs and in the development and optimization of new applications. Developers of performance analysis and prediction tools will find the Tracefile Testbed to be a convenient source of tracefiles for testing the functionality and display capabilities of their tool.

10. Bibliography

[1] R. Eigenmann and S. Hassanzadeh. Benchmarking with Real Industrial Applications: The SPEC High-Performance Group. *IEEE Computational Science and Engineering*, Spring Issue, 1996.

[2] T. Fahringer and A. Pozgaj. P3T+: A Performance Estimator for Distributed and Parallel Programs. *Journal of Scientific Programming*, 7(1), 2000.

[3] K.L. Karavanic and B.P. Miller. Improving Online Performance Diagnosis by the Use of Historical Performance Data. In *Proc. SC'99*, 1999.

[4] B.P. Miller et al. The Paradyn Parallel Measurement Performance Tool. *IEEE Computer*, 28(11):37-46, 1995.

[5] M. Newsome, C.M. Pancake and J. Hanus. 'Split Personalities' for Scientific Databases: Targeting Database Middleware and Interfaces to Specific Audiences. *Future Generation Computing Systems*, 6:135-152, 1999.

[6] S.E. Perl, W.E. Weihl, and B. Noble. Continuous Monitoring and Performance Specification.Technical Report 153, Digital Systems Research Center, June 1998.

[7] D.A. Reed et al. Performance Analysis of Parallel Systems: Approaches and Open Problems. In *Joint Symposium on Parallel Processing*, pages 239-256, 1998.

[8] S. Shende and A. Malony and J. Cuny and K. Lindlan and P. Beckman and S. Karmesin, Portable Profiling and Tracing for Parallel Scientific Applications using C++. In *Proc. SPDT'98: ACM SIGMETRICS Symposium on Parallel and Distributed Tools*, pages 134-145, 1998.

[9] J. Yan, S. Sarukhai, and P. Mehra, "Performance Measurement, Visualization and Modeling of Parallel and Distributed Programs Using the AIMS Toolkit," *Software - Practice and Experience*, 25(4):429-461, 1995.

[10] O. Zaki, E. Lusk, W. Gropp, and D. Swider. Toward Scalable PerformanceVisualization with Jumpshot. *The International Journal of High Performance Computing Applications*, 13(2):277-288, 1999.

EMPOWER: A Scalable Framework for Network Emulation*

Pei Zheng and Lionel M. Ni
Department of Computer Science and Engineering
Michigan State University, East Lansing, MI 48824
{zhengpei, ni}@cse.msu.edu

Abstract

The development and implementation of new network protocols and applications need accurate, scalable, reconfigurable, and inexpensive tools for debugging, testing, performance tuning and evaluation purposes. Network emulation provides a fully controllable laboratory network environment in which protocols and applications can be evaluated against predefined network conditions and traffic dynamics. In this paper, we present a new framework of network emulation EMPOWER. EMPOWER is capable of generating a decent network model based on the information of an emulated network, and then mapping the model to an emulation configuration in the EMPOWER laboratory network environment. It is highly scalable not only because the number of emulator nodes may be increased without significantly increasing the emulation time or worrying about parallel simulation, but also because the network mapping scheme allows flexible ports aggregation and derivation. By dynamically configuring a virtual device, effects such as link bandwidth, packet delay, packet loss rate, and out-of-order delivery, can be emulated.

1. Introduction

New protocols and applications continue to emerge as a result of the explosive growth of the Internet. It is highly necessary to test, debug and tune protocol implementations and network applications before deploying them to a target network. This procedure cannot be neglected especially when the target network is quite dynamic or difficult to access. Both researchers and application developers need a test environment to facilitate this development and deployment. Moreover, Internet Service Providers (ISPs) need tools or small-scale systems to evaluate the performance of their networks in terms of IP routing efficiency, alternative route availability, and link failure recovery time. Furthermore, to enforce system security, an experimental testbed is needed to test Denial of Service (DoS) attacks and other network security breaches.

Five existing approaches are available for this purpose: network simulation, Parallel Discrete Event Simulation

(PDES), a small-scale testbed[1], a large-scale testbed, and network emulation. Network simulation provides a synthetic conceptual network environment in a single operating system kernel. It typically requires real protocol implementation or application code to be converted such that it may be executed in a simulation environment. PDES is proposed to improve the simulation speed by executing a single discrete event simulation program on a parallel computer [1]. A small-scale testbed is a simple laboratory network environment that may resemble some portion of the target network in terms of network topology or traffic characteristics. A large-scale testbed can be the same of the entire target network, or a similar Wide Area Network (WAN). Network emulation is the execution of real network protocol implementation code in a controllable laboratory network environment, usually a Local Area Network (LAN) configured to emulate a real network.

The advantage of network simulation is obvious. As a synthetic network environment, it is easy to simulate a complex network topology. However, the synthetic network environment is based on some simplified assumptions about network conditions and traffic dynamics, and therefore may poorly mimic the real network. Another major drawback of network simulation is that the simulation time will increase dramatically as the complexity of simulated network increases. PDES partially addresses the simulation speed problem with the parallelism of a simulation program. However, PDES is difficult because it is extremely hard to maintain the correct order of computation in a parallel environment [1].

Unlike network simulation, a small-scale testbed and a large-scale testbed are real networks, thus real protocols and applications can be evaluated directly without any modifications. The problem of a testbed is that it cannot generate specific network conditions and traffic dynamics, as well as repeatable network traffic. This is unacceptable when the underlying network protocols, such as routing protocols like OSPF and RIP, are highly sensitive to some kinds of network conditions and network changes. Moreover, a large-scale testbed is often costly.

As a fully controllable laboratory network, network emulation is able to provide a rich set of network conditions and traffic dynamics, which can be applied to the underlying emulation for any specific purposes. In addi-

---

* This research was supported in part by NSF grant EIA-9911074.

[1] In this paper, testbed refers to a system or network environment without any synthetic network conditions and traffic dynamics.

tion, network emulation may mimic a real network more closely than network simulation since network traffic in an emulation environment and the operation of network protocols and applications are "real" instead of logical entities or processes of an operating system. The network protocol code may be directly used without any conversion. Although network emulation has many advantages, it has been criticized with some drawbacks [2] such as expensive to build, difficult to reconfigure and limited flexibility. In addition, existing emulation systems are usually non-scalable in two aspects: First, the maximum number of routers that an emulation system can emulate is bounded to the number of emulator hosts in the system. In particular, some network emulators simply abstract a wide area network to a single "cloud" or gateway with empirical network characteristics [3-5]. Second, the maximum emulated bandwidth that an emulation system can achieve is restricted by the bandwidth of the physical emulation environment.

In this paper, we proposed a new network emulation framework called EMPOWER (EMulation of the Performance Of WidE aRea networks), which can overcome all these drawbacks listed above. EMPOWER provides a powerful and flexible network emulation system that may complement simulation tools. The basic idea of EMPOWER is to map the target network to a fully controllable and scalable laboratory emulation network environment, and then precisely generate certain network conditions and traffic dynamics that can be applied to network traffic within the system. Similar to the use of a "wind-tunnel" to emulate the operation of aircraft wings in flight, EMPOWER uses real network protocol implementations and real application code to evaluate network behaviors. Essentially the emulation environment consists of a number of *emulator nodes* interconnected through hubs or switches. Each emulator node is a low-cost, multi-port PC with commodity components running Linux. Unlike other network emulators, EMPOWER is capable of mapping a network topology to the emulation environment, and making necessary changes to the routing table of the emulator node accordingly. As a result, routing protocols and mechanisms could be examined and tested with EMPOWER. Moreover, each emulator node in EMPOWER can be configured to emulated multiple routers in the target network, making the system highly scalable in emulating large networks.

The organization of the rest of the paper is as follows. The EMPOWER framework is presented in Section 2, as well as such important design issues as network mapping scheme, system and bandwidth scalability problem. Section 3 describes the EMPOWER prototype implementation and some experimental results, which can be regarded as a validation of EMPOWER. Related works to network emulation are outlined in Section 4. Finally, we summarize the paper and describe the future work in the last section.

2. The EMPOWER Framework

2.1 Design Objectives

In contrast to a pure software simulation solution or a single-host emulation solution[2], EMPOWER is actually a unique combination of hardware-software. It offers the following features. First, EMPOWER can emulate multi-host network topologies, which may include multiple routers and links, with automatic subnet and IP address assignment. Second, EMPOWER provides a fully controlled network environment, which can generate workloads and emulate any specific network conditions and traffic dynamics. Third, protocols can be tested in EMPOWER without modifications to the real code. Fourth, EMPOWER is able to emulate large-scale networks without significantly increasing emulation time. Finally, EMPOWER is a scalable emulation environment. Depending on the size and scale of the network topology, EMPOWER may easily increase the number of emulator nodes without worrying about the difficulty encountered in parallel simulation.

To describe the system architecture, some concepts and terminologies need to be defined since we use them frequently in the remaining sections of this paper.

Table 1. Terminologies and concepts used in EMPOWER

Emulator Node (EN)	A machine with one or more network interface cards (NICs). The number of emulator nodes in a specific emulation configuration depends on the target network topology.
Network Port	Each NIC has one or more network ports. In EMPOWER, we use a D-Link DFE-570TX that has 4 100 Base-TX network ports as an NIC.
Physical Port (PP)	A network interface within an emulated network topology, such as a router's interface. Each physical port has its own IP address.
Virtual Port (VP)	The basic emulation component in EMPOWER. Each network port may be configured as one or more virtual ports. Conversely, multiple network ports in the same emulator node may be aggregated as a single virtual port. Each virtual port has a virtual device attached.
Management Port (MP)	A network port on each EN that is used to control and monitor the emulator node.

[2] Almost all known emulators provide an aggregate behavior of the network, such as delay, drop rate, and effective bandwidth, without distinguishing each router's behavior and its influence on other routers.

Virtual Device (VD)	Each virtual port has an associated virtual device. A virtual device is an operating system kernel module that intercepts the outbound packet stream and applies predefined network conditions and traffic dynamics to each packet.
Router	A router in the emulated network. Each router may have several physical ports (interfaces).
Virtual Router	A set of virtual ports and their attached virtual devices. Virtual routers in an emulation configuration are the counterparts of routers in the corresponding emulated network.
Link	A physical link in the emulated network.
Virtual Link	A connection between two virtual routers in an emulation configuration. Virtual links in an emulation configuration are the counterparts of links in the corresponding emulated network.

Note that each EN may have a number of NICs[3]. While most NICs have only one port, we use multi-port NICs (e.g., 2-port NIC from Intel and 4-port NIC from D-Link) to reduce the number of ENs required.

2.2 Virtual Device Module

The basic component of a network emulation configuration is the VD. A VD is a kernel module that resides between the kernel IP layer and the device driver. The key to this module is that it only affects those packets from the IP layer to the network device driver of a network interface. By attaching each network device to one or more VDs, we may flexibly control every packet sent from this network device.

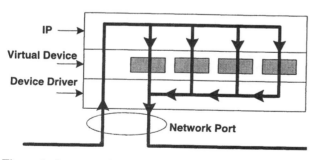

Figure 1. An example of a network port with four virtual ports

As shown in Figure 1, a network port, i.e., an Ethernet port on an NIC is shared by four VPs. A VD module is generated and attached to each VP. We may control the

characteristics of the packets from each VP by simply configuring each VP's VD module. The internal architecture of a VD module is shown in Figure 2. There are six sub-modules exist from the entrance to the exit along a packet's journey inside the module: the MTU sub-module, the delay sub-module, the bandwidth sub-module, the loss sub-module, the out-of-order sub-module and the bit error sub-module. Each sub-module can substantially incur one aspect of IP traffic dynamics and network conditions. In addition, background traffic can be generated within the emulator node according to a set of traffic models such that the impact of the background traffic to the emulation experiment can be studied. Note that the VD module does not affect the packet receiving procedure of an emulator node. Packets entering the underlying network port traverse the network layers of the operating system in its original way. With appropriate routing settings those packets can be routed to the correct VP, where a VD module is attached and configured for predefined traffic dynamics and network conditions. Upon exiting from the VD module, those packets are then redirected to the network port and physically sent out from a network device. The VD module also supports trace-driven emulation, in which a trace file of real network traffic is used as the input to the emulator instead of traffic generated by some applications. In the EMPOWER prototype, the VD modules are implemented as a kernel loadable module on Linux. A GUI interface is also provided to easily configure the network conditions and traffic dynamics and to apply background traffic for each VD module. Useful traffic statistics can also be viewed on this GUI interface.

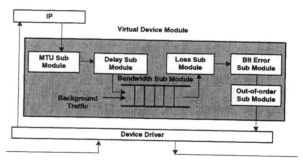

Figure 2. A virtual device module

2.3 EMPOWER Architecture

As a combined hardware-software approach, EMPOWER consists of a certain number of ENs running Linux, and one or more Ethernet switches[4]. In our prototype, each EN has multiple 4-port NICs. Thus each EN may has $4*m$ network ports, where m is the number of 4-

---

[3] We use NICs with PCI bus connection. Most of the low-cost PCs have 4 to 6 PCI slots.

[4] Here we consider 100 BaseT switches and 100 BaseT NICs. We could use Gigabit Ethernet switches and NICs.

port NICs installed. All the ports connect to Ethernet switches. On each EN one network port is designated as a management port (MP).

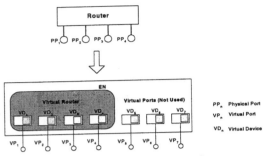

Figure 3. Virtual port mapping

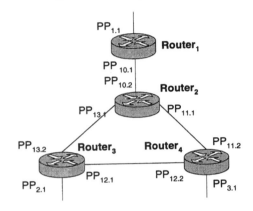

Figure 4. An example of network topology

Figure 3 illustrates the emulation of a 4-port router in an EN with four virtual ports. Each PP in the router maps to a VP. Each VP can be fully controlled by its attached VD. Thus, the four VPs constitute a virtual router.

A network emulator must be able to map a network topology efficiently and accurately. We present such a mapping by using the example topology given in Figure 4. Four routers interconnect through certain PPs (e.g., router 1 connects to router 2 through $PP_{10.1}$). Since there are totally 11 PPs, the same number of VPs (VDs) is needed to form an emulation configuration of those four virtual routers. For simplicity of topology mapping, we assume in this example that each network port only has one VP, although each network port can be derived to multiple VPs at a time. For unidirectional network traffic entering $PP_{1.1}$ and exiting from $PP_{2.1}$, the complete routing path is: router 1, router 2, and router 3. For unidirectional network traffic entering $PP_{2.1}$ and exiting from $PP_{1.1}$, the routing path is: router 3, router 4, router 2, and router 1. To emulate network traffic between these two PPs ($PP_{1.1}$ and $PP_{2.1}$), a sample emulation configuration with two emulator nodes (EN_1 and EN_2) may be setup. EN_1 has two virtual routers that emulate router 1 and router 2, respectively. EN_2 has the other two virtual routers correspond-

ing to router 3 and router 4, respectively. Each virtual router must be configured with the correct number of virtual ports. The routing tables of each emulator node will be modified in accordance with the predefined traffic path in the emulated network such that the behavior of each router can be faithfully emulated by a virtual router. Each VD is assigned an IP address, which is the same as its corresponding PP. In addition, two test nodes are needed to generate network traffic and to measure the end-to-end performance. Performance of each virtual router is measured on the emulator node.

2.4 Design Issues

Given sufficient information of the target network, the mapping scheme in EMPOWER is able to map the target network to an emulation configuration as close as possible. To achieve this, the same number of virtual routers as routers in the target network must be generated, and the same of number of virtual links must be created as well. Presently EMPOWER employs a simple yet effective port-mapping scheme for this purpose. According to this scheme, each PP in the target network is mapped to a VP in an emulation configuration. Consequently the problem of efficiently and accurately mapping PPs to VPs becomes a critical issue, which in turn affects EMPOWER's routing mechanism. The port-mapping algorithm must be efficient enough such that the number of ENs allocated for an emulation configuration is minimal. A preliminary observation is that all VPs of a virtual router must be located in the same EN such that network traffic within a virtual router may be completely controlled by simply configuring the related virtual devices in the virtual router. Otherwise, packets from one VP must traverse the Ethernet switch (which is not under the control of EMPOWER) to reach another VP of the same virtual router on another EN. With this observation, the port mapping problem is reduced to the bin-packing problem [6, 7], which is known to be an NP-hard problem. Presently the Best Fit (BF) algorithm [7] is used in EMPOWER to address this problem.

The flexibility of the mapping scheme in EMPOWER is that a network port in EMPOWER may generate multiple VPs instead of only one. These VPs share the same physical channel of the network port. Thus it is possible for an emulation network with n network ports to emulate a real network with more than n PPs. However, since all virtual ports in the same network port compete for the same network bandwidth, a resource competition problem may occur. This problem also brings a bandwidth constraint to the port-mapping scheme, in which the sum of emulated bandwidth of a set of shared VPs can never exceed the physical bandwidth of the corresponding network port.

Our approach for virtual router allocation makes the task of routing mechanism comparatively easy. A routing decision of a virtual router is made simply by looking up the routing table in that EN. There is no need to look up routing tables in other ENs since all the VPs of a virtual router are located in the same EN. However, the routing mechanism between virtual routers remains a significant challenge. Virtual router routing is completely different from conventional routing mechanisms, in which each host has only one routing table, and all the routing algorithms are based solely on this table. In EMPOWER, each EN has several virtual routers, each must maintain its own routing table. The operation of the route look up in a virtual router's routing table must be the same as in the conventional routing mechanism. With the advanced routing feature of Linux kernel 2.4 or above [8], this can be implemented without any modifications to the traffic generation program, but may need minor changes to the routing protocol implementations [9-11] to support multiple routing tables. In addition, we need to setup virtual links between virtual routers. In the real network, a physical link between two PPs is simply setup by corresponding routing table entries. In EMPOWER, however, the addition of the same routing table entries to those related virtual routers' routing tables fails to setup the virtual link because the operating system kernel of the EN will not forward packets among local network ports. Currently EMPOWER employs an ARP binding approach to setup the virtual link between two VPs.

When one uses network simulation to evaluate a network protocol, the simulation time increases as the size of the simulated network increases. With network emulation, we may increase the number of ENs to reduce the emulation time. However, in practice, it is impractical and costly to have a large number of ENs. As a scalable network emulation framework, EMPOWER is able to emulate more routers than the number of ENs by emulating multiple routers in a single EN. The number of PPs EMPOWER can emulate can also be increased by generating multiple VPs on one network port. However, as previously mentioned, resource competition may become a problem in both cases.

Another issue is that how to emulate a network link whose bandwidth is larger than 100 Mbps given that each network port is a fast Ethernet port. One approach is to aggregate multiple network ports to form a VP, called IP channel bonding [12]. This will reduce the number of VPs available in the emulation system, and is feasible if the target network is small enough. Another possible solution to this problem is to scale down the large bandwidth to below 100 Mbps. We need to investigate as a research issue the accuracy of emulation if we scale down network bandwidths linearly.

3. Prototype Implementation and Experimental Results

3.1 Prototype Implementation

As a combination of a hardware and software system, EMPOWER may be divided into two parts: a hardware system, which consists of a number of PCs with multiple 100BaseTX ports and several 100BaseT Ethernet switches, and a software system, which includes a number of VD modules and virtual router modules, routing control modules, a system operator module, and a traffic generator module.

Current EMPOWER prototype has eight rack-mount PCs. Each PC has four PCI slots. We use D-Link DFE 570TX 4-port NIC cards as the NICs in all ENs. We have an expandable and stackable managed 100BaseT switch (the current system has 96 ports and may be easily expanded) and many 100BaseT hubs. All PCs run Linux with kernel version 2.4.x. In our implementation, each virtual router has one routing table and several VDs. The IP routing look up within a virtual router is simply determined by the virtual router's routing table other than the main routing table. As a result, virtual routers are completely separated from each other in terms of packet forwarding.

3.2 Preliminary Emulation Results

We setup a simple "router chain" scenario for our emulation experiment. Four routers, R_1, R_2, R_3 and R_4 interconnect in a row from R_1 to R_4. In the EMPOWER prototype, these four routers are mapped to four virtual routers, VR_1, VR_2, VR_3 and VR_4, respectively. Since there are totally eight PPs in this topology, one EN with two 4-port 100BaseTX Ethernet card is enough to emulate this topology. Based on the scheme described in the previous section, an experimental emulation configuration is obtained by a simple topology mapping. In this configuration, four virtual routers are generated. Each virtual router has two VPs and a routing table that is exactly the same as the corresponding physical router. Possible IP network traffic dynamics and network conditions can be generated by controlling the VD that is attached to each VP. In addition, TN_1 and TN_2 are setup to generate network traffic and collect test results. IP network traffic between TN_1 and TN_2 will be forwarded from one VP to the other by each virtual router.

To test the maximum throughput of our EMPOWER prototype we executed a program (sender) on TN_1 to generate UDP packets at a specified rate. These packets are routed to TN_2 through VR_1, VR_2, VR_3 and VR_4. Another program (receiver) running on TN_2 receives those UDP packets and calculates the effective bandwidth between these two test nodes. The packet size is set to 1470 bytes to minimize the overhead of protocol headers, to minimize the overhead of protocol headers, yet avoid fragmentation in the Ethernet with a MTU of 1500 bytes. In the first experiment, we do not apply any bandwidth limitation to any links. Thus the test result should show the maximum throughput of our EMPOWER prototype.

Figure 5 shows the UDP throughput experiment result. The X-axis is the packets arrival rate of the EMPOWER prototype. The Y-axis is the UDP throughput. These two curves represent two different ENs using an AMD K6/2 300MHz CPU and an Intel Pentium 4 1.7GHz CPU, respectively. It can be seen that the EMPOWER prototype with an Intel Pentium 4 1.7GHz CPU can forward packets without any packet drops when the packet arrival rate is less than 60Mbps. After that, the kernel will drop packets since the device driver's interrupt handler cannot keep up with a very high packet arrival rate. The problem is not critical since EMPOWER is mostly used as a performance evaluation environment or a test tool for protocol development, in which the major concern is the behavior of the protocol in common network situations instead of those extreme cases. Mogul and Ramakrishnan discussed this problem in [13]. Their approach to maintain high performance of a host-based router is a hybrid of interrupt-driven and polling kernel, in which interrupt is used to avoid latency during low load and polling is used to ensure progress and performance during high load. Figure 5 also shows that with a faster CPU (about 6 times faster), the EMPOWER prototype's maximum network throughput is increased from 45 Mbps to 60 Mbps.

In addition to the UDP throughput experiment, we also want to verify the accuracy of bandwidth emulation of the EMPOWER prototype. We do this verification by applying bandwidth limitation to one of the links between these virtual routers. The bandwidth limitation ranges from 5Mbps to 60Mbps. This experiment is conducted using the EN with an Intel Pentium 4 1.7GHz CPU.

Figure 6 shows the bandwidth emulation experiment result. The effective throughput is quite closed to the theoretical throughput. Thus the EMPOWER prototype is quite accurate in emulating a specified bandwidth.

Figure 7 shows the emulation result with various packet sizes. For a specific bandwidth emulation, the throughput of the emulation configuration first experiences dramatic increase from less than 10Mbps until reaching the emulated bandwidth. The low throughput with small packet size results from the overhead of protocol header, i.e., a large portion of bandwidth is taken up by the transmission of UDP and IP headers instead of the payload. When the packet size is large enough, the effect of protocol headers can be neglected.

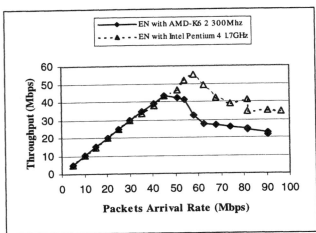

Figure 5. UDP throughput experiment

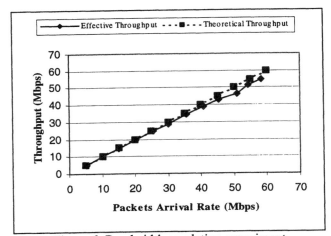

Figure 6. Bandwidth emulation experiment

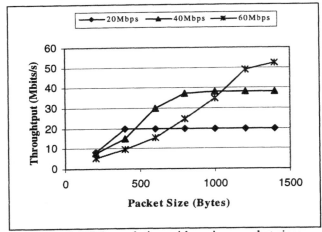

Figure 7. UDP emulation with various packet sizes

In addition to the bandwidth experiments, the accuracy of emulating packet delay with EMPOWER is also tested. We configured one of the virtual routers to incur a fixed delay for each traversing packet. We then executed "ping" on TN_1 to send 1000 ICMP packets to TN_2, and calculated the average roundtrip time of these packets. The original Linux kernel of the EN only provides a rough time accuracy of 1 jiffy, which is 10 ms on an Intel i386 platform. To achieve a better time accuracy, we increase the kernel's default interrupt frequency such that 1 jiffy becomes 1 ms in the modified kernel. The packet delay experiment results show that packet delay accuracy is within 1 ms.

4. Related Work

Modeling and simulation of the network has been extensively studied in the last 30 years. The most known and widely used simulator is ns. ns is derived from REAL [14], which is derived from NEST [15]. Based on ns, the VINT project provides improved simulation tools for network researchers to be used in the design and deployment of new wide-area Internet protocols [16]. The difficulties in simulating the Internet are discussed in [17].

There are some existing approaches to network emulation. NIST NET and Ohio Network Emulator (ONE) [3] emulate a router by loading a network device module into a Linux kernel, which intercepts the outbound packet stream and applies network traffic dynamics conditions to the stream. Dummynet [18] intercepts the communication between the protocol layer under analysis (TCP) and the underlying layer (IP). Delayline [5] is an application-level emulation tool that is capable of changing the characteristics of the underlying network by configuring a set of locally connected hosts. Davies and Blair [19] offered another emulator, specializing in adaptive mobile network applications, which may be used with any UDP-based applications with only a few modifications. ENDE [4] is a network delay emulator that estimates end-to-end delay by sending ICMP (Internet Control Message Protocol) packets to the remote host, while running underlying applications and protocols on the local machine under the control of the emulator.

While all the above approaches address the underlying problem to some extent, they share the same disadvantages: these approaches do not provide means to emulate a network topology. Instead, only one single router may be emulated, or the emulated network has to be aggregately simplified as a *cloud*, which provides controllable network conditions and traffic dynamics such as bandwidth, delay, and packet loss rate. Thus this kind of approach may only be used to test end-to-end applications and protocols. It fails to emulate a complicated network topology that may be used to test some new protocols that involve packet routing and quality of service. As an alternative approach, Fall [20] provides an emulation facility for VINT/NS simulator [21] such that experimental protocols and applications may be tested against repeatable network traffic dynamics generated by network simulator. Although one may use the rich resource of the network

simulator to test protocols and applications, this approach also inherits the limitations of network simulation.

The Utah Emulab, also called the Utah Network Testbed, is a unique type of experimental environment: a universally available "Internet Emulator", which provides a balance between control and realism [22]. Several hundred machines, combined with secure, user-friendly web-based tools, and driven by ns-compatible scripts, allow users to remotely reserve, configure and control machines and links down to the hardware level. Even the operating system disk contents may be securely and fully replaced with custom images. A major limitation of Emulab is that each node in the emulated network must be mapped to a machine in the testbed. Another node is used to shape the traffic between two connected nodes. As a result, the number of the nodes that the system can emulate is restricted by the number of machines in the system. Moreover, this is a very expensive emulation environment, which is unaffordable by most network researchers.

We began our own network emulation project in 1998 [23]. Our focus was on the design and implementation of the VD. We built the first version of a VD, a loadable Linux kernel module that can emulate network bandwidth, packet delay and packet loss. Thus a controllable path can be set and a single link topology (point to point) can be emulated. This work was adopted by a company as a commercial product, which received the 1999 Internet Telephony Magazine Product of the Year Award [24]. The VD module was improved in [25] with a better kernel queue management and extended the functionality, such as out-of-order packets and transmission errors. We also added the feature to support multiple VD modules per single network port to allow emulating the behavior of multiple network traffics by loading multiple VDs. In this approach, incoming packets are forwarded to a VP that has a one-to-one relationship with a VD. Instead of implementing IP routing among VDs, a packet dispatch policy is used to further forward the packets to another physical network interface that has one-to-many relationships with the VDs. While this approach partially solves the topology-mapping problem, strictly speaking, it is not "real" network emulation because it does not emulate the router's internal packet forwarding process, let alone emulating routing algorithms. EMPOWER, on the other hand, employs our previous work on VD and aims to setup a real experimental network emulation environment.

5. Conclusions and Future Work

In this paper we introduced a new scalable network emulation framework EMPOWER that can be regarded as a powerful and flexible supporting tool for the development of new protocols and applications, as well as performance evaluation of existing protocols. Each emulator node in EMPOWER may employ multiple network ports, and each network port can be mapped to one or more

VPs. Thus EMPOWER is highly scalable in terms of emulation capacity. Specific network conditions and traffic dynamics, such as link bandwidth, propagation delay, packet loss rate, link failure and queuing disciplines, are generated by configuring all active VDs. EMPOWER also provides a mapping scheme to map a real network to an emulation configuration.

There are some open research problems in EMPOWER. We plan to investigate the resource competition problem within an emulator node, and its impact on the validity of the emulation result. We need to find the number of network ports that an EN can handle before the processor or the PCI bus becomes the bottleneck. In addition, the scalability of emulation bandwidth remains a challenging research issue. Our future work will focus on these issues.

References

[1] R. M. Fujimoto, "Parallel Discrete Event Simulation," *Communications of the ACM*, vol. 33, pp. 30-53, October 1990.

[2] S. Bajaj, L. Breslau, D. Estrin, K. Fall, S. Floyd, P. Haldar, M. Handley, A. Helmy, J. Heidemann, P. Huang, S. Kumar, S. McCanne, R. Rejaie, P. Sharma, K. Varadhan, Y. Xu, H. Yu, and D. Zappala, "Improving Simulation for Network Research," Department of Computer Science, USC, Tech Report 99-702b, 1999.

[3] M. Allman, A. Caldwell, and S. Ostermann, "ONE: The Ohio Network Emulator," Ohio University, Tech Report TR-19972, August 1997.

[4] I. Yeom and A. L. N. Reddy, "ENDE: An End-to-end Network Delay Emulator," Master's thesis, Texas A&M University, 1998

[5] D. B. Ingham and G. D. Parrington, "Delayline A Wide-Area Network Emulation Tool," Department of Computing Science, University of Newcastle.

[6] J. E. G. Coffman, M. R. Garey, and D. S. Johnson, "Approximation Algorithms for Bin-packing - An Updated Survey," *Algorithm Design for Computer System Design*, pp. 49-106, 1984.

[7] J. E. G. Coffman, M. R. Garey, and D. S. Johnson, "Approximation Algorithms for Bin Packing: A Survey," in *Approximation Algorithms for NP-Hard Problems*, D. Hochbaum, Ed. Boston: PWS Publishing, 1997.

[8] Linux Advanced Routing and Traffic Control, http://www.linuxdoc.org/HOWTO/Adv-Routing-HOWTO.html

[9] Gated Routing Package, http://www.nexthop.com/techinfo/manuals.shtml

[10] Gnu Zebra Routing Package, http://www.zebra.org/

[11] MPLS for Linux, http://sourceforge.net/projects/mpls-linux/

[12] Beowulf Ethernet Channel Bonding, http://www.beowulf.org/software/bonding.html

[13] J. C. Mogul and K. K. Ramakrishnan, "Eliminating Receive Livelock in an Interrupt-driven Kernel," In *Proceedings of the 1996 USENIX Tecnical Conference*, December 1995.

[14] S. Keshav, "REAL: A Network Simulator," University of Califonia, Berkeley, Tech Report CSD-88-472, 1988.

[15] A. Dupuy, J. Schwartz, Y. Yemini, and D. Bacon, "NEST: A Network Simulation and Prototyping Testbed," *Communications of the ACM*, vol. 33, pp. 66-74, October 1990.

[16] L. Breslau, D. Estrin, K. Fall, S. Floyd, J. Heidemann, A. Helmy, P. Huang, S. McCanne, K. Varadhan, Y. Xu, and H. Xu, "Advances in Network Simulation," *IEEE Computer*, vol. 33, pp. 59-67, May 2000.

[17] S. Floyd and V. Paxson, "Difficulties in Simulating the Internet," *IEEE/ACM Transaction on Networking*, February 2001.

[18] L. Rizzo, "Dummynet: a simple approach to the evaluation of network protocols," *ACM Computer Communication Review*, vol. 27, 1997.

[19] N. Davies, G. S. Blair, K. Cheverst, and A. Friday, "A Network Emulator To Support the Development of Adaptive Applications," In *Proceedings of 2nd USENIX symposium on Mobile and Location Independent Computing*, Ann Arbor, U.S.A., April 1995.

[20] K. Fall, "Network Emulation in the VINT/NS Simulator," In *Proceedings of 4th IEEE Symposium on Computers and Communications*, July 1999.

[21] S. Bajaj, L. Breslau, D. Estrin, K. Fall, S. Floyd, P. Haldar, M. Handley, A. Helmy, J. Heidemann, P. Huang, S. Kumar, S. McCanne, R. Rejaie, P. Sharma, S. Shenker, K. Varadhan, H. Yu, Y. Xu, and D. Zappala, "Virtual InterNetwork Testbed: Status and research agenda," University of Southern California, Tech Report 98-678, July 1998.

[22] Emulab: The Utah Network Testbed, http://www.emulab.net

[23] K. K. Dam and L. M. Ni, "Design and Implementation of a Network Emulator," Department of Computer Science, Michigan State University, East Lansing, Michigan, Tech Report MSU-CPS-ACS-98-16, 1998.

[24] Internet Telephony Editors' Choice Award 1999: EMIP-1 Internet Emulator, http://www.tmcnet.com/articles/itmag/0899/0899labs3.htm

[25] M. Huang and L. M. Ni, "Emulation of IP-based Networks," Department of Computer Science and Engineering, Michigan State University, East Lansing, Michigan 2000.

Linux/SimOS - A Simulation Environment for Evaluating High-Speed Communication Systems

Chulho Won and Ben Lee
Electrical and Computer
Engineering Department
Oregon State University
{chulho, benl}@ece.orst.edu

Chansu Yu
Department of Electrical and
Computer Engineering
Cleveland State University
c.yu91@csuohio.edu

Sangman Moh, Yong-Youn Kim, and Kyoung Park
Computer and Software Laboratory
Electronics and Telecommunications
Research Institute (ETRI)
Taejon, Korea
{yykim, smmoh, kyoung}@etri.re.kr

Abstract

This paper presents Linux/SimOS, a Linux operating system port to SimOS, which is a complete machine simulator from Stanford. The motivation for Linux/SimOS is to alleviate the limitations of SimOS, which only supports proprietary operating systems. The contributions made in this paper are two-fold: First, the major modifications that were necessary to run Linux on SimOS are described. Second, a detailed analysis of the UDP/IP protocol and M-VIA is performed to demonstrate the capabilities of Linux/SimOS. The simulation study shows that Linux/SimOS is capable of capturing all aspects of communication performance, including the effects of the kernel, device drivers, and network interface.

1. Introduction

The growing demand for high-performance communication for system area networks (SANs) has led to much research efforts towards low-latency communication protocols, such as Virtual Interface Architecture (VIA) [10] and InfiniBand Architecture (IBA) [11]. As these new protocols emerge, accurate evaluation method is needed to understand how the protocols perform and to identify key bottlenecks. Communication protocols closely interact with the kernel, device driver, and network interface. Therefore, these interactions must be properly captured to evaluate the protocols and to improve on them.

The evaluation of communication performance has traditionally been done using *instrumentation* [3], where data collection codes are inserted to a target program to measure the execution time. However, instrumentation has three major disadvantages. First, data collection is limited to the hardware and software components that are visible to the instrumentation code, potentially excluding detailed hardware information or operating system behavior. Second, the instrumentation codes interfere with the dynamic system behavior. That is, event occurrences in a communication system are often time-dependent, and the intrusive nature of instrumentation can perturb the system being studied. Third, instrumentation cannot be used to evaluate new features or a system that does not yet exist.

The alternative to instrumentation is to perform simulations [1, 4, 6, 13, 14]. At the core of these simulation tools is an *instruction set simulator* capable of tracing the interaction between the hardware and the software at cycle-level. However, they are suitable for evaluating general application programs whose performance depends only on processor speed, not communication speed. That is, these simulators only simulate portions of the system hardware and thus are unable to capture the complete behavior of a communication system.

On the other hand, a *complete machine simulation* environment [3, 2] removes these deficiencies. A complete machine simulator includes all the system components, such as CPU, memory, I/O devices, etc., and models them in sufficient detail to run an operating system. Another advantage of a complete system simulation is that the system evaluation does not depend on the availability of the actual hardware. For example, a new network interface can be prototyped by building a simulation model for the network interface.

Based on the aforementioned discussion, this paper presents *Linux/SimOS*, a Linux operating system port to SimOS, which is a complete machine simulator from Stanford [3]. Our work is motivated by the fact that the current version of SimOS only supports the proprietary SGI IRIX operating system. Therefore, the availability of the popular Linux operating system for a complete machine simulator will make it an extremely effective and flexible open-source simulation environment for studying all aspects of computer system performance, especially evaluating communication protocols and network interfaces. The contributions made in this paper are two-fold: First, the major modifications that were necessary to run Linux on SimOS are described. These modifications are specific to SimOS I/O device models and thus any future operating system porting efforts to SimOS will experience similar challenges. Second, a detailed analysis of the UDP/IP protocol and M-VIA is performed to demonstrate the capabilities of

Linux/SimOS. The simulation study shows that Linux/SimOS is capable of capturing all aspects of communication performance in a non-intrusive manner, including the effects of the kernel, device driver, and network interface.

The rest of the paper is organized as follows. Section 2 presents the related work. Section 3 discusses the Linux/SimOS environment and the major modifications that were necessary to port Linux to SimOS. Section 4 presents the simulation study of UDP/IP and M-VIA, an implementation of the Virtual Interface Architecture for Linux. Section 5 concludes the paper and discusses some future work.

2. Related Work

There exist a number of simulation tools that contain detailed models of today's high-performance microprocessors [1, 2, 3, 4, 6, 13, 14]. SimpleScalar tool set includes a number of instruction-set simulators of varying accuracy/speed to allow the exploration of microarchitecture design space [6]. It was developed to evaluate the performance of general-purpose application programs that depend on the processor speed. RSIM is an execution-driven simulator developed for studying shared-memory multiprocessors (SMPs) and non-uniform memory architectures (NUMAs) [1]. RSIM was developed to evaluate parallel application programs whose performance depends on the processor speed as well as the interconnection network. However, neither simulators support system-level simulation because their focus is on the microarchitecture and/or interconnection network. Instead, system calls are supported through a proxy mechanism. Moreover, they do not model system components, such as I/O devices and interrupt mechanism that are needed to run the system software such as the operating system kernel and hardware drivers. Therefore, these simulators are not appropriate for studying communication performance.

SimOS was developed to facilitate computer architecture research and experimental operating system development [3]. It is the most complete simulator for studying computer system performance. There are several variations of SimOS. SimOS-PPC is being developed at IBM Austin Research Laboratory, which models a variety of uni- and multiprocessor PowerPC-based systems and micro-architectures [16]. There is also a SimOS interface to SimpleScalar/PowerPC being developed at UT Austin [17]. However, these systems only support AIX as the target operating system. Therefore, it is difficult to perform detailed evaluations without knowing the internals of the kernel. Virtutech's SimIC [2] was developed with the same purpose as SimOS and supports a number of commercial operating systems including Linux. The major advantage of SimICS over SimOS is improved simulation speed using highly optimized codes for fast event handling and a simple processor pipeline. How-

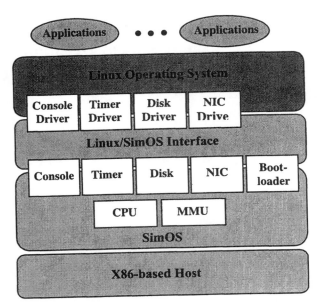

Figure 1. The structure of Linux/SimOS.

ever, SimICS is proprietary and thus the internal details of the simulator are not available to the public. This makes it difficult for users to add or modify new hardware features. The motivation for Linux/SimOS is to alleviate these restrictions by developing an effective simulation environment for studying all aspects of computer system performance using SimOS with the flexibility and availability of the Linux operating system.

3. Overview of Linux/SimOS

Figure 1 shows the structure of Linux/SimOS. An x86-based Linux machine serves as the host for running the simulation environment. SimOS runs as a target machine on the host, which consists of simulated models of CPU, memory, timer, and I/O devices, such as disk, console, and Ethernet NIC. On top of the target machine, a Linux/MIPS kernel version 2.3 runs as the target operating system.

3.1. SimOS Machine Simulator

This subsection briefly describes the functionality of SimOS and the memory and I/O device address mapping. For a detail description of SimOS, please refer to [3].

SimOS supports two execution-driven, cycle-accurate CPU models: Mipsy and MSX. Mipsy models a simple pipeline similar to the MIPS R4000, while MSX models a superscalar, dynamically scheduled pipeline similar to MIPS R10000. The CPU models support the execution of the MIPS instruction set [12], including privileged instructions. SimOS also models a memory management unit (MMU), including the related

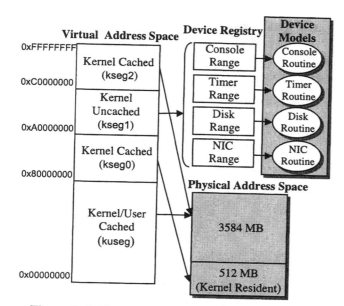

Figure 2. Address mapping mechanism in SimOS.

exceptions. Therefore, the virtual memory translation occurs as in a real machine. SimOS also models the behavior of I/O devices by performing DMA operations to/from the memory and interrupting the CPU when I/O requests complete. It also supports the simulation of a multiprocessor system with a bused-based cache-coherent memory system or a Cache-Coherent Non-uniform Memory Architecture (CC-NUMA) memory system.

Figure 2 represents the SimOS memory and I/O device address mapping. The virtual address space is subdivided into four segments. Segments kseg0 through kseg2 can only be accessed in the kernel mode, while segment kuseg can be accessed either in user or kernel mode. The kernel executable code is contained in kseg0 and mapped directly to lower 512 MB in the physical memory. The segments kuseg and kseg2, which contain user process and per process kernel data structures, respectively, are mapped to the remaining address space in the physical memory. Therefore, communication between CPU and main memory involves simply reading and writing to the allocated memory.

On the other hand, I/O device addresses are mapped to the uncached kseg1 segment, and a hash table called the *device registry* controls its accesses. The function of the device registry is to translate an I/O device register access to the appropriate I/O device simulation routine. Therefore, each I/O device first has to register its device registers with the device registry, which maps an appropriate device simulator routine at a location in the I/O address space. This is shown in Table 1. In response to device driver requests, I/O device models provide I/O services and interrupt the CPU as appropriate.

SimOS provides several I/O device models for con-

sole, timer, SCSI disk, and NIC. These models provide not only the device functionality but also the interface between the simulator and the real world. The console model provides the functionality of allowing a user to read messages from and type in commands into the simulated machine's console. The SimOS NIC model enables a simulated machine to communicate with other simulated machines or real machines through the Ethernet. By allocating an IP address for the simulated machine, it can act as an Internet node, such as an NFS client or a Web server. SimOS uses the host machine's file system to provide the functionality of a hard disk, maintaining the disk's contents in a file on the host machine. Reads and writes to the simulated disk become reads and writes to this file, and DMA transfers require simply copying data from the file into the portion of the simulator's address space representing the target machine's main memory.

Table 1. I/O device address map.

Device	Start address	Size in bytes
Timer	0xA0E00000	4
Console	0xA0E01000	8
Ethernet NIC	0xA0E02000	2852
Disk	0xA0E10000	542208

3.2. Linux/SimOS Interface
In this subsection, the major modifications that were necessary to port Linux to SimOS is discussed, i.e., *Linux/SimOS interface*. Most of the major modifications were done on the I/O device drivers for Linux. Therefore, the description will focus on the interfacing requirements between the Linux device drivers and SimOS I/O device models.

3.2.1. Timer and Console
SimOS provides a simple real-time *clock* that indicates the current time in seconds past since January 1, 1970. The real-time clock keeps the time value in a 32-bit register located at address 0xA0E00000 (see Table 1), and a user program reads the current time using the gettimeofday() system call.

Linux timer driver was modified to reflect the simplicity of the SimOS timer model. The SimOS real-time clock has a single register, while a timer chip in a real system has tens of registers that are accessed by the driver. Also, the Linux timer driver periodically adjusts the real-time clock to prevent it from drifting due to temperature or system power fluctuation. Since these problems are not present in a simulation environment, these features were removed to simplify debugging.

195

The *console model* in SimOS consists of two registers: a control/status register and a data register. In particular, the data register is implemented as a single entry FIFO queue. However, real serial controllers, such as UART, have multiple-entry FIFO queue for faster serial I/O. Therefore, the Linux console driver was modified to support only a single character transfer over the single entry FIFO.

3.2.2. SCSI Disk

The SimOS *disk model* simulates a SCSI disk, which has the combined functionality of a SCSI adapter, a DMA, a disk controller, and a disk unit. Therefore, the registers in the SimOS disk model represent the combination of SCSI adapter registers, DMA descriptors, and disk status and control registers. This is different from a real SCSI disk, which implements them separately, and thus how the Linux disk driver views the disk. In particular, the problem arises when application programs make disk requests. These requests are made to the SCSI adapter with disk unit numbers, which are then translated by the disk driver to appropriate disk register addresses. But, the SimOS disk model performs the translation internally and thus the Linux disk driver is incompatible with the SimOS disk model. Therefore, the SimOS disk model had to be completely rewritten to reflect how the Linux disk driver communicates with the SCSI adapter and the disk unit.

3.2.3. Kernel Bootloader

When the kernel and the device drivers are prepared and compiled, a kernel executable is generated in ELF binary format [15]. It is then responsibility of the SimOS *bootloader* to load the kernel executable into the main memory of the simulated machine.

When the bootloader starts, it reads the executable file and looks for headers in the file. An ELF executable contains three different type headers: a file name header, program headers, and section headers. Each program header is associated a program segment, which holds a portion of the kernel code. Each program segment has a number of sections, and a section header defines how these sections are loaded into memory. Therefore, the bootloader has to use both program and section headers to properly load the program segment. Unfortunately, the bootloader that came with the SimOS distribution was incomplete and thus did not properly handle the ELF format. That is, it did not use both program and section headers to load the program. Therefore, the bootloader was modified to correct this problem.

3.2.4. Ethernet NIC

The SimOS *Ethernet NIC model* supports connectivity to simulated hosts as well as to real hosts. This is achieved using UDP packets of the local host. The Ethernet NIC model encapsulates its simulated Ethernet frames in UDP

packets and sends them through NIC of the local host to a network simulator called EtherSim [4], which runs on a different host. The main function of EtherSim is to forward the received packets to the destination host.

The Ethernet NIC model is controlled by a set of registers mapped into the memory region starting at 0xA0E02000 (see Table 1). The data transfer between the main memory and NIC occurs via DMA operations using descriptors pointing to DMA buffers. Typically, the Linux NIC driver allocates DMA buffers in the uncached kseg1 segment. Since the device registry controls this memory region in SimOS, two modifications were necessary to differentiate between I/O device accesses and uncached memory accesses. First, the Linux Ethernet driver was changed to allocate DMA buffers using the device registry. Second, the device registry was modified to handle the allocated DMA buffer space as an uncached memory space.

4. Simulation Study of UDP/IP and M-VIA

This section presents the simulation results of UDP/IP and M-VIA [12] to demonstrate the capabilities of Linux/SimOS. To evaluate the performance of these two protocols, a test program was run on Linux/SimOS that accepts command-line options specifying send/receive, a message size, and an address. In order to aid the measurement of execution times of send/receive through the protocol layers, a simple program called Echo Server was written. The function of the Echo Server is to receive the network packets generated from a simulated host through the NIC, appropriately modify the headers of the received packets, and send back to the same simulated host. This allowed us to avoid the loop back mode and properly measure the performance of the driver and NIC.

The UDP/IP performance was evaluated by directly sending messages through the legacy protocol stack in Linux/SimOS. On the other hand, M-VIA, which is Virtual Interface Architecture implementation for Linux, requires three components: VI provider library (vipl) is a collection of library calls to obtain VI services; M-VIA kernel module (vipk_core) contains a set of modularized kernel functions implemented in user-level; and M-VIA device drivers (vipk_dev) provide an interface to NIC.

In order to run M-VIA on Linux/SimOS, some modifications were necessary. First, because M-VIA was released only for x86-based Linux hosts, some of the source codes had to be modified to run it on Linux/SimOS. In particular, the code for fast traps (vipk_core/vipk_ftrap.S) had to be rewritten because the MIPS system supports a different system call convention than x86-based systems. Second, the driver for M-VIA had to be modified (as discussed in Subsection 3.2) to work with SimOS Ethernet NIC.

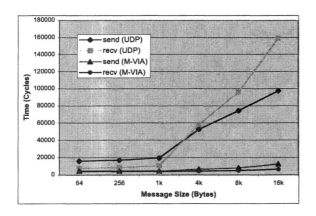

Figure 3. Total execution time vs. message size.

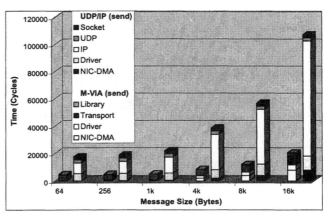

Figure 4. Send execution times for each layer vs. message size.

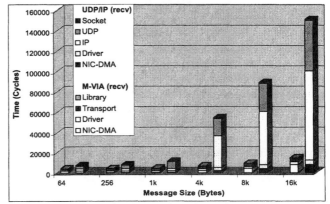

Figure 5. Receive execution times for each layer vs. message size.

The CPU model employed was Mipsy with 32 KB L1 instruction and data caches with 1 cycle hit latency, and 1 MB L2 cache with 10 cycle hit latency. The main memory was configured to have 32 MB with hit latency of 100 cycles, and DMA on the Ethernet NIC model was set to have a transfer time of 240 MB/sec. The results were obtained using SimOS's data collection mechanism, which uses a set of annotation routines written in Tcl [18]. These annotations are attached to specific events of interest, and when an event occurs the associated Tcl code is executed. Annotation codes have access to the entire state of the simulated system, and more importantly, data collection is performed in a non-intrusive manner.

The simulation study focused on the execution time (in cycles) required to perform send/receive using UDP/IP and M-VIA. These simulations were run with a fixed MTU (Maximum Transmission Unit) size of 1,500 bytes and varying message sizes. The total execution times required to perform the respective send/receive for different message sizes are shown in Figure 3. The send results are based on the number of cycles required to perform the socket call sendto() for UDP/IP and VipPostSend() for M-VIA. The receive results are based on the time between the arrival of a message and when the socket call recvfrom() for UDP/IP and VipPostRecv() for M-VIA return. These results do not include the time needed to set up the socket communication for UDP/IP and memory region registration for M-VIA. It also does not include the effects of MAC and physical layer operations. The results in Figure 3 clearly show the advantage of using low-latency, user-level messaging. The improvement factors for send and receive range from 3.5 to 9.3 and 2 to 24 over UDP/IP, respectively.

The cycle times for UDP and M-VIA send/receive were then divided based on the various layers available for each protocol. This allows us to see how much time is spent at each layer of the protocol and how the data size affects the number of cycles required to perform a send/receive. For UDP/IP, the layers are Socket, UDP, IP, Driver, and DMA operations for NIC. For M-VIA, the layers are VI Library calls, Transport layer, Driver, and DMA operations for NIC. These results are shown in Figures 4 and 5, where each message size has a pair of bar graphs representing the execution times of M-VIA (left) and UDP/IP (right).

For UDP/IP send/receive, the amount of cycle time spent on the Socket layer stays relatively constant for all message sizes and represents only a small portion of the total execution time. In contrast, the amount of time spent on the IP layer increases as the message size increases. This is due to the fact that in Linux, in addition to IP fragmentation, data copying from user space to sk_buff buffer during a send is done at the IP layer. In contrast, data copying from sk_buff buffer to user space during a receive is done at the UDP layer. For receive, the time spent on the IP layer increases for message sizes larger than MTU mainly due to defragmentation.

For M-VIA send/receive (i.e., VipPost-Send/VipPostRecv), the Library layer creates a descriptor in the registered memory, adds the descriptor to the send

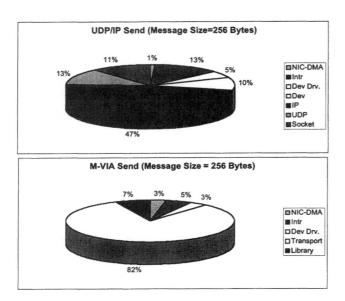

Figure 6. Send time breakdown for UDP/IP and M-VIA for message size 256 bytes.

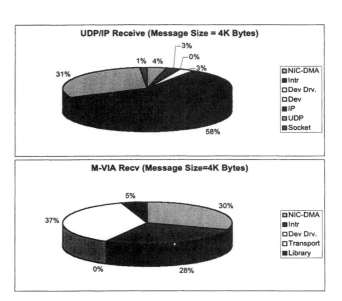

Figure 7. Receive time breakdown for UDP/IP and M-VIA for message size 4K bytes.

queue, and rings the door bell. The Transport layer then performs virtual-to-physical address translation and transfers the control to the Driver layer. As can be seen from the figures, the Library layer has a negligible effect on the overall performance. However, virtual-to-physical address translation and fragmentation/defragmentation in the Transport layer constitute a significant portion of the total execution time.

For Driver and NIC layers, both protocols show similar results. This is because M-VIA uses a similar type of driver to communicate with the Ethernet NIC model. The primary function of the Driver layer is to set up the NIC's DMA and receive interrupts from NIC. As can be seen, the execution time of the Driver layer varies as a function of the message size and represents only a small portion of the total execution time. The DMA transfer in the NIC also varies linearly with the message size. This is consistent since DMA setup and interrupt processing are already reflected in the Driver layer; therefore, DMA transfer time is dependent only on the message size.

The pie charts shown in Figures 6 and 7 give further details about what contributes to the amount of time spent on each layer. The UDP layer has the following operations: UDP header operations, data copy (for receive), sk_buff structure operations, and error processing. For send, data copying and fragmentation occurs at the IP layer and it becomes dominant as message size grows. As a result it constitutes a large portion of the overall send time as shown in Figure 6. In contrast, Figure 7 shows that data copying for a receive operation occurs at the UDP layer and thus represents a large portion of the overall execution time compared to a send operation. How-

ever, due to its large message size (4 Kbytes) IP layer still dominates because of defragmentation.

For UDP/IP, the Driver layer was further subdivided into interrupt handling (Intr), device specific driver functions (Dev Drv.), and general device functions (Dev). Dev Drv. controls NIC hardware functions, such DMA setup, while Dev provides an interface between the IP layer and Dev Drv, such as packet multiplexing/demultiplexing. Thus, for a send operation, the IP layer initiates a DMA operation using Dev Drv. via Dev and Intr is notified of the completion of the DMA transfer. On the other hand, a receive operation is interrupt initiated and thus handled only by Intr and Dev. As shown in Figures 6, all three portions of the Driver layer represent a significant portion of the overall execution time for sending a small message. However, for a large message as shown in Figure 7, the Driver layer becomes relatively insignificant.

For M-VIA, the Driver layer was further subdivided into interrupt handling (Intr) and device specific driver functions (Dev Drv.). There is no Dev in M-VIA since it is a low-latency, user-level messaging. As can be seen in Figure 6, the combined effect of Intr and Dev Drv. is minimal for small messages. However, for a large message as shown in Figure 7, Intr portion is significant but Dev Drv. has no effect. This is because receive operations are completely handled by Intr.

4. Conclusion and Future Work

This paper discussed our efforts to port Linux operating system to SimOS. Moreover, the capability of Linux/SimOS was demonstrated by performing detailed simulation study of UDP/IP and M-VIA. The results confirm that Linux/SimOS is an excellent tool for studying communication performance by showing the details of the various layers of the communication protocols, in particular the effects of the kernel, device driver, and NIC. Moreover, since Linux/SimOS open-source, it is a powerful and flexible simulation environment for studying all aspects of computer system performance.

There are numerous possible uses for Linux/SimOS. For example, one can study the performance of Linux/SimOS acting as a server. This can be done by running server applications (e.g., web server) on Linux/SimOS connected to the rest of the network via EtherSim. Another possibility is to evaluate a new network interface to be implemented. One such example is the Host Channel Adapter (HCA) for InfiniBand [11], which is in part based on Virtual Interface Architecture. Since the primary motivation for InfiniBand technology is to remove I/O processing from the host CPU, a considerable amount of the processing requirement must be supported by the HCA. These include support for message queuing, memory translation and protection, remote DMA (RDMA), and switch fabric protocol processing. The major advantage of Linux/SimOS over hardware/emulation-based methods used in [19, 24] is that both hardware and software optimization can be performed. This prototyping can provide some insight on how the next generation of HCA should be designed for the InfiniBand Architecture.

Acknowledgement

This research was supported in part by Electronics and Telecommunications Research Institute (ETRI) and Tektronix, Inc.

6. References

[1] V. S. Pai *et al.*, "RSIM Reference Manual, Version 1.0," ECE TR 9705, Rice Univ., 1997.

[2] P. S. Magnusson *et al.*, "Simics: A Full System Simulation Platform," *IEEE Computer*, February 2002, Vol. 35, No. 2, pp. 50-58.

[3] S. Harrod, "Using Complete Machine Simulation to Understand Computer System Behavior," Ph.D. Thesis, Stanford University, February 1998.

[4] D. K. Panda *et al.* "Simulation of Modern Parallel Systems: A CSIM-Based Approach," *Proc. of the 1997 Winter Simulation Conference*, 1997.

[5] N. Leavitt, "Linux: At a Turning Point?," *IEEE Computer*, Vol. 34, No. 6, 1991.

[6] D. Burger *et al.*, "The SimpleScalar Tool Set, Version 2.0," *U. Wisc. CS Dept. TR#1342*, June 1997.

[7] M. Beck, *et al.*, *LINUX Kernel Internals, 2nd Edition*, Addison-Wesley, 1997.

[8] Libnet, Packet Assembly System. Available at http://www.packetfactory.net/libnet.

[9] Tcpdump/libpcap. Available at http://www.tcpdump.org.

[10] D. Dunning, *et al.*, "The Virtual Interface Architecture," *IEEE Micro*, March/April, 1998.

[11] Infiniband™ Architecture Specification Volume 1, Release 1.0.a. Available http://www.infinibandta.org

[12] LBNL PC UER, "M-VIA: Virtual Interface Architecture for Linux," http://www.extremelinux.org/activities/usenix99/docs/mvia.

[13] WARTS, Wisconsin Architectural Research Tool Set. http://www.cs.wisc.edu/~larus/warts.html.

[14] SIMCA, the Simulator for the Superthreaded Architecture. http://www-mount.ee.umn.edu/~lilja/SIMCA/index.html.

[15] D. Sweetman, *See MIPS Run*, Morgan Kaufmann Publishers, Inc., 1999.

[16] SimOS-PPC, see http://ww.cs.utexas/users/cart/simOS.

[17] SimpleScalar Version 4.0 Tutorial, *34th Annual International Symposium on Microarchitecture*, Austin, Texas, December, 2001.

[18] M. Rosenblum *et al.*, "Using the SimOS Machine Simulator to Study Complex Computer Systems," *ACM Transactions on Modeling and Computer Simulation*, Vol. 7, No. 1, January 1997, pp. 78-103.

[19] J. Wu *et al.* " Design of An InfiniBand Emulation over Myrinet: Challenges, Implementation, and Performance Evaluation," Technical Report OUS-CISRC-2/01_TR-03, Dept. of Computer and Information Science, Ohio State University, 2001.

[20] M. Banikazemi, B. Abali, L. Herger, and D. K. Panda, "Design Alternatives for Virtual Interface Architecture (VIA) and an Implementation on IBM Netfinity NT Cluster," *Journal of Parallel and Distributed Computing*, Special Issue on Clusters, 2002.

[21] M. Banikaze, B. Abali, and D. K. Panda, "Comparison and Evaluation of Design Choices for Implementing the Virtual Interface Architecture (VIA)," *Fourth Int'l Workshop on Communication, Architecture, and Applications for Network-Based Parallel Computing* (CANPC '00), January 2000.

[22] S. Nagar *et al.*, "Issues in designing and Implementing A Scalable Virtual Interface Architecture," *2000 International Conference on Parallel Processing*, 2000.

[23] A. Begel, "An Analysis of VI Architecture Primitives in Support of Parallel Distributed Communication," to appear in *Concurrency and Computation: Practice and Experience*, 2002.

[24] P. Buonadonna, A. Geweke, and D.E. Culler, "An Implementation and Analysis of the Virtual Interface Architecture," *Proceedings of SC '98*, Orlando, FL, Nov. 7-13, 1998.

[25] A. Rubini, *Linux Device Driver*, 1st Ed., O'Reilly, 1998.

Session 3C

Storage Systems

Introducing SCSI-to-IP Cache for Storage Area Networks

Xubin He, Qing Yang, and Ming Zhang
Department of Electrical and Computer Engineering,
University of Rhode Island, Kingston, RI 02881
{hexb, qyang, mingz}@ele.uri.edu

Abstract

Data storage plays an essential role in today's fast-growing data-intensive network services. iSCSI is one of the most recent standards that allow SCSI protocols to be carried out over IP networks. However, the disparities between SCSI and IP prevent fast and efficient deployment of SAN (Storage Area Network) over IP. This paper introduces STICS (SCSI-To-IP Cache Storage), a novel storage architecture that couples reliable and high-speed data caching with low-overhead conversion between SCSI and IP protocols. Through the efficient caching algorithm and localization of certain unnecessary protocol overheads, STICS significantly improves performance over current iSCSI system. Furthermore, STICS can be used as a basic plug-and-play building block for data storage over IP. We have implemented software STICS prototype on Linux operating system. Numerical results using popular PostMark benchmark program and EMC's trace have shown dramatic performance gain over the current iSCSI implementation.

1. Introduction

As we enter a new era of computing, data storage has changed its role from "secondary" with respect to CPU and RAM to primary importance in today's information world. Online data storage doubles every 9 months due to ever-growing demand for networked information services [8]. In general, networked storage architectures have evolved from network-attached storage (NAS) [2, 13], storage area network (SAN) [7], to most recent storage over IP (iSCSI) [6, 14]. NAS architecture allows a storage system/device to be directly connected to a standard network, typically via Ethernet. Clients in the network can access the NAS directly. A NAS based storage subsystem has built-in file system to provide clients with file system functionality. SAN technology, on the other hand, provides a simple block level interface for manipulating nonvolatile magnetic media. The basic premise of a SAN is to replace the "point-to-point" infrastructure of server

to storage communications with one that allows "any-to-any" communications. A SAN provides high connectivity, scalability, and availability using a specialized network protocol: FC-4 protocol. Deploying such a specialized network usually introduces additional cost for implementation, maintenance, and management. iSCSI is the most recently emerging technology with the goal of implementing the SAN technology over the better-understood and mature network infrastructure: the Internet (TCP/IP).

Implementing SAN over IP brings economy and convenience whereas it also raises performance issues. Currently, there are basically two existing approaches: one carries out SCSI and IP protocol conversion at a specialized switch and the other encapsulates SCSI protocol in TCP/IP at host bus adapter (HBA) level [14]. Both approaches have severe performance limitations. Converting protocols at a switch places special burden to an already-overloaded switch and creates another specialized networking equipment in a SAN. Such a specialized switch not only is costly as compared to off-the-shelf Ethernet switches but also complicates installation, management, and maintenance. To encapsulate SCSI protocol over IP requires significant amount of overhead traffic for SCSI commands transfers and handshaking over the Internet. In addition, packet transfer latency exists over the network, particularly over long distances. Such latency does not reduce linearly with the increase of network bandwidth.

Protocol disparities and network latencies motivate us to introduce a new storage architecture: SCSI-To-IP Cache Storage, or STICS for short. The purpose of STICS is to bridge the disparities between SCSI and IP so that efficient SAN can be built over the Internet. It provides an iSCSI network cache to smooth out the traffic and improve overall performance. Such a cache or bridge is not only helpful but also necessary to certain degree because of the different nature of SCSI and IP such as speed, data unit size, protocols, and requirements. Wherever there is a speed disparity, cache helps. Analogous to *"cache memory"* used to cache memory data for CPU, STICS is a *"cache storage"* used to cache networked storage data for server host. By localizing part of SCSI protocol and filtering out some unnecessary traffic, STICS can reduce the bandwidth requirement of the Internet to implement SAN.

To quantitatively evaluate the performance potential of STICS in real world network environment, we have implemented the STICS under Linux. We have used PostMark benchmark and EMC's trace to measure system performance. PostMark results show that STICS provides up to 4 times performance improvement over iSCSI implementation in terms of average system throughput. For EMC's trace, our STICS shows up to 6 times as fast as the iSCSI in terms of average response time.

2. Architecture

The idea of STICS is very simple. It is just a cache that bridges the protocol and speed disparities between SCSI and IP. Figure 1 shows a typical SAN implementation over IP using STICS. Any number of storage devices or server computers can be connected to the standard Internet through STICS to form a SAN. Instead of using a specialized network or specialized switch, STICS connects a regular host server or a storage device to the standard IP network. Consider STICS 1 in the diagram. It is directly connected to the SCSI HBA of Host 1 as a local storage device. It also acts as a cache and bridge to allow Host 1 to access, at block level, any storage device connected to the SAN such as NAS, STICS 2, and STICS 3 etc. In order to allow a smooth data access from Host 1 to the SAN, STICS 1 provides SCSI protocol service, caching service, naming service, and IP protocol service.

2.1. Cache structure of STICS

Each STICS has a read cache consisting of a large DRAM and a write cache consisting of a 2 levels hierarchy with a small NVRAM on top of a log disk. Frequently accessed data reside in the DRAM that is organized as LRU cache for read operations. Write data are first stored in the small NVRAM. Whenever the newly written data in the NVRAM are sufficiently large or whenever the log disk is free, a log of data is written into the log disk sequentially. After the log write, the NVRAM becomes available to absorb additional write data. At the same time, a copy of the log is placed in the DRAM to speed up possible read operations of the data that have just been written to the log disk. Data in the log disk are organized in the format of *segments* similar to that in a Log-structured File System [15]. A segment contains a number of *slots* each of which can hold one data block. Data blocks in a segment are addressed by their *Segment IDs* and *Slot IDs*.

A Hash table is used to locate data in the RAM buffer including DRAM and NVRAM. DRAM and NVRAM

can be differentiated through their addresses. A LRU list and a Free List are used to keep tracks of the most recently used data and the free slots respectively. Data blocks stored in the RAM buffer are addressed by their *Logical Block Addresses (LBAs)*. The Hash Table contains location information for each of the valid data blocks in the buffer and uses LBAs of incoming requests as search keys. The slot size is set to be the size of a block.

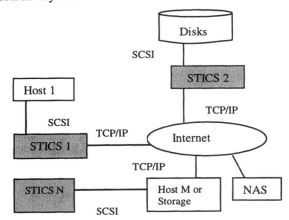

Figure 1. System overview. A STICS connects to the host via SCSI interface and connects to other STICS' or NAS via Internet.

2.2. Basic operations

Write. Write requests may come from one of two sources: the host via SCSI interface and another STICS via the Ethernet interface.

Write requests from the host via SCSI interface: After receiving a write request, the *STICS* first searches the Hash Table by the LBA address. If an entry is found, the entry is overwritten by the incoming write, and is moved to the NVRAM if it is in DRAM. If no entry is found, a free slot entry in the NVRAM is allocated from the Free List, the data are copied into the corresponding slot, and its address is recorded in the Hash table. The LRU list and Free List are then updated. When enough data slots (128 in our preliminary implementation) are accumulated or when the log disk is idle, the data slots are written into log disk sequentially in one large write. After the log write completes successfully, STICS signals the host that the request is complete and the log is moved from the NVRAM to DRAM.

Write requests from another STICS via Ethernet interface: A packet coming from the network interface may turns out to be a write operation from a remote STICS on the network. After receiving such a write request, STICS gets a data block with STICS IP and LBA. It then searches the Hash Table by the LBA and IP. The same writing process as above is then performed.

Read. Similar to write operations, read operations may also come either from the host via SCSI interface or from another STICS via the Ethernet interface.

Read requests from the host via SCSI interface: After receiving a read request, the *STICS* searches the Hash Table by the LBA to determine the location of the data. Data requested may be in one of four different places: the RAM buffer, the log disk(s), the storage device in the local STICS, or a storage device in another STICS on the network. If the data is found in the RAM buffer, the data are copied from the RAM buffer to the requesting buffer. The STICS then signals the host that the request is complete. If the data is found in the log disk or the local storage device, the data are read from the log disk or storage device into the requesting buffer. Otherwise, the *STICS* encapsulates the request including LBA, current IP, and destination IP address into an IP packet and forwards it to the corresponding STICS.

Read requests from another STICS via Ethernet interface: When a read request is found after unpacking an incoming IP packet, the STICS obtains the IP and LBA from the packet. It then searches the Hash Table by the LBA and the source IP to determine the location of the data and sends the data back to the source STICS through the network.

Destages. The operation of moving data from a higher-level storage device to a lower level storage device is defined as *destage* operation [16]. There are two levels of destage operations in STICS: destaging data from the NVRAM buffer to the log disk (*Level 1 destage*) and destaging data from log disk to a storage device (*Level 2 destage*). *Level 1 destage* activates whenever the log disk is idle and there are data to be destaged in the NVRAM. *Level 2 destage* activates whenever one of the following events occurs: 1) the STICS detects a CPU idle period; 2) the size of data in the log disk exceeds a threshold value. *Level 1 destage* has higher priority than *Level 2 destage*. Once the *Level 1 destage* starts, it continues until a log of data in the NVRAM buffer is written to the log disk. *Level 2 destage* may be interrupted if a new request comes in or until the log disk becomes empty. If the destage process is interrupted, the destage thread would be suspended until the STICS detects another idle period. For extreme burst writes, where the log disk is full, *Level 1 destage* forces subsequent writes to the addressed network storage to bypass the log disk to avoid cache overflow [16].

As for *Level 1 destage*, the data in the NVRAM buffer are written to the log disk sequentially in large size (64KB). At the same time, the data are moved from NVRAM to DRAM. The log disk header and the corresponding in-memory slot entries are updated. All data are written to the log disk in "append" mode, which

ensures that every time the data are written to consecutive log disk blocks.

For *Level 2 destage*, we use a "first-write-first-destage" algorithm according to the LRU List. Each time 64KB data are read from the consecutive blocks of the log disk and written to the addressed network storage. The LRU list and free list are updated subsequently. In the future, MQ [18] algorithm may be considered to further increase the performance.

2.3. Cache coherence

There are three ways to configure a distributed storage system using STICS, placing STICS near the host, target storage, or both. If we place a STICS near the host, the corresponding STICS building block is a private cache. If we place a STICS near the storage, we have a shared cache system. There are tradeoffs between shared cache and private cache configurations. From the point of view of cache efficiency, we would like to place cache as close to a host as possible to minimize latency. Such a private cache system allows multiple copies of a shared storage data to reside in different caches giving rise to the well-known cache coherence problem. Shared caches, on the other hand, do not have such cache coherence problem because each cache is associated with target storage. However, each request has to go through the network to obtain data at the target storage side. We have considered both private and shared cache configurations. Shared cache configuration is relatively simple. For private cache configuration, a coherence protocol is necessary. One possible way to implement a cache coherence protocol in private cache system is using the local consistency (LC) model [1], which helps to minimize meta-data network traffic pertaining to coherence protocol. The details of the cache coherence protocol are out of scope of this paper. Interested readers are referred to [3].

2.4. Implementation

There are several ways to implement STICS. A software STICS is a device driver or kernel module that controls and coordinates SCSI host bus adaptor (HBA) and network interface card (NIC). It uses a part of host's system RAM and part of disk to form the cache. STICS can also be implemented at HBA controller level as a STICS card. Such a card has sufficient intelligence with RAM, IDE or SCSI interface, and Ethernet interface. The IDE or SCSI interface is used to connect to a log disk for caching. Finally, STICS can be implemented as a complete cache box with built-in controller, log disks, and local storage.

Currently we have implemented a software prototype of STICS on Linux kernel 2.4.2, and it is implemented as kernel module which can be loaded and unloaded

Table 1. Disk parameters

Disk Model	Manufacture	Interface	Capacity	Data buffer	RPM	Latency (ms)	Transfer rate (MB/s)	Seek time (ms)
O7N3200	IBM	Ultra SCSI	36.7G	N/A	10000	3.0	29.8	4.9
AS010a1	Maxtor	Ultra ATA/100	10.2G	2MB	7200	4.17	16.6	8.5

dynamically. Our implementation uses a part of system RAM and an additional hard disk for caching function. There is no local storage and all I/O operations are remote operations going through the network.

3. Performance evaluations

3.1. Methodology

For the purpose of performance evaluation, we have implemented STICS prototype and deployed a software iSCSI. For a fair performance comparison, both iSCSI and STICS have exactly the same CPU and RAM size. This RAM includes read cache and write buffer used in STICS. All I/O operations in both iSCSI and STICS are forced to be remote operations to target disks through a switch.

Table 2. Machines configurations

	CPU	RAM	IDE disk	SCSI disk
Trout	PII-450	128MB	2 AS010a1	N/A
Cod	PII-400	128MB	AS010a1	N/A
Squid	PII-400	128MB	2 AS010a1	O7N3200

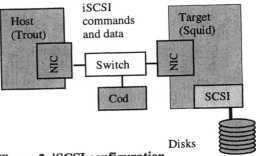

Figure 2. iSCSI configuration

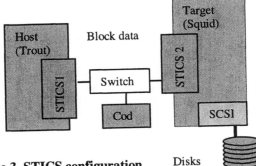

Figure 3. STICS configuration

Our experimental settings are shown in Figures 2 and 3. Three PCs are involved in our experiments, namely *Trout*, *Cod* and *Squid*. *Trout* serves as the host and *Squid* as the storage target. *Cod* serves as a switch console to monitor the network traffic. For STICS experiment, a software STICS is loaded as kernel module. All these machines are interconnected through an 8-port Gigabit switch (Intel NetStructure 470T) to form an isolated LAN. Each machine is running Linux kernel 2.4.2 with a Netgear GA622T Gigabit network interface card (NIC) and an Adaptec 39160 high performance SCSI adaptor. The network cards and switch can be tuned to Gigabit and 100Mbit dynamically. The configurations of these machines are described in Table 2 and the characteristics of individual disks are summarized in Table 1.

For iSCSI implementation, we compiled and run the Linux iSCSI developed by Intel Corporation [6]. The iSCSI is compiled under Linux kernel 2.4.2 and configured as shown in Figure 2.

Our STICS is running on Linux kernel 2.4.2 with target mode support and is loaded as a kernel module as shown in Figure 3. Four MB of the system RAM is used to simulate STICS NVRAM buffer, another 16MB of the system RAM is used as the DRAM read cache in our STICS, and the log disk is a standalone hard drive. When requests come from the host, the STICS first processes the requests locally. For write requests, the STICS writes the data to its write buffer. Whenever the log disk is idle, the data will be destaged to the log disk through level 1 destage. After data is written to the log disk, STICS signals host write complete and moves the data to DRAM cache. When data in the log disk exceeds a threshold or the system is idle, the data in log disk will be destaged to the remote target storage through the network. The hash table and LRU list are updated. When a read request comes in, the STICS searches the hash table, locates where the data are, and accesses the data from RAM buffer, log disk, or remote disks via network.

3.2. Benchmark and workload characteristics

The benchmark we used to measure system throughput is PostMark which is a popular file system benchmark developed by Network Appliance. It measures performance in terms of transaction rates in an ephemeral small-file environment by creating a large pool of continually changing files. PostMark generates an initial pool of random text files ranging in size from a configurable low bound to a configurable high bound.

This file pool is of configurable size and can be located on any accessible file system. Once the pool has been created, a specified number of transactions occur. Each transaction consists of a pair of smaller transactions, i.e. *Create file or Delete file*, and *Read file or Append file*. Each transaction type and its affected files are chosen randomly. The read and write block size can be tuned. On completion of each run, a report is generated showing some metrics such as elapsed time, transaction rate, total number of files created and so on.

In addition to PostMark, we also used a real-world trace obtained from EMC Corporation. The trace, referred to as *EMC-tel* trace hereafter, was collected by an EMC Symmetrix system installed at a telecommunication consumer site. The trace file contains 230370 requests, with a fixed request size of 4 blocks. The whole dataset size is 900M bytes. The trace is write-dominated with a write ratio of 89%. The average request rate is about 333 requests/second. In order for the trace to be read by our STICS and the iSCSI implementation, we developed a program called *ReqGenerator* to convert the traces to high-level I/O requests. These requests are then fed to our STICS and iSCSI system to measure performance.

3.3. Measured results and discussions

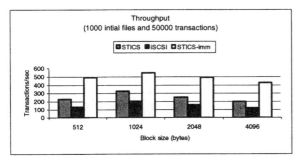

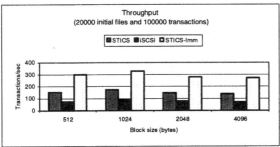

Figure 4. PostMark measurements (100Mbit network)

Throughput. Our first experiment is to use PostMark to measure the I/O throughput in terms of transactions per second. In our tests, PostMark was configured in two different ways. First, a small pool of 1,000 initial files and 50,000 transactions; and second a large pool of 20,000 initial files and 100,000 transactions. The total sizes of

accessed data are 436MB (151.05MB read and 285.08MB write) and 740MB (303.46 MB read and 436.18MB write) respectively. They are much larger than host system RAM (128MB). We left all other PostMark parameters at their default settings. The network is configured as a 100Mbit network.

In Figure 4, we plotted two separate bar graphs corresponding to the small file pool case and the large one, respectively. Each group of bars represents the system throughputs of STICS with report after complete (STICS), iSCSI (iSCSI) and STICS with immediate report (STICS-Imm: host is acknowledged immediately after a write data is in RAM) for a specific data block size. It is clear from this figure that STICS shows obvious better system throughput than the iSCSI. The performance improvement of STICS over iSCSI is consistent across different block sizes and for both small pool and large pool cases. The performance gains of STICS with report after complete over iSCSI range from 60% to 110%. STICS with immediate report outperforms iSCSI by a factor of 2.69 to 4.18.

Table 3. Packet distribution

	# Of packets with different sizes					
	<64 Bytes	65-127	128-255	256-511	512-1023	>1024
iSCSI	7	1,937,724	91	60	27	1,415,912
STICS	4	431,216	16	30	7	607,827

Table 4. Network traffic

	iSCSI	STICS
Total Packets	3,353,821	839,100
Full/Partial Packet Ratio	0.73	1.41
Bytes Transferred	1,914,566,504	980,963,821
Average Bytes/Packet	571	944

To understand why STICS provides such impressive performance gains over the iSCSI, we monitored the network activities at the Ethernet Switch through the console machine *cod* for both STICS and iSCSI implementations. While both implementations write all data from the host to the remote storage, STICS transfers dramatically less packets over the network than iSCSI does. Tables 3 and 4 show the measured network activities for both STICS and iSCSI. Based on our analysis of the numerical results, we believe that the performance gain of STICS over iSCSI can be attributed to the following facts. First, the log disk along with the RAM buffer forms a large cache for the host and absorbs small writes quickly, which reduces the network traffic because many data are overwritten in the local log disk. As shown in Table 4, the number of total bytes transferred over the network is reduced from 1,914,566,504 to 980,963,821 although the total data stored in the target storage is the same. Secondly, STICS eliminates many remote handshaking caused by iSCSI, which in turn reduce the network traffic. We noticed in Table 3 that the small size packets which are mainly used to transfer iSCSI handshaking messages are dramatically reduced from 1,937,724 to 431,216. Thirdly, by combining small writes into large ones, STICS increases the network bandwidth utilization. If we define full packet as the packet with size larger than 1024 bytes of payload data, and other packets are defined as partial packets. As shown in Table 4, STICS improves the ratio of full packets to partial packets from 0.73 to 1.41, and average bytes per packet is increased from 571 in iSCSI to 944 in STICS.

Above results are measured under 100Mbit network, when we configured the switch and network cards as Gigabit network, we observed similar results as shown in figure 5. The performance gains of STICS with report after complete over iSCSI range from 51% to 80%. STICS with immediate report outperforms iSCSI by a factor of 2.49 to 3.07. The reason is as follows. When the network is improved from 100Mbit to 1 Gigabit, the network latency is not decreased linearly. In our test, we found the average latencies for 100Mbit and 1Gigabit network are 128.99 and 106.78 microseconds. The network performance is improved less than 20% in terms of latency from 100Mbit to Gigabit network.

Response times. Our next experiment is to measure and compare the response times of STICS and iSCSI under EMC trace. The network is configured as a Gigabit network. Response times of all individual I/O requests are plotted in Figure 6 for STICS with immediate report (Figure 6a), STICS with report after complete (Figure 6b) and iSCSI (Figure 6c). Each dot in a figure represents the response time of an individual I/O request. It can be seen from the figures that overall response times of STICS are much smaller than that of iSCSI. In Figure 6b, we noticed 4 requests take up to 300ms. These few peak points drag down the average performance of STICS. These excessive large response times can be attributed to the *destaging* process. In our current implementation, we allow the *level 2 destaging* process to continue until the entire log segment is empty before serving a new storage request. It takes a long time to move data in a full log segment to the remote data disk. We are still working on the optimization of the *destage* algorithm. We believe there is sufficient room to improve the *destaging* process to avoid the few peak response times of STICS.

We also plotted histogram of request numbers against response times in Figure 7. In this figure, X-axis represents response time and Y-axis represents the number of storage requests finished at a particular response time. For example, a point (X, Y)=(10, 2500) means that there are 2,500 requests finished within 10 ms. As shown in Figure 7a, for the STICS with immediate

report, most requests are finished within 2 ms, because STICS signals the complete of requests when the data are transferred to NVRAM buffer for write requests. The average response time is 2.7 ms. For the STICS with report after complete as shown in Figure 7b, the response times of the majority of requests fall within the range of 2-5 ms. The rest of requests take longer time to finish but very few of them take longer than 40ms. The average response time is 5.71 ms.

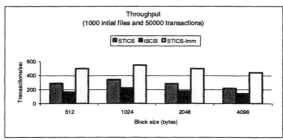

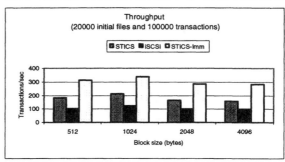

Figure 5. PostMark measurements (Gigabit network)

The iSCSI, on the other hand, has obvious larger response time. The response times of the majority of requests fall within the range of 6-28 milliseconds as shown in Figure 7c. No requests are finished within 5 milliseconds. Some of them even take up to 400ms. The average response time is 16.73ms, which is 2.9 times as much as STICS with report after complete and 6.2 times as much as STICS with immediate report. Such a long responses time can be mainly attributed to the excessive network traffic of iSCSI.

3.4. Costs analysis

As shown in the last subsection, STICS presents significant performance gains over the standard iSCSI implementation. One obvious question to ask is whether such performance improvement comes at extra hardware cost. To answer this question, we have carried out cost analysis as compared to iSCSI. In our experimental implementations, all hardware components such as CPU, RAM, cabling and switches are exactly the same for both iSCSI and STICS except for an additional disk in STICS for caching. With rapid dropping of disk prices, such an

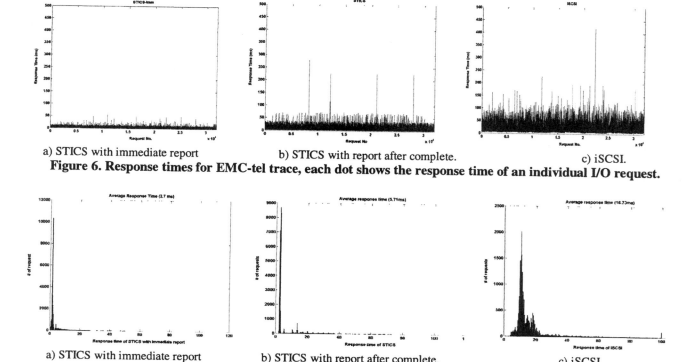

a) STICS with immediate report   b) STICS with report after complete.   c) iSCSI.

Figure 6. Response times for EMC-tel trace, each dot shows the response time of an individual I/O request.

a) STICS with immediate report   b) STICS with report after complete.   c) iSCSI.

Figure 7. Histograms of I/O response times for trace EMC-tel

additional disk is easily justifiable. Typical cost of a 10 GB disk is well under $100 while a typical SAN costs over tens of thousands dollars, implying a very small fraction of additional cost of STICS. Table 5 lists the practical cost of building a minimum SAN configuration with 6 servers and 200 GB using iSCSI and STICS, respectively (all the list prices are as of January 2001). As shown in this table, the cost difference between the two is well under 7%. Considering software cost (*$22,059*) and maintenance cost (*$8,676*) for the same SAN system [10], the cost difference between the two is much less than 3%. We believe trading 3% of additional cost for 6 folds performance gain is certainly worthwhile.

Table 5. Hardware costs comparison

	iSCSI			STICS		
	Qty	Cost	Total	Qty	Cost	Total
HBA	12	$339	$4,068	12	$339	$4,068
Switch	1	$1,229	$1,229	1	$1,229	$1,229
GB NIC	12	$319	$3,828	12	$319	$3,828
OS HDD	12	$85	$1,020	12	$85	$1,020
SCSI HDD	6	$799	$4,794	6	$799	$4,794
Log Disks				12	*$85*	*$1,020*
Total		*$14,939*			*$15,959*	

We have also considered the cost of implementing iSCSI and STICS in hardware. For the same SAN configuration with 6 servers, iSCSI would need an iSCSI to SCSI converter costing $5,083 [10] or iSCSI cards. The additional hardware for each STICS would include an I/O processor with 4-MB NVRAM. We can conservatively estimate the total cost in addition to Table 5 for 12 STICS to be under $5,000.

4. Related work

Existing research that is most closely related to STICS is network attached storage (NAS)[2]. The NAS technology provides direct network connection for hosts to access through network interfaces at file system level. STICS provides a direct SCSI connection to a server host to allow the server to access at block level a SAN implemented over the Internet. In addition to being a storage component of the SAN, a STICS performs network cache functions for a smooth and efficient SAN implementation over IP network.

Another important work related to our research is *Petal* [9], a research project of Compaq's Systems Research Center. Petal uses a collection of NAS-like storage servers interconnected using specially customized LAN to form a unified virtual disk space to clients at block level. *iSCSI* (Internet SCSI) [6,14] emerged very recently provides an ideal alternative to Petal's customized LAN-based SAN protocol. Taking advantage of existing Internet protocols and media, it is a nature way for storage to make use of TCP/IP as demonstrated by earlier

209

research work of Meter et al of USC, *VISA* [12] to transfer SCSI commands and data using IP protocol. iSCSI protocol is a mapping of the SCSI remote procedure invocation model over the TCP/IP protocol [14]. STICS architecture attempts to localize some of SCSI protocol traffic by accepting SCSI commands and data from the host. Filtered data block is sent to the storage target using Internet. This SCSI-in Block-out mechanism provides an immediate and transparent solution both to the host and the storage eliminating some unnecessary remote synchronization. Furthermore, STICS provides a nonvolatile cache exclusively for SCSI commands and data that are supposed to be transferred through the network. This cache reduces latency from the host point of view as well as avoids many unnecessary data transfer over the network, because many data are frequently overwritten.

The idea of using a disk-based log to improve system performance or to improve the reliability of RAM has been used in both file system and database systems for a long time. For example, the Log-structured File System (LFS [15]), Disk Caching Disk (DCD [4]), and other similar systems all use disk-based data/metadata logging to improve file system performance and speed-up crash recovery. Several RAID systems have implemented the LFS algorithm at the RAID controller level [5,11,17]. LFS collects writes in a RAM buffer to form large logs and writes large logs to data disks. While many implementation techniques are borrowed from existing work, the novelty of STICS is the new concept of caching between SCSI and IP.

5. Conclusions

In this paper, we have introduced a new concept STICS to bridge the disparities between SCSI and IP in order to facilitate implementation of SAN over the Internet. STICS adds a new dimension to networked storage architectures allowing any server host to efficiently access a SAN on Internet through a standard SCSI interface. Using a nonvolatile *"cache storage"*, STICS smoothes out the storage data traffic between SCSI and IP very much like the way *"cache memory"* smoothes out CPU-memory traffic. We have implemented a prototype STICS under Linux operating system. We measured the performance of STICS as compared to a typical iSCSI implementation using a popular benchmark (PostMark) and a real world I/O workload (EMC's trace). PostMark results have shown that STICS outperforms iSCSI by up to 4 times in terms of average system throughput. Numerical results under EMC's trace show a factor of 3 to 6 performance gain in terms of average response time. Furthermore, STICS is a plug-and-play building block for storage networks.

Acknowledgements

This research is sponsored in part by National Science Foundation under grants MIP-9714370 and CCR-0073377. Any opinions, findings, and conclusions or recommendations expressed in this material are those of the author(s) and do not necessarily reflect the views of the National Science Foundation. The authors would like to thank the anonymous reviewers for their many helpful comments and suggestions. We would like to thank EMC Corporation for providing trace files to us. We would like to thank Jian Li for his assistance in the experiments and Yinan Liu for his suggestions on graph editing.

References

[1] M. Ahamad and R. Kordale, "Scalable Consistency Protocols for Distributed Services," *IEEE Transactions on Parallel and Distributed Systems*, vol. 10, pp. 888, 1999.

[2] G. Gibson, R. Meter, "Network Attached Storage Architecture," *Communications of the ACM*, Vol. 43, No 11, pp.37-45, 2000.

[3] X. He, Q. Yang, and M Zhang, "Introducing SCSI-To-IP Cache for Storage Area Networks", *Technical Report*, URL: http://ele.uri.edu/~hexb/publications/STICS-Tech-200112.pdf.

[4] Y. Hu and Q. Yang, "DCD-disk caching disk: A New Approach for Boosting I/O Performance," *ISCA'96*, pp.169-178, 1996.

[5] Y. Hu, Q. Yang, and T. Nightingale, "RAPID-Cache --- A Reliable and Inexpensive Write Cache for Disk I/O Systems," *HPCA5*, Jan. 1999.

[6] Intel iSCSI project, URL: *http://sourceforge.net/projects/intel-iscsi*.

[7] R. Khattar, M. Murphy, G. Tarella and K. Nystrom, "Introduction to Storage Area Network," *Redbooks Publications (IBM), SG24-5470-00*, September 1999.

[8] J. Kubiatowicz, et al. "OceanStore: An Architecture for Global-Scale Persistent Storage," *Proceedings of the international conference on Architectural support for programming languages and operating systems (ASPLOS'2000)*, 2000.

[9] E. Lee and C. Thekkath, "Petal: Distributed Virtual Disks," *Proceedings of the international conference on Architectural support for programming languages and operating systems*, pp.84-92, 1996.

[10] B. Mackin, "A Study of iSCSI Total Cost of Ownership (TCO) vs. Fibre Channel and SCSI," *URL: http://www.adaptec.com*, Oct. 2001.

[11] J. Menon, "A Performance Comparison of RAID-5 and Log-Structured Arrays," *Proc. Of 4th IEEE Int'l Symp. High Performance Distributed Computing*, pp. 167-178, 1995.

[12] R. Meter, G. Finn, S. Hotz, "VISA: Netstation's Virtual Internet SCSI Adapter," *Proceedings of the 8th International Conference on Architectural Support for Programming Languages and Operating Systems (ASPLOS)*, pp.71-80, 1998.

[13] E. Miller, D. Long, W. Freeman, and B. Reed, "Strong Security for Network-Attached Storage," Proc. of the *Conference on Fast and Storage Technologies (FAST'2002)*, 2002.

[14] J. Satran, et al. "iSCSI draft standard," *URL: http://www.ietf.org/internet-drafts/draft-ietf-ips-iscsi-12.txt*, 2002.

[15] M. Seltzer, K. Bostic, M. McKusick, C. Staelin, "An Implementation of a Log-Structured File System for UNIX," *Winter USENIX Proceedings*, pp. 201-220, Jan. 1993.

[16] A. Varma and Q. Jacobson, "Destage algorithms for disk arrays with non-volatile caches," *Proceedings of the 22nd annual international symposium on Computer architecture (ISCA'95)*, pp. 83-95, 1995.

[17] J. Wilkes, R. Golding, C. Staelin, T. Sullivan, "The HP AutoRAID Hierarchical Storage System," *Proc. Of the Fifteenth ACM Symposium on Operating System Principles*, pp. 96-108, 1995.

[18] Y. Zhou, J.F. Philbin, and K. Li, "Multi-Queue Replacement Algorithm for Second Level Buffer Caches," *USENIX Annual Technical Conference*, 2001.

Enhancing Write I/O Performance of Disk Array RM2 Tolerating Double Disk Failures

Young Jin Nam, Dae-Woong Kim, Tae-Young Choe, Chanik Park
Department of Computer Science and Engineering/PIRL
Pohang University of Science and Technology
Kyungbuk, Republic of Korea
{yjnam,woong,choety,cipark}@postech.ac.kr

Abstract

With a large number of internal disks and the rapid growth of disk capacity, storage systems become more susceptible to double disk failures. Thus, the need for such reliable storage systems as RAID6 is expected to gain in importance. However, RAID6 architectures such as RM2, P+Q, EVEN-ODD, and DATUM traditionally suffer from a low write I/O performance caused by updating two distinctive parity data associated with user data. To overcome such a low write I/O performance, we propose an enhanced RM2 architecture which combines RM2, one of the well-known RAID6 architectures, with a Lazy Parity Update (LPU) technique. Extensive performance evaluations reveal that the write I/O performance of the proposed architecture is about two times higher than that of RM2 under various I/O workloads with little degradation in reliability.

1. Introduction

With the advent of Storage Area Networks, such as Fiber Channel and Gigabit Ethernet, large-scale storage systems which encompass a large number of disks are commonplace. Such systems are advantageous in terms of scalability and configurability, but they are more susceptible to double disk failures than small-scale systems [6]. Moreover, the rapid growth of disk capacity prolongs the disk recovery time in the event of disk failure. Eventually, this prolonged recovery time will raise the chances of subsequent disk failure during the reconstruction of user data and parity information stored in a faulty disk. In addition, the probability increases that, while reading data which was left unread for a long time, latent sector failures will occur [12]. To recognize these reliability issues associated with recent technology trends, we expect that the need for such reliable storage systems as RAID6 will gain in importance.

A few highly reliable RAID architectures, such as P+Q [6], EVEN-ODD [4], RM2 [8], and DATUM [2], can tolerate double disk failures by elaborately maintaining two distinctive parity data associated with user data. This breed of architectures is formally classified as RAID6 [6]. However, RAID6 suffers from a relatively low write I/O performance compared with other architectures, such as RAID1, 4, 5 [9] due to the maintenance of additional parity information. While RAID5 requires four disk accesses to process a write I/O request, RAID6 demands six disk accesses.

While a myriad of techniques to improve the write I/O performance of RAID5 can enhance that of RAID6 to some extent, none of them can serve as an ultimate solution to resolve the low write I/O performance of RAID6 because they still update two parity information per write I/O request. In [11], Savage and Wilkes proposed *A Frequently Redundant Array of Independent Disks* (AFRAID) which improves the write I/O performance of RAID5 by deferring the update of parity information until the storage system becomes idle. However, the problem of selecting parity groups for the delayed update in RAID5 is straightforward, but not trivial in RAID6. This paper proposes an enhanced RM2 architecture which improves the write I/O performance of RM2, a well-known RAID6 architecture, by employing the *Lazy Parity Update* (LPU). We provide a systematic scheme to determine the parity groups for the delayed update. It is shown that the proposed architecture can double the write I/O performance of RM2 while still providing high reliability under various I/O workloads.

2. The Proposed Architecture

We begin by explaining the nomenclature to be used for the description of the proposed architecture. A stripe unit refers to a group of consecutive disk blocks in a disk. Stripe units which contain user data and parity information are called a data stripe unit and a parity stripe unit, respectively. A parity group is referred to as a set of data stripe units and an associated parity stripe unit where the parity stripe unit is calculated from the set of data stripe units. Data and parity stripe units are stored in different disks, so that faulty stripe units can be reconstructed from other non-faulty stripe units. Let us define $\mathcal{PG}$ as all parity groups within a RAID6 architecture. Next, the $\mathcal{PG}$ is divided into two disjoint parity groups defined as follows.

Definition 1 *Foreground Parity Group* (FPG) refers to the minimum set of parity groups in $\mathcal{PG}$ which can tolerate a single disk failure. *Background Parity Group* (BPG) is defined as $\mathcal{PG} - FPG$.

In addition, the *Background Parity Group List* $(BPGL)$ refers to a list of delayed parity groups. $|BPGL|$ is the number of parity groups in $BPGL$. *Background Parity Group Task* $(BPGT)$ is a background task which processes delayed parity groups in $BPGL$.

2.1. Overview of the RM2 Architecture

Figure 1(a) shows data and parity placements in RM2 [8] which is the base RAID6 architecture of our current work. A data stripe represents a stripe which contains only data stripe units, while a parity stripe contains only parity stripe units. A stripe group is defined as a set of data stripes and a parity stripe which covers all stripe units in a given parity group. Data and parity placements of RM2 are mainly determined based on a Redundancy Matrix, which maps each stripe unit to its corresponding two parity stripe units within a stripe group for the given N disks, as shown in Figure 1(b). A column and a row in the Redundancy Matrix correspond to a disk and a parity group, respectively. Entries in a column have a -1 and a pair of k's where $1 \leq k \leq M - 1$ and M is the stripe group size. An efficient algorithm to determine the maximum M for the given N disks is given in [7]. Note that $M \geq 2$ because a single parity stripe always contains at least a single data stripe. Let us denote $RM_{i,j}$ as the i-th row and j-th column entry in the Redundancy Matrix. If $RM_{i,j} = -1$, then a parity stripe unit of disk j belongs to parity group i, if $RM_{i,j} = 0$, then it has no information, and if $RM_{i,j} = k$ for $1 \leq k \leq M - 1$, then the k-th data stripe unit of disk j belongs to parity group i. PG_i represents the i-th parity group and P_i means the parity stripe unit in the i-th parity group. $D_{i,j}$ indicates that the data stripe unit is involved in computing P_i and P_j, implying the i-th parity group and the j-th parity group. As depicted in Figure 1(a), the parity unit P_5 is related to four data units which encompass $D_{2,5}$, $D_{4,5}$, $D_{5,6}$, and $D_{5,0}$. Conversely, the data unit $D_{2,5}$ is related to P_2 and P_5. More detailed information on RM2 architecture can be found in [8].

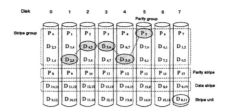

(a) Data/parity placement in a disk

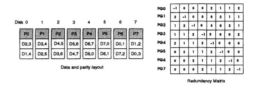

(b) Data/parity layout and Redundancy Matrix

Figure 1. RM2 Architecture: (a) data and parity placements and (b) Redundancy Matrix

2.2. Enhancing Write I/O Performance of RM2

Lazy Parity Update (LPU) Technique: The LPU technique divides all parity groups of $\mathcal{PG}$ into FPG and BPG for the given N disks and serves a write I/O request according to the information from FPG and BPG. Let us

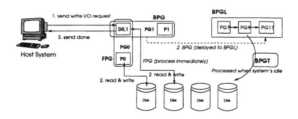

Figure 2. Operation of the Lazy Parity Update technique

denote two parity groups associated with a data block k as pg_k^i, where $i = 0, 1$. Under a normal condition with no disk failures, if pg_k^i belongs to FPG, it will be served before the notification of its completion is delivered to a host. If pg_k^i is included in BPG, its processing will be postponed by registering it into $BPGL$. The request will be processed when the storage system becomes idle. In case that a write-back buffer cache is employed, this behavior occurs when destaging begins. As a result, it can improve the throughput in order to destage the delayed write I/O requests. In the presence of at least one faulty disk, however, two associated parity groups are regarded as being included in FPG. As a result, the processing of parity groups can be delayed no longer. Instead, the storage system is ready to tolerate an additional disk failure by processing all the delayed parity groups in $BPGL$ without a further increase in the $BPGL$ list. Algorithm 1 presents how to manipulate two parity information associated with a write I/O request by using the LPU technique.

Algorithm 1: Manipulating parity information with the LPU technique

> **input** : a write I/O request, r_k
> **begin**
>   **for** *each PG_k^i of two associate parity groups* **do**
>   **if** *# of faulty disks > 0* **or** $PG_k^i \in FPG$ **then**
>   update PG_k^i;
>   **else**
>   delay the updating of PG_k^i by putting it into $BPGL$;
>   **end**
>   **end**
> **end**

Figure 3 depicts the state diagram of the proposed architecture which combines the LPU technique with RM2. Basically, six states exist, which are NORM_safe, NORM_unsafe, DEG1_safe, DEG1_unsafe, DEG2, and FAIL. Each state is determined based on the number of faulty disks and the status of $BPGL$. By delaying the

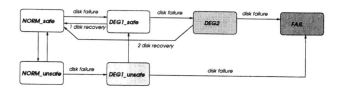

Figure 3. State transition diagram of the proposed architecture

updating of a parity group, NORM_safe is changed into NORM_unsafe if $BPGL = \emptyset$. When all delayed parity groups in $BPGL$ are processed, NORM_unsafe is changed to NORM_safe. If a disk failure occurs in NORM_safe and NORM_unsafe, then the current state is replaced with DEG1_safe and DEG1_unsafe, respectively. With an additional disk failure, DEG1_safe is moved to DEG2. A subsequent disk failure in either DEG1_unsafe or DEG2 results in FAIL. When all faulty parity and data stripe units are recovered at DEG1_safe and DEG2, the current state is moved to NORM_safe.

Initialization of FPG with RM2: In order to make the LPU technique work with RM2, we need to appropriately initialize the two disjoint sets of parity groups – FPG and BPG for the given N disks. Figure 4 provides two examples of initializing parity groups into FPG and BPG with a Redundancy Matrix of a different size. Recall that a Redundancy Matrix plays a key role in manipulating the RM2 architecture. It maintains information on how to place data and parity stripe units within a stripe group. Since a data and/or parity layout within a stripe group is repeated over a storage system, as shown in Figure 1(a) and (b), we focus on a single stripe group rather than consider all parity groups in the storage system. When $N = 7$ and $M = 3$, as shown in Figure 4(a), PG_0, PG_2, PG_4, PG_5, and PG_6 belong to FPG. In case of $N = 8$ and $M = 3$, PG_0, PG_2, PG_4, and PG_6 fall into FPG. Two examples in Figure 4 reveal

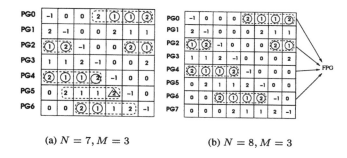

(a) $N = 7, M = 3$ (b) $N = 8, M = 3$

Figure 4. Illustrative examples of configuring FPG and BPG with $N = 7, M = 3$ and $N = 8, M = 3$ within a single stripe group

an interesting tendency, where an $|FPG|$ of $N = 7$ is not smaller than $N = 8$, *i.e.*, the size of FPG is not directly proportional to the number of disks, N. Next, we will solve the problem of how to compute an $|FPG|$ and how to select the set of minimum parity groups of FPG. The following lemma and theorem compute the size of FPG for the given N disks and stripe group size of M.

Lemma 1 *Given RM2 with N disks and a stripe group size of M, $|FPG| \geq \lceil \frac{N}{2} \rceil S$, where S is the total number of stripe groups.*

Theorem 1 *Given RM2 with N disks and a stripe group size of M,*

$$|FPG| = \begin{cases} \frac{N}{2}S & \text{if } N = even \\ (\lceil \frac{N}{2} \rceil + M - 2)S & \text{if } N = odd \end{cases},$$

where S is the total number of stripe groups.

213

Algorithm 2 selects FPG for a single stripe group with the given N disks. Note that a data/parity layout within a stripe group is repeated in the other stripe groups. Thus, a parity group index can be regarded as a relative parity group index at each stripe group, not as an absolute parity group index.

For a stripe group, according to Algorithm 2, the number

Algorithm 2: Selecting the minimum FPG within a stripe group

input	: N disks, M stripe group size
output	: FPG

begin
    /* each stripe group k has a set of parity strip units */
    /* a stripe group denoted by $\{PG_i | 0 \leq i \leq N-1\}$ */
    if N *is even* **then**
        $FPG = \{PG_{2i} | 0 \leq i < \frac{N}{2}\}$
    else
        $FPG = \{PG_{2i} | 0 \leq i < \lceil \frac{N}{2} \rceil\} \cup$
                $\{PG_{2j+1} | 0 \leq j < \lfloor \frac{M-2}{2} \rfloor\} \cup$
                $\{PG_{N-2-2k} | 0 \leq k < \lceil \frac{M-2}{2} \rceil\}$
    end
end

---

of FPG is $\frac{N}{2}$ with an even N and the number of FPG is $\lceil \frac{N}{2} \rceil + M - 2 = \lceil \frac{N}{2} \rceil + \lfloor \frac{M-2}{2} \rfloor + \lceil \frac{M-2}{2} \rceil$ with an odd N.

Theorem 2 *For the given N disks and stripe group size of M, Algorithm 2 provides a valid FPG.*

The proofs of the lemma and the theorems can be found in [7].

2.3. Other Issues

When implementing the proposed architecture on an actual RAID system, some issues arise. First, we need to detect the system idle period in order to process the delayed parity groups in $BPGL$. In our current design, the proposed architecture begins to serve the delayed parity groups immediately when no outstanding I/O requests are incoming from hosts. Second, we must determine how quickly the delayed parity groups in $BPGL$ are to be processed in the event of a single disk failure. As a result, the system moves into a safe state where an additional disk failure can be tolerated. Our current design configures the priority of $BPGT$ as equal to a background task which reconstructs lost data from a faulty disk. Setting the priority of $BPGT$ as that of the normal I/O process will increase the service time of each I/O request until the processing of all delayed parity groups is completed.

2.4. Features of the Proposed Architecture

First, the proposed architecture can considerably improve the write I/O performance of RM2 because it updates only the parity groups to prevent data loss from a single disk failure under no disk failure. However, the write I/O performance of the proposed architecture is identical to that of RM2 in the presence of disk failure.

Second, even if the proposed architecture cannot guarantee the strict reliability requirement of tolerating double disk failure at any given time as RM2, it is expected to still provide extremely high reliability compared with RAID5. Let us consider the event of a disk failure when a storage system is in either DEG1_safe or DEG1_unsafe depending on the $BPGL$ status. We will focus merely on the DEG1_unsafe state as DEG1_safe can tolerate an additional disk failure. At DEG1_unsafe, a recovery path exists from DEG1_unsafe to DEG1_safe in order to reach a state where an additional disk failure can be tolerated in the face of a single disk failure. This path needs to process only the delayed parity groups in the $BPGL$, rather than recover all the parity groups in the storage system, as with RAID5. Consequently, it can be expected that the reliability of the proposed architecture is much higher than that of RAID5, considering the number of parity groups to be processed.

3. Performance Evaluations

This section evaluates the performance of the proposed architecture, which combines the LPU technique with the RM2 architecture.

3.1. Experimental Environment

The proposed architecture is implemented on a real RAID system called PosRAID along with RAID5 and RM2. Hardware components of the PosRAID encompass Pentium IV 1.3GHz, 256MB memory, two QLogic's QLA2200 Fibre Channel HBAs, 32bit/33MHz PCI bus, and six 7200rpm 9GB Seagate Barracuda ST39175FC disks. Note that PosRAID does not support a hardware XOR module. Software components of PosRAID include VxWorks version 5.4 RTOS, a communication module which communicates with hosts and internal disks via Fibre Channel host bus adapters, a RAID engine module which maps a logical block address to a physical block address based on a given RAID architecture and manages a buffer cache, and a resource and/or configuration management module which allocates, deallocates, and configures all hardware and software resources within the storage system. Table 1 shows the configurations of three different architectures under performance evaluations. Note that the number of disks used in both architectures are equal. As a result, the size of RAID5 is larger than RM2 and the proposed architecture which is based on the RM2 architecture. Also, the redundancy rate of RM2 and the proposed architecture is 100 percent because M is set to 2 with $N = 6$.

Table 1. Configurations of three different architectures

Architecture	RAID5	RM2	Proposed
# of disks (N)	6	6	6
Stripe unit size	32KB	32KB	32KB
Buffer cache size	32MB	32MB	32MB
Write cache policy	write back	write back	write back
Parity group size	6	3	3
Stripe group size (M)	–	2	2
Total size	45GB	27GB	27GB
Redundancy ratio	20%	100%	100%

3.2. I/O Performance Measurement

This section measures the I/O performance of the proposed architecture, RAID5, and RM2. Figure 5(a)–(b) show the read I/O performance of RAID5 and the proposed architecture for 4KB and 64KB read I/O workloads with an increase in I/O processes. The read I/O performance of RM2 is the same as that of our proposed architecture. Each I/O has a thinking time which is exponentially distributed with a 10-msec mean which then generates I/O requests and waits until the issued I/O request completes. It then repeats this process of I/O generation. The start block addresses of I/O requests are uniformly distributed in the first 10GB disk space, ranging from black 0 to block 20,971,520. In the

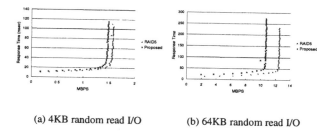

(a) 4KB random read I/O   (b) 64KB random read I/O

Figure 5. Read I/O performance of RAID5 and the proposed architecture with an I/O workload where $N = 6$ and no disk failure exists: (a) 4KB random reads and (b) 64KB random reads

results, the read I/O performance of the proposed architecture is about 93.3 percent and 85.5 percent of the read I/O performance of RAID5 under a 4KB random read I/O workload and a 64KB random read I/O workload, respectively. This performance gap occurs due to the different redundancy rate of each architecture. Table 1 shows that RAID5

requires 120% of $\frac{10GB}{6}$ (2GB) space from each disk in order to provide the 10GB disk space, whereas the proposed architecture needs 200% of $\frac{10GB}{6}$ (3.3GB) space from each disk. This implies that the maximum distance of a disk head movement by the proposed architecture is longer than that of RAID5.

Figure 6(a)–(b) gives the write I/O performance of RAID5, RM2, and the proposed architecture for 4KB and 64KB I/O workloads with an increase in I/O processes. First, we can see that the write I/O performance of the proposed architecture is two times higher than RM2, as expected. However, with the increase of an I/O request size from 4KB to 64KB, the performance gap between the two architectures is slightly reduced because the relative ratio of required disk accesses between the two architectures decreases with the larger I/O request size. However, the write I/O performance of the proposed architecture is still lower than that of RAID5 for the same reason noted above.

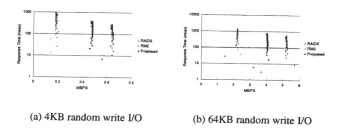

(a) 4KB random write I/O   (b) 64KB random write I/O

Figure 6. The write I/O performance of RAID5, RM2, and the proposed architecture with an I/O workload where $N = 6$ and no disk failure exists: (a) 4KB random writes and (b) 64KB random writes

Figure 7(a)–(d) reveals the write I/O performance and corresponding response times of RAID5, RM2, and the proposed architecture as a write I/O request size varies. As previously shown, the proposed architecture outperforms RM2 by 100% with different write I/O request size under medium and heavy I/O workloads. As mentioned, differences of write I/O performances between the proposed architecture and RM2 are reduced as the I/O request sizes increase.

3.3. Reliability Measurement

The reliabilities of RAID5, RM2, and the proposed architecture are analyzed in terms of *mean time to data loss* (MTTDL). Next, a realistic MTTDL value of the proposed architecture is computed by obtaining realistic values that correspond to theoretical parameters used in the mathematical analysis.

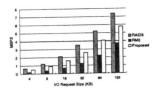

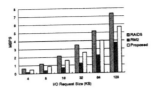

(a) Write I/O performance under medium I/O workload

(b) Write I/O performance under heavy I/O workload

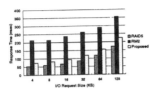

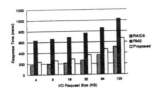

(c) Response time under medium I/O workload

(d) Response time under heavy I/O workload

Figure 7. The write I/O performance and corresponding response times of RAID5, RM2, and the proposed architecture as a function of an I/O request size, where $N = 6$ with no disk failure: the medium I/O workload has 11 I/O processes and the heavy I/O workload has 31 I/O processes

Theoretical Analysis: The analysis assumes that both the failure rate and the repair rate of each disk follow an exponential distribution. The MTTDL of each architecture is computed by using the fundamental matrix M defined as $M = [I - Q]^{-1}$, where Q is a truncated stochastic transitional probability matrix [3]. Then, we can obtain the MTTDL of RAID5 and RM2 as follows. Note that Equation (1) is the same as the reliability equation of RAID5 given in [9].

$$MTTDL_{RAID5} = \frac{(2N - 1)\lambda_1 + \mu_1}{N(N - 1)\lambda_1^2} \quad (1)$$

$$MTTDL_{RM2} = \frac{\lambda_1^2 - 2\lambda_1\mu_1 + \mu_1^2}{N\lambda_1^3} + \frac{\lambda_1^2 - \lambda_1\mu_1 - 2\mu_1^2}{(N - 1)\lambda_1^3} + \frac{\lambda_1^2 + 3\lambda_1\mu_1 + \mu_1^2}{(N - 2)\lambda_1^3} \quad (2)$$

Figure 8 depicts a Markov diagram of the proposed architecture based on the state transition diagram in Figure 3. Finally, the $MTTDL_{proposed}$ of the proposed architecture is obtained as follows:

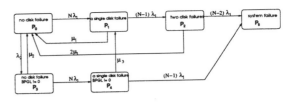

Figure 8. Markov diagram of the proposed architecture

$$MTTDL_{proposed} = \frac{\alpha}{N(N - 1)(N - 2)\lambda_1^3} + \quad (3)$$
$$\frac{\beta}{\gamma} \frac{1}{N(N - 1)(N - 2)\lambda_1^3},$$

where $\alpha = (2\lambda_1^2 - 6N\lambda_1^2 + 3N^2\lambda_1^2 - 4\lambda_1\mu_1 + 5N\lambda_1\mu_1 + 2\mu_1^2)$, $\beta = (2N\lambda_1^4\lambda_2 - 5N^2\lambda_1^4\lambda_2 - N^4\lambda_1^4\lambda_2 + 8\lambda_1^3\lambda_2\mu_1 - 26N\lambda_1^3\lambda_2\mu_1 + 26N^2\lambda_1^3\lambda_2\mu_1 - 8N^3\lambda_1^3\lambda_2\mu_1 - 20\lambda_1^2\lambda_2\mu_1^2 + 40N\lambda_1^2\lambda_2\mu_1^2 - 19N^2\lambda_1^2\lambda_2\mu_1^2 + 16\lambda_1\lambda_2\mu_1^3 - 16N\lambda_1\lambda_2\mu_1^3 - 4\lambda_2\mu_1^4)$, and $\gamma = (2N\lambda_1^3 - 3N^2\lambda_1^3 + N^3\lambda_1^3 + 2\lambda_1^2\lambda_2 - 3N\lambda_1^2\lambda_2 + N^2\lambda_1^2\lambda_2 - 4\lambda_1\lambda_2\mu_1 + 3N\lambda_1\lambda_2\mu_1 + 2\lambda_2\mu_1^2 + 2\lambda_1^2\mu_2 - 3N\lambda_1^2\mu_2 + N^2\lambda_1^2\mu_2 - 2N\lambda_1^2\mu_3 + N^2\lambda_1^2\mu_3 - 2\lambda_1\lambda_2\mu_3 + N\lambda_1\lambda_2\mu_3 - 2\lambda_1\mu_2\mu_3 + N\lambda_1\mu_2\mu_3)$.

Comparisons of Reliabilities: Figure 9 shows the reliability of RAID5 and RM2 architectures, where a MTTF of a single disk ($MTTF_{disk}$) is set to 1,000,000 hours [1] and a MTTR of a single disk ($MTTR_{disk}$) to reconstruct all faulty parity and data blocks is set to 48 hours [11]. That is, $\lambda_1 = 1/1,000,000$ and $\mu_1 = 1/48$. We can see that the reliability of RM2 is higher than that of RAID5 by 10,417 times with 6 disks and by 869 times with 50 disks.

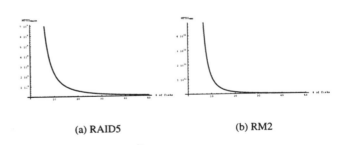

(a) RAID5

(b) RM2

Figure 9. Reliability comparison between RAID5 and RM2

Depending on the increasing and decreasing rates of the delayed parity groups in $BPGL$ (λ_2, μ_2) and the processing rates of delayed parity groups in $BPGL$ in the presence of disk failure (μ_3), the reliability of the proposed architecture

216

ranges from that of RAID5 as the worst case to that of RM2 as the best case. Figure 10 shows two extreme cases. While the first case of $\lambda_2 = 10^4 \mu_2$ and $\mu_3 \simeq \mu_1$ has the same reliability as RAID5, the second case of $\lambda_2 = 10^{-4} \mu_2$ has the same reliability as RM2.

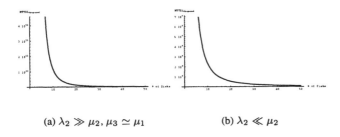

(a) $\lambda_2 \gg \mu_2, \mu_3 \simeq \mu_1$ (b) $\lambda_2 \ll \mu_2$

Figure 10. Two extreme cases of reliability of the proposed architecture

In what follows, we will investigate the effects of the reliability of the proposed architecture as a function of λ_2, μ_2, and μ_3. First, Figure 11(a) presents the effects of λ_2 and μ_2 with a fixed μ_3 on the reliability of the proposed architecture with $N = 6$, where μ_3 is set to $100\mu_1$. If λ_2 is higher than μ_2, then the reliability decreases because the probability of staying at $NORM_{unsafe}$ correspondingly increases. Given a fixed λ_2, the reliability is enhanced with an increase of μ_2. If $\lambda_2 \simeq 0$, then μ_3 does not affect the

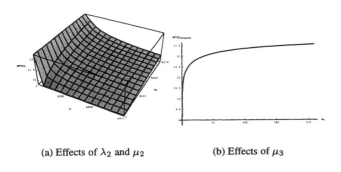

(a) Effects of λ_2 and μ_2 (b) Effects of μ_3

Figure 11. Reliability of the proposed architecture with $\lambda_1 = \frac{1}{1,000,000}$, $\mu_1 = \frac{1}{48}$

reliability of the proposed architecture. In Figure 11(b), λ_2 and μ_2 are set to $\frac{1}{0.01}$ and 100, respectively, i.e., μ_2 is set to much lower than λ_2. As a result, the system is expected to remain at $NORM_{unsafe}$ for most of the time with no disk failure. Next, the value of μ_3 varies from $\frac{1}{48}$ to $\frac{1}{0.0048}$. Figure 11(b) shows that the reliability of the proposed ar-

chitecture is equal to that of RAID5 when μ_3 is small. Conversely, if μ_3 becomes larger, i.e., ≥ 100, then its reliability becomes equal to that of RM2. Note that $\mu_3 = \frac{1}{0.001}$ (hour) means that the expected time to process all delayed parity groups in $BPGL$ will be approximately 4 seconds.

Measurement of a Realistic $MTTDL_{proposed}$ with a Traced I/O Workload: To empirically obtain realistic values for λ_2, μ_2, and μ_3 which were used in the previous analysis, we employ a traced I/O workload of the `cello` system [10]. A Linux system regenerates all I/O requests which were issued to eight disks within the `cello` system on 05/04/92. Note that a different disk in the `cello` system is mapped to a different region of the proposed architecture. When measured, the system remained at $NORM_{safe}$ for 83,176 seconds and $NORM_{unsafe}$ for 3,224 seconds during the 84,400-second observation period. Recall that the RAID system being tested exploits the delayed write scheme with a 64MB write back cache. Thus, the event of inserting the delayed parity groups into $BPGL$ occurs in a bursty manner when dirty data in the write back cache are flushed into physical disks. First, by computing all inter-arrival times between two subsequent times when a parity group is delayed into an empty $BPGL$, we can obtain a realistic value of λ_2, i.e., $\frac{1}{\lambda_2} = 268.01$ seconds, where the maximum inter-arrival time is 3560.78 seconds and the minimum inter-arrival time is 1.11 seconds. Second, by averaging out all elapsed times to process the delayed parity groups in $BPGL$ when $BPGL \neq \emptyset$, it can be calculated that $\frac{1}{\mu_2} = 14.45$ seconds. Third, the maximum value of $|BPGL|$ at $NORM_{unsafe}$ is observed as 934. Recall that the priority of the $BPGT$ is the same as that of the background process which rebuilds faulty data and parity blocks. Then, by deriving a relative relationship between μ_1 and μ_3, we can compute the worst case time to process all delayed parity groups in $BPGL$ in the presence of a disk failure. Since the size of a single disk is 9GB and $M = 2$, reconstructing an entire faulty disk requires rebuilding 147,456 $(= \frac{9GB}{32KB \cdot 2})$ parity groups, which takes $\frac{1}{\mu_1} = 48$ hours. Thus, it can be seen that $\frac{1}{\mu_3}$ is $\frac{1}{\mu_1} \frac{934}{147,456} = 0.30$ hours, implying that processing the delayed parity groups in $BPGL$ is about 160 times faster than reconstructing all of the parity groups in a faulty disk.

Finally, the obtained realistic values for $\frac{1}{\lambda_2}$, $\frac{1}{\mu_2}$, and $\frac{1}{\mu_3}$ by regenerating traced I/O requests of the `cello` system are 0.074, 0.004, 0.30 hours, respectively, where MTTF of a disk $\frac{1}{\lambda_1} = 1,000,000$ hours and MTTR of a disk $\frac{1}{\mu_1} = 48$ hours. Next, Figure 12 shows that the reliability of the proposed architecture when those realistic values are applied to Equation (4). It is revealed that the reliability of the proposed architecture is extremely high, i.e., about 298–436 times that of RAID5 and 0.04–0.34 times that of RM2.

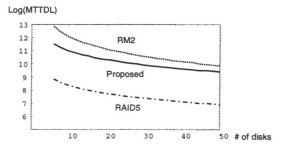

Figure 12. Comparing the reliability of RAID5 and RM2 with the reliability of the proposed architecture configured with the empirically obtained values of $\frac{1}{\lambda_2} = 0.074$, $\frac{1}{\mu_2} = 0.004$, and $\frac{1}{\mu_3} = 0.30$

4. Concluding Remarks

In order to overcome the low write I/O performance of RM2, a well-known RAID6 architecture, we employed a *Lazy Parity Update* (LPU) technique which loosens the strict reliability requirement of tolerating double disk failures at any given time. We implemented the proposed architecture on top of an actual RAID system and then thoroughly evaluated its I/O performance and reliability. I/O throughput measurements revealed that the proposed architecture improves the write I/O performance of RM2 by more than two times. Reliability measurements by theoretical analysis and regeneration of a traced real I/O workload showed that the proposed architecture continuously provides extremely high reliability, *i.e.*, about 298–436 times the reliability of RAID5 and 0.04–0.34 times the reliability of RM2.

In future work, we will conduct more experiments on different testing environments with an odd number of disks which demands a relatively larger *FPG* compared with an even number of disks, a larger number of disks, and different types of traced I/O workloads. In addition, we plan to devise a more sophisticated idle detection mechanism based on previous work [5, 11] and apply the LPU technique to other RAID6 architectures, such as P+Q, EVEN-ODD, and DATUM.

Acknowledgments

The authors would like to thank the Ministry of Education of Korea for its financial support through its BK21 program.

References

[1] St39175fc product manual. Web document. URL: *http://www.seagate.com/support/disc/fc/st39175fc.html*.

[2] G. Alvarez and *et. al*. Tolerating multiple failures in raid architectures with optimal storage and uniform declustering. In *Proceedings of the 24th ISCA*, June 1997.

[3] R. Billinton and R. Allan. *Reliability Evaluation of Engineering System: Concepts and Techniques*. Pitman Advanced Publishing Program, Boston, 1992.

[4] M. Blaum and *et. al*. Evenodd: An efficient scheme for tolerating double disk failures in raid architectures. *IEEE Transactions on Computers*, 44(2), February 1995.

[5] R. Golding and *et. al*. Idleness is not sloth. In *Proceedings of Winter USENIX*, pages 201–212, January 1995.

[6] P. Massiglia. *The RAID Book*. RAID Advisory Board, 6 edition, 1997.

[7] Y. Nam and *et. al*. Enhancing write i/o performance of disk array rm2 tolerating double disk failures. Technical Report CSE-SSL-2002-02, POSTECH, Pohang, Kyungbuk, Republic of Korea, January 2002.

[8] C. Park. Efficient placement of parity and data to tolerate two disk failures in disk array systems. *IEEE Transactions on Parallel and Distributed Systems*, pages 76–86, November 1995.

[9] D. Patterson, G. Gibson, and R. Katz. A case for redundant arrays of inexpensive disks(raid). In *Proceedings of IEEE COMPCON*, pages 112–117, Spring 1989.

[10] C. Ruemmler and J. Wilkes. Unix disk access patters. In *Proceedings of Winter USENIX*, pages 405–420, January 1993.

[11] S. Savage and J. Wilkes. Afraid - a frequently redundant array of independent disks. In *Proceedings of USENIX Technical Conference*, January 1996.

[12] A. Thomasian. Performance analysis of raid5 disk arrays. *Tutorial Material, SIGMETRICS/PERFORMANCE*, June 1998.

An Online Heuristic for Data Placement in Computer Systems with Active Disks

Sumalatha Adabala
School of ECE
Purdue University
adabala@purdue.edu

José A. B. Fortes
Dept. of ECE
University of Florida
fortes@ufl.edu

Abstract

In this paper, an online heuristic is proposed and evaluated, for managing the dynamic memory in a computer system with Active Disks, by physically co-locating in disk memory or main memory, the data pages being accessed by a computation slice. This enables a runtime system that can offload the corresponding computation slice to the appropriate processing unit at the disk memory or main memory. A modified version of SEQUITUR, an online compression algorithm, is used to identify the affinity among sets of pages in a virtual memory page reference stream, and a page allocation and replacement policy that co-locates these sets of pages in memory is presented. The sets of pages identified by the algorithm are shown to closely match the sets of pages referenced by computation slices, using a suite of data access kernels as benchmarks. The paging policy is evaluated with page traces of micro benchmarks and real applications. In memory constrained environments, with additional memory at the disk, most of the benchmarks see improved performance, due to fewer page faults. The paging heuristic can co-locate 50% of the affinity sets on average and can offload up to 100% of the computation to disk, while the number of page faults are comparable to that of the LRU paging policy.

1. Introduction

Active Disks [1, 6, 7, 11] are a proposal for next generation disk drives that provide an environment for executing application code directly at the individual drives. When some of the application processing is offloaded to the disk processor there is an improvement in performance, due to parallel processing across disk processors when the offloaded code is data-parallel, or due to better resource usage when the offloaded code processes large data sets that do not fit in memory. Previous research [1, 6, 7, 11] restricted in-

vestigations to data-intensive applications with out-of-core data sets and system configurations with large numbers of disks. This research looks at exploiting the additional processing available at Active Disks to improve throughput and resource usage of multiprogramming workloads in desktop like configurations, where a few disks are tightly coupled to the main processing unit via a dedicated I/O bus. In such workloads, individual applications often perform better when processed exclusively at the main processing unit, but with processing and memory resource constraints in a multiprogramming environment, they may be able to take advantage of the additional processing and memory available at the Active Disk. Multiple threads of an application may be processed in parallel on the disk processor and the main processor, or a single thread of computation may be invoked on the main processor or disk processor depending on where the data being processed resides. The heuristic presented in this paper, provides the support for dynamic partitioning of application data based on available memory, that is required for these scenarios. It must be complemented by a runtime system that can invoke the corresponding computation at the disk processor or main processor.

In systems with Active Disks, the dynamic memory management policy has the option of allocating and replacing data pages in disk memory, in addition to the main memory. Extending existing paging policies that manage the main memory to effectively manage this additional memory is not straightforward, as the cost of accessing all pages is not the same—some accesses need to cross the I/O interconnect to remote memory. The paging policy must thus try to co-allocate, in disk or main memory, the set of pages being accessed by the corresponding computation at the disk or main processor, to avoid page accesses across the I/O interconnect. Memory management techniques of shared memory multiprocessors, such as the Origin 2000, are not suitable, as they require the Active Disk to be managed separately as a machine running an operating system kernel. This is an inefficient use of the limited resources, processing and memory, on the disk. The paging heuristic proposed in this paper extends page replacement policies, like the LRU

*This work was partially funded by the National Science Foundation under grant CCR-9970728.

(Least Recently Used) policy, which keep track of the temporal locality in page references, to record additional information about references to groups of pages, and uses it to guide co-allocation of pages used by a computation, in disk or main memory. It can be extended to take hints from and give hints to the application runtime system regarding data placement decisions.

The paging heuristic is based on the assumption that the affinity between pages in a page reference stream of an application is associated with them being accessed by a computation slice. A modified version of the SEQUITUR [10] compression algorithm is used for analyzing the page reference stream online and form a grammar based on repeated sequences of pages in it. The paging heuristic uses the grammar to infer affinity among sets of pages and uses this information to extend the LRU (Least Recently Used) paging policy, by trying to co-locate the set of pages in the following ways: (i) A page that is read in from disk is allocated on disk or main memory based on the location of the in-core pages in its set, (b) Since the amount of memory on disks is much smaller than the main memory, sets of pages that do not fit in disk memory are migrated to the main memory, and (c) When large sets (with many pages) that do not fit in the dynamic memory are encountered, an MRU (Most Recently Used) page replacement policy is used, as such sets typically result from streaming reference patterns with poor LRU behavior.

This paper is organized as follows. Section 2, describes the problem of dynamic memory management in computer systems with Active Disks. Section 3, presents the details of the proposed heuristic. Section 4, describes the evaluation of the heuristic. Conclusions and future work are presented in Section 5.

2. Dynamic memory management in systems with Active Disks

The memory hierarchy of a computer system with an Active Disk is shown in Figure 1. The dynamic memory in the system consists of the main memory and the disk memory. A page can reside in the main memory, disk memory or on the disk medium. The latency to access the disk medium, t_d (typically 5-10ms), which includes the disk seek time and time spent in the I/O request queue, is many orders of magnitude larger than the remaining latencies (DRAM access times are ~50ns, PCI bus latencies are ~300ns) encountered when a page is moved around in the memory hierarchy. Current systems are not configured with enough disks to make the I/O bus (PCI and SCSI) a bottleneck and heavy sustained sequential I/O that can saturate the I/O bus is relatively rare. Therefore, the number of page faults to disk is the most significant measure of the performance of a page replacement policy, and cannot be traded-off against

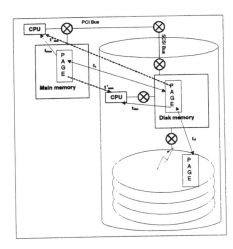

Figure 1. Memory hierarchy in a computer system with an Active Disk

any other performance benefits from processing on disk.

Once the number of page faults is bounded, the effectiveness of a page replacement policy can be measured by the overall improvement in performance due to offloading processing to the disk vs. the other latencies that come into effect when data pages are accessed or moved from different parts of the dynamic memory, i.e. disk memory and main memory. The most significant among the latencies encountered is the latency of data transfer through the I/O bus. As a result data accesses to remote memory (t'_{dm}, t'_{mm}) and page copies (t_t) between disk and main memory degrade performance.

Thus, to evaluate the effectiveness of the the paging policy for systems with Active Disks, the following measures must be determined, (i) the number of page faults, (ii) the number of hits to pages in remote memory, and (iii) the amount of computation offloaded to the disk processor.

3. Using affinity among page references to guide page placement

Paging policies, in current operating systems and database management systems, typically use temporal locality information from a page reference trace or application hints for evicting data pages from memory to disk, e.g. LRU. To co-locate data pages accessed by a computation, the paging policy must be able to identify the sets of pages being accessed by the computation. It can do this by either getting hints from the application, or by observing patterns in the page reference trace of the application. Several proposed branch prediction [2] and data prefetching [14] solutions based on data compression techniques [8, 10, 16], predict future data using models built from patterns in sequences of past data. This information can also be used to predict affinity among sets of pages in a page reference sequence.

The terminology required to understand the information extracted from page references in the proposed approach is presented below.

Page reference sequence: The sequence of (distinct) virtual memory pages that are accessed by an application. There is only one entry in the sequence for multiple consecutive accesses to a page.

Subsequence (of pages): A set of page references that form a subsequence of the page reference sequence.

Spatial affinity (of a set of pages) in the page reference sequence: The property of a set of pages whose references occur close by in the page reference sequence. The pages in a subsequence have spatial affinity.

Temporal affinity (of a subsequence of pages) in the page reference sequence: The property of a subsequence (or any set of pages with spatial affinity), such that an occurrence of the subsequence in the page reference sequence makes it likely that there are occurrences of the same subsequence at a short distance (nearby in time) in the page reference sequence.

Slice of computation: A portion of computation that can be invoked independently on a processor. Depending on the support available from the runtime system, this could be a basic block of code, a procedure, an application, a disklet (code that can run in the disk environment), an applet, etc.

Cluster (of pages): The set of pages referenced by a slice of computation. A cluster shows spatial affinity in the page reference sequence. If the slice of computation is a loop or a procedure, the cluster may also exhibit temporal affinity in the page reference trace.

Affinity set (of pages): A set of pages with spatial and temporal affinity.

3.1. Finding affinity sets using modified SE-QUITUR

The proposed heuristic is based on the assumption that an affinity set (e.g. a repeated subsequence in a page reference sequence) typically corresponds to a cluster. A cluster does not necessarily show up as an affinity set in the page reference sequence. The SEQUITUR algorithm is a linear-time, on-line algorithm for producing a context-free grammar from an input string. The algorithm operates by appending symbols from the input string, in order, to the end of the grammar's start production. After adding each symbol, SEQUITUR manipulates the grammar productions to preserve two invariants:

Digram uniqueness property: A digram is a pair of consecutive symbols on the right side of the grammar production. This property states that a digram occurs at most once in

the rules of the grammar. If adding a symbol introduces a duplicate digram, SEQUITUR replaces both occurrences of the digram with the non-terminal for a rule that has the digram as its right side. For example, after adding symbol c to the grammar:

$$S \rightarrow abcdb$$

The digram bc occurs twice, so both occurrences are replaced with a new non-terminal A:

$$S \rightarrow aAdA$$
$$A \rightarrow bc$$

Rule utility property: All non-terminal symbols in a grammar (except for the start symbol) must be referenced more than once by other rules. SEQUITUR eliminates a rule referenced only once by replacing the reference with the rule's right sid .In the example above, adding another symbol d, results in a new rule to replace the two occurrences of Ad. As the rule A is now used only once, it is eliminated.

$$S \rightarrow aBB$$
$$B \rightarrow bcd$$

The space consumed by SEQUITUR grows linearly with the size of the inferred hierarchy, so to analyze large page reference traces, the bounded space version of SEQUITUR [9] is used.

Additional changes were made to SEQUITUR to simplify the information maintained. Consider the rules generated by the following sequence of symbols abababababababab:

$$S \rightarrow DD$$
$$A \rightarrow ab$$
$$B \rightarrow AA$$
$$C \rightarrow BB$$
$$D \rightarrow CC$$

In general, for every n consecutive occurrences of a symbol x, the SEQUITUR algorithm generates log(n) rules. However, while trying to infer affinity sets of pages from the grammar produced for the page reference sequence, subsequences with distinct pages are required, so the above set of productions is unnecessary information. The complexity of the algorithm and it's space requirements are reduced, by avoiding forming of rules from digrams with identical symbols, and instead replacing the repeated occurrence of the symbol, by a single symbol with an associated repetition count. Thus the previous example results in a smaller grammar that is easier to traverse: grammar:

$$S \rightarrow A^{16}$$
$$A \rightarrow ab$$

The rules in the grammar constructed by the modified SEQUITUR algorithm from a page reference stream correspond to repeated subsequences, i.e. affinity sets. The deeper the occurrence of a rule in the grammar hierarchy inferred by SEQUITUR, the finer is the computation slice accessing the corresponding affinity set. In the proposed heuristic, only affinity sets produced by the rules in the main grammar rule of the inferred grammar are considered, i.e. those corresponding to the coarsest slices of computation. Thus, for the following grammar inferred from a page reference sequence:

$$S \rightarrow CAC$$
$$A \rightarrow bc$$
$$B \rightarrow ef$$
$$C \rightarrow aBdB$$

The affinity sets extracted from the reference stream are: C = {a, e, f, d} and A = {b, c}. Though B = {e, f} is an affinity set in the page reference stream, it is a subsumed in the affinity set C accessed by a coarser slice of computation.

3.2. A paging heuristic that is aware of affinity sets

Every time a page is accessed, it is added to the grammar for the pages referenced so far using the modified SEQUITUR algorithm. Using this information, the paging heuristic tries to accomplish the following: (i) When accessing a page already in memory, mark it as most recently used (MRU), i.e. default LRU policy; When a new page is brought from disk into dynamic memory, (ii) If there are some free pages, co-locate in-core affinity sets by copying between disk memory and main memory, before allocating new page in disk or main memory, or (iii) If there is need for eviction of a page resident in disk or main memory, find a page that does not belong to the affinity set of the new page, because the heuristic predicts that pages in the affinity set are going to be accessed shortly. While searching for a page to evict, co-locate in-core affinity sets, by copying pages between disk and main memory. If all the pages belong to the same affinity set, they are part of a large working set, so eviction is handled with an MRU replacement policy.

PSEUDOCODE FOR THE PAGING HEURISTIC

```
Getnext page reference;
Update page ref grammar with new page;
if page is in dynamic memory then
  mark page as MRU;
end if
// PAGE IS FAULTED IN FROM DISK
if some memory is free on one of the
  disks or in main memory then
  for each disk do
    if some memory is free then
      place page as MRU in disk memory;
    else if MRU or LRU on disk belong to the
      affinity set of MRU in main memory then
      copy MRU or LRU to main memory;
      place page as MRU in disk memory;
```

```
  end if
  end for
  if main memory is free then
    place page as MRU in main memory;
  end if
end if
// A PAGE MUST BE SELECTED FOR EVICTION
if new page belongs to rule R then
  for each disk do
    // AFFINITY SET DOES NOT FIT IN MEMORY
    if all MRU and LRU on disk and memory
    belong to rule R then
      replace MRU on disk;
    else if LRU on disk or main memory OR MRU
    on disk does not belong to rule R then
      replace LRU on disk or main memory;
      OR replace MRU on disk;
    end if
  end for
end if
if new page is not in any rule then
  for each disk do
    find the affinity sets for MRU and LRU
    on disk and main memory;
    co-locate pages by switching between
    disk and main memory;
    if LRU on disk or main memory does not
    belong to the same affinity set as the
    MRU on disk or main memory then
      evict the LRU on disk or main memory;
    end if
  end for
end if
if new page has not been allocated then
  evict LRU on a disk chosen at random;
end if
```

The code in *italics* is associated with looking up information maintained by modified SEQUITUR. These are expensive operations compared to the typical bookkeeping associated with page replacement algorithms, such as LRU. However all of them occur during a page fault, which is an expensive operation, so their overhead should be insignificant. The underlined code involves expensive memory copy operations, which co-locate in-core pages belonging to affinity sets. While all the copies occur during a page fault, the second set of copies that occur when the heuristic is looking for a suitable page to evict can result in up to two copies per disk, so they can generate extensive I/O traffic. Finally, the last **if** condition, which is the default LRU-like policy when co-allocation fails, was monitored when evaluating the heuristic to check if the results were due to this default policy. This code was executed only at data points that were not of interest, i.e. when dynamic memory was unrealistically constrained (very small relative to the working set) and generating large numbers of page faults.

4. Evaluation and Results

Evaluation of the proposed heuristic consists of two parts. The first part consists of showing that the affinity sets in a page reference stream are a good approximation of the clusters corresponding to computation slices in an application. The second part consists of evaluating the paging policy by measuring (i) the number of page faults generated for different memory configurations and comparing them against the number of page faults with the LRU policy, (ii) the degree of co-location of affinity sets achieved, which can be used to get an approximate estimate of data accesses to remote memory, and (iii) the amount of computation offloaded to disk. When the number of page faults generated by the proposed heuristic is comparable to that of the LRU policy, the last two metrics are indicators of the performance of applications when data and computation is offloaded to Active Disks in a computer system.

4.1. Benchmarks

The benchmarks used to evaluate the heuristic are listed in Table 1. They consist of (a) the DIS Stressmark Suite [4], which is a set of small programs that are representative of data-intensive kernels in the DIS benchmarks suite, (b) a set of micro benchmarks that generate the patterns of page references [3] exhibited by relational database operations, (c) multimedia benchmarks from the Berkeley Multimedia Benchmark suite [13] — traces were truncated to a million page references, and (d) application page reference traces collected on UNIX and Windows NT platforms [5]. The page reference sequences for the stressmarks and the benchmarks were collected locally, on a Linux platform with a 4 KB page size, using the VMTrace program [15]. To measure the percentage of processing offloaded to disk, time spent processing a given page is approximated by the time spent by the code referencing the page. The UNIX traces (generated with VMTrace) and the Windows NT traces (generated with Etch) were downloaded from the WWW [15], and reduced in length using the Safely Allowed Drop algorithm [5].

4.2. Matching affinity sets with clusters

The method and measurements used to validate the assumption that pages accessed by a computation slice, i.e. a cluster, translate into an identifiable pattern, an affinity set in the virtual memory page reference sequence are presented in this section. The DIS Stressmark Suite was used to estimate the degree of correspondence between the clusters in the stressmarks and the affinity sets identified by the modified SEQUITUR algorithm, in the virtual page reference sequence.

Computation slices in the stressmarks, typically loops or sections of nested loops, were identified and guard code (i.e.

Table 1. Benchmarks used for evaluation

Benchmarks	Working Set Size (4 K pages)
DIS Stressmarks	
Pointer	17 (small); 65 (large)
Matrix	22 (small); 173 (large)
Neighborhood	9 (small); 129 (large)
Field	9 (small); 23 (large)
Corner-Turn	18 (small); 129(large)
Transitive Closure	8 (small); 32 (large)
Micro benchmarks	
Sequential (S) scan	128
Clustered Sequential (CS) scan	160
Clustered Random (CR) scan	256
Looping Sequential (LS) scan	144
Berkeley Multimedia Suite	
DVJU decode (d)	125
DVJU encode (e)	658
JPEG decode (d)	10
MPEG-2 decode (d)	127
MPEG-2 encode (e)	125
Doom	9
UNIX application traces	
Espresso	77
Gcc	458
Gnuplot	7718
Ghostscript	558
Lindsay	521
P2c	132
Rscheme	2039
Windows NT application traces	
Acroread	1903
CC1	716
Compress	396
Go	267
Netscape	1037
Powerpoint	1000
Vortex	4275
Winword	983

access to a known guard memory page) introduced around each slice by hand. The clusters of pages accessed by the computation slices were easily extracted from the page reference sequence, as they were separated from the remaining page references by accesses to the known guard page. A cluster tree consisting of the clusters as leaves, ordered by the sequence in which the corresponding computation slices were invoked, was built. The grammar generated by the modified SEQUITUR algorithm for the application page access trace (generated without the guard code), was also built into a tree with nodes consisting of the affinity sets in the reference trace. Approximate tree pattern matching [12] was used to determine if the clusters referred to by the computation matched the affinity sets extracted from the page reference trace.

A match between two trees t and t' is exact based on a matching relation R, if t' is a member of R(t), i.e. applying R to t makes it identical to t'. In the case of the cluster and affinity set trees, to test the assumption that every affinity set corresponds to a cluster, the matching relation is defined as, 'every leaf in the affinity set tree must exactly match or be a subset of some leaf in the cluster tree' An exact match is obtained for the DIS stressmarks. By definition, it is not the case that every cluster corresponds to an affinity set. To measure the mismatch between the clusters and the affinity sets being used by the policy, a matching relation, 'every leaf in the cluster tree must match with some leaf, i.e. affinity set, in the affinity set tree,' is defined. When a match between trees, t and t', is approximate [12] the distance between the trees is measured by the edit distance, i.e. the smallest number of changes to t and or t' that result in trees that have an exact match. The edits needed to be made to the affinity sets, so that every cluster in the cluster tree matched an affinity set in the affinity set tree, were measured. Thus, for the heuristic, which aims to co-locate pages in an affinity set together, the edit distance is an upper bound on the number of page accesses by a computation slice that need to go to remote memory, when its cluster does not match any affinity set.

The stressmarks were run with varying sizes of inputs, so that the working set of the application ranged from small (spanning 4-9 pages) to large (spanning 64-128 pages). This resulted in two kinds of virtual page reference traces. With the smaller data sets, where most of the data fits within a page, memory access and reuse patterns are filtered out and do not show up in the page reference trace. These traces represent applications that are not data-intensive. On the other hand, with the larger input sets that span many pages, these memory access patterns do translate into identifiable patterns in the page reference sequence. Further, each stressmark was also run with different parameters (upto 8 variations), so that page access patterns generated by different control flow were evaluated.

In all cases, as tabulated in Table 2, the edit distance between the cluster tree and the affinity set tree (given as the percentage of the number of page inserts in the affinity sets tree with respect to the total number of pages in the cluster tree) is small, indicating a close match between the affinity sets identified from the page reference trace and the clusters of pages accessed by computation slices in the application. The percentage of unmatched rules varies. The large percentage of unmatched affinity sets indicates that there is a high chance that the paging policy may try to co-locate pages that belong together in an affinity set that does not match a cluster for a computation slice in the application. However, the affinity set trees match the cluster tree with an edit distance of zero, implying that these unmatched affinity sets are subsets of other affinity sets.

4.3. Paging

Main memory and disk memory, with sizes varying from zero to the working set size for the benchmarks, and for varying number of disks, were emulated to measure, (a) the number of page faults with the paging heuristic compared against the LRU policy for a system with no Active Disks, (b) the percentage of page hits in main memory and disk memory that are not co-located with their affinity sets, which is an upperbound on the number of page accesses to remote memory, and (c) the percentage of computation offloaded to the disk. The results of the evaluation for different scenarios are presented below.

(i) Total dynamic memory is equal to the working set of the benchmark, and is partitioned between main memory and disk memory. In this case, the number of page faults is the minimum possible, i.e. the number of pages in the working set. The gains from offloading processing and data to the disk processor are traded off against the cost of accessing data from remote memory when data pages are not co-located with the processing. Complete simulation of the system architecture is required to do a proper evaluation of the costs and benefits. Figure 2 shows estimates for the fraction of page accesses to remote memory. The estimates were obtained by measuring the number of hits to pages, that were not co-located with the remaining pages in their affinity sets. The maximum estimate is got by adding these hits at both the disk and the main memory. It is a conservative estimate, as access to any page in an affinity set that is partitioned between disk and main memory, is counted as an access to remote memory. The minimum estimate, is the smaller of the non co-located hits at the disk or main memory. It corresponds to the scenario when all computation is at the disk processor or main processor and the smaller of the possible hits is to the remote memory. The figure shows two sets of estimates for each benchmark, the first when the disk memory is 5% of the dynamic memory, and the second when the dynamic memory is partitioned equally between the disk and main memory. The second configuration, with the larger disk memory, has slightly lower estimates for remote memory accesses, as most of the benchmarks have affinity sets larger than 5% of their working sets. The heuristic achieves 50% co-location on average for all the application benchmarks. The micro benchmarks not shown in the plot, achieved 100% co-location.

(ii) Main memory is smaller than the working set of the benchmark, and is augmented with disk memory, so that the total dynamic memory is equal to the working set of the benchmark. Figure 3 shows the factor of change in the number of page faults for all the benchmarks, when a 5% additional memory is added to the system via an Active Disk. The fraction of application processing that is offloaded to the disk is also shown for the Multimedia Benchmarks. It shows that when main memory is limited, offloading data to any additional disk memory and processing at the disk is beneficial if this enables the working set to fit in dynamic memory. In the case of the UNIX applica-

Table 2. Affinity Evaluation

DIS Stressmarks	Edit distance (%)			% unmatched affinity sets in the affinity sets tree	Average # of pages per unmatched affinity sets
	Max	Min	Avg		
Pointer	2.7	0.09	0.9	63	1
Matrix	0.7	0.3	0.56	28	4.4
Neighborhood	0.0007	0.001	0.00085	25	3.6
Field	3.7	0.02	1.78	16	2
Corner-Turn	0.9	0	0.45	40	3.9
Transitive Closure	0	0	0	24	6.4

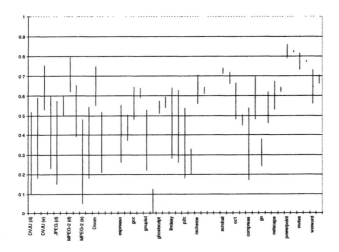

Figure 2. Maximum and minimum estimates of the fraction of hits to pages in dynamic memory that are to remote memory

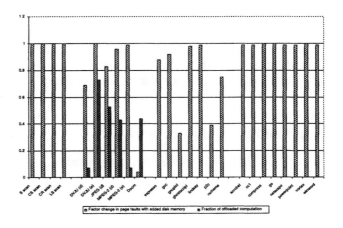

Figure 3. Factor of change in page faults, when dynamic memory of the system is increased by 5% with additional memory at the disk. The corresponding fraction of computation offloaded to the disk processor is also shown for the multimedia benchmarks

tion traces and the multimedia applications, the reduction in page faults and the amount of computation that is offloaded scales with the number of disks and amount of memory per disk. For these applications, offloading processing to Active Disks is always a win.

(iii) Total dynamic memory is less than the working set of the benchmark, and is partitioned between main memory and disk memory. Figure 4 shows the performance of the paging heuristic for this scenario. For each benchmark there is a column (page faults for heuristic normailzed against page faults with LRU) corresponding to the following four configurations: first, with total dynamic memory at 95% of the working set, two configurations are considered (a) 5% of the dynamic memory is disk memory, (b) 50% of the dynamic memory is disk memory; second, with total dynamic memory set at 50% of the working set, two configurations are considered (c) 5% of this memory is the disk memory, and (d) 50% of the memory is from

disk. A column larger than 1, indicates that the heuristic performs poorly for the given partitioning of dynamic memory. The performance of the micro-benchmarks, shows that code with sequential scans, are unaffected by the partitioning of dynamic memory. For the remaining benchmarks, when the total dynamic memory is close to the working set, i.e. configurations (a) and (b), performance is close to LRU, indicating that they may be able to exploit processing at the disk when resources are limited. A few of the benchmarks, see very large reductions in page faults and are clear candidates for further investigation in the context of Active Disks in multiprogramming environments. Figure 5 shows the percentage of computation offloaded to the disk processor in the above four scenarios, for the multimedia benchmarks. In general, for the multimedia benchmarks, the processing offloaded to the disk is proportional to the data offloaded to the disk memory.

225

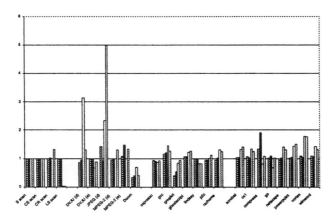

Figure 4. Page faults normalized to LRU, for four different partitionings of dynamic memory between main memory and disk memory

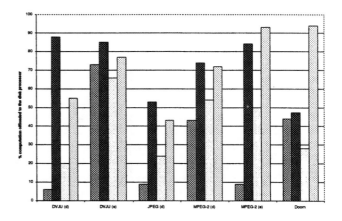

Figure 5. Percentage of processing offloaded to the disk processor for four different partitionings of dynamic memory between the main memory and disk memory

5. Conclusions and future work

In this paper, a paging heuristic that can be used to manage the dynamic memory in computer systems with Active Disks was proposed and evaluated. Evaluation with real application benchmarks shows that applications in multiprogramming environments can definitely benefit from memory and processing at an Active Disk, when resources are limited at the main processing unit. The on-line heuristic presented adaptively partitions the data pages of an application and tries to co-locate pages that are being accessed by a computation slice. The evaluation also identified the potential for significant gains in the performance of some benchmarks in system configurations with Active Disks. Further investigations are planned to, (i) characterize these applications and quantify their performance gains in systems with Active Disks, and (ii) evaluate the heuristic within a real runtime environment.

References

[1] A. Acharya, M. Uysal, and J. Saltz. Active disks: programming model, algorithms and evaluation. *ASPLOS*, pages 81–91, 3-7 October 1998.

[2] I.-C. K. Cheng, J. T. Coffey, and T. N. Mudge. Analysis of branch prediction via data compression. *Proc. of the 7th Intl. Conf. on ASPLOS*, October 1996.

[3] H.-T. Chou and D. J. DeWitt. An evaluation of buffer management strategies for relational database systems. *Proc. of the 11th Intl. Conf. on VLDB*, pages 127–141, 1985.

[4] A. A. E. Corporation. Dis '00 stressmark suite. *Stressmark Specifications Document Version 1.0*.

[5] S. F. Kaplan, Y. Smaragdakis, and P. R. Wilson. Trace reduction for virtual memory simulations. pages 47–58, 1999.

[6] K. Keeton, D. A. Patterson, and J. M. Hellerstein. A case for intelligent disks (IDISKs). *SIGMOD Record*, 27(3), September 1998.

[7] G. Memik, M. Kandemir, and A. Choudhary. Design and evaluation of smart disk architecture for data-intensive applications. *Technical Report*, (CPDC-TR-2000-05-015), 2000.

[8] A. Moffat. Implementing the ppm data compression scheme. *IEEE Trans. on Comm.*, 11(38):1917–1921.

[9] C. G. Nevill-Manning and I. H. Witten. Phrase hierarchy inference and compression in bounded space. *Proc. of Data Compression Conf.*, pages 179–188.

[10] C. G. Nevill-Manning and I. H. Witten. Linear-time, incremental hierarchy inference for compression. *Proc. of Data Compression Conf.*, 1997.

[11] E. Riedel and G. Gibson. Remote execution for network-attached storage. *Technical Report*, (CMU-CS-97-198), December 1997.

[12] D. Shasha and K. Zhang. *Approximate Tree Pattern Matching*, chapter 11, pages 311–369. Oxford University Press, 1997.

[13] N. T. Slingerland and A. J. Smith. Design and characterization of the berkeley multimedia workload. *Technical Report*, (CSD-00-1122), December 2000.

[14] J. S. Vitter and P. Krishnan. Optimal prefetching via data compression. *Proc. of the 23rd Annual IEEE Symp. on Foundations of Computer Science*, October 1991.

[15] The VMTrace tool and page reference traces. www.cs.amherst.edu/~sfkaplan/research.

[16] J. Ziv and A. Lempel. Compression of individual sequences via variable-rate coding. *IEEE Trans. on Information Theory 24*, pages 530–536, September 1978.

Keynote Address

Session 4A

Fault-Tolerant Routing in 2D Tori or Meshes Using Limited-Global-Safety Information

Dong Xiang   Ai Chen
Institute of Microelectronics
Tsinghua University
Beijing 100084, P. R. China

Abstract

A limited-global-safety-information-based metric called local safety is proposed to handle fault-tolerant routing in 2D tori (or meshes). Sufficient conditions for existence of a minimum feasible path between the source and destination is presented based on local safety information in a 2D torus network. An efficient heuristic function is defined to guide fault-tolerant routing inside a $2D$ torus network. Unlike the conventional methods based on the block fault model, our method does not disable any fault-free nodes and fault-free nodes inside a fault block can still be a source or a destination, which can greatly increase throughput and computational power of the system. Techniques for avoidance of deadlocks are introduced. Extensive simulation results are presented.

1 Introduction

Torus and mesh-connected networks have been widely used in the recent experimental or commercial multicomputers. Those machines include the MIT J-machine [5], the Symult 2010, Intel Touchstone, the Cray T3D and T3E systems, M-machine. A $k-$ary $2-$cube network has an $2D$ grid structure with k nodes in each dimension. Each node in a $k-$ary $2-$cube is connected with two different nodes in each dimension. The performance of such multicomputers is highly dependent on the node-to-node communication cost. Fault-tolerant communication in meshes or tori has been extensively studied in [1,2,4,6-9,12,14] recently.

Linder and Harden [11] extended the concept of virtual channel to multiple virtual interconnection networks that provide adaptivity, deadlock-freedom, and

Supported in part by the national science foundation of China under grant 69773030, and in part by the 985 fundamental foundation of national education ministry.

fault-tolerance. Dally and Aoki [4] presented fault-tolerant routing algorithms based on the concept of dimension reversal, which occurs whenever a message takes a hop in a dimension lower compared to that of the previous hop. A message can be routed adaptively if the number of highest virtual channel class or if the message finds a free channel in other outgoing channels of the current host in a finite amount of time. Gaughan and Yalamanchili [8] proposed a misrouting backtracking protocol under pipelined circuit-switching. Pipelined circuit switching needs to set up a path before transmitting messages. Dao, Duato, and Yalamanchili [6] proposed a technique called scouting to handle fault-tolerant routing in a mesh-connected system, which finds a trade-off between the wormhole and the pipelined-circuit-switching techniques by setting a constant k (represents the distance between the header and the data flits). That is, data flits of the message are kept k hops away from the header flit, while the header notifies data flits of the path information in the process of message passing. Glass and Ni [9] presented the negative-first algorithm for meshes without any extra virtual channels.

A dimension-order algorithm for fault-tolerant wormhole routing in torus networks was proposed in [1] recently. The method needs only simple changes to the routing logic and implementation using local fault information. Most of the previous local-information-based methods [1,2] route a message by using only safety information of each node's neighbors, therefore, minimality is not able to be guaranteed although a minimum feasible path is available in many cases. Methods uses global knowledge of faults need to maintain the global fault information and routing tables to study the performance limitations caused by faults.

The extended safety level [12] is the first mechanism using limited-global-information to guide fault-tolerant routing in meshes, which utilizes information about the distance between a node to the closest fault block from the node to all directions. Limited-global-safety-based techniques have been adopted to guide fault-tolerant routing in hypercubes in [3,10,13]. Local safety has been successfully utilized to handle fault-tolerant routing in hypercubes [13], which is adopted to cope with fault-tolerant routing in torus networks in this paper. Local safety is defined as a 4-tuple, which represents the length of the longest feasible path from the node along 4 different directions in $2D$ tori. The block fault model is considered in this paper, which can be extended to arbitrarily shaped faults without disabling any fault-free nodes.

In the rest of this paper, preliminaries of the paper is presented in Section 2. Local safety information is introduced in Section 3. A fault-tolerant algorithm in 2D tori is proposed in Section 4. Techniques to avoid deadlocks are proposed for the fault-tolerant routing algorithm in Section 5. Simulation results are presented in Section 6. The paper is concluded in Section 7.

2   Preliminaries

A $k-$ary $2D$ torus has k^2 nodes, in which each dimension has k nodes. Two nodes (a_1, a_2) and (b_1, b_2) in a $k-$ary $2D$ torus network are connected if they differ exactly at one bit i with $a_i = (b_i + 1) \bmod k$.

Let a node $A = (a_1, a_2)$ be an 2-bit radix k vector. The Lee weight of A can be defined as follows,

$$W_L(A) = L_1(A) + L_2(A)$$

where $L_i(A) = min(a_i, k - a_i)$ for $i = 1, 2$. The Lee distance $L(A, B)$ between two nodes A and $B = (b_1, b_2)$ is defined to be $W_L(A - B)$, that is, the Lee weight of their bitwise difference modulo k. We say a message is sent from a source s to a destination d along a minimum feasible path if length of the path equals Lee distance between the two nodes and there exists no failure in the path.

Assume faults in 2D tori have rectangular shapes. A set of faults F in a 2D torus are block faults if there is one or more than one rectangles such that: (1) There are no faults on the boundary of each rectangle, (2) the interior of the rectangle includes all faulty components in F, and (3) the interior of the rectangle contains no component that is not present in F. A fault-free node is disabled if it has at least two faulty or disabled neighbors along different dimensions for arbitrarily shaped fault models. However, this technique must lose some computational power of the system. A

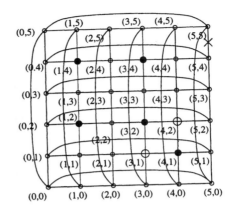

●: faulty node   ○: fault-free node   ◯: unsafe node

Figure 1: 6−ary 2−cube.

new technique is adopted to classify fault-free nodes in the system like [3,10,13].

Definition 1 *Fault-free nodes in a mesh or torus can be classified as follows: A fault-free node is unsafe if it has two faulty or unsafe neighbors along different dimensions; otherwise, it is an enabled node. All faulty nodes, unsafe nodes, and boundary enabled safe nodes between enabled nodes and faulty or unsafe nodes consist of fault blocks.*

Routing between two unsafe nodes can still be completed reliably based on the above technique. Therefore, our method does not lose any computational power. It should be noted that the new definition for fault blocks is quite different from previous ones [1,2,12] because our method does not disable any fault-free nodes. The extended safety level [12] is the first efficient and concise limited-global-safety-based metric to guide fault-tolerant routing in a mesh-connected network in a systematic way. The *extended safety level* is defined as follows: The extended safety level of a node in a given 2D mesh is a 4−tuple (E, S, W, N), where E (S,W,N) stands for the distance from this node to the closest faulty block to its east (south, west, north).

In the next section, we introduce a new definition called local safety to guide fault-tolerant routing in torus-connected networks. Assume the system contains block faults, in which the distance between any two faulty blocks is at least two. This makes the proposed method can handle the case when the system contains much more failures than that in [12].

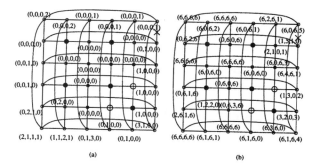

Figure 2: Comparison with the extended safety level: (a) Extended safety level, (b) local safety information.

3 Local Safety Information in 2D Torus Networks

As shown in Fig. 1, the $6-$ary $2-$cube contains 5 faulty nodes $(1, 4)$, $(1, 2)$, $(3, 4)$, $(3, 2)$, and $(4, 1)$, and a link failure $\{(5, 4), (5, 5)\}$. Six fault blocks $\{(0, 5), (0, 3), (2, 5), (2, 3)\}$, $\{(0, 3), (0, 1), (2, 3), (2, 1)\}$, $\{(2, 5), (2, 3), (4, 5), (4, 3)\}$, $\{(2, 3), (2, 0), (5, 0), (5, 3)\}$, and $\{(4, 4), (4, 5), (0, 4), (0, 5)\}$ are formed. For each fault-free node v in a torus network, we define local safety of v as follows:

Definition 2 *Local safety of a node v in a 2D torus network is defined as a $4-$element tuple (v_e, v_s, v_w, v_n), where v_e (v_s, v_w, v_n) is defined as the length of the longest feasible path from v to east (south, west, north).*

It should be noted that a feasible path never go into a fault block. As shown in Fig. 1, local safety of node $(0, 0)$ is $(6, 6, 6, 6)$, and local safety of the node $(2, 2)$ is $(0, 6, 0, 6)$. We have the following lemma.

Lemma 1 *Let (v_e, v_s, v_w, v_n) and (E, S, W, N) be local safety and extended safety level of a node v in a 2D torus network, respectively. We always have $v_e \geq E$, $v_s \geq S$, $v_w \geq W$, and $v_n \geq N$ in any cases.*

The most important reason for the above lemma is that the feasible paths defined by the extended safety level never touch boundaries of fault blocks. Let us consider the faulty $6-$ary $2-$cube as shown in Fig. 1 again. Fig. 2(a) presents the extended safety level of all enabled nodes, while Fig. 2(b) presents local safety information. Clearly, Lemma 1 holds true in all cases. Especially, the extended safety levels of the nodes $(0, 0)$, $(0, 5)$, $(2, 0)$, and $(2, 5)$ are $(2, 1, 1, 1)$, $(0, 0, 0, 2)$, $(0, 1, 3, 0)$, and $(0, 0, 0, 1)$, but local safety of all of them is $(6, 6, 6, 6)$. The extended safety levels of the nodes

$(1, 3)$, $(2, 1)$, $(2, 2)$, and $(2, 4)$ are all $(0, 0, 0, 0)$, but local safety of them is $(6, 0, 6, 0)$, $(0, 6, 3, 6)$, $(0, 6, 0, 6)$, and $(0, 6, 0, 6)$, respectively.

The *spanning submesh* $SM(s, d)$ of two nodes s and d in a 2D torus is defined as the smallest rectangle that connects the nodes by two minimum paths. The minimum paths from the source s to the destination d are composed of nodes and links in the spanning submesh.

Let the spanning submesh $SM(s, d)$ between the source s and destination d in a 2D torus connect s along directions l_1 and l_2, and connect the destination d along directions l_3 and l_4.

Definition 3 *A node s is said to be locally safe with respect to d if $s_{l_1} \geq L_{l_1}(s - d)$ and $s_{l_2} \geq L_{l_2}(s - d)$, where $L_i(s - d)$ and s_i are the Lee weight between s and d with respect to direction i and local safety of s along direction i, respectively. A node is a safe node in the system if it is locally safe with respect to all other fault-free nodes.*

Theorem 1 *There exists a minimum feasible path between a source s and a destination d if s is locally safe with respect to d or d is locally safe with respect to s.*

Proof: We would like to prove the theorem in two different cases: (1) s is locally safe with respect to d; (2) d is locally safe with respect to s. Let us prove case (1), proof of case (2) is similar. Theorem 1 is proved by induction of the Lee distance $L(s, d)$ between s and d. Consider the source s is $(0, 0)$, while the destination is (i, j) with $i > 0$ and $j > 0$. without loss of generality. Assume that $L(s - d) = 2$, there are three separate cases: (1) d is on the X axis; (2) d is on the Y axis; (3) the Lee weights along X and Y axes between s and d are both 1. Local safety of s is at least $(2, 0)$, $(0, 2)$, and $(1, 1)$, respectively, according to the premises. There always exists a minimum feasible path from s to d in all three cases.

Assume that the theorem always holds when $L(s - d) = k$. We should prove the theorem also holds when $L(s - d) = k + 1$. The next node can be found as follows: (1) select the fault-free neighbor v in a minimum feasible path from s to d, where v has the less heuristic value $d_l - L_l(s - v)$ (d_l is the local safety value of the source s along direction l, and $L_l(s - v)$ is the Lee weight between s and v along direction l, $l \in \{N, E\}$; (2) select the unique fault-free neighbor v in the west of d when there is a fault block in the south of s; (3) select the unique fault-free neighbor v in the south of s if there is a fault block in the west of s. A fault-free neighbor v of d as stated above can always be found because d is en enabled node. There always exists a minimum feasible path from v to s according to the assumption. ∎

Lemma 2 *Let $(i, \times)$ and $(\times, j)$ be fault-free rings in a $k-ary$ 2D torus, node (i, j) is a safe node.*

Proof: All fault-free nodes in the fault-free rings $(i, \times)$ and $(\times, j)$ cannot be unsafe nodes because an unsafe node should has at least two faulty or unsafe neighbors along different dimensions. Therefore, local safety of node (i, j) in the 2D torus should be (k, k, k, k). It is clear that node (i, j) is locally safe with respect to all fault-free nodes in the network. That is to say, (i, j) is a safe node in the network. ∎

As shown in the $6-ary$ 2D torus, nodes $(0,0)$, $(2,0)$, $(0,5)$, and $(2,5)$ are safe nodes.

Theorem 2 *There exists a minimum feasible path between s and d if there exists a safe node v in a minimum feasible path between s and d.*

Proof: There exists a minimum feasible path from any fault-free node to v according to Definition 3. There exists a minimum feasible path from s to v, and a minimum feasible path from v to d as stated above. And we have $L(s,v) + L(v,d) = L(s,d)$ because v is in a minimum feasible path from s to d according to the assumption. That is to say, node v is an intermediate node in a minimum feasible path $s \rightarrow v \rightarrow d$ from s to d. ∎

There may still exist a minimum feasible path from a source s to a destination d in many cases even though s is not locally safe with respect to d and d is not locally safe with respect to s.

Lemma 3 *There exists a minimum feasible path from s to d if s has a fault-free neighbor in a minimum path from s to d, and v is locally safe with respect to d or d is locally safe with respect to v.*

Consider the faulty $6-ary$ 2-cube presented in Fig. 1 again. Node $(0,2)$ is not locally safe with respect to $(1,5)$, but $(0,3)$ is locally safe with respect to $(1,5)$, which is an intermediate node in a minimum path from $(0,2)$ to $(1,5)$. A minimum feasible path between $(0,2)$ and $(1,5)$ is thus always available.

Theorem 3 *Let v be an intermediate node in a minimum path from s to d. There always exists a minimum feasible path from s to d if*

- *s is locally safe with respect to v, or v is locally safe with respect to s; and*

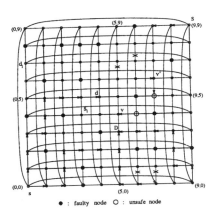

Figure 3: $10-ary$ 2-cube.

- *v is locally safe with respect to d, or d is locally safe with respect to v.*

Proof: Theorem 3 clearly holds true because there exists a minimum feasible path from s to v if s is locally safe with respect to v or v is locally safe with respect to s, and there always exists a minimum feasible path from v to d if v is locally safe with respect to d or d is locally safe with respect to v according to Theorem 1. The node v is an intermediate node in a minimum path from s to d, that is, there exists a minimum feasible path from s to d. ∎

Consider the faulty $10-ary$ 2-cube with 19 faulty nodes and 4 link failures as shown in Fig. 3. There always exists a minimum feasible path from $(0,0)$ to $(3,5)$ although $(0,0)$ is not locally safe with respect to $(3,5)$, and $(3,5)$ is also not locally safe with respect to $(0,0)$. There is an intermediate node $(2,3)$ in a minimum path from $(0,0)$ to $(3,5)$, where $(2,3)$ is locally safe with respect to $(0,0)$, and $(3,5)$ is locally safe with respect to $(2,3)$. Therefore, there exists a minimum feasible path from $(0,0)$ to $(3,4)$.

4 Fault-Tolerant Routing in 2D Tori

Wu [12] proposed a pessimistic routing algorithm, which need to form a minimum feasible path region. Therefore, a message cannot be routed along a minimum feasible path in many cases although it is available. We would like to introduce a systematic routing algorithm route1(), which is quite possible to find a minimum feasible path from the source to the destination by using a heuristic function. The algorithm needs to set up a minimum path before message passing. An important heuristic based on local safety information is used to guide message passing for each dimension inside the $SM(s,d)$,

$$h_i = \begin{cases} 0 & \text{if } d_i \geq L_i(s-d) \\ d_i - L_i(s-d) & \text{otherwise} \end{cases} \quad (1)$$

where d_i is the local safety of the destination d with respect to dimension i, and $L_i(s-d)$ is the Lee weight between s and d with respect to dimension i. The algorithm takes precedence to pass the message along dimension i with less h_i each step. Assume the source does not have knowledge of local safety of the destination. The algorithm randomly selects a dimension to set up the message passing path from the source. If a minimum feasible path has been found from the source to the destination, the destination sends a signal back to the source, and the source passes the message along the selected path; otherwise, try to find a minimum path along dimension i where the source has the less h_i value. Pass the message along the selected path if a minimum feasible path has been found; otherwise, send the message along the dimension i where the destination has the less h_i value. It should be noted that the heuristic function of the source or destination with respect to the current node is a dynamic one in the process of path setup and message passing.

Algorithm route1()

1. Keep local safety of the source s along the corresponding directions that connect s in the spanning submesh. Set up a feasible path from s to d.

2. If a minimum feasible path from s to d has been set up, send a signal from d to s along the setup path. The source s sends the message along the setup minimum feasible path, otherwise (3), (4).

3. Go along the dimension t, where the source s has the less heuristic h_t corresponding to location of the current node v and local safety information of the source if a possible path along dimension t is available, otherwise (4).

4. Go along the other dimension if the current node is on the boundary of a fault block. Continue the above process until $x = 0$ or $y = 0$ is met.

5. If a minimum feasible path has been found, send the message from s along the selected path to d, otherwise (6).

6. Pass the message along the dimension t where d has the less heuristic h_t with respect to local safety information of the destination and location

of the current node if a feasible path from the current node to the destination is available, otherwise (7).

7. If the current node is on the boundary of a fault block, pass the message along the other dimension. Continue the above process until reaching $x = a$ or $y = b$.

8. If there exists a minimum feasible path from the joint node to the destination, pass the message along the feasible path; otherwise (9).

9. Deroute the message to a fault-free neighbor until a fault-free neighbor in a minimum path from the current node to the destination along another dimension is available. Continue the above process until the destination is reached.

The algorithm route1() can find a minimum feasible path from a source s to a destination d if d is locally safe with respect to s or s is locally safe with respect to d. Actually, the algorithm route1() can still find a minimum feasible path from s to d even though neither d is locally safe with respect to s, nor s is locally safe with respect to d in many cases.

Consider a message should be passed from (0,0) to (4,5) in the 10−ary 2D torus as shown in Fig. 3. Let the router randomly select dimension 1, and no minimum feasible path is set up from (0,0) to (4,5). Let the router set up a path from (4,5) to (0,0). We have $h_1 = h_2 = -2$ in this case. The algorithm route1() can select (3,5) or (4,4) as the next node.

Algorithm route1() selects (3,4) as the next node because $h_1 = -1$ and $h_2 = -2$ at this point. The next node of the path selected by the algorithm route1() should be (3,3) because there exists no choice. The next node selected by the algorithm route1() should be (2,3) because $h_1 = -1$ and $h_2 = 0$ at this time. The algorithm can select (1,3) or (2,2) as the next node, which reaches (0,3) and (2,0), respectively. Both cases set up a minimum feasible path from (4,5) to (0,0). It is quite possible for the algorithm route1() to set up a minimum feasible path from the source s to the destination d although s is not locally safe with respect to d and d is locally safe with respect to s.

Algorithm route1() can easily be extended to cases when one of the source and destination is unsafe. As shown in Fig. 3, nodes (6,4) and (7,5) are unsafe. Let a message be sent from (6,4) to (7,5). Node (6,4) tries to set up a minimum path from it to (7,5). The header is routed to (5,4)(v) because both minimum paths are blocked, which is an enabled node. The header is

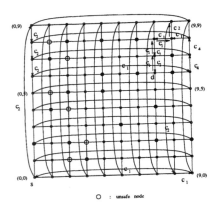

Figure 4: Virtual subnetwork partitioning to avoid deadlocks in a 2D torus.

routed to (7,6) (v') as shown in Fig. 3, where a feasible path from (7,6) to (7,5) is available, and (7,6) is also an enabled node. Both v and v' can be thought of as pseudo-source and pseudo-destination, respectively. Algorithm route1() can be applied to routing between v and v'.

5 Techniques to Avoid Deadlocks

Just like the technique in [11,12], a physical network can be partitioned into several virtual networks. Each virtual network consists of virtual channels arranged in such a way that no cycle exists among channels. Our method supports nonminimal routing unlike the virtual subnetwork partitioning scheme in [11,12].

A 2D torus can be partitioned into four virtual subnetworks (x and y represents two axes of a 2D torus): $+x + y$ ($+c_1, +c_1$), $+x - y$ ($+c_2, -c_1$), $-x - y$ ($-c_1, -c_2$), and $-x + y$ ($-c_2, +c_2$). Two extra virtual channels c_3 and c_4 are utilized for message deroutes along axes x and y, respectively. A virtual subnetwork can be selected for a message based on the relative location of the source and destination. Virtual channels c_1 and c_2 are utilized when a message is routed along a minimal feasible path inside the selected virtual network. Extra virtual channels c_3 and c_4 are used when a message is being derouted. No cycle exists in any virtual network. There also exists no inter-virtual-network cycle. Also, deroutes generate no cycles inside any virtual network.

The faulty 2D torus as shown in Fig. 4 contains 18 faulty nodes, and 6 fault-free nodes are labeled as unsafe. Let a message be sent from (0,0) to (7,6). The algorithm route1() sends the header flit from (0,0) to (7,6). The header flit is routed inside virtual subnet-

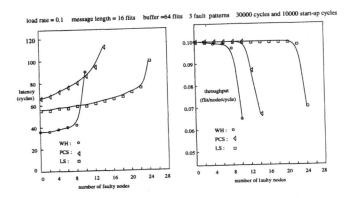

Figure 5: Performance comparison in a 16X16 torus.

work -x-y ($-c_1, -c_2$). The header flit is routed from (0,0) via virtual channel $-c_2$ along the wraparound of dimension y, and then via $-c_2$ along dimension y until reaching node (0,6). The header flit is routed via virtual channel $-c_1$ from (0,6) to (9,6). The only minimal path from (9,6) to (7,6) is blocked by a faulty node. The header flit is derouted from (9,6) along virtual channel $+c_4$ to (9,8), which is then routed via virtual channel $-c_1$ to (7,8), and finally routed from (7,8) to (7,6) via virtual channel $-c_2$. Up to now, the destination (7,6) has the knowledge of local safety of the source (0,0). A signal is sent from (7,6) to (0,0) inside the virtual network +x+y ($+c_1, +c_1$). As shown in Fig. 4, the signal is sent from (7,6) to (7,8) along virtual channel $+c_1$, and along virtual channel $+c_1$ from (7,8) to (8,8). The signal is then sent to (8,9) and (8,0) via virtual channel $+c_1$, which is sent to (0,0) along virtual channel $+c_1$. Up to now, a minimal feasible path has been set up. The message is sent from (0,0) to (7,6) inside the virtual network -x-y ($-c_1, -c_2$) along the set-up path.

6 Simulation Results

The proposed method (LS) has been implemented using a flit-level simulator. Flit-level simulators based on the wormhole routing techniques (WH) in [1] and the pipelined-circuit-switching (PCS) in [8] are also implemented. Two most commonly utilized metrics *throughput* and *latency* are adopted to evaluate three methods. The wormhole-routing-based method needs to disable quite a few fault-free nodes.

Fig. 5 presents performance comparison of three methods in a 16X16 torus with fixed load rate 0.1 (flit/cycle/node). Message length is set as 16 flits, and the buffer size for each node is set as 64 flits. Fig. 5 presents average results of three different fault pat-

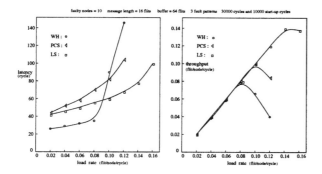

Figure 6: Performance comparison in a 16X16 torus with fixed number of faults.

terns, and each pattern records results of 30000 cycles with 10000 start-up cycles. Results in the start-up cycles are not included. Throughputs of local safety (LS), WH, and PCS in the fault-free network are all 0.1, while latency of three methods is 55, 35, and 65, respectively. Latency of the three methods is 39.1, 58.3 and 75.6, respectively when the system contains 6 faulty nodes, and throughputs of them are 0.1, 0.0988, and 0.1. When the system contains 8 faulty nodes, latency and throughput of the three methods are 59.9 and 0.1, 41.5 and 0.097, and 80.7 and 0.1, respectively. Latency and throughput of LS, WH, and PCS are 60.8 and 0.1, 89.7 and 0.065, and 86.5 and 0.1, respectively when the system contains 10 faulty nodes. When the system contains 14 faulty nodes, latency and throughput of LS and PCS are 63.7 and 0.1, and 112.5 and 0.067, respectively. Latency and throughput of LS are 100.2 and 0.071, respectively when the system contains up to 24 faulty nodes.

Fig. 6 presents performance comparison of the three methods when the system contains 10 faulty nodes. When the load rate of the system is set as 0.06, latency and throughput of LS, WH and PCS are 50.2 and 0.06, 32.5 and 0.058, and 58.4 and 0.06, respectively. Latency and throughput of LS, WH and PCS are 60.2 and 0.1, 89.7 and 0.065, and 81.6 and 0.1, respectively when load rate of the system is set as 0.1. When load rate is set as 0.12, latency and throughput of LS, WH, and PCS are 67.5 and 0.12, 145.3 and 0.039, and 104.9 and 0.083, respectively. Latency and throughput of LS are 100.5 and 0.138 when load rate of the system is 0.16.

Fig. 7 presents performance of local safety when the load rate of the system is fixed or the system contains fixed number of faulty nodes. The left part shows performance of local safety when the load rate is set as 0.13, and the right part is performance of local safety when the system contains 20 faulty nodes. Lo-

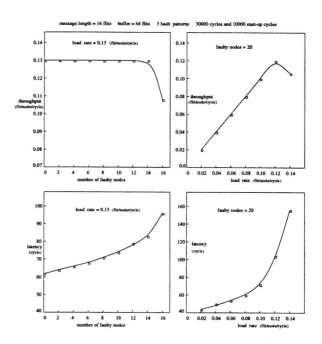

Figure 7: Performance evaluation of local safety in a 16X16 torus.

cal safety gets throughput 0.13 when the system contains no more than 14 faulty nodes and the load rate is 0.13. When the system contains 16 faulty nodes, throughput and latency of local safety are 94.4 and 0.108, respectively. When the load rate of the system is up to 0.12 and the system contains 20 faulty nodes, latency and throughput of the system are 155.8 and 0.12. Latency and throughput of local safety are 155.8 and 0.106, respectively.

Fig. 8 presents performance comparison of three methods in 32X32 torus when the load rate is set as 0.05. When the system contains 24 faulty nodes, latency and throughput of LS, WH, and PCS are

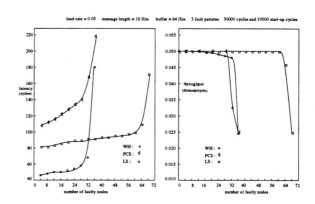

Figure 8: Performance comparison in 32X32 torus.

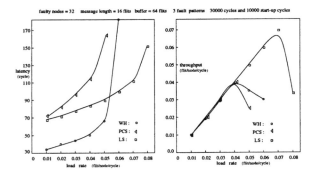

faulty nodes = 32   message length = 16 flits   buffer = 64 flits   3 fault patterns   30000 cycles and 10000 start-up cycles

Figure 9: Performance comparison in 32X32 torus with fixed faulty nodes.

88.7 and 0.05, 55.0 and 0.0493, and 133.1 and 0.0499. When the system contains 36 faulty nodes, latency and throughput of the three methods are 92.2 and 0.05, 180.5 and 0.025, and 218.9 and 0.025, respectively.

Fig. 9 shows performance of LS, WH and PCS when the system contains 32 faulty nodes. Latency and throughput of three methods are 67.4 and 0.01, 35.0 and 0.0098, and 72.5 and 0.01, respectively when load rate is set as 0.01. When load rate is set as 0.05, latency and throughput of LS, WH, and PCS are 90.4 and 0.05, 65.6 and 0.035, and 163.5 and 0.025, respectively. When load rate is set as 0.06, latency and throughput of LS and WH are 100.7 and 0.06, and 181.8 and 0.030, respectively. When load rate is set as 0.08, latency and throughput of LS are 152.6 and 0.035, respectively.

7 Conclusions

Local safety information was utilized to guide fault-tolerant routing in 2D torus multicomputer networks. Fault-tolerant routing with local safety was first studied in 2D torus networks. It is found that a minimum feasible path between a source s and a destination d is available if d is locally safe with respect to s or s is locally safe with respect to d. A heuristic function based on the local safety information was proposed to guide fault-tolerant routing. An efficient algorithm was then proposed to complete fault-tolerant routing in a 2D torus based on local safety information. A new virtual subnetwork partitioning scheme was proposed to avoid deadlocks. Flit-level simulators were implemented by comparing with two previous methods [1,8]. The proposed method can be extended to meshes with a little modification.

References

[1] R. V. Boppana and S. Chalasani, "Fault-tolerant communication with partitioned dimension-order routers," *IEEE Trans. Parallel and Distributed Systems*, vol. 10, no. 10, pp. 1026-1039, 1999.

[2] A. A. Chien and J. H. Kim, "Planar adaptive routing: Low-cost adaptive networks for multiprocessors," *J. of ACM*, vol. 42, no. 1, pp. 91-123, 1995.

[3] G. M. Chiu and P. S. Wu, "A fault-tolerant routing strategy in hypercube multicomputers," *IEEE Trans. Computers*, vol. 45, no. 2, pp. 143-155, 1996.

[4] W. J. Dally and H. Aoki, "Deadlock-free adaptive routing in multicomputer networks using virtual channels," *IEEE Trans. Parallel and Distributed Systems*, vol. 4, no. 4, pp. 466-475, 1993.

[5] W. J. Dally, "The message-driven processor: A multicomputer processing node with efficient mechanisms," *IEEE Micro*, pp. 23-39, Apr., 1992.

[6] B. V. Dao, J. Duato, and S. Yalamanchili, "Dynamically configurable message flow control for fault-tolerant routing," *IEEE Trans. Parallel and Distributed Systems*, vol. 10, no. 1, pp. 7-22, 1999.

[7] J. Duato, "A theory of fault-tolerant routing in wormhole networks," *IEEE Trans. Parallel and Distributed Systems*, vol. 8, no. 8, pp. 790-802, 1997.

[8] P. T. Gaughan, B. V. Dao, S. Yalamanchili, and D. E. Schimmel, "Distributed, deadlock-free routing in faulty, pipelined, direct interconnection networks," *IEEE Trans. Computers*, Vol. 45, No. 6, pp. 651-665, 1996.

[9] C. J. Glass and L. M. Ni, "Fault-tolerant wormhole routing in meshes," Proc. of *IEEE Int. Symp. Fault-Tolerant Computing*, pp. 240-249, 1993.

[10] T. C. Lee and J. P. Hayes, "A fault-tolerant communication scheme for hypercube computers," *IEEE Trans. Computers*, vol. 41, no. 10, pp. 1242-1256, 1992.

[11] D. H. Linder and J. C. Harden, "An adaptive and fault-tolerant wormhole routing strategy for $k-$ary $n-$cubes," *IEEE Trans. Computers*, vol. 40, no. 1, pp. 2-12, 1991.

[12] J. Wu, "Fault-tolerant adaptive and minimal routing in mesh-connected multicomputers using extended safety levels," Proc. of *Int. Conf. on Distributed Computing Systems*, pp. 428-435, 1998.

[13] D. Xiang, "Fault-tolerant routing in hypercube multicomputers using local safety information," *IEEE Trans. on Parallel and Distributed Systems*, vol. 12, no. 9, pp. 942-951, 2001.

[14] J. Zhou and F. C. M. Lau, "Adaptive fault-tolerant wormhole routing in 2D meshes," Proc. of 15-th *IEEE Int. Parallel and Distributed Processing Symp., 2001*.

Routing Permutations with Link-Disjoint and Node-Disjoint Paths in a Class of Self-Routable Networks

Yuanyuan Yang

Department of Electrical & Computer Engineering
State University of New York at Stony Brook, Stony Brook, NY 11794, USA
yang@ece.sunysb.edu

Jianchao Wang

DataTreasury Corporation, Melville, NY 11747, USA
jwang@datatreasury.com

Abstract—High-speed interconnects have been gaining much attention from the computer industry recently as interconnects are becoming a limiting factor to the performance of modern computer systems. This trend will even continue in the near future as technology improves. In this paper, we consider efficiently routing permutations in a class of switch-based interconnects. Permutation is an important communication pattern in parallel and distributed computing systems. We present a generic approach to realizing arbitrary permutations in a class of unique-path, self-routable multistage networks, such as baseline, omega, and banyan networks. It is well-known that this type of interconnect has low hardware cost but can realize only a small portion of all possible permutations between its inputs and outputs in a single pass. In this paper, we consider routing arbitrary permutations with link-disjoint paths and node-disjoint paths in such interconnects in a minimum number of passes. In particular, routing with node-disjoint paths has important applications in the emerging optical interconnects. We employ and further expand the Latin square technique used in the all-to-all personalized exchange algorithms for this class of multistage networks [1] for general permutation routing. As can be seen, our implementation of permutation routing is optimal in terms of the number of passes that messages are transmitted through the network, and it is near-optimal in network transmission time for sufficiently long messages.

Keywords— Routing, permutation, all-to-all personalized exchange, interconnects, optical interconnects, multistage networks, link-disjoint paths, node-disjoint paths, crosstalk-free routing , Latin square.

I. INTRODUCTION AND PREVIOUS WORK

High-speed interconnects have been gaining much attention from the computer industry recently as interconnects are becoming a limiting factor to the performance of modern computer systems [2]. This trend will even continue in the near future as technology improves. In this paper, we consider efficiently routing permutations in a class of switch-based interconnects.

Permutation is an important communication pattern in parallel and distributed computing systems. A permutation represents a one-to-one mapping among the processors in a processor group. In a permutation operation, every processor in a processor group sends a message to one of the processors in the group, and no two processors send their messages to the same processor. A common way to realize a permutation operation in a parallel or distributed computing system is to use a multistage interconnection network (MIN). An MIN usually consists of multiple stages of 2×2 switches with adjacent stages connected by a mapping function. For a detailed survey of various MINs, readers may refer to [3], [4].

Adopting an MIN in a parallel or distributed system enables processors to send their messages concurrently. However, routing must be carefully handled so that there is no conflict during message delivering. In general, there are two types of conflict-free routings in an MIN: routing with *link-disjoint paths* and routing with *node-disjoint paths*. Link-disjoint paths imply that no two different message paths share the same link in the network at a time, which is a mandatory requirement for routing. Node-disjoint paths imply that no two different message paths pass through the same switch in the network at a time. Routing with node-disjoint paths has important applications in guided wave optical switching networks in which optical "crosstalk" between the messages passing the same switch should be avoided [5], [6], [7], [8], [9], [10]. In the rest of this paper, we will simply refer to the routing with link-disjoint paths as routing, and we will consider an $n \times n$ network with n inputs and n outputs.

There has been much research work in the literature on the permutation capability of various multistage networks, see, for example, [3], [4], [5], [7], [8], [9], [10], [11], [12], [13], [14], [15], [16], [17], [18]. In particular, a Benes network [11] can realize arbitrary permutations in $O(n \log n)$ hardware cost and $O(n \log n)$ routing time; Jan and Oruç's self-routing permutation network [13] has $O(n \log n)$ cost and takes $O(\log^2 n)$ routing time; Cheng and Chen's self-routing permutation network [15] was constructed by the reverse banyan networks with $O(n \log^2 n)$ cost and $O(\log^2 n)$ routing time. For a class of unique-path, self-routable multistage networks, such as base-

Research supported in part by the U.S. National Science Foundation under grant numbers CCR-0073085 and CCR-0207999.

line and omega network [3], the hardware cost is $O(n \log n)$ and the routing for permutations is much more efficient (in $O(\log n)$ time complexity), but this type of network can realize only a proper subset of all $n!$ permutations.

Recently, Lai [16] considered using a generalized cube network, a type of unique-path, self-routable MIN, to perform an arbitrary permutation in two passes. The idea is to partition each message into n submessages and then send them independently in each time step. In the first pass, all n submessages are scattered to n processors' appropriate buffer space; and in the second pass, all the submessages are sent to their destinations. How to send these submessages without conflicts on any links relies on so-called switch patterns and tag patterns for the network. The stage control (i.e., all switches in a stage have the same switch setting at any time) is used for routing. As analyzed in a later section, this permutation method is effective for sending sufficiently long messages. A natural question here is whether this permutation method can be generalized to the entire class of unique-path MINs. Although Wu and Feng [3] proved that a class of unique-path MINs were topologically equivalent, from their proofs one cannot directly find a generic and efficient way to generalize the two-pass permutation method in [16] to each individual network. In fact, the correctness proof of the permutation method in [16] depends on the structural property of the generalized cube network that it can be partitioned into two independent subnetworks. However, some network, e.g., an omega network, in the class of unique-path MIN's does not have this structural property. Also, it is not clear whether the permutation method can be extended from the stage control to much easier self-routing control, and whether it can be extended to routing permutations with node-disjoint paths.

In this paper, we propose a generic self-routing permutation algorithm for the entire class of unique-path multistage networks based on the idea in [16] and the theory for realizing all-to-all personalized exchange in multistage networks [1]. We employ and further expand the Latin square technique used in [1]. Our two-pass self-routing permutation algorithm depends on two Latin square matrices for a specific multistage network. We also develop a four-pass self-routing permutation algorithm for node-disjoint paths. Our implementation of permutation routing is optimal in terms of the number of passes that messages are transmitted through the network.

The rest of the paper is organized as follows. Section 2 briefly reviews the results for all-to-all personalized exchange in multistage networks, which will be useful in our generic permutation algorithms. Section 3 further explores some properties of the Latin square discussed in Section 2 related to permutation routing. Then based on these properties, Sections 4 and 5 present the permutation routing algorithms with link-disjoint paths and node-disjoint paths, respectively. Finally, Section 6 compares the permutation algorithms we propose with previous algorithms and concludes the paper.

II. PRELIMINARIES

A. Network structures and permutations

A class of unique-path, self-routable multistage interconnection networks such as baseline, omega, and banyan networks, have been proposed and widely used in parallel processing systems [3], [4]. A typical network structure for this class of network is that each network has $n(= 2^m)$ inputs and outputs and $\log n = m$ stages, with each stage consisting of $\frac{n}{2}$ 2×2 switches and any two adjacent stages connected by n interstage links. Figure 1(a), (b) and (c) illustrate an 8×8 baseline network, omega network and banyan network, respectively.

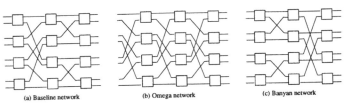

(a) Baseline network   (b) Omega network   (c) Banyan network

Fig. 1. Three typical multistage networks.

A permutation is a one-to-one mapping between the network inputs and outputs. For an $n \times n$ network, suppose there is a one-to-one mapping ρ which maps input i to output d_i (i.e. $\rho(i) = d_i$), where $d_i \in \{0, 1, \ldots, n-1\}$ for $0 \le i \le n-1$, and $d_i \ne d_j$ for $i \ne j$. Let

$$\rho = \begin{pmatrix} 0 & 1 & \ldots & n-1 \\ d_0 & d_1 & \ldots & d_{n-1} \end{pmatrix}$$

denote this permutation. In particular, when $\rho(i) = i$ for $0 \le i \le n-1$, we refer to this permutation as an *identity permutation* and denote it as I. Also, for any permutation ρ there exists its inverse permutation, denoted as ρ^{-1}, such that $\rho \cdot \rho^{-1} = I$.

In the context of a multistage network, each stage in the network can be viewed as a shorter $n \times n$ network, and so does each set of interstage links. Let σ_i $(0 \le i \le m-1)$ denote the permutation represented by stage i, and π_i $(0 \le i \le m-2)$ denote the permutation represented by the set of interstage links between stage i and stage $i+1$. We refer to permutation σ_i as a *stage permutation*, permutation π_i as an *interstage permutation*, and the permutation realized by the entire multistage network as an *admissible permutation* of the network. Clearly, an admissible permutation can be expressed by a composition of stage permutations and interstage permutations. For examples, an admissible permutation of an $n \times n$ baseline network can be expressed as

$$\sigma_{m-1} \pi_{m-2} \sigma_{m-2} \ldots \pi_0 \sigma_0; \qquad (1)$$

and an admissible permutation of an $n \times n$ omega network can be expressed as

$$\sigma_{m-1} \pi_0^{-1} \sigma_{m-2} \pi_0^{-1} \ldots \sigma_1 \pi_0^{-1} \sigma_0 \pi_0^{-1} \qquad (2)$$

where π_0^{-1}, which is called the shuffle function, is the reverse permutation of π_0.

In general, interstage permutations π_i's are fixed by the network topology. However, stage permutation σ_i's are not fixed since each switch can be set to either parallel or cross.

240

B. All-to-all personalized exchange in multistage networks

All-to-all personalized exchange is one of commonly used collective communication operations. In all-to-all personalized exchange, every processor in a processor group sends a distinct message to each of the processors. In [1] a generic algorithm was given for a class of unique-path multistage networks, in which the messages are self-routed on link-disjoint paths. The work has been extended to node-disjoint paths in [6].

B.1 Generating a Latin square

The key idea of the method in [1] is to build a Latin square matrix for a given multistage network, and then any all-to-all personalized exchange on this network can be routed using the tag information represented by the elements in the Latin square matrix.

A *Latin square* [19] is defined as an $n \times n$ matrix

$$A = \begin{bmatrix} a_{0,0} & a_{0,1} & \cdots & a_{0,n-1} \\ a_{1,0} & a_{1,1} & \cdots & a_{1,n-1} \\ \vdots & \vdots & \vdots & \vdots \\ a_{n-1,0} & a_{n-1,1} & \cdots & a_{n-1,n-1} \end{bmatrix} \quad (3)$$

in which the entries $a_{i,j}$'s are numbers in $\{0, 1, 2, \ldots, n-1\}$ and no two entries in a row (or a column) have the same value.

As we know, not all permutations are admissible to a unique-path multistage network. However, in the following, we give a simple way to choose a special set of permutations, which are admissible to a multistage network and can form a Latin square.

First, we introduce a set of basic permutations used for constructing a Latin Square. For an $n \times n$ mapping, where $n = 2^m$, we define m basic permutations ϕ_i $(1 \le i \le m)$ as follows. Let the binary representation of a number $a \in \{0, 1, \ldots, n-1\}$ be $p_{m-1}p_{m-2} \ldots p_1 p_0$. Then

$$\begin{aligned} p_{m-1}p_{m-2} \ldots p_i p_{i-1} p_{i-2} \ldots p_1 p_0 &\overset{\phi_i}{\mapsto} \\ p_{m-1}p_{m-2} \ldots p_i \bar{p}_{i-1} p_{i-2} \ldots p_1 p_0 & \end{aligned} \quad (4)$$

The permutation ϕ_i is actually the operation flipping the ith bit of a binary number.

In the construction of the Latin square used in all-to-all personalized exchange, we are especially interested in ϕ_1, and other ϕ_i's are used only in the correctness proofs. Clearly, the stage permutation of a stage in the network is ϕ_1 if and only if the switches in this stage are all set to cross, and the stage permutation of a stage in the network is I if and only if the switches in this stage are all set to parallel. The following result was obtained in [1].

Theorem 1: Given a unique-path multistage network such as a baseline, an omega, or a banyan network, let the stage permutation of each stage in the network take either ϕ_1 or I. The admissible permutations corresponding to all possible such switch settings form a Latin square.

In Figure 2, we list all possible such switch settings in an 8×8 omega network, and the corresponding Latin square is A

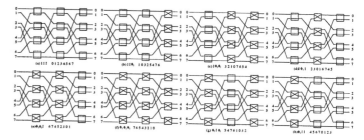

Fig. 2. All possible switch settings, in which each stage is set to either ϕ_1 or I, in an 8×8 omega network and the corresponding overall permutations realized.

in (5).

$$A = \begin{bmatrix} 0 & 1 & 2 & 3 & 4 & 5 & 6 & 7 \\ 1 & 0 & 3 & 2 & 5 & 4 & 7 & 6 \\ 3 & 2 & 1 & 0 & 7 & 6 & 5 & 4 \\ 2 & 3 & 0 & 1 & 6 & 7 & 4 & 5 \\ 6 & 7 & 4 & 5 & 2 & 3 & 0 & 1 \\ 7 & 6 & 5 & 4 & 3 & 2 & 1 & 0 \\ 5 & 4 & 7 & 6 & 1 & 0 & 3 & 2 \\ 4 & 5 & 6 & 7 & 0 & 1 & 2 & 3 \end{bmatrix} \quad (5)$$

An optimal generic algorithm was given in [1] for generating a Latin square for any unique-path multistage network instead of directly using Theorem 1. Latin square A is generated only once for a given multistage network, and can be viewed as a system parameter of the network. Since Latin square A is used for routing in all-to-all personalized exchange algorithm, we call it *all-to-all routing matrix* or simply *routing matrix*.

B.2 All-to-all personalized exchange algorithm using routing matrix A

Given routing matrix A in the form in (3) for an $n \times n$ multistage network, each row $a_{i,0}, a_{i,1}, \ldots, a_{i,n-1}$ $(0 \le i \le n-1)$ of A corresponds to a permutation

$$\begin{pmatrix} 0 & 1 & 2 & \cdots & n-1 \\ a_{i,0} & a_{i,1} & a_{i,2} & \cdots & a_{i,n-1} \end{pmatrix}$$

which is admissible to the multistage network. Under this admissible permutation, the message from processor j $(0 \le j \le n-1)$ reaches processor $a_{i,j}$, and the n processors exchange their messages concurrently through the network without any conflict (i.e. with link-disjoint paths).

The all-to-all personalized exchange algorithm can be briefly described as follows. Performing the n admissible permutations (of the network) corresponding to n rows of routing matrix A one by one, such that in the ith permutation $(0 \le i \le n-1)$ all the processors send their messages in a way that processor j $(0 \le j \le n-1)$ sends its personalized message to processor $a_{i,j}$.

At the end of the algorithm, for any j $(0 \le j \le n-1)$, processor j has sent personalized messages to processors $a_{0,j}, a_{1,j}, \cdots, a_{n-1,j}$, which correspond to the jth column of A (the Latin square); thus each processor has sent personalized messages to all the processors in the processor group.

Also, notice that the all-to-all personalized exchange is a self-routing algorithm in the multistage network, since the routing is based only on the source and destination addresses.

III. MORE PROPERTIES OF ROUTING MATRIX A RELATED TO PERMUTATION

In order to perform an arbitrary permutation in the class of unique-path multistage networks by using all-to-all personalized exchange algorithm discussed above, we need to explore more properties from routing matrix A as a Latin square, which contains all the routing information required for permutation.

As discussed in the last section, routing matrix A for a multistage network represents n special admissible permutations labeled as $0, 1, \ldots, n-1$ corresponding to n rows of A. In general, consider the message from source processor s to destination processor d in the admissible permutation labeled as i, where $s, d, i \in \{0, 1, \ldots, n-1\}$. The following questions are concerning the relationship among the values of three variables s, d and i.

Question 1: For given values of s and i, what is the corresponding value of d?

Question 2: For given values of s and d, what is the corresponding value of i?

Question 3: For given values of d and i, what is the corresponding value of s?

The answer to Question 1 can be obtained directly from the definition of routing matrix A, that is, in the ith permutation, the message from source s reaches destination $a_{i,s}$, thus the unique solution to Question 1 is $d = a_{i,s}$. However, the answers to Question 2 and Question 3 are not so obvious. The following lemma gives the solutions.

Lemma 1: Given $d \in \{0, 1, \ldots, n-1\}$, let all the elements with value d in routing matrix A (as a Latin square) ordered by columns be $a_{i_0,0}, a_{i_1,1}, \ldots, a_{i_{n-1},n-1}$, then there exists a unique solution to Question 2, which is $i = i_s$; and let all the elements with value d in routing matrix A (as a Latin square) ordered by rows be $a_{0,j_0}, a_{1,j_1}, \ldots, a_{n-1,j_{n-1}}$, then there exists a unique solution to Question 3, which is $s = j_i$.

Proof. Consider all elements with value d in Latin square A. By the property of the Latin square, there are exactly n such elements with exactly one at each row and exactly one at each column in A.

For Question 2, let these elements ordered by columns be $a_{i_0,0}, a_{i_1,1}, \ldots, a_{i_{n-1},n-1}$. Clearly $\{i_0, i_1, \ldots, i_{n-1}\} = \{0, 1, \ldots, n-1\}$. Since in the ith permutation, the message of processor s reaches processor $a_{i,s}$ which equals d, $a_{i,s}$ must be one of $a_{i_0,0}, a_{i_1,1}, \ldots, a_{i_{n-1},n-1}$ which are all the elements in A with value d. That is, the unique solution is that $a_{i,s} = a_{i_s,s}$, which yields $i = i_s \in \{0, 1, \ldots, n-1\}$.

Similarly, we can obtain the unique solution to Question 3.

■

Lemma 1 gives solutions to Question 2 and Question 3 by using solely the information in routing matrix A, but the time complexity could be as high as $O(n^2)$. Since the information

is static, we can build another matrix from A so that answering Question 2 or Question 3 takes only $O(1)$ time.

As will be seen later in our generic permutation algorithm, we will only need to answer Question 2. Thus, we build another $n \times n$ matrix B for answering Question 2 as follows.

$$B = \begin{bmatrix} b_{0,0} & b_{0,1} & \cdots & b_{0,n-1} \\ b_{1,0} & b_{1,1} & \cdots & b_{1,n-1} \\ \vdots & \vdots & \vdots & \vdots \\ b_{n-1,0} & b_{n-1,1} & \cdots & b_{n-1,n-1} \end{bmatrix} \tag{6}$$

where

$$b_{i,j} = k \text{ iff } a_{k,i} = j. \tag{7}$$

We have

Lemma 2: Matrix B given in (6) is a Latin square.

Proof. For any element $b_{i,j}$ in B, let $b_{i,j}$ be k. From (7), there must exist some element $a_{k,i} = j$ in A. Thus, $k \in \{0, 1, \ldots, n-1\}$.

For any two elements b_{i,j_1} and b_{i,j_2} in the ith row of B, if they are equal, say, equal to k, then from (7) we must have $j_1 = j_2 (= a_{k,i})$. That is, all n elements in the ith row of B are distinct.

Similarly, for any two elements $b_{i_1,j}$ and $b_{i_2,j}$ in the jth column of B, if they are equal, say, equal to k, then from (7) we must have $a_{k,i_1} = a_{k,i_2} (= j)$. Since A is a Latin square and any two elements in the kth row of A are distinct, we must have $i_1 = i_2$. That is, all n elements in the jth column of B are distinct.

Therefore, B is also a Latin square.

■

The following lemma gives the solution to Question 2 in $O(1)$ time by using matrix B.

Lemma 3: The solution to Question 2 is

$$i = b_{s,d}. \tag{8}$$

Proof. Suppose that the message of source s reaches destination d in the ith permutation. By the definition of Latin square A, we have $a_{i,s} = d$. From (7), we immediately have (8).

■

It is easy to construct Latin square matrix B from A. We give an algorithm $DerivedLatinSquare(.)$ in Table 1. Its correctness can be seen from (7) and Lemma 2, and the time complexity is $O(n^2)$, which is optimal since there are n^2 entries in the matrices. Notice that we only need to build B once (as for A) for a given multistage network, and both A and B can be considered as system parameters used in our permutation algorithm.

An example of Latin square B derived from A in (5) for an 8×8 omega network is given below.

$$B = \begin{bmatrix} 0 & 1 & 3 & 2 & 7 & 6 & 4 & 5 \\ 1 & 0 & 2 & 3 & 6 & 7 & 5 & 4 \\ 3 & 2 & 0 & 1 & 4 & 5 & 7 & 6 \\ 2 & 3 & 1 & 0 & 5 & 4 & 6 & 7 \\ 7 & 6 & 4 & 5 & 0 & 1 & 3 & 2 \\ 6 & 7 & 5 & 4 & 1 & 0 & 2 & 3 \\ 4 & 5 & 7 & 6 & 3 & 2 & 0 & 1 \\ 5 & 4 & 6 & 7 & 2 & 3 & 1 & 0 \end{bmatrix} \tag{9}$$

TABLE 1

THE ALGORITHM FOR DERIVING LATIN SQUARE B

```
Algorithm DerivedLatinSquare(LatinSuare A = (a_{i,j})_{n×n})
Output LatinSuare B = (b_{i,j})_{n×n}
{
    for (k = 0; k < n; k++) {
        for (i = 0; i < n; i++) {
            Let a_{k,i} be j;
            b_{i,j} = k;
        }
    }
}
```

Notice that each row of Latin square A corresponds to an admissible permutation of the multistage network associated. However, each row of Latin square B is generally not admissible to the network. Since matrix B will be used for mapping the buffer index in our generic permutation algorithms, Latin square B is referred to as *buffer mapping matrix* or simply *mapping matrix*.

Given these preparations, we are now in a position to describe the permutation algorithms.

IV. ROUTING PERMUTATIONS WITH LINK-DISJOINT PATHS

Given an $n \times n$ unique-path multistage network with routing matrix $A = (a_{i,j})_{n×n}$ and mapping matrix $B = (b_{i,j})_{n×n}$, we now develop a generic permutation algorithm to realize an arbitrary permutation

$$\rho = \begin{pmatrix} 0 & 1 & \ldots & n-1 \\ d_0 & d_1 & \ldots & d_{n-1} \end{pmatrix}.$$

Consider n processors labeled as $0, 1, \ldots, n-1$, with each processor $j \in \{0, 1, \ldots, n-1\}$ linked to input j of the network and output j of the network. In the algorithm, processor $j \in \{0, 1, \ldots, n-1\}$, as a source, sends its message m_j to processor $d_j \in \{0, 1, \ldots, n-1\}$, as a destination, through the multistage network, and all the n processors perform their operations concurrently.

We make the same assumption as in [16] that each message m_j can be divided into n submessages $m_{0,j}, m_{1,j}, \ldots, m_{n-1,j}$ in order, and all the submessages have the same size. Also, submessage $m_{i,j}$ has a sequence number i.

A submessage always carries its sequence number and final destination so that after the first pass, the final destination of a submessage can still be remembered and when all the submessages of m_j reach their final destination they can be restored to their original order.

Let each processor have two sets of local buffers $c[0 \cdots n-1]$ and $c'[0 \cdots n-1]$ to hold message contents. Each local buffer $c[i]$ (or $c'[i]$) can hold a submessage, its sequence number and its final destination in the buffer's three fields $c[i].data$, $c[i].seq$ and $c[i].dest$, respectively (or in the same fields of $c'[i]$).

The algorithm $PermutationLinkDisjoint(\cdot)$ for realizing any permutation in the multistage network with link-disjoint paths is given in Table 2. In the initialization process, each

TABLE 2

THE PERMUTATION ALGORITHM WITH LINK-DISJOINT PATHS

```
Algorithm PermutationLinkDisjoint((d_0, ..., d_n); (m_0, ..., m_n))
{
    for each processor j (0 ≤ j ≤ n − 1) do in parallel {
        divide m_j into submessages and put into local buffer c[0 ··· n − 1];
    } // end of initialization
    for each processor j (0 ≤ j ≤ n − 1) do in parallel {
        do process1, process2 in parallel {
            {process1:
                for (i = 0; i < n; i++) {
                    send message c[i] to destination processor a_{i,j};
                }
            }
            {process2:
                for (k = 0; k < n; k++) {
                    receive a message r and put into c'[b_{j,r.dest}];
                }
            }
        }
    } // end of the first pass
    for each processor j (0 ≤ j ≤ n − 1) do in parallel {
        do process1, process2 in parallel {
            {process1:
                for (i = 0; i < n; i++) {
                    send message c'[i] to destination processor a_{i,j};
                }
            }
            {process2:
                for (k = 0; k < n; k++) {
                    receive a message r and put into c[r.seq];
                }
            }
        }
    } // end of the second pass
}
```

processor divides the message to submessages and puts them into local buffers $c[0 \cdots n-1]$. At the end of the initialization process, for processor j, $c[i].data$ holds $m_{i,j}$, $c[i].seq$ equals i, and $c[i].dest$ equals d_j, where $0 \leq i, j \leq n-1$.

Then processors perform message transmission through the network in two passes. In each pass, operations similar to all-to-all personalized exchange are performed. That is, in each step i ($0 \leq i \leq n-1$), processor j sends the submessage (in $c[i]$ or $c'[i]$) using destination address $a_{i,j}$ stored in routing matrix A. Thus, at any step, n processors send their messages in parallel through the network with link-disjoint paths due to the fact that any row in A is guranteed to be an admissible permutation to the network. Also, the routing can be either self-routing or stage controlled routing.

One difference from all-to-all personalized exchange is that instead of sending a personalized message of processor j to processor $a_{i,j}$, processor j sends a submessage in the squential order stored in buffers. Another difference is that after receiving a submessage, the processor is responsible to put it in some specific location of the receiving buffers.

The differences between the two passes of data transmissions are that $c[]$ and $c'[]$ are sending buffers and receiving buffers, respectively in the first pass, but the two sets of buffers switch their roles in the second pass; and that the specific location of the receiving buffers in the second pass is simply the sub-message's sequence number, while the location in the receiving buffers in the first pass depends on the final destination of the submessage and the value of an entry in mapping matrix B, which we will explore in more detail later.

Notice that each processor will handle sending messages and receiving messages concurrently. In the algorithm, they are represented as two concurrent processes $process1$ and $process2$ on a processor.

In the following, we will prove the correctness of the algorithm.

Theorem 2: The algorithm $PermutationLinkDisjoint(\cdot)$ performs any permutation among processors correctly.

Proof. We now verify that each message reaches its final destination at the end of the algorithm by tracing down the message sent from processor j.

After the first pass, processor j has sent submessages $m_{0,j}, , m_{1,j}, \ldots, m_{n-1,j}$ to processors $a_{0,j}, , a_{1,j}, \ldots, a_{n-1,j}$, respectively.

On the other hand, when processor j receives a submessage r in the first pass, it will ask Question 2 as in the last section that in which step (admissible permutation) of the second pass the message from source j can reach destination $r.dest$? Lemma 3 gives the solution that it can be done in the i'th step where $i' = b_{j,r.dest}$. This is exactly what $process2$ of the first pass does.

We continue to trace down the message sent from processor j. After processor $a_{i,j}$ receives the submessage $m_{i,j}$ in the first pass, it puts $m_{i,j}$ to the buffer $c'[i'']$ where $i'' = b_{a_{i,j},d_j}$. Therefore, $m_{i,j}$ is sent in the i''th step of the second pass from processor $a_{i,j}$ to destination processor $a_{i'',a_{i,j}}$. We now directly verify that $a_{i'',a_{i,j}}$ cannot be anything else except d_j. In fact, let $a_{i'',a_{i,j}} = k$. From (7), we have $b_{a_{i,j},k} = i'' = b_{a_{i,j},d_j}$, and thus $k = d_j$ due to that B is a Latin square. That is, $m_{i,j}$ finally reaches destination processor d_j; futhermore, submessage $m_{i,j}$ is put into buffer $c[j]$ in a correct sequential order in $process2$ of the second pass. This is true for all submessages $m_{i,j}$ $0 \leq i,j \leq n-1$.

Therefore, all messages $m_0, m_1, \ldots, m_{n-1}$ reach their destinations $d_0, d_1, \ldots, d_{n-1}$, respectively, and are stored in buffers $c[]$ of their destination processors. ∎

Now we give an example of realizing a permutation in an 8×8 omega network by algorithm $PermutationLinkDisjoint(\cdot)$. Suppose the permutation to be realized is

$$\rho = \begin{pmatrix} 0 & 1 & 2 & 3 & 4 & 5 & 6 & 7 \\ 1 & 5 & 7 & 2 & 3 & 4 & 6 & 0 \end{pmatrix}.$$

At the beginning, each of the 8 processors, $P_0, P_1, \ldots, P_7$, holds a message consisting of 8 submessages stored in its buffers $c[]$ as shown in Table 3. After the first pass of the algorithm, the submessages are stored in buffers $c'[]$ of each processor as shown in Table 4. At the end of the algorithm, the submessages are stored in buffers $c[]$ of each destination processor as shown in Table 5.

Now we verify the correctness through the example by tracing down one of the submessages. We take $m_{6,1}$ as an ex-

ample, which is shown in bold in Tables 3-5. Clearly, it is a submessage with sequence number 6 from source processor 1 to destination processor 5. It is originally stored in buffer $c[6]$ of processor 1 (see Table 3). By using the pre-calculated Latin square matrices A and B shown in (5) and (9), respectively, after the first pass of the algorithm, it reaches processor 4 and is stored in its buffer $c'[1]$ since $a_{6,1} = 4$ and $b_{4,5} = 1$ (see Table 4); after the second pass, it (from processor 4) reaches processor 5 in its buffer $c[6]$ since $a_{1,4} = 5$ and the submessage has sequence number 6 (see Table 5).

V. ROUTING PERMUTATIONS WITH NODE-DISJOINT PATHS

In this section we consider realizing an arbitrary permutation in the class of unique-path multistage networks with node-disjoint paths in four passes.

TABLE 3
THE SUBMESSAGES INITIALLY STORED IN BUFFERS $c[]$ OF PROCESSORS

i	P_0's c[]	P_1's c[]	P_2's c[]	P_3's c[]	P_4's c[]	P_5's c[]	P_6's c[]	P_7's c[]
0	$m_{0,0}$	$m_{0,1}$	$m_{0,2}$	$m_{0,3}$	$m_{0,4}$	$m_{0,5}$	$m_{0,6}$	$m_{0,7}$
1	$m_{1,0}$	$m_{1,1}$	$m_{1,2}$	$m_{1,3}$	$m_{1,4}$	$m_{1,5}$	$m_{1,6}$	$m_{1,7}$
2	$m_{2,0}$	$m_{2,1}$	$m_{2,2}$	$m_{2,3}$	$m_{2,4}$	$m_{2,5}$	$m_{2,6}$	$m_{2,7}$
3	$m_{3,0}$	$m_{3,1}$	$m_{3,2}$	$m_{3,3}$	$m_{3,4}$	$m_{3,5}$	$m_{3,6}$	$m_{3,7}$
4	$m_{4,0}$	$m_{4,1}$	$m_{4,2}$	$m_{4,3}$	$m_{4,4}$	$m_{4,5}$	$m_{4,6}$	$m_{4,7}$
5	$m_{5,0}$	$m_{5,1}$	$m_{5,2}$	$m_{5,3}$	$m_{5,4}$	$m_{5,5}$	$m_{5,6}$	$m_{5,7}$
6	$m_{6,0}$	$\mathbf{m_{6,1}}$	$m_{6,2}$	$m_{6,3}$	$m_{6,4}$	$m_{6,5}$	$m_{6,6}$	$m_{6,7}$
7	$m_{7,0}$	$m_{7,1}$	$m_{7,2}$	$m_{7,3}$	$m_{7,4}$	$m_{7,5}$	$m_{7,6}$	$m_{7,7}$

TABLE 4
THE SUBMESSAGES STORED IN BUFFERS $c'[]$ OF PROCESSORS AFTER THE FIRST PASS

i	P_0's c'[]	P_1's c'[]	P_2's c'[]	P_3's c'[]	P_4's c'[]	P_5's c'[]	P_6's c'[]	P_7's c'[]
0	$m_{5,7}$	$m_{1,0}$	$m_{1,3}$	$m_{5,4}$	$m_{1,5}$	$m_{7,1}$	$m_{0,6}$	$m_{6,2}$
1	$m_{0,0}$	$m_{4,7}$	$m_{4,4}$	$m_{0,3}$	$\mathbf{m_{6,1}}$	$m_{0,5}$	$m_{7,2}$	$m_{1,6}$
2	$m_{7,4}$	$m_{3,3}$	$m_{3,0}$	$m_{7,7}$	$m_{4,2}$	$m_{2,6}$	$m_{5,1}$	$m_{3,5}$
3	$m_{2,3}$	$m_{6,4}$	$m_{6,7}$	$m_{2,0}$	$m_{3,6}$	$m_{5,2}$	$m_{2,5}$	$m_{4,1}$
4	$m_{4,6}$	$m_{2,2}$	$m_{5,5}$	$m_{3,1}$	$m_{5,3}$	$m_{1,4}$	$m_{1,7}$	$m_{5,0}$
5	$m_{3,2}$	$m_{5,6}$	$m_{2,1}$	$m_{4,5}$	$m_{0,4}$	$m_{4,3}$	$m_{4,0}$	$m_{0,7}$
6	$m_{1,1}$	$m_{7,5}$	$m_{0,2}$	$m_{6,6}$	$m_{7,0}$	$m_{3,7}$	$m_{3,4}$	$m_{7,3}$
7	$m_{6,5}$	$m_{0,1}$	$m_{7,6}$	$m_{1,2}$	$m_{2,7}$	$m_{6,0}$	$m_{6,3}$	$m_{2,4}$

TABLE 5
THE SUBMESSAGES STORED IN BUFFERS $c[]$ OF PROCESSORS AFTER THE SECOND PASS

i	P_0's c[]	P_1's c[]	P_2's c[]	P_3's c[]	P_4's c[]	P_5's c[]	P_6's c[]	P_7's c[]
0	$m_{0,7}$	$m_{0,0}$	$m_{0,3}$	$m_{0,4}$	$m_{0,5}$	$m_{0,1}$	$m_{0,6}$	$m_{0,2}$
1	$m_{1,7}$	$m_{1,0}$	$m_{1,3}$	$m_{1,4}$	$m_{1,5}$	$m_{1,1}$	$m_{1,6}$	$m_{1,2}$
2	$m_{2,7}$	$m_{2,0}$	$m_{2,3}$	$m_{2,4}$	$m_{2,5}$	$m_{2,1}$	$m_{2,6}$	$m_{2,2}$
3	$m_{3,7}$	$m_{3,0}$	$m_{3,3}$	$m_{3,4}$	$m_{3,5}$	$m_{3,1}$	$m_{3,6}$	$m_{3,2}$
4	$m_{4,7}$	$m_{4,0}$	$m_{4,3}$	$m_{4,4}$	$m_{4,5}$	$m_{4,1}$	$m_{4,6}$	$m_{4,2}$
5	$m_{5,7}$	$m_{5,0}$	$m_{5,3}$	$m_{5,4}$	$m_{5,5}$	$m_{5,1}$	$m_{5,6}$	$m_{5,2}$
6	$m_{6,7}$	$m_{6,0}$	$m_{6,3}$	$m_{6,4}$	$m_{6,5}$	$\mathbf{m_{6,1}}$	$m_{6,6}$	$m_{6,2}$
7	$m_{7,7}$	$m_{7,0}$	$m_{7,3}$	$m_{7,4}$	$m_{7,5}$	$m_{7,1}$	$m_{7,6}$	$m_{7,2}$

In routing with node-disjoint paths, also called crosstalk-free routing in [5][6], no two active message paths are passing through the same switch in the network. Clearly, by this definition, realizing any permutation in a multistage network with node-disjoint paths needs at least two passes. The method used in our previous work [5][6] is to decompose an admissible permutation as an $n \times n$ mapping into two $\frac{n}{2} \times \frac{n}{2}$ mappings so that each of them can be realized in the original $n \times n$ network with node-disjoint paths. Such a $\frac{n}{2} \times \frac{n}{2}$ mapping is called *crosstalk-free semi-permutation* in [6]. However, it is not always achievable to decompose an admissible permutation to two crosstalk-free semi-permutations. Fortunately, it has been proved in [6] that any admissible permutation corresponding to a row of Latin square A for all-to-all personalized exchange can be decomposed to two crosstalk-free semi-permutations. We will show how the results can to extended to the case of realizing any permutation in a unique-path multistage network.

Let $Bits(x)$ be a function of integer x that returns the number of 1's in the binary representation of x. For $n = 2^m$, we define the following sets

$$\mathcal{O} = \{x | x \in \{0, 1, \ldots, n-1\} \text{ and } Bits(x) \text{ is odd }\},$$
$$\mathcal{E} = \{x | x \in \{0, 1, \ldots, n-1\} \text{ and } Bits(x) \text{ is even }\}. \quad (10)$$

Clearly, we have

$$|\mathcal{O}| = |\mathcal{E}| = \frac{n}{2}.$$

$\mathcal{O}$ and $\mathcal{E}$ can also be pre-calculated and stored as system parameters. The following result is summarized from [6].

Theorem 3: Any admissible permutation, as an $n \times n$ mapping that corresponds to a row of routing matrix A for an $n \times n$ unique-path multistage network, can be decomposed to two $\frac{n}{2} \times \frac{n}{2}$ mappings which map from $\mathcal{O}$ and $\mathcal{E}$, respectively. Both the $\frac{n}{2} \times \frac{n}{2}$ mappings are crosstalk-free semi-permutations, i.e. both of them can be realized in the network with node-disjoint paths.

For example, for $n = 8$, we have

$$\mathcal{O} = \{1, 2, 4, 7\} \text{ and } \mathcal{E} = \{0, 3, 5, 6\}.$$

Then an admissible permutation corresponding to the second row of A in (5)

$$\begin{pmatrix} 0 & 1 & 2 & 3 & 4 & 5 & 6 & 7 \\ 1 & 0 & 3 & 2 & 5 & 4 & 7 & 6 \end{pmatrix}$$

can be decomposed to

$$\begin{pmatrix} 1 & 2 & 4 & 7 \\ 0 & 3 & 5 & 6 \end{pmatrix} \text{ and } \begin{pmatrix} 0 & 3 & 5 & 6 \\ 1 & 2 & 4 & 7 \end{pmatrix},$$

which are two crosstalk-free semi-permutations for an 8×8 omega network, i.e. they can be realized with node-disjoint paths (see Figure 3).

To describe our permutation algorithm with node-disjoint paths, we need the following property.

Lemma 4: If the processors which are in set $\mathcal{O}$ (or $\mathcal{E}$) send their submessages according to routing matrix A, each processor will receive $\frac{n}{2}$ submessages.

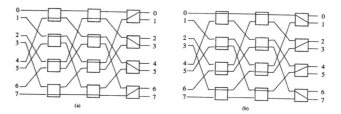

Fig. 3. The two decomposed semi-permutations can be realized in an 8×8 omega network with node-disjoint paths.

Proof. If processor j sends out all its submessages, each processor will receive exactly one submessage since the destination processors are corresponding to the jth column of routing matrix A which is a Latin square. Therefore, after all the processors which are in the set $\mathcal{O}$ (or $\mathcal{E}$) send out their submessages, each processor will receive exactly $|\mathcal{O}| = \frac{n}{2}$ submessages. ∎

Now the algorithm $PermutationNodeDisjoint(\cdot)$ for realizing any permutation in a multistage network with node-disjoint paths is given in Table 6. As can be seen, this algorithm takes four passes to realize a permuattion. Actually, this algorithm is modified from $PermutationLinkDisjoint(\cdot)$ with the first two passes of the former corresponding to the first pass of the latter, and the last two passes of the former corresponding to the second pass of the latter. For the first (or last) two passes in $PermutationNodeDisjoint(\cdot)$, processors in set $\mathcal{O}$ send all their messages in one pass and processors in set $\mathcal{E}$ send in the other pass; and in either pass, all the processors wait to receive submessages. Since the two passes of sending processes of this algorithm are equivalent to one pass of sending processes of algorithm $PermutationLinkDisjoint(\cdot)$, the permutation functionality can be achieved. The node-disjoint property of this algorithm is guaranteed by Theorem 3. Also, notice that in $process2$ this algorithm waits to receive $\frac{n}{2}$ submessages according to Lemma 4 instead of n submessages in $process2$ of $PermutationNodeDisjoint(\cdot)$.

VI. COMPARISONS AND CONCLUDING REMARKS

The permutation algorithms proposed in this paper are based on the idea in [16] and the theory for realizing all-to-all personalized exchange in multistage networks in [1]. Different from the method in [16], which is for a specific multistage network, the results in this paper have the following advantages. Our algorithms are generic for the entire class of unique-path multistage networks including the network used in [16] and the omega network. The routing control in this paper is based on the static information associated with Latin square matrices, and can be either self-routing or stage control. Our method is flexible and much easier than the method in [16], which is suitable only for stage control. Also, our method has been easily extended to permutation with node-disjoint paths, which has important applications in the emerging optical interconnects.

Now we compare the algorithms in this paper to other pre-

TABLE 6

```
Algorithm PermutationNodeDisjoint((d_0, ... , d_n); (m_0, ... , m_n))
{
    for each processor j (0 ≤ j ≤ n - 1) do in parallel {
        divide m_j into submessages and put into local buffer c[0 ··· n - 1];
    } // end of initialization
    for SELECT in {O, E} {
        for each processor j (0 ≤ j ≤ n - 1) do in parallel {
            do process1, process2 in parallel {
                {process1:
                    if j ∈ SELECT {
                        for (i = 0; i < n; i++) {
                            send message c[i] to destination processor a_{i,j};
                        }
                    }// end if
                }
                {process2:
                    for (k = 0; k < n/2; k++) {
                        receive a message r and put into c'[b_{j,r.dest}];
                    }
                }
            }
        }
    } // end of the first two passes
    for SELECT in {O, E} {
        for each processor j (0 ≤ j ≤ n - 1) do in parallel {
            do process1, process2 in parallel {
                {process1:
                    if j ∈ SELECT {
                        for (i = 0; i < n; i++) {
                            send message c'[i] to destination processor a_{i,j};
                        }
                    }// end if
                }
                {process2:
                    for (k = 0; k < n/2; k++) {
                        receive a message r and put into c[r.seq];
                    }
                }
            }
        }
    } // end of the last two passes
}
```

viously proposed permutation algorithms. Since not all permutations can be realized in a unique-path MIN in a single pass, it needs at least two passes to realize an arbitrary permutation. The results in [12] indicated that any permutation can be realized in an omega network in three passes. In our results, any permutation can be realized in a class of unique-path MIN including the omega network in two passes. Thus in our permutation algorithms, the number of passes that each message goes through the network is the minimum. Also, any permutation can be realized with node-disjoint paths in four passes in our algorithm. We believe it is the minimum because for the two semi-permutations decomposed from a permutation, not every semi-permutation can be realized in a unique-path MIN with node-disjoint in one pass. Another advantage is that the routing in our algorithms is as fast as that in [16], which takes a total of $O(n + \log n)$ time (for all n submessages), while the routing in other previously proposed permutation algorithms is much more complex, which takes at least $O(n \log n)$ time.

For network transmission time, since a pipeline can be formed through the stages, for the two passes with each pass transmitting n submessages, the transmission time could be as fast as $2n + \log n - 1$ time steps in the case of link-disjoint paths. However, in the permutation algorithm, we need to wait to receive all n submessages before the next pass starts. So the time steps needed are $2(n + \log n - 1)$. Since the algorithms in this paper require that the messages are divided into n submessages, the transmission time is at least near-optimal for transmitting sufficiently long messages. However, for transmitting short messages, our algorithms as well as that in [16] may not be efficient.

REFERENCES

[1] Y. Yang and J. Wang, "Optimal all-to-all personalized exchange in self-routable multistage networks," *IEEE Trans. Parallel and Distributed Systems*, vol. 11, no. 3, pp. 261-274, 2000.

[2] *InfiniBand Architecture Specification 1.0*, The InfiniBand Trade Association, Oct. 2000, http://www.infinibandta.org.

[3] C.-L. Wu and T.-Y. Feng, "On a class of multistage interconnection networks," *IEEE Trans. Computers*, vol. 29, no. 8, pp. 694-702, 1980.

[4] J. Duato, S. Yalamanchili, and L.M. Ni, *Interconnection Networks: An Engineering Approach*, Morgan Kaufmann Publishers, 2002.

[5] Y. Yang, et al., "Permutation capability of optical multistage interconnection networks," *Journal of Parallel and Distributed Computing*, vol. 60, no. 1, pp. 72-91, 2000.

[6] Y. Yang and J. Wang, "Optimal all-to-all personalized exchange in a class of optical multistage networks," *IEEE Transactions on Parallel and Distributed Systems*, vol. 12, no. 6, pp. 567-582, 2001.

[7] C. Qiao and R. Melhem, "Reconfiguration with time division multiplexed MINs for multiprocessor communications," *IEEE Trans. Parallel and Distributed Systems*, vol. 5, no. 4, pp. 337-352, 1994.

[8] C. Qiao and L. Zhou, "Scheduling switching element disjoint connections in stage-controlled photonic banyans," *IEEE Trans. Communications*, vol. 47, no. 1, pp. 139-148, 1999.

[9] Q. Gu and S. Peng, "Wavelength requirment for permutation routing in all-optical multistage interconnection networks," *Proc. of International Parallel and Distributed Processing Symposium*, pp. 761-768, Cancun, Mexico, May 2000.

[10] Q. Gu and S. Peng, "Efficient protocols for permutation routing on all-optical multistage interconection netowerks," *Proc. of 2000 Interconnation Conference on Parallel Processing*, pp. 513-520, Toronto, Canada, August 2000.

[11] V.E. Benes, "Optimal rearrangeable multistage connecting networks," *The Bell System Technical Journal*, vol. 43, pp.1641-1656, 1964.

[12] D.S. Parker, Jr., "Notes on shuffle/exchange-type switching networks," *IEEE Trans. Computers*, vol. 29, no. 3, pp. 213-222, March 1980.

[13] C.Y. Jan and A.Y. Oruç, "Fast self-routing permutation switching on an asymptotically minimum cost network," *IEEE Trans. Computers*, vol. 45, no. 12, pp. 1369-1379, 1993.

[14] D.M. Koppelman and A.Y. Oruç, "Comlexity of routing in permutation netowrks," *IEEE Trans. Information Theory*, vol. 40, no. 1, pp. 278-284, 1994.

[15] W.-J. Cheng and W.-T. Chen, "A new self-routing permutation network," *IEEE Trans. Computers*, vol. 45, no. 5, pp. 630-636, 1996.

[16] W. K. Lai, "Performing permutations on interconnection networks by regularly changing switch states," *IEEE Trans. Parallel and Distributed Systems*, vol. 11, no. 8, pp. 829-837, 2000.

[17] Y. Yang and J. Wang, "Wide-sense nonblocking Clos networks under packing strategy," *IEEE Trans. Computers*, vol. 48, no. 3, pp. 265-284, 1999.

[18] S.-W. Seo, T.-Y. Feng and H.-I. Lee, "Permutation realizability and fault tolerance property of the inside-out routing algorithm," *IEEE Trans. Parallel and Distributed Systems*, vol. 10, no. 9, pp. 946-957, 1999.

[19] K.P. Bogart, *Introductory Combinatorics, 3rd Edition*, Harcourt Academic Press, 2000.

Fault-Tolerant and Deadlock-Free Routing in 2-D Meshes Using Rectilinear-Monotone Polygonal Fault Blocks

Jie Wu *
Department of Computer Science and Engineering
Florida Atlantic University
Boca Raton, FL 33431
jie@cse.fau.edu

Dajin Wang
Department of Computer Science
Montclair State University
Upper Montclair, NJ 07043
wang@pegasus.montclair.edu

Abstract

We propose a deterministic fault-tolerant and deadlock-free routing protocol in 2-dimensional (2-D) meshes based on Wu's fault-tolerant odd-even turn model and Wang's rectilinear-monotone polygonal fault block model. The fault-tolerant odd-even turn protocol, also called extended X-Y routing, *was originally proposed to achieve fault-tolerant and deadlock-free routing among traditional, rectangular fault blocks. It does not use any virtual channels. The number of faults to be tolerated is unbounded as long as nodes outside fault blocks are connected in the mesh network. The recently proposed rectilinear-monotone polygonal fault blocks (also called* minimal-connected-components *or MCCs) are of the polygonal shapes, and is a refinement of rectangular fault blocks. The formation of MCCs depends on the relative locations of source and destination, and they include much fewer healthy nodes in resultant fault blocks. In this paper, we show that with a simple modification, the extended X-Y routing can also be applied to 2-D meshes using extended MCCs.*

Key words: *Deadlock-free routing, deterministic routing, fault models, fault tolerance, turn models, virtual channels.*

1. Introduction

The mesh topology is one of the most important interconnection networks. This topology possesses many attractive properties. Multicomputer systems using the mesh topology as their underlying architecture have been around for years. Because of its importance to achieving high performance, fault-tolerant computing for the mesh topology has been the focus of an extensive literature. A very important area of mesh fault tolerance concerns its ability to route packets from a source to a destination, avoiding all faulty nodes in the system. Routing algorithms are either *deterministic* or *adaptive*. Deterministic routing uses only one path to route packets from a source to a destination, while adaptive routing makes use of many different routes. Most commercial systems use deterministic routing because of its deadlock freedom and ease of implementation. X-Y routing is an example of dimension-order routing used in 2-dimensional (2-D) meshes and tori. In X-Y routing, the packet is routed first in the x dimension and then in the y dimension. Unfortunately, X-Y routing is not fault-tolerant and it cannot tolerate even a single fault.

Designing a deterministic routing protocol that is both fault-tolerant and deadlock-free poses a major challenge. The *wormhole switching* [8] technique used in the latest generation of multicomputers is subject to deadlock more than packet switching. In addition, wormhole switching tends to support routing with less fault tolerance. Wormhole routing divides a message into packets and packets into flits. It then routes flits through the network in a pipelined fashion. When the header flits reach a node that has no output channel available, all of the flits are blocked where they are (in place). A deadlock occurs when some packets from different messages cannot advance toward their destinations because the channels requested by them are not available. All the packets involved in a deadlocked configuration are blocked forever. Deadlock avoidance is a commonly used approach in which channels are granted to a packet in such a way that a request never leads to a deadlock.

To achieve fault tolerance, faults are normally contained in a set of disjointed rectangular regions called *fault blocks*. The convexity of fault blocks facilitates a simple design for deadlock-free routing. To design a deadlock-free routing, *virtual channels* [5] are usually used to provide a certain degree of routing freedom when routing around a fault block. However, using virtual channels has some disadvantages, for example, the routers based on virtual channels requires more gates and time compared with those not based on virtual channels.

*The work of Jie Wu was supported in part by NSF grants CCR 9900646 and ANI 0073736.

Many studies have been done on deadlock-free routing in 2-D meshes based on the fault block model [1, 2, 7, 9, 11, 14]. Most approaches try to reduce either the number of nonfaulty nodes in a faulty block by considering different types of fault regions or the number of virtual channels. So far the best results can reduce the number of virtual channels to two or three depending on the type of faulty blocks used. To our knowledge, there is no deadlock-free dimension-order routing that can tolerate unlimited number of faults without using virtual channels.

In this paper, we apply Wu's extended X-Y routing to 2-D meshes that use a new fault block model called minimal-connected-component (MCC). The *extended X-Y routing* is a deterministic fault-tolerant and deadlock-free routing protocol in 2-D meshes. It is based on the well-know X-Y routing and the recently proposed *odd-even turn model* [4], which is an extension to Glass and Ni's *turn model* [6] where certain types of turns are prohibited to avoid deadlock. The extended X-Y routing does not use any virtual channels. The number of faults to be tolerated is unbounded as long as nodes outside fault blocks are connected in the resultant mesh network. However, a conservative approach is used in constructing a fault block; that is, many non-faulty nodes are unnecessarily contained in the block in order to form a rectangular shape block.

The MCC model was proposed by Wang [12] as a refinement to the rectangular fault block model. Basically, fault blocks in MCC are of the so-called "rectilinear-monotone" polygonal shapes. The size of fault blocks are greatly reduced by considering the relative locations of source and destination nodes. The original purpose of MCC is to facilitate minimal routing in presence of faults—a node will be included in an MCC block only if using that node in a routing will definitely make the route non-minimal. It turns out that MCC block is the absolutely minimal fault block; that is, no healthy node contained in an MCC will be useful in whatever routing, minimal or non-minimal.

In this paper, we show that the extended X-Y routing can also be applied to 2-D meshes using an extended MCC model through a simple modification. The following are assumptions used in this paper: (1) The fault model is static, that is, no new faults occur during a routing process. (2) Both source and destination nodes are outside any fault block. In addition, the destination is not a boundary node of any fault block. (3) Faults are at least 2 hops away from the four edges of a mesh. (4) A connected 2-D mesh is used with four directions: north (positive x), south (negative x), west (positive y), and east (negative y). (Unlike the convention the north-south axe is used here as the x axe to match the notation used in the odd-even turn model.)

The rest of this paper is organized as follows: Sections 2 and 3 give introduction to odd-even turn, extended X-Y routing, and MCC fault model. Section 4 first extends the definition of MCC model to accommodate to deadlock-free routing and, then, applies the extended X-Y routing to 2-D meshes using extended MCC model. Section 5 concludes the paper and discusses possible future work.

2. Two-dimensional Meshes and Odd-Even Turn Model

In this section, we first briefly review the mesh topology. We then give an introduction to Chiu's odd-even turn model [4], which is an extension to Glass and Ni's turn model.

2.1. 2-dimensional (2-D) meshes

A 2-dimensional (2-D) mesh with $n \times n$ nodes has an interior node degree of 4. Each node u has an address u: (u_x, u_y), where $u_x, u_y \in \{0, 1, 2, ..., n-1\}$. Two nodes u: (u_x, u_y) and v: (v_x, v_y) are connected if their addresses differ in one and only one dimension, say x, and $|u_x - v_x| = 1$. Each non-boundary node in a 2-D mesh has four neighbors, one in each of four directions: east, south, west, and north.

Routing is a process to send *packets* from a source node to a destination node, passing some intermediate nodes. There are basically two types of routing: *deterministic* routing and *adaptive* routing. In deterministic routing, a fixed path is used to send/receive packets for a particular pair of source/destination. The obvious advantages of this routing are its simplicity and ease of implementation. However, it suffers the shortcoming of weak fault tolerability—when one or more nodes on the dedicated path fail, either routing cannot be carried out, or only very limited detours can be taken. In adaptive routing, there is no dedicated path for a pair of source and destination. The path is adaptively constructed in the process of routing. However, the algorithm/implementation for adaptive routing is more complicated.

2.2. Odd-even turn model

Both deterministic and adaptive routings suffer from possible deadlocks when multiple packets are flowing in the mesh. Many strategies, with or without resorting to extra resources, have been proposed. Recently, Chiu [4] proposed an odd-even turn model, an extension to Glass and Ni's turn model [6], to prevent deadlocks without using the popular means of virtual channels. In general, deadlock avoidance tries to avoid the formation of a cycle, which is a necessary condition for deadlock. Such deadlock is also called *communication deadlock* where routing packets are (active) processes and channels are resources. A cycle in a mesh consists of several (at least four) turns. As illustrated in Figure 1, SW (South-West), WN, NE, and ES turns are essential in a clockwise cycle. Likewise, to form a counter-clockwise cycle, SE, EN, NW, and WS turns are necessary.

Figure 1. SW, WN, NE, and ES turns are essential in forming a clockwise cycle. Dually, to form a counterclockwise cycle, SE, EN, NW, and WS turns are necessary.

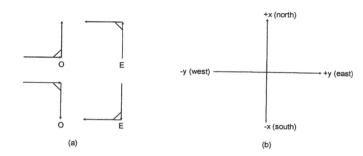

Figure 2. (a) EN, ES turns are permissible only at odd columns; NW, SW turns are permissible only at even columns. (b) The coordinate system used in this paper.

In Chiu's odd-even turn model, certain types of turns are prohibited at certain columns. Refer to Figure 1 again: in clockwise cycle, if we always command an ES turn and an SW turn to take place at different columns, then the essential *rightmost column segment* of a cycle will never be formed. Similarly, in counterclockwise cycle, if we always command EN and NW turns to take place at different columns, then the essential rightmost column segment of a cycle will never be formed. That is the basic idea of the odd-even turn model.

In odd-even turn model, the above four types of turns are disallowed at certain columns: two in a clockwise cycle and two in a counterclockwise cycle. The basic concept behind the turn model is to keep disallowed turns as few as possible to increase the routing adaptivity. Chiu gives two rules for making turns [4]:

> **Rule 1** (To prevent counterclockwise cycle): *Any packet is not allowed to take an EN turn at any node located in an even column, and it is not allowed to take an NW turn at any node located in an odd column.*

> **Rule 2**: (To prevent clockwise cycle) *Any packet is not allowed to take an ES turn at any node located in an even column, and it is not allowed to take an SW turn at any node located in an odd column.*

Figure 2 shows the EN, NW, ES, and SW turns and the columns at which these turns are allowed under above two rules. These four turns are called *sensitive turns*. Turns without restriction are called *insensitive turns*. A small triangle is placed at each sensitive turn that is permissible (as shown in Figure 2). A turn in an even (odd) column is represented by E (O).

3. Extended X-Y Routing and MCC Fault Block Model

3.1. Extended X-Y routing

In the fault-tolerant, deadlock-free routing in [13], called extended X-Y routing, a set of disjointed rectangular fault blocks are first constructed. The distance between two fault blocks along the x dimension (column) is 2 and one along the y dimension (row) is 3. The 3-hop distance requirement along the y dimension is to ensure that two boundary lines (one even column and one odd column) can be constructed at east and west side of each fault block. All faulty and non-faulty nodes are initially labeled *faulty* and *fault-free*, respectively. A fault-free node is changed to *disabled* if it has two faulty or disabled neighbors that are not all in the x dimension; or it has a faulty or disabled neighbor in the x dimension and a faulty or disabled 2-hop neighbor (neighbor's neighbor) in the y dimension. A fault block consists of connected faulty and disabled nodes.

The extended X-Y routing consists of two phases, similar to a regular X-Y routing. In phase 1, the offset along the x dimension is reduced to zero, and in phase 2, the offset along the y dimension is reduced to zero. Assume source and destination nodes are both fault-free. Let $s : (s_x, s_y)$ and $d : (d_x, d_y)$ be the source and destination nodes, respectively. $\Delta_x = |d_x - s_x|$ and $\Delta_y = |d_y - s_y|$ are offsets along dimension x and dimension y, respectively.

The extended X-Y routing protocol, shown in Figure 3, follows the regular X-Y routing (and the packet is in a "normal" mode) until the packet reaches a boundary node of a fault block. At that point, the packet is routed around the block (and the packet is in an "abnormal" mode) clockwise or counterclockwise based on the following rules: When a routing packet routes around a fault block following the boundary ring, the corresponding block is called the *routing block*. During phase 1 (refer to Figure 4 (a) and (b)) the packet is routed around the routing block through the west side of the block. Even columns are used to route the packet along the x dimension (column). In phase 2 (refer to Figure 4 (c) and (d)), odd columns (even columns) will be used to route around a routing block when the packet is east-bound (west-bound). The packet can be routed around the routing block either clockwise or counterclockwise, since either way is permissible. Note that in extended X-Y routing, south-bound corresponds to quadrant III or quadrant IV

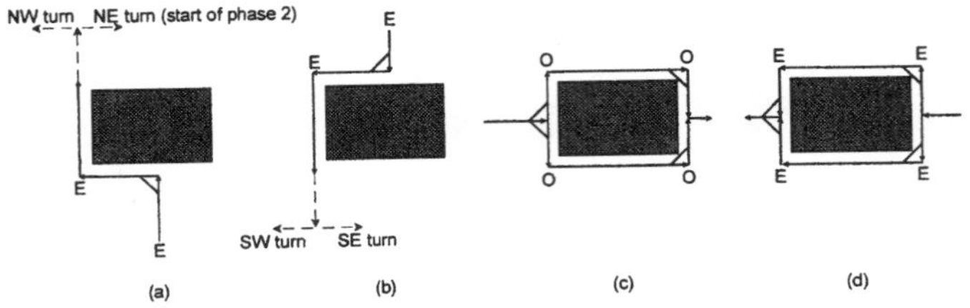

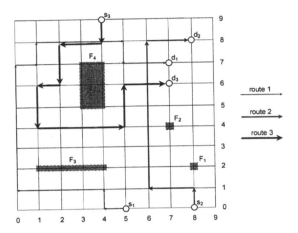

Figure 4. Two cases of routing along the x dimension (column) (a) north-bound and (b) south-bound; and two cases along the y dimension (row) (c) east-bound and (d) west-bound.

Figure 5. Three routing examples in a 10 × 10 mesh with four fault blocks.

Extended X-Y routing:

1. /* the packet is sent to an even column before phase 1 starts */

    (a) If the source is in an odd column and Δ_x is non-zero, then the packet is sent to its west neighbor in an even column.

2. /* phase 1: reduce Δ_x, the offset in the x dimension */

    (a) (Normal mode) reduce Δ_x to zero by sending the packet north (or south).

    (b) (Abnormal mode) when a north-bound (south-bound) packet reaches a boundary node of a fault block, it is routed around the block clockwise (counterclockwise) by following the boundary ring of the fault block as shown in Figure 4 (a) (Figure 4 (b)). The packet takes the first even column turn whenever possible and step (a) is followed.

3. /* phase 2: reduce Δ_y, the offset in the y dimension */

    (a) Once Δ_x is reduced to zero, an NW or NE turn is performed for the north-bound packet (see Figure 4 (a)) and a SW or SE turn is performed for a south-bound packet (see Figure 4 (b)). The selection of a turn depends on the relative location of the destination to the current node.

    (b) (Normal mode) reduce Δ_y to zero by sending the packet east (west).

    (c) (Abnormal mode) when a east-bound (west-bound) packet reaches a boundary node of a fault block, it is routed around the block, clockwise or counterclockwise, along odd columns of the boundary ring as shown in Figure 4 (c) (even columns of the boundary ring as shown in Figure 4 (d)). Routing around the block is completed when Δ_x is again reduced to zero and step (b) is followed.

Figure 3. Extended X-Y routing.

while north-bound corresponds to quadrant I or quadrant II.

Referring to Figure 2 and Figure 4, it can be seen that the rules of turn-making are followed during the block-avoiding manoeuvring. In [13], Wu provided a proof that the extended X-Y routing is both deadlock-free and livelock-free in a 2-D mesh where faults are contained in a set of disjointed fault blocks. Figure 5 shows three routing examples (s_i, d_i), $i \in \{1, 2, 3\}$, in a 10 × 10 mesh with four fault blocks F_1, F_2, F_3, and F_4.

3.2. Minimal-connected-components (MCCs)

In each step of routing, a node can take one and only one direction to its immediate neighbor. Therefore, a routing can be represented as a sequence of directions. Minimal routing in a 2-D mesh can take at most two directions (the corresponding routing is also called *Manhattan routing*). For example, if the destination is in the first quadrant with respect to the source (origin of the coordinate), only north and east directions are used. The formation of MCC fault block is based on the notions of *useless* and *can't-*

250

Labeling procedure for MCC:

1. Initially, label all faulty nodes as *faulty* and all non-faulty nodes as *fault-free*;

2. If node u is fault-free, but its north neighbor and east neighbor are faulty or useless, u is labeled *useless*;

3. If node u is fault-free, but its south neighbor and west neighbor are faulty or can't-reach, u is labeled *can't-reach*;

4. The nodes are recursively labeled until there are no new useless or can't-reach nodes.

Figure 6. Labeling procedure for MCC block for quadrant I destination.

reach nodes: A node labeled useless is such a node that once it is entered in a routing, the next move must take either west or south direction, making a Manhattan routing (in the first quadrant) impossible. A node labeled can't-reach is such a node that to enter it in a routing, a west or south move must be taken, making a Manhattan routing impossible. The node status (faulty, fault-free, useless, and can't-reach) can be determined through a labeling procedure. Connected faulty, useless, and can't-reach nodes form a MCC. The labeling procedure given in Figure 6 is for quadrants I routing, i.e., the destination is in quadrant I (northeast). The labeling procedure for quadrant III (the destination is in southwest) can be obtained just by exchanging the roles of useless and can't-reach. In fact, MCCs generated from quadrant I labeling procedure and from quadrants III labeling procedure are the same, and they are called *type-one MCCs*.

The labeling procedure for quadrant II (the destination is in northwest) can be derived from that for quadrant I by exchanging the roles played by east and west neighbors. Again, the labeling procedure for quadrant IV is from one for quadrant II by exchanging the role of useless and can't-reach. MCCs generated from quadrants II and IV are the same, and they are called *type-two MCCs*. Note that useless and can't-reach nodes correspond to disabled nodes in the regular fault block model. Figure 7 (a) shows the definition of useless and can't-reach nodes (for quadrant I destination), Figure 7 (b) shows sample type-one MCCs (for quadrants I & III destinations). For the same faulty nodes, the corresponding type-two MCCs (for quadrants II & IV destinations) are shown in Figure 7 (c). Figure 8 gives the general shapes of MCCs for routing in the four quadrants.

MCC was originally proposed to facilitate minimal routing (Manhattan routing). An MCC block is a *minimum* connected block, so that a node v of the MCC is either faulty, or if fault-free, then entering v would force a step that violates

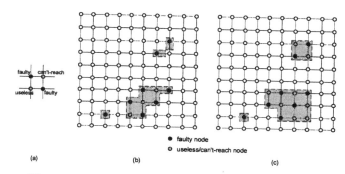

● faulty node
○ useless/can't-reach node

(a)   (b)   (c)

Figure 7. (a) Definition of useless and can't-reach nodes for quadrant I destination. (b) Sample type-one MCCs. (c) Sample type-two MCCs.

(a)   (b)   (c)   (d)

Figure 8. (a) MCC for quadrant I routing (type-one); (b) MCC for quadrant II routing (type-two); (c) MCC for quadrant III routing (type-one); (d) MCC for quadrant IV routing (type-two).

the requirement for a Manhattan route (i.e., a third direction would be used in the route). In other words, the MCC is a fault block model that provides the *maximum* possibility to find Manhattan route among faults. Therefore, if there exists no Manhattan route under MCC fault model, there will be absolutely no Manhattan route. In [12], a sufficient and necessary condition was provided for the existence of Manhattan routes in presence of MCCs.

Experiment results showed that MCC model includes much fewer non-faulty nodes in fault blocks than the conventional rectangular model. Many non-faulty nodes that would have been included in rectangular fault blocks now can become candidate routing nodes. As a matter of fact, MCC block is the "ultimate" minimal fault block; that is, no fault-free node contained in an MCC will be useful in whatever routing, minimal or non-minimal.

4. Extended X-Y Routing in 2-D Meshes with Extended MCCs

4.1. Extended MCCs

By the definition of MCC, the distance between two MCCs is at least 2 along each dimension. To ensure that the distance is at least 3 along the y (row) dimension, we

Labeling procedure for extended MCC:

1. First, generate all original MCCs;

2. If node u is fault-free, but its east neighbor and west neighbor are both MCC nodes, then u is labeled *connector*;

3. If node u is fault-free, but its north neighbor and east neighbor are faulty/useless/connector, u is labeled *useless*;

4. If node u is fault-free, but its south neighbor and west neighbor are faulty/can't-reach/connector, u is labeled *can't-reach*;

5. The nodes are recursively labeled until there are no new useless, can't-reach, connector nodes.

Figure 9. Labeling procedure for extended MCC block for quadrant I destination.

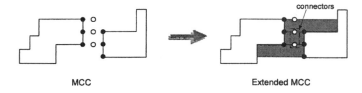

Figure 10. MCCs that are 2-hop apart are merged into one (extended) MCC.

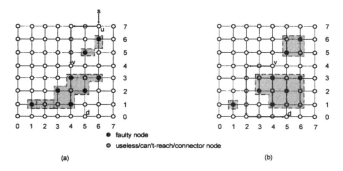

● faulty node
○ useless/can't-reach/connector node

(a)　　　　　　　　　　　　(b)

Figure 11. (a) A quadrant III routing from u to d. (b) A quadrant IV routing from v to d.

give a definition for *extended MCCs* to ensure two boundary columns (at east and west) of each MCC. In the labeling procedure for extended MCC, a new label *connector* is used to connect two MCCs that are two hops away along the y (row) dimension. Again, initially all faulty nodes are labeled *faulty* and non-faulty node *fault-free*. The nodes are recursively labeled until there are no new useless, can't-reach, connector nodes. All useless, can't-reach, and connector nodes are disabled (i.e., included in extended MCCs) and the remaining fault-free nodes are not included in any extended MCCs.

The labeling procedure for extended MCC is given in Figure 9. In Figure 10, the role of connector nodes is illustrated. It can be seen that 2-hop apart MCCs will be merged into one (extended) MCC. Note that the extended MCCs are not minimal fault blocks anymore. However, this modification is necessary to accommodate to the application of odd-even turn model. Also, its rectangular counterparts will undergo the same merge process with even more—as a matter of fact many more—fault-free nodes included. Therefore, in the context of odd-even turn model, the extended MCCs are still the smallest fault blocks.

All nodes included in extended MCCs are *disabled* for routing. Note that in the formation of extended MCCs, certain disabled node can be labeled either useless (can't-reach) or connector. For example, node (5,3) in Figure 11 (a) can be either can't-reach or connector. Since useless, can't-reach, and connector are all disabled, the way each node is labeled will not make any difference on the shape of each extended MCC.

Since a node may have different status (i.e., whether it is an MCC or non-MCC node) for quadrant I/III or quadrant II/IV routing, each node carries two status: $(status_1, status_2)$ where $status_1$ is for quadrant I and III routing and $status_3$ is for quadrant II and IV routing. Refer to Figure 11 again, the status of node (2,3) is (fault-free, fault-free). The one for (3,3) is (fault-free, disabled), for (5,3) is (disabled, disabled), and for (3,1) is (disabled, fault-free). It is assumed that source and destination nodes both have (fault-free, fault-free) status.

4.2. Extended X-Y routing in 2-D meshes with extended MCCs

Once the extended MCCs are defined, the extended X-Y routing for rectangular blocks can be applied with some simple modification. In phase 1, the routing proceeds along the x dimension (vertical) at an even column, until an MCC boundary is hit. At that point, the routing takes a "zigzag" detour along the boundary. Notice that SW and NW turns are sensitive turns and can only be made in even columns. Figure 12 (a), (b) illustrate example north-bound detouring for quadrant I and quadrant II routing, respectively. And Figure 12 (c), (d) illustrate example south-bound detouring for quadrant III and quadrant IV routing, respectively.

In phase 2, when a packet reaches a boundary node of an extended MCC, it is routed around the block *clockwise for quadrants I and III routing*, and *counterclockwise for quadrants II and IV routing*. The above rule is to avoid the formation of the rightmost column of a cycle as shown in

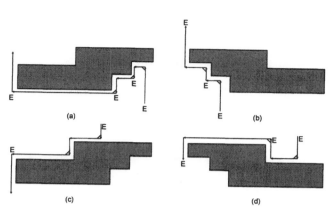

Figure 12. (a) North-bound quadrant I detouring in phase 1; (b) North-bound quadrant II detouring in phase 1; (c) South-bound quadrant III detouring in phase 1; (d) South-bound quadrant IV detouring in phase 1.

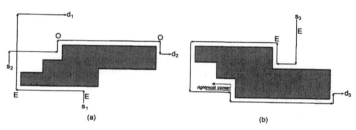

Figure 13. (a) Quadrants I and III routing with extended MCCs. (b) Quadrants II and IV routing with extended MCCs.

Figure 13 (b). Figure 13 (a) shows a quadrant I routing and a quadrant III routing, while Figure 13 (b) shows a quadrant IV routing.

Note that during the routing process, *the selection of block type does not depend on the relative locations of source and destination nodes, but rather relative locations of current and destination nodes!* However, block type of the routing block will not be changed once decided. Figure 11 shows such an example. When a south-bound packet reaches a boundary node u (see Figure 11 (a)), since destination d is in the quadrant III (w.r.t. u), type-one MCC is selected. Once the packet reaches node v which is a boundary node of another MCC, since destination d is in the quadrant IV (w.r.t. v, see Figure 11 (b)), type-two MCC is selected.

Theorem 1: *Using the extended MCC fault block model, the modified extended X-Y routing is deadlock-free and livelock-free.*

Figure 14. A fault block of orthogonal shape.

Proof: In phase 1, assume that the packet is north-bound (the south-bound case can be treated in a similar way), routing around a routing block involves a sequence of the following turns (refer to Figure 12 (a), (b)): NW*, (WS, SW)*, WN, where NW* represents a zero or more repetition of NW turns, and (WS, SW)* represents a zero or more repetition of WS, SW turns. All sensitive turns NW and SW occur at even columns and they are permissible. In the transition between phase 1 and phase 2, either an NW (permissible) or NE (insensitive) turn is performed in an even column.

In phase 2, assume that the packet is east-bound (the west-bound case can be treated in a similar way), routing around a routing block (if any) involves a sequence of the following turns if the packet is routed in the counterclockwise direction: ES, (SE, ES)*, SE, EN. If the packet is routed in the clockwise direction, the following sequence of turns is used: EN, (NE, EN)*, NE, ES. All sensitive turns are performed in odd columns and they are permissible. Once Δ_x is reduced to zero, either an SE or NE turn is performed in an odd column to reduce Δ_y.

Since all involved turns follow the rules of odd-even model, by the result of [4], the modified extended X-Y routing is deadlock-free and livelock-free.

∎

The advantage of MCCs over traditional rectangular fault blocks is obvious—MCCs are much smaller than rectangular fault blocks. Basically, a type-one (type-two) MCC is obtained by removing the unnecessarily included fault-free nodes in the SE (SW) and NW (NE) corner sections of a rectangular block.

The MCC model is not the only effort for reducing the size of fault blocks. In [13], Wu also proposed a similar polygonal-shaped fault model, called *orthogonal fault blocks*, which are fault blocks by removing all four corner sections (see Figure 14). Although an orthogonal fault block is in general smaller than either Type-one or Type-two MCC, it has the following drawbacks, which can be overcome by using MCC model.

- To avoid generating the rightmost column of a cycle, a rather complex process is used in the orthogonal fault block model. In that process, *directional information* is associated with boundary nodes of fault blocks to avoid formation of the rightmost column. Directional information tells direction of routing around the block (clockwise or counterclockwise) and such direction is dependent on the location of current boundary node. No such process is needed in the extended MCC model. In other words, the directional information is already *implied* by the type of the MCC.

- Additional detours may occur in orthogonal fault blocks. For example, additional detours occur whenever the quadrant I routing packet enters the SW corner section of the block. Such case will never occur in the extended MCC model.

The only overhead in the MCC is two different status maintained at an MCC node.

5. Conclusion

We have proposed a deterministic, fault-tolerant and deadlock-free routing protocol in two-dimensional meshes. The protocol is based on Wu's fault-tolerant routing scheme, called extended X-Y routing [13], using odd-even turn model [4] which is a fault-tolerant and deadlock-free routing protocol without using any virtual channels. The recently proposed rectilinear-monotone polygonal model (MCC) [12] has been employed as the fault block model. It has been shown that with a simple modification, the extended X-Y routing can be applied to 2-D meshes using extended MCCs, and the advantage of using MCC model in the context of odd-even turn model has been discussed. Our future work include performance study to verify the effectiveness of the proposed scheme.

References

[1] R. V. Boppana and S. Chalasani, Fault-tolerant wormhole routing algorithms for mesh networks, *IEEE Transactions on Computers*, 44, (7), July 1995, 848-864.

[2] Y. M. Boura and C. R. Das, Fault-tolerant routing in mesh networks, *Proc. of 1995 International Conference on Parallel Processing*, August 1995, I 106-I 109.

[3] S. Chalasani and R. V. Boppana, Communication in multicomputers with nonconvex faults, *IEEE Transactions on Computers*, 46, (5), May 1997, 616-622.

[4] G. M. Chiu, The odd-even turn model for adaptive routing, *IEEE Transactions on Parallel and Distributed Systems*, 11, (7), July 2000, 729-737.

[5] W. J. Dally and C. L. Seitz, Deadlock-free message routing in multiprocessor interconnection networks, *IEEE Transactions on Computers*, 36, (5), May 1987, 547-553.

[6] G. J. Glass and L. M. Ni, The turn model for adaptive routing, *Journal of ACM*, 40, (5), Sept. 1994, 874-902.

[7] S. P. Kim and T. Han, Fault-tolerant wormhole routing in meshes with overlapped solid fault regions, *Parallel Computing*, 23, 1997, 1937-1962.

[8] L. M. Ni and P. K. McKinley, A survey of routing techniques in wormhole networks, *Computer*, 26, (2), Feb. 1993, 62-76.

[9] J. -D. Shih, Adaptive Fault-Tolerant Wormhole Routing Algorithms for Hypercube and Mesh Interconnection Networks, *Proc. of the 11th International Parallel Processing Symposium*, April 1997, 333-340.

[10] P. H. Sui and S. D. Wang, An improved algorithm for fault-tolerant wormhole routing in meshes, *IEEE Transactions on Computers*, 46, (9), Sept. 1997, 1040-1042.

[11] P. H. Sui and S. D. Wang, Adaptive fault-tolerant deadlock-free routing in meshes and hypercubes, *IEEE Transactions on Parallel and Distributed Systems*, 11, 2000, 50-63.

[12] D. Wang, A rectilinear-monotone polygonal fault block model for fault-tolerant minimal routing in mesh, to appear in *IEEE Transactions on Computers*.

[13] J. Wu, A deterministic fault-tolerant and deadlock-free routing protocol in 2-d meshes without virtual channels, Technical Report, Florida Atlantic University, TR-CSE-00-26, Nov. 2000.

[14] J. Zhou and F. Lau, Adaptive Fault-Tolerant Wormhole Routing in 2D meshes, *Proc. of the 15th International Parallel & Distributed Processing Symposium (IPDPS 2001)*, 2001, 56.

Session 4B

Programming Methodologies

Pattern-based Parallel Programming

S. Bromling, S. MacDonald, J. Anvik, J. Schaeffer, D. Szafron, K. Tan
Department of Computing Science, University of Alberta,
Edmonton, Alberta, Canada T6G 2E8
Email: {bromling,stevem,janvik,jonathan,duane,cavalier}@cs.ualberta.ca

Abstract

The advantages of pattern-based programming have been well-documented in the sequential programming literature. However patterns have yet to make their way into mainstream parallel computing, even though several research tools support them. There are two critical shortcomings of pattern (or template) based systems for parallel programming: lack of extensibility and performance. This paper describes our approach for addressing these problems in the CO_2P_3S parallel programming system. CO_2P_3S supports multiple levels of abstraction, allowing the user to design an application with high-level patterns, but move to lower levels of abstraction for performance tuning. Patterns are implemented as parameterized templates, allowing the user the ability to customize the pattern to meet their needs. CO_2P_3S generates code that is specific to the pattern/parameter combination selected by the user. The $MetaCO_2P_3S$ tool addresses extensibility by giving users the ability to design and add new pattern templates to CO_2P_3S. Since the pattern templates are stored in a system-independent format, they are suitable for storing in a repository to be shared throughout the user community.
Keywords: parallel programming environment, design patterns, frameworks, meta-programming.

1 Introduction

Parallel programming is harder than sequential programming. Despite two decades of parallel tools research, many of the ideas that have improved sequential programming productivity have yet to make their way into production parallel tools. Message passing libraries (e.g., MPI) and compiler directives (e.g., OpenMP) represent the state of the art.

There have been numerous attempts to develop high-level parallel programming tools that abstract away much of the parallel complexity. Several tools require the user to write sequential stubs, with the tool inserting all the parallel code [15, 18, 13, 4, 2]. Despite these (often large) efforts, high-level parallel programming tools remain academic curiosities that are shunned by practitioners. There are two main reasons for this (others are explored in [16]):

- Performance. Generic tools generally produce generic parallel code with disappointing parallel performance. Unfortunately, most tools do not provide support for incremental code tuning (e.g., by making all the library code available in a usable form).

- Generality. The tools are usually suitable only for a small class of applications. If an application is not directly supported by the capabilities of the tool, then the developer cannot use the tool at all.

For many developers, these are the main reasons why MPI and OpenMP are so popular: the user has complete control over the performance of their application and the tools are general enough to be usable for most applications.

This paper discusses the CO_2P_3S[1] parallel programming environment, designed specifically to address the performance and generality problems of current parallel programming tools [10, 11]. Three key features of CO_2P_3S contribute to solving these problems: parameterized frameworks, a model that supports multiple layers of abstraction, and a tool that supports the creation of new parallel design pattern templates.

A CO_2P_3S user expresses an application's concurrency by selecting one or more parallel design pattern templates. For each design pattern template, the user selects a series of parameter values that customizes the design pattern template for a specific application. Parameters allow CO_2P_3S to provide general enough design pattern templates to support a wide range of applications, while facilitating the generation of a non-generic efficient code framework. All application-specific code is entered as sequential stubs that are called by the framework.

Most high-level parallel programming tools use a programming model that suffers from a lack of "openness" [16]. The code generated by these tools is often difficult

---

[1]Correct Object-Oriented Pattern-based Parallel Programming System, pronounced "cops".

to tune for performance. In some cases, parts of the code are not available to the user. In other cases, all the code is available, but it is not very human-readable. CO_2P_3S has an open and layered programming model. All of the code is available to the user and it is organized into three layers to make the software architecture understandable at three different levels of abstraction. Performance tuning proceeds from the simplest most abstract top layer to the more detailed lower layers. When sufficient performance is obtained, no further code details need to be learned. This approach provides performance gains that are commensurate with the effort expended.

Current academic tools only support a small number of patterns and, with only a few exceptions, do not allow the creation of new patterns. $MetaCO_2P_3S$ is a graphical design pattern template editor. It supports generality by allowing a pattern designer to both edit existing CO_2P_3S pattern templates and to add completely new pattern templates. New pattern templates are first class in that they are just as general and powerful as the built-in CO_2P_3S patterns. In addition, $MetaCO_2P_3S$ stores pattern templates in an XML format that is independent of CO_2P_3S so they can be used in other parallel programming systems as well. $MetaCO_2P_3S$ also supports performance, by making it easy to design pattern templates with many parameters that can be used to generate efficient code.

This paper makes the following contributions to the evolution of high-level parallel programming environments:

1. CO_2P_3S, a parameterized parallel application development tool that provides a layered programming model with multiple user-accessible abstractions for writing and tuning parallel programs.

2. $MetaCO_2P_3S$, a parallel design pattern development tool. $MetaCO_2P_3S$ supports the development of platform-independent pattern templates that can be imported into CO_2P_3S.

3. The first parallel programming system that supports the creation and usage of tool-independent parallel design patterns.

The CO_2P_3S and $MetaCO_2P_3S$ combination is unique in the parallel computing world. Building a pattern-based parallel programming system is already a difficult task. Ensuring that the same environment can support the addition of new patterns adds further complications. Our community needs a meta-programming tool that enables the creation of new patterns and supports the modification of existing ones. However, we need more than this. If pattern-based programming systems are going to be accepted by the parallel programming community, the patterns must be transferable and re-usable from system to system. This means that the patterns must be expressible in a system-independent

manner, and stored in a central repository. We need "open-patterns" in addition to open-source code. Only in this way can the high-level parallel tools research community create a critical mass of patterns that will interest practitioners. CO_2P_3S and $MetaCO_2P_3S$ is a step towards this vision.

Section 2 presents a sample application that is used throughout the paper. Section 3 describes CO_2P_3S and Section 4 discusses $MetaCO_2P_3S$. Section 5 compares CO_2P_3S and $MetaCO_2P_3S$ to other related systems. Conclusions and future work are presented in Section 6.

2 Case Study: Genetic Sequence Alignment

Throughout this paper, we will use the sequence alignment problem from computational biology to illustrate how CO_2P_3S uses design pattern templates to parallelize applications. This problem is solved by finding an optimal alignment (with respect to a given scoring function) for a pair of DNA or protein sequences [7]. Typical algorithms for sequence alignment construct a dynamic programming matrix with the sequences on the top and left edges. A score is propagated from the top left corner to the bottom right. The value of each entry in the matrix depends on three previously computed values — north or above, west or to the left, and north-west or the above-left diagonal — as shown in Figure 1(a). Once the algorithm has calculated all of the values in the matrix, the maximal cost path (optimal sequence alignment) can be obtained by tracing backwards through the matrix.

This problem was given to a parallel programming expert, who was then asked to parallelize the application using CO_2P_3S. The expert quickly identified a Wavefront parallel design pattern. The Wavefront pattern applies to problems where a computation needs to sweep breadth-first through a tree, with child nodes having data dependencies on their parents. The term *wavefront* describes the edge separating the processed nodes at the top of the tree from the nodes waiting to be processed. The dynamic programming problem is easily expressed as a wavefront due to the dependency of each matrix entry on three neighbors. Figure 1(b) shows how the data dependencies in Figure 1(a) can be transformed to a wavefront computation. Blocks with the same number can be computed concurrently after the blocks with smaller numbers that satisfy the data dependencies have been computed. CO_2P_3S has been used to develop several wavefront-like parallel applications [1].

3 CO_2P_3S

The parallel computing literature is replete with familiar parallel structures. Concepts such as a pipeline, master-slave, work-queue, divide-and-conquer, and wavefront are structures that are well-known to experienced parallel programmers. Each concept immediately conjures up a vision of the concurrency that it represents. A parallel programmer

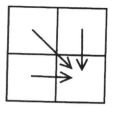 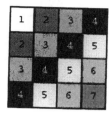

(a) Score propagation. (b) Computation ordering.

Figure 1. Solving the sequence alignment problem with a dynamic programming matrix.

who has used a master-slave structure to solve one application will use that experience to significantly reduce the effort needed to implement another master-slave application. In object-oriented computing, design constructs that can be re-used between applications are often expressed as design patterns [8], which capture design experience at an abstract level. By their nature, design patterns are applicable to different problem domains, each with its own individual characteristics and concerns. A design pattern is a description of a solution to a general design problem that must be adapted for each use. Once a user elects to use a design pattern, most of the basic structure of the application can be inferred.

CO_2P_3S uses object-oriented techniques to simplify parallel programming [10, 11]. Developers begin by identifying the parallel design patterns that describe their application's basic structure. CO_2P_3S takes advantage of this knowledge in a more concrete manner. Specifically, parallel applications that use a similar pattern not only share a design solution, but also have a considerable amount of common code, with only details that vary between applications. CO_2P_3S supports the re-use of this common code by generating a framework of parallel structure code from the selected design pattern. Users then implement their application-specific code within this automatically generated framework that hides the entire parallel infrastructure.

3.1 Frameworks

Frameworks are a set of classes that implement the basic structure of a specific kind of application [9]. This structural code defines the classes in the application and the flow of control through these classes. In general, a user of a framework must subclass the framework classes to provide implementations of key components and compose these classes into an application. In CO_2P_3S, the framework generates placeholders for sequential hook methods that are called by the framework. These methods are the only interface between the application-dependent code and the framework. The user need only implement the few hook methods to

connect the framework to the sequential application code needed to solve the problem.

Frameworks are similar to libraries in some respects. However there is an important difference. When a library is used, a programmer must define the structure of the application and make calls to the library code. Conversely, a framework defines the structure of an application and the programmer supplies code for specific application-dependent routines. Frameworks allow the programmer to reuse the overall design of an application, and capitalize on object-oriented techniques such as encapsulation and code reuse.

We combine frameworks and design patterns by considering the application domain of the framework to be the implementation of a pattern. For instance, consider the description of a Wavefront design pattern. Most wavefront algorithms share the same basic structure with only a few application-dependent properties. We can encapsulate this structure into a framework that implements a basic wavefront. The structural code uses classes that define the application-dependent properties of a wavefront without implementing them, such as the function that computes the value of an element from the value of its predecessors. A user of this wavefront framework supplies these properties by either providing subclasses that contain the needed implementation or by composing framework-supplied classes that modify the basic structure to better fit the application.

3.2 Pattern Templates

It is non-trivial to generate a framework from a design pattern. A design pattern actually represents a family of solutions to a set of related problems. For example, the sequence alignment wavefront problem has specific data dependencies (left, above, and above-left) and the computation shape is an entire rectangular matrix. Other problems can be solved using a Wavefront pattern with different dependencies and a different data shape. It is unreasonable to expect a single design pattern to generate a single code framework that implements a solution to the entire family of problems represented by the design pattern. There appear to be only two options. One option is to specialize the generic design pattern into a series of design patterns that solve specific kinds of problems. However, this approach fails to recognize and take advantage of the common design and code that appears in the specialized patterns and frameworks. The other option is to require a single generic design pattern to generate a single highly-abstracted code framework that can be specialized at run-time using a series of parameter values that describe the application. However, this approach yields code that is complex and inefficient.

The CO_2P_3S solution is to start with a design pattern template instead of a design pattern. A *design pattern template* is a design pattern that has been augmented by a series of parameters whose values span the family of design solutions represented by the design pattern. For example, in the

CO_2P_3S Wavefront design pattern template, two of the parameters are the dependency set and the data shape. This allows the design pattern template to span a large set of application programs while enabling it to generate efficient framework code for each specific application.

CO_2P_3S generates correct framework code from a design pattern description of the program structure. The generated code is specific to the pattern/parameter combination supplied by the user. In contrast, other systems provide the ability to specify the structure with patterns but rely on the user to write application code that matches the specification.

The implementation details of the framework are hidden from the programmer. To change the parallel structure of a program, the user changes a parameter for the pattern template and regenerates the framework code. Although this new framework may introduce additional hook methods that need to be implemented, hooks that were previously implemented are included in the regenerated framework automatically. Alternately, to obtain larger structural changes, the programmer may select a completely different design pattern. In this case, the programmer will need to implement different hook methods; application code will need to be moved from the old hook methods to the new ones.

3.3 A Layered Programming Model

A key aspect of CO_2P_3S is its separation of parallel code from user code. Communication and synchronization constructs are hidden from the user in the generated framework. This helps to prevent the user from writing an incorrect parallel program, and greatly simplifies their implementation effort. To ensure that parallelism hiding does not limit CO_2P_3S users, the programming model is "open", exposing all components of the generated program. CO_2P_3S supports three layers of abstraction, allowing the user to design at a high-level, and move down to lower-levels for performance tuning (if needed).

The *Patterns Layer* promotes the rapid development of structurally correct parallel programs. The user selects a parallel design pattern template from a palette of supported templates. This template represents a family of frameworks for a given design pattern. The user can select the member of this family that is best suited for an application by specifying application–dependent template parameters. Once the parameters have been specified, the template is then used to generate object–oriented framework code implementing the pattern indicated by the template. The result is a correct, functional parallel program. The user supplies the application-dependent hook methods.

The *Intermediate Code Layer* provides a high–level, object–oriented, explicitly-parallel programming language, a superset of an existing object-oriented language. [2] The abstract structural classes are implemented using this lan-

---
[2]Not to be confused with the intermediate code used by compilers.

Figure 2. CO_2P_3S Wavefront pattern template.

guage and are made available to the user. The user can modify the generated structure, write new application code, or tune the structure.

At the *Native Code Layer*, the intermediate language is transformed into code for a native object-oriented language (such as Java or C++). This code provides all libraries used to implement the intermediate code from the previous layer. The user can tailor the libraries for the application requirements or for the execution environment.

The Patterns Layer can be used to quickly build a correct program. The user can then move down to the Intermediate and Native Code Layers to tune the program, if necessary.

3.4 Wavefront Application

Figure 2 shows the main CO_2P_3S window with the Wavefront pattern template selected [1]. Using the pattern window, a CO_2P_3S user can select parameters to customize a pattern template instance so that it matches their application's needs. The Wavefront supports three design parameters and three performance parameters. The design parameters are:

1. The name for the the Wavefront element class.

2. The shape of the element matrix. The default choice is a *full matrix* shape in which all elements of a rectangular matrix are computed. Also supported are *triangular* and *banded* shapes.

3. The dependency set for an element. Figure 1(a) illustrated the dependency set for the sequence alignment application. The user interface prevents a programmer from selecting illegal dependency sets. On the right-hand side of Figure 2, the dependencies graph for the sequence alignment problem is shown.

The performance parameters are:

1. The notification method used to inform elements that a dependency constraint has been satisfied. One choice is to *push* or *pull* the data. Figure 2 shows that the push parameter has been selected.

2. The data type of wavefront elements.

3. Whether the program needs access to non-neighboring elements (not needed for sequence alignment).

In Figure 2, the parameters have been set to the values used for the sequence alignment problem.

The design parameters show the flexibility of the approach, since a large family of different parallel structures can be built from one pattern template. The performance parameters show that the generated code is not generic; they enable the the system to be more specific in the code that is generated, avoiding unnecessary run-time overheads.

After customizing the pattern template by selecting the appropriate set of parameters, the user requests that the framework code be generated. The current pattern templates in CO_2P_3S are configured to generate shared-memory Java code. At the heart of the wavefront implementation is a (hidden) driver that represents the control flow of the parallel code. Figure 3 shows an abstracted version of the wavefront driver. The only class the user implements is the *WavefrontElement* class. This class has three responsibilities: providing an initialization method that is called for each wavefront element (*initialize*), implementing the wavefront operations on a wavefront element (*operateCorner, operateTop, operateLeft, operateInterior*), and supplying a method to be used for reducing the matrix after the computation is complete (*reduce*). The user is supplied with stubs for the appropriate hook methods depending on the parameters specified. The framework invokes the appropriate method based on the location of the element. Each method has appropriate dependent elements as arguments and returns the computed element.

Users are prevented from modifying method signatures. Instead, hyper-links are provided for user-modifiable locations in the code. This is one of the features in the system designed to reduce the chance of programming error.

In Figure 3, note that the generated code skeleton has been specialized to take into account the computation dependencies (above, left, above-left) ensuring that the different cases are called under the right conditions and with the right parameters. This example is intended to emphasize the point that each pattern/parameter combination results in customized code. It also illustrates the need for different layers of abstraction. For example, the code in Figure 3 is non-optimal in the sense that there are far more interior nodes in the matrix than there are corner nodes. Reorganizing the *if* statements to reflect this will result in a (slightly)

```
public void execute(){
    this.initialize();
    while(!queue.isEmpty()){
        /* "work" is a WavefrontElement */
        work = queue.getWork();
        if(work is the corner) /* First element – no neighbors */
            work.operateCorner();
        elsif(work is on top edge) /* Top row – one neighbor */
            work.operateTop(location, leftValue);
        elsif(work is on left edge) /* Left column – one neighbor */
            work.operateLeft(location, aboveValue);
        else /* Interior – three neighbors */
            work.operateInterior(location, aboveValue,
                leftValue, diagonalValue);
    }
    this.reduce();
}
```

Figure 3. Wavefront code skeleton.

faster program. This change cannot be made in the Patterns Layer of CO_2P_3S; the user cannot touch the wavefront driver code. At the Native Code Layer, all the code is exposed to the user, who can then make whatever changes are appropriate. Although this is a trivial example, it does illustrate the need for multiple layers of abstraction in the programming model.

From the pattern designer's point of view, the wavefront can be implemented using a work queue, where nodes at the edge of the wavefront whose data dependencies have been satisfied are available. A user's view into a wavefront framework requires only that they provide the node processing implementation. They need not know about the wavefront driver and how it is implemented. The CO_2P_3S framework includes all the communication and synchronization needed by the application, and automatically divides the matrix into blocks to ensure reasonable granularity. All the user sees is their *initialize, operate,* and *reduce* routines for a single wavefront node.

The Wavefront pattern template in CO_2P_3S was used to implement the dynamic programming matrix algorithm for sequence alignment. Two sequences of 10,000 random proteins each were used as test data. The sequential and parallel implementations of the algorithm were run using a Java 1.3 VM on a four-processor shared-memory SGI O2. The *push* and *pull* notification parameter settings were both used independently as a comparison. The parallel speedups achieved are compared in Figure 4, where each data point is the average over 20 runs. Given a problem large enough to amortize the cost of having a lack of work to do at the beginning and end of a wavefront computation, one would expect to see close to linear speedups.

Given a functional sequential sequence alignment program, a user was able to get the parallel version running using CO_2P_3S in two hours. Of course, this time is not necessarily representative of the cost of doing any application

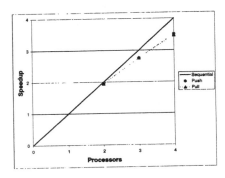

Figure 4. Wavefront speedups.

in CO_2P_3S. Rather it shows that CO_2P_3S has a small learning curve, and that abstraction can have a major impact in the cost of program development. We have performed a user study that confirms these observations [11].

For this particular application, the push/pull choice did not make a significant difference in performance. Was this obvious in advance? The ability to change a fundamental property of the parallelism – pushing versus pulling data – without the user having to write any additional code is a powerful capability. The user can experiment with different parameter combinations to find the settings that offer the best performance. Once this is done, the user then can move to the Intermediate or Native Code Layers of CO_2P_3S to do further performance tuning (e.g., modifying the default blocking algorithm to improve the granularity).

To summarize, compared to previous pattern-based parallel programming efforts performance can be enhanced by:

1. A layered programming model, with the appropriate code exposed to the user at each level. This gives the user the ability to design, develop, test, and experiment at the highest level of abstraction, and move to lower layers of abstraction (if needed) to make incremental improvements.

2. Generalized patterns—pattern templates—that can be customized by parameters. The code generated by a parameter setting is tailored to that particular setting, avoiding the overhead of generic code.

4 MetaCO$_2$P$_3$S

Before the sequence alignment program could be implemented in CO_2P_3S a new parallel design pattern template had to be added. MetaCO$_2$P$_3$S is a tool that supports adding new pattern templates to CO_2P_3S. Any design-pattern-based tool will be limited by the set of patterns that it supports. With most of the parallel pattern-based tools in the literature, if a user's application does not match the suite of patterns available in the tool, then the tool is effectively useless. Programmers are unlikely to invest effort

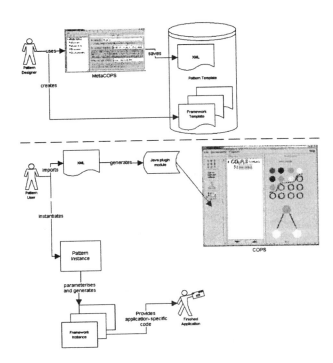

Figure 5. CO$_2$P$_3$S and MetaCO$_2$P$_3$S.

learning an environment that may not meet their needs on future projects.

To address the extensibility problem, we created MetaCO$_2$P$_3$S to enable parallel and object-oriented programming experts, called *pattern designers*, to create new pattern templates. The new pattern templates are *first-class*, meaning they are indistinguishable in form and equivalent in function to the pattern templates included with CO_2P_3S. The tool simplifies the task of building pattern templates. In particular, it facilitates the parameterization and code generation for the templates.

It is the responsibility of the pattern designer to identify new design patterns. This involves isolating a recurring pattern and the various forms that it can take based on pattern parameters, then creating a framework that hides the parallelism details. The designer should take note of the aspects of the framework that are affected by different parameter settings. At this point, the pattern is ready to be formalized as a pattern template using MetaCO$_2$P$_3$S. Analogous to the manner in which CO_2P_3S makes it easier to write parallel programs using pattern templates, MetaCO$_2$P$_3$S makes it easier to write pattern templates for CO_2P_3S.

The following sections provide a summary of the pattern template creation process for CO_2P_3S. Figure 5 illustrates the MetaCO$_2$P$_3$S design process and how this information is used in CO_2P_3S. A more thorough explanation of the process is available in [5].

4.1 Pattern Template Creation with MetaCO$_2$P$_3$S

MetaCO$_2$P$_3$S is launched from the CO$_2$P$_3$S GUI and guides the pattern designer through the pattern template creation process. The pattern designer is required to supply three kinds of information to MetaCO$_2$P$_3$S: class names, parameters, and GUI configuration information.

For each class in the pattern template's framework, a placeholder *class name* must be supplied. Since multiple instances of a single pattern template can be used in a CO$_2$P$_3$S application, the placeholder names are replaced by unique run-time names in framework instances. This is achieved by requiring that CO$_2$P$_3$S users provide at least one user class name for their pattern template instances. The remainder of the framework classes are uniquely named by adding suffixes or prefixes to the user-supplied class name.

There are three types of *parameters* that can affect the framework implementation of a pattern template. Basic parameters are the most common, and consist of an enumerated list of choices supplied by the pattern designer. Extended parameters deal with the less common case where the parameter value is of an arbitrary form. Extended list parameters handle the situation wherein the CO$_2$P$_3$S user supplies a list of values, which may in turn be basic or extended parameters.

The user also has to supply the *GUI configuration*. Figure 2 shows a graphical representation of a CO$_2$P$_3$S pattern template. The GUI configuration section of MetaCO$_2$P$_3$S simplifies the specification of what to display and where.

4.2 Framework Generation

Given a pattern template and a specific parameterization, CO$_2$P$_3$S generates an appropriate object-oriented framework instance. The pattern designer must create a framework template to define the code to be generated for the pattern template. It is the pattern designer's responsibility to ensure that the framework template is set up correctly for code generation, and that the generated frameworks are error-free. An annotated source code template must be written for each of the classes in the framework. The annotations supply the information needed to make the following transformations during framework generation:

- Placeholder class names in the annotated source files must be replaced with the unique names that are supplied by the CO$_2$P$_3$S user.

- Methods or variables may be selectively generated based on the user's basic parameter settings. The pattern designer must specify the combination of parameter settings that allow a given construct to be generated.

- Portions of method bodies may be selectively generated based on the basic parameter settings.

- New methods or sections of method bodies may be generated based on extended or list parameter settings.

- The pattern designer must select at least one framework class that the CO$_2$P$_3$S user can use to add application-specific code. Annotations must be supplied to allow CO$_2$P$_3$S to generate a non-modifiable version of the class, with hyper-links in the user modifiable locations.

4.3 Pattern Template Creation

The pattern descriptions created by MetaCO$_2$P$_3$S are in a system-independent XML format. Pattern designers can also store partially completed pattern descriptions in this format for later completion. A DTD file comes with CO$_2$P$_3$S that describes the format of the XML pattern description file.

When a completed pattern description is imported into CO$_2$P$_3$S, the XML is converted into a compiled plug-in module. XSL is used to transform the pattern description into a Java source file, which is subsequently compiled and loaded into CO$_2$P$_3$S. Since the XML file is system-independent, it can be used in template-based environments other than CO$_2$P$_3$S.

Javadoc is a tool included with the Java distribution whose original purpose was to generate API documentation for Java libraries in HTML. Javadoc runs a modified Java compiler on Java source code files to parse the declarations and specially formatted comments. Javadoc comments have the following format:

```
/**
 * A description
 *
 * @sampleTag a tag that is parsed by Javadoc
 */
public void sampleJavaDeclaration()
```

Javadoc was eventually extended to allow pluggable *doclets*. Doclets are Java programs that satisfy a contract allowing them to receive the parsed data from a given Javadoc execution. This data includes the declarations from each of the parsed classes. Method bodies and field initializations are not provided, since Javadoc ignores them.

CO$_2$P$_3$S framework generation is a source code to source code transformation. There are two inputs to the process. One is a set of Java source code files that have been annotated by the pattern designer for use by Javadoc. The other is the pattern template parameters selected by a CO$_2$P$_3$S user. We have created special tags for the pattern designer, to allow for each of the transformations mentioned in Section 4.2. Default method bodies are provided in separate files, since they are not parsed by Javadoc. The output is a framework instance that has been specialized to match pattern template parameter settings.

4.4 Wavefront Revisited

Since no Wavefront pattern template was available in CO$_2$P$_3$S for the sequence alignment problem, we had an opportunity to use MetaCO$_2$P$_3$S to create a new pattern template. Our parallel programming expert had no involvement in the research on MetaCO$_2$P$_3$S, which also made this exercise a test-bed for the usability of our tool. The following section provides a detailed description of the steps taken by our expert to create the Wavefront pattern template.

The first step was to specify the pattern description using MetaCO$_2$P$_3$S. After launching the tool, the pattern designer named the new Wavefront pattern template and supplied an icon to identify the pattern in CO$_2$P$_3$S. Next, the placeholder framework class names were supplied. One of these, called *WavefrontElement*, was selected as a class to be named by the user. Eight other framework classes were defined, the names of which were made dependent on *WavefrontElement* for their uniqueness, with prefixes and/or suffixes added to indicate their role in the framework. The placeholder class names defined in the pattern description are used to supply run-time names to the code generator.

All the parameters that impact the generated code were specified through the MetaCO$_2$P$_3$S GUI. This was an iterative process. Initially, a parameter set was chosen that met the needs of a specific application (sequence alignment in this case). Later on, as new applications arose that required wavefront parallelism, the pattern was generalized by modifying existing parameters and adding new parameters. MetaCO$_2$P$_3$S provides an interface that facilitates this process, and reduces the likelihood of the pattern designer introducing an error. The result is a Wavefront pattern template that has been used in three different applications [1].

The last step in the pattern description process was providing a GUI configuration (the result is shown in Figure 2). At the top, a textual element is displayed that automatically updates to display the user name for the *WavefrontElement* class. In MetaCO$_2$P$_3$S, the pattern designer needed to provide the location for the text, and the framework class name to display. Below the class name is an image of a wavefront. The pattern designer provided the location and image name. The image below the wavefront and the text element below that are both dynamic representations of the value of the *notification* parameter. Using MetaCO$_2$P$_3$S, the pattern designer defined the images to be used for *push* and *pull* to match the possible values of the parameter.

After providing the pattern description in MetaCO$_2$P$_3$S, the pattern designer needed to provide annotated framework source code for each of the defined classes. This was similar to writing normal Java source code, with a few exceptions:

- Some methods were tagged using Javadoc to be conditionally generated based on a parameter value.

- In the *WavefrontElement* class, some methods were tagged to allow them to be edited by the CO$_2$P$_3$S user.

- Since Javadoc does not parse method bodies, the pattern designer saved them to separate files named after

the method signature. Portions of some methods were set apart to generate for a particular parameter setting.

At this point, the pattern template was completely specified. The pattern designer imported it into the CO$_2$P$_3$S environment, and tested the pattern template prior to implementing the sequence alignment program. The pattern template creation took only a few hours.

To test the coverage and correctness of MetaCO$_2$P$_3$S, we tried to regenerate each of the pattern templates from the original CO$_2$P$_3$S. Every pattern template has been successfully regenerated, and the new standard CO$_2$P$_3$S distribution is the one generated by MetaCO$_2$P$_3$S.

4.5 Pattern Template Repository

For CO$_2$P$_3$S (or any other pattern-based tool) to be accepted as a viable environment for writing parallel programs, its pattern templates must cover a wide variety of parallel problems. If pattern-based programming is to have the impact in the parallel world that it is having in the sequential world, then our community needs to have "open-patterns" (analogous to open-source code). Only in this way can the high-level parallel tools research community create a critical mass of patterns that will interest practitioners. Since MetaCO$_2$P$_3$S enables the creation of new pattern templates, the coverage can be made arbitrarily wide. To facilitate the sharing of pattern templates, we propose that a repository be created. Since the pattern templates consist only of XML and Java files, they are system-independent, and can easily be packaged in a downloadable format for distribution on the Internet.

Another advantage to a central repository is the ability it provides for pattern templates to be refined as new problems identify undiscovered parameters or implementation possibilities. Our Wavefront pattern template went through several such iterations as we applied it to additional applications. For example, when implementing the matrix product chain application, we discovered the need to access non-neighboring elements in the matrix [1]. Our original pattern template did not support this. The modification was accomplished by adding a new parameter to the pattern template, and specifying the effect that this new parameter had on the generated framework code. The Wavefront pattern template has also been copied and modified in the repository by a researcher to generate framework code that runs on a network of workstations rather than a shared-memory machine.

5 Related Work

Although many research groups have studied parallel template-based programming environments, few have addressed the need for extensibility. Most of these environments are not suited for extension. One exception is the DPnDP distributed message-passing programming environment [17]. Like CO$_2$P$_3$S, DPnDP design patterns are modular, and support a pluggable library. However, DPnDP does not provide a tool for creating new patterns, but rather specifies a C++ framework under which patterns can be built. Patterns created using DPnDP can have only a structural specification; all behavioral aspects, such as communication and synchronization, must be supplied by the DPnDP user. However, the patterns supplied with DPnDP automatically implement any pattern-specific behaviors. Therefore, new patterns may not have the same level of functionality and abstraction as those provided with DPnDP.

Another environment that provides template extensibility is Tracs [3]. It provides a tool that allows pattern designers to define architectural models using a formal graph to specify task and communication structures. The architectural model does not include a framework implementation.

Automatic code generation has been studied by many groups with different agendas. Given our parameterization needs and language choice, we took our inspiration from [12, 14]. Also, we studied the COGENT code generator [6], which uses macro expansion to generate framework code for sequential design patterns.

6 Conclusions

In this paper, two obstacles to the widespread acceptance of high-level parallel programming tools are addressed. Although this represents an important step forward towards moving these tools from academia into practice, much work remains to be done.

Performance is an issue with every parallel tool, and this has been particularly acute with high-level parallel programming models. CO_2P_3S resolves many of the performance issues through the use of parameterized parallel design pattern templates, a layered model of abstraction, and a tool to manage the complexities of creating/modifying patterns. The performance will, in part, be constrained by the quality of the code generated by the pattern template. If the ideas presented in this paper catch on, then the community can work towards highly optimizing this process to ensure the best possible performance.

This paper discusses how extensibility, critically lacking in all template-based systems, can be addressed. We have created both a parallel pattern template builder and a structure for framework templates. Our tool generates pattern templates that are first-class, and integrate seamlessly with CO_2P_3S. Through system-independence we have enabled the creation of a pattern template repository. The best chance for making pattern-based parallel programming a reality in practice rests upon whether the research community can work towards realizing the pattern repository vision, regardless of whether CO_2P_3S or $MetaCO_2P_3S$ is used.

Acknowledgments

This research was supported by NSERC and iCORE.

References

[1] J. Anvik, S. MacDonald, D. Szafron, J. Schaeffer, S. Bromling, and K. Tan. Generating parallel programs from the wavefront design pattern. In *HIPS'02*, 2002. On CD-ROM.

[2] B. Bacci, M. Danelutto, S. Orlando, S. Pelagatti, and M. Vanneschi. P^3L: a Structured High–level Parallel Language, and its Structured Support. *Concurrency: Practice and Experience*, 7(3):225–255, 1995.

[3] A. Bartoli, P. Corsini, G. Dini, and C. Prete. Graphical Design of Distributed Applications Through Reusable Components. *Parallel & Distributed Technology*, 3(1):37–51, 1995.

[4] A. Beguelin, J. Dongarra, A. Geist, R. Manchek, and K. Moore. HeNCE: A Heterogeneous Network Computing Environment. Technical Report UT-CS-93-205, Univ. of Tenessee, 1993.

[5] S. Bromling. Meta-programming with parallel design patterns. Master's thesis, Dept. of Computing Science, Univ. of Alberta, 2001.

[6] F. Budinsky, M. Finnie, J. Vlissides, and P. Yu. Automatic Code Generation from Design Patterns. *IBM Systems Journal*, 35(2):151–171, 1996.

[7] K. Charter, J. Schaeffer, and D. Szafron. Sequence Alignment using FastLSA. In *METMBS'2000*, pages 239–245, 2000.

[8] E. Gamma, R. Helm, R. Johnson, and J. Vlissides. *Design Patterns: Elements of Reusable Object-Oriented Software*. Addison-Wesley, 1995.

[9] R. Johnson. Frameworks = (Components + Patterns). *Communications of the ACM*, 40(10):39–42, Oct. 1997.

[10] S. MacDonald. *From Patterns to Frameworks to Parallel Programs*. PhD thesis, Dept. of Computing Science, Univ. of Alberta, Nov. 2001. Available at www.cs.ualberta.ca/~systems.

[11] S. MacDonald, D. Szafron, J. Schaeffer, and S. Bromling. From Patterns to Frameworks to Parallel Programs. *Parallel Computing*, 2002. To appear.

[12] F. Matthijs, W. Joosen, B. Robben, B. Vanhaute, and P. Verbaeten. Multi–level Patterns. In *Object–Oriented Technology (ECOOP'97)*, volume 1357 of *LNCS*, pages 112–115. Springer–Verlag, 1998.

[13] P. Newton and J. Browne. The CODE 2.0 Graphical Parallel Programming Language. In *ACM International Conference on Supercomputing*, pages 167–177, 1992.

[14] M. Pollack. Code Generation using Javadoc. http://www.javaworld.com/javaworld/jw-08-2000/ jw-0818-javadoc_p.html, Aug. 2000.

[15] J. Schaeffer, D. Szafron, G. Lobe, and I. Parsons. The Enterprise Model for Developing Distributed Applications. *Parallel & Distributed Technology*, 1(3):85–96, 1993.

[16] A. Singh, J. Schaeffer, and D. Szafron. Experience with Parallel Programming Using Code Templates. *Concurrency: Practice & Experience*, 10(2):91–120, 1998.

[17] S. Siu. Openness and Extensibility in Design–Pattern–Based Programming Systems. Master's thesis, Dept. of Electrical and Computer Engineering, Univ. of Waterloo, Aug. 1996.

[18] S. Siu, M. D. Simone, D. Goswami, and A. Singh. Design Patterns for Parallel Programming. In *PDPTA'96*, pages 230–240, 1996.

WebGOP: A Framework for Architecting and Programming Dynamic Distributed Web Applications

Jiannong Cao[1], Xiaoxing Ma[1,2], Alvin T.S. Chan[1], Jian Lu[1,2]

[1]Internet Computing and E-Commerce Lab.
Dept. of Computing, Hong Kong Polytechnic University, Hung Hom, Kowloon, Hong Kong
[2]SKLNST, Institute of Computer Software, Nanjing University, Nanjing, China
{csjcao, csxma, cstschan, csjlu}@comp.polyu.edu.hk

Abstract

This paper presents a novel approach, called WebGOP, for architecture modeling and programming of web-based distributed applications. WebGOP uses the graph-oriented programming (GOP) mode, under which the components of a distributed program are configured as a logical graph and implemented using a set of operations defined over the graph. WebGOP extends the application of GOP to the World Wide Web environment and provides more powerful architectural support. In WebGOP, the architecture graph is reified as an explicit object which itself is distributed over the network, providing a graph-oriented context for the execution of distributed applications. The programmer can specialize the type of a graph to represent a particular architecture style tailored for an application. WebGOP also has built-in support for flexible and dynamic architectures, including both planed and unplanned dynamic reconfiguration of distributed applications. We describe the WebGOP framework, a prototypical implementation of the framework on top of SOAP, and performance evaluation of the prototype. Results of the performance evaluation showed that the overhead introduced by WebGOP over SOAP is reasonable and acceptable.

1. Introduction

With the increasing popularity of the Internet and the World Wide Web, more and more web-based distributed systems and applications are built to provide information and business services. Distributed applications are believed to be more complex and difficult to build than centralized applications. Distributed web applications can be even harder to develop because of the underlying dynamic changing network environment, diverse user preferences and ever-evolving functional requirements. Distributed web applications often have dynamic behavior to process new types of information and interact with new environments. They often have to be scalable because of their open user groups. And they should have a flexible internal architecture to support such dynamism and scalability.

How to model and implement flexible and efficient distributed web applications remains a big challenge. One of the promising technologies emerging in software engineering is software architecture. Software architecture, which specifies a software system in terms of its components and the interactions among those components [1], can be a powerful tool to aid the prediction of the system behavior and the management of the system development and maintenance [2]. To build well-defined software architecture for complex distributed web applications, high-level abstract models are required to simplify the architectural design and programming. Underlying middleware support is also needed for component interactions under these models. In this paper, we present a framework for architecting distributed applications that address the above issues. The framework, named WebGOP, adopts a novel approach based on the Graph-Oriented Programming (GOP) model, which was originally proposed as an abstract model for distributed programming [3]. WebGOP extends the application of GOP to the Web environment, providing more powerful programming support for software architecture.

It's GOP's vision that distributed programs can be modeled as a group of functional components coordinating with one another over a logical graph, which depicts the architectural configuration and inter-component communication pattern of the application. Using a message-passing library such as sockets, PVM[4] or MPI [5], the programmer needs to manually translate the graph model into its implementation using low-level primitives. With the GOP model, such a graph metaphor is made explicit in the programming of the distributed system because GOP directly supports the graph construct. By directly using the logical graph construct, the components of a distributed program are configured as a logical graph and implemented using a set of operations defined over the graph. Configuration specification can be separated from the programming of functional components as the naming, communication and cooperation among the components are expressed in terms of graphs.

In WebGOP, the concept of software architecture is reified as an explicit graph object, which provides a locus for addressing architectural issues, separated from programming of the functional components. The WebGOP approach has the following advantages for distributed Web application development. First, the system architecture design can be simplified with the graph abstraction and predefined graph types. Second, the separation of architecture issues from component programming makes the architecture easier to understand and the application easier to reconfigure. It also benefits the reusability of both the components and the architecture. Third, by eliminating direct component referencing, the graph abstraction can be used to make a further decoupling between interacting components, which facilitates the construction of dynamic architectures [9]. With the architecture graph object and the built-in graph-update facilities, dynamic reconfiguration [7][14] of a distributed Web application can be achieved in a reflective way.

A prototype of WebGOP has been developed. It provides both communication middleware support for the interactions of the components of distributed web applications and a graph-oriented framework for the architecture modeling and programming. With the prototype, several example applications have been developed to demonstrate the feasibility of our approach. We also evaluated the performance of several importance aspects of this prototype. The results show that the overhead introduced by WebGOP is reasonable and acceptable.

The rest of the paper is organized as follows: Section 2 introduces the basic GOP model. Section 3 discusses the development of distributed web applications with the WebGOP programming model. A prototype implementation of WebGOP is presented in Section 4. Performance evaluation results of the prototype are described in Section 5. Section 6 describes related work. Finally, in Section 7, we make conclusions and point the directions for our future work.

2. Graph Oriented Programming Model

In GOP [3], a distributed program is defined as a collection of *local programs* (LPs) that may execute on several *processors*. Parallelism is expressed through explicit creation of LPs and communication between LPs is solely via message passing. GOP allows programmers to write distributed programs based on user-specified *graphs*, which can serve the purpose of naming, grouping and configuring LPs, and/or can be used as the underlying structure for implementing uniform message passing and LP co-ordination mechanisms. As illustrated in Figure 1, the GOP model consists of

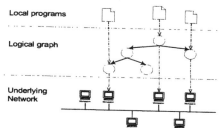

Figure 1: GOP conceptual model

- a *logical graph* (directed or undirected), whose nodes are associated with local programs (LPs), and whose edges define the relationships amongst the LPs.
- a *LPs-to-nodes mapping*, which allows the programmer to bind LPs to specific nodes,
- an optional *nodes-to-processors mapping*: which allows the programmer to explicitly specify the mapping of the logical graph to the underlying network of processors.
- a library of language-level graph-oriented programming primitives.

The programmer first defines variables of the graph construct in a program and then creates an instance of the construct. Once the local context for the graph instance is set up, communication and coordination of LP's can be implemented by invoking operations defined on the specified graph. GOP allows the programmer to exploit the semantics of the graph construct to deal with various aspects of distributed programming. The operations on a user-specified graph can be categorized into several classes

- *Communication and Synchronization.* These operations provide various forms of communication primitives that can be used to pass messages from one node to one or more other nodes in the graph. These primitives can be used by the LPs associated with the nodes to communicate with each other and to synchronize their operations without knowing the low-level details such as name resolution, addressing and routing.
- *Subgraph generation.* These operations derive subgraphs such as the shortest path between two nodes and spanning trees of a graph.
- *Query.* These operations provide information about the graph, such as the number of nodes in a graph, current location of a LP, and whether an edge exists between two nodes.

● *Update.* These operations provide the programmer with the capability to dynamically insert into and/or delete from a graph edges and nodes.

The GOP model has the desirable features of expressiveness and simple semantics. It provides high-level abstractions for programming distributed programs, easing the expression of parallelism, configuration, communication and coordination by directly supporting logical graph operations. Furthermore, sequential programming constructs blend smoothly and easily with distributed constructs in GOP [3][6].

Although the abstract GOP model itself is language and platform independent, our WebGOP is implemented as a Java library. In the rest of the paper, Java-like syntax will be used for presentation of WebGOP interfaces and primitives.

3. The WebGOP framework

In this section we discuss how WebGOP can be used to support architecture modeling and programming for distributed Web application systems. We also address the issues of supporting flexible and dynamic architectures, showing how dynamic reconfiguration of distributed web applications can be achieved in WebGOP.

To illustrate the proposed approach, we use an example application with a Master-Slave architecture consisting of a master node and a set of slave nodes. Such a situation is not uncommon in the real world. For example, in a large enterprise there can be a master server running in the headquarters and multiple regional branch servers distributed across the Internet. Among many functionalities of the application system, the headquarters server may publish business policies for all the regional servers, as well as concurrently initiate query operations on the regional servers for the purpose of, say, data mining.

3.1 Architecture Modeling and Programming

Traditionally, architectures are represented informally as "box and line" drawings. Such drawings however are merely visual aids for understanding. With WebGOP constructs, the designer is required to formally specify the logical graph construct. Figure 2 shows a partial slice of the interface to the graph abstractions in WebGOP. The API includes class definitions for the graph, nodes, edges, as well as WebGOP runtime, together with support operation routines.

With the WebvGOP abstractions, the topology of the graph is precisely specified as a set of nodes and a set of directed edges linking these nodes. For example, a graph depicting a Master-Slave architecture, as shown in Figure 3, is declared as follows:

```
Node master = new Node("Master"),
Node slave1=new Node("Slave1"), ...,
     slave4=new Node("Slave4");
Edge e1 = new Edge(slave1, master),  ... ,
     e4 = new (slave4,master);
```

```
class Graph{     //the logical graph
    // specify a graph
    Graph(String name,Node nodes[],Edge[]
edges);
    // communication primitives
    //unicast
    Usend(Node dest, Message msg);
    Urecv(Node src, Message buf);
    //multicast
    Msend(NodeGroup dests, Message msg);
    Mrecv(NodeGroup srcs, Message[] buf);
    //anycast
    Asend(NodeGroup dests, Message msg);
    Arecv(NodeGroup srcs, Message buf);
    //graph update
    addNode(Node node);
    addEdge(Edge edge);
    delNode(Node node);
    delEdge(Edge edge);
    // bind
    bindLPtoLocalNode(LocalProgram lp);
    unbindLO
    // query and subgraph generation
    ... ...
};

class Node{...}; //graph node
class Edge{    //graph edge
    Edge(Node start, Node end);
    ...
};
class Message{...};//message
class Processor{...};
Interface LocalProgram{...};
class WebGopRuntime{
    static void deployGraph(Graph graph,
Processor[] procs);
    static void deployNode(Node node,
Processor proc);
    static Graph getGraph(String name);
    ...
};
```

Figure 2. Partial WebGOP class definitions

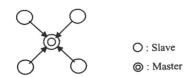

O : Slave

◎ : Master

Figure 3. A simple M/S architecture

```
Graph mygraph = new Graph ("MyGraph",
     {master, slave1, slave2, slave3, slave4},
     {e1, e2, e3, e4 } );
```

In this graph, the master node sits in the center, slaves are distributed around the center, and there is an edge linking each slave to the master.

To deploy the graph, the mapping of the logical graph nodes to the physical processor nodes must be determined. It can be automatically determined by the WebGOP runtime system, or explicitly specified by the programmer. With our example, the mapping is specified as follows:

```
WebGOPRuntime.deployGraph(mygraph,
  { headquarters,
      region1, region2, region3, region4} );
```

where "headquarters" is the reference to the "*Processor*" at the headquarters server and "region*k*" is the "*Processor*" of the *k*th regional server.

Once the graph is deployed, the information about the graph becomes available to WebGOP runtime at each processor for setting up the local execution context for the application. Suppose we have a local program, called "masterLP", running on the master node, and a local program, called "slaveLP", running on the slave nodes. The following statements setup the local context on the headquarters server:

```
// get the graph instance
Graph mygraph =
    WebGOPRuntime.getGraph("MyGraph");
//create a MasterLP instance
LocalProgram masterLP = new MasterLP(...);
// bind masterLP to local node "Master"
mygraph.bindLPtoLocalNode(masterLP);
```

To set up the local context on each regional server, the following statements will be executed:

```
// get the graph instance;
Graph mygraph =
    WebGOPRuntime.getGraph("MyGraph");
//create a SlaveLP instance
LocalProgram slaveLP = new SlaveLP(...);
// bind it to local Node
mygraph.bindLPtoLocalNode(slaveLP);
```

The LPs may be wrapped prefabricated software components or specialized software built from scratch.

LPs can use graph-oriented primitives provided by WebGOP for communications and synchronization. The basis for the graph-oriented communication is the reference to nodes and edges. WebGOP provides built-in references including precedents, successors, closure of precedents, and closure of successors. For example, in mygraph, the "Precedents" of the master are the slave nodes, and the "Successors" of the slaves is the master node. The programmer can also derive new references by carrying out set computations on existing references. For example, reference to neighbor nodes can be derived from the union of the precedents and successors as follows:

```
NodeGroup Neighbors =
```

```
    NodeGroup.union(Precedents, Successors);
```

To further enhance the expressiveness of the graph-oriented reference, a mark and query mechanism is provided. Nodes and edges can be marked with labels that are key-value pairs. New references can be obtained by query on the specified labels.

For communications between the LPs, a set of message passing primitives, including unicast, multicast and anycast, are provided. For example, the master LP may multicast the business policies information to the slave LPs running on the precedent nodes:

```
mygraph.Msend (Precedents, businessPolicy);
```

It can also multicast a message containing a query to all slave LPs, and then wait for the results to come back:

```
mygraph.Msend (Precedents, queryExpression);
mygraph.Mrecv (Precedents, queryResultBuffer);
```

On the other hand, a slave LP can receive the commands from the master LP running on its succeeding node, process the commands, and send back results if required:

```
mygraph.Arecv (Successors, commandBuffer);
if (command is BusinessPolicy) {
    // Apply the Policy
} else if (command is QueryExpression){
    // process the query ...
    mygraph.Asend(Successors, queryResult);
} else if (...) {...} // something else.
```

The class Graph is too general in the sense that it simply specifies the topological configuration of a distributed application in generic terms. It is difficult to express more specific semantics and constrains on a particular architecture. To solve this problem, WebGOP allows the programmer to derive new graph types from the base Graph type, and implement a specific architecture as a specialized graph, such as a "tree" or a "ring" with predefined WebGOP primitives. Specialized graphs provide more architecture-specific semantics information and functionality. For example, for a tree graph, there is one and only one root node and there is not any circle. More specific references, such as parent, children, siblings, and root can be provided for tree nodes. Specialized architecture behaviors are defined in this new graph class and grouped as different interfaces for different nodes of the graph.

For our example, a new graph type, named Star, can be derived as a subclass of Graph:

```
class Star extends Graph
    implements I_Center, I_Leaf
  {... ...};
```

where I_Center and I_Leaf are the interfaces of the star type for the center node and leaf nodes respectively. This graph type will restrict the topology to a star consisting of a center node, a number of leaf nodes, and each leaf node is linked by an edge to the center.

With this new type, local programs can directly use intuitive, architecture-specific communication operations defined in their specific interfaces. In our example, the Master LP at the center makes use of the operations declared in interface I_Center, such as

```
sendToLeaves( queryExpression );
recvFromLeaves( queryResultBuffer );
```

and the slave LPs can use the operations declared in interface I_Leaf, such as

```
recvFromCenter( queryExpBuffer );
sendToCenter( queryResults );
```

As we can see, with WebGOP, the architecture of a distributed application is reified as a runtime graph object. In addition to implementing the topological configuration of the architecture, this specialized graph object also implements architectural behaviors and constraints. The interactions among the components are intermediated by this object, which provide the programmer with a locus for the explicit implementation of constraints on the interactions. For example, the interface I_Leaf of the star object does not provide the leaf LP any operation to communicate with other leaf nodes, which reflects the constraint that leaves in a star are not expected to talk with each other directly. With the interface I_Center, however, the center node is allowed to communicate with all leaves. Many of the constraints can be enforced by the type system of the programming languages. Constraints that cannot be checked statically can be enforced by the graph object at runtime. For example, a node LP may be required to invoke a receive operation after each send operation. Even some global invariants, such as "there should be one and only one token in a token ring architecture", can be implemented as runtime assertions in the graph object.

3.2 Support for dynamic reconfiguration

Web-based distributed applications demand for the ability to dynamically change the system configuration to adapt to the evolving environment and user requirements. WebGOP provides support for dynamic reconfiguration.

Generally, the configuration of a distributed system specifies the system with a) a set of component types; b) the set of component instances of these component types that make up the system; c) the interconnections among the component instances that specify their interactions; d) the mapping of the component instances to the underlying hosts [7][8]. Thus the configuration is roughly corresponding to the concept of software architecture, and dynamic reconfigurable software systems are sometimes called systems with "dynamic architectures" [9].

There are two classes of reconfigurations: planned and unplanned. In the Web environment, software applications often have to process a variety of content types (cf. MIME) so they often dynamically load in corresponding components to process the content.

Distributed web applications also often require dynamic changes in its structure. For example, additional processing nodes may be needed to share the increasing workload. These changes on the system configuration can be anticipated by the programmer and programmed as built-in functionalities. However, there are some unanticipated situations unveiling after the system has been put into operation. For example, we need to remove a node when it fails. Therefore, the system is required to adapt to the needs that have not been accounted for in the original design.

One way to achieve reconfiguration is to have the system shut down, rebuilt, reloaded, and restarted. However, this approach may not work sometimes if it is not allowed or too expensive to completely shutdown the system just for changing a part of it. Dynamic reconfiguration evolves the system without shutting it down. By making the unaffected part of the system continue its operation during the reconfiguration, dynamic reconfiguration techniques help improve system availability.

WebGOP provides support for both planned and unplanned dynamic reconfigurations. First, the graph object decouples the local programs. In terms of configuration, these local programs do not share any information except the graph. They neither directly refer to each other for interactions, and each local program communicates with the rest of the system solely through the interface defined by the graph object. This decoupling makes it possible to make changes to some local programs without affecting other running local programs. Second, the graph object explicitly maintains the current configuration information and provides a collection of query primitives, which can be used to determine the current configuration and identify what must be changed. Third, since the architecture issues are explicitly expressed and managed by the graph object, the scope of the changes can be limited to the graph object and to those nodes that are directly involved. Fourth, with WebGOP abstractions, the changes are described at a high level in terms of a graph, making them easier to understand and manage. At the same time, the predefined graph update primitives facilitate the implementation of the changes. Finally, by reifying the architecture as an object in the system, the runtime evolvement of the architecture can be naturally implemented using polymorphism of graph objects, which suggests a rather systematic way to design and implement dynamic reconfiguration.

I. Programming dynamic architectures with graph updating primitives

WebGOP provides built-in graph update primitives for changing the configuration of a distributed application system built with WebGOP. With these primitives, developers can build flexible architectures for distributed applications conveniently.

Let's return to our example. The master may dynamically add slaves to or remove slaves from the current system configuration according to the current workload. This requires the star graph type to have operations for dynamically adding or removing the leaves (see Figure 4). The operations are declared in the I_Center interface as

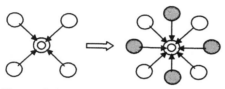

Figure 4. Add new leaves to the star

```
addLeaf(String leafName);
removeLeaf(String leafName);
```

and implemented in the class star. To add a leaf node, one may first create a new node, and then link it to the center node with an edge:

```
Node newLeaf = new Node(leafName);
Edge newEdge = new Edge(newLeaf, center);
Graph.addNode(newLeaf);
Graph.addEdge(newEdge);
WebGOPRuntime.deployNode(newLeaf);
```

With these operations, the star architecture becomes a flexible one, whose topology can be dynamically changed. The resulting graph, however, must remain to be a star, which is a constraint that governs the reconfiguration.

II. Programming unplanned dynamical reconfiguration

With the graph update primitives of WebGOP, unplanned configuration changes can be specified in a straightforward way. However, the most difficult issue is how to ensure the consistency and correctness of the application system during dynamic reconfiguration. WebGOP helps Based on the observation that dynamic reconfigurations can be thought of as evolutionary changes to the target application system, WebGOP treats unplanned reconfiguration itself as new behavior of the application, and achieves reconfigurations by specifying and deriving new architecture behavior of the application.

Since architecture behaviors are implemented in graph types, a new architecture behavior is obtained by deriving new graph types. The new graph type is derived from the current graph type, with the behavior redefined or enhanced. The new configuration of the application can then be achieved from the current configuration by applying the architecture behaviors implemented in the new graph type.

More specifically, in WebGOP, the dynamic reconfiguration process proceeds as follows. First, a new graph type generalizing the original graph type is developed. The original graph object represents the current configuration. The new graph type contains basic evolution behaviors, which specify the minimum steps that translate the configuration from one valid state to another. Using the basic evolution behaviors, an evolution path leading to the specified new configuration is also designed. The WebGOP runtime creates a graph object of the new graph type, initializing it with the current graph object, and redirects the graph object reference used by dependent LPs to the new graph object. Then the evolution path is gradually carried out until the specified new configuration (and new system behavior) is reached.

To certain extend, distributed applications build with WebGOP is reflective because the graph object, which represents the architecture of the application, is an integral part of this application. Reflection makes the dynamic reconfiguration of the architecture easier - architectural changes can be naturally modeled and implemented as the polymorphism of the graph objects.

Let us illustrate the approach with our example. Assume that, as more and more slave nodes are added to the system, the Master itself finally becomes overloaded. Thus we need to add a new Master node into the system. This situation is not foreseen by the system designer and cannot be directly programmer in the system. To handle this in WebGOP, we generalize the Star graph type to allow new "centers" to be added in. Thus we define a new graph type StarMC which represents a star with multiple centers (see Figure 5):

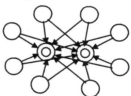

Figure 5. A multi-center star

```
class StarMC extends Star implements
I_MultiCenter {... ...};
```

StarMC implements the new behavior of adding/deleting a new center as defined in the interface I_MultiCenter:

```
addCenter(String newCenterName);
removeCenter(String centerName);
```

Internally, these operations can be implemented by using the graph update primitives. For example, to add a new center, the following primitives may be used:

```
Node newCenter = new Node(newCenterName);
Graph.addNode(newCenter);
for ( ......){ // for each leaf in the graph
  Edge e = new Edge(leaf, newCenter);
  Graph.addEdge(e);
};
WebGOPRuntime.deployNode(newCenter);
```

The addition of new centers will affect the behavior of the application system. So some behaviors defined in Star must be redefined in StarMC. For example, if we want to implement a load balancing strategy, the communication operation SendToCenter for the leaves must be redefined.

The existing local programs running on the leaves are not affected by the dynamic changes, because the communication is automatically adjusted with the polymorphic behavior of the graph object. On the other hand, new local programs that are aware of the new StarMC graph type can make use of new behaviors provided by StarMC.

Once the new graph type StarMC is defined, the WebGOP runtime manager can dynamically load in this class, instantiate new a StarMC object, initialize it with the current Star object, and redirect all graph object references to the new object. The WebGOP runtime manager needs to invoke only once the addCenter operation to add in a new Master program, which is aware of the new graph type StarMC, and can take charge of future tasks of adding and removing of Masters.

4. A prototype implementation of WebGOP

A prototype of WebGOP has been implemented, and several demo applications, including the one directly based on the example discussed in the last section, have

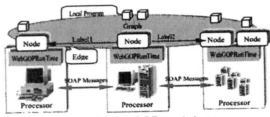

Figure 6. WebGOP prototype

been developed on the prototype. In this section we describe the key issues in implementing the prototype.

As Figure 6 shows , the basic building blocks of WebGOP are the Processors. A *Processor* can be any web-enabled computing device, from wireless PDA to mainframe MPP system, with a WebGOP runtime installed. Processors talk to each other via Simple Object Access Protocol (SOAP) [20], which makes WebGOP compatible with the current web environment.

The WebGOP Runtime provides a container for Nodes of Graphs. A *Node* is an active object running in the context of its Graph. A *Graph*, representing the architecture of an application system, is a shared global object. It is physically implemented with multiple local graph objects distributed over related Processors. There can be multiple Nodes of different Graphs on a single Processor. The WebGOP Runtime is responsible of maintaining the context for each Node by associating it with the local graph object of its Graph. The state of a Graph is co-managed by all of its local graph objects with the support of WebGOP Runtime.

The behavior of each Node is defined by the *Local Program* bound to it. As discussed in the last section, the default type of a graph object is defined by the system, but users can derive their own specialized graph types. Thus a WebGOP application statically consists of a set of LPs, an optional specialized graph type definition, and a configuration specification that declares a Graph and defines the mapping of the Local Programs to the Nodes of the Graph and the mapping of the Nodes to the WebGOP Processors. During execution, the LP instances coordinate with one another by invoking the operations provided by the graph object.

Since our target distributed applications work in the open environment of the Web, unique naming of entities is fundamental. In our prototype, a Processor is uniquely identified with a Unified Resource Locator (URL) and a Unified Resource Name (URN). In fact a WebGOP Processor is implemented as a web service, the URL is the router URL for the SOAP container of the web service, and the URN is the identifier of the web service. A graph is identified by its originating Processor plus a local graph name that is unique on this Processor. A Node is identified by the graph to which it belongs and the node name unique in the graph.

The WebGOP Runtime is built on top of the SOAP API, and provides the WebGOP API for user applications. The core of WebGOP Runtime is the distributed representation and management of graphs, based on which a set of graph-oriented message passing primitives and a set of basic dynamic graph updating primitives are provided. Since graph communication operations are much more frequently used than reconfiguration operations, a fully replicated strategy is chosen for the graph representation. The graph-oriented message passing primitives include synchronous and asynchronous send and receive functions for unicast, multicast and anycast communications. The communication peers are identified with graph nodes and node groups. The Runtime translates these graph nodes and nodes groups into the underlying web communication peer addresses. The dynamic graph-updating primitives modify the graph topology by adding/removing nodes/edges and change the mapping status by binding/unbinding local programs to/from nodes, and nodes to/from processors. To provide dynamic reconfiguration support in this prototype, a simple transactional mechanism for graph updating is implemented. There is also a set of marking and querying primitives. Nodes and edges can be marked with labels of key-value pair. Query for nodes and edges thus can be carried out based on the graph topology and the labels. Several frequently used operations on graph, such as shortest path, minimum spanning tree, are also built in the Runtime.

In addition to the Runtime, a simple system manager is implemented to help the programmer to manage, debug and monitor their WebGOP applications. It also acts as the front-end user interface for application loading, deployment, activation, and management of dynamic reconfigurations.

5. Performance evaluation

This section describes the performance of our prototype implementation of WebGOP. As discussed in Section 2, the GOP model has four classes of operations: communication and synchronization, subgraph generation, query, and update. Since in our prototype a replicated representation of the graph is used, query operations can be done locally. Subgraph generations are in fact implemented as queries. So we concentrate on the communication and graph update operations. The following aspects of the prototype are evaluated: overhead introduced by WebGOP over SOAP for handling message passing, cost of WebGOP multicast, cost of graph update, and cost of graph setup.

Figure 7 compares WebGOP and SOAP in terms of the overhead introduced for handling message passing. Average values of ten measurements are calculated. In the evaluation, we use a WebGOP application with two nodes. One of the nodes sends a message to another node, which, upon receiving the message, immediately sends it back to the sender. During this round trip, the message is encoded and decoded two times. We measure the round-trip time with different sizes of message workload, and compare it with that of a SOAP application doing exactly the same. As we can see from Figure 7, WebGOP's overhead is just a bit more than SOAP. The extra overhead is only 1/3 to 1/2 of the cost of a zero workload SOAP message. While the total cost grows roughly linearly with the message size, the extra overhead caused by WebGOP increases very slowly (from about 10ms to about 20ms while workload increasing from 1 byte to 1e+06 bytes).

Figure 8 shows the graph update cost. In this experiment, we measure the time required for adding a

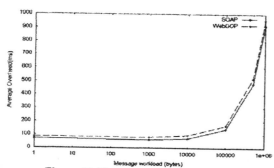

Figure 7. Message passing overhead

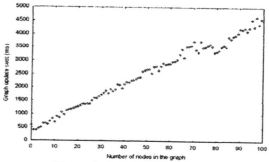

Figure 8. Graph update cost

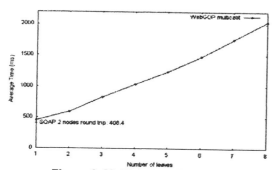

Figure 9. Multicast performance

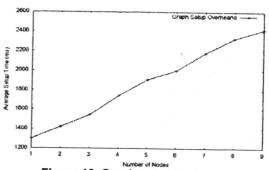

Figure 10. Graph setup cost

We use two experimental environments in the experiments. For evaluating the message passing overhead and graph update cost, we use a controlled sequential environment of Windows 2000 PC workstation with Intel P3 500MHz processor and 256MB memory. For the evaluation of the multicast performance and graph setup cost, we use a NOW environment of 9 Sun Ultra 1 143MHz workstations running Solaris 2.6. These workstations are linked with 100MB/s Ethernet.

node into a graph, which includes the time of linking the new node to an existing node. As shown in Figure 8, the cost is roughly a linear function of the number of nodes in the graph. Recall that in the prototype, a replicated representation of graph is used. All the nodes maintain a copy of the graph information and must be informed of the update.

The performance of WebGOP multicast is shown in Figure 9. In this experiment, we use the graph type "Star" as defined in Section 3. The master LP running on the center multicasts a message to all the leave LPs by calling "sendToLeaves()" and then receives a response from the leaves by calling "recvFromLeaves()". The LPs running on the leaves wait for the message from center by calling "recvFromCenter()" and send the same message back by calling "sentToCenter()". We measure the time spent on this interaction. The results show that while the cost is roughly linear with the number of leaves, the cost per leaf (260ms) when there are 8 leaves is much smaller than SOAP round trip time of 2 nodes (about 400ms). In our prototype implementation, a multicast message is implemented as multiple SOAP messages, but these messages are concurrently sent out.

Figure 10 shows the graph setup cost. In the prototype, a graph must be set up from an initiating node, and information about the graph is transformed from this initial node to other nodes. As we can see, graph setup is an expensive operation. The setup time increase linear with the number of the nodes in the graph.

The results of the performance evaluation as described above show that WebGOP introduces reasonably small and acceptable overhead comparing with the SOAP.

6. Related Work

At the present, most supporting tools and environments for distributed computing do not have architectural support. PVM [4] and MPI [5] provide low-level message-passing facilities. Object-Oriented middleware, such as CORBA [10] and Microsoft's DCOM, focus mainly on the interoperability of distributed objects in heterogeneous environments. Message-Oriented Middleware (MOM) systems provide reliable message queues for cooperating applications. Recently SOAP becomes the de-facto interoperation standard for web services. In terms of software architecture, they only provide support for implementing the "connectors" between the components. With our WebGOP approach, software architectures are reified as runtime graph objects of specialized graph types, which can be designed to provide more comprehensive architectural support with specialized interfaces, functions, and constraints.

As a graph oriented framework for architecture modeling and programming, WebGOP also has a close relationship with software architecture languages. Currently, several architecture description languages have been developed to facilitate architecture specification and formal analysis. A survey can be found in [11]. While architectures specified in these ADLs provide a solid basis for early system analysis and good guidelines for system construction, they are generally abstract descriptions and absent in concrete system implementation. Extra effort must be made to ensure that a system conforms to its architecture specification [12]. Some of the proposals, especially those under the name of "configuration languages" [13][14] and "coordination languages" [15][21], put more emphasis on the dynamism of the system configuration. They attempt to make a clear separation between the local computation of individual components (expressed in common programming languages) and the interaction and coordination among these components (expressed in configuration language or coordination language). Graphs have also been considered intuitively for the expression of software architectures, and this intuition is supported by those works such as [16]. WebGOP is also based on this intuition, and directly support the modeling of architectures as graphs. However, in WebGOP, such graphs are not only abstract architecture descriptions but also concrete constructs for system implementation and explicit objects in final working systems.

As a web computing system with a graph-oriented computing model, WebGOP is related to those wide area distributed and parallel computing environments such as Legion [17] and Globe [18]. Both Legion and Globe provide their own unified object-oriented computing models. Globe proposes a new view of objects in distributed systems: an object can be a distributed shared object that consists of sub-objects distributed in different address spaces. It provides comprehensive replication and caching support that are necessary for developing large-scale distributed applications. The concept of distributed shared object has been adopted to implement the graph object in our WebGOP system. Legion emphasizes the management and sharing of fundamental computing resources on a wide-area-network - CPU, disk, data, etc. - and organizes itself as an operating system in which every entity is encapsulated as an object. In Legion systems, an asynchronous remote method invocation protocol called macro-dataflow (MDF) can be used if some special Legion aware compiler such as MPLC is available. Compared with these works, our approach puts more emphasis on the modeling and implementation of the distributed application architectures. WebGOP can be integrated with those facilities as provided by Globe and Legion to support the development of large scale, high performance distributed web applications.

7. Conclusions and Future Work

In this paper we have proposed WebGOP, a novel approach for architecting distributed Web applications based on a graph oriented programming model. By modeling application system architectures as user defined graphs and operations over graphs, and by reifying architecture issues in explicit graph objects, this approach provide application developers with an intuitively abstraction of system architecture and a set of predefined graph operations to ease system implementation. Further more, this approach provides built-in support for flexible and dynamic architectures. In particular, under this graph-oriented framework, unplanned dynamic reconfiguration can be developed and applied somewhat systematically.

The strength of the WebGOP support for programming flexible and dynamic distributed application is its unifying graph oriented approach to the whole process of application construction and dynamic reconfiguration. On one hand, it decouples the components in a distributed application and facilitates the realization of flexibility and dynamism, and on the other hand, it provides a means to specify and enforce the constraints on dynamic changes, all based on the logical graph construct.

A prototype implementation of WebGOP has been implemented to demonstrate the feasibility of our approach. Results of the performance evaluation of the prototype show that the overhead introduced by WebGOP over SOAP is reasonable and acceptable.

Currently, we are developing a formal foundation for the graph-oriented approach [6]. The Graph Grammar based formalisms such as the approach proposed by Le Meyer [16] is particularly interesting to us. As to the WebGOP system, we are enhancing our prototype with security protection and more functionality for both application development and system management. We are also exploring some real world distributed web applications with WebGOP.

Acknowledgement

This research is partially supported by the Hong Kong Polytechnic University under the research grant H-ZJ80. Jian Lu and Xiaoxing Ma are also partially supported by the Jiansu High Technology Foundation under the grant BG2001012.

References

[1] M. Shaw, R. DeLine, D.V. Klein, et al. Abstractions for Software Architecture and Tools to Support Them, *IEEE Transaction on Software Engineering*, 21(4), April 1995.

[2] D.C. Luckham, J. Vera and S. Meldal, Key Concepts in Architecture Definition Languages, in *Foundations of Component-Based Systems*, Ed. Gary T. Leavens and Murali Sitaraman, Cambridge University Press 2000.

[3] J. Cao, L. Fernando, and K. Zhang, Programming Distributed System Based on Graphs, in *Intensional Programming I*, Ed. Mehmet A. Orgun and Edward A. Ashcroft, World Scientific, 1996.

[4] V. S. Sunderam, PVM: A framework for parallel distributed computing, *Concurrency: Practice and Experience*, 2(4):315-339, December 1990.

[5] Message Passing Interface Forum, *MPI: A message-passing interface standard*, May 1994.

[6] J. Cao, L. Fang, L. Xie, et al., CDG: A Formal Theory for Graph-Oriented Visual Programming of Distributed Systems. *Proc. Visual Methods for Parallel and Distributed Programming, Satellite Workshop at IEEE Symposium on Visual Languages* (VL2000), June 2000, Seattle, Washington.

[7] J. Kramer and J. Magee, Dynamic Configuration for Distributed Systems, *IEEE Transactions on Software Engineering*, 11(4):424-436, April 1985.

[8] J. Cao, E. Chan, C. H. Lee, et al., A Dynamic Reconfiguration Manager for Graph-Oriented Distributed Programs, *Proc 1997 Int'l Conf on Parallel and Distributed Systems* (ICPADS'97), pp. 216-221, IEEE Computer Society Press, Seoul, Korea, Dec 1997.

[9] P. Oreizy and R.N. Taylor, On the Role of Software Architecture in Runtime System Reconfiguration, *IEE Proceedings-Software*, 145(5), October 1998.

[10] Object Management Group, *The Common Object Request Broker: Architecture and Specification* v2.6.

[11] J.A. Stafford and A.L. Wolf, *Architecture-Based Software Engineering*, Technical Report CU-CS-891-99, University of Colorado, Nov., 1999.

[12] M. Moriconi, X. Qian, R. A. Riemenschneider, Correct Architecture Refinement, *IEEE Transactions on Software Engineering*, 21(4), April 1995.

[13] J. Kramer, Distributed Software Engineering, *Proceedings of the 16th International Conference on Software Engineering*, IEEE Computer Society Press, 1994. Los Alamitos, CA, USA.

[14] J. Kramer and J. Magee, Analysing dynamic change in distributed software architectures, *IEE Proceedings-Software*, 145(5), Oct. 1998.

[15] G.A. Papadopoulos and F. Arbab, *Coordination Models and Languages*, CWI Report SEN-R9834 December 31, 1998.

[16] D. Le Metayer, Describing Software Architecture Styles Using Graph Grammars, *IEEE Transactions on Software Engineering*, 24(7):521-533, July 1998.

[17] A. Grimshaw et al., Legion: An Operating System for Wide-Area Computing. *IEEE Computer*, 32(5):29-37, May 1999.

[18] M. Steen, P. Homburg, and A. S. Tanenbaum, Globe: a Wide-Area Distributed System. *IEEE Concurrency*, 7(1):70-78, January-March 1999.

[19] J. Cao, F. Lichuncha and K. Zhang, DIG: A Graph-based Construct for Programming Distributed Systems, *Proc. 2nd International Conference on High Performance Computing*, pp. 417-423, New Delhi, India, Dec, 1995.

[20] Don Box, et al., Simple Object Access Protocol (SOAP) 1.1, W3C Note, May 2000.

[21] N. Carriero and D. Gelernter, Coordination Languages and their Significance, *Communications of the ACM*, 35(2): 97-107, Feb. 1992.

Region Synchronization in Message Passing Systems*

Gurdip Singh and Ye Su
234 Nichols Hall, Computing and Information Sciences
Kansas State University
Manhattan, Kansas 66506
{singh,yesu}@cis.ksu.edu

Abstract

The development of correct synchronization code for distributed programs is a challenging task. In this paper, we propose an aspect oriented technique for developing synchronization code for message passing systems. Our approach is to factor out synchronization as a separate aspect, synthesize synchronization code and then compose it with the functional code. Specifically, we allow the designer of an application to first design the functional code. The designer can then annotate the functional code with *regions* and specify a high-level "global invariant" specifying the synchronization policy. A synchronization policy essentially gives the occupancy rules for the various regions. The solution to this problem, which we term the *region synchronization* problem, involves deriving a set of rules for entering and exiting each region. We provide a systematic the invariant into a message passing algorithm for a point-to-point message passing system. We show that many existing synchronization problems such as group mutual exclusion, reader/writers, committee coordination, and barrier can be specified as instances of the region synchronization problem. Hence, our algorithms can be used to solve a large class of synchronization problems.

1 Introduction

Processes running on different processors in a distributed program may have to communicate with each other to coordinate their activities. To control such interactions, proper synchronization code must be incorporated at appropriate places in such programs. The development of correct synchronization code for distributed systems is a challenging problem. Reports of mission failure due to implementation errors related to synchronization are not uncommon. Therefore, powerful and advanced tools are needed for modular design that can produce verifiable, efficient, and easily maintainable synchronization code.

Many standard synchronization problems such as mutual exclusion, dining philosophers problem, and barrier have been studied extensively, and efficient algorithms are available for different types of distributed platforms [Lam87, RA81, Jou98]. In many applications, however, one may encounter variations of these standard problems. For example, [And91] discusses severals variations of the readers/writers problem such as bounded readers/writers (in which at most k readers are allowed to read concurrently), readers' preference and writers' preference. Common problems defined in operating systems textbooks such as sleeping barbers problem and cigarette smokers problems often involve either variations of standard problems or a combination of two or more standard problems (*e.g.*, the sleeping barbers problem involves both mutual exclusion and producer/consumer synchronization). As a result, solutions to standard synchronization problems may not apply directly to such (ad hoc) problems. Therefore, designers are often confronted with the task of developing synchronization solutions from scratch.

In this paper, we consider an aspect oriented approach for developing synchronization code for distributed programs. We have developed an object-oriented methodology to design shared memory concurrent programs[MSN00]. In our approach, a designer first constructs a high-level solution to the synchronization problem using a formal specification. We then provide an algorithm to implement this high-level solution in a message passing system. Our technique is based on the methodology of global invariants advocated by Andrews [And91]. Specifically, in our technique, the functional code is first developed independently using traditional object oriented design methods such as RUP of UML [JBR99]. Next, we allow a designer to annotate the functional code with synchronization regions. A *region* is essentially a block of code whose execution may require synchronization (for instance, this block of code may have to be executed in an exclusive mode or may represent use of a shared resource). With each region r, we associate

---

*This work was supported by DARPA PCES contract F33615-00-C-3044 and NSF award CCR0098179.

two counters in_r and out_r which are incremented when a process enters and exits the region r respectively. A synchronization policy, which specifies rules for occupancy of regions, is then expressed via a *global invariant* on these counters. We define the *region synchronization* problem as the problem of coming up with synchronization code to control entry and exit into regions to enforce the specified global invariant.

In our methodology, we first derive a coarse-grain solution from the global invariant. This intermediate solution to the region synchronization problem is a mechanical step, and uses atomic test-and-update await statements. The next step is the mapping of the coarse-grain solution to a target platform. In this paper, we present mappings for asynchronous point-to-point message passing systems. The mapping is essentially an algorithm to execute the coarse-grain solution in a distributed manner. The algorithm is an extension of the Lamport's mutual exclusion algorithm [Lam78]. In addition to maintaining the global invariant, our algorithms satisfy the properties of *bounded waiting* and *absence of unnecessary synchronization*. Bounded waiting specifies that each request (either to enter or exit a session) will be eventually satisfied. Absence of unnecessary synchronization specifies that a process must be allowed to enter or exit a region without waiting if there are no pending requests for "conflicting" regions (this notion will be made more precise later). We also give complexity bounds for our algorithms based on the measures defined in [Jou98]. The algorithms presented are simple and provide a base-line solution for a large class of problems. We also discuss several ways in which the algorithm can be systematically modified to exploit problem-specific features.

The significance of our work is two-fold. First, we show that many synchronization problems such as group mutual exclusion, barrier, reader/writers, producer/consumer, and committee coordination can be specified as region synchronization problems. Common problems found in many operating system textbooks such as the cigarette smokers problem, unisex bathroom, and one-lane bridge can be formulated in our framework. Thus, our algorithms can be used to solve a large class of synchronization problems (including ad hoc synchronization problems). Second, our technique also provides a systematic way to develop synchronization code. We believe that this methodology is very well-suited for both developing code for real systems as well as for educational purposes.

2 Comparison to Related Work

Several synchronization problems such as mutual exclusion, barrier synchronization, dining philosophers problem and committee coordination problem have been studied extensively [Lam78, YA95, CM88]. In the mutual exclusion problem, each process alternates between two sections of code: *noncritical section* and *critical section*. At most one process is allowed to be present in the critical section at any given time. A solution to this problem involves coming up with an *entry* and an *exit* protocol to be executed at the entry and exit of the critical section respectively. Joung identified the *group mutual exclusion* problem in which processes of the same type may occupy the critical section concurrently [Jou98] and presented message passing algorithms for point-to-point as well as ring networks [Jou99b, Jou99a]. In [KM01], the GRASP problem was defined in which each process iteratively tries to enter a session with a set of *capabilities*. A process can enter the session only if the combined set of the capabilities of all processes trying to enter that session is sufficient for that session. [KM01] showed that a large number of synchronization problems can be modeled as instances of GRASP problem and presented an algorithm for this problem that is based on wait-free transactions for shared memory systems. [Sch82] discusses the formulation of mutual exclusion and synchronous communication using phase transition predicates and provided a message passing solution. The region synchronization problem proposed in this paper allows a designer to specify regions and then specify occupancy rules for the regions. We show that many problems such as barrier and producer/consumer in addition to mutual exclusion and group exclusion can be modeled as region synchronization problems. Thus, our formulation is similar in spirit to that in [KM01] as it allows a large class of synchronization problems to be modeled. The algorithm in [KM01] is however for shared memory systems whereas our solutions are for message passing systems.

3 Overview of the methodology

Let P be a distributed program with processes $P_1, \ldots, P_n$, where P_i executes at site i. The development of the program P in our methodology is a two-staged process. In the first stage, the functional code is developed for each site i. and writer In the development of the functional code, all aspects (including synchronization) are ignored and only component functionality is implemented.

Identifying synchronization regions:
The next step in the methodology is the identification of regions in the program code. A synchronization region is a code-segment in which a process may have to wait for some event to occur or some condition to hold, or in which a process may trigger an event or change a condition for which another process is waiting. Each region is marked by a starting and an ending control point (these two points may also coincide).

Invariant specification:

A *synchronization policy* constrains the occupancy of the regions. That is, it specifies the rules for entry and exit from the regions. We use a global invariant to describe a synchronization policy. For ease of presentation, we assume that the regions are numbered, $R_1, \ldots, R_m$. For each region R_i, we declare two counters $in[i]$ and $out[i]$ which are incremented when a process enters and exits R_i respectively. Thus, $in[i]$ ($out[i]$) denotes the number of times a process has entered (exited) region R_i so far. A *global invariant GI* is a predicate defined using in and out counters with arithmetic inequalities, arithmetic operators and boolean connectives. For example, for the reader/writers problem, we have two regions, R_1 and R_2 (the *reader* and *writer* regions respectively). Note that although there may be several reader processes, each of which execute a copy of the reader code, there is one *reader* region. Thus, $in[1]$ and $out[1]$ are assumed to the shared counters between the reader processes. Hence, $in[1]$ is incremented any time a reader process enters the reader region in its code. The synchronization policy for the readers/writers problem is then given by the invariant:

$$((in[1] = out[1]) \vee (in[2] = out[2]))$$
$$\wedge (in[2] - out[2] \leq 1)$$

The first conjunct specifies that one of the two regions must always be empty whereas the second conjunct specifies that at most one writer can be in the writer region at any time.

Generation of the coarse grain solution:

The next step is to obtain a coarse-grain solution that increments the in and out counters defined for the regions. A global invariant specification is automatically translated into an implementation independent *coarse-grain* synchronization solution which is represented using atomic test-and-update construct $\langle await(B) \rightarrow S \rangle$. The following two types of synchronization constructs are used in a coarse-grain solution:

1. $\langle S \rangle$: This statement specifies atomic execution of S.
2. $\langle \textbf{await } B \rightarrow S \rangle$: This statement specifies that the process is delayed until B is true; at which point, S is executed atomically. No interleaving occurs between the final evaluation of B and the execution of S.

The coarse-grained solution is obtained as follows: Let $ct++$ be an assignment statement, where ct is $in[i]$ or $out[i]$ for some i. Then, $ct++$ is transformed into $\langle \textbf{await } B \rightarrow ct++ \rangle$, where B is the weakest condition that satisfies the triple $\{GI \wedge B\} \, ct++ \, \{GI\}$. If B is true, the statement $\langle ct++ \rangle$ is used instead. In the following, we give some more examples to illustrate the steps of our technique discussed so far:

Example 1: Consider the group mutual exclusion problem with two regions R_1 and R_2. Each region must be executed in exclusion but several processes may execute in the same region concurrently. The synchronization requirement is specified using the invariant $(in[1] = out[1]) \vee (in[2] == out[2])$. The invariant specifies at least of one the two regions must be empty at any given time. From the invariant, we come up with the following solution:

$\langle await(in[2] = out[2]) \rightarrow in[1] + + \rangle$ // entry protocol
...region R_1...
$\langle out[1] + + \rangle$ // exit protocol

$\langle await(in[1] = out[1]) \rightarrow in[2] + + \rangle$ // entry protocol
...region R_2...
$\langle out[2] + + \rangle$ // exit protocol

This solution solves the group mutual exclusion problem since in a state in which both regions are empty (indicated by $in[1] = out[1] \wedge in[2] = out[2]$), the execution of the entry statement for one of the regions will block the entry to the other region. The invariant can be generalized to specify *Bounded Group Exclusion* in which in addition to exclusion, at most k_i threads are allowed in R_i at any time. This can specified by adding the conjunct $(in[1] - out[1] \leq k_1) \wedge (in[2] - out[2] \leq k_2)$ to the invariant. The readers/writers problem is an instance of bounded group exclusion problem where $k_1 = \infty$ and $k_2 = 1$.

Example 2 In the *group synchronization* problem, there exists N processes who may, from time to time, express interest in forming a group of size M. We model this problem by a single region R_1. When a process wishes to form a group, it requests entry into the region. Subsequently, it tries to exit the region. However, the exit from the region is allowed only when M processes have already entered the region. The following invariant specifies the group synchronization property: $(out[1] \leq (in[1]/M) * M) \wedge (in[1] \leq ((out[1] + M)/M) * M)$, where $/$ is integer division. The first conjunct restricts $out[1]$ so that it can be incremented only after $in[1]$ has been incremented M times. The second conjunct restricts entry of subsequent set of M processes to the region until the previous batch of M processes have left the region. From the invariant, we come up with the following solution:

$\langle await(in[1] < ((out[1] + M)/M) * M) \rightarrow in[1] + + \rangle$
...region R_1...
$\langle await(out[1] < (in[1]/M) * M) \rightarrow out[1] + + \rangle$

The *barrier synchronization* problem is a special case of group formation problem where $N = M$ and each process expresses interest in group formation at the end of each phase. In [Miz01], a number of invariant patterns are given of which group synchronization is one.

Our technique is general enough and several synchronization problems such as barrier synchronization, reader/writers problems, and many synchronization problems found in operating systems texts such as cigarette smokers problem and unisex bathroom problem [And91] can be specified in this framework.

4 Generating synchronization code

The final step is the mapping of the coarse-grain solution to a target platform. Let $\{R_1, \ldots, R_m\}$ be a set of regions and $\{St_1, \ldots, St_p\}$ be a set of statements guarding the entry and exit from regions, where $p = 2m$ (since each region has an entry and an exit statement). We will refer to these as synchronization statements in the following. Each synchronization statement St_i is of the form $\langle await(Cond_i) \rightarrow ct_i++\rangle$ or $\langle ct_i++\rangle$, where ct_i is $in[x]$ or $out[x]$ for some region R_x. We want to develop a distributed algorithm, $Synch$, for executing the coarse-grain solution. As shown in Figure 1, $Synch$ is a distributed program with module $Synch_i$ executing at site i. P_i and $Synch_i$ interact with one another via requests and permissions. In the functional code of P_i, we place code to send a request to $Synch_i$ at the entry and exit point of each region (this essentially is a request to execute the synchronization statement corresponding to that point). After sending a request, P_i awaits permission from $Synch_i$. The $Synch$ modules at different sites must interact via message passing to ensure that statements are executed as specified by the coarse-grain solution. To define the properties to the satis-

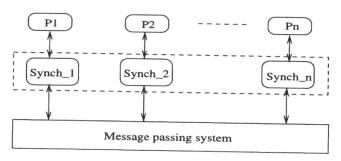

Figure 1: Structure of the Distributed Solution.

fied by $Synch$, we present some definitions:

Definition: St_i and St_j are *conflicting* if (a) there exists a reachable state in P in which both $Cond_i$ and $Cond_j$ are true and (b) in any state s in which both $Cond_i$ and $Cond_j$ are true, executing ct_i++ invalidates $Cond_j$ and executing ct_j++ invalidates $Cond_i$.

Definition: St_i and St_j are *weak conflicting* if (a) there exists a state s in which both $Cond_i$ and $Cond_j$ are true, and executing ct_i++ invalidates $Cond_j$ and executing ct_j++ invalidates $Cond_i$, and (b) St_i and St_j are not conflicting.

Definition: St_i *enables* St_j if there exists a state s in which $!Cond_j \wedge Cond_i$ holds and executing ct_i++ in s makes $Cond_j$ true.

Intuitively, conflicting statements are those that represent competitive synchronization wherein execution of one statement will block the execution of other conflicting statements. For example, in the group exclusion problem stated earlier, the entry statement for region R_1 conflicts with the entry statement for region R_2. The notion is weak conflicting is used to model the case wherein statements may be conflicting depending on the current state. For example, if there exists a upper bound k on the number of processes in R_1 then there will exist states in which processes will be allowed to enter R_1 concurrently. However, there also exists a state (namely, the state in which *k-1* processes are already in R_1) in which only one of the several processes competing to enter the region will be allowed. Note also that a statement may conflict or weak conflict with itself.

We now specify the correctness criteria for $Synch$. Let $s_1 \rightarrow_{a_1} s_2 \rightarrow_{a_2} \ldots$ be an execution of the system, where s_i is a state and a_i is either a local action or a communication action (send or receive).

- **Safety:** We assume that the await statements are derived from an invariant GI as outlined in our technique. Hence, we require that GI be true in all states reachable from the initial state.

- **Absence of unnecessary synchronization:** If P_i requests St_k in state s_x, and in all states s_y, $y \geq x$, there is no pending conflicting request and the set of all pending weak-conflicting requests (excluding $i's$ request) together, if granted, will not invalidate $Cond_k$ then the execution of St_k by $Synch_i$ must not be delayed due to a request by another process (that is, execution of St_k by i must not be delayed due to steps taken to process the request of another process P_j).

- **Bounded waiting:** If P_i requests a statement, say St_k, then $Synch_i$ will eventually execute St_k.

The requirement of absence of unnecessary synchronization, also referred to as concurrent entering, specifies that if more than one process is allowed to occupy a region concurrently then they must be allowed to enter concurrently (that is, without synchronizing among themselves). For example, in the readers/writers problem, if several readers request entry into the reader region and there is no pending writer request then the request of one reader must not be delayed due to the request of another reader. This requirement eliminates lock based solutions wherein each process acquires a lock to evaluate the condition associated with its await statement. Our formulation of this property is somewhat different from the one in [Jou98] due to the presence of weak conflicting statements. For example, consider the statement $\langle await(in[1] - out[1] < 2) \rightarrow in[1]++\rangle$ (specifying that at most 2 process can be in region R_1). If at most two processes request execution of this statement, then they should be allowed to execute without unnecessary waiting. However, if three or more processes request execution of this statement then they may have to synchronize (in this case, the combined set of pending requests invalidates the condition $in[1] - out[1] < 2$). The bounded waiting condition ensures that every request is eventually satisfied. Since our algorithms may impose an ordering (e.g., FIFO) on conflicting and weak conflicting requests, we require the coarse-grain solution to satisfy the following property:

Definition: P is *conflict-live* if in any execution of P, if a request for St_x is pending in any state s then there must exist an execution from state s in which $Cond_x$ becomes true irrespective of the order in which the pending conflicting and weak conflicting requests are ordered.

Essentially, this property requires that $Cond_x$ must be able to become true only via execution of non-conflicting statements (that is, St_x cannot be blocked by a concurrent conflicting request).

We define the message complexity of a program as the number of messages generated for each request. [Jou98] proposed three additional complexity measures to evaluate the algorithms for the group exclusion problem: time complexity, switch complexity and concurrency. In the group exclusion problem, if a process i requests a session, we know that $i's$ entry into the session will be enabled when the current session finishes. However, in our case, if i requests St_x and all regions are empty, i may still not be able to execute St_x as $Cond_x$ may be false. Therefore, we modify the definition of time complexity as follows: We define *time complexity* as the maximum number of execution of conflicting statements while a process i is waiting to execute a statement. We define conflicting regions are those that cannot be occupied simultaneously, and a *session* as a sequence of overlapping execution of the same region (e.g., a reader session would be overlapping executions of the reader region by several readers). Then, the *switch complexity* is defined as the maximum number of times a conflicting session can be established while a process is waiting for a session. Finally, *concurrency* is defined as a maximum number of execution of the same region by processes while a process with a request for a conflicting region is waiting (please refer to [Jou99b] for a detailed definition of these measures).

4.1 A Simple Message Passing Algorithm

In this section, we propose an algorithm that is based on Lamport's algorithm for mutual exclusion [Lam78]. The pseudocode for the algorithm is shown in Figure 2. We assume that each site i maintains a local clock, $clock_i$, which is updated according to Lamport's logical clock rules [Lam78]. When $Synch_i$ receives a request from P_i, it timestamps the request and sends a *request* message to all sites (lines 1-3). Each site responds with a *reply* message on receiving the request (line 7). The timestamp, ts_i, of a

request is a pair $\langle i, clock \rangle$, where $clock$ is the local clock value of i when the request is made. As in the algorithm in [Lam78], we use logical clocks and site ids to impose a total ordering, denoted by $<_t$, on all the requests. Let $seq(req_j)$ denote the sequence number of req_j in the ordering $<_t$.

Each site i maintains a request queue RQ_i in which request messages are stored in the timestamp order. A request req_j is a pair (ts_j, sj), where ts_j is the timestamp of the request and sj is the index of the requested statement (that is, St_{sj} is the requested statement). req_j is *stable* at site i at time t if no request with timestamp lower than ts_j can be received by i after time t. We use two mechanisms for determining when req_j becomes stable at i. If site i has received a message from every other site with timestamp greater than ts_j then req_j is stable at site i. If site i knows $seq(req_j)$ and it has received $seq(req_j)$-1 requests with timestamps lower than ts_j then req_j is stable at i. Also note that i can determine $seq(req_j)$ when req_j becomes stable by maintaining a counter counting the number of requests that have become stable at i prior to req_j.

In our discussion below, we will use $req_i = (ts_i, ri)$ and $req_j = (ts_j, rj)$ to denote the current requests by i and j respectively. As in the algorithm in [Lam78], we want to service requests in the timestamp order (this is required to ensure bounded waiting). However, it may be the case that req_i is ordered before req_j in the timestamp order but $!Cond_{ri} \wedge Cond_{rj}$ may hold in the current state (that is, St_{rj} is enabled but St_{ri} is disabled). Furthermore, it might be the case that executing St_{rj} may enable St_{ri}. In this case, we have to execute req_j before req_i. Therefore, as opposed to the mutual exclusion algorithm of [Lam78] in which requests are serviced in the timestamp order, the actual execution order, denoted by $<_e$, in our algorithm may be different from $<_t$. In our algorithm, we attempt to execute the requests in the timestamp order; however, at certain points, we may need to reorder the requests because the enabling conditions of requests may be false. We do however require that *conflicting requests be serviced in the timestamp order* (this rule is needed to guarantee bounded waiting).

In our algorithm, site i receives all the requests (hence, the queues RQ_i at each site i can be viewed as replicas of each other). Each site i attempts to execute all the requests in RQ_i in the timestamp order. The history of the requests executed so far is encoded in the counter variables (as a counter is incremented whenever a statement is executed). Hence, for each statement St_x, a local copy, $ct[i, x]$, of the counter $ct[i]$ is maintained at each site i (remember that $ct[i]$ is either an *in* or *out* counter incremented in statement St_x). When a request (ts_j, rj) is "enabled" (as discussed below) for execution at site i, $ct[i, rj]$ is incremented. When i executes its own request, a permission signal is sent to the application. Thus, the modules *Synch* perform identical computation at all sites.

```
1  Receive request for St[x] from P[i]
2    clock[i]++; ts = <i,clock[i]>;
3      send request(i, ts, x) to all processes;
4    place request in RQ[i]

5  Receive request(j, ts, y)
6    place <j, ts, y> in RQ[i]; update clock[i];
7    send reply(clock[i]) to j;
8    Check_Stable();

9   Check\_Stable()
10    while (head of RQ[i] is stable)
11    {    Insert_Stable()   }

12 Insert_Stable()
13   (j,ts,rj) = Dequeue(RQ[i]); myseq[i]++;
14   if j = i then Current = myseq[i];
15   if St[rj] conflicts with a request
16      in Stable_List[i] or !Cond[rj] then
17      Enqueue (j,ts,rj) in Stable_List[i];
18   else
19     ct[i,rj]++;
20     if j = i then flag = true;
21            send permission to application;
22              else flag = false;
23     repeat
24      for each request (k,ts1,z) in Stable_List[i]
25       if Cond[z] and St[z] does not conflict with
26       a request ahead of St[z] in Stable\_List[i]
27      then ct[i,z]++;
28              delete (k,ts1,z) from Stable_List[i];
29        if k = i then
30            flag = true;
31            send permission to application
32        else
33         if flag = true then
34             send update(Current) to k;
35    until (no request is executed)
```

Figure 2: Algorithm *Synch*

Consider the case where a request $req_j = (ts_j, rj)$ is received by site i. This request is first placed in RQ_i (line 6), and is further processed at i only when it becomes stable. We maintain an ordered list, $Stable\_List_i$, at i of all stable but pending requests. When req_j becomes stable (line 10), the procedure $Insert\_Stable$ is invoked. In this procedure, we first increment $myseq[i]$ (this variable is used to assign a sequence number to each request in the timestamp order). At this point, i knows of all requests ordered prior to req_j in the timestamp order. Thus, i determines whether req_j can be executed (lines 13-16). If $Cond_{rj}$ evaluates to false or req_j conflicts with a request already in $Stable\_List_i$ then req_j is inserted into $Stable\_List$. For each entry req_j in $Stable\_List_i$, we use an additional field $req_j.conflict$ that points to the request with the largest timestamp in $Stable\_List_i$ that conflicts with req_j. If $Cond_{rj}$ is true and St_{rj} does not conflict with any request in $Stable\_List$

then $ct[i, rj]$ is incremented (line 19). If this request is $i's$ own request then i sends a permission signal to the application (line 21). Incrementing $ct[i, rj]$ may in turn enable other pending requests (these requests may be those that are ahead of req_j in the timestamp order). Therefore, in lines 24-35, we check $Stable\_List$ from the beginning to determine if any request is enabled (we need to check from the beginning to ensure that all sites execute requests in the same order). During this check, a request for St_z becomes *enabled* if $Cond_z$ is true and it does not conflict with an earlier request in $Stable\_List$.

Consider the case in which a request executed by i is its own request (line 20 and line 29). Subsequently, if i finds another request, say req_k, becomes enabled due to its own request being executed, then it sends a *update* message to k contains the sequence number of its current request (line 32). The reason for sending the update message is now explained. Consider the case in which request req_k is stable at k but its condition is false. Also, assume that req_i enables req_k but $ts_k <_t ts_i$. In this case, k needs to wait until req_i is enabled at k before req_k can be executed. However, to execute req_i at k, it must become stable at k. By sending the update message with $seq(req_i)$ to k, we provide a mechanism for k to check when req_i becomes stable. When k receives this message, it uses the sequence number of req_i to determine when req_i becomes stable. This will enable k to execute req_i and subsequently, its own request.

The algorithm satisfies the safety property as all requests will be processed in the same order at all sites. Any reordering of requests due to conditions being false or due to conflicting requests is done in the same manner at all sites. The algorithm also allows concurrent entering and bounded waiting. The property of conflict-live is important in proving bounded waiting. This property requires that starting from state x, it must be possible for $Cond_x$ to become true only via execution of non-conflicting statements. Together with the first-come first-serve discipline on conflicting requests, this property ensures that eventually $Cond_x$ will become true and remain true. Hence, St_x will get executed at i. We now evaluate the complexity of our algorithm. For each request req_i, $N - 1$ request messages and $N - 1$ reply messages are generated. In addition, when req_i is executed, an update message needs to be sent for each request req_j that is enabled by req_i but has a smaller timestamp than that of req_i. This may result in between 0 to *N-1* messages. Hence, the number of messages per request is in the range *2(N-1)* to *3(N-1)*. The time, switch and concurrency complexity of our algorithm are all $O(N)$. Our algorithm has the same complexity with respect to these measures as the group mutual exclusion algorithm of [Jou99b].

5 Optimizations of $Synch$

The algorithm $Synch$ solves the region synchronization problem, which is a very general problem. Our algorithm provides a base-line solution for a large class of synchronization problems, and a starting point to derive more problem specific solutions. We believe that $Synch$ can be further optimized and enhanced with additional properties in a systematic manner. In the following, we discuss some such variations.

5.1 Alternative Scheduling Policies

Our technique is flexible and allows different scheduling policies to be incorporated at two different stages in the development process. A scheduling strategy can be incorporated at the coarse-grain solution level. For example, for the readers/writers problem, policies such as "readers' preference" or "weak readers' preference" can be incorporated in the coarse-grain solution. An alternative scheduling policy can also be incorporated by modifying the algorithm used to execute requests in $Stable\_List$. For example, the algorithm in [Jou99b] allows unbounded concurrency in the group mutual exclusion algorithm as follows: when processes have entered a specific region, a reference philosopher is chosen and as long as the reference philosopher is in the region, all requests for the same region are granted even though conflicting requests with lower timestamp may be pending. This increases the amount of concurrency as more processes are allowed to enter a region concurrently. We can enforce a similar policy by modifying procedure Insert_Stable of $Synch$ by selecting the first process to enter a region as the reference process and allow subsequent requests for the same region as long as the reference process is still in the region.

5.2 Reducing the amount of computation

In $Synch$, identical computation is performed at all sites. In particular, a site needs to perform computation (in addition to sending reply messages) even though it may not have any pending requests. In this section, we show that more information can be piggybacked on the messages to reduce the amount of computation performed by a site. In the algorithm proposed in this section, a site i performs less computation if it does not have a pending request. When a request is issued, the information piggybacked on messages from other sites is used by i to construct the current state.

The algorithm is based on the mutual exclusion algorithm in [RA81]. In this algorithm, the requests are ordered according to logical clocks as in [Lam78]. In response to each request message from j, i sends a $reply$ message to j. However, i delays response to j's request if i's request is ordered earlier than ts_j. When a node has received a reply

message from all sites, it can enter the critical section. The algorithm for group mutual exclusion proposed by [Jou99b] is a modification of this algorithm.

In our algorithm, if a node does not have a pending request, then its behavior is as follows: When a request req_j is received by i, node i sends a reply message immediately (as it does not have a conflicting request). Furthermore, req_j is placed in RQ_i. If there is already an earlier request in RQ_i from j, say to execute St_x, then $ct[i, x]$ is incremented and this earlier request is deleted. The intuition is that since there is at most one pending request per process, j must have already successfully executed its previous request. Furthermore, this request will be ordered before any subsequent request made by i. Hence, node i simply records the execution of j's request by incrementing the corresponding variable. Thus, at most one request per node is maintained in RQ_i.

Consider the case when i receives a request req_i from the application. At this point, the counter values at i record the execution of some of the statements scheduled ahead of i in $<_e$. But, i may not know of all the requests that must be scheduled ahead of its own. Hence, i must reconstruct its state at this point (that is, determine the correct values of the counters and the requests to be placed in RQ_i and $Stable\_List_i$). For this purpose, each site maintains a vector $latest_i[1..n]$ which is updated as follows: Let $last_i$ denote the most recent request by i that has already been executed at i (that is, it is not pending). Then, $latest_i[j]$ indicates the timestamp of the latest request from j that i executed before executing $last_i$. Thus, the vector $latest_i$ contains a record requests that were executed by i prior to i's last request. Note that some of these requests may be ordered after $last_i$ in the timestamp order. When i sends a reply message to j, it includes $latest_i$ in the message.

When i receives a request from the application, it sends a request message to all sites, and waits for the replies. As in the algorithm in [RA81], a reply message is delayed by j if j has a pending conflicting request with a lower timestamp. While waiting for replies, all requests that are received are enqueued in RQ_i. After i sends a request, it computes a temporary vector $wait_i[1..n]$ as follows: $wait_i[j]$ denotes the timestamp of the request from j that i needs to wait for before it processes req_i. Thus, when i receives $reply(latest)$ from j, it updates $wait_i$ by computing the pairwise maximum of the two vectors, $wait_i$ and $latest$. This is done because $latest$ reflects the requests which were ordered before $last_j$ and hence, this set of requests must also be ordered prior to req_i. After i receives all of the replies, the vector $wait_i$ contains information about the requests that must be ordered before its own request and have already been executed (however, $wait_i$ does not give "all" the requests ordered before req_i as some of the pending requests may be ordered before req_i; these request will be present in RQ_i). Site i then waits until it has received all requests indicated in $wait_i$. As it receives these requests, site i simply executes each request by incrementing the corresponding counter (it does not evaluate the conditions). The remaining requests in RQ_i are then processed as in the algorithm $Synch$ in the previous section. All stable requests are moved into $Stable\_List$ and then processed according to method $Insert\_Stable$ of $Synch$ (Figure 2). The only difference is that instead of sending the sequence number in the update message, we need to send the $latest_i$ vector.

The complexity of this algorithm is the same as that of $Synch$ with respect to all the measures except that each message now contains a vector of size N. The advantage of this algorithm is that a site performs less computation when it does not have a pending request. The vector $latest$ is required in the reconstruction of the state in our algorithm because we allow the execution order to differ from the timestamp order. In the mutual exclusion algorithm of Ricart and Agarwala [RA81], all requests are conflicting and are served in the timestamp order. Therefore, it does not require the use of $latest$ vectors. On the other hand, the algorithm in [Jou99b] allows the execution order to be different from the timestamp order and makes use of a vector similar to the latest vector.

5.3 Exploiting the structure of the coarse-grain solution

Since $Synch$ addresses the general region synchronization problem, it is possible that more efficient problem-specific solutions can be designed. We are currently developing techniques to exploit the structure of the coarse-grain solution to optimize $Synch$. Since the coarse-grain solution is problem-specific, this will enable problem-specific optimizations. For example, the total ordering requirement on all requests can be eliminated in certain cases for statements of type $\langle ct_x{+}{+}\rangle$. As another example, consider the barrier synchronization problem of Example 2 in which the coarse-grain solution itself imposes an order on the execution of statements (N entry statements must be executed first followed by N exit statements, and this sequence is repeated). The additional ordering performed by $Synch$ is ensuring that all entry (and exit) statements are executed in the same order in each round. However, since the entry statements do not conflict with each other, the order in which they are executed does not matter. In such cases, we can optimize the $Synch$ algorithm by eliminating the $reply$ messages for requests whose execution order is not important. With this optimization, the barrier problem will require N-1 messages per process per round (which is same as the number of messages that would be required by a problem-specific solution to the barrier problem).

6 Conclusion

In this paper, we describe a methodology for synthesizing synchronization code from high-level specifications in distributed programs. The metholdogy allows specification of synchronization policies via high level global invariants. We provide a systematic way to synthesize a message passing solution from this specification. We showed that a large number of synchronization problems can be formulated in our framework. As a result, our message passing algorithms can be directly applied to solve a large class of synchronization problems.

References

[And91] G.R. Andrews. *Concurrent Programming, Principles and Practice.* Benjamin/Cummings Publishing Co., 1991.

[CM88] M. Chandy and J. Misra. Parallel program design. *Addison-Weslay,* 1988.

[JBR99] I. Jacobson, G. Booch, and J. Rumbaugh. *The Unified Software Development Process.* Addison Wesley, 1999.

[Jou98] Yuh-Jzer Joung. Asynchronous group mutual exclusion. In *ACM Symposium on Principles of Distributed Computing,* 1998.

[Jou99a] Yuh-Jzer Joung. Aynchronous group mutual exclusion in ring networks. In *Proceedings of International Parallel Processing Symposium,* 1999.

[Jou99b] Yuh-Jzer Joung. The congenial talking philosophers problem in computer networks. In *International Symposium on Distributed Computing,* 1999.

[KM01] P. Keane and M. Moir. A general resource allocation synchronization problem. In *IEEE International Conference on Distributed Computing Systems,* 2001.

[Lam78] L. Lamport. Time, clocks, and the ordering of events in a distributed system. *Communications of the ACM,* 21:558–565, 1978.

[Lam87] L. Lamport. A fast mutual exclusion algorithm. *ACM Transactions on Computer Systems,* 9, 1987.

[Miz01] M. Mizuno. A pattern-based approach to develop concurrent programs in uml — part 1/2. In *KSU Technical Report 2001-02 (under review for publication),* 2001.

[MSN00] M. Mizuno, G. Singh, and M. Neilsen. A structured approach to develop concurrent programs in uml. In *Proceedings of the Third International Conference on the Unified Modeling Language,* 2000.

[RA81] G. Ricart and A. K. Agarwala. An optimal algorithm for mutual exclusion in computer networks. *Communications of the ACM,* 24:9–17, 1981.

[Sch82] F. B. Schneider. Synchronization in distributed programs. *ACM Transactions on Programming Languages and Systems,* 4(2), 1982.

[YA95] J-H. Yang and J. Anderson. A fast scalable mutual exclusion algorithm. *Distributed Computing,* 9, 1995.

Session 4C

Web Servers

Streaming Media Caching Algorithms for Transcoding Proxies

Xueyan Tang, Fan Zhang, and Samuel T. Chanson
Department of Computer Science
Hong Kong University of Science and Technology
Clear Water Bay, Hong Kong
E-mail: {tangxy, zhangfan, chanson}@cs.ust.hk

Abstract

Streaming media is expected to become one of the most popular types of web content in the future. Due to increasing variety of client devices and the range of access speeds to the Internet, multimedia contents may be required to be transcoded to match the client's capability. With transcoding, both the network and the proxy CPU are potential bottlenecks for streaming media delivery. This paper discusses and compares various caching algorithms designed for transcoding proxies. In particular, we propose a new adaptive algorithm that dynamically selects an appropriate metric for adjusting the management policy. Experimental results show that the proposed algorithm significantly outperforms those that cache only untranscoded or only transcoded objects. Moreover, motivated by the characteristics of many video compression algorithms, we investigate partitioning a video object into sections based on frame type and handling them individually for proxy caching. It is found that partitioning improves performance when CPU power rather than network bandwidth is the limiting resource, particularly when the reference pattern is not highly skewed.

1 Introduction

Proxy caching is a popular approach to enhance the performance of web content delivery. The proxies are usually deployed much closer to the clients than the content servers. Frequently accessed objects are stored at the proxies so that client requests can be satisfied without having to contact the distant content servers. With the rapid growth of streaming audio and video applications on the web, proxy caching of streaming media objects has become an important research topic in recent years [1, 2, 3, 4].

Meanwhile, network connections and client devices on the Internet are becoming increasingly heterogeneous. New types of client devices such as personal digital assistants (PDAs), mobile phones, palmtop and laptop personal computers continue to emerge. They differ considerably in processing, storage and display capabilities. Different clients may run different playback software requiring different encoding formats. Moreover, the characteristics of access links between the clients and the Internet also vary widely, ranging from narrowband wireless and modem connections (9.6 Kbps – 56 Kbps) to broadband connections (1 Mbps – 100 Mbps). Therefore, in the highly heterogeneous Internet environment, it is difficult to provide a single version of streaming media that can run satisfactorily on all clients. Multimedia contents may need to be converted to a form suitable for display on the target client depending on the availability of resources. This conversion process is called *transcoding*. Possible forms of transcoding include lowering the bit rate of a media stream by reducing the image resolution, size and/or frame rate, converting a media stream from one encoding format to another, and a combination of these. Transcoding can be performed at either the content servers or proxies. In server-based transcoding [5], web objects are transcoded to some predetermined versions in an offline fashion to reduce processing cost when the objects are accessed. However, server-based transcoding is not as flexible as proxy-based transcoding in that it is not as adaptive to changes in the clients' requirements [6]. Proxy-based transcoding [6, 7] relieves content providers from the burden of having to keep track of client device characteristics and maintain multiple versions of the same object. Moreover, it can be deployed without modification to existing content servers. Several transcoding proxy proposals have appeared in the literature recently [8, 9].

Providing transcoding service at the proxies has introduced new challenges on proxy caching. The transcoding process is typically computation intensive. With transcoding, considerable amount of CPU resource at the proxy is required to complete a request. Thus, in addition to the objective of reducing network traffic addressed by existing caching schemes [10, 11], the potential bottleneck of proxy CPU needs to be considered as well. An effective caching scheme for transcoding proxies should deal with network and CPU demands in an integrated fashion. So far, to the best of our knowledge, there has been no related study on caching algorithms for transcoding proxies that take multiple resources into account to improve streaming media delivery.

Multiple versions of the same object are candidates for caching in transcoding proxies. In this paper, we study and compare the performance of a variety of algorithms that keep different object versions in the cache. The focus of our study is the impact on resource demands. In particular, a new adaptive caching algorithm is proposed. The algorithm determines which object versions to cache based on current network and CPU loadings. Our experimental results show that the adaptive algorithm significantly outperforms those algorithms that cache only untranscoded or only transcoded object versions. In addition, we consider a partitioning technique for caching video objects. The motivation came from the fact that frames encoded in different modes (see Section 3.4 for details) have very different characteristics. In MPEG for example, B frames are typically the smallest in size but require the

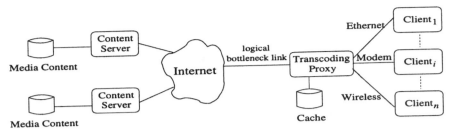

Figure 1. System Architecture

largest CPU time to transcode; while I frames have the largest size but take the least CPU time to transcode. Therefore, it seems desirable to divide a video object into sections based on frame type and handle the sections individually.

The rest of the paper is organized as follows. Section 2 gives an overview of the system architecture we consider. Various caching algorithms for transcoding proxies are presented in Section 3. The simulation model and experimental results are discussed in Sections 4 and 5 respectively. Section 6 describes the related work, and finally, Section 7 concludes the paper.

2 System Architecture

As shown in Figure 1, we consider a media streaming architecture consisting of content servers, transcoding proxies and various types of client devices.

Prerecorded media objects such as audio and video are stored and serviced by the content servers. These objects are referred to as *full object versions*. If the resources required to play a full object version exceed those available at a client, the full object version will have to be transcoded to a version with lower quality (e.g., in terms of display resolution and color depth) to meet the client's capabilities. The transcoding proxy is generally located close to its clients and connected to the content servers via the Internet. The transmission capacity from the content servers to the proxy is modeled by a logical bottleneck link with bandwidth B. For the purpose of this study, we assume B is fixed and known. A variety of client devices can connect to the proxy through different types of networks such as Ethernet, telephone modem and wireless network. To cater for different client capabilities, a full object version may have multiple transcoded versions, one for each class of clients. However, for simplicity, we shall assume a transcoded version can only be produced from the full version. The transcoding capability of the proxy is characterized by its CPU power C. Note that the transcoding proxy in our architecture is considered a logical entity. It could consist of multiple physical entities responsible for different tasks [12].

The request handling procedure proceeds as follows. A user's request for a media object is directed to the proxy. The request in our architecture contains two parts: the name of the media object and the capability of the client device (e.g., specified in the form of User Agent Profile recommended by WAP [13]). Upon receiving the request, the proxy searches its cache for the appropriate object version. One of the following situations can occur:

- *Version Hit*: If the requested object version matching the client's capability is cached, it is sent to the client directly;

- *Content Hit*: If the proxy does not have the requested object version but has the corresponding full version, transcoding

is necessary. The proxy determines the CPU resource (in terms of the proportion of CPU power) required[1]. If there is sufficient CPU power available, the proxy starts transcoding and sends the output stream to the client. The required CPU power is reserved throughout the streaming session. On the other hand, if there is not sufficient CPU power available, the user request is blocked.

- *Cache Miss*: If neither the requested object version nor the full version is in the cache, the full version has to be retrieved from the content server. The proxy determines the bandwidth requirement to fetch the full object version and compares it with the available bandwidth on the bottleneck link. If the available bandwidth is inadequate, the request is blocked. On the other hand, if bandwidth is available, the proxy checks to see whether transcoding is necessary. If transcoding is not needed, the request is accepted and the required link bandwidth is reserved over the lifetime of the stream. Otherwise, the full version has to be transcoded. The decision to accept the request in this case depends on the CPU resource checking process discussed in the situation of content hit. If the request is accepted, the required link bandwidth and CPU power are both reserved for the entire streaming session.

To summarize, depending on the requested object version and the cache status, zero, one or two types of resources may be needed to complete a user request. Table 1 lists the resource demands in the different cases, where the "network" resource refers to that between the content servers and the proxy. The user request is accepted if all required resources are available. Otherwise, the request is blocked.

requested version	cached version			
	full & transcoded	transcoded	full	none
full	none	network	none	network
transcoded	none	none	CPU	network & CPU

Table 1. Summary of Resource Requirements

3 Caching Algorithms

In this section, several caching algorithms for transcoding proxies are discussed. Since web workload changes with time, we concentrate on dynamic caching algorithms that update the cache

---

[1]The issue of estimating the CPU resource requirement is addressed elsewhere (e.g., [14]) and is out of the scope of this paper.

contents continuously at every cache miss rather than static algorithms that reorganize the contents of the entire cache at relatively long and fixed interval (such as days or weeks). Our objective is to minimize the overall request blocking probability.

3.1 Full Version Only (FVO) Algorithm

A common goal of existing caching algorithms for traditional web pages is to reduce the network traffic between the content servers and the proxy [11]. The Full Version Only (FVO) algorithm is a simple extension of this class of algorithms. FVO ignores the existence of transcoded object versions and only caches full object versions. To reduce network demand, the caching gain of a full object version is determined by its bandwidth consumption. Consider a full object version v. Let $f(v)$ be the access frequency[2] of v. Let $b(v)$ and $l(v)$ be the bandwidth requirement to fetch v from the content server and the session duration of v respectively. The caching gain of v is given by $f(v) \cdot b(v) \cdot l(v)$. To maximize the total caching gain, FVO tries to cache full object versions with the highest gain density (i.e., the caching gain per unit cache space occupied)

$$D_{net}(v) = \frac{f(v) \cdot b(v) \cdot l(v)}{s(v)},$$

where $s(v)$ is the size of v. Figure 2 presents the FVO algorithm in pseudo code form.

```
let v be the full version of the requested media object;
if (the request is not blocked) {
    let available space AS = current free space;
    while (AS < s(v)) {
        look for unmarked and idle object version u
            in the cache with the lowest D_net(u);
        if ((u cannot be found) or (D_net(u) > D_net(v))
            break;
        else
            mark u and let AS = AS + s(u);
    }
    if (AS ≥ s(v))
        remove all marked object versions and cache v;
}
```

Figure 2. FVO Algorithm

Since no transcoded object version is cached by FVO, the full version v of the requested media object is always accessed. The FVO algorithm is invoked if v is not in the cache and the request is accepted. If there is not enough cache space to accommodate v, FVO searches for replacement candidates in increasing order of gain density. A cached full version u is eligible for replacement only if u is *idle* (i.e., it is not currently being accessed by any request) and $D_{net}(u) \leq D_{net}(v)$. The second condition ensures that the removed objects have lower gain density than the new object v and hence the replacement operation would not reduce the total caching gain. If sufficient space for v cannot be created even

---

[2]The term "access frequency" in this paper refers to the total rate that an object version is referenced in processing user requests. Note that if a user request is serviced by on-demand transcoding, both the full and the transcoded versions are referenced. An approach to estimate access frequency is presented in Section 4.

by removing all eligible candidates, the cache contents are not updated, i.e., v is streamed to the client without depositing a copy at the proxy.

3.2 Transcoded Version Only (TVO) Algorithm

The Transcoded Version Only (TVO) algorithm aims at reducing CPU demand by only caching the transcoded object versions. The caching gain of a transcoded object version is defined as its CPU consumption to transcode. Suppose v is a transcoded object version and v_F is the corresponding full version. Let $c(v)$ be the required proportion of CPU power to transcode v_F to v. Then the caching gain of v is given by $f(v) \cdot c(v) \cdot l(v)$, where $l(v) = l(v_F)$ is the session duration of v. Similar to FVO, to maximize the total caching gain, TVO tries to cache transcoded object versions with the highest gain density

$$D_{cpu}(v) = \frac{f(v) \cdot c(v) \cdot l(v)}{s(v)},$$

where $s(v)$ is the size of v. Figure 3 presents the TVO algorithm in pseudo code form. The TVO algorithm is invoked every time a transcoded object version v not in the cache is requested and the request is accepted.

```
let v be the transcoded object version being requested;
if (the request is not blocked) {
    let available space AS = current free space;
    while (AS < s(v)) {
        look for unmarked and idle object version u
            in the cache with the lowest D_cpu(u);
        if ((u cannot be found) or (D_cpu(u) > D_cpu(v))
            break;
        else
            mark u and let AS = AS + s(u);
    }
    if (AS ≥ s(v))
        remove all marked object versions and cache v;
}
```

Figure 3. TVO Algorithm

3.3 Adaptive Caching Algorithm

Both the FVO and TVO algorithms have advantages and drawbacks. FVO tries to reduce network demand by caching full object versions. However, it puts much more CPU demand on the transcoding proxy as a transcoded object version needs to be produced on-the-fly every time it is requested. On the other hand, TVO reduces computation demand by caching the transcoded object versions. The drawback is that multiple versions of the same objects may have to be cached, resulting in possibly higher cache miss ratio.

To minimize the overall blocking probability, we propose an adaptive caching algorithm that considers network and CPU resources in an integrated fashion. Notice that a user request may result in one of three actions: (1) request is blocked by the bottleneck link (*network block*); (2) request can be accommodated by the bottleneck link but is blocked by the proxy's CPU (*CPU block*); and (3) request is accepted. The fractions of requests resulting in network blocks and CPU blocks are referred to as the *network blocking probability* p_n and the *CPU blocking probability* p_c respectively. The overall blocking probability is the sum of these two probabilities. Let $p = p_c/(p_n + p_c)$ be the *relative CPU blocking ratio*. A value of p close to 1 implies that CPU capacity rather than network bandwidth is the limiting resource. On the other hand, a value of p close to 0 indicates that network bandwidth is the limiting resource. Our design guideline is to cache appropriate object versions to reduce the burden on the potential bottleneck at the time of caching decision, be it network bandwidth or CPU capacity.

We assign two gain density values for each object version: a network gain density and a CPU gain density. Consider an object version v. The network gain density of v is defined as

$$D_{net}(v) = \frac{f(v) \cdot b(v_F) \cdot l(v)}{s(v)},$$

where v_F is the corresponding full version of v ($v_F = v$ if v is a full object version), and the CPU gain density of v is given by

$$D_{cpu}(v) = \begin{cases} 0 & \text{if } v \text{ is a full object version,} \\ \frac{f(v) \cdot c(v) \cdot l(v)}{s(v)} & \text{if } v \text{ is a transcoded object version.} \end{cases}$$

In our algorithm, the value of p is dynamically estimated based on recent request history. At every accepted request, *all* accessed object versions are considered for caching. A threshold-based policy is employed to decide which gain density metric should be used for making caching decisions. If p exceeds a given threshold α, the CPU gain density is selected. In this way, full object versions are removed from the cache first since they have $D_{cpu}(v)$ values of 0, and transcoded object versions enter the cache to reduce future CPU demand. On the other hand, if p is below the threshold α, the network gain density is selected and full object versions will likely have higher priority to be cached. Having determined the metric, the caching algorithm proceeds similarly to that of TVO or FVO, and is not reproduced here.

3.4 Partitioning Enhancement

Inter-frame techniques are commonly used by video encoding algorithms such as MPEG to achieve a high compression ratio. The rationale is that the difference in information between adjacent pictures is generally much smaller than the amount of data contained in one picture. With inter-frame techniques, the frames of a video stream are encoded in three modes: intra-frame (I), predicted (P) and bidirectional interpolated (B). As shown in Figure 4, an I frame is encoded independently as a still picture, a P frame is encoded with reference to the preceding I or P frame, and a B frame is encoded with reference to both the preceding and following I or P frames.

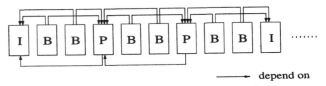

Figure 4. Frame Encoding Dependency

A transcoding process usually consists of two parts: decoding and encoding. Generally, the encoding process requires much

higher CPU time. Furthermore, the CPU time to encode and hence to transcode a frame varies significantly for different frame types. B frames take the most CPU resource to transcode and I frames take the least. On the other hand, B frames are the smallest in size and I frames are the largest. Figure 5(a) shows the average sizes of I, P and B frames relative to one another (normalized by the average size of I frames) for some MPEG-1 video traces [15]. Figure 5(b) shows the CPU time to size ratios of the three frame types (normalized by that of I frames) assuming the ratio of the CPU times to transcode an I, P and B frame is 1 : 3 : 3.5. As can be seen, I, P and B frames have very different CPU time to size ratios. Therefore, they are expected to have different CPU gain densities when cached – B frames are the most beneficial to cache while I frames are the least beneficial.

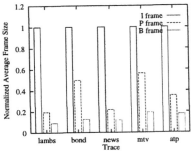

(a) Normalized Average Frame Size

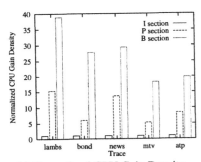

(b) Normalized CPU Gain Density

Figure 5. Comparison of Different Frame Types

Based on these observations, we propose to partition an object version into three sections when inter-frame technique is used: I section, P section and B section. Each section contains all frames of the corresponding type for the entire session and is managed as a caching unit. Let v be an object version and v_X be the X section of v ($X = I, P, B$). The CPU gain density for each section is given by

$$\begin{cases} D_{cpu}(v_I) = \frac{f(v_I) \cdot c(v_I) \cdot l(v)}{s(v_I)} \\ D_{cpu}(v_P) = \frac{f(v_P) \cdot c(v_P) \cdot l(v)}{s(v_P)} \\ D_{cpu}(v_B) = \frac{f(v_B) \cdot c(v_B) \cdot l(v)}{s(v_B)}, \end{cases}$$

where $f(v_X)$ and $s(v_X)$ are the access frequency and size of v_X respectively, $c(v_X)$ is the required CPU power to produce v_X, and $l(v)$ is the session duration of v. For a full object version, we have $c(v_I) = c(v_P) = c(v_B) = 0$ and hence $D_{cpu}(v_I) = D_{cpu}(v_P) = D_{cpu}(v_B) = 0$. For a transcoded object version, since $f(v_I) = f(v_P) = f(v_B)$, as explained above, we have

290

$D_{cpu}(v_I) < D_{cpu}(v_P) < D_{cpu}(v_B)$. With the above definition of CPU gain density, the partitioning technique can be applied in the TVO algorithm in a straightforward manner.

To integrate the partitioning technique into the adaptive algorithm proposed in Section 3.3, we define the network gain density for each section as follows:

$$\begin{cases} D_{net}(v_I) = \frac{f(v_I) \cdot b(v_{FI}) \cdot l(v)}{s(v_I)} \\ D_{net}(v_P) = \frac{f(v_P) \cdot b(v_{FP}) \cdot l(v)}{s(v_P)} \\ D_{net}(v_B) = \frac{f(v_B) \cdot b(v_{FB}) \cdot l(v)}{s(v_B)}, \end{cases}$$

where v_F is the corresponding full version of v, v_{FX} is v_X's corresponding section in v_F, and $b(v_{FX})$ is the bandwidth requirement to fetch v_{FX} from the content server. Notice that for sections belonging to the same transcoded object, v_B needs v_{FB} to encode which in turn depends on v_{FP} and v_{FI} to decode. Similarly, v_P needs v_{FP} to encode which in turn relies on v_{FI} to decode. Thus, v_{FP} would be referenced if v_B or v_P is not available, and v_{FI} would be referenced if at least one of v_I, v_B and v_P is not available. This implies that the caching gain $D_{net}(v_P)$ cannot be achieved unless both v_B and v_P are cached and the caching gain $D_{net}(v_I)$ is not attainable unless all v_B, v_P and v_I are cached. Therefore, when the D_{net} metric is applied, the caching priority order $v_B > v_P > v_I$ should be observed for sections belonging to the same transcoded object. That is, v_P is eligible for caching only if v_B is cached, and v_I is eligible for caching only if both v_P and v_B are cached. This is consistent with the priority order when D_{cpu} metric is used since $D_{cpu}(v_I) < D_{cpu}(v_P) < D_{cpu}(v_B)$ as discussed earlier. Therefore, the partitioning technique can be smoothly integrated into the adaptive algorithm.

The TVO and adaptive algorithms enhanced with the partitioning technique are referred to as the P-TVO and P-Adaptive algorithms respectively.

4 Simulation Methodology

An event-driven simulator has been developed to compare the performance of the caching algorithms discussed in the previous section. The simulator models the architecture described in Section 2 (see Figure 1).

In the simulation, the media objects are assumed to be videos. Each video is characterized by a description vector: $\{duration, size, isize, psize, bsize\}$, where $duration$, $size$, $isize$, $psize$ and $bsize$ are the session duration (in minutes), total size, I section size, P section size and B section size (in bytes) of the video respectively. To use real data for the experiments, we have constructed a library of 250 description vectors using frame size sequences extracted from MPEG-1 video traces [15]. The video traces covered a range of applications such as movies and news. They were encoded at the frame rate of 25 fps with the GOP structure IBBPBBPBBPBB. The session lengths of constructed description vectors were uniformly distributed between 1 and 25 minutes.

A total of N distinct videos were assumed to be stored in the content servers. Each video was assigned a vector randomly selected from the library. The reference frequencies of the N videos followed a Zipf-like distribution [16]. Specifically, the popularity of the ith video was proportional to $1/i^{\alpha}$, where α is the Zipf parameter. The larger the value of α, the more highly skewed the distribution. The default values of N and α were set at 2000 and 0.8 respectively. User requests were generated based on a Poisson process with mean inter-arrival time T which was set to 18 seconds in our simulation.

For simplicity, the bandwidth requirement to fetch a video from the content server is assumed to be its average bit rate i.e., $size/duration$. Similarly, the bandwidth requirements to retrieve the I, P and B sections are set to $isize/duration$, $psize/duration$ and $bsize/duration$ respectively. Figure 6 shows the distribution histogram of the bandwidth requirements of all videos, where each bar represents the fraction of videos in a 50 Kbps interval. Under the default parameter setting, the total bandwidth requirement $TotalB$ on the bottleneck link was about 20 Mbps without caching. We use the *bandwidth coefficient* to describe the capacity of the bottleneck link relative to $TotalB$ in the experiments. The bandwidth coefficient is given by $B/TotalB$, where B is the actual link capacity. Obviously, the smaller the coefficient, the less adequate the bottleneck link bandwidth.

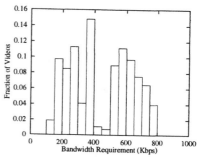

Figure 6. Distribution of Bandwidth Requirement

In the experiments, we used 6 classes of clients with different maximum allowable rate of video streams due to their device characteristics and access bandwidths to the Internet. These range from broadband to modem accesses and from desktop computers to mobile devices under different network conditions. Table 2 shows the maximum allowable rates and accessing probabilities of the client classes.

class	1	2	3
max. allowable rate	1 Mbps	512 Kbps	256 Kbps
accessing probability	0.15	0.2	0.2
class	4	5	6
max. allowable rate	128 Kbps	56 Kbps	19.2 Kbps
accessing probability	0.2	0.15	0.1

Table 2. Classes of Clients

A full video retrieved from the content server has to be transcoded by the proxy if it is to be played on a client with inadequate capability. Thus, a full video v has one transcoded version for each class of clients with capability below v's bandwidth requirement. For instance, a 600 Kbps full video has 5 transcoded versions while a 200 Kbps full video has only 3 transcoded versions. The size of a transcoded video is computed by scaling down the full video size by the bandwidth reduction ratio. For simplicity, we assume that bandwidth reductions are achieved by lowering the image resolution. Since the CPU time required for encoding is proportional to image resolution and the encoding time

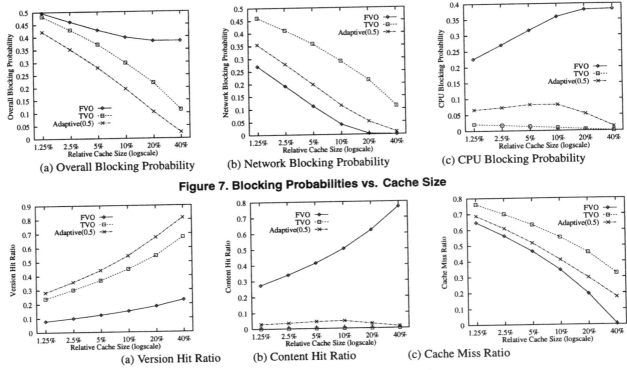

Figure 7. Blocking Probabilities vs. Cache Size

(a) Overall Blocking Probability   (b) Network Blocking Probability   (c) CPU Blocking Probability

(a) Version Hit Ratio   (b) Content Hit Ratio   (c) Cache Miss Ratio

Figure 8. Detailed Cache Hit Ratio Analysis

dominates the overall transcoding time, the CPU requirement of a transcoding task is assumed to be proportional to the image resolution and hence the bit rate of the transcoded video. The ratio[3] of the CPU time to transcode an I, P and B frame was set to 1 : 3 : 3.5. Similar to the bottleneck link capacity, the CPU power of the proxy is described by the *CPU coefficient* in the experiments. The CPU coefficient is a measure of the CPU power of the proxy relative to its transcoding workload without caching, i.e., $1/(\sum_{v \in T} f(v) \cdot c(v) \cdot l(v))$, where T is the set of all transcoded videos, $c(v)$ is the required proportion of proxy CPU power to generate v from the corresponding full video, $f(v)$ and $l(v)$ are the access frequency and session duration of v respectively.

The cache size at the proxy is described relative to the total size of all full and transcoded versions of the videos (about 220 GB). For example, a relative cache size of 10% means the actual cache size is 22 GB. The default relative cache size was set at 10%. A sliding window technique is used to estimate the access frequency of a caching unit (i.e., an object version or a section) dynamically [17]. Specifically, the time-stamps of the most recent K accesses are recorded for the unit. The access frequency is estimated by $K/(t - t_K)$, where t is the current time and t_K is the time-stamp of the Kth most recent access. To make the estimation less sensitive to transient workload, K was set to 2 in our simulation [17]. The access frequency estimate is updated when the caching unit is referenced, and also at reasonably large intervals to reflect aging. For the adaptive algorithms, the value of p, i.e., the relative CPU blocking ratio (see Section 3.3), was dynamically es-

timated by the CPU and network blocking probabilities in the last 200 requests. The default value of threshold α was set to 0.5.

We have performed experiments over a wide range of system characteristics including bandwidth coefficient, CPU coefficient and cache size. The results of the experiments are presented in the following section.

5 Experimental Results

The main objective of the experiments is to compare the *relative* performance of the caching algorithms for transcoding proxies. The overall blocking probability is used as the main performance metric in the experiments. It measures the percentage of user requests that are blocked due to insufficient network or CPU resource. For presentation purposes, the adaptive algorithms employing the threshold α are referred to as Adaptive(α) and P-Adaptive(α).

5.1 Impact of Cache Size

First, we compared the performance of FVO, TVO and Adaptive(0.5) under different cache sizes. Figure 7(a) shows the overall blocking probability when the bandwidth and CPU coefficients were both set to 0.25. As can be seen, the overall blocking probability decreased with increasing cache size for all algorithms. Adaptive(0.5) consistently outperformed FVO and TVO throughout the range of cache sizes examined.

The advantages of the adaptive algorithm are explained with the help of two other sets of figures. Figure 7(b) and (c) shows the network and CPU blocking probabilities, and Figure 8 presents the version hit ratio, content hit ratio and miss ratio of the cache for the three algorithms.

---

[3]We conducted experiments for different ratios and found the general performance trends are not sensitive to the ratio.

From Figure 8(c), it can be seen that FVO had the lowest cache miss ratio. This implies that caching only the full videos is effective in saving network bandwidth, and indeed we see from Figure 7(b) that FVO produced the lowest network blocking probability. However, by comparing Figures 8(a) and (b), it can be observed that most of the hits under FVO were content hits, which require transcoding to complete the requests. As a result, more transcoding activities took place in the proxy, leading to high CPU blocking probability (see Figure 7(c)). On the other hand, TVO only caches transcoded videos thereby reducing the CPU demand at the proxy considerably. Therefore, as shown in Figures 8(a) and 7(c), TVO was able to achieve a much higher version hit ratio than FVO, and its CPU blocking probability was the lowest among the three algorithms. However, caching a transcoded video is useful for a smaller portion of requests than caching a full video, and therefore it is not as effective in saving bandwidth. Furthermore, under TVO, user requests for full videos always result in cache misses. Consequently, TVO is seen to incur the highest cache miss ratio and network blocking probability (see Figures 8(c) and 7(b)). Unlike FVO and TVO, the adaptive algorithm caches both full and transcoded videos. By using a threshold-based policy to dynamically select the suitable gain density metric for use in caching decisions, network and CPU demands are reduced in a balanced fashion. As shown in Figure 7(c), Adaptive(0.5) succeeded in maintaining the CPU blocking probability at a relatively low level. From Figures 8(a) and (c), it can be seen that Adaptive(0.5) obtained the highest version hit ratio among the three algorithms and its miss ratio was close to that of FVO. Consequently, Adaptive(0.5) was able to achieve the least overall blocking probability (see Figure 7(a)).

5.2 Impact of Bandwidth and CPU Coefficients

In this section, we examine the impact of bandwidth and CPU coefficients. The relative cache size was set at 10%. Figure 9 shows the overall blocking probability as a function of the bandwidth coefficient with the CPU coefficient fixed at 0.25.

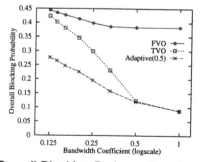

Figure 9. Overall Blocking Prob. vs. Bandwidth Coeff.

As can be seen, the adaptive algorithm produced the lowest blocking probability over a wide range of bandwidth coefficients. In general, the higher the bandwidth coefficient, the lower the blocking probability. Among the three algorithms studied, FVO was the least sensitive to bandwidth coefficient. Its blocking probability decreased slowly with increasing bandwidth coefficient but stopped to improve when the coefficient exceeded 0.3. This is because FVO does not cache transcoded videos to alleviate the CPU bottleneck which is dominant when the bandwidth coefficient is

large. In this case, FVO was unable to make further use of the additional bandwidth and its performance remained fairly constant. In contrast, TVO was the most sensitive to bandwidth coefficient. As discussed in Section 5.1, TVO is not very effective in saving bandwidth. Therefore, from Figure 9, its performance was seen to improve rapidly as the bandwidth coefficient increased. When the coefficient was 1.0, i.e., the bottleneck link was able to accommodate all traffic without caching, its performance was equal to that of Adaptive(0.5).

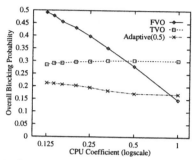

Figure 10. Overall Blocking Prob. vs. CPU Coeff.

Figure 10 shows the impact of the CPU coefficient on the overall blocking probability with the bandwidth coefficient fixed at 0.25. It is seen that the performance of Adaptive(0.5) was much better than those of FVO and TVO over a wide range of CPU coefficients. Since FVO requires all transcoded videos to be dynamically generated at each request, its blocking probability dropped significantly as the CPU coefficient increased. FVO slightly outperformed Adaptive(0.5) when the CPU coefficient was 1.0, i.e., the CPU was powerful enough to dynamically produce all transcoded videos without caching. On the other hand, with a relative cache size of 10%, TVO eliminated most of the transcoding tasks by only caching the transcoded videos, leaving the network as the limiting resource. Consequently, unlike the case of varying bandwidth coefficient, TVO showed fairly constant blocking probabilities under different CPU coefficients.

The results presented in Figures 9 and 10 imply that the proposed algorithm adapts well to changes in available network and CPU resources.

5.3 Impact of Threshold α

The adaptive algorithm reduces CPU demand more aggressively with smaller threshold. In this section, we study the impact of threshold α on performance. Figure 11 shows the experimental results of five different threshold values: 0.01, 0.05, 0.1, 0.5 and 1.0. In these experiments, the bandwidth coefficient was varied from 0.67 to 0.125, the CPU coefficient was set at 0.25, and the relative cache size was 10%. Experimental results with other CPU coefficients and cache sizes showed similar performance trends and are not presented due to space limitation.

At the bandwidth coefficient of 0.67, the CPU resource (at CPU coefficient of 0.25) was relatively less adequate than the network resource. It was therefore desirable to cache more transcoded videos to release the burden on the CPU. Consequently, Adaptive(1.0) is seen to perform worse than others. As the bandwidth coefficient decreased, the network bottleneck became more critical. Thus, the relative performance of Adaptive(1.0) improved.

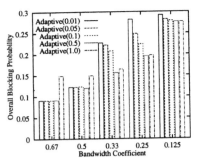

Figure 11. Overall Blocking Prob. vs. Threshold α

For example, Adaptive(0.5) outperformed Adaptive(1.0) by 39% at bandwidth coefficient 0.67, but the advantage was only about 20% when the bandwidth coefficient was 0.5. Meanwhile, the CPU bottleneck became less significant. Hence, the relative performance degraded for algorithms with very small thresholds. As shown in Figure 11, Adaptive(0.01) performed much worse than Adaptive(0.5) at bandwidth coefficients 0.33 and 0.25. When the available bandwidth further decreased, the network became the dominant bottleneck. In this case, the CPU was almost always capable of handling the requests admitted by the bottleneck link, leading to a relative CPU blocking ratio close to 0. Therefore, the value of α had little impact on the overall blocking probability and all adaptive algorithms performed at a similar level (see the case of bandwidth coefficient = 0.125). In these experiments, Adaptive(0.5) was seen to perform well over a wide range of system parameters, indicating that CPU and network demands should be reduced in a balanced fashion.

5.4 Performance of Partitioning Enhancement

Finally, we study the performance of partitioning enhancement. Figure 12 plots the overall blocking probability against the Zipf parameter for four algorithms: TVO, P-TVO, Adaptive(0.5) and P-Adaptive(0.5). In this set of experiments, the bandwidth coefficient, CPU coefficient and relative cache size were set to 1.0, 0.25 and 20% respectively.

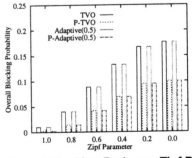

Figure 12. Overall Blocking Prob. vs. Zipf Parameter

In general, P-TVO and P-Adaptive(0.5) performed better than their non-partitioning counterparts, and the improvement increased with decreasing Zipf parameter value. Recall that the partitioning enhancement scheme evaluates the caching benefits of I, P and B sections individually. For large Zipf parameter values (i.e., when the reference pattern is highly skewed), the reference frequency is the dominant factor influencing the gain den-

sity. In this case, $D_{cpu}(v_B)$ of a less popular video v will not likely exceed $D_{cpu}(v'_I)$ of a more popular video v'. Hence, partitioning will not make a significant difference on performance. As shown in Figure 12, the absolute performance difference was small between Adaptive(0.5) and P-Adaptive(0.5) at the Zipf parameter value of 1.0, and the same was true for TVO and P-TVO. In contrast, for small Zipf parameter values (i.e., when the reference pattern is close to uniform), the CPU time to size ratio (i.e., $c(v_X) \cdot l(v)/s(v_X)$) is the dominant factor affecting the gain density. Therefore, partitioning will have significant impact on performance. In Figure 12, it is clearly shown that P-TVO and P-Adaptive(0.5) outperformed TVO and Adaptive(0.5) significantly for Zipf parameter values of 0.0 and 0.2.

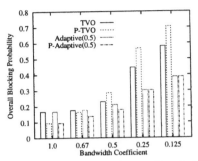

Figure 13. Overall Blocking Prob. vs. Bandwidth Coeff.

Since partitioning reduces CPU demand by taking advantage of different CPU gain densities among sections, it is expected to be more effective when the CPU is the limiting resource. Figure 13 shows the experimental results for different bandwidth coefficients with the Zipf parameter and CPU coefficient set at 0.2 and 0.25 respectively. As can be seen, the advantage of partitioning decreased with decreasing bandwidth coefficient. P-Adaptive(0.5) performed similarly to Adaptive(0.5) at bandwidth coefficients 0.25 and 0.125. On the other hand, since P-TVO does not take bandwidth demand into consideration, its performance deteriorated more rapidly than that of P-Adaptive(0.5) when the bandwidth coefficient decreased. From Figure 13, P-TVO is seen to perform worse than TVO at low bandwidth coefficients.

In summary, partitioning enhances performance when there are sufficient network bandwidth but limited CPU power, particularly when the reference pattern is not highly skewed.

6 Related Work

Some studies on transcoding proxy services for images [7] and videos [8, 9] exist. However, little work has been done on exploring the impact of transcoding on proxy caching. Cardellini *et al.* [18] demonstrated the importance of evenly distributing the computation load of transcoding in a proxy hierarchy to improve response time. Chang *et al.* [19] investigated various caching policies in the context of static web objects transcoding (e.g., HTML pages and images). Their objective was to reduce client access latency. However, they did not take into consideration of CPU contention at the proxy in caching policies. Our work differs from [19] in that we studied streaming media objects which continuously require CPU and network resources throughout the streaming session. We use overall blocking probability as the performance metric and have shown that CPU and network resource demands should be considered in an integrated fashion to improve performance.

While proxy caching of traditional web objects has been well investigated [20, 17, 21, 22], streaming media caching, even without transcoding, is an emerging area not sufficiently explored. Due to the large size of media objects, some research has examined the effectiveness of caching them partially (e.g., prefix caching [1] and segment-based caching [4]). These techniques may be integrated with our proposed scheme to further improve performance for transcoding proxies. Some recent work has studied caching mechanisms for layered encoded multimedia streams [2, 3]. Layered encoding is an alternative to transcoding in order to provide media streams with different resource requirements within the same encoding format. With layered encoding, a media object is encoded into a base layer and one or more enhancement layers. The number of layers to be sent to a client depends on the device characteristics and its access bandwidth to the Internet. However, layered encoding is not currently widely supported by content providers, and it does not preclude the need for inter-format transcoding.

7 Conclusion

The proliferation of different types of client devices and network access methods is making the Internet increasingly heterogeneous. Streaming media objects need to be transcoded to an appropriate version (format) to meet the client's capabilities. With transcoding, both network and CPU are potential bottlenecks for multimedia content delivery. In this paper, we have proposed a new adaptive caching algorithm for transcoding proxies. The algorithm reduces network and CPU demands in an integrated fashion by using a threshold-based policy to select the appropriate gain density metric for use in caching decisions. Extensive simulation experiments have been conducted to evaluate the proposed algorithm. The results show that it significantly outperforms those algorithms that cache only full or only transcoded object versions. Moreover, to take advantage of different CPU times to transcode different types of video frames, we have investigated partitioning a video object into sections based on frame type and handling them individually in proxy caching. It is shown that partitioning enhancement is effective when sufficient network bandwidth but limited CPU power are available, especially when the reference pattern is not highly skewed.

Acknowledgement

The work described in this paper was supported by a grant from the Research Grants Council of the Hong Kong Special Administrative Region, China.

References

[1] S. Sen, J. Rexford, and D. Towsley. Proxy prefix caching for multimedia streams. In *Proc. IEEE INFOCOM'99*, pages 1310–1319, Mar. 1999.

[2] R. Rejaie, H. Yu, M. Handley, and D. Estrin. Multimedia proxy caching mechanism for quality adaptive streaming applications in the internet. In *Proc. IEEE INFOCOM'00*, pages 980–989, Mar. 2000.

[3] J. Kangasharju, F. Hartanto, M. Reisslein, and K. W. Ross. Distributing layered encoded video through caches. In *Proc. IEEE INFOCOM'01*, pages 1791–1800, Apr. 2001.

[4] K.-L. Wu, P. S. Yu, and J. L. Wolf. Segment-based proxy caching of multimedia streams. In *Proc. 10th Int'l WWW Conf.*, pages 36–44, May 2001.

[5] R. Mohan, J. R. Smith, and C.-S. Li. Adapting multimedia internet content for universal access. *IEEE Trans. Multimedia*, 1(1):104–114, Mar. 1999.

[6] E. A. Brewer, R. H. Katz, Y. Chawathe, S. D. Gribble, T. Hodes, G. Nguyen, M. Stemm, T. Henderson, E. Amir, H. Balakrishnan, A. Fox, V. N. Padmanabhan, and S. Seshan. A network architecture for heterogeneous mobile computing. *IEEE Personal Comm.*, 5(5):8–24, Oct. 1998.

[7] R. Han, P. Bhagwat, R. LaMaire, T. Mummert, V. Perret, and J. Rubas. Dynamic adaptation in an image transcoding proxy for mobile web browsing. *IEEE Personal Comm.*, 5(6):8–17, Dec. 1998.

[8] C. K. Hess, D. Raila, R. H. Campbell, and D. Mickunas. Design and performance of mpeg video streaming to palmtop computers. In *Proc. SPIE/ACM MMCN'00*, pages 266–273, Jan. 2000.

[9] T. Warabino, S. Ota, D. Morikawa, M. Ohashi, H. Nakamura, H. Iwashita, and F. Watanabe. Video transcoding proxy for 3gwireless mobile internet access. *IEEE Comm. Magazine*, 38(10):66–71, Oct. 2000.

[10] P. Cao and S. Irani. Cost-aware www proxy caching algorithms. In *Proc. USENIX USITS'97*, pages 193–206, Dec. 1997.

[11] C. Aggarwal, J. L. Wolf, and P. S. Yu. Caching on the world wide web. *IEEE Trans. Knowledge and Data Eng.*, 11(1):94–107, Jan./Feb. 1999.

[12] A. Fox, S. D. Gribble, Y. Chawathe, E. A. Brewer, and P. Gauthier. Cluster-based scalable network services. In *Proc. ACM SOSP'97*, pages 78–91, Oct. 1997.

[13] WAP Forum. User agent profiling specification. *WAP-248-UAProf-20011020-p*, Oct. 2001.

[14] A. C. Bavier, A. B. Montz, and L. L. Peterson. Predicting mpeg execution times. In *Proc. ACM SIGMETRICS'98*, pages 131–140, June 1998.

[15] MPEG-1 Frame Size Traces. http://nero.informatik.uni-wuerzburg.de/MPEG/.

[16] L. Breslau, P. Cao, L. Fan, G. Phillips, and S. Shenker. Web caching and zipf-like distributions: Evidence and implications. In *Proc. IEEE INFOCOM'99*, pages 126–134, Mar. 1999.

[17] J. Shim, P. Scheuermann, and R. Vingralek. Proxy cache algorithms: Design, implementation, and performance. *IEEE Trans. Knowledge and Data Eng.*, 11(4):549–562, July/Aug. 1999.

[18] V. Cardellini, P. S. Yu, and Y.-W. Huang. Collaborative proxy system for distributed web content transcoding. In *Proc. ACM CIKM'00*, pages 69–76, Nov. 2000.

[19] C.-Y. Chang and M.-S. Chen. Exploring aggregate effect with weighted transcoding graphs for efficient cache replacement in transcoding proxies. In *Proc. IEEE ICDE'02*, pages 383–392, Feb. 2002.

[20] S. Williams, M. Abrams, C. R. Standridge, G. Abdulla, and E. A. Fox. Removal policies in network caches for world wide web documents. In *Proc. ACM SIGCOMM'96*, pages 293–305, Aug. 1996.

[21] J. Wang. A survey of web caching schemes for the Internet. *ACM SIGCOMM Computer Comm. Rev.*, 29(5):36–46, Oct. 1999.

[22] L. Rizzo and L. Vicisano. Replacement policies for a proxy cache. *IEEE/ACM Trans. Networking*, 8(2):158–170, Apr. 2000.

Popularity-Based PPM: An Effective Web Prefetching Technique for High Accuracy and Low Storage *

Xin Chen and Xiaodong Zhang
Department of Computer Science
College of William and Mary
Williamsburg, Virginia 23187-8795, USA

Abstract

Prediction by Partial Match (PPM) is a commonly used technique in Web prefetching, where prefetching decisions are made based on historical URLs in a dynamically maintained Markov prediction tree. Existing approaches either widely store the URL nodes by building the tree with a fixed height in each branch, or only store the branches with frequently accessed URLs. Building the popularity information into the Markov prediction tree, we propose a new prefetching model, called popularity-based PPM. In this model, the tree is dynamically updated with a variable height in each set of branches where a popular URL can lead a set of long branches, and a less popular document leads a set of short ones. Since majority root nodes are popular URLs in our approach, the space allocation for storing nodes are effectively utilized. We have also included two additional optimizations in this model: (1) directly linking a root node to duplicated popular nodes in a surfing path to give popular URLs more considerations for prefetching; and (2) making a space optimization after the tree is built to further remove less popular nodes. Our trace-driven simulation results comparatively show a significant space reduction and an improved prediction accuracy of the proposed prefetching technique.

1 Introduction

Accurately predicting Web surfing hyperlink paths based on the historical information of the surfing paths, we are able to reduce the Web access latencies by prefetching to-be-used Web data. Web prefetching is becoming important and demanding, even though the Web caching technique has been improved.

An important task for prefetching is to build an effective prediction model and its data structure for storing highly selective historical information. Prediction by Partial Match (PPM) is a commonly used technique in Web prefetching, where prefetching decisions are made based on historical URLs in a dynamically maintained Markov prediction tree. For a Web server supporting a huge amount of Web pages, a prefetching system built by the traditional PPM model occupies a significant portion of the memory space. We have conducted a comprehensive study to evaluate common Web surfing patterns and regularities related to popularities of URLs [6]. We characterize the surfing behavior of each individual client as an *access session* which consists of a sequence of Web URLs continuously visited by the same client. If a client has been idle for more than 30 minutes, we assume that the next request from the client starts a new access session. We have analyzed the surfing patterns of multiple trace files (to be discussed in the next section), and observed that high percentage of access sessions follow three strong regularities.

- **Regularity 1:** *Majority clients start their access sessions from popular URLs of a server. However, majority of URLs in a server are not popular files.*

- **Regularity 2:** *Majority long access sessions are headed by popular URLs.*

- **Regularity 3:** *The accessing paths in majority access sessions start from popular URLs, move to less popular URLs, and exit from the least URLs. The accessing paths in minority access sessions start from less popular URLs, and remain in the same type of URLs, and exit from the least URLs.*

The popularity information is ignored in existing prediction models, which is their major and common weakness. Building the popularity information into the Markov prediction tree, we propose a new prefetching model, called *popularity-based PPM*, to achieve both high prediction accuracy and low storage requirement.

*This work is supported in part by the National Science Foundation under grants CCR-9812187, EIA-9977030, and CCR-0098055.

Conducting trace-driven simulations, we show that our technique effectively combines the advantages of the existing PPM prefetching approaches, and addresses their limits. Compared with two existing PPM techniques, we show the popularity-based PPM significantly reduces the required space for storing the nodes by 1 to several dozen times. Furthermore, we show that our technique outperforms these techniques by 5 to 10% of hit ratios in most cases. We also demonstrate that the proposed prediction method is highly effective to be used between Web servers and Web proxies.

Our proposed prefetching technique not only reduces storage space significantly and improves the prediction accuracy, but also has the following advantages for Web servers. First, with the efficient data structure of compacted trees, the proposed technique significantly reduces the Web server processing time for prefetching, downloading the server burden. Second, the storage space requirement increases slightly as the number of days for URLs increases. In contrast, the storage requirement for existing PPM techniques increases in a much faster pace, limiting its scalability. Finally, since the popularity of Web files is normally stable over a long period, a prefetching system focusing on popular URLs that are frequently accessed would be relatively reliable. The study in [22] has a similar observation.

2 Evaluation Methodology

The popularity-based PPM model and related performance issues are evaluated by trace-driven simulations. The evaluation environment consists of different Web traces, a simulated server where different PPM models are built to make prefetching decisions, and multiple clients sending requests to the server and receiving requested and prefetched data from the server.

2.1 Traces

The Web traces we have used for performance evaluation are most recently available in public domains:

1. NASA [17]: There are two trace files available in the Internet Traffic Achieve site, which contain HTTP requests of two months to the NASA Kennedy Space Center WWW server in Florida. We have used the trace file of July, collected from 00:00:00 July 1, 1995 through 23:59:59 July 31, 1995, a total of 31 days. The interval of the timestamp is one second.

2. UCB-CS [9]: This trace contains HTTP requests of one week to the Web site (Apache httpd server) of the Department of Computer Science at the University of California at Berkeley. The recorded requests were from July 1, 2000 (Saturday), 00:00 am to July 11,

2000 (Monday) 00:00 am. The internal of the timestamp is one second.

2.2 Simulation

We have built a simulator to construct Web servers connected to clients. The requests to servers can be directly sent from the clients or from proxy caches. Several prefetching PPM models which will be discussed in next sections are built in the server. The server makes prefetching decisions based on the PPM models by sending both requested and prefetched data to the targeted clients. The PPM models are dynamically maintained and updated based on historical data during a period of time.

The simulator consists of two function parts: (1) analyzing traces and building PPM models, and (2) making predictions.

In practice, image files can be embedded in an HTML document. The embedded image files can be in types of ".gif", ".xbm", ".jpg", ".jpeg", ".gif89", ".tif", ".tiff", ".bmp", ".ief", ".jpe", ".ras", ".pnm", ".pgm", ".ppm", ".rgb", ".xpm", ".xwd", ".pcx", ".pbm", and ".pic". An HTML document can be in types of ".html", ".htm", ".shtml". If an HTML file of the same client is followed by image files in 10 seconds, we consider the image file as an embedded file in the HTML file. For these embedded files, we record them with the HTML files.

The simulator assumes both proxies and browsers exist, and are connected to the server. Identifications of users are useful information to construct the prediction structure. Unfortunately, limited HTTP log files identify the users making requests. Although some logs have unique user IDs for clients (for example, by storing HTTP cookies), this type of log files has only been available recently, but not available in the public domain. We have to use IP address which may represent proxy servers. We recognize that this may introduce some inaccuracy in our simulation, but it will not affect evaluation of the principles of different prefetching models.

The simulator makes the following assumption. If an address (or IP) sends requests more than 1000 per day, it is considered as a proxy, otherwise it is a browser. The proxy is assumed to have a disk cache size of 16 GB and a browser is assumed to have a cache of 10 MB. The cache replacement algorithm used in our simulator is LRU.

2.3 Performance Metrics

- *Hit ratio* is the ratio between the number of requests that hit in browser or proxy caches and the total number of requests.

- *Latency reduction* is the average access latency time reduction per request.

- *space* is the required memory allocation measured by the number of nodes for building a PPM model in the Web server for prefetching.

- *traffic increment* is the ratio between the total number of transferred bytes and the total number useful bytes for the clients minus 1.

3 Popularity-based PPM Model

In data compression community, researchers have developed several context models to use m proceeding symbols to determine the probability of next symbol (an m order Markov model). Prediction by Partial Match (PPM) (see e.g. [7]) is one of such context models, which has been actively used in Web predictions. Entropy analysis and empirical studies have shown that the prediction accuracy increases as the increase of the prediction order in each branch, so does the space storing the URL nodes of the PPM model (see e.g. [23]). In this section, we first review two representative methods to build PPM models for prefetching, and then propose our popularity-based PPM model.

3.1 Relative Popularity

The popularity of a Web URL is normally characterized by the number of accesses to it in a given period of time. The popularities of different URLs can be ranked by a server dynamically from time to time. We have calculated the popularities for all the URLs in each trace file collected from different servers by its Relative Popularity, RP. For a given URL, we have

$$RP = \frac{the\ number\ of\ accesses\ to\ the\ URL}{the\ highest\ popularity\ in\ the\ trace}, \quad (1)$$

where the *highest popularity* is the number of accesses to the most popular URL in the trace. This metric compares each URL with the most popular URL in the trace. For example, an URL with $RP = 10\%$ has received 10% accesses relative to the most popular URLs.

We have further ranked the popularities of URLs by 4 grades in a $\log_{10}$ base: Grade 3: $RP = (10\%, 100\%]$, Grade 2: $RP = (1\%, 10\%]$, Grade 1: $RP = (0.1\%, 1\%]$, and Grade 0: $RP \leq 0.1\%$.

The requests from individual client could be divided as *access session* which consists of a sequence of Web URLs continuously visited by the same client. If a client has been idle for more than 30 minutes, we assume that the next request from the client starts a new access session.

3.2 Two Existing PPM Models

There are two representative approaches to build a PPM prediction model. The first approach is to widely create branches from the historical URL files. The PPM tree is given a fixed height so that the length of each branch is not allowed to grow beyond the height. The left figure in Figure 1 shows the prediction tree structure of the standard PPM model for the access sequence of $\{ABCA'B'C'\}$. The advantage of this approach is that the model can be easily and regularly built with a low complexity. There are two major limits associated with this approach. First, the fixed height Markov prediction tree of PPM does not well match the common surfing patterns presented in the previous section. Second, the prediction accuracy can be low if the tree is short in order to save space; and the storage requirement can grow rapidly for a small height increment of the tree. This approach has been used in several prefetching prototypes and systems (see e.g. [26], [12]).

The other approach is to reduce the space requirement by only storing long branches with frequently accessed URLs, which is called LRS (Longest Repeating Subsequences) [23]. Since majority objects in Web servers are accessed infrequently, keeping only frequently accessed paths would not noticeably affect overall performance, but significantly reduce space requirement. Besides the advantage of space reduction, this approach also has high prediction accuracy from the high-order Markov models in a limited number of branches.

There are two limits for this approach. First, since the LRS-PPM model tree only keeps a small number of frequently accessed branches, prefetching for many less frequently accessed URLs is ignored, thus, the overall prefetching hit rates can be low. Second, in order to find the longest matching sequence, the server must have all the previous URLs of the current session, which is maintained by the server and updated based on the accessing information of clients. This process can be expensive.

3.3 Observations from the Two Models

Using popularity grades, we further examine the effectiveness and prefetching behavior of the standard PPM and LRS-PPM models. We have two following observations.

1. Majority hit documents from the prefetched files are popular documents.

Similar to a practical configuration, the height of the prediction tree of the standard PPM model is set to 3 in our experiments (simplified as 3-PPM). We only present the NASA trace here since the experiments with other traces show similar results. The left figure in Figure 2 presents comparisons of the percentage of the hit documents from the prefetched files using the standard PPM model (3-PPM), the LRS-PPM model (LRS), and our proposed popularity-based PPM (PB-PPM) to be discussed in the next section. Although the percentage of prefetched popular files

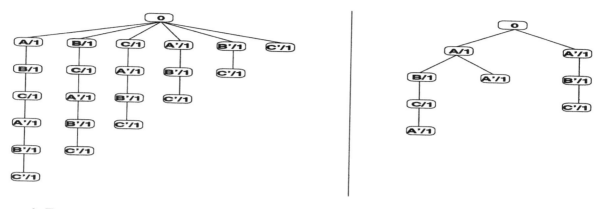

Figure 1. Tree structures of the standard PPM (left) and PB-PPM (right) models for the access sequence of $\{ABCA'B'C'\}$.

decreases as the historical record accumulated by multiple days increases, the percentage is at least 60%. The standard PPM model has the lowest percentage. Our experiments also show that the prediction accuracy on popular documents is higher than that on less popular documents in both 3-PPM and PB-PPM models.

2. A significant amount of predicted branches are unused in the two models.

In the standard PPM and LRS-PPM models, an URL in a session may be recorded multiple times. For example, for a repeated sequence of URL $\{ABCDEF\}$, C will be recorded twice and F will be recorded 5 times if we do not limit the length of prediction trees in both models. Although a large amount of information for prediction is available, the usage of different paths is not equal. If all accesses to C are after AB, the path BC will never be used. This is common due to the hierarchical structure of Web pages. Since only a small amount of paths are used, the tree structures in both models can occupy large memory space for many unused or infrequently used branches. We also evaluate the tree utilization of 3-PPM model and LRS model. We define a path as a URL sequence from the root to an ending leaf. If this path has been used, we mark it useful. The unmarked paths are unused paths. The right figure in Figure 2 presents the path utilization rates in the three models. When we increase the number of days for predictions, the utilization rates of both 3-PPM and LRS structures decrease rapidly. For example, the utilization rate of the 3-PPM model decrease to less than 20%, and LRS decreases to 40% when 7 days are used.

Our observations further confirm the important roles of popular documents in prefetching, and the lack of the utilization in the two existing models.

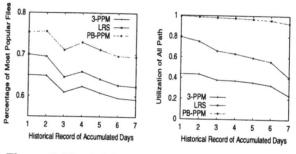

Figure 2. The left figure gives the percentages of popular documents in the total prefetched files. The right figure gives the utilization rates of paths for predictions.

3.4 Constructing a Popularity-based PPM Model

Building the popularity information into the Markov prediction tree, we propose a new prefetching model, called *popularity-based PPM*. In this model, the Markov prediction tree dynamically grows with a variable height in each branch where a popular URL can lead a set of long branches and a less popular document leads a set of short ones. This tree structure combines the advantages of the existing PPM prefetching approaches, and addresses their limits by improving the prediction accuracy from both long branches with popular URLs, while keeping the storage requirement low from only storing less popular documents in a large group of short branches. The popularity-based PPM is built with the following rules.

1. The heights for branches starting from different URLs are proportional to the relative popularity of the URLs. The proportional differences among different branches can be adjusted to adapt the changes of access patterns.

2. The initial maximum height is set by considering the available memory space for PPM model and access session lengths. If the lengths of most access sessions are short, building long branches in the PPM model may not be necessary. The maximum height is a moderate number in practice. Our experiments show that more than 95% of the access sessions have 9 or less URLs (or clicks). This is consistent with the results reported in [13] for a trace file of 3,247,054 Web page requests from 23,692 AOL users on December 5, 1997.

3. If the popularity grade of an URL not immediately following the heading URL in a branch is higher than the heading URL's grade, or is the highest grade, we will create a special link between the heading URL and a duplicated node of this URL. This approach gives popular URLs more considerations for prefetching, to increase the prediction accuracy and access hit ratios.

4. Each URL in a sequence is added only once to the tree unless the the URLs' popularity grade is higher than the node ahead of it. This approach limits the number of root nodes, effectively reducing the space requirement.

If symbols A, B, and C are three different URLs, notation ABC represents an access sequence to the three URLs by one or more clients. The right figure in Figure 1 gives an example on how a popularity-based PPM model is built based on access sequence $ABCA'B'C'$, where URLs A and A' have a predetermined popularity grade of 3, URLs B and B' have a predetermined popularity grade of 2, and URLs C and C' have a predetermined popularity grade of 1. In this example, the maximum height is 4.

We have further made space optimization after the popularity-based PPM tree is built by combining the following two alternatives. The first optimization is based on the relative access probability of non-root nodes in the tree, which is defined as the ratio between the number of accesses to a URL node and the number of accesses to its parent node. We examine each non-root node, and if the relative access probability is lower than a certain level (ranging 5% to 10% in our experiments), we will remove the node and its linked branches. The second space optimization alternative we have used is to remove each node to which the absolute number of accesses is only one. We will show that these two optimization alternatives can significantly reduce space in next section.

The left figure in 2 shows that the popularity-based PPM model significantly increases the usage of popular documents from the prefetched files, ranging from 70% to 75%. The right figure in 2 shows that the method significantly increases the path utilization rate, ranging from 92% to 100%.

4 Comparative Performance Evaluation

4.1 Simulation Parameters

We have implemented the three PPM prediction models for prefetching: (1) the standard PPM model without limiting the height for each branch, (In some experiments, we had to limit the heights due to limited memory space.) (2) the LRS model keeping the longest repeating subsequences in the PPM tree, and (3) our popularity-based PPM model with the space optimization.

In practice, the standard PPM model should be built with a fixed height for each branch. In order to maximize the prediction accuracy of the standard PPM model, we did not limit the height of each branch while building the model. This will give an upper bound of prediction accuracy for the PPM model.

For the LRS model, if an URL sequence is accessed twice or more, the sequence is considered as a frequently repeating one. A longest sequence covers many independent access sessions which can be removed from the PPM tree by keeping the longest sequence. Our implementations follow the original LRS design [23].

For the popularity-based PPM model, the maximum height of branches is set to 7 for heading URLs of grade 3, 5 for grade 2, 3 for grade 1, and 1 for grade 0 in our experiments. After the popularity-based PPM tree is built, we have done space optimization by cutting each branch which has 10% or lower relative access probability. If the absolute number of accesses to a node is no more than 1, we have also removed the node in for some traces (e.g. the UCB-CS trace).

A longest matching method is used in both the standard PPM and the LRS-PPM models, which matches as many previous URLs as possible to make a prediction. In contrast, when the current clicked URL is a root in the tree, the popularity-based PPM model will make additional predictions with the linked nodes which are duplicated popular ones in the branch.

We set two thresholds for predictions. One is used for the possibility of next accesses, which is set to 0.25 in all the models. Another is used for the maximum size of files to be prefetched. The threshold size affects both hit ratios and the amount of traffic increase. A large threshold allows more data to be prefetched, which is beneficial to hit ratios, but may increase traffics. Since the popularity-based PPM model gives more prefetching considerations to popular nodes, we limit its threshold to 30 Kbytes. The threshold for the standard PPM and LRS-PPM is set to 100 Kbytes.

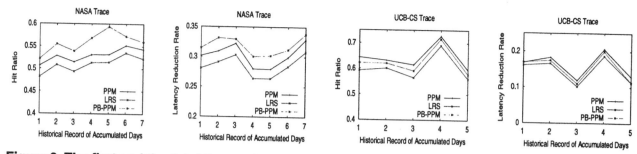

Figure 3. The first and the third figures (from left to right) give the hit ratios of two traces by the three different PPM prediction models. The second and the fourth figures give the comparisons of the latency reduction among the three models.

4.2 Hit Ratios and Latency Reductions

The leftmost figure in Figure 3 presents the changes of the hit ratios using the NASA trace versus the number of days used for predictions in prefetching. Our trace-driven simulation results show that hit ratios of the popularity-based PPM consistently higher than the other two prefetching models. Using historical data of five days to predict data accesses of the sixth day, the hit ratio of the popularity-based PPM is 20% and 13% higher than that of the LRS-PPM and the standard PPM models, respectively.

We estimated connection times and data transferring times by using the method presented in [16], where the connection time and the data transferring time are obtained by applying a least squares fit to measured latency in traces versus the size variations of documents fetched from different remote servers. The second figure in Figure 3 presents the comparisons of latency reductions using the NASA trace versus the number of days used for predictions in prefetching. We show that the popularity-based PPM outperforms both the standard PPM and the LRS-PPM models reducing 4% to 15% more average latency.

The right two figures in Figure 3 presents the performance results using the UCB-CS trace up to 5 days. The third figure in Figure 3 shows that the hit ratio of the popularity-based PPM is slightly lower than the the standard PPM model (a difference of about 2%), and is 6% higher than the LRS-PPM model. The rightmost figure in Figure 3 compares the latency reductions of the three models. The latency reductions of the popularity-based PPM model are slightly lower than the standard PPM (a difference of about 3%), and 4% higher than the LRS-PPM model. Compared with its significant space reduction, the popularity-based PPM model is still the most cost-effective one for the UCB-CS trace although the hit ratios and the latency reductions are not the highest.

4.3 Space and Traffic Overhead

Table 1 compares the number of URLs (nodes) stored by each of the three PPM models for predictions using the NASA trace. We show that number of nodes stored in the standard PPM model dramatically increases as the number files in days used for prediction increases. It is not fair to compare the standard PPM model with other models because we did not limit the height of each branch in the standard PPM model. However, the space requirement comparisons between the LRS-PPM and the popularity-based PPM are reasonable because both models optimize the space usage by different strategies.

The leftmost figure in Figure 4 plots the space requirement in number of nodes for the NASA trace as the number of days used for prediction increases. We show that the number of nodes required for LRS-PPM model proportionally and quickly increases as the number of days increases while the space requirement increases for the popularity-based PPM is in a much slower pace. The LRS quickly increases the space requirement by storing 1.73, 2.9, 3.8, 5.1, 6.4, and 6.9 times more nodes than the popularity-based PPM using 2, 3, 4, 5, 6, and 7 day files for predictions, respectively.

We have two major reasons to explain the quick increase of the number of nodes in LRS-PPM based on our experiments. First, each LRS branch in the model is further cut and paste into multiple sub-branches starting from different URLs. This process will produce node duplications. Second, as the number of day files increases, the number of the longest repeating sequences also proportionally increases, but the numbers of occurrences of subsequences which are also independent sequences decrease. In contrast, the popularity patterns are not changed a lot as the number of day files increases, thus, the popularity-based PPM model only moderately increases the number of nodes stored in the tree structure.

The second figure in Figure 4 compares the traffic in-

Days	1	2	3	4	5	6	7
PPM	424,387	1,008,905	1,674,680	2,588,131	3,115,732	3,575,437	4,133,146
LRS	9,715	19,567	33,233	44,325	56,635	70,247	82,525
PB-PPM	5,527	7,164	8,476	9,156	9,276	9,976	10,411

Table 1. Space size in number of nodes used for each PPM model for the NASA trace.

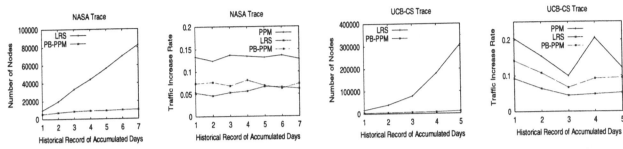

Figure 4. The first and the third figures (from left to right) give the number of nodes using two traces by the LRS-PPM and PB-PPM prediction models. The second and the fourth figures give the comparisons of the traffic increase percentage among the three models.

creases among the three PPM models for the NASA trace. The standard PPM model has the highest traffic increase (around 32%). The traffic increase of the popularity-based PPM model is about 23% while the LRS-PPM model is 22% when up to 4 day files are used. The traffic increases of the two models are quite close when more than 4 day files are used.

Table 2 compares the number of URLs (nodes) stored by each of the three PPM models for predictions using the UCB-CS trace. The two space optimization alternatives have been used in the popularity-based PPM model. Again, the number of nodes stored in the standard PPM model dramatically increases as the number files in days used for prediction increases. The third figure in Figure 4 plots the space requirement in number of nodes for the UCB-CS trace as the number of files in days used for predictions increases. The space reductions by the popularity-based PPM is 1 to several dozen times compared with the LRS-PPM model. The last figure in Figure 4 compares the traffic increases among the three PPM models for the UCB-CS trace. The PPM model has the highest traffic increase (up to 21%). The traffic increase percentage of the popularity-based PPM model is up to 14% which is higher than that the LRS-PPM model (up to 9%). The irregularity of the surfing patterns in the UCB-CS trace is a major reason for this difference. The popularity grades of the starting URLs are evenly distributed in the UCB-CS trace, and some of the popular entries may not lead to long sessions. Thus, some of the branches headed by less popular URLs in the

popularity-based PPM model are given short heights, but may be accessed as frequently as the branches headed by popular URLs.

5 Prefetching between Servers and Proxies

Proxies have been widely used as caching storages in the Internet between Web servers and clients. In this section, we evaluate the effectiveness of the popularity-based PPM prefetching between Web servers and proxies.

In our experiments, we randomly select 1 to 32 clients to connect with a proxy. The total document hits come from three sources: (1) hits on browsers, (2) hits on the cached documents in the proxy, and (3) hits on the prefetched documents in the proxy. Since our PB-PPM is sensitive to the threshold that is the maximum size of documents to be prefetched, we tested two thresholds of 40KB and 100KB in our experiments (simplified as PB-PPM-40KB, and PB-PPM-100KB, respectively). Due to the page limit, we only present the results from the NASA trace in this paper. We obtained similar results from other traces.

The left figure in Figure 5 presents comparative total hit ratios among the standard PPM (PPM), the LRS-PPM (LRS), PB-PPM-40KB, and PB-PPM-100KB as the number of the clients increases from 1 to 32. The hit ratio curve of the LRS is the lowest (from 42% to 71%), while the PB-PPM-100KB curve is the highest (from 61% to 78%). The PB-PPM-40KB and the standard PPM curves are in the middle. As the number of clients increases to 24 and more,

Days	1	2	3	4	5
PPM	3,339,315	8,872,552	10,674,669	21,579,994	43,365,678
LRS	16,200	39,437	78,816	180,521	309,916
PB-PPM	3,840	4,690	6,192	7,684	10,981

Table 2. Space size in number of nodes used for each PPM model for the UCB-CS trace.

the standard PPM hit ratio curve merges to that of the PB-PPM-40KB. This study indicates that the popularity-based PPM can achieve high hit ratios with a moderate threshold size for the prefetched documents, such as 100KB, in the environment of Web servers and proxies.

The right figure in Figure 5 presents the comparative the network traffic increments among the three models. As the number of clients increases, the traffic increment decreases for all the three models. We show that the standard PPM has the highest traffic increment (20% for 32 clients, while the PB-PPM-40KB has the lowest traffic increment (10% for 32 clients), although they have similar hit ratios. We also show that there is a tradeoff between increasing hit ratios and lowering traffic increment in the popularity-based PPM model. By adjusting the threshold size of prefetched documents, we are able to address the tradeoff.

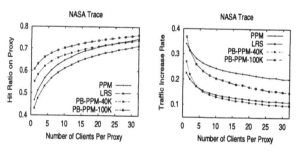

Figure 5. The left figure gives comparative proxy hit ratios among the three prefetching models, and the right figure gives the comparative network traffic increments between Web servers and the proxy among the three prefetching models.

6 Other Related Work

Prefetching methods can be divided into three types: server-initiated, client-initiated, and cooperative prefetching. In server-initiated prefetching, servers always push their popular documents to the clients. The work reported in [2] uses service proxies (agents) to serve for multiple home servers, and the mapping between home servers and ser-

vice proxies can be many-to-many. Markatos and Chronaki [20] propose a Top-10 approach which combines the servers' active knowledge of their popular documents with client access profiles. Web servers regularly push their most popular documents to Web proxies, and proxies then push those documents to the active clients.

In client-initiated prefetching, the information observed by the client side are used to determine the prefetching contents. A simulation study on accesses to two popular UCLA sites is reported to present a client-initiated prefetching software [15]. Wcol [27] is a proxy software that parses HTML and prefetches documents, links and embedded images. Duchamp [11] presents a new implementation of client-based prefetching system which collects the knowledge of popular URLs for clients to initiate prefetching.

A cooperative prefetching between a server and a client/proxy uses the information of the two sides. Cohen et. al. [8] propose an end-to-end approach to improving Web performance by collectively examining servers and clients. Server groups the relative files together, and the proxy prefetches selected files. Server and client/proxy communicates with each other through data piggybacking. Another study in [5] proposes a coordinated proxy-server prefetching technique that adaptively utilizes the reference information and coordinates prefetching activities at both proxy and Web servers.

Using the first-order of Markov models and speculations based on statistical information of servers, other researchers have developed prefetching methods (see e.g. [2], [21], and [25]). Researchers have also proposed hint-based Web clients and servers which can load/store the predicted data objects for future use. (see e.g. [8] and [19]). The access distribution among all Web URLs operated by Google search engine is part a model of "random walks" [3]. These studies do not consider building the common surfing patterns and regularities into prediction models. High orders or variable orders of Markov models are also not concerned issues for prefetching. Related performance evaluation on caching and network effects has been reported in many studies (see e.g. [4, 10, 14]).

7 Conclusion

Building popularity information into the PPM model, we have proposed and evaluated the popularity-based PPM model for Web prefetching with an objective of high accuracy and low space requirement. Conducting trace-driven simulations, we have shown its effectiveness measured by hit ratios, latency reductions, space requirement, and traffic increase percentage. We have also applied the proposed PPM model to the prefetching between servers and proxy caches, and showed that it is effective in this environment to improve the hit-ratios while reducing network traffics.

Acknowledgment: This work is a part of an independent research project sponsored by the US National Science Foundation for program directors and visiting scientists.

References

[1] P. Barford, A. Bestavros, A. Bradley, and M. Crovella, "Changes in Web client access patterns: characteristics and caching implications", *World Wide Web Journal*, 2(1):15-28, January,1999.

[2] A. Bestravos, "Using speculation to reduce server load and service time on the WWW", *Proceedings of the 4th ACM International Conference on Information and Knowledge Management*, (CIKM'95), Baltimore, Maryland, 1995.

[3] S. Brin and L. Page, "The anatomy of a large-scale hypertextual Web search engine", *Proceedings of the 7th International World Wide Web Conference*, Brisbane, Australia, 1998.

[4] R. Caceres, F. Douglis, A. Feldmann, G. Glass, and M. Rabinovich, "Web proxy caching: the devil is in the details", *Proceedings of the Workshop on Internet Server Performance*, Madison, Wisconsin, June 1998.

[5] X. Chen and X. Zhang, "Coordinated data prefetching by utilizing reference information at both proxy and Web servers", *Proceedings of 2nd Performance and Architecture of Web Servers*, PAWS'01, Boston, MA, June 2001.

[6] X. Chen and X. Zhang, "Popularity-based Web surfing patterns", Technical Report, Department of Computer Science, College of William and Mary, Ocotober 2001.

[7] J. G. Cleary and I. H. Witten, "Data compression using adaptive coding and partial string matching", *IEEE Transactions on Communications*, Vol. 32, No. 4, pp. 396-402, 1984.

[8] E. Cohen, B. Krishnamurthy, and J. Rexford, "Improving end-to-end performance of the Web using server volumes and proxy filters", *Proceedings of the ACM SIGCOMM 1998*, 1998, pp. 241-253.

[9] Computer Science Department, University of California, Berkeley, URL: http://www.cs.berkeley.edu/logs/.

[10] M. Crovella and P. Barford, "The network effects of prefetching", *Proceedings of the IEEE INFOCOM'98 Conference*, San Francisco, California, April, 1998.

[11] D. Duchamp, "Prefetching hyperlinks", *Proceedings of the 2nd USENIX Symposium on Internet Technologies and Systems* (USITS'99), October 1999.

[12] L. Fan, P. Cao, W. Lin, and Q. Jacobson, "Web prefetching between low-bandwidth clients and proxies: potential and performance", *Proceedings of ACM SIGMETRICS Conference on Measurement and Modeling of Computer Systems*, May 1999, pp. 178-187.

[13] B. A. Huberman, P. L. T. Pirolli, J. E. Pitkow, and R. M. Lukose, "Strong regularities in world wide Web surfing", *Science*, Vol. 280, April 3, 1998, pp. 95-97.

[14] A. K. Iyengar, E. A. MacNair, M. S. Squillante, and L. Zhang, "A general methodology for characterizing access patterns and analyzing Web server performance", *Proceedings of the International Symposium on Modeling, Analysis and Simulation of Computer and Telecommunication Systems*, Montreal, Canada, July 1998.

[15] Z. Jiang and L. Kleinrock, "An adaptive network prefetch scheme", *IEEE Journal on Selected Areas of Communication*, Vol. 17, No. 4, 1998, pp. 358-368.

[16] S. Jin and A. Bestavros, "Popularity-aware greedyDual-size Web proxy caching algorithms", *Proceedings of 20th International Conference on Distributed Computing Systems*, (ICDCS'2000), April 2000.

[17] Lawrence Berkeley National Laboratory, URL: http://ita.ee.lbl.gov/

[18] J. I. Khan and Q. Tao, "Partial prefetch for faster surfing in Composite Hypermedia", *USENIX Symposium on Internet Technology and Systems*, San Francisco, California, USA, March 2001. USENIX Association.

[19] T. M. Kroeger, D. D. E. Long, and J. C. Mogul, "Exploiting the bounds of Web latency reduction from caching and prefetching", *Proceedings of the USENIX Symposium on Internet Technologies and Systems*, Monterey, California, April 1997.

[20] E. P. Markatos and C. E. Chronaki, "A top-10 approach to prefetching on the Web", Technical Report, No. 173, ICS-FORTH, Heraklion, Crete Greece, August 1996.

[21] V. N. Padmanabhan and J. C. Mogul, "Using predictive prefetching to improve World Wide Web latency", *Computer Communication Review*, 1996, pp. 22-36.

[22] V. N. Padmanabhan and L. Qiu, "The content and access dynamics of a busy Web site: findings and implications", *Proceedings of the ACM SIGCOMM 2000*, Stockholm, Sweden, August 2000.

[23] J. Pitkow and P. Pirolli, "Mining longest repeating subsequences to predict world wide Web surfing", *Proceedings of the 1999 USENIX Technical Conference*, April 1999.

[24] R. Sarukkai, "Link prediction and path analysis using markov chains", *Proceedings of the 9th International World Wide Web Conference*, Amsterdam, Netherlands, May 2000.

[25] S. Schechter, M. Krishnan, and M. D. Smith, "Using path profiles to predict HTTP requests", *Proceedings of the 7th International World Wide Web Conference*, Brisbane, Australia, 1998.

[26] T. Palpanas and A. Mendelzon, "Web prefetching using partial match prediction", *Proceedings of Web Caching Workshop*, San Diego, California, March 1999.

[27] Wcol Group, "Www collector: the prefetching proxy server for WWW", 1997. URL: http://shika.aist-nara.ac.jp/products/wcol/.

Load Balancing in Distributed Web Server Systems with Partial Document Replication[*]

Ling Zhuo   Cho-Li Wang   Francis C. M. Lau

Department of Computer Science and Information Systems
The University of Hong Kong
{lzhuo, clwang, fcmlau}@csis.hku.hk

Abstract

How documents of a Web site are replicated and where they are placed among the server nodes have an important bearing on balance of load in a geographically Distributed Web Server (DWS) system. The traffic generated due to movements of documents at runtime could also affect the performance of the DWS system. In this paper, we prove that minimizing such traffic is NP-hard. We propose a new document distribution scheme that periodically performs partial replication of a site's documents at selected server locations to maintain load balancing. Several approximation algorithms are used in it to minimize traffic generated. The simulation results show that this scheme can achieve better load balancing than a dynamic scheme, while the internal traffic it causes has a negligible effect on the system's performance.

1. Introduction

The increasing popularity of the World Wide Web has resulted in large bandwidth demands which translate into high latencies perceived by Web users. To tackle this latency problem, multiple copies of documents are distributed geographically and placed in caches at optimal locations.

Web caching attempts to reduce network latency by storing the commonly requested documents as close to clients as possible. Simple caches have no information on users' access pattern, and so they would habitually try to keep a copy of any document just requested. This may limit the performance of caches. For example, research in [1] shows that the maximum cache hit rate achievable by any caching algorithm is bounded under 40% to 50%

A proactive Web server on the other hand can decide where to place copies of a document in a distributed Web server (DWS) system where the server nodes are distributed geographically. In most existing geographically DWS systems, each server node keep the entire set of Web documents managed by the system. Incoming requests are distributed to the server nodes via DNS servers [6,9,11]. Although such systems are simple to implement, the caching of IP addresses on the client side or in intermediate DNS servers could easily result in uneven load among the server nodes. Moreover, the full replication leads to much waste of disk space due to those documents that are not frequently requested.

To achieve better load balancing as well as to avoid disk wastage, one can replicate part of the documents on multiple server nodes [5,12,14,15,18,19] and use content-aware distributor software to redirect a client request to a server node that has the requested document [16]. Some rules are then needed in such a geographically DWS system to determine each document's number of replicas and the distribution of these replicas. These rules constitute what we call the *document distribution scheme*, and they should achieve the following goals.

- *Load Balancing*: Since requests tend to target at a small part of the entire collection of documents [3], frequently requested documents should be replicated to avoid bottlenecks. Documents and their replicas should be placed in such a manner that most of the time the load of the participating server nodes is equalized.
- *Reduced Traffic*: To adapt to users' access patterns, documents need to be re-duplicated and re-distributed among the server nodes dynamically or periodically. Communications caused by such actions should be kept to the minimum so that the performance of the geographically DWS system would not be adversely affected.

Existing schemes mainly focus on balancing the load, but not the traffic issues. In this paper, we propose a new document distribution scheme that can improve load balancing performance of geographically DWS systems,

---

[*]This research was supported by CRCG Grant 10203944 and HKU 2001/02 Large Items of Equipment Grants 10003.01/02/001

while minimizing the communication cost needed. We assume that each document has approximately the same popularity in all the server locations. Therefore, we will not consider network proximity to clients in replicating and distributing the documents.

The performance of our scheme is evaluated through simulation using real access log data. The results show that this scheme can balance the load in the DWS system during run-time efficiently, and the internal traffic generated due to these algorithms is reasonably minimal.

The rest of the paper is organized as follows. Section 2 formulates the document distribution problem in the DWS systems and gives a proof of its NP-hardness. Section 3 presents our document distribution algorithms. In Section 4, we describe our simulation methodology and present the performance results. Section 5 surveys related work, and Section 6 concludes the paper and discusses future work.

2. Problem Formulation

In this section, we formulate the document distribution problem in DWS systems. Chen [7] proved that minimizing the maximum load over all server nodes is NP-complete. We will prove that even when the load balancing constraint is removed, the problem of minimizing the communication cost of moving the documents is NP-hard.

Suppose there are N documents and M server nodes in the system. Each server node has storage capacity C. Each document has size of s_i and number of replicas c_i (In this paper, if we don't state otherwise, we assume $i = 1,...N$ and $j = 1,...M$).

A "cost link" is constructed between each document and each server: p_{ij}, associated with the number of bytes to be transferred if document i is assigned to server j. We also have variables t_{ij}^l ($l = 1,...c_i$), which is 1 if lth replica of ith document is placed on jth server; otherwise, it is 0.

The determination of c_i is under the limitation of total storage, i.e., $\sum_{i=1}^{N}(s_i * c_i) \leq M * C$.

After c_i is determined, all the documents and their replicas are placed on the server nodes under these constraints: (1) each server can only hold replicas whose total size does not exceed its disk space; (2) each server can hold at most one replica of a document; (3) no document is left unassigned to any server node; (4) load is equalized among the server nodes.

As we stated at the beginning of the section, we won't include constraint (4) in the formulation. The replica placement problem formulation is therefore as below:

$$\text{minimize } z = \sum_{j=1}^{M}\sum_{i=1}^{N}\sum_{l=1}^{c_i} t_{ij}^l p_{ij}$$

subject to

$$\sum_{i=1}^{N}\sum_{l=1}^{c_i} t_{ij}^l s_i \leq C \qquad (1)$$

$$\sum_{l=1}^{c_i} t_{ij}^l \leq 1, \qquad (2)$$

$$\sum_{j=1}^{M}\sum_{l=1}^{c_i} t_{ij}^l = c_i \qquad (3)$$

$$t_{ij}^l = 0 \text{ or } 1, \quad l = 1,...c_i$$

A replica placement that fulfills all the above constraints is a "feasible placement." Our discussion is under the assumption that a feasible placement always exists. We call this optimization problem the *Replica Placement Problem* (RPP). When $c_i = 1$, the problem is 0-1 RPP.

Lemma *0-1 RPP is NP-hard*

Proof: We reduce the bin-packing problem, which is NP-hard [13], to the 0-1 RPP. For the bin-packing problem, s_i denotes the size of object i and the bin's size is C. We assume that, in any feasible solution, the lowest indexed bins are used. This means that if there are two bins with the same available storage, the object will be placed in the one with the lower index.

Given the bin-packing problem, we can construct a 0-1 RPP with costs p_{ij} as follows.

$$p_{ij} = \begin{cases} 1, & i \in \{1,...N\}, j = 1 \\ (p_{i,j-1}) * N + 1, & i \in \{1,...N\}, j \in \{2,...M\} \end{cases}$$

With such costs, the total cost of any set of replicas assigned to $\{s_1,...s_j\}$ is lower than the total cost of any set of replicas assigned to $\{s_1,...s_{j+1}\}$. It is then obvious that the bin-packing problem gets the minimal number of bins used if and only if the 0-1 RPP gets the minimal total communication cost.

Since the 0-1 RPP is a special case of the RPP, our document placement problem is NP-hard.

3. Document Distribution Scheme

In this section, we propose our document distribution scheme, which periodically re-replicates and re-distributes the documents based on the access pattern in the past period. We first describe an algorithm for determining the number of replicas for each document. Next, we present several heuristics that use available information in different ways in order to achieve minimal communication cost.

3.1. Density Algorithm

Intuitively, we should prefer to duplicate documents that require more work on the part of the DWS system as well as the small-size ones. We use the concept of "density" to represent the workload per unit storage of the document. The larger a document's density is, the more replicas it will have.

```
Input: d_i, s_i, C, M, N,
Variables: S, total size of document
          S_disk, available disk space
          d_min, minimal density
          temp_S, total size of temporary replicas
          temp_c_i, temporary number of replicas
Output: c_i (i = 1, ...N)
   1.compute S, S_disk = M * C - S
   2.sort documents by decreasing density d_i,
      find d_min
   3.for i = 1 to N {
         temp_c_i = d_i / d_min }
      compute temp_S
   4.for i = 1 to N {
         c_i = temp_c_i * S_disk / temp_S
         if (c_i >= M-1){
               c_i = M-1
               temp_S = temp_S − temp_c_i * s_i
               S_disk = S_disk − c_i * s_i }}
   5.finally decide c_i (i = 1,...N)
```

Figure 1. Density algorithm

To compute a document's density, we associate document i with weight w_i, which represents the workload it brings to the server node holding it. In our algorithm, w_i is computed as $s_i * r_i$, where s_i is the document's size and r_i is its access rate in the past period. The density of a document d_i, therefore, equals to w_i / s_i. If a document is duplicated, we assume that the workload is divided evenly among its replicas (true if we assign requests to the replicas in a round-robin manner). Therefore, a replica of document i has weight of w_i / c_i and density of d_i / c_i.

The Density Algorithm is shown in Figure 1. First, the space equal to the total size of documents is reserved to guarantee that each document has at least one copy in the system. Step 2 sorts the documents by their densities decreasingly. In Step 3, each document gets a temporary replica number. The densities of the temporary replicas are nearly equal to the minimal density. Step 4 adjusts the temporary replica numbers under the storage limitation. Replica numbers are computed according to the ratio between available disk space and the total size of the temporary replicas, thus the resulting replicas still maintain similar densities. In Step 5, each replica number is finally decided as an integer not larger than M.

This algorithm replicates the documents according to their densities under the storage limitation. The time complexity of it is $\Theta(N \log N + N)$. From Step 4, we know that for any two documents u and v, if $1 < c_u, c_v \leq M$ and $d_u > d_v$, $d_u / (c_u - 1) \approx d_v / (c_v - 1)$. Thus, we can assume if $d_u > d_v$, $d_u / c_u > d_v / c_v$, for any two documents u and v.

Since we have proved that the minimization problem of communication cost is NP-hard, in the rest of this section, several approximation algorithms for distributing the replicas to the server nodes are proposed. Before we begin the discussion, we need to introduce a new variable, W_j. It denotes the weight of server j and is computed as the sum of the weights of all replicas allocated to it. Also, in the following discussion, we call document i and its replicas "replica set i".

3.2. Greedy-cost Algorithm

```
Input: c_i, s_i, p_ij, C, M, N
Output: t_ij^l (i = 1,...N, j = 1,...M, l = 1,...c_i)
   1.sort (i, j) pairs by increasing cost, p_ij
   2.for each (i, j) in the sorted list{
         if (c_i > 0) {
            allocate a replica to server j if it has
            enough space and t_ij^l = 0 (l = 1,...c_i).
            c_i = c_i − 1 }}
```

Figure 2. Greedy-cost algorithm

Greedy-cost algorithm aims to minimize traffic by keeping as many as documents as they are in the system, without caring if the load of the servers is balanced.

This algorithm is shown in Figure 2. To minimize the cost, it first sorts the (document, server) pairs by the communication cost between the document and the server increasingly. Then in this order, a replica of document i is allocated to server j if it has enough storage space and has not been assigned the same replica in this period. The total time complexity is $\Theta(MN \log MN + MN)$.

3.3. Greedy-load/cost Algorithm

Unlike Greedy-cost algorithm, Greedy-load/cost algorithm considers balancing the load among the server nodes as well as minimizing the cost caused in distributing the documents.

```
Input: c_i, s_i, p_ij, C, M, N
Output: t_ij^l (i = 1,...N, j = 1,...M, l = 1,...c_i)
Variable: D_j, density of server j (j = 1,...M)
    1.sort replica sets by increasing density, d_i / c_i
    2.for i = 1 to N {
        sort servers by increasing communication
        cost, p_ij. Servers having the same p_ij are
        sorted by decreasing density, D_j
        allocate replica set i
        update D_j (j = 1,...M) }
```

Figure 3. Greedy-load / cost algorithm

To achieve load balancing, we expect seeing that after document distribution, the weights of the server nodes are approximately the same. Since the density of a server node D_j equals to W_j / (amount of used disk space in server j), in a homogeneous DWS system, this means that after document distribution, the server nodes have similar densities. Therefore, in Greedy-load/cost algorithm, the replica sets are sorted by decreasing density and are allocated in this order. When choosing server nodes for replica set i, the server nodes are sorted by increasing communication cost p_{ij}. If two server nodes have the same cost, the one with the larger density D_j is chosen.

The time complexity of Greedy-load algorithm is $\Theta(N \log N + NM \log M)$. To simplify it, we can use the sorting result of the Density algorithm, based on the assumption that if $d_u > d_v$, $d_u / c_u > d_v / c_v$. Thus the algorithm only takes $\Theta(NM \log M)$ time.

3.4. Greedy-penalty Algorithm

It is possible that allocating a document at different times generates different traffic. For example, if we allocate document i immediately, we can assign it to server x with $p_{ix} = 0$; if we delay allocating it for a while, however, server x may have become full and the document has to be placed on server y with $p_{iy} = s_i$. In this case, we say we are punished and use f_i to refer to the value of penalty. A penalty-based algorithm hopes to decrease cost by placing documents in certain order. It has been used to solve the General Assignment Problem [13].

We say a placement is "better" if it incurs less communication cost. In Greedy-penalty algorithm, f_i is computed as the difference in the costs of replica set i's best and second best placements, according to the current status of the server nodes. This algorithm iteratively places the replica sets until they are all allocated. Each time it computes f_i for all unassigned replica sets, and the one yielding the largest penalty are placed with its best placement. The time complexity of this algorithm is $\Theta(N^2 \log N + NM \log M)$.

```
Input: c_i, p_ij, s_i, C, M, N
Output: t_ij^l (i = 1,...N, j = 1,...M, l = 1,...c_i)
Variables: f_i, penalty for document i (i = 1,...N)
    while there are unassigned replica sets {
        for each unassigned replica set i{
            if only c_i server nodes have enough
            storage to hold document i{
                allocate replica set i
                goto while }
            else {
                sort servers by increasing cost with
                document i, p_ij.
                compute f_i }}
        sort replica sets in decreasing penalty, f_i
        allocate the replica set with minimal f_i in its
        best placement}
```

Figure 4. Greedy-penalty algorithm

If there are only c_i server nodes having enough storage to hold document i, we need to allocate replica set i immediately. Otherwise, we might leave a replica unassigned and violate constraint (3). In this case, we set f_i to ∞. If there are multiple replica sets with infinite penalty, they are placed in the order of decreasing densities. To do this, we can use the sorting results of the Density algorithm.

4. Simulation Results

4.1. Experimental Setup

We use the CSIM 18 package [21] for our simulation. In our simulation model, requests are redirected to the server nodes that have the requested documents using HTTP redirection. When a document has copies in multiple server nodes, the requests for it are assigned in round-robin fashion. Initially, Web documents are randomly placed on the server nodes without replication. Afterwards, documents are replicated and distributed among the server nodes every 3 hours.

In our simulation, processing a web request comprises (1) redirection (if necessary), (2) waiting in the queue of the serving server node, (3) reading the file from disk. The connection establishment time and teardown time is neglected. The round-trip time of redirection is 100 ms [16]. The disk access time is about 19 ms and the disk transfer time about 21 MB/s [22]. We use two real traces of Web access. One is from a website mainly used for hosting personal homepages, called Data Set 1. Another, called Data Set 2, is obtained from The Internet Traffic Archive [20]. For simplicity, the documents in the same directory are grouped and these groups are used as basic units of replication and distribution.

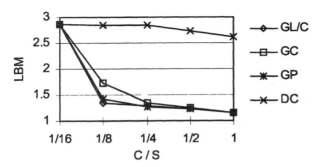

Figure 5. Load balancing performance with Data Set 1 (16 server nodes)

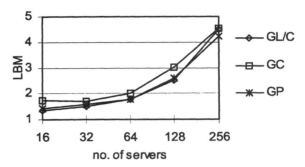

Figure 7. Load balancing performance with Data Set 1 ($C / S = 1/8$)

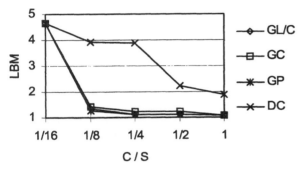

Figure 6. Load balancing performance with Data Set 2 (16 server nodes)

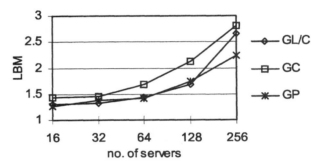

Figure 8. Load balancing performance with Data Set 2 ($C / S = 1 / 8$)

We simulated the algorithms presented in Section 3. Density algorithm is combined with Greedy-cost (GC), Greedy-load/cost (GL/C), Greedy-penalty (GP) respectively. For the purpose of comparison, we added a Dynamic scheme (DS). In this scheme, each server node owns a part of documents. Dynamically it examines the other servers' load and determines if they are under-loaded or overloaded or. It then replicates one of its documents to the under-loaded node or revokes one replica of its documents from the overloaded node. This scheme is similar to the one used in DC-Apache. In our simulation, the servers check load status every 10 minutes.

4.2. Load Balancing Analyses

The Load Balance Metric (LMB) [4] is used as a performance metric for measuring load balancing results. We record the peak-to-mean ratio of server utilization every sampling period (10 minutes) during the simulation. The LBM value is obtained by calculating the weighted average of the peak-to-mean ratios measured, using the total server utilization at the sampling point as the weight. A smaller LBM value indicates better load balancing performance.

Figure 5 and Figure 6 present the load balancing performance of our scheme when the number of servers is

fixed as 16. The y-axis is LBM value. The x-axis is C / S, where C is the storage capacity of each server node and S is the total size of the documents. We can see that DS doesn't improve load balancing much as the storage capacity increases. This is because in DS, each server node can only replicate one document once a time so that the available disk space is not utilized efficiently to remove hot spots. On the contrary, the load balancing performance of our scheme increases as storage capacity increases because the Density Algorithm fully utilizes the disk space. Among the document distribution algorithms, GC performs worst in load balancing while GL/C and GP's performance is similar.

Next, we fix the storage capacity, and increase the number of server nodes from 16 to 256. The results are shown in Figure 7 and Figure 8. We notice that GL/C's and GP's performance is still close when the node number is not very large. When there are more than 128 nodes, however, GL/C appears to deteriorate faster than GP.

4.3. Traffic Analyses

We record the total number of bytes transferred inside the system each period (except the first period, as documents are randomly distributed without duplication initially). At the end of the simulation, the ratio between

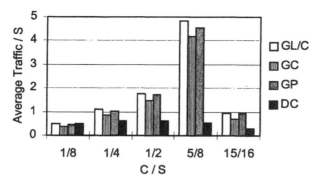

**Figure 9. Average traffic with Data Set 1
(16 server nodes)**

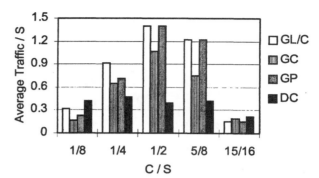

**Figure 11. Average traffic with Data Set 2
(16 server nodes)**

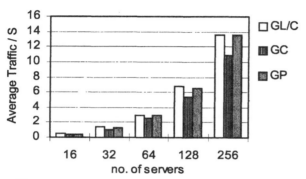

**Figure 10. Average traffic with Data Set 1
(C / S = 1/8)**

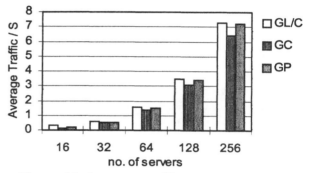

**Figure 12. Average traffic with Data Set 2
(C / S = 1/8)**

the average traffic each period and total size of Web documents S is computed. In the figures, y-axis represents this ratio.

We can see from Figure 9 and Figure 10 that when number of server nodes is fixed, the traffic caused by the algorithms first increases as the storage capacity C increases, and then decreases. This is because when there is more available disk space, more documents are replicated and the numbers of replicas of popular documents are larger. Once the access pattern changes, therefore, more replicas of the past period are revoked and more new replicas of this period need to be distributed. It is easy to understand that GC, which cares most about communication cost, incurs the least cost. We find that when the storage capacity is large, the traffic caused by GL/C and GP is almost the same.

As the number of nodes increases, the total storage space increases, therefore, the traffic in the system increases. From Figure 10 and Figure 11, we can see that GC still causes least traffic, and the traffic caused by GL/C and GP get closer as the number of nodes increases.

The actual time needed to move the documents

$$t \approx total\ bytes\ /(B * M)$$

where M is the number of servers and B is the bandwidth between any two server nodes. Therefore, if we assume that the bandwidth is 1 MB/s and total size of the

documents is 1G, moving documents would take no more than several minutes. Since during this period, the DWS system can continue to serve requests with documents not in the move, its performance would not be substantially affected.

In the figures, DS's average traffic may be smaller than that of our scheme. But since its period is much shorter, its total traffic is actually larger than ours. This may be because that it frequently replicates a document and then revokes it.

From the simulation results, we see that our document distribution scheme can achieve better load balancing in a geographically DWS system and generate less traffic than the dynamic scheme. Among the document distribution algorithms, GC's load balancing performance is not as good as that of GP and GL/C. However, GC generates the least internal traffic. GL/C needs shortest computing time. Its load balancing performance is best in most cases and only generates a little more traffic than GP. When the number of server nodes is large, however, GL/C performs much worse than GP. GP balances the load well but it requires more computation than the others. A suitable algorithm can be chosen according to the practical situation of a geographically DWS system.

5. Related Work

Much research work has been done on ways to keep a balanced load in geographically DWS systems.

Various DNS based scheduling techniques have been proposed. The NCSA scalable web server depends on round-robin DNS to dispatch requests [11], while [9] found that the DNS policies combined with a simple feedback alarm mechanism could effectively avoid overloading the server nodes. Adaptive TTL algorithm [8] was proposed to address the uneven client request distribution and heterogeneity of server capacities. The main problem with these techniques is that DNS only has a limited control on the requests reaching the Web servers, due to the caching of IP address in intermediate DNS servers and client caches.

The content-aware requests distribution strategy LARD [16] makes it possible to balance the load among the server nodes through partitioning the Web documents among the server nodes, with or without replication. DCWS [5] makes use of a graph-based Web document-partitioning algorithm. Each document resides on its home server at first and can be migrated to a co-op server for load balancing reason. To redirect client requests from the home server to the co-op server, all hyperlinks pointing to the document are modified. However, if the system happens to contain many hot spots (i.e., popular Web pages with extremely high request rates), to equalize the load is absolutely non-trivial.

DC-Apache [12] is similar to DCWS, except that documents are replicated instead of migrated among the server nodes. Each document has a home server that keeps its original copy. Every time the number or locations of copies of a document change, the document's home server needs to regenerate all the hyperlinks pointing to this document based on global load information. This operation requires substantial computation.

Riska et. al. observed that directing tasks of similar size to the same server reduces the slowdown in a web server and proposed a load balancing policy ADAPTLOAD [18] which partitions the documents among the server nodes according to their sizes. How to effectively choose parameters of the policy still needs more work.

In RobustWeb [14], each document has the same number of replicas. The replicas are placed on the server nodes based on past access pattern to equalize the servers load. Multiple copies of a document may have different weights of redirection, and the requests are assigned to them in a weighted round-robin way. Instead of moving documents like we do, in RobustWeb, only the weights of the copies are computed periodically. When the access pattern change dramatically, however, it's difficult to maintain load balancing using this method.

Ng at el. [15] included the prefetching feature in their EWS system. In this system, documents that are always accessed together are grouped and placed on the same server node. Only the first request of a session has to go through the redirection server, thus cutting down on the redirection overhead. Load balancing is achieved by using a revised document placement algorithm of the one used in RobustWeb. Our work can be considered a derivative from theirs by taking disk utilization and communication cost into account. The algorithms we propose in this paper can be deployed in EWS.

Recently there has been an increase in interest in replica placement in Content Delivery Networks (CDN) that offer hosting services to Web content providers [2,10,17]. Although the problem formulation in CDN is very similar to ours, it mainly focuses on minimizing clients' latency or total bandwidth consumption, and not balancing the load among the servers.

6. Conclusion and Future Work

In this paper, we study how to replicate and distribute the documents in a geographically DWS system to achieve load balancing. In contrast with existing work, we also take the communication cost caused by distributing the replicas into consideration. We prove that even without load balancing constraint, minimizing this cost in homogeneous DWS systems is NP-hard.

We propose a document distribution scheme which periodically replicates the documents and distributes the replicas. In this scheme, we utilize the concept of "density" of a document to decide number of replicas for each document. Several distribution algorithms are proposed and they use the available information from different perspectives to reduce internal traffic of the geographically DWS system. Our scheme is compared with a dynamic scheme using real log files. The results show that our scheme could balance the load in a DWS system more efficiently during run-time and causes less traffic. We also discuss the difference between the distribution algorithms and the situations for which they are suitable.

Our next step is to incorporate geographical information into our document distribution scheme. We aim at a geographically DWS system which would automatically copy a document to a location where it is in most demand, while maintaining load balancing and minimizing communication cost. Such a geographically DWS system would reduce access latencies and be most suitable for Web sites where different parts of the content are of interest to people from different geographical locations.

References

[1] M. Abrams, C.R. Standridge, G. Abdulla, S. Williams, and E.A. Fox, "Caching Proxies: Limitations and Potentials". In *Proc. of 4th International World Wide Web Conference*, Boston, USA, December 1995, pp 119-133.

[2] A. Aggarwal and M. Rabinovich, "Performance of Dynamic Replication Schemes for an Internet Hosting Service". *Technical Report*, AT&T Labs, October 1998.

[3] M.F. Arlitt, and C.L. Williamson, "Web Server Workload Characterization: The Search for Invariants". In *Proc. of the 1996 SIGMETRICS Conference on Measurement & Modeling of Computer Systems*, Philadelphia, USA, May 1996, pp.160 – 169.

[4] R.B. Bung, D.L. Eager, G.M. Oster, and C.L. Williamson, "Achieving Load Balance and Effective Caching in Clustered Web Servers". In *Proc. of 4th International Web Caching Workshop*, San Diego, USA, March 1999, pp. 159-169.

[5] S.M. Baker, and B. Moon, "Scalable Web Server Design for Distributed Data Management". In *Proc. of 15th International Conference on Data Engineering*, Sydney, Australia, March 1999, pp. 96.

[6] V. Cardellini, M. Colajanni and P.S. Yu, "Dynamic Load Balancing on Web-Server Systems". In *IEEE Internet Computing*, vol. 3, No. 3, May/June 1999, pp 28-39.

[7] L.C. Chen and H.A. Choi, "Approximation Algorithms for Data Distribution with Load Balancing of Web Servers". In *Proc. of the 3rd IEEE International Conference on Cluster Computing (CLUSTER'01)*, Newport Beach, USA, October 2001.

[8] M. Colajanni and P.S. Yu, "Adaptive TTL Schemes for Load Balancing of Distributed Web Servers". In *ACM Sigmetrics Performance Evaluation Review*, 25(2):36--42, September 1997.

[9] M. Colajanni, P.S. Yu, and D.M. Dias, "Analysis of Task Assignment Policies in Scalable Distributed Web-Server Systems". In *IEEE Trans. Parallel and Distributed Systems*, vol. 9, No. 6, June 1998, pp. 585-600.

[10] J. Kangasharju, J. Roberts, and K.W. Ross, "Object Replication Strategies in Content Distribution Networks". In *Proc. of Web Caching and Content Distribution Workshop (WCW'01)*, Boston, USA, June 2001.

[11] T.T. Kwan, R.E. McGrath, and D.A. Reed, "NCSA's World Wide Web Server: Design and Performance". In *IEEE Computer*, vol. 28, No. 11, November 1995, pp. 68-74.

[12] Q.Z. Li, and B. Moon, "Distributed Cooperative Apache Web Server". In *Proc. of 10th International World Wide Web Conference*, Hong Kong, May 2001.

[13] S. Martello and P. Toth, *Knapsack Problems: algorithms and computer implementation*, John Wiley & Sons Ltd, 1990.

[14] B. Narendran, S. Rangarajan, and S. Yajnjk, "Data Distribution Algorithms for Load Balanced Fault Tolerant Web Access". In *Proc. of 16th Symposium on IEEE Reliable Distributed Systems*, Durham, USA, October 1997, pp. 97-106.

[15] C.P. Ng and C.L. Wang, "Document Distribution Algorithm for Load Balancing on an Extensible Web Server Architecture". In *Proc. of 1st IEEE/ACM International Symposium on Cluster Computing and the Grid (CCGrid 2001)*, Brisbane, Australia, May 2001.

[16] V.S. Pai, M. Aron, G. Banga, M. Svendsen, P. Druschel, W. Zwaenepoel, and E. Nahum, "Locality-Aware Request Distribution in Cluster-based Network Servers". In *Proc. of 8th International Conference on Architectural Support for Programming Languages and Operating Systems*, San Jose, USA, October 1998, pp. 205-216.

[17] L. Qiu, V.N. Padmanabhan, and G.M. Voelker, "On the Placement of Web Server Replicas". In *Proc. of 20th IEEE INFOCOM*, Anchorage, USA, April 2001.

[18] A. Riska, W. Sun, E. Smirni, and G. Ciardo, "ADATPTLOAD: effective balancing in clustered web servers under transient load conditions". In *Proc. of 22nd International Conference on Distributed Computing Systems (ICDCS 2002)*, Vienna, Austria, July 2002.

[19] C.S. Yang and M.Y. Luo, "A Content Placement and Management System for Distributed Web-Server Systems". In *Proc. of 20th International Conference on Distributed Computing Systems (ICDCS 2000)*, Taipei, Taiwan, April 2000.

[20] ClarkNet-HTTP, http://ita.ee.lbl.gov/contrib/ClarkNet-HTTP.html

[21] CSIM18, http://www.mesquite.com/htmls/csim18.htm

[22] Seagate ST360020A, http://www.seagate.com

Session 5A

Partitioning Unstructured Meshes for Homogeneous and Heterogeneous Parallel Computing Environments*

PeiZong Lee, Jan-Jan Wu, and Chih-Hao Chang
Institute of Information Science
Academia Sinica
Taipei, Taiwan, R.O.C.
Internet: {leepe,wuj,chchang}@iis.sinica.edu.tw

Abstract

Partitioning meshes is a preprocessing step for parallel scientific simulation. The quality of a partitioning is measured by load balance and communication overhead. The effectiveness of a partitioning significantly influences the performance of parallel computation. In this paper, we propose a quadtree spatial-based domain decomposition method for partitioning unstructured meshes. The background quadtree, which is originally used to represent the density distribution among elements within the computing domain, can be used to obtain an initial partitioning and to do multi-level refinement. As the quadtree implicitly defines hierarchical relationship, which is a natural way to define coarsening and uncoarsening phases, we can repeatedly apply coarsening, partitioning, and uncoarsening multilevel refinement phases, until no improvement can be made. Thus, for most cases, the partitioning results by our method are better than those produced by other graph-based partitioning methods. Experimental studies for the NACA0012 airfoil, the NASA EET wing, and an artillery shell within a shock tube are reported.

1 Introduction

In this paper, we focus on partitioning unstructured meshes. Unstructured meshes are popularly used to facilitate computation with complex geometry. Partitioning unstructured meshes is also called domain decomposition. We use the number of elements in a partition to represent the *load* of its corresponding PE, and the number of boundary elements or the number of cut edges between adjacent partitions to represent *communication overhead*. A good domain decomposition maintains high load balance among PEs while requiring low communication overhead among PEs. Our key contribution is a systematic approach to partition unstructured meshes in terms of complete load balance with low communication overhead for both homogeneous and heterogeneous parallel computing environments.

There is trade-off between minimizing computation time among PEs and minimizing communication time within the interconnection network. The difficulty of partitioning unstructured meshes is to pursue evenly weighted distribution of elements among partitions while minimizing the number of boundary elements between adjacent partitions. (It is necessary for heterogeneous computing environment to do weighted distribution of elements among partitions.) Partitioning unstructured meshes can be treated as a graph-based partitioning problem that is shown to be NP-complete [6], hence optimal solutions are computationally intractable for large problems. However, several heuristic methods were proposed, such as recursive coordinate bisection [5, 8], geometric bisection [16], recursive spectral bisection [18], multi-level recursive spectral bisection [1], recursive Kernighan-Lin min-cut bipartitioning [4], multilevel *k*-way partitioning [11], and other techniques. A complete survey of partitioning irregular graphs can be seen elsewhere [9].

Coordinate bisection approach can achieve complete load balance due to available information of coordinates. However, it may suffer large edge-cut between adjacent partitions when the mesh density is uneven. The graph-based approach treats each element as a node and defines an edge connected to two nodes if the corresponding elements of these two nodes are adjacent. In graph-based approach, more expensive techniques such as maximal matching and maximal independent sets are necessary for generating coarsening graphs due to lack of coordinate information.

In this paper, we present a quadtree spatial-based domain decomposition tool. In our method, the unstruc-

*This work was partially supported by the NSC under Grants NSC 89-2213-E-001-050, NSC 89-2218-E-001-003 and NSC 89-2218-E-001-002.

tured mesh is generated based on a background quadtree which specifies the density distribution among elements within the computing domain [13]. In the quadtree spatial-based partitioning, a specific space-filling curve that passes through every quadtree leaf implicitly defines a sequential order among the two-dimensional quadtree leaves, where the Morton order and the Hilbert-Peano order space-filling curves are frequently used [17, 19]. Deciding an initial (homogeneous or heterogeneous) partitioning of quadtree leaves is reduced to the partitioning of a linear sequence of weighted tasks, where tasks represent quadtree leaves and weights are the number of triangles falling within each quadtree leaf.

The quadtree leaves also can be treated as a coarsening graph. With the implicitly hierarchical data structure of the background quadtree, we can repeatedly apply multi-level, graph-based, and Kernighan-Lin refinement to improve the quality of domain decomposition, where each coarsening graph is also constructed based on the background quadtree. Thus, in most cases, our method is able to achieve better load balance with less communication overhead than other graph-based domain decomposition tools such as METIS.

After performing multi-level refinement for partitioning the coarsening graph (of quadtree leaves), we further use a dynamic diffusion method [20] to move boundary elements among partitions, so that all partitions are completely load balanced. After that, we apply Kernighan-Lin refinement [12] again to decrease the number of cut-edges between adjacent partitions.

It is worthwhile to mention that METIS, which can only partition unstructured meshes into partitions of similar sizes, is only suitable for homogeneous computing environment in which each PE has the same computing power. However, our quadtree spatial-based partitioning tool can decompose unstructured meshes into partitions according to weight parameters for different PEs. Thus, our method is applicable to both homogeneous and heterogeneous environments.

The rest of this paper is organized as follows. Section 2 presents unstructured mesh generation based on a background quadtree. Section 3 proposes our quadtree spatial-based partitioning for domain decomposition. Section 4 presents experimental studies on a workstation cluster and a PC cluster, and Section 5 gives some concluding remarks.

2 Generating Delaunay meshes based on a background quadtree

Since we use a background quadtree to guide the generation of Delaunay triangular mesh and the partitioning of this unstructured mesh, we describe this background quadtree. A quadtree is a rooted tree in which every internal node has four children, which are denoted by SW (south west), NW

(north west), NE (north east), and SE (south east) from left to right. Every node in the quadtree corresponds to a square. We use a *cell* to represent a *leaf* in the quadtree without confusion. A quadtree is called balanced if any two adjacent cells differ at most by a factor of two in size [3]. Figure 1 shows a quadtree and its balanced version.

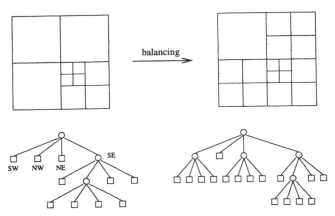

Figure 1. A quadtree and its balanced version.

2.1 Representation of density distribution by a quadtree

While generating Delaunay triangular mesh, we use a background quadtree to specify a smooth change of density distribution of elements (triangles) in the computing domain. Figure 2-(d) shows a sample blunt body in a given flow domain. The domain is decomposed by means of a quadtree representation.

The cell size of the background quadtree influences the number of points planting in that cell. Density ranks among cells are assigned by a dynamic programming algorithm, such that the difference of density ranks between neighboring cells is at most one. First, the initial density constraints are given. Three cells, each containing one extreme point where the curvature of boundary curve is large, are assigned the highest density of density rank 1 as shown in Figure 2-(a). We maintain a balanced quadtree during execution. Figure 2-(b) shows the balanced quadtree for the initial step. We can then use a multi-level priority queue method to determine the density distribution. Figure 2-(c) presents the first intermediate step in assigning the density distribution. The multi-level priority queue method starts from the cells A which have the highest density (and, thus, the smallest density rank number); then, the density ranks of their neighboring cells B, which were not visited before, are assigned to be

$$\min\{\text{original density rank of } B, (\text{density rank of } A) + 1\},$$

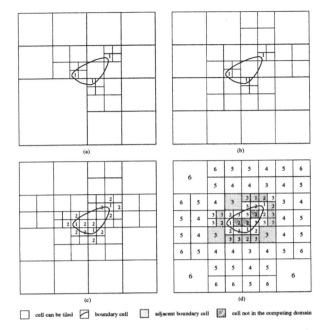

(a)

(b)

(c)

(d)

☐ cell can be tiled ◩ boundary cell ☐ adjacent boundary cell ▨ cell not in the computing domain

Figure 2. Illustration of the background quadtree for the density distribution: (a) The initial density constraints; (b) the balanced quadtree for the initial step; (c) the first intermediate step in assigning the density distribution; (d) the final quadtree for the density distribution.

where the cell rank and the density rank have to satisfy the constraints that each cell contains at most up to some number of elements (triangles). The final density distribution is shown in Figure 2-(d).

The background density quadtree implicitly maintains a well-spaced point placement. Using Bowyer-Watson Delaunay triangulation algorithm along with Steiner point insertion and local refinements to generate unstructured meshes, we can generate high-quality unstructured meshes [13].

2.2 Discussion

The background density quadtree plays three roles. First, in this section, it specifies a smooth change of density distribution of elements in the computing domain, thus, it allows us to generate high quality Delaunay triangular meshes. Second and third, in the next section, we show how this background quadtree can help us obtain an initial partitioning and do multi-level refinement, respectively.

If an unstructured mesh does not associate with a background quadtree, we can construct one such that each (leaf) cell of the quadtree contains at most up to some number of

elements (triangles). Then, this constructed quadtree can be used in the next section to obtain an initial partitioning and to do multi-level refinement.

3 Quadtree spatial-based partitioning

In order to reduce execution time while still maintaining load balance and minimizing communication overhead among PEs, it is practical to apply multi-level refinement techniques to partition unstructured meshes. An unstructured mesh can be treated as a graph. This graph is first coarsened down to a small number of vertices, a partitioning of this much smaller graph is computed, and then this partitioning is projected back toward the original (finer) graph by successively applying Kernighan-Lin refinement algorithms to refine the partitioning at each intermediate level [11]. Since the finer graph has more degrees of freedom, such refinements decrease the edge-cut. The coarsened graph intrinsically represents the structure of the original graph and Kernighan-Lin refinement algorithms can do localized refinement between adjacent partitions; therefore, multi-level refinement techniques do take into account both global view and local view of optimizations [9].

Our partitioning algorithm includes the following three steps.

Step 1: Find an initial partitioning based on a quadtree. This step will be presented in Section 3.1.

Step 2: Repeatedly perform multi-level refinement from Step 2.1 to Step 2.3 until no improvement can be made.

Step 2.1: Coarsening phase, which will be presented in Section 3.2.1.

Step 2.2: Partitioning phase, which will be presented in Section 3.2.2.

Step 2.3: Uncoarsening refinement phase, which will be presented in Section 3.2.3.

Step 3: Apply a dynamic diffusion algorithm to force partitions complete load balance [20], and then apply the Kernighan-Lin refinement algorithm to reduce the edge-cut [12]. This step will be presented in Section 3.3.

3.1 An initial partitioning based on a quadtree

We use a Hilbert-Peano space-filling curve to traverse every quadtree leaf and define a sequential order among all quadtree leaves. Figure 3-(a) shows a Hilbert-Peano space-filling curve traversing through a regular mesh [2]; Figure 3-(b) shows a Hilbert-Peano space-filling curve traversing through a density quadtree of a blunt body that is shown in Figure 2-(d).

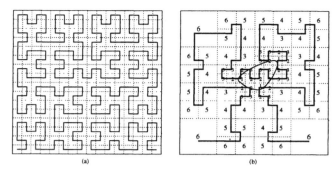

Figure 3. A Hilbert-Peano space-filling curve traverses through (a) a regular mesh and (b) a density quadtree of a blunt body, where each leaf is associated with a density rank.

Then, we identify each triangle falling within a specific quadtree leaf according to the location of its gravity center. After that, we apply a bucket sort for all triangles according to the sequential order defined by the Hilbert-Peano space-filling curve. Now, an initial partitioning of an unstructured mesh can be obtained by partitioning a linear sequence of weighted tasks, where each task represents a quadtree leaf and whose weight is the number of triangles falling within that quadtree leaf. Figure 4-(a) shows that the density quadtree of the blunt body is partitioned into three parts of equal weights.

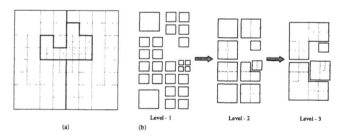

Figure 4. (a) The density quadtree of the blunt body is partitioned into three parts of equal weights. (b) Three consecutive coarsening graphs for the first partition.

3.2 Multi-level graph-based refinement based on a quadtree

The initial partitioning serves as a basis that we are trying to reduce its edge-cut.

3.2.1 Coarsening phase

The quadtree representation implicitly defines hierarchical (parent-child) relationship for a series of coarsening graphs. Originally, each quadtree leaf is represented by a node, whose weight is the number of triangles falling within that quadtree leaf. For each pair of adjacent quadtree leaves, we define an edge connecting their corresponding nodes, and the edge weight is the number of pairs of adjacent triangles falling between these two quadtree leaves.

Let $G_1 = (V_1, E_1)$ be the weighted graph derived from the original quadtree leaves, where the node (vertex) set V_1 represents all quadtree leaves and the edge set E_1 represents all related edges defined in above. Then, a sequence of coarsening graph $G_1, G_2, \ldots, G_m$, where $|V_1| > |V_2| > \cdots > |V_m|$, can be defined by the following rule.

If all four quadrants (children) of an internal node (parent) belong to the same partition in graph G_k, this internal node represents a coarsening node for the next-level coarsening graph G_{k+1}. Otherwise, if four quadrants of an internal node belong to different partitions in graph G_k, then a separate coarsening node will represent all quadrants that belong to each separate partition in the next-level coarsening graph G_{k+1}.

Let V_{k+1}^x be a coarsening node of $\bigcup V_k^a$, where for every a, V_k^a is a coarse node in graph G_k and V_{k+1}^x is a coarser node in graph G_{k+1}. The node weight of V_{k+1}^x is equal to the sum of all node weights of V_k^a. The edge weight of $\langle V_{k+1}^x, V_{k+1}^y \rangle$ is equal to the sum of all edge weights of $\langle V_k^a, V_k^b \rangle$, where $V_{k+1}^y = \bigcup V_k^b$.

The coarsening phase can be done by simply traversing the quadtree bottom up only once. Figure 4-(b) shows three consecutive coarsening graphs for the first partition of the blunt body example.

3.2.2 Partitioning phase

For each pair of adjacent partitions in the graph $G_m = (V_m, E_m)$, we apply a variation of greedy graph growing partitioning algorithm (GGGP) [9] and then followed by applying a variation of coarse-grain Kernighan-Lin refinement algorithm [9] to check whether we can find a new partitioning whose edge-cut is smaller than that of the basis (initial) partitioning. If it is, then the new partitioning is selected and served as the new basis partitioning.

The GGGP algorithm starts from an initial seed node, and then selects adjacent boundary nodes one by one until loads between two partitions are balanced. Because this greedy algorithm is sensitive to the choice of the initial seed node, in our implementation, we select six boundary nodes as the starting points of the algorithm, where three boundary nodes are in the first partition and the remaining three boundary nodes are in the second partition.

While allowing 3% to 5% load imbalance, the coarse-grain Kernighan-Lin refinement algorithm tries to swap a pair of boundary nodes between two partitions or to move one boundary node from one partition to the other partition, subject to minimize edge-cut and maintain load balance between these two partitions.

3.2.3 Uncoarsening refinement phase

During the uncoarsening phase, the partitioning of the coarsest graph G_m is projected back to the original graph by going through the graphs G_{m-1}, G_{m-2}, ..., G_1. Let V_{k+1}^x be a coarsening node of $\bigcup V_k^a$, where for every a, V_k^a is a coarse node in graph G_k and V_{k+1}^x is a coarser node in graph G_{k+1}. Since each node of G_{k+1} contains a distinct subset of nodes in G_k, the partitioning in graph G_k can be obtained by the following rule. If $V_{k+1}^x = \bigcup V_k^a$ is in partition P_j, then for every a, V_k^a is in partition P_j.

Since the graph G_k is finer than G_{k+1}, it has more degrees of freedom that can be used to improve the partitioning by reducing its edge-cut. For each pair of adjacent partitions at the graph $G_k = (V_k, E_k)$, again, we apply a coarse-grain Kernighan-Lin refinement algorithm [9] to check whether we can find a new partitioning whose edge-cut is smaller than that of the basis (initial) partitioning. If it is, then the new partitioning is selected and served as the new basis partitioning.

3.2.4 Discussion

The quadtree implicitly defines hierarchical relationship. Therefore, we can repeatedly apply coarsening, partitioning, and uncoarsening refinement phases, until no improvement can be made. We call this *W-cycle* refinement. W-cycle means a series of *V-cycles* and a V-cycle represents a cycle of coarsening, partitioning, and uncoarsening refinement. Note that, METIS only applies a V-cycle refinement, where their coarsening phase is based on a maximal matching among adjacent nodes. We found that, for many cases, the partitioning results by our method are better than those by METIS. Perhaps it is because our method adopts the W-cycle refinement.

3.3 Load balancing by a dynamic diffusion algorithm

Since the multi-level refinement is applied on a coarse-grain graph, which is derived from the density quadtree leaves, the result partitioning may not be completely load balanced w.r.t. PEs' weights. In the following, we present a variation of dynamic diffusion algorithm [20] to achieve load balance among partitions.

According to PEs' weights, each partition P_i has an arithmetical quota of triangles for complete load balance, say quota(P_i). Let load(P_i) be the number of triangles currently in partition P_i. Therefore, if load(P_i) > quota(P_i), partition P_i is over-loaded; if load(P_i) < quota(P_i), partition P_i is under-loaded. We define diff(P_i) to be $|$load(P_i) − quota(P_i)$|$. We maintain a graph, where each node represents a partition and each edge connects two nodes corresponding to two adjacent partitions.

A dynamic diffusion algorithm

Step 1: Find a node (partition) having the smallest number of degree, say P_i. If there are two or more than two such nodes, then we choose the one having the minimum diff(P_i).

Step 2: If P_i is over-loaded, then we choose an adjacent node P_j such that load(P_j) − quota(P_j) is the smallest number, and move diff(P_i) adjacent boundary triangles from partition P_i to partition P_j.

If P_i is under-loaded, then we choose an adjacent node P_j such that load(P_j) − quota(P_j) is the largest number, and move diff(P_i) adjacent boundary triangles from partition P_j to partition P_i.

Step 3: Eliminate node P_i and its adjacent edges.

Step 4: Repeat Step 1 through Step 3 until there exists only one node.

This algorithm guarantees complete load balance because the graph is always connected. The word *dynamic* reflects the fact that partitons' workload change during execution of the algorithm.

Finally, we apply Kernighan-Lin refinement algorithm [12] again to reduce the edge-cut between all pairs of adjacent partitions. At this time, each node represents a triangle and for each pair of adjacent triangles, we define an edge connecting their corresponding nodes, where each node weight or edge weight is 1. The Kernighan-Lin refinement algorithm tries to swap a pair of boundary nodes between two partitions, subject to minimizing edge-cut between these two partitions.

4   Experimental studies of partitioning

We used two experimental environments for parallel computation. The first one includes four dual-processors Ultrasparc-2 (300 MHz) workstations (running SunOS 5.6) and three single-processor Ultrasparc-1 (165 MHz) workstations (running SunOS 5.5.1) connected by a 100-Mbps (Mega bit per second) fast Ethernet. The second one consists of sixteen dual-processors Pentium-3 (1.0 GHz) PCs (running Red-Hat Linux 6.1) connected by a 1.2 Gbps (Giga bit per second) Myrinet.

We evaluated the effectiveness of our partitioning method with three applications by a Euler flow solver [14]: the NACA0012 airfoil, the NASA EET wing, and an artillery shell within a shock tube.

The NACA0012 airfoil: For the case when inflow Mach number is 0.8 and angle of attack is 3°, iterations are executed until a steady state is reached. The computing domain includes 23791 elements.

The NASA EET wing: For the case when inflow Mach number is 0.2 and angle of attack is 20°, iterations are executed until a steady state is reached. The computing domain includes 26900 elements.

An artillery shell within a shock tube: In the case of a shock tube, when the inflow Mach number is 1.2 and angle of attack is 0°, an incoming shock is moving from left to right, which is an unsteady case. We use 10 sub-iterations in each time step to drive a temporary convergent solution. The computing domain includes 156412 elements.

4.1 Partitioning on two homogeneous environments

Table 1 summarizes the partitioning results and the execution times for each iteration of the parallel Euler flow solver on eight Ultrasparc-2 CPUs. Two sets of partitioning results and times, one for our quadtree spatial-based partitioned mesh, and the other for METIS-partitioned mesh, are shown in each table, respectively. In these tables, the tuple (CE, LIF, LIR, time, comm, SU) represents (number of cut-edges, load imbalance factor, load imbalance ratio, execution time in seconds for each iteration on the workstation cluster of eight Ultrasparc-2 CPUs, communication time in seconds for each iteration, and speed up), where *load imbalance factor* is the difference of the largest number of elements and the smallest number of elements among PEs, and *load imbalance ratio* is the ratio of load imbalance factor dividing by the theoretical average number of elements in each PE.

All execution times for one iteration of the Euler flow solver by our partitioning results are better than those produced by METIS. This is because our partitioning results are completely load balanced, but results produced by METIS aren't. In addition, in most cases, the numbers of cut-edges generated by our method are less than those produced by METIS.

All three tables show speedup; the execution time decreases when the number of PEs increases and the execution time increases when the size of the problem increases. We also observed that the workstation cluster is more suitable for coarse-grained computation: the artillery shell, which consists of 156412 elements, achieves better speedups than the NASA EET wing, 26900 elements, which in turn also outperforms the NACA0012 airfoil, 23791 elements.

Table 2 summarizes the partitioning results and the execution times for each iteration of the parallel Euler flow solver on thirty-two Pentium-3 CPUs. Current implementation of MPICH for PC/Linux platforms does not seem to be as efficient as for Ultrasparc workstations. This results in higher communication overhead on the PC/Linux cluster. The overhead is more evident in larger problem sizes. This may explain why code for the artillery shell performs less efficiently (lower efficiency) than both the NASA EET wing and the NACA0012 airfoil.

In summary, because our spatial-based partitioning tool generates balanced partitions with a relatively lower communication cost than those done by METIS, the execution times based on our tool are smaller (better) than those based on METIS. The performance advantage of our approach is more significant on the PC/Linux cluster due to higher MPI communication overhead in the PC/Linux cluster. This is because higher communication overhead lengthens the waiting time of the processors during the pipelined stages in the parallel Euler flow solver.

4.2 Partitioning on a heterogeneous environment

We have also partitioned unstructured meshes and run the Euler flow solver on a heterogeneous network consisting of eight Ultrasparc-2 workstations and three Ultrasparc-1 workstations. The ratio of processing speed between these two types of machines is about 2. We compare two cases, one is partitioning the mesh into 11 non-equal-sized partitions according to the speed ratio, the other is decomposing the mesh into 11 equal-sized partitions. As shown in Table 3, the execution time of the NACA0012 airfoil is 0.29 seconds per iteration for heterogeneous partitioning, and 0.37 seconds per iteration for homogeneous partitioning. Taking heterogeneity into concern improves the execution time by about 22%. Similarly, for the NASA EET wing, heterogeneous partitioning improves the execution time by 23%. We were not able to get the performance results of the artillery shell, due to insufficient memory space in the slower workstations.

The time on the heterogeneous network of eleven workstations (e.g. 0.30 seconds for the NASA EET wing) is only competitive to that on a homogeneous system of eight Ultrasparc-2 workstations (0.31 seconds). We have observed that the communication time between two different types of workstations is much higher than on homogeneous ones (0.078 seconds on 11 processors vs. 0.057 seconds on 8 processors), an indication that MPICH 1.1.2 (the MPI implementation that we used for message passing between processing nodes) may not handle communication between heterogeneous workstations (under different operating systems) efficiently. We expect that the performance of the solver on the heterogeneous system will be much improved

Table 1. The unstructured meshes are partitioned into 2, 4, 6, and 8 partitions by our method and METIS. The tuple (CE, LIF, LIR, time, comm, SU) represents (number of cut-edges, load imbalance factor, load imbalance ratio, execution time in seconds for each iteration on the workstation cluster of eight Ultrasparc-2 CPUs, communication time in seconds for each iteration, speed up). (a) The NACA0012 airfoil (23791 elements), where uniprocessor time is 1.41 seconds; (b) the NASA EET wing (26900 elements), where uniprocessor time is 1.58 seconds; (c) an artillery shell within a shock tube (156412 elements), where uniprocessor time is 89 seconds.

(a)

#Par.	Our method						METIS					
	CE	LIF	LIR	time	comm	SU	CE	LIF	LIR	time	comm	SU
2	532	1	0.0%	0.91	0.103	1.55	674	5	0.0%	0.97	0.103	1.45
4	1135	1	0.0%	0.46	0.064	3.07	1312	269	4.5%	0.52	0.063	2.71
6	1568	1	0.0%	0.36	0.063	3.92	1671	209	5.3%	0.41	0.061	3.44
8	2023	1	0.0%	0.30	0.060	4.70	2316	169	5.7%	0.34	0.056	4.15

(b)

#Par.	Our method						METIS					
	CE	LIF	LIR	time	comm	SU	CE	LIF	LIR	time	comm	SU
2	421	0	0.0%	0.89	0.112	1.78	528	232	1.7%	0.99	0.111	1.60
4	1012	0	0.0%	0.50	0.066	3.16	1094	281	4.2%	0.56	0.065	2.82
6	1469	1	0.0%	0.37	0.060	4.27	1444	252	5.6%	0.43	0.060	3.67
8	1801	1	0.0%	0.31	0.057	5.10	2058	193	5.7%	0.35	0.059	4.51

(c)

#Par.	Our method						METIS					
	CE	LIF	LIR	time	comm	SU	CE	LIF	LIR	time	comm	SU
2	837	0	0.0%	55.43	2.89	1.61	1091	502	0.6%	56.50	3.01	1.58
4	2138	0	0.0%	29.01	2.11	3.07	2683	890	2.3%	29.88	2.60	2.98
6	3057	1	0.0%	21.53	1.98	4.13	3303	1160	4.4%	22.73	2.38	3.92
8	3702	1	0.0%	16.96	1.36	5.25	4436	1025	5.2%	17.70	1.77	5.03

Table 2. The unstructured meshes are partitioned into two through thirty-two partitions for the PC cluster by our method and METIS. (a) The NACA0012 airfoil (23791 elements), where uniprocessor time is 0.92 seconds; (b) The NASA EET wing (26900 elements), where uniprocessor time is 1.05 seconds; (c) an artillery shell within a shock tube (156412 elements), where Uniprocessor time is 61 seconds.

(a)

#Par.	Our method						METIS					
	CE	LIF	LIR	time	comm	SU	CE	LIF	LIR	time	comm	SU
2	532	1	0.0%	0.88	0.377	1.05	674	5	0.0%	1.09	0.438	0.84
4	1135	1	0.0%	0.69	0.259	1.33	1312	269	4.5%	0.78	0.307	1.18
8	2023	1	0.0%	0.38	0.160	2.42	2316	169	5.7%	0.46	0.213	2.00
16	3079	1	0.1%	0.20	0.108	4.60	3313	76	5.1%	0.31	0.139	2.97
32	4878	1	0.1%	0.10	0.072	9.20	5137	42	5.7%	0.18	0.091	5.11

(b)

#Par.	Our method						METIS					
	CE	LIF	LIR	time	comm	SU	CE	LIF	LIR	time	comm	SU
2	421	0	0.0%	0.90	0.381	1.17	528	232	1.7%	1.17	0.443	0.90
4	1012	0	0.0%	0.73	0.269	1.44	1094	281	4.2%	0.81	0.315	1.30
8	1801	1	0.0%	0.41	0.182	2.56	2058	193	5.7%	0.51	0.211	2.06
16	3051	1	0.1%	0.21	0.114	5.00	3177	92	5.5%	0.34	0.155	3.09
32	4611	1	0.1%	0.11	0.084	9.55	4793	49	5.8%	0.19	0.099	5.53

(c)

#Par.	Our method						METIS					
	CE	LIF	LIR	time	comm	SU	CE	LIF	LIR	time	comm	SU
2	837	0	0.0%	68.17	14.32	0.89	1091	502	0.6%	73.64	16.67	0.83
4	2138	0	0.0%	40.02	8.37	1.52	2683	890	2.3%	58.70	10.65	1.04
8	3702	1	0.0%	27.65	7.92	2.21	4436	1025	5.2%	38.58	9.31	1.58
16	6798	1	0.0%	16.08	5.40	3.79	7703	556	5.7%	19.22	6.93	3.17
32	10304	1	0.0%	8.79	3.92	6.94	11711	279	5.7%	11.26	4.78	5.42

once newer version of MPICH becomes available.

Table 3. (total time, communication time) of the NACA0012 airfoil and the NASA EET wing for homogeneous partitioning and heterogeneous partitioning on a heterogeneous workstation cluster with eleven PEs.

	NACA0012 airfoil	NASA EET wing
homogeneous partitioning	0.37 (0.095)	0.39 (0.099)
heterogeneous partitioning	0.29 (0.073)	0.30 (0.078)

5 Conclusion

In this paper, we have presented a quadtree spatial-based domain decomposition method for partitioning unstructured meshes. We used a background quadtree to represent the density distribution among elements within the computing domain. This background quadtree also can be used to obtain an initial partitioning and to do multi-level refinement. The background quadtree implicitly defines hierarchical relationship. Coarsening and uncoarsening phases can be defined according to this hierarchical relationship. Thus, we can repeatedly apply coarsening, partitioning, and uncoarsening multi-level refinement phases, until no improvement can be made.

We then used a dynamic diffusion algorithm to migrate boundary elements among partitions, so that all partitions were completely load balanced. After that, we applied Kernighan-Lin refinement to decrease the number of cut-edges between adjacent partitions. We have run cases for the NACA0012 airfoil, the NASA EET wing, and an artillery shell within a shock tube on a workstation cluster and a PC cluster to evaluate the effectiveness of our partitioning method. Experimental studies show that our partitioning approach is promising. Because of space limitation, we have to remove some detailed presentation, a complete version of this paper, however, can be seen elsewhere [15].

References

[1] S. T. Barnard and H. D. Simon. Fast multilevel implementation of recursive spectral bisection for partitioning unstructured problems. *Concurrency: Practice and Experience*, 6(2):101–117, Apr. 1994.

[2] G. Breinholt and C. Schierz. Algorithm 781: Generating hilbert's space-filling curve by recursion. *ACM Trans. on Math Soft.*, 24(2):184–189, June 1998.

[3] M. de Berg, M. van Kreveld, M. Overmars, and O. Schwarzkopf. *Computational Geometry: Algorithms and Applications*. Springer, Berlin, 1997.

[4] F. Ercal, J. Ramanujan, and P. Sadayappan. Task allocation onto a hypercube by recursive mincut bipartitioning. *Journal of Parallel and Distributed Computing*, 10(1):35–44, 1990.

[5] C. Farhat and M. Lesoinne. Automatic partitioning of unstructured meshes for the parallel solution of problems in computational mechanics. *International Journal for Numerical Methods in Engineering*, 36:745–764, 1993.

[6] M. R. Garey and D. S. Johnson. *Computers and Intractability*. W. H. Freeman and Co., San Francisco, 1979.

[7] W. Gropp, E. Lusk, and A. Skjellum. *Using MPI: Portable Parallel Programming with the Message-Passing Interface*. The MIT Press, Cambridge, MA, 1994.

[8] M. T. Heath and P. Raghavan. A Cartesian parallel nested dissection algorithm. *SIAM J. Matrix Anal. Appl.*, 16:235–253, 1995.

[9] G. Karypis and V. Kumar. A fast and high quality multilevel scheme for partitioning irregular graph. *SIAM J. Sci. Comput.*, 20(1):359–392, 1998.

[10] G. Karypis and V. Kumar. METIS: A software package for partitioning unstructured graphs, partitioning meshes, and computing fill-reducing orderings of sparse matrices, version 4.0. Dept. of Computer Science, Univ. of Minnesota, Sep. 1998.

[11] G. Karypis and V. Kumar. Multilevel k-way partitioning scheme for irregular graphs. *Journal of Parallel and Distributed Computing*, 48:96–129, 1998.

[12] B. W. Kernighan and S. Lin. An efficient heuristic procedure for partitioning graphs. *Bell Syst. Tech. J.*, 49(2):292–307, Feb. 1970.

[13] P.-Z. Lee and C.-H. Chang. Unstructured mesh generation using automatic point insertion and local refinement. In *Proc. National Computer Symposium*, pages B550–B557, Taipei, Taiwan, Dec. 1999.

[14] P.-Z. Lee, C.-H. Chang, and J.-J. Wu. Parallel implicit Euler solver on homogeneous and heterogeneous computing environments. AIAA paper 2001–2588, American Institute of Aeronautics and Astronautics, June 2001.

[15] P.-Z. Lee, J.-J. Wu, and C.-H. Chang. Partitioning unstructured meshes for homogeneous and heterogeneous parallel computing environments. available via WWW at http://www.iis.sinica.edu.tw/~leepe/PAPER/icpp02.ps.

[16] G. L. Miller, S.-H. Teng, W. Thurston, and S. A. Vavasis. Automatic mesh partitioning. In *Graph Theory and Sparse Matrix Computation*, volume 56 of *The IMA volumes in mathematics and its applications*, pages 57–84. Springer Verlag, 1993.

[17] C. W. Ou, S. Ranka, and G. Fox. Fast and parallel mapping algorithms for irregular problems. *The Journal of Supercomputing*, 10:119–140, 1996.

[18] A. Pothen, H. D. Simon, and K. P. Liou. Partitioning sparse matrices with eigenvectors of graphs. *SIAM J. Matrix Anal. Appl.*, 11:430–452, 1990.

[19] M. S. Warren and J. K. Salmon. A parallel hashed oct-tree N-body algorithm. In *Proc. Supercomputing'93*, 1993.

[20] D.-L. Yang, Y.-C. Chung, C.-C. Chen, and C.-J. Liao. A dynamic diffusion optimization method for irregular finite element graph partitioning. *The Journal of Supercomputing*, 17(1):91–110, Aug. 2000.

Distributed Game-Tree Search Using Transposition Table Driven Work Scheduling

Akihiro Kishimoto and Jonathan Schaeffer
Department of Computing Science, University of Alberta,
Edmonton, Alberta, Canada T6G 2E8
{kishi@cs.ualberta.ca, jonathan@cs.ualberta.ca}

Abstract

The $\alpha\beta$ algorithm for two-player game-tree search has a notorious reputation as being a challenging algorithm for achieving reasonable parallel performance. MTD(f), a new $\alpha\beta$ variant, has become the sequential algorithm of choice for practitioners. Unfortunately, MTD(f) inherits most of the parallel obstacles of $\alpha\beta$, as well as creating new performance hurdles. Transposition-table-driven scheduling (TDS) is a new parallel search algorithm that has proven to be effective in the single-agent (one-player) domain. This paper presents TDSAB, the first time TDS parallelism has been applied to two-player search (the MTD(f) algorithm). Results show that TDSAB gives comparable speedups to that achieved by conventional parallel $\alpha\beta$ algorithms. However, since this is a parallelization of a superior sequential algorithm, the results in fact are better. This paper shows that the TDS idea can be extended to more challenging search domains.

Keywords: *$\alpha\beta$ search, transposition-table-driven scheduling, single-agent search, transposition table.*

1. Introduction

The development of high-performance game-playing programs has been the subject of over 50 years of artificial intelligence research. At the heart of these programs is the $\alpha\beta$ tree search algorithm. The strong correlation between the depth of search and the resulting program's performance prompted researchers to quickly move to parallel solutions, including multi-processor systems (e.g., WAYCOOL using a 256-processor HyperCube [6], CRAY BLITZ using a 16-processor Cray [8], SUN PHOENIX using a network of 32 workstations [19], ZUGZWANG using 1,024 Transputers [4]) and special-purpose hardware (including DEEP BLUE [7]). Of course, the most vivid demonstration of this technology was the 1996 and 1997 matches between DEEP BLUE and World Chess Champion Garry Kasparov.

Many artificial intelligence applications are search based and require real-time responses. Clearly faster hardware enables more computations to be performed in a fixed amount of time, generally allowing for a better quality answer. Dual-processor machines and clusters of inexpensive processors are ubiquitous and are the *de facto* research computing platforms used today.

Single-agent domains (puzzles) and two-player games have been popular test-beds for experimenting with new ideas in sequential and parallel search. This work transfers naturally to many real-world problem domains, for example planning, path-finding, theorem proving, and DNA sequence alignment. There are many similarities in the approaches used to solve single-agent domains (A* and IDA*) and two-player games ($\alpha\beta$). Many of the sequential enhancements developed in one domain can be applied (with modifications) to the other.

Two recent developments have changed the way that researchers look at two-player search. First, MTD(f) has emerged as the new standard framework for the $\alpha\beta$ algorithm preferred by practitioners [15]. Second, TDS is a new, powerful parallel search paradigm for distributed-memory hardware that has been applied to single-agent search [17, 18]. Given that there is a new standard for sequential $\alpha\beta$ search (MTD(f)) and a new standard for parallel single-agent search (TDS), the obvious question is what happens when both ideas are combined.

In MTD(f), all searches are done with a so-called minimal window $[\alpha, \alpha + 1]$. Each search answers a binary question: is the result $\leq \alpha$ or is it $> \alpha$? At the root of the tree, a series of minimal window searches are performed until the result converges on the value of the search tree. MTD(f) has been shown to empirically out-perform other $\alpha\beta$ variants. It has the nice property of searching using a single bound, an important consideration in a parallel search.

TDS is an elegant idea that reverses the traditional view of parallel search. Instead of sending data to the work that needs it, TDS sends the work to the data. This simple reversal of the relationship between computation and data simplifies the parallelism, reduces parallel overhead, and yields impressive results for single-agent search applications.

This paper introduces TDSAB, TDS parallelism adapted to $\alpha\beta$ search (specifically, MTD(f)) [9]. This is the first attempt to integrate TDS parallelism into two-player search. The speedups in two application domains (the game of Awari, small branching factor; Amazons, large branching factor) average roughly 23 on a network of 64 workstations, a result that is comparable to what others have achieved using conventional parallel $\alpha\beta$ algorithms. However $\alpha\beta$ is not the best sequential algorithm for searching game trees; MTD(f) has been shown to be 5-15% better [15]. Parallel performance must always be compared to that of the best sequential algorithm. Given that the game-development community is moving to MTD(f) as their sequential standard, the results in this paper confirm that this algorithm is also suitable for high-performance parallel applications.

Section 2 discusses sequential and parallel game-tree search algorithms. Section 3 introduces TDSAB, while Section 4 presents experimental data on its performance. Section 5 discusses future work on enhancing this algorithm.

2. Game-tree Search

This section gives a quick survey of $\alpha\beta$ searching. Good surveys of the literature are available for sequential [12] and parallel [1] game-tree search.

2.1. Sequential Search

For more than 30 years the $\alpha\beta$ algorithm has been the most popular algorithm for two-player games. The algorithm eliminates provable irrelevant nodes from the search. Two bounds are maintained, α and β, representing the lower and upper bounds respectively on the minimax value of the search tree (the search window). The savings of $\alpha\beta$ come from the observation that once the search proves that the score of the node is outside the search window, then further effort at that node is irrelevant.

Many enhancements have been added to $\alpha\beta$ to (dramatically) improve the search efficiency. The most important of these is the transposition table, a cache of the results from previously searched sub-trees [20]. Its effectiveness is application dependent. For chess, for example, it is worth a factor of 10 in performance. Thus any high-performance implementation must have a transposition table.

MTD(f) is recognized as the most efficient variant of sequential $\alpha\beta$. Figure 1 shows that MTD(f) is just a sequence of minimal window $\alpha\beta$ calls, searching node n to depth d. The initial search is centered around the value f (usually the value returned by the previous iteration in an iterative-deepening search). This result is then monotonically increased or decreased to the correct minimax value. The transposition table is critical to the performance of MTD(f), since the tree is repeatedly traversed, albeit with a different search window. The table prevents nodes that have been proven to be inferior from being searched repeatedly.

```
int MTD(node_t n, int d, int f) {
    int score;
    int lowerbound = -∞; upperbound = ∞;
    if (f == -∞) bound = f + 1;
    else bound = f;
    do {
        /* Minimal window search */
(+)     score = AlphaBeta(n, d, bound-1, bound);
        if (score < bound) upperbound = score;
        else lowerbound = score;
        /* Re-set the bound */
        if (lowerbound == score) bound = score + 1;
        else bound = score;
    } while (lowerbound ≠ upperbound);
}
```

Figure 1. MTD(f)

2.2. Obstacles to Parallel Search

$\alpha\beta$ has proven to be a notoriously difficult algorithm to get good parallel performance with. To achieve a sufficient speedup, we must cope with the following obstacles:

- *Search overhead* is the (usually) larger tree built by the parallel algorithm as compared to the sequential algorithm. This cost is estimated by:

$$Search\ overhead = \frac{parallel\ tree\ size - sequential\ tree\ size}{sequential\ tree\ size}.$$

  Note that this overhead could be negative (super-linear speedups are occasionally observed).

- *Synchronization overhead* occurs when processors have to sit idle waiting for the results from other searches. A good approximation for this is to measure the average percent of idle time per processor. This overhead can be reduced by increasing the amount of concurrency (for example, speculative search), usually at the cost of increasing the search overhead.

- *Communication overhead* is the consequence of sharing information between processors. In a shared-memory environment, this is effectively zero (although there may be some locking overhead). In a distributed-memory environment, communication is done via message passing. Since all messages are small (less than 100 bytes), the overhead can be estimated by counting messages and multiplying this by the average cost of a message send. Note that fast communication is critical to performance; a late message can result in unnecessary work being spawned in parallel. Hence, a faster network can improve the efficiency of the search.

- *Load balancing* reflects how evenly the work has been distributed between the processors. Ideally, each processor should be given work that takes exactly the same amount of time. In practice, this does not happen, and some processors are forced to wait for others to complete their tasks. Note that load balancing is an important influence on synchronization overhead,

None of these overheads is independent of each other. A high-performance $\alpha\beta$ searcher needs to be finely tuned to choose the right mix of parameters and algorithm enhancements to balance the performance trade-offs.

2.3. Parallel Search Algorithms

Numerous parallel $\alpha\beta$ algorithms have been proposed. The PV-Split algorithm invoked parallelism down the leftmost branch of the tree (the *principal variation*) [13]. In the late 1980s, several algorithms appeared that initiated parallelism throughout the tree (Enhanced PV-Split [8], Dynamic PV-Split [19], Young Brothers Wait Concept [5]). Further concurrency could be achieved using speculative search (UIDPABS [14], APHID [3]).

The Young Brothers Wait Concept (YBWC) serves as a suitable framework for describing most of the commonly used parallel $\alpha\beta$ implementations [4]. There are many variants of YBWC, but they only differ in the implementation details (e.g., [10, 21]). Highly optimized sequential $\alpha\beta$ search algorithms usually do a good job of ordering moves from best to worst. A well-ordered $\alpha\beta$ search tree has the property that if a cut-off is to occur at a node, then the first move considered has a high probability of achieving it. YBWC states that the left-most branch at a node has to be searched before the other branches at the node are searched. This observation reduces the search overhead (by ensuring that the move with the highest probability of causing a cut-off is investigated before initiating the parallelism) at the price of increasing the synchronization overhead (waiting for the first branch to return).

To minimize synchronization overhead and improve load balancing, many algorithms (including YBWC) use *work stealing* to offload work from a busy processor to an otherwise idle processor. When a processor is starved for work, it randomly chooses a processor and then "steals" a piece of work from its work queue. Although work stealing improves the load balancing, on distributed-memory machines this can have an adverse impact because of the lack of information available in the transposition table.

2.4. Parallel Transposition Tables

Practical $\alpha\beta$ search algorithms have transposition tables. In a shared-memory environment, transposition tables can be easily shared, making results from one processor available to others as soon as it has been computed. In a distributed memory environment, things are not so simple; the efficient implementation of transposition tables becomes a serious problem. Since processors do not share memory, they cannot access the table entries of other processors without incurring communication overhead.

There are three naive ways to implement transposition tables on distributed-memory machines. With *local transposition tables*, each processor has its own table. No table entries are shared among processors. Therefore, looking up

and updating an entry can be done without communication. However, local transposition tables usually result in a large search overhead, because a processor may end up repeating a piece of work done by another processor.

With *partitioned transposition tables*, each processor keeps a disjoint subset of the table entries. This can be seen as a large transposition table divided among all the processors (e.g., [4]). Let L be the total number of table entries with p processors, then each processor usually has $\frac{L}{p}$ entries. When a processor P needs a table entry, it sends a message to ask the processor Q which keeps the corresponding entry to return the information to P (communication overhead). P has to wait for Q to send back the information on the table entry to P (synchronization overhead). When processor P updates a table entry, it sends a message to the processor that "owns" that entry to update its table entry. Updating messages can be sent asynchronously.

Using *replicated transposition tables* results in each processor having a copy of the same transposition table. Looking up a table entry can be done by a local access, but updating an entry requires a broadcast to *all* the other processors to update their tables with the new information (excessive communication overhead). Even if messages for updates can be sent asynchronously and multiple messages can be sent at a time by combining them as a single message, the communication overhead increases as the number of processors increases. As well, replicated tables have fewer aggregate entries than a partitioned table.

All three approaches may do redundant search in the case of a DAG (Directed Acyclic Graph). A search result is stored in the transposition table *after* having finished searching. If identical nodes are allocated to different processors, then duplicate search may occur, which increases the search overhead. Because the efficient implementation of transposition tables in a distributed environment is a challenging problem, researchers have been looking for better solutions [2, 19].

2.5. TDS

Transposition-table Driven Scheduling (TDS) flips the idea of work-stealing to solve the transposition table problem [17, 18]. Work-stealing moves the data to where the work is located; TDS moves the work to the data. A similar idea also appears in [11].

In TDS, transposition tables are partitioned over the processors like a partitioned transposition table. Whenever a node is expanded, its children are scattered to the processors (called *home processors*) which keep their transposition table entries. Once the work is sent to a processor, that processor accesses the appropriate transposition table information locally. All communication is asynchronous. Once a processor sends a piece of work, it can immediately work on another task. Processors periodically check to see if new work has arrived.

The idea of TDS seems to be easily applied to two-player games. However, there are important differences between single-agent search (IDA*) and two-player search ($\alpha\beta$) that complicate the issue:

(1) **Pruning:** $\alpha\beta$'s scheme for pruning is different from that of IDA*. IDA* uses a single bound; $\alpha\beta$ uses a pair of bounds (the search window).

(2) **Cut-offs:** IDA* only aborts parallel activity when the final search result has been determined. $\alpha\beta$ cut-offs occur throughout the search. When a cut-off occurs at a node, there has to be a way to abort all work spawned from that node.

(3) **Search window:** $\alpha\beta$ can search identical nodes with different search windows.

(4) **Priority of nodes:** The order in which nodes are considered is more important in $\alpha\beta$ than in IDA*. In IDA*, move ordering only affects the efficiency of the last iteration, while in $\alpha\beta$ it impacts every node in the tree. For IDA*, a stack is sufficient to prioritize nodes; for $\alpha\beta$, this is insufficient.

(5) **Saving the tree:** An IDA* tree node does not need to know its parent. In $\alpha\beta$, values must be passed back from child nodes to parent nodes. This requires an $\alpha\beta$ implementation that guarantees the search tree is saved in the transposition table.

However, TDS has several important advantages that can facilitate the parallel performance of $\alpha\beta$:

(1) All transposition table accesses are done locally. All communication is asynchronous.

(2) DAGs are not a problem, since identical positions are guaranteed to be assigned to the same processor.

(3) Given that positions are mapped to random numbers to be used for transposition table processor assignments, statistically good load balancing happens for free.

Since TDS has proven to be so successful in single-agent search, the obvious question to ask is how it would fare in two-player search.

3. TDSAB

This section presents a new parallel $\alpha\beta$ algorithm, TDSAB (Transposition-table Driven Scheduling Alpha-Beta), the first attempt to parallelize MTD(f) using the TDS algorithm. Transposition tables are critical to the performance of MTD(f), and a TDS-like search addresses the problem of an efficient implementation of this data structure in a distributed-memory environment.

3.1. The TDSAB Algorithm

MTD(f) has an important advantage over classical $\alpha\beta$ for parallel search; since all searches use a minimal window, the problem of disjoint and overlapping search windows will not occur (a serious problem with conventional parallel $\alpha\beta$ implementations). The disadvantage is that for each iteration of MTD(f), there may be multiple calls to $\alpha\beta$, each of which incurs a synchronization point (at line "+" in Figure 1). Each call to $\alpha\beta$ has the parallelism restricted to adhere to the YBWC restriction to reduce the search overhead. The distribution of nodes to processors is done as in TDS.

Since TDSAB follows the TDS philosophy of moving work to the data, the issues explained in the last section have to be resolved. The following new techniques are used for TDSAB:

(1) **Search order:** The parallel search must preserve the good move ordering (best to worst) that is seen in sequential $\alpha\beta$. Our solution to this issue is similar to that used in APHID [2]. Each node is given a priority based on how "left-sided" it is. To compute the priority of a node, the path from the root to that node is considered. Each move along that path contributes a score based on whether the move is the left-most in the search tree, left-most in that sub-tree, or none of the above. These scores are added together to give a priority, and nodes are sorted to determine the order in which to consider work (see [9] for details).

(2) **Signatures:** When searching the children of a node in parallel and a cut-off score is returned, further work at this node is not necessary; all outstanding work must be stopped. However, since TDS does not have all the descendants of a node on the same processor, we have to consider an efficient way of tracking down this work (and any work that has been spawned by it) and terminating it. Cut-offs can be elegantly handled by the idea of giving each node a *signature*. When a cut-off happens at a node P, TDSAB broadcasts the signature of P to all the processors. A processor receiving a cut-off signature examines its local priority queue and deletes all the nodes whose signature *prefix* is the same as the signature of P (see Section 3.2).

(3) **Synchronization of nodes:** The search order of identical nodes must be considered carefully in the case of cyclic graphs, in order to avoid deadlock. We have developed a strategy for synchronizing identical nodes that is deadlock-free (see Section 3.3).

Figure 2 gives pseudo code for TDSAB. For simplicity, we just explain TDSAB without YBWC and also do not use the negamax form. The function $ParallelMWS$ does one iteration of a minimal window search $[\alpha, \alpha+1]$ in parallel. The end of the search is checked by the function $FinishedSearchingRoot$, which can be implemented by broadcasting a message when the score for the root has been decided. The function $RecvNode$ checks regularly if new information comes to a processor. $RecvNode$ receives three kinds of information:

1. NEW_WORK: a processor has examined a node and spawned the node's children to be evaluated in parallel.

The new work arrives, assigned a priority, and inserted in the priority queue (lines marked "="). Eventually this work will reach the head of the priority queue (if it is not cut-off). If the work to be searched is terminal or a small piece of work then it is immediately searched locally (the cost of doing it in parallel out-weighs the benefits) and sent back to its parent node (lines marked "-" in the figure). Otherwise, the children of the node are generated and sent to their *HomeProcessors* to be searched (lines marked "!").

2. CUT-OFF: a signature is received and used to remove work from the priority queue. If a processor receives a signature, the function *CutAllDescendants* examines its local queue and discards all nodes with a matching signature prefix (see the pseudo-code at "*").

3. SEARCH_RESULT: the minimax score of a node is being returned to its parent node (lines marked "+").

If new information arrives at a processor, *GetNode*, *GetSignature*, and *GetSearchResult* get information on a node, signature, and score for a node respectively. *GetLocalJob* determines a node to be expanded from its local priority queue, and *DeleteLocalJob* deletes a node from the queue. We note that TDSAB keeps information on nodes being searched unlike the IDA* version of TDS. *SendNode* sends a node to the processor chosen by the function *HomeProcessor*, which returns the id of the processor having the table entry for the node (a function of the transposition table key *TTKey*).

When receiving a search result, TDSAB has to consider two cases (*StoreSearchResult*). If a score proves a fail high (result > α), TDSAB does not need to search the rest of the branches. The fail-high score is saved in the transposition table (*TransFailHighStore*), the node is dequeued from the priority queue, and the score is sent to the processor having the parent of the node (*SendScore*). Only after a processor has completed searching a node is it discarded. Because searching the rest of the branches has already started, the processor broadcasts a signature to abort useless search, then deletes the node. When a fail low happens (result $\leq \alpha$), a processor stores the maximum score of the branches. If all the branches of a node are searched, the fail-low score for the node is stored in the transposition table (*TransFailLowStore*), and the score is reported back to its parent.

3.2. Signatures

Let P be a node and Q be a child of P. When searching the children of P in parallel, if Q returns a score that causes a cut-off at P, searching other children of P is not necessary. If any child of P is currently being searched, then it must be stopped. TDSAB, therefore, has to stop any useless searches in order to avoid increasing the search overhead. However, because all the descendants of P are not always on the same processor in the TDS framework, we

```
int α; /* A search window is set to [α, α + 1]. */
/* Granularity depends on machines, networks, and so on. */
const int granularity;

void ParallelMWS() {
    int type, v;
    node_t p;
    signature_t sig;
    do {
        /* Check if new information arrives. */
        if (RecvNode(&type) == TRUE) {
            switch(type) {
(=)             /* New work is stored in its priority queue. */
(=)             case NEW_WORK:
(=)                 GetNode(&p); Enqueue(p); break;
(*)             /* Obsolete nodes are deleted from its priority queue. */
(*)             case CUT_OFF:
(*)                 GetSignature(&sig); CutAllDescendents(sig); break;
(+)             /* A search result is saved in the transposition table. */
(+)             case SEARCH_RESULT:
(+)                 GetSearchResult(&p,&v); StoreSearchResult(p,v); break;
            }
        }
        GetLocalJob(&p);
        if (p == FOUND) {
(-)         if (p == terminal || p.depth ≤ granularity) {
(-)             /* Local search is done for small work. */
(-)             v = AlphaBeta(p,p.depth,α,α + 1);
(-)             SendScore(p.parent,v);
                DeleteLocalJob(p);
            } else { /* Do one-ply search in parallel. */
(!)             for (int i = 0; i < p.num_of_children; i++) {
(!)                 int pe = HomeProcessor(TTKey(p.child_node[i]));
(!)                 p.child_node[i].depth = p.depth - 1;
(!)                 SendNode(p.child_node[i],pe);
                }
            }
        }
    } while (!FinishedSearchingRoot());
}

void StoreSearchResult(node_t p, int value) {
    if (value > α) { /* Fail high */
        TransFailHighStore(p,value);
        SendScore(p.parent,value);
        SendPruningMessage(p.signature); DeleteLocalJob(p);
    } else { /* Fail low */
        p.score = MAX(p.score,value); p.num_received ++;
        if (p.num_received == p.num_of_children) {
            /* All the scores for its children are received. */
            TransFailLowStore(p,p.score);
            SendScore(p.parent,p.score);
            DeleteLocalJob(p);
        }
    }
}
```

Figure 2. Simplified Pseudo Code for TDSAB

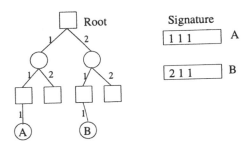

Figure 3. Signatures

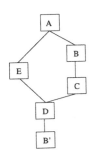

Figure 4. Deadlock with Cycles

have to consider an efficient implementation for cut-offs in TDSAB. In a naive implementation, when a cut-off happens at a node, a message has to be sent to all processors searching that node's children asking them to remove the child node from their priority queue (and, in turn, messages to their children to stop searching, and so on). This approach clearly results in the exchange of many messages which can lead to a large increase in communication overhead, and also a delay in killing unnecessary work (which, in turn, results in more search overhead).

In TDSAB, when a cut-off occurs, we reduce the number of messages exchanged by using a *signature*. Intuitively, the signature for P is the path traversed from the root node to P. Every branch of a node has a tag which differentiates it from other branches at that node; a signature of P is seen as a sequence of these tags from the root to P. Figure 3 illustrates an example of signatures. The decimal number on each branch between two nodes is the tag. The signature of A is 111 derived from the path from the root to A; the signature of B is 211.

When a cut-off happens at a node P, TDSAB broadcasts the signature of P to all the processors. When a processor receives a cut-off signature, it examines its local priority queue and deletes all the nodes which have the same paths from the root to P. For example, in Figure 3, if TDSAB wants to prune all the children of A, the signature 111 is broadcast and each processor prunes all the nodes that begin with the signature "111···".

3.3. Deadlock

The search order of identical nodes has to be carefully handled in order to avoid deadlock. Assume that a processor has two identical nodes. If searching the second node is *always* delayed until after the completion of the first node, then a deadlock may occur. Figure 4 illustrates this problem. Suppose that B and B' are identical nodes. If these nodes are searched in the following order, a deadlock will occur: (1) A is expanded, and B and E are sent to their home processors. (2) B is expanded, and C is sent. If B's processor receives a node B' identical to B, searching B' is

delayed until it receives a score for B. (3) E is expanded, and D is sent. (4) D is expanded, and B' is sent. Searching B' is done after finishing B. (5) C is expanded, and D is sent. In this case, B waits for the score for C, C waits for D, D waits for B', and B' waits for B. Therefore a cyclic wait has been created and a deadlock ensures.

To eliminate the possibility of deadlock, if two identical nodes are encountered and neither of the nodes has been searched yet, then TDSAB searches the shallower one first. When a node n_1 whose search depth is shallower or equivalent to an identical node n_2 whose search has already begun, then n_2 waits until n_1's search completes. When a deeper search has already started, the shallower search of an identical node is also started. This strategy avoids a deadlock by preventing a shallower node from waiting for a deeper node to return its score, which happened in Figure 4. However, some nodes can be searched more than once even if it does not cause a deadlock, when a deeper node is expanded before a shallower identical node. In practice, this additional overhead is small. The correctness of this approach is proven in [9].

3.4. Implementation Details

TDSAB has been implemented for the games of Awari and Amazons (see www.cs.ualberta.ca/~games). The African game of Awari is characterized by a low branching factor (less than 6) and an inexpensive evaluation function. Amazons is a new game that has grown in popularity since it seems to be intermediate in difficulty between chess and Go. It has a very large branching factor (2,176 at the start of the game) and an expensive evaluation function. These games have different properties that exhibit themselves by different characteristics of a parallel search.

Historically, chess has been used to benchmark the performance of parallel $\alpha\beta$ algorithms. Chess is no longer in vogue, and researchers have moved on to other games with interesting research problems. Both Awari and Amazons are the subject of active research efforts and thus are of greater interest.

For Amazons the YBWC strategy was modified. Be-

Number of Processors	Execution Time (seconds)	Speedup	Search Overhead (%)	Synch. Overhead (%)	Comm. Overhead (%)
1	2177.2	-	-	-	-
8	463.81	4.69	18.5	20.3	0.8
16	253.48	8.59	15.3	30.1	1.1
32	152.67	14.26	15.6	40.5	1.5
64	99.80	21.82	15.6	55.0	3.6

Table 1. Awari Performance, 24-ply

Number of Processors	Execution Time (seconds)	Speedup	Search Overhead (%)	Synch. Overhead (%)	Comm. Overhead (%)
1	1604.1	-	-	-	-
8	343.58	4.67	55.8	11.1	0.9
16	180.11	8.90	55.2	15.1	1.0
32	116.11	13.81	79.2	25.4	1.3
64	68.25	23.50	66.4	35.5	3.6

Table 2. Amazons Performance, 5-ply

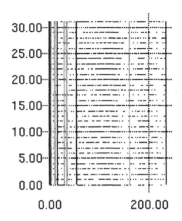

Figure 5. Awari Idle Times

cause of the large branching factor the basic YBWC strategy distributes too many nodes to the processors, resulting in a lot of search overhead. Therefore, if the first branch of a node does not cause a cut-off, a smaller number of children (P where P is the number of processors) are searched in parallel at a time. If none of these branches causes a cut-off then the next P nodes are searched in parallel, and so on.

For Awari, the search was modified to consider all the children of the root node in parallel. Although this is a search overhead versus synchronization overhead trade-off, it solves a serious problem for any domain with a small branching factor: insufficient work to keep the processors busy (*starvation*).

4. Experiments

The Awari and Amazons programs were written in C and used PVM. Tables 1 and 2 show the experimental results. All results were obtained using Pentium IIIs at 933 Mhz, connected by a 100Mb Ethernet. Each processor had its own 200 MB transposition table. Each data point is the average of 20 test positions. The search depths were chosen so that a test position would take 1-2 minutes on 64 processors (i.e., the typical speed seen in tournaments). Awari, with its low branching factor and inexpensive evaluation function, can search 24-ply deep in roughly the time it takes to search Amazons (and its large branching factor and expensive evaluation function) 5-ply deep (one ply is one move by one player).

To measure synchronization and communication overheads, we used an instrumented version of the programs. Therefore, we note that the theoretical speedups calculated by these overheads do not always reflect the observed speedups in each game.

The Awari results can be compared to previous work using checkers, which has a similarly small branching factor. The TDSAB speedup of 21.8 on 64 processors easily beats the APHID speedup of 14.35 using comparable hardware [2]. Analysis of the overheads shows that synchronization is the major culprit. This is not surprising, given that there are 12 iterations (the program iterated in steps of two ply at a time), and an average of 3 synchronization points per iteration. Figure 5 shows a graph of processor idle time (white space) for a typical search. The Y-axis is the processor number (0-31) and the X-axis is time. The vertical lines show where a synchronization point occurred. The last few synchronization points resulted in lots of idle time, limiting the speedup.

Amazons has only slightly better performance (23.5-fold speedup), which may seem surprising given the large branching factor (and, hence, no shortage of work to be done). The very large branching factor turns out to be a liability. At nodes where parallelism can be initiated, many pieces of work are generated, creating lots of concurrent activity (which is good). If a cut-off occurs, many of these pieces of work may have been unnecessary resulting in increased search overhead (which is bad). In this case, search overhead limits the performance, suggesting that the program should be more prudent than it currently is in initiating parallel work. Other parallel implementations have adopted a similar policy of searching subsets of the possible moves at a node, precisely to limit the impact of unexpected cut-offs (for example, [21]).

Multigame is the only previous attempt to parallelize MTD(f) [16] (conventional parallel $\alpha\beta$ was used). Multigame's performance at checkers (21.54-fold speedup) is comparable to TDSAB's result in Awari. For chess, Multigame achieved a 28.42-fold speedup using partitioned transposition tables; better than TDSAB's results in Amazons. However, comparing these numbers is not fair. The Multigame results were obtained using slower machines (Pentium Pros at 200 Mhz versus Pentium IIIs at 933 Mhz), a faster network (Myrinet 1.2Gb/s duplex network versus 100Mb/s Ethernet), longer execution times (roughly 33% larger), and different games.

When comparing TDSAB's parallel performance to that of other implementations (including ZUGZWANG), one must take into account that "standard" $\alpha\beta$ is now an inferior sequential algorithm. MTD(f) builds trees that are 5-15% smaller on average [15]. All speedups should be computed relative to the *best sequential algorithm*. Now that a new standard for sequential $\alpha\beta$ performance has been set, previously published parallel algorithms and results should be re-evaluated.

5. Conclusions

The results of our work on TDSAB are encouraging. Clearly, the TDS framework offers important advantages for a high-performance search application, including asynchronous communication and effective use of memory. However, these advantages are partially offset by the increased synchronization overhead of MTD(f). The end result of this work are speedups that are comparable to what others have reported, perhaps even better when one takes into account the differences between MTD(f) and $\alpha\beta$. This is the first attempt to apply TDS to the two-player domain, and undoubtedly improvements will be found to further enhance performance.

Moving TDS from the single-agent domain to the two-player domain proved challenging. New techniques had to be invented to accommodate the needs of $\alpha\beta$. In many ways, $\alpha\beta$ is a worst-case scenario; most artificial intelligence search algorithms do not need all the parallel capabilities required by $\alpha\beta$. This work generalizes TDS and shows that it can be a powerful parallel paradigm for a wide class of search algorithms.

There are numerous ideas yet to explore with TDSAB including: better priority queue node ordering, reducing MTD(f) synchronization, controlling the amount of parallelism initiated at a node, and speculative search. As well, a TDS implementation of $\alpha\beta$ (not MTD(f)) would be useful for comparison purposes. All these ideas are topics of current research.

6. Acknowledgments

Financial support was provided by the Natural Sciences and Engineering Research Council of Canada (NSERC) and Alberta's Informatics Circle of Research Excellence (iCORE).

References

[1] M. Brockington. A taxonomy of parallel game-tree search algorithms. *International Computer Chess Association Journal*, 19(3):162–174, 1996.

[2] M. Brockington. *Asynchronous Parallel Game-Tree Search*. PhD thesis, Dept. of Computing Science, Univ. of Alberta, 1998.

[3] M. Brockington and J. Schaeffer. Aphid: Asynchronous parallel game-tree search. *Journal of Parallel and Distributed Computing*, 60:247–273, 2000.

[4] R. Feldmann. *Game Tree Search on Massively Parallel Systems*. PhD thesis, Univ. of Paderborn, August 1993.

[5] R. Feldmann, B. Monien, P. Mysliwietz, and O. Vornberger. Distributed game tree search. *Journal of the International Computer Chess Association*, 12(2):65–73, 1989.

[6] E. Felten and S. Otto. Chess on a hypercube. In G. Fox, editor, *Third Conference on Hypercube Concurrent Computers and Applications*, volume II-Applications, pages 1329–1341, 1988.

[7] F. Hsu. IBM's Deep Blue chess grandmaster chips. *IEEE Micro*, (March-April):70–81, 1999.

[8] R. Hyatt and B. Suter. A parallel alpha/beta tree searching algorithm. *Parallel Computing*, 10:299–308, 1989.

[9] A. Kishimoto. Transposition Table Driven Scheduling for Two-Player Games. Master's thesis, Dept. of Computing Science, Univ. of Alberta, 2002.

[10] B. Kuszmaul. *Synchronized MIMD Computing*. PhD thesis, Massachusetts Institute of Technology, 1994.

[11] U. Lorenz. Parallel controlled conspiracy number search. In *13th Annual Symposium on Parallel Algorithms and Architectures (SPAA2001)*, pages 320–321, 2001.

[12] T. Marsland. Relative performance of alpha-beta implementations. In *IJCAI*, pages 763–766, 1983.

[13] T. Marsland and F. Popowich. Parallel game-tree search. *IEEE PAMI*, 7(4):442–452, 1985.

[14] M. Newborn. Unsynchronized iteratively deepening parallel alpha-beta search. *IEEE PAMI*, 10(5):687–694, 1988.

[15] A. Plaat, J. Schaeffer, W. Pijls, and A. de Bruin. Best-first fixed-depth minimax algorithms. *Artificial Intelligence*, 87(1–2):1–38, 1996.

[16] J. Romein. *Multigame - An Environment for Distributed Game-Tree Search*. PhD thesis, Vrije Universitat Amsterdam, 2001.

[17] J. Romein, H. Bal, J. Schaeffer, and A. Plaat. A performance analysis of transposition-table-driven scheduling. *IEEE PDS*, 2002. To appear.

[18] J. Romein, A. Plaat, H. Bal, and J. Schaeffer. Transposition table driven work scheduling in distributed search. *AAAI National Conference*, pages 725–731, 1999.

[19] J. Schaeffer. Distributed game-tree searching. *Journal of Parallel and Distributed Computing*, 6:90–114, 1989.

[20] D. Slate and L. Atkin. CHESS 4.5 - The Northwestern University Chess Program. In P. Frey, editor, *Chess Skill in Man and Machine*, pages 82–118. Springer-Verlag, 1977.

[21] J.-C. Weill. The ABDADA distributed minmax-search algorithm. *International Computer Chess Association Journal*, 19(1):3–16, 1996.

Space and Time Efficient Parallel Algorithms and Software for EST Clustering*

Anantharaman Kalyanaraman
Dept. of CS
Iowa State University
Ames, IA 50011

Srinivas Aluru[†]
Dept. of ECpE
Iowa State University
Ames, IA 50011

Suresh Kothari
Dept. of ECpE
Iowa State University
Ames, IA 50011

Abstract

Expressed sequence tags, abbreviated ESTs, are DNA molecules experimentally derived from expressed portions of genes. Clustering of ESTs is essential for gene recognition and understanding important genetic variations such as those resulting in diseases. In this paper, we present the design and development of a parallel software system for EST clustering. To our knowledge, this is the first such effort to address the problem of EST clustering in parallel. The novel features of our approach include 1) design of space efficient algorithms to keep the space requirement linear in the size of the input data set, 2) a combination of algorithmic techniques to reduce the total work without sacrificing the quality of EST clustering, and 3) use of parallel processing to reduce the run-time and facilitate the clustering of large data sets. Using a combination of these techniques, we report the clustering of 81,414 Arabidopsis ESTs in under 2.5 minutes on a 64-processor IBM SP, a problem that is estimated to take 9 hours of run-time with a state-of-the-art software, provided the memory required to run the software can be made available.

1 The EST Clustering Problem

DNA is a sequence composed of four different types of nucleotides, denoted by A, C, G and T. For computational purposes, it can be considered as a string over the alphabet $\Sigma = \{A, C, G, T\}$. *Genes* are stretches of DNA that encode for protein molecules. They are composed of alternating segments called *exons* and *introns*. A gene is *transcribed* to its corresponding *mRNA*, which is a molecule describing the concatenation of the exons. The mRNA is later translated into its corresponding protein molecule. A cell contains mRNAs from different genes in various concentrations depending on its necessity to produce proteins. Through experimentation, the mRNAs are isolated and converted to the corresponding DNA molecules, known as *cDNA*. Due to experimental limitations, several cDNAs of various lengths

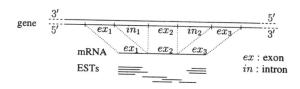

Figure 1. A simplified diagrammatic illustration of a gene, mRNA and ESTs.

are obtained instead of just full-length cDNAs. Part of the cDNA fragments of average length about 500-600 can be sequenced. The sequencing can be done from either end. The resulting sequences are called *Expressed Sequence Tags*, or *ESTs* (see Figure 1).

Given a set of ESTs, **the EST clustering problem** is to partition the ESTs into clusters such that ESTs from each gene are put together in a distinct cluster. The input EST sequences contain errors due to the nature of experiments involved in deriving and sequencing them. A further complication arises due to the fact that DNA is actually a double stranded molecule and a gene could be part of either strand. The two strands are related according to the following nucleotide pairings: $A \leftrightarrow T$ and $C \leftrightarrow G$. The two strands of a DNA have opposite directionality. Thus, one strand can be obtained from the other using a *reverse complementation* operation, where complementation refers to substituting according to the pairing $A \leftrightarrow T$ and $C \leftrightarrow G$.

The motivation for this work stems from the wide range of applications that require EST clustering. Some important applications are gene identification, gene expression studies, differential gene expression studies, Single Nucleotide Polymorphism (SNP) discovery and design of microarrays. A repository of ESTs collected from various organisms is maintained at the National Center for Biotechnology Information (http://www.nicb.nlm.nih.gov/dbEST). With the number of ESTs for some organisms running into a few million, parallel processing is essential to cluster such large collections of ESTs.

The rest of the paper is organized as follows: In Section 2, we present our approach to EST clustering and highlight problems with current software. Section 3 contains details of our parallel algorithms. Experimental results are presented in Section 4. Section 5 concludes the paper.

---

*Research supported by NSF under ACI-0203782.

[†] Also supported by NSF Career under CCR-0096288.

Input	TIGR Assembler	Phrap	CAP3
50,000	X	23 mins	5 hrs
81,414	X	X	X

Table 1. Run-times of TIGR Assembler, Phrap and CAP3 on *Arabidopsis* ESTs using one IBM SP processor with 512 MB memory ('X' denotes insufficient memory to run program).

2   Our Approach

The primary information available to cluster ESTs is the potential overlaps between ESTs from the same gene. The overlap between two sequences can be computed by a pairwise alignment algorithm using dynamic programming [1, 9, 10, 12] in run-time quadratic in the length of the sequences, making it expensive to run for all pairs of ESTs. Hence, approximate overlap detection algorithms are used for fast identification of pairs of ESTs with potential for good quality overlap. The dynamic programming algorithm is then run on the more promising pairs.

The most popular software tools used for EST clustering are Phrap [3], CAP3 [6] and TIGR Assembler [13]. The run-times of each of these three programs on our benchmark *Arabidopsis* EST data sets are shown in Table 1. The programs are run on an IBM SP processor to enable direct comparison of results with our parallel software. We identified the generation of promising pairs as the memory-intensive phase and the computation of pairwise alignments on the promising pairs as the time-intensive phase. As for quality assessment, CAP3 produced the least number of erroneous clusters (see also [7]).

In light of experience with current software, the focus of our research is on developing memory-efficient algorithms and developing algorithmic strategies to minimize run-time without affecting quality. We also focused on parallel processing to achieve the twin objectives of further reducing run-time and facilitating clustering of large EST data sets by taking advantage of scaling of memory with the number of processors.

In our approach, each EST is initially considered a cluster by itself. Two clusters are merged when an EST from each cluster can be identified that show strong overlap using the pairwise alignment algorithm. This process is continued until no further merges are possible. If a pair of identified ESTs do not show strong overlap, the corresponding clusters cannot be merged, and the effort in testing is wasted. Note that it may still be the case that the two clusters should be merged and our choice of the pair does not reflect that.

When two clusters are merged, it is no longer necessary

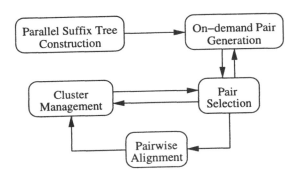

Figure 2. Organization of our Parallel EST Clustering Software.

to test pairs of ESTs where each is drawn from one of the two clusters. As success in merging of clusters depends on the choice of promising pairs being tested, significant savings in run-time can be achieved by generating pairs of ESTs in decreasing order of probability of strong overlap. We use length of a maximal common substring of pairs as the metric for predicting strongly overlapping pairs, and generate pairs of ESTs in the decreasing order of this metric. To minimize the memory requirements, our algorithm remembers its state and produces the next set of pairs on demand.

3   Parallel EST Clustering

The organization of our software is depicted in Figure 2. We first build a distributed representation of the generalized suffix tree data structure in parallel. This is used for on-demand generation of promising pairs in decreasing order of maximal common substring length. The pair generation itself is done in parallel, and the algorithm is such that each processor need only access the portion of the suffix tree within itself. Maintaining and updating of the EST clusters is handled by a single processor, which acts as a master processor directing the remaining processors to both generate batches of promising pairs and perform pairwise alignment on promising pairs. Our algorithms for each of the components of the software are described in the following sections.

3.1   Parallel Construction of Generalized Suffix Tree

The suffix tree of a string is a compacted trie of all its suffixes [4]. Leaves in a suffix tree correspond to suffixes and internal nodes correspond to longest common prefixes shared by two or more suffixes. A Generalized Suffix Tree (GST) is a compacted trie of all suffixes of a set of strings, and can be constructed in time linear in input size [4].

We use the following notation: Let n be the number of ESTs and the set $\mathcal{E} = \{e_1, e_2, \ldots, e_n\}$ denote the ESTs. The total number of characters in all the ESTs is denoted by N. Let l be the average length of an EST, i.e., $l = \frac{N}{n}$. Because of the double stranded nature of DNA, each EST and its reverse complement must be considered. Let $\mathcal{S} = \{s_1, s_2, \ldots, s_{2n}\}$ denote the $2n$ strings such that $e_i = s_{2i-1}$ and $\bar{e}_i = s_{2i}$, where $\bar{e}_i$ denotes the reverse complement of e_i. We use the terms *string* and *sequence*, and *substring* and *subsequence* in an equivalent manner.

We perform a parallel construction of the GST for $\mathcal{S}$, and this data structure is used for on-demand pair generation. Parallel algorithms for construction of suffix trees using the CRCW/CREW PRAM model are presented in [2, 5]. Due to the unrealistic assumptions underlying the PRAM model with respect to accessing remote memory, a direct implementation of these algorithms is unlikely to be practically efficient. Moreover, the average length of an EST is a fixed number (500-600) irrespective of the number of ESTs. Because of this, we use the following approach:

Initially, the ESTs are distributed across processors such that each processor has an approximately equal share of the total input, measured in number of characters. Each processor scans its ESTs and their reverse complements, and partitions their suffixes into at most $|\Sigma|^w$ buckets based on the first w characters. The total number of suffixes in each bucket over all the processors is computed using a parallel summation algorithm in $O(\log p)$ communication steps, where p is the number of processors. The buckets are then distributed to the processors such that 1) all the suffixes in a bucket are allocated to the same processor and 2) the total number of suffixes in all the buckets allocated to a processor is as close to $\frac{nl}{p}$ as possible. Care should be taken in choosing w. While assigning a large value to w may result in the loss of some potential overlapping pairs, assigning a low value will result in a small number of buckets for distribution among processors. Typically a value of 10 will allow us to generate $4^{10} > 1,000,000$ buckets, enough to distribute them in a load-balanced fashion on multiprocessor systems.

For each bucket, the processor responsible for it constructs the tree for all the suffixes in the bucket. Note that a sequential suffix tree construction algorithm can no longer be used because all suffixes of a string do not fall in the same bucket, unless the string is a repetition of a single character. To construct the tree, we use the simple approach of scanning all suffixes of a bucket one character at a time. As a result, a bucket is further subdivided into smaller buckets which are recursively subdivided, until each suffix is assigned a separate bucket. Assuming each processor receives approximately $\frac{nl}{p}$ total suffixes, the run-time for tree construction is $O\left(\frac{nl^2}{p}\right) = O\left(\frac{Nl}{p}\right)$. This algorithm works well in practice because l is independent of n. Note that the tree for each bucket is a subtree in the GST for $\mathcal{S}$. The collection of trees can be thought of as a distributed representation of the GST except for the top portion consisting of nodes with string-depth $< w$.

Because of concern for space-efficiency, each tree is stored as follows: The nodes are generated and stored in the order of the depth-first search traversal of the tree. Each node contains a single pointer to the rightmost leaf node in its subtree. All the children of a node can be retrieved using the following procedure — The first child of a node is stored next to it in the array. The next sibling of a node can be obtained by following the pointer to its rightmost leaf and taking the node in the next entry of the array. If a node and its parent have identical rightmost leaf pointers, the node has no next sibling. A leaf is one whose rightmost leaf pointer points to itself.

3.2 On-demand Pair Generation

Let *promising pair* refer to a pair of strings with a maximal common substring of length $\geq \psi$, a threshold value. The goal of the on-demand pair generation algorithm is to report the promising pairs on-the-fly, in decreasing order of maximal common substring length. We generate at no additional storage cost, a promising pair at most as many times as the number of distinct maximal substrings common to the pair. The algorithm operates on the following idea - If two strings share a maximal common substring α, then the leaves corresponding to the suffixes of the strings starting with α will be present in the subtree of the node with path-label[1] α. Thus the algorithm can generate the pair at that node.

A substring α of a string is said to be *left-extensible* (alternatively, *right-extensible*) by c if c is the character to the left (alternatively, right) of α in the string. If the substring is a prefix of the string, then it is said to be left-extensible by λ, the null character. Let $subtree(v)$ denote the set of nodes in the subtree of node v. Let $leaf(f)$ denote the leaf corresponding to a suffix f. Let $leaf\text{-}set(v) \subseteq \mathcal{S}$ be the set of strings that have a suffix f such that $leaf(f) \in subtree(v)$. The $leaf\text{-}set(v)$ is partitioned into five sets, $l_A(v)$, $l_C(v)$, $l_G(v)$, $l_T(v)$ and $l_\lambda(v)$, referred to as $lsets(v)$. If a string s is in $l_c(v)$ (for $c \in \Sigma \cup \{\lambda\}$), then the string has a suffix f such that $leaf(f) \in subtree(v)$ and f is left-extensible by c. Observe that such a partition need not be unique because a string s could have two suffixes f and f' such that $leaf(f)$ and $leaf(f')$ both are in $subtree(v)$, and f and f' are left-extensible by different characters. Then s could be either in $l_{c_i}(v)$ or $l_{c_j}(v)$. Any of

---

[1] The path-label of a node in GST is the concatenation of the edge labels from root to the node.

Algorithm 1 *Pair Generation*

GeneratePairs(Forest of local GST subtrees with roots of string-depth $< \psi$)
1. Compute the string-depth of all nodes in local GST subtrees.
2. Sort nodes with string-depth $\geq \psi$ in decreasing order of string-depth.
3. For each node v in that order
  IF v is a leaf THEN **ProcessLeaf(v)**
  ELSE **ProcessInternalNode(v)**

ProcessLeaf(Leaf: v)
1. Compute $P_v = \bigcup_{(c_i,c_j)} l_{c_i}(v) \times l_{c_j}(v)$, $\forall (c_i, c_j)$ s.t., $c_i < c_j$ or $c_i = c_j = \lambda$

ProcessInternalNode(Internal Node: v)
1. Traverse all *lsets* of all children $u_1, u_2, \ldots, u_m$ of v. If a string is present in more than one *lset*, all but one occurrence of it are removed.
2. Compute $P_v = \bigcup_{(u_k,u_l)} \bigcup_{(c_i,c_j)} l_{c_i}(u_k) \times l_{c_j}(u_l)$, $\forall (u_k, u_l)$, $\forall (c_i, c_j)$ s.t., $1 \leq k < l \leq m$, $c_i \neq c_j$ or $c_i = c_j = \lambda$
3. Create all *lsets* at v by computing :
  For each $c_i \in \Sigma \cup \{\lambda\}$ do
  $l_{c_i}(v) = \bigcup_{u_k} l_{c_i}(u_k)$, $1 \leq k \leq m$

Figure 3. Algorithm for generation of promising pairs.

these partitions will work for the pair generation algorithm.

The algorithm for generation of pairs is given in Figure 3. The nodes in local subtrees with string-depth[2] $\geq \psi$ are sorted in decreasing order of string-depth, and processed in that order. The *lsets* at leaf nodes are computed directly from the leaf labels. The set of pairs generated at node v is denoted by P_v. If v is a leaf, the cartesian products of *lsets* corresponding to different characters are computed, in addition to a cartesian product of $l_\lambda(v)$ with itself, and their union is taken to be P_v.

If v is an internal node, the *lsets* of the children of v are traversed to eliminate multiple occurrences of the same string in the *lsets* of different children of v. Note that after the elimination, the *lsets* at a child of v may no longer represent a partition of the *leaf-set* of the child. After the elimination, cartesian products of *lsets* corresponding to different characters and different children are computed, in addition to cartesian products of the *lsets* corresponding to λ of different children, and their union is taken to be P_v. The *lset* for a particular character at v is obtaining by taking a union of the *lsets* for the same character at the children of v. Because of the elimination of multiple occurrences, the *lsets* at v constitute a partition of *leaf-set(v)*.

Traversing *lsets* of all child nodes to eliminate multiple occurrences of a string is implemented to run in time proportional to the sum of the cardinalities of those *lsets*.

A global array of size $2n$ indexed by string identifiers is maintained. When a string is encountered in an *lset* at a node, the entry in the array for this string is checked to see if it is marked with the identifier of the internal node being processed. If not, the array entry is marked with the node identifier. If it is already marked, the occurrence of this string from this *lset* is removed. A linked list implementation of the *lsets* allows the union in *Step 3* of *ProcessInternalNode* to be computed using $O(|\Sigma|^2)$ concatenation operations. At this point, the *lsets* at the internal node's children are removed. This limits the total space required for storing *lsets* to $O(N)$, linear in the size of the input.

A pair generated at a node v is discarded if the string corresponding the smaller EST id number is in complemented form. This is to avoid duplicates such as generating both (e_i, e_j) and $(\bar{e}_i, \bar{e}_j)$, or generating both $(e_i, \bar{e}_j)$ and $(\bar{e}_i, e_j)$ for some $1 \leq i, j \leq n$. Thus without loss of generality, we will denote a pair by (s, s'), where $s = e_i$ and s' is either e_j or $\bar{e}_j$ for some $i < j$. The relative orderings of the characters in $\Sigma \cup \{\lambda\}$ and the child nodes, avoid duplicate generation of both (s, s') and (s', s) at the same node.

Let P_v denote the set of unordered pairs generated at any node v. In summary, if v is a leaf,
$$P_v = \{(s_1, s_2) \mid s_1 \in l_{c_1}(v), s_2 \in l_{c_2}(v),$$
$$c_1, c_2 \in \Sigma \cup \{\lambda\}, ((c_1 < c_2) \vee (c_1 = c_2 = \lambda))\}$$
and if v is an internal node,

---

[2]The string-depth of a node in GST is the string length of its path-label.

$$P_v = \{(s_1, s_2) \mid s_1 \in l_{c_1}(u_k), s_2 \in l_{c_2}(u_l),$$
$$c_1, c_2 \in \Sigma \cup \{\lambda\}, u_k < u_l,$$
$$((c_1 \neq c_2) \vee (c_1 = c_2 = \lambda))\}$$

The following lemmas are intended to prove the correctness and run-time characteristics of the algorithm:

Lemma 1 *Let v be a node with path-label α. A pair (s, s') is generated at v only if α is a maximal common substring of s and s'.*

Proof: At a leaf node v, if the algorithm generates a pair (s, s'), it is because the strings are either from $lsets$ representing different characters or from the $lset$ representing λ. In either case, α is a maximal common substring.

For an internal node v, the algorithm implies that $s \in l_{c_i}(u_k)$ and $s' \in l_{c_j}(u_l)$, where u_k and u_l are distinct children of v and $c_i \neq c_j$ unless $c_i = \lambda$. Thus s and s' must have suffixes f and f' respectively, corresponding to leaves $x \in subtree(u_k)$ and $y \in subtree(u_l)$. These suffixes have the prefix α and f is left-extensible by c_i in s and f' is left-extensible by c_j in s'. If $c_i \neq c_j$, then the prefix α is not left-extensible by the same character in s and s'. If $c_i = c_j = \lambda$, then α is a prefix common to both s and s'. Also, since $u_k \neq u_l$, the prefix α is not right-extensible by the same character in s and s'. Thus, the prefix α of f and f' is a maximal common substring of s and s'. Figure 4 illustrates the proof for the case of an internal node. ∎

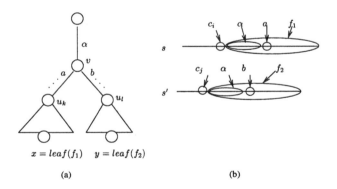

Figure 4. Illustration of the proof of Lemma 1.

Corollary 2 *The number of times a pair is generated is at most the number of distinct maximal common substrings of the pair.*

Proof: Follows directly from Lemma 1 and the fact that a pair is generated at a node at most once. The latter is true because for any internal node, the algorithm retains only one occurrence of a string before generating pairs, and for any leaf there can be at most one occurrence of any string in its $lsets$. While this bounds the maximum number of times a pair is generated, a pair may not be generated as many times. ∎

Lemma 3 *A pair (s, s') is generated at least once if it has a maximal common substring of length $\geq \psi$, where ψ is the threshold value.*

Proof: Consider α, a largest maximal substring of length $\geq \psi$ common to strings s and s'. As α is maximal, there exists either a leaf v or an internal node v with path-label α. Also there exist suffixes f and f' of s and s' respectively that belong to $subtree(v)$ and that have α as a prefix, which is neither left-extensible nor right-extensible by the same characters in both s and s'. Thus if α is the path-label of a leaf, then s and s' will be present in the leaf's $lsets$ corresponding to different characters or the $lset$ corresponding to λ, implying that the algorithm will generate the pair at this leaf. If α is the path-label of an internal node, then the fact that α is a largest maximal common substring ensures that s and s' will be present in the $lsets$ of different children and the $lsets$ will correspond either to different characters or to λ. Thus the algorithm will generate the pair at this internal node. ∎

Lemma 4 *The algorithm runs in time proportional to the number of pairs generated plus the cost of sorting the nodes of the GST.*

Proof: Once the nodes are sorted by string-depth, each node of string-depth $\geq \psi$ is processed exactly once. For every pair generated and reported at any node, there is an equivalent reverse complemented pair which is generated and discarded elsewhere. This increases the run-time by a constant factor of 2. At an internal node, eliminating duplicate string ids reduces the total size of all $lsets$ of all its children by at most a factor of $(|\Sigma| + 1)$. This is because a string is present in at most one $lset$ of each child node and the number of children is bounded by $(|\Sigma| + 1)$. The total size of all the $lsets$ of all the children after duplicate elimination is bounded by the number of pairs generated at the node. Taken together, this implies that the cost of elimination by traversing the $lsets$ of the child nodes is bounded by a constant multiple of the number of pairs generated at the node (assuming $|\Sigma|$ is finite). ∎

Finally, as each processor locally sorts the nodes in its local portion of GST, the order in which the promising pairs are generated is guaranteed to be in the decreasing order of their maximal common substring length only with respect to the local GST. In an ideal greedy approach the order has to be consistent across processors but as the GST is stored in a distributed fashion, this might involve a significant communication overhead. From our experiments we found that a compromise on the ideal greedy approach as opposed to incurring an additional communication overhead to be a better choice in terms of run-time. Note that the quality of clustering is unaffected by the order of pair generation.

3.3 Parallel Clustering

Our parallel clustering algorithm makes use of master-slave paradigm. The master processor is responsible for maintaining and updating clusters, and allocating promising pairs for pairwise alignment. The slave processors generate promising pairs in decreasing order of maximal common substring length and compute pairwise alignment on the pairs provided by the master processor. Pairwise alignment may not be performed for each generated pair because the current set of EST clusters may obviate the need to do so. Hence, the master processor is also responsible for the selection of pairs to be aligned. For load-balancing, a pair generated on a slave processor need not be allocated to the same processor for pairwise alignment.

The master processor has two buffers: 1) $WORKBUF$, a large work buffer of pairs yet to be processed, and 2) $CLUSTERS$, the set of EST clusters. $WORKBUF$ is implemented as a queue and the promising pairs that are added to it for pairwise alignment are dispatched in units of *batchsize* to slave processors. The EST clusters are maintained using the union-find data structure [14]. We require two operations − 1) to find the cluster of an EST (find), and 2) to merge two clusters (union). The amortized run-time per operation using the union-find data structure is given by the inverse Ackermann's function [14], a constant for all practical purposes.

The master processor performs a loop of interactions with the slave processors until all slave processors have run out of pairs and all pairs in $WORKBUF$ have been processed and their results collected. The sequence of operations during each iteration is as follows: A message received from a slave consists of two parts − R results and P promising pairs. R results correspond to the results of the most recent pairwise alignments performed by the slave processor. The master processor updates $CLUSTERS$ for those results that indicate one of the alignment patterns shown in Figure 5b with a score above a certain threshold. Additional processing like detection of alternative splicing and consulting protein databases can be done to improve quality of the results. Following this, the master processor selectively adds a portion (say P') of the P promising pairs reported by the slave processor to $WORKBUF$. A pair is added only if the corresponding ESTs are in two different clusters, eliminating unnecessary work. If a slave processor runs out of pairs it is marked *passive*, and is considered *active* otherwise.

After incorporating a received message, the master processor sends to the slave processor a message containing: W pairs extracted from $WORKBUF$ for pairwise alignment, and the number of pairs to request from the slave processor during their next interaction (E). The value of W is *batchsize*, or fewer if not available. Once a pair is assigned for pairwise alignment it is removed from $WORKBUF$. The value of E is determined as follows: Let $\mu = \frac{P}{P'}$ and δ be the ratio of the total number of slave processors (p) and the number of active slave processors. Let $nfree$ be the number of free slots in $WORKBUF$. Then $E = min(\mu \times \delta \times batchsize, \frac{nfree}{p})$. This is to receive approximately $\delta \times batchsize$ useful pairs from each active slave, without running the risk of overflowing $WORKBUF$. The δ factor ensures that there is enough work supplied to reactivate the passive slave processors for doing alignments. If both E and W are zero, no message is sent but instead, the slave processor is kept on a *wait-queue*. Later in one of the ensuing interactions, when there is excess work in $WORKBUF$, it is assigned to the slave processors in the wait-queue, thus removing such slave processors from the queue.

Each slave processor has three buffers: 1) Γ, the local GST, 2) $PAIRBUF$, to store the promising pairs generated on-demand but not yet sent to the master processor, and 3) $NEXTWORK$, the next batch of pairs for alignment. To get the process started, each slave processor initially generates three equal portions of *batchsize* number of pairs. After pairwise alignment is computed on the first portion, the results along with the third portion are sent to the master processor. The processor then marks the second portion as $NEXTWORK$ and enters a loop of interactions. Henceforth, the processor always has the next batch of pairs to work on, between submitting the results of the previous batch and receiving another set of pairs from the master processor, thus overlapping communication with computation.

The sequence of tasks performed by a slave processor during its interaction with the master processor is as follows: The processor computes pairwise alignment on the set of pairs in $NEXTWORK$. Once the (R) results are obtained, the processor waits for the next message from the master processor. While waiting, it generates more promising pairs until either a message arrives, or $PAIRBUF$ is full, or it runs out of promising pairs. This again ensures that the processor is not idle while waiting for the master processor to respond. A message received from the master processor consists of W pairs and the number E. If E pairs are not available in $PAIRBUF$, more promising pairs are generated on-the-fly from Γ until either E pairs are in $PAIRBUF$ or it runs out of promising pairs. The processor dispatches a message to the master processor consisting of $P (= min(E, \text{pairs in } PAIRBUF))$ promising pairs and the R results, ending the current interaction.

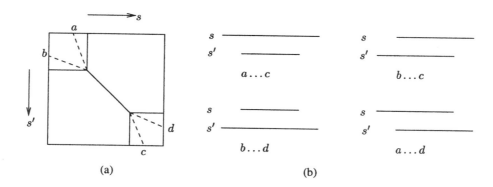

(a)   (b)

Figure 5. Figure showing pairwise alignment computed by extending a maximal common substring match at both ends. Also shown are the four types of alignments accepted as evidence to merge clusters, and their corresponding optimal paths in the dynamic programming table.

n	10,051		30,000		60,018		81,414
	Ours	CAP3	Ours	CAP3	Ours	CAP3	Ours
OQ	94.82	95.74	84.69	86.81	88.12	89.60	87.36
OV	0.04	0.15	7.67	6.70	4.79	4.54	6.02
UN	5.14	4.13	8.90	7.42	7.80	6.42	7.46
CC	97.37	97.83	91.71	92.93	93.69	94.51	93.25

Table 2. Quality assessment results of our software and CAP3 using benchmark data sets. CAP3 could not be run for $n = 81,414$ due to memory limitation.

Pairwise alignment is computed as shown in Figure 5a. Instead of aligning entire strings, we reduce work by merely extending the already computed maximal substring match at both ends using gaps and mismatches. This limits the area of computation as shown in the figure. To further limit work, we use banded dynamic programming, where the band size is determined by the number of errors tolerated. Quality can be controlled by the usual set of parameters, such as match and mismatch scores, gap opening and gap continuation penalties, and the ratio of score obtained to the ideal score consisting of all matches [11].

4 Experimental Results

We implemented our parallel EST clustering algorithms using C and MPI. We report results on the quality of EST clustering produced by the software and its run-time performance on an IBM SP with 375 MHz Power3 processors.

4.1 Quality Assessment

The accuracy of the results is assessed using a benchmark data set consisting of 81,414 ESTs from *Arabidopsis*

thaliana, and their correct clustering. As the complete genome of this plant is available and is relatively small, correct clustering can be obtained through alternative means. We compared the clusters generated by our software and CAP3 against the correct set of clusters generated using the above approach. To make a comparison, we adopted the following approach: For a given cluster of ESTs, generate all pairs of ESTs from the same cluster. Based on the number of such pairs generated the following measurements are defined: A pair according to output is called a true positive (TP) if it is also paired in the correct clustering, and a false positive (FP) otherwise. A pair not in output is called a true negative (TN) if it is also not paired according the correct clustering, and a false negative (FN) otherwise. Based on these measurements quality metrics are defined as follows [8]: *Overlap-quality* is the proportion of TPs over the total number of unique pairs extracted from clusters of both results, and is given by $OQ = \frac{TP}{TP+FP+FN}$. *Over-prediction* is the proportion of over-predicted pairs, and is given by $OV = \frac{FP}{TP+FP}$. *Under-prediction* is the proportion of unpredicted pairs, and is given by $UN = \frac{FN}{TP+FN}$. Overall performance is given by the *correlation-coefficient*,

$$CC = \frac{TP.TN - FP.FN}{\sqrt{(TP+FP).(TN+FN).(TP+FN).(TN+FP)}}.$$

Ideally $OQ = CC = 100\%$ and $OV = UN = 0\%$.

The results of assessing the quality of our software and CAP3 using the benchmark data sets are shown in Table 2. Observing the metrics OQ, OV, UN and CC, our results are very close to the results of CAP3. In general, the under-prediction rate is greater than the over-prediction rate and this is attributable to the conservative nature of clustering criteria used. The results are based on the choice of quality threshold experimentally found to result in the least number of false positives and false negatives.

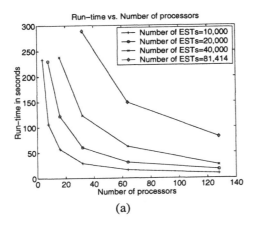
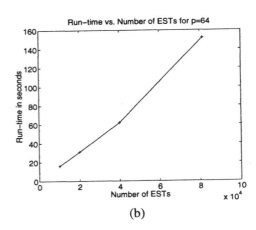

(a)   (b)

Figure 6. The graph to the left shows parallel run-times as a function of the number of processors. The run-times as a function of the data size for a fixed number of processors are shown in the graph to the right.

p	Parti-tioning	Construction of GST	Sorting Nodes	Pairwise Alignment	Total Time
8	3	180	5	42	230
16	1	91	2	27	121
32	1	45	1	13	60
64	0.5	22	0.5	8	31
128	0.5	11	0.5	5	17

Table 3. Time (in seconds) spent in various components of parallel EST clustering for 20,000 ESTs.

4.2 Run-time Assessment

The software is run for various subsets of the *Arabidopsis* EST data set using different numbers of processors (see Figure 6a). A window size of eight is used in partitioning the ESTs into buckets for parallel GST construction and *batchsize* is chosen to be sixty pairs. As can be observed, the run-times scale with the number of processors. Figure 6b shows run-time as a function of the data size for a fixed number of processors. Although the memory required scales linearly with the problem size, the total run-time cannot be analytically determined and depends on the input data set. The run-time spent in various components of the software for 20,000 ESTs is shown in Table 3. Asymptotically, the largest contributor is the time spent in performing the necessary alignments, followed by the time spent in parallel construction of GST. However for smaller data sizes, the alignment phase runs faster than the GST construction phase as seen from Table 3.

The total number of promising pairs and the number of pairs on which the pairwise alignment algorithm is run as a function of the data size are shown in Figure 7. This clearly illustrates the reduction in run-time achieved as a conse-

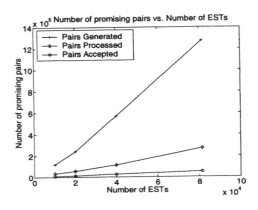

Figure 7. The number of pairs generated and the number of pairs that are aligned as a function of data size.

quence of generating promising pairs in decreasing order of maximal common substring length, as opposed to the traditional way of generating pairs in an arbitrary order.

The effect on the run-time as the *batchsize* is varied for clustering 20,000 ESTs on 32 processors is shown in Figure 8. A small *batchsize* results in more communications between the master processor and the slave processors. With a large *batchsize*, the slave processors become less responsive to pair generation, thus not taking advantage of the latest clustering information available to determine if alignment of a pair is necessary. We found the optimal *batchsize*, which is expected to increase with increase in the number of processors, to be in the range of 40-60 for our experiments. When the *batchsize* is fixed and the number of slave processors is increased, there is a gradual increase in the percentage of the total time the master is busy and the percentage is well under 2% even on 128 processors. Thus using a single

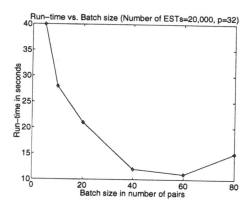

Figure 8. Run-times for parallel clustering as a function of *batchsize.*

master processor will not be a bottleneck even for a large number of slave processors.

5 Conclusions and Future Work

We reported on the development of a parallel software system for EST clustering. In creating this software, our overarching goal has been to facilitate fast and accurate clustering of large EST data sets, which is accomplished through the use of memory-efficient algorithms, algorithmic heuristics and parallel processing. We are working on improving the prediction accuracy of the software by doing additional processing such as detection of alternative splicing. Several interesting problems remain, whose solution can be used to improve the run-time and functionality of the software. Can a parallel GST construction algorithm with optimal parallel run-time be designed for a practical model of parallel computation? Is there a way to incrementally adjust the EST clusters when a new batch of ESTs is sequenced, instead of the current method of clustering all the ESTs from scratch?

Acknowledgments

We wish to thank Volker Brendel for introducing the EST clustering problem to us, providing benchmark data and for many valuable suggestions. We thank Richa Agarwala from National Institute of Health for discussions that led to an improved understanding of the problem characteristics. The run-time measurements are taken using the *Blue Horizon* IBM SP at the San Diego Supercomputer Center.

References

[1] S.F. Altschul, W. Gish, W. Miller, E.W. Myers, and D.J. Lipman. Basic local alignment search tool. *Journal of Molecular Biology*, 215:403–410, 1990.

[2] A. Apostolico, C. Iliopoulos, G. M. Landau, B. Schieber, and U. Vishkin. Parallel construction of a suffix tree with applications. *Algorithmica*, 3:347–365, 1988.

[3] P. Green. *http://www.mbt.washington.edu/phrap.docs/phrap.html*, 1996.

[4] D. Gusfield. *Algorithms on strings, trees and sequences: computer science and computational biology.* Cambridge University Press, Cambridge, London, 1997.

[5] Ramesh Hariharan. Optimal parallel suffix tree construction. *Journal of Computer and System Sciences*, 55(1):44–69, 1997.

[6] X. Huang and A. Madan. CAP3: A DNA sequence assembly program. *Genome Research*, 9(9):868–877, 1999.

[7] F. Liang, I. Holt, G. Pertea, S. Karamycheva, S. Salzberg, and J. Quackenbush. An optimized protocol for analysis of EST sequences. *Nucleic Acids Research*, 28(18):3657–3665, 2000.

[8] P. A. Pevzner M. S. Gelfand, A. Mironov. Gene recognition via spliced alignment. In *Proc. National Academy of Sciences*, volume 93, pages 9061–9066, 1996.

[9] S.B. Needleman and C.D. Wunsch. A general method applicable to the search for similarities in the amino acid sequence of two proteins. *Journal of Molecular Biology*, 48:443–453, 1970.

[10] W.R. Pearson and D.J. Lipman. Improved tools for biological sequence comparison. *Proc. National Academic of Sciences USA*, 85:2444–2448.

[11] J. Setubal and J. Meidanis. *Introduction to computational molecular biology.* PWS Publishing Company, Boston, MA, 1997.

[12] T.F. Smith and M.S. Waterman. Identification of common molecular subsequences. *Journal of Molecular Biology*, 147:195–197, 1981.

[13] G. Sutton, O. White, M. Adams, and A. Kerlavage. TIGR assembler: A new tool for assembling large shotgun sequencing projects. *Genome Science and Technology*, 1:9–19, 1995.

[14] R.E. Tarjan. Efficiency of a good but not linear set union algorithm. *Journal of the ACM*, 22(2):215–225, 1975.

Session 5B

Task Scheduling

A Lower-Bound Algorithm for Minimizing Network Communication in Real-Time Systems

Cecilia Ekelin and Jan Jonsson

Department of Computer Engineering
Chalmers University of Technology
SE–412 96 Göteborg, Sweden
{*cekelin,janjo*}*@ce.chalmers.se*

Abstract

In this paper, we propose a pseudo-polynomial-time lower-bound algorithm for the problem of assigning and scheduling real-time tasks in a distributed system such that the network communication is minimized. The key feature of our algorithm is translating the task assignment problem into the so called k-cut problem of a graph, which is known to be solvable in polynomial time for fixed k. Experiments show that the lower bound computed by our algorithm in fact is optimal in up to 89% of the cases and increases the speed of an overall optimization algorithm by a factor of two on the average.

1 Introduction

An important design objective in distributed systems is to reduce the amount of inter-processor communication among processes. This is true both for high-performance parallel architectures as well as loosely-coupled embedded systems, although for different reasons. The main purpose of high-performance multiprocessor systems is to decrease the runtime of the executed applications. An essential component in reaching this goal is limiting the amount of bus communication because it slows down the execution speed compared to information passing through memory. For embedded systems, low network communication is desired for a number of practical and economical reasons. First, it may enable the use of a slower but cheaper communication medium. Furthermore, the amount of cabling may be reduced altogether which reduces not only the cost but also the size and weight of the system. Second, message transmission over a network increases the power consumption. This is a serious drawback for many embedded systems that run on battery power. Third, a less loaded network can be made more tolerant to failures since spare bandwidth can be used to retransmit corrupted information.

Hence, given a system consisting of communicating processes (tasks) and nodes (processors), connected via a network, it is desired that the tasks are assigned to the nodes such that the amount of communication over the network is minimized. However, in real-time systems the behavior of the tasks is constrained by execution and timing constraints. That is, the assignment is only valid if it is also possible to schedule the tasks (and messages) correctly. This is particularly true for *hard* real-time systems where, for instance, a missed deadline may result in system failure. Therefore, for such systems the assignment and scheduling must be performed off-line. In general, the given optimization problem is NP-hard which means that the runtime of an optimal algorithm is exponential (unless P=NP). This has led to most proposed approaches being based on suboptimal algorithms. However, one cause of the large execution time for an optimal algorithm is that the time *finding* the optimal solution is in many cases only a fraction of the time *verifying* that it is indeed optimal. Hence, a common way to reduce the average computational complexity of an optimization algorithm is to use a *lower-bound* function which estimates the optimum. This estimate is then used by the optimization algorithm to reduce the search space. The lower-bound function typically addresses a simplified version of the original problem and should be both safe (never be worse than the optimum) and tight (close to the optimum).

In this paper we show that the problem of task assignment and scheduling such that the network communication is minimized closely resembles the problem of partitioning a graph into k subgraphs such that the cost of the removed edges is minimized. This problem is known as the k-cut problem and has been shown to be solvable in polynomial time [1] (for fixed k). Therefore, the basic idea behind the lower-bound algorithm that we propose is to solve a number of k-cut problems and interpret the result in the original problem formulation. In addition to proposing the algorithm we also show how it can be integrated in an optimization framework and demonstrate its effect through a number of experiments.

The rest of the paper is organized as follows. We begin in Section 2 with a review of related work. We then state the

343

problem in Section 3 and continue in Section 4 with an explanation of the optimization framework used. Our lower-bound algorithm is presented in Section 5. The experiments we have performed are described in Section 6 where their results are also discussed. Finally, we state our conclusions in Section 7.

2 Related Work

The task assignment problem has been well studied within the area of distributed systems. In this context, the problem is to minimize the turnaround time (or makespan) of the application which is the combined cost of message transmission and task execution. Popular approaches to this problem include both optimal methods such as Branch-and-Bound [2, 3, 4, 5] as well as heuristic methods [6, 7, 8]. This problem has also been addressed in the design of embedded systems [9] where the "cost" is directly related to manufacturing costs. However, for real-time systems that consist of periodic tasks, the makespan is not a meaningful optimization objective. The problem also becomes more complicated due to the introduction of release times and deadlines that affect the scheduling of the tasks. Therefore, optimal methods for these systems usually focus on timing aspects. For instance, Branch-and-Bound algorithms have been used to minimize the maximum lateness [10] or the probability of a dynamic failure [11].

Hence, not many optimal methods for minimizing network communication have been proposed for real-time systems. In a heuristic method presented by Ramamritham [12] it is suggested that pairs of communicating tasks should be grouped together. (We refer to this as communication-clustering.) Tindell, Burns and Wellings [13] present a method based on simulated annealing. Graph-theoretic approaches based on k-cut with *specified vertices* have also been proposed. In this problem there is an additional constraint of a set of vertices $\{v_1, ..., v_k\}$ where each v_i should be in a different subgraph after the cut. It should be noted that this problem is NP-hard for $k \geq 3$ even with k fixed. A pioneer in this field was Stone [14] who presents how to use the Ford-Fulkerson network-flow algorithm to address the (non-real-time) task-assignment problem. Unfortunately, the approach does not easily extend to incorporate additional application constraints. For real-time systems, Tia and Liu [15] present a heuristic algorithm for the k-cut problem with specified vertices which is then used to solve the assignment problem. The algorithm generates clusters from a graph consisting of communicating tasks and available processors, such that each cluster contains one processor. A similar approach is taken by Abdelzaher and Shin [16] who present a heuristic k-cut algorithm which is used to address the problem with specified vertices. (Interesting enough, for 2-cuts the algorithm is in fact a part of the optimal 2-cut algorithm [17].) The algorithm operates in two steps. First, tasks are partitioned into clusters based on their

amount of communication. Second, these clusters are assigned on to the processors in a fashion similar to [15].

A common property of the mentioned algorithms is that they, in the context of optimization, produce an *upper bound* on the optimum. In contrast, the algorithm we propose produces a lower bound which can be used to enhance an optimal algorithm. Hence, our algorithm can be seen as a *static* variant of the lower-bound function used for pruning in Branch-and-Bound algorithms. For instance, Ma and Chung [18] propose such a function based on the exploitation of small graph cuts. The strength of our algorithm is its generality which makes it applicable for a wide range of systems and also enables it to be used in multi-objective optimization.

3 Problem Description

The general assignment and scheduling problem considers the assignment of *tasks* to processing *nodes* and the execution of these tasks in a timely fashion. These actions are restricted by a set of *constraints* that must be satisfied and *objectives* that measure the quality of a solution.

In our model of the hardware architecture we assume that there are m nodes $\eta_1, ..., \eta_m$, which are connected via a *communication network*, and each node contains one *processor*. Each node may also have a number of *resources* that can be used locally by tasks at that node. The application is modeled as a task graph which includes n *periodic* tasks $\tau_1, ..., \tau_n$, that execute on the processors and possibly communicate by *message passing*. The worst-case execution time of task τ_i on processor η_p is $execution\_time(i, p)$ and the size of a message from τ_i to τ_j is $message\_size(i, j)$. Each periodic task is invoked at regular intervals of length $period(i)$. We use τ_i^k to denote the kth invocation of τ_i. Each task invocation must complete its execution within a time interval of length $deadline(i)$ where $deadline(i) \leq period(i)$. Furthermore, all invocations of a task must execute on the same node. That is, migration is not allowed. Due to the periodicity it is sufficient to consider a schedule of length equal to the least-common multiple (LCM) of all task periods, referred to as the lcp.

Note that the transmission delay for a message is defined as follows:[1]

$$delay(i,j) = \begin{cases} 0, \text{if } \tau_i \text{ and } \tau_j \text{ are assigned to the same node} \\ message\_size(i,j) \cdot c_{speed}, \text{otherwise} \end{cases}$$

However, because tasks are periodic, a message may be sent several times during the considered time-span. The number of transmissions is given by $count(i,j) = \frac{lcp}{LCM\{period(i), period(j)\}}$. Our objective function f that is subject to minimization, is the total amount of transmissions over the network. That is, $f = \sum_{\forall(i,j)} count(i,j) \cdot delay(i,j)$.

---

[1]Without loss of generality we assume that $c_{speed} = 1$.

The problem we are addressing in this paper is how a lower bound on f can be computed. That is, a safe estimation on the smallest value f can assume. This value can then be used by an optimization algorithm to reduce the search space. Clearly, a trivial lower bound on f is zero. However, in many cases this will be an overly pessimistic assumption. Thus, if the minimal (network) communication is larger than zero, we would like a lower bound that also is larger than zero but not larger than the optimal value. How can this be achieved? We use the classical lower bound approach in which a simplified version of the original problem is addressed. Before we present the details of our approach, it is necessary to explain the overall optimization framework.

4 Optimization Framework

Our optimization framework is based on constraint programming [19]. That is, the problem is expressed as variables and constraints that are handled by a constraint solver. A solution is an assignment of values to the variables such that the constraints are satisfied. A key feature of the constraint solver is that is employs constraint propagation to reduce the search space. This means that by considering the consequences of the constraints the solver is able to detect infeasible partial solutions. That is, before all variables have been assigned.

Within our framework, scheduling is assumed to be time-triggered and non-preemptive (time-tables for each node are generated) and the communication network is assumed to be a bus (messages have to be scheduled). Hence, the variables represent the start times for the tasks and messages, $start(\tau_i^k)$ and $m\_start(\tau_i^k, \tau_j^l)$, (determining the schedule) and the execution nodes for the tasks, $node(\tau_i)$, (determining the assignment). The constraints are:

- Periodicity: $start(\tau_i^k) \geq period(i) \cdot (k-1)$ and $start(\tau_i^k) + execution\_time(i, p) \leq deadline(i) \cdot k$, (where $node(\tau_i) = \eta_p$)

- Non-preemptiveness: $\forall \tau_i^k, \tau_j^l, i \neq j : \neg(node(\tau_i) = node(\tau_j) \wedge start(\tau_i^k) \leq start(\tau_j^l) < start(\tau_i^k) + execution\_time(i, p))$

- Communication[2]: $start(\tau_i^k) + execution\_time(i, p) \leq m\_start(\tau_i^k, \tau_j^l)$ and $m\_start(\tau_i^k, \tau_j^l) + delay(i, j) \leq start(\tau_j^l)$

- Locality: $node(\tau_i) \in \{\eta_p\}$

The actual modeling of the constraints can be found in [20]. This reference also proposes how to select variables and values to assign in the search for a solution. In particular, it is suggested that communicating tasks should

be grouped together and that symmetry exclusion should be used. A search strategy that is not investigated in [20] is *depth-bounded discrepancy search (DDS)* [21]. This tree-search strategy can be explained as "reverse backtracking". That is, when an infeasible (leaf) node has been detected the search backtracks to the *earliest* choice point instead of the latest (as in chronological backtracking). The rational behind this is that the heuristic used to determine in what order the branches should be traversed, is more likely to make a wrong decision in the beginning of the search when there still are many undetermined problem properties. As a result, DDS, at least to some extent, avoids getting stuck in the wrong part of the search tree. Hence, the advantage of DDS is that it usually finds solutions faster than chronological backtracking. On the other hand, ensuring optimum (or determining that a solution does not exist) can be costly since symmetry exclusion as described in [20] cannot be used. However, combined with a tight lower-bound function, DDS is likely to be an interesting alternative even in an optimization framework. Hence, for assignment, DDS is used (with communication-clustering) whereas the scheduling is performed as in [20][3]. Optimization is performed by iteratively solving the same problem with increasingly tighter bound on the objective function.

It should be noted that the lower-bound computation is independent of the actual problem constraints because it will consider the problem *after* constraint propagation has been carried out. That is, the input is the communication graph. In fact, the lower-bound function can be implemented in any optimization framework and is not limited to constraint programming. However, because we use a single model for the task assignment and scheduling problem, the propagation performed by the constraint solver may provide information about the communication graph that otherwise may not be that easily available. For example, whether two tasks have to assigned the same or different nodes due to scheduling constraints. Furthermore, we can draw on the constraint propagation when determining the validity of a particular assignment because it is a partial solution to the combined problem. Hence, the lower bound produced using a constraint programming framework may very well be superior to other approaches.

5 Lower-Bound Algorithm

In this section we present our major research contribution; the algorithm LB that computes a lower bound on the network communication in a distributed real-time system.

5.1 Basic idea

In the overall task assignment and scheduling problem, it is the assignment that directly determines the amount of network communication (the value of f). However, the scheduling indirectly determines f because an assignment

---

[2]For communication we also require the non-preemptiveness constraint.

[3]It is basically a form of list-scheduling.

is only valid if tasks and messages also can be scheduled. Hence, a proposed assignment may be rejected or accepted based on the subsequent schedulability analysis. Because an *exact* schedulablity analysis in itself in general is NP-complete we would like to be able to make the decision based on a *necessary* schedulability analysis that runs in polynomial time. If assignments then are tried in a suitable order, we may hopefully be able to discard clearly infeasible assignments quickly. That is, we will have a lower-bound function for f. So how should the assignments be ordered for this idea to work? By looking at the communication graph we can detect whether or not the entire task graph is connected. If we then select a cluster (subgraph) in the graph and are unable to assign (using the necessary schedulability analysis) the entire cluster to the same node, we know that the cluster has to be *cut* into (at least) two subgraphs where the cost of this cut equals the amount of network communication. That is, the cut is the messages that have to be sent over the network and the cost is the value of f. Hence, the cheapest way we can cut the cluster into k subgraphs such that all tasks in each subgraph can be assigned to the same node will be a lower bound on the network communication (for this cluster). This is also known as the k-cut problem which has been shown to be solvable in polynomial time for fixed k [1]. Unfortunately, we do not know for what value of k our problem will be solved. However, because we are only interested in a lower bound, we can choose a suitable value for k and either a solution will be found or it will not. Regardless of the scenario, we will have found a value on the lower bound. (Although it will be tighter if a solution is found.) In the following section we go into details of the actual lower-bound algorithm.

5.2 Algorithm

In the description of our algorithm we will use the following notation. The communication (task) graph is denoted $G = (V, E)$ where V are the vertices (tasks) and E the edges (communication links) with associated costs $(count(i, j) \cdot delay(i, j))$. If G is not connected it can be divided into subgraphs $G_i = (V_i, E_i)$ such that $V = \bigcup V_i, E = \bigcup E_i$ and $\forall i, j, i \neq j : V_i \cap V_j = \emptyset, E_i \cap E_j = \emptyset$. A k-cut X_k in a graph G is a set of edges E' which when deleted separates the graph into exactly k (nonempty) subgraphs. The cost of the cut $c(X_k)$ is the sum of the edge costs in E'. The minimum k-cut X_k^* is the cut with the smallest cost. The function $\mathtt{assign}(V)$ performs the necessary schedulability analysis based on the assumption that all tasks in V are assigned to the same node. In our case, it is part of the constraint framework and the constraint solver will reject or accept the assignment based on the result of the constraint propagation. This is possible because the assignment and scheduling is expressed in a single joint model. It should be noted that the tasks always will remain unassigned after the call. That is, a cluster is not fixed to

PROCEDURE: **lower-bound (LB)**
Input: A graph G and a maximum k
Output: A lower bound on the network communication in G

```
(1)    𝒢 := {Gᵢ}
(2)    lb := 0
(3)    FOR each Gᵢ ∈ 𝒢 DO
(4)        k := 2
(5)        IF not assign(Vᵢ) THEN
(6)            ok := false
(7)            WHILE not ok and k ≤ kₘₐₓ DO
(8)                (c, ok) := k-cut-assign(Gᵢ, k)
(9)                k := k + 1
(10)           END
(11)           lb := lb + c
(12)       END
(13)   END
(14)   return lb
```

PROCEDURE: k-**cut-assign**
Input: A connected graph G and a k
Output: A lower bound on the network communication in G and true/false if success/failure.

```
(1)    (X*ₖ, 𝒞) := k-cut-candidate(G, k)
(2)    WHILE 𝒞 ≠ ∅ DO
(3)        𝒞 := 𝒞 − X where c(X) is minimal
(5)        IF c(X) ≤ c(X*ₖ) THEN
(5)            𝒢 := G \ X†
(6)            WHILE 𝒢 ≠ ∅ DO
(7)                𝒢 := 𝒢 − Gᵢ
(8)                IF not assign(Vᵢ) THEN
(9)                    𝒢 := {Gᵢ}
(10)                   exit WHILE
(11)               END
(12)           END
(13)           IF 𝒢 = ∅ THEN
(14)               return (c(X), true)
(15)           END
(16)       ELSE
(17)           𝒞 := ∅
(18)       END
(19)   END
(20)   return (c(X*ₖ), false)
```

† This results in a set $\{G_i\}$ of disconnected graphs.

a particular node. The function $\mathtt{enumerate}(G, c)$ is from [22] and enumerates all 2-cuts in G with cost $< c$. The function $\mathtt{min\text{-}k\text{-}cut}(G, X_{k-1})$ produces a k-cut from a given $k-1$-cut by applying the minimum 2-cut algorithm [23, 17] to each of the graphs in $G \setminus X_{k-1}^*$ and select the best partition.

In words, the algorithm $\mathtt{lower\text{-}bound}$ (LB) operates as follows. Given a connected task graph that cannot be assigned to the same node, the minimum 2-cut is computed. If the subgraphs resulting from this cut still cannot be assigned, the minimum 3-cut is computed. In addition, all 2-cuts with cost less than this cut needs to be examined (in order). This examination is performed by k-$\mathtt{cut\text{-}assign}$. In the next round the minimum 4-cut is computed as well as candidate 2- and 3-cuts. The main part of the work is performed by k-$\mathtt{cut\text{-}candidate}$ which operates recur-

PROCEDURE: *k*-cut-candidate
Input: A connected graph G and a k
Output: X_k^* plus a set $\{X_{k'}\}$ where $k' < k$

(1)	$X_k := \text{min-}k\text{-cut}(G, X_{k-1}^*)^\dagger$
(2)	$\mathcal{A} := \text{enumerate}(G, c(X_k))$
(3)	$\mathcal{C} := \mathcal{A}$
(4)	WHILE $\mathcal{A} \neq \emptyset$ DO
(5)	$\quad \mathcal{A} := \mathcal{A} - X_{k'}$ where $c(X_{k'})$ is minimal
	$\qquad$ and k' is maximal
(6)	$\quad$ IF $k = k'$ THEN
(7)	$\qquad \mathcal{A} := \emptyset$
(8)	$\quad$ ELSE
(9)	$\qquad \mathcal{G} := G \setminus X_{k'}$
(10)	$\qquad c := c(X_k) - c(X_{k'})$
(11)	$\qquad$ FOR each $G_i \in \mathcal{G}$ DO
(12)	$\qquad\quad \mathcal{B} := \text{enumerate}(G_i, c)$
(13)	$\qquad\quad \mathcal{D} := \{X_{k'} \cup X\}$ where $X \in \mathcal{B}^\ddagger$
(14)	$\qquad\quad \mathcal{C} := \mathcal{C} \cup \mathcal{D}$
(15)	$\qquad\quad \mathcal{A} := \mathcal{A} \cup \mathcal{D}$
(16)	$\qquad$ END
(17)	$\quad$ END
(18)	END
(19)	return $(X_{k'}, \mathcal{C})$

$\dagger$ It is assumed that X_{k-1}^* is stored from the previous round (if $k > 2$).
$\ddagger$ Hence, this generates the set $\{X_{k'+1}\}$.

sively in a branch-and-bound fashion. That is, given a k'-cut ($k' < k$) each resulting graph G_i is subject for further cutting, provided that the remaining allowed cut cost is large enough. The largest value of k_{max}, that makes sense, is the number of nodes in the system. (See line (7) in `lower-bound`.) However, any value can be used as a stopping criterion depending on the trade-off between lower-bound improvement and computational complexity. Recall that the lower bound obtained by the algorithm is valid (but not as tight) even in the case when k_{max} is reached (i.e. no feasible assignment has been found).

5.3 Complexity

A main component in our algorithm is the function `enumerate` which generates the set of 2-cuts that we need to consider. The parameter used to limit the cost of the cuts can be expressed as $p\lambda(G)$ where p is a constant and $\lambda(G)$ is the cost of the minimum 2-cut in the graph G. According to [22] `enumerate` runs in $O(ne^2 + en^{2p})$ where e is the number of communication links and an upper bound on the number of cuts generated is $O(n^{2p})$. In our case, $p\lambda(G) = c(X_k)$ where $c(X_k)$ is an upper bound on $c(X_k^*)$. As for this analysis, this bound can be arbitrarily bad and can therefore be computed heuristically.[4] Thus, $p = \frac{c(X_k)}{\lambda(G)}$. Clearly, $p \geq 1$ for $k \geq 2$ and an increase in k also increases p (since $c(X_k)$ increases). This makes the number of cuts exponentially dependent on k. However, the largest value of k is k_{max} which is fixed.

Each of the generated 2-cuts is then separated further until the minimum k-cut has been found. Generally, for the graph G_i resulting from a cut $X_{k'}$, the maximum allowed

---

[4]It is required that $c(X_k) \geq c(X_{k'})$ for $k > k'$.

---

cost for any further cut of G_i is $c(X_k) - c(X_{k'})$. This means that $p_i\lambda(G_i) = p\lambda(G) - p'\lambda(G)$ or $p_i = (p - p')\frac{\lambda(G)}{\lambda(G_i)}$. If $\lambda(G_i) \geq \lambda(G)$ we have $p_i \leq p - p'$ implying $p_i < p$ which means that $O(n^{2p})$ is an upper bound on the number of cuts generated for G_i as well. Unfortunately, if $\lambda(G_i) < \lambda(G)$ the above reasoning does not hold. Instead, assume that $O(n^{2p})$ is *not* an upper bound but that $|\mathcal{B}| > |\mathcal{A}|$. According to this assumption there must then exist a cut $X \notin \mathcal{A}, c(X) \geq c(X_k)$ with a corresponding cut $X_i \in \mathcal{B}$ where $X_i = X \setminus X_{k'}$. We then have that $c(X_i) \geq c(X) - c(X_{k'})$ due to that X may not contain all edges in $X_{k'}$. From the generation of $\mathcal{B}$ we know that $c(X_i) < c(X_k) - c(X_{k'})$ which gives us $c(X) - c(X_{k'}) < c(X_k) - c(X_{k'})$ or $c(X) < c(X_k)$. But this contradicts the very existence of the cuts X and X_i. Hence, our assumption was false and $|\mathcal{B}| \leq |\mathcal{A}|$. Thus, $O(n^{2p})$ can be confirmed to be an upper bound on the number of cuts generated by `enumerate`.

Hence, the total number of 2-cuts for $X_{k'}$ is limited by $O(k'n^{2p})$. Since these $X_{k'+1}$ cuts now are added to the original set of 2-cuts, the WHILE-loop has to iterate for at most $O(n^{2p} + n^{2p}2n^{2p} + ... + n^{2p}2n^{2p} \cdots (k-1)n^{2p})$ or $O(\sum_{j=1}^{k-1} j! n^{2pj})$ times. Based on the complexity of `enumerate`, a call to k-cut-candidate will take at most $O((e^2n + n^{2p}e) \cdot \sum_{j=1}^{k-1} j! n^{2pj})$

The upper bound on the number loops in k-cut-assign is the same as for k-cut-candidate which means that a call to k-cut-assign inherits the same complexity due to the assumption that `assign` runs in polynomial-time. Because `lower-bound` will call k-cut-assign k_{max} times, the overall complexity of LB will be limited by $O((e^2n + n^{2p}e) \cdot \sum_{k=2}^{k_{max}} \sum_{j=1}^{k-1} j! n^{2pj})$. For $k = k_{max}$ the dominating term will be $O(en^{2pk_{max}})$. This makes the runtime complexity of LB pseudo-polynomial because p is a number given by the particular problem (but not related to the input size). In order to get a polynomial-time complexity it it would be possible to introduce p_{max} (similar to k_{max}).

Despite this high computational complexity our experiments will demonstrate that the performance of the overall optimization algorithm will indeed increase with the use of LB. It should be noted that in most cases LB will be considerably faster than the worst-case complexity indicates. In particular, a number of algorithm improvements can be made which will be described in the following section.

5.4 Improvements

In order to increase the performance of the lower-bound algorithm we have made some improvements compared to the version describe above. The enhancements that we present are conceptual ones whereas pure implementation improvements, like using faster data structures, still are possible. Although the improvements decrease the average runtime of LB, they do not improve the worst-case computational complexity.

Good cuts The lower bound on the network communication is established when a k-cut is successfully assigned. This means that the necessary schedulability analysis succeeded as well. Hence, it is likely that this assignment also will be feasible even when the exact schedulability analysis is used. Therefore, instead of just recording the cost of the cut (the lower bound) it would be beneficial to also record the cut itself (the assignment). (See line (14) in `k-cut-assign`.) In case a solution *is* found using the assignment this solution is not only optimal but also probably found rather quickly. This procedure can also be used when the lower bound is zero (i.e. the subgraphs can be assigned to the same node) to indicate a promising assignment.

Bad cuts A significant part of our algorithm is testing whether or not a k-cut can be assigned or not by using the necessary schedulability analysis. The number of candidate cuts to test grows rapidly with k and it would therefore be desired to somehow discard cuts without actually performing the assignment. This can be done by recognizing that if one subgraph G_i, resulting from a cut, cannot be assigned then neither can a subgraph G_j, from another cut, if $G_i \subseteq G_j$. Hence, if it turns out that G_i is infeasible then *all* cuts which results in subgraphs containing G_i are infeasible as well and can be removed. (See line (8) in `k-cut-assign`.)

Redundant cuts In order to compute the minimum k-cut our algorithm starts out with a set of promising 2-cuts which are evolved to k-cuts. Unfortunately, since we iteratively increase k, this set has to be recomputed for each k. This means that set used when computing the k-cut will actually contain the set used to compute the $k-1$-cut. Recall that k'-cuts ($k' < k$) with cost less than the minimum k-cut are candidates for assignment testing (as well as for the minimum k-cut computation). However, the fact that we are computing the minimum k-cut implies that all candidates associated with computing the $k-1$-cut must have failed. Hence, all k'-cuts ($k' < k-1$) with cost less than the minimum $k-1$-cut can be discarded as assignment candidates. They can still be useful for the minimum k-cut computation though. (See line (14) in `k-cut-candidate`.)

Equivalent cuts Consider a graph where there exist a 2-cut where $V_1 = \{\tau_1, \tau_2\}$ and a 3-cut with the same cost where $V_1 = \{\tau_1\}$ and $V_2 = \{\tau_2\}$. Obviously it is possible to separate τ_1 from τ_2 without any cost, which implies that they were not connected in the first place. That is, the cuts are semantically equivalent. In particular, any further partition of the 2-cut is also a partition of the 3-cut (or the 3-cut

itself). This means that the 2-cut can be replaced by the 3-cut. (In practice, the 2-cut is removed from the sets $\mathcal{A}$ and $\mathcal{C}$ in `k-cut-candidate`.) In general, a k-cut is equivalent to a $k-1$-cut if $c(X_k) = c(X_{k-1})$ and $V_i^k + V_j^k = V_l^{k-1}$.

Remaining cut cost In line (10) in `k-cut-candidate` we compute the maximum cost allowed for remaining cuts which is then used in the `enumerate` procedure. However, if the allowed cost is smaller than the minimum edge cost in the graph, `enumerate` will certainly fail. Hence, the FOR-loop can be omitted in this case.

Impossible 2-cuts Explicit assignment constraints will cause trouble for our lower bound algorithm. If two communicating tasks τ_1 and τ_2 are explicitly located on different nodes the corresponding edge *must* be cut but this is not recognized. Hence, a large number of actually impossible assignments may be tried in vain. However, this can be improved by identifying that, in a feasible k-cut, $\tau_1 \in V_i$ and $\tau_2 \in V_j$. If we ensure that this is the case already in the initial 2-cut, a large number of impossible 2-cuts will not even be generated. Therefore, we first collect all such pairs of tasks and then modify `enumerate` (line (3) in `k-cut-candidate`) to only generate 2-cuts where exactly one task in each pair is in V_1. (Trivially, the other task is in V_2.) However, this will result in an empty set of 2-cuts if there exist a "cycle" between three tasks. That is, $node(\tau_1) \neq node(\tau_2), node(\tau_2) \neq node(\tau_3), node(\tau_3) \neq node(\tau_1)$. Hence, if a task conflicts with other tasks in both V_1 and V_2, this rule does not apply.

Intra-node communication A problem similar to the one in the previous paragraph appears if two tasks clearly have to be on the same node (due to explicit locality or scheduling constraints). Their edge cost will be then zero, causing the algorithm to cut at this edge which in fact *must not* be cut. However, this is solved by contracting the two vertices (tasks) into one (as far as the lower bound algorithm is concerned).

5.5 Example

To illustrate the behavior of LB we use the example shown in Figure 1. It is assumed that the system contains 5 (identical) processors. Hence, $k_{max} = 5$. The trace for finding a lower bound on this example can be seen in Figure 2.

The trace shows that, since all tasks could not be assigned to the same node, the minimum 2-cut is computed with cost 6. (Cutting off τ_{16} or τ_{22}.) The tasks can still not be assigned using this partitioning, so the minimum 3-cut is computed with cost 12. (Cutting off τ_{16} and τ_{22}.) The number of 2-cuts that has to be examined in this iteration are 5. The entries $X - Y$ indicate the number of candidate k'-cuts ($k' < k$) with cost less than the minimum k-cut

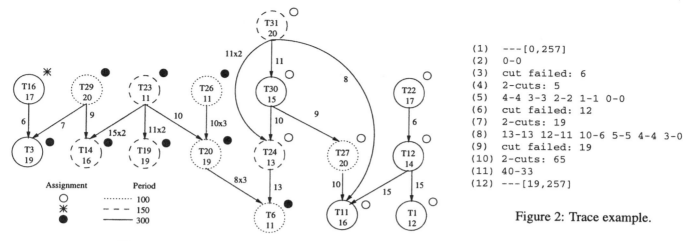

Figure 1: Task communication graph (Ti=τ_i)

```
(1)    ---[0,257]
(2)    0-0
(3)    cut failed: 6
(4)    2-cuts: 5
(5)    4-4  3-3  2-2  1-1  0-0
(6)    cut failed: 12
(7)    2-cuts: 19
(8)    13-13  12-11  10-6  5-5  4-4  3-0
(9)    cut failed: 19
(10)   2-cuts: 65
(11)   40-33
(12)   ---[19,257]
```

Figure 2: Trace example.

cost. Here, X is the initial number of cuts to try and Y the amount remaining when "bad cuts" have been removed. (This also means that the currently minimum candidate already has been selected and found infeasible.) Hence, the number of candidate cuts that are actually tried for assignment correspond to the number of $X - Y$ entries. Obviously, none of the 2-cut candidates works out (e.g., cutting off τ_{29} or $\{\tau_{16}, \tau_3\}$) so the minimum 4-cut (plus 2- and 3-cut candidates) have to be computed with cost 19. (Cutting off τ_{22}, τ_{16} and τ_3.) Here we see that out of 14 candidates only 6 need to be examined. Unfortunately, assignment is still not possible, forcing us to compute the minimum 5-cut. This time the second tried candidate, with cost 19, results in a feasible assignment which then gives the lower bound. As a matter of fact, this assignment is also feasible when scheduling is considered which implies that the lower bound also is the optimal solution. The assignment is also shown in Figure 1. If we had chosen to set $k_{max} = 4$ the algorithm would have aborted after line (9), still with a lower bound of 19 but without any "good cut". If $k_{max} = 3$ it would have aborted after line (7) with 12 as the lower bound. Another observation that can be made is that for $k = 4, p = \frac{19}{6} = 3\frac{1}{6}$. This example takes approximately three seconds to run on an Ultra Sparc with 128 Mbytes of RAM. Using pure DDS, the optimal solution is found after 5.5 minutes.

6 Experiments

To demonstrate the performance and effect of our lower-bound algorithm LB we have made a number of experiments. In this section we describe these experiments and discuss their results.

6.1 Setup

In the experiments we have used two different configurations of the overall optimization algorithm. In the basic configuration, DDS, we do not use LB but the lower bound on the network communication is zero. In the configuration DDS+LB we use DDS together with our lower-bound function.

The layout of the experiments is a number of studies (A, B, C and D), where for each study we randomly generated 100 task sets using the parameters displayed in Table 1. Values indicated using ranges were chosen randomly from a uniform distribution. The task periods in each task set were drawn (with uniform probability) from the set $\{100, 150, 300\}$ to avoid a too large lcp and to get a small deviation in the total number of task invocations for each task set. For each task $deadline(i) = period(i)$. The tasks in each task set were grouped into a number of clusters such that only tasks within a cluster were allowed to communicate. Cyclic or mutual communication was avoided by only allowing a task τ_i to communicate with a task τ_j if $j < i$. The processors had the same speed and a probability of having a resource attached which, with another probability, was required by a task. Hence, if a task requires a resource it must be assigned to a node that has the resource (in enough capacity). In all studies $k_{max} = 6$ where LB is used.

The purpose of study A (B) was to examine the effect of LB in the presence (absence) of resource constraints. In Study C the performance of LB related to the amount of independent subgraphs in the problem was investigated. Study D was performed to illustrate the runtime distribution of the overall optimization algorithm.

The performance of our experiments was measured in terms of *average runtimes* of the search algorithm to find the optimal solution, taken over the 100 task sets in the study. It should be noted that, with the given parameter setup, there was no guarantee that a generated problem was feasible. In our evaluation, we found that about 5% were infeasible. Furthermore, runs that did not finish within one hour were terminated and excluded in the runtime computation.

Table 1: Configuration parameters for the task sets

Parameter	Study			
	A	B	C	D
Number of tasks	32	32	32	8
Average number of task invocations	*64*	*64*	*64*	*16*
Execution times	10–20	10–20	10–20	20–30
Communication probability	0.075	0.075	0.325	0.5
Average number of communication links	*21*	*21*	*25*	*8*
Message sizes	5–15	5–15	5–15	5–15
Number of processors	8	8	8	8
Resource probability	0.5	0	0.5	0
Resource capacity	1–3	-	1–3	-
Task resource usage probability	0.2	0	0.2	0
Task resource usage amount	1–2	-	1–2	-
Clusters	1	1	3	1

Table 2: Algorithm performance (seconds / # time outs)

Study	Algorithm		% optimal LB
	DDS	DDS+LB	
A	205 / 49	11 / 29	70
B	253 / 53	52 / 25	75
C	267 / 45	37 / 36	57
D	8.6 / 1	4.4 / 1	89

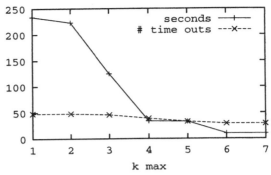

Figure 3: Study A

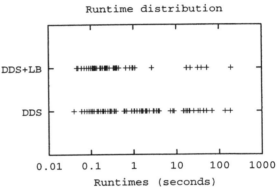

Figure 4: Study D

6.2 Results

The effect of using the lower bound in the studies can be seen in Table 2. The table clearly shows that LB improves the overall performance of the optimization algorithm. An interesting result is that in a large number of runs the lower bound computed by LB also was the optimum.

The task sets used in Study B are actually the same as in Study A, except that all resource constraints have been removed. As the results indicate, the presence of resource constraints aid DDS since the search space becomes reduced. In contrast, LB is hindered by resource constraints since the computed lower bound and "good cut" frequently may be too conservative. Thus, DDS+LB neatly balances the strengths and weaknesses of the two algorithms with respect to the resource constraints in the application.

Recall that $k_{max} = 6$ but in Study C actually $k \leq 4$ in all runs. Hence, if the application consists of separate clusters, which in reality often is the case, it is likely that k_{max} can be set to a smaller value without affecting the quality of the solution. As a consequence, the worst-case computational complexity of LB is reduced. The relation between the performance of DDS+LB and the value of k_{max} is illustrated in Figure 3. As k_{max} increases, more lower-bound computations will reach their "good cut" which results in increased performance. This also means that the improvement eventually reaches a fixpoint.

It should be noted that just considering the average runtime for an algorithm can be misleading since the runtime distribution is rather skewed as illustrated in Figure 4. As indicated by this graph, it is actually the case that 88% of the runs for DDS+LB (in Study D) finish in less than one second. In other words, the probability that an optimal assignment and schedule for a task set (with Study D properties) will be found within one second, is 88%. The corresponding probability for DDS is 59%. This probabilistic view provides more accurate information about the behavior of the algorithm, compared to the arithmetic mean. Especially since the runtime distribution most likely is heavy-tailed [24] which implies that the mean is undefined. In general, the only situation when DDS+LB performs worse than DDS is when the computed lower bound does not affect the pruning made by DDS.

Because the purpose of LB is to improve the lower-bound computation when the optimum is greater than zero, it is interesting to know that in the experiments about 30% of the runs had zero as the optimal solution.

6.3 Discussion

There are some situations where the performance of the lower-bound algorithm may be degraded. First, because the algorithm considers each cluster in isolation, it might be the case that each individual subgraph fits on the same node but they do not fit when considered simultaneously. In particular, this occurs when tasks request resources and two clusters are independently assigned to the same node which in fact only has the capacity for one of the clusters. This phenomena explains the rather poor result for Study C regarding the number of optimal lower-bounds. Second, if the application consists of a single large cluster, the pieces cut off from the graph are likely to be too small to do any good, for low values on k. (See the example.) This forces k_{max} to be rather large which increases the runtime and memory required for the algorithm.

In our experiments we have only used identical speed of the processors. It can be argued that a system with varying processor speeds is likely to have the same effect as the presence of resource constraints and for the same reason.

It should be noted that although an optimal or feasible solution may not be found by the optimization algorithm, the lower bound computed by LB may still be useful. For instance, the best solution found so far may be regarded as sufficiently good when compared to the lower bound. Furthermore, the calculated lower bound may imply that the optimum is too bad, causing the application to be redesigned.

As for the optimization algorithm, it was only when the lower bound was optimal that the performance increased. This suggests that the modeling of the problem within our optimization framework could be improved to provide better pruning based on the lower bound.

7 Conclusions

In this paper, we have considered the problem of optimal task assignment and scheduling. In particular, we focused on how to find a lower bound on the network communication in distributed real-time systems. As a result, we propose a pseudo-polynomial-time algorithm for computing such a lower bound based on the k-cut problem. Despite the high computational complexity of our algorithm, our experiments show that it is indeed capable of reducing the average runtime significantly for the overall optimization problem. Furthermore, in as many as 89% of the runs, the computed lower bound was also the optimum.

References

[1] O. Goldschmidt and D. S. Hochbaum, "Polynomial Algorithm for the k-cut Problem," *Proc. of the IEEE Symposium on Foundations of Computer Science*, 1988, pp. 444–451.

[2] P.-Y. R. Ma, E. Y. S. Lee, and M. Tsuchiya, "A Task Allocation Model for Distributed Computing Systems," *IEEE Trans. on Computers*, vol. 31, no. 1, pp. 41–47, Jan. 1982.

[3] G. H. Chen and J. S. Yur, "A Branch-and-Bound with Underestimates Algorithm for the Task Assignment Problem with Precedence Constraint," *Proc. of IEEE Internatinal Conference on Distributed Computing Systems*, May 28–June 1, 1990, pp. 494–501.

[4] C.-C. Shen and W.-H. Tsai, "A Graph Matching Approach to Optimal Task Assignment in Distributed Computing Systems Using a Minimax Criterion," *IEEE Trans. on Computers*, vol. 34, no. 3, pp. 197–203, Mar. 1985.

[5] T. P. Ajith and C. S. R. Murthy, "Optimal Task Allocation in Distributed Systems by Graph Matching and State Space Search," *Journal of Systems and Software*, vol. 46, no. 1, pp. 59–75, Apr. 1999.

[6] V. M. Lo, "Heuristic Algorithms for Task Assignment in Distributed Systems," *IEEE Trans. on Computers*, vol. 37, no. 11, pp. 1384–1397, Nov. 1988.

[7] C. E. Houstis, "Module Allocation of Real-Time Applications to Distributed Systems," *IEEE Trans. on Software Engineering*, vol. 16, no. 7, pp. 699–709, July 1990.

[8] C.-C. Hui and S. T. Chanson, "Allocating Task Interaction Graphs to Processors in Heterogeneous Networks," *IEEE Trans. on Parallel and Distributed Systems*, vol. 8, no. 9, pp. 908–925, Sept. 1997.

[9] J. Hou and W. Wolf, "Process Partitioning for Distributed Embedded Systems," *Proc. of the International Workshop on Hardware/Software Co-design*, 1996, pp. 70–76.

[10] T. F. Abdelzaher and K. G. Shin, "Optimal Combined Task and Message Scheduling in Distributed Real-Time Systems," *Proc. of the IEEE Real-Time Systems Symposium*, Pisa, Italy, Dec. 5–7, 1995, pp. 162–171.

[11] C.-J. Hou and K. G. Shin, "Allocation of Periodic Task Modules with Precedence and Deadline Constraints in Distributed Real-Time Systems," *IEEE Trans. on Computers*, vol. 46, no. 12, pp. 1338–1356, Dec. 1997.

[12] K. Ramamritham, "Allocation and Scheduling of Precedence-Related Periodic Tasks," *IEEE Trans. on Parallel and Distributed Systems*, vol. 6, no. 4, pp. 412–420, Apr. 1995.

[13] K. W. Tindell, A. Burns, and A. J. Wellings, "Allocating Hard Real-Time Tasks: An NP-Hard Problem Made Easy," *Real-Time Systems*, vol. 4, no. 2, pp. 145–165, June 1992.

[14] H. S. Stone, "Multiprocessor Scheduling with the Aid of Network Flow Algorithms," *IEEE Trans. on Software Engineering*, vol. 3, no. 1, pp. 85–93, Jan. 1977.

[15] T.-S. Tia and J. W.-S. Liu, "Task and Resource Assignment in Distrubuted Real-Time Systems," *Proc. of the Second Workshop on Parallel and Distributed Real-Time Systems*, Apr. 1994, pp. 43–51.

[16] T. F. Abdelzaher and K. G. Shin, "Period-Based Load Partitioning and Assignment for Large Real-Time Applications," *IEEE Trans. on Computers*, vol. 49, no. 1, pp. 81–87, Jan. 2000.

[17] M. Stoer and F. Wagner, "A Simple Min-Cut Algorithm," *Journal of the ACM*, vol. 44, no. 4, pp. 585–591, July 1997.

[18] Y.-C. Ma and C.-P. Chung, "A Dominance Realation Enhanced Branch-and-Bound Task Allocation," *Journal of Systems and Software*, vol. 58, no. 2, pp. 125–134, Sept. 2001.

[19] E. Tsang, *Foundations of Constraint Satisfaction*, Academic Press, 1993.

[20] C. Ekelin and J. Jonsson, "Evaluation of Search Heuristics for Embedded System Scheduling Problems," *Proc. of the International Conference on Principles and Practice of Constraint Programming*, Paphos, Cyprus, Nov. 26–Dec. 1, 2001, pp. 640–654.

[21] T. Walsh, "Depth-bounded Discrepancy Search," *Proc. of International Joint Conference on Artificial Intelligence*, Nagoya, Japan, Aug. 23–29, 1997.

[22] H. Nagamochi, K. Nishimura, and T. Ibaraki, "Computing All Small Cuts in an Undirected Network," *SIAM Journal of Discrete Mathematics*, vol. 10, no. 3, pp. 469–481, Aug. 1997.

[23] H. Nagamochi and T. Ibaraki, "Computing Edge-Connectivity in Multigraphs and Capacitated Graphs," *SIAM Journal of Discrete Mathematics*, vol. 5, no. 1, pp. 54–66, Feb. 1992.

[24] C. P. Gomes, B. Selman, N. Crato, and H. Kautz, "Heavy-Tailed Phenomena in Satisfiability and Constraint Satisfaction Problems," *Journal of Automated Reasoning*, vol. 24, no. 1-2, pp. 67–100, 2000.

LDBS: A Duplication Based Scheduling Algorithm
for Heterogeneous Computing Systems *

Atakan Doğan   and   Füsun Özgüner
Department of Electrical Engineering
The Ohio State University
2015 Neil Avenue
Columbus, OH 43210-1272
email: {dogana, ozguner}@ee.eng.ohio-state.edu

Abstract

Finding an optimal solution to the problem of scheduling an application modeled by a directed acyclic graph (DAG) onto a set of heterogeneous machines is known to be an NP-hard problem. In this study, we present a duplication based scheduling algorithm, namely the levelized duplication based scheduling (LDBS) algorithm, which solves this problem efficiently. The primary goal of LDBS is to minimize the schedule length of applications. LDBS can accommodate different duplication heuristics, thanks to its modular design. Specifically, we have designed two different duplication heuristics with different time complexities. The simulation studies confirm that LDBS is a very competitive scheduling algorithm in terms of minimizing the schedule length of applications.

1. Introduction

A *heterogeneous computing* (HC) system is a suite of geographically distributed machines interconnected by a high-speed network, thereby promising high-speed processing of computationally intensive applications with diverse computing needs. It is envisioned that such a computing system will enable users around the globe to execute their applications on the most suitable computing resources. In order to take advantage of a HC system, an application is first split into coarse-grained communicating tasks, which are represented by a *directed acyclic graph* (DAG), and then, a scheduling algorithm is used to assign the tasks of the application to machines. Since both the performance of a particular application and the utilization of system resources

heavily depend on how applications are scheduled, deploying an efficient scheduling algorithm is crucial. However, finding an optimal solution to the problem of scheduling a directed acyclic graph onto a HC system is not trivial and the problem is NP-hard [3].

The intrinsic high complexity of the scheduling problem has led to the development of a variety of heuristic scheduling algorithms. An important class of scheduling algorithms is *duplication based list scheduling* algorithms where tasks can be duplicated into idle time slots between two already scheduled tasks. In the literature, many task duplication based scheduling algorithms, including the *duplication first and reduction next* (DFRN) algorithm [9], the *task duplication based scheduling* (TDS) algorithm [4], the *critical path fast duplication* (CPFD) algorithm [1], and few other algorithms cited in [9] and [1], share the following assumptions: (1) The computing system is homogeneous. (2) The number of machines is unbounded. (3) The communication network is completely connected and homogeneous. Consequently, these algorithms cannot be used to schedule a DAG-structured application on a heterogeneous computing system where the number of machines is bounded. Recently, Ranaweera and Agrawal [11] have extended the TDS algorithm in [4] so that TDS can be used for a set of heterogeneous machines interconnected by a homogeneous, completely connected network. Thus, the TDS algorithm [11] has a limited applicability to a HC system as well.

Motivated by the facts given above, in this study, our goal is to design a duplication based matching and scheduling algorithm that can be deployed to schedule a DAG-structured application on a heterogeneous computing system, which is composed of a set of heterogeneous machines interconnected by a heterogeneous, arbitrary connected network. In order to achieve this goal, we develop the *levelized duplication based scheduling* (LDBS) algorithm. The modular design of the LDBS algorithm permits the use of different du-

---

*This material is based upon work supported by the National Science Foundation under Award No. CCR-0100633.

plication heuristics in the algorithm. Specifically, we design two different duplication heuristics with different time complexities. We compare the performance of LDBS against HEFT [13] by simulation. Our extensive simulation studies reveal that the average schedule length of LDBS is as much as 36% smaller than that of HEFT, which is a significant improvement over a high performance scheduling algorithm. The rest of the paper is organized as follows.

In Section 2, we define the classical matching and scheduling problem and introduce some notation. The LDBS algorithm is presented in Section 3 and the simulation studies are given in Section 4. In Section 5, finally, we present our conclusions.

2. Matching and Scheduling Problem

The matching and scheduling problem along with the proposed scheduling algorithms will be established based on the following assumptions.

A heterogeneous computing system is assumed to be composed of p heterogeneous machines denoted by $M = \{m_1, m_2, \cdots, m_p\}$ where machine m_j, $1 \leq j \leq p$, is a dedicated one, i.e., m_j executes each task to completion without preemption. Such a computing system is assumed to be controlled by a *centralized scheduler* which allocates system resources to a variety of applications with the goal of minimizing running time of applications.

An application executing on the system is represented by a *directed acyclic graph* $T = (V, E)$, where the set $V = \{v_1, v_2, \cdots, v_n\}$ denotes the set of tasks to be executed and the set of directed edges E represents the communication between pairs of tasks. Let $t_{i,j}^E$ be the expected execution time of task v_i on machine m_j. It is assumed that the expected execution time $t_{i,j}^E$, $1 \leq i \leq n$ and $1 \leq j \leq p$, is known. Techniques such as code profiling/analytic benchmarking [15] and statistical prediction [6] have been devised to estimate $t_{i,j}^E$. Let $e_{k,l} \in E$ indicate communication from task v_k to v_l, where task v_k (v_l) is said to be an immediate predecessor (successor) task of task v_l (v_k). Associated with directed edge $e_{k,l} \in E$ is the volume of data in terms of bytes, which is denoted by $d_{k,l}$, that will be transmitted from task v_k to v_l upon the completion of task v_k.

The classical matching and scheduling problem, where task duplication is not considered, can be formally defined as follows. Let $\mathcal{M} : V \to M$ denote a matching function, where $\mathcal{M}(i)$, $1 \leq i \leq n$, defines the machine to which task v_i is assigned. Let $\mathcal{S}_j : V \to \{0, 1, \cdots, n\}$ be a scheduling function, where $\mathcal{S}_j(i)$, $1 \leq i \leq n$ and $1 \leq j \leq p$, denotes the execution order of task v_i on machine m_j ($\mathcal{S}_j(i) = 0$ defines that task v_i is not assigned to machine m_j). Consequently, a matching function $\mathcal{M}$ and a set of scheduling functions $\{\mathcal{S}_1, \mathcal{S}_2, \cdots, \mathcal{S}_p\}$ can represent a possible assignment of a DAG to machines in a

HC system. Let $\mathcal{X}_i = \{\mathcal{M}(i), \mathcal{S}_{\mathcal{M}(i)}(i)\}$ denote a possible matching and scheduling decision for task v_i and π_i denote all possible matching and scheduling decisions for task v_i. Thus, $\mathcal{X} = \mathcal{X}_1 \times \mathcal{X}_2 \times \cdots \times \mathcal{X}_n$ defines a possible task assignment of tasks in set V to machines in set M and $\pi = \pi_1 \times \pi_2 \times \cdots \times \pi_n$ represents all possible task assignments.

Suppose that task assignment $\mathcal{X}$ is given. Because of the precedence constraints, task v_i cannot start running on machine $\mathcal{M}(i)$ unless all data items from its immediate predecessor tasks have been received by machine $\mathcal{M}(i)$. Let $t_{i,k}^D$ ($e_{k,i} \in E$) denote the time when task v_i has received the data from task v_k and

$$t_{i,k}^D = \begin{cases} t_k^F, & \text{if } \mathcal{M}(k) = \mathcal{M}(i) \\ t_k^F + d_{k,i} c_{\mathcal{M}(k),\mathcal{M}(i)}, & \text{otherwise} \end{cases} \quad (1)$$

where t_k^F denotes the finish time of task v_k and $c_{s,t}$ denotes the expected transmission time of sending one byte of data from machine m_s to m_t. The time when all data items of task v_i have been received by machine $\mathcal{M}(i)$ is referred to as the *data arrival time*. Definition 1 formalizes the data arrival time of a task.

Definition 1 *The data arrival time of task v_i, which is denoted by t_i^D, is defined to be:*

$$t_i^D = \max_{e_{k,i} \in E}\{t_{i,k}^D\} \quad (2)$$

In order for the execution of a task to start on a machine, all data items of the task must be received and the machine must be available. Thus, the start time of task v_i, which is denoted by t_i^S, is defined to be:

$$t_i^S = \max\left\{t_i^M, t_i^D\right\} \quad (3)$$

where t_i^M denotes the time when machine $\mathcal{M}(i)$ will be available to execute task v_i: $t_i^M = 0$, if task v_i is the first task to be executed on machine $\mathcal{M}(i)$; t_i^M equals to the finish time of the $(k-1)$th task, if it is the kth task. Finally, the finish time of task v_i (t_i^F) is defined to be:

$$t_i^F = t_i^S + t_{i,\mathcal{M}(i)}^E \quad (4)$$

The objective in the matching and scheduling problem is to find a possible task assignment $\mathcal{X}$ such that the schedule length (maximum of the finish time of tasks) is minimized. Formally, the matching and scheduling problem is defined to be:

$$\min_{\mathcal{X} \in \pi}\left\{\max_{v_i \in V}\{t_i^F\}\right\} \quad (5)$$

Finding an optimal solution to the problem defined by (5) is known to be an NP-hard problem [3]. Consequently, in this study, we focus on designing heuristic approaches so as to solve this problem.

3. A Duplication Based Scheduling Algorithm

In this section, we propose a new duplication based scheduling algorithm that can produce schedules with very competitive makespan for DAG-structured applications running on HC systems.

3.1 Level sorting

The level sorting process can be expressed recursively as follows: Given a DAG $T = (V, E)$, level 0 contains all tasks with no predecessor tasks. Level i consists of all tasks v_l such that, for all edges $e_{k,l} \in E$, task v_k is in a level less than i, and there exists at least one task v_k with level $i - 1$. Note that the last level will be composed of tasks with no successor tasks. Figure 1 shows a sample DAG that has been level-sorted.

The level sorting technique groups tasks that are independent of each other into a level, that is, there is no data dependency between two tasks with the same level. As a result, all tasks within a level can be executed in parallel. Note that the level sorting technique has been previously used in other scheduling algorithms, such as LMT [5] and hybrid remapper [8].

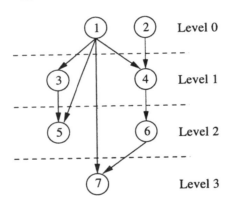

Figure 1. An example of level sorted DAG.

3.2 Rank assignment

The rank of a task can be interpreted as the length of the critical path from that task to an exit task, which is a task with no successor task, of the task graph. Note that the *critical path* of a task is a set of vertices and edges, forming a path from that task to an exit task, of which the sum of computation cost and communication cost is the maximum. The computation of ranks starts from exit tasks and recursively progresses by traversing the task graph upward until all ranks are obtained.

Each task $v_i \in V$ will be associated with a static priority $rank_i$ by using the expression below.

$$rank_i = \bar{t}_i^E + \max_{e_{i,l} \in E}\{rank_l + d_{i,l}\overline{c_{s,t}}\} \tag{6}$$

where $\bar{t}_i^E$ is the average execution time of task v_i and $\overline{c_{s,t}}$ is the average communication cost of sending one byte of data between machines in set M. It should be noted that priority assignment expression (6) is used by the HEFT algorithm [13] as well.

3.3 LDBS algorithm

First, a few definitions on which the proposed algorithms are based will be introduced. With respect to (3), the start time of a task depends on the data arrival time of that task. The predecessor task from which the data arrives at the latest time is referred to as the *Critical Immediate Predecessor* (CIP) of the task. Formally, Definition 2 identifies the CIP of a task.

Definition 2 *The Critical Immediate Predecessor (CIP) of task v_i is defined to be:*

$$CIP(v_i) = \left\{v_k \,\middle|\, t_{i,k}^D = t_i^D\right\} \tag{7}$$

In non-insertion based scheduling algorithms, the time when a machine is assumed to be available to execute a new task is taken as the finish time of the last task assigned to that machine. However, it is also possible that a time slot between two already scheduled tasks on the machine may be large enough to accommodate another task. Formally, Definition 3 rules the selection of a suitable time slot for a task on a particular machine.

Definition 3 *Given that a set of r tasks $\{v_1, v_2, \cdots, v_r\}$ have been assigned to machine m_j, task v_i can be scheduled into time slot l (between tasks v_{l+1} and v_l) on machine m_j, if*

$$t_{l+1}^S - \max\left\{t_l^F, t_i^D\right\} \geq t_{i,j}^E \tag{8}$$

is satisfied, where $0 \leq l \leq r$, $t_{r+1}^S = \infty$, and $t_0^F = 0$.

Definition 4 *The earliest start time of task v_i is defined to be:*

$$t_i^S = \max\left\{t_l^F, t_i^D\right\} \tag{9}$$

where time slot l is the first time slot for which inequality (8) holds. Furthermore, the earliest finish time of task v_i can be computed by using (4) and (9).

```
    1.  level_sort (T);
    2.  Let l_i be the level associated with task v_i;
    3.  Let l = 1, l_x = max_{v_i ∈ V} {l_i} and
        List = {v_i| l_i = 0};
    4.  min_min_heuristic (List);
    5.  while (l ≤ l_x)
    6.      Let List = {v_i| l_i = l};
    7.      duplication_heuristic_vx (List);
    8.      Let l = l + 1;
    9.  endwhile.
```

Figure 2. The LDBS algorithm.

Figure 2 shows the proposed LDBS algorithm. Basically, LDBS uses an existing meta-task scheduling algorithm to schedule tasks with level zero and one of the two duplication heuristics proposed in this study to schedule a set of tasks whose levels are the same and greater than zero. At step 1, task graph T is level sorted. A depth-first search algorithm can be used to level sort an input DAG. Thus, the time complexity of the level sorting process is $O(|V| + |E|)$. At steps 2 and 3, a few variables are introduced, where l_x is the height of task graph T and $List$ is a list of tasks with level zero. The time complexity of step 3 is $O(|V|)$. Since all tasks in $List$ are independent of each other, any meta-task scheduling algorithm can be used to assign these tasks. In this study, the *min-min heuristic*, which has been shown to perform quite well as compared to other meta-task scheduling algorithms [2] and is easy to implement, is chosen. Note that new meta-task scheduling algorithms, *segmented min-min* [7] and *relative cost* [14], have been reported to outperform the min-min heuristic. The time complexity of the min-min heuristic is $O(|V|^2|M|)$. Steps between 5 and 9 will be repeated l_x times, where each iteration of the *while* loop is to schedule a set of tasks with the same level. At step 6, $List$ is set to be composed of tasks with level l. The time complexity of this step is $O(|V|)$. At step 7, a duplication heuristic, either *duplication_heuristic_v1* or *duplication_heuristic_v2*, is used for scheduling the tasks in set $List$. Note that *duplication_heuristic_vx* corresponds to either of these two heuristics. In addition, the duplication heuristics proposed have different time complexities. Consequently, the time complexity of step 7 together with the LDBS algorithm depends on which version of the duplication heuristic is chosen. In the following two sections, the duplication heuristics developed are presented.

3.3.1 Duplication heuristic: Version one

Figure 3 shows the first version of the duplication heuristic. Steps between 2 and 24 will be repeated until all tasks in

$List$ are assigned, where each iteration of the *while* loop is to schedule only one task from set $List$. At step 3, variable $ftime$ is initialized. In the algorithm, there are three *for* loops: The first *for* loop (steps from 4 to 20) is to consider each task in set $List$ as a potential task to be scheduled next. The second *for* loop (steps from 5 to 19) is to consider each machine in set M as a potential machine to which the next task could be scheduled. Inside of these two *for* loops, a task-machine pair (v_i, m_j) with the minimum finish time across all possible task-machine pairs will be found, where task duplication will also be applied to further decrease the finish time of task v_i on machine m_j. At step 6, the earliest start time and finish time of task v_i on machine m_j is found, where task insertion is allowed. At step 7, it is checked if assigning task v_i to machine m_j is the best scheduling decision in terms of minimizing the schedule length so far. If it is, variables $v_i^*, m_j^*, \hat{v}_i^*, \hat{m}_j^*$, and $ftime$ are set accordingly. At step 11, v_k is set to the CIP of task v_i. Up to this point, task duplication is not performed yet. The third *for* loop (steps from 12 to 18) is to introduce task duplication into the algorithm. Inside of the third *for* loop, *minimize_start_time* function is called to duplicate the CIP of task v_i (v_k) on machine m_l, where each machine m_l in set M will be considered. Note that, since task v_k is the one from which a data item will be received the latest by task v_i, duplicating an immediate predecessor task other than the CIP will not decrease the start time of task v_i. Thus, the CIP of task v_i is chosen to be duplicated first among all immediate predecessor tasks of task v_i. In addition, while duplicating task v_k on machine m_l, task insertion is applied, if possible. Basically, *minimize_start_time* function recursively duplicates the CIP of task v_i on machine m_l, where the CIP of task v_i is likely to change after each task duplication, until the start time of task v_i cannot be decreased further. A detailed explanation of *minimize_start_time* function will be given in the next paragraph. At step 14, it is checked if assigning task v_i to machine m_j together with possibly duplicating few of task v_i's immediate predecessor tasks is the best scheduling decision in terms of minimizing the schedule length so far. If it is, at steps 15 and 16, few variables are set accordingly. At step 21, task-machine pair (v_i^*, m_j^*) is found to be the one that minimizes the schedule length the most for the current iteration. Furthermore, if $\hat{v}_i^* \neq \emptyset$, *minimize_start_time* function will duplicate as many of task v_i^*'s immediate predecessor tasks as possible, starting from task $\hat{v}_i^*$, on machine $\hat{m}_j^*$. At step 22, task v_i^* is scheduled into a time slot on machine m_j^* that minimizes its start time. At step 23, task v_i^* is removed from set $List$.

Figure 4 shows the *minimize_start_time* function, which is called by both of the duplication heuristics. At step 2, it is checked if task v_k is a valid task. Note that $v_k = \emptyset$ is possible since, at step 21 (or step 20 in the second version), task duplication may not be necessary, which is indicated by

```
1.  duplication_heuristic_v1 (List)
2.    while (all tasks in List are assigned)
3.      Let ftime = ∞;
4.      for each task v_i ∈ List
5.        for each machine m_j ∈ M, j ≤ p
6.          Compute the earliest start time (t_i^S) and
            finish time (t_i^F) for (v_i, m_j);
7.          if (t_i^F < ftime)
8.            Let v_i* = v_i, m_j* = m_j, v̂_i* = ∅, and
              m̂_j* = ∅;
9.            Let ftime = t_i^F;
10.         endif.
11.         Let v_k = CIP(v_i);
12.         for each machine m_l ∈ M, l ≤ p
13.           stime = minimize_start_time (1, v_i,
                m_j, v_k, m_l, t_i^S);
14.           if (stime + t_{i,j}^E < ftime)
15.             Let v_i* = v_i, m_j* = m_j, v̂_i* = v_k, and
                m̂_j* = m_l;
16.             Let ftime = stime + t_{i,j}^E;
17.           endif.
18.         endfor.
19.       endfor.
20.     endfor.
21.     minimize_start_time (0, v_i*, m_j*, v̂_i*, m̂_j*, ∞);
22.     Schedule task v_i* in a time slot on machine m_j*
          that minimizes its start time;
23.     Remove v_i* from List;
24.   endwhile.
25. end.
```

Figure 3. The first version of the duplication heuristic.

```
1.  minimize_start_time (mode, v_i, m_j, v_k, m_l, stime)
2.    if (v_k ≠ ∅)
3.      if (v_k is not already assigned to m_l)
4.        Duplicate v_k in a time slot on m_l that
          minimizes its start time;
5.        Recompute t_i^S for (v_i, m_j);
6.        if (t_i^S < stime)
7.          Let v_k = CIP(v_i);
8.          stime = minimize_start_time (mode, v_i,
              m_j, v_k, m_l, t_i^S);
9.          if (stime < t_i^S)
10.           t_i^S = stime;
11.         endif.
12.         if (mode)
13.           undo_duplication (v_k, m_l);
14.         endif.
15.       else
16.         undo_duplication (v_k, m_l);
17.       endif.
18.       return (t_i^S);
19.     endif.
20.     return (∞);
21.   endif.
22.   return (∞);
23. end.
```

Figure 4. The start time minimization algorithm.

tion heuristic.

The time complexity of the first version of the duplication heuristic can be computed as follows. The *while* loop iterates $O(V)$ times. Since step 13 is the dominant step of the heuristic, each iteration will take $O(|V||M|^2(|V||E||M|))$ time, where $O(|V||E||M|)$ is the time complexity of *minimize_start_time* function. In order to come up with $O(|V||E||M|)$ as the time complexity of *minimize_start_time* function, note first that *minimize_start_time* function can be called recursively at most $O(|V|)$ times. The dominant steps of the function are steps 4, 5 and 13 (or 16), each of which can be implemented in $O(|E||M|)$ time. Thus, the overall time complexity of *minimize_start_time* function is $O(|V||E||M|)$. Consequently, the time complexity of the first version of the duplication heuristic is $O(|V|^3|E||M|^3)$, which is also the time complexity of LDBS using the first version of the duplication heuristic.

3.3.2 Duplication heuristic: Version two

Figure 5 shows the second version of the duplication heuristic. The main difference between the first version and sec-

$v̂_i^* = ∅$. At step 3, it is checked if task v_k is already assigned to machine m_l. If it is, task duplication is not needed. At step 4, task v_k will be scheduled into such a time slot on machine m_l that its start time is minimized. At step 5, the earliest start time of task v_i on machine m_j will be recomputed. If this task duplication does not decrease the start time of task v_i, at step 16, the task duplication is undone. Otherwise, new CIP of task v_i is found at step 7 and then, *minimize_start_time* function is recursively called at step 8. Thus, *minimize_start_time* function duplicates only the immediate predecessor tasks of a particular task. However, note that since task duplication is used to reduce the finish time of all tasks, a task's predecessor tasks other than immediate predecessor ones could already be duplicated. Between steps 9 and 11, t_i^S is updated accordingly. At steps 13, the current task duplication is undone if $mode = 1$, that is, the impact of the task duplication on the start time of task v_i is just evaluated inside of the third *for* loop in the duplica-

ond version of the duplication heuristic is as follows. In the first version, all tasks within the same level are treated equally by the algorithm. Among the tasks within same level, at each iteration, task-machine pair (v_i, m_j) with the minimum finish time is found and then, task v_i is assigned to machine m_j. However, this may lead to making a scheduling decision where a relatively less important task can be scheduled before a critical task, which may be on the critical path. In order to tackle this problem, in the second version, tasks in $List$ are sorted in the decreasing order of their $ranks$ at step 2. After that, they are considered for scheduling in the sorted order. Thus, a task that is more likely to be on the critical path will be considered first by the algorithm. Note also that, the second version does not have a $while$ loop, thereby making the second version a less complex algorithm. The details of the second version will not be discussed simply because they should be clear after the detailed explanation of the first one. Furthermore, the time complexity of the LDBS algorithm using the second version of the duplication heuristic is $O(|V|^3|E||M|^2)$.

4. Experiments

In order to evaluate the proposed algorithms, a simulation program that can be used to emulate the execution of randomly created or real application task graphs on a simulated computing system was developed.

In the simulation program, a heterogeneous computing system is randomly created based on two parameters, namely the number of *computation machines* p and the number of *communication machines* q. In order to interconnect p machines in set M, a network of q communication machines is employed, where the network topology is randomly generated and each computation machine is randomly connected to a communication machine. This simulation model closely mimics a computing system where a set of machines is interconnected by a switched-based network. Note that the network itself can also be heterogeneous where several networking technologies are simultaneously used. The last parameter of interest of the system model is set as follows. The transmission rates of links are assumed to be uniformly distributed between 1 and 10 Mbits/sec.

The simulation studies performed are grouped into two sets; (1) executing randomly generated task graphs with different number of tasks (between 20 and 100) on a computing system with $p = 20$ and $q = 20$, and (2) executing randomly generated task graphs with 50 tasks on a computing system with p ranging from 10 to 50 and $q = 20$. With respect to the randomly generated task graphs, the execution time of each task of the task graph is assumed to be uniformly distributed between 10 and 120 minutes, where the execution times of a given task are different on different

```
1.  duplication_heuristic_v2 (List)
2.      Sort tasks in List in the decreasing order of
            their ranks into List;
3.      for each task vᵢ ∈ List
4.          Let ftime = ∞;
5.          for each machine mⱼ ∈ M, j ≤ p
6.              Compute the earliest start time (tᵢˢ) and
                    finish time (tᵢᶠ) for (vᵢ, mⱼ);
7.              if (tᵢᶠ < ftime)
8.                  Let vᵢ* = vᵢ, mⱼ* = mⱼ, v̂ᵢ* = ∅, and
                        m̂ⱼ* = ∅;
9.                  Let ftime = tᵢᶠ;
10.             endif.
11.             Let vₖ = CIP(vᵢ);
12.             for each machine mₗ ∈ M, l ≤ p
13.                 stime = minimize_start_time (1, vᵢ,
                        mⱼ, vₖ, mₗ, tᵢˢ);
14.                 if (stime + tᵢ,ⱼᴱ < ftime)
15.                     Let vᵢ* = vᵢ, mⱼ* = mⱼ, v̂ᵢ* = vₖ, and
                            m̂ⱼ* = mₗ;
16.                     Let ftime = stime + tᵢ,ⱼᴱ;
17.                 endif.
18.             endfor.
19.         endfor.
20.         minimize_start_time (0, vᵢ*, mⱼ*, v̂ᵢ*, m̂ⱼ*, ∞);
21.         Schedule task vᵢ* in a time slot on machine mⱼ*
                that minimizes its start time;
22.         Remove vᵢ* from List;
23.     endfor.
24. end.
```

Figure 5. The second version of the duplication heuristic.

machines. Furthermore, the volume of data to be transmitted among tasks are randomly generated such that the *communication to computation ratio* (CCR) is 0.1, 1.0, or 10.0, where the average communication time between a task and its successor tasks is set to the average execution time of the task times CCR. By using a range of CCR values, different types of applications can be accommodated. That is, computation intensive applications may be modeled by assuming CCR = 0.1 whereas data intensive applications may be modeled by assuming CCR = 10.0.

In the simulations, the performance of LDBS is compared against HEFT [13] simply because HEFT has been shown to outperform several other high performance scheduling algorithms, including DLS [12], LMT [5], FCT [10], etc. On the other hand, LDBS is not compared against TDS [11] since TDS is limited to a HC system with homogeneous, completely connected network topology as pointed before. For the first set of simulation studies, the results are shown in Figure 6 where the number of tasks in a randomly generated task graph is fixed to 20, 40, 60, 80, or 100 and each data point is the average of the data obtained in 25 experiments. Note that $LDBS_1$ and $LDBS_2$ in Figures 6 and 7 denote the LDBS algorithm using the first version and the second version of the duplication heuristic, respectively.

For $CCR = 0.1$ in Figure 6 (top figure), HEFT outperforms LDBS by a small margin. Specifically, at best, the average schedule length of HEFT is 5% and 2% smaller than that of $LDBS_1$ and $LDBS_2$, respectively. The reason why HEFT outperforms LDBS can be explained by the fact that HEFT can identify critical path tasks much better as compared to LDBS, where the level sorting of tasks in LDBS can alter the importance of tasks. Note also that, for small values of CCR, the performance of both LDBS and HEFT tend to decrease because the size of time slots between already scheduled tasks is likely to be smaller, which could make it harder to insert new tasks into those time slots.

For $CCR = 1.0$ in Figure 6, LDBS clearly outperforms HEFT. The performance of $LDBS_1$ and $LDBS_2$ are quite close, though $LDBS_2$ takes less time to complete as compared to $LDBS_1$. Specifically, the average schedule length of $LDBS_1$ is 19% on average and 22% at best smaller than that of HEFT. Furthermore, the average schedule length of $LDBS_2$ is 19% on average and 21% at best smaller than that of HEFT.

For $CCR = 10.0$ in Figure 6 (bottom figure), the difference in the performances of LDBS and HEFT is again quite significantly in favor of LDBS. Specifically, the average schedule length of $LDBS_1$ is 27% on average and 30% at best smaller than that of HEFT. In addition, the average schedule length of $LDBS_2$ is 29% on average and 36% at best smaller than that of HEFT.

For the second set of simulation studies, randomly generated task graphs with 50 tasks and $CCR = 1.0$ are assumed to be executed on a heterogeneous computing system with 10, 20, 30, 40, or 50 machines. The results of this simulation study are shown in Figure 7. According to Figure 7, with the increase in the number of machines, the average schedule length of applications under LDBS and HEFT decreases as expected. Besides, LDBS outperforms HEFT by a significant margin and the performance of $LDBS_1$ and $LDBS_2$ are virtually the same. Specifically, the average schedule length of LDBS is 23% on average and 27% at best smaller than that of HEFT. Furthermore, as the number of machines increases, LDBS outperforms HEFT by an increased margin.

In general, the simulation studies confirm that the LDBS algorithm is a much better choice than the HEFT algorithm as far as the minimization of the makespan of applications is concerned. On the other hand, producing better task assignments by LDBS takes much more time as compared to

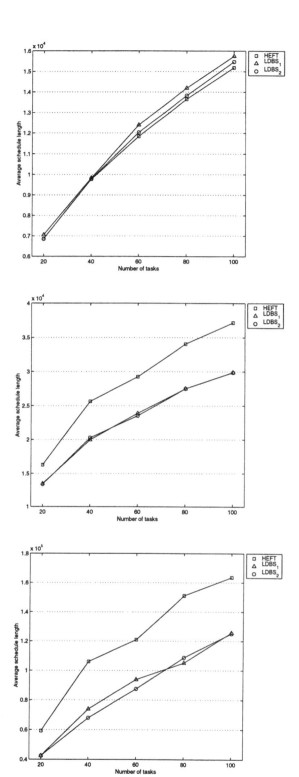

Figure 6. Average schedule length of DAGs with CCR= 0.1, CCR= 1.0, or CCR= 10.0 under the LDBS and HEFT algorithms.

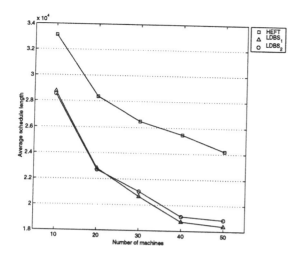

Figure 7. Average schedule length of DAGs with CCR= 1.0 under the LDBS and HEFT algorithms with respect to increasing number of machines.

HEFT. This may be somewhat expected because a task duplication based algorithm is likely to have more time complexity than an insertion based scheduling algorithm with no task duplication.

5. Conclusions

In this study, we have addressed the problem of scheduling of DAG-structured applications on a heterogeneous computing system. In order to solve this problem, we have designed a duplication based scheduling algorithm, namely the LDBS algorithm. LDBS is designed in a modular fashion so that it can employ distinct duplication heuristics easily. With regards to duplication heuristics, we have developed two of them, each having different time complexity.

The primary goal in the design of LDBS is to minimize the makespan of DAG-structured applications. As clearly shown in the previous section, LDBS is a very promising scheduling algorithm in that it outperforms HEFT by a significant margin in most of the simulation scenarios. We have to note that the time complexity of LDBS is rather high. As we have shown in Section 3, high complexity of LDBS is due to the duplication heuristic that is employed. Because of the modular architecture of LDBS, on the other hand, it is possible to decrease the time complexity of LDBS by incorporating a less complex duplication heuristic into the algorithm.

References

[1] I. Ahmad and Y.-K. Kwok. On exploiting task duplication in parallel program scheduling. *IEEE Trans. Parallel and Distributed Systems*, 9(9):872–892, Sept. 1998.

[2] T. D. Braun et. al. A comparison study of static mapping heuristics for a class of meta-tasks on heterogeneous computing systems. In *IPPS/SPDP Workshop on Heterogeneous Computing*, pages 15–29, San Juan, Puerto Rico, Apr. 1999.

[3] P. Chretienne, E. G. Coffman, Jr., J. K. Lenstra, and Z. Liu. *Scheduling Theory and its Applications*. John Wiley & Sons, 1995.

[4] S. Darbha and D. P. Agrawal. Optimal scheduling algorithms for distributed-memory machines. *IEEE Trans. Parallel and Distributed Systems*, 9(1):87–94, Jan. 1998.

[5] M. A. Iverson, F. Özgüner, and G. J. Follen. Parallelizing existing applications in a distributed heterogeneous environment. In *IPPS Workshop on Heterogeneous Computing*, pages 93–100, Santa Barbara, CA, 1995.

[6] M. A. Iverson, F. Özgüner, and L. Potter. Statistical prediction of task execution times through analytic benchmarking for scheduling in a heterogeneous environment. *IEEE Trans. Computers*, 48(12):1374–1379, Dec. 1999.

[7] M-Y.Wu, W. Shu, and H. Zhang. Segmented min-min: A static mapping algorithm for meta-tasks on heterogeneous computing systems. In *IPDPS Workshop on Heterogeneous Computing*, pages 375–385, Cancún, Mexico, May 2000.

[8] M. Maheswaran and H. J. Siegel. A dynamic matching and scheduling algorithm for heterogeneous computing systems. In *IPPS/SPDP Workshop on Heterogeneous Computing*, pages 57–69, Orlando, FL, Mar. 1998.

[9] G.-L. Park, B. Shirazi, and J. Marquis. DFRN: A new approach for duplication based scheduling for distributed memory multiprocessor systems. In *Int'l Parallel Processing Symposium*, Geneva, Switzerland, Apr. 1997.

[10] A. Radulescu and A. J. C. van Gemund. Fast and effective task scheduling in heterogeneous systems. In *IPDPS Workshop on Heterogeneous Computing*, pages 229–238, Cancún, Mexico, May 2000.

[11] S. Ranaweera and D. P. Agrawal. A task duplication based scheduling algorithm for heterogeneous systems. In *Int'l Parallel and Distributed Processing Symposium*, pages 445–450, Cancún, Mexico, May 2000.

[12] G. C. Sih and E. A. Lee. A compile-time scheduling heuristic for interconnection-constraint heterogeneous processor architectures. *IEEE Trans. Parallel and Distributed Systems*, 4(2):175–187, Feb. 1993.

[13] H. Topcuoglu, S. Hariri, and M.-Y. Wu. Task scheduling algorithms for heterogeneous processors. In *IPPS/SPDP Workshop on Heterogeneous Computing*, pages 3–14, San Juan, Puerto Rico, Apr. 1999.

[14] M.-Y. Wu and W. Shu. A high-performance mapping algorithm for heterogeneous computing systems,. In *Int'l Parallel and Distributed Processing Symposium*, San Francisco, CA, Apr. 2001.

[15] J. Yang, A. Khokhar, S. Sheikh, and A. Ghafoor. Estimating execution time for parallel tasks in heterogeneous processing (HP) environment. In *IPPS Workshop on Heterogeneous Computing*, pages 23–28, Cancún, Mexico, Apr. 1994.

An Efficient Fault-tolerant Scheduling Algorithm for Real-time Tasks with Precedence Constraints in Heterogeneous Systems [*]

Xiao Qin   Hong Jiang   David R. Swanson
Department of Computer Science and Engineering
University of Nebraska-Lincoln
Lincoln, NE 68588-0115, {xqin, jiang, dswanson}@cse.unl.edu

Abstract

In this paper, we investigate an efficient off-line scheduling algorithm in which real-time tasks with precedence constraints are executed in a heterogeneous environment. It provides more features and capabilities than existing algorithms that schedule only independent tasks in real-time homogeneous systems. In addition, the proposed algorithm takes the heterogeneities of computation, communication and reliability into account, thereby improving the reliability. To provide fault-tolerant capability, the algorithm employs a primary-backup copy scheme that enables the system to tolerate permanent failures in any single processor. In this scheme, a backup copy is allowed to overlap with other backup copies on the same processor, as long as their corresponding primary copies are allocated to different processors. Tasks are judiciously allocated to processors so as to reduce the schedule length as well as the reliability cost, defined to be the product of processor failure rate and task execution time. In addition, the time for detecting and handling of a permanent fault is incorporated into the scheduling scheme, thus making the algorithm more practical. To quantify the combined performance of fault-tolerance and schedulability, the performability measure is introduced. Compared with the existing scheduling algorithms in the literature, our scheduling algorithm achieves an average of 16.4% improvement in reliability and an average of 49.3% improvement in performability.

1. Introduction

Heterogeneous distributed systems have been increasingly used for scientific and commercial applications, including real-time safety-critical applications, in which the system depends not only on the results of a computation, but also on the time instants at which these results become available. Examples of such applications include aircraft control, transportation systems and medical electronics. To obtain high performance for real-time heterogeneous systems, scheduling algorithms play an important role. While a scheduling algorithm maps real-time tasks to processors in the system such that deadlines and response time requirements are met, the system must also guarantee its functional and timing correctness even in the presence of faults.

The proposed algorithm, referred to as eFRCD (*efficient Fault-tolerant Reliability Cost Driven Algorithm*), endeavors to comprehensively address the issues of fault-tolerance, reliability, real-time, task precedence constraints, and heterogeneity. To tolerate one processor permanent failure, the algorithm uses a Primary/Backup technique to allocate two copies of each task to different processors. To further improve the quality of the schedule, a backup copy is allowed to overlap with other backup copies on the same processor, as long as their corresponding primary copies are allocated to different processors. As an added measure of fault-tolerance, the proposed algorithm also considers the heterogeneities of computation and reliability, thereby improving the reliability without extra hardware cost. More precisely, tasks are judiciously allocated to processors so as to reduce the schedule length as well as the reliability cost, defined to be the product of processor failure rate and task execution time. In addition, the time for detecting and handling of a permanent fault is incorporated into the scheduling scheme, thus making the algorithm more practical.

The rest of the paper is organized as follows. Section 2 briefly presents related work in the literature. Section 3 describes the workload and the system characteristics. Section 4 proposes the eFRCD algorithm and the main principles behind it, including theorems used for presenting the algorithm. Performance evaluation is given in Section 5. Section 6 concludes the paper by summarizing the main contributions of this paper.

[*] This work was supported by an NSF grant (EPS-0091900) and a Nebraska University Foundation grant (26-0511-0019)

2. Related work

The issue of scheduling on heterogeneous systems has been studied in the literature in recent years. A scheduling scheme, STDP, for heterogeneous systems was developed in [16]. In [3,17], reliability cost was incorporated into scheduling algorithms for tasks with precedence constraints. However, these algorithms neither provide fault-tolerance nor support real-time applications.

Previous work has been done to facilitate real-time computing in heterogeneous systems. In [7], a solution for the dynamic resource management problem in real-time heterogeneous systems was proposed. These algorithms, however, cannot tolerate any processor failure. Fault-tolerance is considered in the design of real-time scheduling algorithms to make systems more reliable.

In paper [6], a mechanism was proposed for supporting adaptive fault-tolerance in a real-time system. Liberato et al. proposed a feasibility-check algorithm for fault-tolerant scheduling [8]. The well-known Rate-Monotonic First-Fit assignment algorithm was extended in [2]. However, both of the above algorithms assume that the underlying system either is homogeneous or consists of a single processor.

The algorithm in [1] is a real-time scheduling algorithm for tasks with precedence constraint, but it does not support fault-tolerance. Manimaran et al. [9] and Mosse et al. [4] have proposed dynamic algorithms to schedule real-time tasks with fault-tolerance requirements on multiprocessor systems, but the tasks scheduled in their algorithms are independent of one another and are scheduled on-line. Martin [10] devised an algorithm on the same system and task model as that in [4]. Oh and Son studied a real-time and fault-tolerant scheduling algorithm that statically schedules a set of independent tasks [12]. Two common features among these algorithms [4,8,11, 12] are that (1) tasks are independent from one another and (2) they are designed only for homogeneous systems. Although heterogeneous systems are considered in both [17] and eFRCD, the latter considers fault-tolerance and real-time tasks while the former does not consider either.

Very recently, Girault et al. proposed a real-time scheduling algorithm for heterogeneous systems that considers fault-tolerance and tasks with precedence constraints [5]. This study is by far the closest to eFRCD that the authors have found in the literature. The main differences between [5] and eFRCD are three-fold: (a). eFRCD considers heterogeneities in computation, communication and reliability that will be defined shortly, whereas the former only considers computational heterogeneity. These hetero-geneities. (b). The former does not take reliability cost into consideration, whereas eFRCD is reliability-cost driven; and (c). The former allows the concurrent execution of primary and backup copies of a task while eFRCD allows backup copies of tasks whose primary copies are scheduled on different processors to overlap one another.

In the authors' previous work, both static [14,15] and dynamic [13] scheduling schemes for heterogeneous real-time systems were developed. One similarity among these algorithms is that the *Reliability Cost Driven Scheme* is applied. With the exception of the FRCD algorithm [15], other algorithms proposed in [13,14] cannot tolerate any failure. In this paper, the FRCD algorithm [15] is extended by relaxing the requirement that backup copies of tasks be not allowed to be overlapped.

3. Workload and system characteristics

A real-time job with dependent tasks can be modelled by *Directed Acyclic Graph (DAG)*, $T = \{V, E\}$, where $V = \{v_1, v_2,...,v_n\}$ is a set of tasks, and a set of edges E represents communication among tasks. $e_{ij} = (v_i, v_j) \in E$ indicates a message transmitted from task v_i to v_j, and $|e_{ij}|$ denotes the volume of data being sent. To tolerate permanent faults in one processor, a primary-backup technique is applied. Thus, each task has two copies, namely, v^P and v^B, executed sequentially on two different processors. Without loss of generality, it is assumed that two copies of a task are identical. The proposed approach also is applied when two copies of each task are different.

The heterogeneous system consists of a set $P = \{p_1, p_2,...,p_m\}$ of heterogeneous processors connected by a network. A processor communicates with other processors through message passing. A measure of *computational heterogeneity* is modeled by a function, $C: V \times P \rightarrow Z^+$, which represents the execution time of each task on each processor. Thus, $c_j(v_i)$ denotes the execution time of v_i on p_j. A measure of *communicational heterogeneity* is modeled by a function $M: E \times P \times P \rightarrow Z^+$. Communication time for sending a message e_{sr} from v_s on p_i to v_r on p_j is determined by $w_{ij}*|e_{sr}|$, where $|e_{sr}|$ is the communication cost and w_{ij} is the weight on the edge between p_i and p_j, representing the delay involved in transmitting a message of unit length between the two processors.

Given a task $v \in V$, $d(v)$, $s(v)$ and $f(v)$ denote the deadline, scheduled start time, and finish time, respectively. $p(v)$ denotes the processor to which v is allocated. These parameters are subject to constraints: $f(v) = s(v) + c_i(v)$ and $f(v) \leq d(v)$, where $p(v) = p_i$. A real-time job has a *feasible schedule* if for all $v \in V$, it satisfies both $f(v^P) \leq d(v)$, and $f(v^B) \leq d(v)$.

A *k-timely-fault-tolerant (k-TFT)* schedule is defined as the schedule in which no task deadlines are missed [12], despite k arbitrary processor failures. The goal of eFRCD is to achieve 1-TFT.

The reliability cost of task v_i on p_j is defined as the product of failure rate, λ_j, of p_j and v_i's execution time on p_j. It should be noted that *reliability heterogeneity* is implied in the reliability cost by virtue of heterogeneity in $c_j(v_i)$ and λ_j. Let $RC_0 (R, \Psi)$ and $RC_i(R, \Psi)$ $(1 \le i \le m)$ be the reliability cost when no processor fails and when p_i fails, where Ψ is a given schedule and $R = \{\lambda_1, \lambda_2, ..., \lambda_m\}$ is a set of failure rates for the processors. RC_0 and RC_i are determined by equation (1) and (2), respectively.

$$RC_0(R, \Psi) = \sum_{i=1}^{m} \sum_{p(v^P)=i} \lambda_i c_i(v) \qquad (1)$$

$$RC_i(R, \Psi) = \sum_{j=1, j\ne i}^{m} \sum_{p(v^P)=j} \lambda_j c_j(v) + \sum_{j=1, j\ne i}^{m} \sum_{p(v^P)=i, p(v^B)=j} \lambda_j c_j(v)$$

$$= \sum_{j=1, j\ne i}^{m} \left(\sum_{p(v^P)=j} \lambda_j c_j(v) + \sum_{p(v^P)=i, p(v^B)=j} \lambda_j c_j(v) \right) \qquad (2)$$

In equation (2), the first summation term on the right hand side represents the reliability cost due to tasks whose primary copies reside in fault-free processors, while the second summation term expresses the reliability cost due to the backup copies of the tasks whose primary copies reside in the failed processor.

Reliability, given in the following expression, captures the ability of the system to complete parallel jobs in the presence of one processor permanent failure.

$$RL(R, \Psi) = e^{-RC(R, \Psi)} \qquad (3)$$

4. Scheduling algorithms

In this section, we present the eFRCD algorithm, which has three objectives, namely, (1) total schedule length is reduced so that more tasks can complete before their deadlines; (2) permanent failures in one processor can be tolerated; and (3) The system reliability is enhanced by reducing the overall reliability cost of the schedule.

4.1 An outline

The key for tolerating a single processor failure is to allocate the primary and backup copies of a task to two different processors such that the backup copy subsequently executes if the primary copy fails to complete due to its processor failure. Not all backup copies need to execute, even in the presence of a single processor failure. Since only tasks allocated to the failed processor are affected and need their backup copies to be executed, certain backup copies can be scheduled to overlap with one another. More precisely, a v^B is allowed to overlap with other backup copies on the same processor, if the corresponding primary copies are allocated to the different processors to which the v^P is not allocated. Thus, in a feasible schedule, the primary copies of any two tasks must not be allocated to the same processor if their backup copies are on the same processor and there is an overlap between two the backup copies. This statement is formally described as below.

Proposition 1. $\forall v_i, v_j \in V : \left(p(v_i^B) = p(v_j^B) \right) \wedge$
$$\left(\left(s(v_i^B) \le s(v_j^B) < f(v_i^B) \right) \vee \left(s(v_j^B) \le s(v_i^B) < f(v_j^B) \right) \right) \to p(v_i^P) \ne p(v_j^P)$$

Fig. 1 Primary copies of v_i and v_j are allocated to p_1 and p_3, respectively, and backup copies of v_i and v_j are both allocated to p_2. These two backup copies can be overlapped with each other.

Fig. 1 shows an example illustrating this case. In this example, v_i^P and v_j^P are allocated to p_1 and p_3, respectively, and backup copies of v_i and v_j are both allocated to p_2. These two backup copies can be overlapped with each other because at most one of them will ever execute in the single-processor failure model.

The algorithm schedules tasks in the following three main steps. First, tasks are ordered by their deadlines in non-decreasing order, such that tasks with tighter deadlines have higher priorities. Second, the primary copies are scheduled. Finally, the backup copies are scheduled in a similar manner as the primary copies, except that they may be overlapped on the same processors to reduce schedule length. More specifically, in the second and third steps, the scheduling of each task must satisfy the following three conditions: (1) its deadline should be met; (2) the processor allocation should lead to the minimum increase in overall reliability cost among all processors satisfying condition (1); and (3) it should be able to receive messages from all its predecessors. In addition to these conditions, each backup copy has three extra conditions to satisfy, namely, (i) it is allocated on the processor that is different than the one assigned for its primary copy, (ii) its start time is later than the finish time of its primary copy plus the fault detection time δ and (iii) it is allowed to overlap with other backup copies on the same processor if their primary copies are allocated to different processors. Condition (i) and (ii) can be formally described by the following proposition.

Proposition 2. A schedule is 1-TFT
$$\to \forall v \in V : \left(p(v^P) \ne p(v^B) \right) \wedge \left(s(v^B) \ge f(v^P) + \delta \right).$$

4.2 The eFRCD algorithm

To facilitate the presentation of the algorithm, necessary notations are listed in the following table.

Table 1. Definitions of Notation

Notation	DEFINITION
$D(v)$	The set of predecessors of task v. $D(v) = \{v_i \mid (v_i, v) \in E\}$

$S(v)$	The set of successors of task v, $S(v) = \{v_i \mid (v, v_i) \in E\}$
$F(v)$	The set of feasible processors to which v^B can be allocated, determined in part by **Theorem 2**.
$B(v)$	The set of predecessors of v's backup copy, determined by Expression (7).
VQ_i	The queue in which all tasks are scheduled to p_i, $s(v_{q+1}) = \infty$, and $f(v_0) = 0$
$VQ_i'(v)$	The queue in which all tasks are scheduled to p_i, and cannot overlap with the backup copy of task v, where $s(v_{q+1}) = \infty$, and $f(v_0) = 0$
$v_i \succ v_j$	v_i is *schedule-preceding* v_j, if and only if $s(v_j) \geq f(v_i)$.
$v_i \Rightarrow v_j$	v_i is *message-preceding* v_j, if and only if v_i sends a message to v_j. Note that $v_i \Rightarrow v_j$ implies $v_i \succ v_j$ but not inversely.
$v_i \mapsto v_j$	v_i *execution-preceding* v_j, if and only if both tasks execute and $v_i \Rightarrow v_j$ Note that $v_i \mapsto v_j$ implies $v_i \Rightarrow v_j$ and $v_i \succ v_j$
$EAT_i^P(v)$	The *earliest available time* on p_i for v^P
$EAT_i^B(v)$	The earliest available time on p_i for v^B.
$EST_i^P(v)$	The earliest start time for v^P on processor p_i.
$EST_i^B(v)$	The earliest start time for v^B on processor p_i.

A detailed pseudocode of the eFRCD algorithm is presented below.

The eFRCD Algorithm:

Input: $T = \{V, E\}$, P, C, M, R /* DAG, Distributed System, Computational, Communicational and Reliability Heterogeneity */

Output: Schedule feasibility of T, and a viable schedule Ψ if it is feasible.

1. Sort tasks by the deadlines in non-decreasing order, subject to precedence constraints, and generate an ordered list OL;

2. /* Schedule primary copies of tasks */

for each task v in OL, following the order, schedule v^P **do**

  . 2.1 $s(v^P) \leftarrow \infty$; $rc \leftarrow \infty$; $VQ_i = \varnothing$;

  2.2 **for** each processor p_i **do** /* Check if v can be allocated to p_i */

  /* Calculate $EST_i^P(v)$, where $VQ_i = \{v_1, v_2, ..., v_q\}$ is the queue in */

  /* which all tasks are scheduled to p_i, $s(v_{q+1}) = \infty$, and $f(v_0) = 0$ */

    2.2.1 /*Compute the earliest start time of v on p_i */

    for $(j = 0$ to $q + 1)$ **do**

    /* check if the unoccupied time intervals, interspersed */

    /* by currently scheduled tasks, can accommodate v */

      if $s(v_{j+1}) - MAX\{f(v_j), EAT_i^P(v)\} \geq c_i(v)$ **then**

        $EST_i^P(v) = MAX\{f(v_j), EAT_i^P(v)\}$; **break;**

    end for

    2.2.2 /* Determine the earliest EST_i based on **Equation (6)** */

    if v^P starts executing at $EST_i^P(v)$ and can be completed before $d(v)$ **then**

      Determine reliability cost rc_i of v^P on p_i;

      /* Find the minimum reliability cost */

      if $((rc_i < rc$ **or** $(rc_i = rc$ and $EST_i^P(v) < s(v^P)))$ **then**

        $s(v^P) \leftarrow EST_i^P(v)$; $p \leftarrow p_i$; $rc \leftarrow rc_i$;

  end for

  2.3 **if** no proper processor is available for v^P, **then** return(FAIL);

  2.4 Assign p to v, where the reliability cost of v^P on p is the minimal; $VQ_i \leftarrow VQ_i + v^P$;

  2.5 Update information of messages;

end for

3. /*Schedule backup copies of tasks */

for each task v in the ordered list, schedule the backup copy v^B **do**

  3.1 $s(v^B) \leftarrow \infty$; $rc \leftarrow \infty$;

  /* Determine whether the v^B should be allocated to processor p_i */

  3.2 **for** each feasible processor $p_i \in F(v)$, subject to **Proposition 2** and **Theorem 2,** **do** /* identify backup copies already scheduled */

    3.2.1 **for** $(v_j \in VQ_i)$ **do** /* on p_i that can overlap with v^B */

      if $(v_j$ is a primary copy) **or** $((v_j$ is a backup copy) **and** $(p(v_j) = p(v)))$ **then** /* subject to **Proposition 1** */

        copy v_j into task queue $VQ_i'(v)$;

    3.2.2 Determine if v^P is a strong primary copy (using **Theorem 4**);

    3.2.3 **for** (all v_j in task queue $VQ_i'(v)$) **do** /*check the unoccupied */

/* time intervals, and time slots occupied by backup copies */

/* that *can overlap* with v^B, can accommodate v^B */

      if $s(v_{j+1}) - MAX\{f(v_j), EAT_i^B(v)\} \geq c_i(v)$ **then**

        $EST_i^B(v) = MAX\{f(v_j), EAT_i^B(v)\}$; **break;**

    end for

    3.2.4 /*Determine the earliest EST_i based on **Equation (9)** */

    if v starts executing at $EST_i^B(v)$ and can be completed before $d(v)$ **then**

      Determine reliability cost rc_i of v^P on p_i;

      /* Find the minimum rc */

      if $((rc_i < rc)$ **or** $(rc_i = rc$ and $EST_i^B(v) < s(v^B)))$ **then**

        $s(v^B) \leftarrow EST_i^B(v)$; $p \leftarrow p_i$; $rc \leftarrow rc_i$;

    end if

  end for

  3.3 **if** no proper processor is available v^B, **then** return(FAIL);

  3.4 Find and assign $p \in F(v)$ to v, where the reliability cost of v^B on p is the minimal; $VQ_i \leftarrow VQ_i + v^B$;

  3.5 Update information of messages;

  3.6 **for** each task $v_j \in B(v)$ **do** /* avoid redundant messages */

    v_j sends message to v^B if possible; (based on **Theorem 1** and **Expression (7)**)

  3.7 **for** each task $v_j \in S(v)$ **do** /* avoid redundant messages */

    if $p(v^P) \neq p(v_j^P)$ **or** v^P is not a strong primary copy **then**

      v^B sends message to v_j^P if possible; (based on **Theorem 3**)

end for

return (SUCCEED);

4.3 The scheduling principles

Recall that $EST(v)$ and $EAT(v)$ are important to determine a proper schedule for a given task v. While both EAT and EST indicate a time when all messages from v's predecessors have arrived, EST additionally signifies that the processor to which v is allocated is now available for v to start execution. In the following, we present a series of derivations that lead to the final expressions for $EAT(v)$ and $EST(v)$.

If only one of v's predecessors $v_j \in D(v)$ is considered, then the earliest available time $EAT_i(v, v_j)$ for the primary/ backup copies of task v depends on the finish time $f(v_j)$, the earliest message start time $MST_{ik}(e)$, and the transmission time $w_{ik}*|e|$, for message e sent from v_j to v, where $p_k = p(v_j)$. Thus,

$$EAT_i(v, v_j) = \begin{cases} f(v_j) & \text{if } p_i = p_k \\ MST_{ik}(e) + w_{ik}*|e| & \text{otherwise} \end{cases} \quad (4)$$

Now consider all predecessors of v. Clearly v must wait until the last message from all its predecessors has arrived. Thus the earliest available time for v^P on p_i, $EAT_i^P(v)$ is the maximum of $EAT_i(v, v_j)$ over all the predecessors.

$$EAT_i^P(v) = MAX_{v_j \in D(v)} \{EAT_i(v^P, v_j^P)\} \quad (5)$$

Based on expression (5), $EST_i^P(v)$ on p_i can be computed by checking the queue VQ_i to find out if the processor has an idle time slot that starts later than task's $EAT_i^P(v)$ and is large enough to accommodate the task. This procedure is described in step 2.2.1 in the algorithm. $EST_i^P(v)$ is applied to derive $EST^P(v)$, the earliest start time for v^P on any processor. Expression for $EST^P(v)$ is given below.

$$EST^P(v) = \underset{p_i \in P'}{MIN}\left\{EST_i^P(v)\right\} \qquad (6)$$

where $P' = \left\{ p_i \in P'' \mid c_i(v) \times \lambda_i = \underset{p_{i_j} \in P''}{MIN}\left\{c_j(v) \times \lambda_j\right\}\right\}$, and

$P'' = \{p_i \in P \mid EST_i^P(v) + c_i(v) < d(v)\}$.

$EST^B(v)$, the earliest start time for v^B, is computed in a more complex way than $EST^P(v)$. This is because the set of predecessors of v^P, $D^P(v)$, contains exclusively the primary copies of v's predecessor tasks, whereas the set of predecessors of v^B, $B(v)$, may contain a certain combination of the primary and backup copies of v's predecessor tasks. In order to decide $B(v)$, it is necessary to introduce the notion of *strong primary copy* as follows.

Note that there are two cases in which v^P may fail to execute: (1) $p(v^P)$ fails before time $f(v^P)$, and (2) v^P fails to receive messages from all its predecessors. Case (2) is illustrated by a simple example in Fig. 2 where dotted lines denote messages sent from predecessors to successors. Let v_j be a predecessor of v, and $p(v) \neq p(v_j)$. Suppose at time $t < f(v_j^P)$, $p(v_j^P)$ fails, then v_j^B should execute. Suppose v_j^B is not schedule-preceding v^P, v^P can not receive any message from v_j^B. Hence, even if $p(v^P)$ does not fail, v^P still can not execute. The primary copy of a task that never encounters case (2) is referred to as a *strong primary copy*, as formally defined below.

Definition 1. Given a task v, v^P is a strong primary copy, if and only if the execution of v^B implies the failure of $p(v^P)$ before time $f(v^P)$). Alternatively, given a task v, v^P is a strong primary copy, if and only if no failures of $p(v^P)$ at time $f(v^P)$) imply the execution of v^P.

Recall that one assumption is that only one processor will encounter permanent failures, we observe that if v_i is a predecessor of v_j, and the primary copies of both tasks are strong primary copies, then v_i^B is not message-preceding v_j^B. Fig. 3 illustrates a scenario of the case, which is presented formally in the theorem 1 that is helpful in determining the set of predecessors for a backup copy (See step 3.6).

Theorem 1. Given two tasks v_i and v_j, v_i is a predecessor of v_j. v_i^B is *not message-preceding* v_j^B, meaning that v_i^B does not need to send message to v_j^B, if v_i^P and v_j^P are both strong primary copies, and $p(v_i^P) \neq p(v_j^P)$.

Proof: Since v_i^P and v_j^P are both strong primary copies, according to Definition 1, v_i^B and v_j^B can both execute if and only if both v_i^P and v_j^P have failed to execute due to processor failures. But v_i^P and v_j^P are allocated to two different processors, an impossibility. Thus, at least one of v_i^B and v_j^B will not execute, implying that no messages need to be sent from v_i^B to v_j^B. ☐

Let $B(v) \subset V$ be the set of predecessors of v^B. It is defined as follows.

$B(v) = \{ v_i^P \mid v_i \in D(v)\} \cup \{v_i^B \mid v_i \in D(v) \wedge$
$(v_i^P$ *is not a strong primary copy* $\vee v^P$ *is not a strong primary copy* $\vee p(v_i^P) = p(v^P))\} = D^P(v) \cup D^B(v)$ (7)

In the eFRCD algorithm, the primary copy is allocated before its corresponding backup copy is scheduled. Hence, given a task v and its predecessor $v_i \in D(v)$, two copies of v_i should have been allocated when the algorithm starts scheduling v^B. Obviously, v^B must receive

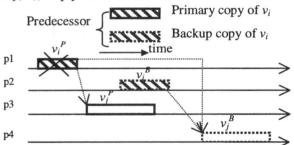

Fig. 2 Since processor p₁ fails, v_i^B executes. Becuase v_j^P can not receive message from v_i^B, v_j^B must execute instead of v_j^P.

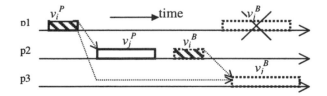

Fig. 4 $(v_i, v_j) \in E$, v_i^B is not schedule-preceding v_j^P and v_i^P is a strong primary copy. v_j^B can not be scheduled on the processor on which v_i^P is scheduled.

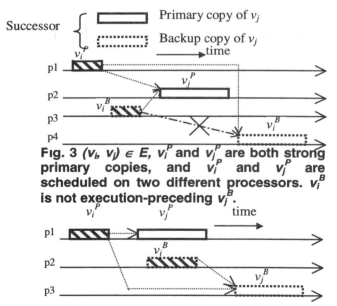

Fig. 3 $(v_i, v_j) \in E$, v_i^P and v_j^P are both strong primary copies, and v_i^P and v_j^P are scheduled on two different processors. v_i^B is not execution-preceding v_j^B.

Fig. 5 v_i is the predecessor of v_j, v_i^P and v_j^P are scheduled on the same processor, and v_i^P is the strong primary copy. In this case, v_i^B is not execution-preceding v_j^B.

message from v_i^P and all $v_i^B \in D^B(v)$. Therefore, the maximum earliest available time of v^B on p_i is determined by the primary copies of its predecessors, the backup copies of tasks in $D^B(v)$ and messages sent from these tasks. $EAT_i^B(v)$ is given in the expression below, where δ is a certain amount of time to detect and handle the fault.

$$EAT_i^B(v) =$$

$$MAX\{f(v^P) + \delta, MAX_{v_j^P \in D^P(v)}(EAT_i(v^B, v_j^P)), MAX_{v_j^B \in D^B(v)}(EAT_i(v^B, v_j^B))\}$$

$$= MAX_{v_j^P \in D^P(v), v_k^B \in D^B(v)}\{f(v^P) + \delta, EAT_i(v^B, v_j^P), EAT_i(v^B, v_j^B)\} \quad (8)$$

$EST_i^B(v)$ and $EST^B(v)$ denote the earliest start time for v^B on p_i, and the earliest start time for v^B on any processor, respectively. The computation of $EST_i^B(v)$ is more complex than that of $EST_i^P(v)$, due to the need to judiciously overlap some backup copies on the same processors. The computation of $EST_i^B(v)$ can be found from step 3.2.3 in the above algorithm. The *backup-overlapping scheme* (BOV) is implemented in step 3.2, which attempts to reduce schedule length by selectively overlapping backup copies of tasks. The expression for $EST^B(v)$ is given below,

$$EST^B(v) = MIN_{p_i \in P'}\{EST_i^B(v)\} \quad (9)$$

where $P' = \left\{p_i \in P'' \mid c_i(v) \times \lambda_i = MIN_{p_{ij} \in P'}\{c_j(v) \times \lambda_j\}\right\}$, and

$P'' = \{p_i \in F(v) \mid EST_i^B(v) + c_i(v) < d(v)\}$.

The candidate processor p_i in P'' is not chosen directly from the set P. Instead, it is selected from $F(v)$, a set of feasible processors to which the backup copy of v can be allocated. Obviously, $p(v^P)$ is not an element of $F(v)$. Given a task v, it is observed that under some special circumstance, v^B cannot be scheduled on the processor where the primary copy of v's predecessor v_i^P is scheduled (Fig. 4 illustrates this scenario). The set $F(v)$ can be generated will help of Theorem 2.

Theorem 2. Given two tasks v_i and v_j, $(v_i, v_j) \in E$, if v_i^B is not schedule-preceding v_j^P, and v_i^P is a strong primary copy, then v_j^B and v_i^P can not be allocated to the same processor.

Proof: Suppose the theorem is incorrect, thus, v_j^B and v_i^P are allocated to the same processor. Assume that v_i^B executes instead of v_i^P. This, combined with the fact that v_i^P is a strong primary copy, implies that $p(v_i^P)$ has failed before time $f(v_i^P)$. Since $f(v_i^P) < f(v_j^B)$, it also implies that $p(v_i^P)$ has failed before time $f(v_j^B)$, indicating that v_j^B will not execute. v_i^B cannot be execution-preceding v_j^P, since v_i^B is not schedule-preceding v_j^P. Hence, v_i^B must be execution-preceding v_j^B, impling that v_j^B does execute. A contradiction. □

Recall that $EAT_i(v, v_j)$ in expression (4) is a basic parameter used to derive $EAT_i^P(v)$ in expression (5) and $EAT_i^B(v)$ in expression (8). $EAT_i(v, v_j)$ is determined by the start time $MST_{ik}(e)$ of message e sent from $p_i = p(v)$ to $p_k = p(v_j)$. A message is allocated to a link if the link has

an idle time slot that is later than the sender's finish time and is large enough to accommodate the message. $MST_{ik}(e)$ is computed by the following procedure, where $e = (v_j, v)$, $MST(e_{r+1}) = \infty$, $MST(e_0) = 0$, $|e_0| = 0$, and $MQ_i = \{e_1, e_2, ..., e_r\}$ is the message queue containing all messages scheduled to the link from p_i to p_k. This procedure behaves in a similar manner as the procedure for computing $EST_i^P(v)$ in step 2.2.1.

Computation of $MST_{ik}(e)$:
1. **for** (g = 0 to r + 1) **do** /* Check whether the idle time slots */
   /* If the idle time slots can accommodate v, return the value */
2. **if** $MST_{ik}(e_{g+1}) - MAX\{MST_{ik}(e_g) + w_{ik}*|e_g|, f(v_j)\} \geq w_{ik}*|e|$ **then**
3. **return** $MAX\{MST_{ik}(e_g) + w_{ik}*|e_g|, f(v_j)\}$;
4. **end for**
5. **return** ∞; /* No such idle time slots is found, MST is set to be ∞ */

In scheduling messages, the proposed algorithm tries to avoid sending redundant messages in step 3.7, which is based on theorem 3. Suppose v_j^P has successfully executed, either v_i^P is execution-preceding v_j^P or v_i^B is execution-preceding v_j^P. We observe that, in some special cases illustrated in Fig 5, v_i^B will never be execution-preceding v_j^P. This statement is described Theorem 3.

Theorem 3. Given two tasks v_i and v_j, $(v_i, v_j) \in E$, if the primary copies of v_i and v_j are allocated to the same processor and v_i^P is a strong primary copy, then v_i^B *is not execution-preceding* v_j^P, meaning that sending a message from v_i^B to v_j^P would be redundant.

Proof: By contradiction: Assume v_i^B *is* execution-preceding v_j^P, thus, both v_i^B and v_j^P must execute (Table 1). Since v_i^P is a strong primary copy, processor $p(v_i^P)$ must have failed before time $f(v_i^P)$ (Def. 1). But v_i^P and v_j^P are allocated to the same processor and v_i^P is schedule-preceding v_j^P, implying that v_j^P also could not execute. A contradiction. □

The notion of strong primary copy appears in Theorems 1-3, it is therefore necessary to be able to determine whether a task has a strong primary copy. Theorem 4, applied to eFRCD in step 3.2.2, suggests an approach to determining whether a task has a strong primary copy. In this approach, we assume that we already know if all the predecessors have strong primary copies or not. By using this approach recursively, starting from tasks with no predecessors, we are able to determine whether a given task has a strong primary copy.

Theorem 4. (a) A task with no predecessors has a strong primary copy. (b) Given a task v_i and any of its predecessors v_j, if they are allocated to the same processor and v_j has a strong primary copy, or, if they are allocated on two different processors and the backup copy of v_j is message-preceding the primary copy of v_i, then v_i has a strong primary copy. That is, $\forall v_j \in V, (v_j, v_i) \in E: ((p(v_i^P) = p(v_j^P) \wedge (v_j^P \text{ is a strong primary copy})) \vee (p(v_i^P) \neq p(v_j^P) \wedge (v_j^B \Rightarrow v_i^P)) \rightarrow (v_i^P \text{ is a strong primary copy}).$

Proof: As the proof of (a) is straightforward from the definition, it is omitted here. We only prove (b). Suppose before time $f(v_i^P)$, processor $p(v_i^P)$ does not fail. Let v_j be a predecessor of v_i. There are two possibilities: (1) $p(v_i^P) = p(v_j^P)$, we have $f(v_j^P) < f(v_i^P)$, implying that processor $p(v_j^P)$ does not fail before $f(v_i^P)$. Because v_j^P is a strong primary copy, v_j^P must execute. (2) $p(v_i^P) \neq p(v_j^P)$ and $v_j^B \Rightarrow v_i^P$, implying that even if one processor fails, v_i^P can still receive message from task v_j (recall that $v_j^P \Rightarrow v_i^P$). Based on (1) and (2), we have proven that v_i^P can receive messages from all its predecessors. Thus, v_i^P must execute since $p(v_j^P)$ has not failed by time $f(v_i^P)$. Therefore, according to Defnition 1, v_i^P is a strong primary copy. $\quad\square$

5. Performance evaluation

In this section, we compare the performance of the proposed algorithm with three other algorithms in the literature, namely, OV [12], FGLS [5], and FRCD [15] by extensive simulations.

Three performance measures are used to capture three important but different aspects of the algorithms. The first measure is *schedulability (SC)*, defined to be the percentage of parallel real-time *jobs* that have been successfully scheduled among all submitted jobs. The second is *reliability (RL)*, defined in expression (3). To combine the performances of the first two measures, the third measure, *performability (PF)*, is defined to be a product of *SC* and *RL*.

It is noted that the four algorithms differ in some aspects. First, OV assumes independent tasks and homogeneous systems, whereas FRCD, eFRCD and FGLS consider tasks with precedence constraints that execute on heterogeneous systems. Second, among FRCD, eFRCD and FGLS, while the former two incorporate computational, communicational and reliability heterogeneities into the scheduling, the latter considers only computational heterogeneity. To make the comparison fair, FGLS, FRCD and eFRCD are downgraded to handle independent tasks that execute on homogeneous systems.

Similarly, in Sections 5.4, the eFRCD algorithm is downgraded by assuming communicational homogeneity, while the FGLS algorithm is adapted to include reliability heterogeneity.

5.1 The workload

Workload parameters are chosen either based on those used in the literature [14,17] or represent realistic workload. In each simulation experiment, 100,000 real-time DAGs were generated independently for the scheduling algorithm as follows: First, determine the number of real-time tasks N, the number of processors m and their failure rates R. Then, the computation time in the execution time vector C is randomly chosen and uniformly distributed in a given range. Third, data communication among real-time tasks and communi-

cation weights are uniformly selected from *1* to *10*. Fourth, the failure rates were uniformly selected from a given range. Finally, the fault detection time δ is randomly computed according to a uniform distribution. Real-time deadlines can be defined in two ways:
1. A single deadline associated with a real-time job, which is a predetermined set of tasks with or without precedence constraints. Such a deadline, referred to as a *common deadline* [10,11,12], was employed in OV. To make a fair comparison, the common deadline is applied to FGLS, FRCD and eFRCD in simulation studies reported in Sections 5.2 and 5.3.
2. Individual deadlines associated with tasks within a real-time job. This deadline definition is often used for the dynamic scheduling of independent real-time tasks [4,8]. In sections 5.4, this deadline definition was adapted for tasks with precedence constraints. More specifically, given $v_i \in V$, if v_i is on p_k and v_j is on p_l, then v_i's deadline is determined by: $d(v_i) = MAX\{d(v_j)\} + |e_{ij}| \times w_{lk} + MAX\{c_k(v_i)\} + t$, where $e_{ij} \in E$, $k \in [1, m]$, t is chosen uniformly from a given range H that represents the individual relative deadline.

5.2 Schedulability

This experiment evaluates performance in terms of schedulability among the four algorithms, namely, OV, FGLS, FRCD and eFRCD, using the *SC* measure. The workload consists of sets of independent real-time tasks that are to be executed on a homogeneous distributed system. The size of the homogeneous system is fixed at 20, and a common deadline of 100 is selected. The failure rates are uniformly selected from the range between $0.5*10^{-6}$ and $3.0*10^{-6}$. Execution time is a random variable uniformly distributed in the range [1, 20]. *SC* is first measured as a function of task set size as shown in Fig. 6.

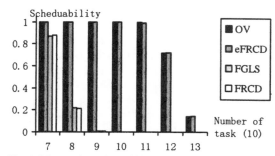

Fig. 6 SC as a function of N. Deadline= 100, m=16.

Fig. 6 shows that the SC performances of OV and eFRCD are almost identical, and so are FGLS and FRCD. Considering that eFRCD had to be downgraded for comparability, this result should imply that eFRCD is more powerful than OV, because eFRCD can also schedule tasks with precedence constraints to be executed on heterogeneous systems, which OV is not capable of.

The results further reveal that both OV and eFRCD significantly outperform FGLS and FRCD in *SC*, suggesting that both FGLS and FRCD are not suitable for scheduling independent tasks. The poor performance of FGLS and FRCD can be explained by the fact that they do not employ the BOV scheme. The consequence is twofold. First, FGLS and FRCD require more computing resources than eFRCD, which is likely to lead to a relatively low *SC* when the number of processors is fixed. Second, the backup copies in FGLS and FRCD cannot overlap with one another on the same processor, and this may result in a much longer schedule length.

5.3 Reliability performance

In this experiment, the reliability of the OV, FGLS, FRCD and eFRCD algorithms are evaluated as a function of maximum processor failure rate, shown in Fig. 7. To stress the reliability performance, *SC*s of all the four algorithms are assumed to be 1.0, by assigning an extremely loose common deadline. The task set size and system sizes are 200 and 20, respectively. Execution time of each task is chosen uniformly from the range between 500 and 1500. The failure rates were uniformly selected from range $[1.0*10^{-6}, MAX\_F]$, where MAX_F varies from $3.5*10^{-6}$ to $7.5*10^{-6}$ per hour with increments of $0.5*10^{-6}$.

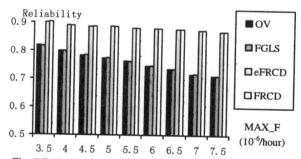

Fig. 7 Reliability as function of MAX_F. N = 50, m = 20.

As can be observed in Fig. 7, the *RL* of OV and FGLS are very close, and so are those of FRCD and eFRCD. FRCD and eFRCD perform considerably better than both OV and FGLS, with *RL* values being approximately from 10.5% to 22.3% higher than those of OV and FGLS. The FRCD and eFRCD algorithms have much better reliability simply because OV and FGLS do not consider reliability in their scheduling schemes while both FRCD and eFRCD take reliability into account. This experimental result validates the use of the proposed FRCD and eFRCD algorithm to enhance the reliability of the system, especially when tasks either have loose deadlines or no deadlines.

5.4 Effect of computational heterogeneity

The computational heterogeneity is reflected by the variance in execution times of the computation time vector *C*, and therefore a metric $\eta=(\alpha,\beta)$ is introduced to represent the computational heterogeneity level, where α =(MIN_E+MAX_E)/2 is the average value for execution time in *C*, and $\beta = \alpha$ - MIN_E is the deviation of *C*. Clearly, the higher the value of β, the higher the level of heterogeneity. To study the effect of the heterogeneity level on the *PF* of FGLS and eFRCD, α is fixed to 20 and β is chosen from 0 to 28 with increments of 4. Fig. 8 shows *PF* as a function of β, the heterogeneity level.

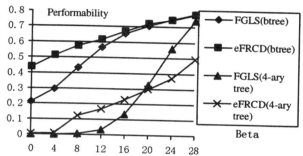

Fig. 8 PF of btree and 4-ary tree as a function of heterogeneity level. H=[1,100], N=150, m=20, alpha=20

The first observation from Fig. 8 is that the value of *PF* increases with the heterogeneity level. This is because *PF* is a product of *SC* and *RL*, and both *SC* and *RL* become higher when the heterogeneity level increases. These results can be further explained by the following reasons. First, though the individual relative deadlines are not affected by the change in computational heterogeneity, high variance in task execution times does affect the absolute deadlines, making the deadlines looser and the *SC* higher. Second, high variance in task execution times also provides opportunities for more tasks to be packed in with the fixed number of processors, giving rise to a higher *SC*. Third, *RC* decreases as the heterogeneity level increases, implying an increasing *RL*.

A second interesting observation is that eFRCD outperforms FGLS with respect to *PF* at low heterogeneity levels while the opposite is true for high heterogeneity levels. This is because when heterogeneity levels are low, both *SC* and *RL* of eFRCD are considerably higher than those of FGLS. On the other hand, eFRCD's *SC* is lower than that of FGLS at a high heterogeneity level, and *RL*s of two algorithms become similar when heterogeneity level increases. Therefore, eFRCD's *PF*, the product of *SC* and *RL*, is lower than that of FGLS at high heterogeneity levels. This result suggests that, if *SC* is the only objective in scheduling, FGLS is more suitable for systems with relatively high levels of heterogeneity, whereas eFRCD is more suitable for scheduling tasks with relatively low levels of heterogeneity. In contrast, if *RL* is the sole objective, eFRCD is consistently better than FGLS. In addition, Fig.8 indicates that performability of FGLS increases much more rapidly with heterogeneity level than that of eFRCD, implying that FGLS is more sensitive to the change in computational heterogeneity than eFRCD.

6. Conclusion

In this paper, an efficient fault-tolerant and real-time scheduling algorithm (eFRCD) for heterogeneous systems executing tasks with precedence constraints is studied. The fault-tolerant capability is incorporated in the algorithm by using a Primary/Backup (PB) model, in which each task is associated with two copies that are allocated to two different processors. eFRCD relaxes the requirement in FRCD [15] that forbids the overlapping of any backup copies to allow such overlapping on the same processor if their corresponding primary copies are allocated to different processors. The system reliability is further enhanced by reducing overall reliability cost while scheduling tasks. Moreover, the algorithm takes system and workload heterogeneity into consideration by explicitly accounting for computational, communicational, and reliability heterogeneity.

To the best of our knowledge, the proposed algorithm is the first of its kind reported in the literature, in that it most comprehensively addresses the issues of fault-tolerance, reliability, real-time, task precedence constraints, and heterogeneity. To assess the performance of eFRCD, extensive simulation studies were conducted to quantitatively compare it with the three most relevant existing scheduling algorithms in the literature, OV [12], FGLS [5], and FRCD [15]. The simulation results indicate that the eFRCD algorithm is considerably superior to the three algorithms in the vast majority of cases. There are two exceptions, however. First, the FGLS outperforms eFRCD marginally when task parallelism is low. Second, when computational heterogeneity is high, the eFRCD algorithm becomes inferior to the FGLS algorithm.

References

[1] T.F. Abdelzaher and K.G. Shin., "Combined Task and Message Scheduling in Distributed Real-Time Systems," *IEEE Transaction on Parallel and Distributed Systems*, Vol. 10, No. 11, Nov. 1999.

[2] Alan A. Bertossi, Luigi V. Mancini, Federico Rossini, "Fault-Tolerant Rate-Monotonic First-Fit Scheduling in Hard-Real-Time Systems," *IEEE Trans. Parallel and Distributed Systems*, 10(9), pp. 934-945, 1999.

[3] A. Dogan,F. Ozguner, "Reliable matching and scheduling of precedence-constrained tasks in heterogeneous distributed computing,"*In Proc. of the 29th International Conference on Parallel Processing*, pp. 307-314, 2000.

[4] S. Ghosh, R. Melhem and D. Mosse, "Fault-Tolerance through Scheduling of Aperiodic Tasks in Hard Real-Time Multiprocessor Systems", *IEEE Trans. On Parallel and Distributed Systems*. Vol 8, no 3, pp. 272-284, 1997

[5] A. Girault, C. Lavarenne, M. Sighireanu and Y. Sorel, "Fault-Tolerant Static Scheduling for Real-Time Distributed Embedded Systems," *In Proc. of the 21st International Conference on Distributed Computing Systems*(ICDCS), Phoenix, USA, April 2001.

[6] O. Gonzalez, H. Shrikumar, J.A. Stankovic and K. Ramamritham, "Adaptive Fault Tolerance and Graceful Degradation Under Dynamic Hard Real-time Scheduling," *In Proc. of the 18th IEEE Real-Time Systems Symposium*, San Francisco, California, December 1997.

[7] E.N. Huh, L.R. Welch, B.A. Shirazi and C.D. Cavanaugh, "Heterogeneous Resource Management for Dynamic Real-Time Systems," *In Proc. of the 9th Heterogeneous Computing Workshop*, 287-296, 2000.

[8] F. Liberato, R. Melhem, and D. Mossé, "Tolerance to Multiple Transient Faults for Aperiodic Tasks in Hard Real-Time Systems," *IEEE Transactions on Computers*, Vol. 49, No. 9, September 2000.

[9] G. Manimaran and C. Siva Ram Murthy, "A Fault-Tolerant Dynamic Scheduling Algorithm for Multiprocessor Real-Time Systems and Its Analysis," *IEEE Transactions on Parallel and Distributed Systems*, 9(11), November 1998.

[10] M. Naedele, "Fault-Tolerant Real-Time Scheduling under Execution Time Constraints," Sixth International Conference on Real-Time Computing Systems and Applications, Hong Kong, China, 13 - 15 December, 1999.

[11] Y.Oh and S.H.Son, "An algorithm for real-time fault-tolerant scheduling in multiprocessor systems," *4th Euromicro Workshop on Real-Time Systems*, Greece, 1992, pp.190-195.

[12]Y. Oh and S. H. Son, "Scheduling Real-Time Tasks for Dependability," Journal of Operational Research Society, vol. 48, no. 6, pp 629-639, June 1997.

[13]X. Qin, and H. Jiang, "Dynamic, Reliability-driven Scheduling of Parallel Real-time Jobs in Heterogeneous Systems," *In Proc. of the 30th International Conference on Parallel Processing*, Valencia, Spain, pp.113-122, 2001.

[14]X. Qin, H. Jiang, C.S. Xie, and Z.F. Han, "Reliability-driven scheduling for real-time tasks with precedence constraints in heterogeneous distributed systems," *In Proc. of the 12th International Conference Parallel and Distributed Computing and Systems,* pp.617-623, November 2000.

[15]X. Qin, H. Jiang, and D.R. Swanson, "A Fault-tolerant Real-time Scheduling Algorithm for Precedence-Constrained Tasks in Distributed Heterogeneous Systems," *Technical Report TR-UNL-CSE 2001-1003*, Department of Computer Science and Engineering, University of Nebraska-Lincoln, September 2001.

[16] S. Ranaweera, and D.P. Agrawal, "Scheduling of Periodic Time Critical Applications for Pipelined Execution on Heterogeneous Systems," *In Proc. of the 2001 International Conference on Parallel Processing*, Valencia, Spain, Sept 4-7, 2001, pp. 131-138.

[17] S. Srinivasan, and N.K. Jha, "Safty and Reliability Driven Task Allocation in Distributed Systems," *IEEE Trans. Parallel and Distributed Systems*, 10(3), pp. 238-251, 1999.

Session 5C

Clusters: Programming

Efficient Global Object Space Support for Distributed JVM on Cluster[*]

Weijian Fang, Cho-Li Wang and Francis C.M. Lau
Department of Computer Science and Information Systems
The University of Hong Kong
{wjfang+clwang+fcmlau}@csis.hku.hk

Abstract

We present the design of a global object space in a distributed Java Virtual Machine that supports parallel execution of a multi-threaded Java program on a cluster of computers. The global object space virtualizes a single Java object heap across machine boundaries to facilitate transparent object accesses. Based on the object connectivity information that is available at runtime, the object reachable from threads at different nodes, named as distributed-shared object, are detected. With the detection of distributed-shared objects, we can alleviate overheads in maintaining the memory consistency within the global object space. Several runtime optimization methods have been incorporated in the global object space design, including an object home migration method that reallocates the home of a distributed-shared object, synchronized method migration that allows the remote execution of a synchronized method at the home node of its synchronized object, and object pushing that uses the object connectivity information to improve access locality.

1. Introduction

A *distributed Java Virtual Machine* (JVM) supports parallel execution of a multi-threaded Java application on a distributed-memory platform like cluster without any modification on the Java program. Java threads created within the program can be transparently distributed among the cluster nodes to achieve a higher degree of execution parallelism and leverage cluster resources to solve large-scale problems.

Due to the popularity of Java [3], distributed JVM has recently become an attractive research problem and several experimental prototypes have emerged. Java/DSM [18], cJVM [2], Hyperion [14], Jackal [17] and JESSICA [13], are some of the well-known examples. The distributed JVM presents a *single system image* (SSI) [8] to Java applications through the creation of a *global*

object space (GOS) that "virtualizes" a single Java object heap across multiple cluster nodes to facilitate transparent object access in a distributed environment. For example, the JESSICA system [13] which uses a page-based DSM systems, JUMP [4], to build the GOS. This approach greatly alleviates the burden of the construction of GOS because all the memory consistency issues, such as object faulting, addressing, replication policy, and transmission mechanism, are all managed by the DSM's cache coherence protocol. Such a design, however, suffered from a mismatch between object-based memory model of Java and the underlying page-based DSM implementation. For example, the false sharing problem occurs because of inconsistent sharing granularity between the variable-sized Java objects and the fix-sized memory pages. As thus, the performance of JESSICA was not satisfactory [5]. More efficient solutions to support object sharing among distributed Java threads is demanded.

In this paper, a new *global object space* support for distributed JVM is proposed. We define two types of Java objects: *node-local object* that is reachable from the threads that are at the same cluster node, and *distributed-shared object* (DSO) that is reachable from at least two threads that are located at different cluster nodes.

We argue that the separation of distributed-shared objects and node-local objects can alleviate overheads in maintaining the memory consistency within the global object space and achieve better performance of distributed JVM. Firstly, only distributed-shared objects suffer from heavy overheads in maintaining the memory consistency since they may have multiple duplicated copies on different nodes. Detection of DSOs could make consistency protocol be more lightweight. Secondly, in Java program, synchronization primitives are not only used to protect critical section but also to maintain memory consistency. Synchronization operations on a node-local object do not need to trigger the distributed operations to maintain consistency, because node-local objects are only reachable from some local threads. Detection of DSO makes consistency maintaining less frequently. Thirdly, it is not necessary to apply the

[*] This research is supported by Hong Kong RGC grant HKU-7030/01E.

distributed garbage collection operations on node-local objects since it is safe to garbage collect node-local objects locally.

We proposed a lightweight solution for detecting the distributed-shared objects. Distributed-shared objects can be detected using an object connectivity graph derived from object reference information that is available at runtime. Our GOS design further leverages the identification of distributed-shared objects and the availability of connectivity information for realizing the Java memory model in a distributed JVM. Such connectivity information was not exploited in most of the previous object-based or page-based DSM systems.

Several areas of optimizations have been proposed in our GOS design: (1) the *object home migration* that reduces communication traffic by migrating the home of a distributed-shared object to a node that need to access the object more frequently; (2) *synchronized method migration* that optimizes critical section execution by shipping a synchronized method to the home node of its synchronized object; (3) *object pushing* that uses connectivity information to prefetch objects for achieving better access locality.

We have tested our design in our JESSICA distributed JVM. The preliminary results show that our approach is promising. With all the optimizations enabled, all four benchmark programs achieved an efficiency of over 84% on four nodes, and all achieved an efficiency of over 75% on eight nodes except one program.

The next section discusses the detection of distributed-shared objects in detail. Section 3 describes our home-based multiple-writer cache coherence protocol that implements the Java memory model. Section 4 discusses various optimizations implemented in GOS. Performance results are reported in section 5. In section 6, several related works are discussed and compared with our GOS. Conclusions are given in Section 7.

2. Distributed-shared Object

In the JVM, each variable, including not only object field that resides in the heap but also thread-local variable that resides in the Java thread stacks, has a type, either a reference type or a primitive type, such as integer, char, or float. This type information is known at compile time and written into class files generated by the compiler. At runtime, the class loader builds up type information from class files. Thus, by looking up runtime type information, we can identify those variables that are of reference type.

2.1 Connectivity Graph and Reachability

If an object's field contains a reference to another object, connectivity exists between these two objects. Instance objects created during runtime will strictly conform to the type information of the class. Therefore, a *connectivity graph* can be built to describe the referential relationship among all objects. The graph is dynamic since connectivity between objects may change from time to time through the reassignment of objects fields.

Reachability describes the relationship between thread and its reachable objects based on the connectivity graph. A thread can reach a subset of objects in the connectivity graph, which include the root objects whose references reside at the thread stack, and all other objects reachable from the root objects via some paths in connectivity graph. Based on the reachability, we can distinguish between *thread-local* objects that can only be reachable from one single thread, and *thread-escaping* objects that can be reachable from multiple threads.

In the context of distributed JVM, Java threads and objects are distributed among different nodes. With the consideration of the relative location between the thread and its reachable objects in a cluster environment, we extend the concepts of thread-local and thread-escaping object and define *node-local* object and *distributed-shared* object: (1) *Node-local object* is an object that is reachable from thread(s) located at the same cluster node. It is either a *thread-local* object or a *thread-escaping* object. (2) *Distributed-shared object* (DSO) is an object that is reachable from at least two threads located at different cluster nodes.

2.2 Detection of DSO

A mechanism to identify distributed-shared objects is essential in the GOS because the accesses on the DSO will initiate a series of thread synchronization and object consistency operations, which involve multiple cluster nodes' collaboration. To minimize the detection overheads, a lightweight DSO detection mechanism is proposed. The detection of DSO in GOS is postponed to the time when a thread is to be migrated or a remote object request is initiated, because not all reachable objects are necessarily accessed during the whole lifetime of the execution.

During the thread migration, we examine the thread context to be transmitted across node boundary. We also examine the object content sent to a remote node. The objective is to identify object references stored in them. The transmitted object reference implies the object is a DSO since it is reachable from the threads located at different nodes. If an object reference is identified, and the object has not been marked as a DSO, it is marked at this moment. On the first appearance of a received remote reference, an empty object of its exact class will be created and associated with it. The object's access state will be set to invalid. When it is accessed later, its up-to-date content will be faulted in. In this scheme, only those objects whose references appear on multiple nodes will be detected as DSOs.

2.3 An Example

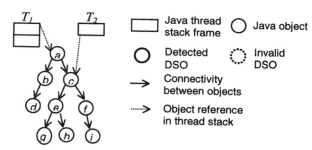

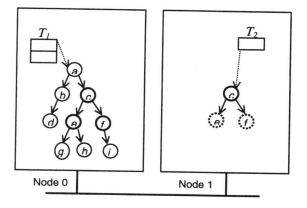

(a) Reachability graph

(b) After thread T_2 is distributed to Node 1

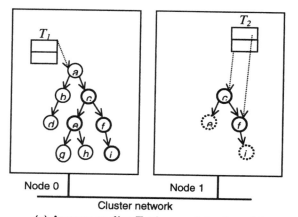

(c) Access on f by T_2 triggers detection of i
Figure 1. Detection of distributed-shared object

Examining the case in Figure 1, a thread T_1 prepares an object tree then passes the reference of object c to another thread T_2 as shown in the reachability graph (Figure 1.a). When T_2 is distributed to another cluster node, i.e. node 1, all the objects reachable from object c become DSOs. Object a, b, and d are not DSOs since they are thread-local to T_1. Instead of detecting all these objects as DSOs at one blow, we detect object c as a DSO and send object c to node 1. Because object e and f are directly connected with object a, we also detect object e and f as DSOs but do not send them to node 1 (Figure 1.b). On node 1, we create two objects whose type are exactly the same as the types of object e and f. Since the contents of object e and f are not available, we set their access state to *invalid*. Next time when object f is accessed by T_2 on node 1 (Figure 1.c), an object fault will occur. An object request message will be sent to node 0. This event will trigger the detection of object i as a DSO. The up-to-date content of object f is copied from node 0 to node 1. Details of how to maintain the coherence of objects located among multiple nodes are discussed in next section. If object e is not accessed by T_2, object e is always invalid on Node 1 and object g and h will never be detected as DSOs.

3. Cache Coherence Protocol

Java memory model (JMM) mainly defines the memory consistency [1] semantics of multi-threaded Java applications. Any implementation of GOS support for distributed JVM must conform to JMM. We follow the JMM proposed in [15], which is very similar to lazy release consistency [10].

In Java, there is a lock associated with each Java object. Java language provides synchronized block facility, either a synchronized method or a synchronized statement, for achieving exclusive access in a critical section. Enter and exit of a synchronized block correspond to acquiring and releasing the lock associated with the synchronized object. The JMM requires that when a thread acquires a lock, all object values modified by threads previously release the same lock, should be visible to the thread acquiring the lock.

Our GOS implements the JMM with a home-based multiple-writer cache coherence protocol. The object is the unit of coherence. Each DSO is associated with a home node, which is the node that creates the object. Since DSOs can be detected at runtime, accesses on invalid copies of DSOs will fault in their contents on demand. Upon releasing a lock, all updated values to non-home copies of DSOs should be forwarded to corresponding home nodes. Upon acquiring a lock, a flush action is required to set the access states of the non-home copies of DSOs invalid, which guarantees the up-to-date contents will be faulted in from the home nodes when they are accessed later. Before the flush, all updated values to non-home copies of DSOs should be forwarded to the corresponding home nodes. Therefore, in such a way, a thread is guaranteed to see the up-to-date content of DSOs after it acquires the proper lock. Since a lock can be regarded as a special field of an object, all the operations on a lock are also executed at the corresponding home node. Thus the home node of the object being locked acts as the lock manager.

The concurrent writes to DSO are permitted by using twin and diff techniques [11]. On the first write to a non-home copy of DSO, a twin of object will be created, which is the exact copy of the object. On lock acquiring and releasing, the diff is created by comparing twin with current object content word by word and sent to the home node.

In addition, we can impose some special coherence protocols on some types of objects. For example, since String objects are read-only, the cached copy of a distributed shared String object can be simply treated as a node-local object. Some objects are considered as node-dependent resources, such as file etc. When these node-dependent objects are detected as DSOs, object replication should be prohibited. Instead, the accesses to them should be transparently redirected to their home nodes. This is an important issue to guarantee complete single system image to Java applications.

4. Optimizations

In this section, we study three optimization techniques coupled with the distributed-shared objects. The first two techniques, *object home migration* and *synchronized method migration*, are the refinements to our memory coherence protocol that implements JMM. The third one, *object pushing*, makes use of object connectivity information to improve access locality and achieve the effect of communication aggregation.

4.1 Object Home Migration

In our home-based protocol, a Java thread can access a DSO with less overhead if the thread is located at the home node of the DSO. Thus, it will be more efficient if we can set the home of a DSO according to thread's runtime object access pattern. In GOS, a mechanism is applied to determine the home of a DSO at runtime. Subsequent object home migration is allowed to adapt to thread's object access pattern.

We take a conservative solution that only those objects written from a single remote node will be applied the home migration. In other words, we only apply this optimization to objects exhibiting single writer access pattern. This scheme was adopted because migrating object home may have negative impacts on performance. For example, to notify a thread that doesn't know the object home has already been migrated, an additional redirection message should be sent.

Under our coherence protocol, non-home object writes are reflected to home node on synchronization points. On home node, object request can be considered as a remote read and the diff received on synchronization point as

remote write. Object accesses on the home node are also recorded.

To minimize the overhead in detecting single writer pattern at runtime, we record only the consecutive writes on an object, which are from the same remote node. Table 1 shows the events and the corresponding actions on the object's current home node when object home migration is enabled. In the table, C denotes the count of consecutive writes from a specific remote node N. The counter C will be reset to 1 if a different remote node issues an object write.

The number of consecutive writes roughly records the number of synchronization iterations during which the object is only updated by that node. We follow a heuristic that an object presents single writer pattern if the count of consecutive writes exceeds a predefined threshold. If single writer pattern is detected, the object home is migrated to the writing node.

Table 1. Events and actions in object home migration

Event	Action
Local read	No action
Local write	$C = 0$
Remote read from a different node from N	No action
Remote write from a different node from N	$C = 1$; $N =$ the writing node
Remote read from N	If $C >$ threshold, migrate home to N
Remote write from N	C++

4.2 Synchronized Method Migration

```
1   class Counter {
2       private int i; // internal counter
3
4       public Counter() {
5           i = 0;
6       }
7
8       public synchronized void inc() {
9           i++;
10      }
11 }
```

Figure 2. Synchronized method migration example

Java's synchronization primitives (e.g., synchronized block, wait and notify methods of Object class) are originally designed for thread synchronization in a shared memory environment. The synchronization constructs built from them may be inefficient in the distributed JVM that is implemented in a distributed memory architecture like cluster.

Considering the Counter class source code in figure 2, we suppose the instance object is a DSO and its home is not the node that invokes inc(). Upon entering and exiting the synchronized inc() method, the invoking node will acquire and release the lock of the instance object. In line 9, the object will be faulted in. In this case, we observe 3 message roundtrips.

It is a common behavior that synchronized object's fields will be accessed in the synchronized method. Thus, all the synchronization requests or object requests will be sent to the home node of the DSO. This will lead to multiple short messages floating between the nodes involving in this synchronization operation.

Migrating synchronized method of DSO to its home node for execution will effectively reduce the number of messages and reduce consistency maintaining overhead incurred in synchronization operations.

4.3 Object Pushing

In Java program execution, after an object is accessed, its reachable objects in connectivity graph are very likely to be accessed afterward. Since object connectivity information is available at runtime, it is possible to prefetch multiple related objects in connectivity graph to improve this kind of access locality.

We use object pushing to improve the prefetching accuracy. While requesting a DSO, the home node will push the requested object together with multiple objects reachable from it to the requesting node. This mechanism provides accurate prefetching since the home node has the up-to-date copies of the objects and the connectivity information maintained in the home node is always valid.

This solution is better than the pull-based one, which relies on the requesting node to fault in the requested objects. In this scenario, the faulting node issues explicit instructions to specify which objects to be pulled. A fatal drawback of this solution is that the connectivity information contained in the invalid object may be obsolete. Therefore, the prefetching accuracy is not guaranteed. Some unneeded objects, even garbage objects, may be prefetched. This will result in the waste of communication bandwidth.

In our implementation, we set an optimal message length, which is the preferred aggregation size of objects to be carried to the requesting node. Reachable objects rooted from the requested object will be selected to copy to the message buffer until the current message length is larger than the optimal message length. Some selection mechanism, either depth-first or bread-first algorithm, can be applied.

To reduce negative impact of pushing unneeded objects, we will not push large objects. For example, the arrays of reference type, e.g., multi-dimension arrays, are usually shared among multiple threads. Object pushing is not performed on the request of an array of reference type.

Overall, the object pushing improves the access locality since objects to be accessed in the future have been moved to the executing thread's local memory. Object pushing can also improve performance by achieving aggregation effect on communication because it can effectively reduce the number of object requests during the execution cycles.

5. Performance Evaluation

In this section, we study the performance of GOS. The GOS is embedded in our JESSICA distributed JVM for supporting object sharing in a cluster environment. All the tests are performed on a cluster of 300MHz Pentium II PCs, running Linux 2.2.14, and connected by a fast Ethernet. The JESSICA is executed under the interpreter mode. In our tests, when the Java applications are started, Java threads are automatically distributed among cluster nodes to achieve maximal parallelism.

5.1 Application Suite

Our application suite consists of four multi-threaded Java programs: All-pair Shortest Path (ASP), Successive Over-Relaxation (SOR), Traveling Salesman Problem (TSP), and Nbody.

ASP calculates the shortest path between any pair of nodes in a graph using a parallel version of Floyd's algorithm. It requires n iterations to solve an n-nodes problem. At iteration k, all threads need the value of the kth row of the distance matrix. There is a barrier at the end of each iteration. The workload is distributed equally among worker threads in row wise.

SOR does red-black successive over-relaxation on a 2-D matrix for a number of iterations. There are two barriers in each iteration. The workload is distributed equally among worker threads in row wise.

Nbody simulates the motion of particles due to gravitational forces over a number of simulation steps. The program follows the algorithm of Barnes & Hut. Each worker thread is computing the motion simulation of a part of particles. A quadtree is constructed at the beginning of each step, which will be accessed by all worker thread.

TSP finds the shortest route among a number of cities using parallel branch-and-bound algorithm, which prunes large parts of the search space by ignoring partial routes already longer than current best solution. We divide the whole search trees to many small ones to form a job queue. Every worker thread will get jobs from this queue until the queue is empty.

5.2 Application Performance

Figure 3 shows the efficiency for each application after all optimizations are enabled. Sequential performance data is measured on the original Kaffe JVM when calculating efficiency.

All 4 benchmark programs have achieved efficiency larger than 84% on 4 nodes and all have achieved efficiency larger than 75% on 8 nodes except Nbody. ASP even achieves an efficiency of 98% on 4 nodes. In ASP, while the cluster size is scaled to 8 nodes, the global synchronization among all threads becomes a primary factor to pull down the efficiency. SOR's situation is similar. In Nbody, there is a construction of quadtree in each simulation step, which cannot be parallelized. When the main thread performs construction of quadtree, all other threads are waiting. The efficiency decreases while the cluster size increases. TSP is a computation intensive program comparing with other benchmark programs. Load imbalance among worker threads is a major factor affecting efficiency.

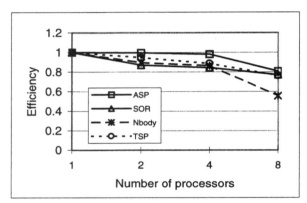

Figure 3. Efficiency

Table 2 shows their communication effort for some given parameters on a 4-node cluster after all optimizations are enabled. Msg column shows the number of messages and the Data column shows the network data volume involved. All the four programs need to access the object heap intensively and involve considerable communication effort except TSP.

Table 2. Communication effort

	Parameters	Msg (K)	Data (MB)
ASP	A graph of 512 vertices	21.5	24.98
SOR	1024 by 1024 matrix for 30 iterations	22.9	42.01
Nbody	400 particles for 10 simulation steps	10.6	4.74
TSP	12 cities	2.9	0.24

Figure 4 shows the normalized execution time break down against number of processors for the four benchmark programs. Obj denotes the time to request an up-to-date copy of a faulting object. Syn denotes the time spent on synchronization operations, such as lock, unlock, and wait. Comp denotes the computation time.

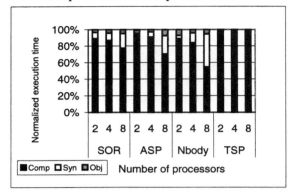

Figure 4. Percentage of execution time break down against no. of processors

Since we insert software checks before object accesses to test object access states, an additional test was conducted to evaluate the overhead of the access checks in our GOS. Comparing the sequential performance on JESSICA with that on Kaffe, the cost of checks can be derived. Since our implementation is based on interpreter model, check cost doesn't contribute significant overhead. In all four benchmarks, check cost is less than 3.5% against execution time on Kaffe.

5.3 Effect of Optimizations

In this subsection, the effect of individual optimizations is studied. Figure 5 shows the effects of optimizations on execution time, message number, and communication data volume when running the benchmark suite on a 4-node cluster. In the below figures, NO means no optimization, HM means object home migration, SMM means synchronized method migration, Push means object pushing. In this test, TSP solves a problem of 8 cities.

As seen from the figures, object home migration greatly improves the performance of ASP and SOR. This is because some DSOs are only written by one thread in some duration of execution in SOR and ASP. The use of synchronized method migration decreases the number of messages by 29.96% for ASP and 4.58% for SOR. Synchronized method migration also results in less synchronization operations. As a result, the execution time decreases by 8.82% for ASP and 1.84% for SOR. Object pushing aggregates small object messages into a larger message. Nbody is a typical application involved with lots of small-sized DSOs. The number of messages is remarkably reduced by 79.83% with object pushing enabled. Since object pushing may push unneeded objects as well, communication data volume increases by 5.23%. Nevertheless, Nbody's execution time decreases by

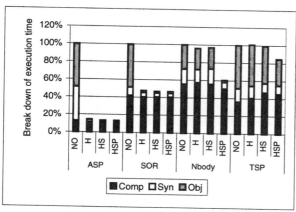

(a) Breakdown of execution time
H: HM, HS: HM+SMM, HSP: HM+SMM+Push

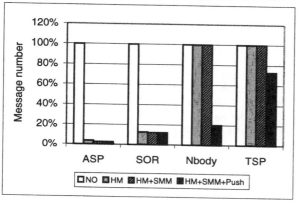

(b) Message number

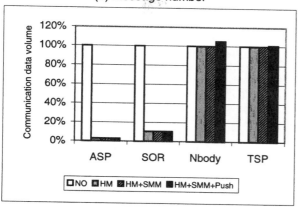

(c) Communication data volume
Figure 5. The effects of optimizations

37.81% as a final result. Object pushing also reduces TSP's message number by 27% and incurs a little more communication data. As a result, TSP's execution time decreases by 14%. Compared with Nbody and TSP, most DSOs used in ASP and SOR are large 2-dimension arrays. Object pushing has little effect on them. Synchronized method migration increases Nbody's execution time by within 2%. Object pushing increases ASP's execution

time by 1%. Overall, the negative impact incurred by these optimizations in our benchmark programs is very limited.

6. Related Work

As a distributed JVM, cJVM [2] uses a proxy object model to implement global object space. Method invocation and fields accessing on the *proxy object* are shipped to its master object in general. Several optimizing techniques were applied to reduce such shipping. This approach is more suitable for the sequential consistency memory model. However, under the proposed Java memory model, i.e., the lazy release consistency, this approach may not be very effective since a more aggressive object caching mechanism, like our global object space, seems more appropriate. In addition, the load distribution in cJVM is determined by object distribution in method shipping approach. Load balance might be difficult to achieve without programmer's effort.

JESSICA [13] leveraged a page-based DSM to build GOS. All objects are allocated into distributed shared memory. Such an approach suffers from false sharing problem that is inherited from the page-based DSM. Since page-based DSM isn't aware of Java runtime connectivity information, it is difficult to detect distributed-shared objects and do further optimizations. The detail analysis of various factors contributing to the efficiency in using page-based DSM for supporting distributed object sharing can be found in [5]. Java/DSM [18] is another similar example that builds global object space on top of page-based DSM.

Some other approaches reply on compiler techniques to transparently run multi-threaded Java applications on a cluster. They directly compile multi-threaded Java program to native code that is able to execute in a distributed platform. In these systems, JVM is not involved in the execution and a software DSM is employed to support global object accesses. Hyperion [14] compiles Java bytecode to C source code, then compiles to native code further. Jackal [17] compiles Java source code to native code. In both cases, most efforts to improve performance are done at compile time. Jackal's compiler enables two optimizations: *object-graph aggregation* and *automatic computation migration*, which are similar to our object pushing and synchronized method migration. Object-graph aggregation uses heap approximation algorithm [6] to identify those related objects. However, heap approximation algorithm cannot distinguish between different runtime objects that are created at the same allocation site. Hence this approach is effective only at the situation when the related objects are from different allocation sites. Comparatively, our object pushing is a runtime approach and has no such drawback.

Both Jackal and Hyperion do not intend to detect distributed-shared objects.

In the DSM field, DOSA [7] implements a fine-grained DSM support for typed language such as Java. Its aim is to keep sharing granularity at object level but still rely on the virtual memory support to do the access state check as in the page-based DSM. It introduces a level of indirection on object accessing. Access to objects will go through a handle table to locate object's actual address. The indirection adds overhead on object accesses and impairs cache locality.

7. Conclusions

This paper presents a global object space support for distributed JVM. Distributed-shared objects are detected with the help of runtime object connectivity information to improve the performance. Only distributed-shared objects are taken care of to maintain consistency in global object space. Several optimizations can be incorporated into the global object space. Among them, home migration and object pushing can effectively improve the performance of applications presenting certain access behaviors. Synchronized method migration can optimize the execution of Java synchronized method in the context of distributed JVM. After all optimizations are enabled, considerable performance is obtainable.

In our future work, we will incorporate the detection of distributed-shared object with our distributed garbage collection algorithm in global object space. To further improve the performance of global object space, an adaptive cache coherence protocol will be implemented, which will automatically adjust to the various access patterns of distributed-shared objects. As object access pattern may change dynamically during the execution lifetime, we believe a runtime solution is more effective to adapt to the access patterns.

References

[1] S. Adve and K. Gharachorloo. Shared memory consistency models: A Tutorial. *IEEE Computer*, 29(12): 66-76, December 1996.

[2] Y. Aridor, M. Factor, and A. Teperman. cjvm: a single system image of a jvm on a cluster. In *Proc. of International Conference on Parallel Processing*, 1999.

[3] Gilad Bracha, James Gosling, Bill Joy, and Guy Steele. The Java Language Specification, Second Edition. Addison Wesley, 2000.

[4] B. Cheung, C.L. Wang, Kai Hwang. A Migrating-Home Protocol for Implementing Scope Consistency model on a Cluster of Workstations. International Conference on *Parallel and Distributed Processing Techniques and Applications* (PDPTA'99), pp. 821-827, 1999, Las Vegas.

[5] W.L. Cheung, C.L. Wang, and F.C.M. Lau. Building a Global Object Space for Supporting Single System image

on a Cluster. To appear in *Annual Review of Scalable Computing*, Volume 4, World Scientific, 2002.

[6] Rakesh Ghiya and Laurie J. Hendren. Putting pointer analysis to work. In *25th Annual ACM SIGACT-SIGPLAN Symposium on the Principles of Programming Languages*, pages 121--133, January 1998.

[7] Y. Charlie Hu, Weimin Yu, Dan Wallach, Alan Cox, and Willy Zwaenepoel. Runtime support for distributed sharing in typed languages. In *Proceedings of the Fifth ACM Workshop on Languages, Compilers, and Run-time Systems for Scalable Computers*, Rochester, NY, May 2000.

[8] K. Hwang, E. Chow, C.L. Wang, H. Jin, and Z. Xu, Desinging SSI Cluster with Hierarchical Checkpointing and Single I/O Space. In *IEEE Concurrency*, 1999.

[9] P. Keleher. Distributed Shared Memory Home Pages. http://www.cs.umd.edu/~keleher/dsm.html.

[10] P. Keleher, A. L. Cox, and W. Zwaenepoel. Lazy release consistency for software distributed shared memory. In Proceedings of the 19th *Annual International Symposium on Computer Architecture*, pages 13--21, May 1992.

[11] P. Keleher, S. Dwarkadas, A.L. Cox, and W. Zwaenepoel. TreadMarks: Distributed Shared Memory on Standard Workstations and Operating Systems. Proceedings of *the Winter 94 Usenix Conference*, pp. 115-131, January 1994.

[12] Tim Lindholm and Frank Yellin. The Java Virtual Machine Specification, Second Edition. Addison Wesley, 1999.

[13] Matchy J. M. Ma, Cho-Li Wang, and Francis C. M. Lau. Jessica: Java-enabled single-system-image computing architecture. *Journal of Parallel and Distributed Computing*, 60, Oct. 2000. (JESSICA source code is available at: http//www.srg.csis.hku.hk/Jessica-src/.)

[14] M. MacBeth, K. McGuigan, and P. Hatcher. Executing java threads in parallel in a distributed-memory environment. In *Proc. of IBM Center for Advanced Studies Conference*, 1998.

[15] Jeremy Manson and William Pugh. Core Semantics of Multithreaded Java. In *Proc. of Joint ACM Java Grande - ISCOPE 2001 Conference*, June 2001.

[16] Transvirtual Technologies Inc. Kaffe JVM. http://www.kaffe.org.

[17] R. Veldema, R. F. H. Hofman, R. A. F. Bhoedjang, and H. E. Bal. Runtime Optimizations for a Java DSM Implementation. In *Proc. Joint ACM JavaGrande-ISCOPE 2001*, Stanford, 2001.

[18] W. Yu and A. Cox. Java/dsm: A platform for heterogeneous computing. In *Proc. of ACM 1997 Workshop on Java for Science and Engineering Computation*, 1997.

A Secure Protocol for Computing Dot-Products in Clustered and Distributed Environments

Ioannis Ioannidis, Ananth Grama, and Mikhail Atallah
Department of Computer Sciences, Purdue University,
W. Lafayette, IN 47907.
{ioannis, ayg, mja}@cs.purdue.edu *

Abstract

Dot-products form the basis of various applications ranging from scientific computations to commercial applications in data mining and transaction processing. Typical scientific computations utilizing sparse iterative solvers use repeated matrix-vector products. These can be viewed as dot-products of sparse vectors. In database applications, dot-products take the form of counting operations. With widespread use of clustered and distributed platforms, these operations are increasingly being performed across networked hosts. Traditional APIs for messaging are susceptible to sniffing, and the data being transferred between hosts is often enough to compromise the entire computation. For example, in a domain decomposition based sparse solver, the entire solution can often be reconstructed easily from boundary values that are communicated on the net. In yet other applications, dot-products may be performed across two hosts that do not want to disclose their vectors, yet, they need to compute the dot-product. In each of these cases, there is a need for secure and anonymous dot-product protocols. Due to the large computational requirements of underlying applications, it is highly desirable that secure protocols add minimal overhead to the original algorithm. Finally, by its very nature, dot-products leak limited amounts of information – one of the parties can detect an entry of the other party's vector by simply probing it with a vector with a 1 in a particular location and zeros elsewhere. Given all of these constraints, traditional cryptographic protocols are generally unsuitable due to their significant computational and communication overheads. In this paper, we present an extremely efficient and sufficiently secure protocol for computing the dot-product of two vectors using linear algebraic techniques. Using analytical as well as experimental results, we demonstrate superior performance in terms of computational overhead, numerical stability, and security. We show that the overhead of a two-party dot-product computation using MPI as the messaging API across two high-end workstations connected via a Gigabit ethernet approaches multiple 4.69 over an un-secured dot-product. We also show that the average relative error in dot-products across a large number of random (normalized) vectors was roughly 4.5×10^{-9}.

Keywords: Secure dot-products, Application-level security protocols, Distributed secure computations.

1 Introduction and Motivation

With the emergence of clustered and distributed platforms as cost-effective parallel programming environments, a number of critical computations are routinely executed over the net. These include scientific simulations, data mining operations, and commercial transactions. Data transferred over the net in such applications is highly susceptible to packet sniffing, and other attacks that compromise the privacy and integrity of the computation. While the problem of packet sniffing can be addressed by secure-tunneling the data (encrypting all communication), the overhead of secure tunneling puts tremendous pressure on already scarce communication throughput. The problem of securing communicated data is much better handled in application level protocols as opposed to general cryptographic protocols.

In yet other computations, entities participating in a parallel program may not trust each other. For example, two competing grocery chains may elect to join forces in mining their sales data. Yet, neither might want to reveal precise sales figures to the other. Most database operations take the form of calculating the dot-product of an external with a resident, database vector. These

*This work is supported in part by National Science Foundation grants EIA-9806741, ACI-9875899, and ACI-9872101, and by CERIAS at Purdue University. Computing equipment used for this work was supported by National Science Foundation and by the Intel Corp.

vectors are valuable to both parties and leaking information has a definite cost. Nevertheless, the popularity of data mining forces a compromise between speed and security. In more malicious environments, two hosts may choose to execute an untrusted computation protocol to guard against the possibility that one of the hosts may have been compromised. In such cases, hosts may agree to participate in a computation so long as their own data is not compromised (revealed) to others.

In addition to lack of trust in the network and other parties, secure and anonymous protocols are subject to traditional constraints of parallel processing – namely that a ten-fold speedup from parallelism must not be cancelled out by a ten-fold slowdown resulting from the secure protocol. With these objectives in mind, we propose, in this paper, a secure protocol for a key computational kernel – dot-products. By its very nature, a dot-product leaks a certain amount of information. If two parties are trying to compute a secure and anonymous dot-product, one of the parties can detect an entry of the other party's vector by simply probing it with a one in the corresponding location. Due to this, we expect a higher-level application protocol to disallow a large number of probes on a single vector. We focus here on securing a single dot-product using a protocol that has low computational (and communication) overhead, good security properties, and excellent numerical stability.

Consider two parties, Alice and Bob, holding a vector each and wanting to compute securely their dot-product. There are two important aspects of this operation. First, no one eavesdropping the communication should be able to derive any information on the nature of the two vectors. Second, the only thing revealed to either party should be the outcome of the operation. Existing protocols meeting the above criteria derive their security from the properties of modular exponentiation and introduce unacceptable overhead unless perfect security is absolutely necessary. On the other hand there is a wide range of environments demanding a fast protocol, secure enough to resist a large repertory of attacks but not necessarily a very powerful, yet unlikely, adversary. For such applications, linear algebraic techniques provide a powerful set of tools for securing, at the application level, the underlying computations. Here, we present one such protocol that has extremely low overhead (shown to tend to a factor of 4.69 on average), excellent numerical stability, and security properties.

The rest of this paper is organized as follows: Section 2 presents three applications of the proposed technique, Section 3 presents an overview of the protocol and discusses existing results in the area, Section 4 outlines the new dot-product protocol, Section 5 provides experimental results of overhead and stability, and Section 6 draws conclusions and outlines ongoing work.

2 Applications

The proposed protocol has been designed with the following specific applications in mind. This list is merely representative of the rich class of applications to which the protocol can be applied.

- *Biometrics and matching.* The heart of all data matching applications is the dot-product. The need for security is heightened when the data contains sensitive information. The most notable example is that of biological or genetic information. The demand for such applications is expected to increase significantly and with it, the need for privacy and efficiency. Anonymity is the main objective but the amount of information involved nullifies any computation-intensive attack, even if it looks feasible in theory.

- *Distributed data mining.* Data mining involves data whose collection has a considerable cost and whose security is essential. The widespread use of data mining techniques and their distributed nature demand fast, secure dot-product protocols. Computation overhead might not be the critical factor in this case, but the limited bandwidth does not allow for a large communication overhead. Any protocol aimed at data mining applications should feature a small number of rounds and a limited bit count.

- *Critical scientific computations.* Such computations usually take place in tightly coupled networks. A typical representative kernel of these applications is an iterative linear system solver. The core of this solver is the sparse mat-vec operation. Matrices are typically row partitioned (typically using a graph partitioner such as Metis or Chaco) and, in this form they are simply multiple dot-products. A defining characteristic of such applications is that data is typically reused over repeated mat-vecs. A protocol exploiting this characteristic, enjoys a huge advantage, because it amortizes most of the overhead over a large number of rounds.

3 Overview of Protocol and Related Results

The most commonly used technique for hiding a number is modular multiplication. This is considered a perfectly secure and efficient operation. Generalizing to higher dimensions is what one would ideally want for a protocol involving vectors. In the case of the dot-product, this is not possible due to the incompatibility of the operation with modular arithmetic. Furthermore, in this protocol a vector would have to be multiplied with a random matrix, which leads to complications. The protocol we present is based on the above principle. It leaks a controlled amount of information, however, this information leakage is negligible compared to the inherent leak in the problem. In experiments our protocol demonstrates ideal numerical stability and an overhead, compared to the simple dot-product operation, of a factor of less than 4.7, in the worst case. If the same vector is reused, subsequent computations can reuse more than half of the computations and exactly half of the communication, for an even lower amortized overhead. These measurements were taken over a Gigabit ethernet and they reveal that the overhead is dominated by the communication. Over a slower network, such as the Internet, the above ratio would be even lower.

3.1 Related research

The first secure multiparty computation problem was described in [1]. Since then, research on such problems has grown significantly to form one of the most active areas of research in computer security. In [2], a general framework for any secure multiparty computation was presented. Although this framework can be applied to the dot-product problem, yielding an algorithm linear in the size of the vectors, its extensive use of *oblivious transfer* ([5]) makes it impractical because of very high constants in computation and communication.

There have not been many protocols specific to the secure multiparty dot-product computations. In [3, 4], such protocols are described in the context of larger constructions. They are based on conventional cryptographic techniques which incur a large overhead since they rely on the difficulty of problems related to modular exponentiation for their security.

4 The Proposed Dot-Product Protocol

We consider here, a two-party computation where each party is *honest-but curious*. In other words, everyone participating in the protocol abides by the rules but if they have the opportunity to find out something more than they are supposed to, they will. We also assume that only one of the parties is interested in the result, a realistic assumption for the range of applications dot-products are associated with. Finally, a random number in the context of real-valued vectors is a uniformly distributed, random integer cast into real.

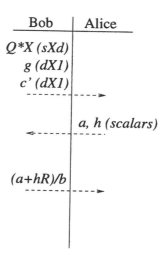

Figure 1. Proposed protocol for secure dot-products.

A formal statement of the problem is as follows: Alice holds vector v and Bob vector w, both in $\Re^{d-1}$, $d \geq 3$. Alice is interested in computing $w^T \cdot v$ without revealing anything about her vector. Bob is willing to participate in such a protocol as long as he does not reveal more than the dot-product to Alice.

Let Q be a random $s \times s$ matrix, $s \geq 2$, where s is a security parameter. Bob chooses a random r, $1 \leq r \leq s$, and $s - 1$ random $d \times 1$ vectors, x_i, $1 \leq i \leq s$, $i \neq r$. Let w' be the vector in $\Re^d$ for which $w_i' = w_i$, for all $1 \leq i \leq d - 1$, and $(w_d)' = 1$. He sets $x_r = w'$ and creates an $s \times d$ matrix X, whose i-th row is x_i^T. We define the following:

$$b = \sum_{i=1}^{s} Q_{ir}$$

$$c = \sum_{i=1,i\neq r}^{s} \left(x_i^T \cdot \sum_{j=1}^{s} Q_{ji} \right)$$

Bob chooses a random $d \times 1$ vector f and three random numbers R_1, R_2, R_3, and makes the following public:

$$Q \cdot X$$

$$c' = c + f^T \cdot R_1 \cdot R_2$$

$$g = f \cdot R_1 \cdot R_3$$

Let v' be in $\Re^d$ such that $v_i' = v_i$, for all $1 \leq i \leq d - 1$, and $v_d = \alpha$, where α is a random number. Alice

381

computes:

$$y = Q \cdot X \cdot v'$$

$$z = \sum_{i=1}^{s} y_i$$

and

$$a = z - c' \cdot v'.$$

She sends a to Bob and also computes and sends to Bob:

$$h = g^T \cdot v'.$$

Bob computes:

$$\beta = \frac{a + h \cdot \frac{R_2}{R_3}}{b}$$

and sends it to Alice. The desired dot-product is finally given by $\beta - \alpha$. This protocol is illustrated in Figure 1.

4.1 Proof of Correctness

A proof that what Bob computes is indeed the desired dot-product is as follows:

$$
\begin{aligned}
c \cdot v' &= \sum_{i=1, i \neq r}^{s} (x_i^T \cdot \sum_{j=1}^{s} Q_{ji}) \cdot v' \\
&= \sum_{i=1, i \neq r}^{s} (x_i^T \cdot v' \cdot \sum_{j=1}^{s} Q_{ji})
\end{aligned}
$$

We also, have:

$$c' \cdot v' = c \cdot v' + h \cdot \frac{R_2}{R_3}$$

$$\Rightarrow a + h \cdot \frac{R_2}{R_3} = z - c \cdot v'$$

$$y = Q \cdot X \cdot v' = Q \cdot (X \cdot v') = Q \cdot u$$

Where,

$$u_i = x_i^T \cdot v'$$

From this, we have

$$
\begin{aligned}
y_j &= \sum_{i=1}^{d} (Q_{ji} \cdot x_i^T \cdot v') \\
\Rightarrow z &= \sum_{j=1}^{s} y_j \\
&= \sum_{j=1}^{s} \sum_{i=1}^{d} (Q_{ji} \cdot x_i^T \cdot v') \\
&= \sum_{i=1}^{d} (x_i^T \cdot v' \cdot \sum_{j=1}^{s} Q_{ji}) \\
\Rightarrow z - c \cdot v' &= x_r^T \cdot v' \cdot \sum_{j=1}^{s} Q_{jr} = b \cdot (w')^T \cdot v'
\end{aligned}
$$

Therefore, $\beta = w^T \cdot v + \alpha$. This verifies the correctness of the protocol.

4.2 Analysis of Security

Due to the nature of multiplication and addition, some information is statistically revealed by the protocol. However, since exposing a vector d times in dot-product calculations will reveal it fully, any such analysis can only have limited success. We analyze here the information flow between Alice and Bob.

- From Bob to Alice

  Bob makes three things public:

  - $Q \cdot X$. Vector w is involved in this $s \times d$ matrix. However, even if Alice can guess which row of X is w, it is impossible to separate the two matrices in any way without further information. Therefore, making this matrix public conveys no information about w to Alice.

  - c'. This is the sum of a random vector and a vector, which could be claimed to leak information, although it is quite debatable whether it does. However, unless the random vector is disclosed, c' is certain not to leak information.

  - g. This vector does not reveal information about the random vector of the previous paragraph, unless one could guess the R_i's. So long as they are random, no information is leaked.

  - a, h. Alice knows that the product is a linear combination of these two. If she uses a linearly independent vector w'' w.r.t. w, to create more equations so that she can deduce the coefficients for a and h, she will introduce a new unknown to the system for each new equation, namely $w''^T \cdot v$. If w'' is linearly dependent w.r.t. w she does not create a new equation. We, also, note that $a = 0$ if and only if $h = 0$. Therefore, she cannot deduce any information about v.

    Sending h to Bob, Alice reveals an equation about her vector. This way, both parties come out of the protocol with the same number of equations. To keep this equation secret from an eavesdropper, Alice and Bob must share a secret random number or use standard encryption to communicate it. Since this is only a scalar, the overhead is insignificant.

- From Alice to Bob.

  Alice sends two things to Bob, after step 1.

– a. This vector cannot reveal anything to Bob, unless he can separate z from $c' \cdot v$.

– h. This gives to Bob an equation about v'. Computing the dot-product gives another equation. He cannot combine a and h to get any more information for w. Totally, Bob has two equations about v'. However, for v itself, he effectively has one equation, as many as Alice has for his vector.

4.3 Stability considerations

Besides the security and efficiency of the scheme, we need to ensure that the error introduced by the extra computations does not affect the accuracy of the result. One can avoid such errors by extending the precision, however, this introduces extra overhead. We present experimental data suggesting that the accuracy of the computation is similar to that of computing an un-secured dot-product without extended precision.

5 Experimental results

As we have indicated earlier, we are interested in two aspects of the protocol behavior: the overhead it introduces and its numerical stability.

- Overhead. There are two types of overhead involved in the protocol. The communication overhead is the amount of extra data that needs to be communicated, compared to the simple protocol. The computation overhead refers to the extra computation performed. We note that both of these overheads depend on the security parameter s. The computation overhead has a quadratic dependence on it, while the communication overhead is only linearly dependent. All measurements presented in this section correspond to $s = 2$. We believe that even for this low value of the security parameter, there is a sufficient measure of security provided by the protocol.

  – Communication. Bob must send four vectors to Alice. Two further rounds of communication are needed, involving in total three scalars.

  – Computation. One of the features of our protocol is that a large part of the data can be reused when the same vector is repeatedly used in different dot-product computations. More specifically, if Alice and Bob have engaged in an execution of the protocol and they want to execute the protocol again with only Alice changing her vector, Bob needs to change only f, R_1, R_2, R_3 and, consequently, c' and g. $Q \cdot X$ and b can remain the same without compromising the security of his vector. This means that the majority of the computation overhead can be amortized over a large number of executions.

  – Total overhead. The protocol was implemented on two PIII/450MHz machines connected over a Gigabit ethernet. The messaging API was MPI. All the measurements were taken over the entire protocol, without any amortization. We used randomly instantiated, normalized vectors of length 10^6. For the generation of random numbers, we used the standard C-library drand48 pseudo-random number generator. The overhead in this case is observed to be ≈ 4.69, on average. We observe that in spite of the relatively fast network, communication overhead dominates total overhead. One can expect this effect to be even more pronounced for slower networks. The use of more sophisticated means for obtaining random numbers should not have significant impact on the above overhead.

- Numerical stability. The average relative error over a large number of random (normal) vectors was measured to be $4.493 \cdot 10^{-9}$. Given that the relative error of the normal computation of the dot-product is of the same order, the results can be considered absolutely satisfactory.

6 Concluding Remarks and Ongoing Research

In this paper, we have presented a secure protocol for computing dot-products. We have demonstrated analytically as well as experimentally the excellent performance characteristics, numerical stability, and security properties of the protocol. Compared to conventional cryptographic techniques, this linear algebraic technique has much lower overhead.

Ongoing work in our group focuses on developing secure computation techniques for a variety of problems in data mining and analysis. Data mining poses the problem of computing the dot-product between two binary vectors, efficiently and securely. The challenge in this case is to avoid the extensive use of number theoretic techniques. Two variations of the problem come from the dot-product between sparse vectors (the difficulty arising from the need to hide which positions are important while not wanting to traverse all of them) and the threshold variation of the problem, where we want to know whether the product exceeds a specified threshold but nothing more.

References

[1] Andrew C.-C. Yao, "Protocols for secure computation", Proc. 23rd IEEE Symposium on Foundations of Computer Science (FOCS), 1982, pp 160 - 164.

[2] Oded Goldreich, Silvio Micali and Avi Wigderson, "How to play any mental game or a completeness theorem for protocols with honest majority", Proc. 19th Annual ACM Symposium on Theory of Computing (STOC), 1987, pp. 218 - 229.

[3] Wenliang Du and Mikhail J. Atallah, "Protocols for Secure Remote Database Access with Approximate Matching", 7th ACM Conference on Computer and Communications Security (ACMCCS 2000), The First Workshop on Security and Privacy in E-Commerce, Nov. 1-4 2000, Athens, Greece.

[4] Wenliang Du and Mikhail J. Atallah, "Privacy-Preserving Cooperative Scientific Computations", In 14th IEEE Computer Security Foundations Workshop, June 11-13 2001, Nova Scotia,Canada.

[5] M. Rabin, "How to exchange secrets by oblivious transfer", Technical report TR-81, Aiken Computation Laboratory, Harvard University, 1981.

A Technique for Adaptation to Available Resources on Clusters Independent of Synchronization Methods Used *

Umit Rencuzogullari and Sandhya Dwarkadas

Department of Computer Science
University of Rochester
Rochester, NY 14627–0226
umit,sandhya@cs.rochester.edu

Abstract

Clusters of Workstations (COW) offer high performance relative to their cost. Generally these clusters operate as autonomous systems running independent copies of the operating system, where access to machines is not controlled and all users enjoy the same access privileges. While these features are desirable and reduce operating costs, they create adverse effects on parallel applications running on these clusters. Load imbalances are common for parallel applications on COWs due to: 1) variable amount of load on nodes caused by an inherent lack of parallelism, 2) variable resource availability on nodes, and 3) independent scheduling decisions made by the independent schedulers on each node. Our earlier study has shown that an approach combining static program analysis, dynamic load balancing, and scheduler cooperation is effective in countering the adverse effects mentioned above. In our current study, we investigate the scalability of our approach as the number of processors is increased. We further relax the requirement of global synchronization, avoiding the need to use barriers and allowing the use of any other synchronization primitives while still achieving dynamic load balancing. The use of alternative synchronization primitives avoids the inherent vulnerability of barriers to load imbalance. It also allows load balancing to take place at any point in the course of execution, rather than only at a synchronization point, potentially reducing the time the application runs imbalanced. Moreover, load readjustment decisions are made in a distributed fashion, thus preventing any need for processes to globally synchronize in order to redistribute load.

1. Introduction

Clusters of Workstations (COWs) are attractive since they provide high compute power at low cost. COWs provide lower maintenance cost by allowing heterogeneous hardware to be put together, enabling partial upgrades and providing the opportunity to spread an upgrade over a period of time. COWs also have lower operating cost as they use readily available hardware and software. Each machine is generally autonomous and runs an independent copy of the operating system, allowing all users equal and uncontrolled access privileges.

Unfortunately, the advantages we enumerated above turn into disadvantages when COWs are used as a parallel computing platform. Since COWs are mostly operated as autonomous systems, scheduling decisions are made independently. Furthermore, since access to individual machines is not regulated, it is likely that some of the nodes running a parallel program will have other programs running on them. Heterogeneous clusters imply variance in resources among nodes. Each of these reasons contribute to the likelihood that some nodes will be overloaded while others are underutilized. Combining these factors with program characteristics, such as inherent lack of parallelism or unpredictable processing requirements, makes running parallel programs in such an environment much less efficient than expected.

In the past, each of these problems has been addressed in isolation. Load balancing has been studied for both COWs and parallel machines [8, 12, 22, 17, 10, 4]. Lowenthal et. al. [12] and Morris et. al. [7] use a global strategy for optimizing the execution path through the data distribution graph of a program, which is executed at runtime and directed by the number of incurred page faults and computation time of each parallel region.

Coscheduling has also been studied extensively, in the form of explicit coscheduling [16, 23] for parallel machines, and in the form of implicit coscheduling [20, 3, 15], for

*This work was supported in part by NSF grants EIA-9972881, EIA-0080124, CCR–9702466, CCR–9988361, and CCR–9705594; by an external research grant from DEC/Compaq; and by the U.S. Department of Energy Office of Inertial Confinement Fusion under Cooperative Agreement No. DE-FC03-92SF19460.

COWs.

Coscheduling works best when the amount of work and the available resources are equal across all nodes. On an autonomous COW it is highly likely that nodes have different numbers of processes running, which reduces the effectiveness of the coscheduling approach. If implicit coscheduling is used, the resulting schedule might also no longer be fair. On the other hand, load balancing takes its motivation from the assumption that each of the nodes has a different load/resource ratio, and tries to make that ratio equal across nodes. Even when load balancing is perfect across nodes, delays caused by multiprogramming will not be addressed, since communicating or synchronizing processes would have to wait for their communication/synchronization partner to be scheduled before they are able to finish their operation.

An obvious solution would seem to be to combine load balancing with a coscheduling scheme. Unfortunately, a trivial combination does not work since it still suffers from message delays, or possible unfairness. For example, consider a parallel application running on two nodes, where one of the nodes, say A, is dedicated, and the other, B, is running another application along with the parallel application. Assume the load is balanced, i.e. the parallel process on node A is getting twice as much work to do as its peer on node B. A coscheduler cannot do anything, since the parallel application is naturally coscheduled. However, in this case it is possible for the process running on A to send a message and wait for its partner to be rescheduled, should the partner process on B be de-scheduled. The wait time could be as high as one quantum.

Our solution to the above problems has been developed in the context of software distributed shared memory (SDSM). An SDSM protocol provides the illusion of shared memory to the programmer. The benefit in our case is that the complexity of the load balancing middleware is reduced since data is automatically moved to where it is accessed rather than having to be explicitly coded. Our earlier study [18] has shown an effective way of coping with load imbalances and scheduling discrepancies for applications using barriers to synchronize. A "barrier" requires all involved processes to arrive at the barrier before anyone may depart from it.

Our new system extends our previous work by being oblivious to the synchronization method used. This permits the exclusive use of locks and flags, which are much more relaxed methods of synchronization. A lock requires an acquirer to wait only if the lock to be acquired is being held by another party. Flags, on the other hand, are an event-based synchronization mechanism that can be used to signal the completion of an event. Further, we explore the scalability of our system and show that our combination of cooperative scheduling and load balancing scales up to 32 processors and provides excellent performance benefits. Our new extensions benefit even barrier-based applications by providing them with ways of balancing load without waiting for a barrier, in cases where the time between barriers is large.

```
int    sh_dat1[N], sh_dat2[N],a,b,c,d;

for (i=lowerbound;i<upperbound;i+=stride)
    sh_dat1[a*i + b] += sh_dat2[c*i + d];
```

Figure 1. Initial parallel loop. Shared data is indicated by the prefix sh_.

The rest of the paper is organized as follows: Section 2 provides information about our former system and how our new system differs and what capabilities are added. Section 3 evaluates the system separating the effects of each component. Finally, Section 4 concludes and outlines our plans for future work.

2. Design And Implementation

Our programming environment is software distributed shared memory (DSM). DSM hides the details of communication from the user by providing a layer below the application that implicitly manages data movement. Data movement due to load reassignment, which would otherwise be needed to be somehow explicitly added to the program, is handled implicitly. Even though it is relatively easy to explicitly code data movement when the data to be moved is known statically, it is much harder when the decision is made dynamically, since the source and destination are hard to determine. We use Cashmere-2L (CSM) [21], as our base DSM system.

Due to relaxing the requirements of the use of barriers, the monitoring and redistribution methods we used in our earlier work must be modified. We elaborate on each of the components and their modifications in the following sections.

2.1. Baseline Load Balancing System

Our baseline system consists of three separate subsystems: static program analysis, runtime system, and operating system scheduling support. Our earlier work [18] presented a scheme to balance load and increase the throughput of COWs for "barrier-based" parallel applications. In that implementation, all synchronizations were pushed into the runtime system, and load was balanced only at synchronization points, which were barriers. Our current extensions, in addition to supporting other classes of applications, also allow barrier-based applications to balance at arbitrary points,

```
Initialize
  sharing types /*STENCIL/INDEPENDENT*/
  load types    /*FIXED/VARIABLE*/
  list of arrays,       /*sh_dat1,sh_dat2*/
  list of access types, /*read/write*/
  list of upper/lower bounds and strides
  coefficients and constants /*a,b,c,d*/

taskSet = partition_tasks();

get a task while there are Tasks in the taskSet
  set lowbound, highbound, stride for that Task

  for (i=lowbound;i<highbound;i+=stride)
     sh_dat1[a*i + b] += sh_dat2[c*i + d]
```

Figure 2. Parallel loop with pseudocode that serves as an interface to the runtime system. The runtime system can then change the amount of work assigned to a process.

hence making it possible to balance load between barriers when the time between successive barriers is large. This in turn reduces the amount of time an application runs unbalanced.

The following sections describe each of the three components separately and explains what had to be changed in order to extend our system to work with a larger class of applications.

2.2. Static Program Analysis

We use static program analysis to identify the access pattern of our parallel program as well as to insert the runtime-system hooks that monitor the process activity. Once a parallel region is identified, there are two dimensions along which load distribution decisions can be made. The first is the amount of work per subtask (where a subtask is identified as the smallest independent unit of work that can be performed in parallel, e.g., a single iteration of a parallel loop). The second is the data accessed by each subtask. For many regular access patterns, the compiler can identify the data accessed by each parallel loop. In addition, the compiler can also attempt to predict whether each parallel loop performs the same or different amounts of work. Our static analysis [9] provides information on the above two dimensions wherever possible.

We illustrate the interface between the compiler and the runtime, as well as the information extracted by the compiler, through a sample parallel loop. Figure 1 shows pseudo-code for the original loop. There are several pieces of information that the compiler supplies to the runtime system. For every shared data structure, the compiler initializes data structures indicating its size and the number and size of each dimension. In addition, for each parallel region,

the compiler supplies information regarding the shared data accessed (in the form of a regular section [6]) per loop (or subtask) in the parallel region. The loop is then transformed as shown in the pseudo-code in Figure 2. In reality, much of the information passed to the runtime task partitioner is initialized only once, with only those variables that change are updated on each invocation.

Once the information on the loop bounds and array dimensions is available, the amount of computation and the locality of access can be deduced (heuristically) for several important classes of applications. For instance, detecting that the amount of work per parallel loop is a function of the parallel loop index implies that in order to achieve a balanced distribution of load while preserving access locality, a cyclic distribution of the parallel loops would be useful[1]. Similarly, detecting a non-empty intersection between the regular sections of adjacent parallel loops implies a stencil-type computation with nearest-neighbor sharing, while detecting an empty or loop-independent intersection among loops implies loop-independent sharing.

Two variables in the data structure for each parallel region encode this information — *load* and *access*. *load* is currently defined to be one of *FIXED* or *VARIABLE*, the default being *FIXED*. A *VARIABLE* load type is currently used as an indication to use a cyclic load distribution, while a *FIXED* load type is used as an indication to use a block load distribution. *Access* is currently defined to be one of *STENCIL* or *INDEPENDENT*. *Access* is intended to influence the type of load distribution used, and to determine the type of redistribution used. *Access* can potentially be updated by the runtime system based on information about data currently cached by the process. An access type of *STENCIL* is treated as a signal to use a blocked load distribution as well as a blocked re-assignment of load (i.e., load is re-assigned by shifting loop boundaries in proportion to the processing power of the individual processors). Using this type of load re-assignment minimizes steady-state communication due to nearest-neighbor sharing. However, the redistribution results in data being communicated among all neighboring processors during each redistribution. An access type of *INDEPENDENT* signals the ability to minimize this communication by assigning a heavily loaded processor's tasks directly to the lightly loaded processors. Since data sharing among loops is iteration-independent, there is no resulting increase in steady-state communication.

For source-to-source translation from a sequential program to a parallel program that is compatible with our runtime system, we use the Stanford University Intermediate Format (SUIF) [1] compiler. The SUIF system is organized as a set of compiler passes built on top of a kernel that de-

---

[1]In the presence of conditional statements, changing load within a parallel loop cannot always be detected at compile-time. Application-specific knowledge could also be easily encoded by the user.

fines the intermediate format. Each of these passes is implemented as a separate program that reads its input from a file and writes its output to another file. SUIF files always use the same format.

We added two passes to the SUIF system for our purposes. The first pass works before the parallel code generation and inserts code that provides the runtime system with information about each parallel region's access patterns. The second pass works on parallelized programs and modifies the loop structure by inserting the required runtime system hooks and modifying the loop structure to use runtime-system provided execution parameters.

The standard SUIF distribution can generate a single-program, multiple-data (SPMD) program from sequential code for many simple loops but lacks the more complex transformations essential to extract parallelism from less easily analyzable loops. While our SUIF passes provide an easy translation mechanism for many programs, it is straightforward to insert the required data structures by hand into an already parallelized program.

2.3. Runtime System

The runtime system is the main component that uses the information provided by the static analysis to partition, distribute and redistribute the work among all cooperating processes. Also, it is the component that using the provided interface, cooperates with the scheduler and other processes. Load distribution is based on the concept of Relative-Power, and guided by the statically provided information and runtime feedback.

2.3.1. Relative Processing Power

As described in [9, 18], in order to partition the load according to available resources we try to estimate available computational resources and communication overhead. In general it is reasonable to assume a node with more resources is capable of doing more work in a given amount of time. We base our load distribution decisions on our estimation of the computing capability of a node, which we call RelativePower. Intuitively, RelativePower is proportional to w/t, where w is the amount of work done and t is the elapsed time. For applications that employ barriers, all processes work in the same parallel region, on their appointed work, until they are done and reach the next barrier. In this scheme, it is trivial to know the amount of work done, since all assigned iterations of all parallel regions have to be executed before a barrier is reached and RelativePower is recomputed. The other component, time, can also be measured easily as well, hence, making the estimation of RelativePower fairly straightforward.

However, we do not rely on existence of barriers in applications in our new runtime system. When no barriers are employed, it is likely that multiple parallel regions are spanned and different number of iterations are executed in each of these parallel regions by each of the processes. In most cases, not all processes have finished their assigned work. This makes estimation of the amount of completed work, harder to obtain. For the purposes of computing the RelativePower, we use the minimum execution time for an iteration as the basis for determining the amount of work for that iteration. Prior to computation of the RelativePower, all processes exchange their number of executed iterations, and the time it took to execute these iterations, for each of the parallel regions. Figure 3 shows the pseudocode of how to compute RelativePower.

```
static float RelativePower[NumProcs]
   //Initialized to 1/NumProcs
float IterTime[NumParRegs][NumProcs]
   //Execution time of parallel region
float NumIters[NumParRegs][NumProcs]
   //Executed Tasks in Each Region
float WorkPerProc[NumProcs]
float PerProcExecTime[NumProcs]
float Power,SumOfPowers=0

//Calculate the amount of work done by each
//process and the time it took to do so.
for all Parallel Regions i
   float AvgTime,WorkDone
   float MinIterTime = LARGENUMBER

   for all Processes j
      PerProcExecTime[j] += IterTime[i][j]
      AvgTime = IterTime[i][j]/NumIters[i][j]
      if (AvgTime < MinIterTime)
         MinIterTime = AvgTime
   for all Processes j
      WorkDone = NumIters[i][j] * MinIterTime
      WorkPerProc[j] += WorkDone

//Calculate RelativePower
for all Processes i
   Power = WorkPerProc[i]/PerProcExecTime[i]
   RelativePower[i] = Power
   SumOfPowers += Power

//Normalize The RelativePower
for all Processes i
   RelativePowers[i] /= SumOfPowers
```

Figure 3. Computing "RelativePower".

2.3.2. Task Distribution Strategy

Upon entrance for the first time to a parallel region, the runtime system partitions the parallel region into tasks based on the access pattern, the load per parallel loop, and the size of the coherence unit. The size of the data elements along with the size of the coherence unit are used to determine the partitioning in an attempt to reduce false sharing. Work is partitioned so that accesses by each individual process are in multiples of the coherence unit in order to avoid false sharing across processors. Consecutive loop iterations are blocked together until their size is a multiple of the coherence unit. This defines the minimum task size. Once the minimum task size has been determined, a fixed number of tasks per parallel region are created and assigned to processors using either a block or cyclic distribution based on whether the load is defined to be *FIXED* or *VARIABLE*, respectively, or whether the access pattern is *STENCIL*. The size of each task is an integral multiple of the minimum task size and enough tasks are created to allow later redistribution when relative processing powers change.

At any time the runtime system has a notion of perceived `RelativePower`. Program execution starts by assuming all processors have equal amount of work to do and they are all equally powerful, i.e. their `RelativePower` is equal. The `RelativePower` is updated regularly as explained in Section 2.3.1. Load reassignment occurs when a significant change in the `RelativePower` is detected[2].

While tasks are being created, if the access pattern is *STENCIL*, then a single task per process, sized proportional to the perceived `RelativePower` of that process is created. If the access pattern is not *STENCIL*, however, many equal-sized fixed tasks are created and they are distributed among processes with numbers proportional to their perceived `RelativePower`. For *STENCIL* regions, load is balanced by changing the size of the task via shuffling its boundaries. Otherwise, load is balanced by moving tasks from processors with decreased `RelativePower` to those with increased `RelativePower`. Even though balancing itself might involve more communication when the access pattern is *STENCIL*, the steady-state communication is reduced by making sure all assignments have the least number of boundaries possible.

Task assignment and execution take the topology of the processors into account. For a cluster of SMPs, work is partitioned in a hierarchical manner in order to account for the fact that intra-node communication is cheaper than inter-node communication. Task redistribution is performed across SMPs. Task stealing is allowed within each SMP. Locality has been shown to be more important than load balancing [14]. Given the continuously increasing speed gap between processors and memory and the use of deeper memory hierarchies, locality management is an even bigger issue in today's processors. In order to preserve locality within an SMP, each processor maintains task affinity — it must finish its own task assignment prior to stealing a task from another processor (similar to [11]). This is done by using a per-processor task queue, and having a processor retrieve tasks from the head of its queue but steal from the tail of another processor's queue. Once a task is stolen from another processor's task queue, it is moved and owned by

the stealing processor.

When any of the processes is not able to proceed due to not finding anything in its task queue, the first attempt is to steal tasks from processes running on the same SMP node. If a *suitable* task is not found there either, a balancing request message is issued. Upon this request, all processes exchange their execution statistics and compute the new `RelativePower`. Exchanged statistics also include the number of times a process iterated over a parallel region. For the purposes of reducing the number of messages and message assembly time, statistics are written directly into network mapped memory.

To accommodate applications without barriers, it is required to decide when a new load reassignment should take effect. Since some processes might be lagging behind, every reassignment of tasks does not take effect immediately for all processes. A process may move a task from another process only when the source and destination processes are at the same phase with respect to the region being processed. If the old owner is lagging behind (the most likely scenario) and a task is moved, a naive approach might skip some computation stages (parallel regions or iterations), resulting in incorrect computation. It is also possible for the old owner to be ahead, for example, when the parallel region's access type is *STENCIL*, in which case work might erroneously be replicated. In order to simplify the implementation and reduce the need for synchronization, for each of the parallel regions we determine the current computation state of the fastest process in terms of the current parallel region and the number of times each parallel region has been executed. Old owners of tasks that are moved use this information to stop processing them when this computation state is reached. The new owners take over at that time.

Guaranteeing the coherence of a task to be moved requires the old and new owner of a task to synchronize after the old owner operates on the data for the last time, if they have not done so already. To guarantee coherence, consistency operations and task modifications are timestamped. The movement of a task is legal if the timestamp of the consistency operation is larger than the modification timestamp of the task being moved. Otherwise, the old owner and the new owner of the task need to exchange updates to bring the copy of the new owner up-to-date.

2.4. Cooperative Scheduling Support

Multiprogramming adds an additional dimension to the problem of imbalanced load. Communication among cooperating processes can result in significant delay if one of the cooperating processes is de-scheduled and unable to respond. Coscheduling [16, 20, 3, 23, 15] approaches have been used in the past, where cooperating processes are scheduled to execute simultaneously on all processors. This

---

[2]At least one of the `RelativePowers` must change enough to make sure some load movement would actually happen

approach is good when the load on all processors is equal. However, in the presence of autonomous nodes with unequal levels of multiprogramming at each processor, a more distributed and cooperative approach is required in order to improve efficiency while retaining autonomy.

Our goal is to reduce the wait time experienced by parallel applications in the presence of multiprogramming through the use of a cooperative scheduler. We modified a priority-based scheduler to achieve this goal while retaining the fairness and autonomy of the individual schedulers on each node. Our implementation is on Compaq's Tru64 (formerly known as DEC Unix) version 4.0F.

2.4.1. Scheduler Modifications

In order to improve response times, the scheduler must be willing to schedule an application's process on demand. However, this cannot be accomplished in traditional schedulers without compromising fairness. To provide the scheduler with the flexibility to handle these conflicting requirements, each process, upon declaration of its interest in cooperating with remote processes, is charged a scheduling quantum of time. This time is held in a *"piggy-bank"* for future use by the process. The *"piggy-bank"* is replenished any time the process voluntarily yields the processor prior to the expiration of its scheduling quantum (by adding an amount less than or equal to the remainder of the quantum, and charging that amount to the process), but is guaranteed not to grow larger than one quantum. This prevents a process from taking over the processor for long periods of time by yielding often. When a scheduling request is received, the scheduler uses the time in the piggy-bank, if any, to schedule the intended process.

2.4.2. OS-Runtime Interface

For a process of a parallel application to be scheduled on demand, the desire to schedule it needs to be communicated to its scheduler. For many networks, receiving a message involves executing some code on the recipient end, in the driver. This code could be modified to implicitly communicate with the scheduler, to express desire for immediate scheduling. Our network, Compaq's Memory Channel, however, is a low latency remote write network, and it does not execute any code on the recipient host CPU, upon receipt of a message. Hence the desire for scheduling a peer need to be communicated explicitly. For that purpose we send a signal. However, sending a signal after each message or at every synchronization point is expensive, and in some cases, where the peer is already scheduled or the message is asynchronous, it is not needed. For the purposes of eliminating excessive signals, we employ other features provided by our network to communicate among cooperating processes.

We provide a system call that allows each process to register a signal and a memory location. The registered signal is used by a cooperating process as a wakeup signal. Upon receiving that signal, rather than delivering it to the application, if the scheduler can schedule the process using the equity in the piggy-bank, while continuing to guarantee fairness, it does so.

The registered memory location has two boolean words. The first ("scheduling status") is written by the scheduler and gives hint to other processes regarding the scheduling status of the registering process. It is set by the scheduler when the process is de-scheduled. The second word ("signaled") is set by signal-sending processes to inform others that a scheduling request has been sent to a particular process, preventing them from sending yet another signal. When the process is scheduled, both words of the registered memory are reset, indicating that the process is scheduled and no scheduling request is pending. These memory locations are placed in network mapped memory, and modifications to these locations are broadcast to all other processes. The additional communication overhead resulting from this sharing is minimal in comparison to the rest of the protocol and data communication overhead for the application. This is especially true for the medium-scale clusters used for such parallel applications.

2.4.3. Runtime Cooperation

In order to give the scheduler the flexibility to respond to on-demand scheduling requests, an application must voluntarily yield the processor in order to build up its piggy-bank. A yield system call[3] is used to free up resources preemptively in order to build up this future "equity". The yield call is made by a process whenever the process would otherwise spin waiting for an external event such as communication or synchronization with a remote process. The yield call takes one argument to indicate the lowest priority that the caller is willing to yield to. The argument specifies a priority relative to the priority of the caller. If no other process within the given priority is available, the call returns immediately with no effect. Otherwise, a runnable process with the highest priority is picked and scheduled. A spin-block strategy [15] is used to avoid unnecessary yields. The spin time is set to be at least twice the round-trip communication time and is doubled each time the yield is unsuccessful.

A complication in implementing this system call is accounting for resource usage. In many operating systems, processes are charged at the granularity of a clock-tick, which is about 1 msec on our platform. If a process yields frequently enough, it might either not be charged at all for its use, or it could be over-charged depending on the rela-

---

[3]While some operating systems already provide this ability, we had to add this system call to Tru64.

tive timing of a clock-tick and the yield call. In order to fix this, we used hardware cycle counters as the basis for accounting.

3. Evaluation

3.1. Experimental Platform

Our experimental environment is a cluster of Compaq AlphaServer 4100 workstations. Each workstation is equipped with four 21164A processors operating at 600 MHz, 2 GB of shared memory, and a Memory Channel network interface. The Memory Channel [5] is a PCI-based crossbar network, with a peak point-to-point bandwidth of approximately 83 MBytes/sec. The network is capable of remotely writing to memory mapped areas, but does not have remote read capability. The one-way latency for a 64-bit remote-write operation is 3.3 μsecs.

All the programs, the runtime library, and Cashmere were compiled with **gcc** version 2.8.1 using the **-O2** optimization flag. On our platform, a scheduling quantum is approximately 10ms and a process runs until the quantum expires, unless there is a higher priority process. A null system call takes approximately 0.5 μs and a context switch takes approximately 6 μs.

3.2. Experimental Results

In order to evaluate our system, we used a set of eight applications as our benchmarks. These benchmarks exhibit a range of sharing patterns and types of parallel regions. Figure 4 shows the execution results of our applications. We ran our applications using 32 processors, under 4 different load schemes as shown in Table 1. For the purposes of loading a processor, we use a program that executes in a tight loop incrementing a variable (a pure computational load). For each load scheme, we present execution times with no support (*None*), with support for task stealing within a node enabled (*Steal*), and with task stealing within a node as well as load balancing across nodes enabled (*Balance*). The case labeled "No Load" is the base case. It is intended to show baseline execution time and the runtime system overhead, and in some cases how the runtime system might help offsetting the anomalies due to the application algorithm, even in the absence of any other load. The "Load-4" case is intended to show the adaptation of the system by shifting the parallel program tasks from an overloaded node and distributing these tasks among other nodes. The "Load-8" case is intended to show the effectiveness of intra node load balancing, by task stealing. Finally, the "Load-16" case shows the effectiveness and scalability of load balancing schemes as well as how scalable the cooperative scheduling is. Note that cooperative scheduling is enabled in all the

experiments. Hence these performance improvements are on top of what cooperative scheduling could achieve. Section 3.2.1 evaluates the effect of cooperative scheduling on performance. Following is a description of our benchmarks and discussion of our results.

Label\Nodes	0	1	2	3	4	5	6	7
No-Load	0	0	0	0	0	0	0	0
Load-4	0	4	0	0	0	0	0	0
Load-8	1	1	1	1	1	1	1	1
Load-16	0	0	0	0	4	4	4	4

Table 1. Number of processors running a sequential program along the parallel program for each of the configurations.

Transitive Closure: A graph algorithm that checks reachability from one vertex to others. The main intuition in the implementation is that if vertex A is reachable by vertex B, then every vertex reachable by vertex A is also reachable by vertex B. We used a random input with any pair of vertices having 60% likelihood of having an edge. The amount of computation depends on whether the pair of vertices picked up could reach each other. Hence, even though the loop structure is regular, the computation within the loop is conditional, creating an application induced (short-term) load imbalance.

Gaussian Elimination: A parallel gaussian elimination algorithm. The solution is computed by using partial pivoting and back substitution, and the row elimination is parallelized. The dataset size in our experiments is a matrix of 8Kx8K floating point numbers. Flags are used for synchronization purposes. A processor sets a flag upon computing the pivot, which in turn signals availability of the pivot to other processors. This implementation has more relaxed synchronization than a barrier implementation, because it allows two processes to be working with different pivots at any time of the computation. Furthermore, flags are known to be less affected by multiprogramming than barriers [13].

Jacobi: An iterative method for solving partial differential equations with nearest neighbor averaging as the main computation. We used a matrix of 8Kx8K floating point numbers. At each iteration, neighboring processors need to exchange their boundary rows of data. Two arrays are employed, where one is used as a scratch pad. Two barriers are required at each iteration, one after doing the averaging and the other after copying the data from the scratch pad to the main array. Since it exhibits nearest neighbor sharing, a single task is created per process to reduce steady state communication. Load balancing is achieved by resizing assigned task rather than changing the number of fixed tasks assigned to each processor.

391

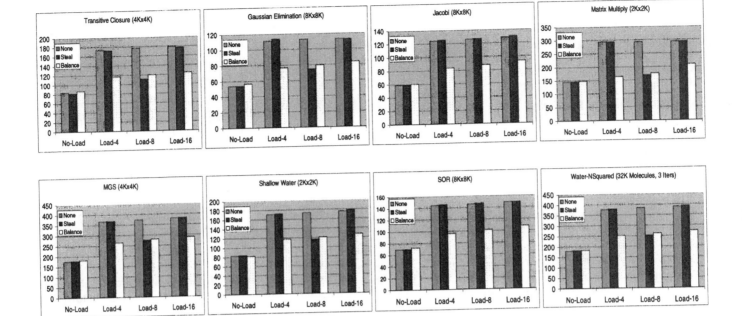

Figure 4. Effectiveness of load balancing. The Y-axis is the execution times in seconds. X-axis labels indicate the load as explained in Table 1. "None" indicates no balancing was done, "Steal" indicates only intra-node task stealing was allowed, and finally "Balance" indicates both intra-node stealing and inter-node balancing were allowed. In all cases scheduling support was on.

Matrix Multiply: A simple matrix multiplication algorithm parallelized by forming tasks with groups of rows and distributing these tasks among processes. The dataset consists of three 2048x2048 matrices of integers — one each for the multiplier, multiplicand, and result. This application has very long periods of computation and very little communication or synchronization. As a result, it is oblivious to lack of coordination.

Modified Gramm Schmidt (MGS): This application computes an orthonormal basis for a set of N-dimensional vectors. At each iteration i, the algorithm first sequentially normalizes the ith vector, then makes all vectors $j > i$ orthogonal to vector i, in parallel. Since the application leaves out a row at each iteration, the created distribution is cyclic.

Shallow: The shallow water benchmark from the National Center for Atmospheric Research. This code is used in weather prediction and solves differential equations on a two dimensional grid. During the execution, 11 parallel regions are spanned, with some of the regions taking only a few milliseconds, involving a single row of the matrix.

SOR: Successive-over-relaxation is a nearest neighbor averaging algorithm from the TreadMarks [2] distribution, that is also used to solve partial differential equations. A matrix of 8Kx8K floating point numbers is used in our experiments.

Water-NSquared: A molecular dynamics simulation from the SPLASH-1 [19] benchmark suite. It is run for 3 steps. The bulk of the interprocessor communication occurs during a phase that updates intermolecular forces using locks, resulting in a migratory sharing pattern. Between each update phase, a barrier operation is performed. We use an input set of 32K molecules. The application acquires a lock to update each of the molecules. Our SDSM system has a maximum number of 4K locks, causing 8 molecules share one lock. Even though contention for a lock is likely, the critical region is very short. Furthermore, if any process holding a lock happened to be de-scheduled, the cooperative scheduling mechanism would reschedule it, reducing the wait time. Despite the high number of locks, the number of barriers executed in the course of the run is small.

As Figure 4 demonstrates, having both intra-node task stealing and inter-node load balancing enabled (i.e. "Balance") reduces the execution time across all application when there is any load, and the overhead in the absence of load is minimal. The reduction in execution time is no less than 26% and it is as high as 44%. Several results are worth noting. First of all, for all the applications with the exception of jacobi and SOR, intra-node task stealing alone achieves slightly better runtime reduction for the "Load-8" (no inter-node imbalance) case. This is mainly due to the fact that task stealing alone has less overhead than inter-node load balancing, and in some cases, load balancing might cause one piece of work to move from one node to another causing slightly more communication in the system. For **transitive closure**, even in the absence of load the execution time is reduced 3% when intra-node task stealing is used. This is due to smoothing the short-term load imbalance induced by application characteristics, by stealing tasks from processes lagging behind. **Gaussian elimination** uses the most relaxed form of synchronization, and the results show that our system handles this type of synchronization correctly and effectively. **Jacobi and SOR** are applications with loops marked as being *STENCIL*. This causes creation of a single task per process, and makes task-stealing impossible. However, load balancing is very effective for both applications. **Matrix multiply** has been shown, in our earlier study [18], to exhibit a reduction of 33% at most when all features were turned on. In this set of experiments the reduction is as high as 44%. This improvement is mainly the result of the ability to balance load before reaching a barrier (there are roughly 20 secs between barriers), and hence reducing the time the application runs imbalanced. **Shallow** benefits from the runtime system even in the absence of any other load, by cutting the execution time by about 1%, despite the overhead of the runtime system. This improvement is the result of localizing computation for loops which involve very little work over a small amount of data. This cuts the cost of communication by having the nodes that currently cache the data perform all the computation.

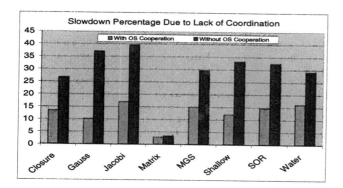

Figure 5. Effectiveness of cooperation. The left bar shows the percentage of overhead due to multiprogramming when the runtime system cooperates with the OS as described in Section 2.4. The right bar is when there is no coordination among parallel processes.

3.2.1. Effectiveness of Cooperative Scheduling

In order to determine how effective our cooperative scheduling is, we conducted experiments with and without cooperation. Results are shown in Figure 5. In all cases, applications were run with "Load-16" configuration as shown in Table 1. None of the load balancing or locality management features were used. Ideally the execution time of each application should be exactly twice as much as the case when all the nodes are dedicated. Any amount above this is a slowdown due to multiprogramming. Not cooperating with the OS leaves the scheduling uncoordinated and hence adds a slowdown of up to 39%. Just turning the cooperation on, which in effect causes interacting processes to be scheduled on demand, reduces this overhead by 50% on average, and in some cases as much as 72%. 72% reduction is achieved in Gaussian Elimination, where it is important to have the process producing the pivot be scheduled while others are fetching the pivot from it. Even though we reduce the effects of lack of coordination in all cases, there are several reasons for not achieving the ideal: 1) There is a delay of several microseconds between sending a signal and actually the signal reaching its destination. 2) Since events are polled by the OS at each hardware clock tick, which is about 833μs, a signal waits on average half of this time to be processed, after being received by the target node. 3) The context switch adds cost. 4) In some cases, it is possible for a scheduling request to be ignored if the recipient process has already used its fair share, and granting that request would be unfair to other processes on the same node. This is an indication that load balancing is needed, and in most cases the runtime system, when enabled, would redistribute the load moving some of the work to other processes.

4. Conclusions

We have presented a system that combines compile-time analysis, runtime load balancing and locality considerations, and cooperative scheduling support for improved performance of parallel applications running on an autonomous COW. The system works regardless of the synchronization method used by the parallel application and at the same time is fair to all processes. Reducing the execution time of the parallel program while being fair to other applications improves the throughput of the COW. Our previous work addressed similar issues for applications that used barrier synchronization. The extensions described in this paper are important not only because of extending the application base we address, but also due to providing opportunities for applications using barriers to be able to adapt to available resources before a barrier is reached. Furthermore, since barriers are known to be more vulnerable to resource mismatches, it provides applications with the opportunity to be implemented using synchronization primitives other than barriers.

For parallel applications that use our system, we have shown that using all the features helps to reduce the execution time by as much as 44% on top of the reduction achieved by cooperative scheduling and on up to 32 processors. Features such as the ability to reshuffle work on the fly without the need to be at a synchronization point benefit applications with long periods of computation between two synchronization points (e.g. matrix multiply). Our run-time system's awareness of the underlying topology of the cluster reduces the amount of communicated data considerably by moving the data within the SMP node first. Data is moved across nodes only when the aggregate load of the collection of processors within the node exceeds the pool of resources within that node.

References

[1] S. P. Amarasinghe, J. M. Anderson, M. S. Lam, and C. W. Tseng. The SUIF compiler for scalable parallel machines. In *Proceedings of the 7th SIAM Conference on Parallel Processing for Scientific Computing*, February 1995.

[2] C. Amza, A.L. Cox, S. Dwarkadas, P. Keleher, H. Lu, R. Rajamony, and W. Zwaenepoel. TreadMarks: Shared memory computing on networks of workstations. *IEEE Computer*, 29(2):18–28, February 1996.

[3] Andrea D. Dusseau, Remzi H. Arpaci, and David H. Culler. Effective distributed scheduling of parallel workloads. In *Proceedings of SIGMETRICS 1996*, pages 25–36, PA, USA, May 1996. ACM.

[4] D. L. Eager and J. Zahorjan. Adaptive guided self-scheduling. Technical Report 92-01-01, Department of Computer Science, University of Washington, January 1992.

[5] Richard B. Gillett. Memory channel network for PCI. *IEEE Micro*, 16(1):12–18, Feb 1996.

[6] P. Havlak and K. Kennedy. An implementation of interprocedural bounded regular section analysis. *IEEE Transactions on Parallel and Distributed Systems*, 2(3):350–360, July 1991.

[7] D. G. Morris III and D. K. Lowenthal. Accurate data redistribution cost estimation in software distributed shared memory systems. In *Proceedings of the 8th Symposium on the Principles and Practice of Parallel Programming*, June 2001.

[8] Sotiris Ioannidis and Sandhya Dwarkadas. Compiler and run-time support for adaptive load balancing in software distributed shared memory system. In *Languages, Compilers, and Run-Time Systems for Scalable Computers*, pages 107–122, May 1998.

[9] Sotiris Ioannidis, Umit Rencuzogullari, Robert Stets, and Sandhya Dwarkadas. Craul: Compiler and run-time integration for adaptation under load. *Journal of Scientific Programming*, August 1999.

[10] C. Kruskal and A. Weiss. Allocating independent subtasks on parallel processors. *IEEE Transactions on Software Engineering*, 11(10):1001–1016, Oct 1985.

[11] Hui Li, Sudarsan Tandri, Michael Stumm, and Kenneth C. Sevcik. Locality and loop scheduling on NUMA multiprocessors. In *1993 International Conference on Parallel Processing*, pages 140–147, August 1993.

[12] D. K. Lowenthal and G. R. Andrews. An adaptive approach to data placement. In *10th International Parallel Processing Symposium*, April 1996.

[13] E. Markatos, M. Crovella, P. Das, C. Dubnicki, and T. LeBlanc. The effects of multiprogramming on barrier synchronization. In *Proceedings of the Third IEEE Symposium on Parallel and Distributed Processing*, pages 662–669, December 1991.

[14] E. P. Markatos and T. J. LeBlanc. Load balancing versus locality management in shared-memory multiprocessors. *1992 International Conference on Parallel Processing*, pages 258–267, August 1992.

[15] Shailabh Nagar, Ajit Banerjee, Anand Sivasubramaniam, and Chita R. Das. A closer look at coscheduling approaches for a network of workstations. In *Proceedings of 11th ACM Symposium on Parallel Algorithms and Architectures*, pages 96–105, June 1999.

[16] John K. Ousterhout. Scheduling techniques for concurrent systems. In *Proceedings of the 3rd International Conference on Distributed Computing Systems*, pages 22–30. IEEE, October 1982.

[17] C. D. Polychronopoulos and D. J. Kuck. Guided self-scheduling: a practical scheduling scheme for parallel supercomputers. In *IEEE Transactions on Computers*, December 1987.

[18] U. Rencuzogullari and S. Dwarkadas. Dynamic adaptation to available resources for parallel computing in an autonomous network of workstations. In *Proceedings of the 8th Symposium on the Principles and Practice of Parallel Programming*. ACM, June 2001.

[19] J.P. Singh, W.-D. Weber, and A. Gupta. SPLASH: Stanford parallel applications for shared-memory. *Computer Architecture News*, 20(1):2–12, March 1992.

[20] Patrick Gregory Sobalvarro. *Demand-based Coscheduling of Parallel Jobs on Multiprogrammed Machines*. PhD thesis, M.I.T., January 1997.

[21] R. Stets, S. Dwarkadas, N. Hardavellas, G. Hunt, L. Kontothanassis, S. Parthasarathy, and M.L. Scott. Cashmere-2L: Software coherent shared memory on a clustered remote-write network. In *Proceedings of the 16th ACM Symposium on Operating Systems Principles*, pages 170–183, October 1997.

[22] P. Tang and P. C. Yew. Processor self-scheduling for multiple nested parallel loops. In *1986 International Conference on Parallel Processing*, August 1986.

[23] Andrew Tucker and Anoop Gupta. Process control and scheduling issues for multiprogrammed shared-memory multiprocessors. In *Proceedings of the 12th ACM SIGOPS Symposium on Operating Systems Principles*, pages 159–166. ACM, December 1989.

Panel Session

Keynote Address

Session 6A

Dynamic Hybrid Routing (DHR) in Mobile Ad Hoc Networks

Seungjin Park

Department of Computer Science
Michigan Technological University
1400 Townsend Drive
Houghton, MI 49931
spark@mtu.edu

Brian VanVoorst

Distributed Architecture and Computing Group
Honeywell Laboratories
3660 Technology Drive
Minneapolis, MN 55418
vanvoorst_brian@htc.honeywell.com

Abstract

The route discovery and maintenance processes in wireless mobile networks are very expensive tasks due to the mobility of the host. Route discovery requires a considerable amount of resources and therefore it is wise to utilize the effort already invested in existing paths. This paper proposes a dynamic hybrid routing (DHR) protocol in ad hoc networks, which constructs paths only upon demand by taking attributes from both proactive and reactive algorithms. The goal of DHR is to re-use, whenever possible, portions of several existing paths when establishing a new path. The reusability is accomplished by using dynamic proactive zones (PZs), through which nearby existing path information is disseminated. By utilizing the information stored in PZs, considerable savings (in time and traffic) can be achieved over other on-demand routing algorithms that use flooding. In other route-finding algorithms, proactive zones are formed throughout the network and remain unchanged, whereas in DHR, routes are created and destroyed dynamically around the existing paths. Even though DHR may not find the shortest path between source and destination, it does reduce the amount of traffic needed to find a path and therefore increases the available bandwidth for data transfer.

1. Introduction

A network that consists of wireless mobile hosts without any centralized control point or fixed infrastructure is called an *ad hoc* network. Ad hoc networks are of interest because they can be quickly deployed and used without prior arrangements. Applications include quick deployment of military communications and rescue missions, where an established network is neither feasible nor available [9].

In wireless networks, radio ranges of wireless hosts (nodes) are limited due to physical and economic constraints. If a node, *u*, is within a radio range of another node, say *v*, then *u* is said to be a *neighbor node* of *v* and

we say that there is a link connecting *u* and *v*. For the simplicity of discussion, we assume that all links are bi-directional in this paper.

Often a node *s* (source node) wants to communicate with another node *d* (destination node) that is not a neighbor of *s*. For successful transmission between the two nodes, there must be a series of *intermediate nodes*, $b_1, b_2, \ldots, b_m$, $m \geq 1$, that relay the packet from *s* to *d*. This ordered set of nodes $(s, b_1, b_2, \ldots, b_m, d)$ is referred to as a *path* (or *route*) from *s* to *d* and is denoted as *P(s, d)*. In the following, we set $s = b_0$ and $d = b_{m+1}$. $v \in P(m, n)$ denotes that node *v* is on *P(m, n)*. Note that every intermediate node, b_i, has exactly two neighbor nodes, b_{i-1}, b_{i+1}, in the path. The geographical position of node *v* is denoted as (x_v, y_v) in a 2-dimensional plane. The physical distance between two nodes, *p* and *q*, is denoted as $|(p, q)| = \text{Sqrt} \left(|x_q - x_p|^2 + |y_q - y_p|^2 \right)$.

Although a wireless node does a physical "broadcast" (all nodes within range can hear) of data when it transmits, there is a significant difference between a *unicast (send)* packet and a *broadcast* packet in wireless networks. The term unicast implies that there is a designated destination node for the packet, whereas in a broadcast all nodes that hear the message are designated to receive it. This is a logical distinction, because physical communication is still accomplished via a wireless broadcast. When a node *s* wants to *unicast* a packet to a node *d* within its range, *s* broadcasts the packet to all nodes in its transmission range, because broadcast is the only method to transfer a packet in a wireless network. However, only *d* reacts to that packet (i.e., relays the packet) in unicast communication, whereas in broadcast all nodes in the range react, resulting in flooding. Therefore, a unicast send consumes much less time and bandwidth than broadcast. In the proposed algorithm, unicast communication will be used, whenever possible, over broadcast.

401

1.1. Taxonomy of routing algorithms

One popular classification of the routing algorithms is based on the time when the route is determined. In *proactive* algorithms [1], each node constantly updates and maintains the routes to all nodes in the network using the well-known link-state or distance-vector routing algorithms. Another classification of routing algorithms is the *reactive* algorithms [2, 3, 4]. Reactive algorithms start finding routes only when necessary. In these protocols, if a node wants to send a packet to a destination node, then it broadcasts a control packet called a *route request packet* (REQ) to its neighbor nodes. If none of them has a route to the destination, each relays the REQ to its neighbor nodes, and so on until the REQ reaches the destination node. (This forwarding of requests from one node to all its neighbors is called "flooding" and can consume a lot of bandwidth.) If the REQ reaches either the destination node or a node that contains a path to the destination, the node sends a control packet called a *route reply packet* (RPY) back to the source by reversing the path found by the REQ. On receiving a RPY, the source knows that the path to the destination has been established and sends its data packet along the path.

Haas [8] has proposed a hybrid routing protocol called Zone Routing Protocol (ZRP), which incorporates desirable features of both reactive and proactive protocols. Routing in ZRP consists of Interzone and Intrazone. Each node in ZRP proactively maintains routes to destinations within a routing zone. Intrazone operation is used inside a routing zone maintained by a node proactively, whereas Interzone routing reactively discovers routes to destinations that are beyond a node's routing zone. Other well-scalable routing schemes based on hierarchical routing can be found in [10, 11, 12].

Routing protocols can be improved if additional information about the nodes is available. Recently, routing algorithms have been proposed based on the assumption that each node can obtain its own geographic information via GPS (or another service) [5, 6, 7]. LAR [5] uses location information to facilitate a reactive route discovery algorithm by searching only the Expected Zone (EZ). Greedy forwarding [6] selects the node geographically closest to the destination as the next hop node. DREAM [7] uses a proactive approach by constantly exchanging location information among nodes of the network. Even though these methods use global flooding to find the destination nodes for the first time, the position information of the nodes can reduce the amount of search space for later searches.

1.2 Motivation for Dynamic Hybrid Routing

As we mentioned earlier, finding a route in a wireless networks is an expensive operation in terms of both time and bandwidth utilization. Therefore, development of efficient routing algorithms with low communication overhead may increase throughput for data traffic in the network. Since we have already invested considerable resources to find routes, it would be wise to take full advantage of these existing paths. Unfortunately, most of the routing algorithms described above do not utilize existing routes enough, and as a result, they waste valuable resources finding routes when an existing route may be near by.

In this paper, we propose a protocol, Dynamic Hybrid Routing (DHR), that is a hybrid of proactive and reactive routing and that utilizes location information. DHR shares information about a route with nodes near that route. When a REQ comes near an existing route, the request can be forwarded to the existing route and travel it, if it will move the REQ closer to the destination. This is only possible because DHR maintains the location information of the destination and the location of nodes on existing routes. To control the propagation of this route information, a *proactive zone* (PZ) is formed around the path, and dissemination of the path information is limited to those nodes inside this PZ.

Our approach differs from ZRP [8] in two important ways: 1) PZs in ZRP are static, whereas DHRs PZs are created and destroyed when the path is created and destroyed, and 2) PZs in DHR help find paths quickly and efficiently by re-using portions of existing paths, whereas the purpose of ZRP is to propagate the REQ efficiently.

The remainder of this paper is organized as follows. Section 2 presents DHR. Simulation results are explained in Section 3. Our conclusions follows in Section 4.

2. DHR (Dynamic Hybrid Routing)

DHR assumes a two-layer structure. The *lower layer* of DHR can be any routing algorithm, such as DSR [4], AODV [2], DSDV [1], TORA [3], any location-related algorithm [5, 13, 14], or even one yet to be developed. The *upper layer* provides services that allow the underlying routing algorithm to re-use paths. The upper layer constructs and utilizes Proactive Zones to improve the performance of the lower layer by guiding it to find the route to the destination faster and more efficiently.

Each path has its own proactive zone. A proactive zone is a geographic region around the path in which information about the existence of the path will be disseminated. Consider a path $P(s,d)$, with a proactive zone called $PZ(s,d)$ (Figure 1). Inside the area of $PZ(s,d)$ there may be a node m which is not a part of $P(s,d)$. DHR will broadcast the existence of $P(s,d)$ to all nodes in $PZ(s,d)$ so that they are aware of $P(s,d)$. If node m receives a REQ going toward the location of d, m can utilize an existing portion of the path $P(s,d)$ to forward the REQ efficiently.

To facilitate node m being able to reach path $P(s,d)$ we break the PZ into sections (sub proactive zones) which we call subPZs. A subPZ is centered around each node along the path of $P(s,d)$. Such nodes are called *pivot nodes*. All nodes inside the subPZ are notified about the subPZ by that subPZ's pivot node (see Figure 2). Later, when a node such as v wants to utilize the existing path $P(s,d)$, it simply routes the message to the pivot node c of its subPZ.

The shape of the PZ may influence the effectiveness of the proposed scheme. A triangle-like shape is adopted in this paper because the nodes closer to source of the path may take more advantage from the path than the nodes closer to the destination node. Other shapes are possible and will be considered in future work.

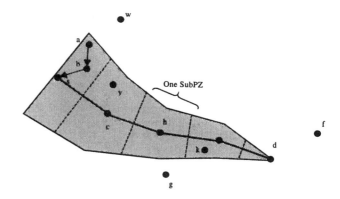

Figure 2. An example of a proactive zone of path $P(s, d)$. Shaded areas surrounded by dotted lines are subPZs, and nodes on the $P(s, d)$, for example c and h, are pivot nodes.

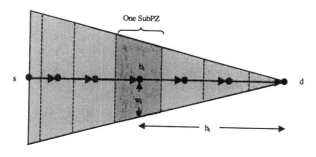

Figure 1: An example of a proactive zone (PZ) formed by the path from s to d. The subPZs are centered in the y-dimension around the pivot nodes. The darker area is the subPZ of b_i. We have chosen to use triangular PZs that get larger in the x-dimension the farther away the intermediate node is from d. Other shapes may be considered in future work.

2.1 Establishing the Proactive Zone

A proactive zone is a region around a path. Conceptually we speak about the PZ as a whole; however, it is created and maintained in a distributed fashion as a series of subPZs. No one node manages (or is aware of) the entire geography of the PZ.

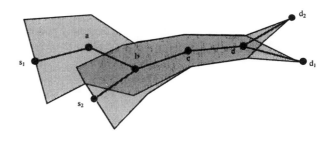

Figure 3. When two paths share a common set of nodes, such as the case of nodes b, c, and d, then their proactive zones will intersect.

Source Location	Destination Location	Pivot Location	subPZ Boundaries	Time To Live	Route Packet Took Through subPZ
$S_{x,y}$	$D_{x,y}$	$V_{x,y}$	$(N_{x,y}, S_{x,y}, E_{x,y}, W_{x,y})$	TTL	$\{v, u_1, u_2, \ldots, u_n\}$

Figure 4: Proactive Zone Packet. PZPs originate at pivot nodes and are flooded inside a subPZ to establish a route back to the main path.

To build the triangular PZ, as shown in Figure 1, we perform the following calculations. Suppose there is an established path from s to d in the network as shown in Fig. 2, where $s = (x_s, y_s)$, $d = (x_d, y_d)$, $b_i = (x_i, y_i)$, $i = 1, 2, \ldots, m$, for all intermediate nodes. For simplicity of explanation, assume that all nodes in $P(s, d)$ have the same value in y-coordinates. For each node, b_i, in the path, let the distance between b_i and d be $h_i = |x_d - x_i|$. (In general cases, this value would be sqrt $(|x_d - x_i|^2 + |y_d - y_i|^2)$.) Then the Proactive Zone (PZ) is defined as the area surrounded by lines formed by connecting points $\{(x_d, y_d), (x_m, y_m + \omega h_m), (x_{m-1}, y_{m-1} + \omega h_{m-1}), \ldots, (x_1, y_1 + \omega h_1), (x_s, y_s + \omega h_s), (x_s, y_s - \omega h_s), (x_1, y_1 - \omega h_1), \ldots, (x_m, y_m - \omega h_m), ((x_d, y_d)\}$ in that order, where ω is a parameter that decides the depth of the PZ.

2.2 Forming subPZs

The purpose of the further division of PZs into subPZs is to restrict the communication information overheard about a path. A PZ is further divided into *subPZs* as follows. *A boundary line* in a PZ for two consecutive nodes, b_i and b_{i+1}, in $P(s, d)$, is the line that is perpendicular to and passing through the midpoint of the link (b_i, b_{i+1}); i.e., (b_i, b_{i+1}) and the boundary line intersect at $((x_i + x_{i+1})/2, y_i)$. Dotted lines in Figure 1 are the boundary lines for the subPZs in this example. The subPZ of intermediate node b_i is the area that is both 1) within the PZ, and 2) between its immediate left and right boundary lines as shown in the darker shaded area in Figure 1. The node b_i of the subPZ is called a *pivot*.

During the period in which a path, say P, is valid, every pivot node, in P calculates its subPZ and periodically broadcasts to all nodes in its subPZ a *Proactive Zone Packet* (PZP), shown in Figure 4. The PZP includes the positions of the source $(S_{x,y})$ and destination $(D_{x,y})$ of P and the position of the pivot node B $(B_{x,y})$, and geographical information about its subPZ $(N_{x,y}, S_{x,y}, E_{x,y}, W_{x,y})$. The PZP also contains the time to live for the path. Once this time expires, this path is invalidated.

The last piece of information contained in the PZP is the route back to the pivot node.

Figure 5 shows the algorithm for forwarding a PZP inside a subPZ. This makes a spanning tree from each pivot node to the nodes inside the subPZ, allowing them to know about and utilize the path the pivot nodes are on.

To keep the subPZ alive, each pivot node b_i should periodically check to make sure it can still communicate with its upstream and downstream neighbors (b_{i-1} and b_{+1}). If the connections are still good, the pivot should re-send its PZP (preferably before the last PZP's TTL field has expired) so as to keep the nodes in the subPZ notified of the path.

Since a node can be involved in more than one PZ in DHR, some of the PZs may overlap as shown in Figure 3. Therefore, it is necessary for each node to maintain a *Pivot Table* (PT), in which each row denotes a single PZ.

2.3 Utilizing the existing paths with subPZs

In DHR, every node knows its geographic position. When a node, s, wants to send a packet to its destination node, d, s must first find a route to d. Remember that DHR is a layer on top of another arbitrary routing algorithm for which we assume REQs are sent out to establish a path. Figure 5 shows the algorithm used by DHR to find a path. In the algorithm, node c is the current node that has the REQ. After receiving the REQ, node c performs the steps in the algorithm shown in Figure 5.

Briefly stated, each node will in turn look to see first if it is the destination, then if it knows how to get to the destination, then if it is in a subPZ to the destination, and finally if can move the REQ on a path (either from its route table or pivot table) that will at least take it closer to the destination. If all else fails, it propagates the REQ according to the lower level protocol.

1. Check to see if node is inside the subPZ represented by the PZP. If not, discard. Otherwise, go to step 2.
2. Check if the PZP is for a path *P(s,d)* for which we already have a PZP. If no, go to step 4. If yes, go to step 3.
3. If the current PZP represents a shorter path (fewer hops) than the path already stored in PT, replace the stored PZP with the current PZP and proceed to step 4. Otherwise, discard the PZP.
4. The current node stores that path in its PT, adds its address to the route in the PZP, and broadcast the packet to its neighbors.

Figure 5: The algorithm a node executes when receiving a PZP. This algorithm forwards PZPs inside a subPZ, forming a spanning tree from pivot nodes to the nodes in the subPZ.

After receiving a REP from *d*, *s* recognizes the existence of the path to *d* and may then send its data packets along the path. Issues of route maintenance, route destruction, and overlapping routes are all issues handled by the underlying routing protocol and will not be discussed in this paper. Similarly, we will not discuss the specifics of the route table that the underlying routing protocol might use.

2.4 Costs of DHR and optimizations

To get the benefits of DHR, one must accept four costs: memory space, additional communication, algorithm execution time, and possible network congestion. The memory space cost is the pivot table, made up of the PZPs, one for each PZ that a node is a part of. The space of a PZP is the space of seven geographic coordinates, the TTL, and the route to the pivot. Because of the TTL field, PT entries will eventually be cleared out if they are not of use. In case of a full PT, a replacement policy of "least recently used", or "soonest to expire" can be used to eliminate an entry. It is not expected that a PT need be very large.

The required additional communication is minimal, because a PZP will be broadcast in a limited area (the subPZ). This overhead happens only when the path is created, and then occurs periodically to keep it alive. The period of updates can be selected dynamically due to network conditions. The execution time of the algorithm

is inconsequential when we consider the difference between today's fast CPU's and relatively slow wireless network speeds.

The most interesting cost is that of possible network congestion. DHR encourages the use of existing paths. This may result in some path segments being utilized as paths for many different source and destination pairs. Conditions that would bring network congestion about are slow moving (or static) nodes with lots of communication taking place on a given vector (say east to west). One suggestion to mediate this problem is to introduce a response delay on behalf of busy nodes and let a node put forth multiple REQs in the event that a RPY is not heard "soon enough." This implements a quality of service control into the network. In this scenario, a busy node which did not want to encourage more traffic on a given path (reducing quality of service) would delay sending on the REQ, resulting in a delay in sending back the RPY and encouraging the possibility that another path to the destination would be found first. The possibility of this case happening, and how it should be handled, is a topic for future research.

3. Simulation results

Our preliminary simulations have concentrated on how often existing paths can be used to transfer REQs to the expected area of the destination. We have focused our initial study on achieving 100% path usage for REQ transfer; that is to say, we have been exploring the situations necessary for no flooding to be needed for an arbitrary source to find a path to the destination's expected area.

All simulations are of a 500x500 unit area with randomly placed nodes. The communication range for all nodes is 100 units. Our simulations vary the number of nodes in the area and the number of existing paths established between nodes in the simulation (both are command line parameters to the simulation). Paths are established at random by choosing two nodes and attempting to build a path between them. There is no guarantee that a path can be found between the randomly chosen nodes, so if a path can not be found, two other nodes are chosen. This process repeats until the number of pre-existing paths requested by the user are built.

After the simulation is established (random nodes placed and random paths selected) the simulator then performs 10,000 experiments in which two nodes are selected at random and an attempt is made to form a path using the DHR algorithm without doing any flooding. (Note this is a more restrictive case of the DHR algorithm described in Figure 6). Success or failure of this experiment is recorded, and then to verify the step, a brute force attempt is made to see if the path could be found by any means (flooding). The number of times DHR succeeds in finding a path in situations in which a path is possible determines the success of the simulation.

---

1. If c has received the same REQ previously, then c discards the REQ. Otherwise, go to step 2.
2. If $c = d$, go to step 5. Otherwise, go to step 3.
3. If $c \in P(x, d)$ for any node x, go to step 5. Otherwise, c is not d, and c is not on a path to d, so go to step 4.
4. If c is in a subPZ of pivot node p such that $p \in P(x, d)$ for any node x (determined by examining the PT), then go to step 5. Otherwise, c is not in a subPZ that will lead to d, so go to step 6.
5. Node c found a path to d. Node c sends a RPY packet back to s along the path stored at intermediate nodes, END.
6. Let R be the set of paths in either c's route table or PT, such that if P is a path $P(x, m)$ in R, then following P to node m would lead the REQ closer to d (closeness is determined by geo-location data). If R is the empty set, go to step 7. Otherwise, if R is non-empty, then choose path q from R such that q is the path that would bring the REQ the closest to d. Node c sends the REQ as a unicast message, and the next hop on the path is next node on the path to q. END.
7. Since c doesn't know any information that would help it reach d, c propagates the REQ as a broadcast according to the lower level protocol. END.

Figure 6: Algorithm for utilizing existing paths in DHR. This algorithm assumes some node c has received a REQ to find a path from node s to d.

Figure 7 shows the result of ten such experiments in which the number of nodes was 100, and the number of

existing paths was 100. In Figure 7 we can see variation of success rates from 45% to 80%. From this, we conclude that success can very greatly depending on node placement, communication pair selection, and established pair selection. Larger simulations may level out these variances.

Figure 8 shows the effect of changing the number of existing paths from 50 to 400 while keeping the number of nodes constant (100). To accommodate the variance in simulation results illustrated in Figure 7, each point in Figure 8 is the average success rate of 10 simulations for that node/path parameter choice. Figure 8 shows that as the number of existing paths increases. This is because we are increasing the ratio of paths to nodes, such that there is a greater chance that a series of paths could be used to find a route from one node to another.

Figure 9 explores DHR's sensitivity to the number of nodes in the simulation. For these experiments, the number of existing paths are held at 100, while the number of nodes increases from 50 to 400. As in Figure 8, each point plotted is the average success rate of 10 different simulations. Figure 10 shows that as the number of nodes increases the success rate of DHR decreases. This makes sense, as this operation decreases the ratio of paths to nodes.

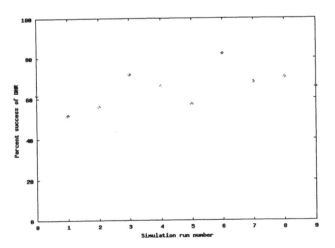

Figure 7: Variation in the success of DHR is seem in simulation results for a repeated experiment with 100 nodes and 100 established paths. Experiments are performed in a 500x500 unit area with randomly placed nodes and randomly selected communicating pairs. Communication range is 100 units.

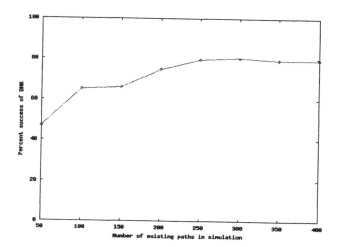

Figure 8: DHR success increases as the number of existing paths increases and the number of nodes is held at 100. Each point plotted is the average success rate of 10 simulations. Experiments are performed in a 500x500 unit area with randomly placed nodes and randomly selected communicating pairs. The communication range is 100 units.

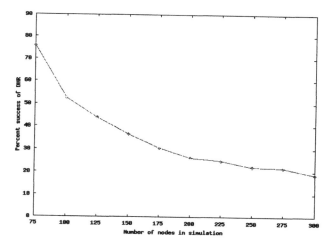

Figure 9: DHR success decreases as the ratio of paths to nodes decreases. In this experiment, the number of nodes increases as the number of existing paths is held at 100. Each point plotted is the average success rate of 10 simulations. Experiments are performed in a 500x500 unit area with randomly placed nodes and randomly selected communicating pairs. The communication range of the nodes is 100 units.

One of the observations we make is that the success of DHR is very dependent on the simulation parameters selected. This is not unique to DHR, but in fact is true for all wireless protocols If there are not enough nodes to build a path between the sender and destination, no protocol will be successful. Similarly, the communication range needs to be sufficiently large, such that enough nodes can talk to each other. Our simulation shows that DHR can be very successful when the ratio of paths to nodes is sufficiently high. A path–to–node ratio of 2.5:1 was enough to give DHR a 80% chance of finding a route without ever needing to perform a broadcast using the parameters for our simulation.

4. Conclusions

We have proposed an efficient routing algorithm, Dynamic Hybrid Routing (DHR), for mobile wireless ad hoc networks that utilizes geographical information. Unlike previous known algorithms, DHR takes advantage of existing active paths when a new route needs to be found. To accomplish this, a proactive zone (PZ) is built around the path. The PZ is broken down and managed in smaller parts called subPZs, where each subPZ is centered around a node on the path. The PZs in DHR are different from those of previously known algorithms. DHR PZs are static; i.e., they are formed and stay permanently. The main purpose of PZs in our algorithm is to inform and guide the REQs to proper paths to reach their destinations quickly and efficiently. As a result, a significant amount of bandwidth can be saved.

Our simulations show that DHR is capable of finding a route using existing paths without ever needing to communicate by flooding. The chance of DHR succeeding at this increases as the ratio of paths to nodes increases. In our simulation, we see that a ratio of 2.5 paths per node (on average) will allow DHR to be 80% successful in finding a route between two arbitrary nodes.

We are interested in studying different shapes and sizes of PZs. The shape of the PZ may have a huge impact on the overall performance of DHR. For example if we assume that the transmission range of nodes in the network is the same, then the links connecting nodes are bi-directional; i.e., both directions of a path can be used. Then, the shape of the PZ will become a rectangle.

Since DHR encourages the use of an existing paths instead of building a new one, it may cause some heavy traffic in certain paths. Increasing the response time to issue RPY at the nodes in the existing path can prevent this congestion.

References

[1] C. Perkins, and P. Bhagwat, "Highly-Dynamic Destination-Sequenced DistanceVector Routing (DSDV) for Mobile computers," *SIGCOM'94*, 1994., pp. 234-244.

[2] C. Perkins, E. Royer, and S. Das, "Ad hoc on Demand Distance Vector (AODV) Routing," Internet draft, IETF, Oct. 1999.

[3] V. Park and M. Corson, "A Highly Adaptive Distributed Routing Algorithm for Mobile Wireless Networks," *Proceedings of IEEE Infocom*, Apr. 1997, pp.1405-1413.

[4] D. Johnson and D. Maltz, "Dynamic Source Routing in Ad-hoc Wireless Networking," *in Mobile Computing*, T. Imielinski and H. Korth, editors, Kluwer Academic Publishing, 1996.

[5] Y. Ko and N. Vaidya, "Location-aide Routing in Mobile Ad Hoc Networks," *Proceedings of the Fourth Annual ACM/IEEE MobiCom '98*, 1998, pp. 66-75.

[6] B. Karp and H. Kung, "GPSR: Greedy Perimeter Stateless Routing for Wireless Networks," ," *Proceedings of the Sixth Annual ACM/IEEE MobiCom '00*, 2000., pp. 243-254.

[7] S. Basagni, I. Chlamtac and V. Syrotiuk, "A Distance Effect Algorithm for Mobility (DREAM)," *Proceedings of the Fourth Annual ACM/IEEE MobiCom '98*, 1998, pp. 76- 84.

[8] J. Haas, "A New Routing Protocol for the Reconfigurable Wireless Network," *In Proceedings of the 1997 IEEE 6th International Conference on Universal Personal Communications, ICUPC '97*, Oct. 1997, pp. 562-566.

[9] C. Perkins, "Ad Hoc Networking," *Addison-Wesley*, 2001.

[10] K. K. Kasera and R. Ramanathan, "A Location Management Protocol for Hierarchically Organized Multihop Mobile Wireless Networks," *IEEE ICUPC '97*, Oct. 1997

[11] G. Pei, M. Gerla and T Chen, "Fisheye State Routing: A Routing Scheme for Ad hoc Wireless Networks," *IEEE International Conference on Communications*, June 2000, pp. 70-74.

[12] A. Iwata, C Chiang, G. Pei, M. Gerla and T.Chen, "Scalable Routing Strategies for Ad hoc Wireless Networks," *IEEE Journal on Selected Areas in Communications, Special Issue on Wireless Ad Hoc Networks*, vol. 17, no 8, Aug. 1999, pp. 1369-1379.

[13] A. Boukerche and S. Roger, "GPS Query Pptimization in Mobile and Ad hoc Networking," *6th IEEE Symposium on Computers and Communications*, 2001, pp. 198-203.

[14] I. Stojmenovic, "Voronoi Diagram and Convex Hull Based Geocasting and Routing in Wireless Networks," SITE, University of Ottawa, TR99-11, Dec. 1999.

Effective Methodology for Deadlock-Free Minimal Routing in InfiniBand Networks *

J. C. Sancho, A. Robles, J. Flich, P. López and J. Duato
Department of Computer Engineering
Universidad Politécnica de Valencia
P.O.B. 22012, 46071 - Valencia, SPAIN
E-mail: {jcsancho,arobles,jflich,plopez,jduato}@gap.upv.es

Abstract

The InfiniBand Architecture (IBA) defines a switch-based network with point-to-point links whose topology is arbitrarily established by the customer. Often, the interconnection pattern is irregular, which complicates routing and deadlock avoidance. Current routing algorithms for NOWs, either achieve a low network performance, such as the up*/down* routing scheme, or cannot be implemented on IBA networks. IBA switches provide support for several virtual lanes, but they are primarily intended for QoS. Hence, its use for other purposes, like deadlock avoidance or performance improvement, should be limited.

In this paper, we propose a simple and effective methodology for designing deadlock-free routing strategies that are able to route packets through minimal paths in InfiniBand networks. This methodology can meet the trade-off between network performance and the number of resources dedicated to deadlock avoidance. Evaluation results show that the resulting routing strategies significantly outperform up*/down* routing. In particular, throughput improvement ranges, on average, from 1.33 for small networks to 4.05 for large networks. Also, it is shown that just two virtual lanes and three service levels are enough to achieve more than 80% of the throughput improvement achieved by the best proposed routing strategy (the one that always provides minimal paths without limiting the number of resources).

1 Introduction

InfiniBand [6] has been recently proposed as a standard for communication between processing nodes and I/O devices as well as for interprocessor communication.

InfiniBand can be used as a platform to build networks of workstations (NOWs) or clusters of PCs [9] which are becoming a cost-effective alternative to parallel computers. Currently, clusters are based on different available network technologies (Fast or Gigabit Ethernet [16], Myrinet [1], ServerNet II [5], Autonet [15], etc...). However, they may not provide the protection, isolation, deterministic behavior, and quality of service required in some environments.

The InfiniBand Architecture (IBA) is designed around a switch-based interconnect technology with high-speed point-to-point links and virtual cut-through switching. Nodes are directly attached to a switch through a Channel Adapter (CA). An IBA network is composed of several subnets interconnected by routers, each subnet consisting of one or more switches, processing nodes and I/O devices.

Routing in IBA subnets is distributed, based on forwarding tables (routing tables) stored in each switch, which only considers the packet destination ID for routing [6]. Also, IBA routing is deterministic as the forwarding tables only store one output link per destination ID. IBA switches support a maximum of 16 virtual lanes (VL). VL15 is reserved exclusively for subnet management, whereas the remaining VLs are used for normal traffic. However, IBA virtual lanes can not be directly selected by the routing algorithm (they are used in a deterministic fashion). In IBA, to route packets through a given virtual lane, packets are marked with a certain Service Level (SL), and SLtoVL mapping tables are used at each switch to determine the virtual lane to be used. The VL returned by the SLtoVL mapping tables does not only depend on the packet SL, but it also depends on the input and output ports through which the packet enters and leaves the switch. Thus, once the output physical port has been provided by the routing table, the virtual lane is obtained by taking into account both the SL of the packet and the input and output physical ports at the current switch. As a consequence, both the output port and the virtual lane are selected in a deterministic way in IBA. According to the

---
*This work was supported by the Spanish CICYT under Grants TIC2000-1151 and 1FD97-2129, and by Generalitat Valenciana under Grant GV00-131-14.

IBA specification [6], service levels are primarily intended to provide quality of service (QoS), deadlock avoidance and traffic prioritization.

2 Motivation

Usually, NOWs are arranged as switch-based networks whose topology is defined by the customer in order to provide wiring flexibility and incremental expansion capability. Often, due to physical constraints, the connection between switches does not follow any regular pattern, being the resulting topology irregular. The irregularity in the topology makes routing and deadlock avoidance quite complicated.

Several routing algorithms have been proposed in the literature for NOWs, such as the up*/down* [15] and its variants [12], the adaptive-trail [10], the minimal adaptive [14], and the smart-routing [2]. However, IBA specifications do not establish any specific routing algorithm to be used, leaving to the user the task of computing the forwarding tables of each switch.

The adaptive-trail and the minimal adaptive routing algorithms allow the existence of cyclic dependencies between channels provided that there exist some channels (escape paths) without cyclic dependencies which avoid deadlocks. Escape paths must be dynamically selected when the rest of virtual lanes are busy. Therefore, they cannot be supported by IBA switches because routing in IBA is deterministic and the selection of virtual lanes is also deterministic. The smart-routing algorithm is deterministic and it has been shown that it can obtain a very high performance [4]. However, its main drawback is the high time required to compute the routing tables.

On the other hand, up*/down* is the most popular routing algorithm currently used in the NOW environment, like Myrinet [1]. The main advantage of up*/down* routing is the fact that it is simple and easy to implement [15]. However, up*/down* routing has several drawbacks that may noticeably reduce network performance. First of all, this routing scheme does not guarantee minimal paths between every pair of nodes. This fact leads to an increase in packet latency and a waste of network resources. Additionally, the concentration of traffic in the vicinity of the root switch causes a premature saturation of the network, thus obtaining a low network throughput and leading to an uneven channel utilization.

The low network performance achieved by up*/down* and the impossibility of applying the adaptive routing schemes on IBA networks justify the necessity of searching new routing schemes specially adapted for IBA. In this paper, we address this issue.

At first sight, it could be thought that routing in IBA is no longer a problem because IBA switches provide enough resources (virtual lanes) to avoid deadlock. As virtual lanes are mainly intended for QoS and traffic prioritization, they will probably be divided into groups and assigned to different traffic flows corresponding to different QoS requirements. Moreover, we have recently shown that virtual lanes can also be used to improve performance by reducing the head-of-line blocking effect [13]. Thus, it would be advisable to use as few VLs as possible to guarantee deadlock-free routing in IBA with the aim of providing enough VLs for other purposes, such as QoS or head-of-line blocking reduction.

In this paper, we propose a simple and effective methodology for designing deadlock-free routing strategies that are able to route packets through minimal paths in InfiniBand networks. Although, a high number of network resources may be required to provide minimal paths between every pair of nodes, the new methodology is able to provide a good trade-off between network performance and the limited number of network resources available for deadlock avoidance. Notice, though, that using a limited number of network resources for deadlock avoidance may prevent some packets from following minimal paths, so affecting network performance.

The rest of the paper is organized as follows. In section 3, the up*/down* routing scheme and its implementation on IBA is described. Section 4 describes the proposed methodology for deadlock-free minimal routing in IBA. In section 5, the IBA simulation model is described, together with the discussion of the simulation results. Finally, in sections 6 and 7, some conclusions are drawn and future works are commented, respectively.

3 Up*/Down* Routing on IBA

Up*/down* is a deadlock-free routing algorithm valid for any network topology. Routing is based on an assignment of direction labels ("up" or "down") to the operational links in the network by building a breadth-first spanning (BFS) tree. To compute a BFS tree a switch must be chosen as the root. Starting from the root, the rest of the switches in the network are arranged on a single spanning tree [15].

After computing the BFS spanning tree, the "up" end of each link is defined as: 1) the end whose switch is closer to the root in the spanning tree; 2) the end whose switch has the lowest identifier, if both ends are at switches at the same tree level. As a consequence, each cycle in the network has at least one link in the "up" direction and one link in the "down" direction. To avoid deadlocks while still allowing all links to be used, this routing scheme uses the following rule: a legal route must traverse zero or more links in the "up" direction followed by zero or more links in the "down" direction. Thus, cyclic channel dependencies are avoided because a message cannot traverse a link in the "up" direction after having traversed one in the "down" direction.

Unfortunately, up*/down* routing cannot be applied to InfiniBand networks in a straightforward manner because it does not conform to IBA specifications. The reason for this is the fact that the up*/down* scheme takes into account the input port together with the destination ID for routing, whereas IBA switches only consider the destination ID. However, Up*/down routing can be implemented on InfiniBand by using any of the strategies recently proposed in [11, 8].

4 New Methodology for Deadlock-free Minimal Routing in IBA

In this section, we describe the methodology to provide deadlock-free routing in InfiniBand networks through minimal paths by using virtual lanes and service levels. Its main goal is to provide a simple and effective routing strategy for IBA that meets the trade-off between a high network performance and a bounded number of network resources (virtual lanes and service levels) used for routing. The proposed methodology is composed of seven different stages as shown in Figure 1.

At the first stage, all the possible minimal paths between every pair of hosts in the network are computed. This includes all the paths whose lengths are equal to the topological distances between hosts. Notice that although several minimal paths will be computed for the same source-destination pair, we will select only one of them at a later stage. Also, notice that the use of these routing paths does not guarantee deadlock freedom because cyclic channel dependencies may arise.

At the second stage, we search for possible cyclic channel dependencies. In particular, we search for those paths that may lead to deadlock for a given routing scheme. We have chosen in this paper the up*/down* routing scheme because of its simplicity. We check whether every computed minimal path contains any forbidden transition according to the up*/down* rule. As known, a forbidden transition occurs when the path uses a link in the "up" direction after having used one in the "down" direction. In order to guarantee deadlock freedom, we must remove these transitions. However, this will be done at a later stage. At this stage we only mark the forbidden transitions.

Cyclic channel dependencies can be removed by using virtual lanes [3]. An easy way of doing this is to route a packet through a new different virtual lane every time a forbidden transition is found. In turn, cyclic channel dependencies between virtual lanes can be removed by forcing their use in a sequential (increasing or decreasing) order.

In our methodology, a packet will be injected into the network through VL0 (Virtual Lane 0). It will continue being routed through VL0 until the first forbidden transition has to be crossed. Then, the packet will be routed through

	Before selecting paths				After selecting paths		
	0	1	2	3	0	1	2
8	82.4	17.6	0	0	82.4	17.6	0
16	64.6	35.2	0.2	0	64.7	35.2	0.1
32	50.6	46.2	3.2	0	52.1	47.6	0.3
64	39.1	52.7	7.1	0.1	42.1	56.5	1.4

Table 1. Average percentage of paths crossing 0, 1, 2, and 3 forbidden transitions for different networks.

VL1. If the packet has not to cross more forbidden transitions, it will continue to be routed through VL1 until it reaches the destination host. Otherwise, the packet will change from VL1 to VL2 when the next forbidden transition is crossed, and so on.

Notice that the paths that cross the highest number of forbidden transitions will impose the upper bound on the number of virtual lanes to be used. This number will depend on the network size and the generated BFS spanning tree. In order to estimate this number, we have analyzed one hundred randomly generated topologies[1] for different network sizes (8, 16, 32, and 64-switch networks with 32, 64, 128, and 256 hosts, respectively), averaging the maximum number of forbidden transitions (see Table 1). As can be seen, the number of forbidden transitions along whatever minimal path is not higher than three.

Notice that we are taking into account all the possible minimal paths. For a particular source-destination pair, it is possible to have several minimal paths and some of them needing more forbidden transitions than others. If we select a subset from all the possible minimal paths (keeping at least one path per source-destination pair), we can decrease even more the maximum number of forbidden transitions. In this case, we have found that the largest number of forbidden transitions along whatever minimal path is only two (as shown also in Table 1). As can be seen, most paths need to cross none or only one forbidden transition. The average percentage of routing paths crossing two forbidden transitions is 1.4%. As a consequence, only 3 VLs seems to be enough to guarantee deadlock-free routing through minimal paths between whatever pair of hosts.

Therefore, at the third stage of the methodology (Figure 1) we will select those paths that minimize the number of forbidden transitions. Notice that after selecting paths there still may be some pair of hosts with more than one minimal path.

In order to carry out the virtual lane transitions in Infini-Band, it is necessary to use service levels (SLs). SLs are

---

[1] For further details, see section 5.1.

411

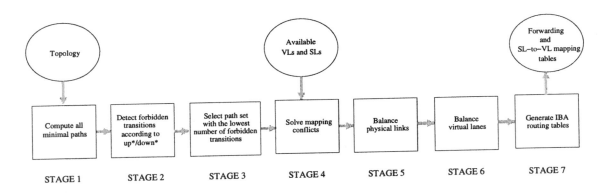

Figure 1. Stages of the proposed methodology.

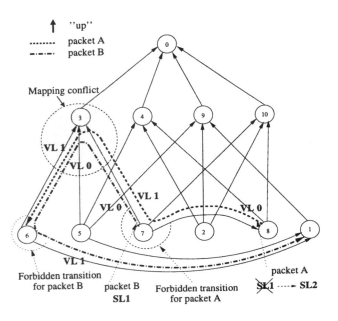

Figure 2. Mapping conflict example for a 16-switch network.

used to decide the VLs to be used at each switch (by using the SL-to-VL mapping tables, which are indexed by the input port, output port, and the service level of the packet). The SL is placed at the header of the packet and it cannot be changed by the switches. Therefore, we must also assign the SL to be used with each possible path.

According to the proposed methodology, every path will be labeled with a different SL depending on the number of forbidden transitions to be crossed. For example, SL0 will be assigned to packets being routed through paths without forbidden transitions (packets will use only VL0), SL1 to packets having to cross one forbidden transition (packets will initially use VL0 and then VL1), and so on.

However, the fact of fixing a path with a unique SL can lead to a mapping conflict. This conflict occurs when two

packets labeled with the same SL having to cross the same number of forbidden transitions enter a switch through the same input port but through different VLs, and they need to be routed to the same output port but also through different VLs. This is because the SL-to-VL mapping table does not use the input VL in order to determine the output VL. The problem arises when the number of forbidden transitions crossed by each path until this moment is different. Notice that this situation may ocur only when both packets are labeled with SL$\neq$0. Figure 2 illustrates this problem. The only minimal path to reach switch 6 from switch 8 is the one that traverses switches 7 and 3 (path length is 3 hops). As can be seen, this path contains only one forbidden transition (down-up transition), which is located at switch 7. For this aim, packets being routed through this path will be labeled with SL1. The same occurs with the packets being routed from switch 7 towards switch 1, whose only minimal path is the one that crosses switches 3 and 6 (path length is 3 hops). In this case, the forbidden transition is located at switch 6 and packets will be also labeled with SL1. As can be observed, both paths lead to a mapping conflict at switch 3. This is due to the fact that one of the packets must be routed through VL0 because it still has not crossed the forbidden transition, whereas the another packet must be routed through VL1 because it has already crossed the forbidden transition.

Hence, at the fourth stage of the methodology (Figure 1), we will solve these mapping conflicts in the following way. Firstly, we will try to find an alternative minimal path for one of the paths causing the conflict. If it is not possible and there is still one additional service level available, then it will be used. Otherwise, a non-minimal path will be computed according to the up*/down* routing algorithm. Notice from the Figure 1 that the methodology admits a bounded number of available SLs to solve mapping conflicts. Let us illustrate this in the example shown in Figure 2. Given that there is no alternative minimal path between both pairs of source-destination switches, one of the pack-

	Network size			
Resources	8	16	32	64
2VL-2SL	100	18	-	-
2VL-3SL	-	75	1	-
2VL-4SL	-	3	5	-
3VL-3SL	-	4	15	-
3VL-4SL	-	-	79	-
3VL-5SL	-	-	-	47
3VL-6SL	-	-	-	50
3VL-7SL	-	-	-	3

Table 2. Percentage of random topologies needing different number of resources to obtain minimal routing.

ets will need to be labeled with a different service level, not used for the purpose of crossing forbidden transitions. In this example, packet A should be injected into the network using SL2 instead of SL1.

As solving mapping conflicts may increase the number of needed service levels, Table 2 shows the number of resources required to provide routing through minimal paths for different network sizes. For each network size we have analyzed 100 randomly generated topologies[2]. The table groups the topologies by the number of needed resources (rows). As can be seen, all the 8-switch networks need only 2 VLs and 2 SLs, whereas most 64-switch networks need 3 VLs and 5, 6 or even 7 SLs. Hence, as network size increases, a significant number of SLs is required to guarantee deadlock-free minimal routing. For this reason, our methodology limits the use of SLs to solve mapping conflicts, at the expense of preventing some packets from being routed through minimal paths.

After solving the mapping conflicts (after stage 4), the methodology has obtained a deadlock-free set of paths with more than one minimal path per each source-destination pair. However, as IBA forwarding tables only provide one output port per destination ID, we will select only one path per source-destination pair. This selection is done at the fifth stage. For this purpose, we apply the traffic balancing algorithm proposed in [12], which tries to balance the number of paths crossing every channel. By doing this, we obtain a balanced and deadlock-free set of paths with one minimal path per each source-destination pair.

At the sixth stage, we will also balance virtual lane utilization. As it was shown in Table 1, most paths do not cross any forbidden transition in small networks. As a consequence, VL0 will be the most utilized virtual lane. On the other hand, in large networks, a significant percentage of

---
[2]For further details, see section 5.1.

	Virtual lane		
	0	1	2
8	91.3 %	8.6%	0
16	83.2 %	16.6 %	0.04 %
32	76.2 %	23.6 %	1.7 %
64	70.0 %	29.1 %	0.75 %

Table 3. Average percentage of paths crossing each virtual lane for different networks.

paths cross a single forbidden transition. However, packets being routed through these paths do not use VL1 until they have to cross the forbidden transition. As a consequence, VL0 will be also the most used virtual lane in this case. Table 3 shows the average percentage of paths crossing each virtual lane for different network sizes. As we can see, there is a traffic unbalance over the virtual lanes. This can negatively influence network performance, as shown in [13]. In order to better balance the traffic over the virtual lanes, we can distribute the traffic initially destined to use only VL0 among the rest of VLs. This can be easily done by modifying the SL level of these packets. Notice that this will be carried out only if it does not introduce new mapping conflicts. These packets do not cross any forbidden transition and they are routed through the same assigned VL until being delivered, without switching to any other VL. In other words, at this point we have several virtual networks mapped into the same physical network, each one using a different VL. Packets are allowed to move from virtual network i to virtual network j only if $j > i$ (this is the case of crossing a forbidden transition). Hence, balancing virtual lane utilization cannot lead to deadlock.

Finally, at the seventh stage, the routing information is generated. This includes the forwarding tables, the SL-to-VL mapping tables, and the tables that map destination ID's with SLs at the source hosts.

The overall computational complexity of the proposed methodology is imposed by the stage that applies the traffic balancing algorithm, whose cost is $O(n^3)$. Notice that, the overall computational complexity could be reduced down to $O(n^2)$ if a simpler traffic balancing algorithm were used.

5 Performance Evaluation

In this section, we will study the influence on performance of the proposed methodology to provide deadlock-free routing through minimal paths in InfiniBand networks. In particular, we are interested in analyzing if the routing strategies resulting from applying the proposed methodology are able to meet the trade-off between network performance and the number of network resources available.

For this purpose, we have developed a detailed simulator that allows us to model the network at the register transfer level following the IBA specifications [6]. First, we will describe the main IBA subnet model features defined in the specs together with the main simulator parameters and the modeling considerations we have used in all the evaluations. Then, we will evaluate the proposed methodology under different topologies and packets lengths.

5.1 The IBA Subnet Model

The IBA specification defines a switch-based network with point-to-point links, allowing any topology defined by the user. The network allows the communication between end-nodes acting as hosts (Host Channel Adapters, HCA) or as I/O devices (Target Channel Adapters, TCA). The end-nodes are attached to switches using the same links used between switches.

Packets are routed at each switch by accessing the forwarding table. This table contains the output port to be used at the switch for each possible destination. If there is sufficient buffer capacity in the output buffer, the packet is forwarded. Otherwise, the packet must wait at the input buffer. In the simulator, each switch will have a crossbar connecting the input ports to the output ports, allowing multiple packets to be simultaneously transmitted without interference. The crossbar will be able to transmit one byte on every cycle per connection.

Switches can support up to a maximum of 16 virtual lanes (VL). Each VL provides separate guaranteed buffering resources in order to support QoS. For this aim, packets are marked with a service level (SL) identifier at the source host which cannot be changed in the subnet. The SL identifier is used at each switch to compute the VL to be used from the SLtoVL table associated to each output port.

Each output port has also two dedicated tables to select the next VL that contains a packet to be transmitted over the physical link. These two tables allow the implementation of any arbitration policy. In the simulator we will implement a VL round-robin arbiter per output port.

We will use a non-multiplexed crossbar on each switch. This crossbar supplies separate ports for each virtual lane. We will use a simple crossbar arbiter based on FIFO request queues per output crossbar port that will select the first request that has enough buffer space in the corresponding output crossbar port. Although more efficient schemes have been proposed [7] they are more complex. In any case, arbitration issues are beyond the scope of this paper. The crossbar bandwidth will be set accordingly to the value of the injection rate of the links. Buffers will be used both at the input and the output side of the crossbar. Buffer size will be fixed in both cases to 1 KB.

The routing time at each switch will be set to 100 ns.

This time includes the time to access the forwarding and SLtoVL tables, the crossbar arbiter time, and the time to set up the crossbar connections. Additionally, the virtual cut-through switching technique is used.

Links in InfiniBand are serial. The link speed is fixed to 2.5 Gbps. Each port can be configured to use 1, 4, or 12 serial links (1X, 4X, or 12X). In the simulator, the link injection rate will be fixed to the 1X configuration. We also model the fly time (time required for a bit to reach the opposite link side). This parameter depends on the link length and the propagation delay of the cable. We will model 20 m copper cables with a propagation delay of 5 ns/m. Therefore, the fly time will be set to 100 ns.

The IBA specification defines a credit-based flow control scheme for each virtual lane. A packet will be transmitted over the link if the number of available credits is enough to store the entire packet (1 credit = 64 bytes). IBA allows the definition of different MTU (Maximum Transfer Unit) values for packets ranging from 256 to 4096 bytes.

We will use two different packet lengths in all the evaluations. We will use short packets with a payload of 32 bytes, and long packets with a payload of 256 bytes.

For each simulation run, we assume that the packet generation rate is constant and the same for all the end-nodes. Once the network has reached a steady state, the packet generation rate is equal to the packet reception rate. We will evaluate the full range of traffic, from low load to saturation. Finally, we will use a uniform distribution of packet destinations in all the evaluations. In all the presented results, we will plot the average packet latency[3] measured in nanoseconds versus the average accepted traffic[4] measured in bytes/ns/switch.

We will analyze irregular networks of 8, 16, 32 and 64 switches. These network topologies will be randomly generated taking into account some restrictions. First, we will assume that every switch in the network has 8 ports, using 4 ports to connect to other switches and leaving 4 ports to connect to end-nodes (HCAs or TCAs). And second, switches will be interconnected by exactly one link. Ten different topologies will be analyzed for each network size. We will show minimum, maximum, and average results for these topologies. We will also plot some detailed results for some representative topologies for every network size.

5.2 Simulation Results

The routing strategies resulting from applying the proposed methodology will be referred to as M_xVLySL (Minimal routing with **x** Virtual Lanes and **y** Service

---

[3]Latency is the elapsed time between the generation of a packet at the source host until it is delivered at the destination end-node.

[4]Accepted traffic is the amount of information delivered by the network per time unit.

Levels). Notice that the routing strategies that use the largest number of VLs and SLs will be the ones that provide minimal routing for all the packets. The rest ones will only provide minimal routing partially, because some packets will need to be routed through non-minimal paths.

For comparison purposes, we have also evaluated the up*/down* routing scheme with the same number of VLs, which will be referred to as UD_xVL, where x represents the number of VLs being used. In this case, traffic will be distributed among all the available VLs. A packet will randomly enter the network through a particular VL and will cross the network through the same VL until it is delivered at the destination host. Notice that, VLs are distinguished by using a different SL per each VL.

Network size	Minimum	Maximum	Average
32-byte packets			
8	1.15	1.9	1.33
16	1.52	2.5	1.93
32	1.84	3.38	2.61
64	2.84	4.77	4.05
256-byte packets			
8	1.19	1.36	1.83
16	1.62	2.39	1.9
32	2.09	3.29	2.65
64	2.88	4.68	4.02

Table 4. Factors of throughput increase with respect to the up*/down* routing when using minimal routing. Packet size is 32 and 256 bytes. Uniform distribution of packet destinations.

5.2.1 Results for an Unbounded Number of VLs/SLs

Firstly, we will analyze the results obtained by the proposed methodology when minimal paths between any pair of hosts are guaranteed.

Table 4 shows minimun, maximum, and average factors of throughput increase with respect to up*/down* routing. Uniform distribution of packet destinations and 32/256-byte packet sizes were used. Ten different topologies for each network size were considered. As it can be seen, the proposed methodology is able to considerably increase network throughput for all the network sizes. Indeed, this improvement becomes higher as network size increases (on average, up to four times more throughput than up*/down* for 64-switch networks).

Figures 3.a, 3.b, 3.c, and 3.d show evaluation results for the selected topologies that exhibit an average behavior for 8, 16, 32, and 64-switch networks, respectively. Although these figures plot results for different combinations of VLs

and SLs, let us consider now only the ones that guarantee minimal paths between any pair of hosts (the ones that use the highest numbers of VLs and SLs).

As it can be seen, the proposed strategy is able to outperform the up*/down* routing algorithm both in terms of network throughput and message latency, despite the fact that both routing algorithms use the same number of virtual lanes. In particular, all the proposed routing strategies achieve a noticeable reduction in latency with respect to up*/down routing for all the traffic range. This reduction is more significant as network size increases (up to a 10% lower latency for low traffic rates and 64-switch networks). This reduction in latency is mainly due to the fact that the proposed routing strategies allow all the packets to be routed through minimal paths.

5.2.2 Results for a Bounded Number of VLs/SLs

In this section, we will analyze at what extent it is possible to maintain a significant throughput improvement with respect to up*/down* when the number of resources used by the proposed routing strategy is bounded. For this aim, we will gradually reduce both the number of VLs and SLs used by the methodology. In both cases, this will lead to a reduction in the number of provided minimal paths, either because some paths have several forbidden transitions (reduction in the number of VLs) or because some minimal paths give rise to mapping conflicts (reduction in the number of SLs). This may reduce network performance. Notice that the number of SLs will be allways larger than or equal to the number of VLs.

In particular, for a 16-switch network (Figure 3.b), reducing one SL (M_2VL2SL) causes network throughput to be reduced by 20%, also slightly increasing latency. However, the factor of improvement in throughput with respect to up*/down* is as high as 1.6. This improvement represents more than 80% of the improvement achieved by M_2VL3SL, which can be considered a very acceptable result.

For the 32-switch network, M_2VL2SL continues to improve throughput with respect to UD_3VL by a factor of 2.39. Again, this improvement represents more than 80% of the improvement achieved by M_3VL4SL.

For the 64-switch network, we can observe that the reduction in the number of resources used by the routing strategies has a greater influence on network performance. This is because in large networks, average distances between switches are longer, thus appearing more forbidden transitions that will prevent some packets from following minimal paths. Two facts draw our attention. First, we observe that throughput dramatically decreases (by 55%) when going from M_2VL3SLs to M_2VL2SLs, also increasing latency for the full range of traffic. This is because

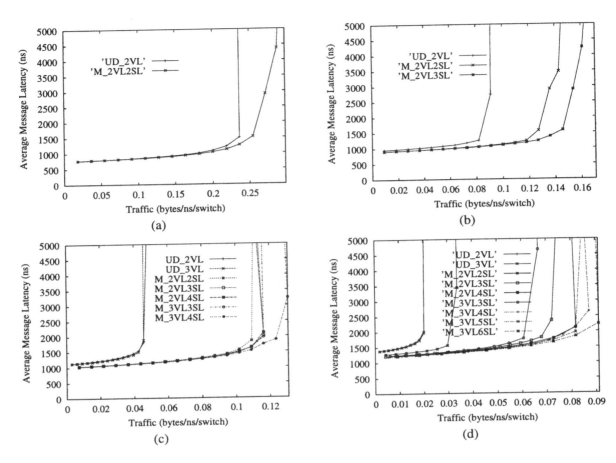

Figure 3. Average packet latency vs. traffic. Network size is (a) 8, (b) 16, (c) 32, and (d) 64 switches. Packet length is 32 bytes. Uniform distribution of packet destinations.

when service levels are restricted to only 2 SLs it is not possible to solve any mapping conflict by using additional SLs. Therefore, a larger number of packets will need to be routed through non-minimal paths. Second, we observe a significant increment in throughput (by 15%) when going from M_3VL3SLs to M_2VL4SLs. Although using only 2 VLs prevents packets crossing two forbidden transitions from following minimal paths, the influence on the average distance is small, because the percentage of these kind of paths is very low, as shown in Table 1. Removing these few minimal paths makes easier to solve mapping conflicts in the network. Indeed, by having an additional SL, more mapping conflicts can be solved without sacrificing minimal routing. On the other hand, the M_3VL3SLs routing apparently provides more minimal paths (by allowing minimal paths with 2 forbidden transitions). However, the number of available service levels is not enough to solve all the mapping conflicts leading to a larger overall number of non-minimal paths.

Table 5 shows minimum, maximum, and average factors of throughput increases with respect to UD_3VL for 10

different topologies for every network size with a bounded number of network resources. We can observe that using 2VLs and 2SLs is enough to achieve more than 80% of the throughput improvement achieved by the routing strategies that allways guarantee minimal paths. However, this is not the case for 64-switch networks where 3 SLs are required to achieve a similar behavior. Therefore, we can conclude that using 2 VLs and 2 SLs is a good choice to provide deadlock-free routing in IBA while allowing most packets to follow minimal paths, except for large networks, where an additional SL is required.

In order to analyze more thoroughly the effect of using a bounded number of resources on performance, Table 6 shows the *average distance* and the *crossing path*[5] metrics, together with their respective standard deviations, for different network sizes (the same topologies selected in Figure 3). We can observe that there is a total correlation between average distance and crossing path metrics. The analysis of these metrics explains the relative performance of the rout-

---

[5]Maximum number of routing paths crossing whatever physical channel in the network.

Network size	2VL-2SL			2VL-3SL			3VL-3SL		
	Min	Max	Avg	Min	Max	Avg	Min	Max	Avg
32-byte packets									
8	1.15	1.9	1.33	-	-	-	-	-	-
16	1.60	2.44	1.84	1.66	2.41	1.88	-	-	-
32	1.73	3.05	2.26	1.76	3.11	2.47	1.89	3.19	2.42
64	1.14	1.99	1.60	2.54	3.16	3.60	2.15	3.23	2.75
256-byte packets									
8	1.19	1.83	1.36	-	-	-	-	-	-
16	1.56	2.39	1.83	1.6	2.29	1.83	-	-	-
32	1.88	2.86	2.28	1.92	3.10	2.55	1.92	3.10	2.42
64	1.61	1.89	1.70	2.34	3.52	2.80	2.22	3.02	2.62

Table 5. Factors of throughput increase for the routing strategies that use a bounded number of resources. Packet size is 32 and 256 bytes. Uniform distribution of packet destinations.

ing strategies shown in Figure 3. In general, it can be observed that increasing the number of VLs causes a reduction in the *average distance* metric. The same conclusion can be observed for SLs. When both parameters (VLs and SLs) are simultaneously considered, we can find out the combination that leads to the best performance. In particular, for 64-switch networks we can see that SLs have more impact on performance. M_2VL4SL and M_2VL3SL have a lower average distance than M_3VL3SL. Hence, they obtain a better performance.

6 Conclusions

Virtual lanes and service levels in InfiniBand are primarily intended to provide QoS. As a consequence, its use for other purposes such as deadlock avoidance and routing should be very restricted. However, using a limited number of network resources could prevent some packets from following minimal paths, which could affect network performance.

In this paper we have proposed an effective methodology to design deadlock-free routing strategies for IBA networks that allows packets to be routed through minimal paths, so improving network performance.

The main advantage of the proposed methodology is that the resulting routing strategies are suitable to meet the trade-off between high network performance and the use of a bounded number of network resources. Therefore, it is able to take advantage of those resources not required by the applications to provide QoS.

Simulation results show that in the worst case (large networks) up to 3 VLs and 6 SLs could be necessary to guarantee deadlock-free minimal routing. The needed network resources decreases as the network size decreases. In particular, only 2 VLs and 3 SLs are needed for 16-switch

networks. Throughput improvement with respect to the up*/down* routing scheme ranges from a factor of 1.33 for 8-switch networks to a factor of 4.05 for 64-switch networks.

However, it is possible to use a smaller number of network resources while maintaining a good level on performance. In this sense, the simulation results show that using 2 VLs and 2 SLs is enough to achieve the 80% of the throughput increase achieved by the routing strategy that guarantees minimal routing. For 64-switch networks, an additional SL can be needed.

7 Future work

As future work, we plan to apply the proposed methodology by using other routing schemes for detecting forbidden transitions, like smart-routing and variants of up*/down*, which impose less routing restrictions.

Also, we are intendeed to develop new strategies to select the initial set of minimal paths (resulting for applying the third stage), so as for solving mapping conflicts, taking into account the traffic balance issue. For example, it would be interesting to analyze the trade-off between using the largest number of minimal paths and achieving a better traffic balance in the network.

References

[1] N. J. Boden et al., Myrinet - A gigabit per second local area network, *IEEE Micro*, vol. 15, Feb. 1995.

[2] L. Cherkasova, V. Kotov, and T. Rokicki, "Fibre channel fabrics: Evaluation and design," in *Proc. of 29th Int. Conf. on System Sciences*, Feb. 1995.

Network size	Average distance $\times 10^3$	Average distance standard dev.	Crossing path	Crossing path standard dev.
8 switches (Average topological distance equal to 1429 $\times 10^{-3}$)				
2VL-2SL	1429	0.49	3	0.50
UD_2VL	1429	0.49	4	1.04
16 switches (Average topological distance equal to 1991 $\times 10^{-3}$)				
2VL-3SL	1991	0.78	12	2.57
2VL-2SL	1996	0.74	12	2.61
UD_2VL	2192	0.96	22	5.23
32 switches (Average topological distance equal to 2483 $\times 10^{-3}$)				
3VL-4SL	2483	0.81	26	3.31
3VL-3SL	2484	0.81	26	3.66
2VL-3SL	2486	0.82	27	3.78
2VL-2SL	2511	0.85	28	4.01
UD_3VL	2931	1.20	85	20.05
64 switches (Average topological distance equal to 3177 $\times 10^{-3}$)				
3VL-6SL	3177	0.98	72	11.16
3VL-5SL	3178	0.98	78	13.22
3VL-4SL	3189	1.00	89	13.78
3VL-3SL	3286	1.14	124	19.57
2VL-4SL	3206	1.03	89	14.50
2VL-3SL	3244	1.08	116	16.60
2VL-2SL	3496	1.35	236	35.45
UD_3VL	4013	1.58	389	73.76

Table 6. Influence of the routing strategy on some behavioral metrics for networks sizes of 8, 16, 32, and 64 switches.

[3] W. J. Dally and C. L. Seitz, Deadlock-free message routing in multiprocessors interconnection networks, *IEEE Trans. on Computers*, vol. C-36, no. 5, pp. 547-553, May. 1987.

[4] J. Flich, P. López, M.P. Malumbres, J. Duato, and T. Rokicki, "Combining In-Transit Buffers with Optimized Routing Schemes to Boost the Performance of Networks with Source Routing," *Proc. of Int. Symp. on High Performance Computing*, Oct. 2000.

[5] D. García and W. Watson, Servernet II, in *Proc. of the 1997 Parallel Computer, Routing, and Communication Workshop*, Jun 1997.

[6] InfiniBand^{TM} Trade Association, *InfiniBand^{TM} architecture. Specification Volumen 1. Release 1.0.a.* Available at http://www.infinibandta.com.

[7] C. Minkenberg and T. Engbersen, A Combined Input and Output Queued Packet-Switched System Based on PRIZMA Switch-on-a-Chip Technology, in *IEEE Communication Magazine*, Dec. 2000.

[8] P. López, J. Flich, and J. Duato, Deadlock-free Routing in InfiniBand^{TM} through Destination Renaming, in *Proc. of 2001 Int. Conf. on Parallel Processing*, Sept. 2001.

[9] G. Pfister, *In search of clusters*, Prentice Hall, 1995.

[10] W. Qiao and L. M. Ni, "Adaptive routing in irregular networks using cut-through switches," in *Proc. of the 1996 Int. Conf. on Parallel Processing*, Aug. 1996.

[11] J.C. Sancho, A. Robles, and J. Duato, Effective Strategy to Compute Forwarding Tables for InfiniBand Networks, in *Proc. of 2001 Int. Conf. on Parallel Processing*, Sept. 2001.

[12] J.C. Sancho and A. Robles, Improving the Up*/down* routing scheme for networks of workstations in *Proc. of Euro-Par 2000*, Aug. 2000.

[13] J.C. Sancho, J. Flich, A. Robles, P. López and J. Duato, "Analyzing the Influence of Virtual Lanes on InfiniBand Networks," in *Proc. of Workshop on Communication Architecture for Clusters*. Apr. 2002.

[14] F. Silla and J. Duato, Tuning the Number of Virtual Channels in Networks of Workstations, in *Proc. of the 10th Int. Conf. on Parallel and Distributed Computing Systems*, Oct. 1997.

[15] M. D. Schroeder et al., Autonet: A high-speed, self-configuring local area network using point-to-point links, *SRC research report 59*, DEC, Apr. 1990.

[16] R. Sheifert, *Gigabit Ethernet*, Addison-Wesley, April 1998.

On-line Permutation Routing on WDM All-Optical Networks

Qian-Ping Gu*

Abstract: *For a sequence $(s_1, t_1), ..., (s_i, t_i), ...$ of routing requests with (s_i, t_i) arriving at time step i on the wavelength-division multiplexing (WDM) all-optical network, the on-line routing problem is to set-up a path $s_i \rightarrow t_i$ and assign a wavelength to the path in step i such that the paths set-up so far with the same wavelength are edge-disjoint. Two measures are important for on-line routing algorithms: the number of wavelengths used and the response time. The sequence $(s_1, t_1), ..., (s_i, t_i), ...$ is called a permutation if each node in the network appears in the sequence at most once as a source and at most once as a destination. Let H_n be the n-dimensional WDM all-optical hypercube. In this paper, we develop two on-line routing algorithms on H_n. Our first algorithm is a deterministic one which realizes any permutation by at most $\lceil 3(n-1)/2 \rceil + 1$ wavelengths with response time $O(2^n)$. The second algorithm is a randomized one which realizes any permutation by at most $(3/2 + \delta)(n-1)$ wavelengths, where δ can be any value satisfying $\delta \geq 2/(n-1)$. The average response time of the algorithm is $O(n(1 + \delta)/\delta)$. Both algorithms use at most $O(n)$ wavelengths for the permutation on H_n. This improves the previous bound of $O(n^2)$. Both algorithms reach the competitive ratio $O(n)$ on the number of wavelengths.*

Key words: On-line routing algorithm, WDM all-optical networks, permutation routing, hypercube, competitive analysis

1 Introduction

Wavelength-division multiplexing (WDM) all-optical networks provide huge bandwidth for bandwidth-intensive communication applications such as web browsing, video on demanding, electronic commerce, and so on. A switched optical network consists of nodes (terminals or switches) and node-to-node links (optical fibers). WDM all-optical networks use optical switches which keep the data stream transmitted in optical form from source to destination to eliminate

the well known electro-optic conversion bottleneck at intermediate nodes. Another bottleneck for realizing the huge bandwidth of optical fiber is the optic-electronic bandwidth mismatch between the fibers and the terminals (e.g., workstations and gateways) in the network. The key for eliminating this bottleneck is the concurrent data transmissions on the same fiber by multiple terminals. Wavelength-division multiplexing is the current favorite multiplexing technology for realizing the concurrency by partitioning the huge bandwidth of the fibers into multiple non-overlapping wavelengths, each wavelength supports a communication channel. Concurrent data transmissions are realized by transmitting each data stream by a distinct wavelength. We refer to the books of [12, 11] for more details of WDM optical networks.

Circuit-switched routing mode is used in the WDM all-optical network. We consider the networks without wavelength converters. For such networks, an optical signal is transmitted from an input to an output on the same wavelength and thus, a message is transmitted on the same wavelength from source to destination. A routing request on the WDM all-optical networks is an ordered node pair (s, t) of the network, where s is *source* and t is *destination*. To realize the connection for a set $R = \{(s, t)\}$ of routing requests on the WDM all-optical network, routing algorithms are required to set up a path from s to t and assign a wavelength to the path for every $(s, t) \in R$ so that the paths with the same wavelength are edge-disjoint. A key problem in developing routing algorithms is to minimize the number of wavelengths used by the algorithms [7, 4, 5, 8, 16, 10, 6, 9, 3, 2].

Routing algorithms can be classified into off-line (or static) algorithms and on-line (or dynamic) algorithms. Let $R = \{(s_i, t_i) | i \geq 1\}$ be a set of routing requests. An off-line algorithm realizes the connection for R when all pairs in R are known. The algorithm is appropriate to deal with the case that the routing requests arrive in batch, e.g., in video conferencing. In many applications, however, routing requests may arrive dynamically and each request should be responded in time. For such applications, on-line algorithms are required. Assume

---

*School of Computing Science, Simon Fraser University, Burnaby B.C. V5A 1S6 Canada (qgu@cs.sfu.ca)

that the requests in R arrive in the order that (s_i, t_i) comes in at time step i ($i \geq 1$). An on-line algorithm realizes the connection for (s_i, t_i) in step i without the knowledge of $(s_j, t_j), j > i$.

A fundamental communication application is permutation R where each node of the network appears in R at most once as a source and at most once as a destination. In this paper, we consider on-line routing algorithms for permutations on the WDM all-optical networks with the directed hypercube topology (with two directed edges, one in each direction, between every pair of adjacent nodes). We denote the n-dimensional directed hypercube by H_n which has $N = 2^n$ nodes. The hypercube is an important interconnection network for parallel computing system and has started to receive attention in optical network community as well due to the growing interest in virtual topology design on optical networks (see Chapter 4 of [12], for example). The advantages of using the hypercube as the virtual topology are that the structure of the hypercube is well understood, and many algorithms are simpler and available in the literature. Routing algorithms on the WDM all-optical hypercube have been studied from both mathematics and networks points of view [14, 1, 13, 4, 5]. For off-line algorithms, it is known that any permutation can be realized by two wavelengths on H_n [4]. However, whether a permutation can be realized by one wavelength on the hypercube is still a challenging open problem (known as Szymanski Conjecture [14]).

A straightforward on-line routing algorithm for permutations on H_n is to connect a request (s_i, t_i) by a shortest path. This approach has small response time of $O(n)$, however, may need up to $2^{n/2}$ wavelengths which could be far beyond the number of wavelengths supported by an optical fiber for the network of large size. The problem with the shortest paths routing on H_n is that too many messages may use the same link. This happens in both circuit-switched and packet-switched routings. To overcome this problem, the following approach was proposed in [15] for packet-switched routing: For each pair (s_i, t_i), an intermediate node u_i is selected at random, and then the message is sent from s_i to u_i and from u_i to t_i via shortest paths. This approach can be applied to the circuit-switched routing as well. The direct implementation of the above approach on H_n gives an on-line randomized algorithm of $O(n)$ response time that realizes any permutation by $O(n^2)$ wavelengths with high probability. To the author's best knowledge, this is the best known upper bound on the number of wavelengths for on-line permutation routing on H_n.

We modify the approach of [15] to develop on-line algorithms for permutations on H_n. We give a deter-

ministic algorithm which realizes any permutation by at most $\lceil 3(n-1)/2 \rceil + 1$ wavelengths on H_n. The response time of the algorithm is $O(2^n)$. We also give a randomized algorithm which realizes a permutation by at most $(3/2 + \delta)(n - 1)$ wavelengths, where δ can be any value satisfying $\delta \geq 2/(n - 1)$. The average response time of the algorithm is $O(n(1 + \delta)/\delta)$. For constant δ, the algorithm uses $O(n)$ wavelengths and has $O(n)$ average response time. Notice that the number of wavelengths supported by an optical fiber can be as large as 2^7 [12]. Our algorithms can realize permutations on the hypercube of practical size. It is known that for off-line routing, any permutation on H_n can be realized by two wavelengths [4]. Both of our algorithms reach a competitive ratio of $O(n)$ over the off-line algorithm on the number of wavelength.

The rest of the paper is organized as follows. Section 2 gives the preliminaries. The routing algorithms are given in Section 3. The performance of the algorithms are analyzed in Section 4. The final section concludes the paper.

2 Preliminaries

The n-dimensional directed hypercube, denoted by H_n, is the directed graph on node set $V(H_n) = \{0,1\}^n$ such that there is an edge from $u \in V(H_n)$ to $v \in V(H_n)$ if and only if u and v differ exactly in one bit position. Figure 1 (a) gives an H_3.

For a binary number $v = x_1 x_2 ... x_n \in \{0,1\}^n$, we call x_i, $1 \leq i \leq n$, the ith bit of v. Given any edge (u, v) in H_n, if u and v differ in the ith bit position, $1 \leq i \leq n$, then we say edge (u, v) is in dimension i. For $u \in \{0,1\}^n$, we denote by $u^{(i)}$ the binary number which differs exactly in the ith bit position from u. In H_n, u and $u^{(i)}$ are adjacent by the edge in dimension i.

For $n \geq 1$, the 0-subcube of H_n, denoted by H_{n-1}^0, is defined to be the subgraph of H_n induced by the set of nodes whose first bit is 0. Define similarly the 1-subcube of H_n. Thus, H_{n-1}^0 and H_{n-1}^1 are both isomorphic to H_{n-1} and are connected to each other by edges of H_n in dimension 1.

The following *projection mapping* will be used frequently. Mapping $\pi : V(H_n) \to V(H_{n-1})$ is defined by $\pi(x_1 x_2 \ldots x_n) = x_2 \ldots x_n$, i.e., it removes the first bit of the n-tuple identifying the node. For $a = 0, 1$, mappings $\pi_a : V(H_n) \to V(H_{n-1}^a)$ are defined by $\pi_a(x_1 x_2 ... x_n) = a x_2 ... x_n$. In other words, π_0 (resp. π_1) maps the nodes of H_n to the nodes of H_{n-1}^0 (resp. H_{n-1}^1).

The n-dimensional butterfly, denoted by B_n, consists of $(n + 1)2^n$ nodes arranged in $n + 1$ stages connecting $N = 2^n$ inputs and N outputs. The stages are num-

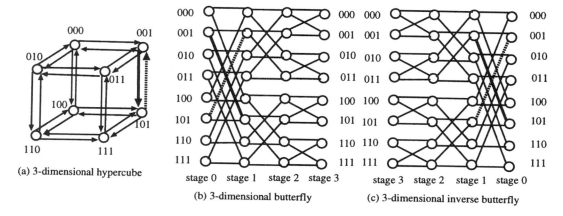

(a) 3-dimensional hypercube   (b) 3-dimensional butterfly   (c) 3-dimensional inverse butterfly

Figure 1: The 3-dimensional hypercube.

bered $0, 1, ..., n$ from left to right. Each node is given a binary label of $\{0,1\}^n$. There is an edge from node u at stage $i-1$ to node u' at stage i ($1 \leq i \leq n$) if and only if either $u' = u$ or $u' = u^{(i)}$. The 3-dimensional butterfly network B_3 is given in (b) of Figure 1. We call an edge from u to u' a *straight edge* if $u = u'$ are identical, and a *cross edge* otherwise. For any input and output pair (u, v) in the butterfly network, there is a unique path from u to v in the network. Similar to the butterfly B_n, we can define the *inverse butterfly IB_n*. The 3-dimensional inverse butterfly IB_3 is given in (c) of Figure 1.

When we connect a butterfly and an inverse butterfly, we get a *Beneš network*. Figure 2 gives the 3-dimensional Beneš network BN_3. We call the butterfly and the inverse butterfly in the Beneš network the *forward part* and the *backward part* of the network, respectively. The nodes which connect the butterfly and the inverse butterfly are called *intermediate nodes*.

The structure of H_n is closely related to BN_n. A node $u \in V(H_n)$ corresponds to a row of nodes with binary label u in BN_n. The edge $(u, u^{(i)})$ in dimension i of H_n corresponds to the cross edge from node u at stage $i-1$ to node $u^{(i)}$ at stage i in the forward part and the cross edge from node $u^{(i)}$ at stage i to node u at stage $i-1$ in the backward part in BN_n (see Figure 1). A path from an input u to an output v in BN_n can be directly mapped to a path from u to v in H_n as follows: A cross edge $(u, u^{(i)})$ in BN_n is mapped to the hypercube edge $(u, u^{(i)})$ and a straight edge (u, u) in BN_n is mapped to node u of H_n (indicates the path staying on the same node).

A set of routing requests on a network is a multiset R of ordered pairs of nodes of the network. For each pair (s, t) in R, s is called source and t is called destination of the pair. R is $h - k$ if each node of the network appears

in R at most h times as a source and at most k times as a destination. R is called a *permutation* if it is $1 - 1$.

Given a set R of routing requests on a network, a *connection* for R is a multiset P of directed paths of the network that contains exactly one path from s to t for every pair $(s, t) \in R$. For any path p in the network, define the conflict number $c(p, P)$ of p with respect to connection P to be the number of paths in $P \setminus \{p\}$ that share a common edge with p. For a connection P, define the conflict number of P to be

$$C(P) = \max\{c(p, P) | p \in P\}.$$

The following proposition can be easily verified.

Proposition 1 *The paths in connection P can be assigned by at most $C(P)+1$ wavelengths so that the paths with the same wavelength are edge-disjoint.*

3   Routing algorithms

A straightforward approach for realizing a sequence of routing requests is the shortest path routing. However, in shortest path routing, too many messages from different sources may use the same edge in the hypercube, resulting in a large number of wavelengths needed. The following approach was proposed in [15] for the synchronous packet-switched routing on H_n: For each pair (s_i, t_i), an intermediate node u_i is selected and the message is sent from s_i to u_i and then from u_i to t_i by shortest paths.

Given a set R of routing requests, let P be the connection for $\{(s_i, u_i)|(s_i, t_i) \in R\}$ and Q be the connection for $\{(u_i, t_i)|(s_i, t_i) \in R\}$ in H_n. It is shown in [15] that for any permutation R on H_n, if u_i is selected randomly, then $C(P) = O(n)$ and $C(Q) = O(n)$ with high

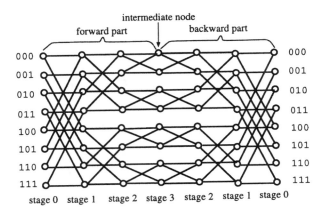

forward part   backward part

000   001   010   011   100   101   110   111

000   001   010   011   100   101   110   111

stage 0   stage 1   stage 2   stage 3   stage 2   stage 1   stage 0

Figure 2: The 3-dimensional Beneš network.

probability. The approach of [15] can be directly applied to on-line routing on H_n: When request (s_i, t_i) arrives, we select an intermediate node u_i, connect s_i to u_i and u_i to t_i by shortest paths and assign the path $s_i \to t_i$ a wavelength. This direct application, however, does not give an algorithm of $O(n)$ wavelengths for our problem. To see this, we diagram the approach in the form of Beneš network: Select an intermediate node in BN_n as u_i and connect s_i to u_i in the forward part and u_i to t_i in the backward part. Let P be the connection for (s_i, u_i) and Q be the connection for (u_i, t_i) in BN_n. Then any path of P and any path of Q are edge-disjoint. Since each edge in H_n corresponds to one edge in the forward part and one edge in the backward part of BN_n, the direct mapping suffers from a problem that a hypercube edge may appear in both a path $p \in P$ and a path $q \in Q$. That is, the paths in H_n obtained from the direct mapping of p and q may not be edge-disjoint. We call this problem the *conflict between the forward part and the backward part*. This conflict does not give any trouble to synchronous packet-switched routing, as the edges in P and the edges in Q are used in different time slots. However, the conflict between the forward part and the backward part gives problems for circuit-switched routing, because all the edges in the paths are used simultaneously. Since the conflict can happen at every dimension, the direct application of the approach of [15] gives an on-line randomized algorithm of $O(n^2)$ wavelengths with high probability for permutations on H_n.

The algorithms proposed in this paper follow a similar approach as that in [15]: Upon the arrival of a request (s_i, t_i), we select an intermediate node u_i and connect (s_i, u_i) and (u_i, t_i) by shortest paths. To avoid the conflict between the forward part and the backward part, we adopt the mapping scheme proposed in [1, 4] to

map the forward part and backward part of the paths in the Beneš network to different subcubes of the hypercube. Roughly speaking, we deal with a routing request (s_i, t_i) on H_n as a request $(\pi(s_i), \pi(t_i))$ on the $(n-1)$-dimensional hypercube H_{n-1} and find the path $p : \pi(s_i) \to \pi(u_i) \to \pi(t_i)$ on BN_{n-1}. Then we map the forward part $\pi(s_i) \to \pi(u_i)$ of p to one subcube (say the 0-subcube) of H_n and the backward part $\pi(u_i) \to \pi(t_i)$ of p to the other subcube (1-subcube) of H_n. More specifically, for $s_i \in V(H_{n-1}^0)$, the path $s_i \to t_i$ in H_n consists of four parts:

1. forward part $\pi_0(s_i) \to \pi_0(u_i)$ which is the direct map of the forward part of p to H_{n-1}^0;

2. backward part $\pi_1(u_i) \to \pi_1(t_i)$ which is the direct map of the backward part of p to H_{n-1}^1;

3. bridge edge $(\pi_0(u_i), \pi_1(u_i))$ which connects the forward part and the backward part; and

4. suffix edge $(\pi_1(t_i), \pi_0(t_i))$ for $t_i \in V(H_{n-1}^0)$ (for $t_i \in V(H_{n-1}^1)$, the suffix edge is empty).

For $s_i \in V(H_{n-1}^1)$, a symmetric mapping is used: The forward part and backward part of p are mapped to H_{n-1}^1 and H_{n-1}^0, respectively. We call the above mapping scheme *Beneš-subcube mapping*.

To make the correspondence between the bridge edges and the Beneš network clear, we modify the Beneš network by connecting each output of the butterfly B_n to the input at the same row of the inverse butterfly IB_n by an edge (see Figure 3).

For the path p in the modified BN_{n-1}, let I_p be the path in H_n consisting of the forward part $\pi_0(s_i) \to \pi_0(u_i)$, the bridge edge $(\pi_0(u_i), \pi_1(u_i))$, and the backward part $\pi_1(u_i) \to \pi_1(t_i)$. Then there is a $1-1$ correspondence between the edges of p and the edges of I_p.

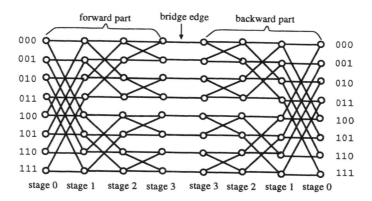

forward part   bridge edge   backward part

stage 0   stage 1   stage 2 stage 3   stage 3 stage 2   stage 1   stage 0

Figure 3: The 3-dimensional modified Beneš network.

From this, we have a nice property of Beneš-subcube mapping stated in the next lemma.

For any set P of paths in the modified BN_{n-1}, let $I(P) = \{I_p | p \in P\}$ be the set of paths in H_n.

Lemma 2 *The conflict number $C(P)$ is the same as the conflict number $C(I(P))$.*

This property gives a base on analyzing the number of wavelengths for permutations on H_n.

Now we give our algorithms. We first introduce some notation. For a set $R = \{(s, t)\}$ of routing requests on H_n and $a = 0, 1$, define

$$R_a = \{(s, t) | s \in V(H_{n-1}^a), (s, t) \in R\}.$$

For a permutation $R = \{(s_i, t_i) | i \geq 1\}$ with (s_i, t_i) arriving at time step i and $a = 0, 1$, define

$$R_a(i) = \{(s_j, t_j) | 1 \leq j \leq i, (s_j, t_j) \in R_a\}.$$

We extend the projection mapping π to a set R of routing requests by defining $\pi(R) = \{(\pi(s), \pi(t)) | (s, t) \in R\}$. Here, the set notation is interpreted as that for multi-set, so that $(\pi(s), \pi(t))$ and $(\pi(s'), \pi(t'))$ are distinct elements of $\pi(R)$ even if they are identical, as long as (s, t) and (s', t') are distinct elements in R. In the algorithms, let $P_a(i)$ denote the connections for $\pi(R_a(i))$ $(a = 0, 1)$ in BN_{n-1}. We also partition the available wavelengths into two disjoint sets W_0 and W_1. The paths in the connection $P_0(i)$ (resp. $P_1(i)$) are assigned with the wavelengths in W_0 (resp. W_1).

We name our deterministic algorithm *D_Routing*. The algorithm is simple: Given a routing request $(s_i, t_i) \in R$, it enumerates the 2^{n-1} paths between $\pi(s_i)$ and $\pi(t_i)$ in BN_{n-1} to find one with the minimum conflict number, maps the path to H_n by Beneš-subcube mapping, and assigns a wavelength to the path. The details of Algorithm D_Routing is given in Figure 4

Procedure D_Routing
Input: A routing request (s_i, t_i) in a permutation
    $R = \{(s_i, t_i) | i \geq i\}$ on H_n in time step i.
Output: A path $s_i \to t_i$ in H_n and a wavelength
    such that the paths in $P_a(i)$ $(a = 0, 1)$ with
    the same wavelength are edge-disjoint.
begin
    1. For $(s_i, t_i) \in R_a$ $(a = 0, 1)$, enumerates the
       2^{n-1} paths from $\pi(s_i)$ to $\pi(t_i)$ on the
       modified BN_{n-1} to find the path
       $p : \pi(s_i) \to \pi(t_i)$ such that
       $c(p, P_a(i))$ is the minimum.
    2. For $(s_i, t_i) \in R_a$ $(a = 0, 1)$, assign path p a
       wavelength in W_a such that the paths in $P_a(i)$
       with the same wavelength are edge-disjoint.
    3. Map path p to H_n by Beneš-subcube mapping.
end.

Figure 4: The deterministic on-line routing algorithm for permutation on H_n.

Our randomized algorithm *R_Routing* finds the path as follows: For (s_i, t_i), we select one path from $\pi(s_i)$ to $\pi(t_i)$ in BN_{n-1} at random. If the conflict number of the path is smaller than a pre-defined threshold then we accept the path, assign the path a wavelength, and map the path to H_n by Beneš-subcube mapping. Otherwise, we repeat the selection process until a path is accepted. The details of Algorithm R_Routing is given in Figure 5. In the algorithm $(3/4 + \delta/2)(n - 1)$ is the pre-defined threshold, where δ can be any value satisfying $\delta \geq 2/(n - 1)$. There is a trade-off between the number of wavelengths and the response time of the algorithm. Decreasing (resp. increasing) the value of δ will reduce the number of wavelengths (resp. response

Procedure R_Routing

Input: A routing request (s_i, t_i) in a permutation
  $R = \{(s_i, t_i) | i \geq 1\}$ on H_n in time step i.

Output: A path $s_i \to t_i$ in H_n and a wavelength
  such that the paths in $P_a(i)$ $(a = 0, 1)$ with
  the same wavelength are edge-disjoint.

begin

1. Pick up a path $p : \pi(s_i) \to \pi(t_i)$
   at random from the 2^{n-1} paths between
   $\pi(s_i)$ and $\pi(t_i)$ in BN_{n-1}.
2. For $(s_i, t_i) \in R_a$,
   if $c(p, P_a(i)) \geq (3/4 + \delta/2)(n - 1)$
   then repeat Step 1.
3. For $(s_i, t_i) \in R_a$ $(a = 0, 1)$, assign path p a
   wavelength in W_a such that the paths in $P_a(i)$
   with the same wavelength are edge-disjoint.
4. Map path p to H_n by Beneš-subcube mapping.

end.

Figure 5: The randomized on-line routing algorithm for permutation on H_n.

time) but may increase the response time (resp. number of wavelengths).

4 Analysis of algorithms

In this section, we derive the number of wavelengths used by and the response times of Algorithms D_Routing and R_Routing. To get the numbers of wavelengths, we work out the conflict numbers of the connections given by the algorithms for R_0 and R_1 and apply Proposition 1.

Lemma 3 *For permutation R and $a = 0, 1$, let P_a be a connection for $\pi(R_a)$ on BN_{n-1} and Q_a be a connection for R_a on H_n obtained by Beneš-subcube mapping of P_a. Then the conflict number $C(P_a)$ is the same as the the conflict number $C(Q_a)$.*

Proof: We only show the lemma on R_0. The proof for R_1 is symmetric. From the definition of R_0 and the fact that R is a permutation, set $\pi(R_0)$ is $1 - 2$ on BN_{n-1}, and at most one suffix edge $(\pi_1(t_i), \pi_0(t_i))$ is appended to each path $\pi_0(s_i) \to \pi_1(t_i)$ in $I(P_0)$. Therefore, the suffix edges in the paths of Q_0 are edge-disjoint. From this and Lemma 2, the conflict number $C(P_0)$ is the same as the conflict number of $C(Q_0)$. $\square$

From the above lemma and Proposition 1, the number of wavelengths for the connection Q_a can be determined by finding $C(P_a)$ $(a = 0, 1)$. For any pair (s, t) in BN_n, there are 2^n paths between s and t. Figure 6

gives the $2^3 = 8$ paths between 110 and 010 in BN_3. Notice that the forward parts of the 2^n paths from s to t form a binary tree with root s. We call this binary tree the *forward tree*. Similarly, the backward parts of the 2^n paths form a binary tree (*backward tree*) with root t. Given any path p in BN_n, p shares common edges with the forward tree from some stage of the butterfly. Similarly, p shares common edges with the backward tree until some stage of the inverse butterfly. Figure 6 shows a path from 010 to 111 that shares common edges with the forward tree from stage 1 and with the backward tree until stage 3. Path $010 \to 111$ blocks two paths from 110 to 010. In general, we have the following result.

Lemma 4 *For the forward and backward trees formed from the 2^n paths between (s, t) in BN_n, if path p shares common edges with the forward tree from stage f and with the backward tree until stage b in BN_n then p blocks 2^r, $r = \max\{n - f - 1, n - b - 1\}$, of the 2^n paths.*

Proof: Due to the unique path property of the butterfly, there is no cycle in the union graph of p and the forward tree. Therefore, p blocks exactly 2^{n-f-1} paths from s to the leaves of the forward tree. Similarly, p blocks 2^{n-b-1} paths from the leaves to t in the backward tree. From this, p blocks 2^r, where $r = \max\{n - f - 1, n - b - 1\}$, of the 2^n paths from s to t. $\square$

Lemma 5 *Given a $1 - 2$ routing requests set R with at most 2^n pairs, for any $(s, t) \in R$ let P be a connection for $R \setminus \{(s, t)\}$ on the modified Beneš network BN_n. Then there is a path $p : s \to t$ in BN_n with $C(p, P) \leq \lceil 3n/4 \rceil - 1$.*

Proof: Given the request $(s, t) \in R$, there are 2^n paths in BN_n to connect s and t. We say a path $q \in P$ gives m blocks to the 2^n paths if q shares a common edge with m of the 2^n paths. The number m can be calculated by Lemma 4 if the source and destination of q are known. We count the total number of blocks from the paths in P and derive the average number of blocks in one path from s to t.

Now, we calculate how many blocks in total the paths in P can contribute. For $1 \leq k \leq n$, let S_k be the set of sources in R that differ from s in at least one of the dimensions $1, ..., k$ and are identical with s in dimensions $k + 1, ..., n$. Then S_1 has at most one node $s^{(1)}$, S_k has at most $2^k - 1$ nodes and $S_k \setminus S_{k-1}$ has at most 2^{k-1} nodes. Similarly, let T_k be the set of destinations in R that differ from t in at least one of the dimensions $1, ..., k$ and are identical with t in dimensions $k + 1, ..., n$. Define T_0 to be the set of destinations in R that have the same binary label as t. Then T_0 has at most one node, T_k has

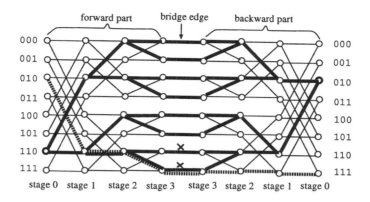

Figure 6: The 8 paths between two nodes on BN_3.

at most $\min\{2^n - 1, 2^{k+1} - 1\}$ nodes, and $T_k \setminus T_{k-1}$ has at most $\min\{2^n - 1, 2^k\}$ nodes.

For any path $q : s' \to t'$ in P, let $j \geq 1$ and $k \geq 0$ be the minimum integers such that $s' \in (S_j \setminus S_{j-1})$ and $t' \in (T_k \setminus T_{k-1})$. Then by Lemma 4, q contributes 2^r blocks, where $r = \max\{n-k-1, n-j-1\}$. For $r = n-1$, we have $k = 0$. Since $|T_0| \leq 1$, there can be at most one path q which contributes 2^{n-1} blocks. For $r = n-2$, we have $k = 1$ and $j \geq 1$ or $j = 1$ and $k \geq 1$. From $|T_1| \leq 2$ and $|S_1| \leq 1$, there can be at most three paths, each of which contributes 2^{n-2} blocks. In general, for $i \geq 2$ and $r = n - i$, we have $k = i$ and $j \geq i$ or $j = i$ and $k \geq i$. From $|T_i \setminus T_{i-1}| \leq \min\{2^n - 1, 2^i\}$ and $|S_i \setminus S_{i-1}| \leq 2^{i-1}$, there can be at most $\min\{2^n - 1, 2^i + 2^{i-1}\}$ paths, each of which contributes 2^{n-i-1} blocks. Summarizing the above and from the fact that R has at most 2^n pairs, the paths in P can contribute at most

$$2^{n-1} + \sum_{i=1}^{n-1} 2^{n-i-1} \times (2^i + 2^{i-1}) = n \times (2^{n-1} + 2^{n-2}) - 2^{n-2}$$

blocks. Since there are 2^n paths between s and t, the average number of blocks on each path is at most

$$\frac{n \times (2^{n-1} + 2^{n-2}) - 2^{n-2}}{2^n} = \frac{3n}{4} - \frac{1}{4}.$$

Therefore, there must be a path p from s to t with $c(p, P) \leq \lceil 3n/4 \rceil - 1$. $\square$

Lemma 5 provides a base for calculating the conflict number of connections given in our algorithms.

Theorem 6 *Algorithm D_Routing realizes any permutation R by at most $\lceil 3(n - 1)/2 \rceil + 1$ wavelengths. The response time for each request in R is $O(2^n)$.*

Proof: Let $R = \{(s_i, t_i)\}$ be a permutation with (s_i, t_i) arriving at time step i. For $R_0 = \{(s_i, t_i)|s_i \in$

$V(H_{n-1}^0), (s_i, t_i) \in R\}$, $\pi(R_0)$ is a 1-2 routing request set on H_{n-1}. From Lemma 5, the conflict number $C(P_0(i))$ of the connection $P_0(i)$ is at most $\lceil 3(n - 1)/4 \rceil - 1$. From Lemma 3, we have a connection Q_0 for $R_0(i)$ on H_n with conflict number $C(Q_0) \leq \lceil 3(n-1)/4 \rceil - 1$ on H_n. From Proposition 1, the paths in Q_0 can be assigned by at most $\lceil 3(n - 1)/4 \rceil$ wavelengths so that the paths with the same wavelength are edge-disjoint. Similarly, $\lceil 3(n - 1)/4 \rceil$ wavelengths are enough for the paths for $R_1(i)$. Thus, Algorithm D_Routing uses at most $2\lceil 3(n - 1)/4 \rceil \leq \lceil 3(n - 1)/2 \rceil + 1$ wavelengths.

Algorithm D_Routing enumerates the 2^{n-1} paths between $\pi(s_i)$ and $\pi(t_i)$ to find the path p with the minimum conflict number. The enumeration can be done by searching the forward and backward trees for $\pi(s_i)$ and $\pi(t_i)$. This can be done in $O(2^n)$ time because there are $O(2^n)$ edges in the trees. $\square$

Theorem 7 *Algorithm R_Routing realizes any permutation R by at most $(3/2 + \delta)(n - 1)$ wavelengths, where δ can be any value satisfying $\delta \geq 2/(n-1)$. The average response time of the algorithm is $O(n(1 + \delta)/\delta)$.*

Proof: For $(s_i, t_i) \in R_0$, from Lemma 5 and $\delta \geq 2/(n - 1)$, there must be a path $p : \pi(s_i) \to \pi(t_i)$ in BN_{n-1} with $c(p, P_0(i)) < (3/4 + \delta/2)(n-1)$. Algorithm R_Routing will finally find such a path p and realize R_0 by at most $(3/4 + \delta/2)(n - 1)$ wavelengths and R by at most $(3/2 + \delta)(n - 1)$ wavelengths.

To get the average response time of the algorithm, we need the average number of selections to get a good path. For each (s_i, t_i), let x be the probability that a randomly selected path is accepted by the algorithm. The average number of selections is

$$\sum_{i=1}^{\infty} i \times (1 - x)^{i-1} x = \frac{1}{x}.$$

425

Since each selection takes $O(n)$ time, the average response time of the algorithm is $O(n/x)$.

Let Q be the set of paths $q : \pi(s_i) \to \pi(t_i)$ in BN_{n-1} with $c(q, P_0(i)) \geq (3/4 + \delta/2)(n-1)$. Then $x = 1 - |Q|/2^{n-1}$. By Lemma 5,

$$|Q|(3/4 + \delta/2)(n-1) \leq 2^{n-1}(3/4)(n-1).$$

From this,

$$x \geq 1 - \frac{3/4}{3/4 + \delta/2} = \frac{\delta}{3/2 + \delta}.$$

Thus, the average response time is $O(n(1 + \delta)/\delta)$. $\square$

Notice that off-line algorithms use smaller number of wavelengths than on-line algorithms because off-line algorithms know all pairs in the set of routing requests while on-line algorithms have no knowledge on the pairs arriving later. One measure for an on-line algorithms is the *competitive ratio* which is the ratio of the performance of the on-line algorithm to the performance of the best known off-line algorithm. It is known that any permutation on H_n can be realized by two wavelengths [4]. From this, both Algorithms D_Routing and R_Routing reach the competitive ratio of $O(n)$.

5 Concluding remarks

A deterministic algorithm and a randomized algorithm are proposed for on-line permutation routing on the WDM all-optical hypercubes. Both algorithms can realize the permutation on H_n by $O(n)$ wavelengths. It is worth to investigate that whether the number of wavelengths can be reduced further for on-line permutation routing on the hypercube. It is also an interesting problem to improve the response time of the deterministic algorithm.

Acknowledgment

This work was partially supported by the NSERC research grant (RGPIN250304), President Research Grant and Endowed Research Fellowship of Simon Fraser University.

References

[1] S.B. Choi and A.K. Somani. Rearrangeable circuit-switched hypercube architectures for routing permutations. *J. of Parallel and Distributed Computing*, 19:125–130, 1993.

[2] Q. Gu and S. Peng. Efficient protocols for permutation routing on all-optical multistage interconnection networks. In *Proc. of 2000 International Conference on Parallel Processing (ICPP00)*, pages 513–520, 2000.

[3] Q. Gu and S. Peng. Wavelengths requirement for permutation routing in all-optical multistage interconnection networks. In *Proc. of International Parallel and Distributed Processing Symposium, IPDPS'2000*, pages 761–768, 2000.

[4] Q.P. Gu and H. Tamaki. Routing a permutation in the hypercube by two sets of edge-disjoint paths. *Journal of Parallel and Distributed Computing*, 44:147–152, 1997.

[5] Q.P. Gu and H. Tamaki. Multicolor routing in the undirected hypercube. *Discrete Applied Mathematics*, 100:169–181, 2000.

[6] J. Kleinberg and A. Kumar. Wavelength conversion in optical networks. In *Proc. of the 10th Annual ACM-SIAM Symposium on Discrete Algorithms SODA'99*, pages 566–575, 1999.

[7] M. Milail, C. Kaklamanis, and S. Rao. Efficient access to optical bandwidth. In *Proc. of the 36th Annual Symposium on Foundations of Computer Science (FOCS'95)*, pages 548–557, 1995.

[8] A. Mokhtar and M. Azizoğlu. Adaptive wavelength routing in all-optical networks. *IEEE/ACM Trans. on Networking*, 6(2):197–206, 1998.

[9] L. Narayanan, J. Opatrny, and D. Sotteau. All-to-all optical routing in optimal chrodal rings of degree four. In *Proc. of the 10th Annual ACM-SIAM Symposium on Discrete Algorithms SODA'99*, pages 695–703, 1999.

[10] R. Ramaswami and G. Sasaki. Multiwavelength optical networks with limited wavelength conversion. *IEEE/ACM Trans. on Networking*, 6(6):744–754, 1998.

[11] R. Ramaswami and K.N. Sivarajan. *Optical Networks A Practical Perspective*. Morgan Kaufmann, 1998.

[12] K.M. Sivalingam and S. Subramaniam. *Optical WDM Networks, Principles and Practice*. Kluwer Academic Publishers, 2000.

[13] A.P. Sprague and H. Tamaki. Routings for involutions of a hypercube. *Discrete Applied Math.*, 48:175–186, 1994.

[14] T. Szymanski. On the permutation capability of a circuit-switched hypercube. In *Proc. Inthernational Conference on Parallel Processing (I)*, pages 103–110, 1989.

[15] L.G. Valiant. A scheme for fast parallel communication. *SIAM J. on Computing*, 11(2):350–361, 1982.

[16] G. Wilfong and P. Winkler. Ring routing and wavelength translation. In *Proc. of the 9th Annual ACM-SIAM Symposium on Discrete Algorithms SODA'98*, pages 333–341, 1998.

Session 6B

Wireless/Mobile Computing

Dynamic Service Composition for Wireless Web Access

Siu-Nam Chuang, Alvin T.S. Chan[1], Jiannong Cao
Department of Computing
The Hong Kong Polytechnic University
Hung Hom, Kowloon
Hong Kong, SAR, China
[1]Email: cstschan@comp.polyu.edu.hk

Abstract

This paper describes a Web proxy architecture called WebPADS, short for "Web Proxy for Actively Deployable Services." The WebPADS was developed to enhance Web applications running on a wireless network. The WebPADS provides mechanisms to automatically locate and configure a flexible and adaptive wireless Web proxy. In addition, it provides a framework that facilitates the development of add-on services, where the services can be actively deployed and migrated across Web proxies, in order to adapt to the changing wireless environment.

1. Introduction

The success of wireless cellular technology has led to the evolution of a highly mobile computing model based on the potentially unconstrained movement of clients using wireless connectivity [1]. However, the wireless environment is drastically different from its wired counterpart. Many design assumptions, upon which existing protocols and applications for fixed network environment are built, are no longer appropriate in a wireless environment. In particular, bandwidth, latency, and error rates are all significantly poorer, varying and asymmetric in nature, which leads to sub-optimal utilization of a wireless link when used by Web applications. Previous proposals [2] have been made on enhancing the Web browsing experience in a wireless environment. Mowgli WWW [3] and WebExpress [4] are both based on an agent-proxy approach. This approach places an agent in the mobile node and another agent in the fixed network, all HTTP requests/responses are intercepted, transformed and optimized for transmission over a wireless network.

The agent-proxy approach has been shown to improve the performance of HTTP over a wireless network. In particular, effort has been directed toward applying specific services to alleviate the poor performance of Web applications in a wireless environment. Importantly, these services are static in nature because they require a priori installation and deployment. However, as the number and variety of services being provided through the Web continues to grow, a static client-intercept architecture that offers fixed functionalities will not be able to cope with the increasing demands placed upon these applications. As a direct result, both updating and adding functionalities to the client-intercept architecture can be complicated, to say the least. The inherent mobility of the mobile node makes it important for the mobile node and all the agents on the fixed network to become capable of being updated dynamically with the newly upgraded functionalities to ensure compatibility and consistent operations.

More importantly, the effects of varying characteristics in a wireless environment require the dynamic reaction of an agent-proxy to counter those effects. As such, it is important that an agent-proxy is able to actively deploy services that best match the operating environment of the wireless network.

In this paper, we propose an active service deployment approach, which is an extension to the agent-proxy approach. In the active service deployment model, the proxy is composed of a chain of service objects called mobilets (pronounced *mo-be-lets*). This model offers flexibility because the chain of mobilets can be dynamically reconfigured [5][6] to adapt to the vigorous changes in the characteristics of a wireless environment, without interrupting the service provision for other mobile nodes. Furthermore, mobilets can also be migrated to a new proxy server when the mobile node moves to a different network domain. We have realized the active service deployment model by crafting its design into a programmable infrastructure that forms the baseline architecture of the WebPADS (short for **Web P**roxy for **A**ctively **D**eployable **S**ervices).

2. System overview

The WebPADS platform, as shown in Figure 1, is an

object-oriented system based on the active service deployment architecture, comprising some system components and mobilets. Core system components provide essential services for the deployment of an agent-proxy that forms a unit of service executing under the WebPADS execution environment. The unit of service is implemented as an agent-proxy mobilet that provides added services to the wireless environment. System components also provide generic facilities that serve mobilets. The mobilets provide services that enhance the Web-browsing experience. These services can be added, removed and updated dynamically. A series of mobilets can be linked together to form a processing chain, allowing the WebPADS to benefit from the aggregated functionality of a group of services.

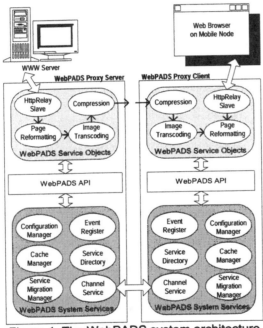

Figure 1. The WebPADS system architecture

The components of the WebPADS system are briefly described as follows:

The configuration manager is responsible for the connection negotiation between the proxy client and the proxy server. It is also responsible for initializing the service objects, and interconnecting the services. The WebPADS employs the use of the *Service Location Protocol (SLP) service agent* (SA) and *user agent* (UA) [7] to perform service discovery between the proxy client and the proxy server.

The *service migration manager* manages the process of importing and exporting services objects, between the WebPADS server and the WebPADS client. It also cooperates with the service directory to activate, to store

and to keep track of the changes made to the active service objects.

The *service directory* records all the known service types. The object codes are stored in a *service repository*, which is used for service activation and service migration.

The *event register* allows objects to register for event sources. When an event occurs, the objects that have registered for that event source are notified. Event sources include various changes in network status, machine resources status and connectivity status.

The *channel service* provides virtual channels for the service objects to communicate. Instead of opening separate TCP connections for each message, messages are multiplexed into a single persistent TCP connection, which then eliminates the overheads of opening new TCP connections and avoids the slow start effect on overall throughput [2].

The mobilet is designed to be a service entity that can be downloaded, pushed or migrated to a WebPADS platform for execution within that environment. The name, mobilet, bears a strong resemblance to applet. Applets are active codes executed within Web browsers whilst mobilets are active mobile codes that run within the agent-proxy WebPADS environment.

Mobilets exist in pairs: a master mobilet resides at the WebPADS client and a slave mobilet resides at the WebPADS server. A pair of mobilets cooperates to provide a specific service. A typical case would be when a slave mobilet shares a major portion of the processing burden. In this situation, the master mobilet instructs the slave mobilet what regarding which actions should be carried out and it also presents the processed output to the WebPADS client.

The service composition of WebPADS follows a nested approach. Each mobilet X performs an encapsulation service in a wireless environment, whilst the corresponding mobilet X′ decapsulates the data. In this case, appropriate headers are added by mobilet X to provide header information used by X′ for peer-to-peer processing. As shown in Figure 2, the architecture consists of more than one mobilet, in which the mobilets are chained together on the proxy client in a specified order, and the corresponding peer mobilets are chained together in nested order on the proxy server. Each mobilet encapsulates the data and adds header information in a well-formed nested order.

In order to support robustness in service configuration, all mobilets can be dynamically deployed across a WebPADS proxy client and server. In other words, it is possible for a mobile node to carry with it relevant mobilets as it travels across foreign domains. As the need arises, mobilets from the client can be dynamically pushed to a WebPADS proxy server and configured to operate in a coordinated manner. Conversely, it is possible for a WebPADS server to push mobilets to a WebPADS client to actively install new services to operate across a wireless link. To provide support for usability of a client as it moves across network domains, it is necessary for the WebPADS to facilitate migration of services. To adapt to changes in locality, network condition, and server availability, mobilets can migrate from one WebPADS server to another. Through service migration, changes in a wireless environment cause minimal interruption to service provision.

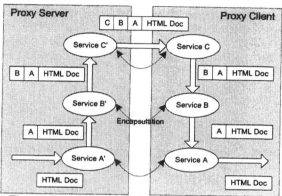

Figure 2. Service chaining

3. The WebPADS framework

In this section, we describe the WebPADS architecture. This framework comprises of six core services that are integrated within the WebPADS executive environment. Before detailing each of these services and its corresponding design, we provide a high-level overview of the services and their interactions within the WebPADS system.

Service Environment. This service allows flexible and robust deployment of an application-level based mobilet. In particular, it defines the execution environment, the programming model of the mobilets and the programming resources that are available to mobilets.

Service Deployment. Service deployment involves: locating and loading of mobilet source code, configuring a mobilet, and the composition of mobilets to form a service chain. To support active deployment, mobilets can be suspended, terminated and replaced at any point during their execution. Mobilets can also be redeployed so that a newer version of the same mobilet replaces the older one seamlessly.

Service Communication. As a network service, one of the major operations of a mobilet is communication. The messaging and event subsystems serve the communications needs of mobilets, which require efficient operation over a wireless environment. These messaging and event subsystems also serve other system components, and represent a standard communication protocol within

the WebPADS execution environment.

Service Adaptation. Once the service composition is established on the WebPADS platform, the entire service chain and the individual mobilets (that are executing) must be able to be automatically re-configured to adapt to the changes in the operating environment. Also, a facility is provided for the user to adjust the configuration of the services dynamically.

3.1. Service environment

An important design requirement of the WebPADS is to facilitate flexible and robust deployment, and migration of mobilets. Towards this end, we have chosen Java as the programming language of the WebPADS platform. Java is an object-oriented, network-savvy, robust, portable, multithreaded and dynamic language, which is an ideal candidate for development of the WebPADS platform.

The Mobilet programming model benefits from the features of Java. In this model, a mobilet is a mobile object that: has its own thread of control, is event-driven, and also communicates by passing messages. This model defines a set of abstractions and behaviors that ease the development of new mobilets. The main abstractions of the programming model are: mobilet, service chain, connector, object identifier and message. These abstractions are defined as follows:

Mobilet. A mobilet is a mobile object that can be dynamically deployed between a WebPADS client and server, and it can migrate between different WebPADS servers. Each mobilet has a separate thread of execution so that it can run autonomously. Mobilet functionality is characterized by customizable methods that react to state transitions and incoming messages.

Service Chain. Each of the services provided to a user consists of multiple mobilet pairs, which form a pair of service chains, with one chain residing in the WebPADS client and the other in the WebPADS server. A *ServiceChain* object is an entity that manages message passing and state transitions of the mobilets within a service chain. The ServiceChain acts as a proxy to the bounded mobilets. This proxy provides an interface that allows other management components to easily regulate the behavior of a group of chained mobilets without the need to directly interact with each mobilet within a service chain.

Connector. One of our design aims for a mobilet is that it need not be aware of the existence of adjacent mobilets. In other words, when forwarding messages within a service chain, a mobilet only has to decide the direction in which to send a message. It does not need to know details concerning the recipient mobilet. The Connector class provides this automatic message forwarding function. An instance of a *Connector* provides a way to connect the mobilets together, and is responsible for forwarding messages within a service chain. Moreover, the *Connector* is also responsible for forwarding the state transition command to the mobilets that it connects. This process is called *state flooding* because an instruction from the service chain is able to spread the state transition command throughout the entire service chain. The *Connector* also exists at the endpoints of a service chain. When a message reaches either of these endpoints and leaves the service chain, the connector will forward the message to its next hop or destination.

Object Identifier. Each mobilet has a unique object identifier, called an *ObjectID*, which is used by other objects to locate the mobilet within the WebPADS system. The ObjectID object is the only reference needed for passing a message and replying to a message, as well as for event registration and notification.

Message. Objects in the WebPADS system communicate by asynchronous message passing. Therefore unless explicitly specified, the message sender will not be blocked while waiting for a reply from the message recipient. The *WpsMesssage* class models a message in the WebPADS system. Each *WpsMessage* instance contains: the source and destination *ObjectID*, a command field that specifies either a command or a type of message, the sequence numbers for the current message and the message that it is replying to, and a content object that can be any serializable object.

The *Mobilet* class is one of the key classes in the WebPADS Application Programming Interface (API). It is an abstract class that the mobilet programmer uses as the base class for developing a customized mobilet. The *Mobilet* class defines methods that must be overridden by the mobilet programmer, so that the behavior of the mobilet is customized to react correctly to state transitions and incoming messages. These methods are systemically called by the WebPADS system when the corresponding events take place in the life cycle of a mobilet. The methods that represent the behaviors of a mobilet are shown in Figure 3.

```
public class Mobilet extends Wps implements Serializable {
//----------------------------//
// Implementation omitted here //
//----------------------------//
    // This method is called when the mobilet is started
    abstract void onStart() {}

    // This method is called before service reconfiguration.
    abstract void onSuspend() {}

    // This method is called before service migration.
    abstract int onMigrate() {}

    // Called after service migration or reconfiguration.
    abstract void onResume() {}

    // This method is called before killing the mobilet.
    abstract void onTerminate() {}

    // This method is called when message is sent to the mobilet.
    abstract void msgHandler(WpsMessage) {}
}
```

Figure 3. The basic behaviors of a mobilet

3.2. Service deployment

Service deployment involves locating and loading mobilet source code, configuration of mobilets, and composition of mobilets that form a service chain. To support active deployment, mobilets can also be terminated at any point during their run-time. Also, mobilets can be redeployed so that a newer version of the same mobilet can replace the older one seamlessly.

3.2.1. Configuration description file. To regulate the service deployment policies, the WebPADS system maintains a configuration description file utilizing XML. Figure 4 shows the document type definitions (DTD) of the configuration:

Referring to line 20 of Figure 4, the *codebase* attribute of a mobilet specifies the location of the packaged mobilet jar archive, which is in the form of a universal resource locator (URL). Line 21 specifies which class file within the jar archive is the extended mobilet class. With these two attributes, the WebPADS system is able to locate the source code of the desired mobilet. Lines 22 and 23 define a client chain map and a server chain map, each composed of multiple mobilets, which specifies the chaining of mobilets on the two corresponding WebPADS platforms.

```
    <?xml version="1.0" encoding="UTF-8"?>
1   <!ELEMENT LOCAL_PORT (#PCDATA) >
2   <!ELEMENT SERVER_ADDRESS_PORT (#PCDATA) >
3   <!ELEMENT SERVER_PORT_HTTP (#PCDATA) >
4   <!ELEMENT DEFAULT_SERVICE_CODEBASE (#PCDATA) >
5   <!ELEMENT DEFAULT_EVENT_CODEBASE (#PCDATA) >
6   <!ELEMENT RECONFIG_DELAY (#PCDATA) >
7   <!ELEMENT MIGRATION_DELAY (#PCDATA) >
8   <!ELEMENT PARAMETER (LOCAL_PORT, SERVER_PORT,
    SERVER_PORT_HTTP, DEFAULT_SERVICE_CODEBASE,
    DEFAULT_EVENT_CODEBASE, RECONFIG_DELAY, MIGRATION_DELAY)>

9   <!ELEMENT EVENT (#PCDATA) >
10  <!ATTLIST EVENT codebase CDATA #IMPLIED>
11  <!ATTLIST EVENT code CDATA #IMPLIED>
12  <!ELEMENT CLIENT_EVENT_LIST (EVENT)+>
13  <!ELEMENT SERVER_EVENT_LIST (EVENT)+>

14  <!ELEMENT RELATION (#PCDATA) >
15  <!ATTLIST RELATION operator CDATA #REQUIRED>
16  <!ELEMENT CONDITION (EVENT, RELATION) >
17  <!ATTLIST CONDITION equivalent CDATA #IMPLIED>
18  <!ELEMENT ENVIRONMENT (CONDITION)+>

19  <!ELEMENT SERVICE (#PCDATA) >
20  <!ATTLIST SERVICE codebase CDATA #REQUIRED>
21  <!ATTLIST SERVICE code CDATA #REQUIRED>
22  <!ELEMENT CLIENT_CHAIN_MAP (SERVICE)+>
23  <!ELEMENT SERVER_CHAIN_MAP (SERVICE)+>

24  <!ELEMENT CHAIN_MAP (ENVIRONMENT, CLIENT_CHAIN_MAP,
    SERVER_CHAIN_MAP)>
25  <!ATTLIST CHAIN_MAP default CDATA "false">
26  <!ELEMENT RECONFIGURATION (CHAIN_MAP)+>

27  <!ELEMENT MIGRATION (ENVIRONMENT) >
28  <!ELEMENT CONFIGURATION (PARAMETER, CLIENT_EVENT_LIST,
    SERVER_EVENT_LIST, RECONFIGURATION, MIGRATION)>
```

Figure 4. The DTD of the configuration file

3.2.2. Creation. After a WebPADS client and server are connected, the system starts to create the pair of service chains at the two ends, according to the service chain maps specified in the configuration file. The WebPADS client queries the service directory for the mobilet classes. The service directory then either loads the mobilet classes from the service repository, if they are cached in the service repository, or loads the classes from the specified location of their jar archive. At the same time, this WebPADS client sends a message to the WebPADS server, containing the server chain map description. The WebPADS server then undergoes a similar procedure to load the mobilet classes. After all the classes are loaded, the mobilets are initialized, together with the service chain and connector objects that chain and interconnect the mobilets. The mobilets now enter the "SERVICE_STARTING" state, and the onStart() method of each mobilet is called. After that, when the service chains receive the "SERVICE_START_READY" messages from all the mobilets, a "SERVICE_CHAIN_ START_READY" message is exchanged between the WebPADS client and server. Subsequently, the execution threads of the mobilets are started. At the time when the onStart() method is called, a mobilet thread is not yet started. No mobilet threads are started until the WebPADS platform receives the "SERVICE_CHAIN_START_ READY" message from its peer. However, once a mobilet is initialized, the mobilet's message queue is ready to receive messages, regardless of the state of the mobilet. This mechanism ensures that the whole service composition starts processing incoming data only after all mobilets complete their preparations for starting.

3.2.3. Suspension and resumption. During the course of operating the service composition, the need for altering the composition arises from time to time. In order to adapt to changes in a wireless environment and to user preferences, mobilets can be migrated, terminated, or even added. Before altering the service composition, the service chain pair is first suspended. The service chains modify the state of each mobilet to "SUSPENDING", allowing the execution thread of a mobilet to pause, provided it has completed processing of the current message. Each mobilet's onSuspend() method is then called. The pair of service chains collects the "SERVICE_SUSPENSION_ READY" message, and then the chains exchange the "SERVICE_CHAIN_SUSPENSION_READY" message. This service composition is then said to be in a suspended state.

The Resumption process contains similar operations. First the states of the mobilets are changed to RESUMING, and the onResume() method is called. The service chains collect the SERVICE_RESUMPTION_READY message, and then exchange the "SERVICE_CHAIN_ RESUMPTION_READY" message. After that, the execution threads of the mobilets are resumed.

3.2.4. Migration. After the service suspension process is finished, the service chain at the WebPADS server is ready for migration. Before migration begins, the state of the mobilets is changed to MIGRATING, and the onMigrate() method is called. After collecting the SERVICE_MIGRATION_READY messages, the service chain sends the "SERVICE_CHAIN_MIGRATION_ READY" message to the service migration manager. The Java object serialization mechanism produces a serialized form of the whole service chain, including the service chain object itself, connectors, mobilets and all the messages in the mobilets' message queue. As all member fields and object references of a mobilet are serialized, the mobilet programmer has to ensure that any objects that it references are serializable, otherwise these object references will become outdated after migrating to a new execution environment. In this respect, if a mobilet keeps a non-serializable object reference to a system component after migrating to a new WebPADS environment it will cause an error. The usual practice is to exercise bookkeeping of these non-serializable object references in the onMigrate() and the onResume() methods. When a mobilet needs to access the system components, it should obtain the references on-demand using the system's static method, and the references should not be reused. After the service chain is migrated to the new WebPADS server, the service resumption process takes place, and then the service composition can be resumed.

3.3. Service communication

Messaging is the essential communication mode for all objects within the WebPADS system, including the system components and mobilets. The messaging model of the WebPADS is designed to be asynchronous, which means that a message sender will not wait for a response to the message it has sent. This allows the message sender to return to its thread of execution as soon as possible. Together with the fact that each mobilet and system component has its own thread of execution, this messaging model automatically forms a message-processing pipeline that allows simultaneous processing of multiple messages.

To enable asynchronous messaging, all system components and mobilets possess a message queue that holds incoming messages, and the messages are processed in a first-in-first-out manner. To create a message, the sender has to provide: its own ObjectID, the receiver's ObjectID, an optional content object that can be any arbitrary serializable object, and an integral command value. The integral command value multiplexes the message command and the data type of the optional content object. When the message is being created, a creation time tag is added and a message sequence number is assigned to the message. If the message is meant to be a reply to a previous message, the sender has to supply the sequence number of that previous message.

There are two ways to send out a message. One way is

for the sender to put the message into the recipient's message queue directly, while the other way is to call the *send()* method of the message. The message's *send()* method resolves the location and object reference of the recipient automatically, and adds itself to the recipient's message queue. Direct access to the message queue is used only when the sender has the recipient's object reference, which means that both sender and recipient must reside on the same platform. The *send()* method can be used regardless of the location of the message recipient.

If the destination ObjectID identifies a remote recipient, the message will be sent to the *ChannelService* object that maintains a transport session to the destination platform. The *ChannelService* object serializes and sends the message to the destination platform's *ChannelService* object, where the message is deserialized, and the *arrived()* method is called. The message then translates the source and destination *ObjectID*s that it carries into the local *ObjectID*s that reference the source and destination. Finally, the message calls its own *send()* method again to deliver itself to the recipient.

3.4. Service adaptation

One of the advantages of the WebPADS system is that the service composition is highly adaptive to the changes in a wireless environment. However, to react to the changes in this environment, the WebPADS system must provide means to both monitor the changes, and to disseminate the changes to interested parties. The event model involves three parties: an event source, event information and an event listener. An event source is an object that extends the *WpsEvent* class. The *WpsEvent* class provides the basic implementation for adding, removing and notifying an event listener. Similar to a mobilet, *WpsEvent* is designed to be actively deployable such that a WebPADS client can push a new event source to a WebPADS server on initialization. Figure 4, lines 9 to 13, show that the class loading mechanism of event sources is virtually the same as that of mobilets. The event register provides a directory for other objects to locate these event sources.

Event information is the object that is sent to the listener when an event occurs, and is modeled by the *EventInfo* class. An *EventInfo* object contains an integral value – *primeValue* that represents the status of the event. This value is customized by the event source, which can take on any semantic and should be understood by the listener. For example, an event source that checks the average network delay of the wireless link can report an event and set the *primeValue* to 100 to represent the delay is 100ms. Besides the *primeValue*, an *EventInfo* object also contains a *HashMap* that can store an arbitrary number of key-value object pairs, which means that the event source can send any additional information to the listener.

To subscribe to an event source, a system component or mobilet has to call the *addListener()* method of an event source, while also passing it the *ObjectID* of the listener. When an event occurs, a message containing the *EventInfo* is sent to each subscribed listener. If a mobilet subscribes to an event, it should call the event source's *removeListener()* method within its *onTerminate()* method, because after service termination the mobilet's *objectID* in the list of listeners is no longer valid.

To monitor the environmental changes in a more structured manner, the environment monitor class, *EnvMonitor*, was created. *EnvMonitor* extends the *WpsEvent* class allowing it to become an event source. An environment monitor can monitor multiple event sources. Within an environment monitor, thresholds and conditions are set and compared to the *primeValue* of each monitored event source. Only when all the specified conditions are fulfilled, will the environment monitor notify its listeners. We can have different environment monitors representing different environment setups. Composite environment monitors can be setup to oversee other environment monitors, allowing hierarchical monitors of event sources. This provides for a flexible and detailed representation of a specific environment setup that can represent a complex environment setup.

When a WebPADS client starts, a default service composition is created based on the description of the XML configuration file. At the same time, a number of reconfiguration service chain maps are also created, each attached to an environment monitor that regulates the time and conditions when the service reconfiguration should take place. Figure 4, lines 14-18, show the description of conditions for events that the environment monitor oversees. Lines 24-26, show the binding between a service chain map and an environment monitor. When all the conditions monitored by an environment monitor are fulfilled, then the current service composition will be reconfigured to the service chain map that is attached to the environment monitor. However there are cases when the continuously changing environment leads to frequent service reconfigurations, which may affect the quality of service provision due to an extreme oscillation. To prevent this, as shown in Figure 4, line 6, an element in the configuration file specifies the minimal time interval between two service reconfigurations.

Automatic service reconfiguration aims to maintain a optimal service composition that adapts to the varying characteristics of a wireless environment. However, the reconfigured service composition might not always be what the user wants. For example, on a slow link, an image transcoding service is activated to reduce the image size, in order to improve the response time. However, the user might want to save a specific image in full detail, which is prohibited by the transcoding service. Thus, it is clear that the reconfiguration of service composition should allow user intervention. To achieve this, a Web Page is generated for a user to dynamically reconfigure the current service composition. The user can enable/disable a list for available mobilets, and each mobilet can also export a list of parameters that can be changed by the user using a specific mobilet Web page.

4. Implementation and evaluation

The WebPADS framework and the HTTP service have been implemented and tested extensively. To demonstrate the service composition of mobilets, two mobilets for HTTP services were developed:

A *text compressor* that compresses html files in the HttpResponse on the WebPADS server, and decompresses the html file on the WebPADS client.

An *image transcoder* that is able to convert images from the JPEG to GIF format, as well as convert images from color into gray scale, and also resize images.

To test the service adaptation feature, we have created three pseudo-event sources that emulate the functions of actual event sources, and report an event using a GUI interface. These pseudo-event sources are:

A bandwidth checker that reports a bandwidth change event, using the *primeValue* of *EventInfo* to represent the bandwidth in Kbps.

A disconnection detector that reports a disconnection from the WebPADS server, using the *primeValue* of *EventInfo* set to 1, which represents a Boolean true value.

A server locator that reports discovery of new WebPADS servers, using the *primeValue* set to true as a flag, and a string added to the *HashMap* of the *EventInfo*, to indicate the IP address and the listening port number, for each new WebPADS server.

One of the major concerns on the WebPADS architecture is that the advantages introduced by WebPADS would not justify the overheads incurred. Initial measurements were taken to investigate the overheads incurred by the architecture. Measurements were taken using three PCs. The WebPADS server and the Linux router were located at the same fixed LAN within the campus network. The mobile node was connected to the second network interface of the Linux router using a different network ID. The mobile node also runs a script-controllable Java Web browser called the MiniBrowser, which was created solely for the purpose of this experiment. The MiniBrowser is HTTP/1.1 compatible, and behaves like a normal Web browser. Importantly, this browser is designed to allow us to accurately test the interactions between the web entities and to collect measurements that are crucial in characterizing the WebPADS system.

The Linux router is configured with a NIST Net network emulator [8] to emulate wireless connections. The NIST Net is a Linux kernel module that can control the bandwidth, the delay, and the drop rate of any connection that passes through. This controlled environment allows us to perform incremental and systematic tests of the framework by adjusting the wireless operating environment through the NIST emulator and to investigate the effects of these changes on the performance of wireless web access.

The setup of our experiment was as follows:

A student was asked to achieve two tasks using a normal Web browser: (a) find the current UV index in Hong Kong and (b) find the opening hours of the campus library and the computer laboratory. The student was allowed to start from any Web page when beginning the search for the desired information.

Step 1. The pages visited by the student are recorded, and compiled into a list of sixteen URLs.

Step 2. The list of URLs was added to the MiniBrowser, which then retrieved the web pages one by one, and the time taken for each page to download was recorded.

Step 3. The bandwidth of the NIST net was initially set to 1Mbps.

Step 4. The MiniBrowser was scripted to get the pages using the WebPADS system, which was configured with a pair of *HttpRelay* mobilets, and two pairs of null mobilets.

Step 5. Step 5 was repeated, using a direct connection to the Internet, instead of using the WebPADS proxy.

Step 6. Step 5 and 6 was repeated five times, using an interleaved WebPADS system.

Step 7. Step 7 was repeated four times, with the bandwidth of NIST Net set to 500Kbps, 100Kbps, and 50Kbps respectively.

Step 8. Step 8 was repeated four times within two days, twice at 00:00 (i.e., midnight), when Internet traffic is off-peak, and twice at 12:00 (i.e., noon), which is the peak hour for Internet traffic.

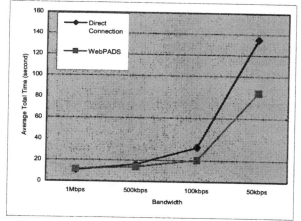

Figure 5. Retrieval time for the testing URLs using a direct connection and a WebPADS connection

Figure 5 shows that the average total time for retrieving

the sixteen pages using WebPADS was slower only at bandwidths above 1Mbps. Therefore the overhead created by the WebPADS system was insignificant for bandwidth under 500Kbps. The sharp rise in retrieval times at 50kbps, was due to a number of pages that caused timeouts under the low bandwidth conditions, which inflated those recorded retrieval times.

5. Conclusion

Even though the World Wide Web has existed for only a relatively short period of time, it has undergone unprecedented growth in terms of the number of Web servers and Web users. Rapid growth is expected to continue and this technology is infiltrating many more aspects of our lives. The extension of Web access to a wireless environment is seen as a natural evolution, as more and more handheld devices with communication facilities become common personal communication devices. This paper addressed the need to augment the existing wireless communication platform to better adapt Web access interactions operating in a wireless environment. Existing Internet protocols, on which the Web is based, were designed under the assumptions of using a fixed network environment that provides a highly stable connectivity and a relatively high bandwidth. These assumptions are invalid when users move to wireless and mobile connectivity, where the operating environment is far more hostile. In this paper, we described the development of the active service deployment model, upon which the WebPADS was built. The WebPADS intercepts Web traffic at the two ends of a wireless link; the web traffic is then transformed and optimized for more efficient use of that wireless link. Services provided by the WebPADS can by migrated from one WebPADS server to another WebPADS server located on another network domain to track the mobility of the mobile node, and to serve the mobile node continuously. Furthermore, the constitution of services provided to any user can be dynamically reconfigured to adapt to vigorous changes in the characteristics of a wireless environment. On the WebPADS system, a set of HTTP services was developed, which served as a fully functional example to verify the feasibility of the WebPADS framework. Interestingly, as noted in our experiments, the WebPADS system did not incur unnecessary overheads, while supporting a highly programmable platform that supports active service deployment across the wireless link to mitigate the effects from hostile characteristics of a wireless environment. The complete framework is constructed using Java as the execution platform, which supports a highly portable system to operate across heterogeneous environments. The initial experiments conducted with the system have revealed promising results that have significantly motivated us to further investigate and characterize the system in terms of its robustness and its ease of deploying active services across a mobile environment. In particular, we are working on the provision of a service chain migration protocol [1] that supports seamless transfer of services between WebPADS servers while maintaining the consistency requirements as service objects are transferred and re-bound in the new environment. The results of this work will be reported in our future publications.

6. Acknowledgments

The authors would like to thank the reviewers for their critical comments and helpful advice. This project is supported by the Central Research Grant under the account code G-V893.

7. References

[1] Perkins, C., "IP Mobility Support", RFC 2002, October 1996.

[2] Nielsen, H. F., Gettys, J., Baird-Smith. A.,Prud'hommeaux, E., Lie , H. W., and Lilley, C.; "Network performance effects of HTTP/1.1, CSS1, and PNG", *Proceedings of the ACM SIGCOMM '97 conference on Applications, technologies, architectures, and protocols for computer communication*, 1997, pp. 155 - 166.

[3] Liljeberg, M., Alanko, T., Kojo, M., Laamanen, H. and Raatikainen, K. "Optimizing Word-Wide Web for Weakly Connected Mobile Workstations: An Indirect Approach," in *Proceedings of the Second International Workshop on Services in Distributed and Networked Environments*, pp. 132 – 139, 1995.

[4] Hausel, B., Lindquist, D., "WebExpress: A System for Optimizing Web Browsing in a Wireless Environment," in *Proceedings of the MobiCom'96*, Rye, New York, USA, November 1996.

[5] Chuang, S. N., Chan, Alvin T. S., Cao Jiannong, "Active Framework Supporting Wireless Web Access," to appear in the *Proceedings of the IEEE Wireless Communications and Networking Conference (WCNC2002)*, Mar 2002, Orlando, Florida, U.S.A.

[6] Amir, E., McCanne, S., and Katz, R., "An active service framework and its application to real-time multimedia transcoding," *Proceedings of the ACM SIGCOMM '98 conference on Applications, technologies, architectures, and protocols for computer communication*, pp. 178 – 189, 1998.

[7] Guttman E., Perkins C., Veizades J., Day M., "Service Location Protocol, Version 2", RFC2608. June 1999.

[8] **NIST Net,** http://snad.ncsl.nist.gov/itg/nistnet/, 2002.

---

[1] Our current implementation supports primitive migration, which does not take into consideration of the consistency requirements as services are moved and re-bound to a new WebPADS server.

MOBY – A Mobile Peer-to-Peer Service and Data Network

Tzvetan Horozov
Motorola Labs.
IL02-2240, 1301, E. Algonquin Road
Schaumburg, IL 60196
horozov@labs.mot.com *

Ananth Grama
Department of Computer Sciences
Purdue University
W. Lafayette, IN 47907
ayg@cs.purdue.edu

Venu Vasudevan
Motorola Labs.
IL02-2240, 1301, E. Algonquin Road
Schaumburg, IL 60196
Venu_Vasudevan-CVV012@email.mot.com

Sean Landis
Motorola Labs.
IL02-2240, 1301, E. Algonquin Road
Schaumburg, IL 60196
Sean_Landis-CSL044@email.mot.com

Abstract

This paper describes the design and implementation of MOBY, a network for mobile peer-to-peer exchange of services and data. Constraints on computing power of mobile devices, limited hardware, networking, and software resources, and ad-hoc nature of mobile clients pose considerable challenges from the points of view of supporting performance goals, ease of service integration, and adaptation. These challenges are addressed in MOBY by dynamic service location and client mapping, surrogates for mobile clients, and standardized interfaces built upon off-the-shelf software components.

1. Introduction.

The emergence of peer-to-peer (P2P) networks for accessing vast amounts of data and diverse services coupled with the heterogeneity of access devices is rapidly re-shaping existing network infrastructure. P2P networks facilitate seamless information flow in a scalable manner without relying on a centralized broker. P2P networks for handheld wireless devices are different from those in wired hosts in two important aspects. The limited resources available to the device have implications for the design of suitable services infrastructure. While it is reasonable to expect a wired host to provide certain underlying software support

for facilitating a peer-to-peer network, this might not be a valid assumption for handheld devices. Consequently, we must either rewrite our services or develop suitable middleware to bridge the gap between the service and the access device. The second major difference is the ad-hoc nature of handheld devices, which requires protocols for seamless integration into the network. While this poses some technical challenges, it also presents opportunities for exposing data and services specific to device location. In order for a wireless peer-to-peer network to utilize this potential, scoped service search mechanisms (based on location predicates in addition to service descriptors) must be developed. Service Networks such as MOBY have tremendous application potential. A driver stuck in traffic can compute alternate routes based on dynamic congestion information using a vehicle routing service. A passenger can download precise weather information and regional maps upon arrival by locating corresponding services. All of this can be done without relying on a central server (such as weather.com or mapquest.com) from a thin client. In the scientific domain, MOBY enables access to services (applications) on large computing platforms at supercomputing centers as well as data repositories around the world. By suitably structuring these services, it is possible to use thin clients both as data sources (instruments, sensors) and as data sinks (output devices). In this framework, each mobile device potentially brings value to the network by providing useful data and services.

The motivating design considerations for MOBY are fourfold: (i) end-user transparency (providing the end user with a seamless view of the network); (ii) ubiquity (facilitating a wide range of wired and wireless components into the network); (iii) ease of application integration (providing API for developers); and (iv) performance. To facilitate

---

*This work is supported in part by National Science Foundation grants EIA-9806741, ACI-9875899, ACI-9872101, and Motorola Labs. Computing equipment used for this work was supported by National Science Foundation, Intel Corp. and Motorola Labs

these design goals, MOBY leverages on two key existing technologies – Jini [3] and the Jini Technology Surrogate Architecture Specification [21]. The key advantage of Jini is that it provides a service broker architecture to clients that do not have a-priori knowledge about the services and ways in which they interact. This technology is ideal for the ad-hoc nature of wireless networks, where peers come and go and where self-healing services must interact with devices that have different capabilities. Unfortunately, most of these devices do not have sufficient resources to support Jini. The *Surrogate Architecture Specification* provides a solution to the resource limitations of hand-held devices such as cell-phones and palm devices. It provides a specification that allows the device to run a surrogate on a wired host. Jini and Jini Surrogates provide a strong foundation for creating a peer-to-peer network such as MOBY but they are not sufficient. There are several major challenges that must be resolved. The first challenge is the lack of class loading functionality in J2ME [2] - Micro Edition of Java 2 for small devices. This is a serious limitation if we want to instantiate different protocol adapters in order to communicate with various services. The second issue relates to service discovery over the internet. While Jini services can be successfully discovered over a LAN, other services may be deployed on hosts that are not multicast reachable. For such services, we must provide mechanisms to extend Jini discovery over the Internet. Yet another issue relates to reliability and security in service discovery. Finally, with respect to performance, service location and client mapping have a critical impact on resource utilization and end-user performance. MOBY provides innovative new schemes for resource allocation, service location, and client mapping. This technique allows increased resources to be allocated to services that are more frequently accessed and positions such services "closer" to the clients that need them.

2. Related Research.

A wide range of projects have focused on various aspects of the MOBY infrastructure. The popularity of peer-to-peer data networks such as Gnutella [1],and Freenet [12], has resulted in their widespread deployment. While the focus of these networks is on information sharing (rather than service sharing), they provide some of the underlying technologies for service location and mapping. Enabling infrastructure for sharing services in distributed object oriented frameworks has been the subject of extensive research and development. Technologies such as RMI [6], CORBA [5], DCOM [11], DOT-NET [18] etc. provide foundational technologies for remote method calls. Several protocols for service location and discovery, such as Jini [3], Salutation [7], eSpeak [9], Service Discovery Service (SDS), Service Location Protocol (SLP) [22], and Wide Area ex-

tension to SLP (WASRV) [19], have also been developed. Application servers such as BEA WebLogic [8] and IBM WebSphere [10] have also been developed.

The Rover [16] software toolkit supports the construction of mobile-transparent and mobile-aware applications. The key objective of this toolkit is to develop develop proxies for services that make the mobile characteristics transparent to applications. The Ninja project [14] targets robust, scalable, distributed internet services for highly heterogeneous devices. Ninja consists of the following components: Bases, which are powerful workstation cluster environments; Units, which are service access devices; Active Proxies, for unit or service based adaptation, and Paths, which tie together units, services, and active proxies. It has been shown that the Ninja architecture provides the needed flexibility, facilitates application integration, and rapid service evolution.

JXTA [13] is a related P2P technology developed at Sun Microsystems with the objective of providing interoperability in data sharing, platform independence (language/OS) in service sharing, and ubiquity across the range of devices covered. JXTA consists of the core, which provides security, monitoring, and group services among peers. The JXTA services layer provides a range of functionality such as indexing, searching, and sharing. The JXTA applications layer allows users to build P2P applications in the JXTA framework. Services and information are 'advertised' in XML descriptors. These descriptors are searched using a peer discovery protocol. Access to these services is provided by the JXTA services layer.

3. MOBY System Architecture.

The general architecture of MOBY, as shown on Figure 1, pieces together a number of Jini domains. Every Jini domain consists of a local area network that allows multicast and contains the following components:

1. Wireless access point through which wireless devices such as cell phones or PDAs connect to the network.

2. Surrogate Host (SH) which is compliant with the *Surrogate Architecture Specification*. The SH provides run-time environment to the surrogates of different wireless devices.

3. *Jini Lookup Service.* One or more (JLUS) which is used for service look-up and registration

4. Jini Services Host (JSH) is a machine that can launch different Jini services by instantiating a downloadable jar-file.

5. A central gateway, called *Mnode*, which has three main functions: establishing secure connection with other

Jini domains, keeping registration information about the local Jini domain, and controlling the launch of Jini services on the (JSH).

6. Jini services, each of which are registered with JLUS.

7. Wireless devices such as PDAs or cell phones, which connect to the network through the wireless access point and launch their own surrogate on the SH.

A device enters the network via a wireless access point closest to it. Upon connection, the device obtains an IP address as well as some initialization data. This requires some modifications to the existing connection protocol but such modifications are beyond the scope of this paper. Initialization data contains information about the Surrogate Host IP address, its registration ports as well as the URL location of the surrogate that needs to be downloaded for the particular device. After obtaining this information, the device runs a start-up application that is downloaded and installed in advance. This application initiates communication with the SH, which results in launching of a surrogate on the SH downloaded from the web. The device then opens a data connection with the surrogate and becomes a peer in MOBY.

As the surrogate runs Java 2 Platform Standard Edition (J2SE), it supports multicast and registers with JLUS in the local domain. After this the surrogate can discover all Jini services that are running locally. One such service is the *Mnode*. An *Mnode* exports important methods that allow the surrogates to participate in MOBY by sending queries in the network or by retrieving information about the local domain. Each *Mnode* serves as a gateway for its LAN and is responsible for connecting to other LANs. This allows the surrogates to browse the entire MOBY network for services. The secure establishment of connection between *Mnodes* as well as their communication is discussed in detail in Section 3.2.

3.1. Services in MOBY.

There are three classes of services in MOBY. The first class comprises of *General Jini Services*. These are services that maintain their registration according to the *Jini* specification. The second class of services is *Peer Services*. These are services that are downloaded in a jar file and instantiated on the surrogate. For example the device/surrogate can download a talk daemon, which allows the user to connect and chat with other devices. The third class of services is called *System Jini Services*. These are *Jini* services, which are managed by the network. They could be launched on demand at any particular *Jini* domain, or terminated if they are not popular among the peers of MOBY. They differ from

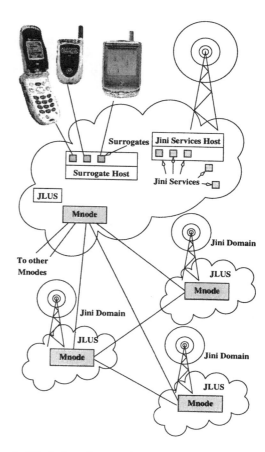

Figure 1. High-level overview of the MOBY architecture.

the *General Jini Services* in that their instantiation or termination is automatically controlled by the network according to a load balancing technique described in Section 7.4.

3.2. Security in MOBY.

MOBY provides extensive safeguards for services and service access. References to malicious services (e.g., a malicious map server advertised on a network) can lead to invalid data (false maps) and wastage of resources (network and processor resources at the wireless client). With the eventual goal of large-scale deployment, MOBY supports secure and reliable service discovery, i.e., if a client gets a reference to a service, the client must be able to identify the owner of that service.

Current versions of Jini do not provide secure service registration; any service can register with any description from anywhere within the domain. Other systems address this drawback using a variety of authentication mechanisms. These mechanisms are beyond the scope of this paper. MOBY simply uses these mechanisms to build upon a lo-

439

cal area network in which services registered with JLUS are secured. Each Jini domain has an associated *Mnode*, which connects it to the rest of MOBY. When users request a service, they get the description of the service along with the ID of the LAN where that service is registered. Thus, prior to using the service, a user can authenticate the ID of the service provider. In addition to the security provided by a given node about the origin of its services, the signed ID of nodes allow them to stay connected in a trusted network that identifies all malicious intrusions. Thus, when an *Mnode* sends a query on the network the result is from a trusted source.

In order to maintain such ID description, each *Mnode* must talk to an authority T, which maintains a database for MOBY and is secure. The associated protocol uses public key cryptography, 512 bits, RSA and is as follows:

1. *Mnode* $\rightarrow T$: $E_T(\text{Ip, Port}, T_i, K_{Mnode})$, where E_T is the public key of T, Ip and Port are the IP address and port of the *Mnode*, T_i is a time stamp, and K_{Mnode} is the public key of the *Mnode*.

2. T looks in its database and verifies that the Port and IP address are of a registered service provider, such as *Mapquest*, for example.

3. $T \rightarrow$ *Mnode*: $E_{Mnode}(S_T(\text{Port, Ip, ID}, T_i, \text{D}))$, where S_T is the public signature key of T, D is the period for which the signature is valid, ID is the identity of the *Mnode* that was obtained from the database in the previous step. This consists of an XML description of the node.

The tuple (Port, Ip, ID, T_i, D) is referred as node ID. After obtaining its signed ID each *Mnode* gets the IDs of some other *Mnodes* (from T, for example) and establishes communication with them. Each pair of nodes confirm each others' IDs after which they select a session key and secure-tunnel all communication between them with that key. In this way queries sent on the network are not subject to sniffing.

3.3. Searching for Services in MOBY.

An XML descriptor is attached to each service. For Jini services this descriptor provides two important pieces of information. The first one is a general service description that is used to match queries sent by peers. The second one supplies the URL from where a protocol adapter for different client devices can be downloaded. For *Peer Services* the XML descriptor provides information that is valuable to other peers that need to contact that service.

Each *Mnode* maintains a database containing information about all running services (of any type) in the local domain and their XML descriptors. Thus searching for a particular service requires propagation of the query to every *Mnode*.

Secure MOBY Search. Search in MOBY is done via broadcast with a fixed TTL of the packet. For example the first search for a service will be with a lower TTL. If no result is returned then the client may decide to repeat the search with a higher TTL, which expands the search diameter. As described earlier each *Mnode* knows of a fixed number of other *Mnodes* with which it communicates via secure tunnels and forwards all queries. The network protocol used is UDP. The reason for this is that UDP does not require expensive connection setup and maintenance which allows a host to send hundreds of queries per second to different hosts [15]. The drawbacks are that UDP packets can get lost or damaged [17]. However if a query that is sent to 20 hosts reaches only 15 of them, the objective of a multicast search is achieved; not to mention that the initiating client can repeat the query. MOBY does not guarantee that there is unique service description for each service but it guarantees that there is a unique *Mnode* description. As there could be services offered by different sources that have the same description, the user of the device may choose the service that he/she needs by the description of the *Mnode* that is returned as a result.

Client/Service Interaction. The user of the device can communicate with services in the following way. Each service has a service proxy which is downloaded from the JLUS where the service is registered. The service proxy is usually in the form of RMI stubs that have a reference to the methods of the service. Each Jini service contains URL references to downloadable protocol adapters for different devices. As suggested in the Service UI project [23], the service proxy should provide only the communication mechanism between the user and the service (RMI, TCP, etc.). Following this principle, the protocol adapter provides the entire logic of the interaction between the user and the service. It is instantiated with a reference to the service proxy and adapts the communication between the service and the user, as it is device specific. This requires service providers to supply downloadable protocol adapters for different devices communicating with their service.

The three types of services in MOBY require three different service search and client instantiation techniques:

General Jini Services. The surrogate searches for a Jini service in the local domain first. If the service is not found, a secure MOBY search is performed as described earlier. The search returns a reference to the JLUS where the Jini service and its proxy are registered, as well as a URL location from where an appropriate protocol adapter for that service can be downloaded. This is sufficient information for the surrogate to launch the client, initializing it with the service proxy, which can communicate with the service.

System Jini Services. Search for *System Jini Services* is similar to the search described above, except that when the service is not found, it must be instantiated. This mechanism is described in detail in section 7.4.

Peer Services. Since these are services that are available as downloadable jar-files the only thing that a device needs as a result of a service search is the URL from where to download the jar-file. Since these services are maintained by MOBY administrators, a centralized server keeps track of the URL storage for each service. Thus the search for a *Peer Service* is performed by contacting a central authority that supplies the required information in order to instantiate the service on the device. Instantiation of services happens only when a service is terminated and restarted at an alternate location, or when a service is replicated. Since this does not happen, the centralized server does not pose a significant bottleneck. In situations where the centralized server becomes a bottleneck, generalizations of this scheme to a distributed server can be developed.

4. Resource Management in MOBY.

The deployment model for MOBY is for phone companies and ISPs to provide access for their wireless subscribers. This would require certain hardware resources at the ISP. A crucial problem in this scenario relates to the service distribution in different Jini domains and the amount of hardware resources that should be allocated to a service.

General Jini Services do not present significant problems for the administrators of the network. If a company decides to make some of its services available to subscribers, it reaches an agreement with MOBY administrators. Subsequently, it is assigned an *Mnode* which connects their services to the rest of the network. In the case of a *Peer Services* MOBY administrators only need to provide verification and storage for the byte-code of the services, which is instantiated on each device/surrogate. The *System Jini Services* however require special handling for launching them at the locations where they are most requested.

System Jini services perform several important functions in MOBY. Introducing services into the network, allocating resources to these services, and deallocating resources when they are no longer accessed requires constant network monitoring and resource management. Access patterns to services may be periodic, (for example, traffic and stock quote servers are likely to be accessed during certain times of the day) or a-periodic. System Jini services attempt to optimize

client latency by moving services closer, replicating them, and terminating them, while satisfying a variety of server resource constraints.

5. Classes of *System Jini Services*.

It is reasonable, at this point, to identify services that are mobile. In contrast to services that are tied to large databases and associated servers (such as search engines), there are other services that can easily take advantage of the dynamic deployment of *System Jini Services*. *Content adapters* are services that provide computational capabilities for thin clients. An example of such a service is a picture editor. Photographs, typically stored in compressed formats such as JPG might not be easily handled by thin clients. For example, the Handspring Platinum under J2ME supports only PNG formatted files. Thus the client requires a service to convert pictures to PNG format. Deploying this service in a specific Jini domain only requires downloading and launching the service. *Database facade* is a second class of *System Jini Services* which includes those that require a small persistent store (database) to perform their function. A good example here is a yellow pages directory service for a particular city. The database could easily be downloaded into a particular Jini domain and the service could be deployed there. A third class of services, called *location-specific cache*, includes those that take advantage of coherence in user interests. For example, when using a Mapquest service, the likelihood of a peer requesting a map of the local area is high. This allows the service to cache and serve information to peers without having to contact the database on every query.

Other classes of services include real-time applications. For example a service could maintain a real-time connection to its central database and provide real-time stock quotes to different users at the same time. All these examples show that *System Jini Services* provide a powerful mechanism for fast and easy access to services.

6. The Need for *System Jini Services*.

Selecting services to be hosted on networks in the face of changing peer interests and demand is an important problem. Allocating hardware resources to these services can be a problem not only in the long-run but in the short-run as well. For example, the demand for different services could vary with the time of day (for example, stock quote servers during the day and entertainment information servers during evening hours). It is highly desirable to allocate larger amounts of resources to more frequently accessed services.

A second issue pertains to the movement of services closer to where they are frequently accessed. In the case

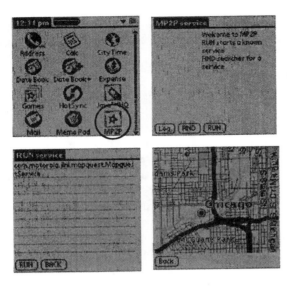

Figure 2. Screen shots of a MOBY client on a Palm emulator.

of RMI, for example, the latency of a method call made by the protocol adapter to the service determines the speed of application execution. Therefore it is desirable that the adapter (or the surrogate on which it is installed) be close to the service. This is especially the case for applications that make frequent calls to the service. Moving services closer to frequently accessed regions has the additional advantages of reducing load on the *Mnodes* (fewer queries) and network traffic. System Jini services allow such resource adaptation and service migration to occur transparently.

7. Prototype MOBY Implementation.

We now discuss specific details of our prototype MOBY implementation. We must note that this implementation has proven extremely stable over long periods of operation in a laboratory environment.

7.1. Terminal Application.

Our prototype implementation is based on Handspring Platinum hand-held devices. However the application will run on any device that has installed J2ME [2] with an MIDP [4] API implementation. The device must be capable of downloading and instantiating a protocol adapter application for each service. However, the current version of MOBY does not support dynamic class loading. There are two reasons for this: security issues and hardware capability.

In order to connect the hand-held device to MOBY we have developed a terminal application that is installed via the HotSync cradle. Terminal applications are not new and provide the most natural solution for controlling applications that are not running on the local machine. In our case, we have an application that runs on the surrogate (a jar file is being downloaded and instantiated) and we would like to get the resulting user interface for that application on the device's screen.

MIDP contains a package *javax.microedition.lcdui* which allows us to create UI on the device. We take the commands from the classes in that package and create user interface called *CommandSender* with matching commands. The surrogate then instantiates an object that implements this interface. Thus programmers can use the reference to the *CommandSender* interface and issue commands at the surrogate which resemble those in the *javax.microedition.lcdui* package. Their invocation results in modification of the terminal application on the device. The mechanics of the communication is hidden from the user by a separate data stream that is opened between the device and the *CommandSender* object on the surrogate.

7.2. Surrogate Architecture.

The surrogate allows the device to communicate with the rest of the network. When the device starts its registration with the SH, it provides a reference to a jar-file where the surrogate's byte code is stored. The SH downloads the jar-file and instantiates the surrogate.

Upon instantiation the surrogate opens two TCP sockets and waits for the device to connect. One of the connections is used to keep the surrogate running and the other is used for sending/receiving data. The surrogate uses the Jini Technology IP Interconnect Specification [20], which allows it to get a reference to the JLUS from the SH.

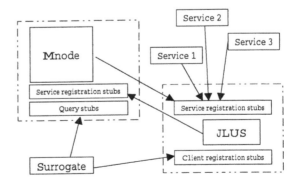

Figure 3. Method calls by various MOBY components.

The surrogate has three main functions, which are described

below:

Class Loading. As described earlier, when a surrogate discovers a service, it must also instantiate an appropriate protocol adapter to serve as a bridge between the service proxy and device client. When the surrogate downloads the adapter, it instantiates it with a reference to the *Command-Sender*. Subsequently the protocol adapter can invoke the methods provided by the interface and install the logic required for its application on the device. At this point, the user can start communicating with the service. Thus the adapter classes will be downloaded and instantiated on the surrogate.

Query Initiation. The main communication between the surrogate and the rest of the network is in the form of RMI calls. Figure 3 shows the RMI usage by various components of MOBY. When the surrogate is instantiated on the SH, it uses RMI to register with JLUS and monitor all Jini services running locally. One such service is the *Mnode*. When the surrogate gets a reference to the *Mnode*, it uses the RMI methods that it exports in order to register the device. When the user initiates a query for a service, the surrogate first contacts JLUS to check if the service is present locally. If not the surrogate invokes the appropriate RMI methods of the *Mnode*, which initiate the search over the entire MOBY network.

Query Response. If the surrogate launches a peer service then that service must be advertised to the participants of the network. In this case, the surrogate uses the appropriate RMI methods of the *Mnode* to register the peer service with its initialization parameters.

7.3. *Mnode*.

The *Mnode* is the router that connects the local Jini domain to the rest of the network. As mentioned earlier, when a service provider decides to make some services available to the mobile devices in MOBY, it is assigned an *Mnode* together with some initialization parameters such as IP address and Port.

Upon start-up, each *Mnode* chooses a 512 bit RSA public/private session key pair. After it gets its identity signed by the central server T, the node stores all information that can uniquely identify it in a file that is made available to the public. This file could be published on the internet or, in our case, it is supplied back to T to be stored in its database.

When an *Mnode* has established its identity, the node requests some identity files from T. As T stores all identity files of the currently running *Mnodes* it is able to supply the files that identify hosts which are physically close to the requesting node. This helps in building an evenly distributed

network around a fixed region and suits our needs as we assume that the user of the mobile device is interested in services that are physically proximate. After receiving some identity files the node connects to the corresponding hosts and establishes tunneled communication.

The *Mnode* serves the clients in the local domain in three ways: it registers with JLUS and monitors all active services, it registers any non Jini services that are started on the devices, and it allows devices to send queries to the rest of the network. Those functionalities are exposed to clients via RMI stubs as shown in Figure 3. In addition, the node also manages launching of *System Jini Services* as described in section 7.4.

7.4. Managing System Jini Services.

System Jini Services (SJS) are key components of MOBY. The architecture on which those service are currently launched is a simple host that downloads the service jar-file and instantiates the service. There are more sophisticated systems, which allow launching of a service remotely by passing it through a set of protocols. At this point, we introduce two methods for launching a service.

Deterministic Launch. As SJS are guaranteed to be found at any time in the system, if a requested service is not found, then it must be launched somewhere on the network. *Deterministic launch* guarantees the instantiation of a service and works as follows: the current *Mnode* tries to launch the service locally. If it succeeds, the result is returned to the device, otherwise, it queries the network for hardware resources and eventually gets a reply from several nodes that either have no SJS service running or have SJS services that are idle and can be terminated. The current *Mnode* picks the "closest" node and asks it to perform the launch of the SJS. If by this time that node had become busy then the next node is picked and the service launched there. Eventually the requested service is instantiated.

Probabilistic Launch. In a probabilistic launch a parameter i is supplied which describes the maximum distance (in terms of number of hops) at which a service should be launched. For example, for $i=2$ the probabilistic launch returns a result if a service could be launched no more than 2 nodes away from the current *Mnode*. Otherwise, a failure is signaled.

7.5. Service Launch.

The algorithm for launching a service at each *Mnode* is shown in Figure 4. When a service request comes from the local domain the *Mnode* first checks if the service is requested often (a table is maintained indicating the frequency

443

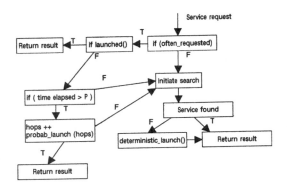

Figure 4. Initiating a service launch in MOBY.

with which each service is requested). If this is not the case, then a regular search for the service is initiated. The search terminates either by finding the service or instantiating it as close as possible to the local domain.

If the service is considered to be requested often, a check is made to see if the service is already instantiated. If this is the case then a reference to it is returned. If not, the *Mnode* tries to instantiate it at distance *hops*. If successful, the result is returned; if not, the number of hops is increased by one and the next instantiation is tried at distance *hops +1*. The parameter P is used to allow some time for the system to change. If a service cannot be instantiated close to the requesting client, then there is no need to try immediately, rather, it should wait some time and then try again. After a predetermined time interval, if a service continues to be requested, then it is instantiated as close as the current resources allow.

8. Concluding Remarks and Current Work.

In this paper, we have described a fully functional wireless peer-to-peer network, MOBY. While only a small number of applications have been integrated into the network at this stage, efforts are under way to standardize a service interface, which would allow a much larger class of services to be made available. Work on the MOBY network is progressing along many avenues of research and development. Quantification of performance is one of the most difficult parts of the development process. While individual components, such as resource discovery across *Mnodes*, remote service invocation overhead, service migration, etc., can be independently quantified, it is difficult to quantify end-to-end performance without a large-scale deployment. With respect to development efforts, ongoing work focuses on making the infrastructure more robust and to extend it to other services and devices

References

[1] Gnutella home page. http://gnutella.wego.com.
[2] Sun Microsystems. $Java^{TM}$ 2 Micro Edition. http://java.sun.com/products/j2mewtoolkit/.
[3] Sun Microsystems. Jini technology specification white paper. http://www.sun.com/jini/specs.
[4] Sun Microsystems. Mobile Information Device Profile ($MIDP^{TM}$). http://java.sun.com/products/j2mewtoolkit/.
[5] Object Management Group. The common object request broker: Architecture and specification, 1995. Tech. Rep. Version 2.0, Object Management Group.
[6] Sun Microsystems. Java Remote Method Invocation, 1997.
[7] Salutation Consortium. Salutation home page, 2000. http://www.salutation.org/.
[8] BEA Systems. BEA WebLogic Application Servers, 2001. http://www.bea.com/products/weblogic/.
[9] Hewlett-Packard Inc. eSpeak: The Universal Language of E-Services, 2001. http://www.espeak. net/.
[10] IBM Corporation. IBM WebSphere Application Server, 2001. http:// www-4.ibm.com/software/webservers/.
[11] N. Brown and C. Kindell. Distributed ComponentObject ModelProtocol- DCOM/1.0, 1996. http://ds.internic.net/internet-drafts/draft-brown-dcom-v1-spec-00.txt.
[12] I. Clarke, O. Sandberg, B. Wiley, and T. Hong. Freenet: A distributed anonymous information storage and retrieval system. In *Proc. of the ICSI Workshop on Design Issues in Anonymity and Unobservability*, Berkeley, CA, 2000, International Computer Science Institute, 2000.
[13] L. Gong. Project jxta: A technology overview, 2001. http://www.jxta.org/project/www/docs/TechOverview.pdf.
[14] S. D. Gribble, M. Welsh, R. von Behren, E. A. Brewer, D. E. Culler, N. Borisov, S. E. Czerwinski, R. Gummadi, J. R. Hill, A. D. Joseph, R. H. Katz, Z. M. Mao, S. Ross, and B. Y. Zhao. The ninja architecture for robust internet-scale systems and services. *Computer Networks*, 35(4):473–497, 2001.
[15] C. Grothoff, T. Horozov, C. Bennett, I. Patrascu, and T. Stef. Gnet – a truly anonymous networking infrastructure, 2001. Technical Report, Purdue University.
[16] A. D. Joseph, J. A. Tauber, and M. F. Kaashoek. Mobile computing with the rover toolkit. *IEEE Transactions on Computers*, 46(3):337–352, 1997.
[17] J. Kurose and K. Ross. *Computer Networking: A Top-Down Approach Featuring the Internet*. Addison-Wesley, 2000.
[18] B. Meyer and S. of. The significance of dot-net. *Software Development*, 8(14):51–60, 2000.
[19] J. Rosenberg, H. Schulzrinne, and B. Suter. Wide area network service location, 1997. IETF Internet Draft, 1997.
[20] K. Thompson. $Jini^{TM}$ technology ip interconnect specification, 2001. http://developer.jini.org/exchange/projects/surrogate/specs.html.
[21] K. Thompson. $Jini^{TM}$ technology surrogate architecture specification, 2001. http://developer.jini.org/exchange/projects/surrogate/specs.html.
[22] J. Veizades, E. Guttman, C. Perkins, and S. Kaplan. Service location protocol, 1997. RFC 2165.
[23] B. Venners. The serviceui project, 2000. http://swww.sartima.scom/sjini/serviceui/index.html.

Performance Comparison of Location Areas and Reporting Centers Under Aggregate Movement Behavior Mobility Models

Huanjing Wang, Guangbin Fan, and Jingyuan Zhang
Computer Science Department
The University of Alabama
Tuscaloosa, AL 35487
{hwang, gfan, zhang}@cs.ua.edu

Abstract

Location management deals with how to track mobile users within the cellular network. It consists of two basic operations: location update and paging. The total location management cost is the sum of the location update cost and the paging cost. Location Areas and Reporting Centers are two popular location management schemes. The motivation for the study is the observation that the location update cost difference between the Reporting Centers scheme and the Location Areas scheme is small whereas the paging cost in the Reporting Centers scheme is larger than that in the Location Areas scheme. The paper compares the performance of the Location Areas scheme and the Reporting Centers scheme under aggregate movement behavior mobility models by simulations. Simulation results show that the Location Areas scheme performs about the same as the Reporting Centers scheme in two extreme cases, that is, when a few cells or almost all cells are selected as the reporting cells. However, the Location Areas scheme outperforms the Reporting Centers scheme at the 100% confidence level with all call-to-mobility ratios when the reporting cells divide the whole service area into several regions.

1. Introduction

In the past decade, cellular communications has experienced an explosive growth due to recent technological advances in cellular networks and cellular phone manufacturing. It is expected that it will experience even more growth in the next decade. In a cellular system, a service area is divided into smaller areas of hexagon shape, called cells [4,11]. Each cell is served by a base station (BS). Each base station is connected to the mobile switching center (MSC) that is, in turn, connected to the public switched telephone network (PSTN). A mobile station (MS) communicates with another terminal, either mobile or fixed, via a base station.

Location management is one of the fundamental issues in cellular networks. It deals with how to track mobile users within the cellular network. Location management consists of two basic operations: location update and paging. Each operation has a cost. The total cost of location management is the sum of location update cost and paging cost. The task of location management is to find a strategy that minimizes the total cost. A location update scheme can be classified as either static or dynamic [3,10,15]. In a static scheme, there is a predetermined set of cells at which a location update must be generated by a mobile station regardless of its mobility. Location Areas [9] and Reporting Centers [2,5] are two popular examples of static schemes. In a dynamic scheme, a location update can be generated by a mobile station in any cell depending on its mobility. Examples of dynamic schemes include time-based [3,12], movement-based [1,3,7] and distance-based [3,6,8].

In the Location Areas approach [9], the service coverage area is partitioned into location areas. Each location area (LA for short) consists of several contiguous cells. The base station of each cell broadcasts the identification of the location area to which the cell belongs. Therefore, a mobile station knows which location area it is in. A mobile station will update its location whenever it moves into a cell that belongs to a new location area. On a call arrival for a particular mobile station, the cellular system will page all cells within the LA reported by the mobile station at its last update. The key issue with the Location Areas scheme is how to define location areas such that the total location management cost is minimized.

Another popular location management scheme is Reporting Centers [2,5]. The Reporting Centers approach designates a subset of cells as reporting centers (or reporting cells). A reporting center (RC for short) periodically transmits a short message to identify its role. A mobile station can learn whether or not it is in a reporting cell by listening to the message. A mobile station will update its location when it enters a new reporting center. When an incoming call arrives for a mobile station, the cellular system will page all cells within the vicinity of the reporting center that was last reported by the mobile station. The vicinity of a reporting center is defined as the collection of all non-reporting cells that are reachable from the reporting cell without crossing another reporting cell plus the reporting center itself. The key issue of the Reporting Centers scheme is how to select a set of reporting cells to minimize the total location management cost.

In this paper, we compare the performance of the Location Areas scheme and the Reporting Centers scheme under aggregate movement behavior mobility models by simulations. The remainder of the paper is organized as follows. Section 2 describes the motivation of the study. Section 3 compares the performance of Reporting Centers generated by Hac and Zhou's algorithm and Location Areas generated by our proposed algorithm. In Section 4, we compare the performance of Reporting Centers and Location Areas under the assumption that the reporting centers are connected, and they divide the whole service area into several regions. Section 5 summarizes the simulation results.

2. Motivation

The motivation of the study is the observation that the location update cost difference between Reporting Centers and Location Areas is small whereas the paging cost in Reporting Centers is far larger than that in Location Areas. Let us consider a one-dimensional network topology as shown in Figure 2-1, where b, d, and e are reporting centers. We define the location area A as consisting of all non-reporting cells between d and b and the location area B as consisting of all non-reporting cells between b and e. Next we will decide the location area to which a reporting cell such as b should belong.

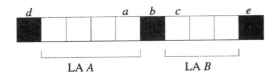

Figure 2-1 A one-dimensional network topology with reporting centers and location areas.

In the long run, the number of times a mobile station (MS for short) enters a cell is about the same as the MS leaves the cell. Let $m_{i \to j}$ denote the number of times a MS moves from cell i to j, then for cell b, we have:

$$m_{b \to a} + m_{b \to c} = m_{a \to b} + m_{c \to b} \qquad (2\text{-}1)$$

The total cost of location management is the sum of location update cost and paging cost. First we consider the paging cost. In the Reporting Centers scheme, the paging cost will be the vicinity of the reporting center. The vicinity of a reporting center is defined as the collection of all non-reporting cells that are reachable from the reporting cell without crossing another reporting cell plus the reporting center itself. In Figure 2-1, the vicinity of reporting cell b consists of 8 cells. The paging cost is 8 when a call arrives for a MS whose last reported cell is b in the Reporting Centers scheme. In the Location Areas scheme, the reporting center b will be assigned to either the left location area A or the right location area B. In either case, the paging cost in the Location Areas scheme is smaller than that in the Reporting Centers scheme. In Figure 2-1, the paging cost is 5 if b belongs to the left location area A or 4 if b belongs to the right location area B. The above argument applies to other reporting centers. So the paging cost in the Reporting Centers scheme is larger than that in the Location Areas scheme.

Next we consider the location update cost. In the Location Areas scheme, a user updates its location when it crosses a boundary between two location areas. In the Reporting Centers scheme, we assume a MS updates its location when it enters a reporting center. (Note that it is different from the actual rule. The actual rule specifies that a MS updates its location when it enters a new reporting cell. We will use the actual rule for simulations.) Suppose reporting center b belongs to left location area A in Figure 2-1, the update cost in the Reporting Centers scheme is $m_{a \to b} + m_{c \to b}$, and the update cost in the Location Areas scheme is $m_{b \to c} + m_{c \to b}$. If the location update cost in Location Areas is smaller than that in Reporting Centers, Equation 2-2 will hold.

$$m_{b \to c} + m_{c \to b} < m_{a \to b} + m_{c \to b} \qquad (2\text{-}2)$$

If Equation 2-2 does not hold, then

$$m_{b \to c} + m_{c \to b} > m_{a \to b} + m_{c \to b} \qquad (2\text{-}3)$$

From Equation 2-3, we get

$$m_{b \to c} > m_{a \to b} \qquad (2\text{-}4)$$

Subtracting Equation 2-4 from Equation 2-1, we get

$$m_{b \to a} < m_{c \to b} \qquad (2\text{-}5)$$

Adding $m_{a \to b}$ to both sides, we get

$$m_{b \to a} + m_{a \to b} < m_{c \to b} + m_{a \to b} \quad (2\text{-}6)$$

The right side is the location update cost in the Reporting Centers scheme, and the left side in the Equation 2-6 is the location update cost in the Location Areas scheme when b belongs to right location area B. From Equations 2-2 and 2-6 we show the location update cost in the Reporting Centers scheme is always larger than that in the Location Areas scheme if a MS updates its location when it enters a reporting cell.

3. Reporting Centers Generated by Hac and Zhou's Algorithm

The idea of the Reporting Centers scheme has been first proposed in [2]. In [5], Hac and Zhou presented an approximate algorithm to select a subset of reporting centers to minimize the total location update and paging costs in a two-dimensional hexagonal cellular network with weighted mobility rates and query rates. In this section, we will first introduce a two-dimensional hexagonal cellular network with weighted mobility rates and query rates. Given a two-dimensional hexagonal cellular network with weighted mobility rates and query rates, we will then generate the reporting centers by Hac and Zhou's approximate algorithm and generate the location areas using our algorithm. Finally the performance of Location Areas and Reporting Centers will be compared.

3.1 Cellular Networks with Weighted Mobility Rates and Query Rates

A two-dimensional hexagonal cellular network topology is used to model a more general service area where mobile stations can move in any directions. Figure 3-1 shows a two-dimensional hexagonal cellular network with 19 cells, where a cell is represented by a hexagon. In such a network, each cell has 6 neighboring cells.

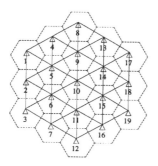

Figure 3-1 A two-dimensional cellular network with 19 cells and its graph representation.

We use a graph G to represent a cellular network [5,13]. A node in G represents a cell, and the link connects two nodes if the corresponding cells those two nodes represent are neighboring cells. The graph representation of the cellular network is imposed on the cellular network in Figure 3-1.

The simulations in this paper use the aggregate movement behavior mobility model introduced in [5]. For that purpose, each node is assigned two weights. One is the mobility weight W_{mi} that represents the frequency the subscribers enter the cell i, in the number of moves per unit of time. Mobility weight is also called mobility rate. The other is the query weight W_{qi} that represents the frequency of incoming calls to the subscribers in the cell i, in the number of calls per unit of time. Query weight is also called query rate.

3.2 Hac and Zhou's Approximate Algorithm to Find Reporting Centers

The cost of Location management is comprised of location update cost and paging cost. The basic idea of the Reporting Centers scheme is to find a subset of cells as reporting centers, such that the total location management cost is minimized. Hac and Zhou's approximate algorithm described in [5] bounds the paging cost and minimizes the updating cost. It is assumed a cellular network is represented by a graph G. The number of nodes in G is N. Each node has two weights, mobility weight W_{mi} and query weight W_{qi}, $1 \leq i \leq N$. To make this paper self contained, Hac and Zhou's algorithm to find the reporting centers is described as follows.

1) Build two lists: the first for the centers list S, the second for the noncenters list V.
2) Initialize S with all nodes in it.
   Sort S in the descending order of the node's mobility weight.
   Mark all nodes that have not been tried yet. Initialize V empty.
3) Pick node with the largest mobility weight from S (i.e., the first node in S).
4) Make x a noncenter node.
   If $z(S\text{-}x) \leq Z$, then do:
      a) $S = S - x$.
      b) Put this node into V.
   else do:
      a) Put this node back to the tail of S, i.e. x is still the center node.
      b) Mark the node as tried.
5) If this is still a node not tried yet, then go to step 3).
6) Else return list S as centers and list V as noncenters.

In this algorithm, Z is the integer that represents the upper bound size of vicinity, and $z(S_i)$ is the largest size of vicinity among all vicinities under the current selection of center nodes S_i. The vicinity of a reporting cell is the set of all nonreporting cells that are reachable from the reporting cell without crossing another reporting cell, and the reporting cell is in the vicinity of itself. The authors also propose a refinement procedure to get a better result. We have used the refined procedure to identify the reporting centers.

3.3 Our Algorithm to Find Location Areas

In the Location Areas scheme, mobile stations will update their location whenever they move into a cell that belongs to a new location area. Under the aggregate movement behavior mobility model, the update cost is the sum of mobility weights of boundary links. The mobility weight of a boundary link is the sum of mobility weights of two related (adjacent) cells divided by 6. For example, in Figure 3-2, if cells 5 and 9 are in different location areas, the link between cells 5 and 9 is a boundary link whose boundary weight is $(W_{m5} + W_{m9})/6$. (For convenience, we will generate the mobility weight for each boundary link. The mobility weight for a node is obtained by adding up the mobility weights of its boundary links.) The paging cost for cell i is the query weight W_{qi} multiplied by the size of location area to which cell i belongs. For example, the paging cost for a MS in cell 5 in Figure 3-2 is $W_{q5}* 5$.

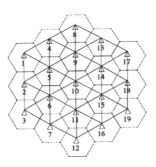

Figure 3-2 A cellular network with 4 location areas and its graph representation.

The call-to-mobility ratio for each cell is the query weight divided by the mobility weight. To reduce the update cost, we try to keep the cell with a low ratio away from the boundary. Therefore, a cell with a lower ratio has a higher probability that it will be combined with neighboring cells to form a new location area.

Given a graph G representing a cellular network, assume the number of nodes in G is N, and each node has two weights, mobility weight W_{mi} and query weight W_{qi} ($1 \leq i \leq N$). In our algorithm, K is used to store nodes in G, and L_i is used to store all cells of the location area to which cell i belongs. Our algorithm will start with each

cell as a location area. The algorithm will continue combining a location area with its neighboring location areas if the total cost will be reduced. The detail of our algorithm is described as follows.

1) Initialize K with all nodes in G.
   Sort the nodes in K in increasing order of the node's call-to-mobility ratio.
   For each node i ($1 \leq i \leq N$), initialize L_i with itself,.
2) While K is not empty
   Let x be the node with the smallest call-to-mobility ratio.
   Compute the total cost C with location areas defined by L_i, ($1 \leq i \leq N$).
   Find a node z that is a neighboring cell of x and is not in list L_x, such that the total cost C' resulting from merging L_x and L_z is minimized.
   If $C' < C$, do the following.
      a) For each node u in L_x, append L_z to L_u.
      b) For each node v in L_z, append L_x to L_v.
   $K = K - x$.
3) Return list L_i, $1 \leq i \leq N$.

3.4 Simulation Results

We use a two-dimensional cellular network with 19 cells as shown in Figure 3-1 for performance comparison under various call-to-mobility ratios. Given a mobility-rate mean and a query-rate mean for boundary links, we generate the mobility rate and the query rate for each boundary link using an exponential random number generator provided by the CSIM simulation software [16]. The mobility rate and the query rate for a node are obtained by adding up the corresponding weights of its boundary links. Based on the mobility rates and the query rates for nodes, we will use Hac and Zhou's algorithm to find the reporting centers, and our algorithm to find the location areas. Finally, we will compare the costs of both schemes. To evaluate both schemes under different call-to-mobility ratios, one method is to retain the mobility-rate mean and change the query-rate mean. The other method is to retain the query-rate mean and change the mobility-rate mean. We will show the simulation results with the first method. The simulations using the other method have similar results [14].

Figures 3-3, 3-4 and 3-5 plot the location management costs of the Reporting Centers scheme and the Location Areas scheme under the aggregate movement behavior mobility model.

Simulation results show when the call-to-mobility ratio is equal to or smaller than 0.015, there is only one reporting cell, and the whole service area is one location area based on the corresponding algorithms. Figure 3-3 illustrates the Location Areas scheme performs about the same as the Reporting Centers scheme when the ratio is equal to or smaller than 0.015.

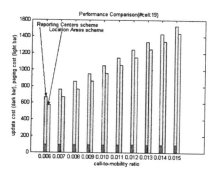

Figure 3-3 Total cost comparison of Location Areas and Reporting Centers schemes under the aggregate movement behavior model (#RC=1).

Simulations show when the ratio is equal to or smaller than 0.05, a few cells are selected as reporting cells, and the whole service area is one location area. Otherwise, at least half of cells are selected as reporting cells, and the number of location areas is more than one. Figure 3-4 shows the Location Areas scheme performs better than the Reporting Centers scheme when the ratio is between 0.02 and 0.26.

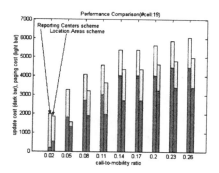

Figure 3-4 Total cost comparison of Location Areas and Reporting Centers schemes under the aggregate movement behavior model (1<#RC<19).

Simulations show when the ratio is equal to or larger than 0.3, every cell is selected as a reporting cell. Figure 3-5 indicates the Location Areas scheme performs better than the Reporting Centers scheme. This is because not every cell is a location area based on our algorithm.

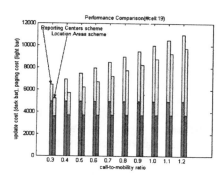

Figure 3-5 Total cost comparison of Location Areas and Reporting Centers schemes under the aggregate movement behavior model (#RC=19).

4. Reporting Centers Divide the Whole Service Area into Several Regions

In the previous section, we have shown the simulation results between Reporting Centers generated by Hac and Zhou's approximate algorithm and Location Areas generated by our algorithm under the aggregate movement behavior mobility model. Hac and Zhou's approximate algorithm tends to identify either a few cells as reporting centers or almost all cells as reporting centers. It is well known, under those two extreme cases, Location Area perform about the same as Reporting Centers. In this section, we assume the reporting centers are connected and they divide the whole service area into several regions.

4.1 Assumptions

We will use a two-dimensional cellular network with 19 cells as shown in Figure 4-1, and we assume cells 3, 6, 8, 9, 10, 15, and 19 are reporting centers, marked by solid triangles in Figure 4-1. The reporting cells are connected and divide the whole service area into three regions. The two reasons for choosing those reporting cells are stated below.

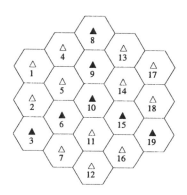

Figure 4-1 A two-dimensional network with 3 regions divided by reporting cells.

First, let us consider an isolated reporting center in a two-dimensional network, as illustrated in Figure 4-2, where cell 10 is the isolated reporting center. In this case, the vicinity of reporting center 10 consists of its six neighboring cells and itself. If we let cell 10's vicinity be a location area, the paging cost in the Location Areas scheme is the same as that in the Reporting Centers scheme, whereas the update cost in the Location Areas scheme could be smaller than that in the Reporting Centers scheme because a mobile station does not need to update its location at cell 10 in the Location Area scheme. Therefore it is not very meaningful to have an isolated reporting center.

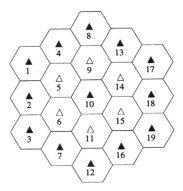

Figure 4-2 A two-dimensional network with an isolated reporting cell.

Second, it is not very meaningful to have a hanging reporting center as shown in Figure 4-3, where cell 10 is a hanging reporting center. In this case, the vicinity of cell 10 has six cells. If we let those six cells be a location area, the paging cost in the Location Areas scheme is the same as that in the Reporting Centers scheme, whereas the update cost in the Location Areas scheme could be smaller than that in the Reporting Centers scheme because a mobile station does not need to update its location at cell 10 in the Location Area scheme.

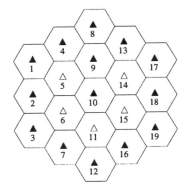

Figure 4-3 A two-dimensional network with hanging reporting cells.

4.2 Simulation Results

We use a two-dimensional cellular network with 19 cells as shown in Figure 4-1 for performance comparison. Because it is not very meaningful to have isolated reporting centers or hanging reporting centers, we assume the reporting centers are connected, and they divide the whole service area into several regions. For example, in Figure 4-1, the reporting cells divide the whole service area into three regions. We will define the regions divided by the reporting centers as location areas. A reporting center can either belong to a neighboring location area or form a location area by itself.

As in the previous section, we first generate the mobility rate and the query rate for each boundary link from a mobility-rate mean and a query-rate mean. We then compute the mobility rate and the query rate for a node by adding up the corresponding weights of its boundary links. Next we run Hac and Zhou's algorithm to find the reporting centers, and our algorithm to find the location areas. Finally, we will compare the costs of both schemes. To evaluate both schemes under different call-to-mobility ratios, we first retain the mobility-rate mean and change the query-rate mean. Then we retain the query-rate mean and change the mobility-rate mean.

Figure 4-4 plots the location management costs of the Reporting Centers scheme and the Location Areas scheme under the aggregate movement behavior mobility model with a fixed mobility-rate mean. The call-to-mobility ratio is the mean of query rates divided by the mean of mobility rates. We perform simulations for different call-to-mobility ratios ranging from 0.2 to 2.4.

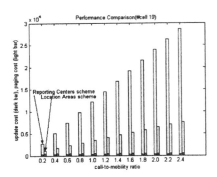

Figure 4-4 Total cost comparison of Location Areas and Reporting Centers schemes under the aggregate movement behavior model with a fixed mobility-rate mean.

From Figure 4-4, we have found that the location update cost difference between the Reporting Centers scheme and the Location Areas scheme is small whereas the paging cost in the Reporting Centers scheme is larger than that in the Location Areas scheme. The total cost in the Location Areas scheme is smaller than that in the Reporting Centers scheme. The Location Areas scheme performs better than the Reporting Centers scheme at the 100% confidence level under the aggregate movement behavior mobility model with the fixed mobility-rate mean and varying query-rate means.

Figure 4-5 presents the location management costs of the Reporting Centers scheme and the Location Areas scheme under the aggregate movement behavior mobility model with a fixed query-rate mean. From the simulations we have found the total cost in the Reporting Centers scheme is larger than that in the Location Areas scheme. The simulation results have shown that the Location Areas scheme outperforms the Reporting Centers at the 100% confidence level under the aggregate movement behavior mobility model with the fixed query-rate mean and varying mobility-rate means.

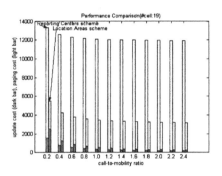

Figure 4-5 Total cost comparison of Location Areas and Reporting Centers schemes under the aggregate movement behavior model with a fixed query-rate mean.

5. Summary

Location Areas and Reporting Centers are two popular location management schemes. In the Location Areas scheme, the service area is partitioned into location areas. A mobile station updates its location whenever it moves into a cell that belongs to a new location area. On a call arrival for a mobile station, the cellular system will page all cells within the location area that was last reported by the mobile station. In the Reporting Centers scheme, a set of cells has been selected as reporting cells. A mobile station needs to update its location whenever it moves into a new reporting cell. When an incoming call arrives for a mobile station, the cellular system will page all cells within the vicinity of the reporting center that was last reported by the mobile station. The total cost of Location Areas and Reporting Centers is the sum of their

corresponding location update cost and paging cost. The paper compares the performance of the Location Areas scheme and the Reporting Centers scheme under the aggregate movement behavior mobility models by simulations.

We perform simulations on a two-dimensional hexagonal cellular network with 19 cells. We first compare the performance between Reporting Centers generated by Hac and Zhou's algorithm and Location Areas generated by our proposed algorithm. Simulation results show that the Location Areas scheme performs about the same as the Reporting Centers scheme. This is mainly because Hac and Zhou's approximate algorithm tends to identify either a few cells as reporting centers or almost all cells as reporting centers. We then compare the performance of Reporting Centers and Location Areas under the assumption that the reporting centers are connected and they divide the whole service area into several regions. Simulation results show the Location Areas scheme outperforms the Reporting Centers scheme at the 100% confidence level with all call-to-mobility ratios when the reporting cells divide the whole service area into several regions. The final conclusion of this paper is that in most cases the Location Areas scheme performs better than the Reporting Centers scheme.

6. References

[1] F. Akyildiz, J. S. M. Ho and Y.-B. Lin, Movement-Based Location Update and Selective Paging for PCS Networks, *IEEE/ACM Transactions on Networking*, vol. 4, no. 4, August 1996, pp. 629-638.

[2] A. Bar-Noy and I. Kessler, Tracking Mobile Users in Wireless Communications Networks, *IEEE Transactions on Information Theory*, vol. 39, no. 6, Nov. 1993, pp. 1877-1886.

[3] Amotz Bar-Noy, Ilan Kessler, and Moshe Sidi, Mobile users: To update or not to update? *Wireless Networks*, vol. 1, no. 2, July 1995, pp. 175-185.

[4] Uyless Black, *Mobile and Wireless Networks*, Prentice Hall, 1996.

[5] Anna Hac and Xian Zhou, Locating Strategies for Personal Communication Networks: A Novel Tracking Strategy, *IEEE Journal on Selected Areas in Communications*, vol. 15, no. 8, Oct. 1997, pp. 1425-1436.

[6] J. S. M. Ho and I. F. Akyildiz, Mobile user location update and paging under delay constraints, *Wireless Networks*, 1 (1995) 413-425.

[7] J. Li, H. Kameda and K. Li, Optimal dynamic location update for PCS networks, *IEEE/ACM Transactions on Networking*, vol. 8, no. 3, June 2000, pp. 319-327.

[8] U. Madhow, M. L. M. Honig and K. Steiglitz, Optimization of Wireless Resources for Personal

Communications Mobility Tracking, IEEE/ACM Transactions on Networking, vol. 3, no. 6, December 1995, pp. 698-707.

[9] M. Rahnema, Overview of the GSM Systems and Protocol Architecture, *IEEE Communications Magazine*, vol. 31, no. 4, April 1993, pp. 92-100.

[10] S. Ramanathan and M. Steenstrup, A survey of routing techniques for mobile communication networks, *Mobile Networks and Applications,* vol. 1, no. 2, Jan. 1996, pp. 89-104.

[11] T. S. Rappaport, *Wireless Communications - Principles and Practice,* Prentice Hall, 1996.

[12] C. Rose, Minimizing the average cost of paging and registration: A timer-based methods, *Wireless Networks*, 2 (1996) 109-116.

[13] I. Stojmenovic, Honeycomb networks: Topological properties and communication algorithms, *IEEE Transactions on Parallel and Distributed Systems*, vol. 8, no. 10, October 1997, pp.1036-1042.

[14] H. Wang, Performance Comparison of Location Areas and Reporting Centers Location Management Schemes, Master's Thesis, Computer Science Department, The University of Alabama, Tuscaloosa, 2001.

[15] J. Zhang, Location Management in Cellular Networks, in *Handbook of Wireless Networks and Mobile Computing*, Ivan Stojmenovic (Editor), John Wiley & Sons, 2002, 27-49.

[16] Mesquite Software, Inc. *User's Guide to CSIM18 Simulation Engine (C++ version)*, 1996, Austin, TX.

Session 6C

Middleware Systems

Neuron — A Wide-Area Service Discovery Infrastructure

Hung-Chang Hsiao   Chung-Ta King*
Department of Computer Science
National Tsing Hua University
Hsinchu Taiwan, 300
hsiao@pads1.cs.nthu.edu.tw

Abstract

A wide-area service discovery infrastructure provides a repository in which services over a wide area can register themselves and clients everywhere can inquire about them. In this paper, we discuss how to build such an infrastructure based on the peer-to-peer model. The proposed system, called Neuron, can be executed on top of a set of federated nodes across the global network and aggregate their resources to provide the discovery service. Neuron is self-organizing, self-tuning, and capable of tolerating failures of nodes and communication links. In addition, it allows the services to be described with arbitrary forms and the system load to be distributed evenly to the nodes. Neuron also supports event notification. We evaluated Neuron via simulation. The preliminary results show that service registration, discovery and service state advertising take at most $O(\log N)$ hops to complete.

1. Introduction

Due to the ubiquity of the Internet, the maturity of wireless networking and the availability of portable and embeddable thin devices, billions of devices, ranging from multitera FLOPS supercomputers to miniature sensors can be interconnected and function together to provide a wide variety of services. Services, no matter where and how they are provided, may be accessed from any place, at any time, via any device. However, with the vast amount of information and resources in the Internet, there is no easy way for a user or program to know all the available services, not to mention to track them.

The problem is further complicated by the fact that the Internet is dynamic, spontaneous, unstable, and unreliable. The deployed services may become unavailable, because the devices or communication links that provide the service may fail. New services or capabilities may be added at any time, and their states may change dynamically. Worse, users may roam about freely and enter environments that are totally strange to them. Discovering services in the new environment becomes a problem. All these point to a need to name and discover services in a robust way, particularly at a global scale.

The task is challenging not only because of the amount of information needed to be tracked, but also because of the dynamic nature of the Internet. Centralized discovery serv-

ers might not be able to provide the level of services required.

In this study, we propose a novel service discovery infrastructure, *Neuron*, which provides a wide-area substrate for service registration, discovery and state advertisement. Neuron is designed based on the *peer-to-peer* (P2P) model [3][7] and aims at utilizing distributed resources in a wide-area network such as the Internet to aid the discovery service. Thus, Neuron must be able to aggregate the resources of nodes across administrative boundaries. In addition, it has to combat the dynamic nature of networked environments, especially the situation when participating nodes dynamically join and leave Neuron. Hence, it must manage dynamic node configuration, utilize untrusting nodes, and tolerate faults, all without centralized administrators.

The second design goal of Neuron is to ensure its accessibility. This requires guarantee of the durability and availability of the service, and optimization in accessing the service across the network. Neuron should allow the participating nodes to self-maintain the aggregated and networked resources to provide reliable and responsive accesses. The load needs to be evenly distributed among the nodes, and the service name should be expressive. The naming system should allow applications to request and register services with arbitrary descriptions for a wide variety of services.

Neuron is implemented on top of Tornado [5], a global-scale P2P data locating, routing and storing infrastructure. The primary design concept of Neuron is the construction of a *virtual shared space* for each service. The virtual shared space permanently stores the service object and manages the end systems that are interested in it. A service provider publishes its service and then a reliable virtual shared space is constructed. If an end system is interested in such a service object, it subscribes to the service. Any change to the service object is posted to the associated end systems.

Compared with previous works [1][6][8][9] on service discovery, Neuron has several unique features. (1) It provides an expressive naming system, which allows services to be expressed in free form. (2) Neuron can utilize untrusted and unreliable resources from the network, which may be across administrative boundaries. It can support wide-area service discovery and accommodate a wide variety of services. It can also support a large number of requests for a particular service without compromising the performance. (3) Neuron can self-configure its architecture and self-tune its performance. It can be scaled to any size according to its current load. (4) Each service registered to Neuron can be stored for an indefinite duration. (5) To dis-

---

* This work was supported in part by National Science Council, R.O.C., under Grant NSC 90-2213-E-007-076 and by Ministry of Education, R.O.C., under Grant MOE 89-E-FA04-1-4.

cover a service, only $O(logN)$ hops of communication are required, where N is the number of active nodes in the system and a *hop* is one end-to-end communication between any two nodes. (6) Neuron can notify the changes of states of services that the end systems are interested in. (7) The load in Neuron can be evenly distributed to the participating nodes while minimizing the utilized resources. (8) Neuron is an application-level solution and thus avoids the need for cumbersome deployments and OS-level supports. It does not need centralized administrative control. To our knowledge, Neuron is the first and the most comprehensive work towards P2P-based service discovery infrastructure.

The remainder of the paper is organized as follows. Section 2 presents the system goals of Neuron. The design of Neuron is detailed in Section 3. Section 4 presents our evaluation methodology and reports the evaluation results. Related works are presented in Section 5 and conclusions of the paper are given in Section 6, with possible future research directions.

2. System Goals

With the ubiquitous Internet, it is possible to aggregate the untrusted or federated resources (e.g., desktop PCs, workstations, and servers) on the Internet to provide distributed and global-scale data and computation services. Neuron is an overlay infrastructure on top of Tornado for service discovery services. Each participating node contributes portion of its storage and computation to Neuron to help discover resources in the system. A participating node can be a client to request particular services from other nodes in Neuron, and at the same time be a server to supply the stored services to other nodes.

Neuron was developed with the following goals in mind:
- **Aggregating resources on the network:** The Internet today has interconnected an enormous amount of computing and storage devices. Resources on these devices, e.g., CPU cycles and storage, are often underutilized. Aggregating these devices not only exploits their idle resources but also allows rapid deployment of desired services.
- **Reliability:** Resources exploited on the Internet may be highly volatile, depending on the environment deployed. For instance, the aggregated resources may be attacked (e.g., denial-of-services attacks) and become unavailable, or they may be linked to the Internet through intermittent wireless links. Our infrastructure must accommodate such instable resources and tolerate possible faults.
- **Self-organization:** Neuron should admit nodes from different administrative domains and allow them to dynamically participate and leave the system. Each node should manage its connectivity to the system and help other nodes to perform their requests without centralized control.
- **Load distribution:** To prevent performance bottleneck in the infrastructure, Neuron has to distribute the system load to participating nodes according to their capabilities, e.g., computation, communication and energy. When service objects are first generated, they should be allocated to the nodes evenly. Popular service objects are epidemically cached and replicated by multiple nodes to alleviate the load imbalance.

- **Security:** Nodes coming from different administrative domains may not be trusted. A malicious node may peek at data items in the infrastructure and alter them. Neuron needs to provide encryption to data to reduce the risk of malicious attacks. Only those nodes with legal keys can access published service objects.
- **Durability:** Since nodes may dynamically leave the system, the published services maintained by those nodes might not be available. To guarantee that every service object is accessible at any time, Neuron should provide high service availability.
- **Scalability:** The entire state of the system should be distributed to the nodes to achieve scalability. The amount of partial states maintained by each node should not scale to the system size.
- **Responsiveness:** Neuron should provide its discovery service promptly. The number of requests and the system size should not influence the response time significantly. In addition, services may change their states to reflect their current situation; these changes should be presented as agile as possible.
- **Characterization:** The service can be described in free form, and clients can discover their desired services via free-style description. Meanwhile, any matched service needs to be responded to clients in fidelity.

3. Neuron

Neuron is built on top of Tornado [5] and supports efficient service registration and discovery. In this section, Neuron is introduced. We first give an overview of Neuron in Section 3.1. Section 3.2 presents basic operations in Neuron. Operations that allow Neuron to adapt to the dynamic environments are described in Section 3.3. Section 3.4 discusses the reliability issues in Neuron and the scalability issue is addressed in Section 3.5.

3.1. Overview

Conceptually, Neuron constructs a *virtual shared space*. Service providers can register their services through the virtual shared space by using free form expressions. Clients can look up the registered services and query service states via similar expressions. Service descriptions are encrypted via the RSA algorithm, for example. Clients intending to acquire a service need to obtain the corresponding public keys first, and only service providers can alter their services with private keys.

Neuron is implemented on top of Tornado and thus built with the hash-based addressing scheme. Neuron is therefore capable of supporting nomadic services by decoupling service location and address. The hash-based scheme also allows the virtual space created by Neuron to support anonymity, i.e., service providers and clients are not necessarily aware where to register and access services. It leverages the overall system reliability and service durability by reducing malicious attacks on particular nodes in Neuron. Applications can thus concentrate on what services they want rather than where and how to accesses services. The states of the services can be promptly updated to the clients that are "*interested*" in such services.

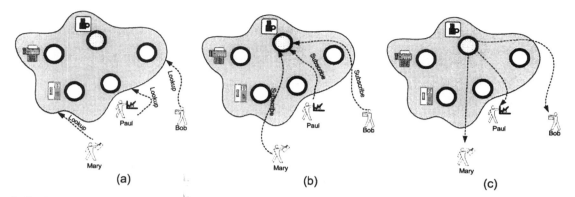

Figure 1. Basic operations in Neuron. (a) Bob, Paul and Mary would like to locate a nearby coffee vending machine, and they perform a service lookup. (b) Bob, Paul and Mary subscribe to the vending machine service that they discovered. (c) The coffee vending machine will report its states, e.g., the number of available cups, to its subscribers.

Figure 1 shows a usage example of Neuron. Note that with the aid of Tornado, Neuron is able to operate in the global network. The example here, which shows service discovery in a localized setting, illustrates the diversity of Neuron. In this example, there are three services presented in the virtual shared space: telephone, printer, and coffee vending machine. Bob, Mary and Paul would like to have a coffee. Therefore, they request a nearby coffee vending machine from the virtual space by issuing the *lookup* operation. After the coffee vending machine is discovered, Bob, Mary and Paul may like to know what coffee drinks are available. Thus, Bob, Mary and Paul *subscribe* to the services provided by the discovered vending machine (see Figure 1(b)). The current state of the vending machine will be published to them (see Figure 1(c)). Suppose further that Paul likes to have a Cappuccino, but the machine runs out of it. The subscription allows Paul to be notified once the drink is refilled. Note that if Bob, Mary and Paul would like to cancel their subscriptions, they need to explicitly *unsubscribe* them.

3.1.1. Naming

Naming in Neuron adopts a free form expression. Each service is characterized by (*service name, attribute$_1$ = value$_1$, attribute$_2$ = value$_2$, attribute$_3$ = value$_3$,…, attribute$_n$ = value$_n$*), where *service name* is the type of the service and *attribute$_i$=value$_i$* indicates the associated attributes. For example, a color display in room 734 of the EECS building can be characterized as (*LCD Display, color depth = 65536, resolution = 1024×768, room = 734, building = EECS*).

To register a service to Neuron, a request is sent to its *service home node*. The service home node is a Tornado node and is responsible for providing a permanent storage for the service and the associated states. It also provides access control for the service. Given a service, its ID is calculated via the following hashing function:

$$H\left(\prod(h_1, h_2, h_3, \cdots, h_n)\right) \quad (1)$$

and

$$\begin{cases} h_i = H(service\,name) & if\ i = 1 \\ h_i = H(attribute_i = value_i) & if\ i \neq 1 \end{cases} \quad (2)$$

where H is the hashing function used by Tornado, and $\prod$ takes the hashed values h_1, h_2, h_3, …, h_n and outputs the concatenation of h_1 and the sorted h_2, h_3, …, h_n. For example, if $h_2 < h_3 < … < h_n$, then the ID of the home node is $H(h_1 \oplus h_2 \oplus h_3 \oplus \cdots \oplus h_n)$, where $\oplus$ denotes the concatenation. Given the ID of the service, it can then be mapped to a Tornado node, which is called the *service home node* of the service.

3.1.2. Leasing

Neuron requires each registered service provide a time contract, which denotes the service's lifetime. The lifetime is determined by the service provider. If a registered service does not renew its contract, this implies to Neuron that the service may be failed or terminated. Its entries will be removed from the virtual shared space. An "active" service is one that periodically or aperiodically advertises its states to Neuron. Neuron guarantees a permanent and durable home node to host the active services. The leasing model allows a service to present its most up-to-date states to the clients.

3.2. Basic Operations

In this section, the data structure used by Neuron is first presented in Section 3.2.1. Section 3.2.2 then describes the operations for service registration, discovery, subscription and renewal.

3.2.1. Data Structure

Assume that a service is expressed as (e_1, e_2, e_3, …, e_n), where e_1 is the hashed value of the service name (i.e., $e_1 = H(service\,name)$) and e_2, e_3, …, e_n are the hashed values of the attributes. For simplicity of presentation, we assume that $e_2 < e_3 < … < e_n$. The ID of the home node is then given by Equations 1 and 2 as $H(e_1 \oplus e_2 \oplus e_3 \oplus \cdots \oplus e_n)$. Figure 2 shows an example in which two services, the printer and the vending machine, are registered to the virtual shared space. The printer is expressed as (X_1, X_2, X_3, …, X_n) and the vending machine as (Y_1, Y_2, Y_3, …, Y_m).

The data structure used by Neuron is a *Neuron tree*. A Neuron tree is a *virtual* binary tree, and each service is associated with one such binary tree. The root vertex of a Neuron tree is stored in the home node of the service. The home

457

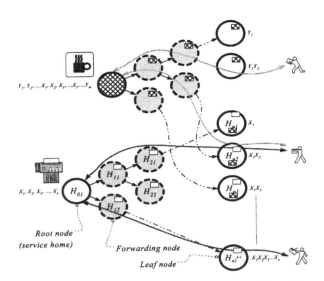

Figure 2. The Neuron trees of two services: the coffee vending machine and the printer. The arrows show how the services are published and refreshed. Three clients subscribe to the services and receive updated states.

node not only provides a permanent store and access control for a service object, but also computes an initial binary tree for it.

The home node calculates the IDs of the leaf vertices of a Neuron tree by applying the hashing function

$$E = \{e_1\} \oplus \{k_2 e_2 \oplus k_3 e_3 \oplus k_4 e_4 \oplus \cdots \oplus k_n e_n\}, \quad (3)$$

where $k_i = 0$ or 1 and $i = 2, 3, \ldots, n$. Thus, the IDs of the leaf vertices are $H(e_1)$, $H(e_1 e_2)$, $H(e_1 e_3)$, $H(e_1 e_4)$,..., $H(e_1 e_2 e_3 \ldots e_n)$. As Figure 2 shows, the leaf vertices of the printer service are those nodes with IDs $H(X_1)$, $H(X_1 X_2)$, $H(X_1 X_3)$, $H(X_1 X_4)$,..., $H(X_1 X_2 X_3 \ldots X_n)$. Given the ID of a leaf vertex, it can be mapped to a Tornado node, where it is stored. That Tornado node will be referred to as a *leaf node*. At a first glance, it seems that the tree requires at least 2^{n-1} Tornado nodes to store. However, these Tornado nodes need not be disjoint, and it actually depends on the mapping from the data addressing space to the node addressing space in Tornado and the load of the Neuron tree (i.e., if the load is continuously increased, more Tornado nodes can be introduced to the Neuron tree to alleviate the load of participating Tornado nodes). In addition, the number of terms in an expression, n, is not expected to be large. Further discussion of this point can be found in [4].

It is possible that several Neuron trees share the same leaf vertices. That is, they have common attribute-value pairs in their service expression. To distinguish the Neuron trees that have common attribute-value pairs, each Neuron tree is associated with a unique tag, which is the hashing key (i.e., $H(e_1 \oplus e_2 \oplus e_3 \oplus \cdots \oplus e_n)$) of the service object.

In addition to calculating the IDs of the leaf vertices, the root node also computes the IDs of the intermediate vertices in the Neuron tree, which are called the *forwarding vertices*. The forwarding vertex at the i-th level and m-th position in a

<table>
<tr><td>(1)</td><td colspan="2">*Input:* the service expression $(e_1, e_2, e_3, \ldots, e_n)$;</td></tr>
<tr><td>(2)</td><td colspan="2">*Output:* the ID of the home node;</td></tr>
<tr><td>(3)</td><td colspan="2">*Procedure Register* **begin**</td></tr>
<tr><td>(4)</td><td colspan="2">Let $o_1 \leftarrow H(e_1)$ and $o_2, o_3, \ldots, o_n$ be the sorted list of the values in the input expression $e_2, e_3, \ldots, e_n$;</td></tr>
<tr><td>(5)</td><td colspan="2">Let $home \leftarrow H(o_1 \oplus o_2 \oplus o_3 \oplus \cdots \oplus o_n)$ and perform *Publish(home)*;</td></tr>
<tr><td>(6)</td><td colspan="2">Let F be the set of forwarding nodes, whose addresses are calculated by initializing $H_{n1} = H(o_1)$, $H_{n2} = H(o_1 o_2)$, $H_{n3} = H(o_1 o_3)$, $H_{n3} = H(o_1 o_4)$,..., $H_{n^{n-1}} = H(o_1 o_2 o_3 \ldots o_n)$;</td></tr>
<tr><td>(7)</td><td colspan="2">**For** $i \leftarrow 0, 1, 2, 3, \ldots, n-1$</td></tr>
<tr><td>(8)</td><td colspan="2">**For each** $v \in \nabla \leftarrow \{H_{it} : 1 \le t \le 2^i\} \subseteq F$</td></tr>
<tr><td>(9)</td><td colspan="2">$OC(v, home) \leftarrow \{H_{(i+1)t}, H_{(i+1)(t+1)}\}$;</td></tr>
<tr><td>(10)</td><td colspan="2">$IC(H_{(i+1)t}, home) \leftarrow v$;</td></tr>
<tr><td>(11)</td><td colspan="2">$IC(H_{(i+1)(t+1)}, home) \leftarrow v$;</td></tr>
<tr><td>(12)</td><td colspan="2">**Return** *home*;</td></tr>
<tr><td>(13)</td><td colspan="2">**End.**</td></tr>
</table>

Figure 3. The service registration and publish algorithm, where $OC(a,b)$ and $IC(a,b)$ are the output and input channel sets, respectively, of the virtual node. The virtual node has an ID a and is responsible for the service object with the unique hashing key b.

Neuron tree is denoted H_{im}, and its ID is obtained as follows.

$$H_{im} = \begin{cases} H\left(\prod(e_1, e_2, e_3, \cdots, e_n)\right) & if\ i = 0 \\ \left\lceil \dfrac{H_{(i+1)m} + H_{(i+1)(m+1)}}{2} \right\rceil & if\ i \ge 1 \end{cases}, \quad (4)$$

where H_{01} is the ID of the root vertex, $H_{n1} = H(e_1)$, $H_{n2} = H(e_1 e_2)$, $H_{n3} = H(e_1 e_2 e_3)$, ..., $H_{n2^{n-1}} = (e_1 e_2 \ldots e_n)$ are the leaf vertices, and $0 \le i \le n$, $1 \le m \le 2^{n-1}$. The forwarding vertex may be mapped to a Tornado node, which is referred to as a *forwarding node*.

3.2.2. Service Access Algorithms

Service registration and publishing. Figure 3 presents the algorithm for service providers to register a service to Neuron. First, the hashed values of the expression of the given service are sorted (see Line 4). Then the service object is stored to the home node with the sorted and concatenated hashing keys (see Line 5). The sorting operation guarantees that there is an identical order of hashed values for a set of expressions. Note that the *publish* operation is provided by Tornado, which routes and stores the designated data items to a Tornado node with the ID numerically closest to the specified hashing value.

To publish the service, the home node then computes the IDs of the forwarding vertices via Equation 4. The forwarding vertices are mapped to Tornado nodes, and the Neuron tree is constructed by setting up the output and input channels between the nodes. The ID of the input/output channel is again a hashed value rather than the stationary IP address of the node. This allows the use of the fault-resilient routing method of Tornado and consequently leverages Neuron's reliability. In addition, to boost performance, it is possible to take a shortcut route between two nodes by employing the *directories* in Tornado.

(1) *Input:* the service expression ($e_1, e_2, e_3, \ldots, e_m$);
(2) *Output:* a set of discovered services, D;
(3) *Procedure Discovery* **begin**
(4) $D = \phi$;
(5) Let $o_1, o_2, o_3, \ldots, o_m$ be the sorted list of the hashed values of the service expression $e_1, e_2, e_3, \ldots, e_m$;
(6) Let $leaf \leftarrow H(o_1 \oplus o_2 \oplus o_3 \oplus \cdots \oplus o_m)$;
(7) **For** each tag $t \leftarrow Tag(node_{leaf})$
(8) **For** each hashed value $v \in IC(leaf, t)$
(9) $D = D \cup ReachRoot(v, t)$;
(10) **Return** D;
(11) **End.**

(a)

Input: the hashed address v and the tag t;
Output: a set of discovered services, D';
Procedure ReachRoot **begin**
$D' \leftarrow \phi$;
If $IC(v,t) = \phi$ **then**
$D' \leftarrow \{service\ object\ in\ node_v\}$
Else
$ReachRoot(IC(v,t), t)$;
Return D';
End.

(b)

Figure 4. The service discovery algorithm that looks up services conforming to the given expression $e_1, e_2, e_3, \ldots, e_m$, where $Tag(x)$ contains the tags in a given virtual node with ID x, and $node_v$ denotes a physical Tornado node with the ID closest to x.

If a Neuron tree is heavily loaded, the cost to build the tree is at most $(n+1) \times \lceil \log N \rceil$ hops of communication without overloading a particular forwarding node in such a Neuron tree. This includes the communication for routing a registration message towards its root node and that for publishing the service down to the nodes storing the leaf vertices, where n is the number of tuples in the expression of the service, N is the number of active nodes in Neuron and $\lceil \log N \rceil$ is the routing overhead in Tornado. However, if the system is lightly loaded, the communication cost may be reduced to $2 \times \lceil \log N \rceil$ hops. The detail is presented in Section 3.3 and [4].

Discovery. To discover a serve, clients issue a free form expression, and all the registered services conforming to the expression are returned. Conceptually, the discovery is performed by backtracking the Neuron trees from a node storing the leaf vertex conforming to the expression. The backtracking is terminated if it reaches the root node (i.e., the service home node). The root node then replies necessary information (e.g., the interface to the object) to the client. Note that it is possible to discover several services satisfying the request. In this case, the backtracking will visit the root nodes of several Neuron trees.

The discovery algorithm is presented in Figure 4. Again, the service expression is sorted first according to the hashed values of the expression. Then the requesting node sends the request message to the node with an ID closest to the hashing address obtained from the concatenation of the hashed values of the expression (see Line 6 in Figure 4(a)). This node stores the leaf vertex conforming to the specified expression. That leaf node then informs the node whose ID is closest to the received hashing address to perform the *ReachRoot* operation to backtrack to the root (see Figure 4(b)). Since services may share common attribute-value pairs, their Neuron trees have common leaf vertices. Thus, the leaf node may need to inform several nodes to do the backtracking. Discovery operation takes $n \times \lceil \log N \rceil$ hops at most in a heavily loaded Neuron space.

Input: the service expression ($e_1, e_2, e_3, \ldots, e_m$);
Procedure Subscribe **begin**
Let $o_1, o_2, o_3, \ldots, o_m$ be the sorted list of the hashed values of the service expression $e_1, e_2, e_3, \ldots, e_m$;
Let $node_{leaf} \leftarrow H(o_1 \oplus o_2 \oplus o_3 \oplus \cdots \oplus o_m)$;
For each $v \leftarrow Tag(node_{leaf})$
$Sub(v) \leftarrow Sub(v) \cup \{client's\ address\}$;
End.

Figure 5. The subscription algorithm, where $Sub(v)$ contains the hashing or network addresses of the clients that subscribe to the service with the hashing address v.

Subscription. Once a client discovers a particular service, it may subscribe to and access the service. The subscription operation in Neuron is shown in Figure 5.

A subscription request is handled by associating the subscription to the leaf vertex of the Neuron tree representing the subscribed service. The ID of the leaf vertex is the hashing key of the expression specified by the client. Again, since multiple Neuron trees may share common leaf vertices, a subscription request may subscribe to several services at once. Note that, a client may not be a Tornado node. For example, it may be a thin-client device. The set *Sub(v)* in Figure 5 is used to handle this problem by recording the network addresses (e.g., the IP addresses) of the clients that subscribe to the service with the hashing address v. It is pos-

Input: the ID of the home node, *home*, and the states to be updated;
Procedure Refresh **begin**
For each $v \in OC(home, home)$ in $node_{home}$
Update the states in $node_{home}$;
$RefreshChild(v, home)$;
End.

(a)

Input: the ID of a child node, v, the ID of the home node *home*, and the states to be updated;
Procedure RefreshChild **begin**
If $OC(v, home) = \phi$ **then**
For each $s \in Sub(home)$ of $node_v$
Forward refreshed states to $node_s$
Else
For each $v' \in OC(v, home)$
$RefreshChild(v', home)$
End.

(b)

Figure 6. The renewal algorithm, where (a) is performed in the root node and (b) is performed in forwarding/leaf nodes

sible to further incorporate the transport protocol used (e.g., HTTP and FTP) in $Sub(v)$. Since Neuron is based on the Tornado infrastructure, the communication cost of the subscription operation is $\lceil log\ N \rceil$ hops at most.

Renewal. Services need to renew their states to Neuron periodically or aperiodically, depending on the implementation of the services. A service will be removed quietly from Neuron if the associated time contract is expired. To renew the states, a service needs to send its up-to-date states to its home node. The home node then forwards the states to nearby forwarding nodes. The forwarding nodes further transmit the states down the Neuron tree until all the leaf nodes and associated subscribers are updated. Note that the renewal operation takes $n \times \lceil log\ N \rceil$ hops at most for a heavily loaded Neuron space. Figure 6 shows the algorithm.

3.3. Optimization and Management

The hash-based naming scheme in Neuron can evenly distribute the load under normal conditions, i.e., the underlying Tornado nodes will store similar amount of service objects. However, some services may be more popular than others and thus are frequently accessed. To handle the increasing system load, Neuron implements an adaptive tree management strategy to recruit unused Tornado nodes. Of course, the load of a particular service may also be decreased. Due to the space limitation, we omit the descriptions for the tree management algorithm. The details can be found in [4].

3.4. Reliability

Since nodes in Neuron may fail and communication links may be broken, Neuron relies on the fault-resilient routing supported from Tornado. This is helped with the hash-based naming, which allows a Neuron vertex to delay the binding of the actual network address (e.g., the IP address) to the name of the overlaying node.

Suppose, for a given service tagged with t, a node c detects that its parent or child node failed. The node will send a recovery request to a Tornado node with an ID closest to the failed parent or child node. Let us assume that it is the parent node of node c that failed, and the contacted Tornado node is p. Node c will send a message containing $root(c,t)$ to p. Other nodes that detect the failure of the parent node will do the same. Eventually, p will receive all the recovery requests from the child nodes of the failed node. Similarly, the parent node p' of the failed node will also detect the failure and send a recovery request with $l = leaf(p',t)$ to p, where $root(p,t) \in OC(l,t)$. With this information, p can construct the virtual Neuron sub-tree it needs to host.

Reliability of Neuron can be further improved with the k-replication mechanism of Tornado, which replicates k identical copies to k Tornado nodes whose IDs are closest to the home node. It follows that each Neuron space is implicitly replicated to k spaces that are deployed over different Tornado nodes. When a Neuron node fails, the contents stored in the failed node can be recovered from the replica nodes. Since the replica node already has the most up-to-date states of the failed node, there is no need to reconstruct the Neuron sub-tree.

3.5. Scalability

Although Neuron can adapt to the changing load by varying the mapping of virtual forwarding nodes to Tornado nodes, the size of a Neuron space for a given service is obviously limited by the number of attribute and value pairs. A further limitation occurs when the Neuron tree is fully loaded, i.e., each virtual forwarding node is mapped to a physical Tornado node, and every node is loaded with excessive requests. One workaround is to forward the requests to the replica nodes. Note that the number of replica k is given by the service provider. However, it can be changed dynamically. In this way, it is possible to guarantee high availability and at the same time ensure scalability.

Intuitively, Neuron introduces a large amount of Tornado nodes to accommodate a great amount of requests while maintaining efficient registration, lookup and states propagation without producing hot spots for those popular services. However, if a service is not popular in demand, the corresponding Neuron tree may be degenerated and consequently hosted by a few of Tornado nodes. The size of a Neuron tree is thus highly dependant on the load of the participated Tornado nodes. Thus the size of a Neuron tree does not exponentially grow with the number of attribute-value pairs. This feature not only helps reduce the number of network hops required to access a particular service but minimize the resources used.

4. Performance Evaluation

We evaluated Neuron via simulation. For the P2P data routing, locating and storage infrastructure, we simulated 125 Tornado nodes initially. Each Tornado node is associated with a randomly and uniformly generated hashing key. All the Tornado nodes are equipped with a routing and a neighbor table. Each routing level in the routing table has two leader nodes, each taking care of a particular region in the node addressing space. Each neighbor table has four numerically closest active nodes. Although Tornado provides caching and directory map for performance optimization, we did not turn on these features in order to concentrate on the performance of Neuron.

Due to a lack of traces for service discovery protocols, we resorted to the simulation of a service object containing 4096 attribute and value pairs. The resultant Neuron tree has 8191 Neuron nodes. The hashing keys of the service object and the associated attribute-value pairs are generated randomly and uniformly. The primary performance metric is the path length, i.e., the number of hops required for routing a given request.

4.1. Scalability

We changed the network size dynamically from 125 Tornado nodes to 150000. There are total 150000 time steps simulated and each simulated node performs at most 10 periodical updates to the associated routing and neighbor tables. In each iteration, a new node is introduced. The measured path length is averaged over routes between randomly generated clients and service home nodes.

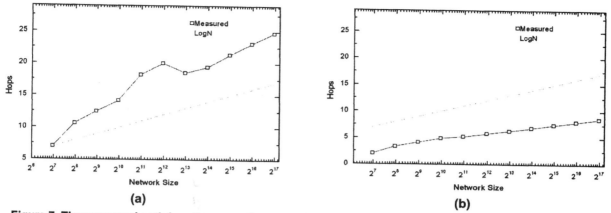

(a)   **(b)**

Figure 7. The measured path length versus the network size for (a) service registration and (b) subscription.

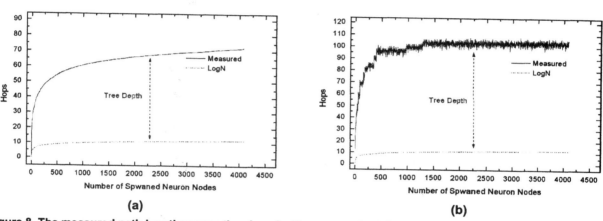

(a)   **(b)**

Figure 8. The measured path length versus the size of a Neuron tree for (a) service lookup and (d) service renewal.

Figure 7 shows the average path length for service registration and subscription. We can see that path length increases nearly linearly with the logarithm of the network size. Note that the path length for registration is measured and averaged over the worst cases in which the registration messages are delivered to the farthest Neuron leaf nodes.

4.2. Stressing

In this experiment, we perform the stressing test by introducing random traffic incrementally. A client with a randomly generated ID is chosen to send a request to a randomly chosen Neuron leaf node in the simulated Neuron tree. The Neuron space is deployed on a Tornado network with 150000 nodes. Each Neuron node is assumed to accommodate only one request at a simulated time step. The requests are doubted continuously with the simulated time steps. Note that the Neuron tree will adapt to the system traffic by spreading the load to more Tornado nodes. The simulation terminated when the Neuron tree grew to a complete binary tree consisting of 8191 Neuron nodes. The performance for lookup and renewal is measured for varying sizes of the Neuron tree.

Figure 8 presents the path length for service lookup and renewal. We can see that the lookup performance scales logarithmically with the number of nodes in the Neuron

space. The depth of the Neuron tree is obviously dominated by the number of attribute-value pairs. The overhead can be optimized by utilizing the directory provided by Tornado to route the messages with shortcuts. This optimization is not evaluated in this study though.

Similarly, the renewal performance also scales logarithmically. This means that additional hops are required to epidemically distribute the up-to-date states from the service object to the root node, plus the hops for distributing the states from the leaf nodes to the subscribers. Figure 8(b) depicts the number of hops required to transmit the states in the longest path of the simulated Neuron tree.

4.3. Fault-Resilience

To explore the robustness of Neuron in providing service availability, Neuron nodes simulated are randomly detached from the Neuron space. Initially, the simulated Neuron space consists of 64000 nodes. Figure 9 presents the service availability with a varying number of replicas for each Neuron node. The replicas will contain the interface of the service object, the internal Neuron tree data structure, and the addresses of the subscribers, etc.

We can see that when 50% of the nodes are failed, up to 80% of randomly generated requests can be served by the Neuron space without replication. When there are three rep-

461

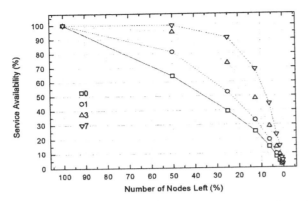

Figure 9. The service availability versus the number of remaining active nodes, where there are 0, 1, 3 and 7 replicas for each Neuron node.

licas, up to 95% of requests can be served. The percentage improves to 99% when there are seven replicas. Even active Neuron nodes are below 10%, the Neuron space can still serve 45%, 29% and 19% of requests with 7-, 3- and 1-replications.

5. Related Works

Sun Jini [6] provides a framework for discovering federated network devices via Remote Message Invocation (RMI). In Jini, services register themselves to the lookup servers, and clients discover desired services by querying the lookup server. Jini adopts the client-server model and thus may not be able to handle large numbers of requests with a single lookup server. Thus, Jini cannot be scaled up for supporting Internet-scale services. The lookup server in Jini may become a single point of failure, which is not adequate for dynamic and distributed environments. Another product similar to Jini can be found in [8]. Neuron adopts the peer-to-peer model rather than the client-server model, which is appealing for providing wide-area services without suffering the single point of failure.

Another representative service discovery protocol is SLP [9] proposed by IETF, which employs centralized directory agents. Similar to Jini, SLP may have performance bottleneck and single point of failure with the centralized approach. Although the directory agents of SLP can be configured via the standard directory protocols (e.g., LDAP), deploying the directory servers is cumbersome. In addition, partitioning the naming space to the directory agents requires extra overhead. This further complicates the system deployment. In contrast, Neuron does not rely on particular servers, and the Neuron nodes cooperate to serve requests.

The Berkeley SDS [2] extends SLP to support secure and authenticated communication with a static hierarchical structure for wide-area services. The hierarchical architecture cannot self-configure to adapt to the changes of distributed environments. SDS shares some common features of SLP and cannot tolerate failure of nodes and communication links. It also needs to partition the naming space.

The work most related to Neuron is perhaps INS [1]. INS is equipped with a self-organizing resolver network, although the resolver network may be highly sensitive to the failure of nodes and communication links. Services in INS

are expressed in a hierarchical fashion and each resolver maintains an identical copy of such a hierarchical tree representation. The results are that (1) the hierarchical presentation for services limits the expressiveness of services, and (2) aggregating the tree presentation for a service into a resolver node constraining INS to support small-area services only. Although it is possible to scale INS to support wide-area services by introducing domain space resolvers, this introduces administrative overheads. Neuron is quite different from INS as Neuron is implemented on top of Tornado, which provides highly reliable and scalable Neuron space for service discovery. Naming in Neuron is relatively free and poses no hierarchical relationship. This gives higher expressiveness. More importantly, the naming space is distributed to the Neuron nodes to share the load.

6. Conclusions

In this paper, a wide-area service discovery infrastructure called Neuron is introduced. Neuron is based on the P2P model and implemented on top of Tornado, a P2P data routing, locating and storing substrate. Neuron is designed for aggregating the resources in a wide-area network, and it becomes more powerful if more resources can be exploited. Neuron can tolerate node or link failure and disconnection, while maintaining high service availability. This helps ensure the durability of registered services. Neuron can adapt to the changing load by distributing the load to the participating nodes. Clients can subscribe to the services of interest and receive their up-to-date states. The services can be described in free forms. Our simulation study shows that Neuron scales logarithmically with the number of active nodes. The cost to perform service registration, discovery, subscription and renewal takes $O(logN)$ hops at most.

References

[1] W. Adjie-Winoto, E. Schwartz, H. Balakrishnan, and J. Lilley. "The Design and Implementation of an Intentional Naming System," In *Proceedings of ACM Symposium on Operating Systems Principles*, pages 186-201, December 1999.

[2] S. E. Czerwinski, B. Y. Zhao, T. D. Hodes, A. D. Joseph, and R. H. Katz. "An Arachitecture for a Secure Service Discovery Service," In *Proceedings of the ACM/IEEE International Conference on Mobile Computing and Networks*, pages 24-35, August 1999.

[3] Gnutella. http://gnutella.wego.com/.

[4] H.-C. Hsiao and C.-T. King. "Neuron — A Global-Scale Peer-to-Peer Server Discovery Infrastructure," *Technical Report*, May 2002.

[5] H.-C. Hsiao and C.-T. King. "Tornado — A Global-Scale Peer-to-Peer Storage Infrastructure," *Submitted for Publication*.

[6] Jini™. http://www.sun.com/jini/.

[7] Napster. http://www.napster.com/.

[8] Universal Plug and Play. "Understanding Universal Plug and Play — a White Paper," June 2000. http://upnp.org/resources/whitepapers.asp.

[9] J. Veizades, E. Guttman, C. Perkins, and S. Kaplan. "Service Location Protocol," June 1997. RFC2165. http://www.ietf.org/rfc/rfc2165.txt.

ART: Robustness of Meshes and Tori for Parallel and Distributed Computation

Chi-Hsiang Yeh
Dept. of Electrical and Computer Engineering
Queen's University
Kingston, Ontario, K7L 3N6, Canada
yeh@ee.queensu.ca

Behrooz Parhami
Dept. of Electrical and Computer Engineering
University of California
Santa Barbara, CA 93106, USA
parhami@ece.ucsb.edu

Abstract

In this paper, we formulate the array robustness theorems (ARTs) for efficient computation and communication on faulty arrays. No hardware redundancy is required and no assumption is made about the availability of a complete submesh or subtorus. Based on ARTs, a very wide variety of problems, including sorting, FFT, total exchange, permutation, and some matrix operations, can be solved with a slowdown factor of $1 + o(1)$. The number of faults tolerated by ARTs ranges from $o(\min(n^{1-\frac{1}{d}}, \frac{n}{d}, \frac{n}{h}))$ for n-ary d-cubes with worst-case faults to as large as $o(N)$ for most N-node 2-D meshes or tori with random faults, where h is the number of data items per processor. The resultant running times are the best results reported thus far for solving many problems on faulty arrays. Based on ARTs and several other components such as robust libraries, the priority emulation discipline, and $X'Y'$ routing, we introduce the robust adaptation interface layer (RAIL) as a middleware between ordinary algorithms/programs (that are originally developed for fault-free arrays) and the faulty network/hardware. In effect, RAIL provides a virtual fault-free network to higher layers, while ordinary algorithms/programs are transformed through RAIL into corresponding robust algorithms/programs that can run on faulty networks.

1. Introduction

A d-dimensional mesh consists of $n_1 n_2 \cdots n_d$ nodes of degree $2d$ arranged in an $n_1 \times n_2 \times \cdots \times n_d$ grid. When wraparound links are used for all dimensions, a d-dimensional torus results. The scalability, compact layout, constant/small node-degree, desirable algorithmic properties, and many other advantages have made meshes, tori, and n-ary d-cubes the most popular topologies for the interconnection of parallel processors. A very large variety of algorithms have been proposed for these networks [3, 10, 11, 13, 16, 15, 17]. These algorithms usually assume that a fault-free mesh or torus is available, and most of them cannot be applied to faulty meshes or tori directly, even in the presence of only a small number of faulty elements.

To utilize in faulty arrays the very large body of ordinary algorithms originally developed for fault-free arrays without redesigning or modifying them one by one, we add the *robust adaptation interface layer (RAIL)* as a middleware between ordinary algorithms/programs and the faulty hardware/network (i.e., faulty meshes, tori, or n-ary d-cubes). In RAIL, no hardware redundancy (e.g., spare processors or links) is necessary and the availability of a complete (fault-free) submesh or subtorus is not required. RAIL can be envisioned as an MPI-like middleware, where the details for tolerating faults are transparent to applications and hidden from the programmers. As a result, from the algorithm/program point of view, the adaptation layer located on top of the hardware layer hides the faulty processors and/or links from the algorithms, so that a virtual fault-free network is provided to higher layers and ordinary algorithms/programs can be executed on such a platform without modifications; from the hardware/network point of view, the adaptation layer in effect incorporates fault tolerance into the design of algorithms so that ordinary algorithms/programs are transformed into robust algorithms/programs that can run on faulty networks. In addition to using RAIL as a middleware, the proposed techniques can also lead to robust algorithms/functions that may be implemented in a library, which can be invoked by programmers and/or the operating system so that the applications have the flexibility to efficiently utilize the fault tolerance features.

Based on RAIL, we formulate the *array robustness theorems (ARTs)*, which show that a wide variety of important problems, such as sorting, permutation routing, unicast, broadcast, total exchange, reduction (e.g., semigroup computation), prefix computation, selection, fast Fourier transform (FFT), matrix multiplication, and ascend/descend algorithms can be executed on faulty arrays (i.e., meshes, tori, or n-ary d-cubes) with a factor of $1 + o(1)$ slowdown relative to a fault-free array of the same type. ARTs classify computing and communication problems into categorizes that can be efficiently supported by RAIL, associate them with the required RAIL techniques and procedures systematically, and quantify the resultant performance. Conventional wisdom is that low-degree networks are less robust than high-degree networks. But our results indicate that low-dimensional meshes and tori are very robust in that an array with a large number of faulty processors and links has, for a large variety of problems, computation and communication powers similar to those of a fault-free array. For example, an N-node 2-D mesh with $N^{1/3}$ faults can execute many algorithms, such as sorting, permutation routing, reduction (e.g., semigroup computation), prefix computation, FFT, matrix multiplication, unicast, broadcast, total-exchange, multinode broadcast, random routing, and dynamic broadcast, almost as fast as a slightly smaller fault-free mesh. Dally [8] and Agarwal [1] have shown that lower-dimensional networks achieve better performance than high-dimensional networks under various constraints, such as constant bisection bandwidth, fixed channel width, and fixed node size. Our robustness results for meshes, tori, and n-ary d-cubes, combined with their previously established cost/performance benefits [1, 8], make the case for low-dimensional architectures even stronger.

2. The robust adaptation interface layer

In this section we present several components for the robust adaptation interface layer (RAIL).

2.1. Basic components of RAIL

Various algorithms have been developed for mesh-connected computers and their variants, such as tori and n-ary d-cubes, based on the assumption that a fault-free mesh (or torus, n-ary d-cube) is available [3, 10, 11, 13, 16, 15, 17]. Since fault tolerance is very important to parallel processing, a variety of techniques for adaptive fault-tolerant routing or reconfiguring faulty arrays have also been proposed [5, 6, 12, 18, 19, 23]. In particular, we propose in [23] $X'Y'$ routing for deadlock-free wormhole routing faulty arrays. Combination of ordinary algorithms and appropriate adaptive or fault-tolerant routing schemes constitutes the first component for RAIL. However, such combined algorithms in general do not guarantee optimal performance, and the resultant performance is highly dependent on the fault patterns, which may lead to very poor performance in the worst case (e.g., degraded by a large nonconstant factor); while the reconfiguration techniques either use redundant links and nodes to restore a complete mesh or require a complete submesh/subtorus for performing parallel algorithms, which may be expensive to build or unavailable.

Since it is impractical to redesign all algorithms for faulty meshes and tori one by one and guaranteed optimal or satisfactory performance is important for some applications or computing environments, several systematic methods for transforming ordinary algorithms to obtain robust algorithms that can run on faulty arrays have been proposed [7, 14, 23]. One general fault tolerance scheme along this line, called the multi-scale self-simulation scheme, was devised by Cole, Maggs, and Sitaraman [7], who showed that an $n \times n$ mesh can be emulated with constant slowdown on an $n \times n$ mesh that has $n^{1-\varepsilon}$ faulty processors for any fixed $\varepsilon > 0$. Due to the robustness of the scheme, we incorporate it into RAIL as another component.

However, the multi-scale self-simulation scheme is relatively complicated, leading to difficult implementation issues, and comes with huge performance penalties in practice, given the significant increase in the leading constants of the running times. In [23], we proposed the robust algorithm-configured emulation (RACE) scheme as a software-based fault tolerance scheme for the systematic transformation of ordinary algorithms to obtain corresponding robust algorithms that are fast and easy to implement. In [23], RACE was used to incorporate fault tolerance into the design of algorithms, and is applicable to many computation and communication problems to obtain robust algorithms that have slowdown factors $1 + o(1)$ relative to the best algorithms for fault-free arrays. As a comparison, the multi-scale self-simulation scheme [7] is applicable to almost any problems, while RACE is only applicable to a (large) subset of them. However, RACE is also a general emulation scheme and is applicable to most important computation and communication problems in parallel computation. Moreover, when RACE is applicable to a certain application, it is usually preferable to use RACE instead of the multi-scale self-simulation scheme, since the former usually achieves considerably better performance (by a moderate to large constant factor) and is easier to implement. In this paper, we propose to use RACE to generate important robust algorithms that can be used as library routines. Such robust lobraries constitute another component of RAIL. Note that algorithms in robust lobraries can be further optimized. They can also be derived/transformed using techniques other than RACE or redesigned from scratch.

In addition to generating robust algorithms, we propose in this paper to use RACE in a way different from [23], by implementing it as a robust middleware between ordinary algorithms/programs and the faulty network/hardware. A difference between RAIL and RACE alone is that RAIL is more versatile and is applicable to any computation or communication problems. In Subsection 2.2 we define in the following subsections the notion of virtual subarrays (VSA) in faulty arrays (with or without wraparound) that can utilize the RAIL middleware for efficient computing and communication on faulty arrays without relying on hardware redundancy. Based on VSA, RACE, and several related techniques, we formulate, the array robustness theorems (ARTs) for solving a wide variety of problems on faulty arrays with negligible overhead. RACE and the associated ARTs become an important component of RAIL. More details can be found in Subsection 2.3 and [23] for RACE and Sections 3, 4, and 5 for ARTs.

The priority emulation discipline is a heuristic strategy that can be used in priority-based schemes for emulating ordinary algorithms with low cost and improved performance (or performance that can be guaranteed probabilisticly). It is another component of RAIL and will be introduced in Subsection 2.4. Other techniques can also be incorporated into RAIL at a later time and will be reported in the future.

Figure 1 illustrates the relationship between RAIL, robust algorithms, hardware-based fault tolerance layer, and their interfacing with algorithm/program and network/hardware layers. VSA denotes virtual subarrays to be defined in Subsection 2.2. SET and CET are the stepwise emulation technique and the compaction/expansion technique to be introduced in Subsections 2.3 and 4, respectively, for performing RACE. Algorithms/programs that conform to ar-

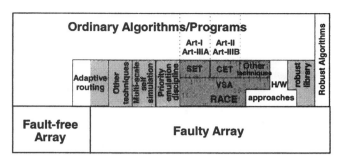

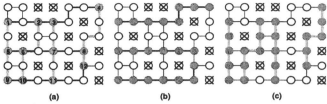

Figure 1. The robust adaptation interface layer (RAIL), associated components, and its interface with related layers. RAIL is represented as shaded areas (including dark and light ones). The dark area is representing the RACE scheme, a component of RAIL.

Figure 2. (a) A 3-by-4 VSM in a faulty 6-by-7 mesh with 9 faults. (b) Virtual rows of the VSM. (c) Virtual columns of the VSM.

ray robustness theorem I (ART-I) or condition A of ART-III can use SET; while algorithms/programs that conform to ART-II or condition B of ART-III can use CET. More details concerning how the various components of RAIL should be used will be presented in Subsection 2.5.

Note that the execution of ordinary algorithms on RAIL usually has negligible degradation compared to fault-free systems (e.g., a factor of $1 + o(1)$ slowdown), and are relatively easy to implement after reconfiguration is performed, which only needs to be done once after a fault occurs or is recovered from. Note also that when the number of faults is small, reconfiguration for RAIL can be performed in a short time, and possible configurations may be precomputed and stored, if so desired, in a distributed manner and broadcast when needed. Moreover, as indicated in Fig. 1, RAIL can also work in combination with previous hardware-based fault tolerance schemes. This can be done by executing ordinary algorithms when the number of faults has not exceeded the limit of the hardware fault tolerance scheme, while activating an appropriate component of RAIL otherwise. In effect, RAIL transform any ordinary algorithms to robust ones, including a very wide variety of important problems at high speed, and converting the faulty array into a virtual fault-free array, even for faulty meshes and tori whose rows and columns are (almost) all incomplete and those without any complete submesh or subtorus.

2.2. Virtual subarrays (VSAs) as a basis for RAIL

A *virtual subarray (VSA)* of a d-dimensional faulty array (with or without wraparound) is obtained by embedding a smaller d-dimensional array in it, where the embedded rows of the same dimension do not overlap and the embedded nodes and links are mapped onto healthy nodes and paths (See Fig. 2a). More precisely, each node of this smaller array is mapped onto a different healthy node of the faulty array; each link of this smaller array is mapped onto a healthy path of the faulty array. The embedded rows (or columns) of a certain dimension i, $i = 1, 2, ..., d$, do not overlap with each other, and are called *dimension-i virtual rows* (or *vir-*

tual columns) of the virtual subarray. Figures 2b and 2c show the virtual rows and virtual columns of a 3×4 virtual subarray.

Node $(x_1, x_2, ..., x_d)$ of the virtual subarray (called a *VSA node*) is located at the intersection of virtual row x_1 of dimension 1, virtual row x_2 of dimension 2, ... , and virtual row x_d of dimension d. Note that the virtual rows of different dimensions are allowed to have more than one node in common, in which case we select one of the nodes at the intersection either arbitrarily or according to certain criteria (e.g., minimizing the dilation of the resultant embedding). Then, VSA nodes $(x_1, ..., x_{i-1}, x_i, x_{i+1}, ..., x_d)$ for certain x_j, $j \neq i$, and all $x_i = 1, 2, ..., m_i$ form a *dimension-i row* of the virtual subarray that has length equal to m_i and is called a *VSA row*. The nodes of a VSA row form a subset of the corresponding dimension-i virtual row. Figure 2a shows a 3×4 virtual subarray in an array with 9 faults and the associated VSA nodes.

A *virtual submesh (VSM)* is a virtual subarray without wraparound; a *virtual subtorus (VST)* is a virtual subarray with wraparound. A *congestion-free virtual subarray* is a virtual subarray embedded in a faulty array with load and congestion both equal to 1 [11]. All the embedded links of a congestion-free virtual subarray correspond to a set of nonoverlapping paths in the faulty array. In other words, a dimension-i virtual row intersects with a dimension-j virtual row at exactly one node if $i \neq j$, while a virtual row does not intersect with another virtual row of the same dimension i. Many important problems can be solved efficiently on congestion-free virtual subarrays. More details concerning VSAs can be found in [23].

2.3. The RACE scheme as a component of RAIL

In RACE, we assume that a preprocessing stage has identified a virtual subarray to be used (perhaps at reconfiguration time using the simple method presented in Subsection 2.2 or a more complicated method). We can then redistribute the data on a faulty network to a virtual subgraph and then uses the virtual subgraph to emulate algorithms developed for a fault-free network. The proposed RACE scheme have three basic stages:

Basic Stages for Robust Emulation

- Stage 1: The data items to be processed are redistributed evenly to the processors on the virtual subarray such that a VSA processor has at most a items. On the virtual subarray, a processor that has fewer than a items may pad its list with suitable "dummy item(s)" (e.g., ∞ for sorting).

- Stage 2: The virtual subarray emulates a corresponding algorithm on an $m_1 \times m_2 \times \cdots \times m_d$ array, each processor of which has at most a items.

- Stage 3: The results are redistributed back to healthy processors of the original $n_1 \times n_2 \times \cdots \times n_d$ faulty array.

More details concerning RACE can be found in [23].

Stage 2 of the RACE scheme can be implemented using various techniques such as SET or CET. In the *stepwise emulation technique (SET)* we directly emulate a transmission over the dimension-i link of a processor by sending the data item along the dimension-i virtual row to which the processor belongs. If the virtual subarray is a complete array, (that is, no faulty processor exists within it and the embedded smaller array has dilation 1), no degradation is caused by Stage 2 using this naive method. On the other hand, under wormhole or cut-through routing, or packet-switching with a large load, the overhead caused by Stage 2, when implemented with SET, is negligible even when the array is faulty. Also, many algorithms, such as semigroup and prefix computations [14], can be emulated using SET with small overhead even if packet-switching is employed and the load is 1. Moreover, SET will be used to formulate the array robustness theorem I (ART-I) for fault-tolerant computing on congestion-free virtual subarrays in Section 3.

We can also use other techniques to implement Stage 2 of the RACE scheme. For example, the compaction/expansion technique leads to the array robustness theorem II (ART-II), presented in Section 4. Moreover, efficient implementation of Stages 1 and 3 extends ARTs I and II to the array robustness theorem III (ART-III), as presented in Section 5. A wide variety of important problems can then be solved efficiently in faulty arrays based on these ARTs.

2.4. The priority emulation discipline for RAIL

In this subsection we propose a heuristic strategy, called the *priority emulation discipline*, for effective implementation of robust algorithms based on RAIL in case where computation-free routing (i.e., routing without any computation steps) is performed or when an average of S or more routing steps separate consecutive computation steps. Our goal is to perform these routing tasks or algorithms on a virtual subarray of the faulty array with small slowdown relative to a fault-free $m_1 \times m_2 \times \cdots \times m_d$ array of the same type, when there exists a congestion-free $m_1 \times m_2 \times \cdots \times m_d$ virtual subarray with small width overhead (e.g., $o(S/b)$) and the routing path for any packet makes at most a small number b of turns (i.e., a routing path changes its dimensions at most b times). The discipline is also applicable to configurations different from virtual subarrays in RACE, but no guaranteed results are described here for such applications.

We first look at several problems that may occur when using naive methods to implement such algorithms on a virtual subarray and then propose strategies to improve the performance. The first problem is that when a packet X is delayed by $o(S)$ steps when it arrives at node V (for example, due to dilation along its routing path), there can be up to $o(dS)$ other packets at node V which are routed after packet X in the original algorithm for fault-free array but arrive at node V before packet X in the faulty array. If the network nodes of the faulty array use a first-come first-serve (FCFS) discipline, then packet X will be delayed by $o(dS)$ steps at node V and the resultant algorithm is suboptimal when d is not a constant. What makes the situation worse is that packet X may then be delayed by $o(d^2 S)$ steps at the next node, $o(d^3 S)$ steps at the following node, and so on. Since some packets may be severely delayed, the performance of the algorithms may degrade considerably when using such a naive method. One may argue that the preceding problem will not occur if the packets of the emulated algorithm are scheduled to arrive at a node right before they can be transmitted. However, this will give rise to accumulated delays of different types: when a packet X is delayed by $o(S)$ steps when it arrives at node V, there can be up to $o(S)$ packets at node V which are routed after packet X in the original algorithm for fault-free array but arrive at node V before packet X in the faulty array. Therefore, packet X will be delayed by $o(S)$ steps at node V, and may be delayed by another $o(S)$ steps at the next node, and so on.

In what follows we present a strategy, called the *priority emulation discipline*, which is easy to implement and can solve the above problems. The central idea of this strategy is that if a packet X_1 should be transmitted before another packet X_2 at a node (and over a link) according to the schedule of the algorithm on the fault-free array being emulated, then packet X_1 has higher priority for transmission over that link in the faulty array. Moreover, when there is at least one packet requiring transmission over a link, that link will not be idle so that the network resources are effectively utilized. An intuitive reason that the priority emulation discipline can improve the performance is that the more a packet is delayed, the higher its priority becomes in its future transmissions so that it is usually not further delayed at (temporarily) congested nodes/links. Therefore, the delay of a packet does not accumulate along its routing path and its slowdown is primarily due to the dilated paths between VSA nodes along its routing path.

Implementation of the priority emulation discipline is simple: all packets are still routed along the same paths as those in the emulated algorithm, and each packet begins its routing at the same time as in the emulated algorithm (though it may be queued at the starting node). We first consider the case where in the emulated algorithm packets arrive at a node right before their transmissions (without queueing). Each packet X begins with a tag that holds the starting timestamp T_X. Whenever packet X is transmitted through a VSA node, the timestamp T_X is increased by one. When there are multiple packets contending a node (or a link under the multi-port communication model), a packet Y that has the smallest timestamp T_Y is transmitted, since T_Y is the time that packet Y should have been transmitted over that node or link if the array were fault-free. Note that there cannot be multiple packets with the same tag at a node (and over a certain link under the multi-port communication model), since T_Y is the time for packet Y to be transmitted over that link in the emulated algorithm and there can be only one packet transmitted over that link at the same time in the emulated fault-free array. In a more general case where packets of the emulated algorithm may arrive at a node before their transmissions and are queued there, we simply set T_X to be the time for packet X to be transmitted at the corresponding node in the emulated fault-free array. Note that the virtual subarray is congestion free, so once we resolve the order for transmissions at a VSA node, packets never compete for links again along the path between two VSA nodes (i.e., along an embedded link).

2.5. Typical operations of RAIL

RAIL is a layer inserted between ordinary algorithms/ programs and the faulty hardware/network (i.e., the faulty array). We can envision RAIL as an MPI-like middleware, where the details for tolerating faults are transparent to the program developers, similar to the way the details for implementing collective communications are hidden from parallel programmers using MPI. In addition to ease of programming, such characteristics also improve the portability of parallel programs across platforms.

RAIL is located on top of the layer corresponding to a faulty array, and below the layer corresponding to ordinary algorithms and programs designed for fault-free arrays. RAIL hides the faulty elements from the algorithms and programs, so that a virtual fault-free network is provided to the algorithm/program layer; RAIL also transforms ordinary algorithms and programs into robust algorithms/programs that can run on the faulty array. Figure 1 illustrates the relationship between RAIL and the algorithm/program and network/hardware layers.

As presented in Subsection 2.1, RAIL consists of various components, including the RACE scheme presented in Subsection 2.3, the priority emulation discipline proposed in Subsection 2.4, as well as other fault tolerance schemes such as adaptive fault-tolerant routing [18, 23] and the multi-scale self-simulation scheme proposed by Cole, Maggs, and Sitaraman [7]. When a new fault occurs, RAIL first checks whether there are spare processors and/or links that can tolerate the fault and resume a complete array. If not, RAIL may estimate and/or measure the performance by using adaptive fault-tolerant routing and/or the priority emulation discipline to get around the fault, before the reconfiguration phase of RACE is completed. If the expected or measured performance is poor, RAIL will switch to RACE, which guarantees an optimal slowdown (within a factor of $1 + o(1)$) for most important computation and communication problems when the total number of faults are not very large. RAIL will select the appropriate techniques, such as SET or CET, to perform the required emulation, according to the switching technique used, the number of items per node, and the categories for the problems being executed. In the unusual case where RACE is not applicable to the problems or perform poorly, RAIL will consider switching to other schemes such as the multi-scale self-simulation

scheme that is applicable to most problems. RAIL can, of course, test these options in a different order according to the specific characteristics of the applications and the parallel system, as well as the information available. We expect that more fault tolerance schemes will be developed and added to RAIL due to the importance of fault tolerance in future parallel and distributed systems. We will report further developments in the future.

3. Fault-tolerant communication and computation on congestion-free virtual subarrays

Recall that a congestion-free virtual subarray is a virtual subarray embedded in a faulty array with congestion 1. In this section, we show that many important problems can be solved efficiently on congestion-free virtual subarrays based on RAIL.

3.1 ART-I for congestion-free virtual subarrays

In this subsection, we focus on a specific class of algorithms, which perform an average of S consecutive routing steps along each of the dimensions without any computation step in between. We propose the *phase synchronization discipline* and show that these algorithms can be emulated on congestion-free virtual subarrays with negligible slowdown under this discipline using the RACE scheme.

When using the phase synchronization discipline, all nodes simply synchronize at the end of a phase (which may perform certain computation steps). If there exists a congestion-free $m_1 \times m_2 \times \cdots \times m_d$ virtual subarray whose width overhead is $o(S)$, then the average slowdown factor for each phase is $1 + o(1)$ relative to a fault-free $m_1 \times m_2 \times \cdots \times m_d$ array of the same type. This is because routing along a dimension of a congestion-free virtual subarray is only delayed by $o(S)$ steps additively. Moreover, if we synchronize each phase, the interaction between delayed packets will never cause excessive accumulation of delay on certain packets, since the delay of one phase has no effect on the next phase. The RACE scheme under the phase synchronization discipline is very easy to implement and is powerful in that many important robust communication and computation algorithms can be performed with a factor of $1 + o(1)$ slowdown, as indicated in the following theorem and corollaries.

Theorem 3.1 (Array Robustness Theorem I (ART-I)) *If an algorithm for an array (i.e., mesh or torus) performs an average of S consecutive routing steps along each of the dimensions (at the same time) without any computation step in between, and there exists a congestion-free $m_1 \times m_2 \times \cdots \times m_d$ virtual subarray whose width overhead is $o(S)$, then the slowdown factor for performing the algorithm on a virtual subarray of the faulty array is $1 + o(1)$ relative to a fault-free $m_1 \times m_2 \times \cdots \times m_d$ array of the same type.*

When the number of faulty processors and/or links in an $n_1 \times n_2 \times \cdots \times n_d$ is $o(n_{min})$, where $n_{min} = \min(n_1, n_2, ..., n_d)$, it is guaranteed that at least an $(n_1 - o(n_{min})) \times (n_2 - o(n_{min})) \times \cdots (n_d - o(n_{min}))$ congestion-free virtual subarray with width overhead $o(n_{min})$ exists and is easy to find, leading to the following corollary.

Corollary 3.2 *If an algorithm for an array (i.e., mesh or torus) performs an average of S consecutive routing steps along each of the dimensions (at the same time) without any computation step in between, and there are $o(\min(S, n_{min}))$ faulty processors in an $n_1 \times n_2 \times \cdots n_d$ array, then the slowdown factor for performing the algorithm on a virtual subarray of the faulty array is $1 + o(1)$ relative to a fault-free $(n_1 - o(n_{min})) \times (n_2 - o(n_{min})) \times \cdots (n_d - o(n_{min}))$ array of the same type.*

Note that the number of faulty processors and links whose tolerance is indicated by ART-I and Corollary 3.2 is not small for low-dimensional arrays (i.e., small d). For example, these results apply to an N-node 2-D mesh/torus with $\Theta(\sqrt{N}/\log N)$ faults for which the size of the virtual subarray is $1 - o(1)$ that of the entire array. Communication algorithms, such as unicast (node-to-node routing), broadcast, total-exchange, and multinode broadcast, are at the heart of many applications [3]. Based on ART-I and Corollary 3.2, we can show that these algorithms as well as a variety of other important algorithms can be executed on congestion-free virtual subarrays with a factor of $1 + o(1)$ slowdown relative to a fault-free array. Since optimal algorithms for total exchange are among the most complicated communication algorithms, we describe, in the following subsection, an asymptotically optimal algorithm for performing total-exchange in faulty n-ary d-cubes as an example of applications of ART-I.

Various other computation or communication problems can also be executed efficiently on top of RAIL over a (possibly) faulty array. In particular, many applications, such as FFT, bitonic sort, matrix multiplication, convolution, and permutation can be formulated as ascend/descend algorithms [11] and performed efficiently based on ART-I [23]. Execution of these and other algorithms based on ART-I will be reported in the near future.

3.2. Total exchange on faulty n-ary d-cubes

In what follows we propose a generally applicable algorithm for executing g total exchange tasks in any fault-free vertex- and edge-symmetric network, where g is the degree of the network. We show that $(N - 1)D_{ave}$ communication time is sufficient in an N-node network and is strictly optimal, where D_{ave} is the average internode distance of the network. We label the nodes of the network as $0, 1, 2, ..., N - 1$ and let dimensions $r_{i,1}, r_{i,2}, ..., r_{i,q_i}$ be the dimensions of links in the order encountered along a shortest path between node 0 and node i, $i = 1, 2, 3, ..., N - 1$. We first present an algorithm $\mathcal{A}_1$ for executing a TE task under the *single-dimension communication (SDC) model* [21], where only links of the same dimension can be used at the same time for the entire network. At stage i of the algorithm $\mathcal{A}_1$, $i = 1, 2, 3, ..., N - 1$, each node successively sends a packet through links of dimensions $r_{i,1}, r_{i,2}, ..., r_{i,q_i}$. Since the network is vertex-symmetric, all the N packets sent by differ-

ent nodes during stage i have different destinations (which is equivalent to a permutation task), and a node sends packets to different destinations during different stages (which is equivalent to a single-node scatter task [3]). Collectively, the network performs a TE task during the $N - 1$ stages, under the SDC model. Since all the packets are sent via shortest paths, the total time required is equal to $(N - 1)D_{ave}$.

To optimally perform g TE tasks under the all-port communication model, we will execute all of them at the same time, each under the SDC model. However, contention over links will occur if we directly apply algorithm $\mathcal{A}_1$ for all the g tasks. In what follows, we show how contention can be completely avoided. We define algorithm $\mathcal{A}_i$, $i = 2, 3, 4, ..., g$, as the algorithm where packets are sent over links of dimension $((j + i - 2) \bmod d) + 1$ during a step if, at the same step of algorithm $\mathcal{A}_1$, packets are sent through links of dimension j, $j \in \{1, 2, 3, ..., g\}$ (along the same direction in networks like n-ary d-cubes). Clearly, algorithms $\mathcal{A}_1, \mathcal{A}_2, \mathcal{A}_3, ... \mathcal{A}_g$ are guaranteed to use links of different dimensions at any given step, and all of them can be simultaneously completed in $(N - 1)D_{ave}$ time.

Since the network is vertex and edge symmetric, the N packets sent during stage i of a certain algorithm $\mathcal{A}_j$ have different destinations, and a node sends packets to different destinations during different stages. As a result, each algorithm $\mathcal{A}_j$, $j = 1, 2, 3, ... g$, performs a TE during the $N - 1$ stages. Therefore, we can perform g TE tasks in $(N - 1)D_{ave}$ time under the all-port communication model.

If we allow packets to be split into mini-packets that can be routed independently without any overhead, then the time required to perform a single TE task becomes $(N - 1)D_{ave}/g$. Many papers have proposed algorithms for executing TE tasks in several popular topologies under several communication models. The result given above applies to general symmetric topologies, and gives optimal execution times for several important topologies, including hypercubes, n-ary d-cubes, generalized hypercubes [4], and star graphs [2]. The preceding algorithm for the all-port communication model is essentially based on finding an algorithm for executing total exchange under the single-dimension communication model and then rotating the dimensions of the single-dimension algorithm by i dimensions for all $i = 1, 2, ..., 2d - 1$ in order to find an algorithm that fully utilizes all dimensions concurrently. This strategy is useful in many routing problems and will be referred to as the *Single-To-All Rotation (STAR)* technique in this paper. The resultant algorithm for performing TE is called a *STAR TE algorithm*.

To apply the STAR TE algorithm to a faulty n-ary d-cube, we first identify a congestion-free virtual m-ary d-subcube in it, which is a virtual subtorus (VST) with the same length m along each VST row. From the notion provided by ART-I, we know that the number of turns in a routing path should be minimized in order to improve the performance and increase the number of faults tolerated without affecting the leading constant of the running time. Therefore, we use a special case of the STAR TE algorithm where links of the same dimension in a shortest path must be a connected subgraph of that path (i.e., they form a unique VSA subrow for that dimension). The resultant path between each of the source-destination pairs has at most $d - 1$ turns and, thus, the length of a path can be increased by at most $dW_{overhead}$ hops, where $W_{overhead}$ is the width overhead. From ART-I, when $W_{overhead} = o(D_{ave}/d) = o(m)$, the slowdown factor for executing $g = 2d$ TE tasks on the virtual m-ary d-subcube is only $1 + o(1)$ compared to a fault-free m-ary d-cube, leading to the following corollary.

Corollary 3.3 *We can execute $2d$ instances of a TE task in an n-ary d-cube that has an arbitrary pattern of $o(n/d)$ faulty processors and/or links in $(N-1)D_{ave} = dnN/4 + o(dnN)$ communication time, which is optimal within a factor of $1 + o(1)$, where D_{ave} is the average distance of a fault-free $(n - o(n/d))$-ary d-cube, $N = n^d - o(n^d)$ is the size of the virtual $(n - o(n/d))$-ary d-subcube, and data items are input/output to/from the virtual $(n - o(n/d))$-ary d-subcube.*

4. Fault-tolerant computation on general virtual subarrays

In this section, we introduce the *compaction/expansion technique (CET)*, derive the array robustness theorem II (ART-II) based on CET, and then present its applications to robust sorting and permutation routing.

4.1. ART-II for general virtual subarrays

Fault-tolerant computing in a virtual submesh using CET is based on the following 4 phases:

The Compaction/Expansion Technique (CET):

- Phase 0 (precalculation): Each dimension-i virtual row performs semigroup and prefix computation to determine the total number t of processors in the virtual row that are not VSM nodes and for each VSM node, the number l of processors to its left that are not VSM nodes.

- Phase 1 (compaction): The items in each VSM node are shifted to the left by $l - \lceil t/2 \rceil$ positions if $l - \lceil t/2 \rceil > 0$ and the items are shifted to the right by $\lceil t/2 \rceil - l$ positions if $\lceil t/2 \rceil - l < 0$.

- Phase 2: The consecutive operations (e.g., routing and computation) along rows of the dimension are performed within each compacted row (i.e., the virtual subrow composed of the m_i neighboring nodes currently holding the data).

- Phase 3 (expansion): The data items in each of the m_i-node compacted rows are shifted back to VSM nodes; this is the inverse of Phase 1.

Phase 0 can be completed in $O(m_i + t_{max})$ time using algorithms for semigroup and prefix computation on a virtual row [14]. This precalculation phase only needs to be executed once after each new processor or link failure. Phases 1 and 3 can each be performed in $a\lceil t/2 \rceil$ time. The integer t is usually small, and is guaranteed to be smaller than f_B and the length of the virtual row. Clearly, Phase 2 can be performed

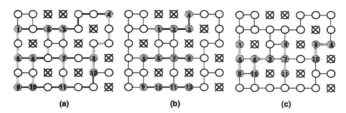

Figure 3. (a) A 3-by-4 VSM. (b) Compacted rows of the VSM. (c) Compacted columns of the VSM.

without any slowdown compared to operations along fault-free m_i-node rows.

Many important problems such as sorting require computation between every few routing steps and thus cannot be solved efficiently in faulty meshes using ART-I. Based on CET, we can solve this class of problems efficiently on a mesh which may contain significantly more faults. Figure 3 provides an example for sorting on compacted rows and columns of a virtual submesh based on CET. The shaded circles in Fig. 3a represent a 3×4 virtual submesh within a 6×7 mesh with 9 faulty processors. The shaded circles in Fig. 3b represent the positions of data items for performing CET row sort upon completion of Phase 1. The processors that hold the data items from a VSM row upon completion of Phase 1 are collectively called a *compacted row*. The number X in a circle represents the position for the data item that was initially held by processor X of the virtual submesh. The shaded circles in Fig. 3c represent the positions of data items for performing CET sort along columns. The processors that hold the data items from a VSM column form a *compacted column*.

The following theorem provides the conditions and characterizes the class of problems that can be solved efficiently based on CET.

Theorem 4.1 (Array Robustness Theorem II (ART-II))
If an algorithm for a mesh performs S consecutive routing and computation steps along the same dimension on the average, and there exists an $m_1 \times m_2 \times \cdots \times m_d$ virtual submesh whose width overhead is $o(S)$, then the slowdown factor for performing the algorithm on a virtual submesh of the faulty mesh is $1 + o(1)$ relative to a fault-free $m_1 \times m_2 \times \cdots \times m_d$ mesh.

In addition to the different requirements for the underlying communication patterns, another important difference of ART-II compared to ART-I is that ART-II can potentially tolerate a significantly larger number of faults with negligible slowdown. For example, it can be shown that, using techniques similar to those used in [9], an N-node 2-D array with $o(N)$ random faults or a p-faulty array with faulty rate $p = o(1)$ contains $(N - o(N))$-node virtual subarrays with probability $1 - o(1)$; such an faulty array, however, is not likely to contain a congestion-free virtual subarray with comparable size, making ART-I inapplicable. (We conjecture that the preceding results can be extended to arrays of

469

higher dimensions $d \geq 3$.) When a congestion-free virtual subarray is available, we can execute d copies of such an algorithm concurrently, leading to the following corollary.

Corollary 4.2 *If an algorithm for a mesh performs S consecutive routing and computation steps along the same dimension on the average, and there are $o(\min(S, n_{min}))$ faulty processors in an $n_1 \times n_2 \times \cdots n_d$ array, then the slowdown factor for performing (up to) d copies of the algorithm on a virtual subarray of the faulty array is $1 + o(1)$ relative to performing a copy of the algorithm on a fault-free $(n_1 - o(n_{min})) \times (n_2 - o(n_{min})) \times \cdots (n_d - o(n_{min}))$ array of the same type.*

A wide variety of algorithms, such as reduction (e.g., semigroup computation), prefix computation [15], FFT [11], sorting (e.g. the algorithms proposed in [10]), and matrix multiplication, have $S = O(n)$, and thus can run with a slowdown factor of $1 + o(1)$ in a mesh with an arbitrary pattern of $o(n)$ faults or in $100 - o(1)$ out of 100 N-node 2-D meshes with $o(N)$ random faults. In what follows, we present robust sorting in faulty meshes and n-ary d-cubes as examples of how ART-II can be applied.

4.2. Sorting in faulty meshes and n-ary d-cubes

In [22], we have shown that 1-1 sorting in an $n \times n$ mesh with $o(n)$ faults can be performed in $2.5n + o(n)$ communication time using the FOE-snake order [22], a variant of the blockwise snakelike order (see Fig. 4). The robust sorting algorithm proposed in [22] is actually a special case of ART-II since we emulate the sorting algorithm proposed in [10], which performs $\Theta(n)$ operations along a dimension on the average. In [14], we have shown that 1-1 sorting in an $n \times n$ bypass mesh with $o(n^{1/4})$ faults can be performed in $2.5n + o(n)$ communication time using row order or snakelike order by emulating the Schnorr/Shamir sorting algorithm [11, 13, 17]). The average number of steps along a dimension in the Schnorr/Shamir sorting algorithm is only $\Theta(n^{1/4})$, so the number of faults that can be tolerated without increasing the leading constant of the running time is only $o(n^{1/4})$ when direct emulation is used. In [20, 24], we have also shown that 1-1 sorting in an $n \times n$ mesh with $o(n)$ faults can be performed in $3n + o(n)$ communication time using row order or snakelike order by emulating a variant of the Schnorr/Shamir sorting algorithm [11, 13, 17]). We increase the number of faults tolerated to $o(n)$ by modifying the Schnorr/Shamir sorting algorithm so that the average number of steps along a dimension is increased to $o(n)$. All the aforementioned sorting algorithms can be viewed as the applications of ART-II to 1-1 sorting in 2-D faulty meshes.

Resorting to ART-II, we can easily extend the results given in these papers from 1-1 sorting to h-h sorting and from 2-D meshes to d-D faulty meshes and tori. These generalizations can be achieved by emulating the sorting algorithm for fault-free meshes and n-ary d-cubes given in [10], which performs $\Theta(n)$ steps along a dimension on the average. In summary, if an $m_1 \times m_2 \times \cdots \times m_d$ virtual submesh with width overhead $o(m_{min})$ exists, h-h sorting on the virtual submesh can be performed in $hm_1/2 + 2\lceil \frac{h}{4} \rceil (m_2 +$

$m_3 + \cdots + m_d) + o(hdm_{min})$ communication steps (excluding precalculation time), where $d = O(1)$, $m_i = \Theta(m_j)$, and $m_{min} = \min(m_1, m_2, ..., m_d)$.

When $h = 1$, we can fold the data items to the middle of the virtual submesh and use 2-2 sorting of preceding method as the algorithms given in [10, 13, 20, 22, 24], leading to the following result: If an $m_1 \times m_2 \times \cdots \times m_d$ virtual submesh with width overhead $o(m_{min})$ exists, 1-1 sorting on the virtual submesh can be performed in $m_1/2 + 2(m_2 + m_3 + \cdots + m_d) + o(dm_{min})$ communication steps (excluding precalculation time), where $d = O(1)$ and $m_i = \Theta(m_j)$ for all i and j. The algorithm we proposed in [22] represents a special case of the preceding results with $d = 2$. The h-h sorting algorithm for fault-free n-ary d-cubes given in [10] requires $\lceil \frac{h}{4} \rceil (d-1)n + o(hdn)$ communication steps that can be emulated using SET with a slowdown factor of $1 + o(1)$, in addition to $\lceil \frac{h}{4} \rceil n + o(hn)$ communication steps and $hn + o(hn)$ computation steps, which can be emulated using CET with a slowdown factor of $1 + o(1)$. These results also lead to efficient permutation routing and the details are omitted in this paper.

5. Fault-tolerant computing in the entire faulty array

Up to now, we have assumed that data items are input/output to/from a virtual subarray. In this section, we formulate the *array robustness theorem III (ART-III)* for fault-tolerant computing and communication on the entire faulty array (in contrast to computing on a virtual subarray, as required by ART-I and ART-II).

An important feature of RAIL, based on ART-III, is that all healthy and connected nodes, rather than only nodes belonging to a virtual subarray, can be used for computation. Thus, computing resources are not wasted unnecessarily, which is particularly important to computation-bound problems. As for communication-bound problems, utilizing all healthy nodes to execute a task does not necessarily increase the performance, since the bisection bandwidth is not increased and a certain amount of communication overhead is required to distribute data items to nodes that do not belong to the virtual subarray. Therefore, ART-I and ART-II, which only use nodes on a virtual subarray for computation in order to facilitate simpler and more efficient communications, may be more suitable for solving communication-bound problems. Note that even when ART-I and ART-II are applied to the execution of communication-intensive subtasks within an application, no healthy node is disabled; rather, all such nodes are kept alive and running at all times. A load balancing policy may improve the system performance by appropriately distributing the subtasks among all healthy nodes.

5.1. ART-III for the entire faulty array

If we map healthy and connected processors in a faulty array to a virtual subarray in row-major order, then the time required for data redistribution is $\Omega(n)$ in usually case, since there usually exists a worst-case scenario where a healthy

1	2	3	4	5	6
12	11	10	9	8	7
13	14	15	16	17	18
24	23	22	21	20	19
25	26	27	28	29	30
36	35	34	33	32	31

Figure 4. An example of blockwise snakelike order in an array with 36 blocks. A processor in block i is ranked before a processor in block j if $i < j$.

processor near the beginning of a row is mapped to a VSA node near the end of a VSA row. If a different mapping from the faulty array to its virtual subarray can be used, such as mapping $\Theta(n^{1-\frac{1}{d}}) \times \cdots \times \Theta(n^{1-\frac{1}{d}})$ blocks of healthy processors in a faulty array to $\Theta(n^{1-\frac{1}{d}}) \times \cdots \times \Theta(n^{1-\frac{1}{d}})$ blocks in a virtual subarray in blockwise snakelike order (see Fig. 4), we can show that the time required for data redistribution can be reduced to $o(dn)$. In [22], we have introduced algorithm *data redistribution (DR)* on 2-D arrays and analyze its performance. The algorithm can be extended to d-D arrays with $d \geq 3$ and the details are omitted.

Lemma 5.1 *Data redistribution from a d-D $n \times \cdots n$ array with $o(n^{1-\frac{1}{d}})$ faulty processors onto an appropriate virtual subarray, or its reverse process, can be performed in $o(hdn)$ steps, where h is the number of data items per healthy processor.*

Algorithm DR and its extensions for higher-dimensional arrays are generally-applicable methods for data redistribution to/from virtual subarrays, and is guaranteed to run in negligible time (e.g., $o(n_{min})$ time) when the number f of faults is small (e.g., $f = o(n_{min}^{1-\frac{1}{d}})$). In practice, comparable performance may also be achieved for much larger f, since worst-case scenarios are unlikely. Moreover, since algorithm DR will be invoked frequently if most problems are computed using all healthy and connected processors of an array, it is usually worth the effort to improve and optimize this process, even if only lower order terms of the total execution time can be improved. When data redistribution can be performed in negligible time, we have the following theorem for fault-tolerant computing in the entire faulty array.

Theorem 5.2 (Array Robustness Theorem III (ART-III)) *Let T be the total time required for performing the algorithm on the fault-free array. If there exists an $m_1 \times m_2 \times \cdots \times m_d$ virtual subarray whose width overhead is $o(S)$, data redistribution and its inverse process can be performed in $o(T)$ time, and*

(A) an algorithm for an array (i.e., mesh or torus) performs an average of S consecutive routing steps along each of the dimensions (at the same time) without any computation step in between and the virtual subarray is congestion-free, or

(B) an algorithm for a mesh performs S consecutive routing and computation steps along the same dimension on the average,

then the slowdown factor for performing the algorithm on the entire faulty array, each healthy and connected processor of which has at most h data items, is $1 + o(1)$ relative to a fault-free $m_1 \times m_2 \times \cdots \times m_d$ array of the same type with load at most $\lceil h(\prod_{i=1}^{d} n_i - f) / \prod_{i=1}^{d} m_i \rceil$.

When the number of faults is small and data items are mapped to blocks of appropriate size nearby, it is guaranteed that data redistribution can be performed in negligible time and that a congestion-free virtual subarray exists, leading to the following corollary.

Corollary 5.3 *Let T be the total time required for performing the algorithm on the fault-free array. If there are f faulty processors in an $n_1 \times n_2 \times \cdots n_d$ array with $f = o$ $(\min(S, T_{min}^{1-\frac{1}{d}}, \frac{n_{min}}{hd}))$ (or $f = o(\min(S, T_{min}^{1-\frac{1}{d}}, \frac{n_{min}}{d}))$), blockwise snakelike mapping from all healthy processors to the virtual subarray is allowed in the emulation, and*

(A) an algorithm for an array (i.e., mesh or torus) performs an average of S consecutive routing steps along each of the dimensions (at the same time) without any computation step in between and the virtual subarray is congestion-free, or

(B) an algorithm for a mesh performs S consecutive routing and computation steps along the same dimension on the average,

then the slowdown factor for performing the algorithm on the entire faulty array, each healthy and connected processor of which has at most h data items, is $1 + o(1)$ relative to a fault-free $(n_1 - o(\frac{n_{min}}{hd})) \times (n_2 - o(\frac{n_{min}}{hd})) \times \cdots (n_d - o(\frac{n_{min}}{hd}))$ array of the same type with load at most $h + 1$ (or $h + o(h)$, respectively).

In what follows, we present results for performing total exchange in faulty meshes, tori, and n-ary d-cubes, as examples of how ART-III can be applied.

5.2. Solving problems based on ART-III

Since mappings similar to blockwise snakelike order [10] are usually allowed for the emulation of communication algorithms, we have the following corollary based on ART-III and Corollary 3.3.

Corollary 5.4 *A total of $2d - 1$ (or $2d - o(d)$) TE tasks can be executed in an n-ary d-cube that has an arbitrary pattern of f faulty processors and/or links in $dnN/4 + o(dnN)$ communication time, which is optimal within a factor of $1 + o(1)$ when d is not a constant, where $f = o(\min(n^{1-\frac{1}{d}}, n/d^2))$ (or $f = o(\min(n^{1-\frac{1}{d}}, n/d))$, respectively), $N = n^d - f$ is the number of healthy processors, and data items are input/output to/from each of the healthy and connected processors in the entire faulty n-ary d-cube.*

471

If we allow a packet to be split into $2d - o(d)$ mini-packets, the time required to perform a single TE task becomes $nN/8 + o(nN)$ communication time when d is not a constant and a mini-packet requires $1/(2d - o(d))$ time for transmission. This time complexity is also optimal within a factor of $1 + o(1)$ for both fault-free and faulty n-ary d-cubes.

Similar results can also be obtained for sorting and permutation routing in the entire faulty array. More details will be reported in the near future.

6. Conclusion

In this paper, we have proposed to add a RAIL middleware for interfacing the large body of ordinary algorithms/programs designed for fault-free arrays with a possibly faulty network/hardware. Based on RAIL, we formulated three array robustness theorems (ARTs), which lead to the fastest known solutions for a variety of important problems such as sorting, permutation routing, total-exchange, and ascend/descend algorithms on faulty arrays. ARTs classify computation and communication problems into several categories, each of which indicates the required RAIL techniques and quantifies the resultant performance according the available parameters such as the total number of faults.

An important implication of our results is that low-dimensional meshes, tori, and k-ary n-cubes are robust in that they can solve many problems with negligible slowdown in the presence of a (relatively) large number of faults. Thus, if low-dimensional meshes, tori, and k-ary n-cubes have comparable or even better performance than hypercubes and high-dimensional k-ary n-cubes (as indicated in [8] under certain assumptions), then the superiority of low-dimensional networks will be even more pronounced when the network/hardware may be faulty. The approach and techniques proposed in this paper can also be applied to a variety of other important problems as well as other network topologies. The details will be reported in the near future.

References

[1] Agarwal, A., "Limits on interconnection network performance," *IEEE Trans. Parallel Distrib. Sys.*, Vol. 2, no. 4, Oct. 1991, pp. 398-412.

[2] Akers, S.B., D. Harel, and B. Krishnamurthy, "The star graph: an attractive alternative to the n-cube," *Proc. Int'l Conf. Parallel Processing*, 1987, pp. 393-400.

[3] Bertsekas, D.P. and J. Tsitsiklis, *Parallel and Distributed Computation – Numerical Methods,* Athena Scientific, 1997.

[4] Bhuyan, L.N. and D.P. Agrawal, "Generalized hypercube and hyperbus structures for a computer network," *IEEE Trans. Comput.,* vol. 33, no. 4, Apr. 1984, pp. 323-333.

[5] Bruck, J., R. Cypher, and C. Ho, "Fault-tolerant meshes and hypercubes with minimal numbers of spares," *IEEE Trans. Comput.,* vol. 42, no. 9, Sep. 1993, pp. 1089-1104.

[6] Bruck, J. and R. Cypher, and C.-H. Ho, "Wildcard dimensions, coding theory and fault-tolerant meshes and hypercubes," *IEEE Trans. Comput.,* vol. 44, no. 1, Jan. 1995, pp. 150-155.

[7] Cole, R., B. Maggs, and R. Sitaraman, "Multi-scale self-simulation: a technique for reconfiguring arrays with faults," *ACM Symp. Theory of Computing*, 1993, pp. 561-572.

[8] Dally, W.J. "Performance analysis of k-ary n-cube interconnection networks," *IEEE Trans. Comput.,* Vol. 39, no. 6, Jun. 1990, pp. 775-785.

[9] Kaklamanis, C., A.R., Karlin, F.T. Leighton, V. Milenkovic, P. Eaghavan, S. Rao, C. Thomborson, and A. Tsantilas, "Asymptotically tight bounds for computing with faulty arrays of processors," *Proc. Symp. Foundations of Computer Science,* vol. 1, 1990, pp. 285-296.

[10] Kunde, M. "Concentrated regular data streams on grids: sorting and routing near to the bisection bound," *Proc. Symp. on Foundations of Computer Science,* 1991, pp. 141-150.

[11] Leighton, F.T., *Introduction to Parallel Algorithms and Architectures: Arrays, Trees, Hypercubes,* Morgan-Kaufman, San Mateo, CA, 1992.

[12] Mazzaferri, R. and T.M. Murray, "The connection network class for fault tolerant meshes," *IEEE Trans. Comput.,* vol. 44, no. 1, Jan. 1995, pp. 131-138.

[13] Nigam, M. and S. Sahni, "Sorting n^2 numbers on $n \times n$ meshes," *IEEE Trans. Parallel Distrib. Sys.,* vol. 6, no. 12, Dec. 1995, pp. 1221-1225.

[14] Parhami, B. and C.-H. Yeh, "The robust-algorithm approach to fault tolerance on processor arrays: fault models, fault diameter, and basic algorithms," *Proc. First Merged International Parallel Processing Symposium and Symp. Parallel and Distributed Processing,* Apr. 1998, pp. 742-746.

[15] Parhami, B., *Introduction to Parallel Processing: Algorithms and Architectures,* Plenum Press, 1999.

[16] Park, A. and K. Balasubramanian, "Reducing communication costs for sorting on mesh-connected and linearly connected parallel computers," *J. Parallel Distrib. Comput.,* vol. 9, no. 3, Jul. 1990 pp. 318-322.

[17] Schnorr, C.P. and Shamir, A., "An optimal sorting algorithm for mesh connected computers," *Proc. Symp. Theory of Computing,* 1986, pp. 255-263.

[18] Su, C.C. and K.G. Shin, "Adaptive fault-tolerant deadlock-free routing in meshes and hypercubes," *IEEE Trans. Comput.,* vol. 45, no. 6, Jun. 1996, pp. 666-683.

[19] Tzeng, N.-F. and G. Lin, "Maximum reconfiguration of 2-D mesh systems with faults," *Proc. Int'l Conf. Parallel Processing,* vol. 1, 1996. pp. 77-84.

[20] Yeh, C.-H. and B. Parhami, "Optimal sorting algorithms on incomplete meshes with arbitrary fault patterns," *Proc. Int'l Conf. Parallel Processing,* Aug. 1997, pp. 4-11.

[21] Yeh, C.-H., "Efficient low-degree interconnection networks for parallel processing: topologies, algorithms, VLSI layouts, and fault tolerance," Ph.D. dissertation, Dept. Electrical & Computer Engineering, Univ. of California, Santa Barbara, Mar. 1998.

[22] Yeh, C.-H., B. Parhami, H. Lee, and E.A. Varvarigos, "2.5n-step sorting on $n \times n$ meshes in the presence of $o(\sqrt{n})$ worst-case faults," *Proc. Merged Int'l Parallel Processing Symp. & Symp. Parallel and Distributed Processing,* Apr. 1999, pp. 436-440.

[23] Yeh, C.-H. and B. Parhami, E.A. Varvarigos, and Theodora A. Varvarigou, "RACE: a software-based fault tolerance scheme for systematically transforming ordinary algorithms to robust algorithms, *Proc. Int'l Parallel and Distributed Processing Symp.*, 2001.

[24] Yeh, C.-H., and B. Parhami, "Efficient sorting algorithms on incomplete meshes," *J. Parallel Distrib. Comput.,* to appear.

Engineering CORBA-Based Systems for High Performance

Wai-Keung Wu and Shikharesh Majumdar
Department of Systems and Computer Engineering,
Carleton University, Ottawa,
CANADA K1S 5B6
majumdar@sce.carleton.ca

Abstract

Inter-operability in heterogeneous distributed systems is often provided with the help of CORBA compliant middleware. Many Distributed Object Computing Systems, however, are characterized by limited heterogeneity. Such systems often contain a subset of components that are written in the same programming language and run on top of the same platform. We present engineering techniques that exploit such limited heterogeneity in systems for achieving high system performance. With these techniques components implemented using diverse programming languages and/or platform use a CORBA compliant middleware, whereas the similar components can use a "Flyover" that employs a separate path between the client and its server and avoids a number of CORBA overheads. Insights into system behavior and performance gained from results of experiments with synthetic workload running on a network of PC's are presented.

1 Introduction

The ability to run distributed applications over a set of diverse platforms is crucial for achieving scalability as well as gracefully handling the evolution in hardware and platform design. Additional components may be added to an existing system for handling an increase in workload or the incorporation of new features in an embedded application for example. Due to the continuous improvement in computing technology, the newly added components are often built using a technology that is different from that used for implementing the legacy components. Moreover, the new feature in the embedded system may require a special platform for execution. An effective middleware system is required to provide inter-operability in such a heterogeneous distributed system. Using such middleware software it is possible for two application components written in different languages and

implemented on top of different operating systems to communicate with one another. This research focuses on heterogeneous systems based on Distributed Object Computing (DOC) which is currently one of the most desirable paradigms for application implementation.

The Common Object Request Broker Architecture (CORBA) is a standard proposed by the Object Management Group for the construction of object oriented client-server systems in which clients can receive service from servers that may run on diverse platforms [9]. Both the clients and servers use a common standard Interface Definition Language (IDL) for interfacing with the Object Request Broker (ORB) that provides client-server inter-communication as well as a number of other facilities such as location and trading of services through the ORB agent. This research focuses on the performance enhancement of systems based on CORBA that is used widely by distributed system builders.

Many distributed systems such as telecommunication systems and various types of real-time embedded systems are characterized by limited heterogeneity. A subset of nodes in such a system is built using the same programming languages and operating systems.

When conventional implementation of CORBA is applied to many telecommunication systems, middleware overheads can degrade performance to such an extent that system specifications are violated [17]. This paper focuses on engineering such CORBA-based systems with limited heterogeneity. The primary motivation is to achieve a performance enhanced system that can meet the requirements of performance demanding application. A flexible architecture called *flyover* that employs a number of performance optimization strategies is presented. In this architecture, the system components that exhibit heterogeneity can communicate through the CORBA compliant ORB, whereas similar components can use a flyover, which communicates through proprietary protocols and bypasses a number of standard CORBA operations. The flyover not only achieves a higher performance by exploiting limited heterogeneity in systems but also preserves application transparency, as well as location transparency, without ORB source code modification. A distributed system may incorporate components implemented using various programming languages and/or platforms. By always using the same CORBA compliant method invocations and with the help of the flyover, the application designers can focus on their core applications rather than developing their own proprietary method to exploit limited heterogeneity and attain a better performance. This can lead to substantial savings in terms of development and testing efforts. Based on a prototype built using Orbix MT-2.3 running on a network of SPARC workstations under a synthetic workload we have compared the performance of flyover-based systems with that of pure CORBA-compliant ORB-based systems. A synthetic workload enables performance comparison under various pre-determined workload conditions. The results of our experiments demonstrate the potential of achieving substantial performance benefits from the use of flyovers.

The main contributions of this research include:

- the design and implementation of a tool prototype for installing flyovers prototype on a commercially available middleware based systems;
- a number of performance optimization techniques that include preventing native to CDR (CORBA specified data format explained in a later section) conversions, avoiding padding bytes, direct socket communication, effective demultiplexing and an optimized GIOP protocol;
- the investigation of the relative performance of the flyover, and two commercial ORB products Orbix-MT 2.3 and Orbix 2000;
- the experimental evidence that the flyover prototype exhibits a significant performance improvement for transferring short messages in systems;
- insights into system behavior that include the impacts of message size and system load on the system performance;
- the demonstration that the flyover prototype can be implemented without source code modification of the middleware product.

Although this research is based on a specific middleware product we believe that the techniques used in the construction of the flyover are general and can be used with other CORBA compliant products for achieving a high system performance. A preliminary set of experiments that were used to investigate the potential of some of the techniques used in the flyover is discussed in [2].

The paper is organized as follows. Section 2 presents a brief overview of CORBA and related work. A description of the design of the flyover is presented in Section 3. Section 4 describes the experiments and the results captured in the performance measurements made on the system. Section 5 presents our conclusions and directions for future work.

2 Overview of CORBA and Related Work

CORBA is a specification for a standard architecture for distributed object oriented systems that uses the client-server paradigm. The interactions among clients and servers in a CORBA system are mediated through an entity called the Object Request Broker (ORB). The ORB core (the communication infrastructure of the ORB), which handles the transmission of requests as well as the reception of results and exceptions, coordinates all inter-communications among clients, servers, and brokers.

A short description of the different steps in the development of a CORBA compliant system using C++ as the programming language is presented [1]. At the beginning, we need to specify, design, and write the object interfaces using the OMG Interface Definition Language (IDL). The IDL source code is translated by an IDL compiler, which produces the client stubs, and server skeletons that serve as the glue at their respective sides between the ORB core and the application implementations. The main programs in the server and client application code are then developed. Before invoking a method on a server object the client process must communicate with the ORB broker that locates the object and obtains the Interoperable Object Reference (IOR). When the client uses the object reference to invoke a method in the server, a marshalling of data takes place inside the client stub that converts the native data representation at the client side into the Common Data Representation (CDR) format specified in CORBA. The data in CDR is demarshalled by the server skeleton into the native data format used at the server side. The object adapter demultiplexes the request to the target object and invokes the appropriate method that executes and uses the skeleton to send the result back to the client. A marshalling and demarshalling of the result take place in the server skeleton and in the client stub respectively. The data in the CDR format is transported through the network in accordance with the General Inter-ORB Protocol (GIOP) specified in the CORBA standard. In addition to interoperability CORBA also provides a number of services that includes trading and naming services (see [11] for details).

2.1. Related Work

A large body of research exists in the field of CORBA-based systems. A representative set of previous work that has focused on CORBA performance is discussed in this section. A detailed survey is available in [23]. The performance comparisons of C socket, C++ wrappers for socket and CORBA are presented in [15]. Different architectures for multithreaded systems and their impacts on performance of CORBA-based systems are described in [13]. The impact of different client-middleware-server interaction schemes on performance is presented in [1]. A growing class of real-time systems requires more stringent end-to-end quality-of-service (QoS) support including bandwidth, latency and priority preservation. To meet this challenge, a Real-Time CORBA (RT CORBA) specification is proposed recently [10][16]. The main characteristics and requirements of Real-Time CORBA specification are summarized in [16]. The architecture, real-time scheduling service and optimizations of the real-time ORB, TAO, are presented in [4] [17] .

CORBA has proven its worth in low speed network to provide a flexible solution for a heterogeneous environment. However, for bulk data transfer on high speed networks such as ATM and Fast Ethernet, empirical studies [5][6] show that, the performance of conventional CORBA is about 30% to 75% lower than the performance achievable using lower-level transport layer interfaces. When CORBA is applied to real-time and embedded systems, which require high bandwidth and low latency, CORBA may degrade the overall system performance and violate the system specification. To overcome these problems, a number of optimization techniques are devised. For example, bypassing the CORBA operations when possible may enhance system performance. Some of the Commodity-Off-The-Shelf (COTS) middlewares provide proprietary protocols to improve performance. However, this is feasible only when both client and server are using the same vendor's ORB. For instance, Orbix provides the "Orbix Protocol" as an option in addition to the standard General Inter-ORB Protocol (GIOP) [7]. The real-time ORB TAO also provides a lightweight version of GIOP by removing some redundant fields in the standard GIOP header [14]. None of these existing works focuses on the general flyover concept for exploiting limited heterogeneity in systems that this paper is concerned with.

3 Design of the Flyover

As mentioned earlier, this paper presents a system called flyover for achieving high performance on systems with limited heterogeneity. Figure 1 shows the general architecture of the flyover. There are two paths through which the client/server pair can communicate. For example, if the client is running on a WinNT and Pentium-based PC workstation and the server process in which the target object resides is running on a Solaris and UltraSPARC workstation, the inter-process communication in this heterogeneous environment can be mediated through the ORB. In accordance with the CORBA standard [9], if the client wants to send a request to the server object through the ORB, the client stub initializes a CORBA::Request object and then passes it through the ORB. Class

CORBA::Request is a CORBA compliant class which is responsible for carrying the request/reply information between the client and server through the ORB.

However, if the client and server use the same OS and hardware platforms, they can communicate directly by a low-level communication interface and proprietary protocols to bypass the ORB. This avoids the additional overhead introduced by the CORBA compliant middleware and achieves a performance gain. In the flyover, the client stub initializes a Message object that is a derived class of CORBA::Request. Class Message has its own marshaling and demarshalling functions which encode/decode the parameters and return value into/from an optimized GIOP message (discussed in Section 3.4). Moreover, the message is sent through a private socket connection between the client and the server, rather than through the ORB core. In the current version of the flyover prototype, before calling an application method, the client must call a method called "Flyover_Disable" if it wants to use the CORBA compliant ORB. Otherwise the application method invocation is handled by the flyover. Another requirement for a system to deploy the flyover mechanism is to use a IDL processing tool that is described in Section 3.5

The flyover itself is neither a self-contained CORBA nor a lightweight-CORBA, but incorporates a low-level communication shortcut between the client and its server into the existing CORBA-based applications. In our research, the prototype of the flyover is implemented on Orbix-MT 2.3 [7]. Orbix is commercially available and one of the most popular ORBs. Orbix-MT 2.3 is a multi-threaded ORB and compliant with the CORBA v.2.1 standard. The same principles can be applied to achieve a flyover on other ORB products.

3.1 Attributes of the Flyover

• **Optimization strategies for enhancing performance:** The main goal of the flyover is to achieve performance gains on systems with limited heterogeneity. The following techniques are used to achieve such performance gains: preventing CDR conversions, removing padding bytes, direct socket-based communication, efficient request demultiplexing, and GIOP optimization.

• **CORBA IDL support:** Most (twenty two) of the IDL data types in the CORBA v.2.3.1 and single inheritance are currently supported in the flyover. The exceptions are: basic data type (Wchar), constructed data type (Wstring), pseudo object type (Type Code, User-Defined Exception, Principal, Context). Supporting these remaining data types and multiple inheritance forms an important direction for our future work.

• **Support for communication and location transparency:** Using a lower level interface (e.g. socket and TLI [19]) to build a robust distributed application is complicated and error-prone. For instance, it requires a good knowledge of communication network issues, such as network address and connection management, process and thread synchronization, and operating system calls. To overcome these problems, the flyover provides communication transparency so that all low-level communication details are hidden from the application programmer.

Moreover, the application programmer has no knowledge of where the target object is located. To preserve location transparency, the flyover uses the object binding provided by CORBA.

- **Flexibility:** The client should be capable of selecting either the ORB or the flyover at run time.

- **Support for client application transparency:** The incorporation of an additional communication path in a CORBA application must require little or no modification to the way CORBA applications are normally developed. Since the flyover prototype is implemented on Orbix-MT 2.3, if the client application uses the Orbix `_bind()` function [7] to get the object reference, there is no modification required on the client application. However, if the client uses the naming service or stringified object reference to obtain the object reference, a small modification on the client application is required because the source codes of the CORBA naming service or ORB interface function `string_to_object` are not available to the ORB users [9]. If the source codes of those functions are available for modification, client application transparency can be preserved completely.

- **Support for IDL specification file, object implementation and server application transparency:** Application programmers need not change the original IDL files, object implementation source files and server applications to facilitate the use of the flyover. This implementation transparency is important because the application programmers do not need to know how the flyover works.

3.2 Methods for Engineering the Flyover in an Application System

Modifying the ORB is applicable only for open source ORB products. We have devised a more general method that modifies the stubs and skeletons which are usually generated by the IDL compiler that processes the IDL specification files provided as its input. Since the stub and skeleton codes are generated as source files, these files can be modified to adapt to the flyover. We have developed a tool called the *Interface Definition Language Processor* (*IDLP*) to deal with all the changes in stub and skeleton codes as well as the IDL source files. A description of the IDLP tool is provided in Section 3.5. Before describing the design of the tool a discussion of how performance

optimization is to be achieved during a CORBA transaction are presented in the following subsections.

3.3 Performance Optimizations

A number of performance optimization techniques are used in the construction of the flyover and are briefly described.

Performance Optimization through Operation ID: In the flyover, the static interface methods and variables are assigned operation IDs by IDLP instead of the commonly used operation names (see [23] for details). The main purpose of using the operation ID instead of the operation name is to reduce the memory footprint of the GIOP message and provide efficient operation dispatching which will be discussed in Section 3.4.

Performance Optimization through Direct Socket Communication: The network communication between the client and server is implemented by a BSD socket. The connection is not shared by other client-server pairs.

Performance Optimization through Disabling CDR Conversion: If the client and the server are running on the same types of hardware and operating systems, the overhead of data conversion can be avoided. Avoiding such unnecessary data conversions can reduce the data marshalling and demarshalling overheads. A similar technique was used to optimize the performance of RPC's in a homogeneous environment.

Performance Optimization through Removing padding bytes: In CDR, all primitive data types must be aligned on their natural boundaries relative to the start of the CDR-byte stream [9]. Any primitive of size n octets must start at an octet stream index that is a multiple of n. In CDR, n is one of 1, 2, 4, or 8. Consider, for example, an IDL structure demo that contains two primitive data types: a character c, followed by a double value d. In accordance with CDR, the character c can occur anywhere in a byte stream, whereas the double must be aligned on a boundary with an index that is a of multiple of 8. The format of the message stream is shown in Figure 2

The unused bytes between c and d are padding bytes that do not have any semantic value. In this example, the number of padding bytes in the request body is 7. This example shows the worst case situation in which 43.75% of the request body is used for transferring padding bytes. Removing these padding bytes can minimize the message size and save communication bandwidth and improve transmission time. Eliminating padding bytes, however, gives rise to an increase in processing times. A tradeoff between the communication bandwidth savings and increase in processing overhead is discussed in [2]. Incorporation of criteria for the selective use of this technique into the flyover warrants investigation. Such a technique will eliminate padding bytes in messages only when the savings in communication time are higher than the processing overheads.

3.4 Optimized GIOP

In CORBA, the communications between the client and the server are through GIOP messages. There are eight types of messages, which are defined in the GIOP specification [9]. To reduce the size of a GIOP message header and request header, the proprietary protocol used in the flyover is highly optimized. Since over 90% of CORBA method calls are Request and Reply messages [22], the optimized GIOP focuses on these two types of messages. All fields such as magic field, version numbers and reserved fields are removed because they are not used in the flyover. This optimization is similar to TAO's GIOPLite protocol [14]. In addition the flyover performs another optimization and the fields such as message type, response expected and byte ordering flags are combined into a single field called `message_properties` to further minimize the message size. Here we assume one GIOP message can carry only one request. Therefore, multiple GIOP messages are required to carry multiple requests.

Moreover, in the optimized GIOP, the object ID replaces the object key in the request header. This step reduces the size of the request message header significantly. In accordance with the CORBA standard [9], the object key is to identify the target object of the invocation. In the flyover, the object ID is used instead of the object key to uniquely identify the object within the server.

In addition, the operation name within the request message is substituted by the corresponding operation ID, which is automatically assigned by IDLP during compilation of the IDL interface specification. Using operation ID instead of operation name not only improves the efficiency of operation dispatching greatly, but also reduces the size of request header. The size of the operation ID is 4 bytes (unsigned long) whereas the length of the operation name is usually more than 3 characters. For space limitations a detailed discussion of how the object ID and the operation ID are used in method dispatching can not be provided (see [23] for details).

The optimized GIOP is lightweight. For example, the total size of the message header and the request header of the method call (e.g. "foobar") is only 17 bytes as compared to 105 bytes for standard GIOP using Orbix-MT 2.3. Thus there is a significant (84%) saving in a request message header. It is important to note that the content of the object key is vendor specific. For example, the size of object key in an ORB called Orbacus 3.0 is 36 bytes. Therefore the byte saving depends on the ORB used in the application.

3.5 The Interface Definition Language Processor

To incorporate the flyover into the CORBA applications, we have developed a prototyping tool called IDLP. This tool is used instead of the original IDL compiler for compiling the IDL interface specification files. Figure 3 describes the procedures of generating client and server executables using IDLP. IDLP (the current version of which supports only C++) consists of two main components: the IDL parser and the C++ parser. The IDL parser analyzes the IDL interfaces defined in the IDL interface specification file and modifies this specification file. It also writes the information (e.g. interface name and interface function name) into the data structures shared by the IDL parser and C++ parser. This information is useful in analyzing the structures of the client stub, server skeleton and the header file. Then IDLP calls the CORBA IDL compiler (supplied by the ORB vendor) to generate the header file, client stub and the server skeleton.

The C++ parser analyzes the structure of the header file, client stub and server skeleton and modifies these to incorporate the flyover into the CORBA applications. From the application programmer's point of view, there is no change in CORBA application development paradigm except that IDLP is used instead of the vendor supplied IDL compiler for compiling the IDL specification files. The IDLP tool presented in this paper is implemented by using the scripting language Perl [18].

4 Experiments and Results

4.1 Experiments

The design and implementation of the flyover have been summarized in the previous section. In order to compare its performance with Orbix-MT 2.3 and its current version Orbix 2000 [8], five types of experiments were conducted. In all the experiments we used a simple server that receives the client request and immediately returns a null result. A synchronous message passing underlies a method invocation on the system.

The first type of experiments is used to measure the response time of a two-way CORBA method call under a "no load" condition. That is, a single client request invokes a single server and there is no resource contention from other clients. The client operates cyclically and generates a single method invocation separated by a significant amount of think time (300ms). Similar relative performance of the flyover and the CORBA compliant ORBs were observed at other values of think time.

The second type of experiments uses an open model with a single server. Client requests arrive at the system following a Poisson process. The client receives the request, and if free, invokes the server method immediately; otherwise the request is queued. In this experiment, the client program consists of two threads of control. One client thread, called the request thread, generates requests with exponentially distributed inter-arrival times. This thread operates cyclically sleeping for an interval of time between creation of two requests. Once a request is generated it is put in a FIFO queue with a time stamp recording the time of arrival. The other client thread, called the execution thread, gets the request from the FIFO queue and invokes the test CORBA method. The thread remains blocked until the reply from the server arrives. This corresponds to an open model used in the literature for characterizing transaction-oriented systems. When the reply arrives from the server, the client execution thread records the time of message reception and repeats the process. The response time of the method call is measured by taking the time difference between the time of reception of the reply from the server and the request arrival time at the client. If the queue is empty, the execution thread waits on the FIFO queue until the next request arrives.

The third type of experiment measures the binding time that is the time required in getting an object reference. Measurement of the binding time is important because the flyover takes one extra remote CORBA call to get the object ID and port number.

The last type of experiment measures the system throughputs in terms of data bytes (not including the GIOP header) transmitted per second over the CORBA compliant ORB or the flyover.

Parameters:

The parameters specifying the characteristics of the applications and the systems are described below.

- Data Types – In this paper, the CORBA IDL data type used for the performance evaluation is the CORBA array. The performance results on other IDL data types that are supported in the flyover are presented in [23].

- Data Sizes – Measurement of the response time of CORBA IDL array is performed for different sizes. The size of the array ranges from 1 to 128K. Varying the data size provides an understanding of system latency in transferring small and large messages.

- Arrival Rate of Requests – This is the rate at which requests arrive at the client following a Poisson distribution. The rate is expressed in number of requests arriving per second. This parameter is used in the second set of experiments for investigation of system performance at different system loads.

- Transport Protocol – The flyover prototype can use a TCP or an UDP transport.

- CORBA Compliant ORB – The flyover prototype is based on Orbix-MT 2.3 which was available from IONA [7] when this research was started. However, another version of the ORB called Orbix 2000 [8] has been released by IONA subsequently. We have included performance measurements made with both the CORBA compliant ORBs, Orbix-MT 2.3 and Orbix 2000 that serve as basis for comparison for the flyover.

Performance Metrics:

- The Mean Client Response Time: Client response time is the elapsed time measured from the moment the request arrives at the client to the time the reply arrives from the server. In the second and third set of experiments, the response time also includes the queuing delay resulting from multiple client requests. The mean response time is a measure of the latency of the system. In the experiments, we use the high-resolution timer gethrtime() Solaris system call[20]. This function returns the current high-resolution real time (as a long long integer) expressed in nanoseconds (ns). The CPU time consumed by this system call is approximately 200 ns. This is very small in comparison to the measured response times that are of the order of milliseconds.

- The Mean System Throughput: This parameter is a measure of the capacity of the system and is measured in terms of the number of data bits transmitted per unit time.

Experiments were performed on the isolated measurement network in our labs, which is dedicated for running the experiments. The measurement network comprises a set of 40 MHz Sparc-2 workstations connected by a 10Mbps Ethernet. Each Sparc-2 workstation contains 32MB RAM and is running under Solaris 7. The Maximum Transmission Unit (MTU) on the Ethernet adapter is 1500 bytes. The Orbix broker is located in a separate 200MHz Ultra-1 workstation. Each experiment consists of a number of repeating client cycles. The number of client cycles is chosen to be large enough to obtain a confidence interval less than or equal to ± 4% of the mean at a confidence level of 99%.

4.2 Results of Experiments

We ran a number of experiments to compare the performance of the flyover, Orbix-MT 2.3 and Orbix 2000 with different system and workload parameters. A representative set of results is presented in this paper. A complete set of experimental results can be found in [23].

4.2.1 Measurement of Response Times under a No Load Condition

Figure 4 and Table 1 show the performance for CORBA array of longs. The array sizes are chosen in such a way that the performance comparisons can be done for a range of response times.

Note that because the upper bound on the size of UDP data packet is 65535 bytes, results for Flyover (UDP) are not available for array sizes of 16K and 32K. As shown in the figure and the table, the flyover exhibits a substantially higher performance in comparison to both Orbix-MT 2.3 and Orbix 2000 in sending an array of long. For example, in transferring an array long[32], the flyover (TCP) achieves a 73.88% and a 49.30% improvement over Orbix-

MT 2.3 and Orbix 2000 respectively. A significant further improvement in flyover performance can be achieved by using UDP instead of TCP as the transport layer protocol. Note that using UDP instead of TCP in the transport layer is expected to give rise to an increase in performance in commercial ORB's as well if IIOP using TCP is not a strict requirement.

Table 1 Performance improvement for CORBA array of long

Array Size	Improvement of Flyover (TCP) over Orbix-MT 2.3	Improvement of Flyover (TCP) over Orbix 2000	Improvement of Flyover (UDP) over Flyover (TCP)
1	77.06%	55.37%	19.99%
32	73.88%	49.30%	24.53%
256	69.77%	45.91%	17.49%
1K	58.51%	34.37%	3.16%
2K	47.94%	26.58%	3.72%
4K	34.44%	18.81%	2.39%
8K	24.05%	9.84%	1.08%
16K	10.94%	5.32%	-
32K	5.94%	2.11%	-

As shown in Table 1, the performance gain is less when a larger array is passing through the flyover. For example, sending an array long[16384] can only produce a 10.94% and a 5.32% performance gain over Orbix-MT 2.3 and Orbix 2000 respectively. The primary reason for this is that the communication (transmission) time becomes the dominant component in the end-to-end response time when the message size increases.

Table 2 presents the average distribution of times in a request-reply transaction corresponding to an array transfer for the Orbix-MT 2.3 and the flyover. Since the return type of the test function is void, the marshalling and demarshalling times of the reply message are zero. Note that the communication time is the sum of the times required to send both request and reply over the network.

From Table 2 one can see that execution times of "Out Request Marshalling" and "In Request Demarshalling" in the flyover are reduced because of preventing CDR conversions that occur in the standard GIOP. The marshalling/demarshalling overheads vary with the numbers of bytes in the messages. For example, the time consumed in demarshalling the input parameter long[32] and long[8192] (reported in [23]) on Orbix-MT 2.3 are 483 μs and 3279 μs respectively. This time difference in demarshalling is because of the larger data size being transferred.

Table 2 also shows the improvement in communication time as a result of using the optimized GIOP and eliminating padding bytes. Optimized GIOP reduces the sizes of GIOP message header and request header (see Section 3.4) while removing padding bytes minimizes the size of the request and reply messages. For example, there

is a significant improvement in communication time (35.63%) in transferring an array long[32] in the flyover (TCP) (3138 μs) in comparison to Orbix-MT 2.3 (4875 μs). However, the transmission time for data increases with the size of the array. Although a large number of padding bytes is removed, the overall response time is dominated by the data transmission time component. Therefore, the response time improvement over Orbix 2000 is only 9.84% in transferring an array long[8192] [23].

Using an UDP transport instead of TCP in the flyover can further reduce communication time because UDP is a connectionless protocol. For example, as shown in Table 1, transferring a small message (e.g. long[32]) in flyover (UDP) (3243 μs) can improve the response time by 24.53% in comparison to the "flyover TCP" (4297 μs). This improvement primarily occurs because of the time saving due to bypassing the establishment and termination of connection, packet sequencing, end-to-end reliability and flow control. An early paper on network performance measurement showed that the maximum throughput of UDP in an Ethernet environment is double than that of TCP [3]. Note that for using UDP, some form of end-to-end acknowledgement may be required at a higher layer. A number of telecommunication applications achieve system reliability by implementing an acknowledgement and re-transmission mechanism at the application layer [12].

It is important to note that in the flyover, there is an upper bound on message size when UDP is used because the maximum IP packet size is 65535 bytes, and the size of a IP header and a UDP header are 20 bytes and 8 bytes respectively [19][21]. For messages with sizes exceeding this UDP upper bound, the flyover generates an user exception (see [23] for details).

The overhead of request dispatching in the flyover is negligible compared to the response time. It only constitutes less than 0.2% of the response time for sending an array long[32] (see Table 2). This time improvement in request demultiplexing and operation dispatching occurs because of using the object ID in the message object. As well, dispatching the request to the corresponding member function of the object implementation is based on comparing the operation IDs, instead of operation names, which is known to be computationally expensive.

4.2.2 Other Performance Measurements

We measured the maximum throughput that can be achieved on the system and the time required to perform a binding operation on the flyover-based system. For the conservation of space we have summarized some of the important performance results in this paper. A more detailed description is available in [23].

• *Throughput Analysis:* High throughput is important for many data intensive applications. The maximum throughput achieved with a flyover is 7.05 Mbps. This is only 11 % lower than that achieved by a raw C socket and is significantly larger than the maximum throughputs achieved with Orbix-MT 2.3 and Orbix 2000.

- *Binding Time:* There is a substantial increase in binding time in the flyover because of the extra overhead of using one extra CORBA method call GET_OBJKEY_ to obtain the port number and object ID of the target object, and establishing the socket connection. The binding operation is observed to take 2246 μs, 3017 μs and 28694 μs in Orbix-MT 2.3, Orbix 2000 and the flyover respectively.

However, in many distributed systems, particularly telecommunication systems, the location of the object is rather static. Therefore, the increase in binding time can be amortized by the time saving from multiple CORBA method invocations on the same object reference in the flyover. For example, four CORBA calls which transfer a double through the flyover are observed to be enough to overcome the extra overhead associated with object binding (see [23] for a more detailed discussion).

- *Degree of Heterogeneity:* The performance improvement data presented so far concern cases in which the request always uses the flyover. Systems with different degrees of heterogeneity are described in [23]. Even on a system with a degree of heterogeneity of 80% (i.e. 20% of the requests take the flyover whereas the rest pass through the CORBA ORB) and for an array[8192] and an arrival rate of 15 requests/sec, the flyover demonstrates a performance improvement of 20.13%. A detailed discussion is provided in [23].

Table 2 Components of response time in a CORBA transaction of long[32]

	Orbix-MT 2.3 (μs)	Flyover (TCP) (μs)	Flyover (UDP) (μs)
Out Request Marshalling	493	331	328
Out Request Processing	1485	168	171
In Reply Processing	2334	317	315
In Reply Demarshalling	0	0	0
Communication time	4875	3138	2086
In Request Dispatching	6434	7.45	7.44
In Request Demarshalling	483	322	322
Out Reply Processing	349	14	13.8
Out Reply Marshalling	0	0	0
Total	16453	4297	3243

4.2.3 Effect of System Load

Figure 5 shows the results of transferring the array long[8192] on the client/server system with Poisson arrival of requests. As the arrival rate increases, the response times of both the flyover prototype and Orbix increase because of the queuing delays experienced by the

requests. This figure shows that the relative performance of the flyover with respect to Orbix improves substantially as the system load increases. For example, when the arrival rate is 4 requests per second and an array long[8192] is transferred, the flyover (TCP) shows a 25.54 % and 9.39 % improvements over Orbix-MT 2.3 and Orbix 2000 respectively. However, at a rate of 14 requests per second, the flyover (TCP) demonstrates a 50.07% and a 18.41% improvements over Orbix-MT 2.3 and Orbix 2000 respectively. This is because when the system load increases, more requests are queued at the client. Since the queuing delay increases non-linearly with load a higher performance improvement is achieved at high load. A similar trend is expected with other kinds of data types.

5. Conclusions

This paper presents a technique called flyover for engineering performance into distributed systems with limited heterogeneity. Results of a number of experiments capturing the performance of the flyover are presented in the previous subsections. Insights into system behavior and performance resulting from these experiments are summarized.

- *Message Size:* The relative performance benefits of the flyover are most evident for small to medium message sizes. A 77.06% performance improvement over Orbix-MT 2.3 is demonstrated by the flyover when a single long integer is transmitted. The performance improvements observed with 8K and 32K messages are 24.05% and 5.94% respectively (see Table 1).

- *Response Time Components:* There are two types of response time components: fixed and variable. The variable components are proportional to the message length. The largest improvement in performance accrues from In Request Dispatching. The next highest contributors to performance improvement are Out Request Processing and In Reply Processing. All the three components seem to be independent of message size (see Table 2). The overall response time, however, is dominated by the variable component called communication time. The performance improvement in the communication time component that accrues from the flyover is rather small for the data captured in Table 2. As message size reaches 8K, communication time becomes almost 10 times that of the next largest response time component. The overall improvement in response time is thus dominated by the communication time component and decreases with an increase in message size. Note that we have considered transmission of simple arrays of a primitive data type. A larger number of padding bytes will be removed by the flyover when arrays of complex data structures are transmitted. A larger performance improvement may be expected in such a case.

- **Impact of Transport Protocol:** Using UDP instead of TCP can lead to a substantial improvement in performance. Up to 24.53% lower response time is achieved at no load by the flyover when the transport protocol is changed from TCP to UDP (see Table 1). UDP is thus recommended for systems that achieve end-to-end acknowledgements through application layer protocols.
- **Throughput:** Flyover not only reduces latency but also it is attractive for data intensive systems. It demonstrates a superior throughput in comparison to Orbix-MT 2.3 and Orbix 2000. For the experimental data presented in Section 4.2.2 the highest throughput achieved by the flyover is only 11% lower than that achieved by a raw C socket.
- **Cost:** Flyover incurs an additional cost when a client binds to an object. But if the same object is invoked multiple times the cost is quickly amortized over the multiple invocations. Experimental data presented in Section 4.2.2 indicates that using the flyover is beneficial if the same object is to be used more than 3 times by a client. In many embedded applications the location of the object may be known a priori and this run time binding cost may be totally avoided.

The IDLP tool used in this research modifies the output of IDL compilers. Achieving the IDLP optimizations directly from an IDL compiler is worthy of further investigation. Performance optimization by information sharing through memory when both the client and server are allocated on the same node is promising and forms a direction for future research.

Acknowledgments

This research was supported by the Communications and Information Technology Ontario (CITO), a Center of Excellence in the Province of Ontario. Diwakar Krishnamurthy's help in preparing this manuscript is gratefully acknowledged.

References

[1] I. Abdul-Fatah, S. Majumdar, "Performance of Architectures for Client-Server CORBA-Based Client-Server Architectures", *IEEE Trans. On Parallel and Distributed. Systems,* 2002 (accepted for publication).

[2] I. Ahmad, S. Majumdar, "Achieving High Performance in CORBA-Based Systems with Limited Heterogeneity," *Proc. IEEE International Symposium on Object Oriented Real Time Computing (ISORC 2001)*, Magdeburg (Germany), May 2001, pp. 350-359.

[3] L. Cabrera, E. Hunter, M. J. Karels, and D. A. Mosher, "User-Process Communication Performance in Networks of Computers," *IEEE Transactions on Software Engineering*, Vol. 14, No. 1, July 1988, pp. 38-53.

[4] C. D. Gill, D. L. Levine and D. C. Schmidt, "The Design and Performance of a Real-Time CORBA Scheduling Service", *International Journal of Time-Critical Computing Systems, special issue on Real-Time Middleware*, Vol. 20, No. 2, Mar 2001, pp. 117-154.

[5] A. Gokhale and D. C. Schmidt, "Evaluating CORBA Latency and Scalability Over High-Speed ATM Networks," in *Proceedings of 17th International Conference on Distributed Computing Systems (ICDCS 97)*, Baltimore, USA, May 1997, pp. 401-410.

[6] A. Gokhale and D. C. Schmidt, "Measuring the Performance of Communication Middleware on High-Speed Networks", in *Proceedings of SIGCOMM '96*, Stanford, California, Aug 1996, pp. 306-317.

[7] IONA Technologies, "Orbix-MT 2.3," 1997.

[8] IONA Technologies, "Orbix 2000," 2000.

[9] Object Management Group, *The Common Object Request Broker: Architecture and Specification*, ver 2.3.1, Oct 1999.

[10] Object Management Group, *The Common Object Request Broker: Architecture and Specification*, ver 2.5, Sept 2001.

[11] R. Otte, P. Patrick and M.Roy, "Understanding CORBA-The Common Object Request Broker Architecture," Prentice-Hall, New Jersey, 1996.

[12] M. Popp, *Personal Communication*, Nortel Networks, May 1999.

[13] D. C. Schmidt, "Evaluating Architectures for multithreaded Object Request Brokers," *Communications of the ACM*, Vol. 41, No. 10, Oct 1998, pp. 54-60.

[14] D. C. Schmidt and C. Cleeland, "Applying Patterns to Develop Extensible ORB Middleware," *IEEE Communications Magazine*, Vol. 37, No.4, Apr 1999, pp. 54-63.

[15] D. C. Schmidt, T. Harrison, E. Al-Shaer, "Object-Oriented Components for High-speed Network Programming," in *Proceedings of 1st Conference on Object-Oriented Technologies*, USENIX, June 1995.

[16] D. C. Schmidt and F. Kuhns, "An Overview of the Real-time CORBA Specification", *IEEE Computer special issue on Object-Oriented Real-time Distributed Computing*, Vol. 33, No. 6, June 2000, pp. 56-63

[17] D. C. Schmidt, D. L. Levine, S. Mungee, "The Design of the TAO Real-Time Object Request Broker," *Computer Communications*, Vol. 21, No. 4, April 1998, pp. 294-324.

[18] R. L Schwartz and T. Christiansen, *Learning Perl*, O'Rielly and Associates, 1998.

[19] W. R. Stevens, *UNIX Network Programming*, Prentice Hall, 1990.

[20] Sun Microsystems, *Solaris 7.0 Reference Manuals*, 1999.

[21] A. S. Tanenbaum, *Computer Networks*, Prentice Hall, 1996.

[22] S. Vinoski and M. Henning, *Advanced CORBA Programming with C++*, Addison Wesley, 1999.

[23] W.-K. Wu, "Flyover – a Technique for Achieving High Performance CORBA-Based Systems," M.A.Sc. Thesis, Aug 2001.

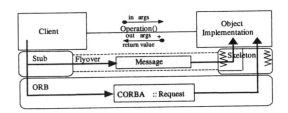

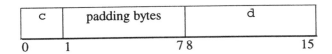

Figure 1 General architecture of the flyover

Figure 2. Padding bytes in a data stream for the IDL struct

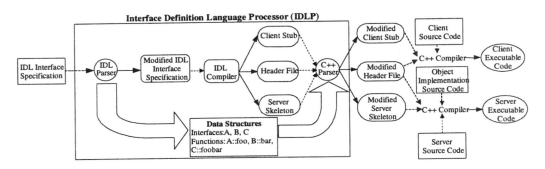

Figure 3. Generation of client and server executable codes using IDLP

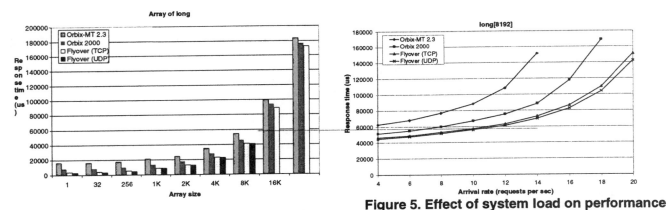

Figure 4. Performance of CORBA array of long

Figure 5. Effect of system load on performance (Data: array long[8192])
[Lines follow the same order as legends with Orbix MT 2.3 at the top and so on]

Session 7A

Algorithms II

A Distributed Algorithm for Knot Detection in a Distributed Graph

D. Manivannan and Mukesh Singhal
Computer Science Dept.
University of Kentucky
Lexington, KY 40506
email: {mani,singhal}@cs.uky.edu

Abstract

Knot detection in a distributed graph is an important problem and finds applications in several areas such as packet switching, distributed simulation, and distributed database systems. This paper presents a distributed algorithm to efficiently detect the existence of a knot in a distributed graph. The algorithm requires 2e messages and a delay of 2(d+1) message hops to detect if a node in a distributed graph is in a knot (e is the number of edges in the reachable part of the distributed graph and d is its diameter). A significant advantage of this algorithm is that it not only detects if a node is in a knot but also finds exactly which nodes are involved in the knot.

Keywords: *Distributed graph, distributed systems, knot detection, deadlock detection, distributed algorithms, distributed simulation.*

1. Introduction

A knot in a directed graph is a subgraph such that every node in the subgraph can be reached from *every* other node in the subgraph and no node outside the subgraph is reachable from any node in the subgraph. The problem of knot detection in a distributed graph arises in several domains. For example in store-and-forward networks, packets at a switching node are blocked if there is no empty buffer at the next switch, and a deadlock occurs if there is a knot in the buffer graph of the switching nodes [6]; in distributed simulation where a process waits for messages from other processes, a knot in the process graph implies a deadlock [1, 8, 12]; in distributed database systems, a transaction waits for response (e.g., a quorum) from remote hosts and a deadlock occurs if the transaction-wait-for graph contains a knot [7]. In general, deadlocks occur in systems due the existence of cycles or knots in the communication graph. A good survey about deadlock detection can be found in [8, 10]. Several algorithms for deadlock detection has been proposed in the literature [2, 11]. To our knowledge, none of the distributed knot detection algorithms proposed in the literature actually find the nodes involved in the knot. Our algorithm not only detects the existence of a knot but also finds the nodes involved in the knot.

1.1. Related Work

Various distributed knot detection algorithms have been proposed to detect knots in graphs of n vertices and e edges. These algorithms can be categorized into three basic classes [3].

1. In the algorithms in the first class, the complete distributed graph is collected at each node by extensive message passing, and knots are detected by a centralized algorithm at each node. The message complexity of one such algorithm is O(ne) [6]. This approach is a simple, but very inefficient.

2. In the algorithms in the second class, each node independently searches to discover whether it is a member of a knot. A distinct search is used at each node [13]. Misra-Chandy algorithm [13], for instance, is based on termination detection of diffusing computation and requires at most 4e messages. Dijkstra [4] proposed a distributed algorithm for detecting whether a network of processes is in a knot. His algorithm is based on his previous work with Scholten [5] on termination detection of diffusing computations. Boukerche and Tropper [1] proposed a knot detection algorithm which requires 2e messages; however, like other algorithms, their algorithm also does not find the nodes involved in the knot.

3. The algorithms in the third class use efficient cycle detection and clustering techniques and merges them into bigger clusters [3]. Cidon's algorithm [3], for instance has message complexity $O(e + n\ log(n))$.

1.2. Paper Objectives

This paper presents an efficient distributed knot detection algorithm in the second class described above. In the previous algorithms of the second class, the initiating node generally sends messages along all edges of the initiating node. These messages propagate along the edges of the graph and are echoed back to the initiating node. Based on the information received in the echoes, the initiating node determines whether it is in a knot. All of the algorithms in the second class except the one proposed by Boukerche and Tropper [1] have the following drawbacks:

1. The node initiating the knot detection and all nodes reached by the algorithm must know their incoming as well as outgoing edges.

2. In these algorithms, knot-detection messages travel along the backward edges of the graph even to nodes that are not reachable from the initiator. However, such unreachable nodes are irrelevant to determine whether the initiator is in a knot, thus increasing the message complexity.

3. When these algorithms terminate, they only detect if the initiating node is in a knot [13]. The initiator discovers no information about what other nodes are involved in the knot.

The algorithm proposed by Boukerche and Tropper [1] does not have the first two drawbacks; however, it still does not discover any information about what nodes are involved in the knot. Our proposed algorithm does not share any of the drawbacks mentioned above. Knot-detection messages sent by the initiator reach only the nodes reachable from the initiator; no knot-detection message is propagated backward along the edges of the graph. Unlike previous algorithms of the second class, our algorithm collects the set of all the nodes involved in the knot, which helps in resolving the deadlock represented by the knot. Our algorithm requires $2e$ messages and $2(d+1)$ message hops delay to detect a knot, where e is the number of edges in the reachable part of the graph and d is the diameter of that part of the graph.

The rest of the paper is organized as follows: In the next section, we present the computational model and definitions. In Section 3, we present the algorithm for knot detection. In Section 4, we prove the correctness of the algorithm. In Section 5, we discuss how the performance of the algorithm can be improved and conclude in Section 6.

2. System Model and Definitions

Computation is organized in spatially separated processes, $\{P_1, P_2,..., P_n\}$, which are connected by a set of bidirectional communication channels. The processes do not share a common memory and communicate with each other solely by passing messages over the communication channels. Messages are delivered reliably with finite but arbitrary time delay. The organization can be described as a graph in which vertices represent the processes and edges represent communication channels.

We also make the following assumptions [13].

1. If a node i sends a message to node j, that message gets appended to the end of $j's$ unbounded length input buffer. This assumption is for ease of exposition.

2. Messages sent from a node i to node j arrive at j's input buffer in the order they are sent.

3. Two messages arriving simultaneously can be ordered arbitrarily and appended to the buffer.

The problem is to detect if a node i is in a knot in the problem graph, which is a directed subgraph of the communication graph. For instance, the problem graph could be a wait-for-graph of a resource allocator. We assume that the problem graph does not change during the execution of the algorithm. For simplicity, we assume that only one process initiates the knot detection. If multiple processes initiate knot detection, the initiations can be distinguished by initiator id and a sequence number associated with the initiation.

3. Our Knot-Detection Algorithm

In this section, we present the basic idea behind our algorithm. Then, we present the algorithm formally and provide a detailed explanation.

3.1. Basic Idea

The initiating node of the algorithm determines if it is in a knot in the graph by checking if every node that is reachable from the initiator node i is on a cycle that passes through the initiator. A node j is said to be reachable from node i if there is a directed path in the graph from i to j. Since no node has complete knowledge of the topology of the graph, the initiator diffuses *detect_knot* message to all nodes in the reachable part of the graph; the *reachable part* of the graph is the set of all those nodes to which there is a directed path from the initiator. In other words, to initiate knot detection, the initiating node sends *detect_knot* message to all its immediate successors; a node j is an immediate successor of a node i in the graph if and only if there is a directed edge (i, j) from node i to node j. Each node receiving the first *detect_knot* message propagates it to all its immediate successors. Thus, *detect_knot* messages propagate to all the nodes that are reachable from the initiator.

The edges along which the first *detect_knot* message is received by each node induce a directed spanning tree (DST) rooted at the initiator.

If the initiator i receives the *detect_knot* message from a node j, i sends a *cycle_ack* reply to j. This *cycle_ack* message informs node j that node j is on a cycle with the initiator. It can be concluded that all the nodes in the DST that lie on a path from the initiator i to node j are also on a cycle with the initiator. In general, if a node k lies on a directed path that joins i and a node that is known to be on a cycle with i, then node k also lies on a cycle with i. The problem is to find an efficient technique to determine if a node in the DST lies on a path that passes from i to a node that is known to be on a cycle with i. This problem is solved as follows:

After a node knows that it is on a cycle with i, it sends *cycle_ack* acknowledgment to all the nodes from which it receives *detect_knot* message thereafter. This message informs the recipients that they are also on a cycle with i. However, after receiving the first *detect_knot* message, a node k may receive a *detect_knot* message from some other node j before knowing if it is on a cycle with i; in this case, node k sends *seen_ack* acknowledgment to node j as soon as it receives *detect_knot*. This message basically informs node j that k has already seen a *detect_knot* message. When j receives the *seen_ack* acknowledgment from k, it includes the ordered pair (j, k) in a local variable. Later, if k is found to be on a cycle with i, it can be concluded from this ordered pair that j is also on a cycle with i. After node j has received acknowledgments from all its immediate successors, it sends a *parent_ack* acknowledgment to its parent. The *parent_ack* lists the nodes that are known to j to be on a cycle with i as well as the set of all ordered pairs of the form (j, l) that j has stored locally as a result of *seen_ack* acknowledgments from its successors. This information about the nodes that are known to be on a cycle with the initiator as well as the set of ordered pairs (j, l) collected are propagated back in the DST until it reaches i.

The initiator i keeps the set of all nodes that are known to be on a cycle with i in a variable called $Incycle_i$. It also keeps the set of all the collected ordered pairs (l, m) in the variable $Seen_i$. For each $j \in Incycle_i$, if $(k, j) \in Seen_i$, then node i concludes that k is on a cycle with i and removes (k, j) from $Seen_i$ and includes k in the set $Incycle_i$. If $Seen_i$ becomes empty, then i concludes that it is in a knot. If i concludes that it is in a knot, then the variable $Cycle\_nodes$ contains exactly the ids of the nodes involved in the knot (see the algorithm in Section 3.2).

3.2. The Algorithm

We now give pseudocode for the knot detection algorithm: As before, we call the initiator i ; it has the following variables:

- OUT_i: A set of node ids, initialized to the set of immediate successors of i in the graph.

- $Seen_i$: A set of ordered pairs of node ids. An ordered pair $(k, j) \in Seen_i$ implies that there is a path from i to k and an edge from k to j in the graph; it also means that both k and j have seen the *detect_knot* message and when j received the *detect_knot* message from k, j did not know if it is on a cycle with the initiator. Initially, $Seen_i$ is empty.

- $Incycle_i$: A set of node ids, initially empty. Node $k \in Incycle_i$ implies k is in a cycle with i.

- $Cycle\_nodes_i$: A set of node ids, initially empty. When the algorithm terminates, if i is in a knot, this variable contains the ids of all the nodes involved in the knot. Initially, it is empty.

- $done_i$: This is a boolean variable, initially set to false.

A node k other than the initiator, has the variables, OUT_k, $Seen_k$, $Incycle_k$ and $done_k$ whose functions are similar to the corresponding variables at node i. In addition, node k also has the following variables.

- has_seen_k: This is a boolean variable which is set to true when node k receives the first *detect_knot* message. Initially, it is set to false.

- $parent_k$: Node k sets this variable to the id of the node from which it received the first *detect_knot* message. Initially, it is set to 0, meaning it has no parent node.

The algorithm at the initiating node i (i.e. Process P_i) and the algorithm at any other node k (i.e., Process P_k) are given below in CSP (communicating sequential processes) [9] like program. We do not strictly adhere to the syntax described in [9] so that the algorithm can be easily understood. The algorithm at the initiating node i is given as a process P_i (Figure 1) with a *repetitive command* having 5 alternative *guarded commands*. The algorithm at any other node k is given as a process P_k (Figure 2) with a *repetitive command* having 5 alternative *guarded commands*. A guarded command is of the form:

$$Guard \longrightarrow Command$$

We call a guarded command an *Action*. An *Action* is enabled if it's *Guard* becomes true. Each enabled *Action*, when executed, is executed atomically. If several *Actions* are enabled at an instant, then only one of these enabled *Actions* is picked randomly and executed. We assume that each enabled action is given a fair chance for execution. Next, we explain the algorithm given in Figure 1 and Figure 2.

Process P_i: /* the knot detection algorithm at the initiator node i */
OUT_i: set of node ids(initially *the set of all immediate successors of* i);
$Seen_i$: set of ordered pairs of node ids(initially *empty*);
$Incycle_i$: set of node ids(initially *empty*);
$Cycle\_nodes_i$: set of node ids(initially *empty*); /* nodes that are in cycle with i */
$done_i$: boolean(initially *false*);

send $detect\_knot(i, i)$ to all nodes in OUT_i;

*[$\neg done_i \wedge$
 receive $\quad parent\_ack(Seen_k, Incycle_k)$
 from P_k
	$\longrightarrow$	$OUT_i := OUT_i - \{k\}$;
		 $Seen_i := Seen_i \cup Seen_k$;
		 if $Incycle_k = \emptyset$ then
		 $\quad\quad Seen_i := Seen_i \cup \{(i,k)\}$;
		 else
		 $\quad\quad Incycle_i := Incycle_i \cup Incycle_k$;
			/*Action 1*/

[]
$\neg done_i \wedge$ receive $seen\_ack(k)$ from P_k $\longrightarrow$ $OUT_i := OUT_i - \{k\}$;   /* Action 2*/
                                                          $Seen_i := Seen_i \cup \{(i,k)\}$;

[]
$\neg done_i \wedge$ receive $cycle\_ack(k)$ from P_k $\longrightarrow$ $OUT_i := OUT_i - \{k\}$;   /*Action 3*/
                                                          $Incycle_i := Incycle_i \cup \{k\}$;

[]
$\neg done_i \wedge$ receive $detect\_knot(i, k)$ from $\longrightarrow$ send $cycle\_ack(i)$ to P_k;   /*Action 4*/
P_k
[]
$\neg done_i \wedge OUT_i = \emptyset$ $\longrightarrow$ for each $j \in Incycle_i$ do   /*Action 5*/]
                                                  $Incycle_i := Incycle_i - \{j\}$;
                                                  $Cycle\_nodes_i := Cycle\_nodes_i \cup \{j\}$;
                                                  for each k do
                                                       if $(k, j) \in Seen_i$ then
                                                             $Incycle_i := Incycle_i \cup \{k\}$;
                                                             $Seen_i := Seen_i - \{(k, j)\}$;
                                              if $Seen_i = \emptyset$ then
                                              Declare *'knot detected'*;
                                              else
                                              Declare *'no knot detected'*;
                                              $done_i := true$

Figure 1. Algorithm at the initiating site i

Process $P_k(k \neq i)$: /* algorithm at any node k other than the initiator i */
has_seen_k: boolean(initially $false$);
OUT_k: set of node ids(initially *the set of all immediate successors of k*);
$Seen_k$: set of ordered pairs of node ids(initially *empty*);
$Incycle_k$: set of node ids(initially *empty*);/* nodes that are in cycle with i */
$parent_k$: a node id (initially 0);
$done_k$: boolean(initially $false$);

```
*[ receive detect_knot(i, j) from Pj      ⟶  if ¬has_seenk then                          /*Action 1*/
                                                 has_seenk := true;
                                                 parentk := j;
                                                 send detect_knot(i, k) to all
                                                 nodes in OUTk;
                                              else
                                                 if Incyclek ≠ ∅ then
                                                     send cycle_ack(k) to Pj;
                                                 else
                                                     send seen_ack(k) to Pj;

[]
¬donek∧                          receive ⟶  OUTk := OUTk − {j};                           /*Action 2*/
parent_ack(Seenj, Incyclej)       from      Seenk := Seenk ∪ Seenj;
Pj                                          if Incyclej = ∅ then
                                                 Seenk := Seenk ∪ {(k, j)};
                                            else
                                                 Incyclek := Incyclek ∪ Incyclej;

[]
¬donek∧ receive seen_ack(j) from Pj   ⟶  OUTk := OUTk − {j};                             /*Action 3*/
                                         Seenk := Seenk ∪ {(k, j)};

[]
¬donek∧ receive cycle_ack(j) from Pj  ⟶  OUTk := OUTk − {j};                             /*Action 4*/
                                         Incyclek := Incyclek ∪ {j};

[]
¬donek ∧ OUTk = ∅ ∧ has_seenk    ⟶  if Incyclek ≠ ∅ then                                /*Action 5*/
                                        Incyclek = Incyclek ∪ {k};
                                     send parent_ack(Seenk, Incyclek) to parentk;
                                     donek := true;

]
```

Figure 2. Algorithm at any non-initiating site k

3.3. An Explanation of the Algorithm

When node i wants to find out if it is in a knot, it sends $detect\_knot(i,i)$ message to all the nodes in OUT_i (*Action 1* of Figure 1). The first parameter of the $detect\_knot$ message is the id of the initiator and the second parameter is the id of the node propagating the message. When node k receives the $detect\_knot(i,j)$ message from node j, it takes one of the following actions (*Action 1* of Figure 2):

1. If it is the first $detect\_knot$ message received, it sets its *parent* to j and propagates the $detect\_knot$ message to all the nodes in OUT_k.

2. If it has already seen a $detect\_knot$ message and $Incycle_k \neq \emptyset$, then it sends $cycle\_ack(k)$ to j. When node j receives this acknowledgment, it includes the id k in the set $Incycle_j$. ($Incycle_k \neq \emptyset$ implies that k is on a cycle with i which implies that j is also on a cycle with i).

3. If it has already seen a $detect\_knot$ message and $Incycle_k = \emptyset$, then it sends $seen\_ack(k)$ acknowledgment to site j. After receiving this message, j includes the ordered pair (j,k) in its local variable $Seen_j$ so that if later k is found to be on a cycle with the initiator, the initiator can conclude that j is also on a cycle with the initiator.

When the initiator receives $detect\_knot$ message back from a node k (*Action 4* of Figure 1), it sends $cycle\_ack(i)$ message to node k so that k knows that it is on a cycle with i (*Action 4* of Figure 1). So, when node k receives $cycle\_ack(i)$ for a $detect\_knot$ message, it includes id i in the set $Incycle_k$ so that k can conclude that it is also in cycle with the initiator (*Action 4* of Figure 2). When node k receives $seen\_ack(j)$ for a $detect\_knot$ message from a node j, it includes the ordered pair (k,j) in the variable $Seen_k$ (*Action 3* of Figure 2). $(k,j) \in Seen_k$ implies j is an immediate successor of k and k is reachable from i. Later, when this information reaches node i, if node i finds that j is on a cycle with i, then it can conclude that node k is also on a cycle with i. When k receives $parent\_ack(Seen_j, Incycle_j)$ message from one of its children in the DST, it updates its variables $Seen_k$ and $Incycle_k$ (*Action 2* of Figure 2).

After a node k has received acknowledgment from all its successors (i.e., when $OUT_k = \emptyset$), it includes its id in the set $Incycle_k$ if it finds at least one of its immediate successors is on a cycle with i (i.e., $Incycle_k \neq \emptyset$) and sends $parent\_ack(Seen_k, Incycle_k)$ message to its parent (*Action 5* of Figure 2).

After receiving acknowledgment from all its immediate successors (i.e., when $OUT_i = \emptyset$), *Action 5* is executed by the initiating node i (Figure 1). Note that after node i has received acknowledgment from all its immediate successors,

for each node j that is reachable from i, either $j \in Incycle_i$ or $(k,j) \in Seen_i$ for some node k, reachable from i (see Observation 5 below). If $j \in Incycle_i$ and $(k,j) \in Seen_i$, then k is also on a cycle with i. Therefore, after the execution of *Action 5* (Figure 1), the variable $Cycle\_nodes_i$ contains the ids of all the nodes reachable from i that are on a cycle with i. If $Seen_i$ becomes empty, which means all the nodes reachable from i are on a cycle with i (see Theorem 1 below), then node i declares '*knot detected*'.

4. Properties of the Algorithm

In this section, we prove the correctness. We also illustrate with examples how the information about the nodes in the knot can be used for deadlock resolution. First, we make the following observations.

4.1. Observations

Observation 1: When an initiator propagates a $detect\_knot$ message, it is eventually received by all nodes of the communication graph that can be reached from node i.

Observation 2: After a $detect\_knot$ message has been received by all nodes reachable from i, *parent* variables at nodes induce a directed spanning tree (DST) of the nodes reachable from i.

Observation 3: Every node in the DST diffuses $detect\_knot$ messages along all its outgoing edges in the communication graph.

Definition: Let $pred(j)$ denote the predecessor node of node j, in the DST.

Definition: *Distance* of a node j, denoted by $dst(j)$, in the DST is defined as:

$$dst(i)= 0$$
$$dst(j)=dst(pred(j))+1 \text{ if } j \neq i$$

Let $dst_{max} = max\{dst(j)\}$. Clearly, $dst_{max} \leq d$, the diameter of the communication graph.

Observation 5: When *Action 5* of process P_i (Figure 1) is enabled, for every node j that is reachable from i, either or both of the following holds:

(i) $j \in Incycle_i$ (ii) $(k,j) \in Seen_i$ for some k that is reachable from i.

This is because of the following: From Observation 2, every node that is reachable from i is in the DST. Also every node $j \neq i$ in the DST sends $parent\_ack(Seen_j, Incycle_j)$ to its parent (*Action 5* of P_j Figure 2). Before sending this acknowledgment, node j includes its id j in the set $Incycle_j$ if $Incycle_j \neq \emptyset$ (*Action 5* of P_j); if $Incycle_j = \emptyset$, then the node k receiving the $parent\_ack(Seen_j, Incycle_j)$ message includes the ordered pair (k,j) in its variable $Seen_k$ (*Action 2* of P_k, $k \neq i$

or *Action 1* of P_i). Thus, for each node j that is reachable from i, either j was included in the variable $Incycle_j$ or an ordered pair (k, j) was included in the variable $Seen_k$ for some node k that is reachable from i. The values of the variables $Incycle_k$ and $Seen_k$ are passed up in the DST with the *parent_ack* message. Each node receiving these values adds them to their corresponding local variables and passes those values to its parent and so on (*Action 2, 5* of P_k). Thus, for each node j that is reachable from i, either j must be included in $Incycle_i$ or an ordered pair (k, j) must be included in $Seen_i$ before P_i executes *Action 5*.

4.2. Correctness Proof

Lemma 1 *If node i is in a knot, then P_i declares* 'knot detected'.

Proof: Note that P_i declares 'knot detected' only after the execution of *Action 5* (Figure 1). Thus, it is sufficient to prove that after the execution of *Action 5*, $Seen_i = \emptyset$; this is because after executing *Action 5*, node i declares '*knot detected*' only if $Seen_i = \emptyset$. Let $(l, m) \in Seen_i$ just before the execution of *Action 5*.
Claim: (l, m) will be removed from $Seen_i$ during the execution of *Action 5*.
Proof of Claim: $(l, m) \in Seen_i$ implies that node m has sent either $seen\_ack(m)$ or $parent\_ack(Seen_m, Incycle_m)$ with $Incycle_m = \emptyset$ to node l (*Action 2* and *3* of P_l, $l \neq i$ or *Action 1* and *2* of P_i, $l = i$). However, since node i is inside a knot, there is a path $\{m_1(= m), m_2, \cdots, m_n(= i)\}$ from node m to node i in the communication graph. Clearly, when i received the $detect\_knot(i, m_{n-1})$ message from node m_{n-1}, it must have sent $cycle\_ack(i)$ acknowledgment to m_{n-1}(*Action 4* of P_i). After receiving this acknowledgment, node m_{n-1} must have included i as well as m_{n-1} in the set $Incycle_{m_{n-1}}$ before sending $parent\_ack$ acknowledgment to its parent (*Action 4* and *5* of $P_{m_{n-1}}$). This means node $m_{n-1} \in Incycle_i$ before *Action 5* was executed at node i. Let j be the smallest integer $(1 \leq j < n - 1)$ such that $m_j \notin Incycle_i$ before the execution of *Action 5* at node i (if there exists no such integer, then $m_j \in Incycle_i \, \forall \, j$ implies that $m_1(= m) \in Incycle_i$ which implies that (l, m) would have been removed from $Seen_i$ during the execution of *Action 5* of P_i and this proves our claim in this case). This means for each integer l $(1 \leq l \leq j)$ node m_l has either received $seen\_ack_{m_{l+1}}$ or $parent\_ack(Seen_{m_{l+1}}, Incycle_{m_{l+1}})$ with $Incycle_{m_{l+1}} = \emptyset$ from m_{l+1} (*Action 2* and *3* of P_{m_l} and *Action 1* of P_i). This means $(m_l, m_{l+1}) \in Seen_i$ for all l such that $(1 \leq l \leq j)$ before the execution of *Action 5*. Since $m_{j+1} \in Incycle_i$, the ordered pairs (m_j, m_{j+1}), (m_{j-1}, m_j), ... $(m_1(= m), m_2)$ and then (l, m) would have been removed from $Seen_i$ during the execution of *Action 5*. This proves our claim.

Since (l, m) is an arbitrary element in $Seen_i$, we have proved that all the elements of $Seen_i$ would have been removed during the execution of *Action 5*. So, $Seen_i = \emptyset$ after the execution of *Action 5* and hence P_i declares '*knot detected*' if i is indeed in a knot. □

Lemma 2 *If P_i declares* 'knot detected', *then node i is in a knot.*

Proof: P_i declares '*knot detected*' only if after the execution of *Action 5*, $Seen_i = \emptyset$. So, it is sufficient to prove that $Seen_i = \emptyset$ after the execution of *Action 5* implies that node i is in a knot. From Observation 5, for each node j that is reachable from i, either j was included in $Incycle_i$ or an ordered pair (k, j) was included in $Seen_i$ for some node k that is reachable from i. Note that during the execution of *Action 5*, every node in the set $Incycle_i$ is on a cycle with i and an ordered pair $(k, j) \in Seen_i$ is removed from $Seen_i$ during the execution of *Action 5* only if $j \in Incycle_i$.

So, after the execution of *Action 5*, $Seen_i = \emptyset$ implies that all the nodes reachable from i are on a cycle with node i. Hence, node i is in a knot. □

Theorem 1 *When Process P_i terminates, P_i declares* 'knot detected' *if and only if node i is in a knot.*

Proof: Follows from Lemmas 2 and 3. □

4.2.1 Deadlock Freedom

When a node receives the first *detect_knot* message, it forwards it to all its immediate successors in the communication graph and waits for their reply to send a *parent_ack* message to its parent. However, upon receiving all successive *detect_knot* messages, it sends a reply immediately; nodes that have no successors also send reply immediately. When the initiator of the knot detection algorithm receives the *detect_knot* message back, it sends a reply immediately. This prevents circular wait from happening. Hence the algorithm is deadlock-free.

On termination of the algorithm, if the algorithm declares 'knot detected', then the variable $Cycle\_nodes_i$ at the initiator contains exactly the ids of the nodes that are involved in the knot. The information about all the nodes involved in the knot is valuable for the purpose of deadlock resolution.

5. Performance of the Algorithm

When we look at *Action 5* of process P_i in the algorithm, it appears as though the algorithm is centralized and not distributed. The amount of work done by the initiator in *Action 5* can be reduced by allowing part of the work to be done by the other processes. To distribute the work more evenly

$$\neg done_k \wedge OUT_k = \emptyset \wedge has\_seen_k \longrightarrow \text{if } Incycle_k \neq \emptyset \text{ then} \qquad\qquad\qquad\qquad /*Action\ 5*/$$

$$Incycle_k = Incycle_k \cup \{k\};$$
$$\text{for each } j \in Incycle_k \text{ do}$$
$$Incycle_k := Incycle_k - \{j\};$$
$$Cycle\_nodes_k := Cycle\_nodes_k \cup \{j\};$$
$$\text{for each } m \text{ such that } (m,j) \in Seen_k \text{ do}$$
$$Incycle_k := Incycle_k \cup \{m\};$$
$$Seen_k := Seen_k - \{(m,j)\};$$
$$Incycle_k := Cycle\_nodes_k;$$
$$\text{send } parent\_ack(Seen_k, Incycle_k) \text{ to } parent_k;$$
$$done_k := true;$$

Figure 3. Modification of *Action 5* of a non-initiating node k

among all the nodes, we can change *Action 5* of process P_k as follows: Like the initiating process P_i, every other process P_k should have a variable $Cycle\_nodes_k$ initialized to the empty set and *Action 5* of process P_k should be changed as in Figure 3. Before sending *parent_ack*, based on the current information, each process computes all the nodes involved in a cycle with the initiator, thus reducing the amount of work done by the initiator.

6. Concluding Remarks

Knot detection in a communication graph is an important problem and finds applications in several domains of distributed systems design, such as store-and-forward networks, distributed simulation, and distributed databases. In this paper, we presented a distributed algorithm to detect if a given node in a communication graph is in a knot. The algorithm requires $2e$ messages and $2(dst_{max}+1)$ message hops delay to detect if a node is involved in a knot (e is the number of edges in the subgraph generated by the nodes reachable from the initiator). The algorithm helps not only in detecting if a node is involved in a knot but also finds exactly which nodes are involved in the knot. We also illustrated with examples on how the information about the nodes involved in the knot can be used for deadlock resolution.

Acknowledgment

We thank the anonymous referees for their valuable comments and suggestions which helped in improving the paper.

References

[1] A. Boukerche and C. Tropper. "A Distributed Graph Algorithm for the Detection of Local Cycles and Knots". *IEEE Transactions on Parallel and Distributed Systems*, 9(8):748–757, August 1998.

[2] J. Brezezinski, J. Helary, M. Raynal, and M. Singhal. "Deadlock Models and a Generalized Algorithm for Distributed Deadlock Detection". *Journal of Parallel and Distributed Computing*, 31(2):112–125, December 1995.

[3] I. Cidon. "An Efficient Distributed Knot Detection Algorithm". *IEEE Trans. on Software Eng.*, 15(5):644–649, May 1989.

[4] E. W. Dijkstra. "In reaction to Ernest Chang's Deadlock Detection.". EWD702, Plataanstraat 5, 5671 AL Nuenen, The Netherlands, 1979.

[5] E. W. Dijkstra and C. S. Scholten. "Termination Detection for Diffusing Computation". *Info. Process. Lett.*, 11(1):1–4, August 1980.

[6] G. Gambosi, D. Bovet, and D. Menascoe. "A Detection and Removal of Deadlocks in Store and Forward Communication Networks". In *Performance of Computer-Communication Systems*, pages 219–229, H. Rudin and W. Bux: editors, 1984. North-Holland.

[7] D. Gifford. "Weighted Voting for Replicated Data". In *Proc. of 7th Symp. on Operating Systems Principles*, pages 150–162, December 1979.

[8] B. Groselj and C. Tropper. "The Distributed Simulation of Clustered Processes". *Distributed Computing*, 4:111–121, 1991.

[9] C. A. R. Hoare. "Communicating Sequential Processes". *Communications of the ACM* , 21(8):666–677, August 1978.

[10] E. Knapp. "Deadlock Detection in Distributed Database Systems". *ACM Computing Surveys*, 19(4):303–328, December 1987.

[11] A. D. Kshemkalyani and M. Singhal. Efficient detection and resolution of generalized distributed deadlocks. *IEEE Transactions on Software Engineering*, 20(1):43–54, Jan. 1994.

[12] J. Misra. "Distributed Discrete-Event Simulation". *ACM Computing Surveys*, 18(1):39–65, March 1986.

[13] J. Misra and K. Chandy. "A Distributed Graph Algorithm: Knot Detection". *ACM Trans. on Programming Languages and Systems*, pages 678–686, 1982.

An Optimal Randomized Ranking Algorithm on the k-channel Broadcast Communication Model *

Koji Nakano
School of Information Science
Japan Advanced Insitute of Science and Technology
Tatsunokuchi, Ishikawa 923-1292, JAPAN
knakano@jaist.ac.jp

Abstract

A Broadcast Communication Model (BCM, for short) is a distributed system with no central arbiter populated by n processing units referred to as stations. The stations can communicate by broadcasting/receiving data packets in one of k communication channels. We assume that the stations run on batteries and expands power while broadcasting/receiving a data packet. Thus, the most important measure to evaluate algorithms on the BCM is the number of awake time slots, in which a station is broadcasting/receiving a data packet. We also assume that the stations are identical and have no unique ID number, and no station knows the number n of the stations. For given n keys one for each station, the ranking problem asks each station to determine the number of keys in the BCM smaller than its own key. The main contribution of this paper is to present an optimal randomized ranking algorithm on the k-channel BCM. Our algorithm solves the ranking problem, with high probability, in $O(\frac{n}{k} + \log n)$ time slots with no station being awake for more than $O(\log n)$ time slots. We also prove that any randomized ranking algorithm is required to run in expected $\Omega(\frac{n}{k} + \log n)$ time slots with at least one station being awake for expected $\Omega(\log n)$ time slots. Therefore, our ranking algorithm is optimal.

1 Introduction

A *Broadcast Communication Model* (BCM, for short) is a distributed system with no central arbiter populated by p processing units referred to as *stations*. The stations are identical and cannot be distinguished by serial or manufacturing numbers. Further, no station knows the number n of

* Work supported in part by the Ministry of Education, Science, Sports, and Culture, Government of Japan, Grant-in-Aid for Young Scientist Research (14780220)

stations in the BCM. For definiteness, the stations are assumed to have the computing power of the random access machine (RAM), and to be synchronous – in particular, they all run the same algorithm and can generate random bits that provide "local data" on which the stations may perform computations. The stations can communicate using k distinct communication channels. We assume that in a unit time slot, each station can broadcast a *data packet* to one of the channels and can receive a data packet from one (possibly the same) channel.

The fundamental characteristic of the model is the broadcast nature of communications. A data packet broadcast in a channel can be received by every station tuned to the channel. The nature of the stations is immaterial: they could be processors in a parallel computing environment or radio transceivers in a wireless network. Likewise, the nature of the broadcast is immaterial: it could be a global bus in a multiprocessor system or a radio frequency channel in a radio network. It is important to note that the BCM model provides a common generalization of bus-based parallel architectures, cluster computing environment, local area networks, and single-hop radio networks. Although the BCM is assumed to be operate in synchronous mode, we do not prescribe a particular synchronization mechanism. We feel that this is best left to the particular application.

We assume that the BCM has the following collision detection capability. In the BCM, the status of a channel is: *NULL:* if no station broadcasts on the channel in the current time slot; *SINGLE:* if exactly one station broadcasts on the channel in the current time slot; and *COLLISION:* if two or more stations broadcast on the channel in the current time slot. The status of a channel can be detected by stations that tune to it. We also assume that broadcasting/receiving a data packet in the BCM is very costly. If the stations run on batteries, saving battery power is exceedingly important, as recharging batteries may not be possible while on mission. It is well known that a station expends power while its transceiver is active, that is, while broadcasting or receiving a packet. Consequently, we are interested in developing algorithms that allow the stations to power their transceiver off (i.e. go to sleep) to the largest extent possible. Accordingly, we judge the goodness of a algorithm by the following two yardsticks: *running time slots*: the overall number of time slots required by the algorithm to terminate, *awake time slots*: for each individual station the total number of time slots when it has to be *awake* in order to broadcast/receive a data packet.

We formalize the *ranking problem* on the BCM as follows: Let $X = \{x_1, x_2, \ldots, x_n\}$ be a set of n distinct keys with total order. The *rank $r(x_i)$* of key x_i $(1 \leq i \leq n)$ is the number of keys in X smaller than x_i. We assume that the n keys are distributed to the n stations so that each station is storing one key. The ranking problem asks each station storing key x_i $(1 \leq i \leq n)$ to compute the rank $r(x_i)$. We also assume that a data packet transferred through a channel can contain at most one key. It is clear that $\Omega(\frac{n}{k})$ time slots are required to solve the ranking problem under this assumption, because every key must be broadcast at least once.

If all of the n stations have unique IDs in $[1, n]$, we can use known efficient parallel sorting algorithms to design energy-efficient ranking algorithms on the BCM. For example, the AKS sorting network [1], which is one of the most efficient parallel sorting algorithms can be implemented on the the k-channel n-station BCM ($k \leq n$) as follows: The AKS sorting network sorts n keys by repeating $\frac{n}{2}$ parallel compare-exchanges for $O(\log n)$ times. Each compare-exchange operation compares two keys and exchanges them if necessary. Since k channels are available, k keys can be transferred in a time slot. Hence, $\frac{n}{2}$ parallel compare-exchanges can be implemented in $\frac{n}{k}$ time slots with each station being awake for two time slots. Since this operation is repeated for $O(\log n)$ times, the AKS sorting network can be implemented on the k-channel BCM to run in $O(\frac{n \log n}{k})$ time slots with no station being awake for more than $O(\log n)$ time slots. Note that, after sorting, each key x_i is stored in station $r(x_i)$. By routing $r(x_i)$ to station i in obvious way, the ranking problem can be solved in $O(\frac{n \log n}{k})$ time slots with no station being awake for more than $O(\log n)$ time slots. However, this algorithm is not time-optimal for the $\Omega(\frac{n}{k})$ lower bound.

Several results of sorting have been obtained in the context on limited bandwidth. Nakano [11] showed that the n-processor network with k global buses, which is essentially the same as the the k-channel n-station BCM, can sort n keys in $O(\frac{n}{k})$ if $k \leq n^{1-\epsilon}$ for any small fixed $\epsilon > 0$. Later, it has shown in [13] that the k-channel n-station BCM can sort n keys in $3\frac{n}{k} + o(\frac{n}{k})$ time slots provided that $k \leq \sqrt{\frac{n}{2}}$. The running time slots of these algorithms are optimal for the $\Omega(\frac{n}{k})$ lower bound. However, these algorithms are not

energy-efficient, because the stations must be awake for almost all the $O(\frac{n}{k})$ running time slots. Further, these algorithms cannot be adapted to the BCM with many channels. The challenge is to find a ranking algorithm which runs on the k-channel BCM, for every k, in $O(\frac{n}{k} + \log n)$ time slots with no station being awake for more than $O(\log n)$. The main contribution of this paper is to present a randomized ranking algorithm that attains this performance with high probability.

We first present a ranking algorithm that runs on the k-channel n-station BCM for every k, with high probability, in $O(\frac{n}{k} + \log n)$ time slots with no station being awake for more than $O(\log n)$ time. We then go on to show the lower bounds of the running and the awake time slots for the ranking on the k-channel n-station BCM. We first prove that, if each station can store a constant number of keys in its local memory, then every randomized algorithm needs to run in expected $\Omega(\frac{n}{k} + \log n)$ time slots with at least one station being awake for expected $\Omega(\log n)$ time slots. Thus, our algorithm is optimal, because it uses a limited size of storage. We also show that, even if every station has unlimited size of local memory and is allowed to perform unlimited number of operations on the local memory in each time slot, the ranking problem requires to run in expected $\Omega(\frac{n}{k} + \frac{\log n}{\log \log n})$ time slots with with at least one station being awake for expected $\Omega(\frac{\log n}{\log \log n})$ time slots.

2 Outline of our ranking algorithm

In this section, we show outline of our ranking algorithm. The detailed implementation will be discussed in Section 5. Throughout this paper, log denotes the logarithm to the base 2 unless otherwise mentioned.

Our ranking algorithm first picks $\frac{n}{\log n}$ keys uniformly at random as *samples* from $X = \{x_1, x_2, \ldots, x_n\}$ and sorts them. Let p_i $(0 \leq i \leq \frac{n}{\log n} - 1)$ denote the i-th smallest sample keys. We take every $\log n$ keys in sorted order as *pivots* from the $\frac{n}{\log n}$ keys. Let $q_j = p_{j \log n}$ $(0 \leq j \leq \frac{n}{(\log n)^2} - 1)$ denote pivots thus obtained. We partition the n keys into $\frac{n}{(\log n)^2} + 1$ groups $Q(0), Q(1), \ldots, Q(\frac{n}{(\log n)^2})$ such that each $Q(j)$ contains the keys larger than or equal to q_{j-1} and smaller than q_j, where $q_{-1} = -\infty$ and $q_{\frac{n}{(\log n)^2}} = +\infty$ for convenience. Let a_i be the index of Q such that x_i is in group $Q(a_i)$. In other words, each key x_i is in the range $[q_{a_i-1}, q_{a_i})$. We compute the *local rank $l(i)$* of each key x_i $(1 \leq i \leq n)$ within the group $Q(a_i)$, which is the number of smaller keys in $Q(a_i)$. We then compute the prefix-sum $|Q(0)| + |Q(1)| + \ldots + |Q(j)|$ for every j $(1 \leq j \leq \frac{n}{(\log n)^2})$. Let $g(i)$ $(1 \leq i \leq n)$ be the prefix-sum $|Q(0)| + |Q(1)| + \ldots + |Q(a_i - 1)|$ if $a_i \geq 1$ and 0 if $a_i = 0$. Finally, each station storing x_i $(1 \leq i \leq n)$ computes $l(i) + g(i)$, which is equal to the desired rank

$r(x_i)$ of x_i.

Figure 1 illustrates the values of local variables computed in our ranking algorithm for $n = 27$ stations. In the figure, for convenience, the log to the base 3 is used, so $\log n = \log_3 n = 3$. The leftmost 9 keys are chosen as samples, and they are sorted. Three pivots 11, 31, and 49 are selected from the samples, and they are used to partition into four groups.

Surprisingly, as we are going to show in Section 5, groups $Q(i)$s are well balanced so that none of the $\frac{n}{(\log n)^2}$ groups has more than $16(\log n)^2$ keys with high probability. Using this fact, stations in $Q(i)$ can concentrate on the task for $Q(i)$ and can sleep during that for the other groups. This idea enables us to obtain an energy-efficient ranking algorithms.

3 A brief refresher of probability theory

We first review elementary probability theory results that are useful for analyzing the performance of our ranking algorithm. For a more detailed discussion of background material we refer the reader to [10]. We then go on to show the analysis of several probabilistic events, which is used to evaluate our ranking algorithm.

Throughout, $\Pr[A]$ denotes the probability of event A. Let X be a random variable denoting the number of successes in n independent Bernoulli trials with success probability p. It is well known that X has a *binomial distribution* and that for every r, $(0 \le r \le n)$,

$$\Pr[X = r] = \binom{n}{r} p^r (1-p)^{n-r}.$$

Further, the expected value of X is given by

$$E[X] = \sum_{r=0}^{n} r \cdot \Pr[X = r] = np.$$

To analyze the tail of the binomial distribution, we shall make use of the following estimates, commonly referred to as *Chernoff bounds* [10]:

$$\Pr[X < (1-\epsilon)E[X]] < e^{-\frac{\epsilon^2}{2}E[X]} \quad (0 \le \epsilon \le 1). (1)$$
$$\Pr[X > (1+\epsilon)E[X]] < e^{-\frac{\epsilon^2}{3}E[X]} \quad (0 \le \epsilon \le 1). (2)$$

For later reference, we state two lemmas which can be obtained using the Chernoff bounds. Due to the stringent page limitation we omit their proofs. The proofs will be shown in the journal version of this paper.

Lemma 3.1 *For every n and m, in order to have n head coins, a fair coin is flipped at most $6n + 10m$ times with probability at least $1 - e^{-m}$.*

Lemma 3.2 *Suppose that, for enough large n, we have $\frac{n}{\log n}$ red and $n - \frac{n}{\log n}$ black bins each of which can store one ball, and have n balls partitioned into $\frac{n}{8(\log n)^2}$ groups with $8(\log n)^2$ balls each. If the n balls are thrown into the n bins at random, every group occupies at least $\log n$ red bins with probability at least $1 - n^{-2}$.*

4 Subalgorithms used in our ranking algorithm

The main purpose of this section is to show fundamental algorithms necessary to implement our ranking algorithm on the BCM.

4.1 PRAM simulation, sorting, and computing prefix-sums

The *CRCW-PRAM* is a parallel machine with synchronous processors and a shared memory [6, 7]. We assume that, if two or more processors write on the same memory cell simultaneously, a special collision symbol is written on it. We are going to show that CRCW-PRAM algorithm can be implemented on the k-channel BCM efficiently. Without loss of generality, we assume that one CRCW-PRAM step is either a *reading step* or a *writing step*. In a reading step, processors can read from one of the shared memory cells, and no processor writes on the shared memory. Similarly, no processor reads from the shared memory in a *writing step*. We will show that reading and writing steps on the PRAM can be simulated by stations on the BCM.

Suppose that an algorithm on the CRCW-PRAM runs in $T(n)$ time using n processors and $M(n)$ shared memory cells. To simulate this algorithm, $M(n)$ shared memory cells are equally assigned to n stations at most $\lceil \frac{M(n)}{n} \rceil$ cells each. Each processor maintains the assigned $\lceil \frac{M(n)}{n} \rceil$ cells stored in its local memory. To simulate a reading step, a station broadcast the values of $\lceil \frac{M(n)}{n} \rceil$ memory cells in turn into k channels. More specifically, the first k stations broadcast the value of the assigned memory cells in $\lceil \frac{M(n)}{n} \rceil$ time slots. The remaining stations repeat the same process. The broadcast by k stations is repeated for $\lceil \frac{n}{k} \rceil$ times at all. Since every memory cell is broadcast, the reading operation by the PRAM processor can be simulated by receiving a data packet on the corresponding channel in an appropriate time slot. Clearly, this task can be done in $\lceil \frac{n}{k} \rceil \lceil \frac{M(n)}{n} \rceil = O(\frac{M(n)}{k} + 1)$ time slots. Further, every station broadcasts in $\lceil \frac{M(n)}{n} \rceil$ time slots and receives a packet in at most one time slot, and thus no station is awake for more than $O(\frac{M(n)}{k} + 1)$ time slots. The writing operation by PRAM processors can be simulated by stations similarly, Thus, we have the following important lemma:

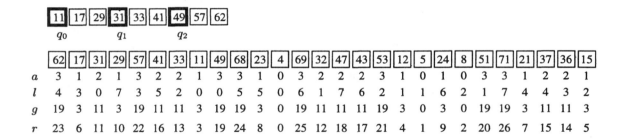

Figure 1. The values of local variables computed in our ranking algorithm

Lemma 4.1 *Any parallel algorithm running on the CRCW-PRAM in $T(n)$ time using n processors and $M(n)$ shared memory cells can be simulated on the k-channel BCM with n stations in $\left(\frac{T(n)M(n)}{k} + T(n)\right)$ time slots with no station being awake for more than $O\left(\frac{T(n)M(n)}{n} + T(n)\right)$ time slots.*

It is well-known that the EREW-PRAM with n processors can sort n keys in $O(\log n)$ time by the AKS sorting network [1]. Since $T(n) = O(\log n)$ and $M(n) = O(n)$, the k-channel BCM with n stations can sort n keys in $O\left(\frac{n \log n}{k} + \log n\right)$ time slots with no station being awake for more than $O(\log n)$ time slots. However, the AKS sorting network has an extremely large constant coefficient in $T(n)$. If our ranking algorithm uses the AKS sorting network as a subroutine, it may have unrealistic large constant factor in time slots. On the other hand, Cole's optimal merge sort, which terminates in $O(\log n)$ time using n processors on the EREW-PRAM [5] has a small constant factor. However, it needs $M(n) = O(n \log n)$ shared memory cells. Alternatively, we use the $\sqrt{n}$ *sample sort* [7, pp.470] which runs, with probability at least $1 - O(n^{-6})$, in $O(\log n)$ time using n-processor and $O(n)$ shared memory cells on the CRCW-PRAM. Using the $\sqrt{n}$ *sample sort* and the simulation result in Lemma 4.1, we have,

Corollary 4.2 *The task of sorting n keys in the k-channel BCM with n stations can be done in $O\left(\frac{n \log n}{k} + \log n\right)$ time slots with no station being awake for more than $O(\log n)$ time slots with probability at least $1 - O(n^{-6})$.*

It is known that, by recursive execution of Column-sort [9], sorting can be done efficiently on limited communication bandwidth models [2, 11]. For example, suppose that, for arbitrary fixed $\epsilon > 0$, $n^{1-\epsilon}$ channels are available to sort n keys. It has been shown in [11] that the sorting can be done in $O(n^\epsilon)$ time slots by repeating the Column-sort. Since the communication of each channel can be simulated by a shared memory cell in an obvious way, the sorting of n keys on the n-processor PRAM can be done in $T(n) = O(n^\epsilon)$ time using $M(n) = n^{1-\epsilon}$ shared memory cells. Thus, from the simulation result in Lemma 4.1, we have

Corollary 4.3 *For every fixed $\epsilon > 0$, the task of sorting n keys in the k-channel BCM with n stations can be done in $O\left(\frac{n}{k} + n^\epsilon\right)$ time slots with no station being awake for more than $O(n^\epsilon)$ time slots.*

It is well known that the n-processor EREW-PRAM can compute the prefix-sums of n numbers in $O(\log n)$ time using $O(n)$ memory cells [6, pp.13]. Thus, by according to the simulation result in Lemma 4.1, we have

Corollary 4.4 *The task of computing the prefix-sums of n numbers in the k-channel BCM with n stations can be done in $O\left(\frac{n \log n}{k} + \log n\right)$ time slots with no station being awake for more than $O(\log n)$ time slots.*

By a complicated implementation of the prefix-sums algorithm, the awake time slots can be reduced to $O(1)$ [15]. We do not have to use this complicated implementation for the ranking.

4.2 Initialization

This subsection is devoted to show initialization algorithms that gives unique IDs in the range to $[1, n]$ to the n stations in the BCM.

We briefly explains a non-energy efficient initialization algorithm, which has presented in [14]. The algorithm repeats partitioning the stations into two subsets by flipping a fair coin as follows. First, every station flip a fair coin and they are partitioned into two subsets. Let P_1 and P_2 be the two subsets with heads and tails, respectively. The stations in P_1 broadcast on the channel. Clearly, the status of the channel is NULL if P_1 is empty, SINGLE if P_1 has one station, and COLLISION if P_1 has two or more stations. If P_1 has one station, then an ID 1 is assigned to it. If P_1 has two or more stations, then, by recursion, IDs are given to all the stations in P_1. After that, the same procedure is executed for P_2.

In order to evaluate the running time slots, we will trace the behavior of stations using a binary tree as follows: Initially, all the stations are in the root. Every station moves to one of the left or right children at random by flipping a coin. The station repeats moving to one of the two children until no other stations are in the same node. If a station is alone in some node it receives an ID and terminates moving. It is easy to see that the running time slots corresponds to the number of nodes that have visited by a station. We say that, after termination of the algorithm, a node is

- *single* if one station has visited it,
- *null* if no station has visited it although two or more stations have visited its parent,
- *good* if two or more station have visited it and both of the children are non-empty,
- *bad* if two or more station have visited it and one of the children is empty.

We are going to evaluate the number of these nodes. Let N_s, N_n, N_g, and N_b denote the number of single, null, good, and bad nodes in the binary tree. It is easy to confirm that $N_s = n$, $N_g = n - 1$ and $N_n = N_b$. Further, one broadcast is performed for each of these four types of nodes. Hence, the running time T satisfies

$$
\begin{aligned}
T &= N_s + N_n + N_g + N_b \\
&= 2N_b + 2n - 1.
\end{aligned}
$$

Thus, we are going to evaluate N_b to get a good estimation of T. If m stations ($m \geq 2$) are visiting a node, then it will be good with probability at least $1 - 2(\frac{1}{2})^m \geq \frac{1}{2}$. Hence, from Lemma 3.1, with probability at least $1 - e^{-m}$, we have no more than $6n + 10m$ internal nodes (i.e either good or bad nodes). It follows that $N_b + N_g \leq 6n + 10m$ with probability at least $1 - e^{-m}$. Hence, we have $N_b \leq 5n + 10m + 1$. Thus, the initialization algorithm runs in $12n + 20m + 1$ time slots with probability at least $1 - e^{-m}$. Note that every station have to be awake for all the time slots in this algorithm.

Lemma 4.5 *The BCM with n stations can be initialized in $12n + 20m + 1$ time slots with probability at least $1 - e^{-m}$ for every $m \geq 1$.*

Using this algorithm, we show an energy-efficient initialization algorithm on the k-channel BCM ($k \leq \log n$) which will be used in our ranking algorithm to initialize each $Q(i)$. We assume that $Q(i)$ has $16(\log n)^2$ stations. Our goal is to initialize stations in $Q(i)$ in $O(\frac{\log n^2}{k})$ time slots with no station being awake for more than $O(\log n)$ time slots with high probability. The idea is to partition the $16(\log n)^2$ stations into $\log n$ subgroups equally at random.

For this purpose, each station in the BCM randomly choose an integer in the range $[1, \log n]$. Let $G(i)$ ($1 \leq i \leq \log n$) denote the set of stations that have selected i. Clearly, $E[|G(i)|] = 16 \log n$. Using the Chernoff bound (2), the probability that a particular $G(i)$ has more than $32 \log n$ stations is at least

$$
\begin{aligned}
\Pr[|G(i)| > 32 \log n] &= \Pr[|G(i)| > (1+1)E[|G(i)|]] \\
&< e^{-\frac{1}{3} 16 \log n} < n^{-7.6}.
\end{aligned}
$$

Thus, all the subgroups have at most $32 \log n$ stations with probability at least $1 - n^{-7.6} \log n > 1 - n^{-7}$. Using Lemma 4.5, a subgroup with less than $32 \log n$ stations can be initialized in $12(32 \log n) + 20(2 \log n) + 1 = 424 \log n + 1$ time slots with probability at least $1 - e^{-2 \log n} > 1 - n^{-2.8}$. Hence, we use $424 \log n + 1$ time slots to initialize a subgroup. Because k ($\leq \log n$) channels are available, k subgroups can be initialized concurrently. Thus, all of the subgroups can be initialized in $\lceil \frac{\log n}{k} \rceil \cdot (424 \log n + 1) = O(\frac{(\log n)^2}{k})$ time slots. The stations in subgroup $G(i)$ are awake for $424 \log n + 1$ time slots to initialize $G(i)$, and they are sleep during the initialization of the other subgroups. Hence, the stations are awake for $424 \log n + 1 = O(\log n)$ time slots. It follows that, no subgroup fails to initialize with probability at least $1 - n^{-2.8} \log n > 1 - n^{-2}$. Thus, we have,

Lemma 4.6 *With probability at least $1 - n^{-2}$, the task of initializing a set of $16(\log n)^2$ stations on the k-channel ($k \leq \log n$) BCM can be done in $O(\frac{(\log n)^2}{k})$ time slots with no stations being awake for more than $O(\log n)$ time slots.*

5 Implementation of our ranking algorithm

We are now in position to show the implementation of our ranking algorithm on the k-channel BCM. The details are spelled out as follows.

Step 1 Initialize the stations in the BCM. Let $S(i)$ ($1 \leq i \leq n$) denote the station with ID i, and x_i denote the key stored in $S(i)$.

Step 2 Let $x_1, x_2, \ldots x_{\frac{n}{\log n}}$ be the sample keys and sort them such that $S(i)$ ($1 \leq i \leq \frac{n}{\log n}$) is storing p_i, the i-th smallest sample keys. After that, each $S(j \log n)$ ($0 \leq j \leq \log n - 1$) is storing a pivot q_j.

Step 3 Each $S(i)$ ($1 \leq i \leq n$) finds an index a_i such that x_i is in $Q(a_i)$.

Step 4 Initialize the stations within each $Q(j)$. At the end of Step 4, the stations in each $Q(j)$ has IDs in the range $[1, |Q(j)|]$.

Step 5 Sort keys within each $Q(j)$ using the local ID obtained in Step 4 to compute the local rank of the keys. At the end of Step 5, every station $S(i)$ knows the local rank $l(i)$.

Step 6 Compute the prefix-sums of $|Q(0)|$, $|Q(1)|$, $\ldots$, $|Q(\frac{n}{(\log n)^2})|$. At the end of Step 5, every station $S(i)$ knows the global rank $g(i)$.

Step 7 Each $S(i)$ $(1 \leq i \leq n)$ computes $l(i) + g(i)$ which is equal to $r(i)$.

We are going to show that each step can be implemented to run for at most $O(\frac{n}{k} + \log n)$ time slots with no station being awake for more than $O(\log n)$ time slots with probability at least $1 - O(n^{-1})$.

Step 1 can be done in $O(\frac{n}{k} + \log n)$ time slots with no station being awake for more than $O(\log n)$ time slots with probability at least $1 - O(n^{-1.83})$ using the initialization algorithm in [3].

By Corollary 4.2, the $\frac{n}{\log n}$ sample keys can be sorted in $O(\frac{\frac{n}{\log n} \cdot \log \frac{n}{\log n}}{k} + \log \frac{n}{\log n})$ time slots with no station being awake for more than $O(\log \frac{n}{\log n})$ time slots with probability at least $1 - O((\frac{n}{\log n})^{-6})$. Thus, Step 2 can be done in $O(\frac{n}{k} + \log n)$ time slots with no station begin awake for more than $O(\log n)$ time slots with probability at least $1 - O(n^{-5})$. Note that the initializing algorithm performed in Step 1 gives unique IDs to the stations uniformly at random. Thus, the $\frac{n}{\log n}$ sample keys stored in $S(1), S(2), \ldots, S(\frac{n}{\log n})$ are randomly chosen from the n keys.

Step 3 can be done by traversing a binary search tree of pivots defined as follows. Imagine a binary search tree of nodes $q_0, q_1, \ldots, q_{\frac{n}{(\log n)^2}-1}$ such that the median $q(\frac{n}{2(\log n)^2} - 1)$ is the root. The left subtree is the binary search tree of $q_0, q_1, \ldots, q_{\frac{n}{2(\log n)^2}-2}$ and the right is that of $q_{\frac{n}{2(\log n)^2}}, \ldots, q_{\frac{n}{(\log n)^2}-1}$. Each station traverses the binary tree from the root to a leaf. Station $S(i)$ moves to the left child if x_i is smaller than the current pivot, and goes to the right child, otherwise. At the leaves each station $S(i)$ can determine the value of a_i. This traverse can be implemented as follows: Station $S(\frac{n}{2(\log n)^2})$ broadcast $q(\frac{n}{2(\log n)^2})$ to the fist channels and every station received it. Next, the left and the right children are broadcast on the first and second channels, respectively. Every station receives one of them. This broadcast is repeated until all of the $\frac{n}{(\log n)^2}$ pivots are broadcast on channels. Let h be the binary tree. Clearly, $h = \log \frac{n}{2(\log n)^2} - 1 = O(\log n)$. The level i $(1 \leq i \leq h)$ of the binary search tree has 2^{i-1} pivots. Using k channels, these 2^{i-1} pivots can be broadcast in $\lceil \frac{2^{i-1}}{k} \rceil$ time slots. Hence all of the pivots can be broadcast in $\sum_{i=1}^{h} \lceil \frac{2^{i-1}}{k} \rceil = O(\frac{n}{k(\log n)^2} + h) \leq O(\frac{n}{k} + \log n)$ time

slots. Further, all stations broadcast a pivot at most once and receive pivots for h times. Thus, no station is awake for more than $O(\log n)$ time slots.

Before showing Step 4, we will evaluate the number of keys in each $Q(i)$ using Lemma 3.2. Recall that the initialization in Step 1 gives the n stations unique IDs in the range $[1, n]$ uniformly at random. This is analogous to throwing the n balls into the n bins. In other words, the n keys are "thrown" into the n stations at random. The stations with IDs in $[1, \frac{n}{\log n}]$ correspond to red bins. Suppose that the n keys are partitioned into $\frac{n}{8(\log n)^2}$ groups $B(1), B(2), \ldots, B(\frac{n}{8(\log n)^2})$ of $8(\log n)^2$ keys each such that the keys in $B(i+1)$ is larger than those in $B(i)$ for every i $(1 \leq i \leq \frac{n}{8(\log n)^2})$. That is, $B(i)$ is a set of keys with ranks in $[8(\log n)^2(i-1)+1, 8(\log n)^2 i]$. From Lemma 3.2, with probability at least $1 - n^{-2}$, every $B(i)$ contains at least $\log n$ samples. If this is the case, then every $B(i)$ includes at least one pivot. It follows that, with probability at least $1 - n^{-2}$, every $Q(i)$ has no more than $16(\log n)^2$ keys Thus, we have the following lemma:

Lemma 5.1 *The probability that $|Q(i)| \leq 16(\log n)^2$ for all i $(0 \leq i \leq \frac{n}{(\log n)^2})$ is at least $1 - n^{-2}$.*

We use the algorithm for Lemma 4.6 to initialize the stations storing $Q(i)$ for each i $(0 \leq i \leq \frac{n}{(\log n)^2})$. If $|Q(i)| \leq 16(\log n)^2$, then using k channels ($k \leq \log n$), stations storing keys in $Q(i)$ can be initialized in $O(\frac{(\log n)^2}{k})$ time slots with no station being awake for more than $O(\log n)$ time slots with high probability. Suppose that we assign k ($\leq \log n$) channels to each group use the algorithm in Lemma 4.6 to initialize each group. Since we have $\frac{n}{(\log n)^2}$ groups, all of the groups succeed in being initialized in $O(\frac{(\log n)^2}{k})$ time slots ($k \leq \log n$) with no station being awake for more than $O(\log n)$ time slots with probability at least $1 - n^{-2} \cdot (\frac{n}{(\log n)^2} + 1) > 1 - n^{-1}$. We assume that all of the groups succeed in being initialized and evaluate the time slots and awake time slots as follows.

Case 1: $\frac{n}{(\log n)^2} + 1 \leq k \leq \frac{n}{\log n}$. We assign $k' = \frac{k}{\frac{n}{(\log n)^2}+1}$ channels to initialize a group. All of the groups can be initialized in $O(\frac{(\log n)^2}{k'}) = O(\frac{n}{k})$ time slots with no station being awake for more than $O(\log n)$ time slots.

Case 2: $k \leq \frac{n}{(\log n)^2}$. We assign $\frac{\frac{n}{(\log n)^2}+1}{k}$ groups to a channel to initialize them. Each channel is used to initialize these groups by the algorithm for Lemma 4.6, in turn, using one channel. Each group is assigned $O((\log n)^2)$ time slots and the stations having the keys in the group execute the initialization algorithm using one channel assigned. The stations in a group are asleep while the initialization for the other groups is executed. Thus, every station is awake for $O(\log n)$ time slots. Further, all the groups can be initialized in $\frac{n}{k(\log n)^2} \cdot O((\log n)^2) = O(\frac{n}{k})$ time slots.

Thus, in Step 4, all the groups can be initialized in $O(\frac{n}{k})$ time slots with no station being awake for more than $O(\log n)$ time slots with probability $1 - n^{-1}$.

Since every station in $Q(i)$ has unique ID in the range $[1, |Q(i)|]$ we can use a deterministic sorting to compute the local ranks. Using the algorithm for Corollary 4.3 with $\epsilon = \frac{1}{2}$, we can sort $16(\log n)^2$ keys in $O(\frac{(\log n)^2}{k} + \log n)$ time slots with no station being awake for more than $O(\log n)$ time slots. In Step 5, we sort the groups concurrently using the k channels similarly to the initialization in Step 4. If $k > \frac{n}{(\log n)^2}$, then all the groups can be sorted in $O(\frac{(\log n)^2}{k'} + \log n) = O(\frac{n}{k} + \log n)$ time slots with no station being awake for more than $O(\log n)$ time slots. If $k \leq \frac{n}{(\log n)^2}$, every group can be sorted in $\frac{n}{k(\log n)^2} \cdot O((\log n)^2) = O(\frac{n}{k})$ time slots with no station being awake for more than $O(\log n)$ time slots. Thus, Step 5 can be done in $O(\frac{n}{k} + \log n)$ time slots with no station begin awake for $O(\log n)$ time slots.

Recall that Step 4 initializes the stations in each $Q(i)$. Thus, at least one station knows the value of $|Q(i)|$. In Step 6, we first move the value of each $|Q(i)|$ to station $S(i)$ and then compute the the prefix-sums of $\frac{n}{(\log n)^2}$ integers $|Q(0)|, |Q(1)|, \ldots, |Q(\frac{n}{(\log n)^2} - 1)|$ using $S(0), S(1), \ldots, S(\frac{n}{(\log n)^2} - 1)$. From Corollary 4.4, the prefix-sums can be computed in $O(\frac{n}{k(\log n)^2} + \log n) < O(\frac{n}{k} + \log n)$ time slots with no station being awake for more than $O(\log n)$ time slots.

Step 7 can be done by broadcasting the prefix-sums in turn using k channels and by local computation. It takes $O(\frac{n}{k(\log n)^2}) < O(\frac{n}{k})$ time slots with each station being awake for $O(1)$ time slots.

Since every step can be done in $O(\frac{n}{k} + \log n)$ time slots with no station being awake for more than $O(\log n)$ time slots with probability at least $1 - O(n^{-1})$, finally, we have

Theorem 5.2 *The task of ranking n keys in the k-channel BCM with n stations can be done in $O(\frac{n \log n}{k} + \log n)$ time slots with no station being awake for more than $O(\log n)$ time slots with probability at least $1 - O(n^{-1})$.*

6   Lower bounds

This section is devoted to discuss the lower bounds for the sorting problem on the initialized BCM. Since the ranking problem can be reduced to the sorting problem easily, the same lower bounds hold for the ranking problem on the uninitialized BCM.

From the bandwidth argument, it is clear that any sorting algorithm takes at least $\Omega(\frac{n}{k})$ time, because every key must be broadcast at least once. We show the limit of acceleration under the following two assumptions in terms of the size of storage of stations: *limited storage*: Each station can store a constant number of keys in its local memory. *unlimited storage*: Each station can store unlimited number of keys in its local memory.

It is well known that any deterministic sorting algorithm needs $\Omega(n \log n)$ comparisons in the worst case as well as the average case [4, pp.172]. We briefly review this argument and related results. Let us consider the sorting problem on input $X = \{x_1, x_2, \ldots, x_n\}$. The sorted sequence of X is one of the possible $n!$ permutations of X. Any deterministic sorting algorithm on X can be represented by a *binary decision tree* such that the leaves are all possible $n!$ permutations and each internal node is associated with comparison of two keys in X. The sorting algorithm traverses the binary decision tree from the root to a leaf. At each internal node, the sorting algorithm moves to one of the two children by the result of the comparison. Clearly, the number of comparisons by the sorting algorithm on a particular input is the number of internal nodes on the path. Thus, the number of comparisons performed in the worst case is the number of internal nodes on the longest path. Since the binary decision tree has $n!$ leaves, there exists a path of length at least $\log n! = \Omega(n \log n)$. Hence, there exists an input X requiring $\Omega(n \log n)$ comparisons by the sorting algorithm. Next, we analyze the average comparisons over all input. We assume that all permutations have equal probability $\frac{1}{n!}$. It is not difficult to confirm that, on any binary tree with $n!$ leaves, the average length of all the $n!$ paths to the leaves is at least $\Omega(n \log n)$. Thus, if all permutations have equal probability, then any deterministic sorting algorithm need to perform expected $\Omega(n \log n)$ comparisons.

Using the *Yao's minimax principle* [16], the average analysis of deterministic algorithms gives a lower bound of the average case analysis of randomized algorithms. More precisely, the expected comparisons of the optimal deterministic sorting algorithm for an arbitrary chosen input distribution is a lower bound on the expected comparisons for the worst input performed by the optimal randomized algorithms. The readers should refer[10, pp.34] for the details of the Yao's minimax principle. It follows that any randomized sorting algorithm has the worst input on which it need to perform expected $\Omega(n \log n)$ comparisons.

On the BCM with limited storage, a station is awake and receives a new key, the station can compare the new key and keys in its local memory. Since it is storing a constant number of keys, it performs only a constant number of comparisons with the new key. In other words, a single awake time slot by a station can involve $O(1)$ comparison. It follows that $\Omega(n \log n)$ total awake time slots are necessary to solve the sorting problem. Hence, any randomized sorting algorithm with limited storage has at least one station that must be awake for expected $\Omega(\log n)$ awake time slots.

Next, we are going to show $\Omega(\frac{\log n}{\log \log n})$ lower bond of awake time slots for the unlimited storage BCM. We will evaluate how many meaningful comparisons can be performed after receiving a new key. Suppose that a station has been awake for s time slots and has received s keys. Thus, it is storing $s+1$ keys in its local storage. Let $y_0, y_1, \ldots, y_s$ ($y_0 < y_1 < \cdots < y_s$) denote the $s+1$ keys and z be a new key received by the station. By comparing z with the $s+1$ keys, the station can find i ($-1 \leq i \leq s$) such that $y_i < z < y_{i+1}$ where $y_{-1} = -\infty$ and $y_{s+1} = +\infty$. Similarly to the proof of the $\Omega(n \log n)$ lower bound, we associate this comparison of key z with the s keys with an internal node having $s+2$ children. Then, any deterministic sorting algorithm can be represented by a *decision tree*. Suppose that a deterministic sorting algorithm on the BCM solves the sorting problem with every station being awake for at most T time slots. Note that an awake time slot by a station is associated with an internal node of the decision tree. Clearly, no internal node has more than $T+1$ children. Further, the total awake time slot is nT, every path from the root to a leaf has nT internal nodes. Since the decision tree have $n!$ leaves, we have $(T+1)^{nT} \geq n!$. It follows that at least one station must be awake for $T = \Omega(\frac{\log n}{\log \log n})$ time slots. By applying the Yao's minimax principle to this lower bound, we have that any randomized sorting algorithm on the BCM with unlimited storage has at least one station that must be awake for expected $\Omega(\frac{\log n}{\log \log n})$ awake time slots. Further, since the running time slot cannot be smaller than the awake time slot any randomized algorithm must be run for expected $\Omega(\frac{n}{k} + \frac{\log n}{\log \log n})$ time slots. Finally, we have,

Theorem 6.1 *Any randomized algorithm that solves the sorting (or ranking) problem of n keys on the BCM with n stations must be run for*

- *expected $\Omega(\frac{n}{k} + \log n)$ time slots with at least one station being awake for expected $\Omega(\log n)$ time slots if storage is limited, and*

- *expected $\Omega(\frac{n}{k} + \frac{\log n}{\log \log n})$ time slots with at least one station being awake for expected $\Omega(\frac{\log n}{\log \log n})$ time slots if storage is unlimited.*

Note that our ranking algorithm is designed for the BCM with limited storage. Thus, our ranking algorithm is optimal under the limited storage assumption.

References

[1] M. Ajtai, J. Komlos, and E. Szemeredi, Sorting in $c \log n$ parallel steps, *Combinatorica*, 3, 1, pp.1–19, 1983.

[2] M. Adler, J. W. Byers, R. M. Karp, Parallel Sorting with Limited Bandwidth, *SIAM Journal on Computing* 29, 6, pp. 1997-2015, 2000

[3] J. L. Bordim, J. Cui, T. Hayashi, K. Nakano, and S. Olariu, Energy-efficient initialization protocols for ad-hoc radio network, *IEICE Trans. on Fundamentals*, E83-A, 9, pp.1796-1803, 2000.

[4] T. H. Cormen, C. E. Leiserson, R. L. Rivest, *Introduction to algorithms*, MIT Press, 1994.

[5] R. Cole, Parallel merge sort, *SIAM J. Computing*, 17, 4, 770-785, 1988.

[6] A. Gibbons and W. Rytter, *Efficient parallel algorithms*, Cambridte University Press, 1988.

[7] J. JáJá, *An introduction to parallel algorithms*, Addison-Wesley, 1992.

[8] D. Krizanc, A survey of randomness and parallelizm in comparison problems, *Advances in Randomized Parallel Computing*, Kluwer Academic Publishers, 25–39, 1999.

[9] F. T. Leighton, Tight bounds on the complexity of parallel sorting, *IEEE Trans. Computers*, 34, 4, 344-354, 1985.

[10] R. Motwani and P. Raghavan, *Randomized Algorithms*, Cambridge University Press, 1995.

[11] K. Nakano, Optimal sorting algorithms on bus-connected processor arrays, *IEICE Trans. Fundamentals*, E-76A, 11, pp.2008–2015, 1994.

[12] K. Nakano, Optimal initializing algorithms for a reconfigurable mesh, *J. Parallel and Distributed Computing*, 24, pp.218–223, 1995.

[13] K. Nakano, S. Olariu, and J. L. Schwing, Broadcast-efficient protocols for mobile radio network, *IEEE Trans. parallel and Distributed Systems*, 10, 12, 1276-1289, 1999.

[14] K. Nakano and S. Olariu, Randomized initialization protocols for ad-hoc networks, *IEEE Trans. on Parallel and Distributed Systems*, 11, 7, pp. 749–759, 2000.

[15] K. Nakano, and S. Olariu, Energy-efficient initialization protocols for single-hop radio networks with no collision detection, *IEEE Trans. on Parallel and Distributed Systems*, 11, 8, 851–863, 2000.

[16] A. C. Yao, Probablistic Computations: Towards a unified measure of complexity, *Proc. of 17th Symposium on Foundations of Computer Science*, pp. 222-227, 1977.

Computational Geometry On The OTIS-Mesh Optoelectronic Computer *

Chih-fang Wang
Department of Computer Science
Southern Illinois University
Carbondale, IL 62901
cfw@cs.siu.edu

Sartaj Sahni
Department of Computer and
Information Science and Engineering
University of Florida
Gainesville, FL 32611
sahni@cise.ufl.edu

Abstract

We develop efficient algorithms for problems in computational geometry—convex hull, smallest enclosing box, ECDF, two-set dominance, maximal points, all-nearest neighbor, and closest-pair—on the OTIS-Mesh optoelectronic computer. We also demonstrate the algorithms for computing convex hull and prefix sum with condition on a multi-dimensional mesh, which are used to compute convex hull and ECDF respectively. We show that all these problems can be solved in $O(\sqrt{N})$ time even with N^2 inputs.

Keywords *and* **phrases:** *optoelectronic computer, OTIS-Mesh, convex hull, smallest enclosing box, ECDF, two-set dominance, maximal points, all-nearest neighbor, closest-pair, prefix sum with condition.*

1 Introduction

It is well known that optical interconnect has superior power, speed, and crosstalk properties compared to electronic interconnect when the interconnect distance is more then a few millimeters [2, 5]. With this knowledge in mind, Marsden *et al.* [8], Hendrick *et al.* [4], and Zane *et al.* [18] have proposed an architecture in which the processors are partitioned into groups. Within each group electronic interconnect is used to connect the processors. Optical interconnect is used to connect processors in different groups.

The optical transpose interconnection system (OTIS) was proposed by Marsden *et al.* [8], where the processors are partitioned into groups of the same size. Processor i of group j is connected to processor j of group i via an optical connection. Krishnamoorthy *et al.* [6] have shown that

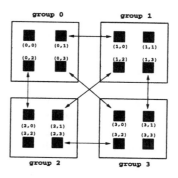

Figure 1. Example of OTIS connections with 16 processors

when the number of groups equals the number of processors within a group, the bandwidth and power efficiency are maximized, and system area and volume minimized. As a result, an N^2 processor OTIS computer is partitioned into N groups of N processors each for our study. Figure 1 shows a 16 processor OTIS architecture. The processor indices are of the form (G, P) where G is the group index and P the processor index within the group.

The OTIS-Mesh optoelectronic computer is a class of OTIS computers in which the electronic interconnect within each group follows the mesh paradigm [18, 13]. A 16 processor OTIS-Mesh computer is shown in Figure 2. The large boxes enclose groups of processors which are denoted by small boxes. The pair of numbers g, p inside a small box represents the group (g) and processor (p) indexes. Groups are numbered in row-major fashion, as they are laid out as a two-dimensional array. The pair (i, j) above a group denotes the row (i) and column (j) in which a group lies. Electronic links are indicated by arrows inside a group, while optical links are shown by arrows among groups. We shall refer to moves utilizing optical links as

---
*This work was supported, in part, by the National Science Foundation under grant CCR-9912395.

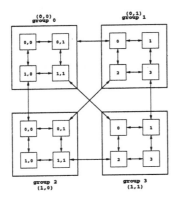

Figure 2. Example of OTIS-Mesh with 16 processors

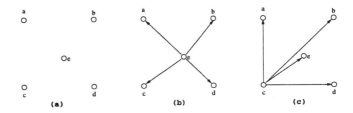

Figure 3. Example for Theorem 1:(a) original layout; (b) $p_i = e$; (c) $p_i = c$.

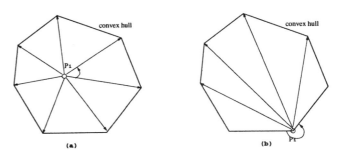

Figure 4. Relations of point p_i and the convex hull: (a) p_i is not an extreme point; (b) p_i is an extreme point.

OTIS moves.

Zane *et al.* [18] have shown that the OTIS-Mesh computer can simulate a $\sqrt{N} \times \sqrt{N} \times \sqrt{N} \times \sqrt{N}$ four-dimensional mesh computer. Sahni and Wang [13] have developed algorithms for data routing algorithms. Wang and Sahni have studied algorithms for basic operations [15] such as prefix sum, consecutive sum, concentrate, sort, and they have also developed algorithms for various matrix multiplication operations [17] and image processing problems [16].

In this paper, we develop algorithms for the following problems that arise in computational geometry: convex hull (CH), smallest enclosing box (SEB), ECDF, two-set dominance (2SD), maximal points (MP), all-nearest neighbor (ANN), and closest-pair for points (CPP). For each problem, we consider the two cases *(a)* An N point problem is to be solved on an N^2 processor OTIS-Mesh and *(b)* an N^2 point problem is to be solved on an OTIS-Mesh with N^2 processors. All of our algorithms run in $O(\sqrt{N})$ time.

2 Convex Hull

We wish to identify the extreme points of a set S of points in a plane. We assume that no three points are collinear.

2.1 $|S| = N$

Our algorithm employs the following result.

Theorem 1 *For any point $p_i \in S$, let $\{p_{j_0}, p_{j_2}, \ldots, p_{j_{N-2}}\} = S - \{P_i\}$ be such that the points $p_{j_0}, p_{j_2}, \ldots$ are sorted by the polar angle made by the vector $\overrightarrow{p_i p_{j_q}}$. Point p_i is an extreme point of S iff there is a k, $0 \leq k < N - 1$, such that the (counterclockwise) angle between $\overrightarrow{p_i p_{j_k}}$ and $\overrightarrow{p_i p_{j_{(k+1) \bmod N-1}}}$ is more than π.*

Proof First consider the example of Figure 3(a). Figure 3(b) shows the case $p_i = e$. For this case, $S - \{p_i\} = \{b, a, c, d\}$ (in polar angle order). The counterclockwise angle between every pair of consecutive vectors is $\pi/2$. According to our theorem, point e is not an extreme point. Figure 3(c) shows the case when $p_i = c$. Now, $S - \{p_i\} = \{d, e, b, a\}$ (in polar angle order). The counterclockwise angle between the consecutive vectors $\overrightarrow{cd}$ and $\overrightarrow{cd}$ is $3\pi/2$, and according to our theorem, point c is an extreme point.

To prove the theorem, note that when p_i is not an extreme point, it must lie inside the convex hull (p_i cannot be on the hull boundary because we have assumed that no three points of S are collinear). Figure 4(a) shows the situation. Since the enclosing convex hull has at least three vertices, the angle between any two vectors originating at p_i and ending at two consecutive vertices of the hull is less than π. Therefore the angle between any two vectors that are adjacent in polar order is all less than π.

When p_i is an extreme point on the convex hull, the angle between the vectors to the hull vertices that immediately precede and follow p_i on the convex hull is more than π. ∎

Theorem 1 results in the following algorithm to determine whether p_i is an extreme point of S.

Step 1: Sort the points $S - \{p_i\}$ by the polar angle of the vectors $\overrightarrow{p_i p_j}$, $p_j \in S - \{p_i\}$. Let $\{p_{j_0}, p_{j_2}, \ldots, p_{j_{N-2}}\}$

be the sorted sequence of points in $S - \{p_i\}$.

Step 2: If there is a k, $0 \leq k < N - 1$, such that the counterclockwise angle between $\overrightarrow{p_i p_{j_k}}$ and $\overrightarrow{p_i p_{j_{(k+1) \bmod N-1}}}$ is more than π, then p_i is an extreme point; otherwise, p_i is not an extreme point.

On an N^2 processor OTIS-Mesh, we can perform the above two steps, concurrently, for all points $p_i \in S$. The points that are determined to be extreme points can then be sorted into polar order with respect to any point in the interior of the convex hull. The resulting sorted order of extreme points defines the convex hull of S. The algorithm is given below. The N points of S are initially distributed, one to a processor, over the processors of group 0.

Step 1: Perform an OTIS move of the points in group 0.

Step 2: Processor 0 of group i, $0 \leq i < N$, broadcasts the point it received in Step 1 to all processors in its group. All processors in a group now have the same point in their A registers.

Step 3: Perform an OTIS move on the points in the A registers. The data is received into B registers. Now, each group i processor has the point p_i in its A register and a point of $S - \{p_i\}$ in its B register.

Step 4: Each processor computes the polar angle of the vector defined by the points in its A and B registers.

Step 5: Each group sorts, into snake-like order, the angles computed by its processors.

Step 6: Each processor in a group checks the condition of Theorem 1 by computing the angle between the vectors defined by p_i, the point in its B register, and the point in the B register of the next processor in the snake like order.

Step 7: Processor 0 of each group is notified by group processors that determine a point p_i is an extreme point.

Step 8: The points that pass the test of Theorem 1 are transmitted to group 0 via an OTIS move.

Step 9: The extreme points accumulated by group 0 are sorted by polar angle order.

Step 2 takes $2(\sqrt{N} - 1)$ electronic moves, Step 5 takes $(4 + \epsilon)\sqrt{N}$ electronic moves [10], and Steps 6 and 7 take up to $2(\sqrt{N} - 1)$ electronic moves each. For Step 9, we must first find a point that is in the interior of the convex hull. This is done by identifying any three of the hull vertices and then computing the centroid of these three vertices. The hull vertices are first moved leftwards in group

0. Then, these vertices are moved downwards to processor (0,0) until processor (0,0) has 3 vertices. The centroid is broadcast to all group 0 processors, the polar angles are computed, and then the hull vertices are sorted by polar angle. The sort takes $(4 + \epsilon)\sqrt{N}$ electronic moves [10] and the remaining operations of Step 9 take $4(\sqrt{N} - 1)$ electronic moves. Overall, our convex hull algorithm takes $(18 + \epsilon)\sqrt{N}$ electronic and 3 OTIS moves.

2.2 $|S| = N^2$

The $|S| = N^2$ $N \times N$ mesh convex-hull-algorithm of [9] is easily generalized to run on an $N^{2/d} \times N^{2/d} \times \cdots \times N^{2/d}$ d-dimensional mesh. The run time is $O(dN^{2/d})$. We simulate the resulting 4-dimensional mesh algorithm on a $\sqrt{N} \times \sqrt{N} \times \sqrt{N} \times \sqrt{N}$ OTIS-Mesh using the simulation strategy described in [18]. This results in an $O(\sqrt{N})$ convex hull algorithm for our N^2 processor OTIS-Mesh. A closer analysis reveals that the resulting algorithm performs $\geq 152\sqrt{N} + o(\sqrt{N})$ electronic moves and $\geq 144\sqrt{N} + o(\sqrt{N})$ OTIS moves.

3 Smallest Enclosing Box

In the smallest enclosing box (SEB) problem, we are given a set S of coplanar points and are to find a minimum area rectangle that encloses all points in S. It is well known [3] that the SEB of S has one side that is collinear with an edge of the convex hull of S and that the remaining three sides of the SEB pass through at least one convex hull vertex each.

3.1 $|S| = N$

Step 1: Compute the convex hull as in Section 2.1.

Step 2: Broadcast the hull vertices from group 0 to all remaining groups.

Step 3: Group i determines the ith hull edge (p_l, p_r) and broadcasts this to all processors within the group.

Step 4: Each group i processor determines the distance h between its hull vertex q (if any) and the ith hull edge (p_l, p_r) as well as the distance w to the perpendicular bisector L of the ith hull edge. If q and p_l are on the same side of L, set $l = -w$ and $r = 0$; otherwise, set $l = 0$ and $r = w$.

Step 5: Processor 0 of each group i computes the maximum of the h's and r's in its group and the minimum of the l's in its group. The area of the SEB that has one side collinear with (p_l, p_r) is $A_i = h_{\max} * (r_{\max} - l_{\min})$.

Step 6: Perform an OTIS move on the A_i's. Now all A_i's are in the group 0 processors.

Step 7: Processor 0 of group 0 determines the minimum A_i.

Step 1 takes $(18 + \epsilon)\sqrt{N}$ electronic and 3 OTIS moves (see Section 2.1), the remaining steps take $8\sqrt{N}$ electronic and 3 OTIS moves. Therefore, the overall complexity of the above SEB algorithm is $(26 + \epsilon)\sqrt{N}$ electronic and 6 OTIS moves.

3.2 $|S| = N^2$

The steps in any SEB algorithm (including the one of Section 3.1) are:

Step 1: Compute the convex hull of S.

Step 2: Find the furthest (*i.e.*, perpendicular distance to the edge) hull vertex for each hull edge.

Step 3: Find the leftmost (*i.e.*, distance is measured from the perpendicular bisector of the hull edge) hull vertex for each hull edge.

Step 4: Find the rightmost hull vertex for each hull edge.

Step 5: Each processor computes the enclosing box defined by the edge and points from the previous steps.

Step 6: Find the box with minimum area.

When $|S|$ equals the number of processors, Step 1 can be done in $O(\sqrt{N})$ time using the algorithm of Section 2.2. Step 5 takes $O(1)$ time, and Step 6 takes $O(\sqrt{N})$ time. Steps 2, 3, and 4 can also be done in $O(\sqrt{N})$ time by adapting the technique of [9].

Let $s(\overline{xy})$ be the slope of the convex hull edge $\overline{xy}$. Let h be the convex hull vertex that is farthest from $\overline{xy}$, let p be the hull vertex that precedes h, and let q be the hull vertex that follows h. In [9] it is shown that $s(\overline{hp}) \leq s(\overline{xy}) < s(\overline{hq})$. Therefore, if the hull edges are sorted by slope, the vertex h is easily identified. The leftmost and rightmost hull vertices may be found in a similar fashion by using the slopes $s(\overline{xy}) \pm \pi/2$. The algorithm to find the hull point h that is farthest from the hull edge $\overline{xy}$ is given below. This algorithm actually finds the farthest hull vertex for all edges $\overline{xy}$ that are on the upper hull (see Step 2.1). The algorithm for all edges of the lower hull is similar. Note that for any upper hull edge, the farthest hull vertex is on the lower hull.

Step 2.1: Let l and r, respectively, be the hull vertices with the least and maximum x-coordinates. Ties are broken arbitrarily. The line $\overline{lr}$ partitions the convex hull into two parts–lower and upper.

Step 2.2: Each processor that has a hull edge computes the slope of this edge and creates a tuple $t = (s, i, u, d)$, where s is the slope of the hull edge, i is the processor index, u is true iff the hull edge is part of the upper hull, and d is empty if u is true, and d is the right end point of the hull edge when u is false.

Step 3: Sort the tuples by the slope s. Ties are broken using the u value (false < true). Note that two edges on the upper (lower) hull cannot have the same slope. The tuple (if any) $t = (s, i, u, d)$ that a processor has is called its t-tuple. This t-tuple originated in processor i.

Step 2.4: Each processor that has a t-tuple with u =false creates a t'-tuple which is a copy of its t-tuple plus the processor's index. That is, $t' = (t, p)$.

Step 2.5: The t'-tuples are first ranked, then concentrated using their ranks, and finally generalized using the p values. Following the generalization, each processor has a t'-tuple.

Step 2.6: Each processor that has a t-tuple T with u =true sets the d value of this t-tuple T to the d value of its t'-tuple. This d value is the hull vertex that is farthest from the edge that resulted in the t-tuple T.

Step 2.7: Route the t-tuples back to their originating processors using the i values of the t-tuples.

Using the rank, concentrate, generalize, and sort algorithms of [15], we can complete the above seven steps in $O(\sqrt{N})$ time. The leftmost and rightmost hull points for each hull edge can similarly be found in $O(\sqrt{N})$ time. Following this, each edge can determine the area of the SEB that has one side collinear to this edge in $O(1)$ time, and the minimum of these area cab be then determined using an additional $O(\sqrt{N})$ time. Therefore, the overall SEB computation takes $O(\sqrt{N})$ time. A closer analysis reveals that the resulting algorithm performs $\geq 375\sqrt{N} + o(\sqrt{N})$ electronic moves and $\geq 144\sqrt{N} + o(\sqrt{N})$ OTIS moves.

4 ECDF

In the ECDF (*empirical cumulative distribution function*) problem, we are given a set S of distinct points in a plane. Point $p_i = (x_i, y_i) \in S$ dominates point $p_j = (x_j, y_j) \in S$ if and only if $x_i \geq x_j$ and $y_i \geq y_j$. For each point $p_i \in S$, we are to determine the number of points that it dominates. Figure 5 shows three points p_1, p_2, and p_3. p_1 and p_2 dominate p_3, p_1 does not dominate p_2, and p_2 does not dominate p_1. The numbers of points dominated by p_1, p_2, and p_3, respectively, are 1, 1, and 0.

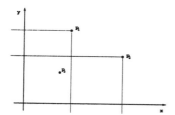

Figure 5. Example of dominating relation

4.1 $|S| = N$

We have enough processes to run the brute force algorithm–perform all N^2 pairs of point comparisons and count the number of points dominated by each point p_i—efficiently. The steps are given below. We begin with point p_i in processor i of group 0; *i.e.*, in processor $(0, i)$.

Step 1: Perform an OTIS move on the points initially in group 0. Now processor $(i, 0)$ has point p_i.

Step 2: Processor $(i, 0)$ broadcasts point p_i to the remaining processors in its group. Each processor saves its point in register A as well as register B.

Step 3: Perform an OTIS move on the register B data. Now, processor (i, j) has point p_i in register A, and point p_j in register B.

Step 4: Each processor sets its C register to 1 if its A register point dominates its B register point; the C register is set to 0 otherwise.

Step 5: Processor $(i, 0)$ computes the sum of the C values in its group.

Step 6: Perform an OTIS move on the sums computed in Step 5.

The complexity of the above algorithm is readily seen to be $4(\sqrt{N} - 1)$ electronic and 3 OTIS moves.

4.2 $|S| = N^2$

We begin with one point in each of the N^2 processors. The strategy is given below.

Step 1: Sort the N^2 points by x-coordinate, and within x-coordinate by y-coordinate.

Step 2: Each point $p_i = (x_i, y_i)$ determines the number of points to its left that have y-coordinates $\leq y_i$.

Step 3: The counts determined in Step 2 are routed back to the originating processors for the individual points.

Steps 1 is done in $O(\sqrt{N})$ time using the OTIS-Mesh sort algorithm of [15]. Step 2 is an example of the general prefix computation (GPC) operation described in [1]. We shall show below, how to do Step 2 in $O(\sqrt{N})$ time. Step 3 may be done in $O(\sqrt{N})$ time by sorting on the originating processor indexes.

Step 2 can be done in $O(\sqrt{N})$ time using a divide-and-conquer algorithm. Let $T = \{p_0, \ldots, p_{N^2-1}\}$ be the sorted point sequence. $C(p_i, T)$ be the number of points to the left of point $p_i = (x_i, y_i)$ that have y-coordinates $\leq y_i$. Let L and R, respectively, denote the left and right halves of T. Let T_y (L_y, R_y) denote the point sequence T (L, R) reordered by y-coordinate and within y-coordinate by x-coordinate. For each $p_i \in L$ (R), let $p_i' \in R_y$ (L_y) be the point with highest index of p_i. The the following equations are easily verified [1]:

$$
\begin{aligned}
C(p_i, S) &= \begin{cases} C(p_i, L), & p_i \in L \\ C(p_i, R) + P(p_i', L_y), & p_i \in R \end{cases} \\
P(p_i, S_y) &= \begin{cases} P(p_i, L_y) + P(p_i', R_y), & p_i \in L \\ P('p_i, L_y) + P(p_i, R_y), & p_i \in R \end{cases}
\end{aligned}
$$

where $P(p_i, S_y)$ is one more than the number of points to the left of p_i in S_y.

We may compute C and P in $O(n)$ time on an n^d processor d-dimensional mesh by partitioning the mesh into $2^d (n/2)^d$ processor submeshes, recursively computing the Cs and Ps of neighboring submeshes until we have the overall C and P. The combining involves sorting, ranking, concentration, and generalization, and takes $O(n)$ time. If $T(n)$ is the time required to compute the Cs and Ps on an n^d processor d-dimensional mesh, then

$$T(n) = T(n/2) + O(n) = O(n)$$

We may simulate the 4-dimensional mesh algorithm on an N^2 processor OTIS-Mesh using the techniques of [18] and compute the Cs and Ps in $O(\sqrt{N})$ time. Therefore, we can solve the N^2 point ECDF problem in $O(\sqrt{N})$ time on an N^2 processor OTIS-Mesh. A closer analysis reveals that the resulting algorithm performs $\geq 192\sqrt{N} + o(\sqrt{N})$ electronic moves and $\geq 136\sqrt{N} + o(\sqrt{N})$ OTIS moves.

5 Two-Set Dominance

In the *two-set dominance* (2SD) problem, we are given two sets S_1 and S_2 of points in a plane. For each point $p \in S_1$ (S_2) we wish to determine the number of points in S_2 (S_1) that are dominated by p. This problem is quite similar to the ECDF problem and is solved in $O(\sqrt{N})$ time by making minor modifications to the ECDF algorithm. Instead of counting all points dominated by p, we only count dominated points that are in a different set from p.

6 Maximal Points

A point $p \in S$ is maximal if and only if p is not dominated by any point in S. In the *maximal points* (MP) problem, we wish to identify all maximal points. This problem may be solved using the ECDF algorithms. Instead of counting the number of points that p dominates, we count the number of points that dominates p. Further simplification comes from realizing that instead of keeping a count of the number of points that dominate p, we can keep a boolean value that is true if and only if at least one point that dominates p has been detected. The complexity of the algorithm remains $O(\sqrt{N})$.

7 All-Nearest Neighbor

In this problem, we are given a set S of points. For each point $p \in S$, we are to find another point $q \in S, q \neq p$, such that the distance between p and q is minimum.

7.1 $|S| = N$

The algorithm for this case is similar to that given in Section 4. Steps 4-6 of that algorithm are changed to

Step 4': Each processor sets its C register to the distance between between the points in its A and B registers (if the points are the same, the C register is set to ∞).

Step 5': Processor $(i, 0)$ computes the minimum of the C values in its group and thereby identifies the nearest neighbor of the point in the group's A registers.

Step 6': Perform an OTIS move on the nearest neighbors computed in the $(i, 0)$ processors.

The overall complexity of the algorithm is the same as that for the ECDF algorithm of Section 4.

7.2 $|S| = N^2$

We use the divide-and-conquer strategy described in [12] and used in [9] to solve the problem on a 2-dimensional mesh. The steps are:

Step 1: Partition the N^2 points into d groups by x-coordinates and solve the all nearest neighbor problem in each group.

Step 2: Partition the N^2 points into d groups by y-coordinates and solve the all nearest neighbor problem in each group.

Step 3: Each point determines the closer of the two neighbors determined in Steps 1 and 2.

Step 4: The partitions of Steps 1 and 2 define d^2 rectangular regions. In each region, label the points that are closer to a corner of the region than to their nearest neighbor as determined in Step 3. There are at most 8 marked points in each region [9].

Step 5: Circulate the at most $8 \times d^2$ marked points through all N^2 processors. During this circulation process, these marked points determine their nearest neighbors.

The correctness of the algorithm has been established in [9] with $d = 5$. The algorithm is easily run on a 4-dimensional N^2 processor mesh with $d > 16$ so as to have complexity of $O(\sqrt{N})$. This results in an $O(\sqrt{N})$ OTIS-Mesh algorithm [18]. A closer analysis reveals that the resulting algorithm performs more than $8340\sqrt{N} + o(\sqrt{N})$ electronic moves and more than $8336\sqrt{N} + o(\sqrt{N})$ OTIS moves!

8 Closest-Pair of Points

The *closest-pair for points* (CPP) in S can be found by first solving the all nearest neighbor problem of Section 7 and then determining the closest pair from the nearest neighbor of each point. The additional effort needed is $2(\sqrt{N} - 1)$ electronic moves when $|S| = N$, and $4(\sqrt{N} - 1)$ electronic plus one OTIS moves when $|S| = N^2$.

9 Conclusion

We have shown that several computational geometry problem—convex hull, smallest enclosing box, ECDF, two-set dominance, maximal points, all-nearest neighbor, and closest-pair of points—can be solved in $O(\sqrt{N})$ time on an N^2 processor OTIS-Mesh. The algorithms for N points have much small constant factors than do the corresponding algorithms for N^2 points.

References

[1] S. Akl. *Parallel Computation: Models and Methods*. Prentice Hall, 1997.

[2] M. Feldman, S. Esener, C. Guest, and S. Lee. Comparison between electrical and free-space optical interconnects based on power and speed considerations. *Applied Optics*, 27(9):1742–1751, May 1988.

[3] H. Freeman and R. Shapira. Determining the minimal-area encasing rectangle for an arbitrary closed curve. *Communications of ACM*, 18:409–413, 1975.

[4] W. Hendrick, O. Kibar, P. Marchand, C. Fan, D. V. Blerkom, F. McCormick, I. Cokgor, M. Hansen, and S. Esener. Modeling and optimization of the optical transpose interconnection system. In *Optoelectronic Technology Center, Program Review*, Cornell University, Sept. 1995.

[5] F. Kiamilev, P. Marchand, A. Krishnamoorthy, S. Esener, and S. Lee. Performance comparison between optoelectronic and vlsi multistage interconnection networks. *Journal of Lightwave Technology*, 9(12):1674–1692, Dec. 1991.

[6] A. Krishnamoorthy, P. Marchand, F. Kiamilev, and S. Esener. Grain-size considerations for optoelectronic multistage interconnection networks. *Applied Optics*, 31(26):5480–5507, Sept. 1992.

[7] M. Kunde. Routing and sorting on mesh-connected arrays. In *Proceedings of the 3rd Agean Workshop on Computing: VLSI Algorithms and Architectures, Lecture Notes on Computer Science*, volume 319, pages 423–433. Springer Verlag, 1988.

[8] G. C. Marsden, P. J. Marchand, P. Harvey, and S. C. Esener. Optical transpose interconnection system architectures. *Optics Letters*, 18(13):1083–1085, July 1 1993.

[9] R. Miller and Q. F. Stout. Mesh computer algorithms for computational geometry. *IEEE Transactions on Computers*, 38(3):321–340, Mar. 1989.

[10] M. Nigam and S. Sahni. Sorting n^2 numbers on $n \times n$ meshes. In *Proceedings of the seventh International Parallel Processing Symposium (IPPS'93)*, pages 73–78, Newport Beach, California, 1993.

[11] M. Nigam and S. Sahni. Computational geometry on a reconfigurable mesh. In *Proceedings of the International Parallel Processing Symposium*, pages 86–93, 1994.

[12] F. P. Preparata and M. I. Shamos. *Computational Geometry: An Introduction*. Springer-Verlag, New York, 1985.

[13] S. Sahni and C.-F. Wang. BPC permutations on the OTIS-Mesh optoelectronic computer. In *Proceedings of the fourth International Conference on Massively Parallel Processing Using Optical Interconnections (MPPOI'97)*, pages 130–135, Montreal, Canada, 1997.

[14] S. Sahni and C.-F. Wang. BPC permutations on the OTIS-Hypercube optoelectronic computer. *Informatica*, 22:263–269, 1998.

[15] C.-F. Wang and S. Sahni. Basic operations on the OTIS-Mesh optoelectronic computer. *IEEE Transactions on Parallel and Distributed Systems*, 9(12):1226–1236, 1998.

[16] C.-F. Wang and S. Sahni. Image processing on the OTIS-Mesh optoelectronic computer. *IEEE Transactions on Parallel and Distributed Systems*, 11(2):97–109, 2000.

[17] C.-F. Wang and S. Sahni. Matrix multiplication on the OTIS-Mesh optoelectronic computer. *IEEE Transactions on Computers*, 50(7):635–646, 2001.

[18] F. Zane, P. Marchand, R. Paturi, and S. Esener. Scalable network architectures using the optical transpose interconnection system (OTIS). In *Proceedings of the second International Conference on Massively Parallel Processing Using Optical Interconnections (MPPOI'96)*, pages 114–121, San Antonio, Texas, 1996.

Session 7B

Communications

Worst Case Analysis of a Greedy Multicast Algorithm in k-ary n-cubes

Satoshi Fujita*

Graduate School of Engineering, Hiroshima University

Kagamiyama 1-4-1, Higashi-Hiroshima, Japan

fujita@se.hiroshima-u.ac.jp

Abstract

In this paper, we consider the problem of multicasting a message in k-ary n-cubes under the store-and-forward model. The objective of the problem is to minimize the size of the resultant multicast tree by keeping the distance to each destination over the tree the same as the distance in the original graph. In the following, we first propose an algorithm that grows a multicast tree in a greedy manner, in the sense that for each intermediate vertex of the tree, the outgoing edges of the vertex are selected in a non-increasing order of the number of destinations that can use the edge in a shortest path to the destination. We then evaluate the goodness of the algorithm in terms of the worst case ratio of the size of the generated tree to the size of an optimal tree. It is proved that for any k ≥ 5 and n ≥ 6, the performance ratio of the greedy algorithm is c × kn − o(n) for some constant 1/12 ≤ c ≤ 1/2.

Keywords: *k-ary n-cube, information dissemination, multicast tree, approximation ratio, analysis of algorithms.*

1 Introduction

A *multicast problem* is the problem of disseminating information from a *source vertex* to a set of *destination vertices* through a given interconnection network [4]. A multicast is used in many important applications such as video-on-demand systems, distance learning systems, and on-line game systems. Although a multicast from a source vertex can be achieved by repeating point-to-point communications to each recipient, such a naive scheme generally takes a long time proportional to the number of destination vertices. Hence, it is widely accepted that the problem should be solved

by flowing a packet through a *tree structure*, that may or may not be a subgraph of the given interconnection network, to have a favorable property depending on the communication model used in the underlying network.

For example, under the store-and-forward model, that is used in several classical parallel computers, the principal objective function to be minimized is the *distance* to the destinations in the derived subtree (in this case, the tree structure must be a subgraph of the original graph that contains the source and all destinations). It is also very important to minimize the *size* of the tree, i.e., the number of links contained in the tree, in order to minimize the traffic congestion caused by the multicast operation. If it adopts the single-port model, i.e., if each processor can access at most one link incident on it at a given time, the time required for a multicast is bounded from below by the logarithm of the number of destinations, since under such model, the number of vertices that have received the source information can at most double in each time unit. Hence in such a case, it is required to complete a multicast within a time that is close to the logarithmic bound as much as possible [8, 6, 7]. Under the wormhole routing model, on the other hand, we can assume that the time required for communication between a sender/receiver pair is independent of the distance between them provided that the transmitted message is long enough [3]. Hence under this model, it is rather easy to construct a tree structure that completes a multicast in a (near) optimal time [9], although it should be carefully addressed the problem of deadlock avoidance since under the wormhole routing model, each communication dynamically occupies much more resources than the store-and-forward model. Reservation of much resources increases the possibility of conflicts among several communications that may occur frequently in a tree-based multicasting. In the literature, there have been proposed several multicast algorithms under the wormhole routing

*This research was partially supported by the Ministry of Education, Culture, Sports, Science and Technology of Japan (# 13680417)

511

model, which address the issue of deadlock avoidance as the principal factor [1, 2].

In this paper, we consider the multicast problem in k-ary n-cubes under the store-and-forward model. The objective of the problem considered here is to minimize the size of the resultant tree by keeping the distance to each destination over the tree the same as the distance in the original graph. In the literature, such a tree is generally referred to as a *multicast tree* [12, 13], and it is known that the problem of finding a *minimum* multicast tree is NP-hard even if we restrict the class of graphs to binary n-cubes [13]. Note that we can always find a multicast tree for any given graph, and the size of any multicast tree is at most the diameter of the graph times the size of an optimal tree. So far, there have been proposed several heuristic algorithms for constructing a multicast tree in binary n-cubes [10, 11, 12, 14, 15, 16] and most of them could be directly applied to k-ary n-cubes. In the following, we first propose an algorithm that grows a multicast tree in a greedy manner, in the sense that for each intermediate vertex of the tree, the outgoing edges of the vertex are selected in a non-increasing order of the number of destinations that can use the edge in a shortest path to the destination. Note that it is an extension of LEN multicast algorithm for binary n-cubes that has been proposed by Lan *et al.* in [12]. We then evaluate the performance of the algorithm in terms of the worst case ratio of the size of the generated tree to the size of an optimal tree. It is proved that for any $k \geq 5$ and $n \geq 6$, the performance ratio of the greedy algorithm is $c \times kn - o(n)$ for some constant $1/12 \leq c \leq 1/2$.

The remainder of this paper is organized as follows. In Section 2, we introduce several necessary definitions. Section 3 describes a greedy multicast algorithm. The analysis of the algorithm in terms of the performance ratio is given in Section 4. Section 5 concludes the paper with future problems.

2 Model

Let $Q_{k,n} = (V(Q_{k,n}), E(Q_{k,n}))$ be a k-ary n-cube, where vertex set $V(Q_{k,n})$ is defined as

$$V(Q_{k,n}) \stackrel{\text{def}}{=} \{0, 1, 2, \ldots, k-1\}^n$$

and two vertices $(a_{n-1}, a_{n-2}, \ldots, a_0)$ and $(b_{n-1}, \ldots, b_0)$ in $V(Q_{k,n})$ are connected by an edge in $E(Q_{k,n})$ if and only if there is an integer $0 \leq i \leq n-1$ such that $a_j = b_j$ for all $j \neq i$ and $|(a_j - b_j) \bmod k| = 1$ for $j = i$. A 4-ary 2-cube $Q_{4,2}$ and ternary 3-cube $Q_{3,3}$ are illustrated in Figure 1. Each vertex in $V(Q_{k,n})$ models a processing element, and each link in $E(Q_{k,n})$ connecting two neighboring vertices in $V(Q_{k,n})$ models a bidirectional

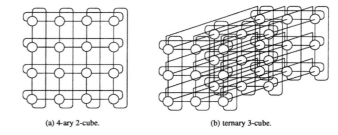

(a) 4-ary 2-cube.   (b) ternary 3-cube.

Figure 1. Example of k-ary n-cube.

communication channel between them. In the following, we often identify each vertex in $V(Q_{k,n})$ with its corresponding k-ary string of length n. Each vertex can directly communicate with an adjacent vertex through a "port" that is associated with the gateway to the link connecting with the neighboring vertex; i.e., for sending a message to a neighbor, it writes the message to the corresponding port, and for receiving a message from the neighbor, it reads it from the port. For $k \geq 3$, ports incident on a vertex are numbered from 0 to $2n - 1$, in such a way that port j is associated with dimension $\lfloor j/2 \rfloor$ and is associated with positive (resp. negative) direction if it is even (resp. odd)[1]. For example, for $k \geq 3$, vertex $(0, 0, 0, 0)$ can send a message to $(0, 0, 1, 0)$ through port 2, since $(0, 0, 1, 0)$ is connected with $(0, 0, 0, 0)$ by a link of the first dimension in the positive direction.

Let U ($\subseteq V(Q_{k,n})$) denote a given set of destination vertices, that contains the source vertex s, without loss of generality. Let $dist_G(u, v)$ denote the distance between u and v in graph G. The problem considered in this paper is described as follows: Given U with a source vertex s, construct a minimum tree T such that $dist_T(s, u) = dist_{Q_{k,n}}(s, u)$ for all $u \in U$. Note that by using the constructed tree, we can achieve a multicast in a straightforward manner by flowing packet through the tree from the source to each destination. In this paper, we assume that the header of each packet contains a subset of U as the *destination list*. A basic scheme for executing a multicast, which dynamically grows a multicast tree, is described as follows. Note that the procedure is locally executed by each vertex $u \in V(Q_{k,n})$.

(1) Receiving Step: Upon receiving a packet from a neighbor (or from itself when $u = s$), it checks the destination list U^* contained in the header of the packet. If $u \in U^*$, then it removes itself from the list, and receives the information contained in

---

[1]For $k = 2$, ports incident on a vertex are numbered from 0 to $n - 1$, in such a way that port j is associated with dimension j.

the body of the packet.

(2) **Assignment Step:** Partition U^* into $2n$ subsets, and assign each subset to a port incident on it. Let U_i ($\subseteq U^*$) denote the subset assigned to the ith port, for $0 \leq i \leq 2n - 1$.

(3) **Forwarding Step:** For all $0 \leq i \leq 2n - 1$, it sends a copy of the packet through the ith port with destination list U_i.

In this paper, for convenience, we will use the following operation $\ominus$ to calculate the relative address of a vertex from the current vertex, and operation $\oplus$ to calculate the name of vertex by the relative address of the vertex:

Definition 1 *Given two vertices* $a = (a_{n-1}, \ldots, a_0)$ *and* $b = (b_{n-1}, \ldots, b_0)$ *in* $V(Q_{k,n})$, $a \ominus b \overset{\text{def}}{=} ((a_{n-1} - b_{n-1}) \bmod k, \ldots, (a_0 - b_0) \bmod k)$ *and* $a \oplus b \overset{\text{def}}{=} ((a_{n-1} + b_{n-1}) \bmod k, \ldots, (a_0 + b_0) \bmod k)$.

Example 1 *Given vertices* $(1, 2, 1, 3)$ *and* $(2, 4, 4, 2)$ *in* $V(Q_{5,4})$, *we have* $(1, 2, 1, 3) \ominus (2, 4, 4, 2) = ((-1) \bmod 5, (-2) \bmod 5, (-3) \bmod 5, 1 \bmod 5) = (4, 3, 2, 1)$, *and given relative address* $(4, 3, 2, 1)$ *and the name of current vertex* $(2, 4, 4, 2)$, *we have* $(4, 3, 2, 1) \oplus (2, 4, 4, 2) = (6 \bmod 5, 7 \bmod 5, 6 \bmod 5, 3 \bmod 5) = (1, 2, 1, 3)$.

Let U be the given set of destination vertices. Let $t_A(U)$ denote the size of a multicast tree generated by algorithm A for given U, and let OPT denote an optimal algorithm. Then, the (worst case) performance ratio of algorithm A, denoted by ρ_A, is defined as follows:

$$\rho_A \overset{\text{def}}{=} \sup_U \rho_A(U) \quad \text{where} \quad \rho_A(U) \overset{\text{def}}{=} \frac{t_A(U)}{t_{OPT}(U)}.$$

3 A Greedy Algorithm

An idea for constructing an efficient multicast tree in terms of the performance ratio would be to merge several delivery paths that are destined to the same direction as much as possible. This intuition can be realized by introducing $2n$ counters one for each port, as follows. Suppose that vertex u receives a list of destinations U^* from a neighbor (or from itself when $u = s$). Assume $u \notin U^*$, without loss of generality. The scheme carries out the following procedure:

Algorithm GREEDY
Let $W := \{v \ominus u : v \in U^*\}$; i.e., W is a collection of relative addresses of the destinations from the current vertex u. Vertex u repeats the following four operations until W becomes empty:

Step 1: For each port $0 \leq j \leq 2n - 1$, calculate the number of destinations in W such that there exists a shortest path from u to the destination that passes through the jth port. Let $c(j)$ denote the number of such destinations for port j. Note that $\sum_{0 \leq j \leq 2n-1} c(j) \geq |W|$ since in general, there could exist several shortest paths to a destination.

Step 2: Let j be an integer that gives the largest value of function c, and W_j ($\subseteq W$) denote the set of relative addresses of vertices that contribute to the count of $c(j)$.

Step 3: Determine U_j as $U_j = \{u \oplus v : v \in W_j\}$.

Step 4: Modify W to $W \setminus W_j$.

Note that it proceeds the assignment of subsets to ports in a *greedy* manner by using $c(j)$ as the cost function.

Example 2 *Consider a multicast in 5-ary 4-cube* $Q_{5,4}$ *with* $5^4 = 625$ *vertices. Suppose that* U *is given as follows:* $U = \{(0,0,0,0), (3,2,4,3), (1,2,3,0), (4,3,2,1), (2,2,1,1)\}$. *At the source vertex* $(0,0,0,0)$, *function* $c(j)$ *is calculated as follows:*

j	$c(j)$	contributing vertices
0	2	$\{(4,3,2,1), (2,2,1,1)\}$
1	1	$\{(3,2,4,3)\}$
2	2	$\{(4,3,2,1), (2,2,1,1)\}$
3	2	$\{(3,2,4,3), (1,2,3,0)\}$
4	3	$\{(3,2,4,3), (1,2,3,0), (2,2,1,1)\}$
5	1	$\{(4,3,2,1)\}$
6	2	$\{(1,2,3,0), (2,2,1,1)\}$
7	2	$\{(3,2,4,3), (4,3,2,1)\}$

Since $c(4) = 3$ *gives the largest value, it selects the fourth port (i.e., positive direction of the second dimension) and assigns destination list* $U' = \{(3,2,4,3), (1,2,3,0), (2,2,1,1)\}$ *to the port; the remaining destination* $(4,3,2,1)$ *will be assigned to an appropriate port, e.g., to port 0. Destination list* U' *is received by adjacent vertex* $(0,1,0,0)$, *and is examined by the vertex in a similar manner to the above. More concretely, at vertex* $(0,1,0,0)$, *function* $c(j)$ *is calculated as follows:*

j	$c(j)$	contributing vertices
0	1	$\{(2,2,1,1)\}$
1	1	$\{(3,2,4,3)\}$
2	1	$\{(2,2,1,1)\}$
3	2	$\{(3,2,4,3), (1,2,3,0)\}$
4	3	$\{(3,2,4,3), (1,2,3,0), (2,2,1,1)\}(= U')$
5	0	$\{\}$
6	2	$\{(1,2,3,0), (2,2,1,1)\}$
7	1	$\{(3,2,4,3)\}$

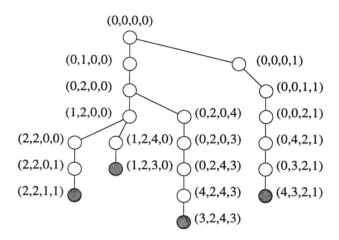

Figure 2. An example of tree generated by GREEDY.

Since $c(4) = 3$ gives the largest value, it selects the fourth port again, and forwards U' to vertex $(0, 2, 0, 0)$ through port 4. At vertex $(0, 2, 0, 0)$, function $c(j)$ is calculated as follows:

j	$c(j)$	contributing vertices
0	1	$\{(2, 2, 1, 1)\}$
1	1	$\{(3, 2, 4, 3)\}$
2	1	$\{(2, 2, 1, 1)\}$
3	2	$\{(3, 2, 4, 3), (1, 2, 3, 0)\}$
4	0	$\{\}$
5	0	$\{\}$
6	2	$\{(1, 2, 3, 0), (2, 2, 1, 1)\} (= U'')$
7	1	$\{(3, 2, 4, 3)\}$

Now, the port that gives the largest value of $c(j)$ changes from 4 to 3 and 6. Suppose port 6 is selected, without loss of generality. Then, $U'' = \{(1, 2, 3, 0), (2, 2, 1, 1)\}$ is forwarded to vertex $(1, 2, 0, 0)$ through port 6, and the remaining destination $(3, 2, 4, 3)$ is forwarded, e.g., to vertex $(0, 2, 0, 4)$ through port 1. A similar operation is repeated until the packet is received by all destinations in U. Figure 2 illustrates the resultant tree.

The goal of this paper is to give a tight bound on the performance ratio of GREEDY. As for the upper bound, we have the following claim: for any multicast tree, each destination is connected with the source vertex by a shortest path with length at most $nk/2$, and an optimal tree must contain at least $|U| - 1$ edges.

Remark 1 *For any $k \geq 2$ and $n \geq 1$, $\rho_{GREEDY} \leq \frac{kn}{2}$.*

In the next section, we prove that the above upper bound is tight in the sense that there is an instance U such that $\rho_{GREEDY}(U) \geq c \times kn$ for some constant c.

4 Lower Bounds

At first, let us consider the case of $n = 2$; i.e., a multicast in tori. The following theorem gives a lower bound on the performance ratio of GREEDY when it is applied to two-dimensional tori.

Theorem 1 *When $n = 2$, the performance ratio of GREEDY is at least $k/6$ for any integer $k \geq 5$.*

Proof. Let $(0, 0)$ be the source vertex, without loss of generality. Let $h = \lfloor (k-1)/2 \rfloor$. Consider the following set of $h + 1$ destinations: $\{(h, 0), (1, h), (2, h), \ldots, (h, h)\}$. An optimal tree for those destinations consists of two path: one is from $(0, 0)$ to $(h, 0)$, and the other is from $(0, 0)$ to (h, h) through $(0, h)$. Figure 3 (b) illustrates an optimal multicast tree for $h = 3$. Observe that the size of this tree is $3h$. On the other hand, GREEDY generates a tree with one backbone path from $(0, 0)$ to $(h, 0)$ and h spines each from $(i, 0)$ to (i, h) for $1 \leq i \leq h$. Figure 3 (a) illustrates a generated tree for $h = 3$. Note that the size of the tree is $h(h + 1)$. Hence we can conclude that the performance ratio of GREEDY is at least $\frac{h(h+1)}{3h} = \frac{h+1}{3} \geq \frac{k}{6}$ which completes the proof. Q.E.D.

We can extend the above construction to general $n \geq 3$, as follows:

Lemma 1 *If there is a set of destinations D ($\subseteq V(Q_{2,n-1})$) in a binary $(n-1)$-cube such that the performance ratio of GREEDY is ρ, then we can construct an instance U ($\subseteq V(Q_{k,n})$) in a k-ary n-cube such that the performance ratio of GREEDY is at least $\rho \times (k-2)/4$.*

Proof. Let $h = \lfloor (k-1)/2 \rfloor$. Note that $0^{n-1} \in D$. First, consider a set D' of vertices in k-ary $(n-1)$-cube, defined as follows:

$$D' \overset{\text{def}}{=} \{(h \times x_{n-2}, h \times x_{n-3}, \ldots, h \times x_1, h \times x_0) : (x_{n-2}, x_{n-3}, \ldots, x_1, x_0) \in D\}.$$

Next, by using set D', consider the following set U of destinations in a k-ary n-cube:

$$U \overset{\text{def}}{=} \{(0, 0, 0, \ldots, 0), (h, 0, 0, \ldots, 0)\}$$
$$\cup \{(y, x_{n-2}, \ldots, x_1, x_0) : y \in \{1, 2, \ldots, h\} \text{ and } (x_{n-2}, \ldots, x_1, x_0) \in D'\}.$$

For example, if D is given as $D = \{(0, 0, 0), (1, 0, 1), (1, 1, 0)\}$ then D' and U are determined as

$$D' = \{(0, 0, 0), (h, 0, h), (h, h, 0)\} \quad \text{and}$$
$$U = \{(0, 0, 0, 0), (h, 0, 0, 0), (1, h, 0, h), \ldots, (h, h, 0, h), (1, h, h, 0), \ldots, (h, h, h, 0)\},$$

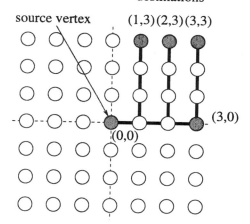

(a) A tree generated by GREEDY.

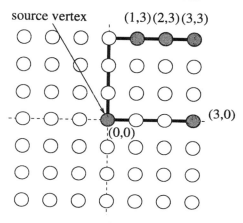

(b) An optimal multicast tree.

Figure 3. Two multicast trees in 7-ary 2-cube.

respectively. By construction, $t_A(D') = h \times t_A(D)$ and $t_{OPT}(D') = h \times t_{OPT}(D)$ hold. Hence, for set U, GREEDY generates a tree with size at least

$$t_A(U) = h + h \times t_A(D') = h + h^2 t_A(D)$$

since all vertices on the path from $(0, 0, \ldots, 0)$ to $(h - 1, 0, 0, \ldots, 0)$ use the positive direction of the $(n - 1)$st dimension as the first port. On the other hand, the size of an optimal tree is at most

$$
\begin{aligned}
t_{OPT}(U) &\leq t_{OPT}(D') + h \times |U| \\
&= h t_{OPT}(D) + h(|D| + 1) \\
&\leq 2h t_{OPT}(D).
\end{aligned}
$$

Hence the performance ratio for U is at least

$$\frac{h + h^2 \times t_A(D)}{2h \times t_{OPT}(D)} \geq \left(\frac{h}{2}\right)\left(\frac{t_A(D)}{t_{OPT}(D)}\right) \geq \left(\frac{h}{2}\right)\rho,$$

which completes the proof.   Q.E.D.

On the other hand, we can prove the following lemma on the performance ratio in binary n-cube $Q_{2,n}$, that is an extension of the argument proposed in [5].

Lemma 2 *There is a set U ($\subset V(Q_{2,n})$) such that $\rho_{GREEDY}(U) \geq (2/7)n - o(n)$.*

Proof. Without loss of generality, let $0^n \in V$ be the source vertex, and assume that $n \geq 4$. Let m be an integer in $\{4, 5, \ldots, n\}$, the value of which will be determined later. For each $m \leq i \leq n$, define set W_i ($\subset \{0, 1\}^i$) as follows:

$$
W_i = \left\{
\begin{array}{ll}
\{1^{m-3}111, 1^{m-3}000, 0^{m-3}111, 0^{m-3}100, \\
\quad 0^{m-3}010, 0^{m-3}001, 0^{m-3}000\} & \text{if } i = m \\
\{w0, w1 : w \in W_{i-1}\} & \text{if } m < i \leq n.
\end{array}
\right.
$$

Note that $|W_m| = 7$ and $|W_i| = 2|W_{i-1}|$ for any $m < i \leq n$; i.e., the size of each subset is represented as

$$|W_i| = |W_m| \times 2^{i-m} = 7 \times 2^{i-m} \qquad (1)$$

for each $m \leq i \leq n$.

By using W_i's, we define a sequence of destination sets $U_m, U_{m+1}, \ldots, U_n$ ($\subset V(Q_{2,n})$) defined as follows:

$$U_i \overset{\text{def}}{=} \{u0^{n-i} : u \in W_i\},$$

and examine the behavior of the algorithm when it is applied to destination list U_n. Let S_i denote the size of the tree constructed for U_i. In the following explanation, since $k = 2$, we assume that each vertex has n ports numbered from 0 to $n - 1$, each of which corresponds to the dimension of a link, and function $c(j)$ is evaluated for those n ports.

At the initial state, U_n is kept by the source vertex 0^n. Hence in the first round, the source vertex examines set U_n, and calculates the values of function $c(j)$ as follows:

$$
c(j) = \left\{
\begin{array}{ll}
(1/2)|W_n| & \text{if } 0 \leq j < n - m \\
(3/7)|W_n| & \text{if } n - m \leq j < n - m + 3 \\
(2/7)|W_n| & \text{if } n - m + 3 \leq j < n.
\end{array}
\right.
$$

Since $1/2 > 3/7 > 2/7$, it selects a port in $\{0, 1, \ldots, n - m - 1\}$ as the first port. Let 0 be the selected port, without loss of generality. After the selection, the source assigns destination list $\{u1 : u \in W_{n-1}\}$ to the selected port. In the second round, the remaining destination list $\{u0 : u \in W_{n-1}\}$ is examined at the source

515

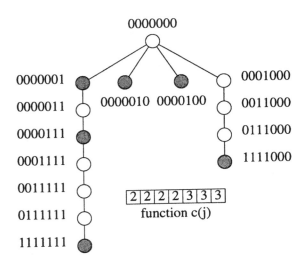

Figure 4. A tree generated by GREEDY for subset W_m.

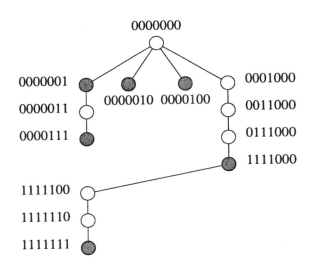

Figure 5. An optimal multicast tree for W_m.

vertex. Note that destination list $\{u1 : u \in W_{n-1}\}$ that is sent to vertex $0^{n-1}1$ will be examined at vertex $0^{n-1}1$ in a similar manner to the processing of $\{u0 : u \in W_{n-1}\}$ $(= U_{n-1})$. After the examination, for example, the source selects port 1 since it gives the largest value $(1/2)|W_{n-1}|$, and then assigns destination list $\{u10 : u \in W_{n-2}\}$ to the selected port. A similar operation is repeated until all ports in $\{0, 1, \ldots, n-m-1\}$ are examined. Since the size of a multicast tree for subset U_i is obtained by connecting two multicast trees, each of which is isomorphic to the multicast tree for U_{i-1}, we have $S_i = 2S_{i-1} + 1$ for $m < i \leq n$; i.e.,

$$S_n = 2^{n-m}(S_m + 1) - 1. \quad (2)$$

Next, for given destination list U_m, function $c(j)$ is calculated as follows:

$$c(j) = \begin{cases} 2 & \text{if } n - m + 3 \leq j < n \\ 3 & \text{if } n - m \leq j < n - m + 3 \text{ and} \\ 0 & \text{if } 0 \leq j < n - m. \end{cases}$$

Hence, in the first three rounds of the examination of U_m, it selects the $(n-m)$th, $(n-m+1)$st, and $(n-m+2)$nd ports in an appropriate order, and then, selects the remaining ports in an appropriate order. The resultant tree for destination list U_m is represented in Figure 4 for $m = 7$ and $n = 7$. From the figure, we can easily observe that the size of the tree is $S_m = 2m - 1$. Hence by Equation (2), we have $S_n = 2^{n-m} \cdot 2m - 1$.

On the other hand, the size of an optimal tree for $U_i = \{u0^{n-i} : u \in W_i\}$ is estimated as follows. Let

T_i denote the size of the tree. By definition, for any $u \in W_i$, there is a vertex $v \in W_{i-1}$ such that $u = v1$. This observation implies that we can construct a tree for i by adding $|W_{i-1}|$ edges to an optimal tree for $i - 1$. In other words, for each $m < i \leq n$, it holds $T_i \leq T_{i-1} + |W_{i-1}|$.

Hence, T_n is represented as $T_n \leq T_{n-1} + |W_{n-1}| \leq T_m + (|W_m| + |W_{m+1}| + \cdots + |W_{n-1}|)$, and by Equation (1), we have

$$\begin{aligned} T_n &\leq T_m + |W_m|(2^{n-m} - 1) \\ &= T_m + 7(2^{n-m} - 1). \end{aligned}$$

Since an optimal tree for W_m grows as in Figure 5; i.e., $T_m = m + 6$, we have

$$\begin{aligned} T_n &\leq (m + 6) + 7(2^{n-m} - 1) \\ &= 7 \cdot 2^{n-m} + m - 1. \end{aligned}$$

Hence, $\rho_{GREEDY}(U)$ is bounded as

$$\begin{aligned} \rho_{GREEDY}(U) &\geq \frac{2^{n-m} \cdot 2m - 1}{7 \cdot 2^{n-m} + m - 1} \\ &= \frac{2m - 2^{m-n}}{7 + (m-1)2^{m-n}}. \end{aligned}$$

By letting $m = n - \log^\alpha n$ for some constant $\alpha > 1$, since it satisfies $2^{n-m} = \omega(n)$, we have $\rho_{GREEDY}(U) \geq \left(\frac{2}{7}\right) n - o(n)$ which completes the proof. Q.E.D.

By Lemmas 1 and 2, we immediately have the following theorem.

Theorem 2 *For any $k \geq 5$ and $n \geq 4$, the performance ratio of GREEDY in $Q_{k,n}$ is at least $nk/14 - o(n)$.*

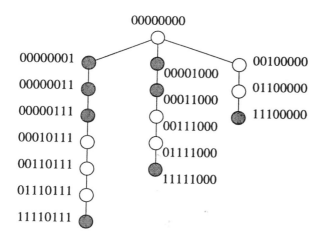

Figure 6. A tree generated by GREEDY for subset W_m in the proof of Lemma 3.

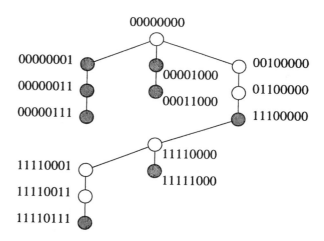

Figure 7. An optimal tree for W_m that is used in the proof of Lemma 3.

Hence we have $\rho_{GREEDY} = c \times nk - o(n)$ for some constant $1/14 \leq c \leq 1/2$, for any $k \geq 5$ and $n \geq 4$. The coefficient of the lower bound could be slightly improved to $1/12$ by using the following lemma.

Lemma 3 *For any $n \geq 6$, there is a set U ($\subset V(Q_{2,n})$) such that $\rho_{GREEDY}(U) = n/3 - o(n)$.*

Proof. Define W_m as follows:

$$W_m \stackrel{\text{def}}{=} \{ \begin{array}{llll} 00\ldots0 & 00000, & 00\ldots0 & 01000, \\ 00\ldots0 & 11000, & 11\ldots1 & 00000, \\ 11\ldots1 & 11000, & 00\ldots0 & 00001, \\ 00\ldots0 & 00011, & 00\ldots0 & 00111, \\ 11\ldots1 & 10111 \}. \end{array}$$

Note that $|W_m| = 9$. For each $i > m$, let us define W_i as $W_i \stackrel{\text{def}}{=} \{w0, w1 : w \in W_{i-1}\}$, as before. Let $U_i \stackrel{\text{def}}{=} \{u0^{n-i} : u \in W_i\}$.

Let S_i be the size of the constructed tree for U_i, and consider the multicast for U_n. Since at the source vertex, it holds

$$c(j) = \begin{cases} (1/2)|W_n| & \text{if } 0 \leq j < n - m \\ (4/9)|W_n| & \text{if } j = n - m \\ (1/3)|W_n| & \text{if } j = n - m + 1 \\ & \text{or } n - m + 3 \leq j < n \\ (2/9)|W_n| & \text{if } j = n - m + 2, \end{cases}$$

we have the same equation to Equation (2) for $m < i \leq n$. On the other hand, for given destination list U_m, function $c(j)$ is calculated as follows; i.e., in the

first round of the examination of U_m,

$$c(j) = \begin{cases} 4 & \text{if } j = n - m \\ 3 & \text{if } j = n - m + 1 \\ & \text{or } n - m + 3 \leq j < n \\ 2 & \text{if } j = n - m + 3 \text{ and} \\ 0 & \text{if } 0 \leq j < n - m. \end{cases}$$

Hence, the source selects the $(n - m)$th port, and assigns $\{0^{m-1}10^{n-m}, 0^{m-2}110^{n-m}, 0^{m-3}1110^{n-m}, 1^{m-5}101110^{n-m}\}$ to the port; in the next round, function $c(j)$ is recalculated as

$$c(j) = \begin{cases} 3 & \text{if } j = n - m + 3 \\ 2 & \text{if } n - m + 4 \leq j < n \\ 0 & \text{if } 0 \leq j < n - m + 3, \end{cases}$$

which causes the selection of the $(n - m + 3)$rd port, and the source assigns $\{0^{m-6}10^{n-m+5}, 0^{m-5}110^{n-m+3}, 1^{m-3}0^{n-m+3}\}$ to the selected port; the remaining destination $1^{m-5}0^{n-m+5}$ will be assigned to the $(n - m + 5)$th port, for example. The resultant tree for destination list U_m is represented in Figure 7 for $m = 8$ and $n = 8$. From the figure, we can easily observe that the size of the tree is $S_m = 3m - 9$. Hence by Equation (2), we have $S_n = 2^{n-m} \times (3m - 9) - 1$.

On the other hand, since an optimal tree for W_m grows as in Figure 4; i.e., $T_m = m + 5$, we have $T_n \leq (m + 5) + |W_m|(2^{n-m} - 1) = 9 \cdot 2^{n-m} + m - 4$. Hence, we have

$$\rho(U) \geq \frac{2^{n-m}(3m - 9) - 1}{9 \cdot 2^{n-m} + m - 4} = \frac{3m - 9 - 2^{m-n}}{9 + (m - 4)2^{m-n}}.$$

Finally, by letting $m = n - \log^\alpha n$ for some constant $\alpha > 1$, we have $\rho(U) \geq \left(\frac{1}{3}\right)n - o(n)$ which completes the proof. Q.E.D.

5 Concluding Remarks

In this paper, we proposed a greedy multicast algorithm in k-ary n-cubes, and evaluated the goodness of the algorithm in terms of the worst case ratio of the size of the generated tree to the size of an optimal tree. It is proved that for any $k \geq 5$ and $n \geq 6$, the performance ratio of the greedy algorithm is $c \times kn - o(n)$ for some constant $1/12 \leq c \leq 1/2$.

An open problem is to find an approximation algorithm that gives a smaller guaranteed performance ratio. A conjecture is that we can apply several techniques developed for related problems to this problem, e.g., the Steiner tree problem and the traveling salesperson problem; for example, a clustering approach that hierarchically partitions the given network is expected to work effectively to give a better guaranteed ratio. Since the problem of finding an optimal multicast tree in k-ary n-cubes is NP-complete, it would also be an interesting direction for future research to find a lower bound on the performance ratio for the class of polynomial time algorithms provided that $P \neq NP$.

References

[1] R. V. Boppana, S. Chalasani, and C. S. Raghavendra. On multicast wormhole routing in multicomputer networks. In *Proc. SPDP '94*, pages 722–729. IEEE, 1994.

[2] R. V. Boppana, S. Chalasani, and C. S. Raghavendra. Resource deadlocks and performance of wormhole multicast routing algorithms. *IEEE Trans. Parallel and Distributed Systems*, 9(6):535–549, June 1998.

[3] W. J. Dally and C. L. Seitz. Deadlock–free message routing in multiprocessor interconnection network. *IEEE Trans. Comput.*, 36(5):547–553, May 1987.

[4] A. J. Frank, L. D. Wittie, and A. J. Bernstein. Multicast communication on network computers. *IEEE Software*, 2(3):49–61, May 1985.

[5] S. Fujita. A note on the size of a multicast tree in hypercubes. *Information Processing Letters*, 54(4):223–227, 1995.

[6] S. Fujita. Neighborhood information dissemination in the star graph. *IEEE Trans. Comput.*, 49(12):1366–1370, 2000.

[7] S. Fujita. Log-time multicast to local vertices in the star graph. In *Proc. IPDPS*. IEEE, Apr 2001.

[8] S. Fujita, S. Perennes, and J. Peters. Neighbourhood gossiping in hypercubes. *Parallel Processing Letters*, 8(2):189–195, 1998.

[9] J. Hromkovič, C.-D. Jeschke, and B. Monien. Optimal algorithms for dissemination of information in some interconnection networks. *Algorithmica*, 10:24–40, 1993.

[10] Y. Lan. Fault-tolerant multi-destination routing in hypercube multiprocessor. In *Proc. ICDCS*, pages 632–639. IEEE, 1992.

[11] Y. Lan. Multicast in faulty hypercubes. In *Proc. ICPP*, pages (I) 58–61. IEEE, 1992.

[12] Y. Lan, A.-H. Esfahanian, and L. M. Ni. Multicast in hypercube multiprocessors. *J. of Parallel and Distributed Comput.*, 8:30–41, 1990.

[13] X. Lin and L. M. Ni. Multicast communication in multicomputer networks. *IEEE Trans. Parallel and Distributed Systems*, 4(10):1105–1117, October 1993.

[14] T. J. Sager and B. M. McMillin. A fast $O(k)$ multicast message routing algorithm. Technical Report CSC-90-2, Dept. of Computer Science, Univ. of Missouri-Rolla, Rolla, Missouli, 1990.

[15] M. Schollmeyer. Multicast routing in unreliable networks. Technical Report CSC-91-16, Dept. of Computer Science, Univ. of Missouri at Rolla, Rola, Missouli, 1991.

[16] J.-P. Sheu and M.-Y. Su. A multicast algorithm for hypercube multiprocessors. In *Proc. ICPP*, pages (III) 18–22. IEEE, 1992.

A Best-Effort Communication Protocol for Real-Time Broadcast Networks

Lakshmi Ramaswamy and Binoy Ravindran
Real-Time Systems Laboratory
The Bradley Department of Electrical and Computer Engineering
Virginia Tech, Blacksburg, VA 24061
Phone: 540-231-3777, Fax: 540-231-3362, E-mail: lramaswa@vt.edu, binoy@vt.edu

Abstract

In this paper, we present a best-effort communication protocol called ABA, that seeks to maximize aggregate application benefit and deadline-satisfied ratio of asynchronous real-time distributed systems that use CSMA/DDCR broadcast networks. ABA considers an application model where end-to-end timeliness requirements of trans-node application tasks are expressed using Jensen's benefit functions. Furthermore, the protocol assumes that the application is designed using CSMA/DDCR feasibility conditions that is driven by a "best" possible estimate of upper bounds on message arrival densities that is possible at design-time. When such design-time postulations get violated at run-time, ABA directs message traffic so that messages that will increase applications' aggregate benefit are only transmitted, buffering others, until such time when the workloads respect their design-time postulated values. To study the performance of ABA, we consider a previously studied algorithm called RBA* as a baseline algorithm. Our experimental results indicate that ABA yields higher aggregate benefit and higher deadline-satisfied ratio than RBA* when message arrival densities increase at faster rates or at the same rates as that of process execution latencies due to the dynamics of the workload.

1. Introduction

Implementing real-time distributed systems using broadcast media networks such as Gigabit Ethernet's and buses internal to ATM switches are becoming highly attractive due to the recently developed CSMA/DDCR (Carrier Sense Multi Access/Deadline Driven Collision Resolution) MAC protocol [5]. Eth-ernet networks are all the more desirable due to their low cost and wide availability.

The IEEE 802.3 Ethernet standard is unsuited for real-time applications due to the random, exponential, back-off strategy of Ethernet's CSMA/CD MAC protocol for resolving access contention to the network media. This is a fundamental limitation of Ethernet networks for real-time applications as it is conceptually equivalent to random scheduling of resources — a highly undesirable feature for satisfying the hard real-time objective of "always meet all timing constraints."

CSMA/DDCR eliminates the randomness of Ethernet's CSMA/CD by emulating a distributed, non-preemptive version of the Earliest Deadline First (EDF) algorithm [10]. Under CSMA/DDCR, when message collisions occur, the collided hosts initiate a deterministic search that is guaranteed to complete earlier for the host with the earliest deadline message. The host that completes the search earlier is then allowed to access the network.

Furthermore, CSMA/DDCR has formally proven timeliness feasibility conditions. The feasibility conditions are established in [5] under upper bounds for message arrival densities—manifestations of application workloads—that are postulated at design-time. Thus, given a hard real-time distributed application, a designer can verify the schedulability of the application by assigning numerical values to the protocol's feasibility condition, and get an "yes" or "no" answer (on the application feasibility).

While CSMA/DDCR (thus) allows hard real-time distributed systems to be built using high performance and low cost broadcast networks, "asynchronous" real-time distributed systems are emerging in many domains for the purpose of strategic mission management. Such systems are fundamentally distinguished by the significant run-time uncertainties that are inherent in their application environment and system resource states [7, 8]. Consequently, it is difficult to postulate upper bounds on application workloads for such systems that will always be respected at runtime. Thus, they violate the deterministic foundations of hard real-time theory that ensures that "all timing constraints are always satisfied" under deterministic postulations of application workloads and execution environment characteristics. Asynchronous real-time distributed systems are emerging in many application domains including defense, telecommunication, aerospace, and industrial automation [8].

To deal with such non-determinism's, recent advances in real-time systems research [6] have produced quality of service (QoS) technologies that allow applications to specify and negotiate real-time requirements. The real-time QoS techniques consider application models where application tasks can operate at multiple, discrete "levels" of service. A level is a strategy for doing a tasks' work and is characterized by a resource usage such as CPU or network utilization, a QoS dimension such as timeliness of computations, and a user-specified benefit.

Thus, if all timing requirements of all tasks cannot be satisfied at run-time (due to the workload hypothesis being violated at run-time), then an adaptation mechanism can determine the "right level" of QoS to optimize a system-wide criteria such as maximizing aggregate benefit. Examples of such QoS techniques for real-time systems are presented in [1].

In this paper, we advance the real-time QoS technology by presenting a best-effort communication protocol called Arrival Density-Driven Best Effort Resource Allocation protocol (or ABA). ABA is a network-layer communication protocol for real-time broadcast networks that use CSMA/DDCR as the MAC protocol.

ABA considers an application model where trans-node application tasks have end-to-end timeliness requirements that are expressed using Jensen's benefit functions [7]. Thus, completing an end-to-end task at anytime will yield a benefit that is specified by the task benefit function. Given such a timeliness model, the objective of ABA is to maximize aggregate task benefit and task deadline-satisfied ratio. Thus, ABA is a "best-effort" protocol in the sense that it seeks to provide the best benefit to the application, where the best benefit that the application can accrue is application-specified (using benefit functions).

ABA regards that the application is designed using CSMA/DDCR feasibility conditions that is driven by a "best" possible postulation of the application workload that is possible at design-time. When such design-time postulations get violated at run-time, due to the non-

determinism inherent in asynchronous real-time distributed systems, ABA directs message traffic so that messages that will increase applications' aggregate benefit and task deadline-satisfied ratio are only transmitted, buffering others, until such time when the workloads respect their design-time postulated values.

The problem of determining a *feasible* message set that will maximize aggregate benefit and task deadline-satisfied ratio can be shown to be NP-hard by mapping it to the problem of determining non-preemptive task schedules that will maximize aggregate task benefit, since transmission of message frames are non-preemptive. In [2], Chen and Muhlethaler show that the non-preemptive task scheduling problem with benefits is NP-hard. Thus, ABA employs a set of heuristics for determining feasible message sets that will maximize aggregate benefit and task deadline-satisfied ratio in polynomial-time.

To determine how well ABA performs, we consider a previously developed algorithm called RBA* [4], for a similar problem as a baseline algorithm. Our experimental results indicate that ABA yields higher aggregate benefit and higher deadline-satisfied ratio than RBA* when message arrival densities increase at faster rates or at the same rates as that of process execution latencies due to the dynamics of the workload.

Thus, the contribution of the paper is the ABA protocol that seeks to maximize aggregate application benefit and deadline-satisfied ratio of asynchronous real-time distributed systems on CSMA/DDCR networks.

The rest of the paper is organized as follows: Section 2 presents the application and system models that we consider in this work. In Section 3, we present the key idea behind ABA. Section 4 presents the core heuristics employed by ABA and the rationale behind the heuristics. We discuss how ABA determines feasible message sets in Section 5. In Section 6, we discuss the experimental evaluation of ABA and RBA*. Finally, the paper concludes with a summary of the work, its contributions, and ongoing efforts in Section 7.

2. The Application and System Model

2.1. Task model

Our application model consists of a set of tasks denoted by $T = \{T_1, T_2, ..., T_n\}$. Each task T_i consists of a set of subtasks (or UNIX-style processes) that execute and communicate to accomplish the function of the task. The connectivity of a task T_i is modeled as a directed acyclic graph, $G(T_i) = (V, E)$, where $v \in V$ denotes a subtask of the task and $(v_i, v_j) \in E$

denotes a pair of subtasks of the task that communicate, where the order of the pair defines the direction of communication. For convenience, we denote the set of subtasks of a task T_i as $ST(T_i) = \{st_1^i, st_2^i, \ldots, st_m^i\}$ and the set of inter-subtask messages of a task T_i as $MS(T_i) = \{m_1^i, m_2^i, \ldots, m_k^i\}$, where an inter-subtask message is simply a message that flows between a pair of communicating subtasks. For convenience, we denote the set of all application messages as the set $M = \bigcup_{\forall i} MS(T_i)$.

We consider the unimodal arbitrary arrival model for messages of the application. Thus, for each application message m_j^i, $a(m_j^i)$ defines the best possible estimate of the upper bound on the number of arrivals of message m_j^i during an interval of time $w(m_j^i)$ that can be postulated at design-time. Thus, $a(m_j^i)/w(m_j^i)$ defines the best estimate of the upper bound on the *arrival density* of the message m_j^i.

A message that is transmitted from an application subtask is packetized by the network protocol stack before transmission. We denote the set of packets or physical network frames of an application message m_j^i as $FR(m_j^i) = \{m_{j,1}^i, m_{j,2}^i, \ldots, m_{j,\alpha}^i\}$ for some constant α.

2.2. Timing Requirements

We use Jensen's benefit functions for expressing application timeliness requirements [7]. We assume "step" benefit functions for all tasks such as the one shown in Figure 1. Thus, completing a task anytime before its deadline will result in uniform benefit; completing it after the deadline will result in zero benefit.

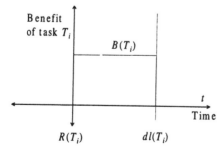

Figure 1. A Step-benefit Function

We denote the maximum (uniform) benefit of a task T_i as $B(T_i)$ and the deadline of task T_i as $dl(T_i)$, respectively.

2.3. System Model

We consider a Local Area Network segment where end-hosts are interconnected using a shared media broadcast network such as Gigabit Ethernet that runs the CSMA/DDCR protocol [5]. Thus, the physical frames of application messages are scheduled by CSMA/DDCR using non-preemptive EDF [10].

We denote the set of end-host processors by the set $H = \{h_1, h_2, \ldots, h_p\}$. We assume that the clocks of the processors are synchronized using a protocol such as [12].

For process scheduling, we consider the DASA best-effort real-time scheduling algorithm [3] that explicitly incorporates benefit functions for scheduling. Our choice of DASA is due to the fact that it outperforms EDF during overloaded situations, and performs the same as EDF during under-loaded situations where EDF is optimal.

3. Overview of ABA

The ABA protocol that we present extends the hard real-time approach for constructing asynchronous real-time distributed systems using broadcast networks that run the CSMA/DDCR protocol. The protocol assumes that the application is designed using CSMA/DDCR feasibility functions that is driven by a best possible estimate of the application workload that is possible at design-time. The best estimate of the application workload is used to postulate upper bounds on arrival densities of messages—and thus message frames—that is needed for the CSMA/DDCR feasibility analysis. However, the protocol regards that such a design-time workload hypothesis can get violated at run-time—and thus the upper bounds on arrival densities—due to the non-determinism that is inherent in asynchronous real-time distributed systems.

ABA counters such violations of workload hypothesis through run-time monitoring and resource allocation. Each host is assume to execute an identical copy of the ABA protocol. Furthermore, under the protocol, each host monitors the application messages that are generated from the host (at run-time) and detect situations when their arrival densities—and thus that of the message frames—exceed the postulated upper bounds. This can cause a high likelihood of task timing failures to occur. When any such condition occurs at a host, the host computes a feasible set of messages that will seek to maximize aggregate application benefit and deadline-satisfied ratio.

The feasible message set is then broadcast system-wide to all hosts. Upon receipt of the broadcast feasible message set, the host buffers all messages that are not part of the feasible set, thereby allowing only the feasible message set to be transmitted. The infeasible messages are buffered until the arrival density of the messages (which increased and exceeded the postulated bounds) decrease and respects the values postulated at design-time.

4. Heuristics and Rationale of ABA

ABA's objective is to maximize aggregate task benefit and task deadline-satisfied ratio. Since determining a *feasible* message set that will maximize aggregate benefit and deadline-satisfied ratio can be shown to be NP-hard, ABA employs a set of heuristics to achieve this objective in polynomial-time. We discuss the heuristics employed by ABA and their rationale in the subsections that follow:

4.1. Decompose Task Deadlines into Message and Subtask Deadlines

Recall that ABA performs resource allocation at the message-level. Thus messages constitute the "input" to the protocol. Therefore, if messages have deadlines, that will enable the protocol to reason about message-level resource allocation that will maximize task deadline-satisfied ratio. Furthermore, the DASA algorithm that we consider for process scheduling requires deadlines for subtasks (for process scheduling). Therefore, task-level deadlines must be decomposed into deadlines for messages and subtasks of the task.

Since we are focusing on step-benefit functions for tasks, the decomposition of task deadlines can be done by assigning deadlines to subtasks and messages of a task from the task deadline in such a way that if all subtasks and messages of the task can meet their respective deadlines, then the task will be able to meet its deadline. Using this heuristic, we can seek to satisfy the task deadline by determining the feasibility of messages of the task that will satisfy the message deadlines. By seeking to satisfy message deadlines, we thus seek to satisfy task deadlines, and maximize aggregate task benefit and task deadline-satisfied ratio (as tasks have step-benefit functions).

We now discuss how task deadlines can be decomposed into subtask and message deadlines in the subsection that follows:

4.1.1 Deadline Decomposition Heuristic

The problem of subtask and message deadline assignment from task deadlines has been studied in a different context [9]. The equal flexibility (EQF) strategy presented in [9] assigns deadlines to subtasks and messages from the task deadline in a way that is proportional to subtask execution times and message transmission times, respectively. The (relative) deadline of a subtask (or that of a message) is simply the sum of the execution time of the subtask (or the transmission time of the message) and a slack value. EQF defines the slack value for a subtask (or that of a message) as a percentage of the total available slack for the subtask (or the message).

The total available slack for a subtask (or a message) is simply the difference between the task deadline and the sum of the execution times and transmission times of all subtasks and messages that "succeed" the subtask (or the message) in the task structure, respectively. The execution times and transmission times of subtasks and messages that precede the subtask (or the message) in the task structure are not considered in the total available slack, since these latencies would already be incurred by the time the subtask starts execution (or the message starts transmission).

Now, the slack value for a subtask (or that of a message) is defined as a percentage of the total available slack for the subtask (or the message), where the percentage is the ratio of the subtask execution time (or the message transmission time) to the sum of the execution times and transmission times of all subtasks and messages that succeed the subtask (or the message) in the task structure, respectively. Thus, higher the subtask execution time (or message transmission time), higher will be the ratio, higher will be the percentage, higher will be the slack value, and higher will be the subtask (or message) deadline.

ABA estimates subtask execution times and message transmission times for the workload upper bound that is postulated at design time. The estimated execution times and message delays are then used to assign subtask and message deadlines, according to EQF, respectively.

4.2. Decompose Message Deadlines into Deadlines for Message Frames

CSMA/DDCR uses deadlines of message frames for resolving collisions on the network media. Thus, deadline of a message must be translated into deadlines for frames of the message. Since frames of a message do not have any precedence relations (unlike the precedences that must be respected by subtasks and messages of a task), the message frames can be transmitted in any order. Furthermore, the benefit of a message is accrued only when all frames of the message arrive at the destination and are reassembled before the message deadline. Thus, a message frame can simply inherit the deadline of its parent message.

4.3. Decompose Task Benefits into Message and Subtask Benefits

Recall that ABA performs resource allocation at the message-level and thus messages constitute the "input" to the protocol. Therefore, if messages have benefits, that will enable the protocol to reason about message-level resource allocation that will maximize aggregate task benefit. Furthermore, the DASA algorithm that we consider for process scheduling requires benefits for subtasks (for process scheduling). Therefore, task-level benefits must be decomposed into benefits for messages and subtasks of the task.

Since we are focusing on step-benefit functions for tasks, a task accrues a benefit only when it completes before the deadline and not when any subset of its subtasks and messages complete before their deadlines. Thus, the subtasks and messages of a task can directly inherit the benefit of their parent task.

4.4. Examine Deadline Feasibility of Messages in Decreasing Order of Message Benefits

By examining messages for determining their feasibility in decreasing order of message benefits, we "greedily" include those messages into the feasible set—if they are feasible—that will yield the largest benefit at any given time, as the message selected next for feasibility analysis is always the one with the largest benefit among the unexamined messages. This will increase the possibility of maximizing aggregate message benefit (and thus the aggregate task benefit).

4.5. Transmit Feasible Messages and Buffer Infeasible Messages

Since we are focusing on step-benefit functions for tasks, transmitting messages that are found to be deadline-feasible will seek to maximize deadline-satisfied ratio of messages and thus maximize task deadline-satisfied ratio.

Furthermore, by buffering infeasible messages, we save network bandwidth, which can be potentially used for satisfying deadlines of lower benefit messages. This will increase the possibility of satisfying the deadlines of greater number of lower benefit messages, resulting in potential contributions of non-zero benefit from them toward aggregate message benefit and thus aggregate task benefit.

Thus, the ABA protocol performs resource allocation according to the heuristics presented here.

5. Determining Feasible Message Sets

To determine a feasible message set that will maximize aggregate benefit and task deadline-satisfied ratio, ABA first sorts the application messages according to message benefits. The protocol then examines the messages in decreasing order of their benefits. For each message, the protocol determines the feasibility of the message using the CSMA/DDCR feasibility condition.

DetFeasibleMessageSet (M)
/* M is the application message set */
1. Sort the set M according to message benefits;
2. FeasibleSet = $\emptyset$;
3. InFeasibleSet = $\emptyset$;
4. For each message $m_j^i \in M$ /* in decreasing order */
   4.1 FeasibleSet = FeasibleSet $\bigcup \{m_j^i\}$;
   4.2 For each message $m_q^p \in$ FeasibleSet
      4.2.1 Let h_k denote source host of message m_q^p;
      4.2.2 If ! CSMA-DDCRFeasible(m_q^p, h_k, FeasibleSet)
        • FeasibleSet = FeasibleSet $- \{m_q^p\}$;
        • InFeasibleSet = InFeasibleSet $\bigcup \{m_q^p\}$;
5. Broadcast FeasibleSet;

Figure 2. Pseudo-Code of *DetFeasibleMessageSet* **Procedure**

The communication delay incurred by a message under the CSMA/DDCR protocol consists of three parts: (1) the *interference time*, which is the amount of time that the message has to wait to access the network due to interference that it suffers from other messages, (2) the *collision resolution time*, which is the amount of time spent by CSMA/DDCR to search the Time Tree and the Static Tree for resolving message collisions, and (3) the actual *physical transmission time*.

The interference time experienced by a message m_j^i that is released for transmission by a host at time t solely depends on the arrival density and bit length of all messages that will be transmitted by all hosts during the interval $[t, dl(m_j^i)]$. Thus, to determine the communication delay of a message, the CSMA/DDCR feasibility condition requires knowledge of the arrival density of all messages generated from all hosts, since they may interfere with the transmission of the message.

When determining the communication delay of a message m_j^i, ABA considers the set of messages that are already present in the feasible set (at the time when m_j^i is examined) since they will interfere with the transmission of m_j^i. Furthermore, if the protocol finds that

m_j^i is feasible and thus decides to include m_j^i in the feasible set, it will reexamine all messages that are in the feasible set since they will now suffer interference from m_j^i.

CSMA-DDCRFeasible(m_j^i, h_k, FS)
/* m_j^i: message; h_k: host of message m_j^i; FS: message set */
1. MD$\left(m_j^i\right)$ = 0;/* message delay bound */
2. MR$\left(m_j^i\right)$ = 0;/* bound on message rank in out queue */
3. TM$\left(m_j^i\right)$ = 0;/* bound on # of messages transmitted
    by all hosts during interval $[t, dl(m_j^i)]$ */
4. For each message $m_q^p \in$ MessgsOfHost(h_k)
    /* MessgsOfHost(h_k): outgoing messages from host h_k */
    4.1 MR$\left(m_j^i\right)$ = MR$\left(m_j^i\right)$ + $\left\lceil \frac{dl\left(m_j^i\right)}{w\left(m_q^p\right)} \right\rceil a\left(m_q^p\right) - 1$;
5. For each message $m_q^p \in FS$
    5.1 TM$\left(m_j^i\right)$ = TM$\left(m_j^i\right)$ +
        $\left\lceil \frac{dl\left(m_j^i\right) + dl\left(m_q^p\right) - \frac{ln\left(m_j^i\right)}{\psi}}{w\left(m_q^p\right)} \right\rceil a\left(m_q^p\right)$;
6. ST$\left(m_j^i\right)$ = $1 + \left\lfloor \frac{\text{MR}\left(m_j^i\right)}{v_k} \right\rfloor$; /* bound on # of static trees
    searched to transmit m_j^i; v_k: # of indices used by h_k */
7. S_1 = ST$\left(m_j^i\right) \times \bar{\xi}^q_{\text{TM}\left(m_j^i\right)/\text{ST}\left(m_j^i\right)}$;/* S_1: bound on
    search times for isolating TM$\left(m_j^i\right)$ over ST$\left(m_j^i\right)$
    consecutive static trees; q: power of m; ξ_k^t: search time
    for isolating k leaves in a t-leaf balanced m-ary tree;
    $\bar{\xi}_k^t$: asymptotic expression of ξ_k^t */
8. S_2 = $\left\lceil \text{ST}\left(m_j^i\right)/2 \right\rceil \times \xi_2^F$;/* S_2: bound on search times for
    isolating ST$\left(m_j^i\right)$ time tree leaves over $\left\lceil \text{ST}\left(m_j^i\right)/2 \right\rceil$
    consecutive static trees; F: # of leaves in time tree */
9. $S = S_1 + S_2$;
10. For each message $m_q^p \in FS$
    10.1 MD$\left(m_j^i\right)$ = MD$\left(m_j^i\right)$ +
        $\left\lceil \frac{dl\left(m_j^i\right) + dl\left(m_q^p\right) - \frac{ln\left(m_j^i\right)}{\psi}}{w\left(m_q^p\right)} \right\rceil a\left(m_q^p\right) \frac{ln\left(m_q^p\right)}{\psi} + xS$;
    /* x: slot time of broadcast media */
11. If MD$\left(m_j^i\right) \le dl\left(m_j^i\right)$
    11.1 Return TRUE;
12. else
    12.1 Return FALSE;

Figure 3. Pseudo-Code of *CSMA-DDCRFeasible* **Procedure**

ABA determines the communication delay of a message using the new arrival density of the message if the arrival density has exceeded the upper bound that was postulated at design time. If there is no change in arrival density, then the protocol uses the design-time postulated upper bound on arrival density.

Thus for each message, ABA tentatively includes the message in the feasible set. The protocol then ex-amines each message in the feasible set (including the newly added message), and analyzes the feasibility of the message by considering the arrival densities of all other messages in the set since they can interfere with the message. If a message is found to be infeasible, then it is removed from the feasible set and buffered until the arrival density of the set of messages that increased reduces back to their design-time postulated values (and thus all messages become feasible). Otherwise, if the message is found to be feasible, it is maintained in the set.

The pseudo-code of a procedure called *DetFeasibleMessageSet* that ABA uses for determining a feasible message set is shown in Figure 2. Note that *DetFeasibleMessageSet* invokes the procedure *CSMA-DDCRFeasible* for determining the communication delay of a message. The pseudo-code of *CSMA-DDCRFeasible* is shown in Figure 3. The procedure *CSMA-DDCRFeasible* is constructed from the CSMA/DDCR feasibility condition presented in [5] and is presented here only for completeness.

6. Experimental evaluation

6.1. Experimental Setup

We conducted application-driven simulation studies to evaluate the performance of ABA. Details of the application parameters used in our experiments were derived from the *DynBench* real-time benchmark described in [13].

As discussed in Section 1, to study how well ABA performs, we consider the RBA* algorithm [4] as a baseline algorithm. RBA* employs a process-replication mechanism, where application processes are dynamically replicated and executed on different hosts for sharing workload increases. The algorithm transparently replicates subtasks of end-to-end tasks and executes replicas on different hosts when workloads of subtasks increase at run-time, causing task response times to increase and cause task timing failures. By replicating subtasks, RBA* seeks to distribute the workload of the subtask among the replicas, exploit concurrency, and thereby reduce task response times.

RBA* employed the replication mechanism for adaptation due to the belief that increases in subtask workloads causing increases in subtask execution times can be best compensated by replicating the subtask and sharing the workload among the replicas. The effectiveness of RBA* was experimentally demonstrated for a broad range of workload conditions in [4].

Since the means of resource allocation for ABA and RBA* are fundamentally different, we considered workload patterns that positively and negatively affect their means. Specifically, we considered three workload scenarios in our study. These include (1) a scenario called "LS-1," where arrival densities of messages increase at a faster rate than execution latencies of subtasks; (2) a scenario called "LS-2," where execution latencies of subtasks increase at a faster rate than arrival densities of messages; and (3) a scenario called "LS-3," where both arrival densities of messages and execution latencies of subtasks increase at the same rate.

6.2. Performance Results

Figure 4 shows the aggregate benefit and deadline-satisfied ratio of ABA and RBA* during the load condition LS-1. From the figure, we observe that ABA yields higher aggregate benefit and higher deadline-satisfied ratio than RBA* during LS-1 when message arrival densities increase at faster rates than subtask execution latencies. This result is intuitive, since ABA performs adaptation at the message-level. In contrast, RBA* performs poorly during such situations when increases in subtask execution latencies is not substantial, thereby diminishing the prospects of the algorithm to make an impact through subtask-level adaptation.

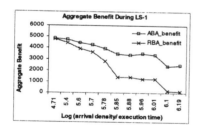

(a) Aggregate Benefit

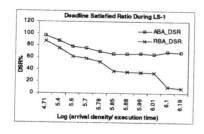

(b) Deadline Satisfied Ratio

Figure 4. Performance During LS-1

Figure 5 shows the aggregate benefit and deadline-satisfied ratio of ABA and RBA* during the load con-

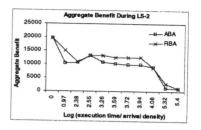

(a) Aggregate Benefit

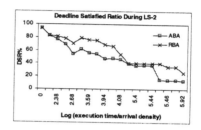

(b) Deadline Satisfied Ratio

Figure 5. Performance During LS-2

dition LS-2. From the figure, we note that RBA* yields higher aggregate benefit and higher deadline-satisfied ratio than ABA during LS-2 when subtask execution latencies increase at faster rates than message arrival densities. This is not surprising, as RBA* exploits increases in subtask execution latencies through replication. On the other hand, the smaller increases in message arrival densities diminishes the ability of ABA to perform effective message-level adaptation.

Finally, in Figure 6, we observe that ABA outperforms RBA* during LS-3, when both subtask execution latencies and message arrival densities increase at the same rate. This is an interesting result as it demonstrates the strong effectiveness of the protocol.

7. Conclusions and Ongoing Work

In this paper, we present a best-effort communication protocol called ABA, that seeks to maximize aggregate application benefit and deadline-satisfied ratio of asynchronous real-time distributed systems that use CSMA/DDCR broadcast networks. ABA considers an application model where end-to-end timeliness requirements of trans-node application tasks are specified using Jensen's benefit functions. Furthermore, the protocol assumes that the application is designed using CSMA/DDCR feasibility conditions that is driven by

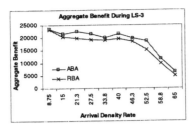

(a) Aggregate Benefit

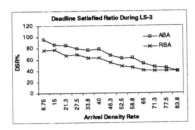

(b) Deadline Satisfied Ratio

Figure 6. Performance During LS-3

a best possible postulation of the application workload that is possible at design-time. When such design-time workload postulations get violated at run-time, ABA directs message traffic so that messages that will increase applications' aggregate benefit are only transmitted, buffering others, until such time when the workloads respect their design-time postulated values.

To study the performance of ABA, we consider a previously studied algorithm called RBA*, for a similar problem. Our experimental results illustrate that ABA yields higher aggregate benefit and higher deadline-satisfied ratio than RBA* when message arrival densities increase at faster rates or at the same rates as that of process execution latencies due to the dynamics of the workload.

Thus, the contribution of the paper is the ABA protocol that seeks to maximize aggregate application benefit and deadline-satisfied ratio of asynchronous real-time distributed systems that use CSMA/DDCR networks.

Several aspects of this work are currently being studied. A serious limitation of ABA is that it assumes that end-hosts and application programs never fail. This is not true in asynchronous real-time distributed systems, which are subject to failures that may arbitrarily occur. Furthermore, ABA considers only step-benefit functions. Non-step benefit functions will allow greater flexibility in adaptation [11]. Thus, we are extending ABA to deal with failures and arbitrary benefit functions.

8. Acknowledgements

This work was supported by the U.S. Office of Naval Research under Grant N00014-00-1-0549.

References

[1] R. Bettati, editor. *Proceedings of The IEEE Workshop on Middleware for Distributed Real-Time Systems and Services.* IEEE Computer Society, December 1997. The 18th IEEE Real-Time Systems Symposium.

[2] K. Chen and P. Muhlethaler. A scheduling algorithm for tasks described by time value function. *Journal of Real-Time Systems*, 10(3):293–312, May 1996.

[3] R. K. Clark. *Scheduling Dependent Real-Time Activities.* PhD thesis, Carnegie Mellon University, 1990. CMU-CS-90-155.

[4] T. Hegazy and B. Ravindran. Using application benefit for proactive resource allocation in asynchronous real-time distributed systems. *IEEE Transactions on Computers*, 2002.

[5] J.-F. Hermant and G. L. Lann. A protocol and correctness proofs for real-time high-performance broadcast networks. In *Proceedings of the Eighteenth International Conference on Distributed Computing Systems*, pages 360–369, 1998.

[6] D. A. R. P. A. IPTO. Quorum. Available at: www.darpa.mil/ipto/research/quorum/projlist.html, August 1997.

[7] E. D. Jensen. Asynchronous decentralized real-time computer systems. In W. A. Halang and A. D. Stoyenko, editors, *Real-Time Computing*, Proceedings of the NATO Advanced Study Institute. Springer Verlag, October 1992.

[8] E. D. Jensen and B. Ravindran. Special issue on asynchronous real-time distributed systems. Call for papers available at: www.ee.vt.edu/~tocsi/, 2000.

[9] B. Kao and H. Garcia-Molina. Deadline assignment in a distributed soft real-time system. *IEEE Transactions on Parallel and Distributed Systems*, 8(12):1268–1274, December 1997.

[10] J. W. S. Liu. *Real-Time Systems.* Prentice Hall, New Jersey, 2000.

[11] C. D. Locke. *Best-Effort Decision Making for Real-Time Scheduling.* PhD thesis, Carnegie Mellon University, 1986. CMU-CS-86-134.

[12] D. L. Mills. Improved algorithms for synchronizing computer network clocks. *IEEE/ACM Transactions on Networking*, pages 245–254, June 1995.

[13] L. R. Welch and B. A. Shirazi. A dynamic real-time benchmark for assessment of qos and resource management technology. In *Proceedings of The Fifth IEEE Real-Time Technology and Applications Symposium*, June 1999.

Reliable MAC Layer Multicast in IEEE 802.11 Wireless Networks

Min-Te Sun, Lifei Huang, Anish Arora, Ten-Hwang Lai
Department of Computer and Information Science
The Ohio State University
2015 Neil Avenue
Columbus, OH 43210-1277
{msun, huangli, anish, lai}@cis.ohio-state.edu

Abstract

Multicast/broadcast is an important service primitive in networks. The IEEE 802.11 multicast/broadcast protocol is based on the basic access procedure of Carrier Sense Multiple Access with Collision Avoidance (CSMA/CA). This protocol does not provide any media access control (MAC) layer recovery on multicast/broadcast frames. As a result, the reliability of the multicast/broadcast service is reduced due to the increased probability of lost frames resulting from interference or collisions. In this paper, we propose a reliable **Batch Mode Multicast MAC** *protocol, BMMM, which substantially reduces the number of contention phases, thus considerably reduces the time required for a multicast/broadcast. We then propose a* **Location Aware Multicast MAC** *protocol, LAMM, that uses station location information to further improve upon BMMM. Extensive analysis and simulation results validate the reliability and efficiency of our multicast MAC protocols.*

1 Introduction

Media Access Control (MAC) remains a fundamental research problems in wireless networks, given the difficulties caused by transmission errors, collisions, and hidden nodes. These difficulties become even more severe when support is provided for multicast/broadcast communication in wireless networks. Such support is necessary for delivering acceptable quality of service in many applications of wireless communications, such as emergency reporting or video conferencing. Moreover, even in scenarios where applications themselves do not demand multicast/broadcast, several higher layer protocols rely heavily on reliable and efficient MAC layer multicast/broadcast, for instance DSR [8], AODV [16] and ZRP [7] routing protocols. It is important to note that multicast/broadcast in the MAC layer refers specifically to the process of sending a data frame to some/all of the *neighbors* of a node. Henceforth in our presentation we treat broadcast as a special case of multicast.

Of the many random access MAC protocols for wireless networks that have been proposed so far, most primarily target unicast communications and do not yield an efficient basis for simulating multicast [9, 6]. In the few that do deal directly with multicast [2, 3], it is apparent that reliability is not a major concern. For instance, in the IEEE 802.11 specification [2], the multicast sender simply listens to the channel and then transmits its data frame when the channel becomes free for a period of time. There is no MAC-level recovery on multicast frame. As a result, the reliability of multicast is reduced due to the increased probability of lost frames resulting from interference or collisions. As another example, in [3], it is simply suggested that the sender transmits a *Request To Send* (RTS) frame immediately followed by the data frame(s). This RTS frame informs the neighbors which are idle to yield their transmissions to somewhat reduce the chance of message collisions. Again, the reliability of this scheme is low.

Recently a few multicast MAC protocols [19, 20, 21] have been proposed to enhance the reliability and the efficiency of the 802.11 multicast protocol. In this paper, we observe that even these protocols have serious reliability and/or efficiency issues. We demonstrate a reliability issue in the first two protocols [19, 20], and show that while the third protocol [21] is logically reliable, it is inefficient and can easily lead to message timeouts. Further, towards redressing these reliability and efficiency issues, we design two multicast MAC protocols based on the IEEE 802.11 *Distributed Coordination Function* (DCF) MAC protocol.

Our first protocol, *Batch Mode Multicast MAC* (BMMM), reduces the number of contention phases from n to 1, where n is the number of intended receivers in a multicast. Essentially, it provides a simple coordination mechanism for avoiding collisions in the transmissions of *Clear To Send* (CTS) and *Acknowledge* (ACK) frames, and ensures that each time the data frame is transmitted, it is received by as many intended receivers as possible. Therefore, BMMM is able to substantially reduce the average total time to complete a multicast MAC request.

Our second protocol, *Location Aware Multicast MAC* (LAMM), uses location information to further improve BMMM. Let S denote the set of intended receivers of a multicast MAC request. We show how the successful transmission of data frame to all nodes in S' using BMMM, where $S' \subseteq S$, is enough to ensure the reception of data by all nodes in S without collision. Assuming that the transmission radius is constant, we provide a necessary and sufficient condition for S'. This significantly reduces the number of

RTS, CTS, RAK and ACK frames in the BMMM protocol. We note that since the US *Federal Communications Commission* (FCC) has requested all wireless service carriers to provide the location service of emergency 911 calls [1], soon each wireless device will be able to identify its own location by means of the geolocation techniques [5]. Indeed, location information has already been used in some routing protocols [10, 4, 22, 12, 15, 17]. But to the best of our knowledge, this paper is the first effort to utilize location information at the MAC layer in wireless networks.

Using the same control and data frame formats in IEEE 802.11 specification, our protocols are able to co-exist with the current unreliable IEEE 802.11 multicast MAC protocol to provide reliable multicast MAC services when needed. To validate the performance of BMMM and LAMM, we have both analyzed and simulated our protocols along with the BSMA protocol in [20] and the BMW protocol in [21]. Our results show that our protocols are substantially more reliable and efficient than the others.

2 Existing Multicast MAC Protocols

As mentioned in Section 1, one purpose of this paper is to report our observations of performances of existing multicast MAC protocols. To this end, we begin with a brief description of CSMA/CA and three other multicast MAC protocols. Note that in IEEE 802.11, the beacon containing the station MAC address is broadcast periodically by each station to announce its presence. A station knows the neighbor's MAC addresses through the exchanges of beacon signals. Each station in the network maintains a routing table containing both the next hop information to the destination and the members of each multicast group. When a multicast request arrives from the network layer, it is assumed that the request indicates the set of neighbors required to reach all the members of the intended multicast group.

2.1 Carrier Sense Multiple Access with Collision Avoidance

The idea of *Carrier Sense Multiple Access with Collision Avoidance* (CSMA/CA) proposed in [11] has been used in many wireless MAC protocols. It works as follows.

Carrier Sense Multiple Access with Collision Avoidance Protocol (CSMA/CA): 1. A node wishing to transmit first listens to the medium.

2. If the medium is idle, transmit the frame.

3. If the medium is busy, then continue to listen until the medium is idle; then backoff for x slots of time, where x is a random number within the contention window.

(a) If the channel is still idle when the backoff timer expires, transmit the frame.

(b) If the channel becomes busy before the timer expires,

stop the timer and listen to the channel again; when the channel is detected idle, restart the backoff timer.

4. After transmission, if the node does not receive an ACK, attempt to retransmit the frame.

5. After receiving a data frame, the receiver returns an ACK.

From the above protocol, we can see that CSMA/CA protocol assumes an Ethernet-like wireless environment and intends to avoid message collision by sensing the medium status at the sender side. When the medium is busy, the node backs off its frame transmission to avoid collision. The step 1, 2 and 3(b) of the CSMA/CA protocol is commonly referred to as the *contention phase*.

The CSMA/CA protocol is known to suffer from the *hidden terminal problem*. Assume stations p and q are within each other's transmission range, and so are stations q and r; but p and r cannot hear from each other. Suppose node p wants to transmit a frame to node q while q's neighbor, r, is transmitting. Using the CSMA/CA protocol, node p will find the medium idle and transmit the frame, causing collisions at q.

Proposed in [3, 6, 9], a common method to solve the hidden terminal problem is to extend the CSMA/CA protocol with a Request-To-Send/Clear-To-Send (RTS/CTS) handshake. Before transmitting a data frame, the sender transmits an RTS frame, with an indication of the amount of time needed. Upon receiving RTS, the receiver returns a CTS, also with an indication of the time needed. All other nodes that hear RTS and/or CTS must back off for the amount of time indicated in RTS/CTS to avoid collisions. This creates a virtual carrier sense at the receiver end and avoids the hidden terminal problem. The IEEE 802.11 *Distributed Coordination Function* (DCF) MAC protocol [2] is essentially the CSMA/CA protocol with the optional RTS/CTS extension.

2.2 Description of Existing Multicast Protocols

In IEEE 802.11, the RTS/CTS extension is not used for broadcast/multicast; and the receivers are not required to return an ACK. As a result, the quality of broadcast/multicast service is not as good as that of unicast.

The protocol in [19] attempts to extend the IEEE 802.11 broadcast/multicast protocol (i.e., the basic DCF MAC) with RTS/CTS handshaking. According to the protocol, when there is a broadcast data frame to send, the sender first executes the contention phase. Once obtaining access to the medium, the sender transmits an RTS frame to its neighbors and waits for CTS frames for WAIT_FOR_CTS time units. If a node receives an RTS frame when it is not in the YIELD phase, it sends back a CTS and then waits for the data frame for WAIT_FOR_DATA time units. If the sender receives any CTS frame before the WAIT_FOR_CTS timer expires, it transmits the data frame. If the sender does not receive any CTS frame before its WAIT_FOR_CTS timer expires, it backs off and enters the contention phase again to retransmit the broadcast data frame.

In [20], the *Broadcast Support Multiple Access* (BSMA)

protocol augments the broadcast MAC protocol in [19] with the NAK frame and the following additional rules:

1. After the sender transmits a data frame, it waits for WAIT_FOR_NAK time units for any possible transmission problem reported by the neighboring nodes.

2. If a receiver does not receive the data frame after it transmitted the CTS frame for WAIT_FOR_DATA time units, it transmits a NAK frame.

3. If the sender does not receive any NAK frame before its WAIT_FOR_NAK timer expires, the broadcast service is complete. Otherwise, the sender backs off and enters the contention phase again to retransmit the broadcast data.

In [21], the *Broadcast Medium Window* (BMW) protocol is introduced to provide a reliable broadcast MAC. The basic idea of the BMW protocol is to treat each broadcast request as multiple unicast requests. Each unicast is processed using the reliable IEEE 802.11 DCF MAC protocol (i.e., CSMA/RTS/CTS/DATA/ACK) with some minor modifications. In BMW, each node maintains three lists: NEIGHBOR, SEND BUFFER and RECEIVER BUFFER. The NEIGHBOR list contains the current neighbors. The SEND BUFFER list contains the ongoing broadcast messages. The node's RECEIVE BUFFER list contains the sequence numbers of the data frames received by the node.

In BMW, when a node has a broadcast data to send, it first executes the contention phase. Afterwards, the sender places the message into its SEND BUFFER and sends out an RTS frame containing the sequence number of the upcoming data frame and the MAC address of the first node in its NEIGHBOR list. When a node receives a RTS intended for it, it checks its RECEIVE BUFFER list to see if it has received all the data frames with sequence number smaller than or equal to the upcoming one. If all the data frames (including the upcoming one) have been received, the receiver sends a CTS with appropriate information to suppress the sender's data frame transmission. Otherwise, the receiver sends a CTS frame with all the missing data frame sequence numbers. The sender, upon receiving the CTS frame from one of the neighbors, checks the CTS frame to transmit all the missing data frames and waits for an ACK. After receiving the data frame, the receiver sends an ACK. The sender moves on to serve the next node on the NEIGHBOR list if either the returned CTS frame indicates all the data frames have been received or an ACK has been received. If all nodes in the NEIGHBOR list have been served, the sender removes the message from its SEND BUFFER.

3 Problems with Existing Multicast MAC Protocols

In [19], the MAC protocol does not coordinate the transmission of the CTS frames. This brings about a serious problem: the collision of CTS frames. Since this protocol is an extension of the IEEE 802.11 DCF MAC, the intended receivers will each send a CTS frame immediately after a short inter-frame spacing (SIFS) if it is not in the YIELD phase. This SIFS is predefined and has the same value for all nodes. For a multicast RTS, if more than one intended receiver replies with a CTS frame, these CTS frames are destined to collide with each other at the sender. To take care of this problem, an assumption is made in [19] that the sender's radio has the *Direct Sequence* (DS) capture ability. That is, when a node receives multiple frames at the same time, the frame with the strongest power can be captured by the node. However, according to [3], in order to successfully capture the frame, the strongest frame's Signal-to-Interference Ratio (SIR) needs to be at least 10dB. If there are only two nodes sending CTS frames with the same power, this requires that one node is at least 1.5 times far away from the sender than the other node is. When more than two nodes are sending CTS frames simultaneously, this SIR is difficult to achieve. In [23], it is reported that when nodes are distributed uniformly, the "capture" effect occurs with a probability at about 0.55 when there are two competing nodes. This probability quickly drops to 0.3 at the presence of 5 nodes and then further drops to 0.2. Thus, in the protocol of [19], the sender is most likely to miss the CTS frames due to collision and the sender's low capture ability. According to the protocol, the sender will back off its transmission of data frame and, after another contention phase, send another RTS. The above process may repeat for several times until a CTS capture is successful or the message times out thus increasing the total time of multicast.

At a first glance, it seems easy to alleviate CTS collisions by allowing each intended receiver to defer its CTS transmission for a random amount of time. That is, instead of sending a CTS after a SIFS time gap, each receiver i defers for a random number, x_i, of time slots, where x_i is an integer within a contention window, say $[0..w]$. This random defer time scheme can reduce the chance of CTS collision at the sender, *if the value of w is not too small*. Unfortunately, as explained below, this is not easy to achieve. According to IEEE 802.11, after the medium is idle for a time equal to *DCF Inter-Frame Spacing* (DIFS), every node can contend for access to the wireless channel. Thus, to implement the above random defer time scheme, the value of w should be *less* than $\frac{DIFS-SIFS}{length\ of\ a\ slot}$ so as to ensure that each CRT is sent before any node has a chance to send any non-CRT frame.

According to the IEEE 802.11 specification, for the *Frequency Hopping Spread Spectrum* (FHSS) medium, the lengths of SIFS and DIFS are 28 and 128 microseconds, respectively, and each slot is 50 microseconds. Thus, the maximum value allowed for w is 1[1], which evidently is too small for the above random defer time scheme to work effectively. One may argue that we can increase the size of w by increasing the value of DIFS. That may be true, but it certainly is unacceptable because a longer DIFS value would considerably slow down all communications in all IEEE 802.11 networks.

---

[1] Actually, there is a value PIFS, defined to be 78 microsecond for FHSS systems. If a medium is idle for PIFS time, a specific node can send a beacon frame to switch to the point coordinated mode. If this feature is available in the wireless network in question, the only value available for w would be 0!

529

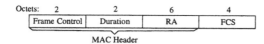

Figure 1. RAK Frame Format

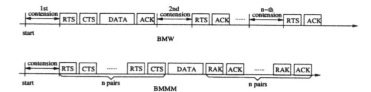

Figure 2. BMW vs BMMM

The BSMA protocol in [20] is essentially the same as the protocol in [19], except that it includes the NAK frame. That means that the BSMA protocol has exactly the same CTS collision problem. The additional NAK frame in [20] does not help resolve the collision of the CTS frame. In fact, since the transmissions of NAK frame are not coordinated either. The same collision problem exists when more than one node send the NAK frames.

The protocols in [19, 20], whether with or without NAK [19, 20], are unreliable in that when a multicast is done, they do not know whether every intended receiver has received the data. These protocols do not improve much in reliability over the current IEEE 802.11 multicast service. In the above sense, the BMW protocol in [21] is reliable because, if necessary, the sender will retransmit the data frame until it has received an ACK from every intended receiver. However, BMW is inefficient for following reasons:

- Contention phase — The BMW protocol requires at least n contention phases for each multicast data frame. Not only is each contention phase lengthy in time, but also the sender has to contend with other nodes for access to the medium. It is possible that some other node wins the contention and thereby interrupts and prolongs the ongoing multicast process.

- Timeout — In many applications (e.g., routing), multicast is time sensitive. If the multicast request can not be fulfilled within a certain amount time, the multicast request will be considered unsuccessful by the higher layer. For such applications, the prolonged multicast process as pointed out above can easily lead to a timeout in the higher layer.

4 Batch Mode Multicast MAC Protocol

In BMW, the sender uses at least n rounds of DCF-like unicasts for a multicast request intended for n neighboring nodes. Each round requires one contention phase before an RTS frame can be sent. If we consolidate the n contention phases into one, then the required time to serve a multicast can be greatly reduced. This is the primary idea of our *Batch Mode Multicast MAC Protocol* (BMMM).

To achieve this goal, the design issue is how to coordinate the transmissions of the control frames, including RTS, CTS and ACK, with no modification of the frame format in IEEE 802.11 specification. First, we want to ensure that there is no collision among control frame transmissions. Second, if one of the sender's neighbors has data to send, it should not pass its contention phase when the sender is exchanging control frames with its intended receivers. To avoid the collisions among CTS and ACK frames, the sender needs to provide a simple coordination among the intended receivers. To prevent a neighbor from passing its contention phase, the protocol needs to ensure the medium will not idle for long when a multicast request is processing. To meet the above requirements, we design the protocol such that the sender instructs its intended receivers (of a multicast) to transmit the control frame in order. The sender uses its RTS frames to sequentially instruct each intended receiver to transmit a CTS. To coordinate ACK transmissions from receivers, a new control frame is required. We therefore propose a new control frame type called RAK (Request for ACK). The RAK frame, as shown in Figure 1, has the same format as the ACK frame. It contains frame control, Duration, receiver address (RA) and frame check sequence (FCS). With the help of the RAK frame, the sender can coordinate the ACK transmissions in the similar manner it coordinates the CTS transmissions. That is, after the transmission of the data frame, the sender uses the RAK frames to sequentially instruct each intended receiver to transmit an ACK. Figure 2 illustrates the difference between BMW and BMMM when the data is received by all intended receivers successfully at the first try.

Our BMMM protocol has several advantages:

- Our protocol greatly reduces the number of contention phases, which will be shown by our analysis and simulation. The time decreased by the reduction of contention phases is much larger than the time increased by the introduction of RAK frames because the transmission of each RAK frame takes one time slot while one contention phase generally takes much more than one time slot. Therefore, our protocol significantly decreases the required time to serve a multicast request.

- Our multicast protocol does not modify any control frame format. This allows our multicast MAC protocol to co-exist with the other IEEE 802.11 protocols, including the unreliable IEEE 802.11 multicast MAC protocol. A multicast request can specify if it needs a reliable service or not from the upper layer to select the appropriate multicast MAC protocol to use.

- In our protocol, the sender transmits RTS frames periodically before sending data and transmits RAK frames periodically after sending the data. This means that the medium will never be idle for more than $2 \cdot SIFS + (T_{CTS} or T_{ACK})$, which is less than DIFS. Since any neighbor wishing to transmit data must listen to ensure the channel is free for at least DIFS, having sender

Batch_Mode_Procedure(Input: S, Output: S_{ACK})

  s executes the contention phase

  for each $p_i \in S$

    s sends RTS containing p_i's MAC address and

      Duration $:= (\|S\| - i) \cdot T_{RTS} + (\|S\| - i + 1) \cdot$

      $T_{CTS} + T_{DATA} + \|S\| \cdot (T_{RAK} + T_{ACK})$

    s waits CTS from p_i for T_{CTS}

  if s received at least one CTS frame

    s sends DATA frame

    for each $p_i \in S$

      s sends RAK containing p_i's MAC address

      s waits ACK from p_i for T_{ACK}

  else /* no CTS was received */

    s backs off and starts the sender's protocol again

  let $S_{ACK} \subseteq S$ be the set of nodes from which S has

  received an ACK

Sender's Protocol:

  if s has a multicast message to send to the nodes in S and

  it is not in yield state

    while $S \neq \emptyset$

      Call Batch_Mode_Procedure(S, S_{ACK})

      $S = S \setminus S_{ACK}$

Receiver's Protocol:

  if a node p receives an RTS frame

    if p's MAC address matches the RTS's receiver address

    and it is not in yield state

      p sends out CTS containing Duration := Duration in

      RTS - T_{CTS}

  if a node p receives a RAK frame

    if p's MAC address matches the RAK's receiver's and

    p has received the data frame and it is not yielding

      p sends ACK containing Duration = Duration in

      RAK - T_{RAK}

  if a node q receives a control frame (RTS/CTS/RAK/ACK)

  not intended for it

    q yields for Duration time specified in the control frame

Figure 3. The Batch Mode Multicast MAC Protocol (BMMM).

transmitting RTS and RAK frames periodically prevents any neighbor from passing its contention phase.

5 Location Aware Multicast MAC Protocol

We pointed out in Section 1 that a node's geographic location can be easily obtained from the Global Position System (GPS). Considering the transmission radius of the IEEE 802.11 (up to 500 feet for 802.11b), the GPS location information is accurate enough to be used for our purpose. In IEEE 802.11 specification, the frame body of the beacon frame format is well enough to accommodate the GPS location information (< 30 bits). If we including the location information in beacons, neighbors will learn each other's location. Location information has been used in some routing protocols. In this section, we investigate the possibility of utilizing location information in medium access control.

The BMMM protocol in Section 3 reduces the number of contention phases by putting $\|S\|$ pairs of RTS/CTS together. The nodes that successfully received the data frame are expected to each return an ACK after it receives a RAK. When the size of S is large, it may be desirable to reduce S's size by considering only a subset of it. That is, when running the BMMM protocol, we send RTS only to the addresses of nodes in a subset, S', of S, and expect only those nodes to return a CTS and, later after receiving the data frame and its RAK frame, return an ACK. Without an explicit ACK from each node in $S \setminus S'$, the sender of course has no way to know whether the nodes in $S \setminus S'$ have received the data frame. But is it possible that by receiving only the ACKs from those nodes in $S' \subseteq S$, the sender is able to conclude that all nodes in S have received the multicast data frame without collision, assuming the transmission error is caused primarily by the collision? In this section, we show that for some subsets S', this is indeed possible. We also establish a necessary and sufficient condition that characterizes all such subsets S'.

Let $A(s)$ denote the coverage area of s, and let $A(S) = \bigcup A(s_i)$ where $s_i \in S$.

Definition 1 *Let S be a set of nodes. A subset S' of S is said to be a cover set of S if $A(S') = A(S)$.*

The following theorem characterizes the above mentioned S'.

Theorem 1 *Let S be the set of all intended receivers of the multicast data frame. In the Batch_Mode_Procedure(), suppose that the sender receives an ACK from every node in a subset S' of S. A node p in $S \setminus S'$ is guaranteed to have received the data frame without collision if and only if S' is a cover set of S.*

Due to length limit, all the proof are omitted in this paper. According to Theorem 1, given a set of intended receivers S, if a minimum cover set of S can be found, then not only the size of the RTS frame but also the number of CTS and ACK frames can be greatly reduced. Computing the minimum cover set is itself an interesting and nontrivial computational geometric problem. In [18], we show that if the sender knows the locations of nodes in S, the minimum cover set of S can be computed in $O(n^{4/3})$ time, where n is the av-

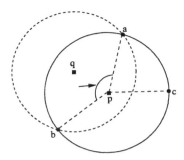

Figure 4. Cover Angle of node p for node q

erage number of intended receivers for a multicast request. For ease of reference, we state this result in the following as a theorem.

Theorem 2 ([18]) *The minimum cover set of a neighbor set S can be computed in $O(n^{4/3})$ time.*

Theorem 1 assumes that every node in S' returns an ACK and all the ACKs are received correctly. The next theorem indicates that even if not every nodes in S' returns an ACK or if not all ACKs are received correctly, we can still tell which nodes in $S \setminus S'$ must have received the data frame without collision.

Theorem 3 *Let S be the set of all intended receivers of the multicast data frame. In the Batch_Mode_Procedure(), suppose that the sender receives an ACK from every node in a subset $S_{ACK} \subseteq S'$, where S' is a cover set of S. Under the assumption that the primary transmission error is caused by collision, a node p in $S \setminus S'$ is guaranteed to have received the data frame without collision if and only if $A(p) \subseteq A(S_{ACK})$.*

To apply Theorem 3, we need an algorithm for easily checking if $A(p) \subseteq A(S_{ACK})$. That is, we want an efficient algorithm to identify if the transmission area of a node is completely covered by the transmission areas of a set of nodes. This is also a non-trivial computational geometry problem. In the following we describe an *angle-based scheme* for this purpose. Before stating the algorithm, we first define the cover angle for the neighboring nodes.

Definition 2 *Assume two nodes p and q are neighbors to each other. Let a and b denote the intersections of $A(p)$ and $A(q)$ boundaries, and c be the intersection of the straight horizontal line passing through p and $A(p)$ boundary to the east of p, the cover angle of p for q is defined to be $\angle apb$ and is denoted as $[\angle cpa, \angle cpb]$, where $\alpha = \angle cpa$ and $\beta = \angle cpb$ (both counter-clockwise). If two nodes are at the same location, their cover angle is defined to be $[0, 360]$. If two nodes are more than R away from each other, their cover angle is defined to be $\emptyset$.*

The arrow in Figure 4 indicates the cover angle of p for q to be $[\angle cpa, \angle cpb]$.

Assuming that the transmission radius is R, the cover angle $[\alpha, \beta]$ of two neighbors can be easily calculated.

Assume that a cover angle $\angle apb$ of p for q is non-zero, according to the definition of the cover angle, it is not difficult to see that the sector of $A(p)$ from $\overrightarrow{pa}$ to $\overrightarrow{pb}$ falls inside

$A(p) \cap A(q)$, hence is covered by $A(q)$. The cover angle provides an efficient way to identify if the transmission area of a node p is completely covered by a set of nodes C.

Theorem 4 *Assume that all nodes have the same transmission radius R. Given a node p and a set of nodes C, if the union of the cover angles $\cup_i [\alpha_i, \beta_i]$ is $[0, 360]$, where $[\alpha_i, \beta_i]$ is p's cover angle for $s_i \in C$, the transmission area of p, $A(p)$, is completely covered by C.*

The *Location Aware Multicast MAC* (LAMM) protocol is a refinement of the Batch Mode Multicast MAC protocol. Assume the intended receiver set of the multicast data frame to be S and the ACK set to be S', we denote MCS(S) the minimum cover set computation procedure that takes S as input and returns the the minimum cover set of S using the algorithm in [18]. Also, we denote UPDATE(S, S') the angle-based procedure that takes both S and S' and returns the set of nodes in S that are not completely covered by S'. The Location Aware Multicast MAC protocol can be formally expressed as following using the Batch Mode Procedure in the BMMM protocol. (The receiver's Location Aware Multicast MAC protocol and the Batch Mode Procedure are exactly the same as in Figure 3.)

Sender's Location Aware Multicast MAC Protocol
    if s has a multicast message to send to the nodes in S
        while $S \neq \emptyset$
            Batch Mode Procedure(MCS(S), S_{ACK})
            $S =$ UPDATE(S, S_{ACK})

6 Analysis

BMMM, LAMM, BMW and BSMA all use the RTS-CTS approach. After sending an RTS frame, if the sender does not receive any CTS frame, it will enter another contention phase to retransmit the RTS. This process is repeated until the sender hears at least one CTS signal and thus sends the data frame. In this section, we analyze the expected number of contention phases needed before the sender sends data for each of the four protocols.

There are five reasons why the sender may not receive a CTS frame from a certain receiver:

- transmission errors in the RTS frame

- collision of the RTS frame

- the receiver is yielding to some other message transmission

- transmission errors in the CTS frame

- collision of the CTS frame

For BMMM, LAMM and BMW the sender receives one CTS frame a time so there is no collision of CTS frames. For BMW, CTS frames may collide.

Combine the first four factors and let q be the probability that the sender does not receive a CTS from a given node due to one or more of these four reasons. Let S be the set of intended receivers and $n = \|S\|$ be its size. Let S' denote

Parameters	BMMM	LAMM	BMW	BSMA
$q = 0.05, n = 5, \|S'\| = 4$	1.00	1.00	1.05	3.27
$q = 0.05, n = 10, \|S'\| = 6$	1.00	1.00	1.05	4.08

Table 1. Expected number of contention phases before the sender sends data

the minimum cover set of S. The probability that at least one CTS frame is successful for BMMM, LAMM and BMW is $1 - q^n$, $1 - q^{\|S'\|}$ and $1 - q$, respectively. If p is the probability for the sender to hear at least one CTS signal, the expected number of contention phases before the sender receives at least one CTS signal is $1 + (1-p) + (1-p)^2 + (1-p)^3 + \cdots = 1/p$. Therefore, the expected numbers of contention phases for BMMM, LAMM and BMW are $\frac{1}{1-q^n}$, $\frac{1}{1-q^{\|S'\|}}$ and $\frac{1}{1-q}$, respectively.

But in BSMA protocol the CTS frames may collide with each other. [20] assumes the DS (direct sequence) capture ability of radio. Since the capture probability is low in general, the sender may still be unable to successfully detect the strongest CTS signal out of the colliding CTS signals. Therefore, to compute the probability of receiving one CTS frame, we need to take the capture probability into account. [23] gives a formula for computing the capture probability C_k for k concurrent signals. For the sender, the probability of receiving exactly k CTS signal is $C(n,k)(1-q)^k q^{n-k}$. Therefore, the probability of receiving one CTS frame is $\sum_{k=1}^{n} C(n,k)(1-q)^k q^{n-k} C_k$ and the expected number of contention phases is its reciprocal. We show two sets of probabilities in Table 1. The BMMM, LAMM and BMW protocols use much fewer contention phases before a data frame can be sent.

Next we analyze the overall numbers of contention phases needed by BMMM, LAMM and BMW. As we already know, the BMW protocol needs at least n contention phases. Considering our BMMM and LAMM protocol, suppose in a round of RTS/CTS/DATA/ACK transmission, the probability for an intended receiver to receive the data successfully is p. Let n denote the number of intended receivers and f_n be the expected number of contention phases for a multicast message that has n receivers. We can easily compute $f_1 = 1 + (1-p) + (1-p)^2 + (1-p)^3 + \cdots = 1/p$. For $n = 2$ we have $f_2 = 1 + C(2,1)p(1-p)f_1 + C(2,2)(1-p)^2 f_2$ and the solution is $f_2 = \frac{3-2p}{p(2-p)}$. For $n = 3$ we have $f_3 = 1 + C(3,1)p^2(1-p)f_1 + C(3,2)p(1-p)^2 f_2 + C(3,3)(1-p)^3 f_3$ and so on. The expected numbers of contention phases are shown in Figure 5 for different n and $p = 0.9$. As can be seen, the expected number of contention phases is far less than n and it increases much slower than the linear function. Therefore, BMMM and LAMM use much less a number of contention phases than BMW. This conclusion will be testified by simulation in the next section. Furthermore, the lines of the expected number of contention phases in Figure 5 coincide with the lines of the average number of contention

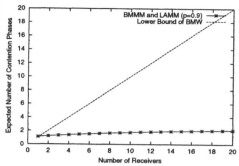

Figure 5. Expected number of Contention Phases in BMW, BMMM and LAMM

Parameter	Value
Signal Time	1 slot
Data Transmission Time	5 slots
Simulation Time	10000 slots
Time Out	100 slots
Radius	0.2
Unicast Message Ratio	0.2
Multicast Message Ratio	0.4
Broadcast Message Ratio	0.4
Message Generation Rate	0.0005/node/slot
Reliability Threshold	90%

Table 2. Parameters Used for Simulations

phases in Figure 9(a) very well.

7 Simulation

To evaluate our multicast MAC protocols, we developed our own wireless LAN simulator. The protocols we simulated include our BMMM and LAMM, as well as BSMA [19] and BMW [20]. We randomly placed 100 nodes in a unit square. Each node is able to send unicast, multicast and broadcast data frames to its neighbors using the simulated protocol. We assume that the time is slotted so that the event (e.g., message sending and receiving) happens at the beginning of a slot. To ensure that BSMA in [20] works as designed, we adopted the direct sequence capture ability for the radio channel. The probability of capturing a collided CTS frame was set according to [23]. All the simulation results were the means of 100 runs of simulations with different random seeds. A multicast message transmission is considered *successful* if the message reaches a certain percentage of the intended receivers. We call such a percentage the *reliability threshold*. If a multicast message either reaches less than the reliability threshold of the intended receivers or times out before completion, the transmission is considered unsuccessful. The following table lists the parameters we used in our simulations, if not mention otherwise:

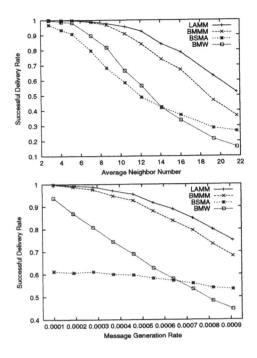

Figure 6. Successful Delivery Rate vs (a) Nodal Density (b) Message Generation Rate

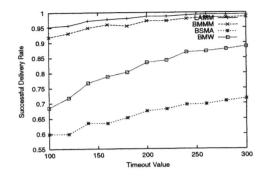

Figure 7. Successful Delivery Rate vs Timeout

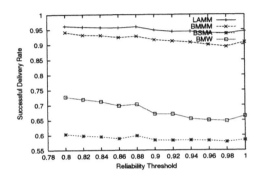

Figure 8. Successful Delivery Rate vs Reliability Threshold

7.1 Reliability

Reliability is the first feature we used to evaluate the protocols. To measure the reliability, we define the *successful delivery rate* to be the number of successful message transmissions divided by the total number of requests. A MAC protocol is reliable if it has a high successful delivery rate. Figures 6 (a) and (b) show the successful delivery rate under different nodal density and message generation rates. The x-axis is the average number of neighbors in Figure 6 (a) and the message generation rate in Figure 6 (b). The y-axis is the successful delivery rate for both Figures 6 (a) and (b).

As can be seen, the successful delivery rate of all protocols degrade when either the number of neighbors or the message generation rate increases. This is due to the fact that the more traffic in a transmission area, the more collisions may occur. Because of collisions, many messages time out before they can reach their destinations. In both Figures 6 (a) and (b), our LAMM and BMMM protocols enjoy the highest and the second highest successful delivery rate, respectively.

As we have pointed out, time-out is one of the major causes of the unsuccessful message transmissions. In Figure 7, we show how timeout value affects the successful delivery rate for different protocols. The x-axis is the timeout value ranging from 100 slots to 300 slots and the y-axis is the successful delivery rate in Figure 7. As expected, the larger the timeout value is, the higher successful delivery rate a protocol produces. No matter what timeout value is used, our BMMM and LAMM protocols constantly produce much higher successful delivery rate than BSMA and BMW protocols.

In the successful delivery rate definition, reliability threshold plays an important role. Next we illustrate how reliability threshold affects the successful delivery rate for different protocols in Figure 8, where the x-axis is the reliability threshold and the y-axis is the successful delivery rate. As can be seen, no matter what reliability threshold we use, our BMMM and LAMM protocols always produce much higher successful delivery rate than BMW and BSMA protocols.

7.2 Efficiency

The second feature we examine is the efficiency. In our simulations, We measure efficiency by the average number of contention phases and the average message completion time.

Figures 9 (a) and (b) show the average number of contention phases (i.e., CSMA/CA) for each protocol under different nodal density and message generation rates. The x-axis is the average number of neighbors in Figure 9 (a) and the message generation rate in Figure 9 (b). The y-axis is the average number of contention phases per message for both (a) and (b). In both Figures 9 (a) and (b), BMW requires the highest number of contention phases. Our BMMM and LAMM protocols are able to produce slightly lower aver-

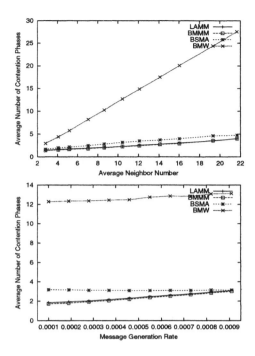

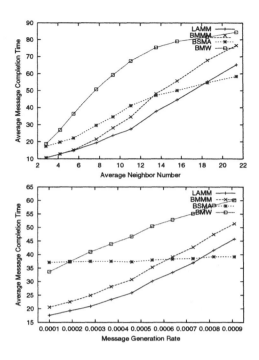

Figure 9. Average Number of Contention Phases vs (a) Nodal Density (b) Message Generation Rate

Figure 10. Average Message Completion Time vs (a) Nodal Density (b) Message Generation Rate

age number of contention phases than BSMA under different nodal density and message generation rates.

Figures 10 shows the average time required to complete a multicast for different protocol. The x-axis is the average number of neighbors in Figure 10 (a) and the message generation rate in Figure 10 (b). The y-axis is the average message completion time for both Figures 10 (a) and (b). As expected, Figures 10 (a) and (b) show that the LAMM protocol requires less time to complete a multicast than BMMM, which in turn requires less time than BMW. This is because of the excessive number of contention phases and control frames in BMW and the smaller number of CTS and ACK frames required by LAMM than by BMMM.

7.3 Comments on Simulation Results

The successful delivery rate is closely related to the average message completion time. The longer average message completion time, the more likely a multicast message may time out and thus lower the successful delivery rate. This explains why the rank of LAMM, BMMM and BMW protocols in Figures 10 (a) and (b) is the same as the rank in Figures 6 (a) and (b).

This simple relationship between the successful delivery rate and the average message completion time can not be applied to the BSMA protocol. In BMW, BMMM and LAMM, when a message is completely multicasted, all intended receivers are guaranteed to receive the message without collision. This is not true for BSMA because in BSMA a mes-

sage can be considered completely transmitted even when the message has not yet reached its intended receivers. This property explains why BMMM and LAMM have a higher successful delivery rate than BSMA even in the case when BSMA's average message completion time is shorter than BMMM and LAMM as shown in Figures 6 and 10.

From the simulation results, we can draw the following conclusions:

- No matter what metric is used, the BMW protocol always incurs the highest overhead. Under most situations, it has the lowest successful delivery rate. Therefore the BMW protocol is not a good multicast MAC protocol.

- As we have said, BSMA itself is not logically reliable. Although BSMA uses just a slightly larger number of contention phases than BMMM and LAMM, it shows much lower successful delivery rate than the latter two even if we allow radio direct sequence capture ability.

- The proposed BMMM and LAMM protocols have the best performance in terms of successful delivery rate and number of contention phases.

8 Conclusion

In this paper, we investigated the existing wireless multicast MAC protocols and showed that they are either unreliable or inefficient. We proposed two reliable multicast

535

MAC protocols: The Batch Mode Multicast MAC protocol and the Location Aware Multicast MAC protocol that can co-exist with the current unreliable IEEE 802.11 multicast MAC protocol. Based on the IEEE 802.11 DCF unicast MAC protocol, BMMM coordinates the receiver's control frame transmissions by sender's RTS and RAK frames. It not only avoids the control frame collisions but also prevents any neighbor from passing its contention phase. This helps noticeably reduce the number of contention phases for a multicast request. As a result, it decreases the average total time required to complete a multicast request and reduce the chance of message timeout. LAMM uses two location-based procedures to further improve upon BMMM. Our analysis and simulation results showed that both BMMM and LAMM exhibit improved reliability and efficiency, with LAMM generally outperforming BMMM.

We conclude with a pointer to future work. Throughout this paper, our focus has been on resolving the hidden terminal problem for multicast. Another problem that is challenging in wireless medium access control is the exposed terminal problem. To the best of our knowledge, no multicast MAC protocol has addressed the exposed terminal problem. With the help of location information, we hope to find an efficient multicast MAC protocol that solves both the hidden and exposed terminal problems.

References

[1] http://www.fcc.gov/e911/

[2] Editors of IEEE 802.11, Wireless LAN Medium Access Control (MAC and Physical Layer (PHY) specification, Draft Standard IEEE 802.11, 1997.

[3] V. Bharghavan et al, "MACAW: A Media Access Protocol for Wireless LAN's," Proc. ACM SIGCOMM 1994, pp. 212-225, Aug. 1994.

[4] P. Bose, et al, "Routing with guaranteed delivery in ad hoc wireless networks," Proc. ACM DIAL M 1999, pp. 48-55, Aug. 1999.

[5] G. M. Djuknic and R. E. Richton, "Geolocation and Assisted GPS," IEEE Computers, Feb, 2001.

[6] C. Fullmer and J. J. Garcia-Luna-Aceves, "Floor Acquisition Multiple Access (FAMA) for Packet Radio Networks," Proc. ACM SIGCOMM 1995, pp. 262-273, Aug. 1995.

[7] Z. J. Haas and M. R. Pearlman, "The Performance of a New Routing Protocol for the Reconfigurable Wireless Networks," Proc. IEEE ICC 1998, pp. 156-160, Jun. 1998.

[8] D. Johnson and D. Maltz, "Dynamic Source Routing in Ad Hoc Wireless Networks," T. Imielinski and H. Korth, Eds. *Mobile Computing*, Ch. 5, Kluwer, 1996.

[9] P. Karn, "MACA - A New Channel Access Method for Packet Radio," ARRL/CRRL Amateur radio 9th Computer Networking Conference, pp. 134-140, Apr. 1990.

[10] B. Karp and H. T. Kung, "GPSR: Greedy Perimeter Stateless Routing for Wireless Networks," Proc. ACM MOBICOM 2000, pp. 243-254, Aug. 2000.

[11] L. Kleinrock and F. A. Tobagi, "Packet Switching in Radio Channels: Part I - carrier sense multiple access modes and their throughput-delay characteristics," IEEE Trans. Commun., vol. COM-23, no. 12, pp. 1400-1416, 1975.

[12] Y. B. Ko and N. H. Vaidya, "Location-Aided Routing (LAR) in Mobile Ad Hoc Networks," Proc. ACM MOBICOM 1998, pp. 66-75, Oct. 1998.

[13] J. Kuri and S. K. Kasera, "Reliable Multicast in Multi-Access Wireless LANs," ACM/Kluwer Wireless Networks, vol 7, pp. 359-369, 2001.

[14] S. Lin and D. J. Costello Jr., "Error Control Coding: Fundamentals and Applications," Prentice-Hall, Englewood Cliffs, NJ, 1983.

[15] S.-Y. Ni, Y.-C. Tseng, Y.-S. Chen, and J.-P. Sheu, "The Broadcast Storm Problem in a Mobile Ad Hoc Network," Proc. ACM MOBICOM 1999, pp. 151-162, Aug. 1999.

[16] C. E. Perkins, E. M. Royer and S. R. Das, "Ad Hoc on Demand Distance Vector (AODV) Routing," http://www.ietf.org/internet-drafts/draft-ietf-manet-aodv-06.tex, IETF Internet Draft, Jul. 2000.

[17] M. Sun, et al, "Location Aided Broadcast in Wireless Ad hoc Networks," Proc. IEEE GLOBECOM 2001, pp. 2842-2846, Nov. 2001.

[18] M. Sun and Ten-Hwang Lai, "Location-aided Geometry-based Broadcast for Wireless Ad hoc Network Systems," submitted for publication.

[19] K. Tang and M. Gerla, "MAC Layer Broadcast Support in 802.11 Wireless Networks," Proc. IEEE MILCOM 2000, pp. 544-548, Oct. 2000.

[20] K. Tang and M. Gerla, "Random Access MAC for Efficient Broadcast Support in Ad Hoc Networks," Proc. IEEE WCNC 2000, pp. 454-459, Sep. 2000.

[21] K. Tang and M. Gerla, "MAC Reliable Broadcast in Ad Hoc Networks," Proc. IEEE MILCOM 2001, pp. 1008-1013, Oct. 2001.

[22] J. Wu and H. Li, "On Calculating Connected Dominating Set for Efficient Routing in Ad Hoc Wireless Networks," Proc. ACM DIAL M, pp. 7-14, Aug. 1999.

[23] M. Zorzi and R. R. Rao, "Capture and Retransmission Control in Mobile Radio," IEEE JSAC, vol. 12, No. 8, pp. 1289-1298, Oct. 1994.

Session 7C

Multimedia Servers

MAC Layer Protocols for Real-time Traffic in Ad-hoc Wireless Networks

Abhishek Pal,   Atakan Doğan,   and   Füsun Özgüner
Department of Electrical Engineering
The Ohio State University
2015 Neil Avenue
Columbus, OH 43210-1272
email: {pala, dogana, ozguner}@ee.eng.ohio-state.edu

Abstract

Providing Quality of Service (QoS) to high bandwidth video, voice and data applications in wireless networks is an important problem. Such applications are in the class of real-time applications; they need communication operations to complete within certain targeted deadlines. Based on this premise, this paper addresses the design of distributed MAC layer protocols that incorporate explicit support for real-time traffic in an ad-hoc wireless network. Specifically, we have developed two new MAC layer protocols, namely the elimination by sieving (ES-DCF) and the deadline bursting (DB-DCF) protocols. Both algorithms use deterministic collision resolution algorithms in order to provide timely delivery guarantees to different classes of real-time traffic. The extensive simulation studies conducted confirmed that ES-DCF and DB-DCF perform well for hard-real-time traffic and soft-real-time traffic, respectively.

1. Introduction

The problem of providing *Quality of Service* (QoS) to high bandwidth video, voice and data applications in wireless networks is still under active research. Applications such as streaming video and voice require a reserved share of the channel capacity over relatively long durations so that their QoS requirements are met; stringent delivery guarantees, particularly on short time scales, need not always be fulfilled for such applications. Other applications such as inter-vehicle communication (IVC) for safety require guaranteed delivery of short bursts of data within certain projected times in the future. Both these classes of applications fall under the broad umbrella of *real-time applications* - they need communication operations to complete within certain targeted deadlines. The way these requirements of

real-time communication are met in a wireless network depends largely on the network architecture (centralized versus distributed) and the medium access protocol (fixed, random, or demand assignment) used.

In distributed wireless networks, which are often referred to as *ad-hoc wireless networks* (AWNs), multiple mobile stations communicate with each other, without the aid of any centralized coordinator station for scheduling or channeling the transmissions. Maintaining QoS guarantees for delay-sensitive traffic is quite difficult in such networks, fundamentally because obtaining a consistent network-wide distributed snapshot of the state of the queues and the channel at the individual nodes at any given instant is an intractable problem.

In order to facilitate the efficient use of a radio channel in AWNs, a variety of *medium access control* (MAC) protocols have been developed. However, most of these MAC protocols, e.g., IEEE 802.11 Distributed Coordination Function (DCF) [7] (referred to henceforth as 802.11 DCF), MACA (Multiple Access with Collision Avoidance) [8], MACAW [2], FAMA-NTR (Floor Acquisition Multiple Access with Non-persistent Transmit Request) [5], etc., are not suitable for supporting real-time traffic on AWNs. This is due to the fact that random back-off techniques implemented in these protocols prevent them from providing deterministic upper bounds on channel access delays. Fortunately, there are also several ideas proposed in the literature for incorporating explicit support for real-time traffic into the MAC layer protocol. Examples of such protocols include 802.11 DCF with Priority Classes (henceforth called PC-DCF) [3], Black-Burst Contention (referred to as BB-DCF) [12], and Real Time-Medium Access Control (RT-MAC) [1]. The reader can refer to [10] for a detailed discussion on the pros and cons of these and some other real-time MAC layer protocols.

This paper focuses on the design of distributed MAC layer protocols that incorporate explicit support for real-time traffic in an ad-hoc wireless network. For the design of a fully distributed MAC layer with real-time communication support, we propose two new protocols, namely the *elimination by sieving* (ES-DCF) and the *deadline bursting* (DB-DCF) protocols. Both algorithms implement deterministic collision resolution algorithms in order to provide timely delivery guarantees to real-time traffic. In particular, ES-DCF is designed to aggressively push hard-real-time (HRT) traffic. DB-DCF, on the other hand, allows nodes with soft-real-time (SRT) traffic to contend along with nodes with HRT traffic during the contention phase. Our extensive simulation studies validate that ES-DCF heavily favors HRT traffic, while DB-DCF delivers good performance for SRT traffic at the expense of increased deadline misses for HRT. Furthermore, both of the proposed protocols are seen to provide consistent good throughput, even under channel overload.

2. Assumptions

We consider an ad-hoc wireless (local area) network in which there are multiple mobile hosts trying to communicate amongst themselves at any given time, and there is no centralized scheduling authority to arbitrate access to a single shared wireless channel over which both transmission and reception, and all messaging (control, data, handshake) take place. The nature of wireless signaling used by the physical layer is of no particular consequence to us; there is, however, some generic functionality provided by the physical layer, e.g., carrier sensing, which the MAC layer needs to utilize. We should emphasize that there are significant differences in the physical layer characteristics of the wired and the wireless communication domains. The unique characteristics of wireless communication media different from traditional wired media include half-duplex operation, multi-path propagation effects (fading and fluctuations in the received signal strength), bursty channel errors, high bit error rate (10^{-3} or even higher), and location dependent reception [6]. In particular, *half-duplex operation*, which prevents a wireless station from transmitting and receiving simultaneously on the same channel, and *location dependent reception*, which results in the well-known *hidden station* and *exposed station* problems, have profound effect on the design and performance of MAC layer protocols.

It is assumed that the wireless channel between any two nodes in the network is *reciprocal* in nature [8], in that both nodes avail of the same data rate and transmission range characteristics. All communication operations between nodes take place in a single hop from a source node to a destination node. Multi-hop wireless networks bring routing issues into the picture; these are beyond the scope of this work. Finally, our initial MAC layer protocol designs neglect the presence of hidden and exposed stations.

3. MAC Layer Protocols for AWNs

In the ensuing sections, we present two new MAC layer protocols that are aimed at providing deterministic deadline-based delivery guarantees to real-time traffic in AWNs. Both of them follow the operational framework specified by 802.11 DCF to a large extent, though the channel access arbitration mechanism differs considerably.

3.1 Elimination by Sieving

This protocol has been named so due to the operation of a dynamic distributed sieve-like mechanism in the collision avoidance phase of the channel access cycle for each real-time node, and will be referred to henceforth as ES-DCF. The MAC layer protocol followed by the non-real-time nodes in the network is the same as that specified by 802.11 DCF, but with the important difference that the non-real-time nodes use a considerably larger value of channel-free-wait-time (DIFS time) than any of the real-time nodes. Thus, this protocol cannot be directly overlaid on an existing IEEE 802.11 AWN implementation. Same technique has been used for non-real-time nodes by PC-DCF [3] and BB-DCF [12] as well. The behavior of the real-time nodes in each data transmission cycle is explained below.

Elimination Phase: In the Elimination phase, similar to the Prioritization phase in HIPERLAN EY-NPMA [4] to a large extent, *graded channel-free-wait-times*, decided by the laxities (closeness to respective deadlines) and the priorities of the corresponding real-time data packets, are used by the real-time nodes in determining when to send their RTS frames. The way the graded channel-free-wait-time is computed will be explained shortly. We should note that the idea of using graded channel-free-wait-times is also hinted by [3], but the basis for determining the grades is different.

The channel-free-wait-time of a real-time packet is a function of its deadline: The closer the deadline of the packet, the smaller is the value of its grade number, and thus the smaller is its channel-free-wait-time. Since it may so happen that two or more real-time packets (at different nodes) have deadlines that are close by, thus causing them to fall into the same grade, finer sub-grades are created by choosing random numbers from a bounded interval (in such a way that the larger grades are still non-overlapping). This is nothing but an anticipatory collision avoidance mechanism. As a real-time packet ages in the MAC layer queue, its grade improves (i.e., its grade number decreases); this helps to avoid the phenomenon of denial of service and helps implement the determinism in the protocol (to be explained). The channel-free-wait-time is also a function of the packet's priority: Two classes of real-time traffic are assumed; packets from the higher priority class always fall into numerically smaller grades.

Channel Acquisition Phase: When a node, after waiting for the requisite channel-free-wait-time as determined by its grade, finds that the channel is still free, it begins its Channel Acquisition phase by transmitting an RTS frame to the intended recipient of its data transmission. Other real-time nodes (that may have been waiting for a larger channel-free-wait-time) defer their accesses upon hearing this transmission; such real-time nodes repeat their elimination phases in the next MAC layer transmission attempt. If this RTS frame is transmitted in the clear, and the node gets back a CTS frame from its intended recipient, it can begin its Data Transmission phase, in which it sends its real-time data packet, packaged in a MAC layer DATA frame, to the intended recipient.

Collision Resolution Phase: If, on the other hand, the RTS frame in the channel acquisition phase is not transmitted correctly, due to some other real-time node(s) having elected the same grade and sub-grade numbers for its (their) real-time packet(s) (or due to transmission errors caused by hidden nodes or channel noise), a Collision Resolution phase is initiated. The collision resolution mechanism, as observed earlier, has to be deterministic in nature, in order to be able to guarantee bounded delays. As such, a window-splitting discipline similar to that used for hard-real-time nodes in [9] could be used. We have instead used, as part of an initial attempt at designing a fully operational protocol, the simpler method of transmitting black-bursts of lengths equal to the (unique) node ID numbers. Note that, in BB-DCF [12], a real-time node transmits a black-burst signal of length proportional to the time that it has been waiting for the channel access. After transmitting its black-burst, when the real-time node turns around and listens to the channel, if it hears a black-burst of longer duration on the channel (transmitted by one or more nodes with larger node ID numbers), it defers its impending transmission attempt; otherwise, it repeats its channel acquisition phase (which would be redundant in the case of an error-free channel and no hidden nodes in the network), followed by the data transmission phase. Whenever a real-time node is forced to defer to another real-time node, the collision resolution phase is repeated after the channel becomes free. It is also important to add here that the collision resolution phase implements the *blocked-access feature* - the nodes that experience a collision in the channel acquisition phase use the smallest channel-free-wait-times, so that they can pre-empt all other nodes during collision resolution. Figure 1 illustrates the operation of the protocol for a real-time node that is made to go through all the above-mentioned phases.

The procedure by which the graded channel-free-wait-times are calculated is explained below, along with the parameters and relationships involved. In ES-DCF, protocol-specific user-adjustable parameters are defined as follows.

max_rel_hrt_ddln: the maximum allowable relative deadline for the higher priority real-time class (beyond which, the node would belong to the lower priority real-time class),

max_rel_srt_ddln: the maximum allowable relative deadline for the smaller priority real-time class (beyond which, the node would be treated as a non-real-time node),

num_hrt_classes: the number of grades of channel-free-wait-times for the higher priority real-time class,

num_srt_classes: the number of grades of channel-free-wait-times for the smaller priority real-time class.

Let *min_rel_ddln* denote the minimum time needed for a complete transmission along with the RTS/CTS handshake, and *min_rel_ddln* is calculated as:

$$min\_rel\_ddln = \tau_{byte} \times (l_{rts} + l_{data} + l_{overhead}$$
$$+ l_{cts} + l_{ack}) + 3.0 \times \text{SIFS\_time} + 4.0 \times \tau_{min} \quad (1)$$

where τ_{byte} is the time taken for the transmission of a complete byte, l_{pckt}, $pckt = \{rts, cts, ack\}$, is the length of a *pckt* packet, l_{data} is the data payload length, $l_{overhead}$ is the data frame overhead, SIFS_time is the SIFS (Short Inter-Frame Spacing) time specified by 802.11 DCF [7], and τ_{min} is the minimum propagation delay. Packets whose deadlines are found to be closer than *min_rel_ddln* can be dropped by the transmission function, as their deadlines would be impossible to meet.

A real-time node, as shown Figure 1, has to wait at least an amount of time equal to (PIFS_time + Slot_time) before the start of Elimination phase, where PIFS_time is the channel-free-wait-time for real-time nodes of the higher priority class that experience collisions in the channel acquisition phase and Slot_time is defined by 802.11 DCF [7]. In addition, Elimination phase must be completed before any non-real-time node is allowed to contend for the channel. As a result, the range of available channel-free-wait-times for real-time nodes is calculated as:

$$free\_time\_range = (\text{DIFS\_time} - \text{Slot\_time})$$
$$- (\text{PIFS\_time} + \text{Slot\_time}) \quad (2)$$

where DIFS_time is the channel-free-wait-time for non-real-time nodes (value greater than that specified by 802.11 DCF).

Using (2), the resolution of the gradation in the channel-free-wait-time, which is denoted by δ, is computed as:

$$\delta = \frac{free\_time\_range}{num\_hrt\_classes + num\_srt\_classes} \quad (3)$$

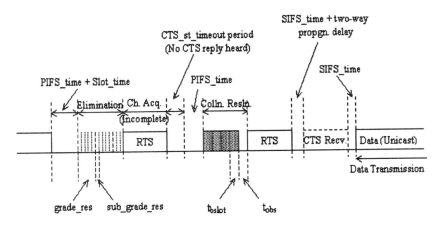

Figure 1. Illustration of the phases of the operation of ES-DCF.

The grade numbers for packets belonging to the two priority classes are computed as:

$$G_{HRT} = \left\lfloor \frac{packet\_laxity}{hrt\_ddln\_res} \right\rfloor$$

$$G_{SRT} = \left\lfloor \frac{packet\_laxity}{srt\_ddln\_res} \right\rfloor \quad (4)$$

where $0 \leq G_{HRT} < num\_hrt\_classes$ and $0 \leq G_{SRT} < num\_srt\_classes$. The term $packet\_laxity$ denotes the closeness to the deadline and equals to

$$packet\_laxity = deadline - current\_time. \quad (5)$$

Note that the grade number depends on the laxity, which in turn, is a function of the current time. In (4), hrt_ddln_res and srt_ddln_res are the deadline resolutions for the real-time nodes of the higher and the smaller priority classes, respectively, and they are computed as:

$$hrt\_ddln\_res = \frac{max\_rel\_hrt\_ddln - min\_rel\_ddln}{num\_hrt\_classes}$$

$$srt\_ddln\_res = \frac{max\_rel\_srt\_ddln - min\_rel\_ddln}{num\_srt\_classes}$$

The resolution of the sub-gradation in the channel-free-wait-time, κ, is determined by system parameters such as the maximum end-to-end propagation delay (τ_{max}) in the network, the carrier-sensing time, the PHY and MAC layer frame processing delays, etc. The random sub-grade number, which is denoted by g, is chosen with equal probability in the range $\lfloor 0, g_{max} \rfloor$ where $g_{max} = \lfloor \frac{\delta}{\kappa} \rfloor$.

Finally, the channel-free-wait-times for packets belonging to the two classes of real-time traffic are calculated as:

$$hrt\_wait\_time = min\_hrt\_wait\_time$$
$$+ \; G_{HRT} \times \delta + g \times \kappa$$
$$srt\_wait\_time = min\_srt\_wait\_time$$
$$+ \; G_{SRT} \times \delta + g \times \kappa \quad (6)$$

where $min\_hrt\_wait\_time$ ($min\_srt\_wait\_time$) is the minimum amount of time for a real-time node of the higher (smaller) priority class for which the node refrains itself from contending for the channel, and $min\_hrt\_wait\_time$ and $min\_srt\_wait\_time$ are defined as:

$$min\_hrt\_wait\_time = \lceil PIFS\_time + Slot\_time \rceil$$
$$min\_srt\_wait\_time = min\_hrt\_wait\_time +$$
$$\lceil grade\_res \times num\_hrt\_classes \rceil \quad (7)$$

It should be emphasized here that the minimum channel-free-wait-time is always greater than the channel-free-wait-time for nodes that experience collisions, which is required to accommodate the blocked-access. Nodes that experience collisions use channel-free-wait-times that are one Slot_time less than the corresponding minimum channel-free-wait-time so that they can always pre-empt any other node with same class that has not experienced a collision.

Again, it should be noted that since G_{HRT} and G_{SRT} vary with time, the corresponding channel-free-wait-times also vary (diminish) with time. The timing specifications for the length of a black-burst slot (t_{bslot}) and the observation duration after the transmission of the black-burst (t_{obs}) remain the same as those used in BB-DCF [12].

A real-time node that gets pre-empted in the elimination phase re-executes its elimination phase after the channel becomes free; as the corresponding real-time packet ages, the node gets numerically smaller grades in each re-execution. Here, there is the danger that a real-time node, after attaining the minimum grade for its class, may remain in the same grade in successive elimination phases and keep getting pre-empted each time; in other words, the elimination phase is still non-deterministic. In order to overcome this problem, we promote the real-time packet to the status of a packet that has experienced a collision, after it has remained in the minimum grade for a certain number of times (χ) calculated according to the relation

$$\chi = \left\lfloor \frac{initial\_packet\_laxity}{min\_rel\_ddln} \right\rfloor - 1. \qquad (8)$$

Once the packet is promoted to the status of a packet that has experienced a collision, the real-time node now uses a channel-free-wait-time equal to either ($min\_srt\_wait\_time$- Slot_time) or ($min\_hrt\_wait\_time$ - Slot_time) depending on whether the packet belongs to the lower priority class or to the higher priority class.

The collision resolution mechanism in our algorithm currently uses node IDs for achieving determinism; these node IDs are assumed unique and need to have numerically small values for the collision resolution to be efficient. Moreover, it is desirable that real-time nodes with higher data-generation rates have numerically greater node IDs, since they need prioritized access to the channel; the ideal situation would be having node IDs assigned in sequential order of data-generation rates. These node IDs can be themselves be considered as "resources available for contention at higher protocol levels" [9]. Specifically, when a real-time node enters an AWN, it may bid for a node ID to be assigned to it, or it may assign itself a value based on its traffic rate and on the real-time node IDs already in use in the AWN. In addition, when a real-time node leaves an AWN (or is powered down), it can broadcast the relinquishment of its node ID to the other nodes in the network.

The non-real-time nodes in the network are always pre-empted by any real-time node that may have a fresh packet to be delivered. In other words, this protocol allows non-real-time nodes to transmit only when the MAC layer queues of all the real-time nodes in the network are empty. This is what happens in BB-DCF also, as explained in [12]. (If this is not desirable, then some form of packet aging could be implemented for the non-real-time data packets also; in such a case, the non-real-time nodes would need to implement the entire protocol, in order to be able to successfully contend with the real-time nodes.)

3.2 Deadline Bursting

As the name implies, this protocol uses measured black-bursts of lengths proportional to the relative-deadlines of the involved packets for the purpose of collision avoidance, and will be referred to henceforth as DB-DCF. Similar to ES-DCF, the non-real-time nodes in the network follow 802.11 DCF [7] as their MAC layer protocol with the exception that the non-real-time nodes use a larger value of channel-free-wait-time (DIFS time) than any of the real-time nodes. Thus, this protocol cannot be directly overlaid on an existing IEEE 802.11 AWN implementation either. The behavior of real-time nodes in each data transmission cycle is explained below.

Black-burst Contention Phase: At the beginning of a transmission cycle, a real-time node that finds the channel already free for the duration (PIFS_time + Slot_time) goes ahead with the transmission of an RTS frame. However, if the channel is found busy at the instant the frame transmission function is called (a much more common occurrence under heavier loads), the real-time node waits for the channel to become free, and remain free for the duration (PIFS_time + Slot_time), and then initiates its Black-burst Contention phase (similar in many ways to the black-burst contention phase of BB-DCF [12]). In this phase, each real-time node that wishes to access the channel transmits a black-burst of length inversely proportional to the urgency (measured in terms of the closeness to the targeted deadline) of its real-time data packet (instead of the contention delay as is done in BB-DCF); black-burst lengths are integral multiples of a black-burst slot time, t_{bslot} (where t_{bslot} is defined in the same way as is done in BB-DCF). After finishing its black-burst transmission, the node turns around and listens to the channel for any longer-duration black-bursts for t_{obs} units of time (again, t_{obs} is defined in the same way as is done in BB-DCF). If it hears another black-burst, which would mean that some other node(s) has (have) a more urgent need to transmit, it defers its channel access till the end of the ensuing transmission; after this, it initiates a fresh black-burst contention cycle with recalculated burst lengths.

Channel Acquisition Phase: If the node does not hear another longer-duration black-burst, it begins its Channel Acquisition phase by transmitting an RTS frame to the intended recipient of its data transmission. If this RTS frame is transmitted in the clear, and the node gets back a CTS frame from its intended recipient, it can begin its Data Transmission phase, in which it sends its real-time data packet, packaged in a MAC layer DATA frame.

Collision Resolution Phase: If, on the other hand, two or more real-time nodes happen to transmit black-bursts of equal length in the black-burst contention phase, and thus, are unable to hear any longer bursts during their observation periods, RTS frame collisions may occur during the channel acquisition phase, with the result that the respective CTS answer frames may not be received. (This could also happen due to transmission errors cause by hidden nodes or channel noise). In such cases, a Collision Resolution phase is initiated; this point onwards, the operation of the protocol is the same as that of the protocol proposed in the previous section, except for the fact that all nodes with packets that experience collisions use a channel-free-wait-time equal to PIFS_time, regardless of whether the corresponding real-time packet belongs to the smaller priority class or the higher priority class. Again, the collision resolution phase implements the blocked-access feature - the nodes that ex-

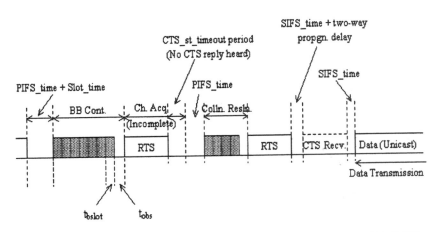

Figure 2. Illustration of the phases of the operation of DB-DCF

perience a collision in the channel acquisition phase use the smallest channel-free-wait-times (PIFS_time), so that they can pre-empt all other nodes during collision resolution.

New protocol-specific user-adjustable parameters, in addition to parameters $max\_rel\_hrt\_ddln$ and $max\_rel\_srt\_ddln$ introduced in the previous section, are defined as follows.

$num\_hrt\_ddln\_steps$: the number of steps of resolution in the deadline range for the higher priority real-time class,

$num\_srt\_ddln\_steps$: the number of steps of resolution in the deadline range for the smaller priority real-time class.

Finally, black-burst lengths (in terms of number of black-burst slots) for the real-time packets belonging to the two priority classes are calculated as:

$$L_{SRT} = num\_srt\_ddln\_steps - i_{SRT}$$
$$L_{HRT} = num\_srt\_ddln\_steps$$
$$+ (num\_hrt\_ddln\_steps - i_{HRT}) \quad (9)$$

In (9), i_{HRT} and i_{SRT} are defined as:

$$i_{HRT} = \left\lfloor \frac{packet\_laxity}{hrt\_ddln\_res} \right\rfloor$$
$$i_{SRT} = \left\lfloor \frac{packet\_laxity}{srt\_ddln\_res} \right\rfloor \quad (10)$$

where

$$hrt\_ddln\_res = \frac{max\_rel\_hrt\_ddln - min\_rel\_ddln}{num\_hrt\_steps}$$
$$srt\_ddln\_res = \frac{max\_rel\_srt\_ddln - min\_rel\_ddln}{num\_srt\_steps}$$

Again, it should be noted that since i_{HRT} and i_{SRT} vary with time, the corresponding black-burst lengths also vary

(increase) with time, up to a maximum limit. The possibility of non-determinism pointed out in the previous section can also arise in this protocol. Here, the problem is solved by promoting any node that has already transmitted the maximum length black bursts for the corresponding priority class once before, to the status of a node that has experienced a collision. Figure 2 illustrates the operation of the protocol for a real-time node.

The non-real-time nodes in the network are always pre-empted by any real-time node that may have a fresh packet to be delivered. In other words, this protocol also allows non-real-time nodes to transmit only when the MAC layer queues of all the real-time nodes in the network are empty.

4. Experiments

We have compared the performance of the new protocols ES-DCF and DB-DCF with that exhibited by 802.11 DCF and PC-DCF in various simulation scenarios that use different kinds of traffic models and varying levels of network traffic load. In this paper, however, we have presented the simulation results for only one simulation scenario due to space limitations. For our simulation studies, we have developed a network simulator coded in C, using the CSIM general-purpose discrete event simulation library [11]. The simulator only models the PHY and the MAC layers of the communication protocol stack. In addition, characteristics of the physical channel have been modeled only to the level of complexity required for a coherent and fairly complete study of the principal MAC layer function - the collision-free scheduling of data transmissions on the shared wireless medium in a fully distributed fashion. In the simulations presented here, error-free channels are used; in addition, only fully connected networks are considered. (By fully connected networks, we mean ad-hoc networks in which all nodes can hear one another at all times, i.e., there are no

544

hidden nodes in the network.) For all parameters regarding the four protocols and other details about the simulation program, we refer reader to [10].

4.1 Persistent fixed-rate real-time data traffic

In this set of simulations, the real-time data sources generate data at regular intervals throughout the simulation run. Two classes of real-time nodes are used - half the nodes belong to the higher priority class with fixed inter-arrival times of 50 ms (i.e., data rates of 320 kbps), and the other half belong to the smaller priority class with fixed inter-arrival times of 125 ms (i.e., data rates of 128 kbps). This is a *worst-case* traffic pattern in that all nodes generate data without any respite, and these packet births occur almost exactly at the same time (in phase) because of the harmonically related data generation rates used for the real-time nodes in the network.

For all the four protocols compared, packets belonging to the higher priority class are dropped, and not transmitted, if they are found to have expired. Packets are checked for deadline expiry at three key points; at the start of each MAC layer transmission attempt, during back-off contention (not applicable to ES-DCF and DB-DCF since they do not have any back-off contention phase) and just before an RTS frame is transmitted. In a sense, the higher priority traffic can be called hard-real-time (HRT) traffic - packets that have expired are useless anyway, so they are dropped. All the HRT packets that do reach the intended recipient do so within their targeted deadlines. Packets belonging to the lower priority class are not dropped and thus may incur overshoots past their targeted deadlines by the time they are actually delivered; we will call this class of traffic as soft-real-time (SRT) traffic.

The number of real-time nodes in the network is varied from 6 to 30. For each case, three separate simulations, with different seeds for the random number generator, are used, and the results are averaged over these three runs. The total offered load on the network exceeds the 2 Mbps capacity of the channel at some point between 6 and 10 nodes (since data packets are being relentlessly generated), i.e., we overload the network. In such a situation, even the best protocol is bound to miss many deadlines.

The graphs in Figures 3 and 4 summarize the performance figures for each of the protocols compared, and perhaps warrant some explanation. Figure 3 shows the *HRT success rate*, which is the ratio of the number of HRT packets delivered successfully (i.e., within their respective deadlines), and the total number of HRT packets offered and the *SRT completion rate*, which is the ratio of the number of SRT packets actually delivered and the total number of SRT packets offered. As far as HRT traffic is concerned, ES-DCF performs better than the rest as it aggressively pushes

HRT data traffic (while neglecting SRT data traffic for the most part). DB-DCF, on the other hand, allows SRT packets to contend along with HRT packets (using equal values of channel-free-wait-times), and thus does not usually give good delivery performance for HRT traffic. For SRT data traffic, DB-DCF attains the best performance, while ES-DCF performs the worst. Figure 4 graphs the average transmit latency and the variation of the overall achieved throughput with the load offered to the network. It is seen from this last graph that all four protocols are stable protocols (at least in the observed load range), in that none of them exhibit a performance breakdown as the network is overloaded. Again, this is due to the fundamental strength of the CSMA paradigm on which 802.11 DCF and the other protocols are based.

Overall, ES-DCF heavily favors HRT data traffic over SRT data traffic, while DB-DCF does the opposite; 802.11 DCF and PC-DCF achieve a balance between the two. We should note that we have observed similar trends for other simulation scenarios too.

5 Conclusions

In this paper, we have proposed two new fully distributed MAC layer protocols that attempt to provide timely delivery guarantees to different classes of real-time data traffic in ad-hoc wireless systems. Of the proposed protocols, ES-DCF is seen to push HRT traffic aggressively, while giving poor service to SRT traffic. This is primarily due to the fact that nodes with SRT packets always use much longer channel-free-wait-times than nodes with HRT packets, even after experiencing collisions in the channel acquisition phase. On the other hand, DB-DCF allows nodes with SRT traffic to contend along with nodes with HRT traffic upon the occurrence of collisions or when SRT packets become urgent, and thus gives good performance for SRT traffic but rather lackluster performance for HRT traffic.

References

[1] R. O. Baldwin, N. J. Davis IV, and S. F. Midkiff. A real-time medium access control protocol for ad-hoc wireless local area networks. *Mobile Computing and Communications Review*, 3(2):20–27, Apr. 1999.

[2] V. Bhargavan, A. Demers, S. Shenker, and L. Zhang. MACAW: A media access protocol for wireless LANs. In *Proceedings of the ACM Conference on Communication Architectures, Protocols and Applications (SIGCOMM)*, pages 212–225, 1994.

[3] D.-J. Deng and R.-S. Chang. A priority scheme for IEEE 802.11 DCF access method. *IEICE Transactions on Communications*, E82-B(1):96–102, Jan. 1999.

[4] European Telecommunications Standards Institute (ETSI). Broadband radio access networks (BRAN); HIgh PErfor-

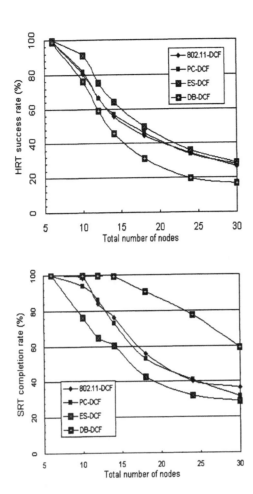

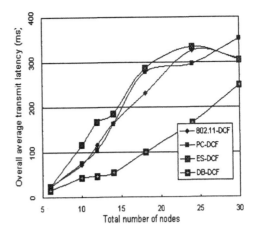

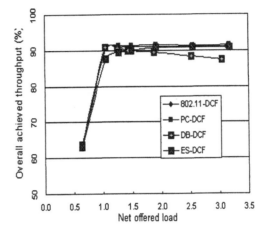

Figure 3. Success rate for HRT packets and completion rate for SRT packets.

Figure 4. Average transmit latency and achieved throughput.

mance Radio Local Area Network (HIPERLAN) Type 1; Functional specification. http://www.etsi.org, EN 300 652 V1.2.1 (1998-07).

[5] C. L. Fullmer and J. J. Garcia-Luna-Aceves. Floor acquisition multiple access (FAMA) for packet-radio networks. In *Proceedings of the ACM Conference on Communication Architectures, Protocols and Applications (SIGCOMM)*, pages 262–273, 1995.

[6] A. C. V. Gummalla and J. O. Limb. Wireless medium access control protocols. *IEEE Communications Society Surveys and Tutorials*, 3(2):2–15, Second Quarter 2000.

[7] The Institute of Electrical and Electronics Engineering (IEEE). Wireless LAN medium access control (MAC) and physical layer (PHY) specifications. http://standards.ieee.org, ANSI/IEEE Std. 802.11 (1999) (a.k.a. ISO/IEC 8802-11:1999(E)).

[8] P. Karn. MACA - A new channel access method for packet radio. In *Proceedings of ARRL/CRRL Amateur Radio Ninth Computer Networking Conference*, pages 134–140, 1990.

[9] M. J. Markowski and A. S. Sethi. Fully distributed wireless MAC transmission of real-time data. In *Proceedings of the Fourth IEEE Real-time Technology and Applications Symposium (RTAS)*, pages 49–57, 1998.

[10] A. Pal. Distributed MAC layer protocols for real-time communication in ad-hoc wireless networks. Master's thesis, The Ohio State University, Columbus, Ohio, 2001.

[11] H. Schwetman. CSIM user's guide: Rev. 1. Technical Report ACT-126-90, Microelectronics and Computer Technology Corporation, June 1991.

[12] J. L. Sobrinho and A. S. Krishnakumar. Quality-of-service in ad-hoc carrier sense multiple access wireless networks. *IEEE Journal on Selected Areas in Communications*, 17(8):1353–1368, Aug. 1999.

Optimal Video Replication and Placement on a Cluster of Video-on-Demand Servers *

Xiaobo Zhou
Department of Computer Science
Wayne State University
Detroit, MI 48202, USA
zbo@cs.wayne.edu

Cheng-Zhong Xu
Department of Electrical & Computer Engg.
Wayne State University
Detroit, MI 48202, USA
czxu@ece.eng.wayne.edu

Abstract

A cost-effective approach to building up scalable Video-on-Demand (VoD) servers is to couple a number of VoD servers together in a cluster. In this article, we study a crucial video replication and placement problem in a distributed storage VoD cluster for high quality and high availability services. We formulate it as a combinatorial optimization problem with objectives of maximizing the encoding bit rate and the number of replicas of each video and balancing the workload of the servers. It is subject to the constraints of the storage capacity and the outgoing network bandwidth of the servers. Under the assumption of single fixed encoding bit rate for all videos, we give an optimal replication algorithm and a bounded placement algorithm for videos with different popularities. To reduce the complexity of the replication algorithm, we present an efficient algorithm that utilizes the Zipf-like video popularity distributions to approximate the optimal solution. For videos with scalable encoding bit rates, we propose a heuristic algorithm based on simulated annealing. We conduct a comprehensive performance evaluation of the algorithms and demonstrate their effectiveness via simulations over a synthetic workload set.

1 Introduction

Early large-scale VoD servers were mostly running on massively parallel computers. For cost-effectiveness and scalability, the research interest in cluster-based streaming servers (briefly, VoD cluster) has increased dramatically in the past few years [2, 9, 10, 12, 15]. A VoD cluster consists of a number of back-end servers controlled by a dispatcher that makes admission decisions. To avoid network traffic jams around the dispatcher, the cluster relies on a TCP handoff protocol to enable servers to respond to client requests directly. There are cluster architectures for VoD servers: shared storage and distributed storage. A shared storage cluster is usually built on RAID systems [10, 14]. Video data is striped into blocks and distributed over the shared disk arrays. Such systems are easy to build and administrate and the cost of storage is low. However, they have limited scalability and reliability due to disk access contention. As the number of disks increases, so do the controlling overhead and the probability of a failure [9].

By contrast, in a distributed storage VoD cluster, each server has its own disk storage subsystem [2, 9, 12]. The servers are linked by a backbone network. Due to the server autonomy, this cluster architecture can offer better scalability in terms of storage and streaming capacity and higher reliability. This type of clusters can also be employed in geographically distributed environments [18].

In this article, we investigate a key issue in the design of this type of clusters, *i.e.* initial placement of videos onto the servers. This is because data placement methods are crucial to the scalability of the VoD cluster and the overhead of video placement is huge. Two complementary approaches are data striping and data replication. The main advantages of striping are high disk utilization and good load balancing ability [2, 9, 10]. However, wide data striping can induce high scheduling and extension overhead [4, 12]. Replication tends to isolate the servers from each other. It can simplify the administration and enhance scalability and reliability of the clusters. In this article, we advocate a video replication strategy that duplicates videos according to their popularities and place the replicas wholly on servers for reliability. Data striping and recovery schemes can be employed within the servers to enhance availability.

A defining characteristic with video streams is that a video can be encoded in different bit rates for different qualities at the cost of different storage and streaming bandwidth requirements. It is this unique feature that distinguishes video replication and placement problem from classical file

* This research was supported in part by NSF grants ACI-0203592 and CCR-9988266.

allocation problems (FAP) [6]. Due to huge storage requirements of videos, full replication is generally inefficient if not impossible. For example, a typical 90-minute MPEG-2 video encoded in a constant bit rate of 6 Mbs requires as much as 4 GB storage. Assuming *a priori* knowledge about video popularities, we intend to find an efficient video placement with partial replication.

The problems are how to determine the encoding bit rates and the replication degree of videos and how to place the video replicas on the distributed storage cluster for high quality, high availability and load balancing under resource constraints. Like many related work [1, 5, 12], it considers videos with constant bit rates (CBR). High quality requires a high encoding bit rate. High availability in this context has two meanings: low rejection rate and high replication degree. The objective of load balancing is to improve system throughput in rush-hours and hence reduce the rejection rate [17]. It is known that increasing the replication degree enhances the flexibility of a system to balance the expected load. Multiple replicas also offer the flexibility in reconfiguration and increase the dynamic load-balancing ability. On the other hand, the replication degree is limited by encoding bit rates of videos and storage capacity of the cluster. Encoding bit rates also are constrained by the streaming bandwidth and the peak request arrival rate. This article presents a solid theoretical framework for the video replication and placement problem. Specifically,

1. We formulate the video replication and placement on distributed storage VoD clusters for high service quality and high service availability as a combinatorial optimization problem.

2. Under the assumption of single fixed encoding bit rate for all videos, we give an optimal replication algorithm and a bounded placement algorithm for videos with different popularities. The placement algorithm achieves a tight bound of load imbalance degree. To reduce the complexity of the replication algorithm, we present a time-efficient algorithm that utilizes the information about Zipf-like video popularity distributions to approximate the optimal solution.

3. For videos with scalable encoding bit rates, we propose a simulated annealing algorithm. We conduct a comprehensive performance evaluation of the algorithms and demonstrate their effectiveness via simulations over a synthetic workload set.

The rest of the article is organized as follows. Section 2 is about background and related work. Section 3 presents the formulation of the problem. Section 4 presents a family of algorithms and their analyses. Section 5 gives performance evaluation. Section 6 concludes the article with remarks on future work.

2 Related Work

VoD applications have long been a research topic. Early server-side studies focused on RAID-based storage subsystem designs as well as disk I/O and network bandwidth scheduling in single servers. The research on storage subsystems has been directed toward: 1) Data striping schemes in storage devices for disk utilization and load balancing [3, 13]; 2) Data retrieval from storage subsystems in order to amortize seek time [14]; 3) Buffering of data segment for disk I/O bandwidth utilization [8]; and 4) Disk scheduling to avoid jitter [14, 16]. There were other complementary studies on hierarchical storage subsystems, admission control and VCR operations. Video streams require huge amount of bandwidth in both disk I/O and network interfaces. Many work focused on reducing I/O requirements by caching, multicasting and broadcasting [1, 7]. Eager *et. al.* give a complete review of these techniques [7]. The research of this topic is out the scope of this paper.

Recent work on VoD applications focused on scalability and reliability in distributed VoD servers [4, 9, 10, 12]. The video replication and placement problem has been studied extensively in the literature [3, 4, 5, 15, 16]. Chervenak *et. al.* argued replication based on Zipf-like distribution access patterns could improve throughput [3]. The authors did not show how to take the advantage of Zipf-like distributions for replication and placement. Chou *et. al.* gave a comparison of scalability and reliability characteristics of servers by the use of striping and replication [4]. The work focused on the tradeoff between the degree of striping and the degree of replication. Dan *et. al.* proposed an online video placement policy based on network bandwidth to storage space ratio of storage devices [5]. The work focused on load balancing between storage devices of a VoD server. The placement policy is heuristic but not optimization-based. Venkatasubramanian *et. al.* proposed a family of heuristic algorithms for dynamic load balancing in a distributed VoD server. Wolf *et. al.* proposed DASD Dancing, for load balancing in a multi-disks server [16]. It employed a replication optimization technique borrowed from the theory of resource allocation problems [11]. In this article, we give an optimal video replication scheme between servers. We then present an efficient algorithm that utilizes the information about Zipf-like video popularity distributions to approximate the optimal solution. In addition, we give a placement strategy that achieves a tight bound for the load imbalance degree. We improve and complement previous work by constructing a theoretical framework for the problem and present a family of efficient replication and placement algorithms. Overall, the defining characteristic with our work is that we consider the tradeoff between the encoding bit rate for service quality and the replication degree for service availability and load balancing.

3 The Optimization Problem

3.1 The Model

We consider a cluster of N homogeneous servers, $S = (s_1, s_2, \ldots, s_n)$, and a set of M different videos, $V = \{v_1, v_2, \ldots, v_m\}$. Each server has a storage capacity C and an outgoing network bandwidth B. Like many other work [1, 15, 16], we consider all videos in set V have the same duration d, say $d = 90$ minutes for typical movies. If a video v_i is encoded in constant bit rate b_i, the storage space for video v_i is calculated as $c_i = d \cdot b_i$.

It is known that the popularity of videos varies with a number of videos that receive most of the requests. We consider the replication and placement for the peak period of length d. This is because one of the objectives of the replication and placement is high service availability during the peak period. Load balancing is critical to improving throughput and service availability during the peak period. Like many other work [1], we consider that outgoing network bandwidth is the major performance bottleneck. We make the following two assumptions, regarding the video relative popularity distributions and the request arrival rates.

1. The popularity of the videos, p_i, is assumed to be known before the replication and placement. The relative popularity of videos follows Zipf-like distributions with a skew parameter of θ. Typically, $0.271 \leq \theta \leq 1$ [1, 15]. The probability of choosing the ith video is $p_i = i^{-\theta} / \sum_{j=1}^{M} j^{-\theta}$.

2. The peak period is same for all videos with various arrival rates. Let $\bar{\lambda}$ denote the average arrival rate during the peak period. Because of the same peak period assumption, the video replication and placement is conservative as it places videos for the peak period. This conservative model provides an insight into the key aspects of the problem and facilitates its formulation.

3.2 The Formulation of the Problem

The objective of the replication and placement is to have high service quality and high service availability. Replication enhances availability and load balancing ability by placement. Load balancing improves system throughput and hence the availability. Increasing the encoding bit rate receives high quality but decreases the replication degree due to the storage constraint. The encoding bit rate of videos is also limited by the outgoing bandwidth constraint of the servers. The objective of the replication and placement hence is to maximize the average encoding bit rate and the average number of replicas (replication degree), and minimize the load imbalance degree of the cluster. Let L denote the communication load imbalance degree of the clus-

ter. Let r_i denote the number of replicas of video v_i. Specifically, we define the optimization objective as:

$$Obj = \sum_{i=1}^{M} b_i / M + \alpha \cdot \sum_{i=1}^{M} r_i / M - \beta \cdot L, \qquad (1)$$

where α and β are relative weighting factors. There are many ways for the definition of load imbalance degree [17]. Two typical examples are

$$L = \max_{\forall s_i \in S} | l_i - \bar{l} |, \qquad (2)$$

and

$$L = \sqrt{\sum_{i=1}^{N} (l_i - \bar{l})^2 / N}, \qquad (3)$$

where $\bar{l}$ is the mean outgoing communication load of the servers, i.e. $\bar{l} = \sum_{i=1}^{N} l_i / N$. Unless otherwise specified, we use the definition of Eq. (2) in the following discussions.

This objective is subject to the following constraints: (1) server storage capacity, (2) server outgoing network bandwidth, and (3) distribution of all replicas of an individual video to different servers. All r_i replicas of video v_i have the same encoding bit rate since they are replicated by the same video. Let $\pi(v_i^j)$ be the index of the server on which the jth of replicas of video v_i, v_i^j, places. And, $\pi(v_i) = k$ means that a replica of video v_i is placed on server s_k. The *communication weight* of each replica of video v_i is defined as $w_i = p_i / r_i$. By the use of a static round robin scheduling policy, the number of requests for video v_i to be serviced by each replica of v_i during the peak period is $w_i \cdot \bar{\lambda} \cdot d$. Let l_k be the outgoing communication load on server s_k. Specifically, we give resource constraints from the perspective of server $s_k (1 \leq k \leq N)$ as:

$$\sum_{\pi(v_i)=k, \forall v_i \in V} b_i \cdot d \leq C, \qquad (4)$$

and

$$l_k = \sum_{\pi(v_i)=k, \forall v_i \in V} w_i \cdot \bar{\lambda} \cdot d \cdot b_i \leq B. \qquad (5)$$

The third constraint is the requirement of distribution of all replicas of an individual video to different servers. That is, all r_i replicas of video v_i must be placed on r_i servers. Specifically,

$$\pi(v_i^{j_1}) \neq \pi(v_i^{j_2}) \qquad 1 \leq j_1, j_2 \leq r_i, j_1 \neq j_2. \qquad (6)$$

Note that if multiple replicas of a video are placed to the same server, it implies that these replicas be merged to one replica. For the same reason, we have one more replication constraint

$$1 \leq r_i \leq N \qquad \forall v_i \in V. \qquad (7)$$

In summary, we formulate the video replication and placement problem as a maximization of Eq. (1) and Eq. (2) or Eq. (3) subject to constraints of Eq. (4) to Eq. (7).

4 Algorithms and Analyses

4.1 Replication of Videos in a Fixed Bit Rate

We first present replication and placement algorithms under the assumption of single fixed encoding bit rate b [1, 15]. Since the storage requirement for each video is a constant, *i.e.* $c_i = d \cdot b$, we re-define the storage capacity of each server C in terms of the number of replicas. Unless otherwise specified, we use the re-definition of C in the following discussions. Note that because the encoding bit rate is fixed, the constraint Eq. (5) may be violated when communication load exceeds the outgoing bandwidth of the cluster.

Replication can achieve fine granularity in terms of communication weight of replicas that offers more flexibility to place replicas for load balancing. We will prove in Section 4.2 that the upper bound of the load imbalance degree L generated by our placement strategy is non-increasing as the replication degree increases. It is desirable to increase the replication degree to saturate the storage capacity of the cluster. The optimization of Eq. (1) is reduced to assigning the number of replicas to each video and minimizing the load imbalance degree L by placement of these replicas.

The objective of the replication is to get fine granularity of replicas in terms of communication weight for later placement. Specifically, we have

$$\text{Minimize} \quad max_{\forall v_i \in V}\{w_i\}, \tag{8}$$

subject to constraints of Eq. (7) and $\sum_{i=1}^{M} r_i = N \cdot C$.

If the video popularity distribution is uniform, a simple round-robin replication achieves an optimal replication scheme with respect to Eq. (8). However, we know the popularity distribution of videos is usually not uniform. The problem of assigning the number of replicas to each video in proportion to its popularity distribution is close to a classical apportionment problem [11]. One known approach is Adams' monotone based divisor method [11, 16]. The difference is the number of replicas of each video is bounded by the number of servers due to constraint Eq. (7).

4.1.1 Bounded Adams' Monotone Divisor Replication

We give the bounded Adams' monotone divisor replication algorithm. It firstly assigns one replica to each video. For the rest replication capacity of the cluster, *i.e.* $N \cdot C - M$ replicas, at each iteration it gives one more replica to the video, whose number of replicas is less than the number of servers and its replica(s) has the currently greatest communication weight.

Figure 1 illustrates the replication of five videos on three servers. Without loss of generality, suppose $p_1 \geq p_2 \geq \cdots p_5$. The storage capacity of each server is three replicas. Initially, each video is given one replica and $w_i = p_i$. For the rest replication capacity of the cluster (4 replicas), at

each iteration a video is chosen to do duplication. Its number of replicas is smaller than the number of servers and the replica(s) of this video has the greatest communication weight currently. For example, in the first iteration, video v_1 is duplicated into two replicas. The communication weight of its each replica is hence $w_1 = p_1/2$. In the second iteration, if $w_1 = p_1/2 = max\{p_1/2, p_2, p_3, p_4, p_5\}$, the two replicas of v_1 will be duplicated into three replicas. The communication weight of the three replicas is $p_1/3, p_1/3$ and $p_1/3$, respectively. In the third iteration, if video v_1 has already three replicas, it won't be duplicated any more. Video v_2 has the greatest communication weight and it is duplicated into two replicas with $w_2 = p_2/2$, and so on.

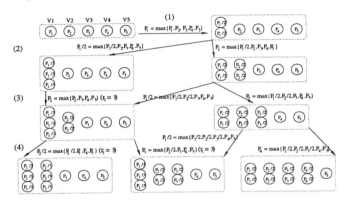

Figure 1: An illustration of the Adams' replication.

Theorem 1. *The bounded Adams' divisor algorithm receives an optimal replication scheme with respect to Eq. (8).*

It can be proved that the algorithm complexity increases with the storage capacity of the cluster. In the worst case, the algorithm complexity is $O(M \cdot N \cdot \log M)$ [11].

4.1.2 Zipf-like Distribution based Replication

The replication algorithms can be applied for dynamic replication during run-time. The disadvantage of the algorithm above is its complexity. To reduce it, we give an efficient algorithm that utilizes the information about the Zipf-like video popularity distributions to approximate the optimal solution. The key idea is to classify the popularities of the videos into N intervals. The videos, whose popularities are within the same interval, are assigned the same number of replicas according to their interval indices. This popularity classification is done in a heuristic way with a Zipf-like distribution. There are two key functions in the algorithm. The function $generate(\psi, u_j)$ partitions the range of $[0, p_1 + p_m]$ into N intervals according to a Zipf-like distribution with a skew parameter of ψ, *i.e.* $\frac{u_j}{p_1+p_m} = j^{-\psi} / \sum_{k=1}^{N} k^{-\psi}, 1 \leq j \leq N$. The boundaries of intervals are given by z_j. Function $assignment(u_j, r_i)$ assigns the number of replicas r_i to video v_i according to the interval index of its popularity. Figure 2 illustrates a replication senario with the setting of 20 videos, 6 servers and popularity parameter $\theta = 0.75$. The storage capacity of the cluster is 24 replicas. The replication algorithm has $\psi = -2.33$.

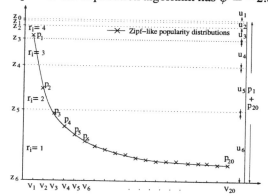

Figure 2: A replication senario.

The parameter ψ determines the total number of replicas generated by the algorithm. we employ a binary search approach to search the parameter ψ. Two key factors of the algorithmic complexity are the search space of parameter ψ and the termination condition of the iterative process.

Lemma 4.1. *In the Zipf-like distribution based replication algorithm, the total number of replicas is non-decreasing as the parameter ψ increases and non-increasing as the parameter ψ decreases.*

Proof: As the parameter ψ increases, the boundary $z_j (1 \leq j \leq N-1)$ decreases due to features of Zipf-like distributions. The total number of replicas is non-decreasing according to function $assignment(u_j, r_i)$. Similarly, we can prove the claim as the parameter ψ decreases.

We give the bounded search space of $[\psi_{min}, \psi_{max}]$ for the parameter ψ. If the first interval $\frac{u_1}{p_1 + p_m} \geq \frac{p_1}{p_1 + p_m}$, we have $r_i = N, \forall v_i \in V$ according to the function $assignment(u_j, r_i)$ and Lemma 4.1. It can be derived that $\psi_{max} = \theta \cdot \log M + \log N$. If the last interval $\frac{u_n}{p_1 + p_m} \geq \frac{p_1}{p_1 + p_m}$, we have $r_i = 1, \forall v_i \in V$ according to the function $assignment(u_j, r_i)$ and Lemma 4.1. It can be derived that $\psi_{min} = -\frac{\psi_{max}}{\log N - \log(N-1)}$.

It is known that $p_{m-1} - p_m = min_{\forall v_i, v_j \in V} \{| p_i - p_j |\}$. The binary search approach terminates when the change of ψ, denoted by ψ_δ, becomes smaller than $\frac{p_{m-1} - p_m}{p_1 + p_m}$. Hence, the bound of ψ_δ is calculated as $\frac{(M-1)^{-\theta} - M^{-\theta}}{1 + M^{\theta}}$. Due to $0.271 \leq \theta \leq 1$, the bound of ψ_δ is minimized when $\theta = 1$ and the minimum approximately equals to M^{-2}. Given the given search space and termination condition for the binary search approach, the complexity of the Zipf-like distribution based replication algorithm is $O(M \cdot \log M)$.

4.2 Video Placement

Video placement is to map all replicas of M videos to N servers to minimize the load imbalance degree L. If the pre-

vious replication leads to a uniform communication weight for all replicas, i.e. $w_i = w_j, \forall v_i, v_j \in V$, a round-robin placement achieves an optimal solution. It supposes that the replicas are arranged in groups in an arbitrary order such as $v_1^1 \ldots v_1^{r_1}, v_2^1 \ldots v_2^{r_2}, \ldots, v_m^1 \ldots v_m^{r_m}$.

However, in most cases, the communication weight of replicas of different videos may be different. For example, the ratio of the highest popularity to the lowest popularity is M^θ. If $M^\theta > N$, $\frac{w_1}{w_m} = \frac{p_1/r_1}{p_m/r_m} \geq \frac{p_1/N}{p_m/1} > 1$ due to constraint Eq. (7). This placement problem is more related to load balancing problems than to bin packing problems [17]. The difference with bin packing problems is that the number of servers for placement is given, rather than to be minimized. The differences with load balancing problems are there are storage limitations for placement and replicas of one video have to be placed to different servers due to constraint Eq. (6). We propose a placement algorithm called *smallest load first placement* in Algorithm 1.

Algorithm 1 Smallest Load First Placement
1: arrange all replicas of each video in a corresponding group;
2: sort these groups in a non-increasing order by the communication weight of the replicas in the groups;
3: **for** each of C iterations (C is the number of replicas that each server can contain) **do**
4:     select N replicas with the greatest communication weights;
5:     distribute these N replicas to the N servers – the distribution should satisfy that the replica with the greatest communication weight should be placed to the server with the smallest load and this server has not been placed with a replica of the same video;
6: **end for**

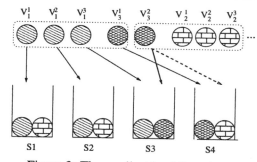

Figure 3: The smallest load first placement.

Figure 3 illustrates the placement strategy in a cluster of 4 servers. The replicas are arranged as $v_1^1, v_1^2, v_1^3, v_3^1, v_3^2, v_2^1, v_2^2, v_3^1 \ldots$ in a non-increasing order according to their communication weights. The first iteration places the first 4 replicas to the 4 servers. In second iteration, the server 4 has the current smallest load and the replica v_3^2 has the greatest communication weight. However, since the server 4 has already been placed with a replica of video v_3, i.e. v_3^1, the replica v_3^2 is placed to the server 3 with the second smallest load, and so on.

Theorem 3. *By the use of the smallest load first placement algorithm, the load imbalance degree defined by Eq. (2) is bounded by the difference between the greatest communication weight and smallest communication weight of the replica(s), i.e.* $L \leq max_{\forall v_i \in V}\{w_i\} - min_{\forall v_i \in V}\{w_i\}$.

Proof: Let $w_1, w_2, \ldots w_n, w_{n+1}, w_{n+2}, \ldots, w_{n \cdot C}$ be the communication weight of the $N \cdot C$ replicas in a non-increasing order. Clearly, $w_1 = max_{\forall v_i \in V}\{w_i\}$ and $w_{n \cdot C} = min_{\forall v_i \in V}\{w_i\}$. In the worse case, the change of L at iteration $j (0 \leq j \leq C - 1)$ of the placement is bounded by $w_{j \cdot n + 1} - w_{j \cdot n + n}$. The summation of these changes would be the worst case for L after the placement. We have $L \leq w_1 - w_n + w_{n+1} - w_{2n} \cdots + w_{n \cdot (C-1)+1} - w_{n \cdot C}$. It follows that $L \leq max_{\forall v_i \in V}\{w_i\} - min_{\forall v_i \in V}$.

Theorem 4. *By the use of the proposed replication and placement algorithms, the upper bound of the load imbalance degree, defined by Eq. (2), is non-increasing as the replication degree increases.*

4.3 Replication and Placement for Videos in Scalable Bit Rate

We consider the general case that the encoding bit rate is scalable and different videos can have different bit rates. The encoding bit rate is a discrete variable and its set is given. This framework provides a flexible way to maintain multiple copies of a video with different encoding bit rates. We propose a heuristic algorithm based on simulated annealing to solve the optimization formulated in Section 3. We construct the algorithm based on the parSA library [18]. The parallelization and generic decisions are connected with parameters of the parSA library itself and are transparent to users. Our implementation focuses on a class of problem-specific decisions. They include:

1. *Cost Function*: The objective function defined in Eq. (1) is the cost function of the simulated annealing.

2. *Initial Solution*: Initial solution place the videos encoded with the lowest possible bit rate to servers in a round-robin way. This makes sense for practical applications as each video can have one replica at least in a low bit rate quality.

3. *Neighborhood Structure:* To compute a neighborhood placement, a server in the cluster is identified by random. The bit rate of one video that has been placed on this server is increased or one new video is placed on the server. If above operation induces that the storage or the outgoing communication capacity of the server exceeds its limitation, the algorithm will decrease the bit rate of one or more videos that have been placed on the server, or delete one or more videos that are placed with the lowest bit rate so that the storage and communication constraints can be satisfied.

5 Performance Evaluation

In this section, we present the simulation results by the use of different replication and placement algorithms with various replication degrees under the assumption of a fixed encoding bit rate. Due to the space limitation, the results of the simulated annealing algorithm are omitted.

We simulated the Zipf-like distribution based replication (Zipf replication) and the bounded Adams' monotone divisor replication (Adams replication). We found that the Zipf replication and the Adams replication achieved nearly the same results in most test cases, except their time complexities. For brevity of the representation, we give the results of the Zipf replication only. To better understand the impact of different replication algorithms on performance, we simulated a feasible and straightforward algorithm called classification based replication [19]. For placement, we compare the round-robin placement algorithm and the smallest load first placement algorithm.

In the simulations, the VoD cluster consisted of 8 homogeneous servers. Each server had 1.8 Gbs outgoing network bandwidth. The storage capacity of each server ranged from 67.5 GB to 202.5 GB. The cluster contained 200 videos with duration 90 minutes each. The encoding bit rate for videos was fixed with the typical one for MPEG II movies, *i.e.* 4 Mbs. The storage requirement of a video hence was 2.7 GB. The storage capacity of the cluster ranged from 200 to 600 replicas and the replication degree ranged from 1.0 to 3.0.

Within the peak period of 90 minutes, the request arrivals were generated by a Poisson process with arrival rate λ [1]. Since the outgoing network bandwidth of the cluster was 3600 streams of 4 Mbs, the peak rate of λ was 40 requests per minute. The video popularity distribution was governed by a Zipf skew parameter θ $(0.271 \leq \theta \leq 1)$ [1, 15].

The simulation employed a simple admission control that a request was rejected if required communication bandwidth was unavailable. We use the rejection rate as the performance metric. In the following, we give some representative results. Each result was an average of 200 runs.

5.1 Impact of Replication on Rejection Rate

First we investigate the impact of replication degree (average number of replicas) on rejection rate. Figure 4 plots the representative results with a set of replication degree $\{1.0, 1.2, 1.6, 2.0, 3.0\}$. Different replication and placement algorithms were employed with popularity parameter $\theta = 1.0$ and 0.5, respectively.

Figure 4 shows that the rejection rate in all subplots decreases with the increase of the replication degree. In the subplot 4(a), the rejection rate decreases dramatically from non-replication to low replication degree 1.2. This is because the most popular videos are given the most replicas, which significantly reduces the granularity of replicas in

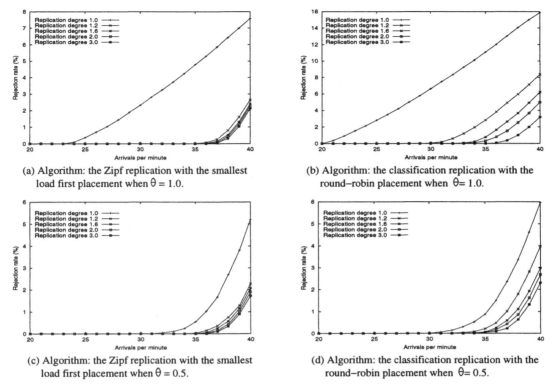

(a) Algorithm: the Zipf replication with the smallest load first placement when θ = 1.0.

(b) Algorithm: the classification replication with the round–robin placement when θ = 1.0.

(c) Algorithm: the Zipf replication with the smallest load first placement when θ = 0.5.

(d) Algorithm: the classification replication with the round–robin placement when θ = 0.5.

Figure 4: Impact of different replication degrees on rejection rate.

terms of communication weight for load balancing placement. There are no dramatic differences between the results of other replication degrees. In the subplot 4(b), the rejection rate gradually decreases with the increase of replication degree, although the change of rejection rate from non-replication to low replication degree 1.2 is still most significant. This means that the Zipf replication with the smallest load first placement can utilize the available storage space more efficiently than the classification based replication with the round-robin placement.

Figure 4 also shows that the Zipf replication with the smallest load first placement yield a lower rejection rate than the the classification based replication with the round-robin placement, especially in the cases with low replication degrees. When the replication degree increases, the difference between the algorithms decreases. It can be expected that as the replication degree reaches full replication, there would be no difference between the algorithms. In comparison with the subplots 4(a) and 4(c), the impact of replication degree decreases as parameter θ decreases. This is because as parameter θ decreases, the video popularity skew decreases which induces the fine granularity of communication weight of replicas for placement. The same conclusion can be made from the comparison between subplots 4(b) and 4(d). It is also agreed by the simulation results with many other θ values in between 0.271 to 1.0.

5.2 Impact of Algorithms on Rejection Rate

Figures 5 depicts the impact of four algorithm combinations on rejection rate when parameter θ is 1.0 and 0.5, respectively. Due to the space limitation, we give the representative results when the replication degree is 1.2 and 3.0.

Figure 5 shows that the algorithm combinations with either the Zipf replication or the smallest load first placement improves over the classification based replication with the round-robin placement significantly. The gap between the subplots of the classification replication with the round-robin placement and the classification based replication with the smallest load first placement shows the improvement of the placement strategy. The gap between the subplots of the classification based replication with the round-robin placement and the Zipf replication with the round-robin placement shows the improvement of the replication strategy. The results also show that the Zipf replication with the round-robin placement and the Zipf replication with the smallest load first placement have nominal differences. This demonstrates the effectiveness of the Zipf replication from another perspective. It can generate finely grained replicas in terms of communication weight for load balancing placement. The difference between algorithm combinations decreases with the increase of replication degrees. It is shown that as the replication degree increases, the curve of the Zipf

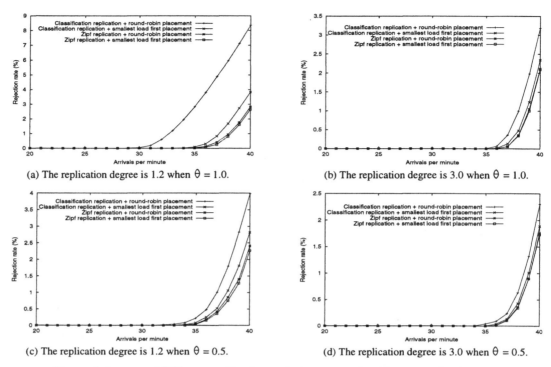

(a) The replication degree is 1.2 when $\theta = 1.0$.   (b) The replication degree is 3.0 when $\theta = 1.0$.

(c) The replication degree is 1.2 when $\theta = 0.5$.   (d) The replication degree is 3.0 when $\theta = 0.5$.

Figure 5: Impact of different replication and placement algorithms on rejection rate.

replication with the round-robin placement and the curve of the Zipf replication with the smallest load first placement are going to merge.

Figure 5 also shows that the curves have the same basic shapes as parameter θ decreases, although the differences in term of rejection rate are progressively less. From the comparisons of the four algorithm combinations, we make the conclusion that the Zipf replication with the smallest load first placement receive the desired result even under a very low replication degree. Other sensitivity analyses varied the number of videos, the video duration, the number of servers, the server outgoing bandwidth, as well as the encoding bit rate. We did not reach any significantly different conclusions regarding to the relative merits of the algorithms.

5.3 Impact of Algorithms on Load Imbalance

Figure 6 shows the change of the load imbalance degree L defined in Eq. (2) with various arrival rates. It helps us understand the performance curves of the four algorithm combinations depicted in Figure 5. Due to the space limitation, we give the results with the setting of $\theta = 1.0$ only.

For the classification based replication with the round-robin placement, the load imbalance degree is affected by the arrival rate significantly. The algorithm combinations with either the Zipf replication or the smallest load first placement receive more stable results with arrival rates.

When system load is light, the load imbalance degree in-

creases as the arrival rate increases. It reaches the peak values when the arrival rate is between 30 to 35 requests per minute. As the arrival rate is close to the outgoing bandwidth capacity of the cluster, the load imbalance degree in all figures decreases. Actually, when the arrival rate exceeds the throughput capacity about 20%, we found that the performance curves of all replication degrees almost merged because all servers were overloaded.

There would be no rejection before the arrival rate reaches the outgoing bandwidth capacity of the cluster, if communication traffic is perfectly balanced within the cluster. The primary reason is that the instances of arrival rate could not always be the mean value. It is the variance of arrival distributions that induces considerable dynamic load imbalance and hence rejections. When the arrival rate is 40 requests per minute, the rejection rate in both figures can be about 2%. We conclude that the Zipf replication with the smallest load first placement receive desirable performance with the accurate prediction of video popularities.

6 Conclusions and Future Work

We have investigated the video replication and placement problem in distributed storage VoD clusters. Under the assumption of single fixed encoding bit rate, we have given an optimal replication algorithm - the bounded Adams' monotone divisor replication and a bounded placement algorithm - the smallest load first placement. We have also presented

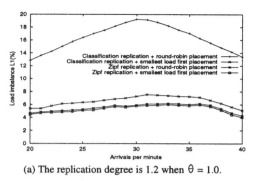
(a) The replication degree is 1.2 when $\theta = 1.0$.

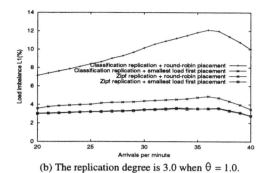
(b) The replication degree is 3.0 when $\theta = 1.0$.

Figure 6: Impact of different replication and placement algorithms on load imbalance degree.

an efficient algorithm utilizing Zipf-like popularity distribution to approximate the optimal replication. For videos with scalable encoding bit rates, a simulated annealing algorithm has been proposed. Comprehensive experiments have demonstrated the effectiveness of the algorithms.

The work in this article was based on the assumptions of a priori knowledge of video popularities and the same peak period of request rates for all videos. To complement the conservative video replication and placement strategies, we have given a request redirection strategy that utilizes the internal backbone bandwidth to balance the outgoing network traffic between the servers during the runtime [19].

The replication and placement framework in this article provides a flexible way to maintains multiple replicas of a video with different encoding bit rates. The flexibility can facilitate providing different qualities to requests for various videos or to requests from various clients/devices. We will report our experience in future work.

References

[1] C. C. Aggarwal, J. L. Wolf, and P. S. Yu. The maximum factor queue length batching scheme for video-on-demand systems. *IEEE Trans. on Computers*, 50(2):97–110, 2001.

[2] W. Bolosky, J. Barrera, R. Draves, G. Fitzgerald, Gibson, M. Jones, S. Levi, N. Myhrvold, and Rashid R. The Tiger video fileserver. In *Proc. NOSSDAV'96*, 1996.

[3] A. L. Chervenak, D. A. Patterson, and R. H. Katz. Choosing the best storage system for video service. In *Proc. ACM Multimedia'95*, pages 109–119, 1995.

[4] C. F. Chou, L. Golubchik, and J. C. S. Lui. Striping doesn't scale: how to achieve scalability for continuous media servers with replication. In *Proc. IEEE ICDCS'00*, pages 64–71, 2000.

[5] A. Dan and D. Sitaram. An online video placement policy based on bandwidth to space ratio (BSR). In *Proc. ACM SIGMOD'95*, pages 376–385, 1995.

[6] L.W. Dowdy and D.V. Foster. Comparative models of the file assignment problem. *ACM Computing Surveys*, 14(2):287–313, 1982.

[7] D. Eager, M. Vernon, and J. Zahorjan. Minimizing bandwidth requirements for on-demand data delivery. *IEEE Trans. on Knowledge and Data Engineering*, 13(5), 2001.

[8] W-C. Feng, B. Krishnaswami, and A. Prabhudev. Proactive buffer management for the streamed delivery of stored video. In *Proc. ACM Multimedia'98*, pages 285–290, 1998.

[9] J. Gafsi and E. W. Biersack. Modeling and performance comparison of reliability strategies for distributed video servers. *IEEE Trans. on Parallel and Distributed Systems*, 11(4):412–430, 2000.

[10] L. Golubchik, R. R. Muntz, C. Chou, and S. Berson. Design of fault-tolerant large-scale VoD servers: with emphasis on high-performance and low-cost. *IEEE Trans. on Parallel and Distributed Systems*, 12(4):363–386, 2001.

[11] T. Ibarkai and N. Katoh. *Resource allocation problem - Algorithmic approaches*. The MIT Press, 1988.

[12] Y. B. Lee and P. C. Wong. Performance analysis of a pull-based parallel video server. *IEEE Trans. on Parallel and Distributed Systems*, 11(12):1217–1231, 2000.

[13] P. J. Shenoy, P. Goyal, S. Rao, and H. M. Vin. Symphony: An integrated multimedia file system. In *Proc. ACM/SPIE Multimedia Computing and Networking*, pages 124–138, 1998.

[14] F. Tobagi, J. Pang, R. Baird, and M. Gang. Streaming RAID: A disk array management system for video files. In *Proc. ACM Multimedia'93*, pages 393–400, 1993.

[15] N. Venkatasubramanian and S. Ramanathan. Load management in distributed video servers. In *Proc. IEEE ICDCS'97*, pages 31–39, 1997.

[16] J. L. Wolf, P. S. Yu, and H. Shachinai. Disk load balancing for video-on-demand systems. *ACM/Springer Multimedia Systems Journal*, 5(6):358–370, 1997.

[17] C. Xu and F. Lau. *Load Balancing in Parallel Computers: Theory and Practice*. Kluwer Academic Publishers, 1997.

[18] X. Zhou, R. Lüling, and L. Xie. Solving a media mapping problem in a hierarchical server network with parallel simulated annealing. In *Proc. 29th ICPP*, pages 115–124, 2000.

[19] X. Zhou and C. Xu. Request redirection and data layout for network traffic balancing in cluster-based video-on-demand servers. In *Proc. IEEE PDIVM Workshop (in conjunction with IPDPS)*, 2002.

A Selection Technique for Replicated Multicast Video Servers

Akihito Hiromori
Graduate School of Eng. Sci.,
Osaka University
hiromori@ics.es.osaka-u.ac.jp

Hirozumi Yamaguchi
Graduate School of Info. Sci.
and Tech., Osaka University
h-yamagu@ist.osaka-u.ac.jp

Keiichi Yasumoto
Graduate School of Info. Sci.,
Nara Inst. of Science
and Technology
yasumoto@is.aist-nara.ac.jp

Teruo Higashino
Graduate School of Info. Sci.
and Tech., Osaka University
higashino@ist.osaka-u.ac.jp

Kenichi Taniguchi
Graduate School of Info. Sci.
and Tech., Osaka University
taniguchi@ist.osaka-u.ac.jp

Abstract

In this paper, we propose a selection technique for replicated multicast video servers. We assume that each replicated video server transmits the same video source as different quality levels' multicast streams. Using an IGMP facility like mtrace, each receiver monitors packet count information of those streams on routers and periodically selects the one which is expected to provide low loss rate and to be suitable for the current available bandwidth of receivers. Moreover, collection of packet count information is done in a scalable and efficient manner by sharing the collected information across receivers. Our experimental results using the network simulator have shown that our method could achieve much higher quality satisfaction of receivers, under the reasonable amount of tracing traffic.

1 Introduction

According to the recent progress of high-speed networks, we can expect that a large number of multimedia contents, especially video contents will be distributed through networks in near future. In general, such multimedia contents consume large amount of bandwidth, therefore the network may be congested if a lot of clients access to a single server. Server replication is one effective solution for such a problem. Service providers can dissolve the network congestion and the convergence of access to a single server, and clients can select suitable servers depending on the network status.

There are a lot of studies investigating how clients collect the network information (bandwidth, network topology, transmission delay and so on) and how they select suitable servers [1, 2]. However, these studies assume unicast servers because their target contents are on-demand contents such as WWW documents. On the other hand, for video broadcasting on scheduled time such as Internet TV, multicast communication is useful to save bandwidth, and new research results of the selection techniques of replicated multicast servers have been proposed [3, 4, 5]. However, these studies assume that much information should be known by each receiver such as (a part of) network topology and available bandwidth on each link, and do not mention how to collect the information. Thus it is not straightforward to adopt them on IP multicast networks.

In this paper, we assume that replicated multicast servers are located on different nodes, and each server transmits the same video source into different quality levels' multicast streams (*i.e.* independent multicast streams of different rates). Under this assumption, we propose a new server selection technique where each receiver monitors packet count information (the numbers of forwarded packets) of those streams on routers using IGMP mtrace query [6] and periodically selects the one which is expected to provide low loss rate and to be suitable for the available bandwidth of the receiver. Furthermore, our selection technique enables receivers to share packet count information in an efficient and distributed manner, in order to avoid significant impact to network load caused by the flood of mtrace query messages sent from a large number of receivers periodically.

We have evaluated the performance of our method using the network simulator *ns-2* [7]. The experimental results have shown that our method could achieve much higher satisfaction in terms of average *quality values* at receivers, keeping the amount of control traffic low enough.

2   Design Concept

For replicated multicast video servers on IP networks, we think that the followings should be considered, (a) how to collect network status, (b) how to deal with heterogeneous receivers and bandwidth fluctuation, and (c) how to keep scalability for a large number of receivers. Regarding (a), some selection methods for unicast servers measure RTT to estimate end-to-end delay and jitter. However, in multicast communication, a delivery tree has been already constructed when a receiver tries to join a group, and the receiver may be able to select the best one by obtaining information about the existing multicast trees in advance. Our method uses IGMP mtrace facility for this purpose. Note that some other methods use this facility for other purposes, for example, Ref. [8] uses it to find paths for local error recovery in reliable multicast. Regarding (c), monitoring routers by a large number of receivers may yield a scalability problem. Considering this trade-off between (a) and (c), we address how to reduce monitoring costs in Section 4. (b) is a common and well-known issue in multicast communication where some receivers in a group using low-speed links may not receive the content while others in the same group may not efficiently use their high-speed links. In this paper, *simulcasting*[9] is assumed where a server is capable of providing a single video source as different quality's streams, and allows receivers to switch quality levels as well as switching servers for rate adaptation. Note that a more sophisticated scheme for the heterogeneity has been known as Receiver-driven Layered Multicast (RLM)[10]. The possibility of RLM in the replicated server architecture is discussed in Section 6.

3   Stream Selection Algorithm

3.1   Replicated Server Architecture

We consider networks where multiple servers on different locations distribute the same video content. Each server encodes the video content into independent L streams, whose *quality levels* are different from each other (e.g., w.r.t. spatial and temporal resolution). We denote each quality level as an integer number where 1 corresponds to the lowest quality and L does the highest quality. Each server transmits the data streams of the video content with 1...L quality levels via independent L multicast groups. Hereafter, we call a data stream transmitted from server S_i with quality level l simply as a *stream*, and denote it as $st_{i,l}$.

3.2   Monitoring Multicast Packet Counts

Most of current IGMP supported routers implement tracing facility of IGMP as specified in [6]. Several tools for monitoring IP multicast traffic using this facility have been proposed so far (see [11] for survey) and among them there is a tool called *mtrace*[6]. Using mtrace with a multicast group address and a source host address, we can obtain a sequential list of routers' addresses on the path from the sender to the receiver with the total numbers of forwarded packets and time stamps on those routers (called *packet count information*).

Multicast routers count the total numbers of forwarded packets during their operation time for every stream(group). We assume that receivers periodically send mtrace query messages for each group. Using the last two query results which include routers' packet counts and their time stamps, the number of forwarded packets per second at each router can be computed. Consequently, each receiver can know the delivering path from a server to the receiver and the number of forwarded packets per second (packet count information) on the intermediate routers of the path.

3.3   Receivers' Knowledge

We assume that each receiver R_j knows the followings as either given information in advance or obtained information by monitoring.

- $path_{i,j}$; the delivery path from server S_i to R_j. We assume that R_j knows $path_{i,j}$ for each server S_i. This is obtained by one time execution of mtrace query for each server.

- $gr_{(i,l),j}$; the *grafting router* (branch router) of $st_{i,l}$ for R_j. It is the router on $path_{i,j}$ that receives $st_{i,l}$ and is the nearest to R_j. We assume that R_j knows $gr_{(i,l),j}$ for each $st_{i,l}$. This router is found as the last router on $path_{i,j}$ where the packet count of $st_{i,l}$ is not zero.

- $ratio_{(i,l)}@r$; the packet arrival ratio of $st_{i,l}$ at router r. We assume that R_j knows $ratio_{(i,l)}@r$ for each pair of $st_{i,l}$ and router r on $path_{i,j}$. Hereafter, $count_{(i,l)}@r$ denotes the number of packets per second at router r obtained by the periodic execution of mtrace queries. $ratio_{i,l}@r$ can be computed by $\frac{count_{(i,l)}@r}{count_{(i,l)}@S_i}$. Note that $count_{(i,l)}@S_i$ denotes the number of transmitted packets of stream $st_{i,l}$ at server S_i and we can not measure this packet count by mtrace. However, this is equal to the number of forwarded packets at the router on the same network as S_i if we assume that packets are rarely discarded on this router. In general,

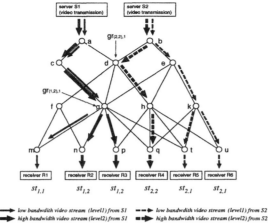

Figure 1. Selecting Streams: Example

congestion rarely occurs at such a router, since there are only a few senders in usual. Therefore this assumption is reasonable.

- $ratio_{(i,l)}@R_j$; the packet arrival ratio of $st_{i,l}$ at receiver R_j where R_j currently receives $st_{i,l}$. $ratio_{(i,l)}@R_j$ can be computed by $\frac{count_{(i,l)}@R_j}{count_{(i,l)}@S_i}$.

3.4 Selecting Streams : Overview by Example

In our technique, each receiver dynamically selects a stream (determines a pair of a server and a quality level) using the packet arrival ratio at each multicast router on the delivery paths from servers to the receiver.

In Fig. 1, two servers S_1 and S_2 transmit the same video content via multicast streams of two different quality levels: level1 (low) and level2 (high) (thus $i = 1, 2$ and $L = 2$). Each receiver $R_j(j = 1..6)$ is receiving one of those multicast streams. For example, R_1 is receiving stream $st_{1,1}$ (the stream of level1 from server S_1) and R_5 is receiving stream $st_{2,1}$ (the stream of level1 from server S_2).

Here, given the packet count information, we think that the following two factors can be used to infer a "good" stream for each receiver; packet arrival ratio at a grafting router (branch router) and the number of hops between the grafting router and the receiver. Now let us suppose that receiver R_1 has been receiving stream $st_{1,1}$ stably for a while (*i.e.*, the packet arrival ratio $ratio_{(1,1)}@R_1$ is high). In order to receive the stream of the higher level (level2), R_1 finds the grafting routers, $gr_{(1,2),1}$ (router g) and $gr_{(2,2),1}$ (router d) ($path_{1,1} = a$-c-g-m and $path_{2,1} = b$-d-f-m). Also let us assume that both $ratio_{(1,2)}@gr_{(1,2),1}$ and $ratio_{(2,2)}@gr_{(2,2),1}$ (packet arrival ratios at grafting routers g and d, respectively) are higher than a certain threshold. The threshold is a lower bound of

packet arrival ratio which is expected to provide stable quality. R_1 selects one of the two streams $st_{1,2}$ and $st_{2,2}$, with minimal number of hops to the grafting router. In this example, since the distance from the grafting router of stream $st_{1,2}$ to R_1 is 1 hop and that of $st_{2,2}$ is 2 hops, R_1 selects $st_{1,2}$.

Similarly, if the packet arrival ratio at a receiver becomes lower than a certain threshold, the receiver selects one of streams of the same or the lower quality levels which are expected to be stable. For example, if $ratio_{(1,2)}@R_3$ becomes lower than a certain threshold, R_3 tries to receive one of $st_{2,2}$, $st_{1,1}$ and $st_{2,1}$. If their packet arrival ratios at their grafting routers are relatively good, R_3 selects $st_{2,2}$ in order to keep the current quality level.

3.5 Selection Algorithm

In our selection procedure, each receiver R_j periodically tries to select a new stream (or keeps receiving the current stream), according to the packet arrival ratio of its receiving stream $st_{i,l}$ ($ratio_{(i,l)}@R_j$).

In selecting streams, each receiver first decides a new quality level suitable than the current level. RLM[10] uses *join-experiment* to decide the number of layers (*i.e.*, receiving rate) to subscribe. *join-experiment* lets a receiver attempt to subscribe the higher layer if she/he wants, and unsubscribe it if significant packet loss is experienced. Additionally, the receiver uses a *join-timer* for every layer, which suggests a time period for a next join-experiment of the layer. This period is increased if a join-experiment is failed, in order to prevent frequent experiments that are likely to fail. Even though our method is different from RLM (we assume independent streams rather than layers), we believe that this scheme is useful for congestion control in our case. Therefore a similar policy can be applied to determine a new quality level in selecting a stream.

In order to describe the selection behavior of a receiver, we define the following three states, (1) *level-up* state, (2) *stable* state and (3) *level-keep-or-down* state, according to $ratio_{(i,l)}@R_j$.

1. A receiver R_j where $ratio_{(i,l)}@R_j \geq P_1$ ($0 < P_1 \leq 1$) is regarded to be in *level-up* state. P_1 is a lower bound ratio by which R_j can infer that there is not significant loss near R_j. In simulation, we have used $P_1 = 0.95$. This value, which is close to 1.00, may yield the better results in our experience, because $ratio_{(i,l)}@R_j$ is likely to fall down greatly (down to about 0.80 or lower) in the event of congestion, and to be close to 1.00 otherwise. R_j selects a new stream $st_{i',l+1}$ if (a) the join-timer expires, (b) $ratio_{(i',l+1)}@gr_{(i',l+1),j} \geq P_2$ holds (this

means that the packet arrival ratio at the grafting router is not less than P_2, and is explained later) and (c) the hop count from $gr_{(i',l+1),j}$ to R_j is the minimum of all the other streams of quality level $l+1$. If there is no such a stream $st_{i',l+1}$, R_j keeps receiving $st_{i,l}$. If this experiment fails (*i.e.* the receiving rate is instable and R_j is back to the current level), R_j extends the join-timer.

Even though the quality level of the new stream is one level higher than the previous stream, there is the possibility that R_j cannot gain the expected quality due to the traffic on the links from S_i to $gr_{(i',l+1),j}$, and also the traffic on the links from $gr_{(i',l+1),j}$ to R_j. By selecting a stream where a certain packet arrival ratio has been already achieved at the grafting router and the distance between the grafting router and the receiver is the shortest of all such streams, the new stream with one level higher is likely to be received stably.

2. A receiver R_j where $P_1 > ratio_{(i,l)}@R_j \geq P_2$ ($P_1 > P_2 > 0$) is regarded to be in *stable* state. P_2 is a lower bound ratio under which R_j cannot tolerate the damage caused by packet loss and by which R_j considers that congestion occurs. In the simulation, we have used $P_2 = 0.85$.

   In this case, R_j keeps receiving $st_{i,l}$.

3. Each receiver R_j where $P_2 > ratio_{(i,l)}@R_j$ is regarded to be in *level-keep-or-down* state.

   In this case, R_j selects a new stream $st_{i',l'}$ ($l' \leq l$) where $ratio_{(i',l')}@gr_{(i',l'),j} \geq P_2$ (the packet arrival ratio at the grafting router is not less than P_2) and l' is the highest level of all such streams. If such a stream is not uniquely determined, R_j selects the one where the hop count from the grafting router $gr_{(i',l'),j}$ to R_j is minimum.

   For streams whose packet arrival ratios at the grafting routers are not less than the threshold P_2, R_j selects the one whose level l' ($l' \leq l$) is the highest of all such streams. In case of $l' = l$, R_j can keep the current quality level, otherwise the quality level is lower than the current level, however, the actual quality is expected to be improved.

4 Improving Scalability in Monitoring Multicast

As stated in the previous section, our technique is a monitoring based approach. Here a reasonable question is that, we may experience the implosion of mtrace packets near a sender, like the NAK implosion problem in feedback-based reliable multicast. Here is a sim-

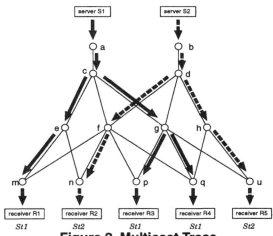

Figure 2. Multicast Trees.

ple analysis of the amount of mtrace packets. Assume that there are 1000 receivers and they periodically send mtrace query packets (at most 0.2KB) for every 2 seconds, for a pair of a multicast group and its sender. These packets are forwarded toward the sender, and thus aggregated at the sender. If each server distributes three streams($L = 3$), the amount of mtrace traffic at each server is $\frac{0.2*8*1,000*3}{2} = 2.4Mbps$. Moreover, the router on the root of the tree needs to process 500 queries per second. Needless to say, these values are impractical and intolerable, and thus some efficient way is desired.

In order to avoid such message explosion, we roughly control receivers in a distributed manner in order to limit the number of queries on networks, and enable to share packet count information. The idea is as follow. We use a multicast group (say C) as a control group where all the receivers are the members. Also every receiver has his/her own timer. One of the servers sends a signalling message to C for every T_m period, for loosely synchronization among receivers. Each receiver sets a random value to the timer and then starts it whenever it receives a synchronization message on C. The random value is determined based on the exponential distribution with parameter λ. When the timer expires, it sends a query message only to the current receiving stream and sends the received response (query result) to C, unless it has received query results from others on C. This enables receivers to share packet count information of the routers on the shared part of delivering paths (*e.g.* if two receivers A and B share a part of their paths to a server and B executes a query, the query result includes packet count information of the routers on the shared part of the paths) and thus the number of queries can be reduced. Due to the limitation of space, we omitted formal description of the method. Readers may refer [12] for the details.

We explain this idea using Fig. 2. There are two servers S_1 and S_2, and they send streams st_1 and st_2, respectively. Receivers R_1, R_3 and R_4 receive st_1, therefore they can send mtrace queries only to st_1 (R_2 and R_5 can do only to st_2). For every T_m, some of R_1, R_3 and R_4 can send mtrace queries to S_1, and now assume that only R_3 and R_4 send queries in this period. Then they know the latest packet counts of the routers on their paths (a-c-g-p and a-c-g-q), and send these query results to the control group C. On the other hand, R_1 can know the latest information on routers a and c which are on its path (a-c-e-m), however cannot know those on e and m. In this case R_1 uses the last information which R_1 knows. Using a random delay generator based on an exponential distribution, the information on the path of each receiver will be updated eventually. As clearly known, the information of a router closer to a sender is updated more frequently at each receiver.

For the information of streams which R_j does not currently receive, R_j knows their information by listening to the control group C. Since R_j does not send mtrace queries to those streams, it never knows the information on the routers which are on the paths to their senders but not included in the multicast trees. For example, R_2 and R_5 send mtrace query results to C and those results do not contain information on m. However, R_1 can know the information of the routers b, d and f which are on the path $path_{2,1}$, and R_1 knows that all the information which is needed to execute our selection procedure (e.g., the grafting router is found as the router which is the closest to the receiver on the path from the server to the receiver and is included in at least one of mtrace query results sent to C).

5 Experimental Results

In order to evaluate the performance of our proposed method, we have designed and implemented a protocol for collecting the number of arrival packets at intermediate routers, as a module of network simulator ns-2[7]. This protocol works in the network layer and is based on the scheme of IP multicast tool mtrace.

In Section 5.1, we have evaluated receivers' *quality satisfaction* which we think is the most important factor in video distribution. Then in Section 5.2 the influence of topologies on the quality satisfaction has been examined. Finally, in Section 5.3, the amount of control traffic (mtrace queries and results) has been measured.

A number of researches have been investigated for modeling traffic patterns in the Internet [13], however, it is still a challenging task. In this paper, we have roughly distinguished the characteristics of background

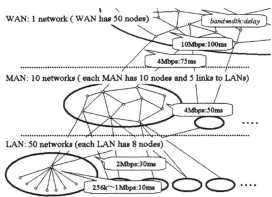

Figure 3. Network Topology

traffic into two typical categories (a) stable case and (b) bursty case, and we have carried out simulations under both cases. In case (a), we have generated no connection. In case (b), we have generated 30 unicast connections of constant bit rates (about 2 Mbps). Their alive time and locations were determined randomly.

As comparison, we consider a method where the nearest server is allocated in advance for each receiver (thus he/she can only select quality levels). This method is called a *fixed server method*. Quality level selection policy in the fixed server method is the same as our method.

We have used networks of a hierarchical topology model called Tiers [14]. The tiers model consists of three types of organizations, WAN, MAN and LAN. In our simulation, we have determined the numbers of nodes in WAN, MAN and LAN as 50, 10 and 8, respectively. Also, the total numbers of WAN, MAN and LAN are 1, 10 and 50, respectively (thus the number of nodes in a network is 550). LAN has a star topology. We have determined link capacities and link delays as specified in Fig. 3.

Servers are located on WAN and receivers are located on LANs. Each server sends three streams ($L = 3$, three quality levels) whose transmission rates are 256kbps, 512kbps and 1Mbps. Also, we have used DVMRP as a multicast routing protocol.

5.1 Receivers' Quality Satisfaction

We define a *quality value* to measure the quality satisfaction of receivers. It represents the quality of video that a receiver receives. If a receiver has received a stream $st_{i,l}$ during a time period (let t_a and t_b denote its starting time and ending time, respectively) and if its packet arrival ratio at time t is p_t, we define the quality value during the time period as the integral of the product of quality level l and arrival ratio p_t (i.e., $\int_{t_a}^{t_b} l * p_t dt$). We have measured average quality values of all the receivers during the simulation time. Note that a quality value may become high not only in the case that the packet arrival ratio is stable and its quality level is suitable but also in the case that the quality level is too high and a lot of packet losses are experienced. In general, quality satisfaction of receivers in the latter case is considered low. Therefore, we also show packet arrival ratios in this section.

Average Quality Value We have measured average quality values in (a) stable cases and (b) bursty cases. Fig. 4 shows those values in our method and the fixed server method. The numbers of receivers are 50, 100 and 150. The vertical axis represents average quality values and the horizontal axis represents simulation cases. Note that in Fig. 4 (a), the theoretically maximum quality values are calculated shown[1].

In stable cases (in Fig 4 (a)), average quality values in our method are around 95 % of those in the fixed server method. This is because of the existence of control traffic (mtrace queries). However, comparing quality values in our method with maximum quality values, our method could achieve 85 % - 95 % (93% in average) of the maximum quality values.

On the other hand, in bursty cases (in Fig 4 (b)), average quality values in our method exceed those in the fixed server method in almost all cases (120% - 140% compared with the fixed server method). Considering the results in both cases, we can see that our method could nicely avoid congested paths.

Average Packet Arrival Ratio In Fig. 5, the average packet arrival ratios in the same experiments above are shown.

Average packet arrival ratios in both methods are similar, and greater than 90 % in stable cases (Fig. 5 (a)). In bursty cases (Fig. 5 (b)), although the ratios were greater than 90 % as in the stable cases, the fixed method could not keep 90%.

From the above results, receivers could select higher quality levels' streams in our method than the fixed server method and avoid congested paths in the event of congestion.

5.2 Network Topology Influence

In our method, receivers select streams based on the two factors: packet arrival ratios at branch routers (grafting routers) and the numbers of hops from them. Even though our method is not designed for specific topology models, the latter factor may differ in different topology models. Therefore, in order to confirm that our selection algorithm works well under typical

---

[1]We have calculated the (theoretically) maximum of average quality values using an integer linear programming (ILP) technique under a fixed allocation of streams to receivers.

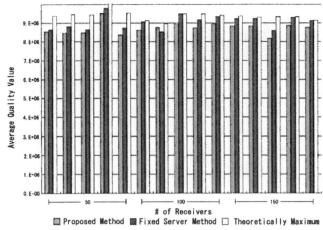

(a) under stable background traffic

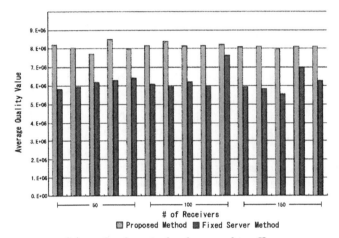

(b) under bursty background traffic

Figure 4. Average Quality Value

network topologies, we have measure average quality values on mesh-like topology networks and pure-tree topology networks as well as on Tiers model (hierarchical topology networks). Note that on pure-tree networks, servers are located near the root node, while they are randomly distributed on mesh-like networks. The results are shown in Fig. 6.

On pure-tree networks, delivering paths from servers are shared in most cases. For this reason, our method and the fixed server method fell into the similar results. On the other hand, on Tiers networks which we have used in the experiments in the previous section, since receivers could have a few different paths, our selection has achieved better performance than the fixed server method by selecting other servers in the event of congestion.

We can find much more striking difference between our method and the fixed server method on mesh-like

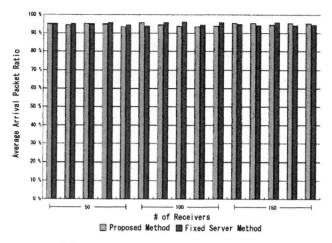

(a) under stable background traffic

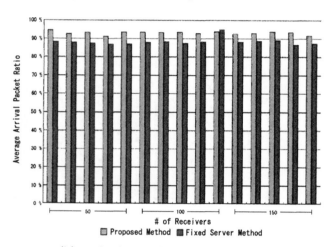

(b) under bursty background traffic

Figure 5. Average Packet Arrival Ratio

topology networks. As we know, since receivers could have a variety of paths, they could adaptively select a feasible server in our method.

5.3 Control Traffic

In Sections 5.1 and 5.2, we have confirmed that our method could totally archive better performance than the fixed server method even in large-scale networks (550 nodes). However, as we stated in Section 4, the number of mtrace queries increases depending on the number of receivers. Even though we have proposed an idea to loosely control the number of queries transmitted, we should confirm that it can actually keep the amount of mtrace query traffic low enough.

In the experiments in Sections 5.1 and 5.2, a server sent a synchronization message for every 1 second, and receivers were controlled where only 25 % of them sent mtrace query in 1 second ($\lambda = 0.3$ in the exponential

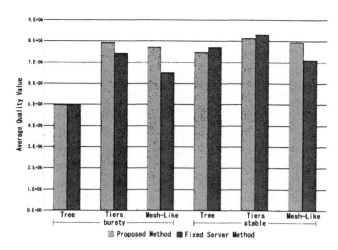

Figure 6. Average Quality Value on Different Networks

distribution used to generate random timer values at receivers). Using this value of $\lambda = 0.3$, we have also carried out experiments to measure the amount of control traffic (mtrace query traffic and traffic on the control group C) varying the number of receivers.

The result is shown in Fig. 7. In this figure, the measured control traffic at a server and a receiver is depicted. The vertical axis represents the number of receivers and the horizontal axis represents the amount of the control traffic. The result has shown that the amount of traffic in both server and receiver sides is less than 12 kbps even in 250 receivers.

Note that we have also proposed a technique to autonomously adjust the control traffic under a certain amount, independent of the number of receivers (see Ref. [12] for details of dynamic λ control). Fig. 8 shows how the technique has automatically adjusted the amount of control traffic in a simulation case. We have examined two cases where λ was fixed to 0.75 in one case, and in another case λ was controlled (initially set to 0.75) so that the traffic could be less than 4kbps. In Fig. 8 we can see that the amount of control traffic is nicely controlled by our dynamic λ control technique.

6 Conclusion

In this paper, we have proposed a new selection technique for replicated video multicast servers. Under the assumption that there exist replicated video servers and each server transmits the same video source as different multicast streams, our technique allows each receiver to monitor packet count information on routers using an IGMP facility and to periodically select the one which is expected to provide low loss rate and to be suitable for the current available bandwidth of the

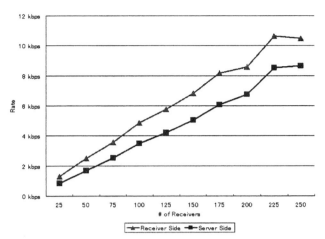

Figure 7. Control Traffic($\lambda = 0.3$)

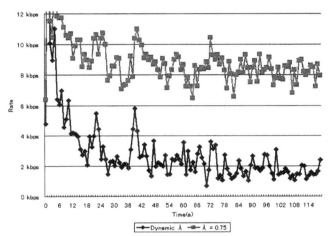

Figure 8. Time vs Control Traffic ($\lambda = 0.75$ and dynamic λ)

receiver.

As briefly mentioned in Section 1, Receiver-driven Layered Multicast [10] on replicated server architecture is also considerable, and is a challenging issue. A receiver is possible to select different servers for subscribing his/her layers, whereas it should consider the differentiation of path characteristics as between layers. This is part of our future work.

References

[1] M. Sayal, Y. Breitbart, P. Scheuermann, and R. Vingralek, "Selection algorithms for replicated web servers," in *Proc. of Workshop on Internet Server Performance (WISP98)*, 1998.

[2] R. L. Carter and M. E. Crovella, "On the network impact of dynamic server selection," *Computer Networks*, vol. 31, no. 23-24, pp. 2529–2558, 1999.

[3] Z. Fei, M. H. Ammar, and E. W. Zegura, "Optimal allocation of clients to replicated multicast servers," in *Proc. of 1999 Int. Conf. on Network Protocols (ICNP'99)*, pp. 69–76, 1999.

[4] G. Riley, M. Ammar, and L. Clay, "Receiver-based multicast scoping: A new cost-conscious join/leave paradigm," in *Proc. of 1998 Int. Conf. on Network Protocols (ICNP'98)*, pp. 254–261, 1998.

[5] A. Hiromori, H. Yamaguchi, K. Yasumoto, T. Higashino, and K. Taniguchi, "Fast and optimal multicast-server selection based on receiver' preference," in *Proc. of 7th Int. Workshop on Interactive Distributed Multimedia Systems & Telecommunication Service(IDMS2000)(LNCS 1905)*, pp. 40–52, 2000.

[6] W. Fenner and S. Casner, "A "traceroute" facility for IP multicast," in *Internet Draft*, 2000.

[7] B. MASH Research Group University of California, "The network simulator ns-2," 2000. http://www-mash.cs.berkeley.edu/ns/.

[8] B. N. Levine, S. Paul, and J. J. Garcia-Luna-Aceves, "Organizing multicast receivers deterministically by packet-loss correlation," *ACM Multimedia*, pp. 210–210, 1998.

[9] S. Fischer, A. Hafid, G. Bochmann, and H. Meer, "Cooperative QoS management for multimedia applications," in *Proc. of Int. Conf. on Multimedia Computing and Systems (ICMCS'97)*, pp. 303–310, 1997.

[10] V. Jacobson, S. McCanne, and M. Vetterli, "Receiver-driven layered multicast," in *Proc. of ACM SIGCOMM'96*, pp. 117–130, 1996.

[11] K. Sarac and K. Almeroth, "Supporting multicast deployment efforts: A survey of tools for multicast monitoring," *Journal of High Speed Networking*, vol. 9, no. 3-4, pp. 191–211, 2000.

[12] A. Hiromori, H. Yamaguchi, K. Yasumoto, T. Higashino, and K. Taniguchi, "A selection technique for replicated multicast video servers," tech. rep., http://www-tani.ist.osaka-u.ac.jp/, 2002.

[13] S. McCreary and K. Claffy, "Trends in wide area IP traffic patterns," tech. rep., CAIDA, 2000. http://www.caida.org/outreach/papers/AIX0005/.

[14] K. Calvert, M. Doar, and E. Zegura, "Modeling internet topology," *IEEE Communications Magazine*, vol. 35, no. 6, pp. 160–163, 1997.

Session 8A

Applications

Minimal Sensor Integrity in Sensor Grids *

Rajgopal Kannan
Department of Computer Science
Louisiana State University
Baton Rouge, LA 70803
rkannan@bit.csc.lsu.edu

Sudipta Sarangi
Department of Economics
Louisiana State University
Baton Rouge, LA 70803

Sibabrata Ray
Department of Computer Science
University of Alabama
Tuscaloosa, AL 35402

S. S. Iyengar
Department of Computer Science
Louisiana State University
Baton Rouge, LA 70803

Abstract

Given the increasing importance of optimal sensor deployment for battlefield strategists, the converse problem of reacting to a particular deployment by an enemy is equally significant and not yet addressed in a quantifiable manner in the literature. We address this issue by modeling a two stage game in which the opponent deploys sensors to cover a sensor field and we attempt to maximally reduce his coverage at minimal cost. In this context, we introduce the concept of minimal sensor integrity which measures the vulnerability of any sensor deployment. We find the best response by quantifying the merits of each response. While the problem of optimally deploying sensors subject to coverage constraints is NP-Complete, in this paper we show that the best response (i.e the maximum vulnerability) can be computed in polynomial time for sensors with arbitrary coverage capabilities deployed over points in any dimensional space. In the special case when sensor coverages form an interval graph (as in a linear grid), we describe a better $O(Min(M^2, NM))$ dynamic programming algorithm.

1 Introduction

Distributed, real-time sensor networks are essential for effective surveillance in the digitized battlefield and for en-

vironmental monitoring. In general, the surveillance zone for the sensors can be viewed as a multidimensional grid with sensors being placed at some of these grid points. Sensors can vary in their monitoring ranges and coverage capabilities of grid points, and have correspondingly different costs. There is a substantial body of literature in sensor networks that addresses techniques for efficient sensor communication [9, 5] and data fusion [8]. With the increasing prevalence of sensor based field operations, research on efficient sensor deployment strategies has also become important [2, 4]. Recently, [3], presented a systematic theory that leads to sensor deployment strategies for effective surveillance and target location. They provide a simplified target location scheme in which every grid point is covered by a unique subset of sensors.

Given the importance of optimal sensor deployment strategies to battlefield commanders and strategists, the converse problem of reacting to a particular deployment by an enemy is equally significant. In particular, issues related to the vulnerability of different deployment strategies must also be examined. In a battlefield environment, for example, one can naturally expect sensors to be the targets of enemy attacks. To the best of our knowledge, there has been no previous work on quantifying the susceptibility of different placement schemes. In [3], optimal sensor deployment is considered only in the context of coverage and cost constraints while the vulnerability of the deployment has been ignored. Clearly from the deployers perspective, a brute force approach to minimizing grid vulnerability is by maximizing coverage of grid points. However this will unnecessarily increase the deployment cost resulting in inefficient utilization of sensor resources. Thus there is need

* This work was supported in part by DARPA and AFRL under grant number F30602-01-1-0551.

for a formal framework relating optimal sensor placement to vulnerability.

In this paper, we introduce for the first time the notion of *minimal sensor integrity*. Sensor integrity is a measure of the vulnerability of any sensor placement strategy to attack. Given that the object of any placement strategy is the maximization of a (point) coverage function, the minimal sensor integrity of a placement strategy is the worst case loss of (point) coverage that can be inflicted at least cost.

Our concept of sensor integrity can be better understood from a game-theoretic viewpoint where there are two players: Player 1 deploys M sensors to cover up to N points in a multidimensional grid while satisfying his coverage and cost constraints. Player 2 attempts to destroy sensors based on her removal costs and point *uncoverage* thereby taking into account the tradeoffs between costs and vulnerability. In this paper, we find our best-response to any deployment by player 1.

We show that for sensors with arbitrary ranges over grids of any dimension, the problem can be solved in $O(\text{Min}(ML^2, NL^2))$ time, where L represents the total coverage by sensors over all points. For the particular case of deployment over a linear grid, we present a dynamic programming solution with a better time complexity of $O(\text{Min}(M^2, NM))$ and $O(N + M)$ storage. In this paper, we do not explicitly find player 1's best-response deployment to player 2's actions. However, since we find player 2's best response to every possible deployment of player 1, our technique can be used to identify sensor deployments and removals that form a sub-game perfect Nash equilibrium [11]. Such sequential move games under different deterministic or probabilistic deployment scenarios will be the subject of future research.

2 Sensor Integrity

We begin by formally defining the problem of computing minimal sensor integrity along with a description of the parameters in our model set up. Let $S = (S_1, S_2, \ldots, S_M)$ be a set of sensors deployed over a region $G = (G_1, G_2, \ldots, G_N)$ of points. Let $\mathcal{P} = \{\mathcal{P}_1, \ldots, \mathcal{P}_r\}$ be the set of all possible sensor placement strategies in the given deployment domain, where strategy P_i induces a given amount of coverage with a corresponding deployment cost. For example, one can consider strategies that minimize the cost while satisfying mandated surveillance accuracy parameters. Alternatively, sensors can be placed in such a way as to simplify target location. $SP_i \subseteq S$ is the set of sensors placed under strategy P_i with $G_i \subseteq G$ the resulting set of points covered by SP_i. Let $U_l \subseteq G_i$ be the set of points left *uncovered* by the loss or destruction of sensor set $SP_i^l \subseteq SP_i$. We represent the advantage to the opponent of uncovering points in G by a benefit function $B : G \to R^+$. To uncover these points, the opponent

pays a sensor removal cost[1] represented by a cost function $C : SP_i \to R^+$.

Then, given sensor placement strategy P_i, the minimal sensor integrity of SP_i is defined as:

$$\min\left(0, \left\{\sum_{S_i \in SP_i^l} C(S_i) - \sum_{G_i \in U_l} B(G_i)\right\}\right)$$

$$\forall \; SP_i^l \; \in \; 2^{SP_i} \quad (1)$$

We denote by S_{opt} the optimal sensor set that must be removed by the enemy to yield the minimal sensor integrity, with G_{opt} the corresponding set of uncovered points. In this paper, we assume that sensor placement has been apriori determined using some independent algorithm, for example, one that considers cost and coverage constraints [3] and only consider the problem of finding S_{opt} and G_{opt} for a given sensor placement strategy.

3 Computing Minimal Sensor Integrity

We consider the problem of computing sensor integrity given an M sensor set S covering a set G of N points with sensor removal cost function C and point uncovering benefit function B. Typically, sensor coverage areas are restricted to be regular polygons, for example, the 2-D problem consists of removing subsets of rectangles or spheres covering a grid. In this and higher dimensional cases, obvious choices of algorithms for computing sensor integrity do not seem to possess either greedy or divide-and-conquer properties. Moreover, the converse problem of optimally deploying sensors subject to coverage constraints is NP-Complete [3] as are the related problems of packing or covering a hyperplane with hyperrectangles [6, 7].

However we are able to develop a polynomial time algorithm by a simple transformation of the sensor integrity problem into a maxflow problem on a directed bipartite graph. Given an instance (G, S, C, B) of the sensor integrity problem, we convert it into a directed bipartite graph $T = (\{A \bigcup S\}, \{G \bigcup X\}, E)$ with edge capacities as follows. We introduce two new vertices A and X along with $N + M$ directed edges $\{(A, P_1), \ldots, (A, P_N)\}$ and $\{(S_1, X), \ldots, (S_M, X)\}$. Each edge (A, P_i) and (S_j, X) are assigned weights of $B(P_i)$ and $C(S_j)$ respectively. Also, for each point $P_a \in G$, we add a directed edge $(P_a, S_b), \forall S_b \in S : S_b$ covers P_a. The weight of such an edge is set to ∞.

Consider a maximum flow in T from A to X. Let $\overline{S} \subseteq S$ and $\overline{G} \subseteq G$ be vertices in the corresponding minimum

---

[1]distinct from the deployment cost paid by the deployer

568

cut. By definition, no point $P_j \in G \backslash \overline{G}$ is covered by any $S_i \in S \backslash \overline{S}$. Moreover since the edges in the middle of bipartite graph are all oriented from G towards S, positive flow cannot be pushed from any node $P_a \in G$ via a path of the form P_a, S_b, P_c, S_d. Thus no points covered exclusively by sensors in $\overline{S}$ can be part of the minimum cut $\overline{G}$ and no sensor that does not cover at least one point in $G \backslash \overline{G}$ can be part of $\overline{S}$. Hence, $\overline{S}$ and $G \backslash \overline{G}$ represents a feasible solution to the minimal sensor integrity problem. Since

$$
\begin{aligned}
A &= \sum_{S_i \in \overline{S}} C(S_i) + \sum_{P_j \in \overline{G}} B(P_j) \\
&\equiv \sum_{S_i \in \overline{S}} C(S_i) + \sum_{P_j \in G} B(P_j) - \sum_{P_j \in G \backslash \overline{G}} B(P_j),
\end{aligned}
$$

is a minimum cut, A also represents the optimal solution to the minimal sensor integrity problem with $S_{\mathrm{opt}} = \overline{S}$ the set of sensors to be removed so that points in $G_{\mathrm{opt}} = G \backslash \overline{G}$ can be uncovered.

Using standard max-flow techniques [1], $\overline{S}$ and $\overline{G}$ can be computed in $O(\mathrm{Min}(M^2 E, N^2 E))$, where E is the edge set of the bipartite graph T. Note that this reduction allows us to compute the minimal integrity even while considering sensors of arbitrary ranges and unrestricted (non-polygonal) coverage areas. Hence this allows us to consider situations such as sensors in a 3-D grid monitoring RF transmissions from arbitrary points on specific wavelengths.

In the special of sensors with linear ranges, we can find a poynomial time solution of much lower complexity by exploiting the order among the sensors. We note that the intersection graph of sensors covering a linear grid forms an interval graph. There are many instances of problems that are more easily solved on interval graphs, for example [10] shows that weighted integrity is polynomial on interval graphs, while it is NP-Complete for comparability graphs.

Note that the optimal solution posseseses the following property.

Observation 1 *Any optimal solution in which point P_i is uncovered will have value*

$$
\tau_{\mathrm{opt}}^{P_i} = \tau_{\mathrm{opt}}^{-P_i} - B(P_i) + \sum_{s \in S^{P_i}} C(s),
$$

where $\tau_{\mathrm{opt}}^{-P_i}$ is the minimum value of the optimal solution computed from $S \backslash S^i$ and $G \backslash P_i$. The overall optimal solutions over S and G are related to the individual optimal solutions as follows:

$$
\tau_{\mathrm{opt}} = \mathrm{Min}_{P_i \in G} \{\tau_{\mathrm{opt}}^{P_i}\}.
$$

$$
\begin{aligned}
G_{\mathrm{opt}} &= \{P_j | \tau_{\mathrm{opt}}^{P_j} = \tau_{\mathrm{opt}}\}. \\
S_{\mathrm{opt}} &= \{\bigcup S^{P_j} | P_j \in G_{\mathrm{opt}}\}.
\end{aligned}
$$

Unlike in higher dimensional grids, a property of linear grids is that removing a point P_i from G and S^{P_i} from S disconnects both sets, leading to two smaller subproblems. The following result suggests a dynamic programming algorithm for computing minimal sensor integrity in a linear grid by exploiting the order among sensors to eliminate sensors and grid points not contributing to the optimal solution. Consider any set of sensors $S = \{S_1, S_2, \ldots S_k\}$, where $S_i = [P_{B_i}, P_{E_i}]$ and ordered such that $P_{E_1} \le P_{E_2} \ldots \le P_{E_k}$. Let $\tau^l(P_j)$ represent the minimal sensor integrity when considering only grid points in $[P_1 \ldots P_j]$ and sensors $S_1, S_2 \ldots S_l, 1 \le l \le k$. Define $\tau^0(P_j) = \sum_{P_1}^{P_j} B(t)$.

For any sensor S_i, we consider the projection of $P_{B_i}^-$ onto ranges of sensors preceding S_i in S. Let S_l denote the latest sensor in S such that either $P_{B_i}^- \in S_l$ or $P_{B_i}^- > P_{E_l}$, $1 \le l < i \le k$. If no such sensor exists, then assign $l = 0$. We have,

Theorem 1 *The minimal sensor integrity for sensor set $S = \{S_1, S_2, \ldots S_i\}$ is given by*

$$
\tau_{P_{E_i}}^i = \mathrm{min} \left(0, \right.
$$
$$
\tau^{i-1}(P_{E_{i-1}}) + C(S_i) - \sum_{P_{E_{i-1}}^+}^{P_{E_i}} B(j),
$$
$$
\left. \begin{cases} \tau^l(P_{B_i}^-) & \text{if } P_{B_i}^- \in S_l \\ \tau^l(P_{E_i}) - \sum_{P_{E_l}^+}^{P_{B_i}^-} B(j) & \text{if } P_{B_i}^- \notin S_l \\ -\tau^0(P_{B_i}^-) & \text{if } l = 0 \end{cases} \right) \quad (2)
$$

Proof: Let $S_{\mathrm{opt}} \subseteq S$ be the optimal subset of sensors to be removed for minimal integrity. Consider sensor S_i, the last element of S. If $S_i \in S_{\mathrm{opt}}$ then points $[P_{E_{i-1}}^+, P_{E_i}]$ are uncovered exclusively by removing S_i. This contributes $C(S_i) - \sum_{P_{E_{i-1}}^+}^{P_{E_i}} B(j)$ to the optimal value of sensor integrity. The remaining contribution to the optimal must be $\tau^{i-1}(P_{E_{i-1}})$. Conversely, if $S_i \notin S_{\mathrm{opt}}$ then points $[P_{B_i}, P_{E_i}]$ are not included in the optimal uncovering. If $P_{B_i}^-$ intersects the range of any preceding sensors, then the optimal solution is $\tau^l(P_{B_i}^-)$, where l is the latest such sensor. Otherwise, the optimal solution is $\tau^l(P_{E_l})$ plus the benefit of removing points from $P_{E_l}^+$ to $P_{B_i}^-$. If no such preceding sensor exists, then the optimal solution only contains the benefits of removing points from P_1 to $P_{B_i}^-$. □

From (2), note that in addition to the endpoints, the optimal solution must also be computed up to any point within the range of a sensor that just precedes the beginning point of any succeeding sensor. Let $P_j \in S_i$. Then,

$$
\tau_{P_j}^i = \min \Bigg(\quad 0,
$$

$$
\left\{
\begin{array}{ll}
\tau^r(P_j) + C(S_i) & \text{if } P_j \in S_r \\
\tau^r(P_{E_r}) + C(S_i) - \sum_{P_{E_r}^+}^{P_j} B(t) & \text{if } P_j \notin S_r \\
C(S_i) - \tau^0(P_j) & \text{if } r = 0
\end{array}
\right\},
$$

$$
\left.
\left\{
\begin{array}{ll}
\tau^l(P_{B_i}^-) & \text{if } P_{B_i}^- \in S_l \\
\tau^l(P_{E_l}) - \sum_{P_{E_l}^+}^{P_{B_i}^-} B(j) & \text{if } P_{B_i}^- \notin S_l \\
-\tau^0(P_j) & \text{if } l = 0
\end{array}
\right\} \right) \quad (3)
$$

where S_r and S_l are the latest sensors preceding S_i in S, which either contain or are to the left of P_j and $P_{B_i}^-$ respectively. The proof is similar to Theorem 1.

To reduce the computation overhead of $\tau_{P_j}^i$, note that the only points of interest at each S_i are the pre-beginning points of succeeding sensors that are within the range of S_i. All such points, along with the optimal solutions at these points can be computed at the time a sensor is first considered for inclusion in the optimal set. For each sensor S_i in the right endpoint ordered set S, define $X^i = \{P_{B_i}^- \bigcup P_{B_p}^- \bigcup P_{E_i}\}, \forall P_{B_p}^- \in S_i, i+1 \leq p \leq M$. These are the points in S_i, where the optimal sensor integrity must be computed. To compute $\tau^i\{X^i\}$, we need to determine the nearest preceding sensor S_r from S, for each point P_j in X^i. We may also need the sum of benefits from $P_{E_r}^+$ to P_j. To avoid repeated computations, we can precompute and store this term for all such points P_j. This can be done by scanning a sorted list of all points in the grid from left to right while keeping a single running sum of point benefits. This sum is initialized to zero at the beginning and whenever we reach a point that is also a sensor endpoint. The current running sum is stored at each pre-beginning point $(P_{B_p}^-)$ that is encountered until the next sensor endpoint is reached.

Algorithm MIN_SENSOR_INTEGRITY

Input:
1. Linear array $G = (P_1, P_2, \ldots P_N)$ of grid points.
2. set $S = \{S_1, S_2, \ldots, S_M\}$ of sensors covering G, where $S_k = [P_{B_k} \ldots P_{E_k}], P_{B_k} \in G, P_{E_k} \in G, 1 \leq k \leq M$.
3. Benefit function $B : G \to R^+$.
4. Cost function $C : S \to R^+$.

Output: Value = Min $(0, C(S_{\text{opt}}) - B(G_{\text{opt}}))$; Optimal set of uncovered points G_{opt}; Optimal set of removed sensors S_{opt}.

Preprocessing:
1. Sort G in increasing order.
2. Sort S in non-decreasing order of right end points.
3. Compute running sum of point benefits from each end-point to all pre-beginning points until the next endpoint.

Procedure:
1. $I_0 = \Phi$;
2. $G_{\text{opt}} = [P_1 \ldots P_{B_1}^-]$;
3. FOR k = 1 to M {
4. $\quad\quad I_k = I_{k-1} \bigcup S_k$; /* Add S_k to set of sensors considered */
5. $\quad\quad G_{\text{opt}} = G_{\text{opt}} \bigcup \{[P_{E_{k-1}}^+ \ldots P_{E_k}]\}$; /* Assume $S_k \in S_{\text{opt}}$ */
6. $\quad\quad$ Compute

$$ X^k = \{P_{B_k}^- \bigcup P_{B_p}^- \bigcup P_{E_k}\}, \forall P_{B_p}^- \in S_k, k+1 \leq p \leq M. $$

7. $\quad\quad \forall P_j \in X^k$, Compute $S_r : r = \text{Max}\{q | P_j \in S_q \text{ or } P_j > P_{E_q}\}, S_q \in I_{k-1}$.
8. $\quad\quad \forall P_j \in X^k$, compute $\tau_{P_j}^i$ as in Equation 3.
9. $\quad\quad$ If $\tau^k(P_{E_k})$ implies $S_k \notin S_{\text{opt}}$, then $G_{\text{opt}} = G_{\text{opt}} - \{[P_{B_k} \ldots P_{E_k}]\}$.
10. $\quad\quad$ } **End FOR**

Theorem 2 *The value of the minimal sensor integrity is $Min(0, \tau^M(P_{E_M}) - \sum_{P_{E_M}^+} B(j))$ and can be computed in $O(Min(M^2, MN))$ time with $O(M + N)$ storage. The optimal set of uncovered points is G_{opt} from which the set of sensors to be removed S_{opt} can be calculated.*

The preprocessing steps in lines 1 and 2 can be completed in $O((N + M) \log(N + M))$ time while the running sums of line 3 can be computed and stored at each point in $O(N)$ time. The For loop in line 3 is executed M times. There are $O(M)$ points in X^k in line 8 for each of which τ values are calculated in $O(1)$ time. Note that if $N < M$, the algorithm can be easily modified to run in $O(NM)$ time by computing the τ values at each point instead of at each sensor.

4 Conclusions

In this paper we have presented a model that takes into account the costs and benefits of sensor removal and point uncoverage. We have shown that the problem of computing the minimal sensor integrity, i.e., the best response to any sensor deployment is polynomial time solvable. This is in sharp contrast to the sensor deployment problem which is NP-Complete. Furthermore, the algorithm remains polynomial when sensors with arbitrary (non-polygonal) coverage areas are deployed over any dimensional grid.

References

[1] R. Ahuja, T. Magnanti and J. Orlin, "Network Flows: Theory, Algorithms and Applications," Prentice-Hall, New York, 1993.

[2] R. R. Brooks, C. Griffin and D. Friedlander, "Self-Organized Distributed Sensor Network Entity Tracking," *Intnl. J. of High-Performance Computing Applications*, to appear.

[3] K. Chakrabarty, S.S. Iyengar, H. Qi and E.C. Cho, "Optimal Sensor Deployment Algorithms for Surveillance and Target Location," *IEEE Tran. on Computers* to appear.

[4] M. Chu, H. Haussecker and F. Zhao, "Scalable Information-Driven Sensor Querying and Routing for Ad Hoc Heterogeneous Sensor Networks," Xerox-PARC Technical Report P2001-10113, July 2001.

[5] D. Estrin, R. Govindan, J. Heidemann, S. Kumar,"Next Century Challenges:Scalable Coordination in Sensor Networks," *Proc.ACM/IEEE International Conference on Mobile computing and Networks*, 1999.

[6] R. Fowler, M. Paterson, and S. Tanimoto, "Optimal Packing and Covering in the Plane," *Information Processing Letters*, vol 12, no. 3, June 1981.

[7] T. Gonzalez, "Covering a Set of Points in Multidimensional Space," *Information Processing Letters*, vol 40, November 1991.

[8] S. S. Iyengar, L. Prasad and H. Min, "Advances in Distributed Sensor Technology," Prentice Hall, Englewood Cliffs, NJ 1995.

[9] J. M. Kahn, R. H. Katz and K. S. Pister,"Mobile Networking for Smart Dust," *ACM/IEEE International Conference on Mobile Computing and Networks*, 1999.

[10] S. Ray, R. Kannan and H. Jiang, "Weighted Integrity Problem is Polynomial for Interval Graphs," under review in *Discrete Applied Mathematics*.

[11] R. Selten, "Reexamination of the Perfectness Concept for Equilibrium Points in Extensive Games." *International Journal of Game Theory*, Vol. 4, pp. 25–55, 1975.

Multithreaded Isosurface Rendering on SMPs Using Span–Space Buckets*

Peter D. Sulatycke and Kanad Ghose
Dept. of Computer Science
State University of New York, Binghamton, NY 13902–6000
email: {sulat, ghose}@cs.binghamton.edu

Abstract

We present in–core and out–of–core parallel techniques for implementing isosurface rendering based on the notion of span–space buckets. Our in–core technique makes conservative use of the RAM and is amenable to parallelization. The out–of–core variant keeps the amount of data read in the search process to a minimum, visiting only the cells that intersect the isosurface. The out–of–core technique additionally minimizes disk I/O time through in–order seeking, interleaving data records on the disk and by overlapping computational and I/O threads. The overall isosurface rendering time achieved using our out–of–core span space buckets is comparable to that of well–optimized in–core techniques that have enough RAM at their disposal to avoid thrashing. When the RAM size is limited, our out–of–core span–space buckets maintains its performance level while in–core algorithms either start to thrash or must sacrifice performance for a smaller memory footprint.

1. Introduction

Isosurface rendering is a well–used technique for visualizing volume data sets that are generated from medical imaging systems (such as CT, MRI, 3–d Ultrasound imaging) and synthesized by computer simulations (such as CFD, FE–modeling, Pharmacology). The volume data set consists of a collection of contiguous data points (voxels) in three (or more) dimensions. Each voxel has an associated spatial or temporal coordinates and a range of values of specific parameters that characterize the volume data. The set of adjacent voxels that form polyhedra within the volume data set are know as cells.

Isosurface rendering displays the surfaces corresponding to a value of a single parameter (or a range of continuous parameter values) of interest. There are three main isosurface rendering steps: (i) cell extraction, which locates the cells that are intersected by the isovalue corresponding to the surface being rendered; (ii) surface computation, which determines how the surface goes through each cell (the well–known marching cubes lookup table [9] is used to perform this step); (iii) rendering of the triangles that correspond to surface elements.

Algorithms to improve the search for intersecting cells can be grouped into three categories: seed algorithms, geometric space algorithms and range based algorithms. Seed algorithms use a data structure to find initial "seed" cells that intersect the isosurface [1, 6, 7]. Starting at these seeds, all remaining intersecting cells are found by visiting adjacent cells that are also intersected by the isosurface. These techniques tend to perform very well but in the worst case can have O(n) complexity.

Geometric space algorithms maintain the original geometric organization of the data while imposing a data structure on this organization. These data structures associate similar neighboring cells together to facilitate the quick location of intersecting cells. In Wilhelms et al [16], branch–on–need octrees were used for this purpose. Other spatial data structures such as Kd–trees can also be used in the same way. This type of algorithm works well for highly coherent data but performs poorly with noisy or highly variable data.

Lastly, range based algorithms have produced some of the best results by using data structures to reorganize the cells according to the range of values within each cell [4, 8, 11]. Data structures such as Kd–trees [8] and lattice subdivisions of span–space [11] have been used to simultaneously sort all cells by maximum and minimum value. In Cignoni et al. [4] binary interval trees were used to achieve a worst case computational complexity of $O(h/2 + K)$, where h is equal to the number of bits used to represent the data values and K is the number of cells intersecting the isosurface.

Algorithms to improve isosurface extraction can be very effective but they have a major limitation – the search optimized data structures that they use require significant amounts of RAM. The transformed data size can easily exceed the available RAM size, causing paging activity to grossly limit performance. As a result, these acceleration algorithms can actually perform worse than brute force techniques. With volume data sets continuing to grow, these in–core acceleration techniques are only practical on

*supported in part by the NSF through award No. EIA–9911099

very high–end computers. Consequently, researchers have turned to out–of–core isosurface rendering solutions.

Out–of–core techniques avoid excessive paging by explicitly storing data on a secondary storage device. However, they present a new challenge for isosurface rendering algorithms – quickly moving the relevant data from the disk to the RAM. Two main techniques have been used to address this problem:

(1) Explicit techniques such as file I/O or page remapping [5] are used to move the out–of–core data in some suitable units (e.g., slice–by–slice) into RAM. The I/O marching cubes variant supplied in the visualization toolkit (vtk) is an example of a slice–by–slice approach [10]. The cells within each such unit are then searched exhaustively within the RAM to locate the intersecting cells, which are then rendered after computing how the surface goes through each such cell. These techniques suffer from high disk I/O overhead and poor cell extraction capabilities, resulting in poor performance.

(2) In–core isosurface extraction algorithms are adapted to out–of–core use [2, 3, 12, 13, 14]. The search–optimized data structures enable the intersecting cells to be located quickly on the disk, which are then moved into the RAM using explicit disk I/O. Surface and rendering computations are then performed on the extracted cells within the RAM. These techniques can be very efficient if care is taken to optimize the disk I/O.

In this paper we present a new isosurface rendering technique, called span–space buckets, that is able to accelerate the visualization of large rectilinear volume data sets. In Section 2, we describe how span–space buckets enables fast cell location while minimizing the factor by which the data set grows. We also show how this algorithm is easily parallelized on SMPs with a variety of static and dynamic load balancing techniques. Section 3 expands on the span–space bucket technique and explains how it can be adapted to out–of–core use. This out–of–core technique not only quickly locates cell of interest but does it in a manner that minimizes head seeking. Additionally, we also show how interleaving on disk is used to reduce disk seeking further. Section 4 then describes how the out–of–core version of span–space buckets can be multithreaded on SMPs. We also show in this section how multiple threads can be used to effectively hide disk I/O. Lastly, Section 5 gives some representative results of the span–space bucket algorithm. With very large data sets our out–of–core span–space buckets maintains its performance level while in–core algorithms either start to thrash or must sacrifice performance for a smaller memory footprint. Additionally, our techniques also scales reasonably well with the number of threads.

2. In–core span–space buckets

The notion of span–space aids greatly in the visualization and design of isosurface extraction algorithms [8]. The span–space, as shown in Figure 1 (a), represents intervals as points in a two dimensional space where the minimum values of intervals correspond to values on the X axis and the maximum value within an interval correspond to values along the Y axis. An interval (a_i, b_i) is represented as a point $(X = a_i, Y = b_i)$. Note that all of the intervals (each representing a cell) correspond to points above or on the diagonal line, $X = Y$. The intervals that intersect the isosurface for an isovalue of Q are points located in the shaded region shown in Figure 1 (a), bounded by the line $X = Q$ and $Y = Q$, as their maximum values (Y–axis) are higher than Q and their minimum values (X–axis) are lower than Q.

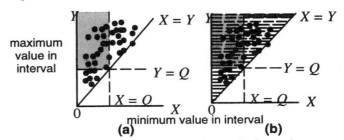

Figure 1. (a) Span–space formulation of the isosurface extraction problem and (b) span–space bucket data structure.

Our span–space formulation is based on the fact that input data values can have a very small fixed data range. For example, most CT data is limited to 12 bits of data which can only represent 4096 different data values. Given this limited range, the span–space can be broken into one bucket for each possible discrete data value; as depicted by the horizontal lines in Figure 1b. Each cell is placed in the bucket that matches the floor of the cell's maximum value. Within each bucket, we sort the cells in ascending order of their minimum value. The bucket–based sorting algorithm used to accomplish this sort is the inspiration for the name, *span–space buckets*. The use of a bucket for every value allows the data to be sorted by maximum and minimum values without having to store the data twice. The buckets sort the data by maximum value while the cells within the buckets are sorted by minimum value.

2.1. Sequential In–core Span–Space Buckets

Our in–core implementation is very straightforward. Instead of storing cell data directly inside the buckets, we store indices to point to the actual cell data represented within the buckets. The cell data itself is spatially organized (i.e., ordered by their coordinate values and in the "raw" 3–d format). All buckets are stored consecutively in RAM. As intersecting cells are located, they are passed to a marching cubes like process to compute the surface passing through them as a set of triangles. No maximum or minimum values are stored within the bucket structures, saving considerable space. Gradients can be precomputed or computed on the fly depending on the amount of RAM.

Span–space buckets can be used for extracting isosurfaces from discrete or non–discrete data sets with equal ease. For discrete data the isosurface extraction process begins with the bucket for the highest possible maximum value. Cells within this bucket, starting with the smallest minimum value cell, are sent to a surface modeling process based on the marching cubes lookup table until a cell with a minimum value of $\lfloor Q \rfloor$ or larger is encountered. This process then continues to the next bucket and so on, ending with and including the bucket corresponding to the value of $\lceil Q \rceil$. Span–space buckets thus process all cells that an isosurface intersects and in the worst case only visits one bad cell in each bucket visited. This gives the near optimal average complexity of $O(K + 2^{h-1})$ for isosurface extraction. Unlike other range based algorithms, span–space buckets does not duplicate the data for a cell (or pointers to data) and thus has half the memory footprint.

For real data the extraction process is identical except processing ends at the bucket corresponding to $\lfloor Q \rfloor$. If Q is also real, a few of the cells encountered while processing bucket $\lfloor Q \rfloor$ will be non–intersecting, having both their maximum and minimum values less than Q. As long as a large number of buckets are used, these extra non–intersecting cells will not affect performance.

The main limitation of this algorithm is that the number of buckets that can be created is limited. To cope with data larger than 20 bit, several consecutive data values could be mapped to the same bucket to allow the scheme to be used with little modification, although this has not been confirmed as of yet. This mapping will only cause the last bucket processed to have non–intersecting cells within it. As long as the number of buckets are sufficiently large, this wasted effort is minimal. For example, using 4096 buckets on a 512 X 512 X 512 data set that uses 32 bit data, with each bucket having the same amount of data, will cause 16,287 cells (on average) to be unnecessarily visited as potential intersecting cells. This corresponds to .012% of the complete data set – a negligible amount.

2.2. Parallel In–core Span–Space Buckets

In–core span–space buckets can be parallelized with a variety of data partitions in the geometric space of the volume data set. However, to produce a well balanced parallel algorithm the volume data set must be broken into partitions that have a data distribution similar to the complete volume data set. Thus partitions in three dimensions, such as cubes, should not be used because they usually exhibit a high degree of coherence and would cause the number of intersecting cells within the regions to vary

widely. A partition based on one or more slices of the volume data is much more representative of the data set's distribution.

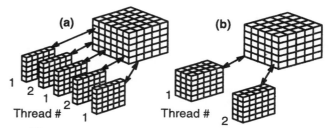

Figure 2. Static data partitions in the geometric space of the volume data set. (a) Round–robin distribution of slice partitions. (b) Slab distribution based on histograms.

Slice partitions may be distributed among a SMP's processors statically or dynamically. Before the slices are distributed a span–space bucket structure is created for each slice partition of the volume data. Static load balancing is simply performed by distributing the structures associated with each partition in a round–robin fashion to the threads. Figure 2(a) depicts this round–robin distribution for the case where one slice is used for each partition. To dynamically assign the slice partitions we use a simple mutex protected counter. Once each of the slice partitions are statically or dynamically assigned to the threads, each thread can perform the search for intersecting cells on their slice partitions independently of the other processors. This duplication of the query process does not significantly hurt performance because the search process is trivial with span–space buckets.

Slice partitions of the volume data set may also be statically assigned to threads using histograms for each slice. During the span–space bucket creation process statistics are gathered on the exact frequency of each maximum–minimum interval associated with each cell. These frequencies are then used to produce a histogram showing how many cells are intersected by each isovalue. This process is then repeated on each span–space bucket structure created. The individual slice histograms can then be used to statically assign consecutive set of slices to each processor, as depicted in Figure 2(b). Consecutive slices are used to take better advantage of the processor cache. This parallel implementation essentially breaks the volume data set into one large slab of slices per thread. The histograms will ensure that each slab will have approximately the same number of intersecting cells within it.

In addition to using geometric space for the partitioning of span–space buckets, partitions within span–space may also be used. Recall that Figure 1(b) shows span–space partitioned into buckets to form the data structure used by the span–space bucket algorithm. Thus, this partition is also ideal for load balancing purposes. All of the cells within each complete bucket can be statically or dynamically assigned to a thread. As with the static distribution of slices, buckets are distributed to the threads using a round–robin technique. Lastly, the buckets can be dynamically distributed by using the mutex counter technique previously described for slice partitions. We show later how each of these five different load balancing techniques compare on a large rectilinear data set.

3. Out–of–core span–space buckets

Even with span–space buckets' reduced memory requirements, the algorithm will eventually degrade as the size of the data and the data structure exceed the available RAM capacity, causing thrashing to occur. Out–of–core techniques that avoid performance degradation due to thrashing must be used and, in addition, the I/O time has to be kept small to get acceptable levels of performance. Span–space buckets is a good structure for minimizing I/O since it minimizes the number of cells checked for isosurface intersection. In addition, optimizing seek time on the disk is equally important for keeping the overall I/O time to a minimum. To keep seek time down, out–of–core implementations of span–space buckets can not use pointer indirections to locate cell data as in the in–core case. Thus all data associated with a cell (including gradients) must be explicitly stored in–line within the span–space bucket structure. This not only minimizes the amount of seeking and data read out but also keeps all disk accesses in consecutive order. On the downside, this causes the volume data to be duplicated within several cells. Since this structure is out–of–core, this duplication is easily tolerated. Note, that this duplication is inevitable in any out–of–core technique that stores data in line to avoid disk seeking.

For out–of–core implementations of the span–space buckets, a *naive implementation* will be to directly use the in–core implementation, as shown in Figure 1 (b), with data for each bucket laid out on the disk from the top to the bottom. In other words, the data for the bucket of cells with a maximum value of *max_value* is stored on the disk, followed by the data for the bucket of cells that have a maximum value of (*max_value* −1) and so on, ending with the data for the bucket of cells that have a maximum value equal to *min_value*. Within each bucket, the data is stored in increasing order of the minimum value of the cells. The top diagram in Figure 3 (a) shows the layout of the first four buckets when written to disk. Each bucket contains cells with the same maximum value and ascending minimum values, while each block within each bucket represents cells with the same minimum value. Cell extraction proceeds in the same manner as used in the in–core implementation, i.e.. reading buckets one at a time and in–order. Even though buckets are read in–order, significant seeking can occur since a trailing region of each bucket must be skipped. In span–space, the trailing section for the first bucket is

shown in dark grey in Figure 1 (b). While the bottom diagram in Figure 3 (a) depicts the disk skipping that must occur due to these trailing sections. We have observed that the seeking needed to skip over this data negatively affects I/O performance even with 8 bit data (255 buckets).

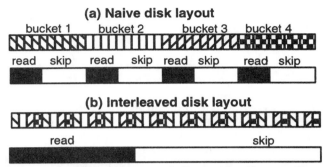

Figure 3 Disk layouts – followed by the reading and head skipping that takes place when reading the first 4 blocks in each bucket.

3.1. Reducing I/O Time With Interleaving

One way of reducing the seeking necessary to retrieve all isosurface intersecting cells is to interleave the buckets when they are written to disk. What results is called *interleaved span–space buckets*. The top part of Figure 3 (b) shows the disk layout of four buckets when their data is interleaved with each other. As in the previous diagram, each block within each bucket represents data with the same minimum value. Thus reading cells from the smallest minimum value to larger minimum values can be done in one sequential read. The lower part of Figure 3 (b) depicts the sequential order of reading of cells contained in the first four blocks of all four buckets. This greatly reduces the seeking required for this particular query but it can worsen the seeking of other queries. For example, if only cells from the first three buckets need to be read in Figure 3 (b), every fourth block of cells (checkered) will have to be skipped or unnecessarily read in.

A solution to this is to break span–space into regions and interleave the buckets within each individual region. Each region is written to disk one after each other, i.e. Region 1 followed by Region 2 and so on. Within each region the horizontal maximum bucket data is interleaved when written to disk. Figure 4 (a) visually shows this interleaving with arrows indicating the ordering of the data as it is written to disk. Each arrow represents cells at the same minimum value within a region and thus each arrow is actually a bucket at a particular minimum value. These buckets are written to disk in a left to right ordering (smallest minimum value to largest). One can think of the regions as being maximum buckets containing vertical minimum buckets. This is somewhere between using only horizontal maximum buckets or only vertical minimum buckets. As will be seen in the results section, significant reduction in total seek time occurs when span–space buckets are interleaved in this fashion.

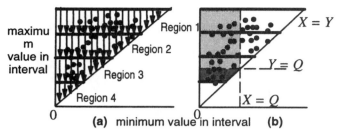

Figure 4.   (a) Regions are written to disk in numerical order, with minimum buckets being written in left to right order and with cells within the bucket being written in the direction of the arrow. (b) Multiple regions reduce the area (darkly shaded) that must be skipped.

The reason for this reduction can be seen if we step though the isosurface processing of Q in Figure 4 (b). The lightly shaded area in Region 1 can be read without any seeking and the unshaded area in Region 1 can be skipped with one seek operation. The total amount of data skipped over hasn't changed but the number of seeks has been reduced, saving a significant amount of time. Processing for Region 2 has the same behavior as Region 1. Processing of subsequent regions continues in this fashion until a region is intersected by the Y = Q line. For the example shown, Region 3 is intersected and must be processed differently. In this region, either the darkly shaded section can be skipped over on disk or it can be read into RAM when each of the vertical minimum buckets are processed. If this data is read into RAM then the unwanted cells can easily be skipped in memory. The extra time required to read in the extra data is insignificant as long as the regions are fairly small, thus this is the preferred approach. On the downside, using small regions means more regions are needed and the time saved can be overshadowed by the extra seeking required for more regions.

The number of regions to use for a particular data set is dependent on the size of the complete out–of–core span–space bucket structure and the number of bits used to represent the data. Through trial and error we determined that a wide range of values are possible. For example, 200–400 regions on a 6.8 Gigabyte span–space bucket structure (12 bit data) all produce equally good results. More data sets need to be tested before clear guidelines can be developed.

3.2. Querying Out–of–Core Span–Space Buckets

As in the in–core case, out–of–core span–space buckets can be used for discrete and real data values. For the sake of brevity, the following description will be limited to the implementation of span–space buckets on the disk when the cell data values are discrete. With slight modifications,

similar to the ones described in the in–core query processing section, non–discrete data values can also be handled. To read in all intersecting cells for any given isovalue, the following pieces of information are needed: the position of the horizontal lines that demarcate the different regions, the length of each vertical minimum bucket in each region and the length of each region. This information naturally comes out of the creation process of the interleaved span–space buckets and is stored on disk until processing begins. It is then brought into memory and stays there until the user is finished with all isosurface extraction. The lengths of the regions do not always have to be stored on disk since they can be calculated from the lengths of the minimum buckets. We will use the notation D_x to designate the horizontal demarcation line of region x, which is denoted as R_x (note the value D_x is the smallest maximum value in R_x). We will also denote $N_{x,y}$ as the length of vertical minimum bucket y in region x. The major processing steps for the out–of–core version are detailed below:

1. Seek to the beginning of the data on disk   (i.e. the beginning of R_1)

2. If the region R_x is completely above or on the horizontal line (Y = Q) for the given isovalue Q, (i.e., the value of D_x is $>= \lceil Q \rceil$), read all cells within R_x that have a minimum value less than Q (i.e. cells left of the X = Q vertical line) as follows:

- compute the sum of the vertical minimum bucket lengths for all minimum buckets less than Q :
$$S_x = \sum_{y=0}^{y=\lfloor Q \rfloor - 1} N_{x,y}$$

- read off the data for S_x cells from the disk into the RAM (these are in consecutive locations, so no disk locations are skipped)

- seek to the beginning of the next region (R_{x+1}) by using the length of R_x and then go to the beginning of step 2.

3. The processing of cells extracted from the disk into the RAM are done in the same order as they were read in. Since all the cells read into RAM from regions above or just on the horizontal line (Y = Q) must be intersected by the isosurface, compute the isosurface going through these cells with a marching cubes like lookup table. For the one region that is intersected by the (Y = Q) line, some of the cells read into RAM are not intersected and must be processed as follows:

- A counter, denoted as w, is used to keep track of the number of cells within each minimum bucket that intersect the isosurface. All isosurface intersecting cells within a bucket are processed in sequential order. Thus when it is determined that a cell does not intersect the isosurface, we can conclude that all of the remaining

576

cells within the same minimum bucket are also non–intersecting. On finding the first non–intersecting cell, $(N_{xy} - w)$ cells are skipped in RAM to get to the start of the next minimum bucket. Processing of the remaining minimum buckets from this one region are done in the same manner.

4. Multithreaded querying of out–of–core span–space buckets

The previous section assumed that one thread performs all I/O operations and isosurface computations. However, there is no reason disk accesses have to block the execution of an out–of–core isosurface extraction algorithm. One thread can be used to perform all I/O operations, while another thread can be used to perform surface modeling computations. This allows I/O times to be effectively reduced by doing useful processing while disk accesses are occurring. Additionally, since I/O times are usually significantly less than computation times, multiple computation threads can be used on a symmetric multiprocessor to achieve a balance of activity with a single I/O thread, improving total performance in the process. The I/O thread and computation threads interact through a set of mutex protected swinging buffers, with the I/O thread acting as a producer and the computation threads acting as consumers. Figure 5 depicts an I/O thread "producing" cell data into a set of mutex protected swinging buffers, with multiple computation threads "consuming" the buffer information. The use of swinging buffers is similar to the multi–threaded implementation of our out–of–core interval trees [12, 13]. We now describe the specific technique used with span–space buckets.

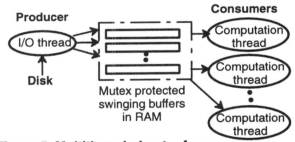

Figure 5. Multithreaded out–of–core isosurface extraction

The I/O thread is only responsible for prefetching all of the intersecting cells in RAM while the computation threads are responsible for isosurface modeling. The multithreaded out–of–core query process is adapted from the sequential query process described in the previous section. The I/O thread processes all regions above the Y=Q line by performing Steps 1 and 2 in the sequential query description in Section 3. However, if S_x is larger than the size of a swinging buffer, which is usually the case, multiple reads equaling the length of the swinging buffer

are performed by the I/O thread. The computation threads then process these cells as soon as a new swinging buffer is full. If no buffer is currently available, the computation threads wait for the file I/O thread to fill in a buffer or for the termination of processing, whichever occurs earlier. The computation threads operate directly on the data within the buffers, no copying or moving of data is performed. This improves performance by avoiding cache misses, page remapping and unnecessary loads and stores. The computation threads render a cell by using the marching cube algorithm [9] to calculate the triangles and corresponding normals that make up the surface within the cell. The triangles are then copied directly into the buffer of a graphics engine where shading and displaying is performed.

The processing of the region intersected by the Y=Q line is directly adapted from Step 3 in the sequential query description in Section 3. As with all the other regions, the I/O thread reads in S_x cells from the intersected region. In this case, some of the cells read into the swinging buffers may be non–interesting. To quickly skip over these non–interesting cells the computation threads uses the w counter and the N_{xy} length as described in Section 3. Specifically, once a computation thread detects a non–intersecting cell it skips $(N_{xy} - w)$ cells to get to the next interesting cell. This process continues until all cells are processed in a buffer. By performing the skips over non–intersecting cells in RAM, disk seeking is kept to a minimum and I/O processing time is improved. The number of non–intersecting read into RAM is kept trivial as long as enough regions are used.

5. Experimental results and discussions

We tested all the parallel implementations on a four processor SUN ES 3500 server, 450 Mhz ULTRASPARC IIi CPUs, with 4 GBytes of RAM and employing a 512 GBytes RAID system (12–way). All multithreading was performed with Solaris threads running on the Solaris 8 operating system. All parallel implementations were tested on the torso of the visible woman CT data set [15], (256 MBytes, 512 X 512 X 512), with gradients precomputed. All in–core algorithms have their gradients precomputed so that there is a fair comparison with their out–of–core counterparts. The data set consists of 12 bit data, representing 4092 different integer isovalues. All results are the harmonic average of 5 runs, with each isovalue being tested consecutively. To avoid spurious results we tested every eighth integer isovalue of the visible woman. The total time plotted in the graphs refers to the time needed to produce the triangles for the surface to be rendered into a RAM buffer. This time does not include the time needed to actually display the triangles, which is mostly a function of the capabilities of the graphics card.

We tested all five in–core parallel span–space buckets algorithms on the visible woman torso using four threads. To highlight the differences between the techniques we plotted some representative isovalues of the data set in Figure 6. The largest sized partitions performed the best for both the static and dynamic algorithms because they have less overhead while still being well balanced. The histogram performed that best out of the static load balancing techniques, performing 15–20% better than buckets partitions and 2–5% better than slice partitions. The best static technique (histograms) performs 1–6% faster than the best dynamic load balancing technique (slices). Even though histograms was the best performing technique its performance is highly variable with the number of threads used. For example, as the number of threads increases the data partition that each thread receives will become more coherent. As the coherency improves, the number of interesting cells per thread will become highly variable, hurting performance. Thus, the preferred technique is dynamic load balancing using slices because it performs well regardless of coherency in the data.

Figure 7 shows how the total execution time of span–space buckets, using dynamic load balancing and slice partitions, varies from one to four threads. This figure shows that two, three and four threads typically perform 1.5, 2.1 and 2.75 times faster than sequential span–space buckets, respectively. For very high isovalues these speedups drop off because the number of intersecting cells quickly drops, making load balancing extremely difficult. In addition, the multithreading overhead starts to become a much larger percentage of the total processing time.

We also compared sequential and parallel span–space buckets to marching cubes [9] with precalculated gradients. The marching cubes algorithm was taken from the Visualization Toolkit (VTK) [10] with optimizations added so that it would not readily thrash. Figure 8 shows the speedup advantage of these implementations over the optimized marching cubes. The speedup of span–space buckets with four threads is very impressive, performing close to any order of magnitude faster than marching cubes for most isovalues. The speedup is only three to five times marching cubes when isovalues with many intersecting (i.e. isovalues 900–1100) are queried. This is due to the number of intersecting cells becoming such a large percentage of the total number of cells that the exhaustive searching of marching cubes performs well.

Figure 9 shows the component times of out–of–core parallel span–space buckets with four computation threads and one I/O thread. Out–of–core span–space buckets requires a lot of disk seeking to visit all of the necessary buckets, increasing I/O time as a result. Consequently, the I/O thread can not always keep up with all of the computation threads. This is evident in Figure 9 where the

I/O time is nearly equal to the computation times. As a result, the I/O thread and the computation threads do not perfectly overlap and the total time is increased. To reduce the effect of these seeks we tested various levels of interleaving with span–space buckets. Interleaving with 250 regions reduced the already low I/O time by approximately 33%. This reduction is less than what was seen on PC platforms (95%) because the RAID system already implements its own type of interleaving. Figure 10 shows the component times of out–of–core interleaved span–space buckets with four computation threads. Even with four threads the I/O time is much less than the time of the computation threads. Thus, nearly all of the I/O time is overlapped with computations and the total time is nearly equal to the computation time.

When less than four computation threads are used the thread computation time is even closer to the total time. The total execution times for one to four computation threads can be seen in Figure 11. Compared to the in–core parallel case, see Figure 7, the speedup of out–of–core span–space buckets is less regular and drops off sooner with high isovalues. The typical out–of–core speedup for two, three and four computation threads is 1.55, 2.0 and 2.25 respectively. The speedup of two and three computation threads is nearly identical to the in–core case. As the number of threads increase, the I/O thread can not always prevent the computation threads from becoming idle. In addition, more synchronization overhead takes place and as a consequence improvement in speedup slows down. For example, out–of–core span–space buckets with four computations threads only performs 2.25 times faster than the sequential algorithm, instead of 2.75 times as in the in–core parallel case. A lower I/O time would enable the computation threads to stay active longer, improving total performance further.

We also compared out–of–core parallel span–space buckets to marching cubes with precalculated gradients. The resulting figure is not shown because it is nearly identical to the parallel in–core case, as seen in Figure 8. On close examination, out–of–core span–space buckets performs 12–17%, 17–24% and 8–12% faster than in–core span–space buckets for one, two and three computation threads, respectively. This performance advantage is due to out–of–core span–space buckets causing less paging and processor cache misses; all data accesses by the computation threads are in–order and require small amounts of RAM. When the number of threads increase to four, this trend reverses with out–of–core span–space buckets performing 2–8% less than the in–core span–space buckets. This is caused by the I/O thread not being able to keep all of the computation threads busy. Even with this difference, out–of–core span–space buckets performs close to an order of magnitude or faster than marching cubes for the majority of isovalues. As in the in–core cases, the speedup is only three to five times marching cubes when isovalues with many intersecting (i.e. isovalues 900–1100) are queried. If the memory requirements of the system were to decrease, the performance of out–of–core span–space buckets would not be affected but the performance of the in–core algorithm would steadily degrade. Likewise, out–of–core span–space buckets would maintain the same relative performance with larger data sets but the in–core algorithm would degrade due to paging.

Examples of images rendered using the out–of–core span–space buckets are depicted in Figure 12. The skin image was taken at isovalue 600 and took 31 seconds to produce the triangles. The bone image was taken at isovalue 1300 and took 18.7 seconds. For these images, the bottleneck was not the triangle generation but the rendering of the triangles. With rapid ongoing advances in graphics card design and improvements in triangle decimation, the display process may become less of a bottleneck. Even with inefficient graphics cards, out–of–core parallel span–space buckets is still useful because it can be used to quickly view in succession many different subsets of a large data set. Thus allowing fast navigation through large data sets and making possible the interactive exploration of the data.

6. Conclusions

We presented a multithreaded implementation of an in–core and out–of–core isosurface rendering system based on span–space buckets. The span–space bucket technique can quickly find all the cells that are needed to construct an isosurface, without visiting many unnecessary cells. This ability not only makes span–space buckets very efficient but also amenable to parallelization. As a result, numerous data partitioning and load balancing techniques can be used to produce excellent speedups. It was determined that dynamically distributed slice partitions is the best choice for in–core parallelization, with a 2.75 speedup over sequential in–core span–space buckets (4 threads). We also showed how span–space buckets can be adapted to out–of–core use and parallelized with mutex protected swinging buffers. With the use of interleaving, I/O times can be further improved by reducing the amount of seeking on the disk. As a consequence, total execution times are improved, producing a 2.25 speedup (4 threads) over sequential out–of–core span–space buckets. This translates to a performance improvement up to an order of magnitude faster than an optimized marching cubes algorithm. Additionally, the out–of–core capability of this algorithm enables data sets to be efficiently visualized without taking up much RAM. This makes parallel out–of–core span–space buckets an excellent technique for isosurface rendering a wide range of volume data set sizes.

7. References

[1] C. Bajaj, V. Pascucci, D. Schikore, "Fast Isocontouring for Improved Interactivity" Proceedings: ACM Siggraph/IEEE Symposium on Volume Visualization, ACM Press, (1996), San Francisco, CA

[2] Y. Chiang, C. Silva, "I/O Optimal Isosurface Extraction", Proceeding of Visualization '97, pp 293–300, Oct 1997

[3] Y. Chiang, C. Silva, W. Schroeder, "Interactive Out–Of–Core Isosurface Extraction", Proc. of Visualization 98, pp 168–174.

[4] P. Cignoni, P. Marino, C. Montani, E. Puppo, R. Scopigno, "Speeding Up Isosurface Extraction Using Interval Trees", Visualization and Computer Graphics, vol. 3, no. 2, pp. 158–170, April 1997

[5] M. Cox, D. Ellsworth, "Application–Controlled Demand Paging for Out–of–Core Visualization", Proceeding of Visualization '97, pp 235–244, Phoenix AZ, Oct 1997

[6] Itoh T., et al., "Volume Thinning for Automatic Isosurface Propagation", Proc. IEEE Visualization '96 , pp. 303–310, 1996.

[7] M. van Kreveld, R. van Oostrum, C. Bajaj, D. Schikore, and V. Pascucci, "Contour Trees and Small Seed Sets for Isosurface Traversal", In Proceedings Thirteen ACM Symposium on Computational Geometry (Theory Track), (Nice, France, June 4–6, (1997), ACM Press, pp. 212–219

[8] Y. Livant, H. Shen, and C. Johnson, "A Near Optimal Isosurface Extraction Algorithm for Structured and Unstructured Grids," IEEE Trans. Visualization and Computer Graphics, vol.2, no. 1, pp. 73–84, Apr. 1996

[9] W.E. Lorensen and H.E. Cline, "Marching Cubes: A High Resolution 3–D Surface Construction Algorithm, Computer Graphics," vol. 21, no. 4, pp.163–169, July 1987

[10] Schroder, W., Martin, K. and Lorensen, B., *The Visualization Toolkit: An Object–Oriented Approach to 3–D Graphics*, 2nd Edition, Prentice–Hall, 1997.

[11] H.Shen, C.D.Hansen, Y. Livnat, and C.R. Johnson, "Isosurfacing in Span Space with Utmost Efficiency (ISSUE)," Visualization '96 Conf. proc., pp. 287–294, Oct. 1996.

[12] P. Sulatycke and K. Ghose, "Out–of–Core Interval Trees for Fast Isosurface Extraction," in Proc. Late Breaking Topics, IEEE VIsualization '98 Conference, pp. 25–28. (Available at: http://opal.cs.binghamton.edu/~sulat.)

[13] P. Sulatycke and K. Ghose, "A Fast Multi–threaded Out–of–Core Visualization Technique," in Proc. IEEE 13–th Intl. Symposium on Parallel and Distributed Systems and the 10–th Symposium on Parallel and Distributed Processing, pp. 569–575.

[14] P. Sutton and C. Hanse, "Isosurface Extraction in Time–varying Fields Using a Temporal Branch–on–Need Tree (T–BON)", in Proc. IEEE Visualization '99, pp. 147–153.

[15] The Visible Human Project, http://www.nlm.nih.gov/research/visible/visible_human.html

[16] J. Wilhelms and A. van Gelder, "Octrees for Faster Isosurface Generation", ACM Transactions on Graphics 11(3):201–227 July 1992

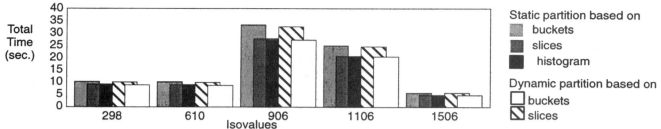

Figure 6. Comparison of parallel in–core span–space bucket techniques using four threads.

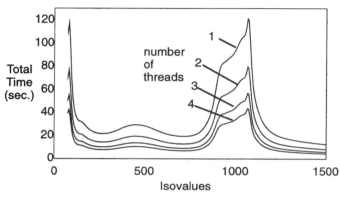

Figure 7. In–core parallel span–space buckets – dynamic load balancing with slice partitions.

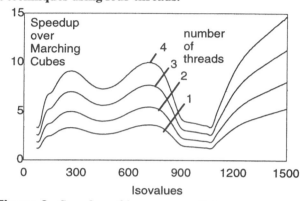

Figure 8. Speedup of in–core parallel span–space buckets over sequential marching cubes. (Dynamic load balancing and slice partitions)

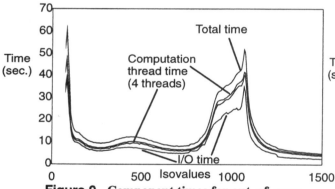

Figure 9. Component times for out–of–core parallel span–space buckets.

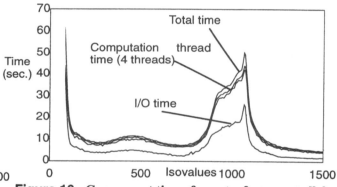

Figure 10. Component times for out–of–core parallel interleaved (250 regions) span–space buckets.

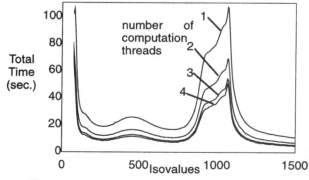

Figure 11. Total execution time of out–of–core parallel interleaved (250) span–space buckets.

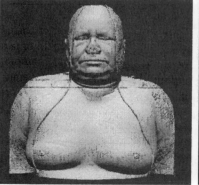

Figure 12. Images rendered of the visible woman.

580

Session 8B

Parallel Job Scheduling

Self-adapting Backfilling Scheduling for Parallel Systems*

Barry G. Lawson
Department of Mathematics and Computer Science
University of Richmond
Richmond, VA 23173, USA
blawson@richmond.edu

Evgenia Smirni, Daniela Puiu
Department of Computer Science
College of William and Mary
Williamsburg, VA 23187-8795, USA
{esmirni,dxpuiu}@cs.wm.edu

Abstract

We focus on non-FCFS job scheduling policies for parallel systems that allow jobs to backfill, i.e., to move ahead in the queue, given that they do not delay certain previously submitted jobs. Consistent with commercial schedulers that maintain multiple queues where jobs are assigned according to the user-estimated duration, we propose a self-adapting backfilling policy that maintains multiple job queues to separate short from long jobs. The proposed policy adjusts its configuration parameters by continuously monitoring the system and quickly reacting to sudden fluctuations in the workload arrival pattern and/or severe changes in resource demands. Detailed performance comparisons via simulation using actual Supercomputing traces from the Parallel Workload Archive indicate that the proposed policy consistently outperforms traditional backfilling.

Keywords: *batch schedulers, parallel systems, backfilling schedulers, performance analysis.*

1. Introduction

In recent years, scheduling parallel programs in multiprocessor architectures has consistently puzzled researchers and practitioners. Parallel systems consist of resources that have to be shared among a community of users. Resource allocation in such systems is a non-trivial problem. Examples of issues that exacerbate the resource allocation problem include the number of users that attempt to use the system simultaneously, the parallelism of the applications and their respective computational and storage needs, the wide variability of the average job execution time coupled with the variability of requested resources (e.g., processors, memory), the continuously changing job arrival rate,

meeting the execution deadlines of applications, and co-scheduling distributed applications across multiple independent systems each of which may itself be parallel with its own scheduler.

Many scheduling policies have been developed with the goal of providing better ways to handle the incoming workload by treating interactive jobs differently than batch jobs [1]. Among the various batch schedulers that have been proposed, we distinguish a set of schedulers that allows the system administrator to customize the scheduling policy according to the site's needs. The Maui Scheduler is widely used by the high performance computing community [7] and provides a wide range of configuration parameters that allows for site customization. Similarly, the PBS scheduler [9] operates on networked, multi-platform UNIX environments, including heterogeneous clusters of workstations, Supercomputers, and massively parallel systems, and allows for the implementation of a wide variety of scheduling solutions. Generally, these schedulers maintain several queues (to which different job classes are assigned), permit assigning priorities to jobs, and allow for a wide variety of scheduling policies per queue. The immediate benefit of such flexibility in policy parameterization is the ability to change the policy to better meet the incoming workload demands. Policy customization to meet the needs of an ever changing workload is a difficult task.

We concentrate on a class of space-sharing run-to-completion policies (i.e., no job preemption is allowed after a job is allocated its required processor resources) that are often found in the heart of many popular parallel workload schedulers. This class of policies, commonly cited as *backfilling* policies, opt not to execute incoming jobs in their order of arrival but rather rearrange their execution order to reduce system fragmentation and ensure better system utilization [8, 13]. Users are expected to provide nearly accurate estimates of the job execution times. Using these estimates, the scheduler rearranges the queue, allowing short jobs to move to the top of the queue provided they do not starve certain previously submitted jobs. Backfilling is ex-

*This work was partially supported by the National Science Foundation under grants EIA-9977030, EIA-9974992, CCR-0098278, and ACI-0090221.

Workload	Mean Exec. Time	Median Exec. Time	C.V. Exec. Time	Mean Number Processors	Median Number Processors	C.V. Number Processors
CTC	10,983.42	946	1.65	10.72	2	2.26
KTH	8,877.07	847	2.34	7.66	3	1.67
PAR	7,000.02	155	1.90	15.16	8	1.47
SP2	6,118.96	514	2.37	10.53	4	1.59

Table 1. Summary statistics of the four selected workloads. All times are reported in seconds.

tensively used by many schedulers, most notably the IBM LoadLeveler scheduler [4] and the Maui Scheduler [7]. Various versions of backfilling have been proposed [5, 8, 10]. [5] characterizes the effect of job length and parallelism on backfilling performance and [10] proposes sorting by job length to improve backfilling.

In this paper, we propose a batch scheduler that is based on the *aggressive* backfilling strategy extensively analyzed in [8]. In contrast to all of the above backfilling-related works, we maintain multiple queues and *separate* effectively short from long jobs. The policy is inspired by related work in task assignment for distributed servers that strongly encourages separation of jobs according to their length, especially for workloads with execution times characterized by long-tailed distributions [11, 12]. Similarly, observed high variance in job execution times in parallel workload traces advocates separating short from long jobs in parallel schedulers.

Our multiple-queue policy assigns incoming jobs to different queues using user estimates of the job execution times. Essentially, we split the system into multiple non-overlapping subsystems, one subsystem per queue. In this fashion, we manage to reduce the average job slowdown by reducing the likelihood that a short job is queued behind a long job. Furthermore, our policy modifies the subsystem boundaries on the fly according to the incoming workload intensities and execution demands. By continuously monitoring the scheduler's ability to handle the incoming workload, the policy adjusts its parameters to guarantee high system utilization and throughput while improving the average job slowdown.

We conduct a set of simulation experiments using trace data from the Parallel Workload Archive [3]. The traces offer a rich set of workloads taken from actual Supercomputing centers. Detailed workload characterization, focusing on how the job arrivals and resource demands *change across time*, guides us into the development of a robust policy that performs well under transient workload conditions.

This paper is organized as follows. Section 2 contains a characterization of the workloads used to drive our simulations. Section 3 presents the proposed policy. Detailed performance analysis of the proposed policy is given in Section 4. Concluding remarks are given in Section 5.

2. Variability in Workloads

The difficulty of scheduling parallel resources is deeply interwoven with the inherent variability in parallel workloads. Because our goal is to propose a robust policy that works efficiently regardless of the workload type, we first closely examine real parallel workloads of production systems. We select four workload logs from the parallel workload archive [3]. Each log provides the arrival time of each job (i.e., the job submit time), the number of processors requested, the estimated duration of the job, the actual duration of the job, the start time of the job, and possible additional resource requests (e.g., memory per node). The selected traces are summarized below.

- **CTC**: This trace contains entries for 79 302 jobs that were executed on a 512-node IBM SP2 at the Cornell Theory Center from July 1996 through May 1997.

- **KTH** : This trace contains entries for 28 487 jobs executed on a 100-node IBM SP2 at the Swedish Royal Institute of Technology from Oct. 1996 to Aug. 1997.

- **PAR**: This trace contains entries for 37 910 jobs that were executed on a 416-node Intel Paragon at the San Diego Supercomputer Center during 1996.

- **SP2**: This trace contains entries for 67 665 jobs executed on a 128-node IBM SP2 at the San Diego Supercomputer Center from May 1998 to April 2000.

Table 1 provides summary statistics for the selected traces[1]. Observe the wide disparity of the mean job execution time across workloads. Also notice the difference (of as much as two orders of magnitude) between the mean and the median within a workload. The high coefficients of variation (C.V.) in job execution times coupled with the large differences between mean and median values suggest the existence of a "fat tail" in the distribution of execution times. Log-log complementary distribution plots confirm the absence of a

---

[1]A common characteristic in many of these traces is that the system administrator places an upper limit on the job execution time. If this limit is reached, the job is killed. Our statistics include the terminated jobs; therefore, some of our output statistics are higher than those reported elsewhere (e.g., see [2]).

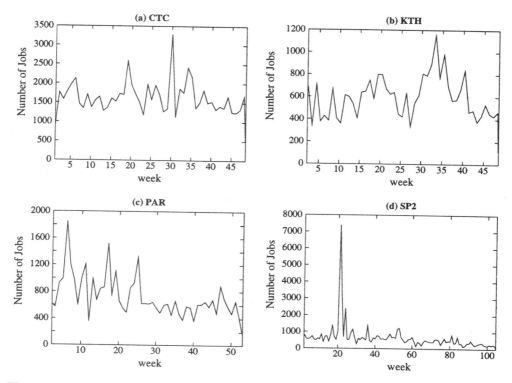

Figure 1. Total number of arriving jobs per week as a function of time (weeks).

heavy tail in the distributions [2], but run times nonetheless remain very skewed within each workload. This type of distribution advocates separating jobs according to their duration to different queues in order to minimize queuing time of short jobs that are delayed behind very long jobs.

Significant variability was also observed in the average "width" of each job, i.e., the number of per-job requested processors. To determine whether job duration and job width are independent attributes, we computed their statistical correlation for each workload. Results were mixed. In some cases, positive correlation was detected, while in other cases there was no correlation at all. Because job duration and job width strongly affect the backfilling ability and performance of a policy, we further elaborate on these two metrics later in this section.

The two parameters that affect performance and scheduling decisions in queuing systems are the arrival process and the service process. To visualize the time evolution of the arrival process, we plot for each trace the total number of arriving jobs per week as a function of time (see Figure 1). We observe bursts in the arrival process[2], but not of the same magnitude as the "flash crowds" experienced by web servers. Significant differences in the per-week arrival intensity exist within each workload, as well as across all

workloads. For this reason we focus not only on *aggregate* statistics (i.e., the average performance measures obtained after simulating the system using the entire workload trace), but also on *transient* statistics within specific time windows.

We now consider the service process. Because Table 1 indicates wide variation in job service times, we classify jobs according to job duration. After experimenting with several classifications, we choose the following four-part classification. Across all workloads, this classification provides a representative proportion of jobs in each class (see Figure 2).

- **class 1**: Short jobs are those with execution times $\leq$ 100 seconds.

- **class 2**: Medium jobs are those with execution times > 100 seconds and ≤ 1000 seconds.

- **class 3**: Long jobs are those with execution times > 1000 seconds and $\leq 10\,000$ seconds.

- **class 4**: Extra-long jobs are those with execution times $> 10\,000$ seconds.

Figure 2 presents the service time characteristics of the four workloads. The left column depicts the overall and per-class mean job execution time as a function of the trace time[3].

---

[2]Bursts also exist relative to smaller time units (e.g., days and hours), but such graphs are omitted for the sake of brevity.

[3]We compute statistics for batches of 1000 jobs, but plot each batch as a function of the arrival time of the first job in the batch.

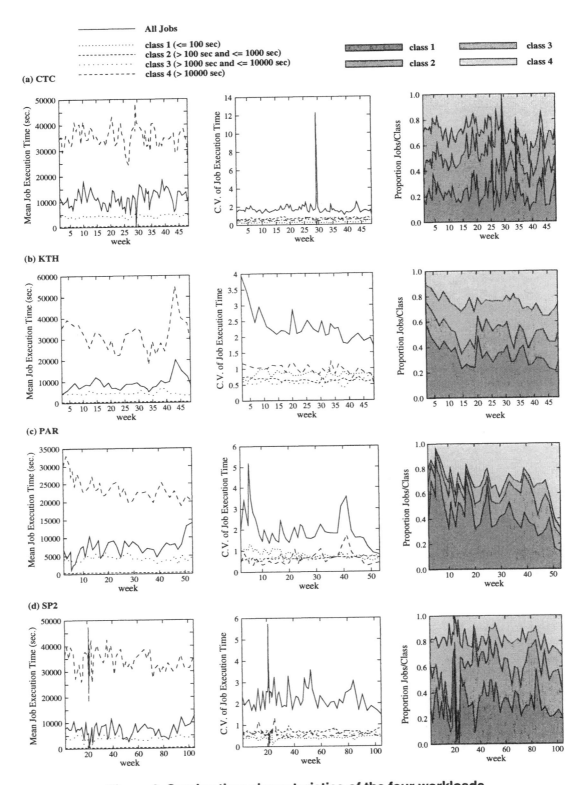

Figure 2. Service time characteristics of the four workloads.

The center column in Figure 2 depicts the overall and per-class C.V. of the average job execution time. Finally, the right column depicts the proportion of jobs per class. Observe that the mean job execution times and the overall C.V. (solid line) vary significantly across time. As expected, for all workloads the per-class C.V. is considerably smaller than the overall C.V. For all traces the proportion of jobs in each class varies dramatically with time.

3. Scheduling Policies

In actual parallel systems, successful scheduling policies use *backfilling*, a non-FCFS approach. Backfilling permits a limited number of queued jobs to jump ahead of jobs that cannot begin execution immediately. Backfilling is a core component of commercial schedulers including the IBM LoadLeveler [4] and the popular Maui Scheduler [7]. Here we propose a new policy, based on backfilling, that adapts its scheduling parameters according to changing workload conditions. Before introducing our new policy, we first describe the basic backfilling paradigm.

3.1. Single-Queue Backfilling

Backfilling is a commonly used scheduling policy that attempts to minimize fragmentation of system resources by executing jobs in an order different than their submission order [5, 8]. A job that is backfilled is allowed to jump ahead of jobs that arrived earlier (but are delayed because of insufficient idle processors) in an attempt to exploit otherwise currently idle processors. The order of job execution is handled differently by two types of backfilling. *Conservative* backfilling permits a job to be backfilled provided it does not delay *any* previous job in the queue. *Aggressive* backfilling ensures only that the *first* job in the queue is not delayed. We use aggressive backfilling for our baseline policy because results have shown its performance superior to conservative backfilling [8].

Basic aggressive backfilling assumes a single queue of jobs to be executed. Jobs enter this queue when submitted by the user. Each job is characterized by its arrival time, by the number of processors required (i.e., the job width), and by an estimate of the expected execution time. Aggressive backfilling is a non-preemptive, space-sharing policy. Any job that attempts to execute for a time greater than its estimated execution time is terminated by the system.

The single-queue backfilling policy always attempts to backfill as many queued jobs as possible. Define the following:

- pivot: the first job in the queue;
- pivot time: the scheduled starting time for the pivot (i.e., the earliest time when sufficient processors will

be available for the pivot);

- extra: the number of idle processors at the pivot time not required for the pivot.

In general, the process of backfilling *exactly one* of these many jobs occurs as follows. If the job is the pivot, the scheduler starts executing the job immediately only if the current time is equal to the pivot time. If the job is not the pivot, the scheduler starts executing the job immediately only if the job requires no more than the currently idle processors *and* will finish by the pivot time, or if the job requires no more than min{currently idle processors, extra processors}.

This process of backfilling exactly one job is repeated until all queued jobs have been considered for backfilling. Hence, the single-queue backfilling policy attempts to backfill as many jobs as possible until no more jobs can be backfilled. This basic single-queue aggressive backfilling algorithm, employed whenever a job is submitted to the system or whenever a job completes execution, is outlined in Figure 3.

Single-queue aggressive backfilling ensures that once a job becomes the pivot, it cannot be delayed further. A job may be delayed in the queue before becoming the pivot, but when the job reaches the front of the queue, it is assigned a scheduled starting time. If a currently executing job finishes early, the pivot may begin executing earlier than its assigned starting time, but it will *never* begin executing after the assigned starting time.

3.2. Multiple-Queue Backfilling

Because the performance of any scheduling policy is sensitive to the transient nature of the impending workload, we propose a multiple-queue backfilling policy that permits the scheduler to quickly change parameters in response to workload fluctuations. Our goal is to decrease the average job slowdown by reducing the number of short jobs delayed by longer jobs.

The multiple-queue backfilling policy splits the system into multiple *disjoint* partitions. The splitting is accomplished by classifying jobs according to the job duration as described in Section 2. We incorporate four separate queues, one per job class (i.e., per system partition), indexed by $q = 1, 2, 3, 4$. As jobs are submitted to the system, they are assigned to exactly one of these queues based on the user estimate of execution time. Let t_e be the estimate (in seconds) of the execution time of a submitted job. Here, we consider that the user provides *accurate* estimates of the expected execution time[4]. The job is assigned to the queue in

---

[4]For details regarding sensitivity of the policy to inaccurate estimates, we refer the interested reader to [6].

```
for (all jobs in queue)
    1. pivot ←— first job in queue
    2. pivot time ←— time when sufficient processors will be available for pivot
    3. extra ←— idle processors at pivot time not required by pivot job
    4. if job is pivot
        a. if current time equals pivot time, start job immediately
    5. else
        a. if job requires ≤ currently idle procs and will finish by pivot time, start job immediately
        b. else if job requires ≤ min{currently idle procs, extra procs}, start job immediately
```

Figure 3. Single-queue aggressive backfilling algorithm.

partition q according to the following equation, consistent with the job classification presented in Section 2.

$$q = \begin{cases} 1, & 0 < t_e \leq 100 \\ 2, & 100 < t_e \leq 1000 \\ 3, & 1000 < t_e \leq 10\,000 \\ 4, & 10\,000 < t_e \end{cases}$$

Note that the assignment of a job to a queue is based solely on the user estimate of job execution time and *not* on the number of requested processors. Initially, the processors are distributed evenly among the four partitions. As time evolves, processors may move from one partition to another (i.e., the partitions may contract or expand) so that currently idle processors in one partition can be used for immediate backfilling in another partition. Hence, the partition boundaries become dynamic, allowing the system to adapt itself to changing workload conditions. We stress that the policy does not starve a job that requires the entire machine for execution. When such a job is ready to begin execution (according to the job arrival order), the scheduler allocates all processors to the partition where the job is assigned. After the job completes, the processors will be redistributed among the four partitions according to the ongoing processor demands of each partition.

The multiple-queue backfilling policy considers all queued jobs (one at a time, in the order of arrival across all queues). Similar to the single-queue backfilling policy, define the following:

- $idle_q$: the number of currently idle processors in partition q ;

- $pivot_q$: the first job in the queue in partition q ;

- $pivot\text{-}time_q$: the scheduled starting time for $pivot_q$ (i.e., the earliest time when sufficient processors will be available for $pivot_q$) ;

- $extra_q$: the number of idle processors in partition q at $pivot\text{-}time_q$ not required for $pivot_q$.

The processors reserved for the pivot at $pivot\text{-}time_q$ consist of $idle_q$ and, if necessary, some combination of idle and/or extra processors from other partitions such that no other pivot that arrived earlier than $pivot_q$ is delayed. The assignment of a scheduled starting time to a pivot job will never delay any current pivot in another partition (i.e., any other pivot that arrived earlier), suggesting that the algorithm is deadlock free.

The policy always attempts to backfill as many queued jobs as possible. In general, *exactly one* of these many jobs is backfilled as follows. Let q be the queue where the job resides. If the job is $pivot_q$, the scheduler starts executing the job immediately only if the current time is equal to $pivot\text{-}time_q$. If the job is *not* $pivot_q$, the scheduler starts executing the job immediately only if there are sufficient idle processors in partition q without delaying $pivot_q$, or if the partition can take idle processors sufficient to meet the job's requirements from one or more other partitions without delaying any pivot.

This process of backfilling one job is repeated, one job at a time in the order of arrival across all queues, until all queued jobs have been considered for backfilling. Hence, the multiple-queue backfilling policy attempts to backfill as many jobs as possible until no more jobs can be backfilled. This multiple-queue aggressive backfilling algorithm, employed whenever a job is submitted to the system or whenever a job completes execution, is outlined in Figure 4.

In both the single-queue and multiple-queue aggressive backfilling policies, the goal is to backfill jobs in order to exploit idle processors and reduce system fragmentation. Both policies ensure that once a job reaches the front of the queue, it cannot be delayed further.

By classifying jobs according to job length, the multiple-queue policy reduces the likelihood that a short job will be overly delayed in the queue behind a very long job. Additionally, because processors are permitted to cross partition boundaries, the multiple-queue policy can quickly adapt to a continuously changing workload. Unlike commercial schedulers that typically are difficult to parame-

```
for (all jobs in order of arrival)
    1. q ⟵ queue in which job resides
    2. pivot_q ⟵ first job in queue q
    3. pivot-time_q ⟵ earliest time when sufficient procs (from this and perhaps other partitions)
                        will be available for pivot_q
    4. extra_q ⟵ idle processors in partition q at pivot-time_q not required by pivot_q
    5. if job is pivot_q
        a. if current time equals pivot-time_q
            I. if necessary, reassign procs from other partitions to partition q
            II. start job immediately
    6. else
        a. if job requires ≤ idle_q and will finish by pivot-time_q, start job immediately
        b. else if job requires ≤ min{idle_q, extra_q}, start job immediately
        c. else if job requires ≤ (idle_q plus some combination of idle/extra procs from other partitions)
                    such that no pivot is delayed
            I. reassign necessary procs from other partitions to partition q
            II. start job immediately
```

Figure 4. Multiple-queue aggressive backfilling algorithm.

terize, multiple-queue backfilling requires only an *a priori* definition of job classes, and then the policy automatically adjusts the processor-to-class allocations. In the following section, we elaborate on the above issues and their effect on performance.

4. Performance Analysis

We evaluate and compare via simulation the performance of the two backfilling policies presented in the previous section. Our simulation experiments are driven using the four workload traces from the Parallel Workload Archive described in Section 2. From each trace record, we extract three values: the job arrival time, the job execution time, and the number of requested processors. Consequently, our experiments fully capture the fluctuations in the average job arrival rate and service demands.

We concentrate both on *aggregate* performance measures, i.e., measures collected at the end of the simulation that reflect the average achieved performance across the entire life of the system, and on *transient* measures, i.e., the average performance measures perceived by the end-user during each time interval corresponding to 1000 job requests[5].

The performance measure of interest that we strive to optimize is the average job slowdown s defined by

$$s = 1 + \frac{d}{\nu}$$

[5]Consistent with Section 2, we use a batch size of 1000 for reasons of statistical significance.

where d and ν are respectively the queuing delay time and actual service time of a job[6].

To compare the single-queue and multiple-queue backfilling results, we define the *slowdown ratio* $\mathcal{R}$ by the equation

$$\mathcal{R} = \frac{s_1 - s_m}{\min\{s_1, s_m\}}$$

where s_1 and s_m are the single-queue and multiple-queue slowdowns respectively[7]. $\mathcal{R} > 0$ indicates the performance gain obtained using multiple queues relative to a single queue. $\mathcal{R} < 0$ indicates the performance loss that results from using multiple queues relative to a single queue.

4.1. Multiple- Versus Single-Queue Backfilling

Figure 5 depicts the aggregate slowdown ratio $\mathcal{R}$ of multiple-queue backfilling relative to single-queue backfilling for each of the four traces. For overall average slowdown (see Figure 5(a)), the multiple-queue policy is superior to the single-queue policy. Figures 5(b)–(e) depict the aggregate *per-class* slowdown ratios (i.e., for short, medium, long, and extra-long jobs). These figures clearly indicate that the multiple-queue algorithm offers dramatic performance gains for all but the extra-long job class.

[6]Bounded slowdown [8] is another popular performance measure. For the sake of brevity, we omit performance results for bounded slowdown that we obtained. Note that the performance of each of the two policies is qualitatively the same using *either* of the two measures.

[7]Because of the $\min\{s_1, s_m\}$ term in the denominator, $\mathcal{R}$ is a *fair*, properly scaled measure of the performance that equally quantifies gain or loss experienced using multiple queues relative to a single queue. If we instead use s_m (or for the same matter s_1) in the denominator, we bias the measure toward gains (or losses).

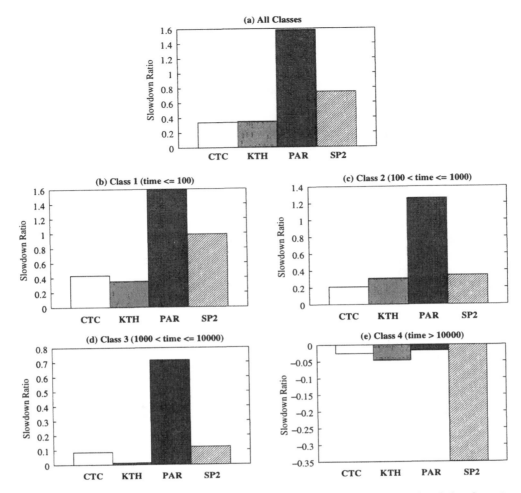

Figure 5. Overall and per-class aggregate slowdown ratio $\mathcal{R}$ for each of the four traces.

Figures 5(b)–(e) confirm that, by splitting the system into multiple partitions, we manage to reduce the number of short jobs overly delayed behind extra-long jobs. Across all workloads, jobs belonging to all but the extra-long job class achieve significant performance gains. Additionally, extra-long jobs experience a decline in average slowdown, but the magnitude of decline is generally much less than the magnitude of improvement seen in the other job classes.

Transient measures illustrate how well each policy responds to sudden arrival bursts. Furthermore, transient measures reflect the end-user perception of system performance, i.e., how well the policy performs during the relatively small window of time that the user interacts with the system. Figure 6 displays transient snapshots of the slowdown ratio versus time for each of the four traces. For all traces, marked improvement (i.e., $\mathcal{R} > 0$) in slowdown is achieved using the multiple-queue backfilling policy. Although the single-queue policy gives better slowdown (i.e., $\mathcal{R} < 0$) for a relatively few batches, multiple-queue backfilling excels with

more frequent and larger improvements.

4.2. Multiple-Queue Backfilling with Delays

Because the decline in average slowdown for extra-long jobs (Figure 5(e)) is typically much less than the improvement for all job classes combined (Figure 5(a)), a natural extension to multiple-queue backfilling is to further impede extra-long jobs. Therefore, we hinder any extra-long job by assigning to it a delay when submitted to the system. Let D be the global delay (in seconds) and let t_s be the time of submission of an extra-long job; the job can begin execution no earlier than $t_s + D$. The goal is to further assist shorter jobs in an attempt to improve the overall average slowdown. To address policy flexibility, we adjust the delay parameter on the fly according to the current perceived performance. By continuously monitoring the average job slowdown of each job class, the policy simply increments or decrements the delay parameter accordingly. Our goal is to increase the delay on extra-long jobs only when short jobs are suffering,

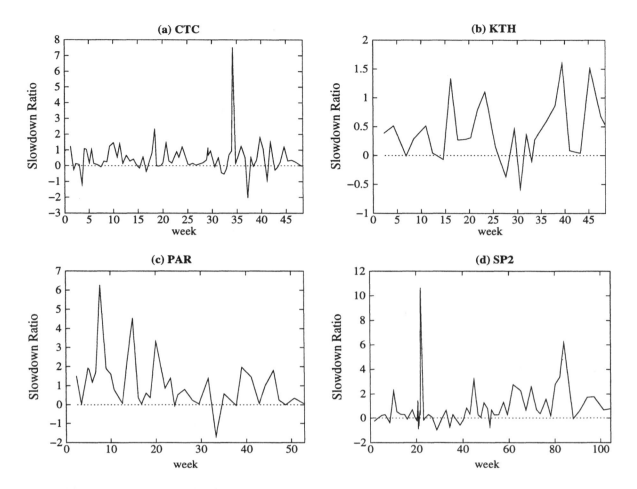

Figure 6. Slowdown ratio $\mathcal{R}$ per 1000-job submissions as a function of time for each of the four traces.

and to reduce the delay when short jobs are overly favored.

More specifically, for batches of 100 completed jobs, we monitor the average slowdown of short jobs in each batch. Let D_k be the global variable delay imposed on extra-long jobs for the kth batch ($k = 1, 2, \ldots$), where D_1 is the *initial* delay. Let s_k represent the average slowdown of short jobs in the kth batch, and let δ_k represent the proportional difference in s_k and s_{k-1} according to the equation

$$\delta_k = \frac{s_k - s_{k-1}}{\max\{s_k, s_{k-1}\}} \qquad \text{for } k > 1$$

with $\delta_1 = s_1$. To avoid too frequent modifications, the delay for batch $k + 1$ is modified only if the proportional difference δ_k is more than 0.25 (i.e., if the difference in average slowdown for short jobs from the previous batch to the current batch changes by more than 25%). If so, we change the global delay by an amount equal to the proportional difference multiplied by the original delay[8]; otherwise, the global

---

[8]Clearly, D_{k+1} must be non-negative.

delay remains unchanged for the next batch. To summarize, the adjusted delay used for batch $k + 1$ is computed via the following algorithmic steps.

---

1. compute δ_k
2. if $|\delta_k| > 0.25$, then $D_{k+1} = \max\{D_k + \delta_k D_1, 0\}$
3. else $D_{k+1} = D_k$

Figure 7 again depicts the aggregate slowdown ratio $\mathcal{R}$ for each of the four traces. For each trace, we show the gain/loss obtained using multiple-queue backfilling with no delay and with variable delay using $D_1 = 2500$. In all cases, multiple-queue backfilling with variable delay clearly surpasses single-queue backfilling (i.e., $\mathcal{R} \gg 0$).

5. Conclusions

We presented a self-adapting, multiple-queue backfilling policy for parallel systems that directs incoming jobs to

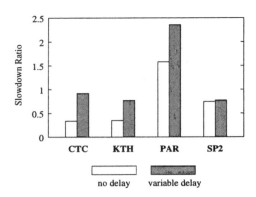

Figure 7. Aggregate slowdown ratio $\mathcal{R}$ using multiple-queue backfilling with no delay and variable delay. All slowdown ratios are computed relative to single-queue backfilling.

different queues according to the user estimated job execution time. By separating short from long jobs, the multiple-queue policy reduces the likelihood that a short job is overly delayed in the queue behind a very long job, and therefore significantly improves the expected job slowdown. Each queue is assigned a non-overlapping partition of system resources on which jobs from the queue can execute. The proposed policy changes the partition boundaries to adapt to evolution of the workload across time.

Multiple-queue backfilling uses minimal parameterization. The policy only requires an *a priori* definition of job classes that regulates the assignment of jobs to queues. This definition of job classes can be easily changed as the system administrator deems appropriate. Furthermore, because of the dynamic nature of the partition boundaries, these external parameters should seldom require modification. Detailed performance comparisons via simulation using actual Supercomputing traces from the Parallel Workload Archive indicate that the proposed policy consistently outperforms traditional single-queue backfilling. Because of its robustness, simplicity, flexibility, and applicability to ever changing workloads, multiple-queue backfilling is an attractive policy for scheduling parallel resources.

Acknowledgments

We thank Tom Crockett for useful discussions that contributed to this work. We also thank Dror Feitelson for making available the workload traces through the Parallel Workload Archive.

References

[1] D. G. Feitelson. A survey of scheduling in multiprogrammed parallel systems. Technical Report RC 19790, IBM Research Division, October 1994.

[2] D. G. Feitelson. Metrics for parallel job scheduling and their convergence. In D. G. Feitelson and L. Rudolph, editors, *Proceedings of the 7th Workshop on Job Scheduling Strategies for Parallel Processing*, volume 2221 of *Lecture Notes in Computer Science*, pages 188–206. Springer-Verlag, 2001.

[3] Parallel Workload Archive. http://www.cs.huji.ac.il/labs/parallel/workload/.

[4] IBM LoadLeveler. http://www.ibm.com/.

[5] P. Keleher, D. Zotkin, and D. Perkovic. Attacking the bottlenecks in backfilling schedulers. *Cluster Computing: The Journal of Networks, Software Tools and Applications*, 3(4), 2000.

[6] B. G. Lawson and E. Smirni. Multiple-queue backfilling scheduling with priorities and reservations for parallel systems, May 2002. Submitted for publication.

[7] Maui Scheduler Open Cluster Software. http://mauischeduler.sourceforge.net/.

[8] A. Mu'alem and D. G. Feitelson. Utilization, predictability, workloads, and user runtime estimates in scheduling the IBM SP2 with backfilling. *IEEE Transactions on Parallel and Distributed Systems*, 12(6):529–543, June 2001.

[9] Portable Batch System. http://www.openpbs.org/.

[10] D. Perkovic and P. Keleher. Randomization, speculation, and adaptation in batch schedulers. In *Proceedings of Supercomputing 2000 (SC2000)*, November 2000.

[11] A. Riska, W. Sun, E. Smirni, and G. Ciardo. AdaptLoad: Effective balancing in clustered web servers under transient load conditions. In *International Conference on Distributed Computing Systems (ICDCS 2002)*, Vienna, Austria, July 2002.

[12] B. Schroeder and M. Harchol-Balter. Evaluation of task assignment policies for supercomputing servers: The case for load unbalancing and fairness. In *Proceedings of the 9th IEEE Symposium on High Performance Distributed Computing (HPDC '00)*, Pittsburgh, PA, August 2000.

[13] D. Talby and D. G. Feitelson. Supporting priorities and improving utilization of the IBM SP2 scheduler using slack-based backfilling. In *Proceedings of the 13th International Parallel Processing Symposium*, pages 513–517, April 1999.

Power Aware Scheduling for AND/OR Graphs in Multi-Processor Real-Time Systems *

Dakai Zhu, Nevine AbouGhazaleh, Daniel Mossé and Rami Melhem
Computer Science Department
University of Pittsburgh
Pittsburgh, PA 15260
{zdk, nevine, mosse, melhem}@cs.pitt.edu

Abstract

Power aware computing has become popular recently and many techniques have been proposed to manage the energy consumption for traditional real-time applications. We have previously proposed two greedy slack sharing scheduling algorithms for such applications on multi-processor systems. In this paper, we are concerned mainly with real-time applications that have different execution paths consisting of different number of tasks. The AND/OR graph model is used to represent the application's data dependence and control flow. The contribution of this paper is twofold. First, we extend our greedy slack sharing algorithm for traditional applications to deal with applications represented by AND/OR graphs. Then, using the statistical information about the applications, we propose a few variations of speculative scheduling algorithms that intend to save energy by reducing the number of speed changes (and thus the overhead) while ensuring that the applications meet the timing constraints. The performance of the algorithms is analyzed with respect to energy savings. The results surprisingly show that the greedy scheme is better than some speculative schemes and that the greedy scheme is good enough when a reasonable minimal speed exists in the system.

1. Introduction

Power aware computing has recently become popular not only for general purpose systems but also for real time systems. For the traditional applications in real-time systems, where a task is *ready* to execute when all its predecessors complete execution, many techniques have been proposed to manage the energy consumption. Such applications are modeled by AND-graphs and the relationship over their tasks is known as AND-only precedence constraints [10]. But this traditional AND model cannot describe many applications encountered in practice, where a task is *ready* to execute when one *or more* of its predecessors finish execution, and one *or more* of its successors are ready to be executed after the task finishes execution. A real life example that falls within this AND/OR model is an automated target recognition (ATR) application, in which the number of regions of interests (ROI) in one frame varies substantially. For some frames, the number of detected ROIs may be maximum and all the tasks need to be executed, while in most cases, the number of detected ROIs in a frame is less than the maximum and part of the application can be skipped. The control flow of most practical applications also have OR structures, where execution of the sub-paths depends on the results of previous tasks. In some applications, the probability of the paths to be executed is also known a priori.

In this paper, we modify the greedy slack sharing algorithm developed in [20] to incorporate the AND/OR features and prove its correctness on meeting the timing constraints. While it achieves some energy savings, the greedy slack sharing algorithm may perform many voltage/speed changes. Considering the timing and energy overhead of voltage/speed adjustment, along with the statistical information about the application and the intuition that minimal energy can be obtained by running all tasks with the same speed, we study a few variations of the speculative scheduling algorithms that intend to save more energy by reducing the number of voltage/speed changes (and thus the overhead) while ensuring that the application's timing constraints will not be violated.

The performance, in terms of energy savings, is analyzed for all the schemes. The results surprisingly show that the greedy scheme is better than some speculative schemes especially when the system has a reasonable minimal speed. All the dynamic schemes perform the best with moderate *load* and α (the ratio of the tasks' average case execution time over worst case execution time).

---
*This work has been supported by the Defense Advanced Research Projects Agency through the PARTS project (Contract F33615-00-C-1736).

1.1. Related Work

For uniprocessor systems, based on dynamic voltage scaling (DVS) technique, Mossé et al. proposed and analyzed several schemes to dynamically adjust processor speed with slack reclamation, and statistical information about task's run-time was used to slow down the processor speed evenly and save more energy [14]. In [16], Shin et al. set the processor's speed at branches according to the ratio of the longest path to the taken paths from the branch statement to the end of the program. The granularity of the proposed schemes is the basic block, which will impose a very high overhead due to too frequent speed changes. Kumar et al. predict the execution time of the task based on the statistics gathered about execution time of previous instances of the same task [12]. Their algorithm is adequate for soft real time operating systems. We note that statistical schemes that predict execution times using history data are not eligible for hard real time systems where the deadlines must be guaranteed. The best scheme is an adaptive one that takes an aggressive approach while providing safeguards that avoid violating the application deadline [2, 13].

When considering the limited voltage/speed levels in the real processors, Chandrakasan et al. have shown that, for periodic tasks, a few voltage/speed levels are sufficient to achieve almost the same energy savings as infinite voltage/speed levels [6]. AbouGhazaleh et al. have studied the effect of the voltage/speed adjustment overhead on choosing the granularity of inserting power management points in a program [1].

For multi-processor systems, with AND-model applications that have fixed task sets and predictable execution times, static power management (SPM) can be accomplished by deciding beforehand the best voltage/speed for each processor [11]. For the system-on-chip (SOC) with two processors running at two different fixed voltage levels, Yang et al. proposed a two-phase scheduling scheme that minimizes the energy consumption while meeting the timing constraints by choosing different scheduling options determined at compile time [17]. Based on the idea of *slack sharing*, for AND-model applications, we have studied the dynamic voltage/speed adjustment schemes on multi-processor systems and proposed two dynamic management algorithms for independent tasks and dependent tasks, respectively [20].

In this paper, we consider the AND/OR model applications that have different execution paths with different task sets taking into account overhead and discrete voltage/speed levels. The paper is organized in the following way. The application model, power model and system model are described in Section 2. The greedy slack sharing algorithm is extended for applications represented by AND/OR graphs in Section 3. Section 4 proposes a few variations of speculative algorithms using the applications' statistical information. Simulation results are given and analyzed in Section 5 and Section 6 concludes the paper.

2. Models

2.1. Application Model: AND/OR Graph

In this paper, we use the AND/OR model [10], which is represented by a graph $G(V, E)$, where the vertices in V represent tasks or synchronization nodes, and the edges $E \subseteq V \times V$ represent the dependence between vertices. The graph represents both the control flow and data dependence between tasks. Only when v_i is the direct predecessor of v_j, is there an edge $e :: v_i \rightarrow v_j \subseteq E$, which means that v_j depends on v_i; in other words, only after v_i finishes execution can v_j become ready for execution. The application also has a deadline D.

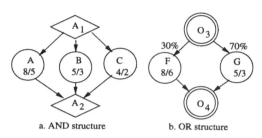

a. AND structure   b. OR structure

Figure 1. The AND/OR Structures

In the extended AND/OR model, there are three different kinds of vertices: computation nodes, AND nodes and OR nodes. A computation node T_i is represented by a *circle*, which has two attributes, c_i and a_i, where c_i is the worst case execution time (WCET) of T_i and a_i is the average case execution time of T_i, all based on maximum processor speed (f_{max}). An AND synchronization node is represented by a *diamond*, which depends on all its predecessors and all its successors depend on it. It is used to explore the parallelism in the applications as shown in Figure 1a. An OR synchronization node is represented by a *double circles*, which depends on only one of its predecessors and only one of its successors depends on it. It is used to explore the different execution paths in the applications as shown in Figure 1b. For simplicity, we only consider the case where an OR node cannot be processed concurrently with other paths. In other words, all the processors will synchronize at an OR node. The synchronization nodes are considered as *dummy* tasks with execution time as 0 ($c = a = 0$).

In the figure, the computation node is labeled by its name and (c_i/a_i). The AND/OR nodes are labeled correspondingly. To represent the probability of taking each execution path after the OR synchronization node v, a number is associated with each successor of v.

Since there is no back edges in our AND/OR model, for the loops in an application, we can treat a whole loop to be one task with the execution time of maximal iterations as c_i and average iterations as a_i. Alternatively, we can expand the loop as several tasks if we know the maximal number of iterations and the corresponding probabilities to have specific number of iterations.

2.2. Power Management Points

In [14], the insertion of power management points (PMP) at the start of each program section is proposed. These points are inserted by the user, or set by the compiler. At each PMP, a new speed is computed based on the time taken so far and an estimation of the time for the future tasks. If the new speed is different from the current processor speed, the speed/voltage setting is invoked.

For the AND/OR model proposed above, there is a PMP before each node. Two values, Π_c and Π_a, are associated with the PMP before the first node in the graph. The values represent the worst case execution time and average case execution time of the application, respectively. For the PMP before an OR node, two values, Π_c^i and Π_a^i, are associated with each path p_i after the OR node. The values represent the worst case execution time and average case execution time for path p_i from the PMP to the end of the program, respectively. All these values can be obtained from profiling and will be used in speculation and computing the new speed. The details are discussed in Sections 3 and 4.

2.3. Power and System Models

We assume that processor power consumption is dominated by dynamic power dissipation P_d, which is given by: $P_d = C_{ef} \times V_{dd}^2 \times f$, where C_{ef} is the effective switch capacitance, V_{dd} is the supply voltage and f is the processor clock frequency. Processor speed, represented by f, is almost linearly related to the supply voltage: $f = k \times \frac{(V_{dd} - V_t)^2}{V_{dd}}$, where k is constant and V_t is the threshold voltage [4, 7]. The energy consumed by a specific task T_i can be given as $E_i = C_{ef} \times V_{dd}^2 \times C$, where C is the number of cycles needed to execute the task. When decreasing processor speed, we also reduce the supply voltage. This reduces processor power consumption cubically and reduces task energy consumption quadratically at the expense of linearly increasing the execution time of the task. For example, consider a task that, with maximum speed f_{max}, needs 10 time units to finish execution. If we have 20 time units allocated to this task, we can reduce the processor speed by half while still finishing the task on time. The new energy consumption would be: $E' = C_{ef} \times (\frac{V_{dd}}{2})^2 \times \frac{f_{max}}{2} \times 20 = \frac{1}{4} \times C_{ef} \times V_{dd}^2 \times f_{max} \times 10 = \frac{1}{4} \times E$, where E is the energy consumption with maximum processor speed. From now on, we refer to *speed change* as both changing the CPU voltage and frequency.

We consider systems that have multiple identical processors with shared memory. The application characteristics and state are kept in the shared memory. All the ready tasks are put into a global queue. Each processor executes the scheduler independently and fetches the tasks from the global queue as needed. We assume that the shared memory is accessed in a mutual exclusive way and access to the shared memory has no extra cost (actually, the cost is part of context switch that we do not consider in this paper).

In this paper, we consider two different power configurations for the processors. First, in the Transmeta model, the voltage/speed setting is given as in Table 1 [18]. There are 16 voltage/speed settings between 700MHz (1.65V) and 200MHz (1.10V). The second power configuration is the Intel XScale model [19], with the voltage/speed setting as shown in Table 2. Note that the speed and voltage do not obey a linear relation in either model, which is different from the assumptions in many published papers.

Table 1. Speed & Voltages of Transmeta 5400

f(MHz)	700	666	633	600
V(V)	1.65	1.65	1.60	1.60
f(MHz)	566	533	500	466
V(V)	1.55	1.55	1.50	1.50
f(MHz)	433	400	366	333
V(V)	1.45	1.40	1.35	1.30
f(MHz)	300	266	233	200
V(V)	1.25	1.20	1.15	1.10

Table 2. Speed & Voltages of Intel XScale

f(MHz)	1000	800	600	400	150
V(V)	1.80	1.60	1.30	1.00	0.75

3. Greedy Algorithm for AND/OR Graph

3.1. Scheduling for Multi-Processor Systems

Since list scheduling is a standard technique used to schedule tasks with precedence constraints [8], we will focus on list scheduling in this paper. List scheduling puts tasks into a ready queue as soon as they become ready and dispatches tasks from the front of the ready queue to processors. When more than one task is ready at the same time, finding the optimal order of the tasks that minimizes execution time is NP-hard [8]. In this paper, we use the same heuristic as in [20] and put into the ready queue first the longest (based on tasks' WCET) among the tasks that become ready simultaneously.

If there is some slack in the system and a task can be allocated more time than its WCET, the system can slow down the

CPU for the task appropriately save energy. Since tasks exhibit a large variation in actual execution time, and in many cases, only consume a small fraction of their worst case execution time [9], any unused time can be considered as *slack*. Furthermore, the execution does not always follow the longest path, and thus there may be some extra slack. For the AND-model applications, *greedy slack sharing* algorithms have been discussed for multi-processor systems, in which part of the slack on processor P_x will be shared with processor P_y if P_x's expected finish time[1] is later than P_y's but actually finishes earlier than P_y. The remaining slack is given to the next task to be run on P_x. See [20] for details.

In the following, we will explore the application's dynamic characteristics both at the task set level (different execution paths) and at the task level (different actual execution time of each task). We extend the greedy slack sharing algorithm for dependent tasks [20] to incorporate the characteristics of AND/OR model and show how it is correct with respect to meeting the timing constraints.

3.2. Greedy Algorithm

The algorithm consists of two phases: an *off-line phase* and an *on-line phase*. The off-line phase is used to collect the execution information about the application with processor speed as f_{max} and it is a two-round phase. In the first round, using list scheduling with longest task first (LTF) heuristics, a *canonical schedule* is generated for each program section separated by OR nodes, in which the tasks use their worst case execution time. The time to finish the application along the longest path (consisting of all the longest program section between OR nodes) is defined as Π_c, which is stored in the PMP at the very beginning. For the PMPs before the OR synchronization nodes, the worst case execution time for remaining tasks on path j is gathered and stored as Π_c^j. For the average case, Π_a and Π_a^j are also analogously collected. The execution order of task T_i is recorded as EO_i and we will maintain the same execution order of tasks in the on-line phase to meet the timing constraints. The execution order of an OR node is the maximal execution order of its predecessors plus 1. For tasks which are on different paths after an OR node and will be executed at the same time, they may have the same execution order.

If $\Pi_c > D$, the algorithm fails to guarantee the deadline; otherwise, the second round of the off-line phase shifts the canonical schedules for all program sections to make them finish exactly on time. Notice that the shifting is a recursive process when there are embedded OR nodes. The start time of T_i in the shifted schedules is called *latest start time LST_i* and is also recorded, it is the time T_i *must* start execution for the

remaining tasks in the shifted schedules to meet the deadline. LST_i will be used to claim the slack for T_i at run time.

Given any heuristic, if the off-line phase does not fail, the following on-line phase can be applied under the same heuristic. The following algorithm will assume that the longest path in the worst case meets the deadline, that is, $\Pi_c \leq D$.

Before presenting the on-line phase of the algorithm, we give some definitions. As in [20], we define the *estimated end time (EET)* for a task executing on a processor as the time at which the task is expected to finish execution if it consumes all the time allocated for it. To determine the *readiness* of tasks, we define the number of *unfinished predecessors (UP_i)* for each task T_i. UP_i will decrease by 1 when any predecessor of task T_i finishes execution. Task T_i is *ready* when $UP_i = 0$.

The speed to execute task T_i using greedy slack sharing reclamation is denoted as f_g^i. To maintain the execution order of tasks as in the canonical schedules, the execution order of the next expected task is defined as EO_{NET}. The current time is represented by t.

Initially, all the root tasks are put into a *Ready-Q*. For all other tasks, UP_i is initialized as the number of predecessors of T_i if the corresponding vertex is not an OR node, and 1 otherwise. The current time t is set to 0 and the execution order of the next expected task EO_{NET} is set to 1.

1 T_k =*Head(Ready-Q)*;
2 If (T_k is OR node $\|$ EO_{NET}==EO_k) && (UP_k == 0))
   Goto Step 4;
3 *wait()*; Goto Step 1;
4 T_k =dequeue(*Ready-Q*);
   $EO_{NET} = EO_{NET} + 1$;
5 If (T_k is Computation node)
   $EET_k = LST_k + c_k$; /* Note that $LST_k \geq t$ */
   $f_g^k = f_{max} \times \frac{c_k}{(EET_k - t)}$; /*compute the speed for T_k*/
   If(P_y is sleep && Head(*Ready-Q*) is next expected and ready)
   signal(P_y);
   Execute T_k at speed f_g^k;
6 If (T_k is Computation node or AND node)
   For each successor T_j of T_k:
   $UP_j = UP_j - 1$;
   If ($UP_j == 0$) enqueue(T_j, *Read-Q*);
   Goto Step 1;
7 If (T_k is OR node)
   $EO_{NET} = EO_k + 1$; /*update the next expected task*/
   If selected path p_i /*the 1st task of path p_i is denoted by T_i*/
   $UP_i = 0$;
   Put T_i into *Ready-Q*;
   Goto Step 1;

Figure 2. The GSS Algorithm invoked by P_{id}

The greedy slack sharing (GSS) algorithm for AND/OR applications is shown in Figure 2. Remember that the execution

---

[1] More accurately, it is the estimated end time (EET) of the task running on processor P_x, as defined later.

order of tasks will be kept the same as in the canonical schedules. From the algorithm, each idle processor tries to fetch the next ready task (Step 1 and 2). If the next expected task is not ready, the processor will go to sleep (Step 3; We use the function *wait()* to put an idle processor to sleep and another function *signal(P)* to wake processor P.). Otherwise, if the task is a computation task, the processor computes a new speed for the ready task, wakes up an idle processor if the task expected after the one the processor is handling is ready and changes the speed if necessary before executing the ready task (Steps 4 and 5). If the task is a dummy task (AND/OR node), the successors of the node are handled properly (Step 6 and 7). The function *enqueue(T,Q)* is used to put the ready task T into Q in the order of tasks' execution order. The shared memory holds the control information, such as *Ready-Q*, UP values, which must be updated within a critical section (not shown in the algorithm for simplicity).

The slack sharing is implicit in the algorithm. In Step 4 and 5, when a processor picks a task that has a earlier LRT than the one it should pick, slack sharing happens implicitly.

3.3. Algorithm Analysis

Theorem 1 *For an application represented by an AND/OR graph with a deadline D and for a given heuristic for assigning priorities to tasks, the greedy slack sharing algorithm will finish by time D if the application can finish before D in the canonical schedules.*

From the off-line phase, after the canonical schedules are shifted, for any execution path if every task uses up the time that GSS algorithm allocates to it, the application will finish just in time. Define FT_i^w as the finish time for T_i in the worst case for the shifted schedule. For any execution path p, we will have $FT_i^w \leq D$ ($T_i \in p$). Notice that EET_i is the latest time T_i should finish, following the same idea as in [20], it is not hard to prove that $EET_i = FT_i^w$ ($T_i \in p$) for any path p. That is, if the application can finish before D in canonical schedules, the execution of all paths under GSS will finish in time. The proof is omitted for lack of space.

While the greedy slack sharing algorithm is guaranteed to meet the timing constraints, there may be many speed changes during the execution since it computes a new speed for each task. It is known that a clairvoyant algorithm can achieve minimal energy consumption for uniprocessor systems by running all tasks at a single speed setting if the actual running time of every task is known. Considering the speed adjustment overhead, the single speed setting is even more attractive. From this intuition, using the statistical information about application, we propose the following speculative algorithms.

4. Speculative Algorithms

Based on different strategies, we developed two speculative schemes. One is to statically speculate the speed for the whole application, the other is to speculate the speed *on-the-fly* to reflect actual behavior of the application, that is, dynamically taking into account the remaining work. For the first scheme, we can speculate a single speed if the speed levels are fine grained, or two speeds otherwise. For the second scheme, we speculate after each OR synchronization node since more slack can be expected from different paths after the branch.

4.1. Static Speculative Algorithms

For static speculative (SS) algorithm, the speed, f_{ss}, at which the application should run is decided at the very beginning based on the statistical information about the whole application, as follows:

$$f_{ss} = f_{max} \times \frac{\Pi_a}{D}$$

where Π_a is the average case finish time of the entire application, which is calculated as[2] $\Pi_a = \sum_p \Pi_a^p \times P_p$, where Π_a^p is the average case finish time for path p, and P_p is the probability of executing path p.

If the speculated speed falls between two speed levels ($f_l < f_{ss} < f_{l+1}$) and the speed levels are fine grained, single speed static speculation will set $f_{ss} = f_{l+1}$. But if the difference between two speed levels is large, two speeds will be speculated for the application. At the beginning, the speculation speed, f_{ss}, is set as the lower speed, f_l. After a certain time point (t_{tp}), f_{ss} is changed to the higher speed level, f_{l+1}. The value of t_{tp} can be statically computed as follows:

$$t_{tp} = \frac{f_{l+1} - f_{ss}}{f_{l+1} - f_l} \times D$$

After f_{ss} is calculated, we will execute the application at f_{ss}, but at the same time ensure that the application finishes on time. This means that we choose the maximum speed between f_{ss} and f_g^i for task T_i, where f_g^i is computed from GSS, guaranteeing temporal correctness.

It is easy to see that, when picking the speed to execute a task, because the SS algorithms never sets a speed below the speed determined by GSS, the SS algorithms will meet the timing constraints if GSS can finish on time. Therefore, from Theorem 1, the SS algorithms can meet the timing constraints if the longest path in canonical schedule under the same heuristics finishes on time.

---

[2]If path p contains OR nodes, the same formula is applied recursively.

4.2. Adaptive Speculative Algorithm

If the statistical characteristics of tasks in the application vary substantially, it may be better to speculate the speed on-the-fly based on the statistical information about the remaining tasks. Considering the speed adjustment overhead and expecting that different paths after the OR synchronization node may result in more slack, the adaptive speculative (AS) algorithm speculates the speed after each OR synchronization node based on statistical information about the remaining tasks, and sets the speculative speed as:

$$f_{as} = f_{max} \times \frac{\Pi_a^r}{D - t}$$

where t is the current time and Π_a^r can be calculated dynamically as the summation of the weighted average of the execution times of all the remaining tasks. Again, to guarantee the deadline, the speed f_i for T_i will be: $f_i = max(f_g^i, f_{as})$.

5. Evaluation and Analysis

In the simulation, we account for both the overhead and discrete speed levels. There are two kinds of overhead, the new speed computation overhead and the voltage/speed adjustment overhead. A detailed discussion about accounting for overheads and discrete speed levels can be found in [20]. The new speed computation overhead used is 300 cycles, obtained by running the code to compute the new speed on the SimpleScalar micro-architecture simulator [5]. With current technology, changing the voltage/speed needs between $5\mu s$ and $150\mu s$ [3, 15], but we expect this overhead to drop with technological advances in the near future. We assume that speed adjustment needs $5\mu s$ (the time needed to change the speed once). We assume that an idle processor consumes 5% of the maximal power level [2].

We consider an application of automated target recognition (ATR) (the dependence graph is not shown due to space limitation) and a synthetic application shown in Figure 3. In ATR, the regions of interest (ROI) in one frame are detected and each ROI is compared with all the templates. For the synthetic application, the time unit for c_i and a_i is in the order of 10^{-4} second. The loops in the graph can be expanded as discussed in Section 2. The numbers associated with each loop are the maximal number of iterations paired with the probabilities to have specific number of iterations. If there is only one number, it is the number of iterations during the execution. We vary the parameters: *load* and α to see how they affect the energy consumption for each scheme. The *load* is defined as the length of the canonical schedule for the longest path p^l over the deadline. The variability of the tasks' execution time α is defined as the average case execution time over worst case execution time for the tasks in the application, which indicates how much dynamic slack there is during tasks' execution. The

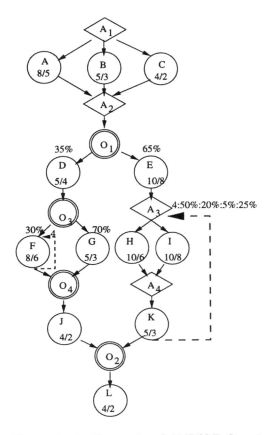

Figure 3. An Example of AND/OR Graph

value of α_i for task T_i is generated from a normal distribution around α and the actual execution time of T_i follows a normal distribution around α_i. Each point in each graph is an average of 1000 runs.

We show results for the following schemes in the graph: static power management (SPM), greedy slack sharing (GSS), static speculation with single speed (SS1), static speculation with two speeds (SS2) and adaptive speculation at each OR node (AS). The energy consumption of each scheme is normalized to the energy consumed by no power management (NPM) where every task runs at f_{max} with idle state energy set as 5% of the maximum power level.

5.1. The Effect of *Load*

When load increases, there is less static slack in the system and therefore energy consumption should increase for all the schemes (since the slowdown capability is smaller) except NPM (since it will consume less idle energy). The results in Figure 4 show the normalized energy consumption for ATR running on dual-processor systems ($\alpha \approx 0.95$, which was measured and means that there is little slack from task's run-time behavior). Note that the normalized energy consumption starts by decreasing with *load*. This is counter-

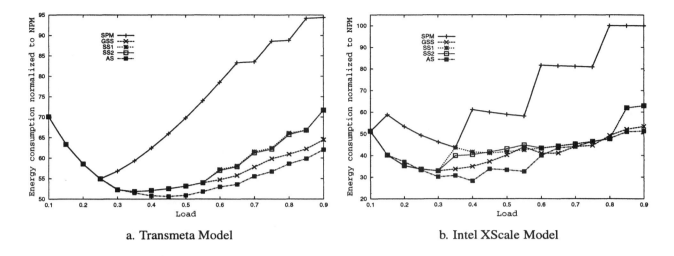

| a. Transmeta Model | b. Intel XScale Model |

Figure 4. Energy vs. *Load* **for ATR running on Dual-Processor systems;** $\alpha \approx 0.95$, *overhead* $= 5\mu s$.

intuitive since, without accounting for the idle energy, normalized energy consumption would increase proportionally with the *load* (since the slowdown capability is smaller). But, at lower *load*, the idle energy consumption has a significant effect: when the desired speed is less than f_{min}, the CPU speed is set to run at f_{min}; the normalized energy consumption curves go down with increased *load* (i.e. decrease in idle time) and starts increasing with *load* when speed is set above f_{min}. When the processors are simulated following the Intel XScale model (Figure 4b), where there are fewer speed levels but wider speed range between levels, the normalized energy for SPM incurs sharp changes. These changes correspond to the upgrade of speed from one level to the next level. For example, when *load* = 0.35, SPM runs at 400MHz and when *load* = 0.4 SPM needs to run at 600MHz (rather than 400MHz) because of speed adjustment overhead. While when *load* = 0.5, SPM still runs at 600MHz and the energy consumption decreases because of less idle energy consumed. For static speculation, when *load* changes from 0.3 to 0.35 or from 0.8 to 0.85, the normalized energy for SS1 and SS2 has a jump, the reason is that the speculative speed is upgraded from one level to the next higher level[3]. Note that the figures show the normalized energy and the energy consumption by NPM decreases with load increasing since less idle energy is consumed.

When ATR is executed on 4 or 6 processor systems, similar results are obtained with more energy consumed by each

---

[3]Note that $f_{ss} = f_{max} \times \frac{\Pi_a}{D} = f_{max} \times \frac{\Pi_a}{\Pi_c} \times \frac{\Pi_c}{D}$ and we defined *load* $= \frac{\Pi_c}{D}$, so $f_{ss} = f_{max} \times load \times \frac{\Pi_a}{\Pi_c}$. For ATR running on dual-processor system, $\frac{\Pi_a}{\Pi_c} \approx 0.48$, when *load* = 0.3 the speculative speed is 150MHz, while when *load* = 0.35 the speculative speed will increase one level and be 400MHz. It is the same for *load* change from 0.8(400MHz) to 0.85(600MHz).

scheme and more sharp changes because of the idle time forced by the scheduler between tasks for the sake of synchronization. Due to the similarity of results, we only show in Figure 5 the results for 6 processors.

We expected the speculative schemes to perform better than the greedy scheme. The reason is that, typically, the greedy behavior tends to run at the least possible speed to use up all the slack for the current task, and consequently the future tasks must run at very high speed [1, 20]. However, the minimum speed is bounded by f_{min}, preventing the greedy scheme from using all the available slack at the very beginning and forcing some slack to be saved for future use. Fewer speed levels also prevents the greedy scheme from using the slack by decreasing the probability of speed changes. As a result, the greedy scheme benefits from the presence of f_{min} and speed levels. The greedy scheme is better than some speculative algorithms when f_{min} is rather high or there are fewer speed levels.

To see how f_{min} and the speed levels affects the performance of the schemes on energy savings, in our future work we plan to experiment with different values of $\frac{f_{max}}{f_{min}}$ and different number of speed levels between f_{max} and f_{min}.

5.2. The Effect of α

For the synthetic application running on a dual-processor system with *load* set at 0.8 and *overhead* at $5\mu s$, when changing α, the normalized energy consumed by each scheme is shown in Figure 6. Since both changing *load* and α have the same effect on the available slack in the system, the shapes of the curves for dynamic schemes are similar to when *load* was changed (the curves for SPM are quite different since SPM can only use static slack that related to *load* only). Notice that, for the Intel XScale model, with *load* = 0.8, SPM runs

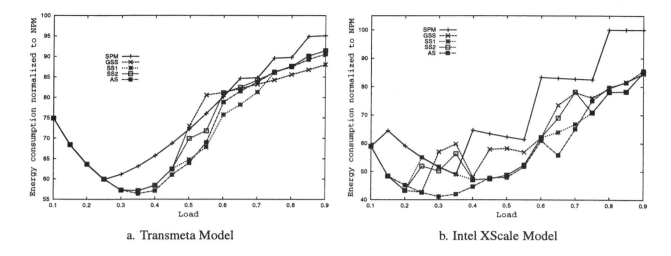

a. Transmeta Model

b. Intel XScale Model

Figure 5. Energy vs. *Load* for ATR running on 6-Processor systems; $\alpha \approx 0.95$, overhead=5μs.

at $f_{max} = 1GHz$ rather than $800MHz$ and consumes the same energy as NPM since SPM does not take into account the actual execution time behavior.

6. Conclusion

In this paper, we extend the AND/OR model by adding probabilities to each execution path after each OR node. This extended model can be used for applications, where a task is ready to execute when one *or more* of its predecessors finish execution and one *or more* of its successors will be ready after the task finishes execution. With the extended AND/OR model, we modify the greedy slack sharing algorithm for dependent tasks on multi-processor systems developed in [20]. Then, using statistical information about the application, we proposed a few variations of speculative algorithms that intend to save more energy by reducing the number of speed change (and thus the overhead) while ensuring that the application meet the timing constraints.

The performance of all the algorithms in terms of energy savings is analyzed through simulations. The greedy algorithm is surprisingly better than some speculative algorithms. The reasons come from two points: one is the minimal speed limitation that prevents the greedy algorithm from using up the slack very aggressively; the other is fewer speed levels that prevents the greedy algorithm from changing the speed frequently. The greedy scheme is good enough when the system has a reasonable minimal speed. The energy consumption for all the power management schemes decreases unexpectedly when the *load* increases at low *load* because of the minimal speed limitation and the idle energy consumption. The dynamic schemes become worse relative to static power management (SPM) when *load* becomes higher and α becomes larger,

since most of the slack will be used to cover the speed adjustment overhead. All the dynamic algorithms perform the best with moderate *load* and α. When the number of processors increases, the performance of the dynamic schemes decreases due to the limited parallelism and the frequent idleness of the processors.

References

[1] N. AbouGhazaleh, D. Mossé, B. Childers and R. Melhem. Toward the Placement of Power Management Points in Real Time Applications. *Workshop on Compilers and Operating Systems for Low Power (COLP)*, Barcelona, Spain, 2001.

[2] H. Aydin, R. Melhem, D. Mossé and P. M. Alvarez. Dynamic and Aggressive Scheduling Techniques for Power-Aware Real-Time Systems. *Proc. of the 22th IEEE Real-Time Systems Symposium*, London, UK, Dec. 2001.

[3] T. D. Burd, T. A. Pering, A. J. Stratakos and R. W. Brodersen. A Dynamic Voltage Scaled Microprocessor System, *IEEE Journal of Solid-State Circuits*, vol.35, no.11, Nov. 2000.

[4] T. D. Burd and R. W. Brodersen. Energy Efficient CMOS Microprocessor Design. *Proc. HICSS Conference*, pp. 288-297, Maui, Hawaii, January 1995.

[5] D. Burger and T. M. Austin. The SimpleScalar Tool Set, version 2.0. Tech. Report 1342, Computer Science Department, University of Wisconsin-Madison, Jun. 1997.

[6] A. Chandrakasan, V. Gutnik and T. Xanthopoulos. Data Driven Signal Processing: An Approach for Energy Ef-

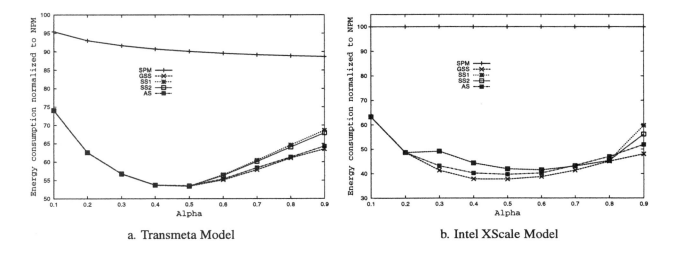

a. Transmeta Model   b. Intel XScale Model

Figure 6. Energy vs. α for the synthetic application of running on 2-Processor systems; $load = 0.8$, $overhead = 5\mu s$.

ficient Computing, *Proc. Int'lSymp. Low-Power Electronic Devicess*, Monterey, CA 1996.

[7] A. Chandrakasan, S. Sheng and R. Brodersen. Low-power CMOS Digital Design. *IEEE Journal of Solid-state circuit*, pp. 473-484, April 1992.

[8] M. L. Dertouzos and A. K. Mok. Multiprocessor on-line scheduling of hard-real-time tasks. *IEEE Trans. On Software Engineering*, SE-15 (12): 1497-1505, 1989.

[9] R. Ernst and W. Ye. Embedded Program Timing Analysis based on Path Clustering and Architecture Classification. *In Computer-Aided Design (ICCAD)97*. pp. 58-604. San Jose, CA, November 1997.

[10] D. W. Gillies and W.-S. Liu, Scheduling Tasks With AND/OR Precedence Constraints. *SIAM J. Compu.*, 24(4): 797-810, 1995.

[11] F. Gruian. System-Level Design Methods for Low-Energy Architectures Containing Variable Voltage Processors. *The Power-Aware Computing Systems 2000 Workshop at ASPLOS 2000*, Cambridge, MA, November 2000.

[12] P. Kumar and M. Srivastava, Predictive Strategies for Low-Power RTOS Scheduling, *Proceedings of the 2000 IEEE International Conference on Computer Design: VLSI in Computers and Processors*

[13] R. Melhem, N. AbouGhazaleh, H. Aydin and D. Mossé. Power Management Points in Power-Aware Real-Time Systems. In *Power Aware Computing*, Ed. by R.Graybill and R.Melhem, Plenum/Kluwer Publishers, 2002.

[14] D. Mossé, H. Aydin, B. Childers and R. Melhem. Compiler-Assisted Dynamic Power-Aware Scheduling for Real-Time Applications, *Workshop on Compiler and OS for Low Power*, Philadelphia , PA, October 2000

[15] P. Pillai and K. G. Shin. Real-Time Dynamic Voltage Scaling for Low-Power Embedded Operating Systems, 18th *ACM Symposium on Operating Systems Principles (SOSP'01)*, Banff, Canada, Oct. 2001

[16] D. Shin, J. Kim and S. Lee, Intra-Task Voltage Scheduling for Low-Energy Hard Real-Time Applications, *IEEE Design and Test of Computers*, March 2001.

[17] P. Yang, C. Wong, P. Marchal, F. Catthoor, D. Desmet, D. Kerkest and R. Lauwereins. Energy-Aware Runtime Scheduling for Embedded-Multiprocessor SOCs, *IEEE Design and Test of Computers*, vol. 18, no. 5, Sep. 2001.

[18] http://www.transmeta.com

[19] http://developer.intel.com/design/intelxscale/

[20] D. Zhu, R. Melhem and B. Childers. Scheduling with Dynamic Voltage/Speed Adjustment Using Slack Reclamation in Multi-Processor Real-Time Systems. *Submitted to IEEE Trans. on Parallel and Distributed Systems*, Nov. 2001. *A preliminary version appeared in the 22th IEEE Real-Time System Symposium, 2001.*

Selective Preemption Strategies for Parallel Job Scheduling*

Rajkumar Kettimuthu   Vijay Subramani   Srividya Srinivasan   Thiagaraja Gopalasamy

D. K. Panda   P. Sadayappan

Department of Computer and Information Science
The Ohio State University
{*kettimut,subraman,srinivas,gopalsam,panda,saday*}@*cis.ohio-state.edu*

Abstract

Although theoretical results have been established regarding the utility of pre-emptive scheduling in reducing average job turn-around time, job suspension/restart is not much used in practice at supercomputer centers for parallel job scheduling. A number of questions remain unanswered regarding the practical utility of pre-emptive scheduling. We explore this issue through a simulation-based study, using job logs from a supercomputer center. We develop a tunable selective-suspension strategy, and demonstrate its effectiveness. We also present new insights into the effect of pre-emptive scheduling on different job classes and address the impact of suspensions on worst-case slowdown.

1 Introduction

Although theoretical results on the effect of pre-emptive scheduling strategies in reducing average job turn-around time have been well established, pre-emptive scheduling is not currently being used for scheduling parallel jobs at supercomputer centers. Compared to the large number of studies that have investigated non-preemptive scheduling of parallel jobs, little research has been reported on empirical evaluation of preemptive scheduling strategies using real job logs [1, 2, 7, 10].

The basic idea behind preemptive scheduling is simple: if a long running job is temporarily suspended and a waiting short job is allowed to run to completion first, the wait time of the short job is significantly decreased, without much fractional increase in the turn-around time of the long job. Consider a long job with runtime T_l. If after time t, a short job arrives with runtime T_s. If the short job were run after completion of the long job, the average job turnaround time would be $\frac{(T_l+(T_l+T_s-t))}{2}$, or $T_l + \frac{(T_s-t)}{2}$. Instead, if the long job were suspended when the short job arrived, the turnaround times of the short and long jobs would be T_s and $(T_s + T_l)$ respectively, giving an average of $T_s + \frac{T_l}{2}$. The average turnaround time with suspension is less if $T_s < T_l - t$, i.e. the remaining runtime of the running job is greater than the runtime of the waiting job.

However, the use of a suspension criterion based simply on comparison of the remaining runtimes of jobs might result in starvation. It is desirable that the suspension strategy bring down the average slowdown without increasing the worst case slowdowns. Even though theoretical results have established that preemption improves the average turnaround time, it is important to perform evaluations of preemptive scheduling schemes using realistic job mixes derived from actual job logs from supercomputer centers, to understand the effect of suspension on various categories of jobs. The primary contributions of this paper are:

- The development of a selective-suspension strategy for pre-emptive scheduling of parallel jobs

- Characterization of the significant variability in the average job slowdown for different job categories

- The study of the impact of suspension on the worst case slowdowns of various categories and development of a tunable scheme to improve worst case slowdowns.

We study the effect of preemption on the performance of various categories of jobs using a locally developed backfill scheduler. The rest of the paper is organized follows. Section 2 presents some basic background on scheduling of parallel jobs. Section 3 discusses the workload characterization. In Section 4, a basic preemptive scheduling scheme is proposed and evaluated. In Section 5, the effect of the preemption scheme on the worst case slowdowns is analyzed and a tunable scheme is proposed and evaluated. In Section 6, the proposed preemption schemes are evaluated under conditions where user estimates of runtime are inaccurate. In Section 7, we evaluate the impact of job-suspension overheads on pre-emptive scheduling. Section 8 presents our conclusions.

2 Background and Related Work

Scheduling is usually viewed in terms of a 2D chart with time along one axis and the number of processors along the other. Each job can be thought of as a rectangle whose height is the user estimated run time and width is the number of processors required. The simplest way to schedule

---
*Supported in part by a grant from Sandia Laboratories

jobs is to use the First-Come-First-Served (FCFS) policy. This approach suffers from low system utilization. Back-filling [8, 9] was proposed to improve the system utilization and has been implemented in most production schedulers [6, 13]. Backfilling works by identifying "holes" in the 2D chart and moving forward smaller jobs that fit those holes. There are two common variations to backfilling - conservative and aggressive. In conservative backfilling, a smaller job is moved forward in the queue as long as it does not delay any previously queued job. In aggressive backfilling, a small job is allowed to leap forward as long as it does not delay the job at the head of the queue.

Some of the common metrics used to evaluate the performance of scheduling schemes are the average turnaround time and the average bounded slowdown. We use the bounded slowdown for our studies. The bounded slowdown of a job is defined as follows:

$$\text{Bounded Slowdown} = \frac{(Waittime + Max(Runtime, 10))}{Max(Runtime, 10)}$$

The threshold of 10 seconds is used to limit the influence of very short jobs on the metric.

Pre-emptive scheduling aims at providing lower delay to short jobs relative to long jobs. Since long jobs have greater tolerance to delays as compared to short jobs, our suspension criterion is based on the eXpansion Factor (XFactor), which increases rapidly for short jobs and gradually for long jobs.

$$\text{XFactor} = \frac{(Waittime + EstimatedRunTime)}{EstimatedRunTime}$$

Although pre-emptive scheduling is universally used at the operating system level to multiplex processes on single-processor systems and shared-memory multi-processors, it is rarely used in parallel job scheduling. A large number of studies have addressed the problem of parallel job scheduling (see [5] for a survey of work on this topic), but most of them address non-preemptive scheduling strategies. Further, most of the work on pre-emptive scheduling of parallel jobs considers the jobs to be malleable [3, 10, 12, 14], i.e. the number of processors used to execute the job is permitted to vary dynamically over time.

In practice, parallel jobs submitted to supercomputer centers are generally rigid, i.e. the number of processors used to execute a job is fixed. Under this scenario, the various schemes proposed for a malleable job model are inapplicable. We address pre-emptive scheduling under a model of rigid jobs, where the pre-emption is "local", i.e. the suspended job must be re-started on exactly the same set of processors on which they were suspended.

In a recent study [2], a pre-emptive scheduling strategy called the "Immediate Service (IS)" scheme was evaluated for shared-memory systems. With this scheme, each arriving job was given an immediate time-slice of 10 minutes, by suspending one or more running jobs if needed. The selection of jobs for suspension was based on their instantaneous-XFactor, defined as (wait time + total accumulated run time)/ (total accumulated run time). Jobs with the lowest instantaneous-XFactor were suspended. The IS strategy was shown to significantly decrease the average job slowdown for the traces simulated. A potential short-coming of the IS scheme is that its preemption decisions are not in any way reflective of the expected runtime of a job. The IS scheme can be expected to provide significant improvement to the slowdown of aborted jobs in the

trace. So it is unclear how much, if any, of the improvement in slowdown was experienced by the jobs that completed normally - however, no information was provided on how different job categories were affected. Chiang et al [1] examine the run-to-completion policy with a suspension policy that allows a job to be suspended at most once. Both these approaches limit the number of suspensions while we use a more selective approach to control the rate of suspensions, without limiting the number of times a job can be suspended. In [10], the design and implementation of a number of multiprocessor preemptive scheduling disciplines are discussed. They study the effect of preemption under the models of rigid, migratable and malleable jobs. They conclude that the preemption scheme that they propose may increase the response time for the model of rigid jobs.

So far, very few simulation based studies have been done on preemption strategies for clusters. If process migration is not allowed (due to the significant practical complications it entails), preemptive scheduling on distributed memory systems imposes an additional constraint that the suspended jobs should be restarted on the same set of physical processors. In this paper we propose tunable suspension strategies for parallel job scheduling in environments where process migration is not feasible.

3 Workload Characterization

From the collection of workload logs available from Feitelson's archive [4], the CTC workload trace was used to evaluate the proposed schemes. This trace was generated by a 430 processors system. In order to reduce the time taken to run the set of simulations, a contiguous 5000 job subset of the trace was used (corresponding to roughly one month's jobs).

Under normal load, with the standard non-preemptive aggressive backfilling strategy, using FCFS as the scheduling priority, the utilization was 51 percent. Although it is known that user estimates are quite inaccurate in practice, as explained above, we first studied the effect of preemptive scheduling under the idealized assumption of exact estimation, before studying the effect of inaccuracies in user estimates of job run time. Also, we first studied the impact of pre-emption under the assumption that the overhead for the suspension and restart is negligible and then studied the influence of the overhead.

3.1 Job Classification

Any analysis that is based on the aggregate slowdown of the system as a whole does not provide insights into the variability within different job categories. Therefore in our discussion, we classify the jobs into various categories based on the runtime and the number of processors requested, and analyze the slowdown for each category.

To analyze the performance of jobs of different sizes and lengths, jobs were classified into 16 categories: four categories based on their run time - Very Short(VS), Short(S), Long(L) and Very Long(VL) and four categories based on the number of processors requested - Sequential(Seq), Narrow(N), Wide(W) and Very Wide(VW). The criteria used for job classification are shown in Table 1. Table 2 shows the percentage of jobs in the trace, corresponding to the sixteen categories.

Job Categorization Criteria

	1 Proc	2-8Procs	9-32Procs	>32 Procs
0-10min	VS Seq	VS N	VS W	VS VW
10min-1hr	S Seq	S N	S W	S VW
1hr-8hr	L Seq	L N	L W	L VW
>8hr	VL Seq	VL N	VL W	VL VW

Table 1. Categorization of jobs based on their runtime and width.

Job Percentage

	1 Proc	2-8 Procs	9-32 Procs	>32 Procs
0-10min	14	8	13	9
10min-1hr	18	4	6	2
1hr-8hr	6	3	9	2
>8hr	2	2	1	1

Table 2. Category based job distribution.

Average Slowdown for Non Preemptive Scheduling

	1 Proc	2-8 Procs	9-32 Procs	>32 Procs
0-10min	2.6	4.76	13.01	34.07
10min-1hr	1.26	1.76	3.04	7.14
1hr-8hr	1.13	1.43	1.88	1.63
>8hr	1.03	1.05	1.09	1.15

Table 3. Average slowdown for various categories with non preemptive scheduling.

Table 3 shows the average slowdowns for the different job categories under a non-preemptive aggressive backfilling strategy. The overall slowdown was 3.58. Even though the overall slowdown is low, from the table it can be observed that one of the Very Short categories has average slowdown as high as 34. Preemptive strategies can be effective in reducing the high average slowdowns for the short categories, without significant degradation for long jobs.

4 Selective Suspension

We first propose a preemptive scheduling scheme, called the Selective Suspension (SS) scheme, where an idle job can preempt a running job if its suspension threshold is sufficiently higher than that of the running job. An idle job attempts to suspend a collection of running jobs so as to obtain enough free processors. In order to control the rate of suspensions, a suspension factor (SF) is used. This specifies the minimum ratio of the suspension threshold of a candidate idle job to the suspension threshold of a running job for preemption to occur. The suspension threshold used is the XFactor of the job.

4.1 Theoretical Analysis

Let T_1 and T_2 be two tasks submitted to the scheduler at the same time. Both tasks are of same length and require the entire system for execution and the system is free when the two tasks are submitted. Let 's' be the suspension factor. Before starting, both tasks have a suspension threshold of 1. The suspension threshold of a task remains constant when the task executes and increases when the task waits. One of the two tasks, say T_1, will be started instantaneously. The other task, say T_2, waits until its suspension threshold τ_2 becomes 's' times the threshold of T_1 before it can preempt T_1. Now T_1 waits until its suspension threshold τ_1 becomes 's' times τ_2 before it can preempt T_2. This occurs repeatedly. The optimal value for SF to restrict the number of repeated suspensions by two similar tasks arriving at the same time can be obtained as follows:

Let τ_w represent the suspension threshold of the waiting job and τ_r represent the suspension threshold of the running job.

Condition for the first suspension: $\tau_w = s$

The preemption swaps the running job and the waiting job. So after the preemption, $\tau_w = 1$ and $\tau_r = s$.

Condition for second suspension: $\tau_w = s * \tau_r$ i.e. $\tau_w = s^2$

Similarly, the condition for n^{th} suspension is $\tau_w = s^n$.

The lowest value of s for which at most n suspensions occur is given by,

$\tau_w = s^{n+1}$, when the running job completes.

When the running job completes,

$\tau_w = \frac{waittime+runtime}{runtime}$ i.e $\tau_w = 2$; since the wait time of the waiting job equals the run time of the running job

$s^{n+1} = 2$, i.e. $s = 2^{\frac{1}{n+1}}$

Thus, if the number of suspensions has to be 0, then s = 2. For at most 1 suspension, we get s as $\sqrt{2}$. With s=1, the number of suspensions is very large, only bounded by the granularity of the preemption routine. With all jobs having equal length, any suspension factor greater than 2 will not result in any suspension and will be same as the suspension factor 2. However, with jobs of varying length, the number of suspensions reduces with higher suspension factors. Thus, in order to avoid thrashing and to reduce the number of suspensions, we use different suspension factors between 1.5 and 5 in evaluating our schemes.

4.2 Preventing Starvation without Reservation Guarantees

An idle job can preempt a running job only if its suspension threshold is at least SF times greater than the threshold of the running job. All the idle jobs that are able to find the required number of processors by suspending lower threshold running jobs are selected for execution by preempting the corresponding jobs. All backfill scheduling schemes use job reservations for one or more jobs at the head of the idle queue as a means of guaranteeing finite progress, thereby assuring freedom from starvation. But the start time guarantees do not make much sense in the presence of preemption. Even if start time guarantees are given to the jobs in the idle queue, they are not guaranteed to run to completion since they can be suspended. However, because the SS strategy uses the expected slowdown as the suspension threshold, there is an automatic guarantee of freedom from starvation - ultimately any job's expected slowdown factor will get large enough that it will be able to preempt some running job and begin execution. Therefore, it is possible to run the backfill algorithm without the usual reservation guarantees. So, we remove the guarantees for all our preemption schemes, since the absence of reservations in the schedule facilitates better backfilling.

Further, jobs in some categories inherently have a higher probability of waiting longer in the queue than a job with comparable XFactor from another job category. For example, consider a VW job needing 300 processors, and a Seq job in the queue at the same time. If both jobs have the same XFactor, the probability that the Seq job finds a running job to suspend is higher than the probability that the VW job finds enough lower threshold running jobs to suspend. Therefore, the average slowdown of the VW category will tend to be higher than the Seq category. To redress this inequity, we impose a restriction that the number of processors requested by a suspending job should be at least half of the number of nodes requested by the job that it suspends, thereby preventing the wide jobs from being suspended by the narrow jobs. The scheduler periodically (once every minute) invokes the preemption routine.

4.3 Algorithm

Let τ_i be the suspension threshold for a task T_i which requests n_i processors. Let N_i represent the set of processors allocated to T_i. Let F_t represent the set of free processors and f_t represent the number of free processors at time 't' when the preemption is attempted.

Let candidates(T_i) represent the set of tasks that can be preempted by task T_i.

candidates(T_i) = { $T_j : \tau_i > $ SF $* \tau_j$ and $\frac{n_j}{n_i} < 2$ }

T_i can be scheduled by preempting one or more tasks in candidates(T_i) if and only if

$n_i \leq (\Sigma n_j + f_t) \, \forall T_j \, \epsilon$ candidates(T_i)

If T_i is itself a previously suspended task attempting reentry, the processor restriction also applies. So the above condition becomes:

candidates(T_i) = { $T_j : \tau_i >$SF$*\tau_j$ and $\frac{n_j}{n_i}<2$ and $N_i \cap N_j \neq \emptyset$ }

T_i can be scheduled by preempting one or more tasks in candidates(T_i) if and only if

$n_i \leq (\Sigma n_j + f_t) \, \forall T_j \, \epsilon$ candidates(T_i)

and

$N_i \subseteq (F_t \cup N_j \, \forall T_j \, \epsilon$ candidates(T_i))

For both of the above scenarios, T_i preempts tasks in candidates(T_i) as given by the following condition:

The set of tasks suspended by T_i is

P = { T_j:$T_j \, \epsilon$ candidates(T_i) and $n_i \leq f_t + \Sigma n_j$ } and (f_t +($\Sigma n_k \, \forall T_k \, \epsilon$ P) - ($n_m : T_m \, \epsilon$ P)) $< n_i$

In essence, the algorithm sorts the list of running jobs in ascending order of the suspension threshold and the list of idle jobs in descending order of suspension threshold. Then for each idle job, a minimal set of running jobs which satisfy the following conditions are chosen for suspension.

- The number of processors used by the running job is less than twice the number of processors requested by the idle job.

- The suspension threshold of the idle job is at least SF times the suspension threshold of the running job.

- The sum of processors of all the running jobs in the minimal set, together with the number of free processors in the system at that instant is greater than or equal to the number of processors requested by the idle job.

4.4 Results

We compare the SS scheme run under various suspension factors with the No-Suspension(NS) scheme with aggressive Backfilling and the IS scheme. From Figure 1, we can see that the SS scheme provides significant improvement for the Very-Short(VS) and Short(S) length categories and Wide(W) and Very-Wide(VW) width categories. For example, for the VS-VW category, slowdown is reduced from 34 for the NS scheme to under 3 for SS with SF=2. For VS and S length categories, lower SF results in lower slowdown. This is because a lower SF increases the probability that a job in these categories will suspend a job in the Long(L) or Very-Long(VL) category. The same is also true for the L length category, but the effect of change in SF is less pronounced. For the VL length category, there is an opposite trend with decreasing SF, i.e. the slowdown increases. This is due to the increasing probability that a Long job will be suspended by a job in a shorter category as SF decreases. In comparison to the base No-Suspension(NS) scheme, the SS scheme provides significant benefits for VS and S categories, a slight improvement for most of the Long categories, but is slightly worse for the VL categories.

The performance of the IS scheme is very good for the VS category. It is better than the SS scheme for the VS length category and worse for the other categories. Even though the overall slowdown for IS (2.06) is considerably less than the No-Suspension scheme (3.58), it is not better than SS (1.69 for SF=2). Moreover, in IS the VW and VL categories get significantly worse.

5   Tunable Selective Suspension (TSS)

From the graphs of the previous section, it can be observed that the SS scheme significantly improves the average slowdown of various job categories. But from a practical point of view, the worst case slowdowns are very important. A scheme that improves the average case slowdowns for most of the categories, but makes the worst case slowdown for the long categories worse, is not a desirable scheme. For example, a delay of 1 hour for a 10 minute job (slowdown = 7) is tolerable whereas a slowdown of 7 for a 24 hour job is unacceptable.

In Figure 2, we compare the worst case slowdowns for SF=2 with the worst case slowdowns of the NS scheme and the IS scheme. It can be observed that the worst case slowdown for the SS scheme is much better than the NS scheme for most of the cases. But the worst case slowdown for some of the long categories is higher than the NS scheme. Even though the worst case slowdown for SS is less than that of NS, the worst case slowdowns are much higher than the corresponding category averages for some of the short categories. For the IS scheme, the worst case slowdown for the very short categories is lower but much higher for the long categories, which is highly undesirable. We next propose a tunable scheme to improve the worst case slowdowns without losing the improvement in the average slowdowns. This is done by controlling the variance

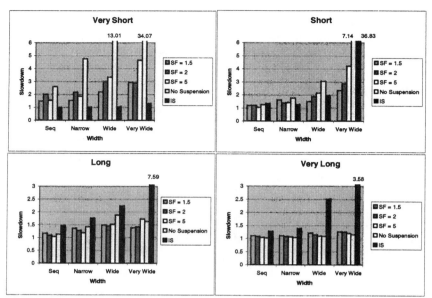

Figure 1. Comparison of the average slowdown of the SS scheme with the NS and IS schemes. Compared to NS, SS provides significant benefit for the VS, S, W and VW categories, slight improvement for most of L categories, but a slight deterioration for the VL categories. Compared to IS, SS performs better for all the categories except for the VS categories.

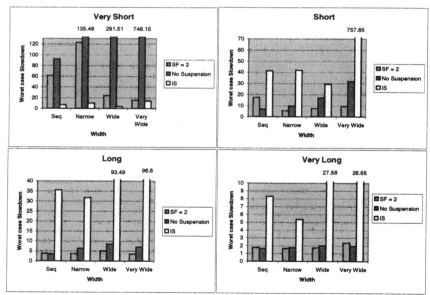

Figure 2. Comparison of the worstcase slowdowns of the SS scheme with the NS and IS schemes. SS is much better than NS for most of the categories and is slightly worse for some of the VL categories. Compared to IS, SS is much better for all the categories except for the VS categories.

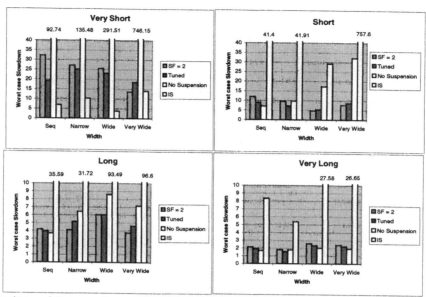

Figure 3. Comparison of the worstcase slowdowns of the TSS scheme with SS, NS and IS schemes. TSS improves the worstcase slowdown for the VL categories and some of the S categories without affecting the other categories.

in the slowdowns by associating a limit with each job. Preemption of a job is disabled when its threshold exceeds this limit. This limit is set to 1.5 times the average slowdown of the category that the job belongs to.

5.1 Control of Variance

Task T_i preempts tasks in candidates(T_i) as given by the following condition:

The set of tasks suspended by T_i is

P = { T_j:$T_j \epsilon$candidates(T_i) and $n_i \leq f_t + \Sigma n_j$ and $\tau_j \leq 1.5$ $*SD_{avg}$(category(T_j))} and $(f_t + (\Sigma n_k \ \forall T_k \ \epsilon \ P) - (n_m :$ $T_m \ \epsilon \ P)) < n_i$

where SD_{avg}(category(T_j)) represents the average slowdown in the SS scheme for the job category to which T_j belongs.

5.2 Results

Figure 3 shows the results for the tunable suspension scheme. It improves the worst case slowdowns for some long categories (VL W, VL VW, L N) and some short categories (VS Seq, VS N, S Seq) without affecting the worst case slowdowns of the other categories. This scheme can also be applied to selectively tune the slowdowns for particular categories.

6 Inaccurate User Estimates

We have so far assumed that the user estimates of job runtime are perfect. Now, we consider the effect of user estimate inaccuracy on the proposed schemes. This is desirable from the point of view of realistic modeling of an actual system workload. In practice, the scheduler only has information about the job wall-clock limit specified by the user, and not the actual execution time. Hence it is important to carry out simulations where the scheduler bases its decisions on the user specified wall-clock limit, which

can often be quite inaccurate. Most simulation based studies on job scheduling have done this, but we believe that there is a problem that has not been recognized by previous studies. Abnormally aborted jobs tend to excessively skew the average slowdown of jobs in a workload. Consider a job requesting a wall-clock limit of 24 hours, that is queued for 1 hour, and then aborts within one minute due to some fatal exception. The slowdown of this job would be computed to be 60, whereas the average slowdown of normally completing long jobs is typically under 2. If even 5% of the jobs have a high slowdown of 60, while 95% of the normally completing jobs have a slowdown of 2, the average slowdown over all jobs would be around 5. Now consider a scheme such as the speculative backfilling strategy evaluated in [11]. With this scheme, a job is given a free time slot to execute in, even if that slot is considerably smaller than the requested wall-clock limit. Aborting jobs will quickly terminate, and since they did not have to be queued till an adequately long window was available, their slowdown would decrease dramatically with the speculative backfilling scheme. As a result, the average slowdown of the entire trace would now be close to 2, assuming that the slowdown of the normally completing jobs does not change significantly. A comparison of the average slowdowns would seem to indicate that the speculative backfill scheme results in a significant improvement in job slowdown from 5 to 2. However, under the above scenario, the change is only due to the small fraction of aborted jobs, and not due to any benefits to the normal jobs. In order to avoid this problem, we group the jobs into two different estimation categories. The jobs that are well estimated (the estimated time is not more than twice the actual runtime of that job) and badly estimated jobs (the estimated runtime

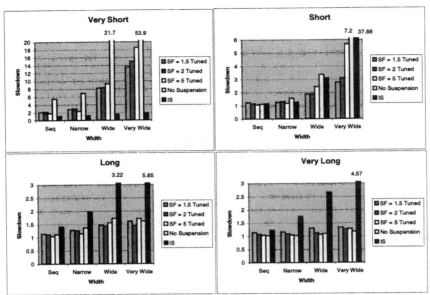

Figure 4. Comparison of the average slowdown of the TSS scheme with NS and IS Schemes with inaccurate user estimates of runtime. The trends are similar to that of the accurate user estimates case.

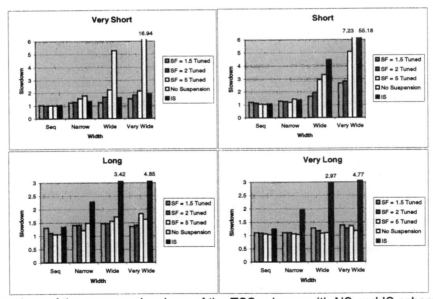

Figure 5. Comparison of the average slowdown of the TSS scheme with NS and IS schemes for the well-estimated Jobs. The trends are similar to that of the accurate user estimate case for the S, L and VL categories. The performance of the SS scheme for the VS categories is better or comparable to that of the IS scheme.

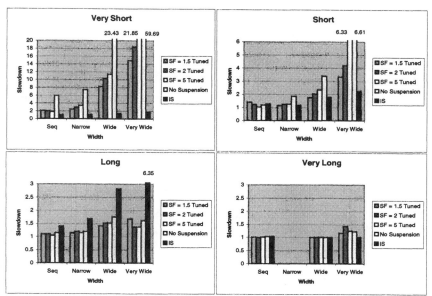

Figure 6. Comparison of the average slowdown of the TSS scheme with NS and IS schemes for the poorly-estimated Jobs. The trends are similar to that of the accurate user estimate case for the S, L and VL categories. The SS scheme tends to penalize very poorly estimated jobs that belong to the VS category.

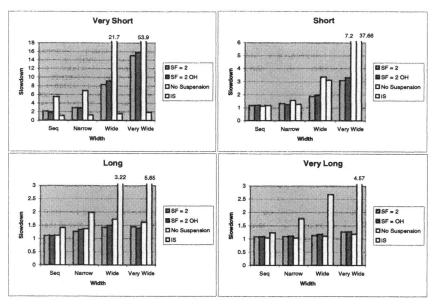

Figure 7. Comparison of the average slowdown of the TSS scheme with IS and NS schemes, with modeling of overhead for suspending/restarting a job. The performance of the TSS scheme in the presence of overhead is comparable to its performance in the absence of overhead.

is more than twice the actual runtime). Within each group, the jobs are further classified into the 16 categories based on their actual run time and the number of processors requested.

It can be observed from Figure 4 that the Selective Suspension scheme improves the slowdowns for most of the categories without affecting the other categories. The slowdowns for the short and wide categories are quite high compared to the other categories and this is mainly because of the over estimation. Since the suspension threshold used by the SS scheme is XFactor, it favors the short jobs. But if a short job was badly estimated, it would be treated as a long job and its suspension threshold would increase only gradually. So it would not be able to suspend running jobs easily and therefore end up with a large slowdown. This does not happen with IS because of the 10 minute time quantum for each arriving job, irrespective of the estimated run time. Therefore, the slowdowns for the very short category (whose length is less than or equal to 10 minutes) are lower with IS than other schemes. However, for the other categories, SS performs much better than IS.

In Figures 5 and 6, the performance data for the various job categories is shown separately for the well estimated jobs and the poorly estimated jobs. It is evident that the higher slowdowns for the VS categories in SS is due to the poorly estimated jobs. It can also be observed that, for the well estimated jobs, SS is comparable to IS for the VS categories and SS outperforms IS for all other categories.

7 Modeling of Job Suspension Overhead

We have so far assumed no overhead for pre-emption of jobs. In this section, we report on simulation results that incorporate overheads for job suspension. Since the job trace did not have information about job memory requirements, we considered the memory requirement of jobs to be random and uniformly distributed between 100MB and 1GB. The overhead for suspension is calculated as the time taken to write the main memory used by the job to the disk. The memory transfer rate that we considered is based on the following scenario: With a commodity local disk for every node, with each node being a quad, the transfer rate per processor was assumed to be only 2 MBps.

Figure 7 compares the slowdowns of the proposed tunable scheme with NS and IS in the presence of overhead for the suspension/restart. It can be observed that overhead does not significantly affect the performance of the Tunable Suspension Scheme.

8 Conclusions

In this paper, we have explored the issue of pre-emptive scheduling of parallel jobs, using a job trace from a supercomputer center. We have proposed a tunable, selective suspension scheme and demonstrated that it provides significant improvement in the average slowdown and the worst case slowdowns of most job categories. It was also shown to provide better slowdown for most job categories over a previously proposed Immediate Service scheme. We also modeled the effect of overheads for job suspension, showing that the proposed scheme provides significant benefits over non-preemptive scheduling and the Immediate Service strategy. We also evaluated the proposed schemes in the presence of over estimations and showed that it produced good results.

Acknowledgments

We would like to thank the anonymous referees for their helpful suggestions on improving the presentation of the paper.

References

[1] S. H. Chiang, R. K. Mansharamani, and M. K. Vernon. Use of application characteristics and limited preemption for run-to-completion parallel processor scheduling policies. In *ACM SIGMETRICS Conference on Measurement and Modeling of Computer Systems*, pages 33–44, 1994.

[2] S. H. Chiang and M. K. Vernon. Production job scheduling for parallel shared memory systems. In *Proceedings of International Parallel and Distributed Processing Symposium*, 2002.

[3] X. Deng, N. Gu, T. Brecht, and K. Lu. Preemptive scheduling of parallel jobs on multiprocessors. In *SODA: ACM-SIAM Symposium on Discrete Algorithms*, 1996.

[4] D. G. Feitelson. Logs of real parallel workloads from production systems. URL: http://www.cs.huji.ac.il/labs/parallel/workload/logs.html.

[5] D. G. Feitelson, L. Rudolph, U. Schwiegelshohn, K. C. Sevcik, and P. Wong. Theory and practice in parallel job scheduling. In D. G. Feitelson and L. Rudolph, editors, *Job Scheduling Strategies for Parallel Processing*, pages 1–34. Springer Verlag, 1997. Lect. Notes Comput. Sci. vol. 1291.

[6] D. Jackson, Q. Snell, and M. Clement. Core algorithms of the Maui scheduler. In D. G. Feitelson and L. Rudolph, editors, *Job Scheduling Strategies for Parallel Processing*, pages 87–102. Springer Verlag, 2001. Lect. Notes Comput. Sci. vol. 2221.

[7] L. T. Leutenneger and M. K. Vernon. The performance of multiprogrammed multiprocessor scheduling policies. In *ACM SIGMETRICS Conference on Measurement and Modelling of Computer Systems*, pages 226–236, May 1990.

[8] D. Lifka. The ANL/IBM SP scheduling system. In D. G. Feitelson and L. Rudolph, editors, *Job Scheduling Strategies for Parallel Processing*, pages 295–303. Springer-Verlag, 1995. Lect. Notes Comput. Sci. vol. 949.

[9] A. W. Mu'alem and D. G. Feitelson. Utilization, predictability, workloads, and user runtime estimates in scheduling the ibm sp2 with backfilling. In *IEEE Transactions on Parallel and Distributed Systems*, volume 12, pages 529–543, 2001.

[10] E. W. Parsons and K. C. Sevcik. Implementing multiprocessor scheduling disciplines. In D. G. Feitelson and L. Rudolph, editors, *Job Scheduling Strategies for Parallel Processing*, pages 166–192. Springer Verlag, 1997. Lect. Notes Comput. Sci. vol. 1291.

[11] D. Perkovic and P. J. Keleher. Randomization, speculation, and adaptation in batch schedulers. *Cluster Computing*, 3(4):245–254, 2000.

[12] K. C. Sevcik. Application scheduling and processor allocation in multiprogrammed parallel processing systems. *Performance Evaluation*, 19(2-3):107–140, 1994.

[13] J. Skovira, W. Chan, H. Zhou, and D. Lifka. The EASY - LoadLeveler API project. In D. G. Feitelson and L. Rudolph, editors, *Job Scheduling Strategies for Parallel Processing*, pages 41–47. Springer-Verlag, 1996. Lect. Notes Comput. Sci. vol. 1162.

[14] J. Zahorjan and C. McCann. Processor scheduling in shared memory multiprocessors. In *ACM SIGMETRICS Conference on Measurement and Modelling of Computer Systems*, pages 214–225, May 1990.

Session 8C

High-Performance Compilers

Optimal Code Size Reduction for Software-Pipelined Loops on DSP Applications *

Qingfeng Zhuge,   Zili Shao,   Edwin H. -M. Sha
qfzhuge@utdallas.edu, zxs015000@utdallas.edu, edsha@utdallas.edu
Department of Computer Science
University of Texas at Dallas
Richardson, Texas 75083

Abstract

Code size expansion of software-pipelined loops is a critical problem for DSP systems with strict code size constraint. Some ad-hoc code size reduction techniques were used to try to reduce the prologue/epilogue produced by software pipelining. This paper presents the fundamental understanding of the relationship between code size expansion and software pipelining. Based on the retiming concept, we present a powerful Code-size REDuction (CRED) technique and its application on various kinds of processors. We also provide CRED algorithms integrated with software pipelining process. One advantage of our algorithms is that it can explore the trade-off space between "perfect" software pipelining and constrained code size. That is, the software pipelining process can be controlled to generate a schedule concerned with code size requirement. The experiment results show the effectiveness of our algorithms in both reducing the code size for software-pipelined loops and exploring the code size/performance trade-off space.

Keywords: *Retiming, DSP processors, Software pipelining, Scheduling*

1 Introduction

Many real-time or high-performance DSP applications, such as telecom and image processing, exhibit intensive computations in loops. Software pipelining is widely used to improve the execution rate of these applications by exploiting the instruction-level parallelism in loops [4, 8]. The compiler of TI's TMS320C6000, a family of high-performance VLIW processors targeted toward Digital Signal Processing (DSP), is a good example of using software pipelining to exploit the multiple functional units [2]. While software pipelining helps to achieve compact schedules, it's disadvantage is the introduction of prologue and epilogue sections, which cause code size expansion. This code size overhead is a significant concern for embedded systems because of the limitation of on-chip memory size. Furthermore, the size of prologue and epilogue grows proportionally as more iterations of the loop

get overlapped in the pipeline [8]. For embedded systems, these two critical requirements, performance and code size, are conflict with each other when using software pipelining to optimize loop schedule. The difficult task of making trade-off between them is left to the compiler.

A simple *for* loop and its transformation after applying software pipelining are shown in Figure 1(a) and Figure 1(b). We can see that the size of prologue and epilogue size is about three times of the kernel code size when the loop schedule length is reduced from four control steps to one control step. Figure 2(a) shows the execution flow of the original loop. Figure 2(b) illustrates the loop pipeline where the execution of the nodes from different iterations are overlapped. The shaded region represents one iteration of the original loop. We can see that a new iteration is initiated in every clock cycle. In the steady state of the pipeline, all the operations can be executed simultaneously within one control step. But the price paid for this significant performance gain is the same significant code size overhead in prologue and epilogue.

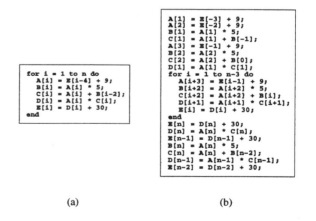

(a)   (b)

Figure 1. (a) Original loop. (b) The loop after applying software pipelining.

Previous work on code size reduction of software-pipelined loop such as code collapsing technique was developed particu-

---

*This work is partially supported by TI University Program, NSF EIA-0103709 and Texas ARP 009741-0028-2001

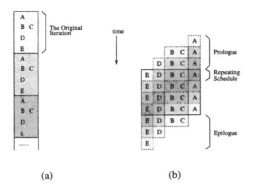

(a)   (b)

Figure 2. (a) A static schedule of original loop. (b) The model of loop pipeline.

larly for TI's TMS320C6000 family [2]. The quality of this approach, however, cannot be guaranteed. Kernel-only code generation schema presented in [8] is specially applied to IA64 processor. It requires special hardware support, and this kind of hardware support is not found in DSP processors. There's no theoretical framework presented in literature for code size control of pipelined loops. More importantly, we believe that by casting a retiming view on the software pipelining, the code size control problems can be unified into one problem of rebuilding the kernel code in prologue/epilogue by using only the retiming functions. We build up a theoretical base to expose the relations between code size of prologue/epilogue and the retiming functions of the computation nodes in the loop.

Our algorithms are developed to remove the iterations of prologue/epilogue by conditionally executing the kernel code. The values of conditional registers are determined by retiming function, which can be known during the software pipelining process. Furthermore, the underlying relationship between the software pipeline depth and the code size increment can be exploited to help compiler exploring the decision space between performance gain and code size control. As we know, even if the loop can be highly pipelined, the generated loop schedule may not be used in a real situation, if it's found that the code size requirement cannot be satisfied. So it is necessary that the software pipelining process can be controlled beforehand to meet a certain code size requirement. We show that our technique can control the software pipelining "degree" to achieve acceptable performance improvement , and at the same time, to cope with the code size requirement.

In this paper, we establish the theory and technique of code size reduction based on retiming concept. The input code description is transformed into a data flow graph, whose nodes represent operations to be performed, and edges represent precedent relations. The cyclic data flow graph can represent iterative algorithms or *for/while* loops in description language. We also depict a loop pipeline as a three-component object: prologue, repeating schedule and epilogue, to reflect the actual repeating pattern of the pipeline schedule. The length of the repeating schedule represents the execution rate of the pipeline at a stable state. We use the

retiming to model software pipelining process, such that the prologue, new loop body and epilogue can be derived directly from retiming functions. A flexible scheduling technique presented by Chao and Sha, Rotation Scheduling [1], is used to generate the pipelined schedule. Because it applies retiming operations implicitly to achieve pipelined schedule with resource constraint.

Our contributions are:

1. Establish the theoretical foundation of code size reduction technique for software-pipelined loops. The retiming concept is used to interpret the software pipelining in our model.

2. Present a general Code-size REDuction (CRED) technique which can be implemented on different types of processors.

3. Explore the trade-off space between the perfect software pipelining and the satisfaction of code size requirement.

4. Present the algorithms of totally or partially removing the iterations in prologue and epilogue.

The experimental results show the effectiveness of our CRED technique in reducing code size of software-pipelined loop. For example, for the 4-stage lattice filter, the software-pipelined code size is 24. But it is significantly reduced to 7 after our CRED technique is applied. The improvement of code sizes is ranged from 57% to 84% from our experiments. We also show the experiments using our algorithms to explore the opportunities in making code size/performance trade-offs.

The rest of the paper is organized as follows: In Section 2, we introduce several basic concepts and principles used in CRED technique. In Section 3, we illustrate the applications of general CRED technique on various types of processors. Section 4 presents the code size reduction theory. Section 5 proposes CRED algorithms. Section 6 provides experimental results.

2 Basic Principles

In this section, we provide an overview of the basic principles related to our code size reduction technique. We demonstrate that retiming and software pipelining are essentially the same concept. In fact, we will use retiming to model software pipelining, and use retiming function to derive the code size of software pipelined loops. First of all, we briefly introduce the data flow graph.

2.1 Data Flow Graph

A data flow graph (DFG) $G = (V, E, d, t)$ is a node-weighted and edge-weighted directed graph, where V is the set of computation nodes, $E \subseteq V * V$ is the set of dependence edges, d is a function from E to the non-negative integers, representing the number of delays between two nodes, and t is a function from V to the positive integers, representing the computation time of each node.

The dependencies within the same iteration are represented by edges without delay. The inter-iteration data dependencies are represented by weighted edges. For an edge $e(u \to v)$ with delays, $d(e)$ means the input data of node v at j^{th} iteration is generated by node u at $(j - d(e))^{th}$ iteration. A loop can be represented by a cyclic DFG. The delay count for any cycle in the cyclic DFG is positive for a legal program. The DFG in Figure 3(a) represents the loop in Figure 1(a). Each iteration corresponds to the execution of each node of DFG for exactly once.

The *cycle period* of a DFG is defined as the computation time of the longest path without delay. The cycle period of a DFG corresponds to the minimum schedule length of one iteration when there are no resource constraint.

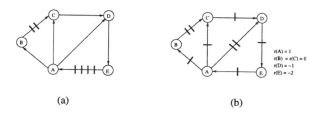

(a)   (b)

Figure 3. (a) A DFG G. (b) A retimed DFG G_R.

2.2 Retiming Technique and Retimed Graph

The *Retiming* technique has been effectively used to obtain the minimum cycle period for a DFG by evenly distributing the delays [1, 5].

On a DFG $G = (V, E, d, t)$, a retiming moves delays around in the following way: a delay is drawn from *each* of the incoming edges of v, and then it is pushed to *each* of the outgoing edges of v, or vice verse. Note that retiming preserves the data dependencies of the original DFG. Only the initial assignments need to be modified after a retiming. The modification of initial assignments is carried out by a *prologue* of statements.

A retiming function $r : V \rightarrow Z$ of a DFG G represents the number of delays moved through node v. Figure 3(b) shows the retimed DFG G_r, where two delays were pushed backward through node E. Therefore, the retiming function $r(E) = -2$.

Let $G_r = (V, E, d_r, t)$ be the DFG retimed by retiming r. A retiming is *legal* iff the delay count d_r is non-negative for any edge in E. That is, $d_r(e) = d(e) + r(u) - r(v) \geq 0$. Also for any cycle l in G, a legal retiming produces $d_r(l) = d(l)$. Since retiming preserves the number of delays in a cycle, it also preserves the iteration bound of a DFG.

We only consider the *normalized* retiming in this paper, which can be obtained by subtracting $min_v r(v)$ from $r(v)$, $\forall v \in V$.

2.3 Retiming and Software Pipelining

Let's use the simple example in Figure 4(a) and Figure 4(b) to have a clearer picture on the effect of retiming. We can retiming the DFG by evenly distributed the delays over the cycle such that the cycle period of the retimed graph is minimized. When a delay is pushed through node A to its outgoing edge, it actually pushed the ith copy of A to be executed with $(i-1)^{th}$ copy of node B, as the dashed rectangular boxes shown in Figure 5(a). And since there's no dependency between A and B within the new iteration, these two nodes can be executed simultaneously in the schedule

of the new iteration if there's no resource constraint. The effect of this new schedule is the same as pipeline the nodes from different iterations as shown in Figure 5(b).

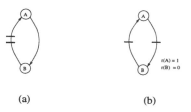

(a)   (b)

Figure 4. (a) A simple DFG. (b) The retimed DFG.

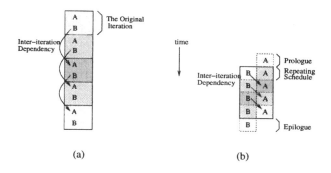

(a)   (b)

Figure 5. (a) A static schedule of original loop. (b) The pipelined loops.

In fact, each retiming corresponds to a software pipelining operation. When a delay is pushed from the incoming edges of node A to its outgoing edges, every copy of node A is shifted up by one iteration, and the first copy of A is shifted out of the first iteration into the prologue. The operations of retiming regroups computation nodes from the different iterations of the original loop body into new iterations.

With normalized retiming function, we can measure the sizes of prologue and epilogue naturally. When $r(v)$ delays are pushed forward through node v, there are $r(v)$ copies of node v appeared in the prologue. The number of copies of a node in the epilogue can also be derived in a similar way. If the maximum retiming value in the data flow graph is $max_u r(u)$, there are $max_u r(u) - r(v)$ copies of node v appeared in epilogue.

For a software-pipelined loop, if the nodes in a static schedule are from k different iterations, we call such k the *depth* of the loop pipeline. From the retiming point of view, if there are k different retiming values, k iterations are pipelined in the static schedule.

615

2.4 Rotation Scheduling

Rotation scheduling is a flexible technique for scheduling cyclic DFGs with resource constraints [1]. In each rotation phase, it implicitly applies retiming operations on a set of nodes, then these nodes are rescheduled to obtain a software-pipelined schedule.

Figure 6(a) to Figure 8(b) illustrate the rotation scheduling progress by simply rotating the first row of the schedule in each rotation phase. For example, in the first rotation phase, node A is rotated and rescheduled as shown in Figure 6(b) and Figure 6(c). The effect on the schedule is the same as pushing the first copy of node A into prologue and the last copy of the other nodes into epilogue. The resulted schedule is optimal. The 4-cycle loop is transformed into a 1-cycle loop. The pipeline depth is four. The italic letters in the schedule show how the second copy of the original loop body are merged with other copies in a new iteration.

In the process of rotation scheduling, the state of rotation can be recorded by retiming functions. For instance, after the last rotation, the retiming functions are $r(A) = 3$, $r(B) = r(C) = 2$, $r(D) = 1$ and $r(E) = 0$. That is, the node A of ith copy, node B and C from $(i+1)^{th}$ copy, node D from $(i+2)^{th}$ copy and node C from $(i+3)^{th}$ copy are overlapped in one iteration of the pipelined loop.

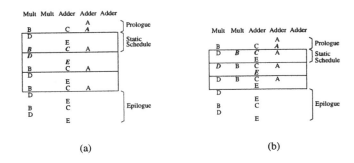

Figure 7. (a) The second phase rotation. (b) Rescheduling.

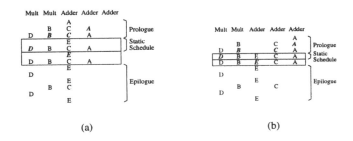

Figure 8. (a) The third phase rotation. (b) The resulted pipeline schedule.

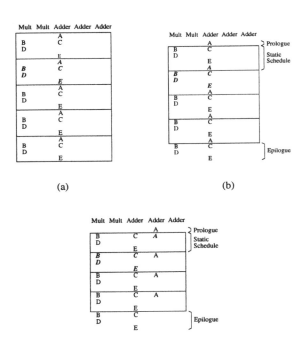

Figure 6. (a) The original loop schedule. (b) The first phase rotation. (c) Rescheduling after rotation.

In this paper, we use rotation scheduling to illustrate the Code-size REDuction (CRED) technique, because it clearly shows the relationship between software pipelining and retiming function, which is a key factor of this technique.

3 Application to Various Processors

Our Code-size REDuction (CRED) technique can be generally applied to various types of processors. We can classify the processors into four classes. **Processor class 1** is the processors without conditional registers, such as Motorola/Agere's StarCore. **Processor class 2** supports conditional execution with conditional registers, such as Philips' TriMedia. Each instruction can be *guarded* by a binary bit. **Processor class 3** implements conditional registers with counters such as TI's TMS320C6000. **Processor class 4** implements special hardware support for conditional execution for software pipelining, such as HP/Intel's IA64. Because of the space limit, we will only focus on the implementation for Processor class 3. The implementations for other classes are similar which are briefly explained in the end of the section.

In this paper, we use the architecture similar to TI's TMS320C6000 DSP processor to illustrate the implementation details. Conditional register and conditional execution are commonly implemented in many architectures [3, 7, 9]. Conditional register is also called predicate register when it holds boolean values, or "guard" register. An instruction guarded by a conditional register is conditionally executed, depending on the value in the conditional register. If it is "true", the instruction is executed. Otherwise, the instruction is disabled.

In TMS320C6000, the conditional register is implemented as a counter [2, 9]. We set the initial value of conditional registers as the maximum retiming value minus the retiming value of the guarded computation node v, i.e. $max_u r(u) - r(v)$. We also specify that the instruction is executed only when $0 \geq p > -LC$, and it is disabled when $p > 0$ or $p \leq -LC$, where LC represents the original loop counter. And the value of conditional register is decreased by 1 in every iteration. We use the notation of [ ] surrounding the conditional register name to indicate the conditional execution. For example,

```
p = 2;
[p]  A[i] = B[i-1] * 5;
p = p - 1;
```

indicates that the computation of A is not executed in the first and second iteration. Instead, it starts to be executed in the third iteration when the value of p is decreased down to 0. Also, the computation of A will not be executed any more when the value of p is less than $-LC$, suppose that $-LC$ is stored in a special register and the value checking of p is done by hardware. The example in Figure 9 illustrates the results after applying CRED on the program in Figure 1(b).

Figure 9(a) shows the code after removing the prologue/epilogue in Figure 1(b). The conditional registers p, q, r and s are used for different retiming values. Each of them starts a backward counting from a different initial value to control the guarded operation. Since there are four different retiming value, we need to use four registers to totally remove prologue and epilogue. A decrement instruction needs to be inserted into the loop body for each register. Suppose that the results of these decrement instructions do not affect the operations out of the loop, these decrements don't need to be guarded. Note that the loop will now be executed for $n - 3 + 3 + 3 = n + 3$ times, since it includes 3 iterations from prologue and the other 3 for epilogue. Figure 9(b) shows the execution sequence after applying CRED technique. Note that each iteration now executes the same static schedule. The numbers in brackets are the values of conditional registers. Figure 9(c) shows that the new code size is the same as kernel code size.

CRED technique can also be applied to the other types of processors. For the processors in class 1, it's obvious that we can use an *if-then* clause to control the execution of the nodes with the same retiming value [6]. Each retiming value needs a counter and a branch control. To implement CRED, class 1 processor also needs a counter and some instructions to manipulate the counter, such as comparison and decrement instructions.

For the processors in class 2, each instruction is guarded by a predicate bit; thus the boolean assignments of predicate bits can be used to control conditional executions [7]. Thus, the performance penalty related to the branches, such as, branch misprediction, and branch delay, can be eliminated. A counter and some counter related instructions should be included to implement CRED. Processor in class 3 have been discussed previously. It uses the counter as a conditional register [9], so the number of inserted

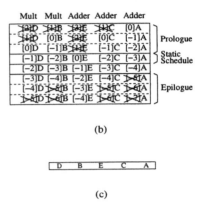

```
p = 0;
q = 1;
r = 2;
s = 3;
for i = 1 to n+3 do
    [p]  A[i] = E[i-4] + 9;
         p = p - 1;
    [q]  B[i-1] = A[i-1] * 5;
    [q]  C[i-1] = A[i-1] + B[i-3];
         q = q - 1;
    [r]  D[i-2] = A[i-2] + C[i-2];
         r = r - 1;
    [s]  E[i-3] = D[i-3] + 30;
         s = s - 1;
end
```

(a)

(b)

(c)

Figure 9. (a) Code after totally removing prologue/epilogue. (b) The execution sequence after applying CRED. (c) The new code size.

instructions are reduced.

Processor in class 4, such as IA64, supplies special hardware support. The conditional register is a 64-bit rotating register, which is controlled by a set of special loop control instructions, such as *brtop*. These instructions are actually the hardware implementations of control logic that deals with the rotating register and the loop counter. For this kind of processor, only one instruction, such as *brtop*, needs to be insert into the loop body. Also, The instructions with the same retiming value are guarded by a one-bit predicate. The number of inserted instructions is the smallest among 4 classes of processors; however, it needs special hardware support that is not yet commonly found in most of processors [3].

4 Code Size Reduction Theorems

In Section 2, we have already demonstrated that software pipelining can be modeled by retiming functions. In this section, we formally present the theorems of code size reduction based on retiming concept. The code size reduction technique is a code transformation that attempts to remove the iterations in prologue and epilogue, so that the code size requirement, i.e., the number of instruction words for a VLIW processor, can be satisfied. The code size reduction technique preserves the correct execution of the removed iterations in prologue/epilogue by conditional operations.

Lemma 4.1. *Given a retimed DFG* $G_r = \langle V, E, d_r, t \rangle$ *of a software-pipelined loop with repeating schedule S. Suppose that there is only one retiming value* $r(v) = k$, *where* $k > 0$ *for all the retimed nodes* $v \in V$, *then, the prologue can be correctly executed by only executing node* v *in schedule S for* k *times.*

Lemma 4.1 can be extended to a general case when multiple iterations are overlapped in the steady stage of pipeline, that is, there are multiple retiming values in the retimed DFG. The following theorem states that all the dependencies in the original code can be preserved by only executing the repeating schedule if we know the retiming value of each node.

Theorem 4.2. *Given a retimed DFG* $G_r = \langle V, E, d_r, t \rangle$ *of a software-pipelined loop with repeating schedule S. The prologue can be correctly executed by:*

- *Executing only S.*
- *Executing node* $u \in V$ *with retiming value* $r(u) = k$ *for* k *times starting from the* $(\max_u r(u) - k + 1)^{th}$ *iteration, where* $k \geq 0$.

For example, if $r(v) = 3$ and $\max_u r(u) = 5$, then node v will not be executed in the first and the second iterations. Instead, it will start to be executed at the third iteration.

Theorem 4.3. *Given a retimed DFG* $G_r = \langle V, E, d_r, t \rangle$ *of a software-pipelined loop with repeating schedule S. Let* n *be the number of iterations in the original loop. The epilogue can be correctly executed by:*

- *Executing only S.*
- *Executing node* $u \in V$ *with retiming value* $r(u) = k$ *for* $(\max_u r(u) - k)$ *times in the last* $\max_u r(u)$ *iterations starting from the* n^{th} *iteration, where* $k \geq 0$.

Theorem 4.2 and Theorem 4.2 establish the theoretical foundation for code size reduction of a software-pipelined loop. They indicate that the code size overhead in prologue or epilogue can be removed by only executing the kernel code after software pipelining, if the computation nodes in the kernel code can be conditionally executed. Figure 9(b) shows the execution sequence of the conditional executions of the repeating schedule.

With the architectural support described in Section 3, the code size reduction technique can be implemented easily with conditional registers and very few hardware support. The following theorem states the number of conditional registers needed for totally removing the prologue and epilogue.

Theorem 4.4. *(Total Code Size Reduction) Given the retimed DFG* $G_r = \langle V, E, d_r, t \rangle$ *of a software-pipelined loop with repeating schedule S. Let* R *be the number of different retiming values in* G_r. *Let* P *be the number of available conditional registers. If* $P \geq R$, *then all the codes in prologue/epilogue can be removed by conditionally executing S. That is, the optimal code size can be achieved.*

Theorem 4.4 defines the maximum software pipelining "degree" allowed for totally removing prologue and epilogue for a given number of conditional registers. For the example, if we have 4 conditional registers, we can remove all three iterations in prologue and epilogue. In the other words, we can produce 3 retiming values greater than zero during software pipelining. To make it clear, we define the software pipelining "degree" as the number of different retiming values produced in the software pipelining. Since the number of different retiming values equals to the pipeline depth, these three terms actually state the same concept from different views.

Since the retiming values in a data flow graph may not be continuous integer sequence, we have the number of different retiming values $R \leq \max_u r(u)$. That is, the number of conditional register P needed is no more than the number of iterations to be removed. So, we use less conditional registers than kernel only method, which use one register for each iteration [8]. Also we use less conditional registers than code collapsing method, which needs two conditional registers for the same computation node, one for removing the copy in prologue, the other for epilogue [2].

Since the resource of conditional registers is very limited in DSP processors, we may not have enough conditional registers to remove all the iterations in prologue/epilogue. The following theorem states the partial code size reduction technique. For example, we have 3 different retiming values $\{0, 3, 4\}$ in a software-pipelined loop, while only 2 conditional registers. Originally, prologue and epilogue each has 4 iterations, since the maximum retiming value is 4. By using partial code size reduction, the nodes in the innermost 3 iterations in prologue and epilogue with retiming value 3 can be removed.

Theorem 4.5. *(Partial Code Size Reduction) Given the retimed DFG* $G_r = \langle V, E, d_r, t \rangle$ *of a software-pipelined loop with repeating schedule S. Let* R *be the number of different retiming values in* G_r, *and* r_P *the* P^{th} *smallest retiming value, where* $P < R$ *is the number of available conditional registers. Then, the innermost* r_P *iterations of prologue and epilogue can be removed by conditionally executing S.*

Suppose that there is a node u in these r_P iterations with retiming value $r(u) > r_P$, we can use the same conditional register for the nodes with retiming value r_P. The initial values of the conditional registers are set as $r_P - r(v)$ for node v with $r(v) \leq r_P$. Figure 10(a) shows the code after removing part of the iterations in prologue/epilogue. Figure 10(b) shows the execution sequence. Figure 10(c) shows the new code size with only the first iteration remains in prologue/epilogue, which usually has a very small number of computation nodes.

Because of the limited number of predicate registers, it's necessary to control the software pipelining "degree" when the code size requirement cannot be satisfied for some deeply pipelined loops. A commonly applied solution for this situation is going back to suppress software pipelining, or simply using another version of the code without pipelining [2, 8]. With CRED-Partial we can avoid the cost of re-doing software pipelining or the brute force solution. As a matter of fact, there is a gray area to be explored between two extreme solutions, that is, the "perfect" software pipelining with the largest prologue/epilogue and no pipelining with the smallest code size. This exploration benefits the compiler in making code

```
q = 0;
r = 1;
s = 2;
A[1] = E[-3] + 9;
for i = 1 to n+1 do
    [q] A[i+1] = E[i-3] + 9;
    [q] B[i] = A[i] * 5;
    [q] C[i] = A[i] + B[i-2];
        q = q - 1;
    [r] D[i-1] = A[i-1] * C[i-1];
        r = r - 1;
    [s] E[i-2] = D[i-2] + 30;
        s = s - 1;
end
E[n] = D[n] + 30;
```

(a)

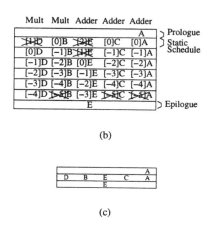

(b)

(c)

Figure 10. (a) The code after reducing part of prologue and epilogue. (b) The execution record. (c) Reduced code size.

size/performance trade-offs.

5   Code Size Reduction Algorithms

In this section, we present CRED algorithms. These algorithms can be used to meet various code size reduction interests of removing prologue and epilogue totally, partially, or removing iterations in either prologue or epilogue. Our CRED algorithms are integrated with rotation scheduling to generate a software-pipelined schedule with minimal code size. As we discussed in Section 3, one decrement instruction needs to be inserted into the loop body for each conditional register, so the schedule length after code size reduction may be increased slightly. However, these inserted nodes can also be retimed during rotation scheduling. Thus, our algorithms are able to generate a minimal schedule length with minimal code size.

1. Total Code Size Reduction Algorithm

The Algorithm 5 is used to totally remove the prologue and epilogue assuming that there's enough conditional registers. Given the DFG G of a loop and its initial schedule, CRED-Total output the optimal schedule with minimal code size. It also reports the number of conditional register used and the new loop counter. If n denotes the original loop counter, the new loop counter will be $n + max_u r(u)$, for $u \in V$.

Algorithm 1 CRED-Total Procedure

Input: Initial schedule S, DFG $G = \langle V, E, d, t \rangle$.
Output: New schedule S_{opt}, the number of conditional registers used j and the new loop counter LC.
    $j \leftarrow 1$;
    for all $i = 0, \ldots, S.length$ **do**
        /* Step 1: Rotate nodes. */
        $Q \leftarrow First\_Row(S)$;
        $S_{opt} \leftarrow ReSchedule(S, Q)$;
        /* Step 2: Guard the nodes v with $r(v) = 0$. */
        $p_0 \leftarrow max_u r(u), \forall u \in V$;
        Insert the decrement instruction of p_0;
        /* Step 3: Guard the nodes with new retiming values. */
        if there's a new retiming value $r(v)$ **then**
            $p_j \leftarrow max_u r(u) - r(v)$;
            Insert the decrement instruction of p_j;
            $j \leftarrow j + 1$;
            $LC \leftarrow LC + 2$;
        end if
        /* Step 4: Update the inserted nodes */
        Update the decrement instructions in S_{opt};
    end for
    return S_{opt}, j, LC;

---

2. Partial Code Size Reduction Algorithm

By given the number of conditional registers, Algorithm 5 can be easily modified to do partial code size reduction (CRED-Partial) as stated in Theorem 4.5. In a practical situation, we may be given a code size requirement and the number of available conditional registers. We'd like to know what is the best schedule length can be achieved within the code size requirement by using these registers. CRED-Partial can be applied to control the software pipelining degree, so that the code size requirement can be satisfied. If we compute the schedule length and the code size in each rotation phase, we will produce a trade-off space between code size and software pipelining degree, which is very useful for designers to make trade-off decisions.

3. Prologue/Epilogue Only Code Size Reduction Algorithm

Since the code sizes in prologue and epilogue are not equal for some application, remove one of them will be good enough for satisfying the code size requirement. Both total and partial CRED algorithms can be modified to fit this request. Because we still have a complete prologue or epilogue in the code, we can use one less conditional register. In case of prologue only CRED, the nodes with retiming value $max_u r(u)$ do not need to be guarded by conditional register. While for epilogue only CRED, the nodes with retiming value 0 do not need to be guarded. Also, the loop counter register is not needed. For epilogue only CRED, the initial value of the conditional register for node v will be set as $-LC + r(v)$, and instead of inserting decrement instructions, we will insert in-

619

crement instructions, so the computation nodes will be disabled when the value of conditional register is greater than 0.

Comparing the effect of prologue/epilogue only CRED technique and that of Code Collapsing technique [2], it's interesting to see that the code size reduced by these two techniques are equal. That is, code collapsing becomes a special case of our CRED technique. Because our technique is based on the fundamental understanding of retiming and code size expansion, it can be generally applied to reduce the code size of any software-pipelined loops.

6 Experiment Results

We have experimented with CRED algorithms on several well-known benchmarks. In most cases, we can use less than three or fewer conditional registers to completely remove all the iterations in prologue and epilogue without incurring performance penalty. The code size improvements are very promising.

Table 1 shows the experimental results of CRED-Total. All the schedules are generated on a simulated architecture with 2 multipliers and 3 adders with conditional registers described in Section 3, assuming that the computation time of each functional unit is one time unit. The data in the second column are the numbers of conditional registers used to remove all the iterations in prologue and epilogue, i.e., the number of different retiming values. The third and forth columns are the code size of "perfectly" software pipelined schedules and the code size after total code size reduction. Here the code size is measured as the number of instruction words. We can see the remarkable code size improvement percentages in the fourth column. The last two columns show the schedule lengths before and after applying CRED-Total. In most cases, except for the all-pole lattice filter, the schedule lengths are the same as pipelined schedule length. The pipelined schedule of all-pole lattice filter has four different retiming values, which means four decrement instructions need to be inserted. It's schedule length is increased by one cycle because its schedule is already very compact. On the other hand, the improvement on the all-pole lattice filter's code size is the largest, since all three iterations in prologue/epilogue are reduced. If the code size requirement of this application can be relaxed to larger than six instruction words, both CRED-Partial and Prologue/Epilogue Only CRED can be applied to achieve the code size target while maintain the schedule length of the tightest pipelined.

Benchmarks	Reg #	Code Size			Sch. Len.	
		SP	CRED	%	SP	CRED
IIR Filter	2	6	2	66.7	2	2
Differential Eq.	3	14	3	78.6	3	3
All-pole Filter	4	39	6	84.6	5	6
Elliptic Filter	2	26	11	57.7	11	11
4-stage Filter	3	24	7	70.8	7	7
Voltera Filter	2	22	9	59.1	9	9

Table 1. The results of CRED-Total.

Table 2 shows the trade-offs between code size and performance for all-pole lattice filter by given two conditional registers. We use CRED-Partial to remove the innermost two iterations of the pipelined loop. The first column shows the software pipeline depth, which is also the software pipeline degree. The second and third columns show the code sizes of software pipelined loop and that after applying CRED-Partial. The fourth column shows the improvement percentage on code size, which is limited by the number of available conditional registers. The last two columns show the schedule lengths before and after applying CRED. In most cases, the schedule lengths produced by CRED are the same as tightest pipelined ones. We can see that when the pipeline depth increases, the code size is increased and the schedule length is decreased. The experimental results show the "gray" area existing between the tightest software pipelining with a large code size and the shallow pipeline with a relatively small code size. By using CRED technique, a compiler can efficiently explore the "gray" area to make code size/performance trade-offs

Pipeline Depth	Code Size			Sch. Len.	
	SP	CRED	%	SP	CRED
2	23	11	52.2	11	11
3	30	19	36.7	7	7
4	39	29	25.6	5	6

Table 2. Experimental Results for All-pole Lattice Filter with 2 conditional registers.

References

[1] L.-F. Chao, A. S. LaPaugh, and E. H.-M. Sha. Rotation scheduling: A loop pipelining algorithm. *IEEE Transactions on Computer-Aided Design of Integrated Circuits and Systems*, 16(3):229–239, Mar. 1997.

[2] E. Granston, R. Scales, E. Stotzer, A. Ward, and J. Zbiciak. Controlling code size of software-pipelined loops on the TMS320C6000 VLIW DSP architecture. In *Proceedings of the 3rd Workshop on Media and Streaming Processorsin conjunction with 34th Annual International Symposium on Microarchitecture*, pages 29–38. ACM, Dec. 2001.

[3] Intel Corporation. *Intel Itanium Architecture Software Developer's Manual Volume 1: Application Architecture*, Dec. 2001.

[4] M. Lam. Software pipelining: An effective scheduling technique for VLIW machines. In *Proceedings of the SIGPLAN'88 Conference on Programming Language Design and Implementation*, pages 318–328. ACM, June 1988.

[5] C. E. Leiserson and J. B. Saxe. Retiming synchronous circuitry. *Algorithmica*, 6:5–35, Aug. 1991.

[6] Motorola Digital DNA & Agere Systems. *StarCore SC140 DSP Core Reference Manual*, Nov. 2001.

[7] Philips, Inc. *TM-1300 Media Processor Data Book*, May 2000.

[8] B. R. Rau, M. S. Schlansker, and P. P. Tirumalai. Code generation schema for modulo scheduled loops. In *Proceedings of the 25th Annual International Symposium on Microarchitecture*, pages 158–169. ACM, Dec. 1992.

[9] Texas Instruments, Inc. *TMS320C6000 CPU and Instruction Set Reference Guide*, 2000.

Software Caching using Dynamic Binary Rewriting for Embedded Devices

Chad M. Huneycutt, Joshua B. Fryman, Kenneth M. Mackenzie
College of Computing Georgia Institute of Technology
Atlanta, GA 30332
{ chadh, fryman, kenmac }@cc.gatech.edu

Abstract

A software cache implements instruction and data caching entirely in software. Dynamic binary rewriting offers a means to specialize the software cache miss checks at cache miss time. We describe a software cache system implemented using dynamic binary rewriting and observe that the combination is particularly appropriate for the scenario of a simple embedded system connected to a more powerful server over a network. As two examples, consider a network of sensors with local processing or cell phones connected to cell towers. We describe two software cache systems for instruction caching only using dynamic binary rewriting and present results for the performance of instruction caching in these systems. We measure time overheads of 19% compared to no caching. We also show that we can guarantee a 100% hit rate for codes that fit in the cache. For comparison, we estimate that a comparable hardware cache would have space overhead of 12-18% for its tag array and would offer no hit rate guarantee.

1 Introduction

Programmability is the primary motivation for automatic management of a memory hierarchy (automatic caching). Programmability enables new functionality, can reduce time to market and improve time in market by strengthening reusability of software in a product line. A memory hierarchy can be managed manually by a programmer but the effort is considerable. General-purpose computers universally employ automatic management of the memory hierarchy via hardware caching and virtual memory mechanisms, but many DSPs and microcontrollers used in embedded systems avoid caching to absolutely minimize its drawbacks.

The drawbacks of caching are added cost, added power and loss of predictable timing. A cache design targeting embedded systems must address these three issues.

A natural target class of embedded applications is one in which the embedded system is in constant communica-

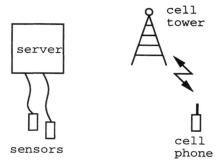

Figure 1. Two examples of networked embedded devices: distributed sensors and cell phones. Both include local processing but are continuously connected to more powerful servers.

tion with a server. In this scenario the server maintains the lower levels of the memory hierarchy for the embedded system. Two examples of this class (Figure 1) include a distributed network of low-cost sensors with embedded processing and distributed cell phones which communicate with cell towers. In each example the embedded device is nearly useless without the communication connection and thus can afford to depend partially on the server for basic functionality. Also in each example, the embedded device is heavily constrained by cost and/or power consumption while the server can be far more powerful.

A specific example of the benefits of caching is illustrated in Figure 2. Consider a sensor with local processing. The sensor operates in one of several modes (initialization, calibration, daytime, nighttime), but only two are performance-critical and the transitions between the modes are infrequent. Figure 2 depicts an idealized view of the memory address space in this system in which the code/data for each mode is disjoint. The key observation is that only the performance-critical modes need to fit entirely in memory and then only one at a time. The local memory can be sized to fit one mode, reducing cost and power over a larger memory.

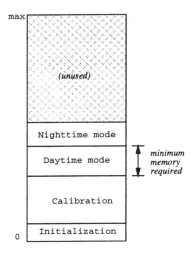

Figure 2. Example: code space for an embedded processor providing local processing to a sensor. The code includes modules for initialization, calibration and two modes of operation, but only one module is active at a given time. The device physical memory can be sized to fit one module.

Software Caching

Implementing caching in *software* helps address the issues of cost, power and predictability. An all-software cache design addresses these issues as follows:

- **Cost:** Software caching requires no die area devoted to caching. A fraction of on-chip memory may be consumed by tags and other overheads but the fraction is an adjustable tradeoff. Software caching can be implemented today on the simplest of microcontrollers.

- **Power:** A hardware cache pays the power penalty of a tag check on every access. The primary performance objective in a software caching design is to avoid cache tag checks. Even though a program using the software cache likely requires additional cycles it can avoid a larger fraction of tag checks for a net savings in memory system power.

- **Predictability:** Software caching offers flexibility to provide predictable timing (zero misses during a section of code) in two ways. At a minimum, one can define manually managed areas of on-chip memory and thus provide predictable modules within the application. More interestingly, a software cache can be fully associative so that a module can be guaranteed free of conflict misses provided the module fits in the cache (Figure 2).

The costs of an all-software cache design versus a hardware design are that, even when all cache accesses are hits, some extra instructions must be executed for cache tag checks, mapping or other overhead.

Software caching may be used to implement a particular level in a multilevel caching system. For instance, the L2 cache could be managed in software while the L1 caches are conventional. For our embedded scenario, we envision a single level of caching at the embedded system chip with a local memory in the range of 1s to 100s of kilobytes.

Dynamic Binary Rewriting

Dynamic binary rewriting in the context of software caching means modifying the instructions of the program at cache miss time. The instructions are rewritten to encode part of the cache state in the instructions themselves. For instance, branches in code can be rewritten to point to the in-cache version of a branch target (if the target is in-cache) or to the miss handler (if the target is not in-cache). Similarly, (some) data accesses can be rewritten to point to in-cache locations.

The key contribution of dynamic rewriting to software caching is that it provides a means to make a fully associative cache with low overhead for hits. Rewritten instructions may be placed anywhere in the cache on a basic-block by basic-block basis. Fully associative hardware caches are impractical unless the cache block size is large.

Rewriting helps reduce the cache hit time and code size at the expense of increased cache miss time. In the target scenario of networked embedded devices, rewriting shifts the cost of caching from the (constrained) embedded system to the (relatively unconstrained) server.

This section has introduced software caching, its application to embedded systems connected by a network to a server and the use of dynamic binary rewriting to improve software caching. The rest of this document is organized as follows. Section 2 describes an instruction cache implementation using dynamic binary rewriting in software. We present two prototypes that were developed and results. Section 3 describes a paper design for a data cache. Section 4 summarizes the range of tradeoffs in implementing a memory hierarchy in software as compared to hardware and discusses related work. Finally, section 5 concludes.

2   Software I-Cache

This section describes a software cache for instructions using binary rewriting and a client-server model. Similar to a hardware cache, a software cache consists of two controller interfaces around the local memories. A software cache controller (CC) sits on the client and handles hits to the remote translation cache, and the memory controller (MC) resides on the server and services misses.

Rewriting

Figure 3 illustrates the basic rewriting mechanism. On

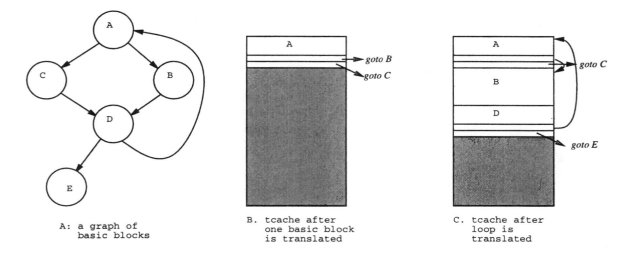

A: a graph of basic blocks

B. tcache after one basic block is translated

C. tcache after loop is translated

Figure 3. Example of Translation Cache (*tcache*) operation. Basic blocks in the original program (A), are copied on demand to the translation cache. As they are copied, branches exiting the blocks are initially rewritten to point to cache miss handlers (B) and eventually, if used, again rewritten to point to other blocks in the *tcache* (C).

the MC instructions from the original program are broken into "chunks" (for our purposes, a chunk is a basic block, although it could certainly be a larger sequence of instructions, such as a trace or hyperblock). These chunks are then sent to the CC, which places them in the translation cache (*tcache*). At translation time, branches are rewritten to point to a cache miss handler. If a branch is subsequently taken, then the target of the original branch is translated, and the branch is rewritten again to point to the now in-cache copy of the target basic block.

The example illustrates both advantages of rewriting. First, after all the basic blocks used in the loop have been discovered, transferred, and rewritten in the cache, the loop runs at full speed on the client with no cache tag checks (but possibly with extra branch instructions). Second, the instruction cache is effectively fully associative. Instructions in the source program may be relocated anywhere in the *tcache*.

Interpreted in conventional caching terms, the rewritten instructions encode cache tags. When an object (*e.g.,* a basic block of instructions) is in the cache, relevant jumps and branches in the cache are adjusted to point to that object. When the object is not in-cache, relevant instructions are adjusted to point to the cache miss handler instead. Instead of tags or a mapping table, the state of the cache is implicit in the branch instructions which, for the most part, are required in the program anyway. Not all tags can be represented this way, but many can be.

Alternatively, interpreted in dynamic compilation lingo, we use binary rewriting to specialize mapping and tag-checking code for the current state of the cache. The spe-

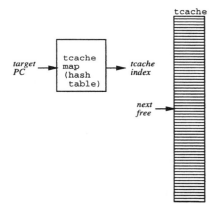

Figure 4. Data structures used for instruction caching. The *tcache* holds the rewritten instructions. The *tcache map* holds mappings from the original address space to indices in the *tcache*.

cialization succeeds in removing the tag check entirely for the common case of branch instructions whose destinations are known at rewriting time.

Invalidation

One invalidates a conventional cache entry by changing the tag or the mapping. With rewriting, we need to find and change any and all pointers that implicitly mark a basic block as valid.

There are two sources of such pointers: pointers embedded in the instructions (the branches) of other basic blocks in the *tcache* and pointers to code stored in data, *e.g.,* in

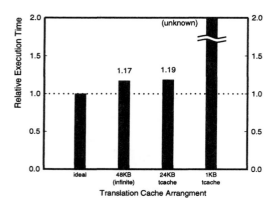

Figure 5. Relative execution time for the software instruction cache. The times are for `129.compress` **from SPEC95 and are normalized to the "ideal" execution time with no software cache.**

return addresses on the stack or in thread control blocks. Pointers in the *tcache* are easy to record at the time they are created. To find pointers in data, the runtime system must know the layout of all such data.

Ambiguous Pointers

Rewriting is limited by pointers that cannot be determined at rewriting time (ambiguous pointers). For instance, computed jumps and returns from subroutines involve pointers to instructions where the pointers are unknown at rewriting time.

There are three approaches to handling ambiguous pointers:

- Use code analysis to determine constant values for pointers (if possible) or to generate useful assertions about pointers. For instance, a computed jump may in fact be provably constant at rewriting time.

- Decree limitations to the programming model in order to provide useful invariants about pointers. For instance, limit the call/return idiom so that the location of return addresses is always known.

- Perform a cache lookup in software at runtime. A runtime cache lookup is always possible as a fallback strategy.

We use the strategy of applying limitations to the programming model combined with cache lookup as a last-ditch approach. The limitations are modest and correspond essentially to code produced by a compiler. A more sophisticated rewriter could employ elaborate analysis [11] or an ISA, such as the Java Virtual Machine, which is more amenable to analysis.

2.1 SPARC Prototype

We have implemented a prototype of a software instruction cache. Our I-cache design uses rewriting for the majority of control transfers, relies on modest restrictions to the programming model to rule out several forms of pointer ambiguity, and resorts to a mapping through a hash table for the remaining ambiguous pointers.

There is no embedded system per se, but instead one program that encompasses both the MC and CC. The MC copies and rewrites the embedded code into a *tcache* in memory and then executes that code directly. Communication between the CC and the MC is accomplished by jumping back and forth in places where a real embedded system would have to perform an RPC to the MC. Since only instruction caching is modeled, the rewritten code accesses data objects in the same memory locations as it would have if it had not been rewritten.

We define the following limitations to the programming model to rule out some forms of ambiguous pointers. The limitations are modest in that they correspond to idioms that a compiler would likely produce anyway.

- Procedure return addresses must be identifiable to the runtime system at all times. Specifically, procedure call and return use unique instructions, the current return address is stored in a particular register and a particular place in the stack frame, the stack layout must be known to the runtime system and any non-stack storage (e.g. thread control blocks) must be registered with the runtime system. The instruction and register requirements are met naturally by the compiler. The stack layout is already defined in SPARC because of SPARC's use of trap-managed register windows. The interface to the thread system is the only new requirement (and we have not yet implemented it).

- Self-modifying programs must explicitly invalidate newly-written instructions before they can be used. For instance, dynamically linked libraries typically rewrite a jump table to the library. SPARC already requires this invalidation as its instruction and data caches are not coherent.

Finally, we do not limit pointers arising from computed jumps:

- For computed jumps, we fall back to a lookup through a hash table. The hash table need only contain the subset of destination addresses that could actually occur at the computed jump – a subset of the *tcache map* in Figure 3.

The implementation runs on UltraSPARC workstations under Solaris 2.7 and Linux 2.2.14. The next subsection describes results.

App.	Dynamic .text	Static .text
`129.compress`	21KB	193KB
`adpcmenc`	1KB	139B
`hextobdd`	23KB	205KB
`mpeg2enc`	135KB	590KB

Table 1. Application dynamically- and statically-linked text segment sizes. `129.compress` **is from the SPEC CPU95 suite,** `adpcmenc` **is from Media-Bench, and** `hextobdd` **is a local graph manipulation application. All were compiled with** `gcc -04`. **The dynamic** `.text` **segment size is an underestimate while the static** `.text size` **is an overestimate.**

2.2 SPARC I-Cache Results

We ran experiments using benchmarks that might appear in an embedded context. The benchmark characteristics are summarized in Table 1. We compare the performance of the software instruction cache with that of a simple hardware cache: a direct-mapped cache with 16-byte blocks. The main point to take away is that the software cache comes close to the performance of the hardware cache in time and space costs, yet the software cache requires no hardware support.

Figure 5 shows the time performance of the software cache. We compare the wall times of `compress95` running under the software cache system with that of `compress95` running natively on the UltraSPARC. The input to `compress95` is large enough that the initial startup time of the cache is insignificant. The result shows that the software cache operates with a slowdown of 19% provided the working set of the code fits entirely in the cache. Of course, if the working set does not fit, performance is awful (the rightmost bar) but the system continues to operate. In our current implementation, we add two new instructions per translated basic block. These extra instructions could be optimized away to provide a performance closer to that of the native binary.

Figures 6 and 7 show the space requirements of software and hardware caches for the benchmarks by looking for the "knee" of the miss rate curve in each case. The result is that, for this coarse test, the cache size required to capture the working set appears similar for the software cache as for a hardware cache.

Finally, note that the working sets observed in the Figures 6 and 7 are a tiny fraction of the program code sizes listed in Table 1. This ratio is an illustration of the benefits of caching depicted earlier in Figure 2: only a fraction of the address space needs to be physical.

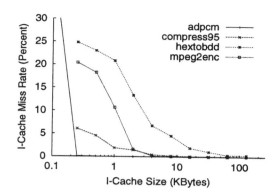

Figure 6. Hardware cache miss rate versus cache size. The cache is a direct-mapped L1 instruction cache with 16-byte blocks. The cache size is the size of data only – tags for 32-bit addresses would add an extra 11-18%.

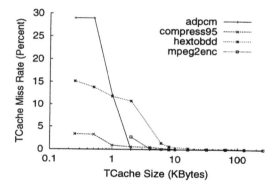

Figure 7. Software cache miss rate versus cache size. The software cache size is the size of the *tcache* in bytes. The software miss rate is the number of basic blocks translated divided by the number of instructions executed.

2.3 ARM Prototype

We have also begun implementation of a softcache for a real embedded system. It operates as follows: when the MC is run, it is provided with an executable file image (the application written for the remote target) and breaks it into small pieces of code and data which can each be sent to the CC as needed. The CC will execute these "chunks" of code, generating exceptions as it tries to use non-resident code targets (*e.g.*, , procedure calls to code which has not been received) or data targets (variables not resident). While the cost of transfer for these chunks between the MC and CC will depend on the interconnect system, as long as the remote node contains enough on-chip RAM to hold the "hot code" and associated data, it will eventually reach steady state in local CC memory. For more details of our implementation,

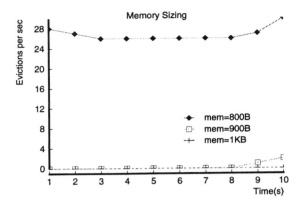

Figure 8. When memory is insufficient to hold the steady state of the application, paging occurs. This can be seen in the topmost line corresponding to 800 bytes of CC memory. When memory is increased to 900 bytes in the CC, the paging falls to zero during steady state, but at the end minor paging occurs to load the terminal statistics routines. This is seen in the light, dotted line on the graph. When the CC memory exceeds the steady state needs, the paging falls off even further as shown in the bottom line for 1024 bytes of CC memory.

see [5].

The MC and CC were written for the Compaq Research Laboratories' Skiff boards. These units contain a 200MHz Intel SA-110, 32MB of RAM, and run the Linux kernel with patches (kernel 2.4.0-test1-ac7-rmk1-crl2). In a real embedded device, the ARM is a popular choice and the Skiff board is well-equipped for testing a variety of embedded programs. For rapid prototyping and debugging, we use the resources of the Skiff boards and Linux kernels. The Skiff boards remotely mount filesystems via NFS and have a 10Mbps network connectivity.

Using cross-hosted gcc 2.95.2 compilers, all development work was done on x86 workstations but run on the Skiff boards. One Skiff board was set up as MC and the other as CC. Debugging was by native ARM gdb running directly on the Skiff boards. For communication between MC and CC we used TCP/IP sockets with standard operations over a 10Mbps network, where all network traffic is accounted for by either the MC, CC, or x86 host telnet sessions to the target Skiff boards. The MC was given a gcc-generated ELF format binary image for input.

The ARM prototype implementation succeeds at splitting the softcache functionality into MC and CC components but is limited in the ways listed below compared to the SPARC prototype from the previous section. These are not fundamental limitations, merely the current state of the

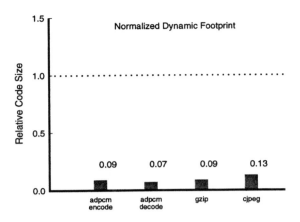

Figure 9. The dynamic footprints above have been normalized so that the static footprint of each benchmark is 1. As can be seen, the hot code is a 7-14X reduction compared to the full program size.

implementation given its different development focus:

- Code is chunked by procedures rather than by basic blocks.
- Procedure call sites use a "redirector" stub as a permanent landing pad for procedure returns to avoid having to walk the ARM's stack at invalidation time.
- Indirect jumps are not supported.

2.4 ARM Results

Using our implementation we were able to determine the network overhead for each code chunk downloaded to be 60 application bytes (not counting Ethernet framing overhead and intermediate protocol overhead) exchanged between CC and MC. This has future implications for the minimum code chunk size we will want to consider. The actual time the MC spends looking up data in tables and preparing the code chunk to be sent will vary with MC host, and could easily be reduced to near zero by more powerful MC systems.

Space Reduction

We then used a combination of static analysis and dynamic execution to find the minimum amount of memory required to maintain steady state in the CC system, which we expected to be a small subset of the entire application code size. Our benchmark applications included gzip, and pieces of MediaBench [8] including ADPCM encode, ADPCM decode, and cjpeg. As expected, we were able to verify the hot code as having a much smaller footprint than the primary application, although we do note that our choice of benchmarks are universally compression-based. We feel that the primary task of the remote devices in the hierarchical context will be to reduce the data set generated and send only reduced amounts to higher systems.

The hot code was initially identified by using gprof to determine which functions constituted at least 90% of the application run time. We then set the CC cache space to be equal to the size of these functions. We observed that varying this size down caused the SoftCache to page more in steady state code, while varying the size up did not increase performance during steady state. Figure 8 shows how the page rate is an indicator to proper sizing of the memory for the CC.

This confirmed that only the gprof identified functions need be resident in the CC cache in steady state. The results from our analysis are shown in Figure 9, which indicates the size of hot code relative to app size. The original code size is not statically linked, and therefore the overhead of libc, crt0, and similar routines are not accounted for. In the real limited hardware system without Linux underneath, libc and similar routines would be considered part of the application image to be cached, and the effective "hot" sizes would be much smaller.

3 Software Caching of Data

This section sketches a paper design for a software data cache to complement the instruction cache presented in the previous section. A data cache can benefit from rewriting but the issues of pointer disambiguation are much more serious than for instructions.

We present one design that has two main features. First, it again exploits some modest limitations to the programming model to eliminate some forms of pointer ambiguity. Second, we define a "slow hit" as a cached data item found on-chip, but with extra effort beyond the case of an ordinary hit. We then can build a fully associative data cache where at least slow hits can be guaranteed provided the data fit in cache.

Basic Caching Mechanism

The basic mechanism for data caching in software is to emulate the action of a hardware cache by implementing mapping, tags or both. Load and store instructions are rewritten as a sequence of instructions to perform the mapping or tag check. The key goal for a software data cache is to reduce the number of tag checks.

Reducing Tag Checks

We reduce tag checks in two ways. First, we rely on limitations to the programming model to treat scalar objects on the stack differently from the rest of data. The stack may thus be treated specially and most tag checks on the stack eliminated. Second, we use rewriting to specialize accesses

```
ld [caddr], %r1  -->          ld [dataaddr(caddr)], %r1
  the constant address is
  known to be in-cache


ld [%r2], %r1 -->             ld [guess(ldaddr)], %r1
  the variable address is     ld [tagbase + %r1], %r3
  not known but we have       srl %r2, NOFFSETBITS, %r4
  a prediction about which    cmp %r3, %r4
  line in cache               bne lmiss
                              sll %r1, NBLOCKBITS - 2
                              and %r2, NBLOCKMASK, %r3
                              add %r1, %r3, %r1
                              ld [database + %r1], %r1
```

Figure 10. Instruction sequences used to implement data caching. If the address is constant, the translated, in-cache address can be rewritten in the code (top). Otherwise, the address is looked up by searching the cache starting with a predicted entry in the cache (bottom).

with constant addresses (scalar global variables).

Additional tag check reductions are possible with additional effort or limitations. For instance, the HotPages system [11] uses a static compiler with sophisticated pointer analysis to selectively create deeper loop nests such that array accesses within the innermost loop all access the same cache line and can thus be checked with one tag check at the beginning of the innermost loop. Alternatively, Java restricts pointers at the language level and passes considerable information down to instruction level in the form of Java Virtual Machine in bytecodes.

Full Associativity

We propose to make a data cache that is fully associative yet includes a fast, predicted common-case path. A fully associative software cache for data will be slow because we cannot get rid of as many tag checks as we can for instructions. We propose to implement the fully associative cache with *predictions* to speed accesses.

3.1 D-Cache Design

We propose to implement data caching in two pieces: a specialized stack cache (*scache*) and a general-purpose data cache (*dcache*). Local memory is thus statically divided into three regions: *tcache*, *scache* and *dcache*.

The stack cache holds stack frames in a circular buffer managed as a linked list. A presence check is made at procedure entrance and exit time. The stack cache is assumed to hold at least two frames so leaf procedures can avoid the exit check.

The data cache is fully associative using fixed-size blocks with tags. The blocks and corresponding tags are kept in sorted order. A memory access has three stages. First, the load/store instruction is expanded in-line into a tag load and check (aided by a block index prediction, described below). A tag match indicates a hit. On a mismatch, a subroutine performs a binary search of the entire *dcache* for the indicated tag. A match at this point is termed a "slow hit". If there is no match in the *dcache*, the miss handler communicates with the server to perform a replacement.

The cache check code must guess the index of the block (and tag) in the fully-associative *dcache*. We use additional variables outside the *dcache* to maintain predictions. The variable predicts that the next access will hit the same cache location. As a variation, the hit code could implement a stride prediction (since the dcache array is in sorted order) or a "second-chance" prediction of index $i + 1$ on a miss to index i before searching the whole *dcache*. The prediction variable does not need to be updated when the *dcache* is reorganized although an update could help.

Figure 10 shows the SPARC assembly for the case of a specialized load/store for a global scalar versus the code for a predicted lookup in the sorted *dcache*.

In summary, the data caching design has two features. First, it uses ISA restrictions and rewriting to specialize a subset of data accesses. Second, it provides for a fully associative data cache with prediction for faster access. The guaranteed memory latency is the speed of a slow hit: the time to find data on-chip without consulting the server.

4 Discussion

Software caching opens up the design space for caching. Software caching appears particularly appropriate for the scenario of a low-cost/low-power embedded system connected to a server where the server actively participates in managing the memory hierarchy. We briefly present issues raised by software caching and novel capabilities enabled by software caching followed by a discussion of related work.

Caching Issues

- *Manual vs. automatic management.* Manual management of the memory hierarchy, like assembly language programming, offers the highest performance but the most difficult programming model.

- *Hardware vs. software.* Viewed in terms of time, hardware mechanisms can afford to check every single memory access while software mechanisms will depend on avoiding such checks. Viewed in terms of power consumption, avoiding checks is always desirable.

- *Binary Rewriting.* Rewriting (applied to software caching) specializes instruction sequences for the current cache state. Trace caching [12] or in-cache branch prediction can be considered hardware versions of rewriting. Software rewriting eliminates tag checks through specialization.

- *Value of Limitations.* Some very useful specializations are illegal under the contract of the instruction set. These specializations may be used either (a) speculatively, (b) when the illegal situation can be proven not to arise or (c) if additional limitations are imposed on the instruction set. A small set of limitations to the instruction set corresponding essentially to the natural idioms of compiler-produced machine code enable a number of important specializations.

- *Language-level help,* e.g., *via Java.* Language-level support is orthogonal but can considerably simplify either manual or automatic memory management. With a manual approach, one can use objects to help delimit the code and data belonging to an operating "mode". With an automatic approach, language-level restrictions on pointers considerably simplify pointer analysis and enable better specialization of data caching.

Novel Capabilities

The software caching system presented here provides a framework for exploring dynamic optimization of memory. To illustrate the power of this approach, here are three novel capabilities of a software cache using rewriting: (1) we could dynamically deduce the working set and shut down unneeded memory banks to reduce power consumption, (2) we can integrate "cache" with fixed local memory at arbitrary boundaries and (3) we could direct memory accesses to multiple parallel memory banks to improve performance.

Since the software cache is fully associative, we can size or resize it arbitrarily in order to shut down portions of memory. In low-power StrongARM devices, the total power in use by the components of the chip we wish to remove are: I-cache 27%, D-cache 16%, Write Buffer 2%. This shows that 45% of the total power consumption lies in the cache alone, before considering other components [10]. By converting the on-chip cache data space to multi-bank SRAM, we can find an optimization for power based on memory footprint. By isolating each piece of code together with its associated variables, it becomes possible to power-down all banks not relevant to the currently executing application subset. By adding architectural support of "power-down" and "power-up" instructions, we can dynamically choose which banks to power at any given moment, leading to a significant potential power savings. Other efforts at enabling partial sleep-mode in on-chip RAM [1, 9, 16] focus on getting the steady-state of the program into just part of the total cache space. We suggest using the entire space and actively selecting which region is currently being powered. This depends on reliable SRAM cells that can be put in sleep mode without data loss [16].

Another facility that the SoftCache enables is a more flexible version of data pinning. With the SoftCache using arbitrarily sized blocks of memory as a "cache-line" model, we can pin or fix pages in memory and prevent their eviction without wasting space. Additionally, we do not lose space by converting part of our cache to pinnable RAM – rather, our entire RAM space can be pinnable or not on arbitrary page sizes. We can also compact regions of pinned pages to be contiguous rather than disjoint, to allow for more efficient memory usage. Whether pinning code (interrupt handlers) or data (cycling buffers), this flexibility allows us to further optimize the memory footprint and usage characteristics of an application in a dynamic manner.

Third, given multiple banks of on-chip memory, software caching can be used to execute multiple load/store operations in parallel. By knowing the dynamic behavior of the system, we can rearrange during runtime where data is located to optimize accesses to different banks and increase overall memory utilization. Additional footprint improvements can be made by finding just the relevant data regions of structures that will be accessed and providing only these items in the CC's local memory.

Related Work

There is related work in all-software caching, fast cache simulation, software-*managed* caches where software handles refills only, dynamic binary rewriting and just-in-time compilation.

Software caching has been implemented using static rewriting mechanisms. The HotPages system uses transformations tightly integrated with a compiler that features sophisticated pointer analysis [11]. In contrast, we focus on the complementary problem of what we can do with dynamic rewriting and without deep analysis. The Shasta shared memory system used static binary rewriting to implement software caching for shared variables in a multiprocessor [13]. Such techniques could be used to implement shared memory between an embedded system and its server.

Dynamic binary rewriting systems have been developed to re-optimize code for improved program performance [7, 2]. In these systems the optimized code is stored in an area that is managed as an instruction cache. For instance, Dynamo [2] identifies hot traces through interpretation, optimizes them and stores them as "fragments" in a fragment cache. We differ from these dynamic optimizers in that caching is our object rather than code optimizations: our goal is to extract the best performance given limited space. Further, we enable separating the rewriting (in the MC) from the cache control (CC) for embedded scenarios.

Fast simulators have implemented forms of software caching using dynamic rewriting. The Talisman-2 [3], Shade [4] and Embra [15] simulators use this technique. Simulators must deal with additional simulation detail which limits their speed. Also, the dynamic rewriters deal with very large *tcache* sizes and avoid the problem of invalidating individual entries by invalidating the *tcache* in its

entirety and infrequently.

As the ratio of processor to memory speed increases, software management of the memory hierarchy creeps upward from the traditional domain of virtual memory management. Software has been proposed to implement replacement for a fully-associative L2 cache [6]. We propose to take an additional step.

A Distributed JVM [14] splits the implementation of a Java just-in-time compiler system between servers and clients to achieve benefits of consistency and performance. We use a similar notion of distributed functionality between a server and an embedded system to minimize memory footprint, system power and cost on the embedded system.

5 Conclusion

This paper described software caching and a particular way of implementing software caching using dynamic binary rewriting. We observe that this system is particularly natural for a class of embedded applications: one where a low-cost, low-power embedded device is continuously connected to a more powerful server. A caching system provides the programmability of a memory hierarchy while the software implementation minimizes system cost and potentially reduces power consumption over a hardware caching implementation. The binary rewriting approach shifts some caching overhead from the embedded device to the more powerful server, matching the characteristics of the scenario. We describe two implementations, one on SPARC with caching on basic-block boundaries, support for indirect jumps and no overhead for procedure calls, the other on ARM that separates the system into memory- and cache-controller pieces. Both systems show that the software cache succeeds at finding the active working set of the test applications.

Acknowledgements

This material is based upon work supported by the National Science Foundation under Grant No. 9876180.

References

[1] D. Albonesi. Selective Cache Ways: On-Demand Cache Resource Allocation. In *Journal of Instruction Level Parallelism*, pages 248–261, 2000.

[2] V. Bala, E. Duesterwakd, and S. Banerjia. Dynamo: A Transparent Dynamic Optimization System. In *PLDI*, 2000.

[3] R. Bedichek. Talisman-2 — A Fugu System Simulator. http://bedichek.org/robert/talisman2/, August 1999.

[4] R. F. Cmelik and D. Keppel. Shade: A Fast Instruction-Set Simulator for Execution Profiling. CSE 93-06-06, University of Washington, 1993.

[5] J. B. Fryman, C. M. Huneycutt, and K. M. Mackenzie. Investigating a SoftCache via Dynamic Rewriting. In *4th Workshop on Feedback-Directed and Dynamic Optimization*, December 2001.

[6] E. G. Hallnor and S. K. Reinhardt. A Fully Associative Software-Managed Cache Design. In *Proceedings of the 27th Annual International Symposium on Computer Architecture*, 2000.

[7] R. J. Hookway and M. A. Herdeg. DIGITAL FX!32: Combining Emulation and Binary Translation. *Digital Technical Journal*, 9(1), 1997.

[8] C. Lee, M. Potkonjak, and W. H. Mangione-Smith. MediaBench: A Tool for Evaluating and Synthesizing Multimedia and Communications Systems. In *MICRO-30*, 1997.

[9] M. Margala. Low-Power SRAM Circuit Design. In *Proceedings of IEEE International Workshop on MemoryTechnology, Design and Testing*, pages 115–122, 1999.

[10] J. Montanaro, R. T. Witek, K. Anne, A. J. Black, E. M. Cooper, D. W. Dobberpuhl, P. M. Donahue, J. Eno, G. W. Hoeppner, D. Kruckmyer, T. H. Lee, P. C. M. Lin, L. Madden, D. Murray, M. H. Pearce, S. Santhanam, K. J. Synder, R. Stephany, and S. C. Thierauf. A 160-MHz, 32-b, 0.5-W CMOS RISC Microprocessor. In *IEEE Journal of Solid-State Circuits, Vol. 31, No. 11*, November 1996.

[11] C. A. Moritz, M. Frank, W. Lee, and S. Amarasinghe. Hot Pages: Software Caching for Raw Microprocessors. MIT-LCS-TM 599, Massachusetts Institute of Technology, 1999.

[12] E. Rotenberg, S. Bennett, and J. Smith. Trace Cache: A Low Latency Approach to High Bandwidth Instruction Fetching. In *Proceedings of the 29th Annual International Symposium on Microarchitecture*, pages 24–34, 1996.

[13] D. J. Scales, K. Gharachorloo, and C. A. Thekkath. Shasta: A Low Overhead, Software-Only Approach for Supporting Fine-Grain Shared Memory. In *Seventh International Conference on Architectural Support for Programming Languages and Operating Systems*, pages 174–185, October 1996.

[14] E. G. Sirer, R. Grimm, A. J. Gregory, and B. N. Bershad. Design and Implementation of a Distributed Virtual Machine for Networked Computers. In *Proceedings of the 17th ACM Symposium on Operating Systems Principles*, pages 202–216, 1999.

[15] E. Witchel and M. Rosenblum. Embra: Fast and Flexible Machine Simulation. In *Proceedings of ACM SIGMETRICS '96: Conference on Measurement and Modeling of Computer Systems*, 1996.

[16] H. Zhou, M. Toburen, E. Rotenberg, and T. Conte. Adaptive Mode Control: A Static-Power-Efficient Cache Design. In *Proceedings of the International Conference on Parallel Architectures and Compilation Techniques*, 2001.

Author Index